Ninth Edition

W9-DJL-606

Criminology TODAY

AN INTEGRATIVE INTRODUCTION

Frank Schmalleger, Ph.D.

Distinguished Professor Emeritus,
The University of North Carolina at Pembroke

 Pearson

330 Hudson Street, New York, NY 10013

For my daughter Nicole,
a next-generation criminologist.

Vice President, Portfolio Management: Andrew Gilfillan
Portfolio Manager: Gary Bauer
Editorial Assistant: Lynda Cramer
Senior Vice President, Marketing: David Gesell
Field Marketing Manager: Bob Nisbet
Director, Digital Studio and Content Production: Brian Hyland
Managing Producer: Cynthia Zonneveld
Content Producer: Holly Shufeldt
Manager, Rights Management: Johanna Burke
Operations Specialist: Deidra Smith
Creative Digital Lead: Mary Siener

Managing Producer, Digital Studio: Autumn Benson
Content Producer, Digital Studio: Maura Barclay
Full-Service Management and Composition: Integra Software Services, Ltd.
Full-Service Project Manager: Abinaya Rajendran
Cover Design: Studio Montage
Cover Photo: A_Lesik/Shutterstock; Gwoeii/Shutterstock; Datskevich Aleh/Shutterstock; TSpider/Shutterstock; Manley099/E+/Getty Images; CribbVisuals/E+/Getty Images
Printer/Binder: LSC Communications, Inc.
Cover Printer: Phoenix Color/Hagerstown
Text Font: Bembo MT Pro 10/13

Credits and acknowledgments for content borrowed from other sources and reproduced, with permission, in this textbook appear on the appropriate page within the text.

Acknowledgements of third party content appear on page with the borrowed material, which constitutes an extension of this copyright page.

Unless otherwise indicated herein, any third-party trademarks that may appear in this work are the property of their respective owners and any references to third-party trademarks, logos or other trade dress are for demonstrative or descriptive purposes only. Such references are not intended to imply any sponsorship, endorsement, authorization, or promotion of Pearson's products by the owners of such marks, or any relationship between the owner and Pearson Education, Inc. or its affiliates, authors, licensees or distributors.

The Internet addresses listed in the text were accurate at the time of publication. The inclusion of a website does not indicate an endorsement by the author or Pearson Education. Pearson Education does not guarantee the accuracy of the information presented at these sites.

Many of the designations by manufacturers and sellers to distinguish their products are claimed as trademarks. Where those designations appear in this book, and the publisher was aware of a trademark claim, the designations have been printed in initial caps or all caps.

Library of Congress Cataloging-in-Publication Data
Schmalleger, Frank, author.
  Criminology today: an integrative introduction / Frank Schmalleger, Ph.D., Distinguished Professor Emeritus, The University of North Carolina at Pembroke.
  Ninth Edition. | Hoboken: Pearson, [2019] | Revised edition of the author's Criminology today, [2017] | Includes bibliographical references and indexes.
  LCCN 2017020526| ISBN 9780134749730 (alk. paper) | ISBN 0134749731 (alk. paper) | ISBN 9780134146386 (perfect bound) | ISBN 0134146387 | ISBN 9780134417110 (loose leaf) | ISBN 0134417119 (loose leaf)
Subjects: LCSH: Criminology. | Criminology—United States.
  LCC HV6025 .S346 2019 | DDC 364—dc23
  LC record available at https://lccn.loc.gov/   2017020526

1   18

Paper bound ISBN-13: 978-0-13-474973-0
ISBN-10:   0-13-474973-1
Loose leaf ISBN-13: 978-0-13-441711-0
ISBN-10:   0-13-441711-9

Brief Contents

PART ONE   Crime and Criminology

CHAPTER 1 | What Is Criminology—Understanding Crime and Criminals   1

CHAPTER 2 | Where Do Theories Come From?—From Idea To Evidence   27

PART TWO   Crime Causation

CHAPTER 3 | Classical and Neoclassical Thought—Choice or Consequences   53

CHAPTER 4 | Early Biological Perspectives on Criminal Behavior—It's What We Are   81

CHAPTER 5 | Biosocial and Other Contemporary Perspectives—Interaction Is Key   101

CHAPTER 6 | Psychological and Psychiatric Foundations of Criminal Behavior—It's How We Think   131

PART THREE   Crime Causation Revisited

CHAPTER 7 | Social Structure Theories—It's Where and How We Live   163

CHAPTER 8 | Theories of Social Process and Social Development—It's What We Learn   193

CHAPTER 9 | Social Conflict Theories—It's How We Relate   233

PART FOUR   The Crime Picture

CHAPTER 10 | Criminal victimization—It's Personal   259

CHAPTER 11 | Crimes Against Persons—It's What We Fear   289

CHAPTER 12 | Crimes Against Property—It's What We Lose   329

CHAPTER 13 | White-Collar and Organized Crime—Crime as a Job   353

CHAPTER 14 | Drug and Sex Crimes—Recreational Offenses   381

CHAPTER 15 | Technology and Crime—It's a Double-Edged Sword   407

CHAPTER 16 | Globalization and Terrorism—Our Small World   427

EPILOGUE   Future Directions—It's What's To Come

Major Theoretical Developments

Classical School

Classical Criminology

1764   **Cesare Beccaria** Deterrence through punishment, free will, social contract

1789   **Jeremy Bentham** Hedonistic calculus, utilitarianism

Neoclassical Criminology

1974   **Robert Martinson** Nothing-works doctrine

1975   **James Q. Wilson** Thinking about crime

1986   **Clarke & Cornish** Rational choice

1988   **Jack Katz** Seductions of crime, emotions and crime

1992   **Clarke & Cornish** Situational choice, situational crime prevention

Biological and Biosocial Theories

Early Positivism

1810   **Franz Joseph Gall** Phrenology, scientific understanding of crime

1830s   **Johann Gaspar Spurzheim** Brought phrenology to America

Criminal Anthropology

1863   **Cesare Lombroso** Atavism, born criminals, criminaloids, Italian School

1913   **Charles Buckman Goring** Challenged Lombroso's theory

1939   **Earnest Hooton** Environment + low-grade human = crime

Criminal Families

1877   **Richard Dugdale** The Juke family

1912   **Henry Goddard** The Kallikak family

1915   **Arthur Estabrook**

Constitutional Theories

1925   **Ernst Kretschmer** Somatotyping

1949   **William Sheldon** Body types, behavioral genetics/twins, heritability, human genome

Twin studies

1968   **Karl Christiansen and Sarnoff Mednick** Genetic determinism

Sociobiology

1975   **Edward O. Wilson** Altruism, territoriality, tribalism, survival of gene pool

Biosocial Criminology

1980   **Darrell J. Steffensmeier**

1997   **Anthony Walsh** Environmental mediation of genetic influences

1990s   **Adrian Raine** Brain dysfunction

2003   **Kevin M. Beaver and Anthony Walsh** Biosocial criminology

2010   **Thomas Bernard** Gender-ratio problem

2010   **Kevin M. Beaver, John P. Wright, and Anthony Walsh** Evolutionary theory

Psychological/ Psychiatric Theories

Modeling Theory

1890   **Gabriel Tarde** Imitation

1973   **Albert Bandura** Aggression is learned, aggression is rewarded, disengagement, social cognition theory, modeling

Psychoanalytic Criminology

1920s–   **Sigmund Freud** Psychoanalysis,

1930s   Id, ego, superego, sublimation

1930s   **August Aichorn** Damaged egos

Personality Theory

1941   **Hervey Cleckley** Psychopathology, psychopath, sociopath

1964   **Hans Eysenck** Traits, supertraits

1968   **DSM-II** Antisocial personality disorder

Behavior Theory

1950s–   **B. F. Skinner** Operant

1970s   Conditioning, operant behavior, rewards/ punishments, stimulus-response

Frustration–Aggression Theory

1939   **J. Dollard** Displacement, catharsis

Cognitive Theory

1955   **Jean Piaget** Stages of human intellectual development

1969   **Lawrence Kohlberg** Stages of moral development

1970   **Stanton Samenow and Samuel Yochelson** The criminal mindset

1979   **Roger Shank and Robert Abelson** Script theory

Crime as Adaptation

1950s   **John Bowlby** Secure attachment, anxious resistant attachment, anxious avoidance attachment

1971   **S. M. Halleck** Alloplastic adaptation, autoplastic adaptation

1995   **Linksy, Bachman, Straus** Societal stress, aggression

1998   **Donald Andrews and James Bonta** Criminogenic needs, criminogenic domains

In Criminology

Social Structure Approaches

Social Disorganization

1920 **Thomas & Znaniecki** Displaced immigrants

1920s **Park & Burgess** Social ecology

1930s Social pathology, concentric zones (Chicago School)

1929 **Shaw & McKay** Cultural transmission (Chicago School)

1973 **Oscar Newman** Defensible space

1982 **James Q. Wilson & George L. Kelling** Broken windows, criminology of place

1987 **Rodney Stark** Theory of deviant neighborhoods

Culture Conflict

1927 **Frederic Thrasher** Gangs and gang typologies

1938 **Thorsten Sellin** Conduct norms, primary conflict, secondary conflict

1943 **William F. Whyte** Subcultures

1955 **Albert Cohen** Gangs, reaction formation

1957 **Sykes & Matza** Techniques of neutralization

1958 **Walter B. Miller** Focal concerns

1960s **Cloward & Ohlin** Illegitimate opportunity structure, delinquent subcultures

1967 **Ferracuti & Wolfgang** Violent subcultures

Strain Theory

1938 **Robert Merton** Anomie, conformity, innovation, ritualism, retreatism, rebellion

1982 **Blau & Blau** Relative deprivation, frustration, distributive justice

1992 **Robert Agnew** General strain theory

1994 **Messner & Rosenfeld** American Dream

Social Process & Social Development Theories

Social Learning Theory

1939 **Edwin Sutherland** Differential association

1960 **Daniel Glaser** Differential identification theory

1966 **Burgess & Akers** Differential association-reinforcement

Social Control Theory

1950s **Walter Reckless** Containment theory, inner and outer containment

1969 **Travis Hirschi** Social bond and self-control: attachment, commitment, belief, involvement

1970s **Howard Kaplan** Self-degradation

1990 **Hirschi & Gottfredson** Social bonds and self-control, general theory of crime

1995 **Charles Tittle** Control-balance, control surplus, control deficit

1995 **Per-Olof H. Wikström** Situational action theory

Labeling Theory

1938 **Frank Tannenbaum** Tagging, dramatization of evil

1951 **Edwin Lemert** Primary deviance, secondary deviance

1963 **Howard Becker** Outsiders, moral enterprise

1997 **John Braithwaite** Reintegrative shaming, stigmatic shaming

Dramaturgy

1960s **Erving Goffman** Dramaturgy, impression management, discrediting information, total institutions, disculturation

Social Development

1920s **Sheldon & Eleanor Glueck** Family dynamics and delinquent careers

1960s **Marvin Wolfgang** Chronic offending

1980s **David P. Farrington** Delinquent development theory

1987 **Terrence Thornberry** Interactional theory

1988 **Lawrence E. Cohen and Richard Machalek** Evolutionary ecology

1993 **Robert J. Sampson and John H. Laub** Life course criminology

1993 **Terrie Moffitt** Life course persisters, adolescence-limited offenders

Social Conflict Theories

Conflict Theories

1848 **Karl Marx** The *Communist Manifesto*

1916 **Willem Bonger** Class struggle

1938 **Thorsten Sellin** Culture conflict

Radical Criminology

1958 **George Vold** Political conflict between groups, conflict is normal

1959 **Ralf Dahrendorf** Conflict is normal, destructive change

1969 **Austin Turk** Social order = pattern of conflict, laws serve to control

1970s **William Chambliss** Power gaps, crime reduces surplus labor

1974 **Richard Quinney** Contradictions of capitalism, socialist principles

Left-realist Criminology

1991 **Jock Young & Walter DeKeseredy** The new criminology

Feminist Criminology

1975 **Adler & Simon** Gender socialization

1977 **Carol Smart** Gender bias in criminology

1988 **Daly & Chesney-Lind** Androcentricity, crime may not be normal

1989 **John Hagan** Power-control theory

Peacemaking Criminology

1986 **Pepinsky & Quinney** Restorative justice, participatory justice

1989 **Lozoff & Braswell** New Age principles

Convict Criminology

2001 **John Irwin, Ian Ross, K. C. Carceral, Thomas J. Bernard, Stephen Richards** Insights from convicted offenders

Theories of Victimology

Victim Precipitation Theory

1947 **Beniamin Mendelssohn** Coined the term "victimology"

1948 **Hans von Hentig** The criminal and his victim

1958 **Marvin Wolfgang** Some victims are positive precipitators in crime

1968 **Stephen Schafer** The victim and his criminal

1970 **Menachem Amir** Victim contribution to victimization

Lifestyle Theory

1970 **Michael J. Hindelang & Michael R. Gottfredson James Garofalo** Demographic variables influence lifestyles and determine victimization risk

Routine Activities Theory (RAT)

1970 **Lawrence Cohen and Marcus Felson** Motivated offenders combine with suitable targets in the absence of a capable guardian

Deviant Places Theory

1980s **Rodney Stark** Stigmatized neighborhoods produce crime

Contents

New to This Edition   xiii

Preface   xv

Acknowledgments   xix

About the Author   xx

PART ONE   Crime and Criminology

CHAPTER 1 | What is Criminology—Understanding Crime and Criminals   1

Introduction   2

What Is Crime?   2

Crime and Deviance   5

What Should Be Criminal?   7

■ **CRIME** | IN THE **NEWS** What Should Be Criminal?   8

What Is Criminology?   9

Defining "Criminology"   9

What Do Criminologists Do?   12

Theoretical Criminology   13

Evidence-Based Criminology   14

Criminology and Evidence-Based Social Policy   15

The Theme of This Text   16

WHO'S TO BLAME—The Individual or Society? Is Criminology Really Just a Form of Academic Excuse Making?   18

The Social Context of Crime   18

Making Sense of Crime: The Causes and Consequences of the Criminal Event   19

Crime and the Offender   20

Crime and the Criminal Justice System   20

Crime and the Victim   20

Crime and Society   21

The Consequences of Crime   22

■ **CRIMINAL** | **PROFILES** Ross Ulbricht—The New Face of Crime?   23

The Primacy of Sociology?   23

Summary   24

Key Terms   25

Questions For Review   25

Questions For Reflection   25

CHAPTER 2 | Where Do Theories Come From?—From Idea to Evidence   27

Introduction   28

Today's Science-Based Criminology   29

The Evolving Science of Criminology   29

Theory Building   30

■ **CRIME** | IN THE **NEWS** Do Violent Video Games Make Kids Kill?   32

The Role of Research and Experimentation   33

Problem Identification   33

Development of a Research Design   34

Choice of Data-Gathering Techniques   38

Problems in Data Collection   40

Review of Findings   41

Quantitative versus Qualitative Methods   42

Values and Ethics in the Conduct of Research   44

The Impact of Criminological Research on Social Policy   46

■ **THEORY** | versus **REALITY** The Stockholm Prize in Criminology   47

The Research Report   48

Writing for Publication   49

Summary   50

Key Terms   50

Questions For Review   51

Questions For Reflection   51

PART TWO   Crime Causation

CHAPTER 3 | Classical and Neoclassical Thought—Choice or Consequences   53

Introduction   54

Major Principles of the Classical School   54

Forerunners of Classical Thought   54

The Demonic Era   55

Early Sources of Criminal Law   56

The Enlightenment   57

The Classical School   59

Cesare Beccaria   59

Jeremy Bentham   60

Neoclassical Criminology   61

■ **THEORY** | versus **REALITY** Three-Strikes Legislation   63

Rational Choice Theory (RCT)   64

The Excitement of Crime   65

Situational Crime-Control Policy   66

■ **THEORY** | in PERSPECTIVE The Classical School and Neoclassical Thinkers   67

Critique of Rational Choice Theory   67

Punishment and Neoclassical Thought   68

Just Deserts   69

Deterrence   69

Capital Punishment   70

PUTTING CRIMINOLOGY TO WORK—Implementing Evidence-Based Policy   71

■ **CRIME** | IN THE **NEWS** Post-Conviction DNA Exonerations Expose Weaknesses in Judicial System   73

Policy Implications of Classical and Neoclassical Thought   74

WHO'S TO BLAME—The Individual or Society? The Excitement of Crime   75

A Critique of Classical and Neoclassical Theories   76

■ **CRIMINAL** | **PROFILES** Gary Steven Krist: The Einstein of Crime?   77

■ **CRIME** | IN THE **NEWS** Crime Pays: Washington, D.C., Considers Paying Off Criminals   78

Summary   79

Key Terms   79

Key Names   79

Questions For Review   80

Questions For Reflection   80

CHAPTER 4 | Early Biological Perspectives on Criminal Behavior—It's What We Are   81

Introduction   82

Traditional Biological versus Modern Biosocial Theories   82

Principles of Biological Theories   83

Early Biological Positivism   84

Physical Features and Crime   84

■ **THEORY** | in PERSPECTIVE Early Biological Theories   85

The Italian School   86

Constitutional Theories   88

■ **THEORY** | versus **REALITY** Positivism: The Historical Statement   89

Criminal Families   90

The XYY Supermale   91

■ **CRIME** | IN THE **NEWS** President of Philippines Says "Criminals Aren't Humanity"   92

Twin Studies and Heredity   93

PUTTING CRIMINOLOGY TO WORK—Implementing Evidence-Based Policy   94

Sociobiology   95

The Biological Roots of Human Aggression   95

The New Synthesis   96

Critique of Early Biological Theories of Criminal Behavior   97

■ **CRIMINAL** | **PROFILES** Richard Benjamin Speck: "Born to Raise Hell"   98

Summary   99

Key Terms   99

Key Names   100

Questions For Review   100

Questions For Reflection   100

CHAPTER 5 | Biosocial and Other Contemporary Perspectives— Interaction Is Key   101

Introduction   102

The Human Genome Project   102

■ **THEORY** | versus **REALITY** The Future of Neuroscience   103

Genetics and Heritability   103

Future Directions in the Study of Genes and Crime   105

The Dysfunctional Brain   107

■ **CRIME** | IN THE **NEWS** Is There a Crime Gene?   107

■ **THEORY** | in PERSPECTIVE Modern Biological Theories   110

Body Chemistry and Criminality   111

Ingested Substances and Nutrition   111

Environmental Pollution   112

■ **CRIME** | IN THE **NEWS** Exposure to Lead, Other Substances Linked to Crime Rate   113

Psychobiotics   114

Hormones and Criminality   115

WHO'S TO BLAME—The Individual or Society? Hormones and Criminal Behavior   117

Low Resting Heart Rate and Crime   118

Galvanic Skin Response   119

Digit Ratio   120

Climate, Weather, and Crime   120

Biosocial Criminology   121

Gender Differences in Criminality   122

Evolutionary Neuroandrogenic Theory   124

Policy Implications of Biological Theories   125

■ **CRIMINAL** | **PROFILES** Jodi Arias—The Petite Killer   126

Critiques of Biological and Biosocial Theories   127

Summary   128

Key Terms   128

Key Names   128

Questions For Review   129

Questions For Reflection   129

CHAPTER 6 | Psychological and Psychiatric Foundations of Criminal Behavior—It's How We Think   131

Introduction   132

Principles of Psychological and Psychiatric Theories   132

History of Psychological Theories   133

Personality Disturbances   133

The Psychopath   134

Antisocial Personality Disorder   136

Trait Theory   137

Cognitive Theories   138

Moral Development Theory   138

Cognitive Information-Processing Theory   139

The Criminal Mind-Set   140

PUTTING CRIMINOLOGY TO WORK—Implementing Evidence-Based Policy   141

The Psychoanalytic Perspective—Criminal Behavior as Maladaptation   142

The Psychotic Offender   144

Frustration–Aggression Theory   145

Crime as Adaptation   145

Criminogenic Needs   146

Attachment Theory   146

■ THEORY | in PERSPECTIVE Types of Psychological and Psychiatric Theories   147

Behavior Theory   148

Behavioral Conditioning   148

Social Cognition and the Role of Modeling   149

Policy and Treatment Implications of Psychological and Psychiatric Approaches   150

WHO'S TO BLAME—The Individual or Society? The Video Game Killer   151

Assessing Dangerousness   152

Predicting Criminality   154

Critique of Psychological and Psychiatric Theories of Crime   154

Criminal Psychological Profiling   155

The Psychological Autopsy   157

Insanity and the Law   157

■ CRIMINAL | PROFILES Andrea Yates—Child Killer   158

Guilty but Mentally Ill (GBMI)   159

Problems with the Insanity Defense   159

Summary   160

Key Terms   160

Key Names   161

Questions For Review   161

Questions For Reflection   161

PART THREE   Crime Causation Revisited

CHAPTER 7 | Social Structure Theories—It's Where and How We Live   163

Introduction   164

Major Principles of Sociological Theories   164

Social Structure Theories   165

■ THEORY | in PERSPECTIVE Types of Social Structure Theories   166

Types of Social Structure Theories   166

Social Disorganization Theory   166

PUTTING CRIMINOLOGY TO WORK—Implementing Evidence-Based Policy   169

PUTTING CRIMINOLOGY TO WORK—Implementing Evidence-Based Policy   171

Strain Theory   172

■ THEORY | versus REALITY The Criminology of Place, Routine Activities, and Crime Mapping   173

■ CRIME | IN THE NEWS The Pros and Cons of "Broken Windows" Policing   174

■ THEORY | versus REALITY The Correlation between Rates of U.S. Unemployment, Interest, and Crime   178

Culture Conflict Theory   179

WHO'S TO BLAME—The Individual or Society? Like Father, Like Son   184

■ CRIMINAL | PROFILES Sanyika Shakur—aka Monster Kody Scott   187

Policy Implications of Social Structure Theories   188

Critique of Social Structure Theories   188

Summary   190

Key Terms   191

Key Names   191

Questions For Review   191

Questions For Reflection   191

CHAPTER 8 | Theories of Social Process and Social Development—It's What We Learn   193

Introduction   194

The Perspective of Social Interaction   194

Types of Social Process Approaches   194

Social Learning Theory   195

■ THEORY | in PERSPECTIVE Types of Social Process Theories   196

Social Control Theories   198

Labeling Theory   205

PUTTING CRIMINOLOGY TO WORK—Implementing Evidence-Based Policy   205

■ **CRIMINAL** | **PROFILES** Dr. Farid Fata—Prescribing Unneeded
Chemotherapy 209
Reintegrative Shaming 210
Dramaturgical Perspective 210

PUTTING CRIMINOLOGY TO WORK— Implementing
Evidence-Based Policy 211
Policy Implications of Social Process Theories 212
Critique of Social Process Theories 213
The Social Development Perspective 214
Concepts in Social Development Theories 214
The Life Course Perspective 215
■ **THEORY** | in **PERSPECTIVE** Social Development
Theories 217
Laub and Sampson's Age-Graded Theory 218
Moffitt's Dual Taxonomic Theory 219
Farrington's Delinquent Development Theory 220
Evolutionary Ecology 221
Thornberry's Interactional Theory 222
■ **THEORY** | versus **REALITY** Social Influences on
Developmental Pathways 223
Developmental Pathways 223
Project on Human Development in Chicago Neighborhoods
(PHDCN) 226
WHO'S TO BLAME—The Individual or Society? Sexual Abuser
Claims Victim Status 227
Policy Implications of Social Development Theories 228
Critique of Social Development Theories 229
■ **CRIMINAL** | **PROFILES** Adam Lanza and the Sandy Hook
School Shootings 229
Summary 231
Key Terms 231
Key Names 232
Questions For Review 232
Questions For Reflection 232

C**HAPTER** 9 | Social Conflict Theories—It's
How We Relate 233
Introduction 234
Law and Social Order Perspectives 234
The Consensus Perspective 234
The Pluralist Perspective 235
The Conflict Perspective 235
■ **THEORY** | in **PERSPECTIVE** Social Conflict Theories 237
Radical Criminology 238
Critical Criminology 240
WHO'S TO BLAME—The Individual or Society? Human
Trafficking, Illegal Aliens, and the American Dream **241**
Radical-Critical Criminology and Policy Issues 242
Critique of Radical-Critical Criminology 242
Emerging Conflict Theories 243
Left-Realist Criminology 243
Feminist Criminology 244

PUTTING CRIMINOLOGY TO WORK—Implementing
Evidence-Based Policy 245
Postmodern Criminology 249
Peacemaking Criminology 250
PUTTING CRIMINOLOGY TO WORK—Implementing
Evidence-Based Policy 253
Moral Time 254
Convict Criminology 254
New Issues in Radical-Critical Thought 255
■ **CRIMINAL** | **PROFILES** Theodore John "Ted" Kaczynski—the
Unabomber 256
Policy Implications of Social Conflict Theories 257
Summary 257
Key Terms 258
Key Names 258
Questions For Review 258
Questions For Reflection 258

PART FOUR The Crime Picture

C**HAPTER** 10 | Criminal Victimization—It's
Personal 259
Introduction 260
Hidden Victims 260
Victimization by the Numbers 261
The National Crime Victimization Survey (NCVS) 261
Critique of the NCVS 262
The Uniform Crime Reporting Program (UCR) 263
Critique of UCR/NIBRS 264
Comparing the UCR/NIBRS and the NCVS 265
Changing Offense Patterns 265
Demographic Correlates of Victimization 267
Revictimization and Polyvictimization 268
WHO'S TO BLAME—The Individual or Society? He Stood His
Ground 269
The Developmental Victimization Survey (DVS) 270
The Personal Impact of Criminal Victimization 270
The Socio-emotional Impact of Victimization 271
The Physical Impact of Victimization 272
The Financial Impact of Victimization 272
Secondary Victimization 272
Victimization as a Risk Factor for Crime 273
Victimology 273
Blaming the Victim: Early Theories of Victim
Precipitation 274
Victimization and Lifestyle 275
■ **THEORY** | in **PERSPECTIVE** Types of Victimization
Theories 276
PUTTING CRIMINOLOGY TO WORK—Implementing
Evidence-Based Policy 279
Deviant Places Theory 279

Victims' Rights 281
  A History of the Victim 281
  Victims' Rights Legislation 282
Restorative Justice: Making the Victim Whole Again 284
  Victim Restitution and Victim Compensation 285
  ■ CRIMINAL | PROFILES Omar Mateen—American Monster 285
Summary 287
Key Terms 287
Key Names 288
Questions For Review 288
Questions For Reflection 288

CHAPTER 11 | Crimes Against Persons—It's What We Fear 289

Introduction 290
Homicide 290
  The Subculture of Violence Theory 292
  Homicide: A Closer Look 293
  Serial Killers 296
  ■ CRIME | IN THE NEWS Why Mass Shootings Won't Go Away 298
  Mass Murder 298
Rape 299
  Theoretical Perspectives on Rape 300
  ■ CRIMINAL | PROFILES Karla Homolka—A Woman Rapist? 301
  Typologies of Rapists 303
  WHO'S TO BLAME—The Individual or Society? Exotic Dancer Claims Rape 304
  Rape: A Closer Look 304
Child Sexual Abuse 307
  Types of Child Sex Abusers 307
Robbery 309
  The Lethal Potential of Robbery 311
  Criminal Careers of Robbers 311
  Robbery and Public Transportation 311
  The Motivation of Robbers 312
  Drug Robberies 313
  The Gendered Nature of Robbery 313
Aggravated Assault 314
  Stranger Assault 314
  Assault within Families 315
Other Forms of Interpersonal Violence 317
  Bullying 317
  Workplace Violence 319
  Hate Crimes 321
  Stalking 322
  ■ CRIMINAL | PROFILES Dylann Storm Roof—The Charleston Church Shooter 325

Summary 326
Key Terms 327
Key Names 327
Questions For Review 327
Questions For Reflection 327

CHAPTER 12 | Crimes Against Property—It's What We Lose 329

Introduction 330
Types of Property Crime 330
Burglary 330
  The Social Ecology of Burglary 331
  ■ THEORY | versus REALITY Ethnographic Research on Active Burglars 333
  A Typology of Burglars 333
  The Locales and Times of Burglary 334
  The Motivation of Burglars 334
  Target Selection for Burglary 335
  The Costs of Burglary 336
  The Burglary-Drug Connection 336
  The Sexualized Context of Burglary 336
Larceny-Theft 337
  Shoplifting and Employee Theft 337
  ■ CRIME | IN THE NEWS "Flash Robs" Become a Troublesome Trend 339
  Flash Mobs and Larceny 339
  Identity Theft 340
Motor Vehicle Theft 342
  Theft of Car Parts 342
  Joyriders: Car Theft for Fun 342
  ■ CRIMINAL | PROFILES Frank W. Abagnale, Jr.—"Catch Me If You Can" 343
  WHO'S TO BLAME—The Individual or Society? Body Parts for Sale 344
  Professional Car Theft 345
Arson 345
  Fire Setters 345
Understanding Property Crimes 346
  Persistent and Professional Thieves 346
  The Criminal Careers of Property Offenders 347
  Property Offenders and Rational Choice 348
Receivers of Stolen Property 348
  The Role of Criminal Receivers 348
  ■ CRIMINAL | PROFILES Colton Harris-Moore—the Barefoot Bandit 350
Summary 351
Key Terms 351
Key Names 351
Questions For Review 351
Questions For Reflection 351

Chapter 13 | White-Collar and Organized Crime—Crime as a Job   353

Introduction   354

A Brief History of White-Collar Crime   354

Understanding White-Collar Crime   355
Definitional Evolution of White-Collar Crime   357
White-Collar Crime Today   357

Corporate Crime   358
■ **THEORY** | versus **REALITY** White-Collar Crime: The Initial
Statement   359
Financial Crime   359
Environmental Crimes and Green Criminology   363
Terrorism and White-Collar Crime   364

Causes of White-Collar Crime   364

Curtailing White-Collar and Corporate Crime   367

Organized Crime   368
Prohibition and Official Corruption   370
Activities of Organized Crime   370

Other Organized Criminal Groups   370
Eurasian Criminal Enterprises   372
Balkan Criminal Enterprises   372
Asian Criminal Enterprises   372
African Criminal Enterprises   373
Middle Eastern Criminal Enterprises   373

Transnational Organized Crime   374
■ **CRIME** | IN THE **NEWS** U.S. Authorities Grapple with the Rise
of Transnational Criminal Organizations   375

Organized Crime and the Law   376

Policy Issues: The Control of Organized Crime   376
■ **CRIMINAL** | **PROFILES** Bernie Madoff—Disgraced
Financier   378
Summary   379
Key Terms   379
KEY NAMES   380
Questions For Review   380
Questions For Reflection   380

Chapter 14 | Drug and Sex Crimes—
Recreational
Offenses   381

Introduction   382

History of Drug Abuse in the United States   382
Extent of Drug Abuse   382
Young People and Drugs   385
Costs of Drug Abuse   386

Types of Illegal Drugs   387
**PUTTING CRIMINOLOGY TO WORK—Implementing
Evidence-Based Policy   388**

Drug Addiction   389

Drug Trafficking   389
Pharmaceutical Diversion and Synthetic Drugs   390
WHO'S TO BLAME—The Individual or Society? His Brother's
Keeper   391
Drugs and Crime   392
Narcoterrorism   392

Social Policy and Drug Abuse   393
Recent Legislation   393
Drug-Control Strategies   394
The Drug Legalization/Decriminalization Debate   395
WHO'S TO BLAME—The Individual or Society? Gangs,
Teenagers, and Peer Pressure   397

Prostitution   397
Morals Legislation   398
A Typology of Prostitutes   398
■ **CRIME** | IN THE **NEWS** International Sex Traffickers Turn Girls
into Slaves   400
Commercial Sexual Exploitation of Children   401
Clients of Prostitutes   401
Prostitution: A Changing Business   402
Exiting the Sex Trade   402
Feminist Perspectives on Prostitution   402
■ **CRIMINAL** | **PROFILES** Heidi Lynne Fleiss—Madame to the
Stars   403
Legalization and Decriminalization of Prostitution   404
Summary   404
Key Terms   405
Questions For Review   405
Questions For Reflection   405

Chapter 15 | Technology and Crime—
It's a Double-Edged
Sword   407

Introduction   408

Technology and Crime   408

High Technology and Criminal Opportunity   409

The Extent of Cybercrime   410

Cybercrime and the Law   411
The History and Nature of Hacking   414

A Profile of Cybercriminals   414
■ **CRIME** | IN THE **NEWS** Cyberbanging   416
Cybercrime as a Form of White-Collar Crime   416
WHO'S TO BLAME—The Individual or Society? Criminal Activity
or Mischievous Gaming?   417

Technology in the Fight against Crime   418
DNA Technology   418
■ **CRIMINAL** | **PROFILES** Kevin Mitnick—Hacker Turned Security
Expert   419
Computers as Crime-Fighting Tools   421

Combating Cybercrime   422

   Police Investigation of Computer Crime   423

   Cybercrime and Internet Security   423

Policy Issues: Personal Freedoms in the Information Age   425

Summary   426

Key Terms   426

Questions For Review   426

Questions For Reflection   426

Chapter 16 | Globalization and Terrorism—Our Small World 427

Introduction   428

Comparative Criminology   428

   Ethnocentrism   429

   Transnational Crimes   430

▪ **THEORY** | versus **REALITY** UN Offense Definitions   431

Human Smuggling and Trafficking   431

   Human Trafficking   433

   Federal Immigration and Trafficking Legislation   434

Terrorism   435

   Domestic Terrorism   436

   International Terrorism   437

▪ **CRIME** | IN THE **NEWS** "Lone-Wolf" Terrorists Remain Difficult to Track Down   438

   Cyberterrorism   439

▪ **CRIMINAL** | **PROFILES** Mohammed Atta—Leader of the 9/11 Attacks   440

WHO'S TO BLAME—The Individual or Society? The Making of a Suicide Bomber   441

   Terrorism and Technology   442

The Radicalization Process   443

Countering the Terrorist Threat   444

   Foreign Terrorist Organizations   445

   The Future of Terrorism   447

International Crime-Fighting Organizations   448

   INTERPOL   448

   Europol   448

▪ **CRIMINAL** | **PROFILES** The Tsarnaev Brothers—The Boston Bombers   449

   The International Criminal Court   450

Summary   451

Key Terms   451

Key Name   451

Questions For Review   451

Questions For Reflection   452

Glossary   G-1

Notes   N-1

Name Index   I-1

Subject Index   I-7

New to This Edition

The ninth edition of *Criminology Today: An Integrative Introduction* continues to offer students a clear, contemporary, and comprehensive introduction to criminology that encourages critical thinking about the causes of crime and crime-prevention strategies. The text's hallmark thematic approach of social problems versus individual responsibility (Is crime a matter of individual responsibility or a symptom of a dysfunctional society?) prompts students to think critically about the causes of crime and helps them see the link between crime theories and crime policies.

New Features in the Ninth Edition

There are many important new features in this ninth edition:

- Start of chapter learning objectives now align with chapter headings, as well as with bulleted summary items and end of chapter discussion questions.

- A series of "Putting Criminology to Work" boxes are now included in the text. Those boxes are based on findings published on **https://www.crimesolutions.gov**. This federal government website strives to evaluate the effectiveness of theory-based practices, and then communicates findings about some of the most effective and promising crime-control and prevention programs.

- The online REVEL version of this text now includes dozens of short author explanatory videos.

- A new series of Criminology Interactive boxes can be found throughout the online REVEL version of this text. These boxes show the relationship between variables of interest in the study of criminology, such as unemployment rates and rates of crime.

New Chapter Content in the Ninth Edition

Chapter 1: What Is Criminology?

The concept of "evidence-based criminology" is now introduced in this chapter, and it continues to be discussed throughout the text.

A "Who's to Blame?" box has been added to this chapter that poses the question of whether criminology is merely a form of academic excuse-making.

The "Criminal Profiles" box at the end of Chapter 1 now focuses on Ross Ulbricht, the mastermind behind the illegal online marketplace known as Silk Road. Ulbricht's case is used to illustrate "the new face of crime."

Varying perspectives on the legalization of marijuana and on the burning of the American flag during political protests are used to illustrate the question of "What Should Be a Crime?" A map showing the legal status of medical and recreational marijuana use in the United States is included.

Chapter 2: Where Do Theories Come From?

The box describing the Stockholm Prize in Criminology has been updated to showcase the work of 2017 award recipient, Richard Tremblay.

Chapter 3: Classical and Neoclassical Thought

The Excitement of Crime section has been expanded to include the recent rash of car burnings throughout Sweden.

The chart used to illustrate prison populations in the United States over time has been simplified and made easier to comprehend.

A description of Washington State's new Swift and Certain Sanctioning model for use in community supervision is now included.

A new "Crime in the News" box describing efforts made by the Washington, D.C., city government to implement a program that pays criminal offenders not to commit any new crimes appears in the chapter.

A new "Putting Criminology to Work" box focusing on the challenges of implementing evidence-based crime policy is now included in the chapter.

Chapter 4: Early Biological Perspectives on Criminal Behavior

A new "Crime in the News" box entitled "President of Philippines Says 'Criminals Aren't Humanity'" has been added.

Chapter 5: Biosocial and Other Contemporary Perspectives

The concept of genetic memory is introduced, defined, and discussed, showing its relevance to human behavior and crime commission.

Richard E. Tremblay's work on the predictors of early and persistent violence is described.

The 2D-4D finger ratio is now discussed in relationship to the likelihood of prenatal androgen exposure and the likelihood of later criminal behavior.

Chapter 6: Psychological and Psychiatric Foundations of Criminal Behavior

The various branches of cognitive theory are discussed and clarified.

A "Putting Criminology to Work" box has been added to the chapter.

The results of a recent meta-analysis of risk assessment modeling have been added to the chapter.

The concept of Serious Violent and Chronic offenders (SVCs) has been added to the chapter.

Chapter 7: Social Structure Theories

A new Criminology Interactive feature has been added to the online REVEL version of this chapter. It examines the correlation between rates of U.S. unemployment, interest, and crime.

Two new "Putting Criminology to Work" boxes have been added to this chapter.

A new key term, crime prevention through environmental design (CPTED), has been added to the chapter.

The "Crime in the News" box on Broken Windows Policing has been updated.

The discussion of Sykes and Matza's "techniques of neutralization" has been expanded.

Added coverage of Arnold S. Linsky and Murray A. Straus, to include their idea that the relationship between the occurrence of stress and the incidence of crime, illness, and other forms of maladaptive behavior was more common in states that had higher levels of social stress, as measured by such factors as business failures, personal bankruptcies, and unemployment claims.

The pattern theory of crime has been added to the chapter. Pattern theory says that the spatial distribution of specific types of crime are determined by the characteristics of the areas in which they occur.

Chapter 8: Theories of Social Process and Social Development

A brief discussion of the "ban the box" movement has been added to the discussion of labeling theory.

A new "Putting Criminology to Work" box has been added to the chapter.

A new "Criminal Profile" box featuring Dr. Farid Fata, the Detroit-area oncologist who dramatically overtreated patients, and received a lengthy prison sentence.

The chapter now ends with a "Criminal Profile" box depicting Adam Lanza.

Chapter 9: Social Conflict Theories

The chapter now opens with a discussion of the growing debate over the legalization of recreational marijuana.

Two new "Putting Criminology to Work" boxes have been added to the chapter.

"Moral time," a concept that is discussed in the chapter, has now been defined and added to the list of key terms.

A new Putting Criminology to Work box has been added to the chapter.

Chapter 10: Criminal Victimization

The chapter opening story has been modified.

Chapter 11: Crimes Against Persons

A new section on bullying and cyberbullying has been added.

The "Stanford rape" case has been written into the chapter.

The criminal profiles box on Dennis Rader has been replaced with a new box about Dylann Roof.

Chapter 12: Crimes Against Property

Now includes the results of a new study of decision-making by burglars. The study showed that burglars burglarize property close to their homes, and that familiarity with the area and with roads influences their choice of targets. The results of a new study of Los Angeles car thieves were added, showing that car types are stolen almost exclusively in response to their environmental availability.

Chapter 13: White-Collar and Organized Crime

A new section on criminal street gangs has been added.

Added discussion of *Why They Do It*, a 2016 book authored by Harvard Business School Professor Eugene Soltes. In the book, Soltes recounts the results of seven years of research and correspondence with 50 convicted white-collar criminals.

Chapter 14: Drug and Sex Crimes

A new story now opens the chapter.

The key term "victimless crimes" is now used and defined in the chapter.

The discussion of medical marijuana has been updated and expanded to include new graphics.

A new "Putting Criminology to Work" box has been added. It describes SAMHSA's National Registry of Evidence-Based Programs and Practices program and discusses the AlcoholEdu for College student-oriented initiative.

A discussion of the commercial sexual exploitation of children (CSEC) and sex trafficking has been added to the chapter.

A new discussion about the sex trade has been added.

Chapter 15: Technology and Crime

Discussion of the Cyberscurity Enhancement Act of 2016 has been added to the chapter.

The line art depicting a timeline of federal research reports on cybercrime has replaced with one showing the enactment of significant federal cybersecurity legislation.

Chapter 16: Globalization and Terrorism

The discussion of international terrorism has been substantially reduced, and the materials on the War on Terrorism have been removed, allowing for a clearer focus on cybercrimes and cyber criminal activity.

Three categories of terrorism are now identified: domestic, international, and cyber.

A new section on terrorist radicalization has been added to the chapter.

A new section on international crime-fighting organizations has been added to include Europol, INTERPOL, and the International Criminal Court.

An end-of-chapter "Criminal Profile" box on the Tsarnev Brothers has been added.

Preface

The opening decade of the twenty-first century was filled with momentous events in the United States, including the destruction of the World Trade Center and an attack on the Pentagon by Islamic terrorists, a fearsome recession, and corporate scandals that cost Americans billions of dollars in lost investments. The second decade saw the advent of a relatively large number of homegrown terrorist efforts to attack American population centers and landmarks, but only the Boston Marathon bombings of 2013 were carried out successfully. The crimes committed by terrorists set a tone for the start of the new century unlike any in living memory. Homeland security became an important buzzword at all levels of American government, while pundits questioned just how much freedom people would be willing to sacrifice to enhance security. Americans felt both physically and economically threatened as stock market losses were traced to the unethical actions of a surprising cadre of corporate executives who had previously been held in high regard in the business world and in the communities where they lived. Soon the media were busily showing a parade of business leaders being led away in handcuffs to face trial on charges of crooked accounting.

Added to the mix by the beginning of 2018 were shocking acts of criminality that emanated from all corners of the world, including mass shootings in the United States; terror attacks in Paris, France; depravities of sex tourism involving human trafficking; sex acts with minors streaming across the Internet in real time; websites like Silk Road selling drugs, hits for hire, sexual services, weapons, and just about anything else; massive copyright-infringement activities like those of New Zealand–based Megaupload; and the theft of hundreds of thousands of personal identities. This in terms of an economic, educational, online, and ever-more-complex social nexus.

Criminologists found themselves wondering what new laws might be enacted to add additional control to handgun sales and ownership; and they also focused on the potential last issue constitutes a very intimate crime that can literally cause a person to face the loss of his or her social self in a complex culture that increasingly defines someone's essence misuse of technology by Internet and energy companies, along with emerging computer capabilities and biotechnologies that, while seeming to hold amazing promise to cure disease and reshape humanity's future, threaten the social fabric in a way not seen since the birth of the atomic bomb or the harnessing of electricity. Similarly, climate changes, violent storms such as Superstorm Sandy, Hurricane Katrina, the Gulf oil spill, our nation's desperate need for alternative and additional energy sources, and the instability in the Middle East contribute to a growing awareness that the challenges facing criminologists in the twenty-first century are unlike any they have previously faced.

It was against this backdrop that the need for a comprehensive revision of *Criminology Today* emerged. This new edition addresses the poignant question of how security and freedom interface in an age of increasing globalism. Chapter 16, in particular, provides substantially enlarged coverage of terrorism and cyberterrorism, including an overview of many types of terrorist groups, such as nationalist, religious, state-sponsored, left-wing, right-wing, and anarchist groups. The findings and recommendations of special committees and government bodies that have focused on terrorism in recent years are also discussed, and online links to the full text of their reports are provided.

The ninth edition, which is now available in a variety of print and electronic formats, presents historical and modern criminological approaches with the aid of real-life stories, up-to-date examples and issues, and interactive media. Key features include

Who's to Blame boxes in each chapter highlight the book's ever-evolving theme of social problems versus social responsibility, a hallmark feature of this text. In each chapter, Who's to Blame boxes build on this theme by illustrating some of the issues that challenge criminologists and policy makers today. Each box includes a case study followed by critical thinking questions that ask readers to ponder to what extent the individual or society is responsible for a given crime.

Theory versus Reality boxes throughout the text showcase selected issues and theories in the field of criminology and invite discussion through thought-provoking questions for consideration.

Criminal Profiles boxes throughout the text offer insights into the lives and criminal motivations of notorious offenders, such as Ross Ulbricht (founder of Silk Road, the underground website); Omar Mateen (the Pulse Nightclub shooter); Jodi Arias, Colton Harris-Moore (the Barefoot Bandit), and Bernie Madoff.

Crime in the News boxes in each chapter present case examples and pose analytical discussion questions about connections between examples and the chapter topics.

Theory in Perspective summary boxes in Parts 2 and 3 outline the main points of various theories for easy reference and study.

In the past few years, crime and criminals have changed in ways that few people had previously imagined would occur, and these changes hold considerable significance for each one of us and for our nation as a whole. It is my hope that this new edition, which is available in a number of formats, will help today's students both to understand the nature of these changes and to find a meaningful place in the social world that is to come.

FRANK SCHMALLEGER, Ph.D.
Distinguished Professor Emeritus
The University of North Carolina at Pembroke

Supplements

Instructor Supplements

Instructor's Manual with Test Bank. Includes content outlines for classroom discussion, teaching suggestions, and answers to selected end-of-chapter questions from the text. This also contains a Word document version of the test bank.

TestGen. This computerized test generation system gives you maximum flexibility in creating and administering tests on paper, electronically, or online. It provides state-of-the-art features for viewing and editing test bank questions, dragging a selected question into a test you are creating, and printing sleek, formatted tests in a variety of layouts. Select test items from test banks included with TestGen for quick test creation, or write your own questions from scratch. Test Gen's random generator provides the option to display different text or calculated number values each time questions are used.

PowerPoint Presentations. Our presentations offer clear, straightforward outlines and notes to use for class lectures or study materials. Photos, illustrations, charts, and tables from the book are included in the presentations when applicable.

Annotated Instructor's Edition (AIE). The AIE of *Criminology Today,* 9e contains notes in the top margins identifying key topics with suggestions for stimulating and guiding class discussion.

To access supplementary materials online, instructors need to request a free instructor access code. Go to **www.pearsonhighered.com/irc**, where you can register for an instructor access code. Within 48 hours after registering, you will receive a confirming email, including an instructor access code. Once you have received your code, go to the site and log on for full instructions on downloading the materials you wish to use.

Alternative Versions

eBooks This text is also available in multiple eBook formats. These are an exciting new choice for students looking to save money. As an alternative to purchasing the printed textbook, students can purchase an electronic version of the same content. With an eTextbook, students can search the text, make notes online, print out reading assignments that incorporate lecture notes, and bookmark important passages for later review. For more information, visit your favorite online eBook reseller or visit **www.mypearsonstore.com**.

REVEL for Criminology Today, Ninth Edition by Frank Schmalleger

Designed for the way today's Criminal Justice students read, think and learn
REVEL offers an immersive learning experience that engages students deeply, while giving them the flexibility to learn their way. Media interactives and assessments integrated directly within the narrative enable students to delve into key concepts and reflect on their learning without breaking stride.

REVEL seamlessly combines the full content of Pearson's bestselling criminal justice titles with multimedia learning tools. You assign the topics your students cover. Author Explanatory Videos, application exercises, and short quizzes engage students and enhance their understanding of core topics as they progress through the content.

Instead of simply reading about criminal justice topics, REVEL empowers students to think critically about important concepts by completing application exercises, watching Point/CounterPoint videos, and participating in shared writing (discussion board) assignments.

Track time-on-task throughout the course The Performance Dashboard allows you to see how much time the class or individual students have spent reading a section or doing an assignment, as well as points earned per assignment. This data helps correlate study time with performance and provides a window into where students may be having difficulty with the material.

Learning Management System Integration Pearson provides both Blackboard Learn™ and Canvas™ integration, giving institutions, instructors, and students easy access to Revel. Our Revel integration delivers streamlined access to everything your students need for the course in the Blackboard Learn and Canvas environments.

The REVEL App The REVEL App further empowers students to access their course materials wherever and whenever they want. With the REVEL App, students can access REVEL directly from their tablet or mobile device, offline and online. Reminders and notifications can be set so you never miss a deadline. Work done on the REVEL app syncs up to the browser version, ensuring that no one misses a beat. Visit **www .pearsonhighered.com/revel/**

Acknowledgments

A book like *Criminology Today* draws on the talents and resources of many people and is the end result of much previous effort. This text could not have been written without the groundwork laid by previous criminologists, academics, and researchers; hence, a hearty thank-you is due everyone who has contributed to the development of the field of criminology throughout the years, especially to those theorists, authors, and social commentators who are cited in this book. Without their work, the field would be that much poorer. I would like to thank, as well, all the adopters—professors and students alike—of my previous textbooks, for they have given me the encouragement and fostered the steadfastness required to write this new edition of *Criminology Today*.

The Pearson team members, many of whom I have come to know very well and all of whom have worked so professionally with me on this and other projects, deserve special thanks. The team includes Gary Bauer, Lynda Cramer, Maura Barclay, Bob Nisbet, and Heather Taylor. My thanks to the photo researcher Amanda Larkin, whose efforts have helped make *Criminology Today* both attractive and visually appealing. Finally, my sincere thanks to project manager Abinaya Rajendran at Integra for her very capable handling of numerous details.

My friends and professional colleagues Ellen G. Cohn at Florida International University, Cassandra Renzi at Keiser University, and Karel Kurst-Swanger at Oswego State University helped in many ways. Dr. Cohn graciously used her deep personal creativity in enhancing the supplements package and creating quality products; she has the exceptional ability of building intuitively on concepts in the text. Thanks also to Bob Winslow at California State University–San Diego for insight and encouragement on a number of important issues and to Jack Humphrey at St. Anselm College and Stephen J. Schoenthaler for their valuable suggestions in the preparation of this new edition.

This book has benefited greatly from the quick availability of information and other resources through online services and in various locations on the Internet's World Wide Web. I am grateful to the many information providers who, although they are too numerous to list, have helped establish such useful resources.

I am thankful as well for the assistance of Prof. Bill Tafoya (retired FBI) and Nancy Carnes of the Federal Bureau of Investigation; E. Ann Carson at the Bureau of Justice Statistics; William Ballweber at the National Institute of Justice; David Beatty, director of public affairs with the National Victim Center; Kris Rose at the National Criminal Justice Reference Service; Marilyn Marbrook and Michael Rand at the Office of Justice Programs; Mark Reading at the Drug Enforcement Administration; and Barbara Maxwell at *USA Today*.

Many manuscript reviewers have contributed to the development of *Criminology Today*. I offer my thanks to the following reviewers for the ninth edition:

Elizabeth Bondurant, Mercer County Community College
Tomasina Cook, Erie Community College
Eugene Matthews, Park University

I also thank the following reviewers for previous editions:

Reed Adams, East Carolina State University
Michael P. Brown, Ball State University
Gregg Buchholz, Keiser University
Bryan D. Byers, Ball State University
Dianne Carmody, Old Dominon University
Steven M. Christiansen, Joliet Junior College
Myrna Cintron, Texas A&M University
Patrick G. Donnelly, University of Dayton
Ronald D. Hunter, State University of West Georgia
Steven Johnson, Eastern Arizona College
Daniel D. Jones, University of Washington
John Kirkpatrick, University of New Hampshire
Joan Luxenburg, University of Central Oklahoma
M. Joan McDermott, Southern Illinois University
William McGovern, Sussex County Community College
Darrell K. Mills, Pima Community College (East Campus)
Robert Mutchnick, Indiana University of Pennsylvania
Michael Pittaro, Lehigh Valley College
Glen E. Sapp, Central Carolina Community College
Jennifer L. Schulenberg, Sam Houston State University
Louis Shepard, West Georgia Technical College
John Siler, Georgia Perimeter College
Tamson L. Six, Lock Haven University
Dianne Williams, North Carolina A&T State University
Jeffrey Zack, Fayetteville Technical Community College
Anthony W. Zumpetta, West Chester University

Finally, but by no means least, I am indebted to a small but very special group of contemporary criminologists who have laid the foundation for our discipline's presence on the Internet. Among them are Cecil Greek at Florida State University, whose online lecture notes (**www.criminology.fsu.edu/crimtheory**) are massively informative; Tom O'Connor of Austin Peay State University, whose Megalinks in Criminal Justice site provides an amazingly comprehensive resource; Matthew Robinson at Appalachian State University, whose Crime Theory links allow visitors to vote on what they think are the causes of crime; and Bruce Hoffman, whose former Crime Theory site at the University of Washington offers many great insights into the field. All of these excellent resources were very useful in writing this book—and it is to these modern-day visionaries that *Criminology Today* owes much of its technological depth.

About the Author

Frank Schmalleger, Ph.D., is Professor Emeritus at The University of North Carolina at Pembroke, where he also was recognized as Distinguished Professor. Dr. Schmalleger holds degrees from the University of Notre Dame and The Ohio State University; he earned both a master's (1970) and a doctorate (1974) in sociology, with a special emphasis in criminology, from The Ohio State University. From 1976 to 1994, he taught criminology and criminal justice courses at The University of North Carolina at Pembroke, and for the last 16 of those years, he chaired the university's Department of Sociology, Social Work, and Criminal Justice. As an adjunct professor with Webster University in St. Louis, Missouri, Schmalleger helped develop the university's graduate program in security administration and loss prevention and taught courses in that curriculum for more than a decade. He has also taught in the New School for Social Research's online graduate program, helping build the world's first electronic classrooms in support of distance learning through computer telecommunications.

Schmalleger is the author of numerous articles as well as many books: *Criminal Justice Today: An Introductory Text for the 21st Century* (Pearson, 2016), now in its 14th edition; *Juvenile Delinquency*, 9th edition (with Clemmens Bartollas; Pearson, 2014); *Criminal Justice: A Brief Introduction*, 11th edition (Pearson, 2016); *Criminal Law Today*, 6th edition (Pearson, 2016); *Corrections in the Twenty-First Century* (with John Smykla; McGraw-Hill, 2015); *Crime and the Justice System in America: An Encyclopedia* (Greenwood Publishing Group, 1997); *Trial of the Century: People of the State of California vs. Orenthal James Simpson* (Prentice Hall, 1996); *Career Paths: A Guide to Jobs in Federal Law Enforcement* (Regents/Prentice Hall, 1994); *Computers in Criminal Justice* (Wyndham Hall Press, 1991); *Criminal Justice Ethics* (Greenwood Press, 1991); *Finding Criminal Justice in the Library* (Wyndham Hall Press, 1991); *Ethics in Criminal Justice* (Wyndham Hall Press, 1990); *A History of Corrections* (Foundations Press of Notre Dame, 1983); and *The Social Basis of Criminal Justice* (University Press of America, 1981). He is also the founding editor of the journal *Criminal Justice Studies* (formerly *The Justice Professional*).

Schmalleger's philosophy of both teaching and writing can be summed up in these words: "In order to communicate knowledge we must first catch, then hold, a person's interest—be it student, colleague, or policy maker. Our writing, our speaking, and our teaching must be relevant to the problems facing people today, and they must—in some way—help solve those problems." Visit Schmalleger's Amazon author page at: **http://amazon.com/author/frankschmalleger**. Follow his tweets **@schmalleger.**

Fox/Getty Images

CHAPTER 1

WHAT IS CRIMINOLOGY

Understanding Crime and Criminals

LEARNING OUTCOMES

After reading this chapter, you should be able to answer the following questions:

- What is crime? What is the definition of crime that the author of this text has chosen to use?

- What is deviance? How are crime and deviance similar? How do they differ?

- Who decides what should be criminal? How are such decisions made?

- What is criminology? What are its many roots?

- What do criminologists do?

- What is evidence-based criminology? How does it complement theoretical criminology?

- How does criminology, and especially criminological research, influence social policy? What is translational criminology?

- What is the theme of this text? Upon what two contrasting viewpoints does it build?

- What is the social context of crime? What are crime's consequences?

- What social science has traditionally provided a central theoretical basis for criminology? Why?

Introduction

According to social commentators, people are simultaneously attracted to and repulsed by crime—especially gruesome crimes involving extreme personal violence. The popularity of today's TV crime shows, Hollywood-produced crime movies, true-crime books and magazines, and Web sites devoted exclusively to the coverage of crime supports that observation. The CBS TV megahit *NCIS*, for example, was recently named the number one TV drama and received an impressive three nominations for TV's People's Choice Award.[1] The show was also nominated as the "Favorite TV Crime Drama," with individual episodes drawing more than 24 million viewers.[2] Earlier, *CSI: Miami*, which ran for ten seasons until ending in 2012, garnered 50 million regular viewers in more than 55 countries. By its eighth season it had become the most popular television show in the world.[3]

Other widely followed TV crime series, both past and present, include shows such as *True Detective* (HBO), *American Crime* (ABC), *Backstrom* (Fox), *Battle Creek* (CBS), *Bosch* (Amazon Prime), *Fargo* (FX), *Bones* (Fox), *Grimm* (NBC), *Castle* (ABC), *Criminal Minds* (CBS), *Blue Bloods* (CBS), *Without a Trace* (CBS), *CSI: Cyber* (CBS), *Lucifer* (Fox), *Magic City* (HBO), *The Unit* (CBS), *The Killing* (AMC), *White Collar* (USA), *The District* (CBS), *Boardwalk Empire* (HBO), *The Shield* (FX), *The Wire* (HBO), *Cold Case* (CBS), *NCIS* (CBS), *Homeland* (Showtime), and *Law and Order* (NBC)—along with the *Law and Order* spin-offs, *Law and Order: Criminal Intent* and *Law and Order: Special Victims Unit*. American TV viewers are hungry for crime-related entertainment and have a fascination with criminal motivation and detective work.

Most crimes cry out for explanation. Yet one of the things that fascinates people about crime—especially violent crime—is that much of it seems to be inexplicable. Some crimes are especially difficult to understand, but our natural tendency is to seek out some reason for the unreasonable. We search for explanations for the seemingly unexplainable. How, for example, can the behavior of child killers be understood, anticipated, and even prevented? Why don't terrorists acknowledge the emotional and personal suffering they inflict? Why do some robbers or rapists kill and even torture, utterly disregarding human life and feelings?

People also wonder about "everyday" crimes such as burglary, robbery, assault, vandalism, and computer intrusion. Why, for example, do people fight? Does it matter to a robber that he may face prison time? How can people sacrifice love, money, careers, and even their lives for access to illegal drugs?

A photo from the highly popular CBS TV show *NCIS*. Shown from left to right are Sean Murray, Brian Dietzen, and Pauley Perrette. Why do many people like to watch TV crime shows like *NCIS*?

What motivates terrorists to give up their own lives to take the lives of others? Why do gifted techno-savvy teens and preteens hack sites on the Internet thought to be secure? While this text may not answer each of these questions, it examines the causative factors in effect when a crime is committed and encourages an appreciation of the challenges of crafting effective crime-control policy.

What Is Crime?

As the word implies, *criminology* is clearly concerned with *crime*. As we begin our discussion of criminology, let's consider just what the term *crime* means (Table 1-1). Like anything else, crime can be defined in several ways, and some scholars have suggested that at least four definitional perspectives can be found in contemporary criminology. These diverse perspectives see crime from (1) legalistic, (2) political, (3) sociological, and (4) psychological viewpoints. How we see any phenomenon is crucial because it determines the assumptions that we make about how that phenomenon should be studied. The perspective that we choose to employ when viewing crime determines the kinds of questions we ask, the nature of the research we

■ **crime** Human conduct in violation of the criminal laws of the federal government, a state, or a local jurisdiction that has the power to make such laws.

■ **criminalize** To make illegal.

TABLE 1-1 | **What Is Crime?**

Depending on how we look at it, "crime" can be understood in various ways. The four major perspectives useful in defining crime are:

The Legalistic
According to the legalistic perspective, crime is:
human conduct in violation of the criminal laws of a state, the federal government, or a local jurisdiction that has the power to make such laws. Seen this way, if there is no law against it, there can be no crime, no matter how deviant or socially repugnant the behavior in question may be.

The Political
According to the political perspective, crime is:
the result of criteria that have been built into the law by powerful groups which are then used to label selected undesirable forms of behavior as illegal. Seen this way, laws serve the interests of the politically powerful, and crimes are merely forms of behavior that are perceived by those in power as direct or indirect threats to their interests.

The Sociological (aka sociolegal)
According to the sociological (or sociolegal) perspective, crime is:
an antisocial act of such a nature that its repression is necessary for the preservation of the existing social order. From this viewpoint, crime is primarily an offense against human relationships, and secondarily a violation of the law.

The Psychological
According to the psychological point of view, crime is:
a form of social maladjustment, especially one which is against the law, that can be seen as a difficulty that an individual has in remaining in harmony with his or her social environment. Seen this way, crime is problem behavior for both the individual and for society.

Source: Pearson Education, Inc.

---

conduct, and the type of answers that we expect to receive. Those answers, in turn, influence our conclusions about the kinds of crime-control policies that might be effective.

> Without a law that circumscribes a particular form of behavior, there can be no crime....

Seen from a legalistic perspective, **crime** is *human conduct in violation of the criminal laws of a state, the federal government, or a local jurisdiction that has the power to make such laws.* Without a law that circumscribes a particular form of behavior, there can be no crime, no matter how deviant or socially repugnant the behavior in question may be.

The notion of crime as behavior[4] that violates the law derives from earlier work by criminologists like Paul W. Tappan, who defined crime as "an intentional act in violation of the criminal law committed without defense or excuse, and

penalized by the state as a felony or misdemeanor."[5] Edwin Sutherland, regarded by many as a founding figure in American criminology, said of crime that its "essential characteristic is that it is behavior which is prohibited by the State as an injury to the State and against which the State may react by punishment."[6]

For purposes of this text, we will employ a legalistic approach because it allows for relative ease of measurement of crimes committed. Official statistics on crime, such as those shown in Figure 1–1, report crime in terms of legislatively established categories, and the number of offenses shown reflect statutory definitions of crime categories.

A serious shortcoming of the legalistic approach to crime, however, is that it yields the moral high ground to powerful individuals who are able to influence the making of laws and the imposition of criminal definitions on lawbreakers. By making their own laws, powerful but immoral individuals can escape the label "criminal." While we have chosen to adopt the legalistic approach to crime in this text, it is important to realize that laws are social products, so crime is *socially relative* in the sense that it is created by legislative activity. Hence, sociologists are fond of saying that "crime is whatever a society says it is." In Chapter 8, we will explore this issue further and will focus on the process of criminalization, which is the method used to **criminalize** some forms of behavior—or make them illegal—while other forms remain legitimate.

A second perspective on crime is the political one, where crime is the result of criteria that have been built into the law by powerful groups and are then used to label selected undesirable forms of behavior as illegal. Those who adhere to this point of view say that crime is a definition of human conduct created by authorized agents in a politically organized society. Seen this way, laws serve the interests of the politically powerful, and crimes are merely forms of behavior that are perceived by those in power as direct or indirect threats to their interests. Thus, the political perspective defines crime in terms of the power structures that exist in society and asserts that criminal laws do not

Per 100,000 population

1980 Crime rate peaks at 5,950

1991 Second high of 5,898

1992 First baby boomers reach age 45, leaving the crime-prone years

1963 First baby boomers reach age 17, entering the crime-prone years

2016 Crime rates drop to a 40-year low

Dollar limit for larceny is removed; measurement change results in rate increase

FIGURE 1-1 │ Crime Rates in the United States, 1933–2016

Source: FBI, Uniform Crime Reports, various years.

necessarily bear any inherent relationship to popular notions of right and wrong.

Even though political processes that create criminal definitions are sometimes easier to comprehend in totalitarian societies, the political perspective can also be meaningfully applied to American society. John F. Galliher, a contemporary criminologist, summarized the political perspective on crime when he wrote, "One can best understand crime in a class-structured society such as the United States as the end product of a chain of interactions involving powerful groups that use their power to establish criminal laws and sanctions against less powerful persons and groups that may pose a threat to the group in power."[7] Galliher points out that, because legal definitions of criminality are arrived at through a political process, the subject matter of criminality will be artificially limited if we insist on seeing crime solely as a violation of the criminal law.

Some criminologists insist that the field of criminology must include behaviors that go beyond those defined as crimes through the political process; not doing so, they say, restricts rather than encourages inquiry into relevant forms of human behavior.[8]

Adherents of the third perspective, the sociological (also called "sociolegal") viewpoint, would likely agree with this statement, seeing crime as "an antisocial act of such a nature that its repression is necessary or is supposed to be necessary to the preservation of the existing system of society."[9] Some

criminologists have gone so far as to claim that any definition of crime must include all forms of antisocial behavior.[10] Ron Claassen, a modern-day champion of restorative justice (discussed in more detail in Chapters 9 and 10), suggested, for example, that "crime is primarily an offense against human relationships, and secondarily a violation of a law—since laws are written to protect safety and fairness in human relationships."[11]

A more comprehensive sociological definition of crime was offered by Herman Schwendinger and Julia Schwendinger in 1975: Crime encompasses "any harmful acts," including violations of "the fundamental prerequisites for well-being, [such as] food, shelter, clothing, medical services, challenging work and recreational experiences, as well as security from predatory individuals or repressive and imperialistic elites."[12] The Schwendingers challenged criminologists to be less constrained in what they see as the subject matter of their field, saying that violations of human rights may be more relevant to criminological inquiry than many acts that have been politically or legally defined as crime. "Isn't it time to raise serious questions about the assumptions underlying the definitions of the field of criminology," asked the Schwendingers, "when a man who steals a paltry sum can be called a criminal while agents of the State can, with impunity, legally reward men who destroy food so that price levels can be maintained whilst a sizable portion of the population suffers from malnutrition?"[13]

Criminal behavior is typically associated with personal features such as impulsivity, risky decision making, antisocial demeanor, and aggression, as well as biological and social risk factors that are mediated by genes and by the social and physical environments.

Jeffrey H. Reiman, another contemporary criminologist, asked similar questions. "The fact is that the label 'crime' is not used in America to name all or the worst of the actions that cause misery and suffering to Americans," said Reiman. "It is primarily reserved for the dangerous actions of the poor." Writing about unhealthy and unsafe workplaces, Reiman asked, "Doesn't a crime by any other name still cause misery and suffering? What's in a name?"[14] While a sociolegal approach to understanding crime is attractive to many, others claim that it suffers from wanting to criminalize activities that cause only indirect harm; that is, it is easier for most people to appreciate the criminality involved in a holdup or a rape than in cost-cutting efforts made by a businessperson.

Finally, a psychological (or maladaptive) perspective says that "crime is a form of social maladjustment which can be designated as a more or less pronounced difficulty that the individual has in reacting to the stimuli of his environment in such a way as to remain in harmony with that environment."[15] Seen this way, crime is problem behavior, especially human activity that contravenes the criminal law and results in difficulties in living within a framework of generally acceptable social arrangements. According to criminologist Matthew B. Robinson, "[t]he maladaptive view of crime does not require any of the [traditional] elements in order for an act to be a crime: no actual harm to others; no prohibition by law before the act is committed; no arrest; and no conviction in a court of law. Any behavior which is maladaptive would be considered crime. If criminologists adopted this view of crime," said Robinson, "the scope of criminology would be greatly expanded beyond its current state. All actually or even potentially harmful behaviors could be examined, analyzed, and documented for the purpose of gaining knowledge about potentially harmful behaviors and developing strategies to protect people from all harmful acts, not just those that are called 'crime' today."[16]

A young woman smoking marijuana. What is crime? Is her behavior against the law?

As this discussion shows, a unified or simple definition of crime is difficult to achieve. The four points of view that we have discussed here form a kind of continuum, bound on one end by strict, legalistic interpretations of crime and on the other by much more fluid, behavioral, and moralistic definitions.

No matter which definition we choose, it is important to recognize that most criminal behavior is typically associated with personal features such as impulsivity, risky decision making, antisocial demeanor, and aggression, as well as biological and social risk factors that are mediated by genes and by the social and physical environments.[17] Hence, in seeking to understand crime and its causes, we must also examine the various kinds of behavior that are most likely to be associated with it. In other words, while aggression and risk taking are not necessarily against the law, they are also characteristic of many types of crime, and their understanding can provide insight into criminal motivation.

Crime and Deviance

Sociologically speaking, many crimes can be regarded as deviant forms of behavior—that is, as behaviors that are in some way abnormal. Piers Beirne and James Messerschmidt, two contemporary criminologists, defined deviance as "any social behavior or social characteristic that departs from the conventional norms and standards of a community or society and for which the deviant is sanctioned."[18] Their definition does not count as deviant, however, any sanctionable behavior that is not punished or punishable. Hence, we prefer another approach to defining

■ **deviant behavior**   Human activity that violates social norms.

■ **delinquency**   A term often used in conjunction with crime and deviance, it refers to violations of the criminal law and other misbehavior committed by young people.

deviance. The definition of **deviant behavior** that we will use in this text is as follows: *Deviant behavior is human activity that violates social norms.*

Abnormality, deviance, and crime are concepts that do not always easily mesh. Some forms of deviance are not violations of the criminal law, and the reverse is equally true (see Figure 1–2). Deviant styles of dress, for example, although perhaps outlandish to the majority, are generally not circumscribed by criminal law unless (perhaps) decency statutes are violated by a lack of clothing. Even in such cases, laws are subject to interpretation and may be modified as social norms change over time.

Some years ago, for example, a judge in Palm Beach County, Florida, held that a city ordinance barring the wearing of baggy pants was unconstitutional.[19] County Judge Laura Johnson ruled that no matter how "tacky or distasteful" baggy pants might be to others, they were merely a fashion statement and that wearing them, especially when no nudity is involved, is a freedom protected under the Fourteenth Amendment to the U.S. Constitution. The ordinance had been overwhelmingly approved by voters only two years earlier. More recently, San Francisco's Board of Supervisors voted to ban total public nudity in their city.[20] The vote came in late 2012 after a series of complaints had been received about men and women strolling through the city's Castro neighborhood without any clothes, and sipping drinks at the city's coffee shops. The local legislation, however, exempted nudity at private beaches and within permitted special events.

Some types of behavior, although quite common, are still against the law, even though those who engage in them might not think of them as deviant. Living and working in the United States as an undocumented alien, for example, although relatively common, is a violation of federal law; but most people who engage in such behavior probably don't think of themselves as "deviant" or "criminal" (although they may still worry about getting "caught" and being deported). Complicating matters still further is the fact that certain behaviors are illegal in some jurisdictions but not in others.

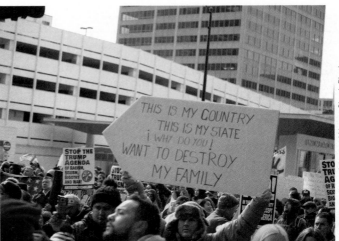

The Perspective of James/Alamy Stock Photo

Protestors in San Francisco demanding that the city retain its "sanctuary" status, which allows undocumented migrants to remain in the city without fear of deportation by federal authorities. Why do some people call undocumented migrants "illegals"?

For example, commercialized gambling, especially gambling involving slot machines and games of chance, is against the law in many parts of the United States but has been legitimized in Nevada, on some Indian reservations, on cruise ships operating outside U.S. territorial waters, on some Mississippi riverboats, and in some state-sponsored locales. Even state governments, seeking to enhance revenues, have gotten into the gambling business through state lotteries, which now operate in 44 states,[21] and many states have laws specifically forbidding participation in online gambling, due largely to their interest in protecting their own lottery revenues. Similarly, prostitution, which is almost uniformly illegal in the United States, is an activity that is fully within the law in parts of Nevada as long as it occurs within licensed brothels and as long as those engaged in the activity meet state licensing requirements and abide by state laws that require condom use and weekly medical checkups. The criminal status of recreational marijuana use also varies between states—a situation discussed in more detail in a Crime in the News box in this chapter.

Finally, we should add that **delinquency**, a term often used in conjunction with crime and deviance, refers to violations of the criminal law and other misbehavior committed by young people. The laws of many states proclaim that "youth" ends at a person's eighteenth birthday, although others specify the sixteenth or seventeenth birthday as meeting that requirement. All states, however, specify certain offenses, like running away from home, being ungovernable, and drinking alcohol, as illegal for children, but not for adults.

Illegal   Illegal and Deviant   Deviant

FIGURE 1-2 | **The Overlap between Deviance and Crime**

Source: Schmalleger, Frank, *Criminology.* Printed and Electronically reproduced by permission of Pearson Education, Inc., Upper Saddle River, New Jersey ISBN 0132966751.

■ **consensus perspective**   A viewpoint that holds that laws should be enacted to criminalize given forms of behavior when members of society generally agree that such laws are necessary.

■ **pluralist perspective**   A viewpoint that says that behaviors are typically criminalized through a political process only after debate over the appropriate course of action.

What Should Be Criminal?

By now, you have probably realized that the question "What is crime?" differs from the question "What should be criminal?"

The consensus viewpoint holds that laws should be enacted to criminalize given forms of behavior when members of society generally agree that such laws are necessary.

While the question "What should be criminal?" can be answered in many different ways, the social and intellectual processes by which an answer is reached can be found in two contrasting points of view: (1) the consensus perspective and (2) the pluralist perspective.

The **consensus perspective** holds that laws should be enacted to criminalize given forms of behavior when members of society generally agree that such laws are necessary. The consensus perspective (described in greater detail in Chapter 9) is most applicable to homogeneous societies, or those characterized by shared values, norms, and belief systems. In a multicultural and diverse society like the United States, however, a shared consensus may be difficult to achieve. In such a society, even relatively minor matters may lead to complex debates over the issues involved, and these debates show just how difficult it is to achieve a consensus over even relatively minor matters in a society as complex as our own.

The second perspective, the **pluralist perspective** of crime (also described in more detail in Chapter 9) recognizes the importance of diversity in societies like ours. It says that behaviors are typically criminalized through a political process only after debate over the appropriate course of action. The political process often takes the form of legislation and may involve appellate court action (by those who don't agree with the legislation). In 2017, for example, President Donald Trump tweeted that "Nobody should be allowed to burn the American Flag."[22] The president threatened loss of citizenship or jail for anyone who burned a U.S. flag.

Protesters burning an American flag. President Trump has sought to make flag-burning a crime, while the U.S. Supreme Court has held that it is a form of protected free speech. Which is it? Which *should* it be?

Years earlier, however, the U.S. Supreme Court held that flag burnings are protected under the constitution as a form of free speech. Similarly, legislatures at both the state and federal levels continue to reexamine gun laws to see if new laws are needed to keep guns out of the hands of potential mass killers. Given the diversity of perspectives that characterize our society, however, agreement over gun laws is not easy to reach. Learn more about both sides of the gun-control debate via **http://www.bradycampaign.org** and **http://home.nra.org**.

CRIME | in the NEWS

What Should Be Criminal?

Most people agree that certain forms of behavior, such as murder, rape, burglary, and theft, should be against the law, but there is far less agreement about the appropriate legal status of things like abortion, gay marriage, gambling, gun ownership, drug use, and other controversial forms of behavior.

One issue that has been trending both in the political arena and on social media is the legalization of marijuana. While drug use and abuse will be discussed in greater detail in Chapter 14, the present wave of legislation to legalize marijuana for both medical and recreational purposes (Figure 1–3) provides a good example of the difficulty in deciding what should or should not be considered criminal.

While existing federal law provides strict penalties for marijuana possession, production, sale, or use, a number of U.S. jurisdictions have recently modified their laws to legalize the possession of small amounts of marijuana for personal use. Most of these new laws, while they permit either recreational or medical marijuana use, prohibit the substance from being consumed in public, and limit the amount (and sometimes the form) allowed. As with other substances that may affect reaction time and judgment, jurisdictions that have expanded the legal availability of marijuana prohibit operating a motor vehicle while under the influence, and do not permit marijuana intoxication to be used as a defense against criminal charges.

Although many observers expect marijuana legalization to soon expand to additional states, disparities between federal and state laws, and battles between opposing sides in state and federal courts, may yet lead to a rolling back of the movement toward marijuana legalization. See Chapter 14 for more details on both the historical and current issues involved in marijuana legalization.

Discussion Questions

1. How do you feel about the legalization of marijuana for personal recreational use?

2. Would you want to live in a state in which marijuana is legal? Why or why not?

Source: Sara G. Miller, "3 More States Legalize Recreational Use of Marijuana; How the Map Looks Now," Live Science, November 9, 2016, http://www.livescience.com/56807-recreational-marijuana-california-massachusetts-nevada.html; and Statista, "The States Where It's Legal to Smoke Marijuana, Statista, August 14, 2017 (https://www.statista.com/chart/6681/the-states-where-its-legal-to-smoke-marijuana).

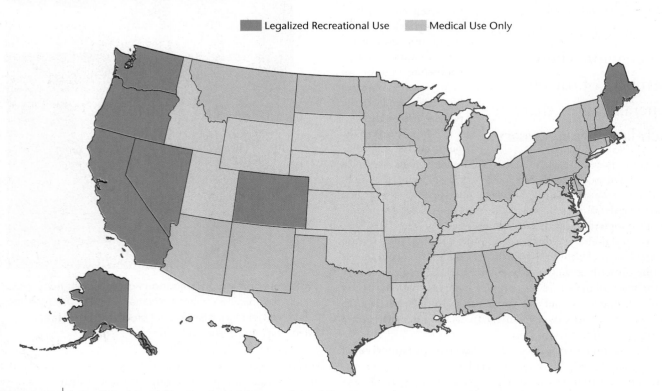

■ Legalized Recreational Use   ■ Medical Use Only

FIGURE 1-3 | Legal Status of Medical and Recreational Marijuana Use in the United States

Sources: Niall McCarthy, Statista, "The States Where It's Legal to Smoke Marijuana", Statista, August 14, 2017 (https://www.statista.com/chart/6681/the-states-where-its-legal-to-smoke-marijuana).

■ **social policy** A government initiative, program, or plan intended to address problems in society. The war on crime, for example, is a kind of generic (large-scale) social policy—one consisting of many smaller programs.

What Is Criminology?

The attempt to understand crime and deviance predates written history. Prehistoric evidence, including skeletal remains showing signs of primitive cranial surgery, seems to indicate that preliterate people explained deviant behavior by reference to spirit possession. Primitive surgery was an attempt to release unwanted spiritual influences. In the thousands of years since, many other theoretical perspectives on crime have been advanced. This text describes various criminological theories and covers some of the more popular ones in detail.

Defining "Criminology"

Before beginning any earnest discussion, however, it is necessary to define the term *criminology*. As our earlier discussion of the nature of crime and deviance indicates, not only must criminologists deal with a complex subject matter—consisting of a broad range of illegal behaviors committed by frequently unknown or uncooperative individuals—but they also must manage their work under changing conditions mandated by ongoing revisions of the law and fluctuating **social policy**. In addition, as we have already seen, a wide variety of perspectives on the nature of crime abound and new ones are entering the literature all the time. All this leads to considerable difficulties in defining the subject matter under study.

There is some evidence that the term *criminology* was coined by a Frenchman, Paul Topinard, in 1889;[23] he used it to differentiate the study of criminal body types within the field of anthropology from other biometric pursuits.[24] While he may have coined the term, Topinard did little to help define it. As with the concept of crime, various definitions of criminology can be found in the literature today. About two decades ago, criminologist Joseph F. Sheley wrote, "There seem to be nearly as many definitions of *contemporary criminology* as there are criminologists."[25]

One straightforward definition can be had from a linguistic analysis of the word *criminology*. As most people know, *-ology* means "the study of something," and the word *crimen* comes from the Latin, meaning "accusation," "charge," or "guilt." Hence, linguistically speaking, the term *criminology* literally means "the study of criminal accusations," that is, "the study of crime." In addition to this fundamental kind of linguistic definition, three other important types of definitions can be found in the literature: (1) disciplinary, (2) causative, and (3) scientific. Each type of definition is distinguished by its focus. Disciplinary definitions are those that, as their name implies, focus on criminology as a discipline. Seen from this viewpoint, criminology is a field of study or a body of knowledge. Some of the earliest criminologists of the past century, including Edwin H. Sutherland, who is often referred to as the "dean of American criminology," offered definitions of their field that emphasized its importance as a discipline of study. Sutherland, for example, wrote in the first edition of his textbook *Criminology* in 1924, "Criminology is the body of knowledge regarding the social problem of crime."[26] Sutherland's text was to set the stage for much of American criminology throughout the rest of the twentieth century. Reprinted in 1934 with the title *Principles of Criminology*,[27] it was to become the most influential textbook ever written in the field of criminology.[28]

Although Sutherland died in 1950, his revered text was revised for many years by Donald R. Cressey and later by David F. Luckenbill. By 1974, Sutherland's classic definition of criminology had been modified by Cressey: "Criminology is the body of knowledge regarding delinquency and crime as a social phenomenon. It includes within its scope the processes of making laws, of breaking laws, and of reacting toward the breaking of laws."[29]

Causative definitions emphasize criminology's role in uncovering the underlying causes of crime. In keeping with such an emphasis, contemporary criminologists Gennaro F. Vito and Ronald M. Holmes stated, "Criminology is the study of the causes of crime."[30]

> There is some evidence that the term *criminology* was coined by a Frenchman, Paul Topinard, in 1889....

Finally, some point to the scientific nature of contemporary criminology as its distinguishing characteristic. According to Clemens Bartollas and Simon Dinitz, for example, "[c]riminology is the scientific study of crime."[31] Writing in 1989, Bartollas and Dinitz seemed to be echoing an earlier definition of criminology offered by Marvin E. Wolfgang and Franco Ferracuti, who wrote in 1967, "Criminology is the scientific study of crime, criminals, and criminal behavior."[32]

One of the most comprehensive definitions of the term *criminology* that is available today comes from the European Society of Criminology (ESC), which in its constitution defines *criminology* as "all scholarly, scientific and professional knowledge concerning the explanation, prevention, control and treatment

■ **criminology**   An interdisciplinary profession built around the scientific study of crime and criminal behavior, including their forms, causes, legal aspects, and control.

■ **criminality**   A behavioral predisposition that disproportionately favors criminal activity.

■ **criminal behavior**   Human activity, both intentional and negligent, that violates the criminal law. It may include a failure to act when there is a legal obligation to do so.

of crime and delinquency, offenders and victims, including the measurement and detection of crime, legislation, and the practice of criminal law, and law enforcement, judicial, and correctional systems."[33] ESC's emphasis is on "knowledge"; even though it mentions the "practice" of what many would call criminal justice (i.e., policing, courts, and corrections), it is the study and knowledge of such practice that form the crux of the ESC perspective.

For our purposes, we will use a definition somewhat simpler than that of the ESC but one that brings together the works of previous writers and also recognizes the increasingly professional status of the criminological enterprise. Throughout this text, then, we will say that **criminology** is *an interdisciplinary profession built around the scientific study of crime and criminal behavior, including their forms, causes, legal aspects, and control.* As this definition indicates, criminology includes consideration of possible solutions to the problem of crime. Hence, this text (in later chapters) describes treatment strategies and social policy initiatives that have grown out of the existing array of theoretical explanations for crime.

Our definition is in keeping with the work of Jack P. Gibbs, a notable contemporary criminologist, who writes that the *purpose* of criminology is to offer well-researched and objective answers to four basic questions: (1) "Why do crime rates vary?" (2) "Why do individuals differ as to criminality?" (3) "Why is there variation in reactions to crime?" and (4) "What are the possible means of controlling criminality?"[34] It is important to note that our definition and Gibbs's guiding queries encompass a number of different terms that are sometimes easily confused. Criminology, **criminality**, crime, deviance, and **criminal behavior** are five concepts used in this chapter and throughout this text, and learning the definition of each provides a good start for anyone studying in this field.

As a field of study, criminology in its present form is primarily a social scientific discipline. Contemporary criminologists generally recognize, however, that their field is *interdisciplinary*—that is, it draws upon other disciplines to provide an integrated approach to understanding the problem of crime in contemporary society and to advance solutions to the problems crime creates. Hence, anthropology (especially cultural anthropology or ethnology), biology, sociology, political science, psychology, psychiatry, economics, ethology (the study of character), medicine, law, philosophy, ethics, and numerous other fields all have something to offer the student of criminology, as do the tools provided by statistics, computer science, and other forms of scientific and data analysis (see Figure 1–4).

FIGURE 1-4 | **Criminology's Many Roots**

Source: Printed and Electronically reproduced by permission of Pearson Education, Inc., Upper Saddle River, New Jersey.

The interdisciplinary nature of criminology was well stated by Jim Short, past president of the American Society of Criminology (ASC), who said, "The organization of knowledge by traditional disciplines has become increasingly anachronistic, as the generation of knowledge has become more interdisciplinary. From its earliest beginnings, when philosophers grappled with relationships between human nature and behavior and biologists sought to relate human physiology to behavior, criminology's concerns have reached across virtually all disciplines that focus on the human condition. Additionally, much of the impetus for criminology has come from concerns that crime be controlled. Criminology thus cuts across professions as well as disciplines."[35]

It is important to note that, although criminology may be interdisciplinary as well as cross-professional, few existing explanations for criminal behavior have been successfully or fully integrated. Just as physicists today are seeking a unified field theory to explain the wide variety of observable forms of matter and energy, criminologists have yet to develop a

■ **criminal justice** The scientific study of crime, the criminal law, and components of the criminal justice system, including the police, courts, and corrections.

generally accepted integrated approach to crime and criminal behavior that can explain the many diverse forms of criminality while also leading to effective social policies in the area of crime control. The attempt to construct criminological theories that are relevant to the problems of today is made all the more difficult because, as discussed earlier, the phenomenon under study—crime—is very wide-ranging and is subject to arbitrary and sometimes unpredictable legalistic and definitional changes.

A successfully integrated field of criminology must bring together the contributions of various theoretical perspectives and disciplines, but it must also—if it is to have any relevance—blend the practical requirements of our nation's judicial system with emotional and rational calls for morality and justice. Is the death penalty, for example, justified? If so, on what basis? Is it because it is a type of vengeance and therefore deserved? Can we say that it is unjustified because many sociological studies have shown that it does little to reduce the rate of serious crime such as murder? Just what do we mean by "justice," and what can criminological studies tell us—if anything—about what is just and what is unjust?

The editors of the journal *Theoretical Criminology*,[36] which began publication over a decade ago, wrote in the inaugural issue that "criminology has always been somewhat of a haphazardly-assembled umbrella-like structure which nevertheless usefully shelters a variety of theoretical interests that are espoused and employed by different disciplinary, methodological and political traditions." Such a structure, they said, "has obvious advantages, notably that it facilitates an interdisciplinary and inclusivist formation rather than supposing an exclusive but contentious 'core'. But one of its weaknesses is that its inhabitants, many of whom shuttle backwards and forwards between it and their parent disciplines, tend to communicate honestly and meaningfully only with those who speak the same theoretical language."[37] In other words, while the field of criminology can benefit from the wide variety of ideas available via a multiplicity of perspectives, all of which seek to understand the phenomenon we call "crime," successful cross-disciplinary collaboration can be quite difficult.

As our earlier definition of criminology indicates, however, it is more than a field of study or a collection of theories; it is also a discipline and a profession.[38] More than a decade ago, in his presidential address to the ASC, Charles F. Wellford identified the "primary purposes" of the criminology profession: "Controlling crime through prevention, rehabilitation, and deterrence and ensuring that the criminal justice system reflects the high aspiration we have as a society of 'justice for all' characterize the principal goals that in my judgment motivate the work of our field."[39]

Notably, criminology also contributes to the discipline of **criminal justice**, which emphasizes application of the criminal law and study of the components of the justice system, especially the police, courts, and corrections. As one author stated, "Criminology gives prominence to questions about the *causes of criminality*, while the *control of lawbreaking* is at the heart of criminal justice."[40] Learn more about the interdisciplinary

A criminalist at work. Crime-scene investigators, like the person shown here, can provide crucial clues needed to solve crimes. How does the work of a criminologist differ from that of a criminalist? Would you like either kind of work?

nature of criminology via **http://www.csudh.edu/dearhabermas/osgood.htm**. Read a few articles describing the nature of contemporary criminology at **http://westerncriminology.org/documents/WCR/v02n1/currie/currie.html, http://westerncriminology.org/documents/WCR/v02n2/hil/hil.html,** and **http://westerncriminology.org/documents/WCR/v02n2/currie/currie.html**.

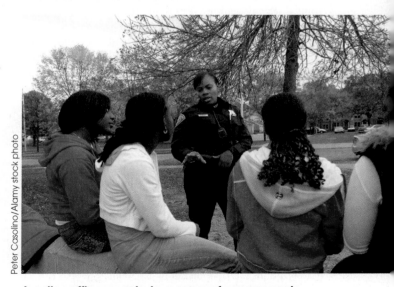

A police officer speaks to a group of young people. Criminology examines the causes of crime and seeks ways to prevent or control it. Criminal justice examines the criminal justice system, including police, courts, and corrections. How do the two disciplines complement one another?

■ **criminologist**   One who is trained in the field of criminology; also, one who studies crime, criminals, and criminal behavior.

■ **criminalist**   A specialist in the collection and examination of the physical evidence of crime.

What Do Criminologists Do?

A typical dictionary definition of a **criminologist** is "one who studies crime, criminals, and criminal behavior."[41] Occasionally, the term *criminologist* is used broadly to describe almost anyone who works in the criminal justice field, regardless of formal training. There is a growing tendency, however, to reserve application of the term *criminologist* to academics, researchers, and policy analysts with advanced degrees who are involved in the study of crime and crime trends and in the analysis of societal reactions to crime. Hence, it is more appropriate today to describe specially skilled investigators, crime-laboratory technicians, fingerprint experts, crime-scene photographers, ballistics experts, and others who work to solve particular crimes as criminalists. A **criminalist** is "a specialist in the collection and examination of the physical evidence of crime."[42] Police officers, corrections professionals, probation and parole officers, judges, district attorneys, criminal defense attorneys, and others who do the day-to-day work of the criminal justice system are best referred to as criminal justice professionals.

Academic criminologists and research criminologists generally hold doctoral degrees (PhDs) in the field of criminology or criminal justice from an accredited university. Some criminologists hold degrees in related fields like sociology and political science but have specialized in the study and control of crime and deviance. Most PhD criminologists teach either criminology or criminology-related subjects in institutions of higher learning, including universities and two- and four-year colleges. Nearly all criminology professors are involved in research or writing projects by which they strive to advance criminological knowledge. Some PhD criminologists are strictly researchers and work for federal agencies like the National Institute of Justice (NIJ), the Bureau of Justice Statistics (BJS), and the National Criminal Justice Reference Service (NCJRS) or for private (albeit often government-funded) organizations with names such as RAND and the Search Group, Inc.

The results of criminological research in the United States are generally published in journals like *Criminology* (the official publication of the American Society of Criminology [ASC]), *Theoretical Criminology, Justice Quarterly* (the Academy of Criminal Justice Sciences), *Crime and Delinquency*, the *American Journal of Criminal Justice* (the Southern Criminal Justice Association), the *Journal of Qualitative Criminology, Social Problems*, and *Victimology*.[43] International English-language journals are numerous and include the *Canadian Journal of Criminology*, the *Australian and New Zealand Journal of Criminology*, and the *British Journal of Criminology*. Read some of these journals and visit the organizations that sponsor them at **http://cj.ua.edu/resources**. The *Crime Science Journal*, a Springer Open Journal, is web-available at **http://crimesciencejournal.springeropen.com**.

> Private security provides another career track for individuals interested in criminology and criminal justice.

People who have earned master's and bachelor's degrees in the field of criminology often find easy entrance into police investigative or support work, probation and parole agencies, court-support activities, and correctional (prison) work. Criminologists also work for government agencies interested in the development of effective social policies intended to deter or combat crime. Many criminologists with master's degrees also teach at two- and four-year colleges and schools.

Private security provides another career track for individuals interested in criminology and criminal justice. The number of personnel employed by private security agencies today is twice that of public law enforcement agencies, and the gap is widening. Many upper- and mid-level private managers working for private security firms hold criminology or criminal justice degrees. The same may soon be true for the majority of law enforcement personnel, especially those in managerial positions.

Anyone trained in criminology has many alternatives (see Table 1–2). Some people with undergraduate degrees in criminology or criminal justice decide to go on to law school. Some teach high school, whereas others become private investigators. Many criminologists provide civic organizations (such as victims' assistance and justice advocacy groups) with much-needed expertise, a few work for politicians and legislative bodies, and some appear on talk shows to debate the pros and cons of various kinds of social policies designed to fight crime. Some criminologists become police officers, investigate crimes and arrest fugitives (Figure 1–5), and some even write texts like this one! For more thoughts on the role of criminologists in the twenty-first century, read **http://westerncriminology.org/documents/WCR/v04n3/article_pdfs/robinson.pdf**.

■ **theory** A series of interrelated propositions that attempts to describe, explain, predict, and ultimately control some class of events. A theory gains explanatory power from inherent logical consistency and is tested by how well it describes and predicts reality.

■ **general theory** A theory that attempts to explain all (or at least most) forms of criminal conduct through a single overarching approach.

■ **unicausal** Having one cause. Unicausal theories posit only one source for all that they attempt to explain.

■ **theoretical criminology** A subfield of general criminology, it posits explanations for criminal behavior.

TABLE 1-2 | **What Do Criminologists Do?**

The term *criminologist* is usually applied to credentialed individuals, such as those holding advanced degrees in the field, who engage in the study of crime, criminal behavior, and crime trends. The word *criminalist* is used to describe people who specialize in the collection and examination of the physical evidence associated with specific crimes. Others working in the criminal justice system are called *criminal justice professionals*. This table and Figures 1–6 and 1–7 illustrate these differences.

Activities of Criminologists	
Data gathering	Public service
Data analysis	Analysis of crime patterns and trends
Theory construction	Scholarly presentations and publications
Hypothesis testing	Education and training
Social policy creation	Threat assessment and risk analysis
Public advocacy	Service as an expert witness at trial or in other court proceedings
Teaching	Public speaking
Jobs in the Field of Criminalistics	
Forensics examiner	Crime-scene photographer
Crime-laboratory technician	Polygraph operator
Ballistics expert	Fingerprint examiner
Crime-scene investigator	
Jobs in the Field of Criminal Justice	
Law enforcement officer	Judge
Probation or parole officer	Defense attorney
Correctional officer	Prosecutor
Prison program director	Jailer
Cybercrime investigator	Private security officer and supervisor
Juvenile justice worker	Victims' advocate

Source: Pearson Education, Inc.

Theoretical Criminology

Theoretical criminology, a subfield of general criminology, is the type of criminology most often found in colleges and universities. Theoretical criminology, rather than simply describing crime and its occurrence, posits explanations for criminal behavior. As Sutherland stated, "The problem in criminology is to explain the criminality of behavior. However, an explanation of criminal behavior should be a specific part of [a] general theory of behavior and its task should be to differentiate criminal from noncriminal behavior."[44]

To explain and understand crime, criminologists have developed many theories. As we shall see in Chapter 2, A **theory**, at least in its ideal form, is made up of clearly stated propositions that posit relationships, often of a causal sort, between events and things under study. An old Roman theory, for example, proposed that insanity was caused by the influence of the moon and may even follow its cycles—hence the term *lunacy*.

Theories attempt to provide us with explanatory power and help us understand the phenomenon under study. The more applicable a theory is found to be, the more generalizable it is from one specific instance to others—in other words, the more it can be applied to other situations. A **general theory** of crime is one that attempts to explain all (or at least most) forms of criminal conduct through a single overarching approach. Unfortunately, as Don M. Gottfredson, past president of the ASC, observed, "Theories in criminology tend to be unclear and lacking in justifiable generality."[45] When we consider the wide range of behaviors regarded as criminal—from murder to drug use to white-collar crime to cybercrime—it seems difficult to imagine one theory that can explain them all or that might even explain the same type of behavior under varying circumstances. Still, many past theoretical approaches to crime causation were **unicausal** while attempting to be all-inclusive; that is, the approaches posited a single identifiable source for all serious deviant and criminal behavior.

■ **integrated theory**   An explanatory perspective that merges (or attempts to merge) concepts drawn from different sources.

FIGURE 1-5 | **The FBI's Ten Most Wanted Fugitives**

An **integrated theory**, in contrast to a general theory, does not necessarily attempt to explain all criminality but is distinguishable by the fact that it merges (or attempts to merge) concepts drawn from different sources. As noted criminologist Gregg Barak stated, "An integrative criminology seeks to bring together the diverse bodies of knowledge that represent the full array of disciplines that study crime."[46] Hence, integrated theories provide potentially wider explanatory power than narrower formulations. Don C. Gibbons, professor of sociology at Portland State University, noted, "The basic idea of theoretical integration is straightforward; it concerns the combinations of single theories or elements of those theories into a more comprehensive argument. At the same time, it would be well to note that in practice, integration is a matter of degree: some theorists have combined or integrated more concepts or theoretical elements than have others."[47]

Both the general applicability and the theoretical integration of criminological theories to a wide variety of law-violating behaviors are intuitively appealing concepts. Even far more limited attempts at criminological theorizing, however, often face daunting challenges. "As we shall see," noted Gibbons, "criminologists have not managed to articulate a large collection of relatively formalized arguments in a general or

integrated form."[48] So, although we will use the word *theory* in describing the many explanations for crime covered by this text, it should be recognized that the word will only loosely apply to many of the perspectives on crime causation that we will discuss.

As we shall learn in Chapter 2, many social scientists insist that, to be considered theories, explanations must consist of sets of clearly stated, logically interrelated, and measurable propositions. The fact that only a few of the theories described in this text rise above the level of organized conjecture—and those offer only limited generalizability and have rarely been integrated—is one of the greatest challenges facing criminology today.

Evidence-Based Criminology

Criminologists make use of contemporary social scientific research methods in the development of criminological theories. The use of rigorous social scientific techniques to develop knowledge in the field of criminology is referred to as **evidence-based criminology** (also called *knowledge-based criminology*). The research conducted by today's criminologists results in a body of scientific evidence applicable to the problems and realities of today's world.

- Forensics examiner
- Crime-scene photographer
- Crime-laboratory technician
- Crime-scene investigator
- Polygraph operator
- Ballistics expert
- Fingerprint examiner

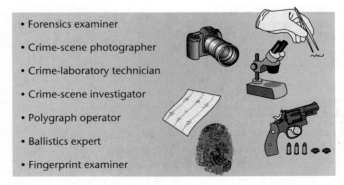

FIGURE 1-6 | **Jobs in the Field of Criminalistics**

Source: Schmalleger, Frank, *Criminology*. Printed and Electronically reproduced by permission of Pearson Education, Inc., Upper Saddle River, New Jersey.

■ **evidence-based criminology**   A form of contemporary criminology that makes use of rigorous social scientific techniques, especially randomized controlled experiments, and the systematic review of research results; also called *knowledge-based criminology*.

■ **translational criminology**   A form of criminology whose purpose it is to translate the results of research into workable social policy.

- Law enforcement officer
- Judge
- Community corrections worker
- Reentry facilitator
- Defense attorney
- Correctional officer
- Prosecutor
- Prison program director
- Jailer
- Computer crime investigator
- Private security officer
- Juvenile justice worker
- Victims' advocate

FIGURE 1-7 | **Jobs in the Field of Criminal Justice**

Source: Schmalleger, Frank, *Criminology*. Printed and Electronically reproduced by permission of Pearson Education, Inc., Upper Saddle River, New Jersey.

Because contemporary criminology is built on a social scientific approach to the subject matter of crime, the discipline has much to offer as we attempt to grapple with the problems of crime and crime control.

In 2009, in recognition of the growing significance of evidence-based criminology, the executive board of the American Society of Criminology (ASC) established a new division of experimental criminology; the division's purpose is "the promotion and improvement of experimental evidence and methods in the advancement of criminological theory and evidence-based crime policy."[49]

Six years later, in 2015, ASC joined with the Academy of Criminal Justice Sciences (ACJS) to establish the Crime and Justice Research Alliance. The Alliance, based in Washington, D.C., works to promote the use of objective research on crime and justice–related issues. Visit the American Society of Criminology on the Web at **http://www.asc41.com**.

Today, evidence-based criminology is given added voice by the Academy of Experimental Criminology, which is

based at the University of Pennsylvania, and by a number of important new journals including the *Journal of Experimental Criminology*, which is the first journal in the field of criminology to focus directly on experimental methods.[50] (See Chapter 2 for a further discussion of evidence-based criminology and of experimental methods in criminology.)

Criminology and Evidence-Based Social Policy

The ultimate outcome of successful criminological theorizing is a set of meaningful social policies based on scientific evidence that proves the theory's usefulness (see Chapter 2). Translating the results of research in the field of criminology into workable social policy is sometimes referred to as **translational criminology**. The National Institute of Justice (NIJ), an arm of the U.S. Department of Justice, explains it this way: "The idea of translational criminology is simple, yet powerful: If we want to prevent, reduce and manage crime, we must be able to translate scientific discoveries into policy and practice."[51]

It is not always easy to translate research into practice, however, even when solid evidence points to needed changes in policy. Some policy implications, such as those relating to the physical environment, for example, are relatively easy to implement. Not only do most criminologists agree that such changes, such as installing brighter lighting in crime-prone areas, can be effective at preventing crime, but they are also easy to implement.

Other policy innovations, especially those calling for cultural or social changes, can be difficult to implement, even when there is strong evidence for their likely success. In a recent example, an editorial in the highly regarded British magazine *New Scientist* asked this question: "Why are we so reluctant to accept that on-screen violence is bad for us?"[52] The article entitled "In Denial" noted that "by the time the average U.S. schoolchild leaves elementary school, he or she will have witnessed more than 8,000 murders and 100,000 other acts of violence on television." For children who play computer games and watch cable TV, the numbers will be far higher. Scientific studies show the obvious detrimental effects of media violence,

■ **social problems perspective**   The belief that crime is a manifestation of underlying social problems, such as poverty, discrimination, pervasive family violence, inadequate socialization practices, and the breakdown of traditional social institutions.

according to the article, "yet every time a study claims to have found a link between aggression, violence, educational, or behavioral problems and TV programs or computer games, there are cries of incredulity...."[53]

A number of professional groups—including the American Medical Association, the American Academy of Pediatrics, the American Psychological Association, and the American Academy of Child and Adolescent Psychiatry—agree that violence in television, music, video games, and movies leads to increased levels of violent behavior among children.[54] A joint statement issued by those organizations says that the effects of violence in the media "are measurable and long-lasting." The groups reached the conclusion "based on over 30 years of research...that viewing entertainment violence can lead to increases in aggressive attitudes, values and behaviors, particularly in children." Moreover, "prolonged viewing of media violence can lead to emotional desensitization toward violence in real life." Similarly, some years ago the Federal Trade Commission (FTC) issued a report[55] on teenage violence that concluded that "Hollywood aggressively markets violent movies, music and electronic games to children even when they have been labeled as appropriate only for adults."[56] The complete FTC report *Marketing Violent Entertainment to Children* is available at **http://www.justicestudies.com/pubs/ftcreport.pdf**.

Even after such findings, however, policy makers are reluctant to slow the production of violent media. For this reason, violence on TV and in video games is still prominent in the United States. *New Scientist* says media vendors dissuade "any criticism of a multibillion-dollar business" where they would lose profits resulting from any policies aimed at crime reduction.[57]

Anyone interested in the creation of sound social policy must respect the well-researched findings of today's criminologists. In the words of NIJ, "Successful dissemination of the results of criminological research requires that the evidence is implemented correctly. In other words, it is not just about finding evidence that something works; it is figuring out why it works and how to implement the evidence in real-world settings."[58]

Professional criminologists are acutely aware of the need to link sound social policy to the objective findings of well-conducted criminological research. A meeting of the ASC, for example, focused on the need to forge just such a link. At the meeting, ASC president Alfred Blumstein, of Carnegie Mellon University, told criminologists gathered there that "an important mission of the ASC and its members involves the generation of knowledge that is useful in dealing with crime

and the operation of the criminal justice system, and then helping public officials to use that knowledge intelligently and effectively."[59] Blumstein added, "So little is known about the causes of crime and about the effects of criminal justice policy on crime that new insights about the criminal justice system can often be extremely revealing and can eventually change the way people think about the crime problem or about the criminal justice system."[60]

The Theme of This Text

At the core of today's thinking about crime exists a crucial distinction between those who believe that crime is a *manifestation of underlying social problems* beyond the control of individuals (the social problems perspective) and those who emphasize that crime is a matter of *individual responsibility* (the individual responsibility perspective).

Building upon this distinction, this text contrasts two perspectives now popular in U.S. society and in much of the rest of the world (see Figure 1–8). One point of view, termed the **social problems perspective**, holds that crime is a consequence of underlying social problems such as poverty, discrimination, inequality of opportunity, breakdown of traditional

FIGURE 1-8 | The Theme of This Text: Social Problems versus Individual Responsibility

Individual Responsibility

Social Problems

■ **individual responsibility perspective** The belief that individuals are fundamentally responsible for their own behavior and that they choose crime over other, more law-abiding courses of action.

social institutions, low level of formal education among some disadvantaged groups, pervasive family violence experienced by some during the formative years, and inadequate socialization practices that leave too many young people without the fundamental values necessary to contribute meaningfully to the society in which they live. Advocates of the social problems perspective, while generally agreeing that crime and violence are serious social problems, advance solutions based on what is, in effect, a public-health model. Adherents of that model say that crime must be addressed in much the same way as public-health concerns like AIDS, herpes, or avian flu.

Proponents of the social problems perspective typically see solutions to the crime problem as coming in the form of large-scale government expenditures in support of social programs designed to address the issues that are perceived to lie at the root of crime. Government-funded initiatives, designed to enhance social, educational, occupational, and other opportunities, are perceived as offering programmatic solutions to ameliorate most causes of crime. The social problems approach to crime is characteristic of what social scientists term a *macro approach* because it portrays instances of individual behavior (crimes) as arising out of widespread and contributory social conditions that enmesh unwitting individuals in a causal nexus of uncontrollable social forces.

A contrasting perspective lays the cause of crime squarely at the feet of individual perpetrators. This point of view holds that individuals are fundamentally responsible for their own behavior and maintains that offenders choose crime over other, more law-abiding courses of action. Perpetrators may choose crime, advocates of this perspective say, because it is exciting, because it offers illicit pleasures and the companionship of like-minded thrill seekers, or because it is simply personally less demanding than conformity. This viewpoint, which we shall call the **individual responsibility perspective**, has a close affiliation with what is known in criminology as rational choice theory (discussed in detail in Chapter 3). It is also closely associated with a strongly held belief in the importance of free will, which is common to Western societies.[61] The individual responsibility perspective stresses individual responsibility above all else.

Advocates of the individual responsibility perspective, with their emphasis on individual choice, tend to believe that social programs do little to solve the problem of crime because, they say, a certain number of crime-prone individuals, for a variety of personal reasons, will always make irresponsible choices. Hence, advocates of the individual responsibility approach suggest highly personalized crime-reduction strategies based on firm punishments, imprisonment, individualized rehabilitation, and increased security as well as a wider use of police powers. The individual responsibility perspective characteristically emphasizes a *micro approach* that tends to focus on individual offenders and their unique biology, psychology, background, and immediate life experiences.

Over time, the individual responsibility perspective has substantially influenced national crime-control policy. Examples of conservatism in our nation's approach to criminals abound. The Violent Crime Control and Law Enforcement Act of 1994, for example (which is discussed in detail later in this text), expanded the number of capital crimes under federal law from a handful of offenses to 52.[62] The law also made billions of dollars available to municipalities to put 100,000 new police officers on the streets and allocated billions for states to build and operate prisons and incarceration alternatives like "boot camps." Prison funding was intended to ensure that additional prison cells would be available to put—and keep—violent offenders behind bars. A subchapter of the 1994 Violent Crime Control and Law Enforcement Act created a federal three-strikes-and-you're-out law that mandated life imprisonment for criminals convicted of three violent federal felonies or drug offenses. Similarly, the law increased or created new penalties for over 70 federal criminal offenses, primarily covering violent crimes, drug trafficking, and gun crimes. Since the 1994 federal legislation was passed, many states have moved to toughen their own laws against violent criminals; violent juveniles and repeat offenders have been especially targeted. The USA PATRIOT Act—enacted in 2001 and renewed with modifications in 2006—targets terrorism and crimes committed in support of terrorist activity. The PATRIOT Act, which was reauthorized again by Congress in 2011, has been criticized by many for going too far in limiting individual freedoms and restricting personal choice, although its supporters argue that its provisions are needed to fight the war on terrorism effectively. The PATRIOT Act and the crime of terrorism are discussed in more detail in Chapter 16.

We should note, however, that the implementation of any social policy can result in unforeseen consequences—such as the massive increase in American prison populations over the past 30 years that resulted from get-tough-on-crime policies. Today, states and the federal government are straining under the financial burden of incarcerating huge numbers of felons, many of whom have been convicted of nonviolent and drug crimes, and efforts are being made to reduce the number of people behind bars.

Advocates of the individual responsibility approach suggest crime-reduction strategies based on firm punishments, imprisonment, individualized rehabilitation, and increased security.

WHO'S TO BLAME—The Individual or Society?

Is Criminology Really Just a Form of Academic Excuse Making?

Three teenage boys were arrested in the small town of Hillsboro, Maine, and charged with beating a homeless man to death with a baseball bat in an underground parking garage on a cold January evening. A surveillance camera captured the beating, and the youngsters were identified by residents who watched the video clip on local TV news.

Because the boys were juveniles, a storm of controversy swarmed around a local judge's decision to charge them as adults and to bind them over for trial in criminal court—something that state law allows for serious crimes if the suspected offenders were over 14 years of age at the time of the alleged offense.

Soon opinions were being heard from many quarters, and the news media arranged to interview a criminology professor, Dr. Roy Humbolt, at a local college to see if he might be able to shed some light on the boys' behavior.

Cultural Creative/Alamy Stock photo

A news conference held to provide insight into a seemingly senseless killing. What value do criminological explanations hold for the understanding of criminal activity? How can we benefit from such explanations?

The first question came from a reporter holding a digital voice recorder toward Professor Humbolt. "What happened here? How do you explain this kind of senseless killing?"

"Well," Humbolt began, "it's not senseless. Crime is a social event, not just an isolated instance of individual activity. And in much youth crime we see patterns of co-offending."

Humbolt felt as though he was hitting his stride and started lecturing as though he was in the classroom with his undergraduates. "Criminal behavior is often attributable to social failings rather than to individual choice. Consider, for a moment, the backgrounds of these young men. Were they subjected to physical abuse while they were growing up? Did they learn violence at the hands of older siblings or parents? Were they, in this instance, involved in some adolescent rite of passage, maybe even an initiation into a gang? Did they feel forced to behave this way because of peer pressure? Was it something they saw on television or in video games that they might have played and then decided to reenact?"

"Dr. Humbolt," the reporter asked, bringing the professor back from his reverie, "even if you find that some of those things are true, isn't criminology just an exercise in excuse making for criminals?"

Think About It

1. What do you think of the explanations offered by Professor Humbolt for the boys' behavior? Which of his explanations, if any, makes the most sense? How can we know for sure if those explanations are accurate?

2. What do you think of the reporter's stinging criticism of the professor? Is the reporter right that criminology is "just an exercise in excuse making for criminals"? Explain your answer.

3. Generally speaking, does understanding absolve responsibility? In other words, if we can understand why someone does something, then should we hold him or her less responsible for doing it? Why or why not?

Note: Who's to Blame boxes provide critical-thinking opportunities based on actual cases.

The Social Context of Crime

Crime does not occur in a vacuum. Every crime has a unique set of causes, consequences, and participants. Crime affects some people more than others, having a special impact on those who are direct participants in the act itself—offenders, victims, police officers, witnesses, and so on. Crime, in general, provokes reactions from its victims, from concerned groups of citizens, from the criminal justice system, and sometimes from society as a whole, which manifests its concerns via the creation of new social policy. Reactions to crime, from the everyday to the precedent-setting, may color the course of future criminal events.[63]

In this text, we shall attempt to identify and examine some of the many social, psychological, economic, biological, and other causes of crime while expounding on the many differing perspectives that have been advanced to explain both crime

■ **social relativity**   The notion that social events are interpreted differently according to the cultural experiences and personal interests of the initiator, the observer, or the recipient of that behavior.

and criminality. Popular conceptions of criminal motivation are typically shaped by media portrayals of offender motivation, which often fail to take into consideration the felt experiences of the law violators. By identifying and studying this diversity of perspectives on criminality, we will discover the characteristic disjuncture among victims, offenders, the justice system, and society about the significance that each assigns to the behavior in question—and often to its motivation. It will not be unusual to find, for example, that sociological or psychological initiatives with which the offenders themselves do not identify are assigned to those offenders by theorists and others.

Making Sense of Crime: The Causes and Consequences of the Criminal Event

This text recognizes that criminal activity is diversely created and variously interpreted. In other words, this text depicts crime not as an isolated individual activity but as a *social event*.[64] Like other social events, crime is fundamentally a social construction.[65] To say that crime is a social construction is not to lessen the impact of the victimization experiences that all too many people undergo in our society every day, nor does such a statement trivialize the significance of crime-prevention efforts or the activities of members of the criminal justice system. Likewise, it does not underplay the costs of crime to individual victims and to society as a whole. It does recognize, however, that although a given instance of criminal behavior may have many causes, it also carries with it many different kinds of

meanings—at least one for offenders, another (generally quite a different meaning, of course) for victims, and still another for agents of the criminal justice system. Similarly, a wide range of social interest groups, from victims' advocates to prisoner "rights" and gun-control organizations, all interpret the significance of law-breaking behavior from unique points of view, and each arrives at different conclusions about what should be done about the so-called crime problem.

For these reasons, it is important to apply the concept of social relativity to the study of criminality.[66] **Social relativity** means that social events are interpreted differently according to the cultural experiences and personal interests of the initiator, the observer, or the recipient of that behavior. Hence, as a social phenomenon, crime means different things to the offender who commits it, to the criminologist who studies it, to the police officer who investigates it, and to the victim who experiences it firsthand.

Figure 1–9 illustrates both the causes and the consequences of crime in rudimentary diagrammatic form. In keeping with the theme of this text, it depicts crime as a social event. The figure consists of a foreground, or setting, which describes those features that immediately determine the nature of the criminal event (including responses to the event as it is transpiring), and a background, in which generic contributions to the crime can be seen along with interpretations of the event after it has taken place. We call the background causes of crime *contributions* and use the word *inputs* to signify the more immediate propensities and predispositions of the actors involved in the situation. Inputs also include the physical features of the setting in which a specific crime takes place. Both background contributions and immediate inputs contribute to and shape the criminal event.

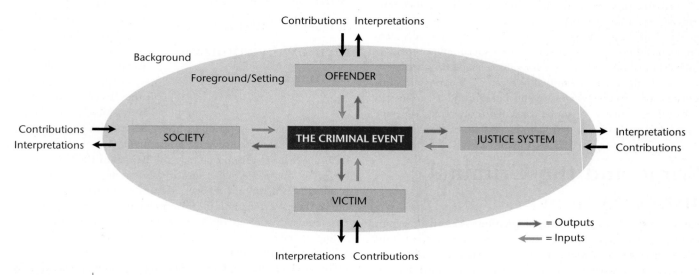

FIGURE 1-9 | Interpreting the Criminal Event

■ **criminal justice system**   The various agencies of justice, especially the police, courts, and corrections, whose goal is to apprehend, convict, punish, and rehabilitate law violators.

The more or less immediate results or consequences of crime are termed *outputs*, whereas the term *interpretations* appears in the diagram to indicate that any crime has a lasting impact both on surviving participants and on society. As Figure 1–9 shows, although the criminal event may occur at a particular point in time and within a given setting, it is ultimately a result of the coming together of inputs provided by (1) the offender, (2) the criminal justice system, (3) the victim, and (4) society (including other individuals who do not fit in any of the first three categories).

Crime and the Offender

Offenders bring with them certain background features, such as personal life experiences, a peculiar biology and genetic inventory (insofar as they are unique organisms), a distinct personality, personal values and beliefs, and various kinds of skills and knowledge (some of which may be useful in the commission of crime). Background contributions to crime can be vitally important. Research, for example, tends to cement the existence of a link between child-rearing practices and criminality in later life. Joan McCord, reporting on a 30-year study of family relationships and crime, found that self-confident, nonpunitive, and affectionate mothers tend to insulate their male children from delinquency and, consequently, later criminal activity.[67] Difficulties associated with the birthing process have also been linked to crime in adulthood.[68] Negative familial relationships and birth trauma are but two of the literally thousands of kinds of experiences individuals may have. Whether individuals who undergo trauma at birth and are deprived of positive maternal experiences will turn to crime depends on many other things, including their own mixture of other experiences and characteristics, the appearance of a suitable victim, the failure of the justice system to prevent crime, and the evolution of a social environment in which criminal behavior is somehow encouraged or valued.

Each of the parties identified in Figure 1–9 contributes immediate inputs to the criminal event. Foreground contributions by the offender may consist of a particular motivation, a specific intent (in many cases), or a drug-induced state of mind.

Crime and the Criminal Justice System

Like the offender, the **criminal justice system** (meaning the various agencies of justice such as the police, courts, and corrections) also contributes to the criminal event, albeit unwillingly, through its failure to (1) prevent criminal activity, (2) adequately identify and inhibit specific offenders prior to their involvement in crime, and (3) prevent the release of convicted criminals who later become repeat offenders. Such background contributions can be seen in prisons (a central component of the justice system) that serve as "schools for crime," fostering anger against society and building a propensity for continued criminality in inmates who have been "turned out." Similarly, the failure of system-sponsored crime-prevention programs—ranging from the patrol activities of local police departments to educational and diversionary programs intended to redirect budding offenders—helps set the stage for the criminal event.

On the other hand, proper system response may reduce crime. A study by Carol W. Kohfeld and John Sprague, for example, found that police response (especially arrest) can, under certain demographic conditions, dramatically reduce the incidence of criminal behavior.[69] Kohfeld and Sprague also found that arrest "constitutes communication to criminals in general," further supporting the notion that inputs provided by the justice system have the power to either enhance or reduce the likelihood of criminal occurrences. Immediate inputs provided by the justice system typically consist of features of the situation such as the presence or absence of police officers, the ready availability (or lack thereof) of official assistance, the willingness of police officers to intervene in precrime situations, and the response time required for officers to arrive at a crime scene.

Crime and the Victim

Few crimes can occur without a victim. Sometimes the victim is a passive participant in the crime, such as an innocent person killed on the street outside his or her home by random gunfire from a drive-by shooting. In such cases, the victim is simply in the proverbial wrong place at the wrong time. Even then, however, merely by being present the victim contributes his or her person to the event, thereby increasing the severity of the incident (i.e., the random shooting that injures no one may still be against the law but is a far less serious crime than a similar incident in which somebody is killed). Sometimes, however, victims more actively contribute to their own victimization by appearing defenseless (having characteristics such as old age, drunkenness, or disability), by failing to take appropriate defensive measures (leaving doors unlocked or forgetting to remove the key from a car's ignition), by unwisely displaying wealth (flashing large-denomination bills in a public place), or simply by making other unwise choices

> Sometimes victims actively contribute to their own victimization by making unwise choices.

■ **socialization**   The lifelong process of social experience whereby individuals acquire the cultural patterns of their society.

(walking down a dark alley off Times Square at 3 A.M.). In a study of Canadian victimization, Leslie W. Kennedy and David R. Forde found that violent personal victimization "is contingent on the exposure that comes from following certain lifestyles," which was especially true "for certain demographic groups, particularly young males."[70]

Although lifestyles may provide the background that fosters victimization, a more active form of victimization characterizes "victims" who initiate criminal activity, such as the barroom brawler who picks a fight but ends up on the receiving end of the ensuing physical violence. Victim-precipitated offenses are those that involve active victim participation in the initial stages of a criminal event and that take place when the soon-to-be victim instigates the chain of events that ultimately results in the victimization. Victimization and victim-precipitation are discussed in greater detail in Chapter 10, *Criminal Victimization*.

Crime and Society

Finally, the general public (termed *society* in Figure 1–9) contributes to the criminal event both formally and informally. Society's formal contributions sometimes take the form of legislation, whereby crime itself is defined. Hence, as we shall discuss in considerable detail in Chapter 15, society structures the criminal event in a most fundamental way by delineating (through legislation and via statute) which forms of activity are to be thought of as criminal.

Society's less formal contributions to crime arise out of generic social practices and conditions like poverty, poor and informal education, and various forms of discrimination by which pathways to success are blocked as well as **socialization** (the process whereby people acquire the cultural patterns of their society). Socialization has an especially important impact on crime causation because it provides the interpretative foundation used to define and understand the significance of particular situations in which we find ourselves, and it is upon those interpretations that we may (or may not) decide to act. Date rape, for example, can occur when a man concludes that his date "owes" him something for the money he has spent on her. That feeling, however inappropriate from the point of view of the victim and the justice system, probably has its roots in early learned experiences—including values communicated from television, the movies, and popular music—about gender-related roles under such circumstances. In other words, society, through the divergent values and expectations it places on people, property, and behavior under particular conditions, may provide the motivational basis for many offenses.

The contributions society makes to the backgrounds of both offender and victim and to the structure of the justice system and the influences each, in turn, has upon the general social order provide for a kind of "feedback loop" in our vision of crime (even though the loop is not shown in Figure 1–9 for fear of unnecessarily complicating it). Through socialization, for example, individuals learn about the dangers of criminal victimization, but when victimization occurs and is publicized, it reinforces the socialization process, leading to an increased wariness of others and so on. An example can be seen in the fact that fear of random violence is much higher today than it was decades ago. The idea of random violence entered cultural awareness following a number of horrendous and well-publicized mass shootings, and is now a shared part of the socialization process in the United States.

The contributions made by society to crime are complex and far reaching. Some say that the content of the mass media (Web sites, television, movies, newspapers, popular music, etc.) can lead to crime by exposing young people to inappropriate role models and to the kinds of activity—violence and unbridled sexuality, for example—that encourage criminality.

Society's foreground contributions to crime largely emanate from the distribution of resources and the accessibility of services, which are often the direct result of economic conditions. In a study of the availability of medical resources (especially quality hospital emergency services), William G. Doerner found that serious assaults may "become" homicides when such resources are lacking but that homicides can be prevented through the effective utilization of capable medical technology.[71] Hence, societal decisions leading to the distribution and placement of advanced medical support equipment and personnel can effectively lower homicide rates in selected geographic areas, but homicide rates will be higher in areas where such equipment is not readily available. In Doerner's words, "[t]he causes of homicide transcend the mere social world of the combatants."[72]

The moments that immediately precede any crime are ripe with possibilities. When all the inputs brought to the situation by all those present coalesce into activity that violates the criminal law, a crime occurs. Together, the elements, experiences, and propensities brought to the situation by the offender and the victim, and those that are contributed to the pending event by society and the justice system, precipitate and decide the nature, course, and eventual outcome of the criminal event. As one well-known criminologist explained, "An understanding of crime and criminality as constructed from the immediate interactions of criminals, control agents, victims, and others, and therefore as emerging from a tangled experiential web of situated dangers and situated pleasures, certainly refocuses theories of criminal causality on the criminal moment."[73] While certain circumstances contribute to the criminal event as it unfolds, it is also important to note that some of the inputs brought to the situation may be inhibiting; that is, they may tend to reduce the likelihood or severity of criminal behavior.

The Consequences of Crime

As mentioned earlier, the causes of crime, however well documented, tell only half the criminological story. Each and every crime has consequences. Although the immediate consequences of crime may be relatively obvious for those parties directly involved (e.g., the offender and the victim), crime also indirectly affects society and the justice system over the longer term. Figure 1–9 terms the immediate effects of crime *outputs*. As with the causes of crime, however, the real impact of such outputs is mediated by perceptual filters, resulting in what the figure terms *interpretations*. After a crime has taken place, each party to the event must make sense out of what has transpired. Such interpretations consist of cognitive, emotional, and (ultimately) behavioral reactions to the criminal event.

Interpretations are ongoing. They happen before, during, and after the criminal event and are undertaken by all those associated with it. In an interesting and detailed study of the interpretative activity of criminal justice system personnel, James F. Gilsinan documented what happens when callers reach the 9-1-1 operator on police emergency lines.[74] Because many prank calls and calls for information are made to 9-1-1 operators, the operators must judge the seriousness of every call that comes through. What the caller says was found to be only a small part of the informational cues that an operator seeks to interpret before assigning the call to a particular response (or nonresponse) category. Honest calls for help may go unanswered if the operator misinterprets the call. Hence, quite early in the criminal event, the potential exists for a crucial representative of the justice system to misinterpret important cues and to conclude that no crime is taking place.

Other interpretative activities may occur long after the crime has transpired, but they are at least as significant. The justice system, taken as a whole, must decide guilt or innocence and must attempt to deal effectively with convicted offenders. Victims must attempt to make sense of their victimization in a way that allows them to testify in court (if need be) and to pick up the pieces of their crime-shattered lives. Offenders must come to terms with themselves and decide whether to avoid prosecution (e.g., if escape is possible), accept blame, or deny responsibility. Whatever the outcome of these more narrowly focused interpretative activities, society—because of the cumulative impact of individual instances of criminal behavior—will also face tough decisions through its courts and law-making agencies. Society-level decision making may revolve around the implementation of policies designed to stem future instances of criminal behavior, the revision of criminal codes, or the elimination of unpopular laws.

Our perspective takes a three-dimensional integrative view of the social event termed *crime*. We will (1) attempt to identify and understand the multiple causes that give rise to criminal behavior, (2) highlight the processes involved in the criminal event as it unfolds, and (3) analyze the interpretation of the crime phenomenon, including societal responses to it.

From this perspective, crime can be viewed along a temporal continuum as an emergent activity that (1) arises out of past complex causes; (2) assumes a course that builds on immediate interrelationships among the victim, offender, and others that exist at the time of the offense; and (3) elicits a formal response from the justice system, shapes public perceptions, and (possibly) gives rise to changes in social policy after it has occurred.

The advantages of an integrative perspective can be found in the completeness of the picture that it provides. The integrative point of view results in a comprehensive and inclusive view of crime because it emphasizes the personal and social underpinnings as well as the consequences of crime. The chapters that follow employ the integrative perspective advocated here to analyze criminal events and to show how various theoretical approaches can be woven into a consistent perspective on crime. For a different point of view, one that describes crime in terms of the five dimensions of (1) law, (2) offender, (3) target and/or victim, (4) location, and (5) time of the incident, read **http://westerncriminology.org/documents/WCR/v03n2/verma/verma.html**.

Corepics VOF/Shutterstock

A group of young people hanging out. The influence of groups can be strong on their members, explaining why sociological theories of crime causation have long been at the forefront of criminological thinking. What other kinds of explanations might help us understand crime?

CRIMINAL | PROFILES

Ross Ulbricht—The New Face of Crime?

In 2015, 31-year-old Ross Ulbricht, the mastermind behind the illegal online marketplace known as Silk Road, was sentenced in Manhattan federal court to spend the rest of his life in prison. He was also ordered to forfeit $183,961,921 in illegal profits. Silk Road, which offered sex, firearms, illegal drugs, pharmaceuticals, hacking services, and even killings-for-hire, was created in 2011 and operated on what's known as the dark Web. Participants used sophisticated and secretive Web browsers, and conducted transactions in untraceable Bitcoins. Officials estimated that the site, before it was shut down, had nearly a million users and raked in over $1.2 billion in sales through millions of transactions.

Online, Ulbricht used the pseudonym Dread Pirate Roberts. Before his true identity was known, the media described him as a "virtual criminal mastermind" and an "online mob boss" who became the new face of organized crime. Ulbricht was said to have personally used his creation to fund a $150,000 hit on a Canadian man who tried to extort him. Investigators said that he later followed up by ordering the killing of the blackmailer's four friends. Ulbricht, however, was ultimately held responsible for the crimes that others committed through the Silk Road portal. U.S. Attorney Preet Bharara says that "Ulbricht bears responsibility for the overdoses, addictions, and other foreseeable repercussions of the illegal drugs sold on Silk Road." It doesn't matter, Bharara said, "that he did not personally handle those drugs; neither would a traditional kingpin."

Silk Road was the first massive online marketplace for illegal goods and services, and it provided a blueprint for other criminals wanting to conduct business autonomously. At sentencing, federal Judge Katherine B. Forrest told Ulbricht that "as the first person" to create a virtual world in which any kind of illegal business could be conducted, he had to pay the price. Anyone who was thinking of following in Ulbricht's footsteps, said the judge, needs to know clearly "and without equivocation that if you break the law this way, there will be very serious consequences." In a footnote to Ulbricht's trial and sentencing, the website bitbet.us took bets (only in Bitcoins, of course) favoring

Silk Road founder, Ross Ulbricht. In 2015, Ulbricht was sentenced to life in prison for creating the anything-goes Internet site.

odds of a successful appeal by Ulbricht, or a presidential pardon of Ulbricht by Donald Trump before mid 2018.

The case of Ross Ulbricht raises a number of interesting questions. Among them are the following:

1. What does the conviction of Ross Ulbricht have to say about the nature of crime in America today?
2. Why did Ulbricht receive such a harsh sentence?

Notes

FBI Press Release, "Ross Ulbricht, AKA Dread Pirate Roberts, Sentenced in Manhattan Federal Court to Life in Prison," May 29, 2015, https://www.fbi.gov /newyork/press-releases/2015/ross-ulbricht-aka-dread-pirate-roberts-sentenced-in-manhattan-federal-court-to-life-in-prison; and "Silk Road: How One Virtual "Mob Boss' Became the New Face of Organized Crime," News.com.au, July 14, 2015, http://www.news.com.au/technology/online /silk-road-how-one-virtual-mob-boss-becamethe-new-face-of-organised-crime/story-fnjwnj25-1227441204850

The Primacy of Sociology?

This text recognizes the contributions made by numerous disciplines, including biology, economics, psychology, psychiatry, physiology, and political science, to the study of crime and crime causation. It is important to recognize, however, that the primary perspective from which many contemporary criminologists operate is a sociological one. Hence, a large number of today's theoretical explanations of criminal behavior are routinely couched in the language of social science and fall within the framework of sociological theory. The social problems versus individual responsibility theme, around which this text is built, is in keeping with such a tradition.

Many would disagree, however, with those who claim that the sociological perspective should be accorded heightened importance in today's criminological enterprise. Those who argue in favor of the primacy of sociology emphasize the fact that crime, as a subject of study, is a social phenomenon. Central to any study of crime, they say, must be the social context of the criminal event because it is the social context that brings victims and criminals together.[75] Much of contemporary criminology rests on a tradition of social scientific investigation into the nature of crime and criminal behavior that is rooted in European and American sociological traditions that are now well over 200 years old.[76]

One of sociology's problems, however, has been its apparent reluctance to accept the significance of findings from other fields as well as its frequent inability to integrate such findings into existing sociological understandings of crime. Another has been its seeming inability to demonstrate conclusively effective means of controlling violent (as well as other forms of) crime. As Diana Fishbein, professor of criminology at the University of Baltimore, said, "Sociological factors play a role. But they have not been able to explain why one person becomes violent and another doesn't."[77]

> The primary significance of crime and of criminal behavior is fundamentally social in nature, and any control over crime must stem from effective social policy.

While sociological theories continue to develop, new and emerging perspectives ask to be recognized. The role of biology in explaining criminal tendencies, for example, appears to be gaining strength as investigations into the mapping of human DNA continue. Charles F. Wellford, past president of the ASC, explained the current state of affairs, saying, "I strongly believe that the future development of causal theory is dependent upon our movement toward integrated theories that involve biological, social, and cultural dimensions. Our failure to achieve much in the way of understanding the causal sequences of crime is in part a reflection of our slowness in moving toward multidisciplinary, integrated theoretical structures. The fact is that for two-thirds of the twentieth century, as criminology developed, we remained committed to a small number of sociological models for which there is extensive proof of their important but limited value. Fortunately in the last 20 years, this has begun to change. Today we see under way substantial research efforts that are based upon models of explanation that far exceed the traditional sociological approaches."[78]

Nonetheless, whatever new insights may develop over the coming years, it is likely that the sociological perspective will continue to dominate the field of criminology for some time to come. Such dominance is rooted in the fact that crime—regardless of all the causative nuances that may be identified in its development—occurs within the context of the social world. As such, the primary significance of crime and of criminal behavior is fundamentally social in nature, and any control over crime must stem from effective social policy.

SUMMARY

- At the start of this chapter, the term *crime* was defined as a violation of the criminal law. Near the end of this chapter, we recognized the complexity of crime, calling it an "emergent phenomenon." In the process, crime was shown to be a law-breaking event whose significance arises out of an intricate social nexus involving a rather wide variety of participants.

- Deviance, or deviant behavior, refers to a violation of social norms. Some forms of behavior (such as murder, rape, and most serious crimes) are both criminal and deviant. Others may be deviant but not criminal (e.g., nudity under certain circumstances), or may be criminal but not regarded as deviant by many members of society (e.g., the use of marijuana).

- Decisions about what should be criminal are generally made by legislatures, at both the state and federal levels. Such decisions are made through a political process that involves input from social interest groups, including those in favor of criminalizing certain behaviors and those opposed to criminalizing them.

- *Criminology* is "an interdisciplinary profession built around the scientific study of crime and criminal behavior, including their forms, causes, legal aspects, and control." Criminology has evolved from a long historical tradition and borrows features from psychology, economics, sociology, and other disciplines.

- The term *criminologist* is applied to credentialed individuals who engage in the study of crime, criminal behavior, and crime trends. *Criminalist* describes people who specialize in the collection and examination of the physical evidence associated with specific crimes. *Criminal justice professionals* include law enforcement officers, judges, criminal defense attorneys, prosecutors, cybercrime investigators, victims' advocates, jailers, correctional officers, and so on.

- Evidence-based criminology refers to the use of rigorous social scientific research methods in the development and testing of criminological theories. Evidence-based criminology offers the promise of building a valuable collection of evidence-based knowledge that can be of service to policy makers and individuals concerned about the fight against crime.

- Criminologists are acutely aware of the need to link sound social policy to the objective findings of well-conducted criminological research. Unfortunately, political considerations and long-standing traditional solutions have formed the basis for much crime-control policy in the past, and the situation is only slowly changing.

- This text builds on a social policy theme by asking what the sources of crime and criminality are and what we can do to control crime. The theme contrasts two perspectives: The *individual responsibility perspective* holds that crime is a matter of individual responsibility; the *social problems perspective* holds that crime is a manifestation of underlying social problems beyond the control of individuals.

- This text sees crime as a social event, not an isolated individual activity. A given instance of criminal behavior may have many causes and many different kinds of meanings. Social relativity holds that social events are interpreted differently according to the cultural experiences and personal interests of the initiator, the observer, and the recipient of that behavior.

- The discipline of sociology has had the most impact on theoretical understandings of crime and crime causation, so a large number of today's theoretical explanations of criminal behavior are routinely couched in the language of social science and fall within the framework of sociological theory. Nonetheless, it is important to recognize the contributions made by numerous other disciplines (biology, economics, psychology, psychiatry, physiology, political science), making the study of crime and crime causation interdisciplinary.

KEY TERMS

consensus perspective, 7

crime, 3

criminal behavior, 10

criminalist, 12

criminality, 10

criminalize, 3

criminal justice, 11

criminal justice system, 20

criminologist, 12

criminology, 10

delinquency, 6

deviant behavior, 6

evidence-based criminology, 14

general theory, 13

individual responsibility perspective, 17

integrated theory, 14

pluralist perspective, 7

socialization, 21

social policy, 9

social problems perspective, 16

social relativity, 19

theoretical criminology, 13

theory, 13

translational criminology, 15

unicausal, 13

QUESTIONS FOR REVIEW

1. What is crime? What is the definition of *crime* that the author of this text chose to use? How might the notion of crime change over time? What impact does the changing nature of crime have on criminology?

2. What is deviance? How are crime and deviance similar? How do they differ?

3. Who decides what should be criminal? How are such decisions made?

4. What is criminology? What are its many roots?

5. What do criminologists do? How does the work of a criminologist differ from that of a criminalist?

6. What is evidence-based criminology? How does it complement theoretical criminology?

7. How does criminology, and especially criminological research, influence social policy? What is translational criminology?

8. What is the theme of this text? On what two contrasting viewpoints does it build?

9. What is the social context of crime? What are crime's consequences?

10. What social science has traditionally provided a central theoretical basis for criminology? Why?

QUESTIONS FOR REFLECTION

1. This text emphasizes the theme of social problems versus individual responsibility. How would you describe both perspectives? How might social policy decisions based on these perspectives differ?

2. Do you think you might want to become a criminologist? Why or why not?

3. Are there any crimes today that you think should be legalized? If so, what are they? Why do you feel this way?

4. Can you think of any advances now occurring in the social or physical sciences that might soon have a significant impact on our understanding of crime and criminality? If so, what would those advances be? How might they affect our understanding of crime and criminal behavior?

5. How would you describe the various participants in a criminal event? How does each contribute to an understanding of the event?

6. In what way is contemporary criminology interdisciplinary? Why is the sociological perspective especially important in studying crime? What other perspectives might be relevant? Why?

7. How does contemporary criminology influence social policy? Do you think that policy makers should address crime as a matter of individual responsibility and accountability, or do you think that crime is truly a symptom of a dysfunctional society? Why?

CHAPTER 2

WHERE DO THEORIES COME FROM?—

From Idea to Evidence

LEARNING OUTCOMES

After reading this chapter, you should be able to answer the following questions:

- What is the role of social scientific research methods in the development of criminological theories? How does the meaning of the word evidence in evidence-based criminology differ from the evidence found at a crime scene or the evidence used in criminal trials?

- What is a theory? What purposes do theories serve? What role do research and experimentation play in theory building in criminology?

- What is internal validity? External validity? How can threats to internal and external validity be addressed?

- What are the differences between quantitative and qualitative methods in the social sciences? What are the advantages and disadvantages of each method?

- What are some of the ethical considerations involved in conducting criminological research?

- How do criminological research and experimental criminology affect social policy?

- What sections might a typical research report contain?

■ **Follow the author's tweets about the latest crime and justice news at @schmalleger.**

Introduction

In 2012, 31-year-old Rudy Eugene was shot to death by Miami police officers on the McArthur Causeway after he attacked a homeless man under an overpass on the six-lane highway and ate the man's face.[1] A bicyclist who observed the frenzied attack alerted police, who intervened and ordered Eugene to the ground, but reports show that he growled at them and continued chewing on his victim. After an initial round into Eugene's torso failed to have any effect, officers shot him four more times, killing him. His victim, 65-year-old Ronald Poppo, who was critically injured, was taken to Miami's Jackson Memorial Hospital where physicians revealed that 80% of his face above his beard had been gnawed away. One of his eyes had been gouged out, and his other eye had been badly damaged, leaving him blind.[2]

Video taken by a surveillance camera on the nearby *Miami Herald* building captured the entire incident. It showed that Eugene, whom the press later dubbed the Miami Cannibal, had spent about 30 minutes before the attack walking around his car that had broken down. He then left the disabled vehicle, stripping clothing from his body as he walked. The last thing he discarded was a Bible that he'd been clutching. Eugene then came across a prone Poppo lying underneath an overpass and began to beat him. The video showed Eugene pulling off Poppo's pants and hitting and biting him in an attack that lasted for 18 minutes before police arrived.

Although no one knows what drove Eugene to attack Poppo, some experts speculated that he had consumed bath salts, designer drugs with an effect similar to amphetamine and cocaine, prior to the attack. Bath salts have been known to raise body temperature to dangerous levels and to cause the brain to overheat, resulting in intense hallucinations. Evidence gathered from Eugene's car, including numerous water bottles that he had apparently consumed before the incident, and his behavior in removing all of his clothing seemed to support the bath salts theory. Toxicology studies of Eugene's remains, however, did not reveal the presence of any exotic drugs in his system, although they showed that he had smoked marijuana.[3]

In an interview given some time after the incident, Eugene's girlfriend suggested that he might have been possessed by the devil or acting under a curse.[4] Eugene, who was from Haiti, apparently believed in voodoo. "That wasn't him," his girlfriend told CBS news reporters. "That was his body but it wasn't his spirit." She said that Eugene had been studying the Bible and texting Bible verses to friends shortly before the attack. "Rudy was battling the devil," she concluded.

The remarks of Rudy Eugene's girlfriend reminded me of the first criminology class that I taught years ago at a small southern college in the heart of what was then referred to as

Rudy Eugene, also known as the "Miami Cannibal," was killed by police in 2012 while apparently attempting to eat a homeless man alive. Can criminological theories explain his actions?

the Bible belt. Many of my students were devoutly religious and thoroughly churched in hallowed concepts such as good and evil, sin, salvation, and redemption. When the three-month course was nearly over and a detailed discussion of biological, psychological, and sociological theories of crime causation had ended, I decided to do some research. I wanted to see which of the theories we had discussed most appealed to the majority of my students. On the last day of class, I took a brief survey. After explaining what I was about to do, I started with the question "How many of you think that most criminal behavior can be explained by the biological theories of crime causation we've studied?" Only one or two students raised their hands. This was a very small number because the class, a popular one, held 131 students and was taught in a small auditorium. "How many of you," I continued, "think psychological theories explain most crime?" Again, only a handful of students responded. "Well, then, how many of you feel sociological theories offer the best explanation for crime?" I asked. A few more hands went up. Still, the majority of students had not voted one way or the other. Fearing that my teaching had been for naught and not knowing what else to ask, I blurted out, "How many of you believe that 'the devil made him do it' is the best explanation for crime that we can offer?" At that, almost all the students raised their hands.

I realized then that an entire semester spent trying to communicate the best thoughts of generations of criminologists had had little impact on most students in the class. They had listened to what I had to say, considered each of the perspectives I presented, and then dismissed all of them out of hand as so much

■ **evidence based**   Built on scientific findings, especially practices and policies founded upon the results of randomized, controlled experiments.

idle conjecture—assigning them the status of ruminations sadly out of touch with the true character of human nature and lacking in appreciation for the true cosmic temper of human activity.

That class held a lesson for me greater than any that the students had learned: It taught me that contemporary criminological theory cannot be fully appreciated until and unless its fundamental assumptions are comprehended. Until students can be brought to see the value of scientific criminology and unless they can be shown why today's criminologists think and reason the way they do, it is impossible to convince them that the criminological enterprise is worthy of serious attention.

> Even the best scientific evidence is rarely accorded the significance that it deserves by policy makers.

The lesson I learned that day was given voice by noted criminological researcher Lawrence W. Sherman, who, upon realizing that even the best scientific evidence the field has to offer is rarely accorded the significance that it deserves by policy makers, wrote, "The mythic power of subjective and unstructured wisdom holds back every field and keeps it from systematically discovering and implementing what works best."[5]

Today's Science-Based Criminology

In Chapter 1 we discussed how today's criminology is **evidence based.** This chapter describes how criminologists use contemporary social scientific research methods in the development of criminological theories, policies, and practices. It is my way of showing to those embarking upon the study of criminology why the modern-day science of criminology has both validity and purpose—that is, how it is applicable to the problems and realities of today's world. Were it not, the study of criminology would be pointless, and the criminological enterprise would become irrelevant.

Evidence-based criminology, a concept that was introduced in Chapter 1, is an increasingly popular form of contemporary criminology that is founded upon the experimental method. The method utilizes the techniques of the social sciences (especially randomized, controlled experiments) in

theory testing. When used in this context, the word *evidence* refers to scientific findings, *not* to the kind of evidence gathered by the police or used in criminal trials.

Some authors credit David Farrington, Lloyd Ohlin, and James Q. Wilson with helping to popularize the use of randomized experiments in the field of criminology.[6] In the mid-1980s, their influential book *Understanding and Controlling Crime* recommended the use of such experiments whenever possible to test assumptions in the justice field.[7] Shortly afterward, the National Institute of Justice (NIJ), under then-Director James C. Stewart, funded more than two dozen criminology-related experiments.[8] A decade later, Anthony Petrosino and his colleagues found that 267 criminological experiments had been conducted and published in English.[9] Today, that number is in the thousands.

Learn more about the growing body of evidence-based findings in the field of criminology at **http://expcrim.org.**

The Evolving Science of Criminology

In his seminal 2003 presidential address to the ASC, John H. Laub used the framework of life course theory (discussed in Chapter 7) to describe the history of criminological thought.[10] Laub identified three eras that he says have characterized the field of criminology over the past 100 years. The first era, said Laub, covered the years 1900 to 1930 and can "be thought of as the 'Golden Age of Research.'"[11] It was a time when data on crime and criminal behavior were largely gathered and evaluated independent of any particular ideational framework.

The second era, the period from 1930 to 1960, Laub called the "Golden Age of Theory" and described it as a time when intellectual theorizing "dominated the scene." Strangely, said Laub, during this second period, "there was no systematic attempt to link criminological research to theory."[12]

Era three extended from 1960 to 2000 and was "characterized by extensive theory testing of the dominant theories, using largely empirical methods." In other words, the third era identified by Laub was a time of scientific examination of the accuracy of criminological theories that had been advanced previously. Although he didn't address it directly, Laub indicated that the current era (i.e., twenty-first-century criminology, or fourth era) is heir to the first three eras and contains "all possible offspring" of what came before.

As Laub's remarks show, criminologists over the past half century have undertaken the task of building a scientific or evidence-based criminology, as distinguished from what had been the "armchair criminology" of earlier times. Armchair criminologists offered their ideas to one another as conjecture—fascinating "theories" that could be debated (and sometimes were) *ad nauseam*. Although the ruminations of armchair criminologists may have achieved a considerable degree of popular acclaim through (1) the involvement of distinguished lecturers, (2) the association of such ideas with celebrated bastions of higher learning, and (3) their publication in prestigious essays, they were rarely founded on anything other than mere speculation.

The ideas of armchair criminologists followed in the intellectual tradition of medieval Christian theologians, who sometimes busied themselves with debates over questions like how many angels could fit on the head of a pin or whether Noah had forgotten to take certain types of insects on board the ark. They were the kinds of things one could probably never know with certainty, no matter how much the ideas were debated, and the ideas being debated were rarely amenable to real-world tests. Under such circumstances, one person's theory was another's fact and still another's wishful thinking.[13]

Although it is easy to dispense with armchair criminology as the relaxed musings of carefree intellectuals undertaken almost as sport, it is far more difficult to agree on the criteria necessary to move any undertaking into the realm of serious scientific endeavor. Present-day criminology is decidedly more scientific, however, than its intellectual predecessor—which means that many of its theories and policy recommendations are amenable to objective scrutiny and systematic testing.

> Criminologists over the past century have undertaken the task of building a scientific or evidence-based criminology.

A variety of criteria have been advanced for declaring any endeavor "scientific." Among them are:[14]

- The systematic collection of related facts (as in the building of a database)
- An emphasis on the availability and application of the scientific method
- "The existence of general laws, a field for experiment or observation, and control of academic discourse by practical application"

- "The fact that it has been accepted into the scientific tradition"
- An "emphasis on a worthwhile subject in need of independent study even if adequate techniques of study are not yet available" (as in the investigation of paranormal phenomena)

Probably all the foregoing could be said of today's criminology. For one thing, criminologists do gather facts (Laub's "Golden Age of Research"). However, the mere gathering of facts, although it may lead to a descriptive criminology, falls short of offering satisfactory explanations for crime. Hence, most contemporary criminologists are concerned with identifying relationships among the facts they observe and with attempting to understand the many diverse causes of crime. This emphasis on unveiling causality moves criminology beyond the merely descriptive into the realm of conjecture and theory building. A further emphasis on measurement and objectivity gives contemporary criminology its scientific flavor.

Theory Building

A few years ago, Inspector Andy Parr, of the Sussex Police Department in England, reviewed crime statistics for the town of Brighton and found that violent crime was higher on nights when the moon was full.[15] "I compared a graph of full moons and a graph of last year's violent crimes and there is a trend," Parr told the United Kingdom's *Telegraph* newspaper. "People tend to be more aggressive" when the moon is full, Parr concluded. His findings were supported, he said, by his patrol experience. "When you try to reason with people on a full moon they become more aggressive and less rational," he told reporters. "When you try to reason with them on a full moon they become more argumentative."

Ultimately, the goal of research in criminology is the construction of theories or models that allow for a better understanding of criminal behavior and that permit the development of strategies intended to address the problem of crime. Simply put, a theory consists of a set of interrelated propositions that provides a relatively complete form of understanding (see Figure 2-1). Hence, even if we find that crime is higher when the moon is full, we must still ask why. Is it because the light from a full moon makes it possible for those who want to commit a crime to see better at night? If so, then we would expect crime to be higher in areas where there is no cloud cover than in areas with clouds. Likewise, lighted cities should show less of a rise in crime during a full moon than rural areas and small

■ **hypothesis**   A tentative explanation accounting for a set of facts that can be tested by further investigation.

■ **theory**   A series of interrelated propositions that attempts to describe, explain, predict, and ultimately control some class of events. A theory gains explanatory power from inherent logical consistency and is "tested" by how well it describes and predicts reality.

FIGURE 2-1 | **The Theory Building Process**

Source: Pearson Education, Inc.

towns. In any event, a complete lunar theory of crime causation would contain specific propositions about the causal nature of the phenomena involved. For viewpoints on another issue, the influence of violent video games on adolescents' behavior, see the Crime in the News box.

The word *theory* can be defined in many ways. One cogent definition comes from Don M. Gottfredson, a well-known contemporary criminologist: "Theories consist of postulates [assumptions], theoretical constructs, logically derived hypotheses, and definitions. Theories can be improved steadily through hypothesis testing, examination of evidence from observations, revisions of the theory, and repetitions of the cycle, repeatedly modifying the theory in light of the evidence."[16] (A **hypothesis** is an explanation that accounts for a set of facts

and that can be tested by further investigation.) Another well-known methodologist describes theories this way: "A theory is a set of related propositions that suggest why events occur in the manner that they do. The propositions that make up theories are of the same form as hypotheses: they consist of concepts and the linkages or relationships between them."[17]

These definitions both have something to offer. In fact, the definition of the term *theory* that we choose to use in this text combines aspects of both. For our purposes, then, a **theory** is a series of interrelated propositions that attempts to describe, explain, predict, and ultimately control some class of events. Theories gain explanatory power from inherent logical consistency and are "tested" by how well they describe and predict reality. In other words, a good theory provides relatively complete understanding, is supported by observations, and stands up to continued scrutiny.

Theories serve a number of purposes. For one thing, they give meaning to observations, explaining what we see in a particular setting by relating it to other things already understood. Hence, a theory of physics can explain the behavior of light by saying that light has properties of both waves and particles. Such a theory is immediately useful because we can easily grasp ideas like waves and particles, even if we have trouble conceptualizing light's essence.

Theories within criminology serve the same purpose as those within the physical sciences, but they are often more difficult to test. For example, few people can intuitively understand the motivation of "lust murderers" (a term developed by the Federal Bureau of Investigation and popularized by the media to refer to men who sexually abuse and kill women, often sadistically). Some psychiatric theories (discussed in Chapter 5) suggest that lust murderers kill because of a deep-seated hatred of women. Hate is something that most minds can grasp, and a vision of lust murder as an extreme example of the age-old battle between the sexes provides an intellectual "handle" that at least some people can comprehend.

CRIME | in the NEWS

Do Violent Video Games Make Kids Kill?

Mass shooters have been known to play violent video games before their sprees, killing people like so many icons on the screen. The two killers at Columbine High School in 1999 were addicted to Mortal Kombat, and Anders Breivik, the Norwegian gunman who killed 77 people in 2011, said he played Call of Duty to train himself.

But did video games make these people violent? Ninety percent of teenage boys play video games—often violent ones like Mortal Kombat and Grand Theft Auto—and yet the juvenile arrest rate for violent crimes declined sharply from 1994 to 2003 and has remained relatively stable since then.

Even so, video games seem to be getting even more savage, with titles like Super Columbine Massacre, Splatterhouse, and Thrill Kill. Manufacturers have set up a rating system to identify violent video games, but it has no teeth. Stores are expected to withhold violent games from younger kids voluntarily. Almost all violent games are in the Mature category, appropriate for ages 17 and up. The next level is an Adults Only (AO) rating, for ages 18 and over. Manufacturers consider an AO rating a sales killer, and very few violent games ever get it.

Some concerned parents have called for an outright ban on selling violent video games to minors, but that would mean removing free speech protections from video games, which courts refuse to do. In 2011, in what might well be the deathblow for the opposition, the U.S. Supreme Court completely struck down a California law that would have banned sales of violent video games to anyone under age 18. The Court rejected the argument that the interactive nature of video games has a stronger impact on young minds than, say, violent movies, which have free speech protections. Justice Antonin Scalia argued that even literature is interactive, writing: "Grimm's Fairy Tales, for example, are grim indeed."

Most Americans, however, did not agree with the ruling. A Rasmussen poll taken afterward found that 67% of the public thought states should have the right to prohibit sales of video games. In addition, several studies have concluded that violent video games cause higher rates of aggression in teenagers. A number of researchers have challenged those conclusions, however, arguing that other causes of aggression were not ruled out.

Source: Pearson Education, Inc.

Thomas Frey/Glow Images

A young man plays a game in a video arcade. Some say that violent electronic games can make young people act out their violent fantasies. Other studies, however, seem to show that such is not the case. What do you think?

Meanwhile, two new studies show that multiplayer video games can actually reduce aggressiveness when the players work together. The studies found that college students who teamed up to play violent video games later showed more cooperative behavior than those who played the games competitively.

Discussion Questions

1. Do you think that violent video games can affect a player's emotions and influence his or her view of the world? Might they also influence his or her real-life behavior? If so, how?

2. What kind of social scientific experiment might be devised to test the assertion that violent video games influence their players' behavior in the real world?

Theories provide understanding in a number of ways. Kenneth R. Hoover identified four "uses of theory in social scientific thinking":[18]

1. Theories provide patterns for the interpretation of data. Population density, for example, tends to be associated with high crime rates, and maps showing high population density tend to be closely associated with diagrams that reflect high rates of crime, so some theorists suggest that overcrowding increases aggression and therefore crime. "People," said Hoover, "like to think in terms of images, analogies, and patterns; this helps to simplify complex realities and to lighten the burden of thought."

2. Theories link one study with another. Some years ago, a case study of women's prisons in California found the

existence of artificially constructed "families" around which women's lives centered. A similar but later study of a Chinese prison also found that the female inmates had created family-like groups. As a result, some theorists suggested that women feel a need to nurture and be nurtured and that they carry this need with them into prison. The fact that cross-cultural support was found for this suggestion provided a linkage between the two studies, which tended to lend further support to it.

3. Theories supply frameworks within which concepts and variables acquire special significance. The death penalty, for example, although especially significant to individuals condemned to die, acquires special significance when seen as a tool employed by the powerful to keep the powerless under their control.

■ **research**   The use of standardized, systematic procedures in the search for knowledge.

■ **applied research**   Research based on scientific inquiry that is designed and carried out with practical applications in mind.

■ **pure research**   Research undertaken simply for the sake of advancing scientific knowledge.

■ **primary research**   Research characterized by original and direct investigation.

■ **secondary research**   Research based on new evaluations of existing information that has been collected by other researchers. Also referred to as **secondary analysis.**

4. Theories allow us to interpret the larger meaning of our findings for ourselves and for others. Hence, the death penalty has become a moral issue for many Americans today, shrouded as it is in ethical considerations and images of national identity and ultimate justice.

Learn more about the nature of modern social scientific thought and theory construction at **http://www.stolaf. edu/people/leming/soc371res/theory.html** and **http:// tinyurl.com/5s7zq5f**.

The Role of Research and Experimentation

The objective of criminology is the development of a body of general verified principles.

More important than the claims made by theories and by the theorists who create them are findings of fact that either support those claims or leave them without foundation. Hence, theories, once proposed, need to be tested against the real world via a variety of research strategies, including experimentation and case studies. This is equally true whether the proposed theory is relatively simple or dauntingly complex.

In his 2009 presidential address to the ASC, incoming president Todd Clear told listeners that "if the evidence-based movement means anything, it means that we want to avoid undertaking programs based on stereotypes and cherished pet theories about crime." Clear described the current state of criminology as focused on the "what works model," and said that "the question '[W]hat works?' might be rewritten as 'How effective is a given program or intervention?'"[19]

Reliable determinations of program effectiveness are made through research. **Research** can be defined as the use of standardized, systematic procedures in the search for knowledge.[20] Some researchers distinguish between applied research and nonapplied, or pure, research. **Applied research** "consists of scientific inquiry that is designed and carried out with practical application in mind."[21] In applied research, the researcher is working toward some more or less practical goal. It may be the reduction of crime, the efficient compensation of victims of crime, or an evaluation of the effectiveness of policies implemented to solve some specific aspect of the crime problem. **Pure research**, on the other hand, is undertaken simply for the sake of advancing scientific knowledge and "does not carry the promise or expectation of immediate, direct relevance."[22]

Another type of research, secondary research or secondary analysis, can be distinguished from primary research.[23] **Primary research** "is characterized by original and direct investigation,"[24] whereas **secondary research** consists of new evaluations of existing information that has already been collected by other researchers.

Scientific research generally proceeds in stages, which can be divided conceptually among (1) problem identification, (2) development of a research design, (3) choice of data-gathering techniques, and (4) review of findings (which often includes statistical analysis).

Problem Identification

Problem identification, the first step in any research, consists of naming a problem or choosing an issue to study. Topics may be selected for a variety of reasons. Larry S. Miller and John T. Whitehead, for example, said that "the choice of what criminologists study is influenced by political decisions,"[25] meaning that the availability of government grant monies frequently determines the focus of much contemporary research in the area of crime. It may also be that private foundation monies have become available to support studies in a specific area. Perhaps the researcher has a personal interest in a particular issue and wants to learn more, or maybe a professor or teacher has assigned a research project as part of the requirements for a class. Whatever the reason for beginning research, however, the way in which a research problem is stated and conceptualized will help narrow the research focus and will serve as a guide to the formulation of data-gathering strategies.

Although some criminological research undertaken today is purely descriptive, the bulk of research in criminology

■ **variable**   A concept that can undergo measurable changes.
■ **operationalization**   The process by which concepts are made measurable.

■ **research design**   The logic and structure inherent in an approach to data gathering.

is intended to explore issues of causality, especially the claims made by theories purporting to explain criminal behavior. As such, much contemporary research is involved with the testing of hypotheses. The *Free Oxford English Dictionary* defines the word hypothesis as follows:[26] "A supposition or proposed explanation made on the basis of limited evidence as a starting point for further investigation."

Within the modern scientific tradition, a hypothesis is a possible explanation for an observed correlation that can be tested in the real world. Some criminologists, as mentioned earlier, have observed what appears to be a correlation, or relationship, between the phases of the moon and the rate of crime commission. Such observers may propose the following hypothesis: The moon causes crime. Although this is a useful starting hypothesis, it needs to be further refined before it can be tested. Specifically, the concepts contained within the hypothesis must be translated into measurable variables. A **variable** is simply a concept that can undergo measurable changes.

Scientific precedent holds that only measurable items can be satisfactorily tested. The process of turning a simple hypothesis into one that is testable is called **operationalization**. An operationalized hypothesis is one that is stated in such a way as to facilitate measurement, and it is specific in its terms and in the linkages it proposes. For example, we might move a step further toward both measurability and specificity in our hypothesis about the relationship between the moon and crime by restating it as follows: Rates of murder, rape, robbery, and assault rise when the moon's fullness increases and are highest when the moon is full. Now we have specified what we mean by crime (i.e., murder, rape, robbery, and assault), rates of which can be calculated. The degree of the moon's fullness can also be measured. Once we have operationalized a hypothesis and made the concepts it contains measurable, those concepts have, in effect, become variables.

Once the concepts within our hypothesis are measurable, we can test the hypothesis itself; that is, we can observe what happens to crime rates as the moon approaches fullness, as well as what happens when the moon is full, and see whether our observations support our hypothesis. As our dictionary definition tells us, once a hypothesis has been operationalized, it is assumed to be true for purposes of testing. It is accepted, for study purposes, until observation proves it untrue, at which point it is said to be rejected. As two renowned research methodologists have stated, "The task of theory-testing is predominantly one of rejecting inadequate hypotheses."[27]

The full moon over New York City. It is the job of researchers to determine the validity of claimed relationships—and of theorists to explain why such relationships hold. Are phases of the moon correlated with changes in the rate of occurrence of certain crimes? If so, why?

Development of a Research Design

Research designs structure the research process. They provide a kind of road map to the logic inherent in one's approach to a research problem, and they also serve as guides to the systematic collection of data (see **http://ssrn.com/abstract=1464994**).

Research designs consist of the logic and structure inherent in any particular approach to data gathering. A simple study, for example, might be designed to test the assertion that the consumption of refined white sugar promotes aggressive or violent tendencies. One could imagine researchers approaching prison officials with the proposal that inmate diets be altered to exclude all refined white sugar. Under the plan, cafeteria cooks would be instructed to prepare meals without the use of sugar. Noncaloric sweeteners would be substituted for sugar in recipes calling for sugar, and sweetened beverages and carbonated drinks containing sugar would be banned. Likewise, the prison canteen would be prohibited from selling items containing sugar for the duration of the experiment.

> The central principle of experimentation is that we must accept the outcome whether or not it is to our liking.

- **confounding effect**   A rival explanation or competing hypothesis that is a threat to the internal or external validity of a research design.

- **internal validity**   The certainty that experimental interventions did indeed cause the changes observed in the study group.
- **external validity**   The ability to generalize research findings to other settings.
- **controlled experiment**   An experiment that attempts to hold conditions (other than the intentionally introduced experimental intervention) constant.

To determine whether the forced reduction in sugar consumption actually affected inmates' behavior, researchers might look at the recorded frequency of aggressive incidents (sometimes called "write-ups" in prison jargon) occurring within the confines of the prison before the experiment was initiated and compare such data with similar information on such incidents following the introduction of dietary changes. A research design employing this kind of logic can be diagrammed as follows:

$$O_1 \times O_2$$

Here O_1 (termed a *pretest*) refers to the information gathered on inmate aggressiveness prior to the introduction of dietary changes (which themselves are shown as X, also called the *experimental intervention*), and O_2 (termed the *posttest*) signifies a second set of observations—those occurring after dietary changes have been implemented. Researchers employing a strategy of this type, which is known as a "one-group pretest-posttest," would likely examine differences between the two sets of observations, one made before introduction of the experimental intervention and the other after. The difference, they may assume, would show changes in behavior resulting from changes in diet—in this case, the exclusion of refined white sugar.

Although this basic research design illustrates the logic behind naïve experiments, it does not provide a good research structure because it does not eliminate other possible explanations of behavioral change. For example, during the time between the first and second observations, inmates may have been exposed to some other influence that reduced their level of aggression. A new minister may have begun preaching effective sermons filled with messages of love and peace to the prison congregation; television cable service to the prison may have been disrupted, lowering the exposure inmates received to violent programming; a new warden may have taken control of the facility, relaxing prison rules and reducing tensions; a transfer or release of especially troublesome inmates, scheduled at some earlier time, may have occurred; a new program of conjugal visitation may have been initiated, creating newfound sexual outlets and reducing inmate tensions; and so on. The possibilities for rival explanations (i.e., those that rival the explanatory power of the hypothesis under study) are nearly limitless. Rival explanations like these, called by some researchers "competing hypotheses" and **confounding effects** by others, make the results of any single series of observations uncertain.

Validity in Research Designs

Confounding effects, which may invalidate the results of research, are of two general types: those that limit the certainty that internal interventions caused the changes in research findings, which is called **internal validity**, and those that affect the ability of researchers to generalize the research findings to other settings, which is called **external validity**. Often, when external validity is threatened, researchers do not feel confident that interventions that "worked" under laboratory-like or other special conditions will still be effective when employed in the field. Hence, researchers achieving internal validity may be able to demonstrate that diets low in refined white sugar lower the number of instances of overt displays of aggressiveness in a single prison under study. They may not feel confident (for the reasons shown in Figure 2-2), however, that similar changes in diet, if implemented in the general nonprison population, would have a similar effect. Most researchers consider internal validity the most vital component of any planned research because, without it, considerations of external validity become irrelevant.

Factors that routinely threaten the internal validity of a design for research are found in Figure 2-2.[28] Threats to external validity are shown in Figure 2-3.

Experimental and Quasi-Experimental Research Designs

To have confidence that the changes intentionally introduced into a situation are the real cause of observed variations, it is necessary to achieve some degree of control over factors that threaten internal validity. In the physical sciences, controlled experiments often provide the needed guarantees. **Controlled experiments** attempt to hold conditions (other than the intentionally introduced experimental intervention) constant. Some researchers have defined the word *experiment* simply as "controlled observation."

Whereas constancy of conditions may be possible to achieve within laboratory settings, it is far more difficult to come by in the social world, which by its very nature is in an ongoing state of flux. Hence, although

Self-selected subjects may be more interested in participation than others, and they may respond more readily to experimental treatment.

■ **quasi-experimental design**   An approach to research that, although less powerful than experimental designs, is deemed worthy of use when better designs are not feasible.

■ **control group**   A group of experimental subjects that, although the subject of measurement and observation, is not exposed to the experimental intervention.

Threats to the Internal Validity of a Research Design

History (or Competing Cause)
Specific events that occur between the first and second observations that may affect measurement.

Maturation
Processes occurring within the respondents or subjects that operate as a result of the passage of time. Fatigue along with decreases in response time due to age are examples.

Repeated Testing (or Testing Effects)
Effects of taking a test upon the scores of a later testing. When respondents are measures in some way that requires them to respond, they tend to do better (i.e., their scores increase) the next time they are tested. In effect, they have learned how to take the test or how to be measured, even though they may not have acquired more knowledge about the subject matter that the test intends to measure.

Instrumentation (or Instrument Change)
Changes in measuring instruments or in survey takers that occur as a result of time. Batteries wear down, instruments need to be recalibrated, interviewers grow tired or are replaced with others, and so on—all of which can change the nature of the observations made.

Statistical Regression (or Regression Toward the Mean)
Return to more average scores. When respondents have been selected for study on the basis of extreme scores (as may be the case with personality inventories), later testing will tend to show a regression toward the mean because some extreme scores are inevitably more the result of accident or luck than anything else.

Differential Selection
Built-in biases that result when more than one group of subjects are involved in a study and when the groups being tested are initially somehow different. The random assignment of subjects to test groups greatly reduces the chances that such significant differences will exist.

Experimental Mortality (or Differential Attrition)
Differential loss of respondents from comparison groups that may occur when more than one group is being tested. For example, one group loses members at a greater rate than another group, or certain kinds of members are lost from one group but not from another.

Experimenter Bias
Inadvertent and nonconscious effects caused by the experimenters, including favoritism or biased behavior toward selected subjects.

FIGURE 2-2 | Threats to the Internal Validity of a Research Design
Source: Pearson Education, Inc.

criminologists sometimes employ true experimental designs in the conduct of their research, they are more likely to find it necessary to use **quasi-experimental designs**, or approaches to research that "are deemed worthy of use where better designs

are not feasible."[29] Quasi-experimental designs are especially valuable when aspects of the social setting are beyond the control of the researcher. The crucial defining feature of quasi-experimental designs is that they give researchers control over the "when and to whom" of measurement, even though others decide the "when and to whom" of exposure to the experimental intervention.

Sometimes, for example, legislators enact new laws intended to address some aspect of the crime problem, specifying the kinds of crime-prevention measures to be employed and the segment of the population to receive them. Midnight basketball, intended to keep young people off the streets at night, provides an example of a legislatively sponsored intervention. During debate on the 1994 Violent Crime Control and Law Enforcement Act, midnight basketball became a point of contention, with senators asking whether money spent in support of such an activity would actually reduce the incidence of serious street crime in our nation's inner cities. Unfortunately, no good research data that could answer the question were then available. Now, however, federally funded midnight basketball programs, which have existed for a number of years, could be studied by researchers. Hence, although criminologists were not politically situated to be able to enact midnight basketball legislation, they are able to study the effects of such legislation *after* it has been enacted.[30]

Whether criminologists decide on experimental or quasi-experimental designs to guide their research, they depend on well-considered research strategies to eliminate rival explanations for the effects they observe. One relatively powerful research design that criminologists frequently employ can be diagrammed as follows:

$$\text{Experimental group} \quad O_1 \times O_2$$
$$\text{Control group} \quad O_3 \times O_4$$

The meaning of the notation used here is similar to that of the one-shot case study design discussed earlier. This approach, however, called the "pretest-posttest control group design," gains considerable power from the addition of a second group; it is called a **control group** because it is not exposed to the experimental intervention.

Critical to the success of a research design like this is the use of randomization in the assignment of subjects to both

■ **randomization**   The process whereby individuals are assigned to study groups without biases or differences resulting from selection.

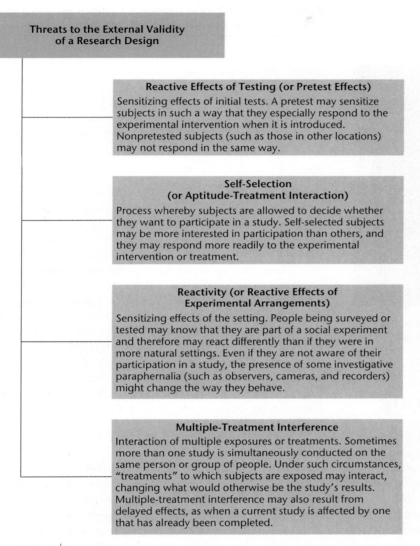

Threats to the External Validity of a Research Design

Reactive Effects of Testing (or Pretest Effects)
Sensitizing effects of initial tests. A pretest may sensitize subjects in such a way that they especially respond to the experimental intervention when it is introduced. Nonpretested subjects (such as those in other locations) may not respond in the same way.

Self-Selection (or Aptitude-Treatment Interaction)
Process whereby subjects are allowed to decide whether they want to participate in a study. Self-selected subjects may be more interested in participation than others, and they may respond more readily to the experimental intervention or treatment.

Reactivity (or Reactive Effects of Experimental Arrangements)
Sensitizing effects of the setting. People being surveyed or tested may know that they are part of a social experiment and therefore may react differently than if they were in more natural settings. Even if they are not aware of their participation in a study, the presence of some investigative paraphernalia (such as observers, cameras, and recorders) might change the way they behave.

Multiple-Treatment Interference
Interaction of multiple exposures or treatments. Sometimes more than one study is simultaneously conducted on the same person or group of people. Under such circumstances, "treatments" to which subjects are exposed may interact, changing what would otherwise be the study's results. Multiple-treatment interference may also result from delayed effects, as when a current study is affected by one that has already been completed.

FIGURE 2-3 | Threats to the External Validity of a Research Design
Source: Pearson Education, Inc.

the experimental and the control groups. **Randomization** is the process whereby individuals are assigned to study groups without biases or differences resulting from selection. Self-selection (when some individuals volunteer for membership in either the experimental or the control group) is not permitted, nor are researchers allowed to use personal judgment in assigning subjects to groups.

Control over potential threats to internal validity is achieved by the introduction of a properly selected control group because it is assumed that both experimental and control groups are essentially the same at the start and that any threats to internal validity will affect both groups equally as

the experiment progresses—effectively canceling out when final differences between the two groups are measured. If some particular historical event, for example, affects the experimental group and modifies the measurable characteristics of that group, that event should have the same impact on the control group. Hence, in the previous design, when O_4 is subtracted from O_2, the remaining observable *net effects* are assumed to be attributable to the experimental intervention.

In the prison study discussed earlier, randomization would require that all inmates be systematically but randomly divided into two groups. Random assignments are typically made by using a table of random numbers. In this simple study, however, something as easy as the flip of a coin should suffice. Members of one group (the experimental group) would no longer receive refined white sugar in their diets, while members of the other group (the control group) would continue eating as before. With this one exception in diet, both groups would continue to be exposed to the same environment, so it can be assumed that any other influences on the level of violence within the prison will cancel out when final measurements are taken and that measurable differences in violence between the two groups can be attributed solely to the effects of the experimental variable (in this case, removal of refined white sugar from the diet).

The use of experimental design in the field of criminology sets a "gold standard" for researchers to follow.

According to Shawn Bushway and David Weisburd at the University of Maryland, criminology is the only field within the social sciences to "show a marked increase in the use of experimental designs over the past 40 years."[31] And the movement has powerful friends. No less an authority than Lawrence W. Sherman, director of the Institute of Criminology at Cambridge University and the former director of research at the Police Foundation, says that the use of experimental design in the field of criminology is the "gold standard" to which evaluations of both theory and practice should be held.[32]

■ **survey research**   Research using a social science data-gathering technique that involves the use of questionnaires.
■ **case study**   A form of research that employs detailed analysis of a person, group, or situation—often over a period of time.

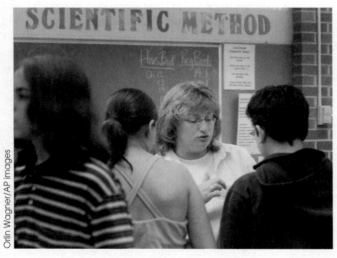

Orlin Wagner/AP Images

A high school science fair booth pays homage to the scientific method. What is evidence-based criminology? How does it make use of the scientific method?

Choice of Data-Gathering Techniques

The combination of (1) hypothesis building, (2) operationalization, and (3) systematic observation in the service of hypothesis testing has made modern-day criminology scientific and has facilitated scientific theory building within the field. Hence, once a research problem has been identified, concepts have been made measurable, and a research design has been selected, investigators must then decide on the type of data to be gathered and the techniques of data gathering they wish to employ. Ultimately, all research depends on the use of techniques to gather information, or data, for eventual analysis. Like research designs, which structure a researcher's approach to a problem, data-gathering strategies provide approaches to the accumulation of information needed for analysis to occur.

Many first-time researchers select data-gathering techniques on the basis of ease or simplicity, and some choose according to the cost or the amount of time the techniques require. The most important question to consider when beginning to gather information, however, is whether the data-gathering strategy selected will produce information in a usable form. The kind of information needed depends on the questions to be answered. Surveys of public opinion about the desirability of the death

penalty, for example, cannot address issues of the punishment's effectiveness as a crime-control strategy.

Five major data-gathering strategies typify research in the field of criminology: surveys, case studies, participant observations, self-reporting, and secondary analysis (also called secondary research).

Surveys

Survey research typically involves the use of questionnaires, or surveys. Respondents may be interviewed in person or over the telephone or queried via e-mail or be directed to online surveys. Mail surveys are common, although they tend to have a lower response rate than other types of social surveys. The information produced through the use of questionnaires is referred to as "survey data." Polling companies like Gallup, CNN, and Roper gather data on public opinion, voting preferences, and so forth, and the U.S. Census Bureau data are gathered by trained survey takers. Survey data also inform the National Crime Victimization Survey (NCVS) and result in publications such as *Crime and the Nation's Households, Criminal Victimization*, and other NCVS-related reports produced by the Bureau of Justice Statistics. Surveys have also been used to assess fear of crime, attitudes toward the police, and extent of unreported crime.

Case Studies

Case studies are built around in-depth investigations into individual cases. The study of one (perhaps notorious) offender, the scrutiny of a particular criminal organization, and the analysis of a prison camp may all qualify as case studies. Case studies are useful for what they can tell us to expect about other similar cases. If a study of a street gang, for example, reveals the central role of a few leaders, then we would expect to find a similar organizational style among other gangs of the same kind.

When one individual (a single subject) is the focus of a **case study**, the investigation may take the form of a subjective life history, which involves gathering as much historical data as possible about a given individual and his or her life experiences. Life histories may also be gathered on groups of individuals, and similarities in life experiences that are thereby discovered may provide researchers with clues to current behavior or with points at which to begin further investigations.

Case studies, although they may suffer from high levels of subjectivity in which feelings cannot be easily separated from fact, provide the opportunity to investigate individual cases—an element lacking in both surveys and participant observations.

■ **participant observation**   A data gathering strategy in which the researcher observes a group by participating, to varying degrees, in the activities of the group.

■ **self-report**   A test or measure about one own's behavior, feelings, or other personal knowledge and characteristics.

Participant Observations

Participant observation "involves a variety of strategies in data gathering in which the researcher observes a group by participating, to varying degrees, in the activities of the group."[33] Some participant researchers operate undercover, whereas others make their identity and purpose known from the outset. As one criminologist stated, participant observation "means that criminologists must venture inside the immediacy of crime."[34]

One of the earliest and best-known participant observers in the field of criminology was William Foote Whyte, who described his 1943 study of criminal subcultures in a slum district that he called "Cornerville" this way:

> My aim was to gain an intimate view of Cornerville life. My first problem, therefore, was to establish myself as a participant in the society so that I would have a position from which to observe. I began by going to live in Cornerville, finding a room with an Italian family. It was not enough simply to make the acquaintance of various groups of people. The sort of information that I sought required that I establish intimate social relations. This active participation gave me something in common with them so that we had other things to talk about besides the weather. It broke down the social barriers and made it possible for me to be taken into the intimate life of the group.[35]

It is possible to distinguish between at least two additional kinds of participant observation: (1) the participant as observer and (2) the observer as complete participant. When researchers make their presence known to those whom they are observing without attempting to influence the outcome of their observations or the activities of the group, they fit the category of participants who are observers. But researchers who make their presence known may inadvertently influence outcomes because people tend to act differently when they know they are being watched.

When they become complete participants in the group they are observing, researchers run the risk of influencing the group's direction. As Whyte explained, "I made it a rule that I should try to avoid influencing the actions of the group. I wanted to observe what the men did under ordinary circumstances; I did not want to lead them into different activities."[36] Another problem facing the participant observer is that of "going native," assuming too close an identification with the subjects or the behavior under study (e.g., an undercover police officer who may be tempted to participate in the illegalities he or she is supposed to be monitoring). When that happens, all sense of the research perspective may be lost, and serious ethical problems may arise.

On the other hand, some researchers may feel disgust for the subjects of their research. Data gatherers with a particular dislike of drug abuse, for example, may be hard put to maintain their objectivity when working as participant observers within the drug subculture. Hence, as noted social science researcher Frank Hagan observed, "The researcher must avoid not only over identification with the study group, but also aversion to it."[37]

Self-Reporting

Another subjective data-gathering technique is the self-report that investigates aspects of a problem not otherwise amenable to study. When official records are lacking, research subjects may be asked to record and report rates of otherwise secretive behavior. Self-reports may prove especially valuable in providing checks on official reports consisting of statistical tabulations gathered through channels such as police departments, hospitals, and social services agencies.

Self-reports may also be requested of subjects in survey research, so self-reporting is sometimes considered simply another form of survey research. However, many self-reporting techniques require the maintenance of a diary or personal journal and request vigilant and ongoing observations of the study subject's own behavior. Hence, sex researchers may ask subjects to maintain an ongoing record of their frequency of intercourse, the variety of sexual techniques employed, and their preference in partners—items of information that are not easy to come by through other means or that cannot be accurately reconstructed from memory.

Self-reporting enters the realm of the purely subjective when it consists of introspection, or personal reflection. Introspective techniques intended to gather data on secretive feelings and felt motivations are often used by psychologists seeking to assess the mental status of patients. Criminologists have at times used introspective techniques to categorize criminal offenders into types and to initiate the process of developing concepts more amenable to objective study.

Secondary Analysis

Not all data-gathering techniques produce new data. Secondary analysis (or secondary research) purposefully culls preexisting information from data that have already been gathered (possibly for another purpose) and examines it in new ways. The secondary analysis of existing data and the use of previously acquired information for new avenues of inquiry are strategies that can save researchers a considerable amount of time and expense.

One important source of data for secondary analysis is the National Archive of Criminal Justice data located in the

■ **intersubjectivity**   A scientific principle that requires that independent observers see the same thing under the same circumstances for observations to be regarded as valid.

■ **replicability**   A scientific principle that holds that valid observations made at one time can be made again later if all other conditions are the same.

Institute for Social Research at the University of Michigan. In the words of the U.S. Department of Justice, the archive's sponsoring agency, "The Archive continually processes the most relevant criminal justice data sets for the research community,"[38] maintaining information on victimization, various aspects of the criminal justice system, and juvenile delinquency. Access to archive data is by request, and data sets are available to individual researchers. Visit the archive via **https://www. icpsr.umich.edu/icpsrweb/**.

The use of secondary data rarely alerts research subjects to the fact that they (or the data they have provided) are being studied, although they may have been aware of it when the data were first gathered, making secondary analysis "nonreactive." For example, the use of archival records in data analysis constitutes a virtual "goldmine of information waiting to be exploited."[39] Nonetheless, it is important to keep in mind that secondary analysis usually involves the use of information that was collected for a purpose outside the interests of the current researcher.

Problems in Data Collection

Scientific data gathering builds on observations of one sort or another. Observation is not unique to science—individuals continuously make observations and draw a plethora of personal conclusions based on what they see or hear. Scientific observation, however, generally occurs under controlled conditions and must meet the criteria of intersubjectivity and replicability. **Intersubjectivity** means that, for observations to be valid, independent observers must report seeing the same thing under the same circumstances. "Do you see what I see?" is a question that highlights the central role of intersubjectivity in scientific observation. If observers cannot agree on what they saw, then the raw data necessary for scientific analysis have not been acquired. **Replicability** of observations, at least in the field of scientific experimentation, means that when the same conditions exist, the same results can be expected to follow; hence, valid experiments can be replicated. The same observations made at one time can be made again at a later time if all other conditions are the same.

> "Do you see what I see?" is a question that highlights the central role of intersubjectivity in scientific observation.

In the physical sciences, replicability is easy to achieve. Water at sea level, for example, will always boil at 100° Celsius. Anyone can replicate the conditions needed to test such a contention. When replicability cannot be achieved, it casts the validity of the observation into doubt. Some years ago, for example, a few scientists claimed to have achieved nuclear fusion at room temperature. Their supposed accomplishment was dubbed "cold fusion" and was hailed as a major breakthrough in the production of nuclear energy. However, when scientists elsewhere attempted to replicate the conditions under which cold fusion was said to occur, they could find no evidence that the initial experimenters were correct. Intersubjectivity and replicability are critical to the scientific enterprise, with one researcher stating that "science rests its claim to authority upon its firm basis in observable evidence."[40]

It is important to recognize, however, that some observations—even those that stand up to the tests of intersubjectivity and replicability—can lead to unwarranted conclusions. For example, spirit possession, an explanation for deviance that was apparently widely held in primitive times, must have appeared to be well validated by the positive behavioral changes that became apparent in those who submitted to the surgery called for by the theory, which was a craniotomy intended to release offending spirits from the head of the afflicted person. The actual cause of behavioral reformation may have been brain infections resulting from unsanitary surgical conditions, slips of the stone knife, or the intensity of pain endured by those undergoing the procedure without anesthetics. To the uncritical observer, however, the theory of spirit possession as a cause of deviance and cranial surgery as a treatment technique would probably appear to have been supported by the evidence of induced behavioral change.

Some methodologists noted that "theories are as much involved in the determination of fact as facts are in establishing a theory."[41] Theories are intimately involved in the process of data collection: They determine what kinds of data we choose to gather, what we look for in the data, and how we interpret the information we have gathered. In short, theories determine what we see as well as what we ignore. In the late 1700s, for example, when a meteor shower was reported to the French Academy of Sciences, observers reported that some fragments had struck the ground, causing tremendous explosions. The learned scientists of the academy quickly dismissed these accounts, however, calling them "a superstition unworthy of these enlightened times."[42] Everyone, they said, knows that

■ **descriptive statistics**   Statistics that describe, summarize, or highlight the relationships within data that have been gathered.
■ **inferential statistics**   Statistics that specify how likely findings are to be true for other populations or in other locales.
■ **correlation**   A causal, complementary, or reciprocal relationship between two measurable variables.
■ **test of significance**   A statistical technique intended to provide researchers with confidence that their results are, in fact, true and not the result of sampling error.

stones don't fall from the sky. For additional information on measurement problems in criminal justice research, visit **http://www.nap.edu/catalog.php?record_id=10581**.

Review of Findings

Some data, once collected, are simply archived or stored, but most data are subject to some form of analysis. Data analysis generally involves the use of mathematical techniques intended to uncover correlations between or among variables and to assess the likelihood that research findings can be generalized to other settings. These are statistical techniques, and their use in analyzing data is called *statistical analysis*. Some theorists, for example, posit a link between poverty and crime. Hence, we might suspect that low-income areas would be high-crime areas. Once we specify what we mean by "low-income" and "crime" so that they become measurable variables, and we gather data on income levels and the incidence of crime in various locales, we are ready to begin the job of data analysis.

Statistical techniques provide tools for summarizing data and also provide quantitative means for identifying patterns within the data and for determining the degree of correlation that exists between variables. Statistical methods can be divided into two types: descriptive and inferential. **Descriptive statistics** describe, summarize, or highlight the relationships within the data that have been gathered. **Inferential statistics**, on the other hand, attempt to generalize findings by specifying how likely they are to be true for other populations or in other locales.

Descriptive statistics include measures of central tendency, commonly called the mode, median, and mean. *Mode* refers to the most frequently occurring score or value in any series of observations. If, for example, we measure the age of all juvenile offenders held in a state training facility, it may be that they range in age from 12 to 16, with 15 being the most commonly found age; 15, then, would be the modal age for the population under study.

Median defines the midpoint of a data series—half of the scores will be above the mean and the other half will be below. It may be, for example, that in our study of juveniles, we find equal numbers in each age category, so the median age for those offenders would be 14.

Mean is the mathematical average of all scores within a given population and is the most commonly used measure of central tendency. It is calculated by simply adding together all the scores (or ages, in our example) and dividing by the total number of observations. Although calculations of the mode, median, and mean will often yield similar results, such will not

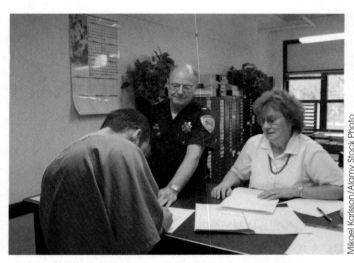

Social science research within a criminal justice setting.
Inmate surveys may increase our knowledge of crime causation. What might such surveys tell us?

Mikael Karlsson/Alamy Stock Photo

be the case with populations that are skewed in a particular direction. If our population of juveniles, for example, consisted almost entirely of 16-year-olds, then the mode for that population would inevitably be 16 while other measures of central tendency would yield somewhat lower figures.

Other descriptive statistics provide measures of the standard deviation of a population (i.e., the degree of dispersion of scores about the mean) and the degree of **correlation** or interdependence between variables (i.e., the extent of variation in one that can be expected to follow from a measured change in another). Although the degree of correlation may vary, the direction of correlation can be described. We say, for example, that if one variable increases whenever another, upon which it is dependent, does the same, a positive correlation (or positive relationship) exists between the two; when one variable decreases in value as another rises, a negative correlation (or inverse relationship) exists.

Another statistical technique, one that provides a measure of the likelihood that a study's findings are the results of chance, is commonly found in criminological literature. **Tests of significance** are designed to provide researchers with confidence that their results are, in fact, true and not the result of sampling error. We may, for example, set out to measure the degree of gun ownership. Let's say that the extent of gun ownership in the area under study is actually 50%. (We have no way of knowing this until our study is complete.) We may decide to use

■ **quantitative method**   A research technique that produces measurable results.

door-to-door surveys of randomly selected households because cost prohibits us from canvassing all households in the study area. Even if we have made our best survey effort, however, some slight probability remains that the households we have chosen to interview may all be populated by gun owners. Although it is very unlikely, we may—by chance—have excluded those without guns. Assuming that everyone interviewed answers truthfully, we would come away with the mistaken impression that 100% of the population in the study area is armed!

The likelihood of faulty findings increases as sample size decreases. Were we to sample only one or two households, we would have little likelihood of determining the actual incidence of gun ownership. The larger the sample size, however, the greater the confidence we can have in our findings. In other words, a positive correlation exists between sample size and degree of confidence we can have in our results. Even so, in most criminological research, it is not possible to study all members of a given population, so samples must be taken. Statistical tests of significance, expressed as a percentage, assess the likelihood that our study findings are due to chance. Hence, a study that reflects a 95% confidence level can be interpreted as having a 5% likelihood that the results it reports are mere happenstance. To put it another way, for every hundred such studies, five yield misleading results. The problem is that it would be impossible to know (without further research) which five that would be.

> Tests of significance are designed to provide researchers with confidence that their results are, in fact, true.

Learn more about statistics and statistical methods from the American Statistical Association and the American Association for the Advancement of Science via **http://www.amstat. org/index.cfm?fuseaction=main** and **http://www.aaas. org/**. Read about statistical tools on the World Wide Web via **http://www.amstat.org/publications/tas.cfm**.

Quantitative versus Qualitative Methods

Years ago, during the Clinton administration, then–Attorney General Janet Reno addressed researchers, criminologists, and professors gathered at the annual meeting of the ASC in Miami, Florida. "Let's stop talking about numbers," Reno exhorted the crowd, "and start talking about crime in human terms."[43] With her admonition, Reno placed herself squarely on the side

of those who feel that there has been a tendency in American criminology over the past half century to overemphasize **quantitative methods** or techniques, that is, those that produce measurable results that can be analyzed statistically. To be sure, as such critics would be quick to admit, a considerable degree of intellectual comfort must be achieved in feeling that one is able to reduce complex forms of behavior and interaction to something countable (as, say, the frequency of an offense). Intellectual comfort of this sort derives from the notion that anything expressible in numbers must be somehow more meaningful than that which is not.

It is crucial to realize, however, that numerical expression is mostly a result of how researchers structure their approach to the subject matter and is rarely inherent in the subject matter itself. Such is especially true in the social sciences, where attitudes, feelings, behaviors, and perceptions of all sorts are subject to quantification by researchers who impose upon such subjective phenomena artificial techniques for their quantification.

One highly quantitative study, reprinted in the journal *Criminology*, reported on the relationship between personality and crime and found that "greater delinquent participation was associated with a personality configuration characterized by high Negative Emotionality and Weak Constraint."[44] It may seem easy to quantify "delinquent participation" by measuring official arrest statistics (although official statistics may not be a good measure of delinquent behavior because many law violations go undiscovered), but imagine the conceptual nightmares associated with trying to make measurable concepts such as "Negative Emotionality" and "Weak Constraint." In such studies, even those replete with numerical data derived through the use of carefully constructed questionnaires, questions still remain of precisely what it is that has been measured.

Not everyone who engages in social science research labors under the delusion that everything can and must be quantified. Those who do, however, are said to suffer from the "*mystique of quantity*." As some critics have pointed out, "[t]he failure to recognize this instrumentality of measurement makes for a kind of mystique of quantity, which responds to numbers as though they were repositories of occult powers. The mystique of quantity is an exaggerated regard for the significance of measurement, just because it is quantitative,

> Not everyone who engages in social science research labors under the delusion that everything can and must be quantified.

■ **qualitative method**   A research technique that produces subjective results, or results that are difficult to quantify.

without regard either to what has been measured or to what can subsequently be done with the measure."[45] The "mystique of quantity" treats numbers as having intrinsic scientific value. Unfortunately, this kind of thinking has been popular in the social sciences, where researchers, seeking to make clear their intellectual kinship with physical scientists, have been less than cautious in their enthusiasm for quantification.

Qualitative methods, in contrast to those that are quantitative, produce subjective results, or results that are difficult to quantify. Even though their findings are not expressed numerically, qualitative methods provide yet another set of potentially useful criminological research tools. Qualitative methods are important for the insights they provide into the subjective workings of the criminal mind and the processes by which meaning is accorded to human experience. Introspection, life histories, case studies, and participant observations all contain the potential to yield highly qualitative data.[46]

Consider, for example, how the following personal account of homicidal motivation conveys subjective insights into the life of a Los Angeles gang member that would otherwise be difficult to express:

Wearing my fresh Pendleton shirt, beige khakis, and biscuits [old men's comfort shoes, the first shoe officially dubbed "Crip shoe"], I threw on my black bomber jacket and stepped out into the warm summer night. I walked up Sixty-Ninth Street to Western Avenue and took a car at gunpoint. Still in a state of indecision, I drove toward the hospital.

I intentionally drove through Sixties' hood. Actually, I was hoping to see one of them before I had made it through, and what luck did I have. There was Bank Robber, slippin' [not paying attention, not being vigilant] hard on a side street. I continued past him and turned at the next corner, parked and waited. He would walk right to me.

Sitting in the car alone, waiting to push yet another enemy out of this existence, I reflected deeply about my place in this world, about things that were totally outside the grasp of my comprehension. Thoughts abounded I never knew I could conjure up. In retrospect, I can honestly say that in those moments before Bank Robber got to the car, I felt free. Free, I guess, because I had made a decision about my future.

"Hey," I called out to Robber, leaning over to the passenger side, "got a light?"

"Yeah," he replied, reaching into his pants pocket for a match or lighter. I never found out which.

I guess he felt insecure, because he dipped his head down to window level to see who was asking for a light.

"Say your prayers, muthaf."

Before he could mount a response I blasted him thrice in the chest, started the car, and drove home to watch *Benny Hill*. Bangin' was my life. That was my decision.[47]

The passage was written by Sanyika Shakur, once known as "Monster Kody" to fellow South Central Los Angeles Crips members. Monster, named for his readiness to commit acts of brutality so extreme that they repulsed even other gang members, joined the Crips at age 11. Sent to a maximum-security prison while still in his teens, Monster learned to write, took on the name Sanyika Shakur, and joined the black nationalist New Afrikan Independence Movement. Shakur's prison-inspired autobiography, *Monster*, provides a soul-searching account of the life of a Los Angeles gang member. The purpose of the book, said Shakur, is "to allow my readers the first ever glimpse at South Central from my side of the gun, street, fence, and wall."[48]

Although Shakur's book is a purely personal account and may hold questions of generalizability for researchers, imagine the difficulties inherent in acquiring these kinds of data through the use of survey instruments or other traditional research techniques. Autobiographical accounts, introspection, and many forms of participant observations amount to a kind

A 22-year-old gang member who identified himself as "Criminal." Some researchers doubt that quantitative methods can adequately assess the subjective experiences of certain kinds of offenders. What is the nature of such "subjective experiences"?

■ **verstehen**   The kind of subjective understanding that can be achieved by criminologists who immerse themselves in the everyday world of the criminals they study.

■ **data confidentiality**   The ethical requirement of social scientific research to protect the confidentiality of individual research participants while preserving justified research access to the information participants provide.

■ **informed consent**   The ethical requirement of social scientific research that research subjects be informed about the nature of the research to be conducted, their anticipated role in it, and the uses to which the data they provide will be put.

of phenomenological reporting in which description leads to understanding, and intuition is a better guide to theory building than volumes of quantifiable data.

Jeff Ferrell of Texas Christian University uses the term **verstehen** to describe the kind of subjective understanding that can be achieved by criminologists who immerse themselves in the everyday world of the criminals they study. Criminological *verstehen*, a term derived from the early writings of sociologist Max Weber, means, said Ferrell, "a researcher's subjective understandings of crime's situational meanings and emotions—its moments of pleasure and pain, its emergent logic and excitement—within the larger process of research"; Ferrell adds, "It further implies that a researcher, through attentiveness and participation, at least can begin to apprehend and appreciate the specific roles and experiences of criminals, crime victims, crime control agents, and others caught up in the day-to-day reality of crime."[49] Learn more about *verstehen* at "Max Weber's Home Page" via **http://www.faculty.rsu.edu/~felwell/Theorists/Weber/Whome.htm**. You can learn more about the techniques of social science research at **http://sru.soc.surrey.ac.uk/** and **http://ssrn.com/abstract=1452620**.

Values and Ethics in the Conduct of Research

Research, especially research conducted within the social sciences, does not occur in a vacuum. Values enter into all stages of the research process, from the selection of the problem to be studied to the choice of strategies to address it. In short, research is never entirely free from preconceptions and biases, although much can be done to limit their impact.

The most effective way of controlling the effects of biases is to be aware of them at the outset of the research. For example, if researchers know that the project they are working on elicits strong personal feelings but necessitates the use of interviewers, then it would be beneficial to strive to hire interviewers who are relatively free of biases or who can control the expression of their feelings. Data gatherers who are prejudiced against subgroups of potential respondents can represent a threat to

the validity of the research results, and they may turn off some respondents, perhaps through racial innuendo, personal style, mannerisms, and so forth.

Of similar importance are ethical issues. Although they may not affect the validity of research results, these issues can have a significant impact on the lives of both researchers and research subjects. The protection of human subjects from harm, the provision of privacy, the need for disclosure of research methods, and **data confidentiality**—which embraces the principle of protecting the confidentiality of individual research participants while preserving justified research access to needed information provided by them—are all critical ethical issues.

To address these and other concerns, the Academy of Criminal Justice Sciences (ACJS) has adopted an official code of ethics. The ACJS Code of Ethics says that researchers "should seek to anticipate potential threats to confidentiality." It goes on to state, "Techniques such as the removal of direct identifiers, the use of randomized responses, and other statistical solutions to problems of privacy should be used where appropriate. Care should be taken to ensure secure storage, maintenance, and/or destruction of sensitive records."[50]

The ACJS code also says, "Confidential information provided by research participants should be treated as such by members of the Academy, even when this information enjoys no legal protection or privilege and legal force is applied. The obligation to respect confidentiality also applies to members of research organizations (interviewers, coders, clerical staff, etc.) who have access to the information. It is the responsibility of administrators and chief investigators to instruct staff members on this point and to make every effort to [ensure] that access to confidential information is restricted."[51]

Informed consent, a strategy used by researchers to overcome many of the ethical issues inherent in criminological research, means that research subjects are informed about the nature of the research to be conducted, their anticipated role in it, and the uses made of the data they provide. Ethics may also require that data derived from personal interviews or the testing of research subjects be anonymous (not associated with

> Ethical issues can have a significant impact on the lives of both researchers and research subjects.

the names of individual subjects) and that raw (unanalyzed) data be destroyed after a specified time interval (often at the completion of the research project).

Federal regulations require a plan for the protection of human subjects as part of grant proposals submitted to federal agencies. For example, the NIJ, a major source of grant support for researchers in the area of criminology, has this to say:

> All NIJ employees, contractors and award recipients must be cognizant of the importance of protecting the rights and welfare of human subject research participants. All research conducted at NIJ or supported with NIJ funds must comply with all Federal, U.S. Department of Justice (DOJ), Office of Justice Programs and NIJ regulations and policies concerning the protection of human subjects and the DOJ confidentiality requirements.[52]

Learn more about NIJ requirements for confidentiality and the protection of human subjects at **http://www.nij.gov /funding/humansubjects/welcome.htm**.

Some universities, research organizations, and government agencies have established institutional review boards with the task of examining research proposals to determine whether expectations of ethical conduct have been met before these proposals are submitted to funding organizations. Institutional review boards often consist of other researchers with special knowledge of the kinds of ethical issues involved in criminological research.

Participant observation sometimes entails an especially thorny ethical issue: Should researchers themselves violate the law if their research participation appears to require it? Those researching gang activities, for example, have sometimes been asked to transmit potentially incriminating information to other gang members, to act as drug couriers, and even to commit crimes of violence to help establish territorial claims important to members of the gang. Researchers who refuse may endanger not only their research but also themselves. Compliance with the expectations of criminal groups evokes other kinds of dangers, including the danger of apprehension and prosecution for violations of the criminal law. As one criminologist explained, "Criminological (and other) field researchers cannot conveniently distance themselves from their subjects of study, or from the legally uncertain situations in which the subjects may reside, in order to construct safe and 'objective' studies. Instead criminological field research unavoidably entangles those who practice it in complex and ambiguous relations to the subjects and situations of study, to issues of personal and social responsibility, and to law and legality."[53]

Although the dilemma of a participant observer, especially one secretly engaged in research, is a difficult one, some of the best advice on the subject is offered by Frank E. Hagan: "In self-mediating the potential conflicting roles of the criminal justice researcher, it is incumbent on the investigator to enter the setting with eyes wide open. A decision must be made beforehand on the level of commitment to the research endeavor and the analyst's ability to negotiate the likely role conflicts. Although there are no hard and fast rules *the researcher's primary role is that of a scientist.*"[54]

Hagan also suggested that a code of ethics should guide all professional criminologists in their research undertakings, requiring each researcher to do the following:[55]

- Avoid procedures that may harm respondents.
- Honor commitments to respondents and respect reciprocity.
- Exercise objectivity and professional integrity in performing and reporting research.
- Protect confidentiality and the privacy of respondents.

Hagan's admonition "Exercise objectivity and professional integrity" became especially important in the mid-1990s when supporters of Project D.A.R.E. (Drug Abuse Resistance Education) blocked publication of research results that showed the program to be ineffective.[56] D.A.R.E., a widely popular antidrug program common in the nation's schools, is a favorite of educational administrators because of the funding it provides. The study, a review of most prior D.A.R.E. research, was conducted by the Research Triangle Institute, a respected research firm in North Carolina, and was paid for by the NIJ.[57] When results showed that D.A.R.E. programs did not significantly reduce drug use among student participants, however, NIJ decided not to publish the findings. "We're not trying to hide the study," said NIJ's Ann Voit. "We just do not agree with one of the major findings."[58] By contrast, Research Triangle Institute researcher Susan T. Ennett proposed that results of the study should be used to decide how to spend drug-education money. Other studies have since supported the finding that D.A.R.E. does not have a significant impact on actual drug use, drug-related outcomes, or attitudes toward drugs.[59] Learn more about the D.A.R.E. study via **http://www .wolfe411.org/adolSA/DARENoEffectsat10-Yr.htm**.

Scientific research demonstrating that popular—and often widely supported—programs are ineffective will inevitably fuel controversy. Such was the case in 2006, when a group of Italian researchers published findings purporting to show that the 12-step method used by Alcoholics Anonymous (AA) to prevent future problem drinking doesn't work. The researchers concluded that "no experimental studies unequivocally demonstrated the effectiveness of A.A. or professional 12-step theory for reducing alcohol dependence or problems."[60] The research left some people claiming that AA worked for them and others saying that more (and better) studies were needed.

Because criminological research can affect social policy, which often involves the expenditure of public funds, the ethical code of the ASC mandates that criminologists be "committed to enhancing the *general* well-being of societies and of the individuals and groups within them," further stating that "criminologists have an obligation not to re-create forms of social injustice such as discrimination, oppression, or harassment in their own work."[61]

Learn more about ethics in criminological research directly from the ASC and the ACJS via **http://www.asc41.com/ ethicspg.html** and **http://www.acjs.org/page/Code_Of_ Ethics**. To read a comprehensive code of ethical standards for general survey research, visit the Council of American Survey Research Organizations via **http://www.casro.org/**. The U.S. Department of Justice's policy on scientific and research integrity is available at **http://www.justice.gov/open/doj-scientific -integrity-policy.pdf**.

The Impact of Criminological Research on Social Policy

Ideally, research results in the field of criminology should have both practical implications that can guide daily practice in relevant areas and a significant impact on those who formulate public crime-control policy. Faye S. Taxman of the University of Maryland's Center for Applied Policy Studies explained that "the normative educative model assumes that a rational use of data by policy makers, practitioners, and scientists will be of value to the field."[62] For example, after studies showed that arrests (rather than mere warnings) of domestic violence perpetrators proved effective in reducing the likelihood of reoffending, many police departments across the country began advising their officers to make such arrests, and some state legislators advocated passage of mandatory arrest laws.[63]

Unfortunately, publicly elected officials are often ignorant of current criminological research or do not heed the advice of professional criminologists, seeking instead to create politically expedient policies, which has led some to proclaim the "irrelevance" of criminology. James Austin of George Washington University bemoaned the lack of attention politicians give to the results of research in criminology: "Despite the annual publication of hundreds of peer-reviewed articles and textbooks proudly displayed at our annual conventions, policy makers are paying little if any attention to us. When Congress or state legislatures debate new crime bill legislation or the effectiveness of past actions, their first question is not, 'What do the criminologists think?' I would venture that one would be hard pressed to cite another discipline that has been so ignored for such a long time."[64] Should criminological research influence policy?

> Research results in the field of criminology should have a significant impact on those who formulate public crime-control policy.

Read more about the issue at **http://ssrn.com/abstract=1504983**.

Three-strikes laws provide an interesting example of the kind of dilemma facing criminologists who hope to influence social policy on the basis of statistical evidence. Three-strikes laws, which became popular with legislatures near the end of the twentieth century, require that felons receive lengthy prison sentences (often life without possibility of parole) following their third felony conviction. Such laws were built on the seemingly commonsense notion that "getting tough" on repeat offenders by putting them in prison for long periods should reduce the crime rate. After all, logic seems to say that lengthy prison sentences for recidivists will reduce crime by removing the most dangerous offenders from society.

One early study of the three-strikes laws in 22 states concluded, however, that such legislation results in clogged court systems and crowded correctional facilities and encourages three-time felons to take dramatic risks to avoid capture.[65] A wider-based study, dubbed "the most comprehensive study ever of crime prevention,"[66] later found that "much of the research on prisons was inadequate or flawed, making it impossible to measure how much crime was actually prevented or deterred by locking up more criminals."[67] The central finding of the massive study, sponsored by the federal Office of Justice Programs and carried out by researchers at the University of Maryland's Department of Criminology and Criminal Justice, was that current government-sponsored crime-prevention initiatives—which at the time totaled over $3 billion annually—were poorly evaluated, leading to uncertainty over whether funded programs actually work.

Nikasha Dicks/ZUMAPRESS/Newscom

Project D.A.R.E. participants at A. Dorothy Hains Elementary School in Atlanta, Georgia. More than a decade ago, studies of Project D.A.R.E. questioned its effectiveness, but government officials decided not to publish the results. How can the objectivity of social scientific research be ensured?

■ **meta-analysis**   A study that combines the results of other studies about a particular topic of interest. Also a comprehensive and systematic review of other studies.

THEORY | versus REALITY

The Stockholm Prize in Criminology

The 2017 Stockholm Prize in Criminology, presented by Stockholm University and the Stockholm Prize in Criminology Foundation, was awarded to Canadian criminologist Richard Tremblay, who is Professor Emeritus of Pediatrics, Psychiatry and Psychology at the University of Montreal. The prize, which carries a cash award of 1.3 million Swedish kronor (about $140,000), was awarded to Tremblay in recognition of his work as "the leading scholar in the world in developing basic science connections between biological, family and social factors in human development." He was also recognized for combining his "research with rigorous tests of policies that may alter these factors to reduce crime and violence." Tremblay's work began in the 1980s in Montreal and continues today in Paris, France, and Dublin, Ireland.

The Stockholm Prize is awarded annually for research achievements in the field of criminology. It is financed by the Jerry Lee Foundation in the United States, with support from the Japanese Correctional Association, the Hitachi Mirai Foundation, and the Söderberg Foundation of Sweden. Visit **www.su.se/english/about /prizes-awards/the-stockholm-prize-in-criminology** for further information about the prize and award recipients and to learn more about the annual Stockholm Criminology Symposium.

Felix Choo/Alamy Stock Photo

An idylic scene at Stockholm University in Sweden. The University is home to the Stockholm Prize in Criminology. What accomplishments does the prize recognize?

"Richard Tremblay Gets Stockholm Criminology Prize," *The Crime Report*, November 30, 2016, (accessed November 30, 2016).

The study, a **meta-analysis** (i.e., a study of other studies), reviewed more than 500 impact evaluations of local crime-prevention programs and practices throughout the nation. Due to largely ineffective evaluation efforts that were often only loosely tied to funded programs, researchers concluded that "the current [government-sponsored research] plan does not provide effective guidance to the nation about what works to prevent crime." Although criminological research had long shown the impracticality of three-strikes provisions, it was not until the financial crisis that began in 2008 that public opinion began to soften on criminal punishments.

One especially important source that evaluates crime-related research is a federal initiative called CrimeSolutions.gov. CrimeSolutions.gov organizes evidence on what works in crime-reduction efforts, including the areas of juvenile justice and crime victim services. The program has become a central resource that policy makers can turn to in order to find an evidence-based program for their community, or if they want to know whether a program they might implement has been determined to be effective. The site currently contains information about hundreds of programs and is constantly updated as new research becomes available.

One of the primary goals of CrimeSolutions.gov is to encourage practitioners to replicate programs with a track record of success. Replicating programs that have been shown to

work and that fit a community's needs can save valuable time and resources.[68]

On CrimeSolutions.gov, users can find answers to essential questions, such as:

● Is there a program that meets my needs?

● Did the program work?

● How was the program designed and implemented?

● Where can I get more information about the program?

CrimeSolutions.gov provides the source of a number of *Putting Criminology to Work* boxes that appear throughout this text.

Another especially important repository of crime- and justice-related literature today can be found at the Campbell Crime and Justice Coordinating Group, a subsidiary project of the Campbell Collaboration, which focuses on what works in the areas of education, social welfare, and criminal justice. The Campbell Collaboration began in 2000 to make systematic reviews of research on the effects of social interventions accessible. You can access the Campbell Collaboration via **http://www .campbellcollaboration.org/**. The Campbell Collaboration Crime and Justice Coordinating Group, can be reached via **https://www.campbellcollaboration.org/crimeandjus-tice.html**.

The Research Report

Findings from research and analysis of data are typically presented in the form of a report or paper in which suggestions for further study may be made. Policy issues or strategies for addressing the problems identified by the researcher are also frequently discussed. Charts, graphs, and tables may be included in the body of a research report. Most reports are professional-looking documents prepared on a word processor with grammar and spelling checkers and printed on a laser or ink-jet printer. Some are eventually published in professional journals, and a few become staples of the field—frequently cited works that illustrate fundamental criminological or methodological principles.

Most research reports follow a traditional professional format with the following component features:

- **Title page:** The title page contains the names of the report's authors, their institutional or professional affiliations, the date of the report, and its title. Many report titles consist of a main title and a subtitle, which generally gives additional information about the report's subject matter. Some report titles seem all-inclusive: "The Impact of Family Structure and Quality on Delinquency: A Comparative Assessment of Structural and Functional Factors";[69] others are relatively straightforward: "Comparing Criminal Career Models."[70]

- **Acknowledgments:** Often, the author wishes to express appreciation to individuals and organizations that facilitated the study or whose help made the study possible in the first place. Sources of grant support, including funding agencies and foundations, individuals and organizations that either participated in the study or were themselves studied, and people who facilitated various aspects of the study or the production of the report are all frequently acknowledged.

- **Table of contents:** Reports of any length (say, beyond ten pages) often contain a table of contents that helps readers find the needed material quickly and provides structure to the report itself. A table of contents that is helpful for readers lists section headings within the body of the report.

- **Preface (optional):** The purpose of a preface is to allow the author to make observations (often of a personal nature) that might not be appropriate within the body of the report. Reasons for choice of the study's subject, observations about the promise held by the field of study, and wide-ranging statements about the future of criminological research are all frequent topics of prefaces found in research reports.

- **Abstract:** An abstract is a brief (usually one-paragraph) summation of the report's findings, allowing readers to gauge whether the subject matter will be of interest to them without reading the entire report. In this day of electronic information, abstracts serve the additional function of providing a quick synopsis that can be made readily available to those searching large databases containing many research articles.

- **Introduction:** Most authors write an introductory section as part of their research report. The introduction describes the aim and purpose of the study, provides a general statement of the problem studied, and furnishes a general conceptual framework for the remainder of the report. The introduction may also outline issues that are related to the problem under study and could benefit from further investigation.

- **Review of existing literature:** Most research builds on existing knowledge and makes use of previous findings. To cite a few proverbial observations, it is not true that "there is nothing new under the sun" when conducting research, it is also not necessary to "reinvent the wheel." In other words, the relevant works of other researchers should be discussed in any report, and the bearing that previous studies have on the present one should be explained. Sometimes researchers who are engaged in literature reviews discover that the questions they wish to study have already been answered or that someone else has found a more concise way of stating their concerns. Hence, new investigators can avoid concept development that is merely repetitive and even data gathering that has already been undertaken.

- **Description of existing situation:** Sometimes a description of the existing situation is combined with a report's introduction. If not, then it is appropriate to elaborate on the problem under study by providing details that describe the conditions existing at the beginning of the study.

- **Statement of hypothesis:** Research etiquette in criminology frequently requires the statement of a hypothesis to be tested. Most researchers have an idea of what they expect to find and set out to test a theory or a proposition derived from a theory. For example, researchers may wish to test whether the Brady Law, a federal statute that limits handgun sales, has effectively met its goal of reducing the number of deaths by firearms. A hypothesis should be a clear and concise statement of what the study purports to test. As mentioned previously, hypotheses useful in guiding research are always operationalized, or expressed in terms that are in some way measurable. Descriptive studies, on the other hand, are not designed to prove or disprove assumptions (although they may not be free of them), and such studies may not contain hypotheses.

- **Description of research plan:** The research design, data-gathering strategies, and plans for statistical analysis should all be described. This section, although it may be elaborate and lengthy, simply provides an overview of the methodology employed by the researcher and explains how the problem was investigated and why particular research strategies were chosen.

- **Disclaimers/limitations:** All research is subject to limitations. Shortages of money, time, personnel, and other resources impose limitations on research undertakings, as do shortcomings in statistical techniques and restrictions on the availability of data. Limitations should be honestly appraised and presented in the research report so that readers will be able to assess their impact on the results reported.

- **Findings/results:** Along with an overview of the research as it was actually conducted, the findings provide a statement of research results, and many regard this section as the heart of the report. The manner in which results are presented can be crucial for ease of understanding: Bar charts and pie charts are probably the most commonly employed types of diagrams (although the type of data collected will determine the appropriate format for its presentation). Some researchers choose to employ tables containing raw numbers when pictorial forms of representation like charts and graphs would better facilitate comprehension.

- **Analysis/discussion:** Once findings have been presented, they should be analyzed and discussed. Not all analyses need be of a quantitative sort; however, much of today's criminological literature is replete with statistical analyses, some of them quite sophisticated. Unfortunately, poorly conceptualized research cannot be helped by later analysis, no matter how sophisticated that analysis may be. Therefore, it is crucial to the success of any research endeavor that early planning—including conceptual development, strategies for data collection, and research designs—be undertaken with an eye toward producing data that will lend themselves to meaningful analysis and discussion after data gathering has been completed. The analysis section should also focus on whether the data, as analyzed, support the study's guiding hypothesis.

- **Summary/conclusions:** The summation section encapsulates the study's purpose and findings in a few paragraphs and may also contain suggested improvements or recommended solutions to the problem studied based on the evidence produced by the report. Policy implications are also discussed (if at all) in the conclusion of the report because they are simply broad-based solutions to problems that have been identified.

- **Endnotes/footnotes:** Endnotes or footnotes may be used to reference quoted sources or to refer readers to supporting documents. Sometimes a combination of endnotes and footnotes is employed. Endnotes, as their name implies, appear at the conclusion of a report (often after the summary but before the appendixes), whereas footnotes are found at the bottom of the pages containing the referenced material.

- **Appendixes:** Not all reports contain appendixes. Those that do may place sample questionnaires, accompanying cover letters, concise exhibits from literature reviews, detailed statistical tables, copies of letters of support, detailed interview information, and so forth, near the end of the document. Appendixes should be used only if they serve the purpose of further explicating the report's purpose, methods, or findings. Otherwise, appendixes may appear to pad the report and can discredit the researcher's efforts in the eyes of readers.

- **List of references:** No report is complete without a list of references or a bibliography used in planning the study and in preparing the document. Although all items listed in the bibliography may not be referenced within the body of the report, source material should still be provided if it was reviewed and served some purpose in study development. Literature that is examined, for example, may guide the researcher to other material or may provide useful insights during the study's overall conceptual formation.

Writing for Publication

Criminologists often seek to publish the results of their research to share them with others working in the field. The primary medium for such publication consists of refereed professional journals, those that employ the services of peer reviewers to gauge the quality of the manuscripts submitted to them. Although the review process can be time-consuming, it is believed to result in the publication of manuscripts that make worthwhile contributions to the field of criminology and in the rejection of those of lesser quality.

> The primary medium for research papers consists of refereed professional journals.

Perhaps the best-known professional journals in the field of criminology today are *American Journal of Criminal Justice, British Journal of Criminology, Crime and Delinquency, Crime and Social Justice, Criminal Justice and Behavior, Criminal Justice Ethics, Criminal Justice Policy Review, Criminal Justice Review, Criminology, Criminology and Public Policy, Critical Criminology, Journal of Contemporary Criminal Justice, Journal of Crime and Justice, Journal of Criminal Justice Education, Journal of Criminal Law and Criminology, Journal of Quantitative Criminology, Journal of Research in Crime and Delinquency, Justice Quarterly*, and *Theoretical Criminology*.[71] For a comprehensive list of journals in the field of criminology, including many that are Web-based, visit **http://www.tamut.edu/academics/tjordan /rsrchhlp/CJJOURNALSv2.htm**.

Each journal has its own requirements for manuscript submission. Some require a single copy of a manuscript, others ask for multiple copies, a few journals request manuscript files on disk along with hard copies, and still others are moving toward electronic submission via the Internet. An increasing number of journals have established submission fees, usually in the $10 to $20 range, to help defray the costs associated with the review process.

Submission etiquette within the field of criminology demands that an article be sent to only one journal at a time. Simultaneous submissions are discouraged and create difficulties for both authors and editors when articles are accepted by more than one publication. Given the complexities of the review and publication processes, it is probably best to write the editor of any journal to which submission is being contemplated to inquire about that journal's particular expectations.

Most journals require that manuscripts be prepared according to a particular style, meaning that citations, capitalization, footnoting, abstracts, notes, headings, and subheadings are all expected to conform to the style of other articles published in the same journal. Two of the most prevalent styles are the American Psychological Association (APA) style and the American Sociological Association (ASA) style.

Most criminological journals, however, utilize a modification of one of these styles. When considering submission of a manuscript for publication review, it is advisable to write to the editor of the journal in question requesting a style sheet or general style guidelines. Style guides are also available from the APA[72] and the ASA, with third-party publishers making style guides available through university and special-purpose bookstores.

If a research report is not intended for publication, other styles may be acceptable. Answers to general questions about report writing and style can be found in publications like William Strunk, Jr., and E. B. White's *The Elements of Style*[73] and Mary-Claire van Leunen's *A Handbook for Scholars*.[74]

SUMMARY

- Criminology is a social science that endeavors to apply the techniques of data collection and hypothesis testing through observation and experimentation. Successful hypothesis testing can lead to theory building and a more complete understanding of the nature of crime and crime causation. Evidence-based criminology, a concept that was introduced in the first chapter, offers the promise of building a valuable collection of evidence-based knowledge that can be of service to policy makers and individuals concerned about the fight against crime.

- A theory is a series of interrelated propositions attempting to describe, explain, predict, and ultimately control some class of events. Theories gain explanatory power from inherent logical consistency, are "tested" by how well they describe and predict reality, provide relatively complete understanding, are supported by observations, and stand up to continued scrutiny.

- Research refers to the use of standardized, systematic procedures in the search for knowledge. Determinations of program effectiveness are made through research. Threats to the internal and external validity of research designs refer to confounding effects that might invalidate the results of research.

- Quantitative methods tend to produce results that are easy to measure, whereas qualitative methods produce subjective results that are difficult or impossible to quantify. Quantitative methods are useful in objectively assessing hypotheses and measuring the effects of an experimental intervention; qualitative methods are important for the insights they provide into the subjective workings of the criminal mind and the processes by which meaning is accorded to human experience.

- Values enter into all stages of the research process. Protection of human subjects from harm, need for privacy, disclosure of research methods, and data confidentiality are all critical ethical issues. To address these and other concerns, the Academy of Criminal Justice Sciences (ACJS) has adopted an official code of ethics for research in the field of criminology.

- Ideally, research results in the field of criminology should have a significant impact on public crime-control policy. Unfortunately, publicly elected officials are often ignorant of current criminological research or do not heed the advice of professional criminologists, seeking instead to create politically expedient policies.

- A typical research report might contain the following sections: title page, acknowledgments, table of contents, preface, abstract, introduction, review of existing literature, description of existing situation, statement of hypothesis, description of research plan, disclaimers/limitations, findings/results, analysis/discussion, summary/conclusion, endnotes/footnotes, appendixes, and list of references. Research findings in the field of criminology are published in professional journals.

KEY TERMS

applied research, 33	evidence based, 29
case study, 38	external validity, 35
confounding effect, 35	hypothesis, 31
control group, 36	inferential statistics, 41
controlled experiment, 35	informed consent, 44
correlation, 41	internal validity, 35
data confidentiality, 44	intersubjectivity, 40
descriptive statistics, 41	meta-analysis, 47

operationalization, 34

participant observation, 39

primary research, 33

pure research, 33

qualitative method, 43

quantitative method, 42

quasi-experimental design, 36

randomization, 37

replicability, 40

research, 33

research design, 34

secondary research, 33

self-report, 39

survey research, 38

test of significance, 41

theory, 31

variable, 34

verstehen, 44

QUESTIONS FOR REVIEW

1. What is the role of social scientific research methods in the development of criminological theories? What does it mean to say that criminology is evidence based? How does the meaning of the word *evidence* in evidence-based criminology differ from the evidence found at a crime scene or the evidence used in criminal trials?

2. What is a theory? What purposes do theories serve? What role do research and experimentation play in theory building in criminology?

3. What is internal validity? External validity? How can threats to internal and external validity be addressed?

4. What are the differences between quantitative and qualitative methods in the social sciences? What are the advantages and disadvantages of each method?

5. What are some of the ethical considerations involved in conducting criminological research? How can researchers make sure that such considerations are met?

6. How do criminological research and experimental criminology affect social policy?

7. What sections might a typical research report contain? Where are research findings in criminology published?

QUESTIONS FOR REFLECTION

1. This text emphasizes the theme of social problems versus individual responsibility. How might a thorough research agenda allow us to decide which perspective is more fruitful in combating crime?

2. What does it mean to operationalize a hypothesis? Why is operationalization necessary?

3. Why is the task of criminological theory construction so demanding? How do we know if a theory is any good?

4. What is a meta-analysis? For what purposes might a meta-analysis be conducted?

5. What are the various types of data-gathering strategies discussed in this chapter? Describe them. Is any one technique better than another? Why? Under what kinds of conditions might certain types of data-gathering strategies be most appropriate?

6. A few years ago, the Bureau of Justice Statistics announced findings that male military veterans were less than half as likely as male nonveterans of the same age to be in prison (the rates reported were 630 versus 1,390 per 100,000 male prisoners, respectively). Does this mean that we can say with confidence that military service decreases a male's likelihood of committing a criminal offense? What other influences might be operating to lower the likelihood of crime commission by male military veterans? (See the full report at http://www.justicestudies.com/pubs/veterans.pdf.)

Jc Berger/Alamy Stock Photo

CLASSICAL AND NEOCLASSICAL THOUGHT—

Choice or Consequences

LEARNING OUTCOMES

After reading this chapter, you should be able to answer the following questions:

- What are the major principles of the Classical School of criminology?

- What were some forerunners of classical thought in criminology?

- Who were some important thinkers of the Classical School of criminology, and what was their legacy?

- What is neoclassical criminology, and how does it differ from the classical perspective? How does it build on it?

- What is the role of punishment in neoclassical criminology?

- What are the policy implications of the Classical School and of neoclassical thought?

- What are the criticisms of classical and neoclassical perspectives on crime?

■ **mores** Behavioral proscriptions covering potentially serious violations of a group's values. Examples include strictures against murder, rape, and robbery.

■ **folkways** Time-honored customs. Although folkways carry the force of tradition, their violation is unlikely to threaten the survival of the group.

Introduction

A number of crimes are relatively spontaneous unplanned events that occur in the heat of passion or when an unanticipated opportunity presents itself. A wallet left on the seat of an unlocked car whose window is rolled down, for example, is an invitation for anyone walking by to steal the wallet, and some people will be unable to resist the temptation to reach out and grab it. The majority of crimes, however, are likely planned—at least to some degree. Crime planning, which involves rational decision making on the part of the offender, means not only that criminals assess the pros and cons of perpetrating offenses (i.e., the benefits versus the likelihood of being caught and punished), but also the means of crime commission. An example of clear thinking in support of criminal activity was recently available on listverse.com, a site that touts itself as "focused on lists that intrigue and educate."[1] One list featured among the site's crime and mystery series is "Top 10 Tips to Commit the Perfect Crime."[2] Among the tips offered are ensuring that anyone contemplating an offense not leave any discoverable DNA at the scene of the crime. Because DNA is ubiquitous, the list author explains that "[t]he best solution … is to commit your crime in a place that is likely to have a lot of DNA from strangers." A park, a shopping mall, or "anywhere that a lot of people tend to gather" is recommended as an offense location. The list author opines that "[f]inding your DNA will be like finding a needle in a haystack."[3]

This chapter examines the belief that at least some illegal activity is the result of rational choices made by individuals seeking various kinds of illicit rewards. The perspectives presented in this chapter form the basis for strict policies of social control—those based on punishment as a primary means for curtailing continued criminality. As you read through this chapter, however, you might ask yourself how the theoretical approaches that it describes can effectively counter the rewards of crime that might be imagined by those who are considering violating the law.

> Some illegal activity is the result of rational choices made by individuals seeking various kinds of illicit rewards.

Major Principles of the Classical School

The first part of this chapter summarizes the central features of the Classical School of criminological thought, while a later section describes the neoclassical perspective—a modern day offshoot of that early school. The eight key principles of classical and current-day neoclassical criminology are shown in Figure 3-1.

Forerunners of Classical Thought

The notion of crime as a violation of established law did not exist in most primitive societies. Lack of law-making bodies, absence of formal written laws, and loose social bonds precluded the concept of crime as law violation, but all human societies, from the simplest to the most advanced, did evidence their own widely held notions of right and wrong. Sociologists call such fundamental concepts of morality and propriety *mores* and *folkways*. *Mores, folkways,* and *law* are terms used by **William Graham Sumner** to describe the three basic forms of behavioral strictures imposed by social groups upon their members.[4] Mores and folkways govern behavior in relatively small primitive societies, whereas in large complex societies, they are reinforced and formalized through written laws.

Mores consist of proscriptions covering potentially serious violations of a group's values (e.g., murder, rape, and robbery). **Folkways** are time-honored customs; although they carry the force of tradition, their violation is less likely to threaten the survival of the social group. The fact that American men have traditionally worn little jewelry illustrates a folkway that has given way in recent years to various types of male adornment, including earrings, gold chains, and even makeup. Mores and folkways, although they may be powerful determinants of behavior, are nonetheless informal because only laws have been codified into formal strictures wielded by institutions and created specifically for enforcement purposes.

Another method of categorizing socially proscriptive rules is provided by some criminologists who divide crimes into the

■ **mala in se**   An act that is thought to be wrong in and of itself.

■ **mala prohibita**   An act that is wrong only because it is prohibited.

Key Principles of Classical and Neoclassical Criminology

- Human beings are fundamentally rational, and most human behavior results from free will coupled with rational choice.

- Pain and pleasure are the two central determining factors of human behavior.

- Punishment serves to deter law violators and serves as an example to others who might contemplate violating the law.

- The principles of right and wrong are inherent in our nature and cannot be denied.

- Society exists to provide benefits to individuals that they would not receive living in isolation.

- When people band together for the protection offered by society, they forfeit some of their personal freedoms in order to enjoy the benefits of living among others cooperatively.

- Certain key rights of the individual are necessary of the enjoyment of life, and governments that restrict and prohibit the exercise of those rights should be disbanded.

- Crime lessens the quality of the contractual bond that exists between individuals and their society. Therefore, criminal acts cannot be tolerated by any members if everyone wants to receive the most benefit from living in a cooperative society.

FIGURE 3-1 | **Key Principles of Classical and Neoclassical Criminology**

Source: Schmalleger, Frank, *Criminology*. Printed and Electronically reproduced by permission of Pearson Education, Inc., Upper Saddle River, New Jersey.

dual categories of **mala in se** and **mala prohibita**. Acts that are *mala in se* are said to be fundamentally wrong, regardless of the time or place in which they occur (e.g., forcing someone to have sex against his or her will and the intentional killing of children). Those who argue for the existence of *mala in se* offenses usually point to some fundamental rule, such as religious

Good and evil are shown attempting to influence a man. Crime and other social evils have always begged for explanation. What would today's criminologists think of the claim that "the devil made him do it"?

teachings (the Ten Commandments, the Koran, and so on), to support their belief that some acts are inherently wrong.

Offenses termed *mala prohibita* are said to be wrong in areas where they are prohibited (e.g., prostitution, gambling, drug use, and premarital sexual behavior). The status of such behaviors as *mala prohibita* is supported by the fact that they are not necessarily crimes in every jurisdiction; prostitution, for example, is legal in parts of Nevada, as is gambling.

The Demonic Era

Since time began, humankind has been preoccupied with what appears to be an ongoing war between good and evil. Evil has often appeared in impersonal guise, as when the great bubonic plague (the "black death") ravaged Europe and Asia in the fourteenth century, leaving as much as three-quarters of the population dead in a span of 20 years. At other times, evil has seemed to wear a human face, as when the Nazi Holocaust claimed millions of Jewish lives during World War II.

Whatever its manifestation, the very presence of evil in the world has begged for interpretation, and sage minds throughout human history have advanced many explanations for the evil conditions that individuals and social groups have at times been forced to endure. Some forms of evil, like the plague and the Holocaust, appear cosmically based, whereas others—including personal victimization, criminality, and singular instances of deviance—are the undeniable result of individual behavior. Cosmic-level evil has been explained by ideas as diverse as divine punishment, karma, fate, and vengeful activities of

■ **Code of Hammurabi**   An early set of laws established by the Babylonian king Hammurabi, who ruled the ancient city of Babylon from 1792 to 1750 B.C.

■ **retribution**   The act of taking revenge upon a criminal perpetrator.

■ **Twelve Tables**   Early Roman laws written approximately 450 B.C. that regulated family, religious, and economic life.

■ **common law**   Law originating from usage and custom rather than from written statutes. The term refers to nonstatutory customs, traditions, and precedents that help guide judicial decision making.

---

offended gods. Early explanations of personal deviance ranged from demonic possession to spiritual influences, to temptation by fallen angels.

Early Sources of Criminal Law

Code of Hammurabi

Modern criminal law is the result of a long evolution of legal principles. The **Code of Hammurabi** is one of the first known bodies of law to survive for study today. King Hammurabi ruled the ancient city of Babylon from 1792 to 1750 B.C. and created a legal code consisting of strictures that were originally intended to establish property and other rights and that were crucial to the continued growth of Babylon as a significant commercial center. Hammurabi's law spoke to issues of theft, property ownership, sexual relationships, and interpersonal violence. Well-known criminologist Marvin Wolfgang observed, "In its day, 1700 B.C., the Hammurabi Code, with its emphasis on retribution, amounted to a brilliant advance in penal philosophy mainly because it represented an attempt to keep cruelty within bounds."[5] Prior to the code, captured offenders often faced barbarous **retribution**, frequently at the hands of revenge-seeking victims, no matter how minor their transgressions had been. Learn more about the Code of Hammurabi at **http://avalon.law.yale.edu/subject_menus/hammenu.asp**.

Early Roman Law

Of considerable significance for our own legal tradition is early Roman law. Roman legions under Emperor Claudius I (10 B.C.–A.D. 54) conquered England in the middle of the first century, and Roman customs, law, and language were forced upon the English population during the succeeding three centuries under the Pax Romana—a peace imposed by the military might of Rome.[6]

Early Roman law derived from the **Twelve Tables**, a collection of basic rules regulating family, religious, and economic life written around 450 B.C. They appear to have been based on common and fair practices generally accepted among early tribes existing prior to the establishment of the Roman Republic; only fragments of the tables survive today.

The best-known legal period in Roman history occurred during the reign of Emperor Justinian I (A.D. 527–565). By the end of the sixth century, the Roman Empire had declined substantially in size and influence and was near the end of its life. Possibly to preserve Roman values and traditions, Justinian undertook the laborious process of distilling Roman laws into a set of writings. This Justinian Code consisted of three lengthy legal documents—the Institutes, the Digest, and the Code itself—and distinguished between two major legal categories: public laws and private laws. Public laws dealt with the organization of the Roman state, its Senate, and governmental offices; private law concerned itself with contracts, personal possessions, legal status of various people (citizens, free people, slaves, freedmen, guardians, husbands, and wives), and injuries to citizens. It contained elements of our modern civil and criminal law, and it influenced Western legal thought up through the Middle Ages. Learn more about early Roman law at **http://www.crystalinks.com/romelaw.html**.

Common Law

Common law refers to a traditional body of unwritten legal precedents that was created through everyday practice in English society, was based on shared traditions and standards, and was supported by court decisions during the Middle Ages. As novel situations arose and were handled by British justices, their declarations became the start for any similar future deliberations.

> Common law refers to a traditional body of unwritten legal precedents that was created through everyday practice in English society.

Common law was given considerable legitimacy in the eleventh century with the official declaration that it was the law of the land by King Edward the Confessor (A.D. 1042–1066). The authority of common law was further reinforced by the decision of William the Conqueror to use popular customs as the basis for judicial action following his subjugation of Britain in A.D. 1066.

Eventually, court decisions were recorded and made available to barristers (English trial lawyers) and judges. As criminologist Howard Abadinsky wrote, "Common law involved the transformation of community rules into a national legal system. The controlling element [was] precedent."[7] Today,

■ **Enlightenment**   A social movement that arose during the eighteenth century and that built upon ideas like empiricism, rationality, free will, humanism, and natural law.

■ **social contract**   The Enlightenment-era concept that human beings abandon their natural state of individual freedom to join together and form society. In the process of forming a social contract, individuals surrender some freedoms to society as a whole, and government, once formed, is obligated to assume responsibilities toward its citizens and to provide for their protection and welfare.

common law forms the basis for much of our statutory and case law and has been called *the* major source of modern criminal law in English-speaking countries around the world. Learn more about common law at **https://www.law.berkeley. edu/library/robbins/CommonLawCivilLawTraditions. html**.

Magna Carta

The Magna Carta (literally, "great charter"), another important source of modern laws and legal procedure, was signed on June 15, 1215, by King John of England at Runnymede, under pressure from British barons who took advantage of his military defeats to demand a pledge to respect their traditional rights and to be bound by law. At the time of its signing, the Magna Carta (63 chapters in length) was little more than a feudal document listing specific royal concessions.[8] Its original purposes were to ensure feudal rights, to guarantee the king would not encroach on landowning barons' privileges, to guarantee the freedom of the church, and to ensure respect for the customs of towns.

Its wording was later interpreted during a judicial revolt in 1613, however, to support individual rights and jury trials. Sir Edward Coke, chief justice under James I, held that the Magna Carta guaranteed basic liberties for all British citizens and ruled that any acts of Parliament that contravened common law would be void, a famous ruling that possibly became the basis for the rise of the U.S. Supreme Court, with its power to nullify laws enacted by Congress.[9] Similarly, a specific provision of the Magna Carta, designed originally to prohibit the king from prosecuting the barons without just cause, was expanded into the concept of due process of law, a fundamental cornerstone of modern legal procedure. Because of these later interpretations, the Magna Carta has been called "the foundation stone of our present liberties."[10]

The Enlightenment

The **Enlightenment** (or the Age of Reason), a highly significant social movement occurring during the seventeenth and eighteenth centuries, was built upon ideas developed by many important thinkers. Because of their indirect contributions to classical criminological thought, it will be worthwhile to spend a few paragraphs discussing the writings of a few of these historical figures. Learn more about the Enlightenment and the intellectual figures who gave it life at **http://www.philosopher.org .uk/enl.htm**.

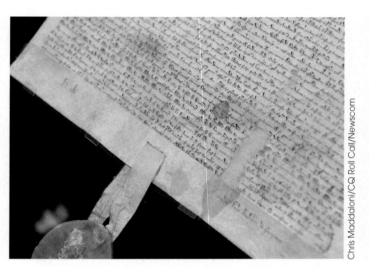

Chris Maddaloni/CQ Roll Call/Newscom

The Magna Carta, an important source of modern Western laws and legal procedure. What are some other significant sources of modern criminal law?

Thomas Hobbes

English philosopher **Thomas Hobbes** (1588–1679) developed what many writers regard as a negative view of human nature and social life, which he described in his momentous work, *Leviathan* (1651). Fear of violent death, he said, forces human beings into a **social contract** with one another to create a state that demands the surrender of certain natural rights and submission to the absolute authority of a sovereign while offering protection and succor to its citizens. The social contract concept significantly influenced many of Hobbes's contemporaries, but much of his writing was condemned for an overly pessimistic view of both human nature and existing governments.

John Locke

In 1690, English philosopher **John Locke** (1632–1704) published his *Essay Concerning Human Understanding*, putting forth the idea that the natural human condition at birth is like a blank slate upon which interpersonal encounters and other experiences indelibly inscribe the traits of personality. In contrast to earlier thinkers, who assumed that people are born with certain innate propensities and rudimentary intellectual concepts and ideas, Locke ascribed the bulk of adult human qualities to life experiences.

In the area of social and political thought, Locke further developed the Hobbesian notion of the social contract and contended that human beings, through a social contract, abandon

■ **natural law**   The philosophical perspective that certain immutable laws are fundamental to human nature and can be readily ascertained through reason. Human-made laws, by contrast, are said to derive from human experience and history—both of which are subject to continual change.

■ **natural rights**   Rights that, according to natural law theorists, individuals retain in the face of government action and interests.

their natural state of individual freedom and lack of interpersonal responsibility to join together and form society. Although individuals surrender some freedoms to society, government—once formed—is obligated to assume responsibilities toward its citizens, to provide for their protection and welfare, and to guarantee them certain inalienable rights such as the right to life, health, liberty, and possessions. A product of his times (the dictatorial nature of monarchies and the Roman church were being much disparaged), Locke stressed the duties that governments have toward their citizens while paying very little attention to the responsibilities of individuals to the societies of which they are a part, and he argued that political revolutions, under some circumstances, might become an obligation incumbent upon citizens.

Locke also developed the notion of checks and balances between divisions of government, a doctrine elaborated on by French jurist and political philosopher **Charles-Louis de Secondat Montesquieu** (1689–1755). In *The Spirit of Laws* (1748), Montesquieu wove Locke's notions into the concept of a separation of powers between divisions of government. Both ideas later found a place in the U.S. Constitution.

Jean-Jacques Rousseau

Swiss-French philosopher and political theorist **Jean-Jacques Rousseau** (1712–1778) further advanced the notion of the social contract in his treatise of that name (*Social Contract*, 1762), stating that human beings are basically good and fair in their natural state but historically were corrupted by the introduction of shared concepts and joint activities like property, agriculture, science, and commerce. As a result, the social contract emerged when civilized people agreed to establish governments and systems of education to correct the problems and inequalities brought on by the rise of civilization.

Rousseau also contributed to the notion of **natural law**, a concept originally formulated by Saint Thomas Aquinas (1225–1274), Baruch Spinoza (1632–1677), and others to provide an intuitive basis for the defense of ethical principles and morality. Submissive to the authority of the church, secular rulers were pressed to reinforce church doctrine in any laws they decreed. Aquinas wrote in his *Summa Theologica* that any human-made law that contradicts natural law is corrupt in the eyes of God. Hence, natural law was incorporated into English common law throughout the Middle Ages.

Rousseau agreed with earlier writers that certain immutable laws are fundamental to human nature and can be readily ascertained through reason. Human-made law, by contrast, derives from human experience and history, both of which are subject to continual change, so human-made law (or "positive law") changes from time to time and from epoch to epoch. Rousseau expanded the concept of natural law to support emerging democratic principles.

Natural Law and Natural Rights

Thomas Paine (1737–1809), an English-American political theorist and the author of *The Rights of Man* (1791 and 1792), defended the French Revolution, arguing that only democratic institutions could guarantee individuals' **natural rights**. At the Second Continental Congress, Thomas Jefferson (1743–1826) and other congressional representatives (many well versed in the writings of Locke and Rousseau) built the U.S. Constitution around an understanding of natural law as they perceived it. Hence, when Jefferson wrote of inalienable rights to "life, liberty, property," he was following in the footsteps of his intellectual forebears and meant that such rights were the natural due of all men and women because they were inherent in the social contract between citizens and their government.

Natural law and natural rights have a long intellectual history. In a *National Review* article subtitled "If Natural Law Does Not Permit Us to Distinguish between Men and Hogs, What Does?" Harry V. Jaffa, director of the Claremont Institute's Center for the Study of the Natural Law, called an 1854 speech given by Abraham Lincoln "the most moving and compelling exhibition of natural-law reasoning in all political history."[11] In that speech, Lincoln argued in favor of freedom for slaves by succinctly pointing out there is no difference between people, whatever their color: "Equal justice to the South, it is said, requires us to consent to the extending of slavery to new countries. That is to say, inasmuch as you do not object to my taking my hog to Nebraska, therefore I must not object to your taking your slave. Now, I admit this is perfectly logical, if there is no difference between hogs and Negroes."[12] Lincoln's point, of course, was that there is a huge difference between human beings and animals by virtue of their nature and that such a difference cannot be denied by logic.

Other commentators have cited the "crimes against humanity" committed by Nazis during World War II as indicative of natural law principles. The chilling testimony of Rudolf Hess,[13] Hitler's deputy, during the 1945 war crimes trial in Nuremberg, Germany, as he recalled the Fuehrer's order to exterminate millions of Jews, indicates the extent of the planned "final solution": "In the summer of 1941, I was summoned to Berlin to Reichsfuehrer SS Himmler to receive personal orders. He told me something to the effect—I do not remember the exact words—that the Fuehrer had given the order for a final solution of the Jewish question. We, the SS, must carry out that order. If it is not carried out now then the Jews will later on destroy the German people. He had chosen Auschwitz on account of its easy access by rail and also because the extensive site offered space for measures ensuring isolation."[14] Although Hitler's Nazi Party made the law in Germany at the time, natural law supporters (largely in other countries) argued that Hitler's final solution to the Jewish "question" was inherently

■ **Classical School** A criminological perspective of the late 1700s and early 1800s that had its roots in the Enlightenment and that held that humans are rational beings, that crime is the result of the exercise of free will, and that punishment can be effective in reducing the incidence of crime to the degree it negates the pleasure to be derived from crime commission.

wrong and that any laws passed in furtherance of it were immoral and should have been struck down.

Although the concept of natural law has waned somewhat in influence over the past half century, many people today still hold that the basis for various existing criminal laws can be found in immutable moral principles or some other identifiable aspect of the natural order. Modern-day advocates of natural law claim that it comes from outside the social group and that it is knowable through some form of revelation, intuition, or prophecy.

The debate over abortion is an example of the modern-day use of natural law arguments to support both sides in the dispute. Antiabortion forces, frequently called "pro-lifers" or "right-to-lifers," claim that an unborn fetus is a person, that he or she is entitled to all the protection we would give to any other living human being, and that such protection is basic and humane and lies in the natural relationship of one human being to another within the relationship of a society to its children. Abortion (also called "pro-choice") advocates, who are striving for passage of a law or for a reinterpretation of past Supreme Court precedent that would support their position, maintain that abortion is a right of any pregnant woman because she is the only one who should be in control of her body and claim that the legal system must address the abortion question by offering protection for this natural right.

Perhaps the best-known modern instance of a natural law debate occurred during confirmation hearings for U.S. Supreme Court Justice Clarence Thomas. Thomas, who was confirmed in 1991, once wrote an opinion in which he argued from a natural law point of view, but that opinion was later challenged by Senate Judiciary Committee members who felt it reflected an unbending judicial attitude. Learn more about natural law at **http://www.iep.utm.edu/natlaw**.

The Classical School

The Enlightenment fueled the fires of social change, leading eventually to the French and American Revolutions and providing many of the intellectual underpinnings of the U.S. Constitution. It also inspired other social movements and freed innovative thinkers from the chains of convention. As a direct consequence of Enlightenment thinking, superstitious beliefs were discarded and men and women began to be perceived, for the first time, as self-determining entities possessing a fundamental freedom of choice; free will and rational thought came to be recognized as the linchpins of all significant human activity. In effect, the Enlightenment inspired the reexamination of existing doctrines of human behavior from the point of view of rationalism.

Every Human is Naturaly selfish.

Everett Collection Historical/Alamy Stock Photo

Thomas Paine (1737–1809), an important contributor to the concept of natural law. What are the central tenets of natural law?

Within criminology, the Enlightenment led to the development of the **Classical School** of criminological thought. Crime and deviance, which had previously been explained by reference to mythological influences and spiritual shortcomings, took their place in Enlightenment thought alongside other forms of human activity as products of the exercise of free will. Once people were seen as having control over their own lives, crime came to be explained as a particularly individualized form of evil—that is, as moral wrongdoing fed by personal choice.

Cesare Beccaria

Cesare Beccaria (1738–1794) was born in Milan, Italy, the eldest of four children; he was trained at Catholic schools and had earned a doctor of law degree by the time he was 20. In 1764, Beccaria published his *Essay on Crimes and Punishments*, which consisted of 42 short chapters covering a few major themes to communicate his observations on the laws and justice system of his time. In *Essay*, Beccaria distilled the notion of the social contract into the idea that "laws are the conditions under which

Cesare Beccaria claimed that "[t]he more promptly and the more closely punishment follows upon the commission of a crime, the more just and useful will it be."

independent and isolated men united to form a society."[15] More than anything else, his writings consisted of a philosophy of punishment. Beccaria claimed that the purpose of punishment should be deterrence rather than retribution, and punishment should be imposed to prevent offenders from committing additional crimes. Beccaria saw punishment as a means to an end, not an end in itself, and crime prevention was more important to him than revenge.

To help prevent crimes, Beccaria argued, adjudication and punishment should both be swift and, once punishment is decreed, it should be certain: "The more promptly and the more closely punishment follows upon the commission of a crime, the more just and useful it will be." Punishment that is imposed immediately following crime commission, claimed Beccaria, is connected with the wrongfulness of the offense, both in the mind of the offender and in the minds of others who might see the punishment imposed and thereby learn of the consequences of involvement in criminal activity.

Beccaria concluded that punishment should be only severe enough to outweigh the personal benefits to be derived from crime commission and that any additional punishment would be superfluous. "In order," he said, "for punishment not to be, in every instance, an act of violence of one or of many against a private citizen, it must be essentially public, prompt, necessary, the least possible in the given circumstances, proportionate to the crimes, [and] dictated by the laws."

Beccaria distinguished among three types of crimes: those that threaten the security of the state, those that injure citizens or their property, and those that run contrary to the social order. Punishment should fit the crime—theft should be punished through fines, personal injury through corporal punishment, and serious crimes against the state (such as inciting revolution) via application of the death penalty. (Beccaria was opposed to the death penalty in most other circumstances, seeing it as a kind of warfare waged by society against its citizens.)

Beccaria condemned the torture of suspects, a practice still used in the eighteenth century, saying that it was a device that ensured that weak suspects would incriminate themselves, whereas strong ones would be found innocent. Torture was also unjust because it punished individuals before they had been found guilty in a court of law. In Beccaria's words, "No man can be called guilty before a judge has sentenced him, nor can society deprive him of public protection before it has been decided that he has in fact violated the conditions under which such protection was accorded him. What right is it then, if not simply that of might, which empowers a judge to inflict punishment on a citizen while doubt still remains as to his guilt or innocence?"

Beccaria's *Essay* also touched upon a variety of other topics. He distinguished between two types of proof: "perfect proof," where there was no possibility of innocence, and "imperfect proof," where some possibility of innocence remained. Beccaria also believed in the efficacy of a jury of one's peers, recommending that half of any jury panel consist of the victim's peers and the other half of the accused's peers.

Beccaria's ideas were widely recognized as progressive by his contemporaries. His principles were incorporated into the French penal code of 1791 and significantly influenced the justice-related activities of European leaders like Catherine the Great of Russia, Frederick the Great of Prussia, and Emperor Joseph II of Austria. Evidence suggests that Beccaria's *Essay* influenced framers of the U.S. Constitution, and some scholars claim that the first ten amendments to the Constitution, known as the Bill of Rights, might not have existed were it not for Beccaria's emphasis on individuals' rights in the face of state power. Perhaps more than anyone else, Beccaria is responsible for the contemporary beliefs that criminals have control over their behavior, that they choose to commit crimes, and that they can be deterred by the threat of punishment. Learn more about Cesare Beccaria at **http://www.iep.utm.edu/beccaria**.

Jeremy Bentham

Jeremy Bentham (1748–1832), another founder of the Classical School, wrote in his *Introduction to the Principles of Morals and Legislation* (1789) that "nature has placed mankind under the governance of two sovereign masters, pain and pleasure."[16] To reduce crime or, as Bentham put it, "to prevent the happening of mischief," the pain of punishment must outweigh the pleasure to be derived from criminal activity. Bentham's claim rested upon his belief, spawned by Enlightenment thought, that human beings are fundamentally rational and that criminals will weigh in their minds the pain of punishment against any pleasures thought likely to be derived from crime commission.

Jeremy Bentham said "Nature has placed mankind under the governance of two sovereign masters, pain and pleasure."

Bentham advocated neither extreme nor cruel punishment—only punishment sufficiently distasteful to the offender that the discomfort experienced would outweigh the pleasure to be derived from criminal activity. The more serious the offense is, the more reward

■ **hedonistic calculus**   The belief, first proposed by Jeremy Bentham, that behavior holds value to any individual undertaking it according to the amount of pleasure or pain it can be expected to produce for that person.
■ **utilitarianism**   Another term for Jeremy Bentham's concept of hedonistic calculus.

■ **Panopticon**   A prison designed by Jeremy Bentham that was to be a circular building with cells along the circumference, each clearly visible from a central location staffed by guards.
■ **positivism**   The application of scientific techniques to the study of crime and criminals.
■ **hard determinism**   The belief that crime results from forces beyond the control of the individual.

---

it holds for its perpetrator and therefore the more weighty the official response must be. "Pain and pleasure," said Bentham, "are the instruments the legislator has to work with" in controlling antisocial and criminal behavior.

Bentham's approach has been termed **hedonistic calculus** or **utilitarianism** because of its emphasis on the worth any action holds for an individual undertaking it. Bentham stated, "By the principle of utility is meant that principle which approves or disapproves of every action whatsoever, according to the tendency which it appears to have to augment or diminish the happiness of the party whose interest is in question; or, what is the same thing to promote or to oppose that happiness." In other words, Bentham believed that individuals could be expected to weigh the consequences of their behavior before acting to maximize their pleasure and minimize their pain, based on intensity, duration, certainty, and immediacy (or remoteness) in time.

Like Beccaria, Bentham focused on the potential held by punishment to prevent crime and to act as a deterrent for those considering criminal activity. Regarding criminal legislation, he wrote that "the evils of punishment must be made to exceed the advantage of the offence." Bentham distinguished among 11 types of punishment:

1. Capital punishment (death)
2. Afflictive punishment (whipping and starvation)
3. Indelible punishment (branding, amputation, and mutilation)
4. Ignominious punishment (public punishment involving use of stocks or pillory)
5. Penitential punishment (censure by the community)
6. Chronic punishment (banishment, exile, and imprisonment)
7. Restrictive punishment (license revocation and administrative sanction)
8. Compulsive punishment (restitution and appointment with probation officer)
9. Pecuniary punishment (fine)
10. Quasi-pecuniary punishment (denial of services otherwise available)
11. Characteristic punishment (mandates such as wearing prison uniforms)

Utilitarianism is a practical philosophy, and Bentham was quite practical in his suggestions about crime prevention. He recommended the creation of a centralized police force focused on crime prevention and control—a recommendation that resulted in the English Metropolitan Police Act of 1829 establishing London's New Police under the direction of Sir Robert Peel.

Bentham's other major contribution to criminology was his suggestion that prisons be designed along the lines of what he called a "Panopticon House." The **Panopticon** was to be a circular building with cells along the circumference, each clearly visible from a central location staffed by guards, constructed near or within cities so that it might serve as an example to citizens of what would happen to them should they commit crimes. He also wrote that prisons should be managed by contractors who could profit from the labor of prisoners and that each contractor should "be bound to insure the lives and safe custody of those entrusted to him." Although a Panopticon was never built in Bentham's England, French officials funded a modified version of such a prison, which was eventually built at Lyons, and three prisons modeled after the Panopticon concept were constructed in the United States.

Bentham's critics have been quick to point out that punishment often does not seem to work and that even punishment as severe as death appears not to have any effect on the incidence of crimes like murder (discussed in greater detail later in this chapter). Such critics forget Bentham's second tenet: For punishment to be effective, "it must be swift and certain." Learn more about Jeremy Bentham from the Bentham Project via **http://www.ucl.ac.uk/Bentham-Project**.

Neoclassical Criminology

The Classical School was to influence criminological thinking for a long time to come, from the French Revolution and the U.S. Constitution to today's emphasis on deterrence and crime prevention. By the end of the 1800s, however, classical criminology, with its emphasis on free will and individual choice as the root causes of crime, had given way to another approach known as positivism. **Positivism** (discussed in greater detail in Chapter 4) made use of the scientific method in studying criminality and was based on an acceptance of **hard determinism**, the belief that crime results from forces beyond the control of the individual. The original

> Positivism made use of the scientific method in studying criminality.

■ **neoclassical criminology**   A contemporary version of classical criminology that emphasizes deterrence and retribution, with reduced emphasis on rehabilitation.

■ **nothing-works doctrine**   The belief popularized by Robert Martinson in the 1970s that correctional treatment programs have little success in rehabilitating offenders.

■ **justice model**   A contemporary model of imprisonment in which the principle of just deserts forms the underlying social philosophy.

■ **three-strikes legislation**   A criminal statute that mandates life imprisonment for criminals convicted of three violent felonies or serious drug offenses.

Jeremy Bentham (1748–1832), whose work is closely associated with the Classical School of criminology. What are the key features of the Classical School?

Stateville Correctional Center in Illinois. The prison, built with cells circling a control area, was based on the Panopticon design proposed by Jeremy Bentham. What did Bentham mean when he said that, for punishment to be effective, "it must be swift and certain"?

positivists completely rejected the notion of free will and turned their attention to the impact of socialization, genetics, economic conditions, peer group influences, and other factors that might determine criminality. Acceptance of the notion of hard determinism implied that offenders were not entirely (if at all) responsible for their crimes and suggested that crime could be prevented by changing the conditions that produced criminality (see Figure 3-2).

While positivism remains an important component of contemporary criminology, many of its assumptions were undermined in the 1970s by (1) studies that seemed to show that offenders could not be rehabilitated no matter what was tried, (2) a growing and widespread public fear of crime that led to "get tough on crime" policies, and (3) a cultural reaffirmation of the belief that human beings had a rational nature. The resulting resurgence of classical ideals, called **neoclassical criminology**, focused on the importance of character (a kind of middle ground between total free will and hard determinism) and the dynamics of character development, as well as the rational choices that people make when faced with opportunities for crime. The neoclassical movement appears to have started with a number of publications produced in the 1970s, such as **Robert Martinson's** national survey of rehabilitation programs.[17] Martinson found that, when it came to the rehabilitation of offenders, nothing seemed to work because most resumed their criminal careers after release from prison. "Nothing works!" became a rallying cry of conservative policy makers, and the **nothing-works doctrine** received much public attention. Many conservative politicians and some criminologists began calling existing notions of crime prevention and rehabilitation into question amid claims that enhanced job skills, increased opportunities for employment, and lessened punishment did nothing to stem what was a rising tide of crime.

In 1975, Harvard political scientist James Q. Wilson wrote *Thinking about Crime*, suggesting that crime is not a result of poverty or social conditions and cannot be affected by social programs;[18] he argued for the lengthy incarceration

| Free Will —— Soft Determinism —— Hard Determinism |
| Classical Criminology ——— Nineteenth-Century Positivist Criminology |

FIGURE 3-2 | Classical Criminology versus Positivism—The Role of Free Will

Source: Schmalleger, Frank, *Criminology*. Printed and Electronically reproduced by permission of Pearson Education, Inc., Upper Saddle River, New Jersey.

THEORY | versus REALITY

Three-Strikes Legislation

Near the end of the twentieth century, many states jumped on the "get tough on crime" bandwagon and adopted the justice model in their approach to crime-control legislation. In the spring of 1994, for example, California legislators passed the state's now-famous "three strikes and you're out" law. Amid much fanfare, then-Governor Pete Wilson signed the three-strikes legislation into law, calling it "the toughest and most sweeping crime bill in California history." California's law, which is retroactive (in that it counts offenses committed before the date the legislation was signed), required a 25-year-to-life sentence for three-time felons with convictions for two or more serious or violent prior offenses. Criminal offenders facing a "second strike" could receive up to double the normal sentence for their most recent offense. Under the law, parole consideration was not available until at least 80% of an offender's sentence has been served.

In 2003, in two separate cases, the U.S. Supreme Court upheld the three-strikes California convictions of Gary Ewing and Leandro Andrade.[i] Ewing, who had four prior felony convictions, had received a 25-year-to-life sentence in a California courtroom following his conviction for felony grand theft of three golf clubs. Andrade, who also had a long record, had been sentenced to 50 years in prison for two petty-theft convictions.[ii] In writing for the Court in the Ewing case, Justice Sandra Day O'Connor noted that states should be able to decide when repeat offenders "must be isolated from society to protect the public safety," even when nonserious crimes trigger the lengthy sentence. In deciding these two cases, both of which were based on Eighth Amendment claims, the Court found that it is not cruel and unusual punishment to impose a possible life term for a nonviolent felony when the defendant has a history of serious or violent convictions.

Practically speaking, California's three-strikes law had a dramatic impact on the state's criminal justice system. "'Three strikes and you're out' sounds great to a lot of people," says Alan Schuman, president of the American Probation and Parole Association. "But no one will cop a plea when it gets to the third time around." In one study conducted by RAND, it was estimated that full enforcement of the law cost as much as $5.5 billion annually—or $300 per California taxpayer per year.

Recently, however, 16 states have modified their three-strikes laws in response to difficult economic conditions; this means that the high cost of imprisonment is leading legislatures to rethink long prison terms. Modifications have included giving judges more discretion in sentencing and narrowing the types of crimes that count as a "strike."

In November 2012, California voters overwhelmingly approved a change to their state's three-strikes law.[iii] The changes mean that now only two categories of offenders can be sentenced as three-strikers: (1) those who commit new "serious or violent" felonies as their third offense, and (2) previously released murderers, rapists, or child molesters who are convicted of a new third strike, even if it is not a "serious or violent" felony. Under the 2012 provision, inmates sentenced under earlier versions of the law are allowed to petition for early release. Estimates are that around 3,000 such inmates will ultimately be released as a result of the 2012 change.

Finally, in 2014, voters in California approved Proposition 47, which reduced around 400 felony offenses to misdemeanors and also made drug possession for personal use a misdemeanor.[iv] The change has led to far fewer three-strikes convictions in the state. However, by 2017, more than 13,500 low-level offenders who had been freed by Proposition 47 found themselves on the streets, with few opportunities for employment—causing critics to say that changes in the law had led to a cycle of homelessness, drug abuse, and petty crime.[v] Learn more about crime-control policy at the Center for Law and Social Policy via **http://www.clasp.org**.

Discussion Questions

1. Some people suggest that three-strikes sentences should be imposed only on offenders who commit violent crimes, such as murder, rape, armed robbery, and certain types of arson. What do you think?

2. How is three-strikes legislation in keeping with the spirit of the justice model described in this chapter?

3. What do you think led to the 2012 and 2014 modifications in the state's three-strikes law that California voters approved?

4. Critics have said that Proposition 47 leads to homelessness, drug abuse, and petty crime. How could such charges have been avoided?

Notes

i. *Ewing* v. *California*, 583 U.S. 11 (2003); *Lockyer* v. *Andrade*, 583 U.S. 63 (2003).

ii. Under California law, a person who commits petty theft can be charged with a felony if he or she has prior felony convictions. The charge is known as "petty theft with prior convictions." Andrade's actual sentence was two 25-year prison terms to be served consecutively.

iii. Tracey Kaplan, "Proposition 36: Voters Overwhelmingly Ease Three Strikes Law," *Mercury News*, November 7, 2012.

iv. Kristina Davis, "What You Need to Know About Prop 47," *U-T San Diego*, October 25, 2014, http://www.utsandiego.com/news/2014/oct/25/proposition-47-drug-possession-misdemeanor-theft (accessed March 5, 2015).

v. Jill Castellano et al., "Two Years After Prop. 47, Addicts Walk Free with Nowhere to Go," *The Desert Sun*, http://www.desertsun.com/story/news/crime_courts/2016/12/14/prop-47-california-addiction/94083338 (accessed January 17, 2017).

---

of offenders and the elimination of criminal opportunity. Also in 1975, David Fogel published a book called *We Are the Living Proof: The Justice Model of Corrections*.[19] His **justice model**, predicated on the growing belief that prisons do not rehabilitate or cure and that criminal offenders *deserve* punishment because of the choices they make, was proposed to the Illinois state legislature as a model for prison reform. Fogel argued that, for the criminal justice process to work, offenders must be treated "as responsible as well as accountable, that is, volitional."[20] **Three-strikes legislation**, a reflection of the justice model, is discussed in the Theory versus Reality box in this chapter.

■ **rational choice theory**   A perspective that holds that criminality is the result of conscious choice and that predicts that individuals choose to commit crime when the benefits outweigh the costs of disobeying the law.

■ **situational choice theory**   A brand of rational choice theory that views criminal behavior "as a function of choices and decisions made within a context of situational constraints and opportunities."
■ **soft determinism**   The belief that human behavior is the result of choices and decisions made within a context of situational constraints and opportunities.

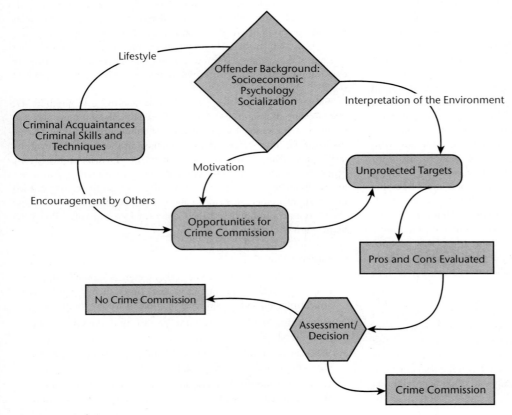

FIGURE 3-3 | Rational Choice and Crime

Source: Schmalleger, Frank, *Criminology*. Printed and Electronically reproduced by permission of Pearson Education, Inc., Upper Saddle River, New Jersey.

Rational Choice Theory (RCT)

Rational choice theory (RCT), a product of the late 1980s, mirrors many of the principles found in classical criminology. The theory, as described by **Ronald V. Clarke** and **Derek B. Cornish**,[21] rests upon the belief that criminals make a conscious, rational, and at least partially informed choice to commit crime and employs cost–benefit analysis (as in the field of economics), viewing human behavior as the result of personal choices made after weighing both the costs and benefits of available alternatives. "[Rational choice] predicts that individuals choose to commit crime when the benefits outweigh the costs of disobeying the law. Crime will decrease when

opportunities are limited, benefits are reduced, and costs are increased."[22] Figure 3-3 diagrams the steps that are likely to be involved in making a choice to commit a property crime. A somewhat different model can be applied in the case of drug offenders since most people who decide to deal drugs do so with an entrepreneurial spirit and often see their activities as a kind of rational business undertaking. Some, in fact, have been known to keep records of their transactions, to include profit-and-loss statements—and even computer-based spreadsheets in an effort to maximize profits.

Situational choice theory, an extension of RCT, provides an example of **soft determinism**, which views criminal behavior "as a function of choices and decisions made within a context of situational constraints and opportunities."[23] The theory holds that "crime is not simply a matter of motivation; it is also a matter of opportunity."[24] Situational choice theory suggests that the probability of criminal activity can be reduced by changing the features of the environment. Clarke and Cornish, collaborators in the development of the situational choice perspective, analyzed the choice-structuring properties of a potentially criminal situation, defining them as "the constellation of opportunities, costs, and benefits attaching to particular kinds of crime."[25] Clarke and Cornish suggested the use of situational strategies to lower the likelihood of criminal victimization in given instances. They also recognized that the rationality of criminal offenders is inevitably bounded or limited, as it is for all of us, by the amount and accuracy of information available to them at the time they are weighing the costs and consequences of future actions.[26]

In brief, rational choice theorists concentrate on "the decision-making process of offenders confronted with specific

Objective: Increase the effort	Example: Close streets
Objective: Increase the risks	Example: Strengthen surveillance
Objective: Reduce the rewards	Example: Identify property
Objective: Reduce provocations	Example: Reduce emotional arousal
Objective: Remove the excuses	Example: Control drugs/alcohol

FIGURE 3-4 | **Situational Crime Control Objectives with Examples**

Source: Schmalleger, Frank, Criminology. Printed and Electronically reproduced by permission of Pearson Education, Inc., Upper Saddle River, New Jersey.

contexts," and have shifted "the focus of the effort to prevent crime from broad social programs to target hardening, environmental design or any impediment that would [dissuade] a motivated offender from offending."[27] Twenty-five techniques of situational crime control can be identified, and each can be classified according to the five objectives of situational prevention. Figure 3-4 outlines those objectives and provides examples of each. All 25 techniques can be seen in the interactive Web graphic available at **http://www.popcenter.org/25techniques**. As shown in the figure, the five objectives are as follows:

1. increase the effort involved in committing a crime,
2. increase the risks associated with crime commission,
3. reduce the rewards of crime,
4. reduce the provocations that lead to criminal activity, and
5. remove the excuses that facilitate crime commission.

Earlier approaches focused largely on the balance between pleasure and pain as the primary determinant of criminal behavior, whereas rational choice theory tends to place less emphasis on pleasure and emotionality and more on rationality and cognition. Some rational choice theorists distinguish among the types of choices offenders make as they move toward criminal involvement. One type of choice, known as involvement decisions, has been described as "multistage" and is said to "include the initial decision to engage in criminal activity as well as subsequent decisions to continue one's involvement or to desist."[28] Another type of choice, event decisions, relates to particular instances of criminal opportunity (such as the decision to rob a particular person or let him or her pass by unmolested); in contrast to involvement decisions, which may take months or even years to reach, these are usually made quickly. Learn more about rational choice theories via **http://criminal-justice.iresearchnet.com/criminology/theories/rational-choice-theory**. You can read about the use of environmental design techniques to reduce crime at **http://www.ncpc.org**. Learn more about crime prevention in general via **http://www.aic.gov.au/media_library/publications/rpp/31/rpp031.pdf**.

The Excitement of Crime

In 2016 and 2017, a wave of car burnings swept across Sweden, a country that prides itself on its low levels of crime. More than 2,000 vehicles were damaged or destroyed, leaving the police with few clues and only a handful of arrests. A Stockholm police spokesperson offered an explanation for the arsons. "There are a few major reasons," he said. "One is that …. that these youth or young men, when interviewed, say it is fun or exciting."[29] One criminologist who focuses on the excitement of crime is **Jack Katz**, whose book *Seductions of Crime* explains crime as the result of the "often wonderful attractions within the lived experience of criminality."[30] Crime, Katz said, is often pleasurable for those committing it, and pleasure is the major motivation behind crime, even if the kind of pleasure to be derived from crime is not immediately obvious. According to Katz, criminologists have often depicted crime as something to be avoided and have failed to understand just how good crime *feels* to those who commit it:

The social science literature contains only scattered evidence of what it means, feels, sounds, tastes, or looks like to commit a particular crime. Readers of research on homicide and assault do not hear the slaps and curses, see the pushes and shoves, or feel the humiliation and rage that may build toward the attack, sometimes persisting after the victim's death. How adolescents manage to make the shoplifting or vandalism of cheap and commonplace things a thrilling experience has not been intriguing to many students of delinquency. The description of "cold-blooded, senseless murders" has been left to writers outside the social sciences. Neither academic methods nor academic theories seem to be able to grasp how it makes sense to them to kill when only petty cash is at stake. Sociological and psychological studies of robbery rarely focus on the distinctive attractions of robbery, even though research has now clearly documented that alternative forms of criminality are available and familiar to many career robbers.[31]

For criminal offenders, crime is indeed rewarding, according to Katz. It is exciting and feels good: "The particular seductions and compulsions [which criminals] experience may be unique to crime," he stated, "but the sense of being seduced and compelled is not. To grasp the magic in the criminal's sensuality, we must acknowledge our own."[32] Katz described the almost sexual attraction shoplifting held for one young offender: "The experience was almost orgasmic for me. There was a buildup of tension as I contemplated the danger of a forbidden act, then a rush of excitement at the moment of committing the crime, and finally a delicious sense of release."[33]

■ **situational crime prevention**   A social policy approach that looks to develop a greater understanding of crime and more effective crime-prevention strategies through concern with the physical, organizational, and social environments that make crime possible.

A glittering jewelry store display window. Rational choice theory says that offenders make a conscious, rational choice to commit crimes. Might some crimes also be irrational?

Criminologists have often depicted crime as something to be avoided and have failed to understand just how good some crime *feels* to those who commit it.

Katz's approach stresses the sensual dynamics of criminality, arguing that crime is sensually compelling for many people. As one writer noted, "Jack Katz argues for a redirection of the criminological gaze—from the traditional focus on background factors such as age, gender, and material conditions to foreground or situational factors that directly precipitate criminal acts and reflect crimes' sensuality."[34] Learn more about the excitement of crime at **http://www.slideshare.net/mattyp99/2013-seductionsof-crimejackkatz**.

Situational Crime-Control Policy

Building on the work of rational and situational choice theorists, Israeli criminologist David Weisburd described the advantages of a situational approach to crime prevention. "Crime prevention research and policy have traditionally been concerned with offenders or potential offenders. Researchers have looked to define strategies that would deter individuals from involvement in crime or rehabilitate them so they would no longer want to commit criminal acts. In recent years, crime prevention efforts have often focused on the incapacitation of high-rate or dangerous offenders so they are not free to victimize law-abiding citizens. In the public debate over crime prevention policies, these strategies are usually defined as competing approaches."[35] However, Weisburd said that "they have in common a central assumption about crime prevention research and policy: that efforts to understand and control crime must begin with the offender. In all of these approaches, the focus of crime prevention is on people and their involvement in criminality."

A new approach developed in large part as a response to the failures of traditional theories and programs. "Although this assumption [the focus on people] continues to dominate crime prevention research and policy," said Weisburd, "it has begun to be challenged by a very different approach that seeks to shift the focus of crime prevention efforts." For many scholars and policy makers, this meant having to rethink assumptions about criminality and the ways offenders might be prevented from participating in crime, with some suggesting that a more radical reorientation of crime-prevention efforts was warranted. They argued that the shift must come not in terms of the specific strategies or theories that were used but in terms of the unit of analysis that formed the basis of crime-prevention efforts and called for a focus not on people who commit crime but on the context in which crime occurs.

This approach, which is called **situational crime prevention**, looks to develop greater understanding of crime and more effective crime-prevention strategies through concern with the physical, organizational, and social environments that make crime possible.[36] The situational approach does not ignore offenders; it merely sees them as one part of a broader crime-prevention equation centered on the context of crime. It demands a shift in the approach to crime prevention from one concerned primarily with why people commit crime to one looking primarily at why crime occurs in specific settings. It moves the context of crime into central focus and sees the offender as only one of a number of factors that affect it. Situational crime prevention is closely associated with the idea of a "criminology of place," which is discussed in more detail in Chapter 7.

Weisburd suggested that a "reorientation of crime prevention research and policy from the causes of criminality to the context of crime provides much promise. At the core of situational prevention is the concept of opportunity."[37] In contrast to offender-based approaches to crime prevention, which usually focus on the dispositions of criminals, situational crime prevention begins with the opportunity structure of the crime

■ **target hardening**   The reduction in criminal opportunity for a particular location, generally through the use of physical barriers, architectural designs, and enhanced security measures.

THEORY | in PERSPECTIVE

The Classical School and Neoclassical Thinkers

The Classical School is a criminological perspective developed in the late 1700s and early 1800s. It had its roots in the Enlightenment and held that men and women are rational beings and that crime is the result of the exercise of free will and personal choices based on calculations of perceived costs and benefits. Hence, punishment can be effective in reducing the incidence of crime when it negates the rewards to be derived from crime commission.

Classical Criminology

Approach: Application of Classical School principles to problems of crime and justice

Period: 1700s–1880s

Theorists: Cesare Beccaria, Jeremy Bentham, others

Concepts: Free will, deterrence through punishment, social contract, natural law, natural rights, due process, Panopticon

Neoclassical Criminology

Approach: Modern-day application of classical principles to problems of crime and crime control in contemporary society, often in the guise of "get tough" social policies

Period: 1970s to the present

Theorists: Ronald V. Clarke, Derek B. Cornish, Jack Katz, many others

Concepts: Rational choice, situational crime prevention, target hardening, just deserts, determinate sentencing, specific deterrence, general deterrence

---

situation, meaning the immediate situational and environmental components of the context of crime. This approach to crime prevention tries to reduce the opportunities for crime in specific situations, which involves efforts as simple and straightforward as **target hardening** or access control.

The value of a situational approach lies in the fact that criminologists have found it difficult to identify who is likely to become a serious offender and to predict the timing and types of future offenses that repeat offenders are likely to commit. Weisburd explained that "legal and ethical dilemmas make it difficult to base criminal justice policies on models that still include a substantial degree of statistical error." Weisburd added that "if traditional approaches worked well, of course, there would be little pressure to find new forms of crime prevention. If traditional approaches worked well, few people would possess criminal motivation and fewer still would actually commit crimes."

Situational prevention advocates argue that the context of crime provides a promising alternative to traditional offender-based crime-prevention policies.[38] They assume that situations provide a more stable and predictable focus for crime-prevention efforts than do people, based on commonsense notions of the relationship between opportunities and crime. Shoplifting, for example, is by definition clustered in stores and not residences, and family disputes are unlikely to be a problem outside the home. High-crime places, in contrast to high-crime people, cannot flee to avoid criminal justice intervention, and crime that develops from the specific characteristics of certain places cannot be easily transferred to other contexts.

In short, situational crime control works by removing or reducing criminal opportunity. If we accept that opportunity is a cause of crime equal in importance to the personal and social characteristics that other researchers point to as causes, then, much of the crime-prevention work that is already being done by police agencies, private security, and businesses aimed at reducing criminal opportunity directly affects the basic causes of crime.

Learn more about situational crime prevention and target hardening via **https://www.newark.rutgers.edu/news/crime-prevention-numbers**.

Critique of Rational Choice Theory

Rational and situational choice theories can be criticized for overemphasizing the importance of individual choice with relative disregard for the role of social factors in crime causation, such as poverty, poor home environment, and inadequate socialization.

According to one study, RCT does not adequately consider the impact of emotional states on cognitive ability and the role of psychopharmacological agents in decision making.[39] The study examined the effects of alcohol and anger on aggression and found that "alcohol diminishes individuals' perceptions of the costs associated with aggression and, in some instances, actually increases the perceived benefits." Similarly, high arousal

■ **displacement**   A shift of criminal activity from one location to another.

Rational choice theory can be criticized for an overemphasis on individual choice and a relative disregard for the role of social factors in crime causation.

levels, such as those associated with anger and other emotions, appear to impair judgment. So, when acting under the influence of alcohol or when experiencing strong emotions, "the individual's capacity to anticipate gratification and aversion, success and failure, and cost is diminished."[40] The authors note that other studies show that approximately 40% of offenders are under the influence of alcohol when committing the crimes for which they are arrested, and suggest that future research involving the rational choice perspective should include the role of emotions and the potential impact of psychopharmacological agents such as drugs or alcohol on the decisions made by people who commit crimes.

One 2005 study that explored the deterrent effect of punishment offers insight into the potential that rational choice theory holds for social policy. In that study, David Lee and Justin McCrary, both at the University of California–Berkeley, examined how juvenile offenders respond to the likelihood of significantly higher sanctions associated with criminality when they reach adulthood.[41] They found that a 230% increase in expected sentence length was associated with only a 1.8% reduction in the likelihood of arrest, so they reasoned that even enormous increases in sentence length seem to do little to reduce the probability of repeat offending: "The small behavioral responses that we estimate suggest that potential offenders are extremely impatient, myopic, or both."[42]

A 2009 study conducted by Italian researchers focused on the large number of Italian inmates who were released in 2006 as efforts were made to reduce the prison population in that country.[43] A condition of release was that anyone who reoffended would face new sanctions *and* have to finish the term they were serving at the time of their release. The possibility of added time was found to have a "substantial effect" on the average prisoner, but the most serious offenders (those whose original sentences were 69 months or longer) appeared not to be deterred by the threat of enhanced sentences. The researchers concluded that career offenders were far less likely to be affected by penalty enhancements than offenders who were not as far down the path of criminality.

Rational choice theory assumes that everyone is equally capable of making rational decisions, which is probably not the case. Some individuals are more logical than others by virtue of temperament, personality, or socialization; some are emotional, hotheaded, and unthinking. Empirical studies of RCT have added scant support for the perspective's underlying assumptions, tending to show instead that criminal offenders are often unrealistic in their appraisals of the relative risks and rewards facing them.[44] Similarly, rational and situational choice theories seem to disregard individual psychology and morality, with their emphasis on external situations. Moral individuals, say critics, when faced with easy criminal opportunities, may rein in their desires and turn their backs on temptation.

Finally, the emphasis of rational and situational choice theories on changing aspects of the immediate situation to reduce crime has been criticized for resulting in the **displacement** of crime from one area to another.[45] Target hardening,[46] a key crime-prevention strategy among such theorists, has sometimes caused criminals to find new targets of opportunity in other areas.[47]

Punishment and Neoclassical Thought

Punishment is a central feature of both classical and neoclassical thought. Whereas punishment served the ends of deterrence in classical thought, its role in neoclassical thinking has been expanded to support the ancient concept of retribution, with those advocating retribution seeing the primary utility of punishment as revenge.

Modern neoclassical thinkers argue that, if a person is attracted to crime and chooses to violate the law, then he or she *deserves* to be punished because the consequences of crime were known to the offender before the crime was committed. The criminal *must* be punished so that future criminal behavior can be curtailed.

Punishment is a central feature of both classical and neoclassical thought.

Notions of revenge and retribution are morally based, built on a sense of indignation at criminal behavior and on the righteousness inherent in Judeo-Christian notions of morality and propriety. Both philosophies of punishment turn a blind eye to the mundane and practical consequences of any particular form of punishment. Hence, advocates of retributive philosophies of punishment easily dismiss critics of the death penalty, who frequently challenge the efficacy of court-ordered capital punishment on the basis that such sentences do little to deter others. Wider issues, including general deterrence, become irrelevant when a person focuses narrowly on the emotions that crime and victimization engender in a given instance. From the neoclassical perspective, some crimes cry out for vengeance while others demand little more than a slap on the wrist or an apology from the offender.

■ **deterrence**   The prevention of crime.
■ **specific deterrence**   A goal of criminal sentencing that seeks to prevent a particular offender from engaging in repeat criminality.
■ **general deterrence**   A goal of criminal sentencing that seeks to prevent others from committing crimes similar to the one for which a particular offender is being sentenced.
■ **recidivism**   The repetition of criminal behavior.
■ **recidivism rate**   The percentage of convicted offenders who have been released from prison and who are later rearrested for a new crime, generally within five years following release.

■ **just deserts model**   The notion that criminal offenders deserve the punishment they receive at the hands of the law and that punishments should be appropriate to the type and severity of the crime committed.

Just Deserts

The old adage "He got what was coming to him" well summarizes the thinking behind the **just deserts model** of criminal sentencing, which refers to the concept that criminal offenders deserve the punishment they receive at the hands of the law and that any punishment imposed should be appropriate to the type and severity of the crime committed. The idea of just deserts has long been part of Western thought, dating back at least to Old Testament times. The Old Testament dictum of "an eye for an eye, and a tooth for a tooth" has been cited by many as divine justification for strict punishments, although some scholars believe that "an eye for an eye" was intended to *reduce* the barbarism of existing penalties, whereby an aggrieved party might exact the severest of punishments for only minor offenses (even petty offenses were often punished by whipping, torture, and sometimes death).

One famous modern-day advocate of the just deserts philosophy was Christian thinker C. S. Lewis. Lewis said that we could ask many questions about punishment, such as whether or not it is an effective deterrent. But, he wrote, the only important question is whether it is deserved:

> The concept of desert is the only connecting link between punishment and justice. It is only as deserved or undeserved that a sentence can be just or unjust…. Thus when we cease to consider what the criminal deserves and consider only what will cure him or deter others, we have tacitly removed him from the sphere of justice altogether.[48]

According to the neoclassical perspective, doing justice ultimately comes down to an official meting out of what is deserved. Justice for an individual is nothing more or less than what that individual deserves when all the circumstances surrounding that person's situation and behavior are taken into account.

Deterrence

True to its historical roots, **deterrence** is a hallmark of modern neoclassical thought. In contrast to early thinkers, however, today's neoclassical writers distinguish between general and specific deterrence: **Specific deterrence** is a goal of criminal sentencing seeking to prevent a particular offender from engaging in repeat criminality. **General deterrence** works by way of example, seeking to prevent others from committing crimes similar to the one for which a particular offender is being sentenced.

Following their classical counterparts, modern-day advocates of general deterrence frequently stress that, for punishment to be an effective impediment to crime, it must be swift, certain, and severe enough to outweigh the rewards flowing from criminal activity. Unfortunately, those who advocate punishment as a deterrent are often frustrated by the complexity of today's criminal justice system and by the slow and circuitous manner in which cases are handled and punishments are meted out. Punishments today, even when imposed by a court, are rarely swift in their imposition; the wheels of modern criminal justice are relatively slow to grind to a conclusion, given the many delays inherent in judicial proceedings and the numerous opportunities for delay and appeal available to defense counsel. Certainty of punishment is also anything but a reality. Certain punishments are those that cannot be easily avoided, but today even when punishments are ordered, they are frequently not carried out—at least not fully. In contemporary America, offenders sentenced to death, for example, are unlikely to have their sentences finalized; for those who do, an average of nearly 12 years passes between the time a death sentence is imposed.[49]

If the neoclassicists are correct, criminal punishments should ideally prevent a repetition of crime, but punishments in the United States rarely accomplish that goal, as high rates of contemporary **recidivism** (repetition of criminal behavior by those already involved in crime) indicate. Recidivism, when used to measure the success of a given approach to the problem of crime, is referred to as a **recidivism rate**, expressed as the percentage of convicted offenders who have been released from prison and who are later rearrested for a new crime, generally within five years following release. Studies show that recidivism rates are high indeed, reaching levels of 80 to 90% in some instances, meaning that eight or nine of every ten criminal offenders released from confinement are rearrested for new law-breaking activity within five years of being set free. Such studies do not

■ **capital punishment**   The legal imposition of a sentence of death upon a convicted offender.

measure the numbers of released offenders who return to crime but who are not caught and ignore those who return to crime more than five years after release from prison; if such numbers were available, recidivism rates would likely be even higher.

One reason U.S. criminal justice seems so ineffectual at preventing crime and reducing recidivism may be that punishments that contemporary criminal law provides are rarely applied to the majority of offenders. Statistics show that few lawbreakers are ever arrested and that, of those who are, fewer still are convicted of the crimes with which they have been charged. After a lengthy court process, most offenders processed by the justice system are released, fined, or placed on probation. Relatively few are sent to prison, although short of capital punishment, prison is the most severe form of punishment available to authorities today. To represent this situation, criminal justice experts often use a diagram known as a "crime funnel." See Figure 3-5 for the 2017 crime funnel, which shows that less than 1% of criminal law violators in the United States can be expected to spend time in prison as punishment for their crimes.

Exacerbating the situation is the fact that few people sent to prison ever serve anything close to the sentences that have been imposed on them. Many inmates serve only a small fraction of their sentences due to early release made possible by time off for good behavior, mandated reentry training, and practical considerations necessitated by prison overcrowding.

Capital Punishment

Notions of deterrence, retribution, and just deserts all come together in **capital punishment**, the legal imposition of a death sentence. The many different understandings of crime and crime control, along with arguments over free will and social determinism, combine with varying philosophies of punishment to produce considerable disagreement over the efficacy of death as a form of criminal sanction.

Opponents of capital punishment make ten claims:

1. Capital punishment does not deter crime.
2. The death penalty has been imposed on innocent people, and no workable system is currently in place to prevent the accidental execution of innocents.
3. Human life, even the life of a murderer, is sacred.
4. State-imposed death lowers society to the same moral (or amoral) level as the murderer.
5. The death penalty has been (and may still be) imposed in haphazard and seemingly random fashion.
6. The death penalty is imposed disproportionately upon ethnic minorities.
7. Capital punishment goes against the most fundamental precepts of almost every organized religion.
8. The death penalty is more expensive than imprisonment.
9. Capital punishment is widely viewed as inhumane and barbaric internationally.
10. There is a better alternative (usually said to be life in prison without possibility of parole). Read more about arguments against the death penalty at **http://www .aclu.org/capital-punishment/case-against-death -penalty** and **http://papers.ssrn.com/sol3/papers .cfm?abstract_id=914162**.

FIGURE 3-5 | The Crime Funnel

Felonies
Committed Annually:
38 Million (Estimate)

Serious Crimes Reported
to the Police Yearly:
10.3 Million

Annual Felony Arrests:
3.8 Million

Annual Felony
Convictions:
1.1 million

People Sent to
Prison Annually:
700,000

Note: Includes drug crimes.
Source: University at Albany, Hindelang Criminal Justice Research Center, *Sourcebook of Criminal Justice Statistics*, http://www.albany.edu/sourcebook (accessed May 25, 2017).

Advocates of capital punishment generally discount each of these claims, countering abolitionist arguments with the proposition that death is *deserved* by those who commit especially heinous acts and that anything short of capital punishment

PUTTING CRIMINOLOGY TO WORK—Implementing Evidence-Based Policy

To make a difference in the real world, criminological theories must first be tested and evaluated. Once evidence has been developed that theory-based practices work, then programs based on them can be implemented to reduce or prevent crime, or to help make victims' lives better. One federal initiative, CrimeSolutions.Gov, strives to evaluate the effectiveness of theory-based practices, and then communicates its findings via the Web. Some of the most effective and promising programs are highlighted in boxes such as this one that appear throughout the text.

PROGRAM: Focused Deterrence Strategies

EVIDENCE RATINGS FOR OUTCOMES: Promising

PROFILE

Focused deterrence strategies (also referred to as "pulling levers" policing) are problem-oriented policing strategies that follow the core principles of deterrence theory. The strategies target specific criminal behavior committed by a small number of chronic offenders who are vulnerable to sanctions and punishment (i.e., youth gang members or repeat violent offenders). Offenders are directly confronted and informed that continued criminal behavior will not be tolerated. Targeted offenders are also told how the criminal justice system (such as the police and prosecutors) will respond to continued criminal behavior; mainly that all potential sanctions, or levers, will be applied. The deterrence-based message is reinforced through crackdowns on offenders, or groups of offenders (such as gangs), who continue to commit crimes despite the warning. In addition to deterring violent behavior, the strategies also reward compliance and nonviolent behavior among targeted offenders by providing positive incentives, such as access to social services and job opportunities.

Relevant Theory: Neoclassical Deterrence

Deterrence theory suggests that crime can be prevented if potential offenders believe the costs of committing a crime outweigh the benefits. Three key concepts play an important role in deterrence theory: the certainty, severity, and swiftness of punishment. The deterrent effects of crime prevention programs and policies are a function of a potential offender's perceptions of the certainty, severity, and swiftness of punishment. Focused deterrence strategies combine elements of classic deterrence with additional elements thought to prevent crime. First, focused deterrence strategies typically begin with an intense focus on particular types of crime and the chronic offenders most responsible for carrying out those crimes. Second, focused deterrence strategies are often referred to as "pulling levers" strategies because they seek to apply every lever available, whether formal or informal, in deterring offenders. Third, focused deterrence strategies work to directly influence *perceived* sanction risks among offenders by communicating directly with them about the consequences of their actions. An important part of altering perceived risks among offenders is administering sanctions swiftly so potential offenders can observe the immediate consequences of their actions on others who have already broken the law.

Evidence-Based Review

These sources were used in the development of this profile:

Meta-Analysis 1

Anthony A. Braga and David L. Weisburd, "The Effects of 'Pulling Levers' Focused Deterrence Strategies on Crime," *Campbell Systematic Reviews*, Vol. 6, http://campbellcollaboration.org/lib/project/96

Source: Adapted from https://www.crimesolutions.gov/PracticeDetails.aspx?ID=11

Note: Putting Criminology to Work features are based on information published online by the National Institute of Justice's (NIJ) Crime Solutions Website. The program ratings shown are those provided by NIJ.

under certain circumstances is an injustice in itself; some people deserve to die for what they have done. Such arguments have evolved from a natural law perspective, are sometimes supported on religious grounds, and are based on the notion of just deserts (discussed earlier).

Strong feelings on both sides of the issue have generated a plethora of studies of the efficacy and fairness of capital punishment as a criminal sanction. The extent to which the death penalty acts as a general deterrent has been widely examined. Some researchers have compared murder rates between states that have eliminated the death penalty and those that retain it, finding little variation in the rate at which murders are committed.[50] Others have looked at variations in murder rates over time in jurisdictions that have eliminated capital punishment, with similar results.[51] A now-classic 1988 Texas study provided a comprehensive review

of capital punishment by correlating homicide rates with the rate of executions within the state between 1930 and 1986;[52] the study, which was especially important because Texas has been quite active in the capital punishment arena, failed to find any support for the use of death as a deterrent.

Similarly, in an important recent study of the deterrent effect of capital punishment, Tomislav V. Kovandzic and colleagues found "no empirical support for the argument that the existence or application of the death penalty deters offenders from committing homicide."[53] Kovandzic's study made use of homicide data from all 50 states and the District of Columbia between the years 1977 and 2006, and the study's design allowed researchers both to assess the impact of changes in capital punishment laws and to compare murder rates in death-penalty jurisdictions with those without capital punishment laws.

Punishments that are both swift and certain hold the potential to prevent even the most serious crimes.

Regardless of studies to the contrary, many death-penalty advocates remain unconvinced that the sanction cannot be an effective deterrent, saying that a death penalty that is swift and certain is likely to deter others. In a succinct summary of studies on the deterrent effect of the death penalty, the Committee on Law and Justice of the National Academies of Sciences released *Deterrence and the Death Penalty*—a publication that included a detailed analysis of previous death penalty research.[54] The committee found that "research to date is not informative about whether capital punishment decreases, increases, or has no effect on homicide rates." It concluded that "claims that research demonstrates that capital punishment decreases or increases the homicide rate or has no effect on it should not influence policy judgments about capital punishment."

Learn more about how capital punishment is seen in contemporary America from the Death Penalty Information Center at **http://www.deathpenaltyinfo.org**. Read about the current state of the death penalty at **http://www.iep.utm.edu/punishme**. A balanced approach to the subject can be read at **http://www.mass.gov/courts/docs/lawlib/docs/5-3-04governorsreportcapitalpunishment.pdf**.

Capital Punishment and Race

According to the Washington-based Death Penalty Information Center, the death penalty has been imposed disproportionately on racial minorities throughout most of U.S. history.[55] Statistics maintained by the center show that "since 1930 nearly 90% of those executed for the crime of rape in this country were African Americans. Currently, about 50% of those on the nation's death rows are from minority populations representing 20% of the country's population." The center, a fervent anti–capital punishment organization, claims that "evidence of racial discrimination in the application of capital punishment continues." Thirty-four percent of those executed since 1976 have been black, even though blacks constitute only 12% of the population. And in almost every death-penalty case, the race of the victim is white. Of the 1,446 executions that have occurred since the death penalty was reinstated [in 1976], the center says, that "only one has involved a white defendant for the murder of a black person." Figures 3-6 and 3-7 show the ethnicity of defendants executed in the United States, as well as the ethnicity of murder victims, over the past 41 years.

On the other hand, capital punishment advocates say that the real question is not whether ethnic differences exist in

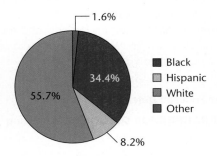

FIGURE 3-6 | **Ethnicity of Defendants Executed in the United States, 1976–2017**

Source: DEATH PENALTY INFORMATION CENTER, Facts about the Death Penalty, May 12, 2016; http://www.deathpenaltyinfo.org/documents/FactSheet.pdf

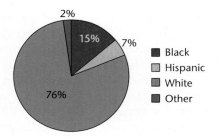

FIGURE 3-7 | **Ethnicity of Victims in Death Penalty Cases in the United States, 1976–2017**

Source: DEATH PENALTY INFORMATION CENTER, Facts about the Death Penalty, May 12, 2016; http://www.deathpenaltyinfo.org/documents/FactSheet.pdf

the rate of imposition of the death penalty but whether the penalty is *fairly* imposed. They argue that if 50% of all capital punishment–eligible crimes were committed by members of a particular (relatively small) ethnic group, then anyone anticipating fairness in imposition of the death penalty would expect to see 50% of death-row populations composed of members of that group (no matter how small the group). In like manner, one would also expect to see the same relative ethnicity among those executed. In short, if fairness is to be a guide, those committing capital crimes should be the ones sentenced to death regardless of race, ethnicity, gender, or other social characteristics.

Although evidence may suggest that African Americans and other minorities in the United States have in the past been unfairly sentenced to die,[56] the present evidence is not so clear. For an accurate appraisal to be made, any claims of disproportionality must go beyond simple comparisons with racial representation in the larger population and must somehow measure both the frequency and the seriousness of capital crimes between and within racial groups. Following that line of reasoning, the Supreme Court, in the 1987 case

CRIME | in the NEWS

Post-Conviction DNA Exonerations Expose Weaknesses in Judicial System

By mid-2017, 349 previously convicted people had been exonerated through the use of DNA evidence. At the time that many of them had been convicted, DNA analysis was either not available or was too costly and impracticable to use. One such story involves Michael Phillips who, in September 2014, became the 321st person in the United States to be exonerated based on DNA evidence, according to the Innocence Project. Phillips was exonerated more than a decade after having served the entire 12 years of a prison sentence that he was handed in 1990. Phillips's exoneration came when the Dallas County (Texas) District Attorney's Conviction Integrity Unit examined previously untested DNA evidence from a rape of which Phillips had been accused. The DNA, which came from semen that had been collected but never analyzed, matched another man known to live close to the crime scene. In 1990, Phillips had been the only suspect in the rape of a 16-year-old girl that took place at the motel where he worked. He was misidentified by the girl during a photo lineup, and—fearing a criminal trial—agreed to plead guilty in hopes of a reduced sentence.

Post-conviction DNA exonerations extend back at least to 1993, when Kirk Bloodsworth was exonerated for the 1984 rape and murder of a 9-year-old girl. Bloodsworth had been linked to the crime by the testimony of five eyewitnesses, but DNA analysis of biological evidence from the crime scene showed that he could not have been the person who committed the crime.

Since Bloodsworth's time, DNA evidence has torn a hole in the U.S. criminal justice system. The 321 prisoners granted DNA exonerations so far served a total of 4,337 years in prison. The Innocence Project says that the leading cause of their wrongful convictions is false eyewitness identification, a factor in 72% of cases, followed by improper forensic procedures in 50% of cases, false confessions in 27% of cases, and false information from informants in 18%.

False eyewitness identifications come up again and again. Witnesses have only fleeting recollections of the crime, which can get blurred when they are asked to pick the perpetrator from many photos at once. David Lee Wiggins was convicted and sentenced to life in prison in 1989 for rape, based on his identification by a rape victim who had just a few glimpses of her assailant. In August 2012, a Texas judge released Wiggins based on DNA evidence.

The Innocence Project reports that it pursues just 1% of the 6,000 to 10,000 cases it reviews at any given time. While DNA has freed many prisoners, advocates say thousands more have persuasive evidence of wrongful prosecution but may never be freed due to lack of DNA evidence. Samples were degraded, thrown out, or never collected.

Forty-nine states now allow a prisoner access to DNA testing, but many of them still put up substantial legal barriers to obtaining tests,

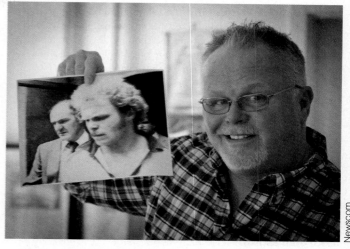

Newscom

Kirk Noble Bloodsworth (born October 31, 1960) holds a picture of himself as a young man. Bloodsworth is the first American sentenced to death row who was exonerated by DNA evidence. How can innocent people be wrongly convicted of serious crimes?

place time limits on DNA access, and have no consistent guidelines for evidence retention. Only about half the states require automatic preservation of DNA evidence after conviction.

There are signs of progress, though. The National Institute of Justice, the research arm of the Justice Department, is funding the development of guidelines for evidence retention. Eleven states have created commissions to study wrongful convictions and recommend changes in the system. And some states have considered improvements in witness identification, such as requiring investigators to show one photo at a time.

Discussion Questions

1. What are your feelings about capital punishment? Provide reasons to support the way you feel.

2. What do you think are the most significant arguments against the death penalty? What do you consider to be the most convincing arguments in favor of it?

3. How do cases of exoneration, like the ones described in this box, affect public opinion about capital punishment?

Sources: The Innocence Project, "DNA Exonerations Nationwide," http://www.innocenceproject.org/Content/DNA_Exonerations_Nationwide.php (accessed May 15, 2017); Molly Hennessy-Fiske, "Texan Wrongly Convicted of Rape Freed after 24 Years in Prison," *Los Angeles Times*, August 25, 2012, http://articles.latimes.com/2012/aug/25/nation/la-na-nn-rape-texas-exonerated-20120824; Kevin Johnson, "Storage of DNA Evidence Crucial to Exonerations," *USA Today*, March 28, 2011, http://usatoday30.usatoday.com/news/nation/2011-03-28-crimelab28_ST_N.htm; Jason Morris, "From Convicted Sex Offender to Millionaire, Man Gets New Life," *CNN* July 31, 2014, http://www.cnn.com/2014/07/31/us/texas-rape-exoneration/index.html.

of *McCleskey* v. *Kemp*,[57] held that a simple showing of racial discrepancies in the application of the death penalty does not amount to a constitutional violation.

To reduce the likelihood that capital punishment decisions will be influenced by a defendant's race, the Washington-based Constitution Project[58] recommended that "all jurisdictions that

impose the death penalty should create mechanisms to help ensure that the death penalty is not imposed in a racially discriminatory manner."[59] The project said that two approaches are especially appropriate in building such mechanisms: (1) the gathering of statistical data on the role of race in the operation of a jurisdiction's capital punishment system, and (2) the active

■ **determinate sentencing**   A criminal punishment strategy that mandates a specified and fixed amount of time to be served for every offense category. Under the strategy, for example, all offenders convicted of the same degree of burglary would be sentenced to the same length of time behind bars.

■ **truth in sentencing**   A close correspondence between the sentence imposed upon those sent to prison and the time actually served prior to prison release.

■ **incapacitation**   The use of imprisonment or other means to reduce the likelihood that an offender will be capable of committing future offenses.

involvement of members of all races in every level of the capital punishment decision-making process. Read the entire report of the Constitution Project at **http://www.deathpenaltyinfo .org/node/1634**, and view more than 1,000 capital punishment–related Web links at **http://www.clarkprosecutor.org/html/ links/dplinks.htm**.

Policy Implications of Classical and Neoclassical Thought

During the past 40 years or so, American justice philosophy has been strongly influenced by the punishment practices of determinate sentencing and truth in sentencing. Because both determinate sentencing and truth in sentencing are rational forms of justice, most criminologists see them as natural consequences of a classical view of crime and punishment.

Determinate sentencing is a strategy that mandates a specified and fixed amount of time to be served for every offense category. Under determinate sentencing schemes, for example, judges might be required to impose seven-year sentences on armed robbers, but only one-year sentences on strong-armed robbers (who use no weapon). Determinate sentencing schemes build on twin notions of classical thought: (1) The pleasure of a given crime can be somewhat accurately assessed, and (2) a fixed amount of punishment necessary for deterrence can be calculated and specified. **Truth in sentencing** requires judges to assess and make public the actual time an offender is likely to serve, once sentenced to prison, and many recently enacted truth-in-sentencing laws require that offenders serve a large portion of their sentence (often 80%) before they can be released.

> Truth in sentencing requires judges to assess and make public the actual time an offender is likely to serve, once sentenced to prison.

Because of the widespread implementation of determinate sentencing strategies and the passage of truth-in-sentencing laws during the last quarter century, prison populations today are larger than ever before. By early 2016, the nation's state and federal prison population (excluding jails) stood at more than 1.5 million inmates, representing an increase of over 700% since 1970.[60] Figure 3-8 shows the U.S. prison population growth rate from 1924 to 2015. Today, for the first time in nearly a century, prison populations appear to have peaked and started to decline, largely as a result of the huge financial burden associated with such numbers.

Imprisonment is one component of a strategy of **incapacitation** (the use of imprisonment or other means to reduce the likelihood that an offender will be capable of committing future offenses). Proponents of modern-day incapacitation often distinguish between the terms *selective incapacitation*, in which crime is controlled via the imprisonment of specific individuals, and *collective incapacitation*, whereby changes in legislation and/or sentencing patterns lead to the removal from society of entire groups of individuals judged to be dangerous. Advocates of selective incapacitation as a crime-control strategy point to studies that show the majority of crimes are perpetrated by a small number of hard-core repeat offenders. The most famous of those studies, conducted by University of Pennsylvania Professor Marvin Wolfgang, focused on 9,000 men born in Philadelphia in 1945.[61] By the time this cohort of men had reached age 18, Wolfgang was able to determine that 627 "chronic recidivists" were responsible for the large majority of all serious violent crimes committed by the group. Other, more recent studies have similarly shown that a small core of criminal perpetrators is probably responsible for most criminal activity in the United States.

Such thinking has led to the development of incapacitation as a modern-day treatment philosophy and to the creation of innovative forms of incapacitation that do not require imprisonment—such as home confinement, use of halfway houses or career training centers for convicted felons, and psychological and/or other treatments designed to reduce the likelihood of future crime commission.

In one example of recent policy changes, Washington state built upon the neoclassical principles of swift-and-certain (SAC)

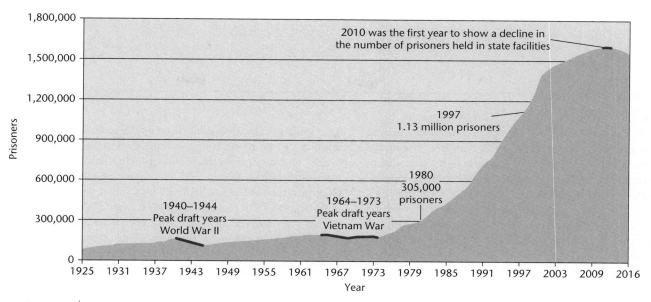

FIGURE 3-8 | **U.S. Prison Populations, 1924–2016**

Source: Bureau of Justice Statistics, *Crime and Justice Atlas 2000* (Washington, DC: Bureau of Justice Statistics, 2001), pp. 42–43; Bureau of Justice Statistics, *Prisoners in 2016* (Washington, DC: Bureau of Justice Statistics, 2017); and other years.

WHO'S TO BLAME—The Individual or Society?

The Excitement of Crime

Following his arrest for the theft of a police car, Moonbeam Kittaro met with one of his friends in the visiting area of the local jail. Here's what he said:

> I stole a cop car and s***, was it exciting!
>
> I mean, the thing was just sitting there running in the parking lot. Who wouldn't take it?
>
> I've never been so high on pure adrenaline. It was an adrenaline rush being behind the wheel of that f***ing car.
>
> It turned my girlfriend on too.
>
> I drove over to her place with the lights and siren on, and as soon as she saw the car she wanted to go for a ride.
>
> We must have hit 140 on the Interstate!
>
> Then we pulled into a rest stop and made love in the back seat.
>
> It was the whole illegal thing that got her so excited.
>
> But that's when we got arrested.
>
> The cops surrounded the car, guns drawn and all that s***.
>
> We didn't even hear them coming.

A police car like the one stolen in this story. What kinds of crimes hold the most excitement for offenders?

Think about it

1. Why did Kittaro steal the car? Do you think he knew, before he stole it, that the theft would lead to so much excitement?

2. Can the desire for excitement explain crimes like Kittaro's? Can the same desire explain other kinds of crimes? If so, what might they be?

3. If excitement explains crime commission, then why doesn't everyone commit crime for the excitement it brings?

4. What kinds of crime-prevention programs might be based on the principles illustrated here?

Note: Who's to Blame boxes provide critical-thinking opportunities based on actual cases.

punishments and enacted a SAC deterrence-based sanctioning model to deal with probation supervision violators. The model calls for the use of immediate short-term jail confinement (about three days) after *every* violation of probation conditions. It also gives community corrections officers (CCOs) the ability to deliver sanctions immediately upon discovering a second low-level violation, rather than after a violation hearing. A three-year evaluation that followed the 2012 implementation of Washington's SAC sanctioning policy found support for the SAC model.[62] Findings showed SAC participants were significantly less likely to be reconvicted of any felony than were members of a control group.

A Critique of Classical and Neoclassical Theories

Classical and neoclassical thought represents more a philosophy of justice than it does a simple theory of crime causation. As Randy Martin, Robert J. Mutchnick, and W. Timothy Austin have observed, "The true test of Beccaria's essay can be judged by the influence it has had over time on our justice system."[63]

Pleasant Valley Prison in Fresno, California. "Law and order" approaches have led to dramatically overcrowded prisons. How can prison overcrowding be reduced?

ZUMA Press/Alamy Stock photo

The influence of Beccaria, the Enlightenment, and classical thinkers can be found today in the U.S. Constitution, in "get tough" approaches to crime, and in a continuing emphasis on individual rights. Martin and colleagues concluded that the Classical School "has left behind a legacy that we see in almost every aspect of our present-day justice system."[64]

As we observed in Chapter 2, any perspective gains credence if actions taken on the basis of its assertions appear to bear fruit. Not surprisingly, advocates of today's neoclassical approaches to crime control take much of the credit for the drop-off in crime rates that have occurred over the past two decades. After all, following the implementation of "get tough on crime" policies like the determinate sentencing schemes called for by the just deserts model, official rates of crime declined substantially.

That decrease led mayors, police chiefs, and politicians throughout the country to declare victory in the battle against crime, and many took personal credit for crime's decline. Notable among such politicians have been then-New York City mayor Rudy Giuliani, Los Angeles mayor Antonio Villariagosa, and former Los Angeles police chief William J. Bratton.

However, the situation is not so simple. As one journalist recently explained it, taking "responsibility for crime trends depends entirely on whether those trends are good or bad. When crime statistics decline, everyone rushes to take credit. The mayor boasted his new initiative is working exactly as he said it would. The police chief proudly declared that the strategy he implemented was a great success. Social service agencies insisted their programs were responsible. And so it goes in city after city. The only thing that varies is the identity of the initiatives, strategies, and programs said to be the cause of the crime drop.... Which suggests pretty strongly that all these claims are empty."[65]

The fact that crime has declined significantly in almost every U.S. jurisdiction over the past 20 years means that it has gone down in areas that instituted "get tough" policies, as well as in areas that saw little change in their approach to crime prevention. Realistically, those who take credit for actively reducing crime in their cities and towns must also somehow account for crime's decline in other locations over which they had no control. Recently, for example, after the mayor and police chief in Los Angeles claimed that their crime-fighting policies had been responsible for an 8% drop in homicides throughout the city, one Los Angeles politician looked at murder rates throughout the region and found that while murder *inside* the city was down 8%, a decline of 15%

CRIMINAL | PROFILES

Gary Steven Krist: The Einstein of Crime?

Born in Aberdeen, Washington, in 1945, Gary Steven Krist was raised in the small fishing village of Pelican, Alaska. His father was a poor salmon fisherman, and Krist himself described his mother as "a well-intentioned scatterbrain."[i]

During his parents' absence, Gary and his brother, Gordon, were left in the care of others. As a preteen, Gary showed a propensity for violence, and he once fired a shotgun over his babysitter's and brother's heads because the babysitter made him angry.

He soon became known throughout the tiny Pelican community as a troublemaker. Krist's parents, however, seemed to view this behavior as simply displays of typical youthful exuberance.

As he entered his teens, Krist's delinquency bloomed into full-fledged criminality. At the age of 14, Krist was arrested with a friend for a series of burglaries, various sexual conquests, and much drinking. He later wrote in a memoir that their "crimes arose, I believe, more from an overpowering hungry curiosity coupled with excess physical energy than from any defined hostility or malice toward others."

While on probation for these offenses, Krist stole a car, which got him sent to a reform school in Ogden, Utah. He unsuccessfully tried to escape on two different occasions yet later recalled that he was "happy" in this reform school because he was "accepted."

After being released in 1961, Krist served a series of short jail terms for crimes such as auto theft. In 1965, he married; then he was arrested a year later, again for auto theft. Eight months into a five-year sentence, he engineered an escape during which guards shot his accomplice to death. Since California law permitted capital punishment when an escape led to someone's death, Krist worried that he'd get the gas chamber if he were found, so he moved his young family to Boston and created a new identity as George Deacon, an aspiring scientist.

The undeniably intelligent Krist obtained a job as a lab technician at MIT, which led to his participation in a September 1968 marine science expedition where the still-married Krist began an affair with a female student named Ruth Eisemann Schier. Before the expedition was over Krist confessed his true identity and criminal past to her, and they formed a plan to run off to Australia.

To finance their planned new life together, Krist and Eisemann Schier plotted to kidnap Emory University student Barbara Jane Mackle, the daughter of a prominent Miami family, and bury her in a homemade box, where she would remain until they received a $500,000 ransom.

Krist and Eisemann Schier did abduct and bury Mackle, who ultimately survived 83 hours underground before police, informed by Krist of the burial site, were able to find and release her. The kidnappers were subsequently caught and tried in Decatur, Georgia, in May 1969.

Before his trial, Krist's intellect was evaluated by a psychiatrist as "if not at the genius level, then certainly in the near genius category." Found guilty, the 23-year-old Krist received a life sentence.

Bettmann/Getty Images

A bearded Gary Steven Krist is escorted from an elevator by a DeKalb County (Georgia) deputy sheriff en route to jail in 1969. Krist had been found guilty for his part in the kidnapping of Barbara Jane Mackle and was sentenced to life in prison. Paroled after ten years, he entered a new life of crime. Why didn't he reform?

Paroled after ten years, Krist set about lobbying for a complete pardon, which he eventually obtained in 1989. He then enrolled in a medical school in the West Indies and completed his M.D. degree. Several states denied him a medical license before the state of Indiana finally granted him a probationary license in 2001.[ii] That license was revoked two years later when Krist's past criminal record and allegations of sexual assaults on patients surfaced.[iii]

In January 2007, 61-year-old Gary Krist, who once described himself as the "Einstein of crime," was on his way back to prison to serve a five-year five-month sentence. A federal sting operation busted Krist and his 41-year-old stepson in early 2006 for conspiracy to bring cocaine and illegal aliens into the United States.[iv]

The case of Gary Krist raises a number of interesting questions. Among them are the following:

1. Krist had trouble with the law from a young age. What might have been the cause of early law violations?

2. Could Krist's parents have changed the course of his life while he still lived at home? If so, how?

3. Krist was undeniably intelligent. Is there any link between intelligence and crime? If so, what might it be?

Notes

i. Steve Fennessy, "The Talented Dr. Krist." *Atlanta Magazine* Online, http://www.atlantamagazine.com/article.php?id=299, (accessed May 21, 2011).

ii. *Cincinnati Enquirer, The Enquirer*, Online Edition, "Doctor Found to Have Been Imprisoned for Kidnapping," November 16, 2002, http://www.enquirer.com/editions/2002/11/16/loc_in-felondoc16.html (accessed July 10, 2011).

iii. Wishtv.com, "Doctor's License Revoked," August 29, 2003, http://www.wishtv.com/Global/story.asp?S=1423007 (accessed May 21, 2011).

iv. MSNBC, "Georgia Man in 1960s Buried Alive Case Gets 5 Years in Drug Case," http://www.msnbc.msn.com/id/16710294/ (accessed May 21, 2011).

■ **dangerousness** The likelihood that a given individual will later harm society or others. Dangerousness is often measured in terms of recidivism, or the likelihood of new crime commission or rearrest for a new crime within a five-year period following arrest or release from confinement.

CRIME | in the NEWS

Crime Pays: Washington, D.C., Considers Paying Off Criminals

In ancient times, towns and villages would pay barbarians "Tribute" in order to avoid attack. More recently, organized crime families extorted "protection money" from businesses who they threatened to vandalize. In 2016, the city of Washington, D.C., considered a similar form of self-protection—paying known criminals a "stipend" not to commit any more crime. The legislation was modeled after a program in Richmond, California, that pays violent offenders up to $1,000 a month not to violate the criminal law after they are released from prison.

The Washington, D.C., city council legislation, known as the Neighborhood Engagement Achieves Results (NEAR) Act of 2016, adapted what some said was a public health approach to crime prevention. It was enacted in response to a 53 percent annual increase in homicides throughout the city in 2015; and in early 2016, city council members unanimously approved it.

One provision of the NEAR Act was to create an Office of Neighborhood Safety and Engagement (ONSE). The goal of the office was to identify teenagers and young adults at high risk for committing violent crimes—or of becoming victims of violent crime. Sponsors of the act were hoping to fund it through lessened justice system involvement—meaning that fewer police officers would be required to patrol the city's streets and that courts and jails would process a reduced number of offenders.

The program required participants to create and execute a successful life plan, moving them away from criminal influences and toward gainful employment. Mentorship, life planning, and trauma informed therapy were all part of the plan.

Even though the Richmond program, which gets its funding from private donations, appears to have successfully lowered violent crime in that community, the NEAR Act has met with resistance from citizens concerned about its moral premise. One critic notes that "Instead of handing their hard-earned money over to a mugger on the street, taxpayers will just give it to the DC government, which will then make sure that it gets into the hands of the most deserving potential criminals who promise to curtail their criminal activities."

Although it was passed by the city council, Washington's NEAR Act hasn't been implemented. That's because Mayor Muriel Bowser, who holds the power to craft city budgets, refused to fund it. Instead, Bower supported a plan to hire community outreach officers to identify troubled youths. Under the mayor's plan, stipends are provided to at-risk residents allowing them to enroll in job training programs and to seek employment.

Discussion Questions

1. Do you think that Washington, D.C.'s NEAR Act should have been funded and implemented? Why or why not?

2. Might programs like the one proposed in Washington, D.C., that pay known criminals to avoid future law violations encourage others to become criminal?

3. If programs like the NEAR Act were shown to be cost-efficient, allowing cities to reduce spending on law enforcement, courts, jails, and prisons, would you support them? Why or why not?

Sources: Monica Potts, "Should Cities Pay Criminals to Not Commit Crimes?," *Time*, April 13, 2016; Aaron C. Davis, "Paying Criminals to Stay Out of Trouble? D.C. Could Be Next City to Try Experiment," *Washington Post*, February 7, 2016; Aaron C. Davis, "Cities Begin to Challenge a Bedrock of Justice: They're Paying Criminals Not to Kill," *Washington Post*, March 16, 2016; Aaron C. Davis, "D.C. Abandons Plan to Pay Criminals to Stay Out of Trouble," *Washington Post*, May 5, 2016; and Petula Dvorak, "Paying Criminals Not to Commit Crime May Not Be So Funny After All," *Washington Post*, February 8, 2016.

---

had taken place in surrounding cities. "If [Mayor] Villariagosa were doing things better than surrounding cities," he asked, "wouldn't the percentage reduction *inside* the city be greater than the reduction *outside* the city?"[66]

Critics also note that the extent of crime's decline might not be as substantial as many people think. Publicized statistical declines may be due at least partially to demographic changes in the American population (i.e., downtown Detroit might have higher rates of reported crime were it not for the movement *out* of the city of many people over the past decade or two) or might be attributed to the changing nature of crime over time (i.e., an increase in virtual or online thefts versus a decline in actual holdups).

Dangerousness (the likelihood that an individual will later harm people or society), is a concept that can be used to decide the value of incarceration in individual cases, but it is not always

> Critics charge that classical and neoclassical thought lacks comprehensive explanatory power over criminal motivation.

recognized by "get tough on crime" strategies that seek to make examples of law violators based more on what they have done rather than the likelihood that they will reoffend. Such critics say that it would make more sense to assess the future dangerousness of a convicted offender rather than impose punishment based on the nature of his or her offense. Assessing dangerousness will be discussed in more detail in Chapter 6.

Critics also charge that classical and neoclassical thought lacks comprehensive explanatory power over criminal motivation, other than to advance the relatively simple claim that crime is the result of free will, the personal attractions of crime, and individual choice (see the Criminal Profiles box). Such critics point out that classical theory is largely bereft of meaningful explanations about how a choice for or against criminal activity is made. Similarly, classical theory lacks any appreciation for the deeper fonts of personal motivation, including those represented by aspects of human biology and psychology as well as the social environment. The Classical School, as originally detailed in the writings of Beccaria and Bentham, lacked any scientific basis for the claims it made. Although neoclassical writers have advanced the scientific foundation of classical claims (via studies like those showing the effectiveness of particular forms of deterrence), many still defend their way of thinking by referring to what are purely philosophical ideals, such as just deserts.

SUMMARY

- The Classical School of criminology posits that at least some illegal activity is the result of rational choices made by individuals seeking various kinds of illicit rewards. The classical perspective sees human beings as fundamentally rational, portrays pain and pleasure as the two central determinants of human behavior, and sees punishment as necessary to deter law violators and to serve as an example.

- The Classical School grew out of the Enlightenment. Notions of free will, individual choice, deterrence as a goal of the justice system, and punishment as a natural consequence of crime owe much of their contemporary influence to the Classical School. Influential thinkers of the Enlightenment era include Thomas Hobbes, John Locke, Thomas Paine, Charles-Louis de Secondat Montesquieu, and Jean-Jacques Rousseau.

- Two important thinkers of the Classical School of criminology, Cesare Beccaria and Jeremy Bentham, saw crime as providing pleasure to those who commit it and believed in punishment as the way to prevent it.

- Neoclassical criminology is a contemporary perspective built on classical principles emphasizing the importance of character and character development as well as the choices people make when faced with opportunities for crime. Rational choice theory recognizes the opportunities for crime and the important role that capable guardians play in preventing it.

- In neoclassical criminology, punishment is seen as providing both a deterrent and just deserts. Just deserts implies that criminal offenders deserve the punishment they receive and that any criminal punishment meted out should be appropriate to the type and severity of the crime committed.

- Policy implications of classical and neoclassical thought build on the idea of a rational offender punished by a system working purposefully toward the goals of crime reduction and the prevention of recidivism. Determinate sentencing and truth in sentencing as well as capital punishment are all strategies that flow from Classical School principles.

- Classical perspectives can be criticized for their lack of comprehensive explanatory power over criminal motivation, and they also largely lack both meaningful explanations about how a choice for or against criminal activity is made and any appreciation for the deeper fonts of personal motivation.

KEY TERMS

capital punishment, 70	natural rights, 58
Classical School, 59	neoclassical criminology, 62
Code of Hammurabi, 56	nothing-works doctrine, 62
common law, 56	Panopticon, 61
dangerousness, 78	positivism, 61
determinate sentencing, 74	rational choice theory, 64
deterrence, 69	recidivism, 69
displacement, 68	recidivism rate, 69
Enlightenment, 57	retribution, 56
folkways, 54	situational choice theory, 64
general deterrence, 69	situational crime prevention, 66
hard determinism, 61	social contract, 57
hedonistic calculus, 61	soft determinism, 64
incapacitation, 74	specific deterrence, 69
just deserts model, 69	target hardening, 67
justice model, 62	three-strikes legislation, 63
mala in se, 55	truth in sentencing, 74
mala prohibita, 55	Twelve Tables, 56
mores, 54	utilitarianism, 61
natural law, 58	

KEY NAMES

Cesare Beccaria, 60	Robert Martinson, 62
Jeremy Bentham, 60	Charles-Louis de Secondat Montesquieu, 58
Ronald V. Clarke, 64	
Derek B. Cornish, 64	Thomas Paine, 58
Thomas Hobbes, 57	Jean-Jacques Rousseau, 58
Jack Katz, 65	William Graham Sumner, 54
John Locke, 57	

QUESTIONS FOR REVIEW

1. What are the major principles of the Classical School of criminology?

2. What were some forerunners of classical thought in criminology?

3. Who were the important thinkers of the Classical School of criminology, and what was their legacy?

4. What is neoclassical criminology, and how does it differ from the classical perspective? How does it build on the classical perspective?

5. What is the role of punishment in neoclassical criminology?

6. What are the policy implications of the Classical School and of neoclassical thought. What kinds of punishment might work best to prevent crime?

7. What are the criticisms of the Classical School? Of neoclassical thinking about crime and crime control?

QUESTIONS FOR REFLECTION

1. This text emphasizes a theme of social problems versus individual responsibility. Which perspective is more clearly supported by classical and neoclassical thought? Why?

2. How would you define *natural law*? Do you believe that natural law exists? If so, what types of behaviors would be contravened by natural law? If not, why not?

3. What is meant by a social contract? How does the concept of a social contract relate to natural law?

4. What are the central concepts that defined the Classical School of criminological thought? Which of those concepts are still alive? Where do you see evidence for the survival of those concepts?

5. How would you define *recidivism*? What is a recidivism rate? Why are recidivism rates so high? What can be done to lower them?

EARLY BIOLOGICAL PERSPECTIVES ON CRIMINAL BEHAVIOR

It's What We Are

godfer/Fotolia

LEARNING OUTCOMES

After reading this chapter, you should be able to answer the following questions:

- What are the differences between historical biological and contemporary biosocial theories of crime?

- What are the basic principles of biological theories of crime?

- How does the Positivist School explain criminality?

- Explain the importance of altruism, territoriality, and tribalism from the sociobiological perspective on crime.

- Identify some criticisms of early biological theories of criminal behavior.

■ **biological theories** Theories that maintain that the basic determinants of human behavior, including criminality, are constitutionally or physiologically based and often inherited.

Introduction

A few years ago, the Dutch Ministry of Justice implemented a program of nutritional supplements in 14 prisons across the Netherlands. Under the program, nearly 500 inmates were provided with healthy diets, devoid of added sugar and supplemented with vitamins and important micronutrients.[1] According to Ap Zaalberg, the project's director, the link between good nutrition and lower levels of antisocial behavior had already been clearly established by studies published in England only a few years earlier, and the Dutch wanted to see if good eating habits could lower levels of violence in their prisons. Zaalberg's interest came from reading an article published in the *British Journal of Psychiatry* in 2002 by Oxford University professor C. Bernard Gesch.[2] Gesch reported on the results of work he had done in recruiting 231 young British prisoners. He assigned half of them to receive carefully selected dietary supplements while the other half received a placebo. Before Gesch's nutritional program was implemented, the placebo and active-treatment groups had been matched according to the number of disciplinary incidents in which each had been involved. There were no significant individual or psychological differences between the two groups in terms of IQ, verbal ability, anger, anxiety, or depression. After Gesch's experimental subjects took specially formulated vitamins, minerals, and essential fatty acids for 142 days, he found that prisoners taking the supplements committed an average of 26.3% fewer offenses compared with the placebo group. He also observed a 35.1% reduction in overall offenses in the group receiving the supplements and a 37% drop in violent incidents. According to Gesch, "… evidence is mounting that putting poor fuel into the brain significantly affects social behavior. We need to know more about the composition of the right nutrients. It could be the recipe for peace."[3] Figure 4-1 shows the levels of some of the nutrients in the disadvantaged youths studied by Gesch.

Traditional Biological versus Modern Biosocial Theories

The field of criminology has been slow to give credence to biological theories of deviant behavior.

The field of criminology has been slow to give credence to **biological theories** of deviant behavior. One reason for this, as noted in Chapter 1, is that contemporary criminology's academic roots are grounded in the social sciences. As

FIGURE 4-1 | Selected Nutrient Levels in Diets of a Sample of Disadvantaged Youth

Source: Based on John Bohannon, "The Theory? Diet Causes Violence. The Lab? Prison," *Science*, Vol. 325 (September 25, 2009), p. 1616, http://www.ifbb.org.uk/files/Science-25-9-09.PDF

Criminality?

■ **traits**   Notable features or qualities of a biological entity. Traits may be classified as physical, behavioral, or psychological. Traits are passed from generation to the next.

well-known biocriminologist **C. Ray Jeffery**, commenting on the historical development of the field, observed, "The term *criminology* was given to a social science approach to crime as developed in sociology. Sutherland's [1924] text *Criminology* was pure sociology without any biology or psychology; beginning with publication of that text, criminology was offered in sociology departments as a part of sociology separate from biology, psychology, psychiatry, and law. Many of the academicians who call themselves criminologists are sociologists."[4]

Fortunately for those studying criminology today, the field of criminology is interdisciplinary, recognizing contributions from many different disciplines. This chapter and the next (Chapter 5, "Biosocial and Other Contemporary Perspectives") review both historical and contemporary biological perspectives on crime, including modern-day biosocial

theories. Many older biological theories, as we will see in this chapter, were relatively simplistic in their approach to explaining human behavior and crime. Newer biosocial perspectives hold that genes and related biological features are more likely to be facilitators rather than determinants of behavior—an idea that we will explore more fully in the chapter that follows.

Principles of Biological Theories

Generally speaking, biological theories focus on the brain as the center of the personality and the major determinant in controlling human behavior. As one biocriminologist explains it, "no matter the source of human behavior, it is necessarily funneled through the brain …"[5] Unlike the classical and neoclassical traditions, however, which consider free will and external forces as the cause of behavior, biological theories look to internal sources, including genetic and physical makeup, as they influence mental processes.

Early biological theorists (generally, prior to the 1960s or 1970s) focused primarily on physical features and heredity as the source of criminal behavior. They considered physical **traits** such as facial features, body type, and shape of the skull as significant causes of criminality. Several early theorists proposed that criminality ran in families and could be inherited, or passed down from one generation to another. Such early approaches, while appropriate for the time in which they were developed, appear relatively simplistic when compared with modern biosocial perspectives.

By contrast, contemporary biological theorists (mostly after 1990) have taken a more in-depth look at human biology, leading them to examine a variety of influences on behavior, including genes and chromosomes, diet, hormonal issues, environmental contaminants, and neurophysical conditions. Nonetheless, both early and contemporary biological perspectives share a number of fundamental assumptions, which are shown in Figure 4-2.

One of the major distinguishing features between historical and contemporary biological theories of criminality is the degree of emphasis that each puts on the last item listed in Figure 4-2 (the interplay between biology and the social and physical environments). While most early biological theories of crime ascribed at least some importance to the role of the social environment in producing behavior, that role was relatively minor. By contrast, contemporary biosocial theorists see the *interaction* between the organism and its environment as the crucial determining factor in almost all behavior.

Joe Carini/The Image Works

A mother reads to her child. The following question forms the essence of the "nature versus nurture" controversy: Are the choices that people make determined more by their biology or by what they have learned?

FIGURE 4-2 | **Fundamental Assumptions of Biological Theories of Crime Causation**

Source: Schmalleger, Frank, *Criminology*. Printed and Electronically reproduced by permission of Pearson Education, Inc., Upper Saddle River, New Jersey.

Early Biological Positivism

Early biological theories of crime, while not as sophisticated as their modern counterparts, are especially significant because they are built on the scientific tradition of positivism. Positivism, which is both discussed and defined in Chapter 3, is associated with the belief that all valid knowledge is acquired only through observation and not through the mere exercise of reason or blind adherence to belief. As mentioned in that previous chapter, early positivism was built on two important principles: (1) an unflagging acceptance of social determinism, or the belief that human behavior is determined not by the exercise of free choice but by causative factors beyond the control of the individual, and (2) the application of scientific techniques to the study of crime and criminology.

The term *positivism* had its roots in the writings of Auguste Comte (1798–1857), who proposed use of the scientific method in the study of society in his 1851 work *A System of Positive Polity*.[6] Comte, who later became known as the father of sociology, believed that social phenomena could be observed, explained, and measured in objective and quantitative terms. For a strict positivist, reality consists of a world of clearly defined facts that can be scientifically measured and—some would hope—controlled.[7] As a framework for thought and analysis, positivism was a giant leap forward because it established a scientific basis for the burgeoning field of criminology.

Physical Features and Crime

Some of the earliest studies in the field of criminology used data from the fields of biology and anthropology to identify physical abnormalities that early criminologists thought could be used to distinguish criminal offenders from other people. One of the earliest attempts to use bodily features to identify criminals was proposed by European anatomist **Franz Joseph Gall** (1758–1828) in his theory of **phrenology** (also

■ **phrenology** The study of the shape of the head to determine anatomical correlates of human behavior.

THEORY | in PERSPECTIVE
Early Biological Theories

Biological theories adhere to the principle that many predispositions relating to human behavior, including aggression, risk-taking, and criminality, are constitutionally or physiologically influenced and inherited. This chapter discusses early biological approaches to crime.

Early Positivism

Early positivism used data from the fields of biology and anthropology to identify physical abnormalities that early criminologists thought could be used to distinguish criminal offenders from other people.

Period: 1790s–1880s

Theorists: Franz Joseph Gall, Johann Gaspar Spurzheim

Concepts: phrenology

Criminal Anthropology

Criminal anthropology is the scientific study of the relationship between human physical characteristics (in particular, bodily features) and criminality. Today the word is mostly applied to the Italian School of Criminology, whose contributors were built on scientific, or positivistic, principles like the use of measurement and observation in applying evolutionary concepts to the study of crime and criminals. Criminal anthropology saw criminals as throwbacks to earlier evolutionary epochs.

Period: 1860s–1930s

Theorists: Cesare Lombroso, Enrico Ferri, Raffael Garofalo, Charles Buckman Goring, Earnest A. Hooton

Concepts: Italian School, Positivist School of criminology, positivism, criminal anthropology, atavism, born criminals, criminaloids, masculinity hypothesis

Constitutional Theories

These biological theories, sometimes called constitutional theories, explain criminality by reference to offenders' body types, inheritance, genetics, or external observable physical characteristics.

Period: Classical constitutional theories, 1930s–1940s; modern constitutional theories, 1960s to the present

Theorists: Ernst Kretschmer, William H. Sheldon

Concepts: somatotyping, mesomorph, ectomorph, endomorph

Criminal Families

In the late 1800s the focus of criminal anthropology turned to the identification of criminal families, or those family groups that appeared to exhibit criminal tendencies through several generations. The study of criminal families built on developing notions of heredity and genetics.

Period: 1870s–1940s

Theorists: Sir Francis Galton, Richard Louis Dugdale, Arthur H. Estabrook, Henry Herbert Goddard

Concepts: heredity, behavioral genetics, criminal families (Jukes and Kallikaks), genetic determinism, eugenics, eugenic criminology

Sociobiology

This theoretical perspective applies evolutionary theory to social behavior and says that most social behaviors are shaped by natural selection. Sociobiology includes the systematic study of the biological basis of all social behavior, which is a branch of evolutionary biology and particularly of modern population biology.

Period: 1975 to the present

Theorist: Edward O. Wilson

Concepts: altruism, tribalism, survival of the gene pool

Twin Studies and Heredity

Genetics and heredity, combined with processes of natural selection, including sexual selection, can produce biologically based differences in behavior. Studies of twins attempted to identify the role that heredity played in criminal behavior, especially among twins who were separated at birth and raised in vastly different environments.

Period: 1920s to the present

Theorists: Karl O. Christiansen, Sarnoff Mednick, and others

Concepts: twin studies (dizygotic and monozygotic twins), genetic determinism

---

called craniology). Gall believed that the shape of the human skull was related to personality and could be used to distinguish criminals from normal men and women. Gall's approach was built on four themes:

1. The brain is the organ of the mind.
2. Particular aspects of personality are associated with specific locations in the brain.

3. Portions of the brain that are well developed cause personality characteristics associated with them to be more prominent in the individual under study, whereas poorly developed brain areas lead to a lack of associated personality characteristics.
4. The shape of a person's skull corresponds to the shape of the underlying brain and is therefore indicative of the personality.

■ **atavism**   A term used by Cesare Lombroso to suggest that criminals are physiological throwbacks to earlier stages of human evolution.

Gall was one of the first Western writers to locate the roots of personality in the brain. Prior to his time, it was thought that aspects of personality resided in various organs throughout the body—a fact reflected in linguistic anachronisms that survive to the present day (e.g., when someone is described as being "hard-hearted" or having "a lot of gall"). Greek philosopher Aristotle was said to believe that the brain served no function other than to radiate excess heat from the body, so Gall's perspective, although relatively primitive by today's standards, did much to advance physiological understandings of the mind–body connection in Western thought.

Although Gall's theory depended on physical measurements of the skull and comparisons of such measurements between individuals, it was never tested using today's rigorous methodological standards (including the research designs discussed in Chapter 2). Nonetheless, it was widely accepted by many of his contemporaries because it represented a shift away from the theological perspectives prevalent at the time toward scientific measurement—a trend that was well under way by the time of his writings. Phrenology also provided systematic evaluation of suspected offenders and was intriguing for its ease of use.

One of Gall's students, German physician **Johann Gaspar Spurzheim** (1776–1853), brought phrenological theory to the United States and helped to spread its influence through a series of lectures and publications on the subject. Phrenology's prestige in the United States extended into the twentieth century, finding a place in classification schemes employed to evaluate newly admitted prisoners. Even Arthur Conan Doyle's fictional character Sherlock Holmes was described as using phrenology to solve a number of crimes. It is still popular today among palm readers and fortune-tellers, some of whom offer phrenological "readings"—although a few states have outlawed such activities. Learn more about phrenology at **http://www.neurosurgery .org/cybermuseum/pre20th/phren/phrenology.html**.

The Italian School

One of the best-known early scientific biological theorists—nineteenth-century Italian army prison physician **Cesare Lombroso** (1836–1909)—coined the term **atavism** to suggest that criminality was the result of primitive urges that survived the evolutionary process in modern-day human throwbacks. Lombroso, whose work had consisted mostly of postmortem studies of the bodies of executed

> Cesare Lombroso coined the term *atavism* to suggest that criminality was the result of primitive urges that survived the evolutionary process.

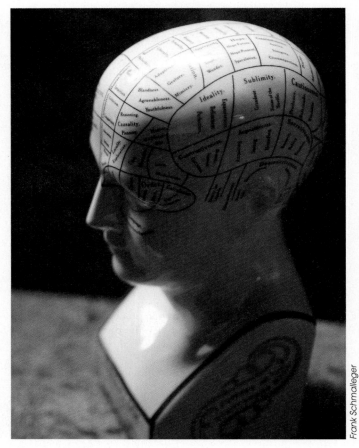

Frank Schmalleger

A phrenological map of the skull. Early criminologists believed that the shape of the skull reflected the brain's ability. Do you think biology plays a significant role in crime?

offenders and deceased criminals, measured the bodies in many different ways.[8] He claimed that, using his system, not only could criminal offenders be separated from the general population, but also specific types of criminals could be identified.

Discussing murderers, for example, Lombroso wrote, "He has a cold concentrated look; sometimes the eye appears injected with blood; the nose is often aquiline or hooked, always large; the ears are long; the jaws powerful; the cheekbones widely separated; the hair is crisp and abundant; the canine teeth well developed, and the lips thin; often a nervous tic or contraction, upon one side of the face only, uncovers the canine teeth, producing the effect of a threatening look or a sardonic laugh."[9]

Lombroso believed that thieves could be recognized because they have "less cranial capacity" and "a remarkable mobility of countenance, the eye small and restless, the eye-brows thick and meeting, the nose flat, and the forehead always low and retreating."

■ **Italian School of Criminology**   A perspective on criminology developed in the late 1800s that held that criminals can be identified by physical features and are throwbacks to earlier stages of human evolution. The Italian School was largely based on studies of criminal anthropology.

■ **criminal anthropology**   The scientific study of the relationship between human physical characteristics (in particular anthropometric features, or bodily measurements) and criminality.

■ **born criminal**   An individual who is born with a genetic predilection toward criminality.

■ **criminaloid**   A term used by Cesare Lombroso to describe the occasional criminal who is enticed into criminality primarily by environmental influences.

Lombroso called physical features that he thought to be indicative of criminality *stigmata of degeneration,* and suggested that they could be used to predict later criminal behavior among individuals who possessed them. He described "the nature of the criminal" as "an atavistic being who reproduces in his person the ferocious instincts of primitive humanity and the inferior animals."[10] Writing around the same time as Lombroso, Italian Raffael Garofalo noted that "[o]ne has but to go into a prison, and by the aid of this description one can distinguish almost at a glance those condemned for theft from those condemned for murder."

Lombroso's ideas gave rise to the **Italian School of Criminology**, also referred to today as criminal anthropology. **Criminal anthropology** is the scientific study of the relationship between human physical characteristics (in particular anthropometric features, or bodily measurements) and criminality. Criminal anthropology probably derives from earlier subjective feelings, prominent for millennia, that unattractiveness, deformity, and disfigurement are somehow associated with evil, spiritual malaise, and general uncleanliness.

Although the earlier works of Gall and others might be subsumed under the umbrella of criminal anthropology, the term is usually reserved in today's criminological literature for the work of Lombroso and other members of the Italian School of Criminology, especially **Enrico Ferri** and **Raffael Garofalo**.

At about the time that Lombroso's ideas were becoming popular, Charles Darwin was making a substantial impact on the scientific world with his theory of biological evolution. Darwin proposed that human beings and other contemporary living organisms were the end products of a long evolutionary process governed by rules such as natural selection and survival of the fittest. Lombroso adapted elements of Darwin's theory to suggest that primitive behavioral traits survived in present-day human populations and led to heightened criminal tendencies among individuals who harbored them. Darwin himself had proposed this idea when he wrote, "With mankind some of the worst dispositions which occasionally without any assignable cause make their appearance in families, may perhaps be reversions to a savage state, from which we are not removed by very many generations."[11]

Lombroso has been called "the father of modern criminology" because he was the first criminologist of note to employ the scientific method—particularly measurement, observation, and generalization—in his work. Other writers have preferred to limit his influence, referring to him simply as the father of the Italian School of Criminology in recognition of the fact that nineteenth-century positivism began in Italy under his tutelage.

Pictorial Press Ltd/Alamy Stock Photo

Comedian Jay Leno, showing off his strong chin. Cesare Lombroso believed that people with weak chins were especially prone to criminality. How might physical features relate to criminality?

Lombroso's most famous term, *atavism*, implies that criminals are born that way. Lombroso was continuously reassessing his estimates of the proportion, from among all offenders, of **born criminals**. At one point, he asserted that fully 90% of offenders committed crimes because of atavistic influences; he later revised the figure downward to 70%, admitting that normal individuals might be pulled into lives of crime. In addition to the category of born criminal, Lombroso described other categories of offenders, including the insane, "criminaloids," and criminals incited by passion. The insane were said to include mental and moral degenerates, alcoholics, drug addicts, and so forth. **Criminaloids**, also called "occasional criminals," were described as people who were enticed into breaking the law by virtue of environmental influences. Nevertheless, most criminaloids were seen by Lombroso as exhibiting some degree of atavism and hence were said to "differ from born criminals in degree, not in kind." Those who became criminals by virtue of passion were said to have surrendered to intense emotions,

■ **Positivist School**   An early criminological perspective that employed scientific objectivity, measurement, and observation in the study of crime and its causation.
■ **masculinity hypothesis**   An early belief in criminology that criminal women exhibit masculine features and mannerisms.

■ **constitutional theories**   Theories that explain criminality by reference to offenders' body types, inheritance, genetics, or external observable physical characteristics.

including love, jealousy, hatred, or an injured sense of honor. To read excerpts of a member of the **Positivist School** of criminology criticizing the classical criminology viewpoint, see the Theory versus Reality box in this chapter (positivism is also discussed in Chapter 3).

In 1893, Lombroso published *The Female Offender.* [12] In that book, he expressed his belief that women exhibited far less anatomical variation than do men, but he insisted that criminal behavior among women, as among men, derived from atavistic foundations. Violence among women, although a rarity in the official statistics of the late 1800s, was explained by the **masculinity hypothesis**, or the belief that criminal women exhibited masculine features and mannerisms. Lombroso saw the quintessential female offender, however, as a prostitute, who was "the genuine typical representative of criminality" among women.[13] Prostitutes, he claimed, act out atavistic yearnings and, in doing so, return to a form of behavior characteristic of humankind's primitive past. Learn more about Lombroso and the theory of atavism via **http://www.encyclopedia.com/topic/Cesare_Lombroso.aspx.**

Evaluations of Atavism

Following in Lombroso's positivistic footsteps around the turn of the twentieth century, English physician **Charles Buckman Goring** (1870–1919) conducted a well-controlled statistical study of Lombroso's thesis of atavism. Using newly developed but advanced mathematical techniques to measure the degree of correlation between physiological features and criminal history, Goring examined nearly 3,000 inmates at Turin prison beginning in 1901. Enlisting the aid of London's Biometric Laboratory, he concluded that "the whole fabric of Lombrosian doctrine, judged by the standards of science, is fundamentally unsound."[14] Goring compared the prisoners with students at Oxford and Cambridge Universities, British soldiers, and noncriminal hospital patients and published his findings in 1913 in his lengthy treatise *The English Convict: A Statistical Study.*[15]

A similar study was conducted between 1927 and 1939 by **Earnest A. Hooton**, a professor of anthropology at Harvard University. In 1939, Hooton published *Crime and the Man,*[16] in which he reported having evaluated 13,873 inmates from ten states, comparing them along 107 physiological dimensions with 3,203 nonincarcerated individuals who formed a control group; his sample consisted of 10,953 prison inmates, 2,004 county jail prisoners, 743 criminally insane, 173 "defective delinquents," 1,227 "insane civilians," and 1,976 "sane civilians." Hooton concluded that criminals showed an overall physiological inferiority to the general population and that crime was the result

of "the impact of environment upon low-grade human organisms."[17] Learn more about the life and work of Earnest Hooton at **http://www.nasonline.org/publications/biographical-memoirs/memoir-pdfs/hooton-earnest.pdf.**

Today the ideas of the Italian School, which linked observable physical abnormalities to crime, are largely seen as a dead end in criminological thinking. However, as Nichole Hahn Rafter says, "Because criminal anthropologists' doctrine of the criminal as a physically anomalous human has long been discredited, we tend to ignore their work, at the same time overlooking the legacy of professional that they, as the first criminologists, bequeathed to us."[18]

Even though mainstream criminology is no longer concerned with claims that physical abnormalities may be linked to crime, some contemporary researchers have examined the link between criminality and minor physical abnormalities (MPAs), including neuro-deficits, fetal alcohol syndrome, and hormone deficits. In a study of teenage boys reported in 2000, for example, Canadian researchers L. Arseneault, Richard E. Tremblay, and colleagues conducted hormonal, anthropometric, psychophysiological, neuropsychological, and psychiatric evaluations of 1,037 boys who had attended kindergarten in 1984 in a socially and economically disadvantaged area of Montreal.[19] Using evaluations provided years later by parents, teachers, classmates, and the children themselves, Arseneault and Tremblay concluded that subtle physical abnormalities, including minor abnormalities in the shape of the ears, tongue, and teeth, were associated with an increased risk of behavioral and psychiatric problems in later years. The researchers suggested that such minor physical abnormalities might have resulted from genetic problems or prenatal insults associated with exposure to toxins. They concluded that "both the total count of minor physical anomalies and the total count of minor physical anomalies of the mouth were significantly associated with an increased risk of violent delinquency in adolescence, beyond the effects of childhood physical aggression and family adversity." Arseneault and Tremblay recognized, however, that abnormalities of the type they identified might be associated with neurological deficits and that abnormalities of the mouth could lead to feeding problems in the first months after birth, which might somehow cause problems in development or socialization.

Constitutional Theories

Constitutional theories explain criminality by reference to offenders' body types; genetics; or external, observable physical characteristics. A constitutional, or physiological, orientation

■ **somatotyping** The classification of human beings into types according to body build and other physical characteristics.

■ **endomorph** A body type originally described as soft and round or overweight.
■ **mesomorph** A body type described as athletic and muscular.
■ **ectomorph** A body type originally described as thin and fragile, with long, slender, poorly muscled extremities and delicate bones.

THEORY | versus REALITY

Positivism: The Historical Statement

In 1901, Enrico Ferri, one of the founders of the Positivist School of criminology, was invited to deliver a series of lectures at the University of Naples. Ferri used the occasion to admonish classical criminologists and to advance the principles of positivism. Following are excerpts from those lectures:

> Let us speak of this new science, which has become known in Italy by the name of the Positive School of Criminology. The 19th century has won a great victory over mortality and infectious diseases by means of the masterful progress of physiology and natural science. But while contagious diseases have gradually diminished, we see on the other hand that moral diseases are growing more numerous. And this makes it very evident that the science which is principally, if not exclusively, engaged in studying these phenomena of social disease should feel the necessity of finding a more exact diagnosis of these moral diseases of society, in order to arrive at some effective and more humane remedy.

> The science of positive criminology arose in the last quarter of the 19th century. [T]he positive school of criminology arises out of the very nature of things, the same as every other line of science. It is based on the conditions of our daily life.

> The general opinion of classic criminalists and of the people at large is that crime involves a moral guilt, because it is due to the free will of the individual who leaves the path of virtue and chooses the path of crime, and therefore it must be suppressed by meeting it with a proportionate quantity of punishment. And the illusion of a free human will (the only miraculous factor in the eternal ocean of cause and effect) leads to the

assumption that one can choose freely between virtue and vice. How can you still believe in the existence of a free will, when modern psychology armed with all the instruments of positive modern research denies that there is any free will and demonstrates that every act of a human being is the result of an interaction between the personality and the environment of man?

And how is it possible to cling to that obsolete idea of moral guilt, according to which every individual is supposed to have the free choice to abandon virtue and give himself up to crime? The positive school of criminology maintains, on the contrary, that it is not the criminal who wills; in order to be a criminal, it is rather necessary that the individual should find himself permanently or transitorily in such personal, physical and moral conditions, and live in such an environment which become for him a chain of cause and effect, externally and internally, that disposes him toward crime. This is our conclusion and it constitutes that vastly different and opposite method, which the positive school of criminology employs as compared to the leading principle of the classic school of criminal science.

Discussion Questions

1. Why did Ferri link control over contagious diseases with the study of crime?
2. If Ferri had been asked to define positive criminology, what kind of definition do you think he would offer?
3. How are notions of moral guilt and free will associated in Ferri's line of thought?

Source: Ernest Unterman, trans., *The Positive School of Criminology: Three Lectures Given at the University of Naples, Italy, on April 22, 23, and 24, 1901, by Enrico Ferri* (Chicago: Charles H. Kerr, 1912).

---

that found its way into the criminological mainstream during the early and mid-twentieth century was that of **somatotyping** (classifying according to body types), primarily associated with the work of **Ernst Kretschmer** and **William H. Sheldon**. Kretschmer, a professor of psychiatry at the German University of Tubingen, proposed a relationship between body build and personality type and created a rather detailed "biopsychological constitutional typology."

Influenced by Kretschmer, Sheldon utilized measurement techniques to connect body type with personality.[20] Sheldon studied 200 boys between the ages of 15 and 21 at the Hayden Goodwill Institute in Boston and concluded that four basic body types characterized the entire group (Figure 4-3):

1. The **endomorph** is soft and round, with "digestive viscera [that] are massive and highly developed" (the person is overweight and has a large stomach).
2. The **mesomorph** is muscular and athletic, with "somatic structures [that] are in the ascendancy" (the person has larger bones and considerable muscle mass).
3. The **ectomorph** is thin and fragile and has "long, slender, poorly muscled extremities, with delicate, pipestem bones."
4. The balanced type is a person of average build, not overweight, thin, or exceedingly muscular.[21]

Individuals (excluding the balanced type) were ranked along each of the three major dimensions using a seven-point

■ **behavioral genetics**   The study of genetic and environmental contributions to individual variations in human behavior.
■ **Juke family**   A well-known "criminal family" studied by Richard L. Dugdale.

■ **heredity**   The passing of traits from parent to child.

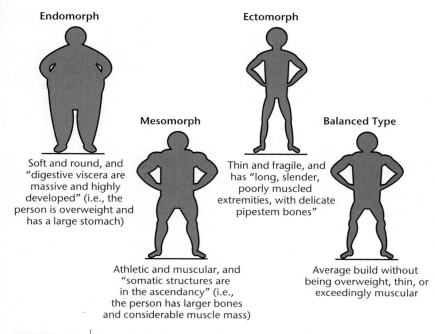

Endomorph

Soft and round, and "digestive viscera are massive and highly developed" (i.e., the person is overweight and has a large stomach)

Ectomorph

Thin and fragile, and has "long, slender, poorly muscled extremities, with delicate pipestem bones"

Mesomorph

Athletic and muscular, and "somatic structures are in the ascendancy" (i.e., the person has larger bones and considerable muscle mass)

Balanced Type

Average build without being overweight, thin, or exceedingly muscular

FIGURE 4-3 | **Sheldon's Body Types**

Source: Schmalleger, Frank Criminology. Printed and Electronically reproduced by permission of Pearson Education, Inc., Upper Saddle River, New Jersey.

scale. Sheldon claimed that varying types of temperaments and personalities were closely associated with each of the body types he identified: Ectomorphs were said to be "cerebrotonic," or restrained, shy, and inhibited; endomorphs were "viscerotonic," or relaxed and sociable. Mesomorphs, or muscular body types, were most likely to be associated with delinquency or "somatotonia," which he described as "a predominance of muscular activity and vigorous bodily assertiveness." Learn more about early theories of body types via **http://ssrn.com/abstract=894062** and **http://www.innerexplorations.com/catpsy/t1c4.htm.**

Criminal Families

Sir Francis Galton (1822–1911) was the first Western scientist to systematically study **heredity**, or the passing of traits from parent to child, and its possible influence on human behavior.[22] In 1907, Galton wrote that "the perpetuation of the criminal class by heredity is a question difficult to grapple with on many accounts. It is, however, easy to show that the criminal nature tends to be inherited…. The criminal population receives steady accessions from those who, without having strongly marked

criminal natures, do nevertheless belong to a type of humanity that is exceedingly ill suited to play a respectable part in our modern civilization, though it is well suited to flourish under half-savage conditions, being naturally both healthy and prolific."[23] Galton's work contributed to the development of the field of **behavioral genetics**, the study of genetic and environmental contributions to individual variations in human behavior. See **http://ssrn.com/abstract=984985** for more about behavioral genetics and crime.

Beginning in the late 1800s, and supported by burgeoning notions of heredity, researchers in the field of criminal anthropology focused on criminal families, or families that appeared to exhibit criminal tendencies across decades. In 1877, American sociologist **Richard Louis Dugdale** (1841–1883) published a study of the **Juke family**, which he described as criminogenic by nature.[24] Dugdale traced the Juke lineage back to a notorious character named Max, a Dutch immigrant who arrived in New York in the early 1700s. Two of Max's sons married into the notorious "Juke family of girls," six sisters, all of whom were said to be illegitimate. Max's male descendants were reputed to be vicious, and one woman named Ada had an especially bad reputation and came to be known as "the mother of criminals." By the time of the study, Dugdale was able to identify approximately 1,200 of Ada's descendants; included among their numbers were 7 murderers, 60 habitual thieves, 90 or so other criminals, 50 prostitutes, and 280 paupers. Dugdale compared the crime-prone Jukes with another family, the pure-blooded progeny of Jonathan Edwards, a Puritan preacher and one-time president of Princeton University. Descendants of Edwards included American presidents and vice presidents as well as many successful bankers and businesspeople, and no one was identified among the Edwards lineage who had had a run-in with the law. In 1916, **Arthur H. Estabrook** published a follow-up to Dugdale's work in which he identified an additional 715 Juke descendants, including 378 more prostitutes, 170 additional paupers, and 118 other criminals.[25] Estabrook, however, was later criticized for neglecting to mention that many Juke descendants were, in fact, not deviant, and that there were a reasonable number of socially successful descendants. For more information about genetics and crime see **http://www .sagepub.com/upm-data/54473_McLaughlin_paperback_ handbook_ch_1.pdf.**

■ **Kallikak family**   A well-known "criminal family" studied by Henry H. Goddard.
■ **eugenics**   The study of hereditary improvement by genetic control.
■ **eugenic criminology**   A perspective that holds that the root causes of criminality are passed from generation to generation in the form of "bad genes."

■ **genetic determinism**   The belief that genes are the major determining factor in human behavior.
■ **supermale**   A male individual displaying the XYY chromosome structure.

Following in the tradition of family tree researchers, **Henry Herbert Goddard** (1866–1957) published a study of the **Kallikak family** in 1912.[26] Goddard attempted to place the study of deviant families within an acceptable scientific framework via the provision of a kind of control group, so for comparison purposes he used two branches of the same family. One branch began as the result of a sexual liaison between Martin Kallikak, a Revolutionary War soldier, and a barmaid whose name is unknown; as a result of this union, an illegitimate son (Martin, Jr.) was born. After the war, Kallikak returned home and married a righteous Quaker girl, and a second line of descent began. The legitimate branch produced only a few minor deviants, but the illegitimate line resulted in 262 feebleminded births and various other epileptic, alcoholic, and criminal descendants. (The term *feebleminded*, which was much in vogue at the time of Goddard's study, was later recast as "mentally retarded," and people exhibiting similar characteristics today might be referred to as "mentally handicapped" or "mentally challenged.") Because feeblemindedness appeared to occur with some predictability in Goddard's study, but criminal activity seemed to be only randomly represented among the descendants of both Kallikak lines, Goddard concluded that a tendency toward feeblemindedness was inherited but that criminality was not.

Like the ideas of the Italian School, constitutional theories and studies of criminal families have largely been discarded today as biosocial researchers develop more sophisticated perspectives on criminology. That's because early criminologist who studied criminal families tended to focus mostly on the idea of inherited natural tendencies without adequately considering the role that social and physical environments play in influencing behavior. Social circumstances, for example, typically conspire to support romantic and physical relationships between people who are alike—meaning that those with lowered abilities might be unsuccessful at finding mates who could change the life-course of their offspring. Another challenge to early theories of criminal families came from their association with the **eugenics** movement of the late 1880s and early 1900s. That movement was vigorously opposed by many in the criminological community throughout the latter part of the twentieth century because it proposed selective human breeding as a course to improvement of the species. **Eugenic criminology**, an offshoot of the movement,[27] held that the root causes of criminality were largely passed from generation to generation in the form of "bad genes."

Eugenic criminology, which accepted the idea of **genetic determinism**, or the belief that genes are the major determining factor in human behavior, replaced the idea of the "feebleminded criminal" with the "defective delinquent," and social policies developed during the eugenics movement called for the sterilization of mentally handicapped women to prevent their bearing additional offspring.[28] Those policies were supported by the federal Eugenics Record Office, which funded studies of "cacogenic," or "bad-gened," families and were endorsed by the 1927 U.S. Supreme Court case of *Buck* v. *Bell*.[29] In *Buck*, Justice Oliver Wendell Holmes, Jr., writing in support of a Virginia statute permitting sterilization, said, "It is better for all the world, if instead of waiting to execute degenerate offspring for crime, or to let them starve for their imbecility, society can prevent those persons who are manifestly unfit from continuing their kind." The eugenics movement continued in the United Kingdom into the 1960s but was largely discredited in this country by intense condemnation of Nazi genetic research, mass sterilization, and eugenics programs, including those that led to the Holocaust. Learn about the consequences of *Buck* v. *Bell* which, although memory of it has faded, has not been overturned, at **http://www.hsl.virginia.edu/historical/eugenics/3-buckvbell.cfm.**

The XYY Supermale

The first well-known study of the modern era to focus on genetic differences as an explanation for criminality was undertaken by **Patricia A. Jacobs**,[30] a British researcher. Jacobs and her colleagues examined 197 Scottish prisoners in 1965 for chromosomal abnormalities through a relatively simple blood test known as karyotyping.[31] Twelve members of the group displayed chromosomes that were unusual, and seven were found to have an XYY chromosome. Normal male individuals possess an XY chromosome structure; normal female individuals are XX. Some other unusual combinations might be XXX, wherein a woman's genetic makeup contains an extra X chromosome, and XXY (also called Klinefelter's syndrome), in which a man might carry an extra X, or female, chromosome. Klinefelter's men often have male genitalia but are frequently sterile and have evidence of breast enlargement and intellectual retardation.[32] The XYY man, however, whose incidence in the prison population was placed at around 3.5% by Jacobs, was quickly identified as potentially violent and was termed a **supermale**.

CRIME | in the NEWS

President of Philippines Says "Criminals Aren't Humanity"

In 2017, Philippines President Rodrigo Duterte dismissed a report by Amnesty International that called his campaign against drug dealers a crime against humanity.

Duterte's regime had been waging a strict and often violent war against drug users and suppliers since he took office in 2016. Allegations circulated throughout the island nation that people suspected of drug crimes were being summarily shot by police, without the benefit of trial—or, in some cases, even evidence.

The Amnesty International report accused Philippines police of murdering defenseless people—some as young as 8 years old—merely on suspicion of involvement in the drug trade. "The police are behaving like the criminal underworld that they are supposed to be enforcing the law against," said the report. Amnesty International accused Duterte's supporters and the police of "fabricating evidence" against those killed.

In the first seven months of Duterte presidential reign, more than 2,500 people officially died in police raids—most of them targeting drug suppliers. Filipinos have long complained that government-sanctioned death squads were murdering accused criminals, and that many suspicious killings had taken place without the police identifying or arresting the killers.

When reporters asked Duterte about the Amnesty International report, he replied: "The criminals, the drug lords, drug pushers, they are not humanity. They are not humanity!"

In describing "drug lords, drug addicts, and drug pushers" he said, "You consider them humanity? I do not!"

Prior to his election as president, Duterte boasted of personally killing 1,700 armed criminals while mayor of Davo City, a metropolis of around 1.5 million people on the island of Mindanao. Many voters thought that his claims were fictitious, and police said they could find no evidence to support them. During his presidential campaign, however, he said that he planned an all-out assault on criminal gangs. "It is going to be bloody....Kill them all and end the problem." He also promised to kill 100,000 criminals in his first six months in office and to feed their bodies to fish in Manila Bay.

Tirana Hassan, Amnesty International's Crisis Response Director accused Duterte's government of paying assassins to murder drug users, and stealing from the dead. In a statement issued along with the report, Hassan said that "people accused of using or selling drugs are being killed for cash in an economy of murder."

Phelim Kine, deputy director of Human Rights Watch for Asia, warned that president Duterte was sending a message that "extrajudicial vigilante-style killings of suspected criminals is a legitimate approach to crime control."

Duterte, who was a hard-line prosecutor before becoming the mayor Davo City in 1998, has never been charged with a crime.

Nippon News/Aflo Co. Ltd/Alamy Stock Photo

Philippines President Rodrigo Duterte. Duterte recently proclaimed a war on drug dealers, telling the news media that "They are not humanity." What did he mean? Do you agree?

Admitting that "the buck stops here," he adds "I accept no criminal responsibility."

Investigations by Human Rights Watch, the United Nations and the Philippines' own Commission on Human Rights, have all supported the Amnesty International report.

Discussion Questions

1. President Duterte's perspective on crime seems dangerously similar to ideas proposed during the eugenics movement of the early 1900s. Although it may not have a biological basis, how is Duterte's thinking like that of the Nazis who attempted the elimination of an entire race of people living within German society?

2. Most would likely admit that Duterte's crime control methods are barbaric, and not acceptable in a civilized world. But some people say that others don't understand the desperation that characterizes Filipino society after it's infiltration by drug cartels. They suggest that "the end justifies the means." What would you say to them?

3. Would a "crime control program" that dehumanizes criminal offenders be possible in the United States? Why or why not?

4. If you were president of the Philippines how would you address that nation's drug problem?

Sources: "'Criminals aren't humanity': Philippines shrugs off Amnesty's 'war on drugs' report," *Russia Today*, February 1, 2017, https://www.rt.com/news/375952-philippines -drugs-amnesty-report/ (accessed February 1, 2017); Floyd Whaley, "Rodrigo Duterte's Talk of Killing Criminals Raises Fears in Philippines," *The New York Times*, May 17, 2016, https://www.nytimes.com/2016/05/18/world/asia/rodrigo-duterte-philippines.html (accessed February 1, 2017).

Following the introduction of the supermale notion into popular consciousness, a number of offenders attempted to offer a chromosome-based defense. In 1969, for example, Lawrence E. Hannell, who was adjudged a supermale, was acquitted of murder in Australia on the grounds of insanity.[33] Such a defense did not work, however, for Richard Speck, who also claimed to be an XYY man but was convicted of killing eight Chicago nursing students in 1966; it was later learned that Speck did not carry the extra Y chromosome. See the Criminal Profiles box for more on Richard Speck.

■ **dizygotic (DZ) twin**   A twin who develops from a separate ovum and who carries the genetic material shared by siblings.
■ **monozygotic (MZ) twin**   One of two twins who develop from the same egg and who carry almost identical genetic material.

The supermale phenomenon (also called the XYY syndrome) appears to have been based more on sensationalism than on fact. Today, little evidence exists to suggest that XYY men actually commit crimes of greater violence than do other men, although they may commit somewhat more crimes overall. A 1976 Danish study of 4,000 men born in Copenhagen between 1944 and 1947 may have helped put the issue to rest with its finding that the incidence of XYY men was less than 1% in the general male population.[34] More recent researchers have similarly concluded that "studies done thus far are largely in agreement and demonstrate rather conclusively that males of the XYY type are not predictably aggressive."[35]

Twin Studies and Heredity

More recently, studies of the criminal tendencies of fraternal and identical twins have provided a methodologically sophisticated technique for ferreting out the role of heredity in crime causation. Fraternal twins, or **dizygotic (DZ) twins**, develop from different fertilized eggs and share only the genetic material common among siblings; identical twins, or **monozygotic (MZ) twins**, develop from the same egg and carry virtually the same genetic material. Hence, if human behavior has a substantial heritable component, twins would display similar behavioral characteristics despite variations in their social environment,

Identical twins. The study of twins is used to show the influence of inheritance on human behavior. Does biology determine behavior?

Kenneth Sponsler/Fotolia

with any observed relationship being stronger among MZ twins than among DZ twins.

One of the first studies to link MZ twins to criminality was published in the 1920s by German physician Johannes Lange.[36] Examining 13 pairs of MZ twins and 17 pairs of DZ twins, he found that in 10 of the 13 MZ twins, both were criminal, whereas only 2 of the 17 DZ twins exhibited such similarity. Lange's findings drew considerable attention, even though his sample was small and he was unable to separate environmental influences from genetic ones adequately. A much larger twin study was begun in 1968 by European researchers **Karl O. Christiansen** and **Sarnoff Mednick**, who analyzed all twins (3,586 pairs) born on a selected group of Danish islands between 1881 and 1910.[37] Christiansen and Mednick found significant statistical support for the notion that criminal tendencies are inherited: 52% of identical twins and 22% of fraternal siblings displayed the

> Christiansen and Mednick found significant statistical support for the notion that criminal tendencies are inherited....

same degree of criminality within the twin pair. Such similarities remained apparent even among twins separated at birth and raised in substantially different environments. Mednick noted, however, that genetic influences appeared to be stronger in the commission of petty, nonviolent offenses than in more violent types of crime. He and Christiansen also found that the genetic risk for criminal behavior was enhanced by the environment in cases where one of the twins was raised in a family with at least one criminal adoptive parent.

The Minnesota Twin Family Study began in 1983.[38] The study's original goal was to establish a registry of all twins born in Minnesota from 1936 to 1955 for psychological research purposes but expanded to include twins born between 1961 and 1964. The Minnesota registry conducted personality and interests tests with more than 8,000 twin pairs and family members (by mail), and its findings seemed to show that MZ twins reared apart are about as similar as MZ twins reared together in personality and temperament, occupational and leisure-time interests, and social attitudes. Study authors warned, however, that "this evidence for the strong heritability of most psychological traits, sensibly construed, does not detract from the value or importance of parenting, education, and other ... interventions."[39]

The study of twins is still common practice in criminology today, and the area of twin studies provides something of an overlap between this chapter and the next; that is, between early and contemporary biological theories. In 1996, for example, British researchers studying 43 MZ and 38 DZ same-sex twins through the use of self-report questionnaires stated that "common bad behaviors of the sort admitted to by the majority of adolescents have a substantially heritable component. Additive genetic effects account for most of the variation, with no evidence of a contribution from shared environment."[40] The researchers also determined that genetic effects on behavior appear to increase with age. The British research was supported by the findings of a joint U.S.–Australian examination of 2,682 adult twin pairs; in that study, researchers found "a substantial genetic influence on risk for conduct disorder" (defined to include chronic stealing, lying, bullying, arson, property destruction, weapons use, cruelty to animals or people, fighting, aggression, truancy, and running away from home).[41]

In 2003, researchers examined the behavior of 1,116 pairs of five-year-old twins participating in a longitudinal study and asked mothers, teachers, study examiners, and the children themselves to evaluate the degree of the children's level of antisocial behavior.[42] Findings showed that antisocial children can be identified early in life, that their behavior can be nearly impossible to control by the time they reach kindergarten, and that heredity plays a far greater role in determining such behavior

PUTTING CRIMINOLOGY TO WORK—Implementing Evidence-Based Policy

To make a difference in the real world, criminological theories must first be tested and evaluated. Once evidence has been developed that theory-based practices work, then programs based on them can be implemented to reduce or prevent crime, or to help make victims' lives better. One federal initiative, CrimeSolutions.Gov, strives to evaluate the effectiveness of theory-based practices, and then communicates its findings via the Web. Some of the most effective and promising programs are highlighted in boxes such as this one that appear throughout the text.

PROGRAM: Nutritional Supplements for Young Adult Prisoners

EVIDENCE RATINGS FOR OUTCOMES: Promising

PROFILE

One notable experiment provided young adult inmates in a British prison with vitamin/mineral supplements as well as supplements of omega-6 and omega-3 essential fatty acids. There were no standards of daily intake that were used to determine the dosage of the four capsules providing the essential fatty acids, However, a replication study involving Dutch prisoners used similar potency of vitamins and minerals from the earlier British study, and included a dosage for omega-3 fatty acids based on research from the International Society of the Study of Fatty Acids and Lipids.

Prisoners in both studies were provided with supplemental nutrients at lunchtime by prison staff. Lunchtime was chosen to minimize the possible side effects of the supplements, such as nausea and belching.

To date, researchers have examined the effects of nutritional supplements on prisoners' antisocial behavior and have included samples of incarcerated juvenile and young adult offenders. This allowed for a controlled environment with a sample of offenders who are prone to aggressive and violent behaviors.

Relevant Theory: Biological Theory—Diet and Nutrition

Providing nutritional supplements to offenders in a controlled environment, like a prison, is based on the assumption that dietary deficiencies, especially diets lacking in vitamins, minerals, and essential fatty acids, may have negative effects on behavior. Therefore, providing prisoners with nutritional supplements to decrease this deficiency may, in turn, lead to a noticeable reduction in negative, antisocial behavior.

Essential nutrients, such as vitamins and minerals, have an indirect effect on behavior, because they are connected to changes in neurochemicals in the brain and body, which ultimately influence behavior. For instance, omega-3 fatty acids have been shown in medical research to have important biological roles in cardiovascular health. These fatty acids may, however, also play a critical role in the neurodevelopment of individuals, because they are concentrated in the brain. An omega-3 fatty acid deficiency during important developmental periods, such as prenatal and early childhood, may then increase an individual's risk for aggressive behaviors later on in life.

Evidence-Based Review

These sources were used in the development of this profile:

Study 1

C. Bernard Gesch, Sean M. Hammond, Sarah E. Hampson, Anita Eves, and Martin J. Crowder, "Influence of Supplementary Vitamins, Minerals and Essential Fatty Acids on Antisocial Behaviour of Young Adult Prisoners: Randomised, Placebo-Controlled Trial," *The British Journal of Psychiatry*, Vol. 181 (2002), pp. 22–28.

Study 2

Ap Zaalberg, Henk Nijman, Erik Bulten, Luwe Stroosma, and Cees van der Staak, "Effects of Nutritional Supplements on Aggression, Rule-Breaking, and Psychopathology Among Young Adult Prisoners," *Aggressive Behavior*, Vol. 36 (2010), pp. 117–126.

Source: https://www.crimesolutions.gov/ProgramDetails.aspx?ID=151

Note: Putting Criminology at Work features are based on information published online by the National Institute of Justice's (NIJ) Crime Solutions Website. The program ratings shown are those provided by NIJ.

■ **sociobiology**   The systematic study of the biological basis of all social behavior.
■ **paradigm**   An example, a model, or a theory.

than does home life or parenting. Because of similar behavior among twin pairs, the researchers concluded that genetic influences were extremely powerful determinants of antisocial behavior across diverse social settings, writing that "research and theory on the etiology of childhood antisocial behavior must look beyond the current focus on socioeconomic contexts and parenting processes, to incorporate genetic explanations and develop new theories of nature-nurture interplay."[43] Also in 2003, Florida State University researcher Jeanette Taylor and colleagues studied two separate groups of teenage male twins—142 MZ and 70 DZ twin pairs—and concluded that antisocial traits among study subjects existed prior to adulthood and that they stemmed to a significant degree from genetic factors.[44] Finally, a recent meta-analysis (i.e., a study of other studies) that combined the results of 51 research publications on twins and adoption purported to show that 41% of behavioral problems could be attributed to genetic influences, while the remaining 59% were due to environmental factors.[45]

Sociobiology

In the introduction to his insightful article summarizing **sociobiology**, Arthur Fisher wrote, "Every so often, in the long course of scientific progress, a new set of ideas appears, illuminating and redefining what has gone before like a flare bursting over a darkened landscape." To some, sociobiology—which burst upon the social science scene in 1975—held the promise of just such a new **paradigm**, or model. The development of this novel paradigm, however, was preceded by the work of ethnologists, including John H. Cook, Sir Julian Huxley, and Austrian Konrad Lorenz, who studied the social behavior of both people and animals and laid the groundwork for later sociobiological perspectives.

The Biological Roots of Human Aggression

In 1966, Austrian animal-expert **Konrad Lorenz** published his now-famous work *On Aggression*.[46] In it, Lorenz described how aggression permeates the animal kingdom and asked, "What is the value of all this fighting?" He wrote, "In nature, fighting is such an ever-present process, its behavior mechanisms and weapons are so highly developed and have so obviously arisen under the pressure of a species-preserving function, that it is our duty to ask this question."[47]

Lorenz accepted the evolutionary thesis of nineteenth-century biologist **Charles Darwin** that aggression within a species favored the strongest and best animals in the reproductive

Kane513/Shutterstock

Two male wolves prepare to fight for pack dominance. Sociobiologists tell us that certain traits, such as territoriality, are common to both animals and humans. How might territoriality lead to crime?

process, but he concluded that aggression serves a variety of other purposes as well. Aggression, said Lorenz, ensures an "even distribution of animals of a particular species over an inhabitable area" and provides for a defense of the species from predators.[48] Human aggression, he claimed, meets many of the same purposes but can take on covert forms, and the drive to acquire wealth and power, which was so characteristic of Western men at the time of his writing, is part of the human mating ritual whereby a man might "win" a prized woman through displays of more civilized forms of what could otherwise be understood as intraspecies aggression.

Lorenz's greatest contribution to the study of human behavior may have been his claim that all human behavior is, at least to some degree, "adapted instinctive behavior"; in other words, much of human conduct is fundamentally rooted in instinctive behavioral responses characteristic of biological organisms everywhere and present within each of us in the form of a biological inheritance from more primitive times. Even rational human thought derives its motivation and direction from instinctual aspects of human biology, and the highest human virtues, such as the value placed on human life, "could not have been achieved," said Lorenz, "without an instinctive appreciation of life and death."[49]

Building on the root functions of aggression, Lorenz concluded that much of what we today call "crime" is the result of overcrowded living conditions combined with a lack of legitimate opportunity for the effective expression of aggression. Crowding increases the likelihood of aggression, while

■ **altruism**   Selfless, helping behavior.
■ **gene pool**   The total genetic information of all the individuals in a breeding population.

■ **tribalism**   The attitudes and behavior that result from strong feelings of identification with one's own social group.

contemporary socialization works to inhibit it. In the words of Lorenz, "In one sense we are all psychopaths, for each of us suffers from the necessity of self-imposed control for the good of the community."[50] When people break down, said Lorenz, they become neurotic or delinquent, and crime may be the result of stresses that have been found to typically produce aggression throughout the animal kingdom.

Lorenz's explanations, like many of the biologically based theories, appear to be more applicable to certain forms of crime than to others, but it is important to recognize that modern frustrations and accompanying manifestations of aggression may be symbolically—rather than directly—expressed. Hence, a stockbroker who embezzles a client's money, spurred on by the need to provide material goods for an overly acquisitive family, may be just as criminal as a robber who beats his victim and steals her purse to have money to buy liquor.

The New Synthesis

Evolutionist **Edward O. Wilson** is credited with coining the term *sociobiology*. In his groundbreaking book, *Sociobiology: The New Synthesis*, Edwards defined *sociobiology* as "the systematic study of the biological basis of all social behavior [that is] a branch of evolutionary biology and particularly of modern population biology."[51] Because of the important role of biology in social evolution that Wilson was able to demonstrate, his work brought renewed attention to biological theories throughout the social sciences.

Through studies of primates, Wilson was able to demonstrate that the human brain and mind are the products of natural selection that occurred early in human evolution as developing hominids overcame the limits to sociality posed by weak social ties, which are characteristic of most primates. In so doing, they were able to develop close-knit social groups based on strong social ties. Wilson then showed how the ability to form large-scale societies contributed to the long-term survival of the social group.

Through his entomological study of social insects (especially ants), Wilson provided examples of **altruism** (selfless, helping behavior) in multiple species and, contrary to the beliefs of some evolutionary biologists, he found that helping behavior facilitated the continuity of the **gene pool** among altruistic individuals. The primary determinant of behavior, including human behavior, said Wilson, was the need to ensure the survival and continuity of genetic material from one generation to the next—and altruism played a role in survival.

Territoriality, according to Wilson's writings, explained many of the conflicts, including homicide, warfare, and other forms of aggression, between and among species, especially human beings. In Wilson's words, "Part of man's problem is that

his intergroup responses are still crude and primitive, and inadequate for the extended extraterritorial relationships that civilization has thrust upon him." The "unhappy result," as Wilson terms it, may be **tribalism**, expressed through the contemporary proliferation of street gangs, racial tension, and hardened encampments of survivalist and separatist groups, as well as the resilience of ethnic divides in the Middle East and throughout Europe and Asia.

Sociobiological theory not only tells us that the violence and aggressiveness associated with territoriality are often reserved for strangers but also explains intragroup aggression (violence occurring within groups). Wilson's theory suggested that within the group "a particularly severe form of aggressiveness should be reserved for actual or suspected adultery. In many human societies, where sexual bonding is close and personal knowledge of the behavior of others detailed, adulterers are harshly treated. The sin is regarded to be even worse when offspring are produced."

Hence, territoriality and acquisitiveness extend to location, possessions, and even other people. Human laws, explained Wilson, are designed to protect genetically based relationships that people have with one another, as well as their material possessions and their claimed locations in space; thus, violations of these intuitive relationships result in crime and in official reactions by the legal system.

Wilson's writings propelled social researchers into a flurry of studies intended to test the validity of his assertions. One Canadian study of violence in the homes of adoptive children found that stepchildren run a risk 70 times greater of being killed by their adoptive parents than do children living with their natural parents. Some writers concluded that "murderous behavior, warfare, and even genocide were unavoidable correlates of genetic evolution, controlled by the same genes for territorial behavior that had been selected in primate evolution."[52]

Others have suggested that biological predispositions developed during earlier stages of human evolution color contemporary criminal activity. Male criminals, for example, tend toward robbery and burglary—crimes in which they can continue to enact their "hunter" instincts developed long ago—but the criminality of women often involves shoplifting and simple theft, more typical of "gatherer" instincts.

Human behavioral predilections can be studied in a variety of ways. In the 1989 book *Evolutionary Jurisprudence*, John H. Beckstrom reported on his examination of over 400 legal documents, as well as legal claims and court decisions spanning over 300 years of judicial activity, that showed support for Wilson's contentions that humans tend to act to preserve their territorial claims, their likelihood of successful reproduction, and the continuation of their own particular genetic material.[53] Other theorists have gone so far as to imply that, among humans, there may be a gene-based tendency to experience guilt and to develop a conscience and that notions of right and wrong, whether embodied in laws or in social convention, may flow from such a naturalistic origin. Learn more about sociobiology in general and the sociobiology of sociopathy at **http://webspace.ship.edu/cgboer/ sociobiology.html** and **http://pathwhisperer.wordpress .com/2011/08/07/the-sociobiology-of-sociopathy-an- integrated-evolutionary-model-linda-mealey.**

As sociobiology began to receive expanded recognition from U.S. investigators, some social scientists, believing the basic tenets of their profession to be challenged by the movement, began to treat it as "criminology's antidiscipline." By the early 1980s, sociobiology presented such a significant threat to U.S. criminology that it could no longer be ignored. Criticisms were quick and included the following:

- Sociobiology fails to convey the overwhelming significance of culture, social learning, and individual experiences in shaping the behavior of individuals and groups.

- Sociobiology is fundamentally wrong in its depiction of the basic nature of humans; there is no credible evidence of genetically based or determined tendencies to act in certain ways.

- Sociobiology is just another empirically unsupported rationale for the authoritative labeling and stigmatization of despised, threatening, powerless minorities.

- Humans are so thoroughly different from other animal species, even other primates, that there is no rational basis for the application to humans of findings from animal studies.

Many such criticisms were advanced by old-guard academics in an effort to prevent their own discipline's decline in influence in the face of otherwise convincing sociobiological claims. Most criminologists, like most academicians, were wedded to the belief that only social theories could explain nearly all human behavior. The importance of Wilson's work was its recognition that human nature is not so much an inherent quality of our species, but rather the "result of culture workings its ways on a biology that somewhat channeled (but did not fix) the subsequent nature of our species."[54]

Today, many open-minded scholars are beginning to sense the growing need for a new synthesis, a way to integrate the promise of biological theories like sociobiology and insights drawn from studies of twins with other long-accepted perspectives, like sociology and psychology, in explaining human behavior. Recently, for example, a statistical analysis of data on twins using the National Longitudinal Study of Adolescent Health (Add Health) database found that as much as 64% of

the variance in low levels of self-control could be explained by genetic factors.[55] The study, based on Gottfredson and Hirschi's General Theory of Crime (see Chapter 8), was designed to determine how levels of self-control were related to biological factors. Studies like these seem to indicate that the field of criminology is ripe for a new integrative approach. Some say that this approach can be found in contemporary biosocial explanations of criminal behavior, to which we turn our attention in the next chapter.

Critique of Early Biological Theories of Criminal Behavior

A central concern with all early biological theories of criminal behavior has to do with the fact that they seemed to relegate the role of free will in human behavior to a kind of philosophical dustbin. If a person's behavior is largely determined, for example, by inherent and unchangeable atavistic features, then he or she may be condemned to a life of crime, and efforts at reformation can be expected to have little positive effect on future behavior. Consequently, some people continue to shy away from biological explanations for criminality and disordered behavior because phrases like "genetic determinism," which are often voiced by the popular media, have come to be synonymous with inevitability. People unschooled in criminology or modern biology tend to believe that "biological" equals "hopeless"[56]— after all, the physical makeup of a person is hard to change.

Other concerns stem from aligning the concept of crime with biological variables because crime is itself a social construction and its meaning varies from place to place and from time to time. Years ago, for example, it was illegal to own physical gold for investment purposes in the United States, but today such ownership is permitted. Similarly, Islamic law in Saudi Arabia makes it a crime for a woman to drive a car while unaccompanied by a male relative, but in the United States (and much of the rest of the world) such activity is far from criminal. While it is possible to hypothesize, for example, that a particular biological trait leads to a desire for gold ownership (or for ownership of shiny things of value) or produces the urge to drive a motor vehicle, the fact that such ownership (or driving) may or may not be criminal makes it hard to link specific biological features with potential criminality. It seems unlikely that any biological feature (or a combination of features) could explain the wide variety of criminal offending today—from insider stock trading and white-collar crime to violent attacks, rape, and murder.

CRIMINAL | PROFILES

Richard Benjamin Speck: "Born to Raise Hell"

In an appalling crime ranked number ten on *Time*'s list of the top 25 crimes of the twentieth century,[i] Richard Speck committed the mass murder of eight nurses from a community hospital in Chicago on the night of July 14, 1966.

Born the seventh of eight children on December 6, 1941, Speck had an early upbringing in Kirkwood, Illinois, that included strict adherence to Baptist religious teachings. When he was just six years old, his father died, and his mother subsequently married a hard-fisted drinker with an arrest record. After the family relocated to Dallas, Texas, Speck performed poorly in school and began sinking into increasingly serious delinquent behavior. His drunken stepfather's response was typically the administration of severe physical punishment for each of Speck's continuing transgressions.[ii] Speck himself became a heavy drinker, an affliction that would haunt him for the remainder of his life.

In spite of incarcerations for various burglaries, thefts, check forgeries, and other low-level crimes, 18-year-old Speck married 15-year-old Shirley Malone in November 1962. Their brief marriage was marked by his repeated absence while imprisoned, punctuated by his physical abuse of both his wife and his mother-in-law whenever he was not in jail. The abuse of his wife included frequent instances of rape at knifepoint.[iii]

In January 1966, the couple divorced, and Speck left Texas to return by bus to Illinois, ending up in Monmouth, a small town near the Iowa border. Following the rape of a 65-year-old woman in early April and the murder of a barmaid 11 days later, Speck was interrogated. He was let go when he became physically ill, but he promised to return for further questioning. When he failed to show up, investigators who went looking for him found he had fled on a bus headed east, presumably to the Chicago area. Before leaving, he had the phrase *Born to Raise Hell* tattooed on his forearm.

Late on the evening of July 13, 1966, a drunken Speck invaded a townhouse where nursing students from nearby South Chicago Community Hospital resided. Within the first hour, he was able to capture and tie up nine women. After securing all the victims, Speck spent the next three hours systematically taking each student to another room within the townhouse and killing her. Each was violently murdered by strangulation, multiple stab wounds, and/or a cut throat; one was also raped.

Speck lost count of the number of women he had captured, and as a result, one of the women survived by rolling under a bed and hiding there. Speck left the townhouse at approximately 3:30 A.M. The survivor, Corazon Amurao, huddled in terror under the bed until almost 6 A.M. before she finally crawled out a window and began calling for help.[iv]

Speck was soon arrested and tried in Peoria, Illinois. The jury returned a guilty verdict in just 49 minutes, and Speck was sentenced to death.[v]

Bettmann/Getty Images

Mass murderer Richard Speck, killed eight young nurses in 1966, and he admitted during the interview that they would have lived if one of the women had not spit in his face as he raped her. Speck's case helped popularize the notion of supermales—predators with a distinctive genetic makeup. Do contemporary understandings of biology support the idea of a supermale?

Speck achieved notoriety in the national press when his lawyers offered the claim that he was an XYY supermale, apparently hoping that the claim could provide a defense to the charges against him. At the time the claim was made, the XYY theory was being debated in academic circles and had become popular with the public. Later tests showed, however, that Speck did not carry the extra Y chromosome.

Speck's death sentence was commuted to 50 to 100 years in prison when the U.S. Supreme Court voided the death penalty in 1972. He died of a heart attack on December 5, 1991.

The case of Richard Speck raises a number of interesting questions. Among them are the following:

1. What caused Richard Speck to go on a murderous crime spree? Do you think it was his background or his biology, or a combination of both?

2. How is the Speck case illustrative of the current debate between advocates of biological theories of crime causation and those who advocate sociological theories?

3. How might a psychologist explain Speck's crimes? A sociologist?

Notes:

i. Howard Chua-Eoan, "The Top 25," *Crimes of the Century, Time,* http://www.time.com/time/2007/crimes/9.html (accessed May 22, 2007).

ii. David Lohr, "Richard Speck," *Crime Magazine: An Encyclopedia of Crime,* August 2003, http://www.crimemagazine.com/richard-speck-0 (accessed August 19, 2015).

iii. Connie Fillippelli, "Richard Speck: Born to Raise Hell," Chapter 11, *Court TV Crime Library,* 2007, http://www.crimelibrary.com/serial_killers/predators/speck/hell_11.html (accessed May 22, 2007).

iv. Ibid., Chapter 16, http://www.crimelibrary.com/serial_killers/predators/speck/hell_16.html (accessed May 22, 2007).

v. Ibid.

A more sensible approach might be to work to identify biological influences on characteristics that most criminals share. Such characteristics could include the level of aggression, risk taking, and danger seeking that individuals demonstrate. Possession of these characteristics may be found to increase the likelihood that some people will gravitate toward criminal activity or to related behaviors. Even if that is true, however, such characteristics might be shared by people who routinely violate the law as well as by those who enforce it. Many on both sides of the law, for example, may be risk takers, danger seekers, and aggressive personalities. Consequently, in some ways criminals and enforcement agents may share any number of characteristics, and even some genes related to behavior propensities, but differ significantly in their orientation toward social life. What separates one from the other might be the nature of the social environment to which people are exposed when growing up.

Given the difficulty in sorting out this kind of complex relationship, it may be impossible to identify any biological features shared solely by criminals. As today's theorists understand, the influence of biology on behavior of any kind is more often the result of an interaction among genetic, hormonal, and other biological features of an individual and his or her social and physical environments. In other words, as the following chapter will show, biological influences are not likely to be the direct cause of crime or conformity but are mediated through a person's surroundings to produce human behavior.

SUMMARY

- Early proponents of biological theories argued that at least some human behavior is the result of biological propensities inherited from more primitive developmental stages in the evolutionary process. Today's biosocial theories, on the other hand, look to the interaction between human physiology and the physical and social environments in an attempt to explain behavior. These newer perspectives, which will be discussed in the next chapter, hold that genes and related biological features are more likely to be facilitators rather than determinants of human behavior.

- Biological theories of crime causation adhere to the principle that many behavioral predispositions, including aggression and criminality, are constitutionally or physiologically influenced. According to some criminologists, human behavior is, to some degree, adapted instinctual behavior, and aggression is a form of biological inheritance from more primitive times. Aggression today may manifest as criminal behavior when environmental conditions conspire to elicit such instinctive responses.

- The Positivist School, which was also discussed in the previous chapter, sees human behavior as determined not by the exercise of free choice, but by causative factors beyond the control of the individual. It was built upon scientific techniques that were applied to the study of criminal behavior.

- Sociobiology is a theoretical perspective developed by Edward O. Wilson that can be described as "the systematic study of the biological basis of all social behavior." Wilson believed that the primary determinant of human behavior was the need to ensure the survival and continuity of genetic material from one generation to the next. Sociobiologists often focus on explaining the violence and aggression associated with territoriality. Sociobiology has been employed to explain intergroup and intragroup aggression.

- Critics of early biological theories of crime point to the fact that it is difficult to associate biological factors with crime because the very meaning of what is criminal changes over time. Moreover, say such critics, early biological theories depicted human beings as helpless in the face of their own biology—a perspective that is now rejected.

KEY TERMS

altruism, 96

atavism, 86

behavioral genetics, 90

biological theories, 82

born criminal, 87

constitutional theories, 88

criminal anthropology, 87

criminaloid, 87

dizygotic (DZ) twins, 93

ectomorph, 89

endomorph, 89

eugenic criminology, 91

eugenics, 91

gene pool, 96

genetic determinism, 91

heredity, 90

Italian School of Criminology, 87

Juke family, 90

Kallikak family, 91

masculinity hypothesis, 88

mesomorph, 89

monozygotic (MZ) twins, 93

paradigm, 95

phrenology, 84

Positivist School, 88

sociobiology, 95

somatotyping, 89

supermale, 91

traits, 83

tribalism, 96

KEY NAMES

Karl O. Christiansen, 93	Earnest A. Hooton, 88
Charles Darwin, 95	Patricia A. Jacobs, 91
Richard Louis Dugdale, 90	C. Ray Jeffery, 83
Arthur H. Estabrook, 90	Ernst Kretschmer, 89
Enrico Ferri, 87	Cesare Lombroso, 86
Franz Joseph Gall, 84	Konrad Lorenz, 95
Sir Francis Galton, 90	Sarnoff Mednick, 93
Raffael Garofalo, 87	William H. Sheldon, 89
Henry Herbert Goddard, 91	Johann Gaspar Spurzheim, 86
Charles Buckman Goring, 88	Edward O. Wilson, 96

QUESTIONS FOR REVIEW

1. What are the differences between historical biological and contemporary biosocial theories of crime?

2. What basic principles characterize biological theories of crime causation? How do such theories differ from other perspectives that attempt to explain the same phenomena?

3. What is the Positivist School of criminology, and what is the historical importance of positivism?

4. Describe sociobiology; include the role of concepts such as altruism, territoriality, and tribalism.

5. How can early biological theories of crime be critiqued?

QUESTIONS FOR REFLECTION

1. This text emphasizes the theme of social problems versus individual responsibility. Which perspective is better supported by the early biological theories of crime causation discussed in this chapter? Why?

2. What can early biological theories of criminology tell us about the state of social science at the time?

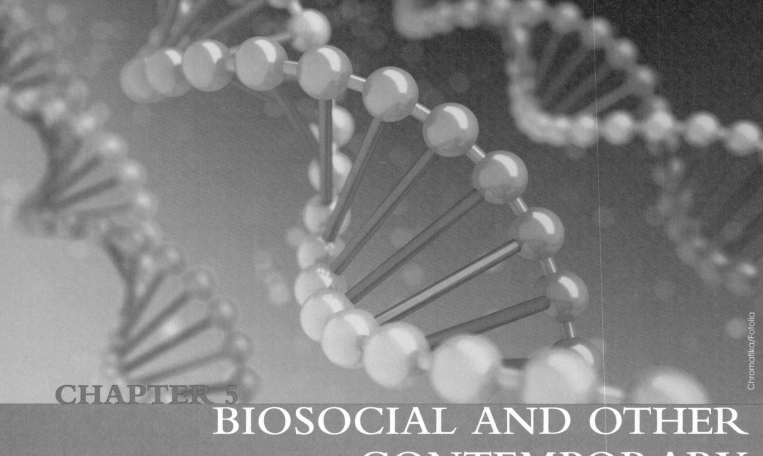

CHAPTER 5

BIOSOCIAL AND OTHER CONTEMPORARY PERSPECTIVES

Interaction is Key

LEARNING OUTCOMES

After reading this chapter, you should be able to answer the following questions:

- What was the purpose of the Human Genome Project (HGP), and what is its significance for modern biological theories of crime?

- What role do genetics and heritability play in contemporary explanations for crime?

- How does brain dysfunction relate to criminality?

- How do body chemistry theories—including those involving diet, blood sugar levels, environmental contaminants, and hormones—explain crime?

- What are biosocial theories, and what role does the gender ratio problem play in contemporary criminology?

- What are the policy implications of modern biological theories of crime?

- What are some criticisms of biological and biosocial theories?

■ **human genome**   A complete copy of the entire set of human gene instructions.

■ **genes**   Distinct portions of a cell's DNA that carry coded instructions for making everything the body needs.
■ **chromosomes**   Bundles of genes.

Introduction

In 2013, Connecticut Chief Medical Examiner, H. Wayne Carver, ordered the testing of Newton, Connecticut, school shooter Adam Lanza's DNA in an effort to determine "if he possessed any genetic abnormalities that could have led to his violent behavior."[1] In issuing that order, Carver was relying on new technologies that have recently been developed to map and explore the biological mechanisms that underlie human behavior. The results of the tests were inconclusive.

The Human Genome Project

One of the most important recent efforts in understanding human nature is the Human Genome Project (HGP), an international research program designed to construct detailed maps of the **human genome**. The HGP began in the United

States in 1990 through a joint effort of the Department of Energy and the National Institutes of Health. It had as its goal the determination of the complete chemical sequence of human DNA. Researchers participating in the project worked together to localize the nearly 100,000 genes within the human genome and to determine the sequences of the 3 billion chemical base pairs that make up human DNA. The HGP was officially declared completed on April 14, 2003[2]— almost exactly 50 years after James Watson and Francis Crick published their historic findings on the double helix, three-dimensional structure of DNA.[3]

The HGP marked the beginning of a new era of research into human biology and recast understandings of human nature, disease, cognition, and behavior. Because the HGP offered radical new insights into fundamental human qualities, we use it as the point of demarcation between earlier biological theories of criminality and those that have been recently developed.

The human genome refers to a complete copy of the entire set of human gene instructions.[4] **Genes** are made of DNA and carry coded instructions for making everything the body needs. **Chromosomes** are bundles of genes.[5] After completion of the HGP, which resulted in the sequencing of the entire genome sequence of a "reference human genome," the focus of genomics research turned to finding individual differences or variants from that reference sequence.[6] Ongoing research projects include the HapMap Project and the Encyclopedia of DNA Elements (ENCODE), which became operational in 2007. The second phase of ENCODE, the 1,000 Genomes Project, has only recently begun.

The use of genetic knowledge developed by the HGP is likely to have momentous implications for both individuals and society. Many of the questions criminologists have raised about the role of genetics in criminal behavior may be answered by the results of research begun by the HGP.[7] In the area of crime-control policy, HGP-related information is expected to support the development of public policy options related to crime prevention and the treatment of offenders.

Learn more about the federal government's involvement in genetic research from the National Human Genome Research Institute (NHGRI) at **http://www.genome.gov/Issues** and learn more about human DNA research from the international HapMap Project at **http://www.genome.gov/10001688**. NHGRI also sponsors a YouTube channel, called GenomeTV, at **http://www.youtube.com/user/GenomeTV**.

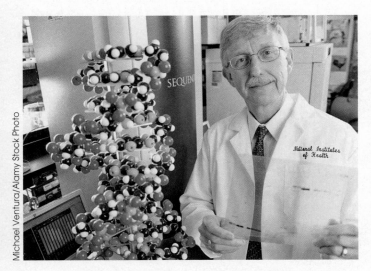

Michael Ventura/Alamy Stock Photo

Dr. Francis Collins, former Director of the Human Genome Project and current Director of the National Institutes of Health. The National Center for Human Genome Research at the National Institutes of Health supported the international Human Genome Project, a research program that determined the complete nucleotide sequence of human DNA. What ethical, legal, and social implications are inherent in such a project?

THEORY | versus **REALITY**

The Future of Neuroscience

In 2013, President Barack Obama announced a new U.S.-led initiative modeled after the Human Genome Project.[i] Known as the Brain Activity Map, the initiative seeks to learn specific details down to a molecular level about how regions and cells in the brain interconnect and function, and how the brain processes information.[ii] "There's this enormous mystery, waiting to be unlocked," Obama said in announcing the project.[iii]

The project, which is anticipated to last decades, will involve federal agencies, private foundations, and teams of neuroscientists and nanoscientists working together to advance knowledge of the brain's billions of neurons in an effort to gain greater insights into perception, actions, and consciousness.[iv] Similar projects are underway in Europe and elsewhere. Europe's Human Brain Project, an extension of the Blue Brain Project at Switzerland's École Polytechnique Fédérale de Lausanne, started a year ago. According to documents released by the project, "It will bring together everything we know and everything we can learn about the inner workings of the brain's molecules, cells and circuits, collect the knowledge in massive databases and use it to build biologically detailed simulations of the complete human brain."[v]

Neurons in a human brain, shown here magnified hundreds of times. How might the Brain Mapping Project described here be applicable to criminology?

Notes

i. Clive Cookson, "Science: Contours of the Mind," *Financial Times*, February 22, 2013, http://www.ft.com/intl/cms/s/0/06568de8-7cc2-11e2-afb6-00144feabdc0.html#axzz2LmTokbXz (accessed March 3, 2013).

ii. "Obama's Brain Activity Map Could Be the Future of Neuroscience Research," *Huffington Post*, February 23, 2013, http://www.huffingtonpost.com/2013/02/23/obamas-brain-activity-map_n_2747159.html (accessed February 25, 2013).

iii. Ibid.

iv. Da vid Jackson, "Obama Unveils Brain Mapping Project to Unlock Mysteries," *USA Today*, April 2013, http://www.usatoday.com/story/news/2013/04/02/obama-brain-mapping-project/2045167 (accessed July 4, 2013).

v. Clive Cookson, "Human Brain and Graphene Projects Win Funding," *Financial Times*, January 27, 2013, http://www.ft.com/cms/s/0/0334040a-6706-11e2-8b67-00144feab49a.html#ixzz2LwHLxWpa (accessed March 2, 2013).

Genetics and Heritability

In 1993, only three years after the launch of the HGP, Dutch criminologists caught worldwide attention with their claim that they had uncovered a specific gene with links to criminal behavior. Researcher **H. Hilger Ropers**, geneticist **Han Brunner**, and collaborators studied what media sources called "the Netherlands' most dysfunctional family." Although members of the unnamed family displayed IQs in the near-normal range, they seemed unable to control their impulses and often ended up being arrested for violations of the criminal law. The arrests, however, were always of men. Tracing the family back five generations, Brunner found 14 men whom he classified as genetically driven to criminality, but none of the women in the family displayed criminal tendencies, although they were said to have often been victimized by their crime-prone male siblings.

■ **neurotransmitters**   Chemical substances that facilitate the flow of electrical impulses from one neuron to the next across nerve synapses.

■ **allele**   An alternate form of a gene, or any of several forms of a gene, sometimes occurring through mutation.

Some criminologists claim that the evidence is very clear about a genetic factor involved in crime.

According to Ropers and Brunner, because men have only one X chromosome, they are especially vulnerable to any defective gene, whereas women (with two X chromosomes) have a kind of backup system in which one defective gene may be compensated for by another correctly functioning gene carried in the second X chromosome. After a decade of study, Ropers and Brunner announced that they had isolated the specific mutation that caused the family's criminality.[8] This gene, they said, is responsible for the production of an enzyme called monoamine oxidase A (MAO-A), which is crucially involved in the process by which signals are transmitted within the brain. MAO-A breaks down the chemicals serotonin (a hormone that plays the role of a neurotransmitter, and which we discuss in more detail later in this chapter) and noradrenaline (another neurotransmitter). **Neurotransmitters** are the chemicals that facilitate the flow of electrical impulses from one neuron to the next across nerve synapses, and the presence or absence of both serotonin and noradrenaline has been linked to aggressive behavior in human beings. Because men with the mutated gene do not produce enough of the enzyme necessary to break down a lot of chemical transmitters, the researchers surmised, their brains are overwhelmed with stimuli, resulting in uncontrollable urges and, ultimately, criminal behavior.

Also in the 1990s, researchers at the University of Texas Health Science Center in San Antonio announced the discovery of a pleasure-seeking gene that, they suspected, plays a role in deviant behavior, addictions, and maybe even murder and violence. The gene, which is a variation (also called an **allele**) of a gene known as "DRD2 A1," is normally involved in controlling the flow of dopamine (a powerful brain chemical that gives people a sense of well-being). When defective, however, the DRD2 A1 allele diminishes dopamine function, which may drive a person to take drugs, drink, or engage in activity that provides a dopamine-like experience. "We think they're seeking out ways of fixing the lack of pleasure," said researcher Kenneth Blum. "You might be a pleasure seeker for alcohol, drugs, sex or maybe you get it from violence or murder."[9]

In 2002, **Avshalom Caspi** and **Terrie E. Moffitt** and their colleagues offered a model of *gene–environment interaction* that recognized that childhood maltreatment appears to be a "universal risk factor for antisocial behavior" in adulthood. Previous research had demonstrated that children who experience abuse—especially those exposed to erratic, coercive, and punitive parenting—frequently develop conduct disorders and display antisocial personality symptoms, and they are

Childhood maltreatment appears to be a "universal risk factor for antisocial behavior" in adulthood.

known to be at greater risk of becoming violent adult offenders than are children who do not experience such maltreatment.[10] Earlier research had also shown that the younger the children are when they experience maltreatment, the more likely they are to display such problems in later life.

Using data from the Dunedin Multidisciplinary Health and Development Study—a longitudinal study of 1,037 children born in the maternity hospital in Dunedin, New Zealand, between April 1, 1972, and March 31, 1973—Caspi and Moffit noted that not all maltreated children grow up to become criminal,[11] but they hypothesized that the development of antisocial behavior is mediated by an interaction between a gene responsible for the production of the enzyme MAO-A and an environment variable (maltreatment). Researchers demonstrated a significant biosocial interaction between MAO-A and early child abuse, leading to violence later in life.[12] Their findings showed that maltreatment "has lasting neurochemical correlates in human children" and that deficient MAO-A activity may cause "neural hyperreactivity" in children in response to threats. The researchers concluded that "childhood maltreatment predisposes most strongly to adult violence among children whose MAO-A is insufficient to constrain maltreatment-induced changes to neurotransmitter systems."[13] Maltreated children with high MAO-A activity did not develop antisocial behavior. The finding was supported by two separate Swedish studies published in 2007.[14]

A 2008 analysis of data from the National Longitudinal Study of Adolescent Health (also known as Add Health) by **Kevin M. Beaver** of Florida State University and associates found that low MAO-A activity can interact with neuropsychological deficits (defined in this study as poor scores on verbal skills tests) to produce low self-control and delinquency. Hence, according to Beaver, data analysis findings "are supportive of an interdisciplinary scientific approach to the study of crime and delinquency, which views antisocial behavior as a multifactorial phenotype that is the result of genetic factors, neural substrates, and environmental factors working independently and synergistically."[15] In other words, in at least some cases, genetic predispositions plus interaction with the surrounding social and physical environments combine to produce delinquency.

Continued focus on the gene related to MAO-A production led to the announced finding of a "warrior gene," and in 2010 National Geographic Television produced a show entitled "Inside the Warrior Gene" that featured men who felt that their lives were controlled by a deep-seated and constant anger that

■ **heritability** The proportion of variation in traits within a group of people that can be attributed to variations in their genes rather than to their environment. Also, a measure of the extent to which genes influence a trait.

■ **GxE** A simple formula intended to highlight the fact that neither genes nor the environment is sufficient by themselves to explain antisocial behavior, but that it is the interaction between the two that determines what happens in most circumstances.

■ **epigenetics** The study of the chemical reactions that occur within a genome, and which switch parts of the genome on or off at strategic times and locations.

■ **gene expression** The process by which the coded information that is stored within a gene is used to create a biological product, usually a protein. Also, the manifestation of a trait in an individual carrying the gene or genes that determine that trait.

might be ascribed to such a biological condition.[16] Variants of the gene were found in boys more likely to engage in violence, to use weapons, and to join gangs.

In 2007, researchers at the University of Texas Southwestern Medical Center discovered that mice carrying certain mutations in what is called the clock gene exhibited manic behaviors, such as recklessness and hyperactivity, and also displayed a preference for addictive substances, such as cocaine, but that treatment with the antipsychotic medicine lithium caused them to behave normally. Somewhat later, Francis McMahon of the National Institute of Mental Health in Bethesda, Maryland, reported finding a number of specific genes that act by influencing how the brain responds to neurotransmitters such as dopamine and that might be associated with bipolar disorder.[17]

In 2008, researchers with the National Institute on Drug Abuse announced that "as much as half of an individual's risk of becoming addicted to nicotine, alcohol, or other drugs depends on his or her genes."[18] The researchers stated, "Pinning down the biological basis for this risk is an important avenue of research for scientists trying to solve the problem of drug abuse."

In 2011, making a genetic argument for at least some forms of callous-unemotional behavior, **Nathalie Fontaine** of Indiana University and colleagues reported that **heritability** (which is a statistical construct that estimates the amount of variation in the traits of a population that is attributable to genetic factors) leads to persistently high levels of such behavior among twin boys.[19] The data on which Fontaine reported were derived from the United Kingdom's ongoing Twin Early Development Study (TEDS), which uses information gathered from over 15,000 families to explore how people change through childhood and adolescence.[20] A similar study, conducted at about the same time, examined differences in self-control between male and female twins. The study authors concluded that "there are genetic differences in self-control that are operating across the sexes in adolescence and adulthood."[21] The results of the study showed that "the same genetic factors influence levels of self-control in males and females," meaning that the "genetic influences on self-control are not gender-specific."

Some of the studies discussed here may appear to point to criminal genes that, once inherited, inevitably produce antisocial behavior. Such a conclusion, however, is not warranted. As we shall see later in this chapter, genes may simply influence the way in which people respond to their surroundings. As one researcher puts it, "genes and environments operating in tandem

[are] required to produce significant antisocial behavior."[22] Hence, so-called criminal genes may be nothing more than genetic predispositions to respond in certain ways to a criminogenic environment. Biosocial criminologists have created a simple formula, expressed as **GxE**, to highlight the fact that neither genes nor the environment is sufficient by itself to explain antisocial behavior, but that it is the interaction between the two that determines what happens in most circumstances.

The study of the chemical reactions that occur within a genome, and which switch parts of the genome on or off at strategic times and locations, is referred to as **epigenetics**. Epigenetics is informed by the principle that "the genome dynamically responds to the environment. Stress, diet, behavior, toxins, and other factors activate chemical switches that regulate **gene expression**."[23] When genes are "expressed," they are used as blueprints for making proteins. The term *epigenetics,* however, means something quite different. It refers to the way in which our genes interact with the surrounding environment and to produce changes in ourselves and in our behavior. In 2017, for example, **Richard E. Tremblay**, whose work is also described in Chapter 3, was awarded the prestigious Stockholm Prize in Criminology for showing that "the predictors of early and persistent violence are epigenetic as well as genetic."[24] Significantly, Tremblay, who studied cohorts of young children in Montreal and elsewhere, found that birth trauma is a reliable predictor of early childhood violence and of continued violence later in life. Tremblay noted that the peak age for violent behavior is not age 20, as some have argued, but rather age three—meaning that early intervention strategies can be effective in turning young people away from future criminal involvement. Implications of other epigenetic studies are discussed in the section that follows. A video explaining epigenetics can be found at **http://www.youtube.com/watch?v=1pcevcmFTbg.**

Future Directions in the Study of Genes and Crime

The HGP, the Brain Activity Mapping project, and studies like those cited here notwithstanding, behavioral geneticists examining the crime problem face some daunting issues: coming up with a generally acceptable definition of criminality, determining how best to measure criminality once it has been defined, separating the influences of the social and physical environments from genetic influences on behavior, and distinguishing

■ **genetic memory**   or *transgenerational memory*, is inherited memory present from birth, that exists in the absence of learned experience, and which is incorporated into the genome over long periods of time. Also referred to as *ancestral memory*, it is passed down through generations in the absence of socialization or training, and may provide the basis for phobias, anxiety, and other psychological states.

among the multiple and potentially interrelated influences of many genes. In the final analysis, the explanatory power of heritability appears to be limited by the fact that it may apply only to specific environments that existed at the time of a given study. For example, red roses grown under optimal conditions will likely all be similar in size, shape, and color, but grow the same roses in a desert or put food coloring in their water, and their appearance is likely to change substantially. As one noted geneticist says, "If the population or the environment changes, the heritability most likely will change as well. Most important, heritability statements provide no basis for predictions about the expression of the trait in question in any given individual."[25] In other words, even red roses watered with blue food coloring are unlikely to end up being red.

New understandings about how genes operate also seem to call into question previous notions that genes are strong determinants of human behavior. Researchers in the field of neurobiology, for example, have found 17 genes, known as CREB genes, that are switched on and off in response to environmental influences. The CREB genes lay down neural pathways in the brain and form the basis of memory; the act of learning turns the CREB genes on and is made possible by them.[26] Hence, the CREB genes respond to human experience rather than determine it. One writer explains it this way: "These genes are at the mercy of our behavior, not the other way around."[27] The FOXP2 gene on chromosome 7 allows the development of language skills in human beings. The CREB and FOXP2 genes have taught researchers that genes are not just carriers of heredity; they are active during life and respond to the environment.

Genes not only shape us, but also can be influenced by our environment. The result is a kind of feedback loop in which genes determine physical and psychological features at both the individual and group level, but are then themselves influenced by our surroundings and by the experiences we encounter.

One of the most important processes involved in the loop of influences is DNA methylation.[28] DNA methylation refers to the addition of a methyl (CH_3) group to the nucleic acid chains that comprise DNA. Methylation results in modifications to DNA and alters which genes are expressed in cells when they divide and differentiate. Methylation is not always a harmful process and is in fact a normal experience that some genes typically undergo. Generally speaking, methylation deactivates affected genes. In other words, *methylation is the process by which our bodies turn off genes*, and that's why methylation plays an important role in the regulation of gene expression. Studies show that patterns of variation in normal methylation, however, can be induced by stress, which produces methylated genes in regions of the DNA where they might not normally be found.

Researchers have found that DNA methylation is a vicious cycle. Not only can it be caused by stresses in the environment,

but it also makes an individual with methylated genes more susceptible to stress later on.[29] Not being well cared for in infancy, for example, leads to changes in genes, which can then be inherited by the next generation. In short, research shows that child abuse and neglect lead to methylation of genes and make people more subject to stress and possibly to disease later in life. This susceptibility is then passed on to future generations making it more difficult for stressed individuals to parent well once they have their own children.[30]

At least one recent study has found that methylation of the oxytocin receptor gene can produce callous and unemotional states in human beings.[31] Another study found that the same organic process can lead to distrust and conflict between groups.[32] Finally, in important research recently presented at a meeting of the Society for Neuroscience, studies confirmed that memories could be passed from one generation of mice to another independent of animal interaction, learning, or socialization. One study, for example, showed that mice inherit specific smell memories from their fathers—even when the offspring have never previously experienced that smell, nor had even met their fathers.[33] Another study showed that female mice trained to avoid an aversive stimulus passed that behavior on to their offspring, even though those offspring were produced long after the stimulus had ended. This phenomenon, in which memories pass between generations, is also thought to affect humans. It is known as **genetic memory**, and may influence phobias, anxiety, and personal characteristics.

> The interaction of genes and the behavioral possibilities that they represent, with features of the social and physical environments, produce meaningful human activity.

In sum, it is important to recognize that genes are both the cause and the consequence of actions—and that they do not so much *determine* human action as *enable* it. Nonetheless, as one researcher puts it, "Single genes can have quite large effects, though, when they are paired with criminogenic environments."[34]

You might want to visit the U.S. Department of Energy's Human Genome Program site at **http://www.genome .gov/10001772.** You can read about how DNA and genetics might influence human behavior at **http://www.scientificamerican.com/article.cfm?id=partial-to-crime** and **http://phenomena.nationalgeographic.com/2014/06/04/my-dna-made-me-do-it-how-behavioral-genetics-is-influencing-the-justice-system** and **http://www.edge.org/3rd_culture/ridley03/ridley_print.html.**

The Dysfunctional Brain

A number of contemporary researchers have explored brain dysfunction as it relates to criminality. For example, studies using positron emission tomography (PET) of the prefrontal cortex of subjects' brains have shown interesting results. Among other things, PET technology can measure the uptake of glucose by the brain. In a 1994 study conducted by University of Pennsylvania professor **Adrian Raine** and his colleagues, PET scans of the brains of 22 murderers (including some who had only attempted murder) revealed that the study subjects showed much lower levels of glucose uptake in the prefrontal cortex than did members of a control group.[35] "The differences that Raine observed were not related to age, gender, handedness, ethnicity, motivation, history of head injury, or presence of schizophrenia. In addition, no subjects were taking psychoactive drugs at the time of the test."[36] Raine observed that their data strongly suggested that "deficits localized to the prefrontal cortex may be related to violence" in some offenders (Figure 5-1). He also noted that "frontal damage is associated with impulsivity, loss of self-control, immaturity, lack of tact, inability to modify and inhibit behavior appropriately, and poor social judgment."[37]

> PET scans of the brains of murderers showed much lower levels of glucose uptake in the prefrontal cortex than did the controls.

CRIME | in the NEWS

Is There a Crime Gene?

After Dale Vincent Bogle, a lifelong criminal, died in 1998, researchers counted 28 members of his immediate family—including brothers, sons, daughters, and grandchildren—who served prison time. "Rooster," as he was called, shepherded his sons into crime, teaching them to shoplift at an early age. But according to scientific research, genes might also explain why so many Bogle family members took up crime.

A study released in 2012 found that genetic influences were even more significant than environmental factors in producing lifelong criminals. Surveying identical twins, fraternal twins, nontwin siblings, halfsiblings, and first cousins, University of Texas at Dallas criminologist J. C. Barnes and colleagues found that genetic factors explained 56% to 70% of the variance for lifelong criminals.

The role of genes in criminality still makes some researchers nervous. It harkens back to eugenics, a theory that viewed criminals as hereditary degenerates. Harvard criminologist Earnest A. Hooton, who died in 1954, linked physical features such as sloping foreheads to criminal traits, and he advocated sterilization for those who had these traits.

Today, criminologists exploring genetics have a very different attitude. Barnes and others do not examine physical characteristics and believe genes cannot fully predetermine crime. Rather, they think genetic predispositions have to be triggered by several environmental factors, such as a chaotic home life and reprobate friends. "Criminals are not born, but the odds at the moment of birth of becoming one are not even," said Irving Gottesman, a psychologist at the University of Virginia.

Researchers like Barnes do not believe there is a specific "crime gene." "There are likely to be hundreds, if not thousands, of genes that will incrementally increase your likelihood of being involved in a crime, even if it only ratchets that probability by 1 percent," Barnes said. This theory may not help us predict crime, but it does help explain why so many members of Rooster Bogle's extended family gravitated to crime.

Barnes's stipulation that people can defy the genetic odds is also readily apparent. When James "Whitey" Bulger, a Boston gang leader, was arrested in 2011, after a 16-year manhunt, his life of crime was contrasted with the life of his younger brother, William "Billy" Bulger, who served as president of the Massachusetts Senate for 18 years. While a young Whitey Bulger was serving time in Alcatraz, Billy was going to law school.

Discussion Questions

1. This article seems to say that crime runs in families. Is that assertion likely to be true? If so, why?

2. What kinds of social policies might be built on the ideas expressed in this article?

3. How might *genetic memory* (a concept discussed earlier in this chapter) influence certain kinds of behavior?

Sources: Patricia Cohen, "Genetic Basis for Crime: A New Look," *New York Times*, June 19, 2011, http://www.nytimes.com/2011/06/20/arts/genetics-and-crime-atinstitute-of-justice-conference.html?pagewanted=all&_r=0; Fox Butterfield, "Father Steals Best: Crime in an American Family," *New York Times*, August 21, 2002, http://www.nytimes.com/2002/08/21/us/father-steals-best-crime-in-an-american-family.html?pagewanted=all&src=pm; and Rick Klein, "Tale of Two Brothers: Whitey and Billy Bulger's Rise to Power in Crime and Politics," *ABC News* January 23, 2011, http://abcnews.go.com/Politics/james-whitey-bulger-billy-bulger-powerful-brotherspowerful/story?id=13915585#.UKPMkBzhO_F.

■ **prefrontal cortex dysfunction**   A condition of the brain that may negatively impact social skills and moral reasoning. Such dysfunction may occur as the result of physical injuries to the brain, disease, or other factors.

■ **neurocriminology**   A perspective that examines the neurological links between the organism, social factors, and criminal behavior.

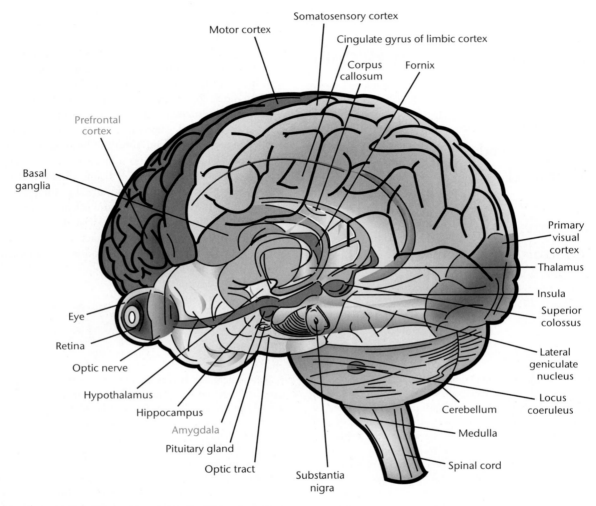

FIGURE 5-1 | The Human Brain Showing the Prefrontal Cortex and the Amygdala

Source: Schmalleger, Frank, *Criminology*. Printed and Electronically reproduced by permission of Pearson Education, Inc., Upper Saddle River, New Jersey.

Raine and other researchers who were involved in the study explained that **prefrontal cortex dysfunction** must be evaluated in terms of how individuals who exhibit the condition interact with features of the environment, including social and psychological influences. Because prefrontal cortex dysfunction may result in failure in school, inability to hold a job, problems in relationships, and so forth, it may not be a direct cause of crime but might predispose someone afflicted with the condition to "a criminal and violent way of life."[38] Raine later replicated the study using 41 murderers who had claimed to be not guilty by reason of insanity (NGRI), and who were matched with 41 "normal" controls. Similar results were obtained, leading Raine to conclude "that murderers pleading NGRI are characterized by ... reduced glucose metabolism in (the) bilateral prefrontal cortex."[39] Still later, Raine and

his colleagues used PET studies to show that differences exist between the brains of people prone to impulsive violence and those who preplan violent crimes.[40]

Seventeen years later, in a 2011 presentation made to the American Association for the Advancement of Science, Raine identified an 18% reduction of the volume of the portion of the brain called the amygdala in psychopaths when compared to nonpsychopaths, along with reductions in the size of the prefrontal cortex.[41] Raine claimed that by examining the brains of children as young as three years, criminologists could already see signs indicating the potential for troubled behavior in the future.[42] Today, Raine's approach has become known as **neurocriminology**, a perspective that examines the neurological links between the organism, social factors, and criminal behavior.

■ **frontal brain hypothesis** A perspective that references physical changes in certain parts of the brain to explain criminality.

■ **neuroplasticity** The ability of the brain to alter its structure and function in response to experience.

Other researchers, using less sophisticated techniques, have been able to show that "violent psychopathology in youth is associated with structural and functional damage" to the brain's orbital cortex.[43] The orbital cortex is that part of the brain that is directly over the orbits of the eyes. Some researchers have termed the neuroanatomical findings from studies like these the **frontal brain hypothesis**.[44]

In 2010, researchers from Columbia University's Medical Center were able to show how a gene defect that leads to a communications breakdown in the brain predisposes people with the defect to schizophrenia.[45] Maria Karayiorgou, Chief of the Division of Medical Genetics in the Department of Psychiatry at Columbia University, first noticed the relationship between the genetic variant and schizophrenia more than ten years earlier and was able to identify a definite pathophysiological mechanism of how the risk of schizophrenia is enhanced by a small deletion of genetic material on a specific chromosome shared by all human beings. She found that 30% of people with the missing genetic material go on to develop schizophrenia, making it one of the biggest genetic risk factors for the disease.

Other brain mechanisms may also be involved in aggression. Allergic reactions to common foods, for example, have been reported as the cause of violence and homicide by a number of investigators.[46] Some foods—including milk, citrus fruit, chocolate, corn, wheat, and eggs—are thought to produce allergic reactions in sensitive individuals, leading to a swelling of the brain and the brain stem. Such swelling is thought to impede the higher faculties, reducing people's sense of morality and creating conditions that support impulsive behavior. Involvement of the central nervous system in such allergies may reduce the amount of learning that occurs during childhood and may contribute to delinquency as well as to adult criminal behavior.

Physical injuries, emotional trauma, disease, and even long-term exposure to stress can also lead to changes in the brain. One 2010 study found that the brains of monkeys whose mothers had the flu while they were pregnant exhibited physical changes similar to those in people with schizophrenia.[47] Researchers noted that their findings supported the suggestion that flu in human mothers-to-be can affect brain development.

Similarly, in 2010, Princeton University's Douglas S. Massey discovered a link between stressors in the social environment and brain structure. Massey, who studied the impact of social stratification on thought processes among residentially segregated minorities, found that "people who are exposed to high levels of stress over a prolonged period of time are at risk of having their brains re-wired in a way that leaves them with fewer cognitive resources."[48] Massey concluded that residential segregation based on race produces life-long stressors, including exposure to violence, social disorder, and poverty, that result in high-risk behavior, including criminality, among deprived minorities.

An infrared image of a human head showing the brain. How might changes in the physical structure of the brain affect behavior? What is meant by the term *brain plasticity*?

Science Source

Recently, some scientists have advanced the term **neuroplasticity** (sometimes called *brain plasticity* or *cortical plasticity*) to mean that the brain can alter its structure and function in response to experience or injury, and to explain why some people experience significant changes in personality when undergoing powerful new experiences. It is well known, for example, that when portions of the brain are physically damaged through trauma, stroke, or other types of injury, adjacent parts of the brain can assume some of the psychological or motor functions that would have otherwise been lost.

In 2003, Harvard University Medical School researchers discovered that the normally thick cable of nerve cells (the *corpus callosum*) connecting the right and left hemispheres in the brain is generally smaller in children who have been abused than in children who were free from abuse.[49] Brain scans show that neglect also reduces the size of the connector, as does constant and severe verbal abuse. According to Martin Teicher, associate professor of psychiatry at Harvard Medical School, "These changes are not limited to physical and sexual abuse; there's growing evidence that even verbal assault can alter the way a developing brain is wired." Teicher and other psychiatrists who conducted the scans concluded that "a smaller *corpus callosum* leads to less integration of the two halves of the brain, and that this can result in dramatic shifts in mood and personality."[50]

Similarly, in 2011, researchers at University College London scanned the brains of dozens of children and found that those who had experienced physical violence at the hands of caregivers showed extra activity in the amygdala and the anterior insula—regions of the brain involved in threat perception and the anticipation of pain. The changes were the same, the researchers said, as those found in soldiers exposed to combat. Eamon McCrory, one of the researchers explained, "Maltreated kids and active soldiers are adapting to survive in a threatening or dangerous environment."[51]

In 2013, researchers in New Mexico reported on scanning the brains of 96 male prisoners just prior to their release to assess impulsivity and inhibitory control.[52] They found that prisoners who showed less activity in the anterior cingulate cortex (ACC)—which is located in the front of the brain—were about twice as likely to reoffend over the next four years compared with those who showed more activity in that specific region of the brain.

In a recent symposium, researchers with the U.S. National Academy of Sciences and the Canadian Institute for Advanced Research reported advances in research on biological *embedding*, or the process by which social experiences change neural circuitry in the brain.[53] Changes in brain structure brought about

THEORY | in PERSPECTIVE
Modern Biological Theories

Modern biological theories of criminality stress the interaction between biological influences and the surrounding social and physical environments. Unlike earlier biological theories, modern biosocial perspectives recognize the role of the environment in shaping both biological processes and behavioral propensities that are related to those processes.

Genetics and Heritability

Genetic characteristics and variations in human chromosomes are thought to play a role in aggression and crime causation. Although contemporary criminologists do not believe that there is one single and identifiable "criminal gene," they do believe that individuals who are genetically predisposed to certain types of behavior may become aggressive or criminal through interaction with the surrounding physical and social environments. Sex-linked chromosomes have special explanatory power by virtue of the fact that the majority of violent offenders are male.

Period: 1965 to the present

Theorists: Patricia A. Jacobs, Nathalie Fontaine, H. Hilger Ropers, Han Brunner, Adrian Raine, Darrell J. Steffensmeier, Thomas Bernard, Richard Tremblay

Concepts: genes, genome, chromosomes, heritability

Brain Dysfunction

Organic problems with the brain may lead to behavioral anomalies, including crime and deviance.

Period: 1990s to the present

Theorists: Adrian Raine and others

Concepts: neurocriminology, frontal brain hypothesis, prefrontal cortex dysfunction, neuroplasticity, embedding

Body Chemistry Theories

Violent or disruptive behavior can sometimes be linked to nutrition, vitamin deficiencies, and other conditions that affect the body. Studies of eating habits, endocrinology, and environmental contaminants have all contributed to advances in understanding such behavior.

Period: 1940s to the present

Theorists: Adrian Raine, Stephen Schoenthaler, Alexander G. Schauss, David Fergusson

Concepts: hypoglycemia, frontal brain hypothesis, psychobiotics, environmental pollution, toxic metals, vitamins, food allergies, environmental pollution, prenatal exposure to toxins, galvanic skin response (GSR)

Hormones, Enzymes, and Criminality

These biological theories explain violent or disruptive and criminal behavior by identifying hormonal influences on human cognition and action.

Period: 1940s to the present

Theorists: Alan Booth, D. Wayne Osgood, Paul C. Bernhardt, Kevin Beaver, Anthony Walsh, Lee Ellis

Concepts: testosterone, evolutionary perspective, evolutionary neuroandrogenic theory (ENA), serotonin, premenstrual syndrome (PMS), hormones (testosterone, cortisol, norepinephrine), neurotransmitters (dopamine), monoamine oxidase A (MAO-A)

Biosocial Criminology

This theoretical perspective sees the interaction between biology and the physical and social environments as key to understanding human behavior, including criminality.

Period: 1987 to the present

Theorists: James Q. Wilson, Richard J. Herrnstein, Hans J. Eysenck, Anthony Walsh, Avshalom Caspi, Terrie E. Moffitt, Kevin M. Beaver,

Concepts: biosocial perspectives incorporate many of the concepts previously listed in this box, including genetics, the gender ratio problem, heritability, hormones, brain dysfunction, body chemistry, natural and sexual selection. Neuroplasticity, genetic memory, and epigenetics are additional associated concepts. The most important contribution from this perspective, however, comes in recognizing the influence of biological factors as they are mediated through the physical and social environments in producing criminal behavior. Biosocial criminologists use the simple formula GxE to represent that interaction.

■ **hypoglycemia**   A medical condition characterized by low blood sugar.

by embedded stressful and traumatic childhood experiences were found to influence a child's development and to persist throughout life. In the words of the researchers, "experiences of childhood adversity affect cellular pathways and translate into the molecular and genetic changes that result in biological effects on development and health."[54]

Researchers have also found positive changes: Neural circuitry in the brains of practiced meditators changes—apparently in response to thousands of hours spent meditating—as evidenced by the fact that the brain waves of meditators were significantly different from those of nonmeditators.[55] Scientists who study neuroplasticity now believe not only that the brain changes in response to external stimuli or physical trauma but also that it is malleable in response to internal stimuli (thoughts). If true, simple self-improvement techniques—such as positive thinking and silently repeated self-affirmations—may foster positive alterations in personality and produce an increased likelihood of socially approved behaviors. A few years ago, for example, UCLA psychiatrist Jeffrey M. Schwartz demonstrated that patients suffering from obsessive-compulsive disorder (OCD) are capable of consciously rechanneling compulsive urges into more socially acceptable activities and that by doing so, they could actually alter their brains' neuronal circuitry.[56] Hence, physical changes to the brain in response to experiences that were once thought possible only in the very young can also characterize adults in some situations. One writer explained that "the brain physically 'captures' the environment as it wires itself in response to environmental experience."[57] The same writer noted, however, that "the brain has many assumptions built into it over eons of evolutionary time; it is no *tabula rasa*."[58] With these considerations in mind, some suggest that the interplay among heredity, biology, and the social and physical environments, may be much more complicated than once thought and may provide the key nexus in any consideration of crime causation.

> Biological theories are theories of criminality, not crime.

Body Chemistry and Criminality

> "You are what you eat" may contain more than a grain of truth.

Today's biological theorists have made significant studies in linking violent or disruptive behavior to body chemistry. Body chemistry is influenced by factors such as eating habits, vitamin deficiencies, environmental contaminants, and the endocrine system. We now turn to those issues.

Ingested Substances and Nutrition

One of the first studies to focus on chemical imbalances in the body as a cause of crime was reported in the British medical journal *Lancet* in 1943.[59] The authors of the study linked murder to **hypoglycemia**, or low blood sugar. Low blood sugar, produced by too much insulin in the blood or by near-starvation diets, was said to reduce the mind's capacity to reason effectively or to judge the long-term consequences of behavior. More recent studies have linked excess consumption of refined white sugar to hyperactivity, aggressiveness, excitability, and impairment of the ability to make reasoned decisions, and popular books like *Sugar Blues* provide guides for individuals seeking to free themselves from the negative effects of excess sugar consumption.[60]

Even the courts have accepted the notion that excess sugar consumption resulting in hyperglycemia may be linked to crime. In the early 1980s, for example, Dan White, a former San Francisco police officer, was given a reduced sentence after his lawyers used what came to be known as the "Twinkie Defense."[61] They argued that White's nightlong binge on large amounts of Coca-Cola and Twinkies before he murdered San Francisco Mayor George Moscone and City Councilman Harvey Milk was evidence of White's unbalanced mental state; the consumption of junk food was presented as evidence of depression because White was normally very health conscious.

More than ten years later, however, a well-conducted 1994 study reported in the *New England Journal of Medicine* seemed to contradict the notion that sugar may lead to hyperactivity;[62] neither sugar nor artificial sweeteners were shown to have any link to an increase in learning disabilities. In the study, researchers at Vanderbilt University and the University of Iowa varied the diets of supposedly sugar-sensitive youngsters from a diet that was high in sugar to a diet that was low in sugar but that contained the artificial sweetener aspartame, and a third experimental diet contained very little sugar but had added saccharin. After surveying parents, teachers, and babysitters and testing the study group for changes in memory, concentration, and math skills, the researchers concluded, "We couldn't find any difference in terms of their behavior or their learning on any of the three diets."[63] Hence, to date, the evidence concerning sugar's impact on behavior is unclear.

Some studies have implicated food additives, such as the flavor enhancer monosodium glutamate, dyes, and artificial flavorings, in producing criminal violence.[64] Other research has found that coffee and sugar may trigger antisocial behavior;[65] researchers were led to these conclusions through finding that inmates consumed considerably greater amounts of coffee, sugar, and processed foods than others.[66] It is unclear, however, whether inmates drink more coffee because of boredom or whether "excitable" personalities feel a need for the kind of stimulation available through coffee consumption. On the other hand, habitual coffee drinkers in nonprison populations have not been linked to crime, and other studies, like the one conducted by Mortimer Gross of the University of Illinois, showed no link between the amount of sugar consumed by inmates and hyperactivity.[67] Nonetheless, some prison programs have been designed to limit intake of dietary stimulants through nutritional management and substitution of artificial sweeteners for refined sugar.

Other studies appear to show that diets deficient in various vitamins and other nutrients can increase aggressiveness and agitation, and can open the door to crime. In recent years, for example, **Stephen Schoenthaler**, a researcher at the California State University in Stanislaus, has demonstrated significant declines in bad behavior in incarcerated adults and in schoolchildren receiving specifically designed vitamin-mineral supplementation.[68] In one of Schoenthaler's studies, for example, schoolchildren receiving vitamin supplements showed a 47% lower rate of antisocial behavior than children who received placebos.[69] More important, the drop in disciplinary infractions among children taking the supplements was due mostly to a decrease in infractions by those who had been identified as habitual offenders before entering the study.

Other nutrients have been studied to assess their possible behavioral impact. In 2003, for example, Ingrid Bergliot Helland reported that maternal diet during pregnancy can strongly affect IQ and early infant behavior, and concluded that it might also determine the risk of delinquency and criminality in later life.[70] Helland and her colleagues supplemented the diets of pregnant and lactating women with either omega-3 (DHA) or omega-6 fatty acids and followed the development of their offspring for years after the supplementation program had ended. They found that children receiving dietary omega-3 supplementation had significantly higher IQ levels by age four and performed better on problem-solving tests than those receiving omega-6 fatty acids.

High dietary intake of DHA and consumption of fish rich in omega-3 fatty acids may be related to less hostility in young adulthood.

A year later, a study of the relationship between omega-3 intake levels and chronic hostility among 3,600 urban young adults concluded that higher consumption of omega-3 fatty acids was related to significantly lower levels of hostility, with researchers stating that "high dietary intake of DHA and consumption of fish rich in omega-3 fatty acids may be related to lower likelihood of high hostility in young adulthood."[71] A 2007 study conducted in the United Kingdom found that antisocial behavior could be reduced in children through dietary supplementation with polyunsaturated fatty acids.[72]

Finally, a 2013 study reported in *Pediatrics*—a journal of the American Medical Association—revealed a clear link between the length of time a child is breast fed and later intelligence, with longer breast-feeding times being correlated with higher intelligence in the developing child.[73] The study controlled for environmental factors, including the mothers' intelligence and diet, and seemed to indicate that nutrients which are found only in breast milk, including fatty acids linked to brain development, are responsible for the observed increase in intelligence. Read more about diet and its possible contribution to criminal behavior at **https://www.psychologytoday.com/blog/evolutionary-psychiatry/201105/diet-and-violence**.

Environmental Pollution

Various substances found in our environment have been shown to be linked to criminal behavior. In 1997, British researchers Roger D. Masters, Brian Hone, and Anil Doshi published a study purporting to show that industrial and other forms of environmental pollution cause people to commit violent crimes.[74] The study used statistics from the FBI's Uniform Crime Reporting Program and data from the U.S. Environmental Protection Agency's Toxic Release Inventory. A comparison between the two data sets showed a significant correlation between juvenile crime and high environmental levels of both lead and manganese. Masters and his colleagues suggested an explanation based on a *neurotoxicity hypothesis*. Another author stated, "According to this approach, toxic pollutants—specifically the toxic metals lead and manganese—cause learning disabilities, an increase in aggressive behavior, and—most importantly—loss of control over impulsive behavior. These traits combine with poverty, social stress, alcohol and drug abuse, individual character, and other social and psychological factors to produce individuals who commit violent crimes."[75] See the Crime in the News box for more information on lead exposure and its effects.

The largest study of lead contamination and its effects on behavior was an examination of 1,000 black children in Philadelphia. It showed that the level of exposure to lead was

CRIME | in the NEWS

Exposure to Lead, Other Substances Linked to Crime Rate

Courtesy of Prof. Kim M. Cecil

Composite MRI images of about 160 members of the Cincinnati Lead Study show that childhood exposure to lead causes gray matter loss (orange areas), especially in frontal areas of the brain.

A set of environmental laws that Congress passed in the late 1970s and 1980s may have done more to reduce the U.S. crime rate than any advance in crime detection. These laws removed lead from paint, gasoline, and plumbing in response to growing evidence that lead harms the body in a wide variety of ways—including leading people into crime.

It has long been established that lead is a potent neurotoxin, and that lead poisoning causes increased aggression, especially among young children, whose small, growing bodies are sensitive to even tiny amounts of lead. Lead interferes with normal brain development in children by destroying the myelin sheaths that surround brain cells, which in turn interferes with neurotransmission.

In 2012, a study published in *Environment International* measured the impact of lead poisoning on crime rates over more than two decades, as affected children grew up and became criminals. In the study,

researchers examined the amounts of lead released in six cities from 1950 to 1985. They correlated these rates with levels of aggravated assaults 22 years later, after the exposed children had grown up. The study found that for each 1 percent increase in the amount of environmental lead, aggravated assaults rose 0.46 percent. "Up to 90 percent of the variation in aggravated assault across the cities is explained by the amount of lead dust released 22 years earlier," researchers wrote.

The study seemed to confirm a prediction that Mark A. R. Kleiman, a professor of public policy at the University of California, Los Angeles, made in 2007: "It's quite plausible that the removal of lead from gasoline in the 1980s had more to do with the crime collapse of the late 1990s than any other single factor."

About the same time, Rick Nevin of the National Center for Health Housing reported results from more recent international studies. He found that "the relationship between lead exposure, arrest, and crime trends … is evident across many crime categories and across nations with divergent preschool blood lead and crime rate trends." The Nevin study shows what appears to be a strong correlation between childhood lead exposure and index crime rates, albeit with a 19-year lag between the two.

Researchers have also connected manganese—used in gasoline, aluminum products, and disposable batteries—to heightened aggression and crime. For example, a study in Australia found that the incidence of severe crime was highest near the country's largest manganese mine. Unlike lead, however, manganese cannot be banned because it is an essential part of the human body. Low doses are harmless, but excessive amounts may be found at work sites, where the U.S. government has set standards on acceptable levels.

Mercury and copper have been linked to aggressiveness, but many other substances have not been tested yet for their effect on the brain. Researchers writing in the British medical journal *Lancet* in 2006 reported that more than 1,000 industrial chemicals show evidence of neurotoxicity in animal tests and need more study about their effect on humans. "Of the thousands of chemicals used in commerce, fewer than half have been subjected to even token laboratory testing for toxicity," the researchers wrote.

Discussion Questions

1. What does this feature say is the likely link between childhood lead exposure and later criminality?

2. What steps can be taken to reduce childhood exposure to environmental lead? What steps have already been taken?

Sources: Rick Nevin, "Understanding International Crime Trends: The Legacy of Preschool Lead Exposure," *Environmental Research*, February 2007, Vol. 104, pp. 315–336; Whet Moser, "Youth Violence: The Lead Cause?," *Chicago Reader*, October 20, 2009, http://www.chicagoreader.com/Bleader/archives/2009/10/20/youth-violence-the-lead-cause.; Noah Schultz-Byard, "Study Links Lead Exposure to Violent Crimes," *ABC Broken Hill*, April 12, 2012, http://www.abc.net.au/local/stories/2012/04/12/3475505.htm.; Jim Haner, "Studies Suggest Link between Lead, Violence," *Baltimore Sun*, May 9, 2000, http://www.baltimoresun.com/news/maryland/bal-te.lead09may09,0,584142.story.

a reliable predictor of the number of juvenile offenses among the exposed male population, the seriousness of juvenile offenses, and the number of adult offenses. More recent studies, including many that Masters was unaware of, seem to support his thesis.[76]

The researchers reasoned that toxic metals affect individuals in complex ways. Because lead diminishes a person's normal ability to detoxify poisons, it may heighten the effects of alcohol

and drugs. Industrial pollution, automobile emissions, lead-based paints, and aging water-delivery systems are all possible sources of lead contamination. In a recent interview, Roger D. Masters, Research Professor at Dartmouth College, noted, "The presence of pollution is as big a factor [in crime causation] as poverty. It's the breakdown of the inhibition mechanism that's the key to violent behavior."[77] When brain chemistry is altered by exposure to heavy metals and other toxins, people

■ **prenatal substance exposure**   Fetal exposure to maternal drug and alcohol use. Prenatal substance exposure can significantly increase a child's risk for developmental and neurological disorders.

■ **psychobiotics**   The study of the psychological and behavioral effects that bacteria can have on the mind, feelings, emotions, and behavior.

lose the natural restraint that holds their violent tendencies in check. In 2016 high lead levels in the public water supply of Flint, Michigan, lead to an investigation by the Environmental Protection Agency, and calls for the governor's resignation. Exposed children were expected to be monitored for years in the hopes that any negative health impacts could be successfully addressed. Six state employees were arrested and charged with crimes related to the lead contamination.

Many recent studies have focused on **prenatal substance exposure** to substances like marijuana, tobacco smoke, and alcohol. In 2000, for example, L. Goldschmidt and colleagues reported the results of a 10-year study that monitored the development of children of more than 600 low-income women. The study, which began during the women's pregnancies, found that prenatal marijuana use was significantly related to increased hyperactivity, impulsivity, inattention, increased delinquency, and externalizing problems;[78] the findings remained significant even when researchers controlled for other lifestyle features.

In 1998, **David Fergusson** and colleagues, in a study of 1,022 New Zealand children who had been followed for 18 years, found that "children whose mothers smoked one pack of cigarettes or more per day during their pregnancy had mean rates of conduct disorder symptoms that were twice as high as those found among children born to mothers who did not smoke during their pregnancy."[79] The observed relationship was twice as strong among male teens as among females. Similar relationships between prenatal smoking and both aggression and hyperactivity in later life have been reported by Dutch researchers.[80] A similar 2006 meta-analysis by researchers at Washington State University found that smoking by pregnant mothers contributed slightly to their children's subsequent antisocial behavior.[81]

Prenatal alcohol exposure also seems to be linked to delinquency and psychiatric problems later in life. A 1999 study of 32 children by Tresa M. Roebuck and colleagues found that alcohol-exposed children exhibited greater delinquency and less intelligence than a control group of children who had not suffered from alcohol exposure while in the womb. The researchers concluded that their findings, which are consistent with the work of other researchers,[82] showed that "alcohol-exposed children, although less impaired intellectually, are more likely than children with mental retardation to exhibit antisocial behaviors, lack of consideration for the rights and feelings of others, and resistance to limits and requests of authority figures."[83] Learn more about fetal alcohol exposure and its effects on children at **http://www.justicestudies.com/pubs/fae.pdf.** Read about pollution's possible link to crime and toxic threats to child development at **http://www.psr.org/assets/pdfs /air-pollution-effects-nervous.pdf.**

Psychobiotics

Within the last few years, a new field of study called **psychobiotics** has begun to emerge that looks at the psychological and behavioral effects that bacteria can have on the mind, feelings, emotions, and behavior.[84] The central focus of study is what are referred to as gut bacteria—or those bacteria that live in the digestive system. Although bacteria are single-celled organisms, they are generally far smaller than human tissue cells; and there are far more bacteria living in a symbiotic relationship in any mammal than that animal has body cells. In human beings, gut bacteria, taken in total, weigh more than the human brain. Recent research has demonstrated that gut bacteria carry a vast array of genes that can produce thousands of chemicals. Many of these chemicals, once produced, are absorbed through the digestive system into the blood. Some of them are linked to brain signaling and include bacteria-produced dopamine, serotonin, and gamma-aminobarytic acid (GABA).[85] In other words, gut bacteria appear to produce chemical messengers that interact with the brain and nervous system. Some studies have even led to the notion that chemicals from gut bacteria help to build and shape the physical structure of the developing brain. Studies of mice raised in the absence of gut bacteria showed that memory, emotional state, and behavior were far different among the subject mice than those exposed to normal environmental bacteria. These studies give support to earlier reports that the absence of the bacterium *Bifidobacterium infantis* in the intestines of human beings can lead to depression. Animal studies have shown that wiping out gut bacteria through ingestion of antibiotic-infused drinking water can produce serious brain impairment and can halt the growth of new neurons.[86] Further, neuroimaging studies show that an identifiable mixture of specific digestive bacteria are associated with "the reduced response of a brain network involved in the processing of emotion and sensation."[87]

Scientists now speculate that a chemical gut–brain axis exists within the body, with the two body regions involved in a constant form of chemical communication. They suggest that introducing the proper bacteria into the digestive system could produce positive results in mood and behavior by reducing blood levels of the stress hormone cortisol and by fighting inflammatory molecules produced by the immune system. The study of the interaction between gut bacteria and behavior is still in its infancy, and more studies will be required before any definitive statements can be made about the relationship between such bacteria and neurobiological conditions.

■ **hormone**   A chemical substance produced by the body that regulates and controls the activity of certain cells or organs.

■ **testosterone**   The primary male sex hormone. It is produced in the testes, and its function is to control secondary sex characteristics and sexual drive.

Hormones and Criminality

A **hormone** is a chemical substance produced by the body that regulates and controls the activity of certain cells or organs. Hormones have come under scrutiny as potential behavioral determinants. The male sex hormone **testosterone**, for example, has been linked to aggression and appears to play an important role in increasing the propensity toward violence and aggression among men. Testosterone is a steroid hormone from the androgen group that is primarily secreted by the testes. Although females produce some testosterone, it is normally present in far higher quantities in the blood and tissues of males.

A few authors have suggested that testosterone is the agent *primarily* responsible for male criminality and that its relative lack in women leads them to commit fewer crimes. A growing body of evidence supports just such a hypothesis. Studies have shown, for example, that female fetuses exposed to elevated testosterone levels during gestation develop masculine characteristics, including a muscular build and a demonstrably greater tendency toward aggression later in life.[88] Other studies show that testosterone continues to influence behavior strongly and that it creates what some have called "sexually dismorphic brains."[89]

Most studies on the subject have consistently shown a relationship between high blood testosterone levels and increased aggressiveness in men, and focused studies have unveiled a direct relationship between the amount of the chemical present and the degree of violence demonstrated by sex offenders.[90] Other researchers have linked anabolic steroid abuse among bodybuilders to destructive urges and psychosis.[91] Anabolic steroids are human-made drugs that have similar effects to testosterone in the body.

Some contemporary investigations have demonstrated a link between testosterone levels and aggression in teenagers,[92] and others have shown that adolescent problem behavior and teenage violence rise in proportion to the amount of testosterone in the blood of young men.[93] In 1987, for example, a Swedish researcher, Dan Olweus, reported that boys aged 15 to 17 showed levels of both verbal and physical aggression that correlated with the level of testosterone present in their blood. He stated that boys with higher levels of testosterone "tended to be habitually more impatient and irritable than boys with lower testosterone levels."[94] He concluded that high levels of the hormone led to increased frustration and habitual impatience and irritability.

In what may be the definitive work to date on the subject, **Alan Booth** and **D. Wayne Osgood** concluded that there is a "moderately strong relationship between testosterone and adult deviance" but suggested that the relationship "is largely

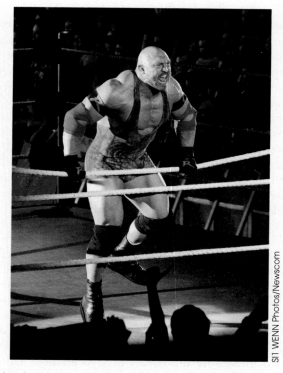

A photo of professional wrestler Ryback Reeves, participating in the 2013 WWE Revenge Tour in Dublin, Ireland. Sex hormones, such as testosterone, have been linked to aggressive behavior; testosterone also enhances secondary sexual characteristics like body hair and muscle mass in males. What kinds of crimes might be hormonally influenced?

mediated by the influence of testosterone on social integration and on prior involvement in juvenile delinquency."[95] In other words, measurably high levels of testosterone in the blood of young men may have some effect on behavior, but that effect is likely to be moderated by the social environment.

Similar conclusions were reached in 1998 by Swedish researchers who evaluated 61 men undergoing forensic psychiatric examinations for blood levels of free testosterone, total testosterone, and sex hormone–binding globulin (SHBG).[96] SHBG is known to determine the level of testosterone concentration in the blood and in body tissue. The Swedish researchers found that blood levels of total testosterone and SHBG were closely related to the extent of antisocial personality, alcoholism, and criminality exhibited by the subjects under study.

A 2007 study by University of Michigan researchers showed a relationship between testosterone, vigilance, and facial

■ **serotonin**   A neurotransmitter that is commonly found in the pineal gland, the digestive tract, the central nervous system, and blood platelets.

expressions of anger (considered to be signals of an impending dominance challenge). People with higher levels of testosterone were more prone to respond aggressively to displays of anger in others. According to the researchers, higher levels of testosterone "may generally decrease aversion to threatening stimuli, and/or may specifically facilitate approach towards signals of dominance challenge ... [and that] a signal of an impending dominance challenge could be rewarding to individuals [who] have a history of success in such encounters."[97] The researchers concluded that the "relationship between testosterone and dominance appears to be reciprocal: winners of dominance challenges show increases in [testosterone], and in turn, higher [testosterone] leads to a greater likelihood to aggress and/or to pursue further dominance challenges, in nonhuman animals and potentially also in humans."[98] See the Who's to Blame in this chapter box in this chapter for a hypothetical example of the possible influence of testosterone on crime causation.

A few limited studies have attempted to measure the effects of testosterone on women. Although women's bodies manufacture roughly one-tenth the amount of the hormone secreted by men, subtle changes in testosterone levels in women have been linked to changes in personality and sexual behavior.[99] One such study showed that relatively high blood levels of testosterone in female inmates were associated with "aggressively dominant behavior" in prison.[100]

Another study whose results were reported in 2003 attempted to measure the impact of high levels of androgens (male hormones, including testosterone) on both males and females.[101] The study examined the "externalizing behavior" of eighty-seven 14-year-olds (51 females and 36 males); other data on externalizing behavior, including aggression, were available from information gathered when the children were 8, 11, and 14 years old. Findings showed that boys with the highest blood plasma levels of androgens exhibited the most persistent aggression, but no association was found between aggression and androgen levels in females.

Fluctuations in the level of female hormones may also bear some relationship to law violation. In 1980, a British court exonerated Christine English of charges that she murdered her live-in lover after English admittedly ran him over with her car following an argument; English's defense rested on the fact that she was suffering from PMS at the time of the homicide. An expert witness, Dr. Katharina Dalton, testified at the trial that PMS had caused English to be "irritable, aggressive, and confused, with loss of self-control."[102]

Serotonin

A 1997 study by **Paul C. Bernhardt** found that testosterone might not act alone in promoting aggression.[103] Bernhardt discovered that aggressive behavior in men may be influenced by high testosterone levels combined with low brain levels

> Aggressive behavior in men may be influenced by high testosterone levels combined with low brain levels of the neurotransmitter serotonin.

of the neurotransmitter **serotonin**. Serotonin, a neurotransmitter, is a hormone that is commonly found in the pineal gland, the digestive tract, the central nervous system, and blood platelets. Serotonin plays an important role in the regulation of learning, mood, and sleep, and in the constriction of blood vessels. Most of the body's serotonin is in the intestines, where it regulates intestinal movements. The rest is found in the neurons of the central nervous system.

Bernhardt postulated that testosterone's true role is to produce dominance-seeking behavior but not necessarily overt aggression. According to Bernhardt, when individuals are frustrated by their inability to achieve dominance, serotonin acts to reduce the negative psychological impact of frustration, producing calmer responses. Men whose brains are lacking in serotonin, however, feel the effects of frustration more acutely and therefore tend to respond to frustrating circumstances more aggressively, especially when testosterone levels are high.

In 1999, researchers set out to test the hypothesis that enhancing brain levels of serotonin might reduce aggression and impulsivity in aggressive male criminals.[104] In the volunteer-only study, ten young male offenders were given daily injections of d,l-fenfluramine, a drug that makes serotonin more available to brain cells. Findings showed that "the drug produced a significant, dose-dependent decrease in aggressive responding 2 to 4.5 hours after dosing ... [and that] all ten subjects decreased their aggressive responding following the highest 0.8 mg/kg dose."[105] Subjects exhibiting the highest rates of aggression showed the greatest decreases in aggression levels after being treated with d,l-fenfluramine, impulsivity similarly decreased.

Serotonin has been called a "behavior-regulating chemical," and animal studies have demonstrated a link between low levels of serotonin in the brain and aggressive behavior. For example, monkeys with low serotonin levels in their brains have been found to be more likely to bite, slap, and chase others of their kind. Studies at the National Institute on Alcohol Abuse and Alcoholism have linked low serotonin levels in humans to impulsive crimes. Men convicted of premeditated murder, for example, have been found to have normal serotonin levels, whereas those convicted of crimes of passion had lower levels.[106]

Other studies have found that the presence of excess manganese lowers brain levels of serotonin and dopamine, both of which are associated with impulse control and planning.[107] Roger D. Masters, whose work was discussed previously in

WHO'S TO BLAME—The Individual or Society?

Hormones and Criminal Behavior

Lamont Ridgeway, 22, was arrested and charged with rape after 21-year-old Nicole Bachman called police to her Minneapolis home at 2:00 A.M. Ridgeway and Bachman had met in an evening art class at the local community college, and Bachman invited Ridgeway to her apartment for a glass of wine after the class was over. Officers couldn't help but notice that Bachman was an unusually attractive young woman whose clothes were in disarray and that she was visibly intoxicated and slurred her words as she spoke; Ridgeway was passed out on her couch, apparently after having had far too much to drink.

"He raped me!" Bachman told the two officers who responded to her call for help. "I told him to stop, and he wouldn't," she said.

Ridgeway was roused from sleep, arrested, searched, handcuffed, and taken to jail, where he was booked and charged with rape. After being advised of his rights not to speak and to have a lawyer represent him, he decided to tell the officers who were questioning him that it wasn't really rape. "She came on to me," he said. "She took her blouse off, then her pants. And she gave me a lot to drink. Yeah, she said 'No,' but by then we were already there. I couldn't stop. Why would she want to, anyway?"

When Ridgeway's lawyer arrived, he advised Ridgeway not to say anything more. The lawyer, hired by Ridgeway's wealthy parents, read the statement that he had given to the police and then hired a neurophysiologist to help in building a defense that might stand up in court.

Kanzefar/Fotolia

A man shows off his massive biceps. How do hormones influence human behavior?

When the case went to trial two months later, the neurophysiologist testified as an expert witness for the defense. He told the jury that blood tests showed that Ridgeway had abnormally large amounts of testosterone naturally occurring in his blood, that testosterone was the chemical messenger responsible for the male sex drive (which, he said, differed substantially from that of women), and that Ridgeway had consequently been unable to control his behavior on the night of the alleged rape. "The young man was simply doing what his hormones made him do," the neurophysiologist testified. "It's my professional opinion," he concluded, "that with that amount of testosterone affecting his judgment, he really didn't have much choice in his behavioral responses once he was offered alcohol and was then visually stimulated by the young woman's removal of her clothes. If this was my patient," the neurophysiologist added, "I'd treat him with the testosterone antagonist Depo-Provera, and we would see the strength of his sex drive substantially diminished. You could be sure that this kind of thing wouldn't happen again."

In response, the prosecution called their own expert, a noted biochemist who, citing various studies, said that there was no clearly established link between blood levels of testosterone and aggressive sexual behavior in human beings. "Even if there were," he said, "people are not mindless animals. We have free choice. We are not so driven by our blood chemistry that we cannot decide what we are going to do in any given situation."

Think about it

1. With which expert witness do you agree more—the neurophysiologist or the biochemist? Why?

2. Do you believe that blood chemistry can ever be an explanation for behavior? For crime?

3. If you answered yes to the previous question, do you think that blood chemistry can ever be an effective excuse for criminality? If you answered no to the previous question, why is blood chemistry not an explanation for behavior?

4. How do our understandings of criminal motivation and crime causality influence our policies on the treatment, punishment, and reformation of those who violate the law?

Note: Who's to Blame boxes provide fictionalized critical thinking opportunities based on actual cases.

this chapter, also claimed that children raised from birth on infant formula rather than breast milk absorb five times as much manganese as breast-fed infants; calcium deficiency is known to increase the absorption of manganese, and "a combination of manganese toxicity and calcium deficiency adds up to 'reverse' Prozac."[108]

One 1998 study of 781 men and women age 21 found a clear relationship between elevated *blood* levels of serotonin (which correspond to lower *brain* levels of the chemical) and violence in men.[109] The study controlled for a host of possible intervening factors, including gender, diet, psychiatric medications, illicit drug use, season of the year (during which the blood test was done), plasma levels of tryptophan (dietary precursor of serotonin), alcohol and tobacco use, psychiatric diagnoses, platelet count, body mass, socioeconomic status, IQ, and history of suicide attempts. The relationship held true when both court records and self-reports of violence were assessed. No relationship between serotonin levels and aggression was seen in female subjects. According to the study's authors, "This is the first study to demonstrate that a possible index of serotonergic function is related to violence in the general population. The epidemiological serotonin effect was not small [but rather] indicated a moderate effect size in the population."[110]

Similar research by Swedish neuropsychiatrists in 2003 found that a "dysregulation of serotonin" in the brain and central nervous system could lead to increased impulsivity, irresponsibility, aggression, and need for stimulation.[111] The researchers examined the cerebrospinal fluid (CSF) of 28 violent and sexual offenders and noted that an imbalance between levels of serotonin and dopamine was highly associated with psychopathic traits.

Hormones, such as testosterone and the thyroid hormone T_3, along with the neurotransmitter dopamine and the stress hormones cortisol and norepinephrine, have all been implicated in delinquency and poor impulse control.[112] In 2000, for example, Keith McBurnett and colleagues reported the results of a study that evaluated 38 boys between the ages of seven and 12 who had been referred to a clinic for the management of behavioral problems.[113]

> Low cortisol levels were associated with early onset of aggression.

The children were studied for four years, using various medical and psychological assessment tools. McBurnett and fellow researchers found that the "meanest" boys had the lowest levels of the hormone cortisol in their saliva: "Low cortisol levels were associated with persistence and early onset of aggression. Boys with lower cortisol concentrations exhibited triple the number of aggressive symptoms and were named as most aggressive by peers three times as often as boys who had higher cortisol concentrations." Although the researchers did not explain why low cortisol levels might be linked to aggression, they suggested that "children with persistent conduct disorder may have genes that predispose them to produce certain hormones differently, or their hormone production may have been altered before or soon after birth."[114]

A few years ago, two separate Swedish studies found evidence suggesting that elevated levels of the thyroid hormone T_3 were related to alcoholism, psychopathy, and criminality.[115] Blood serum levels of the thyroid hormone T_4 (thyroxine), on the other hand, were negatively related to antisocial behavior. The researchers concluded that the results of their studies indicate an intimate relationship between T_3 and T_4 and abuse and antisocial behavior. They emphasize the importance of further studies on T_3 as a biological marker for abuse, social deviance, and repeated violent behavior.

Not all hormones produce aggression or are linked to violence, of course. A 2012 study of what has been billed as the trust molecule showed that increased levels of a chemical messenger known as oxytocin helps to explain why some people are routinely giving and altruistic, while others are seen as coldhearted and stingy.[116] In the brain, oxytocin appears to be the chemical that creates bonds of trust in all types of human relationships. Although oxytocin is primarily a female reproductive hormone that controls contractions during labor, it is also responsible for the bond that forms between mothers and their babies. It is even thought to be responsible for the warm feelings that people feel during lovemaking, or when giving and sharing hugs. The study found that when oxytocin levels rise in the blood, people respond generously and caringly, even to strangers.

As Georgia State University criminologist Leah E. Daigle points out, however, "changes in hormone levels alone do not account for aggressive behavior. Instead, these hormonal changes may affect a third, unspecified variable (such as self-control or social bonds) that lead to aggressive responses."[117] In other words, says Daigle, "rather than directly affecting behavior, hormones may instead interact with social factors to produce criminal behavior."

Low Resting Heart Rate and Crime

One of the most pervasive findings in the area of biological criminology shows that people who consistently engage in antisocial behavior tend to exhibit low resting heart rates.[118] Studies of children as young as three that measured heart rates have been able to predict with considerable accuracy which children will become antisocial in their early to mid-teens.[119] As one noted criminologist observes, "low resting heart rate is considered the best-replicated biological correlate of antisocial behavior."[120]

Heart rate is determined by the body's autonomic nervous system (ANS), and studies consistently show that low rates of autonomic arousal are closely associated with psychopathy, aggression, and other forms of antisocial behavior. Some have proposed that sensation-seeking and fearlessness may help explain the relationship. The relationship between low resting heart rate and crime, while well established, has not

> Low resting heart rate is considered the best-replicated biological correlate of antisocial behavior.

been fully explained. Some researchers suggest that low resting heart rate is a marker of low autonomic arousal, and that low arousal is an unpleasant physiological state akin to boredom—causing people who routinely experience it to seek added stimulation and excitement. Noted biosocial criminologist Adriane Raine, for example, claims that those with a low resting heart

■ **galvanic skin response (GSR)**   A measure of the skin's resistance to electrical current, detectable through simple test instruments. Variations in GSR are often caused by an emotional reaction to stimuli.

rate feel bored and seek out stimulating experiences, which often gets them into trouble.[121] Raising their level of excitement, it's argued, brings people with a normally low rate of autonomic arousal back into a more pleasant physiological state.[122] Others say that a low heart rate reflects a relative lack of fear, and that fearlessness can lead to poor choices and be reflected in increased aggression.[123] It should be noted that low resting heart rate appears to be associated with antisocial behavior only among males and not females; and that low heart rates are frequently found in well-conditioned athletes—and that no one has suggested that athletic conditioning plays a role in crime causation.

One 2014 study examined the relationship between resting heart rate and antisocial behavior in a sample of 335 adolescent boys.[124] Along with heart rate measurements in various settings, subjects completed self-report surveys designed to measure fear, impulsive sensation-seeking, and various forms of antisocial behavior. As with numerous other studies, increased levels of aggression and delinquency were found to be closely associated with a low resting heart rate. Impulsive sensation-seeking, however, was found to have the highest association with low heart rate. Surprisingly, measures of fearlessness did not correlate as well with heart rate. The investigators concluded by suggesting that "children with low resting heart rates may require specialized intervention"[125] to prevent them from becoming involved in antisocial activity. They recommended "encouraging children to participate in prosocial, stimulating behaviors that can partly fulfill their need for stimulation."

Finally, a 2017 study published in *Criminology*, found that lower heart rates in males partly explain their higher levels of offending.[126]

It should be mentioned that certain physiological conditions with no relationship to antisocial behavior might also result in low resting heart rate. People with certain some medical conditions and those with heart rhythm disturbances can also have low heart rates.

Galvanic Skin Response

Researchers have documented a direct relationship between sympathetic nervous system activity and emotional arousal, regardless of the specific emotion being elicited.[127] One significant physiological feature that is under the control of the sympathetic branch of the autonomic nervous system is skin conductivity, also known as **galvanic skin response (GSR)**. GSR (which can also stand for "galvanic skin resistance") is of special interest to criminologists because many studies have determined that GSR readings can be used to assess physiological responses to stress and other environmental stimuli.[128] Such findings have led to GSR measurements being incorporated into devices meant to detect lying (i.e., lie detectors).

The ease with which human skin conducts electricity can be measured with inexpensive low voltage devices that cause no discomfort. Low levels of skin resistance, which are usually associated with high moisture levels produced by sweat glands in the skin, have been found to be indicative of physical and emotional arousal. For most normal people, when frightened, startled, or exposed to a traumatic event, autonomic sympathetic changes occur without consciousness awareness and include increased heart rate, rapid breathing, sweating, decreased salivation, and increased electrical conductivity of the skin.[129] This is why many people report feelings of a tight chest, labored breathing, and sweaty palms during stressful events. These automatic responses to threat and fright are commonly referred to as the "flight or fight" response. Tests reveal, however, that some individuals maintain heightened skin resistance to the flow of electricity (or low GSR), even when exposed to stimuli that would produce profuse sweating in normal subjects. Most importantly, low GSR levels in the face of startling stimuli have been found to be associated with antisocial and aggressive tendencies. Similar to findings that resting heart rate is low among those likely to offend, researchers suggest that low GSR is a proxy measure for low arousal, and that people who demonstrate it are likely to seek stimulation and excitement in order to overcome feelings of boredom and lethargy.

In a recent study to investigate the relationship between GSR and problem behavior, Brazilian researchers tested forty adolescents aged 13 to 16, using questionnaires designed to measure such negative personal qualities as "oppositionality," "headstrongfulness," "hurtfulness," and "bullying."[130] GSR readings were recorded by measuring electrical impulses on the skin. As anticipated, results showed that heightened skin resistance was correlated with the presence of negative and antisocial qualities in the subjects under study.

Electrodes used to measure galvanic skin response (GSR).
Why might varying levels of GSR be indicative of behavioral tendencies among study subjects?

■ **Digit ratio**   The comparative length of index and ring fingers; also known as the 2D-4D ratio.

Finally, some studies have shown that psychopaths demonstrate a higher level of skin resistance (than other people) when viewing emotional facial expressions,[131] or when presented with offers that can easily be recognized as inherently unfair.[132]

Digit Ratio

It has long been known that men tend to have index fingers that are closer in length to their ring fingers than do women. The comparative length of index and ring fingers is known as the 2D-4D ratio (where the "D" stands for "digit"). Evidence from both human and animal studies shows that the 2D-4D ratio is strongly influenced by exposure to androgens during fetal development. The higher the level of exposure to testosterone during fetal development, the smaller the difference in the 2D-4D ratio. Various studies have shown that the 2D-4D ratio is related to fetal growth, hand preference, autism, arm length (especially relative to trunk length), the occurrence of Asperger's syndrome, sperm counts, family size, age at first myocardial infarction in men, and the likelihood of breast cancer in women.

Some criminologists have suggested that, at least in men, low 2D-4D ratios, in which index finger length is close to (or longer than) the ring finger are indicative of what some writers call stereotypical male characteristics—including such behavioral expressions as assertiveness, aggression, risk-taking, and even criminal behavior. At least one recent study appears to have demonstrated that greater differences in digit length in men are predictive of "men's agreeableness with women" (i.e., is associated with "nice guys).[133]

In 2015, Lee Ellis and Anthony W. Hoskin, in a study of 2,059 college students in Malaysia, and 1,291 college students in the U.S., concluded "that high exposure to androgens during prenatal development contributes to most forms of offending following the onset of puberty." Ellis and Hoskin used the 2D-4D ratio as an indirect measure of prenatal androgen exposure.[134]

Inbreeding has been shown to reduce the 2D-4D ratio; although, critics of using such ratio comparisons point out that ethnicity influences such ratios more than gender. In short, while the 2D-4D ratio makes for interesting comparisons, it is likely far too simplistic to be a reliable indicator of criminality.

Climate, Weather, and Crime

A few years ago, as temperatures hovered around 11 degrees Fahrenheit, New York City went without a single murder for more than nine days. Newscasters opined that "the cold, perhaps, pacified a city accustomed, on average, to more than a murder a day."[135] Research on crime and weather has looked at everything from sunshine and humidity to wind speed, barometric

pressure, and rainfall. After reviewing both published and unpublished research in this area, **James Rotton** and **Ellen G. Cohn** of Florida International University concluded that temperature is the only weather variable that is consistently and reliably related to criminal behavior[136] (see Figure 5-2). In general, field research has found a definite positive correlation between temperature and violent crime—more violent crime is reported to the police on warm days than on cold days. However, the relationship between temperature and criminal behavior is more complex than it first appears. Rotton and Cohn's research incorporated not only temperature but also a variety of time-based variables, such as time of the day and day of the week. Their findings suggested that relationships between temperature and various types of criminal behavior are affected, or moderated, by time of day, day of the week, and season of the year.

In a study of assaults in Minneapolis, Cohn and Rotton found that relationships between temperature and assaults were strongest during evening and early hours of the night.[137] A replication conducted in Dallas also found that temperature's correlation with assaults was strongest during evening hours, which are usually the coolest time of day.[138] Other studies conducted in Minneapolis found that temperature was significantly correlated with certain property crimes (burglary, larceny, and robbery),[139] with domestic violence,[140] and with disorderly conduct.[141]

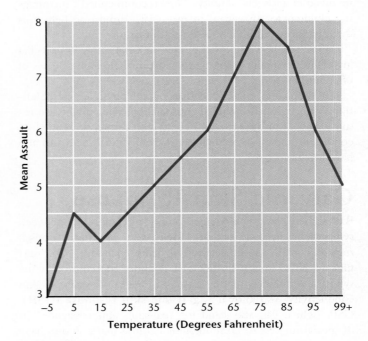

FIGURE 5-2 | **Assault as a Function of Temperature**

Source: E . G. Cohn and J. Rotton, "Assault as a Function of Time and Temperature: A Moderator-Variable Time-Series Analysis," Journal of Personality and Social Psychology, Vol. 72 (1997), pp. 1322–1334.

■ **biosocial criminology** A theoretical perspective that sees the interaction between biology and the physical and social environments as key to understanding human behavior, including criminality.

Cohn and Rotton's findings are consistent with predictions that might be derived from routine activities theory (discussed in Chapter 10). They suggested that uncomfortably hot and cold temperatures keep people apart, resulting in less opportunity for victims and motivated offenders to come in contact with one another. Temporal variables, such as time of day and day of the week, moderate the relationship between temperature and crime by also affecting opportunity; offenders and victims are more likely to come in contact with each other during evening and weekend hours than during the day, when many people are busy at work or school or are engaged in other routine activities.

Other researchers have found an apparent link between barometric pressure and violent criminal offending. Using data on suicides and violent crimes during 1999 in the Louisville, Kentucky, area, Thomas J. Schory and colleagues discovered that "the total number of acts of violence and emergency psychiatry visits are significantly associated with low barometric pressure";[142] low pressure appears to be associated with changes in cerebral blood flow and may lead to increased impulsivity.

Finally, in 2013, University of California Berkeley researchers analyzed data on ancient wars, road rage, and other forms of aggressive behavior and found an historical correlation between high temperatures, extreme rainfall patterns, and violence. Extrapolating their findings into the future, they concluded that the incidence of war and civil unrest may increase by up to 56% between now and 2050 due to global warming and the changes in weather patterns that are expected to accompany it.[143]

Biosocial Criminology

In the mid-1980s, criminologist **James Q. Wilson** and psychologist **Richard J. Herrnstein** teamed up to write *Crime and Human Nature*, a book-length treatise that restated and refined many of the arguments proposed by biological criminologists over the preceding century.[144] Part of their purpose was to reopen discussion of biological causes of crime. "We want to show," Herrnstein said, "that the pendulum is beginning to swing away from a totally sociological explanation of crime."[145] Their avowed goal was "not to state a case just for genetic factors, but to state a comprehensive theory of crime that draws together all the different factors that cause criminal behavior."[146]

Wilson and Herrnstein cited several constitutional factors that they believed made important and undeniable contributions to criminal behavior:[147]

- **Gender.** "Crime has been predominantly male behavior."
- **Age.** "In general, the tendency to break the law declines throughout life."
- **Body type.** "A disproportionate number of criminals have a mesomorphic build."

- **Intelligence.** Criminality is said to be clearly and consistently associated with low intelligence.
- **Personality.** Criminals are typically aggressive, impulsive, and cruel.

Although personality, behavioral problems, and intelligence may be related to and at least partially determined by environment, the authors said that "each involves some genetic inheritance." Wilson and Herrnstein recognized social factors in the development of personality but suggested that constitutional factors predispose a person to specific types of behavior and that societal *reactions* to such predispositions may determine, to a large degree, the form of continued behavior.

In the 1990s, **Anthony Walsh** of Boise State University, who is one of today's best known proponents of **biosocial criminology**, continued the movement toward recognizing biology's contributions to understanding criminal behavior. Walsh emphasized the importance of the *interaction* between biology and the environment in the formation of behavioral responses to given situations. "Biological factors do not operate in an environmental vacuum," said Walsh, "nor do environmental factors operate in a biological vacuum, and we must cease formulating our theories as if they do."[148]

> Biological factors do not operate in an environmental vacuum, nor do environmental factors operate in a biological vacuum.

Walsh became one of the founders of contemporary biosocial criminology—a scientific endeavor that attempts to take all that is known about the biological underpinnings of human behavior and to use that knowledge to assess how human biology interacts with the surrounding physical, cultural, and social environments in producing a criminal event. Biosocial criminology is not so much a theory about crime as it is a perspective on criminality that recognizes the importance of the interaction between biology and the surrounding physical and social environments.

Walsh observes that biosocial perspectives are theories of criminality, not crime.[149] He goes on to explain that crime is a "legal label" that is placed on specific behaviors that violate the criminal law. Criminality, on the other hand, says Walsh, "is a property of individuals, a continuous trait that is itself an amalgam of other continuous traits, and thus belongs to a more inclusive kind of criminology."[150] According to Walsh, criminality can be seen as the willingness to violate individual rights and social norms, whether or not such behavior is against the law. Criminality, says Walsh, consists of "a relative lack of empathy, conscience, self-control, and fear, as well as self-centeredness, and a penchant for risky behavior."[151] Seen this way, biosocial

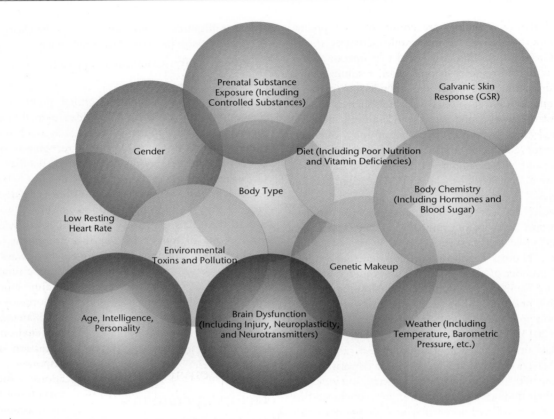

FIGURE 5-3 | Selected Biological Factors Recognized by Biosocial Theory

explanations of criminality are more likely to be couched in terms of a propensity for violence, aggression, deceit, recklessness, fearlessness, and so on, and features of the surrounding environment determine how such propensities are expressed.

Behavioral science expert Diana Fishbein of the Research Triangle Institute (RTI) puts it this way: "[N]umerous behavioral science subdisciplines, including molecular and behavioral genetics, neurobiology, physiology, psychology, cognitive neuroscience, endocrinology, and forensic psychiatry, provide substantial evidence" that certain traits possessed by individuals lead to increased risk for antisocial behavior.[152]

Fishbein notes that "the vast range of studies from these disciplines on vulnerability to antisocial personality disorder, violence, and drug abuse … reveal a pattern that may characterize vulnerable individuals." These patterns, which include individual biological differences in heart rate, hormone levels, and EEG recordings, demonstrate that "vulnerability to antisocial behavior is partially a function of genetic and biological makeup" that is expressed, says Fishbein, "during childhood as particular behavioral, cognitive, and psychological traits, such as impulsivity, attention deficits, aggressiveness, and conduct disorder."

Echoing Walsh, Fishbein notes that "biological differences do not function in a vacuum to increase risk." Instead, she writes that biological factors interact dynamically with many social and environmental conditions "to contribute to or protect from social dysfunction." It is this emphasis on *interaction* between biology and the environment—especially culture and the social environment—that differentiates biosocial criminology from other biological perspectives on crime.

Researchers are beginning to understand just how complex the relationship between biology, behavior, and the social environment can be. Biosocial criminology attempts to recognize this complexity by embracing the role of a multitude of factors leading to criminality (Figure 5-3) and including the interaction of those factors with the surrounding environment.

Gender Differences in Criminality

A number of contemporary writers argue that criminologists must recognize that "the male is much more criminalistic than the female."[153] With the exception of crimes such as

■ **gender ratio problem** The need for an explanation of the fact that the number of crimes committed by men far exceeds the number of crimes committed by women in almost all categories.

prostitution and shoplifting, the number of crimes committed by men far exceeds the number of crimes committed by women in almost all categories, and when women commit crimes, they are far more likely to assume the role of followers than leaders.[154] Leading biosocial researcher **Kevin Beaver** explains it this way: "In virtually every study ever conducted, males are much more likely than females to engage in violence, aggression, and serious crimes. As the seriousness of the offense/behavior increases, the gender gap also tends to increase, such that the most violent criminal acts are almost exclusively a male phenomenon." Beaver calls the differences between female and male rates of offending the *gender gap*. He and other writers also refer to it as the **gender ratio problem** and call for its explanation.[155]

The data on the extent of male–female criminality in the United States show surprising regularity over time: The proportion of homicides committed by men versus women has remained more or less constant for decades—with about 96% of all murders committed by men. Similarly, the proportion of men murdered by men versus the proportion of women murdered by women has been consistent, indicating a much greater propensity for men to murder one another.

If culture exercises the major role in determining criminality, as many social scientists today believe, then we would expect to see recognizable increases in the degree and nature of female criminality over time, especially as changes in socialization practices, cultural roles, and other ethnographic patterns increase the opportunity for women to commit what

had previously been regarded as traditionally male offenses. With the exception of a few crimes, such as embezzlement, drug abuse, and liquor-law violations, such has not been the case. Although women comprise 51% of the population of the United States, they are arrested for less than 20% of all violent crimes and almost 38% of property crimes[156]—a proportion that has remained surprisingly constant since the FBI began gathering crime data nearly a century ago—in spite of all the cultural changes creating new possibilities for women to commit crimes. These gender differences can also be seen in cross-cultural studies (Figure 5-4).

Such findings contrast with the suggestions of authors like **Freda Adler**, who, in her classic 1975 book *Sisters in Crime*, proposed that as women entered nontraditional occupations and roles, there "would be a movement toward parity with men in the commission of crime in terms of both incidence and type."[157] **Darrell J. Steffensmeier**, who studied changes in women's criminality following publication of Adler's book, found almost no evidence to support the belief that a new female criminal is emerging or that female criminality is undergoing the kind of increase Adler expected.[158] The lack of contemporary validation for Adler's thesis suggests that something else is occurring, that some element other than cultural inhibition or equality of opportunity is preventing women from taking their place alongside men as equals in crime.

Penn State criminologist **Thomas Bernard** and colleagues Jeffrey Snipes and Alexander Gerould have advanced

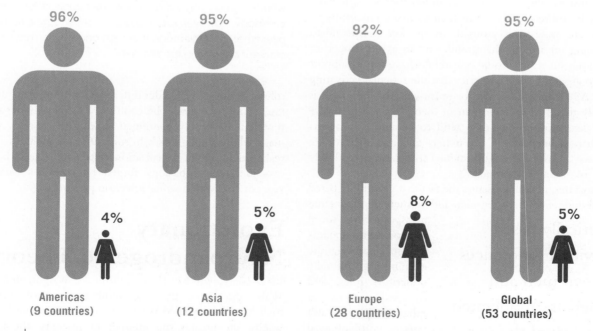

FIGURE 5-4 | Percentage Distribution of Persons Convicted of Homicide, by Sex and by Region, 2012

Source: Global Study on Homicide 2013 (Vienna: UNDOC, 2014), p. 166. http://www.unodc.org/documents/gsh/pdfs/2014_GLOBAL_HOMICIDE_BOOK_web.pdf. United Nations Office on Drugs and Crime.

■ **sexual selection**   A form of natural selection that influences an individual's ability to find or choose a mate.

the proposition that "the issue of why always and everywhere males commit more criminal acts than females is the 'single most important fact that criminology theories must be able to explain.'"[159] Biosocial criminologists suggest that the organic correlates of gender provide the needed explanation. Walsh, for example, says that the gender ratio problem is only a problem "if we are constrained to operate under sociology's strict environmentalist paradigm, which is suspicious of psychological or biological factors that differentiate among individuals and categories of individuals..."[160] If we admit, Walsh writes, that "there is something about gender per se" that is responsible for the observed differences, the problem is resolved.[161]

One of the primary contemporary paradigms useful in understanding gender differences in criminality is the concept of **sexual selection**. Sexual selection, which is a form of natural selection that influences an individual's ability to find or choose a mate, derives from Charles Darwin's theory of evolution.[162] While Darwin was most concerned with explaining how the process of natural selection (survival of the fittest) determines trait differences between species, the concept of sexual selection seeks to explain male female differences within species. Contemporary writers, for example, claim that the important roles of child bearing, child protection, and child rearing created evolutionary pressures for females to become sensitive to immediate environmental stimuli—or what is happening in their immediate vicinity. Such awareness, they claim, provided the ability to identify threats and to shield their offspring from danger. Consequently, because of evolutionary forces, females today may be more sensitive than men to many environmental stimuli, are more easily aroused, are quicker to respond to what is going on around them, and tend to avoid dangerous or threatening situations. Some researchers have found support for such an argument in discoveries that the reticular activating system (RAS), which accounts for sensitivity and response, is more finely tuned in women than in men.[163] To compensate for lower levels of arousal, men tend to be more sensation-seeking than women, these researchers say, and their desire for increased arousal and environmental stimulation are closely linked to risk-taking and crime.[164]

None of this, of course, denies the fact that genetically based behavioral differences between men and women are moderated

> Genetically based behavioral differences between men and women are moderated by aspects of the social environment.

by aspects of the social environment, including socialization, the learning of culturally prescribed roles, and the expectations of others. Still, as Walsh puts it, criminological theories that continue to deny the important

Women's boxing champion, Chungneijang Mary Kom Hmangte of India, after winning a quarter-finals match in the 2012 Olympic Games. Women's boxing, a relatively new sport, reflects women's changing social roles. Male–female differences in criminality, however, seem to display considerable regularity over time. Does this mean that men and women have inherently different behavioral tendencies?

Newscom

role of biology and gender differences in criminality are akin to the "drunk who knew he hadn't lost his keys under the lamppost, but perversely continued looking there anyway because that's where the light is." In sum, Walsh concludes, "we must realize that gender socialization rests on the solid bedrock of sex-differentiated biology forged by countless thousands of years of contrasting sexual selection pressures."[165]

Evolutionary Neuroandrogenic Theory

In 2010, Kevin M. Beaver, John P. Wright, and Anthony Walsh discovered that the number of sexual partners that men have is associated with criminal involvement.[166] In other words, the greater the number of partners, the higher the likelihood of criminal behavior. The researchers noted, however, that "the question ... is why there is a high degree of

■ **evolutionary perspective** A theoretical approach that (1) seeks to explain behavior with reference to human evolutionary history and (2) recognizes the influence that genes have over human traits.

■ **evolutionary neuroandrogenic (ENA) theory** A perspective that holds that (1) the propensity for crime commission evolved among humans beings as part of the male reproductive strategy, and (2) a particular neurochemistry, which is characteristic of males, increases the probability of criminality among males relative to females.

covariation between criminal involvement and the number of sexual partners."

Utilizing an **evolutionary perspective**—or one that (1) seeks to explain behavior with reference to human evolutionary history[167] and (2) recognizes the influence that genes have over human traits—they came to the conclusion that behavioral traits are "manifestations of multiple genes working independently and synergistically" in response to the environment. They proposed that some of the same genes must be involved in both reproductive activity and criminality. Through an analysis of data from the National Longitudinal Study of Adolescent Health (Add Health), they concluded that differing versions of the dopamine transporter gene known as DAT1 were "related to both a greater number of sexual partners and to increased involvement in antisocial behavior for adult males."

Different versions of the same gene are referred to as *polymorphism*, and the word *allele* (used earlier in this chapter) is used to describe an alternative form of a gene that is located at a given position on a specific chromosome. Men who possessed what is known as the 10R allele were determined to be more likely to have multiple sex partners and to demonstrate greater criminal involvement. Hence, the 10R allele was described as the "risk allele for a number of maladaptive outcomes."

In 2005, Minot State University professor **Lee Ellis** added his **evolutionary neuroandrogenic (ENA) theory** to the growing body of biosocial perspectives.[168] Ellis's theory consists of two propositions: (1) the propensity for crime commission evolved among human beings as part of the male reproductive strategy and (2) a particular neurochemistry, which is characteristic of males, "increases the probability of criminality among males relative to females." In other words, criminality is a crude form of competitive behavior over resources, status, and mating opportunities, and "males have been selected for resource acquisitiveness as a result of female preferences for mates who are successful at resource provisioning."[169] Ellis believes that reproductive strategies have guided human evolution, with human males seeking to produce multiple offspring in order to ensure the survival of their genetic material, while human females developed a much different strategy to achieve the same goal—that is, finding a reproductive partner who could ensure the resources necessary over time for the survival of her and her offspring. Ellis argues that early men learned to engage in what he terms "competitive/victimizing behavior" (or CVB), including that aggression thought necessary to win over a mate, or to forcibly mate with her. CVB, argues Ellis, is largely fueled by the male sex hormones, or androgens (including testosterone

and androsterone). "Androgens," says Ellis, "have the ability to affect the brain in ways that increase the probability of" CVB. In primitive societies, Ellis says, CVB probably took the form of direct physical intimidation and victimization. As society became more sophisticated, however, expressions of CVB took sophisticated "commercial" form.

In 2015, researchers confirmed at least part of Ellis's thesis when they found that exposing the developing fetal brain to high levels of testosterone and other androgens elevated the probability of offending later in life.[170]

Policy Implications of Biological Theories

In 1992, the term *standard social science model* (SSSM) was introduced to the general public by Jerome H. Barkow and his colleagues in the edited volume *The Adapted Mind*.[171] The SSSM—which assumes that human beings come into this world like blank slates and acquire almost all of their values, behavioral patterns, and modes of thought through socialization into their surrounding cultures—was identified as the perspective that had characterized much social scientific thought during the twentieth century. According to Barkow, the SSSM provided the underpinnings for the work of many famous sociologists, social psychologists, and social anthropologists of the 1900s, including anthropologists Margaret Mead and Leslie White and sociologist Ellsworth Faris.

Only in the last decade or two has the SSSM largely given way to broader perspectives that include an examination of the role of biology and genetic influences on human behavior. In a more recent book, *The Blank Slate: The Modern Denial of Human Nature*,[172] MIT cognitive scientist Steven Pinker told readers that today's social scientists still continue to ignore unjustly the biological basis of human behavior, replacing it instead with three myths: (1) the blank slate, (2) the Noble Savage, and (3) the Ghost in the Machine. The blank slate myth (mentioned above) holds that the human mind has no innate traits and that the human personality is fully malleable by society. The Noble Savage myth says that human nature is essentially good; and the Ghost in the Machine myth holds that each person has an individual soul-like quality that allows him or her to make choices that can be completely independent of any biological predispositions. These three myths, according to Pinker, comprise the SSSM of the modern era and have led to misguided social and political policies, but it is only when the

CRIMINAL | PROFILES

Jodi Arias—The Petite Killer

How could a petite, soft-spoken woman who had no record of past violence shoot her former lover in the face, slit his throat from ear to ear, and stab him 27 times?

Jodi Arias first denied any role in the 2008 killing and then confessed, claiming she did it in self-defense. At the end of a four-month trial, however, a jury found her guilty of first-degree murder, deciding the killing was so brutal that it could merit the death penalty.

The victim, Travis Alexander, was a leader of the Mormon Church in the Phoenix area who hid his steamy sexual relationship with Arias even from friends. Arias's trial was attended by many and was punctuated with photos of the couple engaging in several different sex acts; a 30-minute tape of phone sex between them; and photos of them both naked, apparently just moments before the murder was committed.[i]

The prosecution portrayed Arias as an obsessed stalker who went out of control when Alexander wanted to date other women. Before the murder, witnesses said she slashed his tires, looked into his windows, and hacked into his Facebook account.[ii]

However, an examination of Arias's past revealed little evidence of the sex-crazed stalker that seemed to emerge after she met Alexander. She claimed her parents had beaten her, but she had no problems with previous boyfriends, at work, or with friends. She had no arrests, convictions, or other legal issues.

Arias grew up in the small town of Yreka, California. "She was a sweet girl, you know, the kind of girl that you just always wanted to be around," her best friend told the Headline News Network. She "definitely wasn't" promiscuous, she added.[iii]

The obsessive, on-again, off-again relationship between Arias and Alexander ended up in murder. They met in Las Vegas in September 2006 at a conference for Prepaid Legal Services, a nationwide company where they both worked. They were both single and about the same age. In addition to being a company salesperson, Alexander worked as a motivational speaker. Arias had recently discovered the Mormon faith. Two months later, Alexander baptized her into the faith and they had sex afterward.[iv]

Alexander's image as a devout Mormon virgin, which he projected to friends, clashed with the erotic adventures he had with Arias. A friend who lived with Alexander testified he did not know he was having sex, saying it could have led to excommunication from the church. Arias's defense attorney said Arias was "his dirty little secret."[v] The prosecution speculated that Arias took pictures of Alexander in sex acts to blackmail him if he tried to leave her.

The couple carried on a long-distance romance between her home in California and his in Mesa, Arizona. They broke up in June 2007 but continued to see each other for sex. Arias moved to Mesa that summer, waiting tables and cleaning Alexander's home for income, then moved back to California in the spring of 2008.

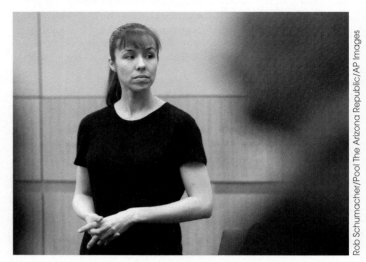

Jodi Arias, convicted in 2013 of the brutal murder of her boyfriend, Travis Alexander. Why did the televised trial draw such large media audiences?

"I want you to understand how evil I think you are," Alexander wrote her in an e-mail a week before he died.[vi] He had invited another woman to go to Cancun, Mexico, with him. In early June, Arias drove to Mesa, arriving at Alexander's home at 4 A.M., and killed him later that day.

Friends found Alexander's mangled body slouched in his shower. Arias's palm print was found in blood at the scene, along with nude photos of them from the day of the killing. When she was later arrested, Arias denied any involvement and blamed it on masked intruders. It was two years later that she first admitted to killing Alexander, saying he became violent after she dropped his new camera, which she was using to take pictures of their sex play.

At the trial, Arias showed little emotion when asked about the killing. The jurors didn't accept Arias's plea of self-defense and wrote to her: "After all the lies you have told, why should we believe you now?" During a later sentencing phase, two sets of jurors were unable to agree upon a death sentence, and Arias is now serving life in prison without the possibility of parole.

The case of Jodi Arias raises some interesting questions. Among them are the following:

1. How could a woman who had no record of past violence commit such a gruesome murder?

2. What aspects of Arias and Alexander's relationship led to the killing?

Notes

i. Tamara Holder, "Four Reasons Why Jodi Arias Should Be Found Guilty of Murder," *FoxNews*, April 2, 2013, http://www.foxnews.com/opinion/2013/04/02/four-reasons-why-jodi-arias-should-be-found-guilty-murder/.

ii. Dale Archer, "Is Jodi Arias a Sociopath?" *Psychology Today*, March 11, 2013, http://www.psychologytoday.com/blog/reading-between-the-headlines/201303/is-jodi-arias-sociopath.

iii. Kat McCullough and Beth Carey, "Arias' Childhood Best Friend: 'She Was a Sweet Girl,'" *HLN*, April 17, 2013, http://www.hlntv.com/article/2013/04/17/jodi-arias-childhood-best-friend-she-was-sweet-girl.

iv. "Timeline of Events in Jodi Arias Murder Case," *ABC News*, May 15, 2013, http://abcnews.go.com/US/wireStory/timeline-events-jodi-arias-murder-case-19185819#.UZPcUXCCMUU.

v. Ryan Owens, "Jodi Arias: Who Is the Admitted Arizona Killer?," *ABC News*, January 8, 2013, http://abcnews.go.com/US/jodi-arias-admitted-arizona-killer/story?id=18159181#.UZPvN3CCMUU.

vi. Brian Skoloff, "Prosecutor Calls Jodi Arias a Manipulative Liar," Associated Press, May 2, 2013, http://news.yahoo.com/prosecutor-calls-jodi-arias-manipulative-liar-195750776.html.

■ **Follow the author's tweets about the latest crime and justice news @schmalleger.**

impact of biology on human behavior is fully recognized that effective social policies—including those aimed at controlling crime—can be developed.

In 1997, in an attempt to bring biological theorizing into the criminological mainstream, Lee Ellis and Anthony Walsh expanded on the theme of genetic predispositions, noting that "in the case of behavior, nearly all of the effects of genes are quite indirect because they are mediated through complex chains of events occurring in the brain. This means that there are almost certainly no genes for something as complex as criminal behavior. Nevertheless, many genes may affect brain functioning in ways that either increase or reduce the chances of individuals learning various complex behavior patterns, including behavior patterns that happen to be so offensive to others that criminal sanctions have been instituted to minimize their recurrence."[173] More than a decade later, Terrie Moffitt, through a meta-analysis of more than 100 studies of genetic influences on antisocial behavior, was able to conclude that "genes influence 40% to 50% of population variation in antisocial behavior."[174]

Critiques of Biological and Biosocial Theories

This chapter discusses a variety of biological and biosocial approaches to explaining crime, including those related to genetics, brain dysfunction, body chemistry, and contemporary understandings of evolutionary theory. Many such perspectives have been criticized because they fail to predict criminality accurately while purporting to understand its causes. For example, if a particular defect in the brain is associated with a greater tendency toward law violation, then why would such theories fail to predict which individuals with those deficits will offend and which will obey the law? The same questions could be asked about genetic attributes and differences in body chemistry. Many of the critiques identified in regard to chemical precursors can be applied to perspectives involving hormones and criminal behavior. Hormones, after all, are chemicals that are made by the body (or are sometimes injected into the bloodstream). As is the case with chemical precursors, hormones apparently don't affect everyone the same way. Not all men with high testosterone levels, for example, are violent or aggressive.

Biosocial theories, for their part, can be criticized in a number of ways.[175] Some critics claim, for example, that biosocial research is fraught with methodological problems because studies in the area have often been based on small, nonrepresentative samples.[176] Also, most research in the area of biosocial theory has been done on offenders who have been placed in clinical treatment settings, making it impossible to tell if study findings are relevant only to convicted criminals in correctional facilities or to the criminal population as a whole. Findings from such studies are difficult to generalize to other settings, and it may be difficult to draw definitive conclusions from small samples that have been studied under unique conditions.

Other critics note that biosocial theories fail to explain regional and temporal variations in crime rates. Biosocial theories, for example, do not seem to explain adequately why one country has higher rates of violent crime than others, or why one region of a city has different rates of property crime. Similarly, biosocial theories cannot totally account for changes in crime rates over time or among different age groups within the same population.

Biological theories that focus on environmental and chemical precursors to crime cannot explain why certain kinds of crime are more likely to occur in certain parts of the country, in particular types of communities, and among members of specific subcultures rather than in others. Such differences imply that much more is at work than chemicals themselves and suggest that cultural differences play a significant role in criminality.

Critics also claim that theories involving chemical precursors cannot account for changes in crime rates over time. Crime rates have trended substantially downward over the past two or three decades, during the same time period that exposure to chemical substances of all types throughout the general population has expanded.

Some biosocial criminologists have been accused of racial and class bias for failing to explain why a disproportionate number of certain kinds of crime are committed by poor people and by racial and ethnic minorities.[177] Critics say that it would be more useful to focus on social settings rather than on biological variables to explain such differences and that characteristics of the social environment—including racism, oppression, discrimination, and economic strain—are more effective at explaining differences in criminality between racial and ethnic groups and social classes. These critics also note that some people may try to use biosocial perspectives to support their own biases and to justify continued social inequality.

SUMMARY

- This chapter began with a discussion of the Human Genome Project (HGP), which was completed in 2003, and recognizes it as corresponding to the start of a new era of biosocial theories in criminology.

- Genetic characteristics and variations in human chromosomes are thought to play an important role in aggression and crime causation. The contemporary study of human genetics builds on a model of gene–environment interaction and employs the concept of heritability to help explain law-breaking behavior. Although contemporary criminologists do not believe that there is one single and identifiable "criminal gene," they do believe that individuals who are genetically predisposed to certain types of behavior may become aggressive or criminal through interaction with the surrounding physical and social environments.

- Some criminologists have explored brain dysfunction and developed the frontal brain hypothesis, which references physical changes in certain parts of the brain to explain criminality. Neuroplasticity, or the ability of the brain to alter its structure and function in response to experience or injury, may be useful in explaining changes in personality and behavior.

- Body chemistry theories say that violent or disruptive behavior can sometimes be linked to poor nutrition, vitamin deficiencies, and other conditions that affect the body. Studies of eating habits, endocrinology, and environmental contaminants have all contributed to advances in understanding such behavior. Criminologists have also studied hormone levels in the blood to explain violent or disruptive behavior by identifying hormonal influences on human cognition and action. Specific hormones studied include neurotransmitters.

- Biosocial criminology sees the interaction between biology and the physical and social environments as key to understanding human behavior, including criminality. It holds that genetic predispositions and their interaction with the surrounding social and physical environments may combine to produce criminality. Biosocial criminologists use the simple formula GxE to highlight the importance of gene–environment interaction in determining behavior. Neuroplasticity, a concept that is central to some biosocial perspectives, may influence and facilitate much of human behavior.

- In the past, biology was often seen as deterministic. The eugenics movement, Nazi extermination programs, and enforced sterilization all resulted from an inaccurate assessment of the power of genes or other physical factors to determine behavior. At the same time, the once widely held belief that the human organism was a blank slate at birth appears now to be a fallacy. A contemporary crime-prevention program needs to be based on modern understandings of the link between biology and crime. A medical perspective could replace the current legalistic interpretation of criminality, leading to the right to treatment for criminal offenders.

- Establishing a workable definition of criminality has been a problem. Few biological studies adequately conceptualize criminality, methodological problems have been found in many studies attempting to evaluate the role of genetics in crime, and results obtained outside the United States may not be applicable within this country. Many criminologists continue to believe that biology provides a context for human behavior, but biological predispositions are overshadowed by the role of volition, mechanisms of human thought, and undeniable influences of socialization and acculturation.

KEY TERMS

allele, 104
biosocial criminology, 121
chromosomes, 102
digit ratio, 120
epigenetics, 105
evolutionary neuroandrogenic (ENA) theory, 125
evolutionary perspective, 125
frontal brain hypothesis, 109
galvanic skin response (GSR), 119
gender ratio problem, 123
gene expression, 105
genes, 102
genetic memory, 106

GxE, 105
heritability, 105
hormone, 115
human genome, 102
hypoglycemia, 111
neuroplasticity, 109
neurotransmitters, 104
prenatal substance exposure, 114
psychobiotics, 114
prefrontal cortex dysfunction, 108
serotonin, 116
sexual selection, 124
testosterone, 115

KEY NAMES

Freda Adler, 123
Kevin M. Beaver, 104
Thomas Bernard, 123
Paul C. Bernhardt, 116
Alan Booth, 115
Han Brunner, 103
Avshalom Caspi, 104
Ellen G. Cohn, 120
Lee Ellis, 125
David Fergusson, 114
Nathalie Fontaine, 105

Richard J. Herrnstein, 121
Terrie E. Moffitt, 104
D. Wayne Osgood, 115
Adrian Raine, 107
H. Hilger Ropers, 103
James Rotton, 120
Stephen Schoenthaler, 112
Darrell J. Steffensmeier, 123
Richard Tremblay, 105
Anthony Walsh, 121
James Q. Wilson, 121

QUESTIONS FOR REVIEW

1. What was the purpose of the Human Genome Project (HGP), and what is its significance for modern biological theories of crime?

2. What role do genetics and heritability play in contemporary explanations for crime?

3. How does brain dysfunction relate to criminality?

4. How do body chemistry theories explain crime?

5. What is biosocial criminology? How is criminality explained from a biosocial perspective?

6. What are the social policy implications of biological and biosocial theories of crime? What modern-day social policies reflect the biological and biosocial approaches to crime causation?

7. What are the shortcomings of biological theories of criminal behavior? Why have many biological approaches to crime causation encountered stiff criticism?

QUESTIONS FOR REFLECTION

1. This text emphasizes the theme of social problems versus individual responsibility. Which perspective is better supported by biosocial theories of crime causation? Why?

2. Past president of the American Society of Criminology C. Ray Jeffery once said: "Open inquiry requires objective consideration of all points of view and an unbiased examination of each for its ability to shed light on the subject under study". Do you agree or disagree with this assertion? Why is it especially relevant to biosocial theorizing in criminology?

3. What is the gender ratio problem in criminology? What traditional explanations had been offered for the problem? Why is the gender ratio problem not a problem from the point of view of biosocial criminology?

Albert Foster Mirrorpix/Newscom

CHAPTER 6

PSYCHOLOGICAL AND PSYCHIATRIC FOUNDATIONS OF CRIMINAL BEHAVIOR

It's How We Think

LEARNING OUTCOMES

After reading this chapter, you should be able to answer the following questions:

- What are the major principles of psychological and psychiatric perspectives on criminal behavior?

- What two major ideas characterized early psychological theories, and what was the difference between them?

- How do personality disturbances explain criminality?

- What are cognitive theories, and what three types of cognitive theories does this chapter discuss?

- What insights into criminal behavior does the psychoanalytic perspective offer?

- How does behavior theory explain the role of rewards and punishments in shaping behavior?

- What are the policy and treatment implications of psychological and psychiatric understandings of criminality?

- How can psychological and psychiatric theories of crime be critiqued?

- What are some assumptions underlying the practice of criminal psychological profiling?

- How does the legal concept of insanity differ from behavioral understandings of the same concept?

■ **forensic psychology**   The application of the science and profession of psychology to questions and issues relating to law and the legal system; also called *criminal psychology*.

■ **criminal psychology**   The application of the science and profession of psychology to questions and issues relating to law and the legal system; also called *forensic psychology*.

Introduction

A number of studies appear to show that most mentally ill people do not commit crimes,[1] and a direct link between mental illness and crime is difficult to demonstrate. Nonetheless, American correctional institutions are filled with persons suffering from psychiatric issues, and many of them never receive the care they need.[2] When some mentally ill people do become violent, however, their crimes can have horrific consequences. Take, for example, the strange case of 61-year-old John Waszynski of Wethersfield, Connecticut.[3] In 2016 Waszynski was found not guilty by reason of insanity in the strangling death of his 86-year-old mother, Krystyna. Waszynski had long been known to residents of his small hometown as "strange." One neighbor told reporters, "Everyone thought he was strange. You just got a creepy feeling from him."[4] Waszynski, who had been diagnosed as a schizophrenic, had been known to wander around his yard naked, and neighbors thought that he lived by himself. After authorities were called by his brother to do a welfare check on Waszynski, they found that he had been living with his mother's decomposing corpse for five or six months after he killed her. Following the "not guilty by reason of insanity" verdict, Waszynski was ordered committed to a state psychiatric hospital.[5]

Mugshots.com

John Waszynski, 61, who was found not guilty by reason of insanity after killing his mother and living with her corpse for five months. What role did Waszynski's mental state likely play in the murder?

Principles of Psychological and Psychiatric Theories

We might ask whether Waszynski was sane at the time he killed his mother; or, more importantly, we might inquire into the nature of insanity itself. What does the term mean, and how is it relevant to criminology? Can we identify features of Waszynski's personality that led to crime commission? If so, might he have been stopped? Questions like these concern all criminologists, but they are especially relevant from a psychological perspective.

Psychological determinants of deviant or criminal behavior are couched in various terms, as *exploitative personality characteristics, poor impulse control, emotional arousal, an immature personality*, and

so forth. Before beginning a discussion of psychological theories, however, it is necessary to provide a brief overview of the terminology used to describe the psychological study of crime and criminality. **Forensic psychology**, one of the fastest-growing subfields of psychology, is the application of the science and profession of psychology to questions and issues relating to law and the legal system.[6] Forensic psychology is sometimes referred to as **criminal psychology**, and forensic psychologists are also called criminal psychologists, correctional psychologists, and police psychologists. Unlike forensic psychologists (who generally hold PhDs), forensic psychiatrists are medical doctors,

> Forensic psychiatry is a branch of psychiatry having to do with the study of crime and criminality.

■ **forensic psychiatry**   A branch of psychiatry having to do with the study of crime and criminality.

■ **personality**   The characteristic patterns of thoughts, feelings, and behaviors that make a person unique, and that tend to remain stable over time. Personality influences an individual's thoughts, behavior, and emotions.

■ **behaviorism**   A psychological perspective that stresses observable behavior and disregards unobservable events that occur in the mind.

■ **conditioning**   A psychological principle that holds that the frequency of any behavior can be increased or decreased through reward, punishment, or association with other stimuli.

■ **psychoanalytic theory**   A perspective developed by psychiatrist Sigmund Freud in the early 1900s that explains the structure of personality and behavior in terms of both conscious and unconscious components and the conflicts between them.

■ **psychopathy**   A personality disorder characterized by antisocial behavior and a failure to feel remorse or guilt.

■ **schizophrenia**   A serious mental illness that distorts the way a person thinks, feels, and behaves. Primary features of schizophrenia include the inability to distinguish between real and imagined experiences and the inability to think logically.

FIGURE 6-1 | **Assumptions of Psychological and Psychiatric Theories of Crime Causation**

Source: Schmalleger, Frank, *Criminology*. Printed and Electronically reproduced by permission of Pearson Education, Inc., Upper Saddle River, New Jersey.

and **forensic psychiatry** is a medical subspecialty that applies psychiatry to the needs of crime prevention and solution, criminal rehabilitation, and issues of criminal law.[7] The assumptions that characterize psychological and psychiatric theories of crime causation are shown in Figure 6-1.

History of Psychological Theories

Two major ideas characterized early psychological theories: **personality** and **behaviorism**. Personality theory built on the burgeoning area of cognitive science, including personality disturbances, the process of moral development, and diseases of the mind, whereas behaviorism (also known as *behavior theory*) examined social learning with an emphasis on behavioral **conditioning**. Together, these two areas formed the early foundation of psychological criminology. This chapter discusses theories of cognitive science and behaviorism as they relate to criminality. A separate discussion of **psychoanalytic theory**, an outgrowth of personality theory, rounds out this chapter.

Personality Disturbances

Psychologists working in the first half of the twentieth century adapted the disease model—a paradigm that had worked so well in the field of medicine—in an effort to cure mental and emotional problems. Consequently, early cognitive perspectives in psychology were couched in terms of mental disease, personality disorder, and **psychopathy**.

Psychologists and psychiatrists today distinguish between the terms *psychopathy* and *psychopathology*. In the psychological literature, psychopathology "refers to any sort of psychological disorder that causes distress either for the individual or for those in the individual's life."[8] Today, depression, **schizophrenia**,

■ **psychopath**   An individual who has a personality disorder, especially one manifested in aggressively antisocial behavior, and who is lacking in empathy. Psychopaths are thought to have been born that way.

attention deficit hyperactivity disorder, alcoholism, and bulimia are all considered forms of psychopathology, or mental disease. One of the most serious of mental diseases is psychopathy, "a very specific and distinctive type of psychopathology."[9]

The Psychopath

Psychopathy is a personality disorder characterized by antisocial behavior and by a lack of sympathy, empathy, and embarrassment. Psychopaths, many of whom are known as effective manipulators, and who clearly understand the motivations of others, are said to dissociate emotionally from their actions and lack empathy or sensitivity toward others.

The concept of psychopathy, called "one of the most durable, resilient and influential of all criminological ideas,"[10] may have evolved from the work of French physician Philippe Pinel (1745–1826), who described a form of "insanity without delirium." The concept is summarized in the words of Nolan D. C. Lewis, who wrote that "the criminal, like other people, has lived a life of instinctive drives, of desires, of wishes, of feelings, but one in which his intellect has apparently functioned less effectually as a brake upon certain trends. His constitutional makeup deviates toward the abnormal, leading him into conflicts with the laws of society and its cultural patterns."[11]

The term *psychopathy* comes from the Greek words *psyche* (meaning "soul" or "mind") and *pathos* (meaning "suffering" or "illness"). The word, which appears to have been coined by German neurologist Richard von Krafft-Ebing (1840–1902),[12] made its way into English psychiatric literature through the writings of Polish-born American psychiatrist Bernard H. Glueck (1884–1972)[13] and British psychiatrist William Healy (1869–1963).[14]

The **psychopath** has been historically viewed as perversely cruel, often without thought or feeling for his or her victims.[15] By World War II, the role of the psychopathic personality in crime causation had become central to psychological theorizing. The concept of a psychopathic personality, which by its very definition is antisocial, was fully developed by neuropsychiatrist **Hervey M. Cleckley** in his 1941 book *The Mask of Sanity*[16]—a work that had considerable impact on the field of psychology. Cleckley described the psychopath as a "moral idiot," or as one who does not feel empathy for others, even though that person may be fully aware of what is happening around him or her. The central defining characteristic of a psychopath is described as a "poverty of affect," or the inability to accurately imagine how others think and feel. Therefore, it becomes possible for a psychopath to inflict pain and engage in cruelty without appreciation for the victim's suffering. Charles Manson, for example, whom some regarded as a psychopath, once told a television reporter,

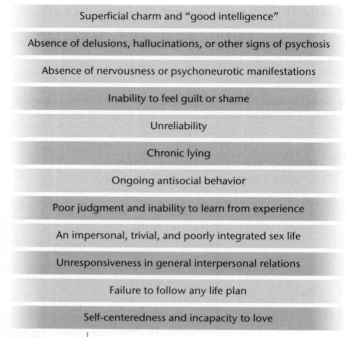

- Superficial charm and "good intelligence"
- Absence of delusions, hallucinations, or other signs of psychosis
- Absence of nervousness or psychoneurotic manifestations
- Inability to feel guilt or shame
- Unreliability
- Chronic lying
- Ongoing antisocial behavior
- Poor judgment and inability to learn from experience
- An impersonal, trivial, and poorly integrated sex life
- Unresponsiveness in general interpersonal relations
- Failure to follow any life plan
- Self-centeredness and incapacity to love

FIGURE 6-2 | **Selected Characteristics of the Psychopathic Personality**

Source: Schmalleger, Frank, *Criminology*. Printed and Electronically reproduced by permission of Pearson Education, Inc., Upper Saddle River, New Jersey.

"I could take this book and beat you to death with it, and I wouldn't feel a thing. It'd be just like walking to the drugstore."[17]

In *The Mask of Sanity*, Cleckley describes numerous characteristics of the psychopathic personality, some of which are shown in Figure 6-2. For Cleckley, "psychopathy was defined by a constellation of dysfunctional psychological processes as opposed to specific behavioral manifestations."[18] Cleckley noted that in cases he had observed, the behavioral manifestations of psychopathy varied with the person's age, gender, and socioeconomic status.

Even though psychopaths have a seriously flawed personality, they can easily fool others into trusting them—hence the title of Cleckley's book. According to Cleckley, indicators of psychopathy appear early in life, often in the teenage years. They include lying, fighting, stealing, and vandalizing. Even earlier signs may be found, according to some authors, in bedwetting, cruelty to animals, sleepwalking, and fire setting.[19] Others have described psychopaths as "individuals who display impulsiveness, callousness, insincerity, pathological lying and deception, egocentricity, poor judgment, an impersonal sex life, and an unstable life plan."[20]

Cleckley believed that there were two kinds of psychopaths: primary and secondary. In later work, psychologist David

■ **sociopath**   An individual who has a personality disorder, especially one manifested in aggressively antisocial behavior, and who is lacking in empathy. Also called "secondary psycohpaths," sociopaths may have been born "normal," but personal experiences they have early in life cause them to develop psychopathic characteristics.

Lykken refined those terms, saying that *primary psychopaths* are somehow neurologically different from other people, and that makes them behave the way they do.[21] Hence, primary psychopaths are born with psychopathic personalities, whereas *secondary psychopaths* (sometimes called **sociopaths**) are born with a "normal" personality, but personal experiences (frequently physical and emotional abuse or trauma) when they are young cause them to develop psychopathic characteristics.

Other types of psychopaths have also been identified, including the *charismatic psychopath* and the *distempered psychopath*. Charismatic psychopaths are charming and attractive, but also habitual liars. They manipulate others to achieve their personal goals, without considering others' feelings. Distempered psychopaths are easily offended and fly into rages even at slight provocations. They have been characterized as having strong urges, including sexual drives, that often lead to addiction.

A definitive modern measure of psychopathy can be found in the Psychopathy Checklist (PCL), developed by Robert Hare (sometimes called the Hare Psychopathy Checklist).[22] The checklist, when used by qualified experts employing information from subject interviews and official records, produces a series of ratings assessing degree of psychopathy. The checklist uses two kinds of indicators: affective and interpersonal traits (glibness, emotional detachment, egocentricity, superficial charm, shallow affect) and traits associated with a chronic unstable and antisocial lifestyle (irresponsibility, impulsivity, criminality, proneness to boredom).[23] Hence, psychopathy has both emotional and behavioral components. A number of studies have demonstrated that the presence of callous unemotional traits, when present in adolescence, reliably predicts later antisocial behaviors.[24]

One study of eight Canadian maximum-security male prisoners classified as psychopaths according to the PCL found that the men were not only impaired emotionally but also unable to efficiently process abstract words, perform abstract categorization tasks, understand metaphors, and process emotionally weighted words and speech.[25] During a test on abstract concepts, the men's brains were scanned using functional magnetic resonance imaging (fMRI), and scans showed that a section of each of their brains did not activate as it should have. The researchers concluded that their findings "support the hypothesis that there is an abnormality in the function of the right anterior superior temporal gyrus in psychopathy."[26] Other studies in neurobiology have linked this part of the brain with abstract problem solving and insight.[27] Deficiencies in this part of the brain may also be associated with autism and the development of childhood schizophrenia.[28]

Some have questioned whether psychopaths merely lack empathy or really don't know the difference between right and wrong. Recent research seems to show that the ability to tell right from wrong is something that human beings are born with, that the human brain is hard-wired to make moral distinctions,

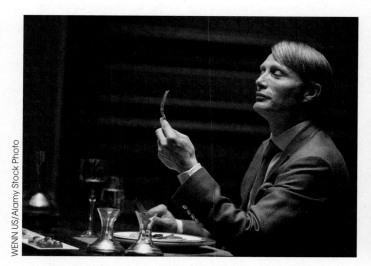

WENN US/Alamy Stock Photo

Mads Mikkelsen as Dr. Hannibal Lecter in the NBC-TV series *Hannibal*. What are the characteristics of a psychopath?

and that the same distinctions tend to be made across cultures.[29] You can test your own sense of right and wrong by taking the Moral Sense Test (MST) online. The MST, which researchers are using to detail the nature of moral psychology, is accessible through Harvard University's Cognitive Evolution Laboratory online at **http://www.moralsensetest.com**.

Traditionally, psychopathology has been regarded as difficult or impossible to treat. But a recent study of adolescent psychopaths found that "youth with psychopathic features who received intensive treatment" in sanction-based programs that held youth accountable for their actions "had significantly lower rates of violent recidivism and a longer time to rearrest for violent behavior" than those who received treatment in a typical juvenile correctional facility.[30] In 2007, the United Kingdom launched an unprecedented treatment and research program focused on "Dangerous People with Severe Personality Disorder" (DPSPD).[31] Although not everyone placed in the program had been diagnosed as a psychopath, in order to be eligible for the program participants had to be diagnosed with a severe personality disorder, and there had to be a demonstrable link between that disorder and the risk of violent offending. Some stated that the program "holds the best chance yet of showing whether violent psychopaths can be reformed." Learn more about the concept of the psychopath as a clinical construct by visiting the Society for Research in Psychopathology via **http://www .psychopathology.org**. Read about the issues involved in identifying criminal psychopaths via **http://www.csc-scc.gc.ca/ publications/forum/e012/e012l-eng.shtml** and see a detailed yet concise FBI discussion of the psychopath at **http:// justicestudies.com/pubs/FBI_Psychopathy.pdf**.

■ **antisocial personality**   An individual who is unsocialized and whose behavior pattern brings him or her into repeated conflict with society.

■ **antisocial personality disorder (ASPD)**   A psychological condition exhibited by individuals who are basically unsocialized and whose behavior pattern brings them repeatedly into conflict with society.

■ **electroencephalogram (EEG)**   The electrical measurement of brain wave activity.

Antisocial Personality Disorder

In recent years, the terms *sociopath* and *psychopath* have fallen into disfavor. In an attempt to identify sociopathic individuals, some psychologists have come to place greater emphasis on the type of behavior exhibited rather than on identifiable personality traits. By 1968, the American Psychiatric Association's (APA's) *Diagnostic and Statistical Manual of Mental Disorders* (DSM) had completely discontinued use of the words *sociopath* and *psychopath*, replacing them with the terms *antisocial personality* and *asocial personality*.[32] In that year, the APA manual changed its description of **antisocial personality** types to "individuals who are basically unsocialized and whose behavior pattern brings them repeatedly into conflicts with society. They are incapable of significant loyalty to individuals, groups, or social values. They are grossly selfish, callous, irresponsible, impulsive, and unable to feel guilt or to learn from experience and punishment. Frustration tolerance is low. They tend to blame others or offer plausible rationalization for their behavior."[33] In most cases, individuals exhibiting an antisocial personality through their behavioral patterns are said to be suffering from **antisocial personality disorder** (sometimes referred to in clinical circles as APD, ASPD, or ANPD). Although the incidence of ASPD is estimated at 2% in the general population, studies have shown that as many as 60% of male prisoner populations may be suffering from the condition.[34]

> **Individuals exhibiting an antisocial personality are said to be suffering from antisocial personality disorder.**

The DSM-IV-TR (text revision) divides personality disorders into three behavioral clusters: A, B, and C. Cluster A personality disorders are those that encompass "odd or eccentric behavior"; Cluster B disorders show "dramatic, emotional, or erratic behavior"; and Cluster C disorders center on "anxious, fearful behavior." Psychologists who work with criminal offenders typically focus on Cluster B disorders, which include what the DSM-IV-TR calls narcissistic, borderline, antisocial, and histrionic personality disorders. In addition, the DSM-IV-TR diagnosis of oppositional defiant disorder (ODD) and conduct disorder (CD) are thought applicable to criminals. However, the American Psychiatric Association does not consider ODD and CD to be personality disorders, even though they show strong continuity and often lead to an adult diagnosis of antisocial personality disorder. Nonetheless, ODD and CD are often considered prerequisites for an adult diagnosis of antisocial personality disorder.[35]

Individuals exhibiting Cluster B disorders can also be diagnosed as having "borderline personality disorder." Some studies have found that borderline patients are more likely to engage in aggressive acts against other people than those diagnosed with only antisocial personality disorder. The most likely explanation is that borderline personalities demonstrate elevated impulsivity.[36]

The causes of ASPD are unclear. Somatogenic causes (those based on physiological features) are said to include a malfunctioning of the central nervous system, which is characterized by a low state of arousal driving the sufferer to seek excitement, and brain abnormalities, which may have been present since birth. Some studies show that an **electroencephalogram (EEG)** taken of an individual diagnosed as having ASPD is frequently abnormal, reflecting "a malfunction of some inhibitory mechanisms" that makes it unlikely that someone characterized by ASPD will "learn to inhibit behavior that is likely to lead to punishment."[37] It is difficult, however, to diagnose ASPD through physiological measurements because similar EEG patterns show up in patients with other types of disorders. Psychogenic causes (those rooted in early interpersonal experiences) include inability to form attachments to parents or other caregivers early in life, sudden separation from the mother during the first six months of life, and other forms of insecurity during the first few years of life. In short, a lack of love or the sensed inability to unconditionally depend upon one central loving figure (typically the mother in most psychological literature) immediately following birth is often posited as a major psychogenic factor contributing to the development of ASPD.

Most studies of ASPD have involved male subjects. Only rarely have researchers focused on women with antisocial personalities, and it is believed that only a small proportion of those afflicted with ASPD are women.[38] What little research there is suggests that females with ASPD possess many of the same definitive characteristics as their male counterparts, and that they assume their antisocial roles at similarly early ages.[39] The lifestyles of antisocial females, however, appear to include sexual misconduct and abnormally high levels of sexual activity, but

■ **traits (psychological)**   Stable personality patterns that tend to endure throughout the life course and across social and cultural contexts.

■ **Five Factor Model**   A psychological perspective that builds on the Big Five core traits of personality.

such research can be misleading because the cultural expectations of female sexual behavior inherent in early studies may not always have been in keeping with reality—that is, early researchers may have had so little accurate information about female sexual activity that the behavior of women judged to possess antisocial personalities may have actually been far closer to the norm than originally believed.

Trait Theory

In 1964, **Hans J. Eysenck**, a British psychologist, published *Crime and Personality*, a book in which he explained crime as the result of fundamental personality characteristics, or **traits**, which he believed are largely inherited.[40] Psychological traits are stable personality patterns that tend to endure throughout the life course and across social and cultural contexts. They include behavioral, cognitive, and affective predispositions to respond to a given situation in a particular way. According to trait theory, as an individual grows older or moves from one place to another, his or her personality remains largely intact—defined by the traits that comprise it. Trait theory links personality (and associated traits) to behavior and holds that it is an individual's personality, combined with his or her intelligence and natural abilities,[41] that determines his or her behavior in a given situation.[42]

Eysenck believed that the degree to which just three universal supertraits are present in an individual accounts for his or her unique personality. He termed these supertraits (1) introversion/extraversion, (2) neuroticism/emotional stability, and (3) psychoticism. Eysenck thought that people who score high on extraversion, neuroticism, or psychoticism are not easily conditioned or socialized, and thus commit more crime in adulthood. Like many other psychologists, he accepted the fact that personality holds steady throughout much of life, but stressed that it is largely determined by genetics. He argued that what we call *personality* is a reflection of variations in the component operating systems of the major behavioral pathways of the brain.

In support of his idea of the genetic basis of personality, Eysenck pointed to twin studies showing that identical twins display strikingly similar behavioral tendencies, whereas fraternal twins demonstrate far less likelihood of similar behaviors. Eysenck also argued that psychological conditioning occurs more rapidly in some people than in others because of biological differences, and that antisocial individuals are difficult to

condition (or to socialize) because of underlying genetic characteristics. He believed that up to two-thirds of all "behavioral variance" could be strongly attributed to genetics.[43]

Of Eysenck's three personality dimensions, one in particular—psychoticism—was thought to be closely correlated with criminality at all stages.[44] According to Eysenck, psychoticism is defined by such characteristics as lack of empathy, creativeness, tough-mindedness, and antisociability. Extroverts, Eysenck's second personality group that was associated with criminality, are described as carefree, dominant, and venturesome, operating with high levels of energy. "The typical extrovert," Eysenck wrote, "is sociable, likes parties, has many friends, needs to have people to talk to, and does not like reading or studying by himself."[45] Neuroticism, the third of the personality characteristics Eysenck described, is said to be typical of people who are irrational, shy, moody, and emotional.

According to Eysenck, psychotics are the most likely to be criminal because they combine high degrees of emotionalism with similarly high levels of extroversion; individuals with such characteristics are especially difficult to socialize and to train and do not respond well to the external environment. Eysenck cited many studies in which children and others who harbored characteristics of psychoticism performed poorly on conditioning tests designed to measure how quickly they would respond appropriately to external stimuli. Because conscience is fundamentally a conditioned reflex, Eysenck said, an individual who does not take well to conditioning will not fully develop a conscience and will continue to exhibit the asocial behavioral traits of a very young child. In essence, criminality can be seen as a personality type characterized by self-centeredness, indifference to the suffering and needs of others, impulsiveness, and low self-control—which, taken together, lead to law-violating behavior.

Today, trait theories of personality have expanded beyond Eysneck's basic three-trait model to encompass five basic traits: (1) openness to experience, (2) extraversion, (3) conscientiousness, (4) neuroticism, and (5) agreeableness. People are said to possess more or less of any one trait, and the combination of traits and the degree to which they are characteristic of an individual define that person's personality. Psychologists call these traits the *Big Five*, and they form the basis of the **Five Factor Model** of psychology (see Figure 6-3). According to many psychologists, "the Big Five are strongly genetically influenced, and the genetic factor structure of the Big Five appears to be invariant across European, North American, and East Asian samples,"[46] which suggests that personality traits, to a

■ **moral development theory**   A perspective on crime causation holding that individuals become criminal when they have not successfully completed their intellectual development from child- to adulthood.

FIGURE 6-3 | **The Big Five Personality Dimensions**

greater or lesser degree, are universally shared by all peoples. Conscientiousness, for example, is related to self-control and is unlikely to be associated with criminality.

Cognitive Theories

Theories of cognition form a third subarea of personality theory. Cognitive approaches are learning theories that examine thought processes and seek to explain how people: (1) learn to solve problems, including those that involve questions of value and morality, and (2) perceive and interpret the social environment. Cognitive theory has a number of branches, three of which are discussed here. The first focuses on moral and intellectual development, while the second is based on information processing theory. The third branch, suggests that experienced offenders share a criminal mind set—or world view. another that examines how people process information. Each of these three perspectives will now be explored.

Moral Development Theory

The first branch of cognitive theory, **moral development theory**, holds that individuals become criminal when they have not successfully completed their intellectual development from child- to adulthood. One of the first comprehensive maps of human psychological development was created by Swiss developmental psychologist **Jean Piaget**. Piaget believed that human thinking and intellectual processes went through a number of biopsychological stages of development—something that

Piaget saw as a natural extension of evolutionary adaptation. Just as a species adapts to its environment, Piaget believed, individual human beings respond to their environment by developing intellectually. He posited four stages of human intellectual development:[47]

1. The *sensory-motor stage*, which lasts from birth to age two. During this stage, children are extremely egocentric (or focused on themselves and their personal experiences) and learn about the world through the physical senses and the movement of their bodies.

2. The *preoperational stage*, which lasts from ages two to seven. During this stage, children are not able to reason well or to use logical thinking, but egocentrism begins to weaken, and motor skills are acquired. Piaget said that this stage was dominated by magical thinking, explaining why beliefs in Santa Claus, the Easter Bunny, and similar mythical characters are typical among younger children.

3. The *concrete operational stage*, which runs from ages 7 to 11. In this stage, children start to develop the ability to reason and to think logically, although they are very concrete in their thinking, and often require practical aids such as buttons or coins to aid in counting and arithmetic. By the time children reach the end of this stage, they are no longer egocentric and are able to appreciate the needs and feelings of others.

4. The *formal operational stage*, which lasts from ages 11 to 16 and continues into adulthood. During this stage, the developing adolescent acquires abstract reasoning skills and learns how to think and reason without the need for external aids.

Central to Piaget's perspective on moral development is the idea that as children grow and learn, they become able to reflect on their own actions—acquiring a sense of the unspoken rules that govern human interaction. According to Piaget, children apply their burgeoning ability to reflect and use it to examine themselves; in the process, they learn right from wrong. In his words, "the child is someone who constructs his own moral world view, who forms ideas about right and wrong, and fair and unfair, that are not the direct product of adult teaching and that are often maintained in the face of adult wishes to the contrary."[48]

Once a child has moved through the four developmental stages, said Piaget, he or she would have moved from moral absolutism (in which the child unquestioningly accepts the dictates of his or her parents or caregivers) to moral relativism (where actions are seen as right or wrong depending on the circumstances in which they are undertaken).

Following Piaget, **Lawrence Kohlberg** offered an expanded cognitive structural theory of morality in a six-stage

■ **cognitive information-processing theory (CIP)**
A psychological perspective that involves the study of human perceptions, information processing, and decision making.
■ **scripts**   Generalized knowledge about specific types of situations that is stored in the mind.

typology (Figure 6-4).[49] In Kohlberg's first stage, people only obey the law because they are afraid of being punished if they don't. By the final, or sixth, stage, however, obedience to the law becomes an obligation that is willingly assumed, and people chose not to violate the law because they value the principle of fairness and believe in interpersonal justice. Those who have evolved to higher stages of moral reasoning are unlikely to commit crimes because they appreciate not only their own needs, but also the needs and interests of others as well.

Kohlberg argued that a preference for higher levels of moral thinking must be universal in human beings, although not necessarily inborn. He believed that people who have successfully moved through all stages of moral development have developed the ability to objectively evaluate opinions and either accept them or reject them without irrationally clinging to their own beliefs. Kohlberg posited that people may turn to crime if they are unsuccessful at making the normal transition between developmental stages of moral reasoning.

Research based on Kohlberg's work has demonstrated that offenders have less ability in making moral judgments than do noncriminals, even when they have similar backgrounds and experiences. In 2015, for example, researchers associated with the Pathways to Desistance project at the Office of Juvenile Justice and Delinquency Prevention found that youths experience protracted maturation, into their mid-twenties, of brain systems responsible for self-regulation. Researchers concluded that "Youth whose antisocial behavior persisted into early adulthood were found to have lower levels of psychosocial maturity in adolescence and deficits in their development of maturity (i.e., arrested development) compared with other antisocial youth."[50]

Cognitive Information-Processing Theory

A second major area of cognitive theory applicable to criminology is **cognitive information-processing theory (CIP)**. CIP involves the study of human perceptions, information processing, and decision-making. Psychological research suggests that people make decisions by engaging in a series of complex thought processes, or steps. In the first step, they encode and interpret the information they are presented with or the experiences they

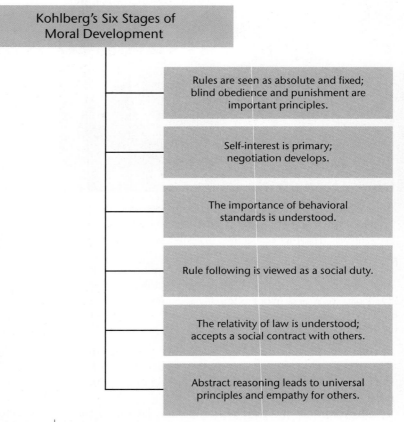

FIGURE 6-4 | **Kohlberg's Six Stages of Moral Development**

have. In the next stage, they search for an appropriate response; in the third stage, they act on their decision.[51]

Some information-processing theorists believe that violent individuals may be using information incorrectly when making decisions. Violence-prone individuals, for example, may see people as more aggressive or threatening than they actually are. Such a view may result in violence even at the slightest provocation. Supportive research suggests that some people engage in violent attacks on others because they believe that they are actually defending themselves, even in the face of misperceived threat.[52] Because of the way that some people process information, they are unable to recognize the harm they are doing to others.[53]

Script Theory

In the late 1970s, **Roger C. Schank** and **Robert P. Abelson** of Yale University developed script theory in order to explain the understanding process that occurs during a situation or event.[54] **Scripts** refer to generalized knowledge about specific types of situations that is stored in the mind. More formally,

Anders Behring Breivik clenches his fist as he arrives in the courtroom for the first day of his trial in Oslo, Norway, April 16, 2012. Breivik, a militant anti-Islamic extremist, was convicted of killing 77 people in Norway and was given a 21-year prison sentence by an Oslo court. Breivik claimed that he acted in self-defense and said that his victims were traitors for embracing multiculturalism. How might moral development theory apply to Breivik?

Schank and Abelson described a script as "a predetermined, stereotyped sequence of actions that define a well-known situation." Script theory is an offshoot of cognitive information processing theory.

People use ready-made scripts in everyday life to anticipate an appropriate sequence of events in a given context. We build scripts in our minds to allow for a number of different roles for those actors (others than ourselves) whose presence is anticipated to play out in the script, and we allow for possible variations in the physical scene and in the progression of events. In this sense, scripts are like stories that we use to structure our expectations of and reactions to circumstances that we expect to typically encounter. Take, for example, the internal script that we might use for restaurant dining. We know that when we arrive at a restaurant we should check with the host or hostess to see if a table is available. We expect that he or she will take us to our table and that a server will arrive soon after we are seated to present us with a menu and to take our drink order. We have similar expectations as to what will occur as our dinner progresses, including the eventual arrival of the check or bill, and the amount or percentage of a tip to be left at the completion of the evening. Because most events play out according to the scripts that we have in mind, things typically go smoothly. Sometimes, however, we can be surprised and find ourselves forced to innovate. In our restaurant example, we might

unexpectedly be served the wrong meal, or (worse) the server might trip and spill food onto us. Unless we are surprised, however, things generally go according to plan and events fit with previous experiences we have had involving the same kind of activity.

According to Helen Gavin and David Hockey, two British criminologists writing in 2010, "scripts are used to guide behavior because the script provides the holder with a set of expectations about what will happen during the unfolding of an event, thus offering a way of predicting the outcome and aid[ing] the individual to act accordingly."[55] Gavin and Hockey recognize that people develop scripts based on the learning opportunities and experiences that are presented to them within their social environment. The idea is similar to that involved in role-playing, whereby children engage in role play as a kind of practice for the adult roles they will assume later in life.

The applicability of scripts to criminal behavior can be seen in the fact that career offenders routinely develop scripts to guide them through criminal activity. Gavin and Hockey say that these particular kinds of scripts "consist of a goal aim, a criminal belief system, a criminally motivated perception, and a self-serving set of distorted cognitions that protect the individual's low self-esteem." Criminals use scripts in their approach to crime commission, much of which becomes routine over time. Consequently, criminal motivations and drives underpin criminal scripts.

In their 2010 study of criminal scripts, Gavin and Hockey detailed the scripts of career offenders and found that they could "be acquired through.... various relevant psychological processes,"[56] along with other more conservative scripts that most people use in their daily lives. Moreover, they concluded that criminal scripts help to form a criminal identity once they have been internalized.

The Criminal Mind-Set

The third branch of cognitive theory focuses on the world view that often characterizes established criminal personalities. In 1970, **Stanton E. Samenow**, a young clinical psychologist, began working with psychiatrist **Samuel Yochelson** in the Program for the Investigation of Criminal Behavior at St. Elizabeth's Hospital, a large federal psychiatric facility in Washington, D.C. Yochelson had abandoned a lucrative psychiatric practice in New York and moved to Washington to direct the criminal behavior research project, which studied and treated serious criminal offenders. After Samenow joined the program, he and Yochelson began to realize that many of the patients they were seeing "were in conflict with society [and] not suffering from internal psychological conflicts."[57]

The two came to believe that criminals make entirely different assumptions about living and behaving than noncriminals do because of ingrained and pervasive errors of thinking. Those errors, combined with other cognitive features, form a criminal world view.

After more than six years of working together, Yochelson and Samenow published a three-volume series, *The Criminal Personality*, in which they wrote that many offenders share an identifiable mind-set that is largely immune to environmental influences and that, for the most part, develops independently of social experience.[58]

In 1984, Samenow published the book *Inside the Criminal Mind*, which was republished 20 years later in a revised edition. The criminal personality, Samenow claims, develops early in childhood and consists of ways of thinking that are characteristic of many types of criminals, but are not shared by noncriminals. In the theoretical model that Samenow developed, he focuses largely on the criminal mind-set and

PUTTING CRIMINOLOGY TO WORK—Implementing Evidence-Based Policy

To make a difference in the real world, criminological theories must first be tested and evaluated. Once evidence has been developed that theory-based practices work, then programs based on them can be implemented to reduce or prevent crime, or to help make victims' lives better. One federal initiative, CrimeSolutions.Gov, strives to evaluate the effectiveness of theory-based practices, and then communicates its findings via the Web. Some of the most effective and promising programs are highlighted in boxes such as this one that appear throughout the text.

PROGRAM: Infant—Parent Psychotherapy

EVIDENCE RATINGS FOR OUTCOMES: Promising

PROFILE

Infant—parent psychotherapy (IPP) is a relationship-based treatment program for parents and infants that aims to improve the parent–child relationship in the wake of incidences of domestic violence and trauma, including maltreatment and neglect of the child. To prevent compromised development that can lead to later maladaptation and psychopathology, IPP seeks to intervene in the early life course of maltreated infants. It does this by examining the insecurities that have developed in maltreating parents from negative experiences during their own childhoods.

During treatment, a therapist meets weekly with mothers and their young children. Sessions are conducted in the home, usually over the course of a year. The therapy sessions are designed to be supportive and nondirective, and include developmental guidance on the basis of concerns from the mothers. The therapeutic relationship that is established between the therapist and the mother provides the mother with a corrective emotional experience, which allows her to differentiate current from past relationships and to form positive representations of herself and of herself in relationship to others, especially her child.

Relevant Theory: Psychotherapy, developmental psychology, attachment theory

IPP is an adaptation of child—parent psychotherapy (CPP), which is a treatment for parents and young children that helps restore normal developmental functioning in the wake of domestic violence and trauma. Designed to use with mothers of maltreated infants, IPP is based on attachment theory but combines and integrates principles from multiple theories (developmental, trauma, social-learning, psychodynamic, and cognitive-behavioral theories) to improve the relationship and attachment between the mother and her infant. The IPP model is guided by the idea that problems in the parent—infant relationship are not just the result of deficits in parenting knowledge and skills. Rather, the problems stem from insecurities that developed from the mother's own experiences in childhood. The infant may remind the mother of negative childhood relationship experiences; in the process, a mother's unresolved feelings can be projected onto her infant, resulting in insensitive care and maltreatment.

Evidence-Based Review

These sources were used in the development of the program profile:

Study 1

Dante Cicchetti, Fred A. Rogosch, and Sheree L. Toth, "Fostering Secure Attachment in Infants in Maltreating Families through Preventive Interventions," *Development and Psychopathology*, Vol. 18 (2006), pp. 623–649.

Source: Adapted from https://www.crimesolutions.gov/ProgramDetails.aspx? ID=106

Notes: Putting Criminology to Work features are based on information published online by the National Institute of Justice's (NIJ) Crime Solutions Website. The program ratings shown are those provided by NIJ.

■ **psychiatric criminology**   A theory that is derived from the medical sciences (including neurology) and that, like other psychological theories, focuses on the individual as the unit of analysis. Psychiatric theories form the basis of psychiatric criminology.

■ **psychoanalysis**   The theory of human psychology founded by Sigmund Freud on the concepts of the unconscious, resistance, repression, sexuality, and the Oedipus complex.

notes that criminals think differently than do noncriminals. Characteristics of the criminal mind-set include anger as a way of life, a focus on excitement without any real consideration of the cost to others, a lack of any feelings of obligation to others, lack of empathy, and prejudgment with which offenders approach most situations. The mind-set of a criminal is not "caused" by poverty, mental illness, or social conditions, Samenow argued, but rather by the need for excitement. It manifests, Samenow said, through personal choices made by offenders.

Although offenders come from a diversity of backgrounds, and although they engage in many different patterns of criminal behavior, Samenow argued that almost all criminal offenders are alike in the way they think. "A gun-toting, uneducated criminal off the streets of Southeast Washington, D.C., and a crooked Georgetown business executive are extremely similar in their view of themselves and the world," he wrote. The difference between a person with a criminal worldview and one with a conformist worldview is so different, said Samenow, that "it's as though the criminal were a different breed."

Samenow wrote that "the criminal chooses crime; he chooses to reject society long before society rejects him." Seen this way, crime resides within the person, Samenow said, and is "caused" by the way the individual thinks, not by his or her environment.[59] Criminal offenders are driven by excitement and self-interest, Samenow believed, and he suggested that if certain forms of criminal behavior were legalized they would lose their excitement, causing people committed to a life of law violations to engage in some other form of forbidden behavior. "No matter how many victims he has and how much damage he does," Samenow argues, "the criminal has little, if any, remorse and continues to regard himself as a good person."

Samenow believed that "behavior follows in the wake of thought,"[60] so the only way to rehabilitate an offender, he said, is to force the individual to see him- or herself realistically and develop responsible patterns of thought. Changed thoughts will lead to a reassessment of the criminal worldview and, hopefully, to positive behavioral change. Writing in 1995, Glenn D. Walters developed a psychological assessment technique based on Yochelson and Samenow's theory. Walters's technique, known as the Psychological Inventory of Criminal Thinking Scales (PICTS), attempted to measure criminal thinking styles. Walters suggested that PICTS scores could be used to guide offender treatment and to set targets for change in order to reduce recidivism.[61]

The Psychoanalytic Perspective—Criminal Behavior as Maladaptation

Psychiatric criminology (also called *forensic psychiatry*) envisions a complex set of drives and motives operating from hidden recesses deep within the personality to determine behavior.

> Psychiatric criminology envisions a complex set of drives and motives operating from hidden recesses deep within the personality to determine behavior.

Perhaps the best-known psychiatrist of all time is **Sigmund Freud** (1856–1939). Freud coined the term **psychoanalysis** in 1896 and based an entire theory of human behavior on it.

Freud said nothing about criminal behavior, and it wasn't until later that other psychoanalysts began to apply concepts that Freud had developed to the study of criminal behavior. From the point of view of psychoanalysis, criminal behavior is maladaptive, or

Sigmund Freud (1856–1939) in the office of his Vienna home, circa 1930. How have Freud's theories influenced contemporary criminology?

■ **neurosis**   A functional disorder of the mind or of the emotions involving anxiety, phobias, or other abnormal behavior.

■ **psychosis**   A form of mental illness in which sufferers are said to be out of touch with reality.

■ **sublimation**   The psychological process whereby one aspect of consciousness comes to be symbolically substituted for another.

■ **psychotherapy**   A form of psychiatric treatment based on psychoanalytical principles and techniques.

■ **id**   The aspect of the personality from which drives, wishes, urges, and desires emanate. More formally, this division of the psyche is associated with instinctual impulses and demands for immediate satisfaction of primitive needs.

■ **ego**   The reality-testing part of the personality; also called the *reality principle*. More formally, this personality component is conscious, most immediately controls behavior, and is most in touch with external reality.

■ **superego**   The moral aspect of the personality, much like the conscience. More formally, this division of the psyche develops by the incorporation of the perceived moral standards of the community, is mainly unconscious, and includes the conscience.

> Sublimation is the psychological process whereby one item of consciousness is symbolically substituted for another.

the product of inadequacies in the offender's personality. Significant inadequacies may result in full-blown mental illness, which can be a direct cause of crime. The psychoanalytic perspective encompasses diverse notions such as personality, **neurosis**, and **psychosis**, and more specific concepts such as transference, **sublimation**, and repression.

Psychotherapy, referred to in its early days as the "talking cure" because it relied on patient–therapist communication, is the attempt to relieve patients of their mental disorders through the application of psychoanalytic principles and techniques.

According to Freud, the personality is made up of three components—the id, the ego, and the superego—as shown in Figure 6-5. The **id** is the fundamental aspect of the personality from which drives, wishes, urges, and desires emanate.

Freud focused primarily on love, aggression, and sex as fundamental drives in any personality. The id operates according to the pleasure principle, seeking full and immediate gratification of its needs. Individuals, however, according to Freud, are rarely fully aware of the urges that manifest (occasionally into awareness) from the id because it is a largely unconscious region of the mind. Nonetheless, from the Freudian perspective, each of us carries within our id the prerequisite motivation for criminal behavior. We are, each one of us, potential murderers, sexual aggressors, and thieves—our drives and urges kept in check only by other controlling aspects of our personalities.

The **ego** is primarily charged with reality testing. Freud's use of the word *ego* should not be confused with popular usage, whereby a person might talk about an "inflated ego" or an "egotistical person." For Freud, the ego was primarily concerned with how objectives might be best accomplished. The ego tends to effect strategies for the individual that maximize pleasure and minimize pain. It lays out the various paths of action that can lead to wish fulfillment. The ego inherently recognizes that it may be necessary to delay gratification to achieve a more fulfilling long-term goal.

The **superego** is much like a moral guide to right and wrong. If properly developed, it evaluates the ego's plans, dismissing some as morally inappropriate while accepting others as ethically viable. The id of a potential rapist, for example, might be filled with lustful drives, and his ego may develop a variety of alternative plans whereby those drives might be fulfilled, some legal and some illegal. His superego will, if the individual's personality is relatively well integrated and the superego is properly developed, turn the individual away from law-violating behavior based on his sensual desires and guide the ego to select a path of action that is in keeping with social convention. When the dictates of the superego are not followed, feelings of guilt may result. The superego is one of the most misunderstood of Freudian concepts. In addition to elements of conscience, the superego also contains what Freud called the "ego-ideal," which is a symbolic representation of what society values. The ego-ideal differs from the conscience in that it is less forceful in controlling behavior in the absence of the likelihood of discovery.

Although, as previously mentioned, Freud did not directly address crime, he did spend much of his time examining abnormal behaviors, many of which might lead to violations of the criminal law. One way in which a person might be led into crime, according to the perspective of psychoanalysis, is as the result of a poorly developed superego. In the individual without

FIGURE 6-5 | **The Psychoanalytic Structure of Personality**

Source: Schmalleger, Frank Criminology. Printed and Electronically reproduced by permission of Pearson Education, Inc., Upper Saddle River, New Jersey ISBN 0132966751.

■ **repression** The psychological process through which a person rejects his or her own desires and impulses toward pleasurable instincts by excluding them from consciousness, thereby removing them from awareness and rendering them unconscious.

■ **paranoid schizophrenic** A schizophrenic individual who suffers from delusions and hallucinations.

a fully functional superego, the mind is left to fall back on the ego's reality-testing ability. To put it simply, the ego, operating without a moral guide, may select a path of action that, although expedient at the time, violates the law. Consequently, without a fully functioning superego, offenders come to be characterized by id-dominated personalities, and the id's need for instant gratification determines their behavior. Individuals suffering from poor superego development are unlikely to give thought to the long-term consequences of the choices they make.

Although Freud actually wrote very little about criminality, **August Aichorn**, another psychoanalyst, did. Aichorn saw the behavior of violent criminals as dominated by the id, leaving them unable to control their impulsive and pleasure-seeking drives stemming from the id.[62] Aichorn believed that as a result of negative life experiences, especially at an early age, violence-prone individuals suffer from damaged egos that are too weak to be able to deal with stressful circumstances and urges that well up from the id.

Another path to criminality from a psychiatric viewpoint is through repressed needs. The psychoanalytical concept of **repression** holds that a person may seek to reject his or her own desires and impulses toward pleasurable instincts by excluding them from his or her own consciousness, thereby removing them from awareness and rendering them unconscious.

One secret need of many criminals, according to some psychologists, is the need to be punished, which arises, according to psychiatric theory, from a sense of guilt. Psychiatrists who suggest that the need to be punished is a motivating factor in criminal behavior are quick to point out that this need may be a closely guarded secret, unknown even to the offender. Hence, from the psychiatric point of view, many drives, motives, and wishes are unconscious or even repressed by people who harbor them. The concept of repression holds that the human mind may choose to keep certain aspects of itself out of consciousness, possibly because of shame, self-loathing, or a simple lack of adequate introspection.

> The need to be punished is a motivating factor in some criminal behavior.

Freudian theory was very popular during the middle part of the twentieth century, but by the 1980s, the notions of ego and id were considered antiquated by most psychiatrists. Attention shifted to the study of chemical imbalances in the brain, and psychopharmacology supplemented—if not replaced—the earlier ideas of Freud and his followers. Marti Olsen Laney, a neuroscience researcher in Portland, Oregon, found that the brains of introverted children functioned somewhat differently from those of extroverts. Brain scans of introverted kids found much more overall activity—especially in the brain's frontal lobes, which are areas associated with problem solving, introspection, complex thinking, and planning.[63]

The field of psychiatry has seen a rekindling of interest in Freudian psychology, however, because psychopharmacology (the use of drugs to treat psychiatric symptoms and disorders) has been unable to provide an alternative grand theory of personality, emotion, and motivation.[64] Moreover, today's neuroscientists are busily creating a chemical map of the mind that seems to validate the general sketch that Freud provided decades ago, and soon a new unified perspective that reconciles the work of neurologists and psychiatrists may emerge. The recognition of just such a possibility prompted Eric R. Kandel of Columbia University, the 2000 Nobel laureate in physiology and medicine, to say that psychoanalysis is "still the most coherent and intellectually satisfying view of the mind."[65]

The Psychotic Offender

Some seemingly inexplicable forms of criminality may be the result of psychosis. People with psychotic disorders are out of touch with reality in some fundamental way, possibly suffering from hallucinations, delusions, or other breaks with reality. Psychoses may be either organic (resulting from physical damage to or abnormalities in the brain) or functional (having no known physical cause). Canadian criminologist Gwynn Nettler said, "Thought disorder is the hallmark of psychosis. People are called crazy when, at some extremity, they cannot 'think straight.'"[66] She identified three characteristics of psychotic individuals: "(1) a grossly distorted conception of reality, (2) moods, and swings of mood, that seem inappropriate to circumstance, and (3) marked inefficiency in getting along with others and caring for oneself."[67]

Psychiatrists today recognize at least nine different types of psychotic disorders, and one important category is schizophrenia. Schizophrenics (mentioned earlier) are characterized by disordered or disjointed thinking, in which the types of logical associations they make are atypical of other people. **Paranoid schizophrenics**, one of the four major subgroups of schizophrenics, also suffer from delusions and hallucinations. Schizophrenia is a disorganization of the personality, and in its most extreme form, it may manifest itself in seemingly irrational behavior as well as hallucinations and delusions.

A recent study of male schizophrenics found that 37% started a criminal career, and 13% had committed their first violent crime, before any contact with the psychiatric hospital system. Study authors concluded that "the criminality committed [by schizophrenics] before first contact to the psychiatric hospital system is substantial, especially among males with schizophrenia."[68] Many studies confirm the association between violence and schizophrenia, but recent evidence from a study conducted in the United Kingdom suggests that the proportion of violent crime directly attributable to schizophrenia is below 10%.[69] When substance abuse is added to the mix, however,

■ **risk assessment**   The practice of using a structured instrument that combines information about individuals in order to classify them as being low, moderate, or high risk for violent behavior, reoffending, or continued criminal activity.

■ **alloplastic adaptation**   A form of adjustment that results from changes in the environment surrounding an individual.

■ **autoplastic adaptation**   A form of adjustment that results from changes within an individual.

the amount of violence associated with schizophrenia increases considerably. Consequently, a 2009 article in the *Journal of the American Medical Association* (JAMA) found that schizophrenics are four to six times as likely as members of the general population to commit a violent crime, and noted that current medical guidelines "recommend that violence **risk assessment** should be conducted for all patients with schizophrenia."[70]

Not all people who are psychotic commit crimes, and many remain law abiding throughout their entire lives. Psychoses, however, may lead to crime in a number of ways. Following the Vietnam War, for example, several American soldiers suffering from a kind of battlefield psychosis killed friends and family members, thinking they were Vietcong soldiers (the enemy). These men, who had been traumatized by battlefield experiences in Southeast Asia, relived their past on American streets. In other crimes committed by psychotics, thought disorders may be less obvious or may exist only temporarily.

Frustration–Aggression Theory

In his early writings, Freud suggested that aggressive behavior is a natural response to frustration and limitations imposed upon a person. This *frustration–aggression thesis* was later developed more fully in the writings of **J. Dollard**, **Albert Bandura**, **Richard H. Walters**, and others. Dollard's frustration–aggression theory held that although frustration can lead to various forms of behavior—including regression, sublimation, and aggressive fantasy—direct aggression toward others is its most likely consequence.[71] Because everyone suffers frustration at times in life (beginning with weaning and toilet training), aggression is a natural consequence of living, but that aggression can be manifested in socially acceptable ways (contact sports, military or law enforcement careers, simple verbal attacks) and/or engaged in vicariously by observing others who are acting violently (in movies, on television, in fiction).

Dollard applied the psychoanalytical term *displacement* to the type of violence that is vented on something or someone who is not the source of the original frustration and suggested that satisfying one's aggressive urges via observation was a form of "catharsis."

Some psychologists have tried to identify what it is that causes some individuals to displace aggression or to experience it vicariously, whereas others respond violently and directly toward the immediate source of their frustrations. Andrew F. Henry and James F. Short, Jr., for example, suggested that child-rearing practices are a major determining factor in such a causal nexus.[72] Restrictive parents who both punish and love their children, said Henry and Short, will engender in their children the ability to suppress outward expressions of aggression, but when one parent punishes and the other loves, or when both punish but neither shows love, children can be expected to show anger directly and perhaps even immediately because they will not be threatened with the loss of love. Physical punishment rarely threatens the loss of love, and children so punished cannot be expected to refrain from direct displays of anger.

In 1960, Stewart Palmer studied murderers and their siblings to determine the degree of frustration to which they had been exposed as children.[73] He found that male murderers had experienced much more frustration than their brothers and that more than twice as many frustrating experiences—ranging from difficult births to serious illnesses, childhood beatings, severe toilet training, and negative school experiences—were reported by the murderers than by their law-abiding siblings.

Crime as Adaptation

Some psychiatrists see crime as an adaptation to life's stresses. According to **Seymour L. Halleck**, a psychiatrist and adjunct professor of law at the University of North Carolina at Chapel Hill, turning to crime can provide otherwise disenfranchised individuals with a sense of power and purpose.[74] Halleck says that crime can also provide "excellent rationalizations" for perceived inadequacies—especially for those whose lives have been failures when judged against the benchmarks of the wider society. "The criminal is able to say …, 'I could have been successful if I had not turned to crime. All my troubles have come to me because I have been bad.'" Thus, crime, according to Halleck, provides "a convenient resource for denying, forgetting or ignoring … other inadequacies."[75]

Insofar as the choice of crime reduces stresses the individual faces by producing changes in the environment (empowerment), it is referred to as **alloplastic adaptation**. When crime leads to stress reduction as a result of internal changes in beliefs, value systems, and so forth, it is called **autoplastic adaptation**.

■ **criminogenic needs**   Dynamic attributes (also known as dynamic risk factors) of offenders and their circumstances that are associated with rates of recidivism.

■ **attachment theory**   A social-psychological perspective on delinquent and criminal behavior holding that the successful development of secure attachment between a child and his or her primary caregiver provides the basic foundation for all future psychological development.

The offender who is able to deny responsibility for other failures by turning to crime is said to be seeking autoplastic adaptation. Because other forms of behavior also may meet many of the same needs as crime, Halleck points out, an individual may select crime over various other behavioral alternatives only when no reasonable alternatives are available or when criminal behavior has inherent advantages—as might be the case under instances of economic or social oppression. (i.e., individuals who are actively discriminated against may find personal and political significance in violating the laws of the oppressing society.)

From Halleck's point of view, crime "has many advantages even when considered independently of the criminal's conscious or unconscious needs for gratification."[76] Even though crime can be immediately rewarding or intensely pleasing, such a reward is more like a "fringe benefit"; its central significance is that it "is an action which helps one survive with dignity."[77] Halleck explained that "we cannot understand the criminal unless we appreciate that his actions are much more than an effort to find a specific gratification."[78]

In another approach to stress as a causative agent in crime commission, **Arnold S. Linsky**, **Ronet Bachman**, and **Murray A. Straus** suggested that stress may lead to aggression toward others and toward oneself (self-destructive behavior like suicide, smoking, and abuse of alcohol).[79] Linsky and his colleagues measured stress at the societal level, arguing that although the relationship between stress and aggression has been studied at the individual level, "the neglect of social stress as an explanation for society-to-society differences in aggression may be partially due to a lack of an objective means of comparing the stressfulness of life in different societies."[80] Concluding that societal stress levels heighten levels of aggression, the authors suggested that social policies should be created to reduce the impact of such stressful events as having to stop work, foreclosing on a mortgage, and dropping out of school.

Finally, we should recognize that perceptions vary and that although criminal behavior may appear to be a valid choice for some individuals who are seeking viable responses to perceived stresses and oppression, their perceptions may not be wholly accurate.

Criminogenic Needs

In 1998, **Donald A. Andrews** and **James Bonta** identified major risk factors associated with criminal conduct that they termed **criminogenic needs**.[81] Criminogenic needs, which Andrews and Bonta referred to in later writings as "criminogenic domains,"[82] can be described as dynamic attributes of offenders and their circumstances that are associated with rates of recidivism.[83] Among the "needs" or risk factors that Andrews and Bonta listed are (1) antisocial attitudes, values, and beliefs; (2) antisocial

personality, including low self-control; (3) antisocial associates and friends; (4) low levels of social achievement, including a lack of educational, vocational, or financial achievement; (5) family factors, including marital instability, a criminal family, and poor parenting skills; (6) substance abuse; and (7) a lack of prosocial pursuits. Criminogenic needs, because they are dynamic or amenable to change, can be targeted by treatment strategies intended to reduce criminality and recidivism.

In their writings, Andrews and Bonta developed the term "criminogenic domain" to refer to major risk factors for continuing criminality. They identified criminal history as a major criminogenic domain and noted that together in combination with antisocial attitudes, criminal associates, and antisocial personality, these represent the "big four" risk factors. Andrews and Bonta were careful, however, not to include criminal history as a criminogenic need because it is a static element unamenable to change.[84]

Attachment Theory

Another psychological approach to explaining crime and delinquency is **attachment theory**, first proposed by English child psychiatrist **John Bowlby** (1907–1990), who observed children during his tenure at the London Child Guidance Clinic after World War II.[85] Bowlby was especially interested in the maladjusted behavior of children who lacked a solid relationship with a mother figure, and he concluded that for healthy personality development to occur, "the infant and young child should experience a warm, intimate, and continuous relationship with his mother (or permanent mother substitute) in which both find satisfaction and enjoyment."[86]

> The successful development of secure attachment provides the basic foundation for future psychological development.

Bowlby identified three forms of attachment: secure attachment, anxious–avoidant attachment, and anxious–resistant attachment.[87] Only the first is healthy, and it develops early in life when a child is confident that the mother figure will be responsible and available when needed. The successful development of secure attachment between children and their primary caregivers, Bowlby said, provides the basic foundation for all their future psychological development, with children developing a secure psychological base when they are "nourished physically and emotionally, comforted if distressed [and] reassured if frightened."[88]

According to attachment theory, delinquent behavior arises when nonsecure attachments are created. Anxious–avoidant

THEORY | in PERSPECTIVE
Types of Psychological and Psychiatric Theories

Psychological and psychiatric theories of criminology are derived from the behavioral sciences and focus on the individual as the unit of analysis. This chapter breaks their discussion down into a number of areas as shown in this box.

Personality Theory

This approach envisions a complex set of drives and motives operating from recesses deep within the personality to determine behavior.

Period: 1930s–present

Theorists: Hervey M. Cleckley, Hans J. Eysenck, many others

Concepts: personality, psychopath, sociopath, antisocial personality, personality, traits, Five Factor Model

Frustration–Aggression Theory

Frustration is a natural consequence of living and a root cause of crime in this theory, where criminal behavior can be a form of adaptation when it results from stress reduction.

Period: 1940s–present

Theorists: J. Dollard, Albert Bandura, Richard H. Walters

Concepts: frustration, aggression, displacement

Crime as Adaptation

Criminal activity facilitates individual adaptation to the environment by reducing life stresses and by producing environmental changes.

Period: 1970s–present

Theorists: Seymour L. Halleck, Donald A. Andrews, James Bonta, John Bowlby Arnold S. Linsky, Ronet Bachman, Murray A. Straus

Concepts: alloplastic and autoplastic adaptation, criminogenic needs, criminogenic domains, attachment theory

Behavior Theory

From a psychological perspective, behavior theory posits that individual behavior that is rewarded will increase in frequency and behavior that is punished will decrease in frequency.

Period: 1940s–present

Theorists: B. F. Skinner, others

Concepts: operant behavior, operant conditioning, classical conditioning, stimulus-response, reward, punishment

Modeling Theory

This theory states that people learn how to behave by modeling themselves after others whom they have the opportunity to observe.

Period: 1950s–present

Theorists: Gabriel Tarde, Albert Bandura, others

Concepts: imitation, interpersonal aggression, social cognition theory, modeling, disengagement

Cognitive Theory

Cognitive theory, also known as moral development theory, holds that individuals become criminal when they have not successfully completed their intellectual development from child- to adulthood.

Period: 1930s–present

Theorists: Jean Piaget, Lawrence Kohlberg, Roger C. Schank, Robert P. Abelson, Stanton E. Samenow, Samuel Yochelson

Concepts: moral development, cognitive-information processing, scripts, criminal mind-set

Psychoanalytic Criminology

This psychiatric approach, developed by Austrian psychiatrist Sigmund Freud, emphasizes the role of personality in human behavior and sees deviant behavior as the result of dysfunctional personalities or maladaptation to the social environment.

Period: 1920s–present

Theorists: Sigmund Freud, August Aichorn, others

Concepts: psychiatric criminology, id, ego, superego, sublimation, psychoanalysis, psychotherapy, neurosis, psychosis, paranoid schizophrenia

attachment develops when children feel rejection and lack confidence concerning parental support and care. Anxious-resistant attachment develops from similar experiences and results in feelings of uncertainty, causing the child (and later, the adult) to feel anxious, to be fearful of his or her environment, and to cling to potential caregivers or partners. Bowlby called delinquents "affectionless," meaning they did not form intimate attachments as children and cannot form such attachments later in life. Attachment theory predicts that the most problematic individuals will be those who were abandoned at an early age, who experienced multiple placements (in foster homes and so on), who had to deal with the early absence of one or both

■ **behavior theory**   A psychological perspective positing that behavior that is rewarded will increase in frequency and behavior that is punished will decrease in frequency.

■ **operant behavior**   Behavior that affects the environment so as to produce responses or further behavioral cues.
■ **reward**   A desirable behavioral consequence likely to increase the frequency of occurrence of that behavior.
■ **punishment**   An undesirable behavioral consequence likely to decrease the frequency of occurrence of that behavior.

parents, and who faced traumatic conditions (physical, sexual, or other abuse) in early childhood.

Tests of attachment theory seem to confirm that difficulties in childhood (especially before the age of eight) produce criminality later in life.[89] Studies have shown that children who were raised in insecure environments are likely to engage in violent behavior as adults and that childhood insecurity leads to a relative lack of empathy.[90] Some attachment theorists believe that the development of empathy is the single most important factor leading to conformity. When children do not receive empathy from those around them, they appear to also be unable to see others as deserving of empathy and become more likely to inflict injury on others. Learn more about attachment theory by visiting the Attachment Research Center via **http://www.psychology.sunysb.edu/attachment**, and read about the development of attachment theory at **http://www.psychology.sunysb.edu/attachment/online/inge_origins.pdf**.

Behavior Theory

Behavior theory, the second main thrust of early psychological theorizing, built upon the concept of conditioned behavior. The idea that behavior could be "conditioned" or *shaped*

> The concept of conditioned behavior was popularized through the work of Russian physiologist Ivan Pavlov.

was popularized through the work of Russian physiologist Ivan Pavlov (1849–1936), whose work with dogs won the Nobel Prize in physiology or medicine in 1904. The dogs, which salivated when food was presented to them, were always fed in the presence of a ringing bell. Soon, Pavlov found, the dogs would salivate as if in preparation for eating when the bell alone was rung, even when no food was present. Hence, salivation, an automatic response to the presence of food, could be conditioned to occur in response to some other stimulus, demonstrating that animal behavior could be predictably altered via association with external changes arising from the environment surrounding the organism. The kind of conditioning that Pavlov demonstrated, which is the association of a particular response to a conditioned stimulus, is referred to today as *classical conditioning*.

Behavioral Conditioning

Behavior theory has sometimes been called the "stimulus–response theory of human behavior." When an individual's behavior results in rewards or feedback that the individual regards as pleasurable and desirable, then that behavior will likely become more frequent. Under such circumstances, the behavior in question is reinforced, and the rewards themselves are referred to as *reinforcements*. Conversely, when punishment follows behavior, chances are that the frequency of that type of behavior will decrease. The individual's responses are termed **operant behavior** because a person's behavioral choices effectively operate on the surrounding environment to produce consequences for the individual.

Behavior theory is often used by parents seeking to control children through a series of **rewards** and **punishments**. Young children may be punished, for example, by being spanked, by having a favored toy taken away, and by the television being turned off. Older children are often told what rules they are expected to obey and what rewards they can anticipate if they adhere to those rules. They also know that punishments will follow if they do not obey the rules.

Rewards and punishments have been further divided into four conceptual categories: (1) positive reinforcements, which increase the frequency of approved behavior by adding something desirable to the situation—as when a "good" child is given a toy; (2) negative reinforcements, which increase the frequency of approved behavior by removing something distressful from the situation—as when a "good" child is permitted to skip the morning's chores; (3) positive punishments, which decrease the frequency of unwanted behavior by adding something undesirable to the situation—as when a "bad" child is spanked; and (4) negative punishments, which decrease the frequency of unwanted behavior by removing something desirable from the situation—as when a "bad" child's candy is taken away. According to behavior theory, it is through the application of rewards and punishments that behavior is shaped.

Behavior theory differs from other psychological theories in that the major determinants of behavior are envisioned as existing in the environment surrounding the individual rather than within the individual. Perhaps the best-known proponent of behavior theory is **B. F. Skinner** (1904–1990), who created the term *operant conditioning*. Skinner, a former Harvard professor, rejected unobservable psychological constructs, focusing instead on patterns of responses to external rewards and stimuli. Skinner did extensive animal research involving behavioral

■ **social cognition theory**   The perspective that people learn how to act by observing others.

■ **modeling**   A form of learning where individuals imitate actions or performances by observing other people in order to add those actions to their own behavioral repertoire.

concepts and created the notion of programmed instruction, which allows students to work at their own pace and provides immediate rewards for learning accomplishments.

Behavior theory is important in the study of criminology because much human behavior is the result of conditioning, and people can be conditioned to respond to situations with either prosocial or antisocial conduct. It's important, too, because it is the foundation on which social cognition theory (which is discussed in the following section) is built. In fact, teachers and parents often use punishments and rewards in an effort to condition their students and children, respectively, to engage in appropriate or desired behavior. Consequently, from the perspective of behavior theory, crime can be explained as the result of inappropriate behavioral conditioning.

Social Cognition and the Role of Modeling

One of the earliest attempts to explain crime and deviance as learned behavior can be found in the work of **Gabriel Tarde** (1843–1904), a French social theorist of the late 1800s. Tarde discounted the biological theories of Lombroso and others. The basis of any society, Tarde believed, was imitation, the tendency of people to pattern their behavior after the behavior of others. Tarde developed a theory of human behavior that built upon three laws of imitation and suggestion.[91] Tarde's first law held that individuals in close intimate contact with one another tend to imitate each other's behavior. His second law stated that imitation moves from the top down. This means that poor people tend to imitate wealthy people, youngsters tend to emulate those who are older, lower-class people tend to imitate members of the upper class, and so forth. The third law of imitation is the law of insertion, which says that new acts and behaviors tend to either reinforce or replace old ones. Hence, the music of each generation replaces the music of the one that preceded it, the politics of young people eventually become the politics of the nation, faddish drugs are substituted for traditional ones, and new forms of crime tend to take the place of older ones (e.g., when computer criminals become a more serious threat to financial institutions than bank robbers).

More recently, **Albert Bandura** developed a comprehensive **social cognition theory** of aggression that depends for its explanatory power on cognitive processes. Bandura believed that reinforcement theory could not account for all types of learning. Although everyone is capable of aggression, Bandura

said, "people are not born with … repertories of aggressive behavior. They must learn them."[92] Bandura, a psychology professor at Stanford University and past president of the American Psychological Society, is often referred to as the creator of *social learning theory* in the field of psychology (a parallel tradition of social learning theories in sociology will be discussed in later chapters). Because of the central role of cognition in Bandura's learning theory, however, he preferred to call his approach *social cognition theory*. Central to Bandura's theory are the ideas of observation, imitation, and modeling.

The concept of **modeling** acknowledges the fact that people learn how to act through their life experiences, and especially by observing others. Bandura wrote that "Most human behavior is learned observationally through modeling: from observing others, one forms an idea of how new behaviors are performed, and on later occasions this coded information serves as a guide for action."[93] In some of his early work, Bandura experimented with children who observed adult role models striking inflatable cartoon characters. When the children were observed after their encounter with adult behavior, they, too, exhibited similarly aggressive behavior. Bandura also studied violence on television and concluded that "television is an effective tutor. Both laboratory and controlled field studies in which young children and adolescents are repeatedly shown either violent or nonviolent fare disclose that exposure to film violence shapes the form of aggression and typically increases interpersonal aggressiveness in everyday life."[94] A later study by other researchers showed that even after ten years, the level of violence that young adults engaged in was directly related to the degree of violent television they had been exposed to as children.[95]

Aggression can be provoked, Bandura suggests, through physical assaults and verbal threats and insults, as well as by thwarting a person's hopes or obstructing his or her goal-seeking behavior. Deprivation and "adverse reductions in the conditions of life" (a lowered standard of living, the onset of disease, a spouse leaving or caught cheating, for example) are other potential triggers of aggression. Bandura adds, however, that a human being's ability to foresee the future consequences of present behavior adds another dimension to the activation of learned patterns of aggression. That is, aggressive behavior can be perceived as holding future benefits for individuals exhibiting it. In short, it can be seen as a means to a desired end.

Bandura also says that individuals sometimes become aggressive because they are rewarded for doing so. The early twentieth-century American concept of a "macho"—virile and

■ **correctional psychology** The branch of forensic psychology concerned with the diagnosis and classification of offenders, the treatment of correctional populations, and the rehabilitation of inmates and other law violators.

masculine—male figure, for example, was often associated with the expectation of substantial reward. Whether this perception was accurate, a significant proportion of American men subscribed to it nonetheless, and for many decades, it served as a guide to daily behavior.

Another form of reward can flow from aggression. Bandura called it the "reduction of aversive treatment." By this, he meant that simply standing up for oneself can improve the way one is treated by others. For example, standing up to a bully may be the most effective way of dealing with the harassment one might otherwise face. Bandura recognized that everyone has self-regulatory mechanisms that can inhibit the tendency toward aggression. People reward or punish themselves, Bandura said, according to internal standards they have for judging their own behavior. Thus, aggression may be inhibited in people who, for example, value religious, ethical, or moral standards of conduct such as compassion, thoughtfulness, and courtesy. Bandura concluded that people who devalue aggression may still engage in it via a process he called *disengagement*. Disengagement may result from (1) "attributing blame to one's victims"; (2) dehumanization through bureaucratization, automation, urbanization, and high social mobility; (3) vindication of aggressive practices by legitimate authorities; and (4) desensitization resulting from repeated exposure to aggression in any of a variety of forms.

Policy and Treatment Implications of Psychological and Psychiatric Approaches

No discussion of social policy as it relates to the insights of criminal psychology would be complete without mention of correctional psychology. **Correctional psychology** is concerned with the diagnosis and classification of offenders, the treatment of correctional populations, and the rehabilitation of inmates and other law violators.

Various forms of psychological and psychiatric treatments for criminal offenders have been developed based on the theories discussed in this chapter. In 2006, John C. Norcross and colleagues used a panel of 101 experts to generally assess the effectiveness of differing psychological assessments and treatments.[96] Fifty-nine treatments and 30 assessment techniques were evaluated, with the experts scoring each on a scale of 1 (not at all discredited) to 5 (totally discredited). Discredited assessment measures included the Luscher Color Test, the Szondi

Test, and the Lowenfeld Mosaic Test for personality assessment, along with handwriting analysis (graphology). Similarly, voice stress analysis for lie detection received a failing grade from the experts. Although it is beyond the scope of this chapter to discuss these and most other techniques in detail, the panel of experts found that the Myers-Briggs Type Indicator and the Rorschach inkblot test, along with some others, were useful assessment techniques.

The most successful techniques for psychological treatment were identified as behavior therapy for sex offenders, cognitive behavioral interventions (discussed later in this chapter), psychodrama, and laughter or humor therapy (for treatment of depression). The least successful treatment techniques included "fringe" methods, such as the use of pyramids for energy restoration, orgone therapy (use of an orgone energy accumulator), crystal healing, rebirthing, and past lives therapy.

Although there are many different psychological and psychiatric treatments available today, including psychotherapy, guide group interaction, behavioral modification, parent training, peer programs, and individual counseling, some of the most successful have aimed to change impulsivity and other offender personality characteristics. One of the most effective correctional techniques, as the Norcross study (mentioned previously) showed, is *cognitive behavioral intervention (CBI)*. CBI is based on the belief that offenders need to acquire better social skills in order to become more prosocial. Cognitive skill-building enables offenders to modify their cognitive processes to control themselves and interact positively with others. According to one source, "the goal of cognitive skills is to teach offenders to manage their own behavior by engaging in processes that develop self-control, making them responsible for and in charge of their actions no matter how stressful the situation. These specific skills include problem solving, social skills training (learned behaviors that enable one to interact with others in ways that elicit positive responses), anger management, and empathy training."[97]

CBI programs not only target the offender's environment, behavioral responses, and skill development, they also seek to increase the offender's reasoning skills and problem-solving abilities, and expand the offender's empathy toward others.

CBI is based, in part, on the work of Stanton Samenow (discussed earlier in this chapter) and was first outlined in a six-part video series entitled *Commitment to Change* that Samenow created. The first three parts of the series emphasize the value of looking at one's own thinking and help to define and identify thinking errors. The next video addresses specific thinking errors that are crucial in problem solving, and the last part outlines various methods useful in overcoming thinking errors.

Finally, it should be noted that psychopathology has been regarded as notoriously resistant to treatment of any kind. One of the first comprehensive studies of treatments intended for psychopaths, conducted by the NATO Advanced Study Institute, concluded that "no demonstrably effective treatment has been found." However, a more recent survey by Friedrich Lösel, a psychology professor at the University of Erlangen–Nuremberg (Germany) found that only a small proportion of 500 English psychiatrists shared that viewpoint.[98] Lösel concluded that effective treatment with psychopaths should involve behavior modification techniques, educational measures, involvement in therapeutic communities, and pharmacological agents.

WHO'S TO BLAME—The Individual or Society?

The Video Game Killer

In early 2018, 17-year-old Jason Sutter was pulled over in a small midwestern town for various traffic offenses, including going 70 mph in a 35-mph zone, running a red light, failing to yield for a blue light and siren, and driving recklessly. When officers discovered that he didn't have a driver's license, Sutter was handcuffed, briefly searched, placed in the back of a patrol car, and driven to the local police station for booking.

After he was photographed and fingerprinted, detective Joe Lockman sat down with him in a small interrogation room. Lockman, a 25-year veteran of the force, was working late and was in the station at 2:00 A.M. when Sutter arrived. The building was nearly empty, so Lockman decided to remove Sutter's handcuffs for what he hoped would be an informal chat. Sutter, who stood only 5 feet 4 inches tall and weighed 135 pounds, reminded Lockman of his son, and the detective hoped that he could teach the boy something about right and wrong.

As Lockman leaned forward to unshackle Sutter, a number of unfortunate events came together with deadly results. Sutter was a high school dropout and video game fanatic who spent most of his waking hours playing violence-themed games—including three in which the "heroes" killed pursuing police officers. Sutter had been improperly handcuffed with his hands in front, giving him easy access to Lockman's service revolver. Lockman carried an older model .38-caliber revolver (instead of a 9-mm semiautomatic pistol), which was loaded with deadly hollow-point ammunition and did not have a safety. When Sutter grabbed the weapon, he was able to immediately pull the trigger and fire two shots into Lockman's chest, killing him instantly.

Sutter fled out the front door of the police station past the surprised desk sergeant. The sergeant, realizing what had happened, pursued Sutter through the front door, and the two exchanged shots. Sutter was wounded in the exchange and captured; he was taken to an area hospital where he underwent surgery and recovered. He was charged with the murder of Detective Lockman, and the district attorney said that he would seek to have Sutter put away for the rest of his life.

Students playing games on their cell phones. Do you think that video games can influence real world behavior?

Auremar/Fotolia

Sutter's parents hired an attorney to defend their son. The lawyer held a press conference during which he announced his defense strategy—that Sutter had been brainwashed by video games and that at the time of the shooting he had been unable to distinguish reality from fantasy. "Jason was confused by all that happened. He thought that he was playing a game," the attorney said. "He didn't realize that someone might really get hurt." He also announced that he was filing a lawsuit against the two media companies that had made the games Sutter played.

Think about it

1. Who is primarily responsible for the murder of Detective Lockman, Sutter or the video game manufacturers? Do both bear at least some responsibility?

2. What role, if any, did society play in Detective Lockman's death? Should government regulations control the content of video games?

3. What role did free will and individual choice play in Sutter's quick decision to take Lockman's gun and shoot him? How much control did Sutter have over his own behavior, and how much of his behavior was merely a response to experiences he had in the past?

Note: Who's to Blame boxes provide fictionalized critical thinking opportunities based on actual cases.

■ **selective incapacitation**   A social policy that seeks to protect society by incarcerating those individuals deemed to be the most dangerous.

Assessing Dangerousness

In 2011, the U.S. Supreme Court rejected the significance of the argument that violence in the media can lead to criminal behavior via imitation, saying that any such concerns were trumped by the free speech rights of video game manufacturers guaranteed under the First Amendment to the U.S. Constitution.[99] In the words of the Court, "This country has no tradition of specially restricting children's access to depictions of violence. And California's claim that 'interactive' video games present special problems, in that the player participates in the violent action on screen and determines its outcome, is unpersuasive."

If, as the Court says, violent media content is protected by the Constitution, the same is not true of violent behavior. Consequently, those who violate the law can be apprehended and punished, and those who persist in law violation can be effectively removed from society. **Selective incapacitation**, although it is not a crime-prevention policy developed by psychologists, is based on the notion of career criminality and predicated upon the use of psychological techniques to effectively identify likely future offenders and those who are likely to reoffend.[100] Career criminals, also called "habitual offenders," are people who repeatedly violate the criminal law. A special type of habitual offender is the serious, violent, and chronic (SVC) offender. SVCs comprise a small group of offenders who are responsible for a disproportionate amount of *violent* crime. Research has shown that only a small percentage of all offenders account for most of the crimes reported to the police. Some studies have found that as few as 8% of all offenders commit as many as 60% serious crimes each year.[101]

A recent Wisconsin study found that imprisonment of individuals determined to be career offenders saved the state approximately $14,000 per year per offender when the cost of imprisonment was compared with the estimated cost of new crimes.[102] Researchers in the Wisconsin study concluded that "prison pays" and suggested that the state continue pursuing a policy of aggressive imprisonment of career offenders, even in the face of escalating costs and vastly overcrowded prisons. The strategy of selective incapacitation, however, depends on accurately identifying potentially dangerous offenders in existing criminal populations. Consequently, in recent years, a central focus of correctional psychologists has been on the development of a number of empirically based risk assessment and classification tools. Such tools have gone through four generations of development, as follows:[103]

- **First generation:** For most of the twentieth century, professional judgment or intuition was the most common method used to predict criminal behavior. Clinical

professionals and correctional psychologists were guided by their own training and experiences, and the lessons they learned were often anecdotal.

- **Second generation:** Beginning in the 1970s, the assessment of risk began to depend more upon actuarial, evidence-based science and less on professional judgment and intuition. Second-generation risk assessments are often referred to as actuarial risk assessments, and consider individual indicators (e.g., a history of substance abuse) that have been demonstrated to increase the risk of reoffending and assign these items quantitative scores.

- **Third generation:** In the early 1980s, risk-assessment instruments began to take into consideration dynamic risk factors and are commonly referred to as risk-need assessments. Third-generation instruments combine the static predictor variables of the second-generation instruments with measured changes in an offender's circumstances.

- **Fourth generation:** Beginning in the early 2000s, fourth-generation risk-assessment instruments began to assess a broader range of risk factors along with what are referred to as "responsivity factors," which many regard as important to treatment. Responsivity factors include reading and cognitive abilities, race, gender, and motivation to change, as well as external factors such as treatment setting and counselor characteristics.

Some of the most commonly used classification instruments in use today are the Level of Service Inventory–Revised (LSI-R), the Static Risk Offender Needs Guide–Revised (STRONG–R), the Psychopathy Checklist–Revised (PCL–R), the Sex Offender Risk Appraisal Guide (SORAG), the Violence Risk Appraisal Guide (VRAG), and the Correctional Offender Management Profiling for Alternative Sanctions (COMPAS). The LSI-R scores offenders as low, moderate, or high risk based on 54 items about the offender that are categorized into ten sublevels: criminal history, education/employment, financial situation, family/marital relationships, accommodation, leisure and recreation, companions, alcohol or drug use, emotional/mental health, and attitudes and orientation.[104] A 2007 study of Iowa offenders showed "that the total LSI-R score is significantly related to the prediction of future criminal behavior."[105] The higher the total risk score, the study showed, the more likely that the client would reoffend.

COMPAS is a risk-assessment tool that was created to measure risks in adult correctional populations in order to provide information to aid in decision making with regard to placement of offenders in the community.[106] COMPAS provides an Overall

Risk Potential, which is a composite score of individual risk estimates for violence, recidivism, failure to appear, and community failure as measured by the instrument. Evaluation studies of both LSI-R and COMPAS vary, and have produced mixed results—especially with nonwhite or female populations.[107] Studies, however, reveal support for previous empirical evidence that criminal history is strongly related to future offending.

Two other important risk-assessment models used in corrections are the risk-need-responsivity (RNR) model and the Good Lives Model (GLM).[108] The RNR model works to match the intensity of treatment interventions to assessed risk levels, and "specifically target(s) criminogenic needs" while tailoring "treatment to the personal and interpersonal needs and capacities of participants."[109] The risk principle of the RNR model holds that the intensity of correctional interventions must match the level of risk represented by the offender. The needs aspect asks that treatment programs target an offender's problems that lead the individual into crime. The responsivity principle requires treatment providers to examine offender idiosyncrasies in designing interventions and treatment plans, and says that treatment must be presented in a style and mode that is responsive to the offender's learning style and abilities.[110]

A recent meta-analysis of risk assessment tools, however, found that "even after 30 years of development, the view that violence, sexual, or criminal risk can be predicated in most cases is not evidence based."[111] Not only do risk assessment measures not live up to expectations, but the study authors found that expert courtroom testimony based on such tools cannot be used "to safely determine criminal prognosis in an individual case." At best, the authors concluded, risk assessment tools should be used as "part of a wider clinical assessment process."

Of course past criminal records may also provide a guide to future criminal offending, at least in some cases. For that reason, the federal 1984 Comprehensive Crime Control Act,[112] which established the U.S. Sentencing Commission, targeted career offenders. Guidelines created by the commission contain, as a central feature, a "criminal history" dimension, which substantially increases the amount of punishment an offender faces based on his or her history of law violations. The sentencing guidelines originally classified a defendant as a career offender if "(1) the defendant was at least 18 years old at the time of the ... offense, (2) the ... offense is a crime of violence or trafficking in a controlled substance, and (3) the defendant has at least two prior felony convictions of either a crime of violence or a controlled substance offense."[113] The definition, however, later came under fire for casting individuals with a history of minor drug trafficking into the same category as serial killers and the like.

> Dangerousness is not an objective quality like obesity or brown eyes; rather, it is an ascribed quality like trustworthiness.

Definitions of dangerousness are fraught with difficulty because, as some have pointed out, "dangerousness is not an objective quality like obesity or brown eyes, rather it is an ascribed quality like trustworthiness."[114] Dangerousness is not necessarily a personality trait that is stable or easily identifiable. Even if it were, some studies of criminal careers seem to show that involvement in crime decreases with age.[115]

Nonetheless, *assessing dangerousness* is a central issue in criminology and is especially true of psychological approaches to criminality.[116] Consequently, those who score high on dimensions meant to measure dangerousness are often committed to mental or forensic hospitals or other controlled facilities, even in the absence of overt criminal behavior.

One decade-long study of violence risk factors among people with mental disorder is the MacArthur Violence Risk Assessment Study.[117] The MacArthur study examined psychiatric patients who had been released from hospitals and evaluated 134 risk factors that study authors had previously identified as possible indicators of later violence. Although a total of 70 factors were found to have a relationship to later violence, a few stood out as especially important during the first 20 weeks following hospitalization. They included:

- **Psychopathy.** Psychopathy, as measured by the Hare Psychopathy Checklist, was more strongly associated with violence than any other risk factor studied.

- **Prior violence.** All measures of prior violence—self-report, arrest records, and hospital records—were strongly related to future violence.

- **Violent thoughts.** Thinking or daydreaming about harming others was associated with later violence, particularly if the thoughts or daydreams were persistent.

- **Anger.** The higher a patient scored on a proprietary anger scale in the hospital, the more likely he or she was to be violent later in the community.

- **Childhood experiences.** The seriousness and frequency of having been physically abused as a child predicted subsequent violent behavior, as did having a parent—particularly a father—who was a substance abuser or a criminal.

- **Diagnosis.** A diagnosis of a major mental disorder—especially a diagnosis of a personality or adjustment disorder—was strongly predictive of violence if it co-occurred with a diagnosis of substance abuse.

- **Suspiciousness:** A generally "suspicious" attitude toward others was found to be related to later violence.

Risk factors that bore no special relationship to later violence included:

- **Delusions.** The presence of delusions—or the type of delusions or the content of delusions—was not associated with violence.
- **Hallucinations.** Hallucinations in general did not elevate the risk of violence. If voices specifically commanded a violent act, however, the likelihood of violence was increased.
- **Diagnosis of schizophrenia.** A diagnosis of schizophrenia was associated with a lower rate of violence than a diagnosis of a personality disorder.

Similarly, the MacArthur study found little relationship between neighborhood, race, or gender and violent behavior following release. Learn more about risk assessment at **http://www.bmj.com/content/bmj/345/bmj.e4692.full.pdf**.

Predicting Criminality

In terms of assessment, it is one thing to be able to identify offenders after they have already violated the law; but it is another to predict beforehand which individuals are likely to offend so that they can be prevented from harming others. One recent study found a strong relationship between childhood behavioral difficulties and later problem behavior.[118] According to the authors of the study, "Early antisocial behavior is the best predictor of later antisocial behavior. It appears that this rule holds even when the antisocial behavior is measured as early as the preschool period." Prediction, however, requires more than generalities. It is one thing to say, for example, that generally speaking, 70% of children who evidence aggressive behavior will show violent tendencies later in life and quite another to be able to predict which individuals will engage in future violations of the criminal law.

To that end, one 2016 study identified four significant modifiable risk factors in late childhood for any type of violent behavior. The factors identified were (1) physical abuse, (2) parental stress, (3) bad friends, and (4) low school motivation. Study authors found that "the higher the number of early risk factors, the higher the probability of later conviction for violence offenses including homicide."[119]

Similarly, a few years ago, psychologists were able to demonstrate a clear relationship between a constellation of personality factors termed "hyperactivity-impulsivity-attention-deficit" (HIA) and offending. Studies found that the future delinquency of children who were characterized by HIA disorder at ages eight through ten could reliably be predicted.[120]

Critique of Psychological and Psychiatric Theories of Crime

Critics say that by focusing on the individual, psychological and psychiatric theories of criminality do not sufficiently take into account social or environmental conditions that produce crime. In fact, if social conditions are the primary cause of crime, as some claim, then individual change brought about by psychological or psychiatric interventions will not necessarily reduce levels of criminal offenses or lower rates of crime.

Similarly, psychological and psychiatric theories place the locus of control within the individual by positing a sense of moral reasoning. However, effective social control may actually stem from within social and physical arrangements that comprise the environment in which the individual functions. In other words, physical and social barriers to crime (such as the presence of a police officer) may be more effective at preventing crime than the sense of right or wrong that psychological theories find so important. Moreover, "some criminologists have an ideological aversion to locating the blame for criminal behavior on individuals and not on inequities in the social structure."[121]

Freudian theory, discussed earlier, has been criticized on several levels. The first and most fundamental criticism of this perspective is its lack of scientific support. Critics point out that Freud's theories are not based on research and that there is no substantial support for his concepts. As such, Freudian theory has been seen as less of a scientific explanation for human behavior based on sound methodology and more of a belief system, valuable as a tool for literary and philosophical interpretation.[122]

Moreover, some claim that psychiatric theories, as distinguished from psychological ones, are appropriate only for explanations of abnormal cognition and do not apply well to otherwise normal people who turn to crime. In fact, some criminologists point to the fact that criminological predicators such as offense history are more accurate in forecasting future offenses than are psychological assessments and diagnosis, even among individuals characterized as mentally disordered.[123]

Freudian theory was very popular during the middle part of the twentieth century. By the 1980s, however, the notions of ego and id were considered antiquated by most psychiatrists. Attention shifted to the study of chemical imbalances in the

■ **psychological profiling** The attempt to categorize, understand, and predict the behavior of certain types of offenders based on behavioral clues they provide; also called criminal profiling and behavioral profiling.

brain, and psychopharmacology, or the use of drugs to treat psychiatric symptoms and disorders, has supplemented—if not replaced—the earlier ideas of Freud and his followers. Recently, however, the field of psychiatry has seen a rekindling of interest in Freudian psychology. The reason, according to some contemporary thinkers, is that psychopharmacology has been unable to provide an alternative grand theory of personality, emotion, and motivation.[124] Moreover, today's neuroscientists are busily creating a chemical map of the mind that seems to validate the general sketch that Freud provided decades ago. As noted earlier, it is possible that soon a new and unified perspective that reconciles the work of neurologists and psychiatrists may emerge.

Behavior theory has been criticized for ignoring the role that cognition plays in human behavior. Martyrs, for example, persist in what may be defined by the wider society as undesirable behavior, even in the face of severe punishment—including the loss of their own lives. Rewards and punishments as controls over human behavior seem to lose any explanatory power because even the most severe punishment is unlikely to deter a martyr who answers to some higher call. Similarly, criminals who are punished for official law violations may find that their immediate social group interprets criminal punishment as status-enhancing—meaning that punishment actually becomes a reward.

Modeling theory, a more sophisticated form of cognitive theory, has been criticized for lacking comprehensive explanatory power. How, for example, can striking differences in sibling behavior, when early childhood experiences were likely much the same, be explained? Similarly, why do apparent differences exist between the sexes with regard to degree and type of criminality, irrespective of social background and early learning experiences? More recent versions of modeling theory, sometimes called "cognitive social learning theory,"[125] attempt to account for such differences by hypothesizing that reflection and cognition play a significant role in interpreting what one observes and in determining responses. Hence, few people are likely to behave precisely as others do because they will have their own ideas about what observed behavior means and about the consequences of imitation.

> Modeling theory, a form of social learning theory, asserts that people learn how to act by observing others.

Criminal Psychological Profiling

During World War II, the U.S. War Department recruited psychologists and psychiatrists in an attempt to predict the future moves that enemy forces might make. In addition, psychological and psychoanalytic techniques were applied to the study of German leader Adolf Hitler, Italian leader Benito Mussolini, Japanese general and prime minister Hideki Tojo, and other Axis leaders. Such psychological profiling of enemy leaders may have given the Allies the edge in battlefield strategy.

After the war ended, little work was done in the field until the 1970s when Federal Bureau of Investigation (FBI) special agent Howard Teten and others began to apply psychological profiling techniques to violent criminal behavior. In July 1984, the Bureau opened the National Center for the Analysis of Violent Crime (NCAVC) on the grounds of the FBI National Academy in Quantico, Virginia. One division within the NCAVC, the Behavioral Sciences Unit (later renamed the Behavioral Analysis Unit, or BAU), began to look for unique psychological patterns in the behavior of serial rapists and killers and launched the practice of routinely profiling high-interest criminal offenders.

Today, **psychological profiling** (also called *criminal profiling* and *behavioral profiling*) is used to assist police investigators seeking to better understand individuals wanted for serious offenses. Psychological profiling is built on the idea that behavioral clues left behind at a crime scene may reflect the personality of the offender.

During an interview, famed profiler John Douglas, the retired FBI special agent who became the model for the Scott Glenn character in Thomas Harris's *Silence of the Lambs*, described criminal profiling: "It is a behavioral composite put together of the unknown subject after analyzing the crime scene materials, to include the autopsy protocol, autopsy and crime scene photographs, as well as the preliminary police reports. It is also a detailed analysis of the victim and putting that information together. To me, it's very much like an internist in medicine who now attempts to put a diagnosis, say, on an illness; I'm trying to put a diagnosis on this particular case that's relative to motive, as well as the type of person(s) who would perpetrate that type of crime."[126]

Profilers develop a list of typical offender characteristics and other useful principles by analyzing crime-scene and autopsy data, in conjunction with interviews and studies of past offenders, in the belief that almost any form of conscious behavior (including behavior the offender engaged in during a criminal episode) is symptomatic of the individual's personality. The way a kidnapper approaches victims, the type of attack used by a killer, and the specific sexual activities of a rapist—all of these might help paint a picture of the offender's motivations, personal characteristics, and likely future behavior. Sometimes psychological profiles can provide clues as to what an offender might do following an attack: Some offenders have been arrested after returning to the crime scene, a behavior typically predicted by specific behavioral clues left behind, and a remorseful type can be expected to visit the victim's grave, permitting fruitful stakeouts of a cemetery.

Although criminal profiling may not be useful in every case, it can help narrow the search for an offender in repetitive crimes involving one offender, such as serial rape or murder. Knowledge gleaned from profiling can also help in the interrogation of suspects and can be used to identify and protect possible victims before the offender has a chance to strike again.

Criminal profiling techniques have also been used in hostage negotiation, where law enforcement officers need to know as much as possible about the hostage taker, and in the analysis of anonymous communications—especially when those communications contain threats of violence. To analyze such communications, profilers have developed a "threat dictionary," in which words contained in the message are weighted and compared to standard speech patterns.[127] An analysis of the communications may indicate the educational level, gender, financial standing, and the social group to which the writer belongs. Similarly, "signature" words or phrases that appear unique to the writer may help to identify him or her.

Profilers have also contributed significantly to the criminological literature. In a well-known study of lust murderers (men who kill and often mutilate victims during or following a forced sexual episode), FBI Special Agents Robert R. Hazelwood and John E. Douglas distinguished between the organized nonsocial and the disorganized asocial types.[128] The organized nonsocial lust murderer exhibits complete indifference to the interests of society and is completely self-centered, methodical, cunning, and "fully cognizant of the criminality of his act and its impact on society."[129] The disorganized asocial lust murderer was described this way: "[He] exhibits primary characteristics of societal aversion. This individual prefers his own company to that of others and would be typified as a loner. He experiences difficulty in negotiating interpersonal relationships and consequently feels rejected and lonely. He lacks the cunning of the nonsocial type and commits the crime in a more frenzied and less methodical manner. The crime is likely to be committed in close proximity to his residence or place of employment, where he feels secure and more at ease."[130]

Orion Picture Album/Newscom

Scott Glenn, starring as Jack Crawford in the crime thriller *Silence of the Lambs,* which publicized the practice of criminal profiling. How can psychological profiling assist criminal investigations?

Critics of psychological profiling say that it is still more art than science. In a recent article published on the American Psychological Association's website, for example, psychologist Lea Winerman says that psychological profiling "is still a relatively new field with few set boundaries or definitions. Its practitioners don't always agree on methodology or even terminology."[131] Moreover, many early FBI profilers were not psychologists, and the techniques they developed were not necessarily based on accepted psychological perspectives or accepted methodology.

Terms like *offender profiling* and *crime-action profiling* are used today to describe the work of profilers. Today's profilers tend to analyze crime-scene data and offender interviews, searching for commonalities that can be used to distinguish between types of offenders. Another term commonly used today is *investigative psychology,* which can be defined as "the scientific discipline of applying, analyzing, or developing psychological principles, theories or empirical findings to aid investigations and the legal process."[132]

Some contemporary psychologists discount the value of profiling. In 2007, a meta-analysis of profiling studies found that "trained profilers did only slightly better

■ **psychological autopsy**   A procedure for investigating a person's death by reconstructing what the person thought, felt, and did before death, based on information gathered from personal documents, police reports, medical and coroner's records, and face-to-face interviews with families, friends, and others who had contact with the person before the death. Used primarily in cases of suicide or murder-suicide.

■ **insanity (legal)**   A legally established inability to understand right from wrong or to conform one's behavior to the requirements of the law.

than non-profilers at estimating the overall characteristics of offenders from information about their crimes."[133] The studies compared the ability of profilers with nonprofilers to gauge an offender's physical characteristics, thinking processes (including motives), and personal habits.[134] Nonetheless, profiling remains highly visible in today's media and continues to be popular with the public. Visit the International Research Center for Investigative Psychology at the University of Liverpool at **https://www.hud.ac.uk/ research/researchcentres/ircip.** In 2014, the FBI's BAU was merged into other operational divisions.

The Psychological Autopsy

Criminal psychologists may sometimes be called upon to perform a **psychological autopsy**, which is "a procedure for investigating a person's death by reconstructing what the person thought, felt, and did before death, based on information gathered from personal documents, police reports, medical and coroner's records, and face-to-face interviews with families, friends, and others who had contact with the person before the death."[135] Psychological autopsies are often conducted in cases of murder-suicides, or in suspected suicides in an attempt to reconstruct the life and character of the suicidal individual—information that might be useful in further criminal investigation. The process focuses on identifying the deceased's state of mind at the time of death and on discovering preexisting behavioral patterns that might have contributed to suicidal or homicidal intent. It includes an attempt to identify interpersonal relationships, cognitions related to them, and affective states of mind, as well as behavioral characteristics that might have contributed to the crime. Psychological autopsies focus particularly on identifying patterns consistent with personality disorders or mental illnesses.[136]

A psychological autopsy can help determine why a particular mode of death resulted and may be able to identify contributing factors. Those constructing a psychological autopsy might ask, "Why did the perpetrator do this? Why now? Why with this particular victim, and in this manner?" Finally, a complete psychological autopsy provides a reflective analysis to help

determine and predict future violent behavior for others who may be similarly situated.

Insanity and the Law

Unfortunately for criminologists, psychological conceptions of mental illness, antisocial personality, and even psychopathy are not readily applicable to the criminal justice system, which relies instead on the legal concept of insanity.[137] **Insanity**, for purposes of the criminal law, is strictly a legal, not a clinical, determination. Seen this way, *insanity* is a term that refers to a type of defense allowable in criminal courts. Although the legal concept of insanity is based upon claims of mental illness, it has no precise counterpart in the jargon of contemporary psychologists or psychiatrists, who speak instead in terms of mental status or, at most, psychosis and personality disorder. As a consequence, legal and psychiatric understandings of mental impairment rarely coincide.

> The legal concept of insanity has no precise counterpart in the jargon of psychologists.

One of the first instances within the Western legal tradition where insanity was accepted as a defense to criminal liability can be found in the case of Daniel M'Naughten (also spelled "McNaughton" and "M'Naghton"). M'Naughten was accused of the 1843 killing of Edward Drummond, the secretary of British prime minister Sir Robert Peel. By all accounts, M'Naughten had intended to kill Peel, but because M'Naughten was suffering from mental disorganization, he shot Drummond instead, mistaking him for Peel. At his trial, the defense presented information to show that M'Naughten was suffering from delusions, including the belief that Peel's political party was persecuting him. The court accepted his lawyer's claims, and the defense of insanity was established in Western law. Other jurisdictions were quick to adopt the M'Naughten rule, as the judge's decision in the case came to be called. The **M'Naughten rule** holds that individuals cannot be held criminally responsible for their actions if at the time of the offense

CRIMINAL | PROFILES

Andrea Yates—Child Killer

David J. Phillip/AP Images

Andrea Yates (center), who admitted drowning her five children in a bathtub at the family home, leaving the Harris County (Texas) Criminal Justice Center with her attorney. Yates was sent to a maximum-security mental hospital where she will be held until she is cured. What do you think should have been done with Yates?

Few crimes have shocked American society as deeply as the drowning of five young children by their mother, Andrea Pia (Kennedy) Yates, in a bathtub in their suburban Houston, Texas, home on June 20, 2001. Her subsequent trial, conviction, life sentence, successful appeal, and second trial brought under intense scrutiny the insanity defense based on a claim of postpartum psychosis.

Yates's early life showed promise for future success. High school valedictorian and swim team captain, she went on to earn an undergraduate degree in nursing from the University of Texas. After obtaining a job as a registered nurse, she met Rusty Yates. Their shared deep Christian faith was a significant factor in their attraction to each other.

When Andrea and Rusty finally married, they planned on having as many children as God intended. The birth of their first child, Noah, a year after their marriage, however, brought unexpected difficulties.

Unaware of the extent of mental illness that had plagued her own family, the new mother was tormented when she began to have violent visions of stabbings and came to believe that Satan was speaking directly to her. Yates hid these frightening experiences from everyone, including her husband. The Yates's had two more children, after which Andrea miscarried. She then had their fourth child, but the birth was followed by pronounced depressive manifestations—including chewed fingers, uncontrollable shaking, hallucinations, voices in her head, suicidal and homicidal thoughts, and two suicide attempts. Soon she entered into a series of psychiatric counseling sessions with various doctors. A wide variety of drug therapies were tried, many of which Andrea rejected by flushing the prescriptions down the toilet.

Despite extensive hospitalizations and medication for her ongoing depression and emerging psychosis—and against the advice of her psychiatrist—Yates became pregnant again, delivering her fifth child, Mary, in November 2000. The pregnancy had resulted from the urging of her husband, who also ignored the strong medical opposition to the birth of another child.[i]

When Yates's father died just four and a half months after her fifth child was born, her mental health declined dramatically.[ii] Both a hospitalization at the end of March and her medication, however, were terminated by her psychiatrist, Dr. Mohammed Saeed, because, he claimed, she did not seem psychotic. Yates returned to the hospital again for ten days in May. Upon her release, she was advised to think positive thoughts and to see a psychologist.

Two days later, she systematically drowned each of her five children.

Following a sensational trial, Yates was convicted and sentenced to life in prison. That conviction was subsequently overturned. In July 2006, Yates was retried, but this time she was acquitted of capital murder charges and found not guilty by reason of insanity. She was immediately ordered to be committed to a mental hospital, where she will remain until she is no longer considered a threat to herself or others.[iii] Today, Yates is held at the Kerrville State Hospital, located 70 miles south of San Antonio. She has been diagnosed with bipolar disorder and is medicated by daily injection.[iv]

The case of Andrea Yates raises a number of interesting questions. Among them are the following:

1. Could Yates be considered a psychopath? Why or why not?

2. How could Yates's mental issues be seen in light of the theories presented in this chapter?

3. Could the irresistible-impulse test be applicable to Yates's case? The M'Naughten rule? Which seems to fit best?

Notes

i   Charles Montaldo, "Profile of Andrea Yates," About.com: Crime/Punishment, 2007, http://crime.about.com/od/current/p/andreayates.htm (accessed June 16, 2010).

ii Ibid.

iii "Jury: Yates Not Guilty by Reason of Insanity," July 26, 2006, MSNBC/Associated Press, http://www.msnbc.msn.com/id/14024728 (accessed June 16, 2007).

iv Andrew Cohen, "How Andrea Yates Lives, and Lives with Herself, A Decade Later," The Atlantic, March 12, 2012, http://www.theatlantic.com/national/archive/2012/03/how-andrea-yates-lives-and-lives-with-herself-a-decade-later/254302 (accessed July 3, 2013).

■ **M'Naughten rule**   A standard for judging legal insanity that requires that offenders did not know what they were doing, or if they did, that they did not know it was wrong.

■ **irresistible-impulse test**   A standard for judging legal insanity that holds that a defendant is not guilty of a criminal offense if the person, by virtue of his or her mental state or psychological condition, was not able to resist committing the crime.

■ **guilty but mentally ill (GBMI)**   A finding that offenders are guilty of the criminal offense with which they are charged, but because of their prevailing mental condition, they are generally sent to psychiatric hospitals for treatment rather than to prison. Once they have been declared cured, such offenders can be transferred to correctional facilities to serve out their sentences.

(1) they did not know what they were doing or (2) they did not know that what they were doing was wrong.

Today, the M'Naughten rule is still followed by many states when insanity is at issue in criminal cases. Critics of the M'Naughten rule say that although the notion of intent inherent within it appeals greatly to lawyers, "it is ... so alien to current concepts of human behavior that it has been vigorously attacked by psychiatrists. An obvious difficulty with the M'Naughten rule is that practically everyone, regardless of the degree of his [mental] disturbance, knows the nature and quality and rightness or wrongness of what he is doing."[138]

The M'Naughten ruling opened the floodgates for other types of insanity claims offered as defenses to charges of criminal activity. One interesting claim is that of irresistible impulse. The **irresistible-impulse test**—employed by 18 states, some of which also follow the dictates of the M'Naughten rule—holds that a defendant is not guilty of a criminal offense if the person, by virtue of his or her mental state or psychological condition, was not able to resist committing the action in question.

Guilty but Mentally Ill (GBMI)

A verdict of **guilty but mentally ill (GBMI)** means that a person can be held responsible for a specific criminal act, even though a degree of mental incompetence may be present. In most GBMI jurisdictions, a jury must return a finding of "guilty but mentally ill" if (1) every statutory element necessary for a conviction has been proved beyond a reasonable doubt, (2) the defendant is found to have been mentally ill at the time the crime was committed, and (3) the defendant was not found to have been legally insane at the time the crime was committed. The difference between mental illness and legal insanity is crucial because a defendant can be mentally ill by standards of the medical profession but sane for purposes of the law.

Upon return of a GBMI verdict, a judge may impose any sentence possible under the law for the crime in question. Offenders who are declared GBMI are, in effect, found guilty of the criminal offense with which they are charged

Several states permit findings of guilty but mentally ill (GBMI).

but, because of their mental condition, are generally sent to psychiatric hospitals for treatment rather than to prison. Once they have

Insanity can be used as a defense against criminal charges. Lorena Bobbitt sobs on the witness stand before acquittal on charges she severed her husband's penis with a kitchen knife; Bobbitt claimed a kind of irresistible impulse. Should she have been acquitted?

been declared "cured," however, such offenders can be transferred to correctional facilities to serve out their sentences.

Problems with the Insanity Defense

Although insanity defenses are popular in courtroom fiction, they are rarely used in the real world. When they are raised, they must be brought before the court and proven by the defense. Studies show that fewer than 1% of all criminal defendants adopt an insanity defense.[139] Even when employed, the defense rarely works, and 75% of those who claim insanity are convicted anyway.[140] And if a defendant is found "not guilty by reason of insanity," he or she is likely to spend a long time in court-ordered institutional psychiatric treatment. Only 15% are immediately set free.[141]

Finally, some critics ask whether the idea of mental illness, or the legal concept of insanity, is even useful in the study of criminology. Confusion, they charge, arises when considering whether mental illness should be seen as a cause, an explanation, or an excuse for criminal behavior.[142]

SUMMARY

- Psychological and psychiatric theories of criminal behavior emphasize individual propensities and characteristics in explaining criminality. Whether the emphasis is on conditioned behavior, human cognition, or the psychoanalytic structure of the human personality, these approaches see the wellsprings of human motivation, desire, and behavioral choice as being firmly rooted in the individual.

- Two major ideas characterized early psychological theories: personality and behaviorism. Personality theory built on the burgeoning area of cognitive science, including personality disturbances and diseases of the mind; behaviorism examined social learning with an emphasis on behavioral conditioning.

- The psychopathic personality, one that is cunning and self-serving but without empathy, offers an explanation for personality found in the unrestrained desires of offenders. The antisocial personality, by contrast, is essentially unsocialized and generally in conflict with society.

- Cognitive theories are learning theories that examine thought processes, and seek to explain how people learn to solve problems and how they perceive and interpret their social environment. Cognitive theory has a number of branches, including one that focuses on moral and intellectual development, and another that examines how people process information.

- Psychiatric criminology, or forensic psychiatry, sees crime as caused by biological and subconscious psychological urges mediated through consciousness. From the point of view of psychoanalysis, criminal behavior is maladaptive, the product of inadequacies in the offender's personality. The psychoanalytic perspective, advanced by Sigmund Freud in the early 1900s, encompasses diverse notions such as personality, neurosis, and psychosis as well as transference, sublimation, and repression. Some psychiatric perspectives see criminality as a form of adaptive behavior to stresses, holding that law violation represents an individual's most satisfactory method of adjustment to inner conflicts that he or she cannot otherwise express.

- Behavior theory (or the stimulus–response approach to human behavior) holds that behavior is directly determined by the environmental consequences it produces for the individual exhibiting the behavior. When an individual's behavior results in rewards or positive feedback, that behavior will increase in frequency; when punishment follows behavior, that behavior will decrease.

- Some theorists now consider that psychological criminology can be used for the development of consistent and dependable social policy in the prediction of dangerousness, the treatment and rehabilitation of offenders, and

selective incapacitation as a workable policy to prevent future criminality.

- Critics say that by focusing on the individual, psychological and psychiatric theories of criminality do not sufficiently take into account social or environmental conditions that produce crime.

- Psychological profiling of criminal offenders, based on the belief that almost any form of conscious behavior is symptomatic of the individual's personality, is a serious crime-fighting undertaking that may change the nature of localized crime-prevention strategies.

- Psychological and psychiatric conceptions of mental illness, antisocial personality, and even psychopathy are not readily applicable to the criminal justice system, which relies instead on the legal concept of insanity. Although the legal concept of insanity is based upon claims of mental illness, it has no precise counterpart in the jargon of contemporary psychologists or psychiatrists.

KEY TERMS

alloplastic adaptation, 145

antisocial personality, 136

antisocial personality disorder (ASPD), 136

attachment theory, 146

autoplastic adaptation, 145

behavior theory, 148

behaviorism, 133

cognitive information-processing theory (CIP), 139

conditioning, 133

correctional psychology, 150

criminal psychology, 132

criminogenic needs, 146

ego, 143

electroencephalogram (EEG), 136

Five Factor Model, 137

forensic psychiatry, 133

forensic psychology, 132

guilty but mentally ill (GBMI), 159

id, 143

insanity (legal), 157

irresistible-impulse test, 159

M'Naughten rule, 157

modeling, 149

moral development theory, 138

neurosis, 143

operant behavior, 148

paranoid schizophrenic, 144

personality, 133

psychiatric criminology, 142

psychoanalysis, 142

psychoanalytic theory, 133

psychological autopsy, 157

psychological profiling, 155

psychopath, 134

psychopathy, 133

psychosis, 143

psychotherapy, 143

punishment, 148

repression, 144

reward, 148

risk assessment, 145

schizophrenia, 133

scripts, 139

selective incapacitation, 152

social cognition theory, 149

sociopath, 135

sublimation, 143

superego, 143

traits, 137

KEY NAMES

Robert P. Abelson, 139

August Aichorn, 144

Donald A. Andrews, 146

Ronet Bachman, 146

Albert Bandura, 145

James Bonta, 146

John Bowlby, 146

Hervey M. Cleckley, 134

J. Dollard, 145

Hans J. Eysenck, 137

Sigmund Freud, 142

Seymour L. Halleck, 145

Lawrence Kohlberg, 138

Arnold S. Linsky, 146

Jean Piaget, 138

Stanton E. Samenow, 140

Roger C. Schank, 139

B. F. Skinner, 148

Murray A. Straus, 146

Gabriel Tarde, 149

Richard H. Walters, 145

Samuel Yochelson, 140

QUESTIONS FOR REVIEW

1. What are the major principles of psychological perspectives on criminal behavior?

2. What two major ideas characterized early psychological theories, and what was the difference between them?

3. How do personality disturbances explain criminality?

4. What are cognitive theories, and what three types of cognitive theories does this chapter discuss?

5. What insights into criminal behavior does the psychoanalytic perspective offer?

6. How does behavior theory explain the role of rewards and punishments in shaping behavior?

7. What are the policy and treatment implications of psychological understandings of criminality?

8. How can psychological and psychiatric theories of criminality be critiqued?

9. What are some assumptions underlying the practice of criminal psychological profiling?

10. How does the legal concept of insanity differ from behavioral understandings of the same concept?

QUESTIONS FOR REFLECTION

1. This book emphasizes the theme of social problems versus individual responsibility. Which perspective is better supported by psychological theories of crime causation? Why?

2. How do psychological theories of criminal behavior differ from other types of theories presented in this book? How do the various psychological and psychiatric approaches presented in this chapter differ from one another?

3. How would the perspectives discussed in this chapter suggest that offenders might be prevented from committing additional offenses? How might they be rehabilitated?

4. How can crime be a form of adaptation to one's environment? Why would an individual choose such a form of adaptation over others that might be available?

5. Which of the various standards for judging legal insanity discussed in this chapter do you find the most useful? Why?

CHAPTER 7

SOCIAL STRUCTURE THEORIES

It's Where and How We Live

LEARNING OUTCOMES

After reading this chapter, you should be able to answer the following questions:

- What is the nature of sociological theorizing, and what are the assumptions upon which sociological perspectives on crime causation rest?

- What do sociologists mean by the term social structure, and how might the organization and structure of a society contribute to criminality?

- What are the three types of social structure theories of crime that are discussed in this chapter, and what are the characteristics of each?

- What are the policy implications of the theories discussed in this chapter?

- What are the shortcomings of the social structure approaches to understanding and preventing crime?

■ **Follow the author's tweets about the latest crime and justice news @schmalleger.**

■ **sociological theory**   A perspective that focuses on the nature of the power relationships that exist between social groups and on the influences that various social phenomena bring to bear on the types of behaviors that tend to characterize groups of people.

■ **social structure**   The pattern of social organization and the interrelationships among institutions characteristic of a society.

Introduction

There's an old saying, something to the effect that you can take the criminal out of a bad environment, but you can't take the bad environment out of the criminal. Although we don't necessarily believe this to be true, some suggest that the negative influences of the social environment—especially things like poverty, lack of education, broken families, disorganized neighborhoods, episodes of discrimination, and socialization into unproductive values—predispose certain people to lives of crime and that such

> Cutting California's dropout rate in half would prevent 30,000 juvenile crimes and save $900 million yearly in enforcement costs.

negative influences may remain active even when people's circumstances change. Central to this perspective is the idea that crime is a social phenomenon, and central to any understanding of crime is the role that society, social institutions, and social processes play in its development and control.

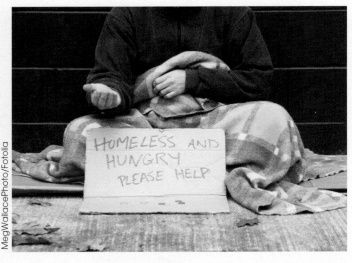

MegWallacePhoto/Fotolia

A homeless man asks for assistance. Ecological theories suggest that crime shows an unequal geographic distribution. Why might certain geographic areas be associated with identifiable patterns of crime?

Major Principles of Sociological Theories

Theories that explain crime by reference to social structure are only one of three major sociological approaches to crime causation. The other two are social process theories and social conflict approaches (which we describe in Chapters 8 and 9). Although sociological perspectives on crime causation are diverse, most build upon the principles shown in Figure 7–1.

Sociological theories examine both institutional arrangements within a **social structure** (i.e., interrelationships

Major Principles of Sociological Theories of Crime

- Social groups, social institutions, the arrangements of society, and social roles all provide the proper focus for criminological study.

- Group dynamics, group organization, and subgroup relationships form the causal nexus out of which crimes develop.

- The structure of society and its relative degree of organization or disorganization are important factors contributing to criminal behavior.

- Although it may be impossible to predict the specific behavior of a given individual, statistical estimates of group characteristics are possible. Hence, the probability that members of a certain group will engage in a specific type of crime can be estimated.

FIGURE 7-1 | **Major Principles of Sociological Theories of Crime**

Source: Schmalleger, Frank, *Criminology*. Printed and Electronically reproduced by permission of Pearson Education, Inc., Upper Saddle River, New Jersey.

■ **social process**   The interaction between and among social institutions, groups, and individuals.
■ **social life**   The ongoing (typically) structured interaction—including socialization and social behavior in general—that occurs between persons in a society.

■ **social structure theory**   A theory that explains crime by reference to the economic and social arrangements in society. This type of theory emphasizes relationships among social institutions and describes the types of behavior that tend to characterize groups of people rather than individuals.

among society's institutions) and **social processes** (i.e., interactions between and among different social institutions, groups, and individuals) as they affect socialization and have an impact on **social life** (i.e., social interaction). In contrast to more individualized psychological theories, which have what is called a "micro" focus, sociological approaches utilize a "macro" perspective, stressing the type of behavior likely to be exhibited by group members rather than attempting to predict the behavior of specific individuals. As noted in Chapter 1, sociological thought has influenced criminological theory construction more significantly than any other perspective during the past half century, due (at least in part) to a widespread concern with social problems including civil rights, the women's movement, issues of poverty, and the decline in influence experienced by many traditional social institutions, such as the family, government, organized religion, and educational systems.

Although all sociological perspectives on crime share some characteristics, particular theories give greater or lesser weight to selected components of social life. We can identify three key sociological explanations for crime:

1. **Crime is the result of an individual's location within the structure of society.** This approach focuses on the social and economic conditions of life, including poverty, alienation, social disorganization, weak social control, personal frustration, relative deprivation, differential opportunities, alternative means to success, and deviant subcultures and subcultural values that conflict with conventional values. (These are the primary features of *social structure theories*, which are discussed in this chapter and in Chapter 10 in the section "Structural Explanations for Homicide.")

2. **Crime is the end product of various social processes.** This approach stresses inappropriate socialization and social learning as well as interpersonal relationships, strength of the social bond, lack of self-control, and personal and group consequences of societal reactions to deviance as they contribute to crime. (These are the primary characteristics of *social process theories* and *social development theories*, which are discussed in Chapter 8, and in Chapter 10 where the subculture of violence thesis is described.)

3. **Crime is the product of class struggle.** This perspective emphasizes existing power relationships between social groups, distribution of wealth within society, ownership of the means of production, and

economic and social structures of society as they relate to social class and social control. (These are the primary features of *social conflict theories*, which are discussed in Chapter 9.)

Social Structure Theories

Social structure theories explain crime by reference to the economic and social arrangements (or structure) of society. They see the various formal and informal arrangements between social groups (i.e., the structure of society) as the root causes of crime and deviance. Structural theories predict that negative aspects of societal structure, such as disorganization within the family, poverty or income inequality within the economic arrangements of society, and disadvantages due to lack of success in the educational process, produce criminal behavior.

Although different kinds of social structure theories have been advanced to explain crime, they all have one thing in common: They highlight those arrangements within society that contribute to the low socioeconomic status of identifiable groups as significant causes of crime. Social structure theorists view members of socially and economically disadvantaged groups as being more likely to commit crime, and they see economic and social disenfranchisement as fundamental causes of crime. Poverty, lack of education, absence of salable skills, and subcultural values conducive to crime are all thought to be predicated on the social conditions surrounding early life experiences, and they provide the causal underpinnings of social structure theories. Environmental influences, socialization, and traditional and accepted patterns of behavior are all used by social structuralists to portray the criminal as a product of his or her social environment, and the immediate social environment is viewed as a consequence of the structure of the society to which the offender belongs. Although criminality is recognized as a form of acquired behavior, it is depicted as the end result of social inequality, racism, and feelings of disenfranchisement to which existing societal arrangements give rise. Similarly, social structure, insofar as it is unfair and relatively unchangeable, is believed to perpetuate the fundamental conditions that cause crime. Consequently, viewed from a social structure perspective, crime is seen largely as a lower-class phenomenon, while the criminality of the middle and upper classes is generally discounted as less serious, less frequent, and less dangerous.

■ **social disorganization theory** A perspective on crime and deviance that sees society as a kind of organism and crime and deviance as a kind of disease, or social pathology. This type of theory is often associated with the perspective of social ecology and with the Chicago School of criminology, which developed during the 1920s and 1930s.

■ **human ecology** The interrelationship between human beings and the physical and cultural environments in which they live.

THEORY | in PERSPECTIVE
Types of Social Structure Theories

Social structure theories emphasize poverty, lack of education, absence of marketable skills, and deviant subcultural values as fundamental causes of crime. These theories, which portray crime as the result of an individual's location within the structure of society and focus on the social and economic conditions of life, are divided into three types.

Social Disorganization

Depicts social change, social conflict, and the lack of social consensus as the root causes of crime and deviance; an offshoot, social ecology, sees society as a kind of organism and crime and deviance as a disease or social pathology.

Period: 1920s–1930s with continued influence on current research

Theorists: Robert Park, Ernest Burgess, W. I. Thomas, Florian Znaniecki, Clifford Shaw, Henry McKay, Oscar Newman, James Q. Wilson, George L. Kelling

Concepts: Social ecology, ecological theories, social pathology, social disorganization, Chicago School, Chicago Area Project, demographics, concentric zones, delinquency areas, cultural transmission, collective efficacy, social cohesion (criminology of place, crime prevention through environmental design [CPTED], environmental criminology, defensible space, crime pattern theory, and the broken windows theory represent, at least in part, a contemporary reinterpretation of early ecological notions.)

Strain Theory

Points to a lack of fit between socially approved success goals and the availability of socially approved means to achieve those goals. As a consequence, according to the perspective of strain theory, individuals who are unable to succeed through legitimate means turn to other avenues (crime) that promise economic and social recognition.

Period: 1930s–present

Theorists: Robert K. Merton, Steven F. Messner, Richard Rosenfeld, Peter Blau and Judith Blau, Robert Agnew

Concepts: Anomie, goals, means, innovation, retreatism, ritualism, rebellion, differential opportunity, relative deprivation, distributive justice, general strain theory (GST)

Culture Conflict

Sees the root cause of crime in a clash of values between variously socialized groups over what is acceptable or proper behavior.

Period: 1920s–present

Theorists: Thorsten Sellin, Frederic M. Thrasher, William F. Whyte, Walter B. Miller, Gresham Sykes, David Matza, Franco Ferracuti, Marvin Wolfgang, Richard A. Cloward, Lloyd E. Ohlin, Albert Cohen, many others

Concepts: Subculture, violent subcultures, socialization, focal concerns, delinquency and drift, techniques of neutralization, illegitimate opportunity structures, reaction formation, conduct norms

Types of Social Structure Theories

This chapter describes three major types of social structure theories: (1) social disorganization theory (also called the *ecological approach*), (2) strain theory, and (3) culture conflict theory (also called *cultural deviance theory*). All have a number of elements in common, and the classification of a theory into a subcategory is often a matter of which aspects a writer chooses to emphasize rather than any clear-cut definitional elements inherent in that theory (see the Theory in Perspective box in this chapter).

Social Disorganization Theory

Social disorganization theory (which depicts social change, social conflict, and lack of social consensus as the root causes of crime and deviance) is closely associated with the ecological school of criminology. Much early criminology in the United States was rooted in the study of urban settlements and communities[1] as well as the human ecology movement of the early twentieth century. *Ecology* is a term borrowed from biology that describes the interrelationships between living organisms and their environment, and social scientists use the term **human ecology**

■ **social disorganization**   A condition said to exist when a group is faced with social change, uneven development of culture, maladaptiveness, disharmony, conflict, and lack of consensus.

■ **social ecology**   An approach to criminological theorizing that attempts to link the structure and organization of a human community to interactions with its localized environment.

■ **social pathology**   A concept that compares society to a physical organism and that sees criminality as an illness.

to describe the interrelationship between human beings and the physical and cultural environments in which they live.[2] Pioneers in the human ecology movement saw cities as "superorganisms" that incorporated areas adapted to specific groups, including ethnic groups (e.g., "Little Italy," "Chinatown"), which were functional enclaves within a larger organized whole that possessed its own dynamics.

The idea of the community as a functional whole that directly determines the quality of life for its members was developed and explored around the beginning of the twentieth century by sociologists such as Emile Durkheim (1858–1917),[3] Ferdinand Toennies (1855–1936),[4] and Georg Simmel (1858–1918).[5] Durkheim believed that crime was a normal part of all societies and that law was a symbol of social solidarity, so an act was "criminal when it offends strong and defined states of the collective conscience."[6]

Some of the earliest sociologists to study American communities were **W. I. Thomas** and **Florian Znaniecki**. In *The Polish Peasant in Europe and America*, Thomas and Znaniecki described the problems Polish immigrants faced in the early 1900s when they left their homeland and moved to American cities.[7] The authors noted that crime rates rose among displaced people and hypothesized that the cause was the **social disorganization** that resulted from immigrants' inability to successfully transplant guiding norms and values from their home cultures into the new one (see **http://www.apa.org/topics/immigration/immigration -psychology.aspx**). Learn more about early social disorganization perspectives via **http://www.csiss.org/classics/ content/66/.** Learn more about social structure theories at **https://communitiesandplace.org.**

The Chicago School

Some of the earliest sociological theories to receive widespread recognition can be found in the writings of **Robert Park** and **Ernest Burgess**. In the 1920s and 1930s at the University of Chicago, they developed what became known as **social ecology**, or the ecological school of criminology.[8] The social ecology movement, influenced by the work of biologists on the interactions of organisms with their environments, concerned itself with how the structure of society adapts to the quality of natural resources and to the existence of other human groups.[9] One writer stated that social ecology is "the attempt to link

Some of the earliest sociological theories to receive widespread recognition were found in the Chicago School and focused on what became known as social ecology.

the structure and organization of any human community to interactions with its localized environment."[10] Because ecological models build on an organic analogy, it is easy to portray social disorganization as a disease or pathology.[11] Hence, social ecologists who studied crime developed a disease model built around the concept of **social pathology**, defined as "those human actions which run contrary to the ideals of residential stability, property ownership, sobriety, thrift, habituation to work, small business enterprise, sexual discretion, family solidarity, neighborliness, and discipline of will."[12] Over time, the concept of social pathology changed and came to represent the idea that some aspects of society are pathological, or "sick," and produce deviant behavior among groups and individuals who are exposed to such social conditions.

Social disorganization and social pathology may arise when a group is faced with "social change, uneven development of culture, maladaptiveness, disharmony, conflict, and lack of consensus."[13] Due to the rapid influx of immigrant populations at the beginning of the twentieth century, American cities were caught up in swift social change, and Park and Burgess saw in them an ideal focus for the study of social disorganization. They viewed cities as having five concentric zones, much like the circles on a target, each with unique characteristics and populations (see Figure 7–2): Zone I, or the "loop," contained retail businesses and light manufacturing; Zone II, also referred to as "zone in transition," surrounding the city center, was home to impoverished immigrant groups, and was characterized by deteriorating houses and factories and abandoned buildings; Zone III, also known as the "working-class" zone, contained the second group of immigrants who escaped the poverty conditions of Zone II. Zone IV was occupied by middle-class citizens with single-family homes; and Zone V, the suburbs, was called the "commuter zone." Park and Burgess noticed that residents of the inner zones tended to migrate to outer zones as their economic positions improved.

■ **cultural transmission**   The idea that delinquency is transmitted through successive generations of people living in an area through the same process of social communication by which languages, social roles, and attitudes are transmitted.

■ **ecological theory**   A type of sociological approach that emphasizes demographics (the characteristics of population groups) and geographics (the mapped location of such groups relative to one another) and that sees the social disorganization that characterizes delinquency areas as a major cause of criminality and victimization.

■ **Chicago School of criminology**   An ecological approach to explaining crime that examines how social disorganization contributes to social pathology.

■ **criminology of place**   A perspective that emphasizes the importance of geographic location and architectural features as they are associated with the prevalence of criminal victimization; also called *environmental criminology*.

■ **environmental criminology**   A perspective that emphasizes the importance of geographic location and architectural features as they are associated with the prevalence of criminal victimization; also called *criminology of place*.

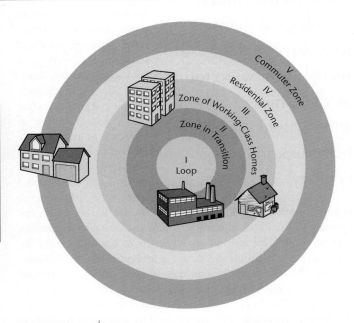

FIGURE 7-2 | Chicago's Concentric Zones
Source: Based on data from Robert E. Park, Ernest W. Burgess, and R. D. McKenzie, The City (Chicago: University of Chicago Press, 1925), p. 55.

Cultural transmission theory says that delinquency is transmitted to new generations in the same way that languages, roles, and attitudes are.

Clifford Shaw and **Henry McKay**, other early advocates of the ecological approach, applied the concentric zones to the study of juvenile delinquency, conducting empirical studies of Chicago juveniles' arrest rates in 1900–1906, 1917–1923, and 1927–1933 (years associated with high rates of neighborhood transition). Shaw and McKay found that rates of offending remained relatively constant over time within zones of transition and concluded that delinquency was caused by the nature of the environment in which immigrants lived rather than by characteristics of the immigrant groups themselves.[14] Shaw and McKay saw social disorganization as the inability of local communities to solve common problems and believed that the degree of disorganization in a community was largely predicated upon the extent of residential mobility and racial heterogeneity present in that community. As a result of their studies, they developed the idea of **cultural transmission**: Traditions of delinquency were transmitted to successive generations in the same zone in the same way that languages, roles, and attitudes were communicated.

Because early **ecological theories** focused on selected geographic areas, their methodology came to be known as "area studies." Because 1920s Chicago served as the model for most such studies, they became collectively referred to as the **Chicago School of criminology**. Although the applicability of these early studies to other cities or other time periods was questionable, the Chicago School had demonstrated the tendency for criminal activity to be associated with urban transitional zones, which were typified by social disorganization, turmoil, lower property values, poverty, and lack of privacy.

The greatest contribution the ecological school made to criminological literature can be found in its claim that society wields a major influence on human behavior.[15] Ecological theorists of the Chicago School used two sources of information: (1) population statistics and official crime and (2) ethnographic data. Population statistics (demographics), when combined with crime information, provided empirical material that gave scientific weight to ecological investigations; ethnographic information, gathered in the form of life stories (ethnographies), described the lives of city inhabitants. By comparing one set of data with the other—demographics with ethnographies—ecological investigators were able to show that life experiences varied from one location to another and that personal involvement in crime was strongly associated with place of residence. Learn more about the Chicago School of criminology at **http://sociology.uchicago.edu/content/history-culture**.

The Criminology of Place

Ecological approaches to crime causation have found a modern rebirth in the **criminology of place** (also called **environmental criminology**), which builds on the contributions of routine activities theory and situational crime prevention

■ **pattern theory**   The idea that specific types of crime are associated with certain areas—and that it is the characteristics of those areas that contribute to crime's concentration.

PUTTING CRIMINOLOGY TO WORK—Implementing Evidence-Based Policy

To make a difference in the real world, criminological theories must first be tested and evaluated. Once evidence has been developed that theory-based practices work, then programs based on them can be implemented to reduce or prevent crime, or to help make victims' lives better. One federal initiative, CrimeSolutions.Gov, strives to evaluate the effectiveness of theory-based practices, and then communicates its findings via the Web. Some of the most effective and promising programs are highlighted in boxes such as this one that appear throughout the text.

PROGRAM: Improved Street Lighting

EVIDENCE RATINGS FOR OUTCOMES: Promising

PROFILE

Interventions that focus on improving street lighting aim to prevent crime by modifying an environment and reducing opportunities for offenders to commit crimes. These interventions may occur in public or private settings, such as residential neighborhoods, parking lots, shopping malls, campuses, hospitals, or various other facilities. Installation and street light components vary by setting. For example, in a neighborhood or residential setting, improved street lighting may include trimming bushes so that lights are more visible, or replacing old or broken lamps with new light fixtures to achieve the street light's intended purpose. Through

modifying and improving environmental measures in various settings, the overall goal of these interventions is crime prevention.

Relevant Theory: Situational Crime Prevention, Crime Prevention through Environmental Design (CPTED)

Improving street lighting to prevent crime is grounded in the idea of situational crime prevention, which involves the associated concept of crime prevention through environmental design (CPTED). Situational crime prevention (discussed earlier in Chapter 3) holds that crime is influenced by environmental conditions in interaction with resident and offender characteristics. Therefore, by improving street lighting, the offender is believed to perceive greater risks of apprehension. It is believed that modifying the nighttime visibility within urban areas should reduce opportunities for crime by increasing the perceived risk of detection.

Evidence-Based Review

These sources were used in the development of the practice profile:

Meta-Analysis 1

Brandon C. Welsh, and David P. Farrington, *Effects of Improved Street Lighting on Crime*. The Campbell Collaboration. **http://www.campbellcollaboration.org/news_/improved_street_lighting_reduce_crime.php**.

Source: Adapted from https://www.crimesolutions.gov/PracticeDetails.aspx?ID=37

Notes: Putting Criminology to Work features are based on information published online by the National Institute of Justice's (NIJ) Crime Solutions Website. The program ratings shown are those provided by NIJ.

(which are discussed in Chapters 3 and 10). It emphasizes the importance of geographic location and architectural features in terms of prevalence of victimization. Such "hot spots" of crime, including neighborhoods, specific streets, and even individual houses and businesses, have been identified by recent writers. Lawrence W. Sherman, for example, and colleagues tell of a study that revealed that 3% of places (addresses and intersections) in Minneapolis produced 50% of all calls to the police. Crime, noted Sherman, although relatively rare in Minneapolis and similar urban areas, is geographically concentrated.[16] Later researchers, using the *pattern theory of crime diversity* have found that not only is crime concentrated in certain areas, but that "the spatial distribution of environmental cues and opportunities plays a central role in regulating crime diversity."[17] In other words

pattern theory shows that specific types of crime are associated with certain geographic areas—and that it is the characteristics of those areas that contribute to crime's concentration.

Policing hot spots, also known variously as *place-based policing* and *place-based crime prevention*, is a concept that was popularized by George Mason University's David Weisburd, University of Maryland's John Eck, Harvard University professor Anthony Braga, and others.[18]

Place-based crime prevention has been shown to be a potentially effective crime-reduction technique. In a 2004 report, the National Research Council Committee to Review Research on Police Policy and Practices concluded that "[t]here has been increasing interest over the past two decades in police practices that target very specific types of crimes, criminals, and

■ **broken windows theory**   A perspective on crime causation that holds that physical deterioration in an area leads to increased concerns for personal safety among area residents and to higher crime rates in that area.

■ **defensible space**   The range of mechanisms that combine to bring an environment under the control of its residents.
■ **Crime Prevention Through Environmental Design (CPTED)**   A crime prevention technique that modifies features of the physical environment to accomplish its goals.

crime places. In particular, policing crime hot spots has become a common police strategy for reducing crime and disorder problems....[A] strong body of evidence suggests that taking a focused geographic approach to crime problems can increase the effectiveness of policing."[19]

Reflecting the questions first addressed by Shaw and McKay, researcher **Rodney Stark** asked, "How is it that neighborhoods can remain the site of high crime and deviance rates despite a complete turnover in their populations? There must be something about places as such that sustains crime."[20] Stark developed a *theory of deviant neighborhoods* consisting of 30 propositions, including the following:[21]

- To the extent that neighborhoods are dense and poor, homes will be crowded.
- Where homes are more crowded, there will be a greater tendency to congregate outside the home in places and circumstances that raise levels of temptation and offer opportunity to deviate.
- Where homes are more crowded, there will be lower levels of supervision of children.
- Reduced levels of child supervision will result in poor school achievement, with a consequent reduction in stakes in conformity and an increase in deviant behavior.
- Poor, dense neighborhoods tend to be mixed-use neighborhoods.
- Mixed use increases familiarity with and easy access to places offering the opportunity for deviance.

The broken windows theory says that neighborhood physical deterioration leads to increased delinquency, vandalism, and crime.

Central to the criminology of place is the **broken windows theory**, which holds that physical deterioration such as increases in unrepaired buildings leads to greater concerns for personal safety among area residents.[22] These concerns lead to further decreases in maintenance and repair; to increased delinquency, vandalism, and crime; and to even further deterioration in safety and the physical environment—all resulting in offenders from other neighborhoods being increasingly attracted by the area's perceived vulnerability. Physical disorder, left unchecked, leads to crime by driving residents indoors and sending a message to would-be offenders that a neighborhood is out of control.[23]

The broken windows perspective, first advanced in a 1982 article by **James Q. Wilson** and **George L. Kelling** titled "Broken Windows: The Police and Neighborhood Safety,"[24]

led to an increase in the use of "order maintenance policing" and a crackdown on quality-of-life offenses, such as panhandling, graffiti, littering, and prostitution, in some of our nation's cities. In 2000 in New York City, (then) Mayor Rudolph Giuliani announced a new police campaign using computer mapping to track crime and to target offenses such as jaywalking, public urination, panhandling, graffiti, public drinking, and prostitution.

Even within high-crime neighborhoods and neighborhoods characterized by urban decay, crimes tend to be concentrated at specific locations, such as street blocks or multiple-family dwellings, and some units within specific apartment buildings are more likely to be the site of criminal occurrences. The criminology of place employs the concept of **defensible space**. The concept was developed by architect **Oscar Newman** in 1972,[25] and means "the range of mechanisms—real and symbolic barriers, strongly defined areas of influence, and improved opportunities for surveillance—that combine to bring an environment under the control of its residents."[26] Newman's publication *Creating Defensible Space* can be accessed via **www.justicestudies.com/pubs/defensible-space.pdf.**

The criminology of place holds that location can be as predictive of criminal activity as the lifestyles of victimized individuals or the social features of victimized households. (*Place* has been defined by researchers as "a fixed physical environment that can be seen completely and simultaneously, at least on its surface, by one's naked eyes."[27]) Places can be criminogenic because they have certain routine activities associated with them or because they provide the characteristics that facilitate crime commission (see, Chapter 10).

Another concept associated with defensible space is the idea of **Crime Prevention Through Environmental Design (CPTED)**.[28] CPTED is based on the belief that offenders decide whether to commit a crime in a particular location after they evaluate the area's physical features. Architects who employ CPTED in their planning, design public areas that are always in plain view, and whose opportunities for criminal activity are limited by physical features such as walls and points of entrance or exit.

Sometimes it is the public or city governments that take the initiative in crime prevention using environmental design. Recently, for example, the Washington, D.C, Metropolitan Police Department was asked to appoint environmental design experts to a planning committee being created by the city to develop two new projects—the Anacostia River front and the Wharf.[29] City officials believed that embedding crime-prevention architects with developers in the planning team would help in the construction of safety-oriented developments.

Some crime-prevention programs are combining ideas derived from the criminology of place with spatial-mapping techniques to fight crime (the Theory versus Reality box

■ **collective efficacy**   The collective ability of residents to produce social action to meet common goals and preserve shared values.

provides information about crime-mapping techniques). Visit the National Institute of Justice's MAPS program via **http://www.ojp.usdoj.gov/nij/maps/**to learn more about crime mapping, and see **http://www.hunchlab.com** for insight into computer algorithms used in predictive policing.

More recent studies of the broken windows concept have cast doubt on the assertion, made by Wilson and Kelling, that police intervention into the process that links disorder and crime can be effective in reducing crime.[30] It may be that disorder and crime have common roots and that one is more associated with the other than produced by it.[31] Hence, efforts to target quality-of-life offenses in urban areas experiencing high levels of social disorganization may not have the desired effect of reducing crime. David Thacher, professor of public policy

and urban planning at the University of Michigan, explained that "these challenges to the broken windows theory have not yet discredited order maintenance policing with policymakers or the public. But among criminologists, order maintenance is clearly under siege."[32] See the Crime in the News box in this chapter for more on broken windows theory.

Collective Efficacy and Crime

Although order maintenance policies implemented by policy makers may have only limited efficiency in reducing crime, efforts to empower residents to exert positive social control within their own neighborhoods may be a workable strategy. The concept of **collective efficacy** grew out of the social disorganization literature and refers to the "collective ability of

PUTTING CRIMINOLOGY TO WORK—Implementing Evidence-Based Policy

To make a difference in the real world, criminological theories must first be tested and evaluated. Once evidence has been developed that theory-based practices work, then programs based on them can be implemented to reduce or prevent crime, or to help make victims' lives better. One federal initiative, CrimeSolutions.Gov, strives to evaluate the effectiveness of theory-based practices, and then communicates its findings via the Web. Some of the most effective and promising programs are highlighted in boxes such as this one that appear throughout the text.

PROGRAM: Safer Cities Initiative

EVIDENCE RATINGS FOR OUTCOMES: Promising

PROFILE

The main goal of the Safer Cities Initiative (SCI) was to reduce crime in the Los Angeles, California, area known as "Skid Row"—a section of the city with a large homeless population concentrated in a densely packed area of economic disadvantage. Skid Row had high rates of crime and victimization, including open-air drug markets, prostitution, theft, robbery gangs, and vandalism. As an attempt to combat rising levels of crime and improve public order in the Skid Row area, the Los Angeles Police Department (LAPD) implemented the SCI program starting in 2006.

Fifty full-time officers were stationed on the streets of Skid Row, where they broke up homeless encampments, issued citations, and made arrests for various offenses. In conjunction with this effort, portable toilets were removed from the area to

deter homeless people from loitering. The LAPD also targeted crimes, such as public intoxication, drug use, and prostitution, all of which were believed to make the area more inviting to criminals. In addition, four to five officers were placed on foot patrol in the area to concentrate exclusively on handling nuisance offenses and maintaining order. Undercover vice teams were also used to target open-air drug markets and prostitution. Lastly, a special undercover squad concentrated on local robberies.

Relevant Theory: Broken Windows Theory

SCI was based on the "broken windows" theory of crime, which posits a connection between neighborhood disorder and serious crime. The premise of this theory is that public order offenses signal that neighborhood residents either do not care to maintain their neighborhood or do not have the resources to do so. Thus, if a window is broken and left unrepaired in a neighborhood, it is a sign that no one cares about the area. According to the theory, if public order offenses are left unchecked, then social order in the neighborhood will decline and lead to an increase in serious criminal behavior.

Evidence-Based Review

These sources were used in the development of the program profile:

Study 1

Richard Berk and John MacDonald, "Policing the Homeless: An Evaluation of Efforts to Reduce Homeless-Related Crime," *Criminology and Public Policy*, Vol. 9 (2010), pp. 813–840.

Source: Adapted from https://www.crimesolutions.gov/ProgramDetails.aspx?ID=182

Notes: Criminology at Work features are based on information published online by the National Institute of Justice's (NIJ) Crime Solutions Website. The program ratings shown are those provided by NIJ.

■ **social cohesion**   An emotional and social investment in a neighborhood and a sense of shared destiny among residents.

■ **strain theory**   A sociological approach that posits a disjuncture between socially and subculturally sanctioned means and goals as the cause of criminal behavior.

■ **anomie**   A social condition in which norms are uncertain or lacking.

residents to produce social action to meet common goals and preserve shared values."[33] Studies show that social interaction between neighborhood residents holds the potential to create a strong sense of **social cohesion** and common interests. When people share common goals and trust each other, quality of life rises and feelings of empowerment emerge. In effect, research shows that grassroots efforts to increase levels of effective community functioning can work, with or without formal intervention from the police, policy makers, or other parties. One study in 2014 that examined both the impact of collective efficacy and social cohesion on crime found that they represented distinct processes but that decreases in either social cohesion or collective efficacy are associated with increases in homicide in the areas studied.[34] Researchers concluded that a community-based collective efficacy effort could be effective at preventing crime.

In what may seem like a contrary finding, Arizona State University criminologists discovered that youth are more likely to co-offend in neighborhoods with peers of their own race/ethnicity, that are less disadvantaged, and that have greater residential stability—all of which, say the researchers, "promote trust among neighbors." In other words "many of the same neighborhood characteristics that reduce crime lead to a greater proportion of co-offending."[35]

Strain Theory

The second type of social structure theory discussed in this chapter is strain theory. *Strain* can be defined as the pressure that individuals feel to reach socially determined goals.[36] The classic statement of **strain theory**—which depicts delinquency as a form of adaptive problem-solving behavior committed in response to problems involving frustrating and undesirable social environments—was offered in 1938 by **Robert K. Merton**, who also refined the concept of **anomie** (a French word meaning "normlessness").

> Robert K. Merton popularized the term *anomie*, a French word meaning "normlessness."

Anomie was popularized by Emile Durkheim in his 1897 book *Suicide*, in which he used the term to explain how a breakdown of predictable social conditions can lead to feelings of personal loss, dissolution, and lack of a sense of belonging.[37] Merton's use of the term *anomie* was somewhat different and meant a disjunction between socially approved means to success and legitimate goals.[38] Merton maintained that legitimate goals, such as wealth, status, and personal happiness, are generally portrayed as desirable for everyone, but the widely acceptable means to these goals, such as education, hard work, and financial savings, are not equally available. As a consequence, crime and deviance tend to arise as alternative means to success when individuals feel the strain of being pressed to succeed in socially approved ways but find that the tools necessary for such success are not available to them and that strain increases as the gulf between the goals and the means available to achieve them widens. Merton's emphasis on the felt strain resulting from a lack of fit between goals and means led to his approach being called *strain theory*.

Complicating the picture further, Merton maintained that not everyone accepts the legitimacy of socially approved goals. Merton diagrammed possible combinations of goals and means as shown in Table 7–1. The first row, labeled *conformity*, signifies acceptance of the goals that society holds as legitimate for everyone, with ready availability of the means approved for achieving those goals; the mode of adaptation associated with this combination of goals and means typifies most middle- and upper-class individuals.

Innovation arises when an emphasis on approved goal achievement combines with a lack of opportunity to participate fully in socially acceptable means to success, which is experienced by many lower-class individuals who have been socialized to desire traditional success symbols (expensive cars, large homes, big bank accounts) but do not have ready access to approved means of acquiring them (educational opportunity);

TABLE 7-1 | Goals and Means Disjuncture

	GOALS	MEANS
Conformity	+	+
Innovation	+	−
Ritualism	−	+
Retreatism	−	−
Rebellion	±	±

Source: Adapted from Robert K. Merton, "Social Structure and Anomie," *American Sociological Review*, Vol. 3, No. 5 (October 1938), pp. 672–682.

THEORY | versus REALITY

The Criminology of Place, Routine Activities, and Crime Mapping

Today's law enforcement agencies are using the criminology of place and routine activities theories (discussed in Chapter 10) to develop situational crime-prevention techniques (see Chapter 3) that combine technology with crime mapping. One implementation of this approach is the Mapping and Analysis Program (MAPS) of the National Institute of Justice. Crime mapping, used in conjunction with geographic information systems (GISs), makes effective use of law enforcement resources by helping police administrators direct patrols to places where they are most needed.

In the routine activities interpretation, crimes are seen as needing three ingredients: a likely offender, a suitable target, and the absence of a guardian capable of preventing the criminal act. Then comes the term *density paradox*: On the one hand, high population densities create a high potential for crime because people and property are crowded in small spaces, resulting in many likely offenders and suitable targets; on the other hand, surveillance is plentiful, so criminal acts in public spaces are likely to be observed by others (guardians). Crime can be reduced or prevented by making people less likely to offend (by increasing guilt and fostering development of the "inner policeman" who tames criminal impulses), by making targets less available (also called *situational crime prevention*), and by making guardians more numerous or effective. Putting the routine activities approach and situational crime prevention into a geographic context involves asking how each element is distributed in geographic space. Where are the likely offenders? (What is the geography of the youthful male population?) Where are the suitable targets? (What is the geography of convenience stores, malls, ATMs, poorly illuminated pedestrian areas?) Where are the guardians? (What is the potential for surveillance, both formal and informal, of targets or areas that may contain targets?)

The perspective that focuses on criminal spatial behavior develops a scenario in which the motivated (potential) criminal uses cues, or environmental signals, to assess victims or targets. Clusters and sequences of cues relating to the social and physical aspects of the environment are seen as a *template*, which the offender uses to evaluate victims or targets; tied to this process is the concept of *activity space*, the area where the offender customarily moves about that is familiar to him or her.

Activity spaces vary with demographics. Historically, younger persons tended to have more constricted activity spaces, not having resources to travel far, and women had more geographically limited activity areas than men because men worked farther from home and their jobs gave them greater mobility; both are less true today.

Analysts considering crime patterns from a theoretical perspective might ask some "filter" questions: How important is geography in explaining a pattern? Is the pattern random or not? If not, why not? Can routine activities theory or criminal spatial behavior theory help explain this pattern? Is this pattern normal or unusual for this area? If the pattern is an anomaly, why is this? What resources can be used to better understand the social and other environmental dynamics of the area of interest?

For a list of websites displaying interactive crime maps, see **http://www.crimemapping.com.** Situational crime prevention was discussed earlier in Chapter 3.

Discussion Questions

1. How does routine activities theory support the concepts involved in the spatial analysis of crime?

2. What is the density paradox? What implications does it have for crime prevention?

3. What "filter" questions are discussed in this box? Can you think of any others that might be asked?

Source: National Institute of Justice, "Mapping and Analysis for Public Safety (MAPS)," http://www.ojp.gov/nij/maps (accessed May 28, 2007); and Keith Harries, *Mapping Crime: Principles and Practice* (Washington, DC: National Institute of Justice, 1999), http://www.ojp.usdoj.gov/cmrc (accessed December 15, 2005).

---

innovative behavioral responses, including crime, can be expected to develop when individuals find themselves deprived. Merton said that "poverty as such, and consequent limitation of opportunity, are not sufficient to induce a conspicuously high rate of criminal behavior. Even the often mentioned 'poverty in the midst of plenty' will not necessarily lead to this result."[39] It is when those who find themselves in poverty are pressured to achieve material success and acquire other associated symbols of status that innovation results.

The third row, *ritualism*, refers to the type of behavior arising when members of society participate in socially desirable means but show little interest in goal achievement. A ritualist may get a good education, work every day in an acceptable occupation, and appear to be leading a solid middle-class lifestyle, yet care little for the symbols of success, choosing to live an otherwise independent lifestyle.

Retreatism describes the behavior of those who reject both the socially approved goals and the means. They may become dropouts, drug abusers, or homeless persons or participate in alternative lifestyles, such as communal living; they are often socially and psychologically quite separate from the larger society around them.

Olli Scarff/Getty Images

London's Metropolitan Police officers view displays from closed circuit television (CCTV) cameras around London in the Special Operations Room of their Central Communications Command. Defensible space can be defined in terms of barriers to crime commission and preventive surveillance opportunities. How might such features be enhanced in high-crime areas?

CRIME | in the NEWS

The Pros and Cons of "Broken Windows" Policing

JAMES Q. WILSON is credited with co-authoring one of the most influential policing theories of all time. His "broken windows" theory posits that crime develops from small things, such as shattered windows, spray-painted gang signs, and panhandling. These outward signs tell criminals that a community is ripe for the picking.

When the theory was first published in 1982, it broke with the orthodoxy of the time, which focused on giving would-be criminals economic incentives to become law-abiding citizens. Wilson, who viewed himself as politically independent, was heralded as a new conservative voice. Republican Mayor Rudy Giuliani of New York City endorsed Wilson's theory when he entered office in 1993.

Rather than just focusing on major crimes, New York City police started going after small crimes in a big way. Misdemeanor arrests increased 70% during the rest of the decade, and Giuliani faced complaints of police harassment. But New York City's crime rate dropped dramatically, much more than a corresponding drop in the nationwide rate. Violent crime in the city declined by more than 56%, compared with a 28% U.S. drop, and property crimes fell by about 65%, compared with 26% nationally.

Los Angeles, Chicago, and Boston also adopted aspects of broken windows, and the theory has led to hot-spot policing, which focuses patrols on areas with high crime. This technique is currently used in several U.S. cities, from Oakland, California, to St. Louis, Missouri.

Similarly, a recent police program piloted in a Detroit neighborhood specifically referenced the theory. The city partnered with the Manhattan Institute, a conservative think-tank that brought in George L. Kelling, Wilson 's co-author on the original 1982 broken windows paper and an executive at the institute.

In the Detroit project, police officers spent extra time interacting with the community, and community members were encouraged to report suspicious activity. At the end of the 120-day pilot, the community noted 32% fewer home invasions in the area compared to the same time last year. At the time, Detroit police planned to extend the program to other Detroit neighborhoods.

Recently, however, some of the principles behind broken windows policing have been called into question. That's because a number of highly publicized police use-of-force incidents grew out of the

An abandoned house in a run-down neighborhood. What does broken windows theory say about places like this?

Carol Dembinsky / Dembinsky Photo Associates / Alamy Stock Photo

heightened vigilance these kinds of programs require. In one example, a man was placed into a choke hold by NYPD officers and died as a result of selling cigarettes on a city street without a license. In another, a convicted felon who had been selling CDs outside of a convenience store in Baton Rouge, Louisiana, was shot and killed by police after he allegedly resisted a pat down search.

Discussion Questions

1. How would you describe the broken windows theory of policing?

2. What implications does the broken windows theory hold for crime-prevention policy? Do you know of any communities in which you'd like to see it applied?

3. Do you agree with recent criticisms of broken windows theory regarding its possible link to excessive use of force by the police? If so, how can the issue be addressed?

Sources: Brian Dickerson, "Broken Windows Theory of Community Policing Will Get Major Test in Detroit," *Detroit Free Press*, May 24, 2012, http://www.freep.com/apps/pbcs.dll/article?AID=2012205240458; Joan Petersilia, "Remembering James Q. Wilson," *The Crime Report*, March 18, 2012, http://www.thecrimereport.org/news/inside-criminal-justice/2012-03-remembering-james-q-wilson; and Ivana Hrynkiw, "Man Shot, Killed by Police Outside Baton Rouge Convenience Store," *Alabama News*, July 6, 2016, http://www.al.com/news/index.ssf/2016/07/man_shot_killed_by_police_outs.html.

Merton's last category, *rebellion*, describes the actions of a person who wishes to replace socially approved goals and means with some other system; political radicals, revolutionaries, and antiestablishment agitators fit into this category. Merton believed that conformity is the most common mode of adaptation prevalent in society and that retreatism is the least common.

A 2006 study by sociologists Thomas M. Arvanites and Robert H. Defina at Villanova University tested the idea that negative economic conditions and declining business cycles can increase social strain, resulting in heightened rates for certain kinds of crimes, especially property crimes. By comparing society's economic conditions over time with rates for such crimes, the researchers concluded that "an improving economy has a negative and statistically significant effect on all four index

property crimes and robbery." Because financial gain is the primary purpose of robbery, they noted that "a finding that robbery is the only violent crime to be influenced by the business cycle was not surprising."[40]

Relative Deprivation

Another version of Merton's anomie theory has been proposed by Steven F. Messner and Richard Rosenfeld, who suggested that inconsistencies in the American Dream are to be blamed for most criminal activity: "Our thesis is that the American Dream itself exerts pressures toward crime by encouraging an anomic cultural environment, an environment in which people are encouraged to adopt an 'anything goes' mentality in the pursuit of personal goals."[41]

■ **relative deprivation** A sense of social or economic inequality experienced by those who are unable, for whatever reason, to achieve legitimate success within the surrounding society.

■ **distributive justice** The rightful, equitable, and just distribution of rewards within a society.

■ **general strain theory (GST)** A perspective that suggests that law-breaking behavior is a coping mechanism that enables those who engage in it to deal with the socioemotional problems generated by negative social relations.

It is often said that Americans are the richest people on earth and that even the poorest Americans are far richer than the average citizen of many Third World nations, but even if such an assertion is true, it means little to someone who is living in the United States and is poor when judged in terms of U.S. standards. Deprivation has an important psychological component and cannot be accurately assessed in absolute terms.

Relative deprivation refers to the economic and social gaps that exist between rich and poor who live in close proximity to one another. According to sociologists Judith Blau and Peter Blau, two proponents of the relative deprivation concept, people assess their position in life by way of comparison with things and people they already know.[42] According to the Blaus, relative deprivation creates feelings of anger, frustration, hostility, and social injustice on the part of those who experience it. According to **distributive justice**, which refers to people's perceptions of their rightful place in the reward structure of society, even wealthy and socially privileged individuals may feel slighted or shortchanged if they feel inadequately rewarded for their behavior or accomplishments. But the perception of the rightful distribution of rewards appears to be highly dependent upon cultural expectations; for example, even successful Americans sometimes feel they deserve more, whereas studies show that Japanese society has been able to accommodate rapid socioeconomic growth without generating a felt sense of economic injustice, even among its least successful members, and without experiencing a substantial increase in crime.[43]

Surveys provide evidence for distinguishing between two types of relative deprivation: personal and group.[44] Personal relative deprivation is characteristic of individuals who feel deprived compared with other people; group relative deprivation is a communal sense of injustice that is shared by members of the same group. People who experience personal deprivation are likely to feel socially isolated and personally stressed, and those who believe their entire social group is deprived relative to other groups are more prone to participate in social movements and may actively attempt to change the social system, making group relative deprivation a powerful force for social change.

General Strain Theory

In 1992, strain theory was reformulated by **Robert Agnew** and others who molded it into a comprehensive perspective called **general strain theory (GST)**.[45] GST sees law-breaking behavior as a coping mechanism enabling those who engage in it to deal with the socioemotional problems generated by negative social relations

> GST sees law-breaking as a coping mechanism for dealing with socioemotional problems.

(Figure 7–3). In 2006, Agnew restated the six central propositions of GST, as shown in Figure 7–4.[46]

Agnew explained that the strains most likely to cause crime in Western societies include child abuse and neglect; negative secondary school experiences; abusive peer relations; chronic unemployment; marital problems; parental rejection; erratic, excessive, and or/harsh supervision or discipline; criminal victimization; homelessness; racial, ethnic, or gender discrimination; and failure to achieve selected goals. Factors that increase the likelihood of criminal coping include poor conventional coping skills and resources; availability of criminal skills and resources; low levels of conventional social support; routine association with criminal others; personal beliefs and values favorable to crime; frequent exposure to situations where the costs of crime are low; low levels of social control, including weak bonds to conventional others; and lack of investment in conventional institutions. Agnew's strategies for reducing exposure to strains include eliminating strains conducive to crime, altering strains to make them less conducive to crime, removing individuals from exposure to strain, and equipping individuals with the traits and skills needed to avoid strains conducive to crime.

GST expands on traditional strain theory in several ways. First, it significantly widens the focus of strain theory to include all types of negative relations between an individual and others; second, GST maintains that strain is likely to have a cumulative effect on delinquency after reaching a certain threshold; third, general strain theory provides a more comprehensive account of the cognitive, behavioral, and emotional adaptations to strain than traditional strain approaches; and finally, GST more fully

■ **negative affective state** An adverse emotion such as anger, fear, depression, or disappointment that derives from the experience of strain.

FIGURE 7-3 | A Visual Representation of Strain Theory

Source: Schmalleger, Frank, *Criminology*. Printed and Electronically reproduced by permission of Pearson Education, Inc., Upper Saddle River, New Jersey.

describes the wide variety of factors affecting the choice of delinquent adaptations to strain.

Agnew saw the crime-producing effects of strain as cumulative and concluded that whatever form it takes, "strain creates a predisposition for delinquency in those cases in which it is chronic or repetitive."[47] Predispositions may be manifested in

the form of **negative affective states**, meaning emotions such as anger, fear, depression, and disappointment.

An analysis by Agnew of other strain theories found that all such theories share at least two central explanatory features.[48] Agnew said that strain theories focus (1) "explicitly on negative relationships with others, relationships in which the individual is

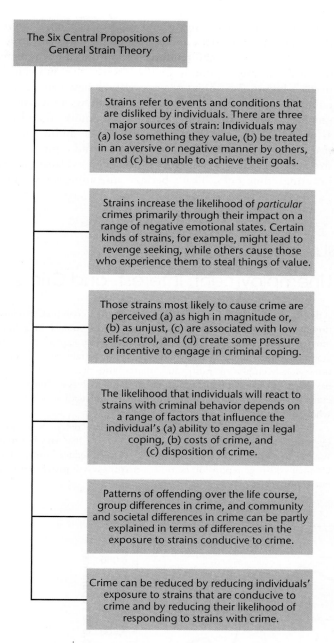

The Six Central Propositions of
General Strain Theory

Strains refer to events and conditions that are disliked by individuals. There are three major sources of strain: Individuals may (a) lose something they value, (b) be treated in an aversive or negative manner by others, and (c) be unable to achieve their goals.

Strains increase the likelihood of *particular* crimes primarily through their impact on a range of negative emotional states. Certain kinds of strains, for example, might lead to revenge seeking, while others cause those who experience them to steal things of value.

Those strains most likely to cause crime are perceived (a) as high in magnitude or, (b) as unjust, (c) are associated with low self-control, and (d) create some pressure or incentive to engage in criminal coping.

The likelihood that individuals will react to strains with criminal behavior depends on a range of factors that influence the individual's (a) ability to engage in legal coping, (b) costs of crime, and (c) disposition of crime.

Patterns of offending over the life course, group differences in crime, and community and societal differences in crime can be partly explained in terms of differences in the exposure to strains conducive to crime.

Crime can be reduced by reducing individuals' exposure to strains that are conducive to crime and by reducing their likelihood of responding to strains with crime.

FIGURE 7-4 | **The Six Central Propositions of General Strain Theory**

Source: Based on The Six Central Propositions of General Strain Theory by Robert Agnew from Pressured Into Crime: An Overview of General Strain Theory. (Los Angeles: Roxbury, 2006).

more broadly as exposure to negative stimuli, general strain was found to be significantly related to delinquency.

Contrary to Agnew's hypothesis, however, Paternoster and Mazerolle found no evidence that the effects of strain were enhanced when they were experienced for longer periods of time or that they were diminished when adolescents classified the area of their life in which they experienced strain as "unimportant." Consistent with earlier findings,[51] Paternoster and Mazerolle found that feelings of general strain were positively related to later delinquency—regardless of the number of delinquent peers, moral beliefs, self-efficacy, and level of conventional social support—and that general strain leads to delinquency by weakening the conventional social bond and strengthening the unconventional bond with delinquent peers.

In a more recent test of GST, Lisa M. Broidy of the University of New Mexico examined the intervening role of negative emotions and legitimate coping strategies as they impact the relationship between strain and crime and found that strain can produce anger and other negative emotions and that different sources of strain tend to produce different emotions.[52] "Hence, although evidence of a relationship exists between strain and negative emotions, the nature of this relationship depends on the specific type of strain and negative emotions considered."[53] Strain-induced anger was more likely to lead to criminal outcomes among men than among women, even though members of both genders experienced anger equally under certain specific types of strained circumstances. Broidy also discovered that "negative emotional responses to strain other than anger are associated with a significant increase in legitimate coping and significant decrease in illegitimate/criminal outcomes."[54]

A 2002 study by Robert Agnew and associates further refined GST by explaining why some individuals are more likely than others to react to strain with delinquency.[55] They found that juveniles who measured high in negative emotionality and low in constraint were more likely to react to strain with delinquency and noted that the "incorporation of such traits into GST represents an integration between strain theory and the rapidly growing research on behavioral genetics and crime."[56] Hence, it may be that certain biological factors make some individuals particularly susceptible to the effects of strain in their lives.

In 2010, Joan R. Hipp at the University of California, Irvine, reporting on a study of crime rates in 352 American metropolitan areas over a 30-year period, reinforced the notion of strain as a cause of crime.[57] Hipp, whose study focused on the effect of economic resources and racial/ethnic composition on the change in crime rates, found that economic inequality increases the amount of crime in cities, but that the distribution of inequality across the census tracts of a city has important interaction effects. In cities with high levels of inequality, Hipp discovered, higher levels of economic segregation actually lead to much higher levels of the types of crime that she studied (including aggravated assaults, robberies, burglaries, and motor vehicle thefts). By contrast, Hipp found, in cities with low levels of inequality, it is mixing of households in neighborhoods with varying levels of income that leads to higher levels of crime.

In 1986, sociologists Arnold S. Linsky and Murray A. Straus, developed a State Stress Index (SSI) that provides a quantitative measure of stress for each state and region in the

not treated as he or she wants to be treated," and he argued that (2) "adolescents are pressured into delinquency by the negative affective states—most notably anger and related emotions—that often result from negative relationships."[49]

In 1994, Raymond Paternoster and Paul Mazerolle tested some of the assumptions underlying GST through an analysis of data from the National Youth Survey.[50] They found partial support for GST and discovered that negative relations with adults, feelings of dissatisfaction with friends and school life, and experiences of stressful events were positively related to delinquency, as was living in an unpleasant neighborhood (with social problems and physical deterioration). When conceived of

United States.[58] Linsky and Straus used the index to evaluate the relationship between the occurrence of stress and the incidence of crime, illness, and other forms of maladaptive behavior. They found that states with higher homicide and suicide rates had higher levels of social stress, as measured by such factors as business failures, personal bankruptcies, and unemployment claims.

Finally, in 2016, criminologist James Austin and Sociologist Gregory D. Squires found strong support for GST by determining that financial interest rates constitute one of the best predictors of crime rates.[59] Simply put, when interest rates go up, crime goes up; when rates come down, crime goes down. As Austin and Squires explain, "Crime Rates are linked to social and economic pressures and structures.... They reflect and reinforce various social phenomena that are not subject simply to the choices that individuals make." Figure 7-5 shows the correlation between interest rates and rates of crime over time. It also shows a measure of unemployments rates, which Austin and Squires found not as predictive of crime as interest rates. The authors noted that the correlation between interest rates and crime is very strong—and offers a potentially powerful explanation for lowering crime rates. That's because, the authors say, "low

THEORY | versus REALITY

The Correlation between Rates of U.S. Unemployment, Interest, and Crime

In 2016, criminologists James Austin and Gregory D. Squires demonstrated an "almost perfect correlation" between financial interest rates and crime in the United States (Figure 7-5). They found that "interest rates constitute one of the best predictors of crime" over time, noting that as interest rates rise so do rates of crime. Although Austin and Squires acknowledged that interest rates do not directly cause crime, they explained that the two are linked through the impact of interest rates on things like employment, income, and economic prosperity. Austin and Squires say that the key to understanding the relationship between interest rates and crime is "stress"—and it is the social stress produced by lessened economic activity that impacts lives and leads to choices in which criminal activity is seen as profitable, or as a way to supplement or even supplant income derived from more legitimate

activities. Increased interest rates lead to decreased economic production because businesses find it harder to borrow money in a high interest rate environment. Thus, they are unlikely to expand their operations, and less likely to hire additional staff or to raise the salaries of those already employed. Austin and Squires write that "Criminologists have long known that when individuals find themselves in difficult circumstances they are more tempted to resort to unlawful activities than when their lives are more routine and stable."

Findings by Austin and Squires support recent recommendations by the President's Council of Economic Advisors that says boosting wages—in particular the minimum wage—"could reduce crime." The Council's 80-page report can be read at **http://www.justicestudies.com/pubs/cea.pdf**.

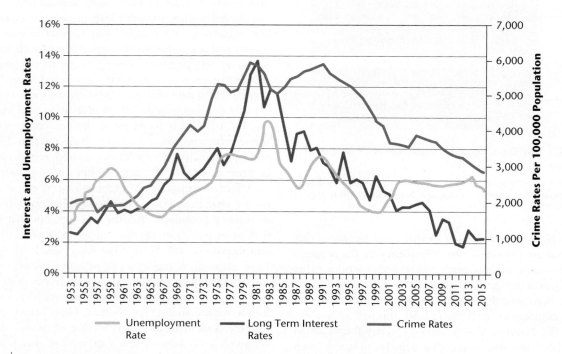

FIGURE 7-5 | Unemployment Rates, Interest Rates, and Rates of Crime in the United States

References: James Austin and Gregory D. Squires, "The 'Startling' Link Between Low Interest Rates and Low Crime," *The Crime Report*, December 6, 2016; and President's Council of Economic Advisors, *Economic Perspectives on Incarceration and the Criminal Justice System* (Washington, DC: The White House, April 2016).

■ **culture conflict theory**   A sociological perspective on crime that suggests that the root cause of criminality can be found in a clash of values between variously socialized groups over what is acceptable or proper behavior; also called *cultural deviance theory.*

■ **conduct norms**   Shared expectations of a social group relative to personal conduct.
■ **subculture**   A collection of values and preferences that is communicated to subcultural participants through a process of socialization.
■ **subcultural theory**   A sociological perspective that emphasizes the contribution made by variously socialized cultural groups to the phenomenon of crime.

interest rates translate into greater economic prosperity," and economic prosperity lowers stressors that would otherwise lead to crime. High interest rates, they say, can dampen economic prosperity and lead to a loss of jobs as businesses are forced to pay more to borrow money, and are able to afford fewer employees. Even so, while the correlation between interest rates and crime seems strong on the surface, saying that low interest rates mean economic prosperity may not be entirely correct. In fact, during the early part of this century, interest rates were kept artificially low by Federal Reserve intervention in an effort to stimulate the economy—not because the economic environment was healthy. In fact, were the unemployment rate to be correlated with interest rates, one would likely find an inverse, but similarly strong correlation.

Culture Conflict Theory

The third type of social structure theory discussed in this chapter is **culture conflict theory** (also called *cultural deviance theory*), which suggests that the root cause of criminality can be found in a clash of values between differently socialized groups over what is acceptable or proper behavior. The culture conflict concept is inherent in ecological criminology (discussed earlier in this chapter) and its belief that zones of transition tend to be in flux and harbor groups of people whose values are often at odds with those of the larger society.

> Conduct norms are acquired early in life through childhood socialization.

The culture conflict perspective found its clearest expression in the writings of **Thorsten Sellin** in his 1938 book *Culture Conflict and Crime*, where he stated that the root cause of crime could be found in different values for what is acceptable or proper behavior.[60] According to Sellin, **conduct norms**, which provide the valuative basis for human behavior, are acquired early in life through childhood socialization, and it is the clash of norms between variously socialized groups that results in crime. Because crime is a violation of laws established by legislative decree, the criminal event itself is nothing other than a disagreement over what should be acceptable behavior.

Sellin described two types of culture conflict. *Primary conflict* arises when a fundamental clash of cultures occurs, as when an immigrant father kills his daughter's lover following an Old World tradition that demands a family's honor be kept intact.[61] *Secondary conflict* occurs, according to Sellin, when smaller cultures within the primary one clash, as when middle-class values (on which most criminal laws are based) find fault with inner-city or lower-class norms, resulting in the social phenomenon we call *crime*.

Subcultural Theory

Fundamental to the notion of culture conflict is the idea of a **subculture**, a collection of values and preferences that is communicated to subcultural participants through a process of socialization. Subcultures differ from the larger culture in that they claim the allegiance of smaller groups of people. For example, the wider American culture may proclaim that hard work and individuality are valuable, but a particular subculture may espouse the virtues of deer hunting, male bonding, and recreational alcohol consumption. Countercultures, which tend to reject and invert the values of the surrounding culture, and criminal subcultures, which actively espouse deviant activity, represent extremes. **Subcultural theory** is a sociological perspective that emphasizes the contributions made by variously socialized cultural groups to the phenomenon of crime.

Early writings on subcultures include *The Gang* by **Frederic M. Thrasher**.[62] Thrasher studied 1,313 gangs in Chicago in 1927, and his descriptive work led to a typology in which he described different types of gangs. In 1943, **William F. Whyte**, drawing on Thrasher's work, published *Street Corner Society*.[63] Whyte, in describing his three-year study of the Italian slum he called "Cornerville," further developed the subcultural thesis, showing that lower-class

■ **focal concerns**   The key values of any culture, especially a delinquent subculture.

residents of a typical slum could achieve success through the opportunities afforded by slum culture, including racketeering and bookmaking. Read more on culture in conflict at **http://ssrn.com/abstract=1325347.**

Focal Concerns

In 1958, **Walter B. Miller** attempted to detail the values that drive members of lower-class subcultures into delinquent pursuits, describing lower-class culture as "a long established, distinctively patterned tradition with an integrity of its own."[64] According to that article, titled "Lower Class Culture as a Generating Milieu of Gang Delinquency," a large body of systematically interrelated attitudes, practices, behaviors, and values characteristic of lower-class culture are designed to support and maintain the basic features of the lower-class way of life. In areas where these differ from features of middle-class culture, action oriented to the achievement and maintenance of the lower-class system may violate norms of the middle class and be perceived as deliberately nonconforming. "This does not mean, however, that violation of the middle-class norm is the dominant component of motivation; it is a by-product of action primarily oriented to the lower-class system."

Miller also outlined what he termed the **focal concerns** (key values) of delinquent subcultures: trouble, toughness, smartness, excitement, fate, and autonomy. Miller concluded that subcultural crime and deviance are not the direct consequences of poverty and lack of opportunity but emanate from specific values characteristic of such subcultures. According to Miller, *trouble* is a dominant feature of lower-class culture. Getting into trouble, staying out of trouble, and dealing with trouble when it arises become focal points in the lives of many members of lower-class culture. Miller recognized that getting into trouble is not necessarily valued in and of itself but is seen as a necessary means to valued ends.

Like many theorists of the time, Miller was primarily concerned with the criminality of men. The lower-class masculine concern with *toughness* may have been due to many men in the groups he examined being raised in female-headed families and may have reflected an almost obsessive concern with masculinity as a reaction to the perceived threat of overidentification with female role models.

Miller described *smartness* as the "capacity to outsmart, outfox, outwit, dupe, take, [or] con another or others and the concomitant capacity to avoid being outwitted, taken or duped oneself. In its essence, smartness involves the capacity to achieve a valued entity—material goods, personal status—through a maximum use of mental agility and a minimum of physical effort." *Excitement* was seen as a search for thrills—often necessary to overcome the boredom inherent in lower-class lifestyles. Fighting, gambling, picking up women, and making the rounds were all described as derivative aspects of the lower-class concern with excitement. *Fate* is related to the quest for excitement and to the concept of luck. As Miller stated, "Many lower-class persons feel that their lives are subject to a set of forces over which they have relatively little control. These are not supernatural forces or organized religion but relate more to a concept of 'destiny' or man as a pawn. This often implicit worldview is associated with a conception of the ultimate futility of directed effort toward a goal."

Autonomy, manifested in statements like "I can take care of myself" and "No one's going to push me around," produces behavioral problems from the perspective of middle-class expectations when it surfaces in work environments, public schools, or other social institutions built on expectations of conformity.

Miller's work on subcultures and their focal concerns is derived almost entirely from his study of black inner-city delinquents in the Boston area in the 1950s and may have less relevance to members of lower-class subcultures in other places or at other times.

Delinquency and Drift

Members of delinquent subcultures are, to varying degrees, participants in the larger culture that surrounds them. Why do subcultural participants choose behavioral alternatives that seemingly negate the norms and values of the larger society? How can a person give allegiance to two seemingly different sets of values—those of the larger culture and those of a subculture—at the same time? **Gresham Sykes** and **David Matza** provided an answer to this question in their 1957 article "Techniques of Neutralization."[65] Sykes and Matza suggested that offenders and delinquents are aware of conventional values, understand that their offending is wrong, but engage in neutralizing self-talk before offending to mitigate the anticipated shame and guilt associated with violating societal norms.[66] Offenders can overcome feelings of responsibility when involved in crime commission by using one or more of these types of justification:

■ **techniques of neutralization** Culturally available justifications that can provide criminal offenders with the means to disavow responsibility for their behavior.

1. **Denying responsibility.** They point to their background of poverty, abuse, and lack of opportunity: "The trouble I get into is not my fault."

2. **Denying injury.** They explain that everyone does it or that individuals or companies can afford it: "They're so rich, they'll never miss it." (See Figure 7–6.)

3. **Denying the victim.** They justify the harm done by claiming that the victim deserved the victimization: "I only beat up drunks."

4. **Condemning the condemners.** They assert that authorities are corrupt or are responsible for their own victimization and that society has made them what they are and must now suffer the consequences: "They're worse than I am. They're all on the take."

5. **Appealing to higher loyalties.** They use defense of their family honor, gang, girlfriend, or neighborhood: "I have to protect myself."

6. **The metaphor of the ledger**, where individuals feel entitled to indulge in misbehavior because they feel that they have accrued credits in the past for good behavior.

7. **Claim that everybody does it**, meaning that the behavior in question is not really deviant.

8. **Claim of entitlement**, by which a person reasons that he or she has special privileges which make the behavior in question acceptable.

The first five of the techniques in this list were described by Sykes and Matza, but others have been added to the list since then. In the words of Sykes and Matza, "It is our argument that much delinquency is based on what is essentially an unrecognized extension of defenses to crimes, in the form of justifications for deviance that are seen as valid by the delinquent but not by the legal system or society at large."[67]

A few years later, Matza went on to suggest that delinquents tend to drift into crime when available **techniques of neutralization** combine with weak or ineffective values espoused by the controlling elements in society, stating that the delinquent "drifts between criminal and conventional action,"[68] choosing whichever is more expedient at the time. By employing techniques of neutralization, delinquents need not be fully alienated from the larger society because these techniques provide an effective way of overcoming their feelings of guilt so that they can commit crimes. Matza used the phrase "soft determinism" to describe drift, saying that delinquents are neither forced to make choices because of fateful experiences early in life nor entirely free to make choices unencumbered by the realities of their situation. Soft determinism is also discussed in Chapter 3 in conjunction with Classical theory.

More recent studies have found that whereas "only a small percentage of adolescents generally approve of violence or express indifference to violence, [a] large

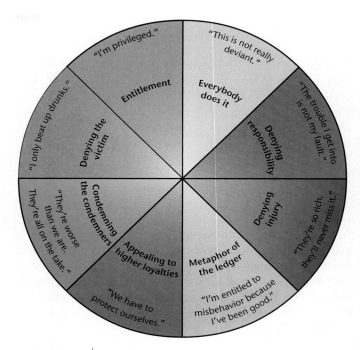

FIGURE 7-6 | Techniques of Neutralization
Source: Based on Criminology (Justice Series), 4e: ISBN-10: 0-13-454864-7.

percentage of adolescents accept neutralizations justifying the use of violence in particular situations."[69] Studies have found that young people who disapprove of violence but associate with delinquent peers often use neutralization techniques as justifications for violence in which they personally engage.[70]

Hard-core, active, noninstitutionalized drug dealers, street robbers, and carjackers have also used neutralization techniques.[71] Sociologist Ken Levi found that professional contract killers, or hit men, tend to begin adapting to the role of professional killer by learning to view killing as "just a job" or as "just business," which allows them to deny responsibility for contracted killings and to view themselves as "hired guns," and their victims as "targets" rather than people.[72]

A 2003 study by sociologist Lois Presser of the University of Tennessee on remorse and neutralization among violent male offenders, based on interviews with 27 men who had committed serious violent crimes, found that the men excused or justified their violent actions through five rationalizations: (1) Victims were to blame for harms that resulted from provoking the offender, (2) victims were themselves offenders or deserving of harm, (3) harm to a victim that was not premeditated or intended carried no blame, (4) the legal sanctioning of an offender negated any harm, and (5) harms to the offender and his or her family stemming from the crime negated any harms caused by the offender.[73]

In innovative research published in 2008, Orly Turgeman-Goldschmidt of Israel's Bar-Ilan University conducted 54 unstructured, in-depth, face-to-face interviews with malicious Israeli computer vandals (hackers) in order to determine what kinds of neutralization techniques they employ and found that the hackers used neutralization techniques common to other offenders, although their language reflected the cyber-realm.[74] Some hackers were found to be similar to political criminals, assuming responsibility by means of internal justifications (by attacking al-Qaeda Web sites or bringing down computers of the Arab news network Al-Jazeera and seeing the activity as a positive contribution to their sociopolitical environment); these "hacktivists" defined themselves as hackers with political consciences.[75] Other hackers justified illegal hacking as simply being fun, rewarding, or self-fulfilling and argued that anyone or anything affected (financial institutions) could afford it and that no one was physically hurt.

Violent Subcultures

Some subcultures are decidedly violent and built around themes and values supporting violent activities. In 1967, **Franco Ferracuti** and **Marvin Wolfgang** published their seminal work *The Subculture of Violence: Toward an Integrated Theory of Criminology*,[76] which drew together many of the sociological perspectives previously advanced to explain delinquency and crime. Ferracuti and Wolfgang's main thesis was that violence is a learned form of adaptation to certain problematic life circumstances and that learning to be violent takes place within the context of a subcultural milieu emphasizing the advantages of violence over other forms of adaptation. These subcultures of violence both expect violence from their members and legitimize it when it occurs: "The use of violence is not necessarily viewed as illicit conduct, and the users do not have to deal with feelings of guilt about their aggression."[77]

Ferracuti and Wolfgang based their conclusions on an analysis of data that showed substantial differences in the rates of homicides between racial groups in the Philadelphia area—nonwhite men had a homicide rate of 41.7 per 100,000 versus a homicide rate of only 3.4 for white men, and nonwhite women showed a homicide rate of 9.3 versus 0.4 for white women. Explaining these findings, Ferracuti and Wolfgang stated, "Homicide is most prevalent, or the highest rates of homicide occur, among a relatively homogeneous subcultural group in any large urban community. The value system of this group … constitutes a subculture of violence. From a psychological viewpoint, we might hypothesize that the greater the degree of integration of the individual into this subculture, the higher the probability that his behavior will be violent in a variety of situations."[78]

Ferracuti and Wolfgang extended their theory of subcultural violence with the following "corollary propositions":[79]

- No subculture can be totally different from or totally in conflict with the society of which it is a part.
- To establish the existence of a subculture of violence does not require that the actors sharing in these basic value elements should express violence in all situations.
- The potential resort or willingness to resort to violence in a variety of situations emphasizes the penetrating and diffusive character of this culture theme.
- The subcultural ethos of violence may be shared by all ages in a subsociety, but this ethos is most prominent in a limited age group, ranging from late adolescence to middle age.
- The counternorm is nonviolence.
- The development of favorable attitudes toward violence and its use in a subculture usually involves learned behavior and a process of differential learning, association, or identification.
- The use of violence in a subculture is not necessarily viewed as illicit conduct, and the users therefore do not have to deal with feelings of guilt about their aggression.

Other writers have commented on geographic distinctions among violent subcultures in different parts of the United States. For example, there are claims that certain forms of criminal violence are more acceptable in the southern United States than in northern portions of the country.[80] Some writers referred to variability in the degree to which interpersonal violence has been accepted in the South over time, whereas others suggested that violence in the South might be a traditional tool in the service of social order.[81]

In 1998, James W. Clarke, a political science professor at the University of Arizona, posited that the high rate of black underclass homicide in the United States flows from a black subculture of violence created by generations of white-on-black violence that first emerged with the "generation of black males that came of age after emancipation."[82] According to Clarke, many black males learned from earlier generations to seek status through their ability to "harm, intimidate, and dominate others."[83]

The wider culture often recognizes a violent subculture's internal rules, so when one member of such a subculture kills another, the wider society may take the killing less seriously than if someone outside the subculture had been killed. Franklin Zimring and his associates described what they called "wholesale" and "retail" costs for homicide: Killings that are perceived to occur within a subculture of violence (when both the victim and the perpetrator are seen as members of

■ **illegitimate opportunity structure**   A subcultural pathway to success that the wider society disapproves of.

a violent subculture) generally result in a less harsh punishment than do killings that occur outside that subculture.[84] Punishments relate to the perceived seriousness of the offense; if members of the subculture in which a crime occurs accept the offense as part of the landscape, so will members of the wider culture.

Differential Opportunity Theory

In 1960, **Richard A. Cloward** and **Lloyd E. Ohlin** published *Delinquency and Opportunity*.[85] Their book, a report on the nature and activities of juvenile gangs, blends the subcultural thesis with ideas derived from strain theory and identifies two types of socially structured opportunities for success: legitimate and illegitimate. Legitimate opportunities are generally available to individuals born into middle-class culture, but participants in lower-class subcultures are often denied access to them, so illegitimate opportunities f or success are often seen as quite acceptable by participants in so-called illegitimate subcultures.

Cloward and Ohlin used the term **illegitimate opportunity structure** to describe preexisting subcultural paths to success not approved of by the wider culture. Where illegitimate paths to success are not already in place, alienated individuals may undertake a process of ideational evolution through which "a collective delinquent solution" or a "delinquent means of achieving success" may be decided upon by members of a gang. Because the two paths to success—legitimate and illegitimate—differ in their availability to members of society, Cloward and Ohlin's perspective has been called "differential opportunity."

> Illegitimate opportunity structures are preexisting subcultural paths to success not approved of by the wider culture.

According to Cloward and Ohlin, delinquent behavior may result from the ready availability of illegitimate opportunities and the effective replacement of the norms of the wider culture with expedient and "legitimate" subcultural rules. "A delinquent subculture is one in which certain forms of delinquent activity are essential requirements for the performance of the dominant roles supported by the subculture."[86] Its most critical elements are the "prescriptions, norms, or rules of conduct that define the activities required of a full-fledged member."[87] They continued, "A person attributes legitimacy to a system of rules and corresponding models of behavior when he accepts them as binding on his conduct."[88] They concluded, "Delinquents have withdrawn their support from established norms and invested officially forbidden forms of conduct with a claim to legitimacy."[89]

Cloward and Ohlin noted that there are two necessary parts to a delinquent act—"It is behavior that violates basic norms of the society, and, when officially known, it evokes a judgment by agents of criminal justice that such norms have been violated."[90] For Cloward and Ohlin, however, crime and deviance are just as normal as any other form of behavior supported by group socialization: "Deviance and conformity generally result from the same kinds of social conditions, [and] deviance ordinarily represents a search for solutions to problems of adjustment." In their view, deviance is just as much an effort to conform (albeit to subcultural norms and expectations) as conformity to the norms of the wider society. "[I]t has been our experience that most persons who participate in delinquent subcultures, if not lone offenders, are fully aware of the difference between right and wrong, between conventional behavior and rule-violating behavior. They may not care about the difference, or they may enjoy flouting the rules of the game, or they may have decided that illegitimate practices get them what they want more efficiently than legitimate practices."[91]

Cloward and Ohlin described three types of delinquent subcultures: (1) criminal subcultures, in which criminal role models are readily available for adoption by those being socialized into the subculture; (2) conflict subcultures, in which participants seek status through violence; and (3) retreatist subcultures, in which drug use and withdrawal from the wider society predominate. These delinquent subcultures have at least three identifiable features: "acts of delinquency that reflect subcultural support are likely to recur with great frequency, access to a successful adult criminal career sometimes results from participation in a delinquent subculture, and the delinquent subculture imparts to the conduct of its members a high degree of stability and resistance to control or change."[92]

Cloward and Ohlin divided lower-class youths into four types based on the degree of commitment to middle-class values and material achievement: Type I youths desire entry to the middle class via improvement in their economic position, Type II youths desire entry to the middle class but not improvement in their economic position, Type III youths desire wealth but not entry to the middle class and are seen as the most crime-prone, and Type IV youths are dropouts who retreat from the cultural mainstream through drug and alcohol use (see the Who's to Blame box in this chapter).

Reaction Formation

Another criminologist whose work is often associated with both strain theory and the subcultural perspective is **Albert Cohen**, who focused primarily on the gang behavior of delinquent youths: "When we speak of a delinquent subculture, we speak of a way of life that has somehow become traditional among certain groups in American society. These groups are the boys' gangs that flourish most conspicuously in the 'delinquency neighborhoods' of our larger American cities. The members of these gangs grow up, some to become law-abiding citizens and others to graduate to more professional and adult forms of criminality, but the delinquent tradition is kept alive by the age-groups that succeed them."[93] Cohen argued that youths from all backgrounds are generally held accountable to the norms of the wider society through a "middle-class measuring rod" of expectations related to school performance, language proficiency, cleanliness, punctuality, neatness, nonviolent behavior, and allegiance to other similar standards, but noted that not everyone is prepared, by birth circumstances and subsequent socialization, to effectively meet such expectations.

In an examination of vandalism, Cohen found that "nonutilitarian" delinquency, in which things of value are destroyed rather than stolen or otherwise used for financial gain, is the result of middle-class values turned upside down.[94] Delinquent youths, often alienated from middle-class values and lifestyles through deprivation and limited opportunities, can achieve

WHO'S TO BLAME—The Individual or Society?

Like Father, Like Son

Reginald Barfield, age 22, was arrested for driving under the influence (DUI) of alcohol and taken to jail. A judge set bail at $500, and his mother came to the jail to post bond for her son. She didn't have much money, so she used the services of a bondsman, who charged her a $70 fee and arranged for Reginald's release. As she drove her son home,

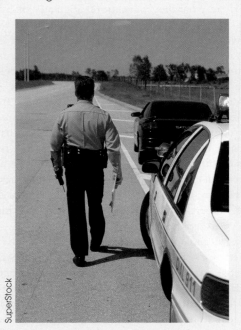

A police officer stops a motorist. Do people learn from the behavior of others?

she began yelling at him, telling him that he had turned out just like his father, who had had a long-standing problem with alcohol.

"You're just like your father, and if you don't change, you'll end up just like him—dead."

Reginald became angry and blurted out that he drank because that was all he had known as a child. "What do you mean?" his mother asked.

"Whenever Dad had a problem or when you two fought," Reginald said, "Dad broke open a bottle and killed the pain. It worked for him. It works for me. So you're right. I'm just like him. But it's not my fault. I learned it from him. You didn't stop him. And you didn't stop me."

Think about it

1. Is Reginald right? Did he learn his problem behavior from his father? What other factors might have contributed to his excessive use of alcohol?

2. Might the concept of reaction formation help explain Reginald's behavior? If so, how?

3. If you were Reginald's mother, to what degree would you hold your son responsible for his problem drinking? To what degree would you hold him responsible if you were a judge hearing his case in court?

4. Are questions about responsibility merely exercises in blame shifting? Is blame shifting ever appropriate when assessing criminal responsibility?

Note: Who's to Blame boxes provide fictionalized critical thinking opportunities based on actual cases.

■ **reaction formation**   The process by which a person openly rejects that which he or she wants or aspires to but cannot obtain or achieve.

status among their subcultural peers via vandalism and other forms of delinquent behavior.

Children from deprived backgrounds turn to delinquency because they experience status frustration when judged by adults and others according to middle-class standards and goals that they are unable to achieve, Cohen claimed. Because it is nearly impossible for them to succeed in middle-class terms, they also may overcome anxiety through the process of **reaction formation**, in which hostility toward middle-class values develops. (Cohen adapted reaction formation from psychiatric perspectives and used it to mean "the process in which a person openly rejects that which he wants, or aspires to, but cannot obtain or achieve."[95])

> Reaction formation means the process in which a person openly rejects that which he or she wants, or aspires to, but cannot obtain or achieve.

Cohen discovered the roots of delinquent subcultures in what he termed the "collective solution to the problem of status."[96] When youths who experience the same kind of alienation from middle-class ideals band together, they achieve a collective and independent solution and create a delinquent subculture. "The delinquent subculture, we suggest, is a way of dealing with the problems of adjustment. These problems are chiefly status problems: certain children are denied status in the respectable society because they cannot meet the criteria of the respectable status system. The delinquent subculture deals with these problems by providing criteria of status which these children can meet."[97]

Cohen's approach is effectively summarized in a theoretical scenario offered by Donald J. Shoemaker, who said that lower-class youths undergo a working-class socialization combining lower-class values and habits with middle-class success values.[98] Lower-class youths experience failure in school because they cannot live up to the middle-class norms operative in American educational institutions, suffer a consequent loss of self-esteem and increased feelings of rejection, drop out of school and associate with delinquent peers, and experience hostility and resentment toward middle-class standards through reaction formation. Such alienated youths achieve status and a sense of improved self-worth through participation in a gang of like-minded peers; delinquency and crime are the result.

The Code of the Street

Work by Elijah Anderson, who studied African American neighborhoods along Philadelphia's Germantown Avenue and published the results in his book titled *The Code of the Street*, offered a subcultural ethnography of the social mores operating in some American inner cities today.[99] In *The Code*, Anderson detailed aspects of street code that stress a hyperinflated notion of manhood resting squarely on the idea of respect: "At the heart of the code is the issue of respect, loosely defined as being treated 'right' or being granted one's 'props' (or proper due) or the deference one deserves." In street culture, a man's sense of worth is determined by the respect he commands when in public.

A crucial distinction between both families and individuals in inner-city neighborhoods like Germantown is expressed by what residents call the "decent family" and the "street family," marking people as either trying to uphold positive values or being oriented toward the street. Street life, Anderson explained, involves displays of physical strength and intellectual prowess meant to demonstrate that "I can take care of myself" and "I can take care of my own." Those who wholeheartedly embrace the street code are proud to live the "thug life," they identify with role models like Tupac Shakur and Young Jeezy, and they see people and situations as obstacles to be subdued or overcome, learning to outsmart or hustle others while avoiding being hustled themselves. See the Criminal Profiles box on gang member Sanyika Shakur, aka Monster Kody Scott.

Gangs Today

Gangs have become a major source of concern in contemporary American society. Although the writings of investigators like Cohen, Thrasher, and Cloward and Ohlin focused on the illicit activities of juvenile gangs in the nation's inner cities, most gang-related crimes involved vandalism, petty theft, and battles over turf. Today the ethnic distinctions that gave rise to gang culture in the 1920s through the 1950s are largely forgotten, and Italian, Hungarian, Polish, and Jewish immigrants, whose children made up many of the early gangs, have been successfully integrated into modern America.

> Gangs have become a major source of concern in contemporary American society.

Today's gangs are quite different from the gangs of the first half of the twentieth century. One-third of jurisdictions covered by the National Youth Gang Survey (NYGS) conducted by the National Gang Center (NGC) reported experiencing gang problems in 2012.[100] Overall, an estimated 3,100 jurisdictions served by city and county law enforcement agencies reported gang problems. Survey results also indicated that an estimated 850,000 gang members and 30,700 gangs were active in the United States during 2012.

The 2012 NYGS confirmed previous findings that gang members are often involved in a variety of serious and violent

Three young men in the Sunset Park section of Brooklyn, New York, displaying gang signs. What would ecological theories say about gangs?

crimes. Almost half of the law enforcement agencies reporting gang problems are involved in collaborative efforts with other law enforcement and criminal justice agencies to combat youth gangs and the serious and violent crimes they commit. The number of gang-related homicides that NYGS respondents reported in the 2012 survey increased by more than 20 percent over the prior five years. This increase was largely due to higher counts of reported gang homicides in larger cities like Chicago.

In addition to conducting surveys, the NGC provides a compilation of gang-related legislation, maintains a repository of gang-related literature, analyzes gang-related data and statistics, and coordinates the activities of the Youth Gang Consortium; you can visit the NGC via **http://www .nationalgangcenter.gov/Publications**. Another group of special interest to anyone wanting to know more about gangs is the National Alliance of Gang Investigators Associations; see **http://www.nagia.org/**

Although its data are older than those available through the NYGS, the National Gang Crime Research Center's Project Gangfact provides a profile of gangs and gang members nationwide, based on data collected by 28 researchers in 17 states:[101]

- The average age for joining a gang nationally is 12.8 years of age.
- Over half who joined gangs have tried to quit.
- More than two-thirds of gangs have written rules for members to follow.
- Over half of all gangs hold regular weekly meetings.
- Nearly 30% of gangs require their members to pay dues.
- Approximately 55% of gang members were recruited by other gang members; the remainder sought out gang membership.
- Most gang members (79%) say they would leave the gang if given a second chance at life.
- Four-fifths of gang members report that their gangs sold crack cocaine.

- Most gangs (70%) are not racially exclusive and consist of members drawn from a variety of ethnic groups.
- One-third of gang members report that they have been able to conceal their gang membership from their parents.
- Most gangs (83%) report having female members, but few allow female members to assume leadership roles.
- Many gang members (40%) report knowing male members of their gangs who had raped females.

Gangs can also be big business. In addition to traditional criminal activities like burglary, extortion, vandalism, and protection rackets, drug dealing has become a mainstay of many inner-city gangs. Los Angeles police estimate that at least four city gangs earn over $1 million each per week through cocaine sales.[102] The potential for huge drug-based profits appears to have changed the nature of the gangs, making them more prone to violence and cutthroat tactics; gang killings, including the now-infamous drive-by shootings, have become commonplace in our nation's cities.

Rodney Dailey, a self-avowed former Boston-area drug dealer and gun-wielding gang member who is now the founder of Gang Peace, an outreach group that tries to reduce gang-related violence, said of today's gang world that "shoot before you get shot is the rule" and that today "things that normally people would have had fistfights about can get you shot or stabbed."[103]

Contemporary researchers are drawing some new distinctions between gangs and violence. G. David Curry and Irving A. Spergel, in a study of Chicago communities, distinguished between juvenile delinquency and gang-related homicide.[104] They found that communities characterized by high rates of delinquency do not necessarily experience exceptionally high rates of crime or of gang-related homicides, and they concluded that although gang activity may be associated with homicide, "gang homicide rates and delinquency rates are ecologically distinct community problems." Gang-related homicide seems to be well explained by classical theories of social disorganization and is especially prevalent in city areas characterized by in-migration and the "settlement of new immigrant groups." In their study, high rates of juvenile delinquency seemed to correlate more with poverty, which they defined as "social adaptation to chronic deprivation." According to Curry and Spergel, "Social disorganization and poverty rather than criminal organization and conspiracy may better explain the recent growth and spread of youth gangs to many parts of the country. Moreover, community organization and social opportunity in conjunction with suppression, rather than simply suppression and incapacitation, may be more effective policies in dealing with the social problem."[105] In proposing a national gang strategy, Finn–Aage Esbensen reminded policy makers that many gang members are delinquent before they become associated with gangs.[106] Esbensen stated that "concerns with gang suppression should not supplant efforts to implement effective delinquency intervention and prevention strategies."[107]

The term *co-offending* refers to the fact that youthful offenders tend to commit crimes in the company of their peers and is especially prevalent in the lives of gang members—about 40% of juvenile offenders commit most of their crimes with others.

CRIMINAL | PROFILES

Sanyika Shakur—aka Monster Kody Scott

It is tempting to rely on Sanyika Shakur's compelling autobiography, *Monster: The Autobiography of an L.A. Gang Member*, as the primary reference for this box. But although much of the material is drawn from his memoir—Shakur is undeniably the world's expert on his alter ego Monster Kody Scott—there is more to this story than can be gleaned from his own writings.

Shakur repeatedly justifies brutal assaults he has committed as being the only reasonable solution "[w]hen the police and other government agencies don't seem to care about what is going on in our communities, those of us who live in them must take responsibility for their protection and maintenance."[i] Yet he also chillingly recounts other assaults, and even murders, as being a form of self-administered therapy to relieve his tensions from such terrible pressures as his mother telling him she disapproved of his lawless lifestyle and use of drugs.

For example, his need "to shoot somebody, eager to vent my anger," after being scolded by his mother for his criminality and marijuana use compelled him (at age 16) to go on the prowl on a bicycle, looking for suitable victims. Upon encountering "three cats who looked about my age leaning against a van, talking and drinking beer," he circled past them and opened fire with a .45-caliber pistol, leaving one victim "motionless in the street." Shakur said he went home, "put the bike in the garage, went to my room [and] fell asleep. I slept very well."[ii]

Born in the tumultuous 1960s (1963), 11-year-old Kody Scott (he adopted the name Sanyika Shakur in prison years later) earned initiation into the infamous Crips street gang with eight blasts from a shotgun aimed at a group of the notorious Bloods, a rival gang. His teen years were an odyssey of violent crime, interspersed with repeated stays in various juvenile detention centers and, ultimately, the California State Penitentiary.

His "Monster" moniker came from one such crime. After being robbed and beaten, the victim had the audacity to strike Shakur in the face, so Shakur "beat him, and stomped him and disfigured him," leaving the young man in a coma.[iii] The severity of the damage caused one investigating police officer to use the word *monster* to refer to the perpetrator, and Shakur decided to adopt the name. "[I]t was just power," he says, proudly. "And I felt it. And I just took that name."[iv]

Feared even by his fellow Crips, Shakur rose through the gang's leadership ranks until he eventually became one of its top leaders and achieved status as an Original Gangster (O.G.), the highest "honor" a gang member can receive.

Shakur calls his behavior inevitable, asserting there are no other options available to him and those like him to achieve success legitimately, portraying himself as the "inevitable product of a hellish environment."[v]

Shakur has been dubbed an "iconic figure" of the hip-hop culture by independent filmmaker Billy Wright, stating that Shakur's "real life

Sanyika Shakur (born Kody Scott), aka Monster Kody Scott, photographed at Pelican Bay prison in June 1993 through Plexiglas. The gangster thug of the literary set was sent back to prison in 2008 for beating a man and stealing his car while out on parole. Is Shakur a villain or a hero?

encapsulates what hip hop imagery is all about."[vi] Wright's current project, titled *Can't Stop, Won't Stop*, tells Shakur's life story.

In December 2006, out on parole from yet another term in the California State Penitentiary, Shakur broke into a man's home and beat him in order to steal his car. In May 2008, as a result of those charges, he was sentenced to six years in prison. He had faced a possible life sentence without the possibility of parole as a persistent felon under California's three-strikes law.[vii] He was paroled again in 2012.

The case of Sanyika Shakur raises a number of interesting questions. Among them are the following:

1. What approach to crime offered in this chapter might best explain Shakur's criminality?

2. How might differential association explain Shakur's criminality? Strain theory?

3. Shakur refers to his criminal behavior as "inevitable." Why would he say that? What does he mean?

Notes:

i. Sanyika Shakur, *Monster: The Autobiography of an L.A. Gang Member* (reprint, New York: Grove Press, 2004), p. 379.

ii. Ibid., pp. 173–174.

iii. Mandalit Del Barco, "Gang Member Turned Author Arrested in L.A.," *Morning Edition*, National Public Radio, March 9, 2007, http://www.npr.org/templates/story/story.php?storyId=7793148 (accessed July 14, 2007).

iv. Ibid.

v. Mark Horowitz, "In Search of a Monster," *Atlantic Monthly*, December 1993, http://www.theatlantic.com/doc/199312/monster (accessed July 14, 2009).

vi. "America's O.G. Gangster—Monster Kody (aka Sanyika Shakur)," http://www.rapindustry.com/monster_cody.htm (accessed September 14, 2009).

vii. Del Barco, "Gang Member Turned Author Arrested in L.A."

■ **Chicago Area Project**   A program originating at the University of Chicago during the 1930s that focused on urban ecology and that attempted to reduce delinquency, crime, and social disorganization in transitional neighborhoods.

Co-offenders are also more likely to be recidivists; when young co-offenders were compared with young solo offenders, the co-offenders had high recidivism rates and committed high numbers of violent crimes. In a 2005 study of co-offending made with grant support from the National Institute of Justice, Temple University Professor Joan McCord and fellow researchers found that violence appears to be learned in the company of others: "Co-offending actually may increase the likelihood that offenders will commit violent crimes. When young offenders affiliate with offenders who have previously used violence, the result appears to be an increase in the likelihood that they will subsequently commit a violent crime? [Y]oung offenders pick up attitudes and values from their companions."[108] Learn more about gangs from Professor Mike Carlie's online book *Into the Abyss* via **http://people.missouristate.edu/MichaelCarlie.**

Policy Implications of Social Structure Theories

Theoretical approaches that fault social structure as the root cause of crime point in the direction of social action as a panacea. In the 1930s, for example, Clifford Shaw, in an effort to put his theories into practice and to reduce delinquency in transitional neighborhoods, established the **Chicago Area Project**. Shaw analyzed oral histories gathered from neighborhood citizens to determine that delinquents were essentially normal youngsters who entered into illegal activities at early ages, often through street play, so he worked to increase opportunities for young people to embark on successful work careers.

> The Chicago Area Project attempted to reduce social disorganization in slum neighborhoods through the creation of community committees.

The Chicago Area Project attempted to reduce social disorganization in slum neighborhoods through the creation of community committees staffed with local residents rather than professional social workers. The project had three broad objectives: (1) improving the physical appearance of poor neighborhoods, (2) providing recreational opportunities for youths, and (3) involving project members directly in the lives of troubled youths through school and courtroom mediation.

Although no effective assessment programs were established to evaluate the Chicago Area Project during the program's tenure, in 1984 RAND Corporation published a 50-year review of the program, declaring it "effective in reducing rates of juvenile delinquency."[109]

Mobilization for Youth (a programmatic outgrowth of Cloward and Ohlin's theory of differential opportunity) provides a bold example of the treatment implications of social structure theories, seeking not only to provide new opportunities but also through direct social action to change the fundamental arrangements of society and thereby address the root causes of crime and deviance. Leaders of Mobilization for Youth decided that "what was needed to overcome formidable barriers to opportunity was not community organization but community action" that attacked entrenched political interests, so the program promoted "boycotts against schools, protests against welfare policies, rent strikes against 'slum landlords,' lawsuits to ensure poor people's rights, and voter registration."[110] A truly unusual government-sponsored program for its time, Mobilization for Youth was eventually disbanded amid protests that "the mandate of the President's Committee was to reduce delinquency, not to reform urban society or to try out sociological theories on American youths."[111]

The War on Poverty declared by the Kennedy and Johnson administrations during the 1960s and subsequent federal and state-run welfare programs that provided supplemental income assistance have been cited[112] as examples of programs that at least held the potential to reduce crime rates by redistributing wealth in American society.[113] Such programs, however, came under fire for perpetuating injustices and for financially penalizing responsible citizens who had to fund the programs. The federal Welfare Reform Reconciliation Act of 1996[114] reduced or eliminated long-term benefits that had previously been available through avenues like the federal Aid to Families with Dependent Children (AFDC) program and established stricter work requirements for welfare recipients through a new Welfare-to-Work program under the Personal Responsibility and Work Opportunity Reconciliation Act of 1996.[115]

Critique of Social Structure Theories

The fundamental assumption of social structure approaches is that social inequality, racism, and poverty are the root causes of crime. Hence, the social structure perspective is intimately associated with the first part of this text's theme, the social problems approach (described in Chapter 1). If the assumptions that inform

The fundamental assumption of social structure approaches is that social inequality, racism, and poverty are the root causes of crime.

social structure theories are true, they largely negate the claims of those who advocate our theme's other part, the individual responsibility perspective.

Social structural explanations for criminality received an enormous boost during the 1960s with the report of President Lyndon B. Johnson's Commission on Law Enforcement and Administration of Justice, a widely disseminated and highly influential document that portrayed social inequality and stifled opportunity as fundamental causes of crime. Later, a number of social commentators began to question the nature of the relationship among poverty, apparent social inequities, and crime.[116] Some argued the inverse of the root causes argument: Poverty and social inequality are produced by crime rather than the other way around; disorder, fear, and crime undermine positive social and economic institutions; and families, schools, churches, businesses, and other institutions cannot function properly in social settings where crime is a taken-for-granted part of the social landscape. If this proposed inverse relationship is even partially true, then addressing poverty and social inequality as the root causes of crime is not only an ineffective crime-prevention strategy but also an unnecessarily costly one.

This chapter has identified three types of social structure theory, and each can be critiqued. Some authors have suggested that ecological theories give too much credence to the notion that spatial location determines crime and delinquency because the nature of any given location changes over time, and evolutions in land-use patterns (such as movement away from homeownership and toward rental or low-income housing) may seriously affect the nature of a neighborhood and the concomitant quality of its social organization. Rates of neighborhood crime and delinquency may be "an artifact of police decision-making practices" and may bear little objective relationship to the actual law violations in an area.[117] If police bias (focus on low-income inner-city areas) exists, it may seriously mislead researchers into categorizing certain areas as high in crime when enforcement decisions made by police administrators merely make them appear that way.

Another critique of the ecological school can be found in its seeming inability to differentiate between the condition of social disorganization and the things it is said to cause. What is the difference between social disorganization and high rates of delinquency? Isn't delinquency a form of the very thing said to cause it? Stephen J. Pfohl observed that early ecological writers sometimes used the incidence of delinquency as "both an example of disorganization and something caused by

disorganization,"[118] making it difficult to gauge the efficacy of their explanatory approach.

Similarly, those who criticize the ecological approach note that many crimes occur outside of geographic areas said to be characterized by social disorganization. Murder, rape, burglary, drug use, and assault all occur in affluent, well-established neighborhoods; white-collar crime, cybercrime, and environmental crime may actually occur *more often* in well-established neighborhoods. Hence, the ecological approach is clearly not an adequate explanation for all crime or for all types of crime.

From an individual responsibility perspective, those who criticize strain theory noted that Merton's strain theory is probably less applicable to American society today than it was in the 1930s because in the ensuing decades considerable effort has been made toward improving success opportunities for all Americans, regardless of ethnicity, race, or gender. Travis Hirschi criticized contemporary strain theory for its inability "to locate people suffering from discrepancy" and noted that human beings are naturally optimistic—a fact that "overrides [the] aspiration-expectation disjunction," concluding that "expectations appear to affect delinquency, but they do so regardless of aspirations, and strain notions are neither consistent with nor required by the data."[119] More recent studies have found that "delinquents do not report being more distressed than other youth."[120] Delinquent youths who are not afforded the opportunities for success available to others appear to be well shielded from sources of stress and despair through their participation in delinquency, so "although strain theorists often have portrayed the lives of delinquents in grim terms, this depiction does not square well with the lived world of delinquency."[121]

Subcultural approaches (the last of the three types of social structure explanations for crime discussed in this chapter) have been questioned by some criminologists who see them as lacking explanatory power. Canadian criminologist Gwynn Nettler called the notion of violent subcultures tautological, or circular, arguing that saying that people "are murderous because they live violently" does little to explain their behavior and that attributing fighting to "other spheres of violence" may be true but that it is fundamentally "uninformative."[122]

The subcultural approach has also been criticized for being racist because many so-called violent subcultures are said to be populated primarily by minorities. Margaret Anderson stated that "the problem with this explanation is that it turns attention away from the relationship of black communities to the larger society and it re-creates dominant stereotypes about blacks as violent, aggressive, and fearful. Although it may be true that rates of violence are higher in black communities, this observation does not explain the fact."[123] In sociological jargon, an observed correlation between race and violence does not necessarily provide a workable explanation for the relationship.

There are other problems with social structure theories that routinely link low levels of socioeconomic status to high levels of delinquency. Empirical studies have consistently found weak or nonexistent correlations between an individual's economic standing and his or her self-reported delinquency.[124] Although low socioeconomic status may promote delinquency by increasing social alienation and financial strain and by decreasing educational opportunity and occupational aspiration, high socioeconomic status may also promote delinquency by increasing a person's willingness to take risks and by decreasing the influence of conventional values. Parental monitoring (knowing where the child is and what he or she is doing) and parental discipline are far more effective predictors of the degree of delinquent involvement.[125]

According to Nettler, social structure theories suffer from another shortcoming that generally affects most other sociological perspectives on crime causation: "The conceptual bias of social scientists emphasizes environments—cultures and structures—as the powerful causes of differential conduct. This bias places an intellectual taboo on looking elsewhere for possible causes as, for example, in physiologies. This taboo is strongly applied against the possibility that ethnic groups may have genetically transmitted differential physiologies that have relevance for social behavior."[126] In other words, social scientists unnecessarily downplay the causative role of nonsociological factors. Many outside of sociology believe that such factors are important, but because sociological theorizing has captured the lion's share of academic attention over the past few decades, the role of other causative factors in the etiology of criminal behavior is in danger of being shortchanged.

Some also see the inability of social structure theories to predict which individuals—or what proportion of a given population—will turn to crime as a crucial failure of such perspectives. Although the large majority of people growing up in poverty-ridden inner-city areas probably experience an inequitable opportunity structure firsthand, only a relatively small number of them become criminal. Even if substantially more people living under such conditions become criminal compared to those living in other types of social environments, a large proportion of people being raised in deviant subcultures and experiencing strain still embrace noncriminal lifestyles. In his book *The Moral Sense*, James Q. Wilson suggested that most people—regardless of socialization experiences and structural aspects of their social circumstances—may still carry within them an inherent sense of fairness and interpersonal morality.[127] If what Wilson suggested is even partially true, then the explanatory power of social structure theories will inevitably be limited by human nature itself. Read a PBS interview with Wilson at **http://www.pbs .org/fmc/interviews/jwilson.htm**.

SUMMARY

- Sociological theories explore relationships among groups and institutions and envision crime as the result of social processes, as the natural consequence of aspects of social structure, or as the result of economic and class struggle. Sociological theories examine institutional arrangements within society and interactions among individuals, groups, and social institutions that affect socialization and have an impact on social behavior.

- Although different kinds of social structure theories have been advanced to explain crime, they all have one thing in common: They highlight those arrangements within society that contribute to the low socioeconomic status of identifiable groups—poverty, lack of education, absence of marketable skills, and subcultural values—as significant causes of crime and view members of socially and economically disadvantaged groups as being more likely to commit crime.

- Three subtypes of social structure theories can be identified: social disorganization theory, strain theory, and culture conflict theory. Social disorganization theory encompasses social pathology, seeing society as a kind of organism and crime and deviance as a kind of disease (or social pathology), and is often associated with social

ecology and the Chicago School of criminology. Strain theory points to a lack of fit between socially approved success goals and the availability of socially approved means to achieve those goals, so individuals unable to succeed through legitimate means turn to other avenues (crime) that promise economic and social recognition. Culture conflict theory suggests that the root cause of criminality can be found in a clash of values between differently socialized groups over what is acceptable or proper behavior.

- Because theories of social structure look to the organization of society for their explanatory power, intervention strategies based on them typically seek to alleviate the social conditions thought to produce crime through social programs that increase socially acceptable opportunities for success and availability of meaningful employment.

- Social structure theories are open to criticisms. Social structure approaches assume that social inequality, racism, and poverty are the root causes of crime, but some argue the inverse: Poverty and social injustices are produced by crime rather than the other way around. If this proposed inverse relationship is even partially true, then addressing poverty and social inequality as the root causes of crime is not only an ineffective crime-prevention strategy but also an unnecessarily costly one.

KEY TERMS

anomie, 172

broken windows theory, 170

Chicago Area Project, 188

Chicago School of criminology, 168

collective efficacy, 171

Crime Prevention Through Environmental Design (CPTED), 170

conduct norm, 179

criminology of place, 168

cultural transmission, 168

culture conflict theory, 179

defensible space, 170

distributive justice, 175

ecological theory, 168

environmental criminology, 168

focal concern, 180

general strain theory (GST), 175

human ecology, 166

illegitimate opportunity structure, 183

negative affective state, 176

pattern theory, 169

reaction formation, 185

relative deprivation, 175

social cohesion, 172

social disorganization, 167

social disorganization theory, 166

social ecology, 167

social life, 165

social pathology, 167

social process, 165

social structure, 164

social structure theory, 165

sociological theory, 164

strain theory, 172

subcultural theory, 179

subculture, 179

technique of neutralization, 181

KEY NAMES

Robert Agnew, 175

Ernest Burgess, 167

Richard A. Cloward, 183

Albert Cohen, 184

Franco Ferracuti, 182

George L. Kelling, 170

David Matza, 180

Henry McKay, 168

Robert K. Merton, 172

Walter B. Miller, 180

Oscar Newman, 170

Lloyd E. Ohlin, 183

Robert Park, 167

Thorsten Sellin, 179

Clifford Shaw, 168

Rodney Stark, 170

Gresham Sykes, 180

W. I. Thomas, 167

Frederic M. Thrasher, 179

William F. Whyte, 179

James Q. Wilson, 170

Marvin Wolfgang, 182

Florian Znaniecki, 167

QUESTIONS FOR REVIEW

1. What is the nature of sociological theorizing? What are the assumptions on which sociological perspectives on crime causation rest?

2. What do sociologists mean by the term *social structure*? How might the organization and structure of a society contribute to criminality?

3. What are the three types of social structure theories that this chapter describes? What are the major differences among them?

4. What are the policy implications of the theories discussed in this chapter? What kinds of changes in society and in government policy might be based on the theories discussed here? Would they be likely to bring about a reduction in crime?

5. What are the shortcomings of the social structure approaches to understanding and preventing crime? Can these shortcomings be overcome?

QUESTIONS FOR REFLECTION

1. This text emphasizes the theme of social problems versus individual responsibility. Which of the theoretical perspectives discussed in this chapter best support the social problems approach? Which support the individual responsibility approach? Why?

2. What do we mean by the term *ecological*? Do you believe that ecological approaches have a valid place in contemporary criminological thinking? Why or why not?

3. How does the notion of a criminology of place differ from more traditional ecological theories? Do you see the approach of criminology of place as capable of offering anything new over traditional approaches? If so, what?

4. What is a violent subculture? Why do some subcultures seem to stress violence? How might participants in a subculture of violence be turned toward less aggressive ways?

Gina Sanders/Fotolia

CHAPTER 8
THEORIES OF SOCIAL PROCESS AND SOCIAL DEVELOPMENT

It's What We Learn

LEARNING OUTCOMES

After reading this chapter, you should be able to answer the following questions:

- How does the perspective of social interaction contribute to understandings of criminal behavior?
- What are the various social process approaches discussed in this chapter?
- What kinds of social policy initiatives might be based on social process theories of crime causation?

- What are the shortcomings of social process theories?
- What are the various social development perspectives discussed in this chapter?
- What are the central concepts of social development theories?
- What kinds of social policy initiatives might be suggested by social development perspectives?
- What are the shortcomings of social development theories of criminality?

■ **social process theories**   Theories that assert that criminal behavior is learned in interaction with others and that socialization processes that occur as the result of group membership are the primary route through which learning occurs; also called interactionist theory.

■ **social development theories**   Perspectives on human development that simultaneously examine many different levels of development—psychological, biological, familial, interpersonal, cultural, societal, and ecological.

Introduction

In 2012, 24-year-old Joran van der Sloot stood before a Peruvian judge and pled guilty to the 2010 murder of 21-year-old Stephany Flores in a Lima, Peru, hotel room. "Yes, I want to plead guilty. I wanted from the first moment to confess sincerely," he told the judge. "I truly am sorry for this act. I feel very bad."[1] Van der Sloot, who gained notoriety as the prime suspect in the 2005 disappearance of 18-year-old Alabama cheerleader Natalee Holloway while she was vacationing on the island of Aruba, fled to Chile after the murder but was extradited to face prosecution in Peru. Prior to sentencing, attorneys for Van der Sloot asked the judge for leniency, saying that their client killed Flores as a result of "extreme psychological trauma" that he had suffered as

Social process theories draw their explanatory power from the process of interaction between individuals and society.

a result of the intense negative publicity he had received in the international news media following Holloway's disappearance. Rejecting his pleas, the judge imposed a sentence of 28 years in prison and ordered him to pay the Flores family $75,000 in reparations. He will be eligible for parole in 2026.[2]

The Perspective of Social Interaction

The theories discussed in the first part of this chapter are called **social process theories**, or interactionist perspectives, because they depend on the process of interaction between individuals and society for their explanatory power. The various types of social process theories include social learning theory, social control theory, and labeling theory. The second part of this chapter focuses on **social development theories**, which tend to offer an integrated perspective and place a greater emphasis on changes in offending over time. Figure 8–1 details the principles of social process and social development theories.

Social process theories of crime causation assume that everyone has the potential to violate the law and that criminality is not an innate human characteristic; instead, criminal behavior is learned in interaction with others, and the socialization process occurring as the result of group membership is seen as

Joran van der Sloot in a Peruvian courtroom. Van der Sloot, who plead guilty to the murder of a 21-year-old Peruvian woman, remains the main suspect in the disappearance of Alabama cheerleader Natalee Holloway. How would social process theories explain his behavior?

Paolo Aguilar/EPA/Newscom

the primary route through which learning occurs. Among the most important groups contributing to the process of socialization are the family, peers, work groups, and reference groups with which one identifies because they instill values and norms in their members and communicate their acceptable worldviews and patterns of behavior.

Social process perspectives hold that the process through which criminality is acquired, deviant self-concepts are established, and criminal behavior results is active, open-ended, and ongoing throughout a person's life. They suggest that individuals who have weak stakes in conformity are more likely to be influenced by the social processes and contingent experiences that lead to crime, and that criminal choices tend to persist because they are reinforced by the reaction of society to those whom it has identified as deviant.

Types of Social Process Approaches

A number of theories can be classified under the social process umbrella: social learning theory, social control theory, labeling theory, reintegrative shaming, and dramaturgical perspective.

■ **Follow the author's tweets about the latest crime and justice news @schmalleger.**

■ **social control theory**   A perspective that predicts that when social constraints on antisocial behavior are weakened or absent, delinquent behavior emerges. Rather than stressing causative factors in criminal behavior, social control theory asks why people actually obey rules instead of breaking them.

■ **differential association**   The sociological thesis that criminality, like any other form of behavior, is learned through a process of association with others who communicate criminal values.

■ **social learning theory**   A perspective that places primary emphasis on the role of communication and socialization in the acquisition of learned patterns of criminal behavior and the values that support that behavior; also called learning theory.

FIGURE 8-1 | **Principles of Social Process and Social Development Theories**

Source: Schmalleger, Frank, *Criminology*. Printed and electronically reproduced by permission of Pearson Education, Inc., Upper Saddle River, New Jersey.

Social learning theory places primary emphasis on the role of communication and socialization in the acquisition of learned patterns of criminal behavior and the values supporting that behavior, whereas **social control theory** focuses on the strength of the bond people share with individuals and institutions around them, especially as those relationships shape their behavior. Labeling theory points to the special significance of society's response to the criminal and sees the process through which a person comes to be defined as a criminal, along with society's imposition of the label "criminal," as a significant contributory factor in future criminality. Reintegrative shaming, a contemporary offshoot of labeling theory, emphasizes possible positive outcomes of the labeling process; the dramaturgical perspective focuses on how people can effectively manage the impressions they make on others. It is to different social learning theories that we now turn our attention.

Social Learning Theory

Social learning theory (also called learning theory) says that all behavior is learned in much the same way and that such learning includes the acquisition of norms, values, and patterns of behaviors conducive to crime, meaning that crime is also learned and that people learn to commit crime from others. Criminal behavior is a product of the social environment, not an innate characteristic of particular people.

Differential Association

One of the earliest and most influential forms of social learning theory was advanced by **Edwin Sutherland** in 1939, who stated that criminality is learned through a process of **differential association** with others who communicate criminal values and who advocate the commission of crimes.[3] He emphasized the role of social learning as an explanation for crime because he believed that many concepts popular in the field of criminology at the time—including social pathology, genetic inheritance, biological characteristics, and personality flaws—were inadequate to explain the process by which an otherwise normal individual turns to crime. Sutherland was the first well-known criminologist to suggest that all significant human behavior is learned and that crime is not substantively different from any other form of behavior.

Although Sutherland died in 1950, the tenth edition of his famous book, *Criminology*, was published in 1978 under the authorship of Donald R. Cressey, a professor at the University of California at Santa Barbara. The 1978 edition of *Criminology* contained the finalized principles of differential

THEORY | in PERSPECTIVE

Types of Social Process Theories

Social process theories (also called interactionist theories) depend on the process of interaction between individuals and society for their explanatory power. They assume that everyone has the potential to violate the law and that criminality is not an innate human characteristic; instead, criminal behavior is learned in interaction with others, and the socialization process that occurs as the result of group membership is seen as the primary route through which learning occurs.

Social Learning Theory

Social learning theory (also called learning theory) says that all behavior is learned in much the same way and that crime is also learned. It places primary emphasis on the roles of communication and socialization in the acquisition of learned patterns of criminal behavior and the values supporting that behavior.

> **Period:** 1930s–present
>
> **Theorists:** Edwin Sutherland, Robert Burgess, Ronald L. Akers, Daniel Glaser
>
> **Concepts:** Differential association, differential association–reinforcement (including operant conditioning), differential identification

Social Control Theory

Social control theory focuses on the strength of the bond people share with the individuals and institutions around them, especially as those relationships shape their behavior, and seeks to identify those features of the personality and of the environment that keep people from committing crimes.

> **Period:** 1950s–present
>
> **Theorists:** Walter C. Reckless, Howard B. Kaplan, Travis Hirschi, Michael Gottfredson, Charles R. Tittle, Per-Olof H. Wikström, and others
>
> **Concepts:** Inner and external containment, self-derogation, social bond, control–balance, general theory of crime (GTC), situational action theory (SAT)

Labeling Theory

Labeling theory (also called social reaction theory) points to the special significance of society's response to the criminal and sees continued crime as a consequence of limited opportunities for acceptable behavior that follow from the negative responses of society to those defined as offenders.

> **Period:** 1938–1940, 1960s–1980s, 1990s
>
> **Theorists:** Frank Tannenbaum, Edwin M. Lemert, Howard Becker, John Braithwaite, others
>
> **Concepts:** Tagging, labeling, outsiders, moral enterprise, primary and secondary deviance, reintegrative shaming, stigmatic shaming

Dramaturgical Perspective

The dramaturgical perspective depicts human behavior as centered around the purposeful management of impressions and seeks explanatory power in the analysis of social performances.

> **Period:** 1960s–present
>
> **Theorists:** Erving Goffman, others
>
> **Concepts:** Total institutions, impression management, back and front regions, performances, discrediting information, stigma, spoiled identity

The Social Development Perspective

The social development perspective provides an integrated view of human development that examines multiple levels of maturity simultaneously, including the psychological, biological, familial, interpersonal, cultural, societal, and ecological levels.

> **Period:** 1980s–present
>
> **Theorists:** Sheldon and Eleanor Glueck, Terrie E. Moffitt, Robert J. Sampson, John H. Laub, Glen H. Elder, Jr., David P. Farrington and Donald J. West, Marvin Wolfgang, Lawrence E. Cohen and Richard Machalek, Terrence Thornberry, and others
>
> **Concepts:** Human development, social development perspective, life course criminology, career criminal, life course, human agency, turning points, social capital, life course–persistent offenders, adolescence-limited offenders, persistence, desistance, evolutionary ecology

---

association (which, for all practical purposes, were complete as early as 1947). Nine in number, the principles read as follows:[4]

1. Criminal behavior is learned.
2. Criminal behavior is learned in interaction with others in a process of communication.
3. The principal part of the learning of criminal behavior occurs within intimate personal groups.
4. When criminal behavior is learned, the learning includes (a) techniques of committing the crime, which are sometimes very complicated and sometimes very simple, and (b) the specific direction of motives, drives, rationalizations, and attitudes.
5. The specific direction of motives and drives is learned from definitions of the legal codes as favorable or unfavorable.
6. A person becomes delinquent because of an excess of definitions favorable to law violation over definitions unfavorable to law violation.
7. Differential associations may vary in frequency, duration, priority, and intensity.

8. The process of learning criminal behavior by association with criminal and anticriminal patterns involves all mechanisms involved in any other learning.

9. Although criminal behavior is an expression of general needs and values, it is not explained by those general needs and values because noncriminal behavior is also an expression of the same needs and values.

Differential association found considerable acceptance among mid-twentieth-century theorists because it combined then-prevalent psychological and sociological principles into a coherent perspective on criminality. Crime as a form of learned behavior became the catchword, and biological and other perspectives were largely abandoned by those involved in the process of theory testing.

Differential Association–Reinforcement Theory

In 1966, **Robert Burgess** and **Ronald L. Akers** published an article titled "A Differential Association–Reinforcement Theory of Criminal Behavior."[5] The perspective, often termed differential reinforcement theory or sociological learning theory, expands on Sutherland's original idea of differential association by adding the idea of reinforcement, the concept of the power of punishments and rewards to shape behavior (see the heading "Behavior Theory" in Chapter 5). In developing their perspective, Burgess and Akers integrated psychological principles of operant conditioning with sociological notions of differential association, and they reorganized Sutherland's nine principles into seven, the first of which stated, "Criminal behavior is learned according to the principles of operant conditioning."[6] Fundamental to this perspective is the belief that human beings learn to define behaviors that are rewarded as positive and that an individual's criminal behavior is rewarded at least sometimes by individuals and groups that value such activity.

Although the 1966 Burgess–Akers article only alluded to the term *social learning*, Akers began to apply that term to differential association–reinforcement theory with the 1973 publication of his book *Deviant Behavior: A Social Learning Approach*.[7] According to Akers, "The basic assumption in social learning theory is that the same learning process, operating in a context of social structure, interaction, and situation, produces both conforming and deviant behavior."[8] Akers identified two primary learning mechanisms: differential reinforcement (also called instrumental conditioning), in which behavior is a function of the frequency, amount, and probability of experienced and perceived contingent rewards and punishments, and imitation, in which the behavior of others and its consequences are observed and modeled. These learning mechanisms, said Akers, operate in a process of differential association involving direct and indirect verbal and nonverbal communication, interaction, and identification with others. As with Sutherland's theory of differential association, the relative frequency, intensity, duration, and priority of associations remain important because they determine the amount, frequency, and probability of reinforcement of behavior that is either conforming or deviant. Interpersonal association also plays an important role because it can expose individuals to deviant or conforming norms and role models.

Akers continued to develop learning theory and in 1998 published the book *Social Learning and Social Structure*, in which he explained crime rates as a function of social learning that occurs within a social structure.[9] He called this explanation of the model of crime the social structure–social learning model (SSSL) and summarized it in seven concise propositions:[10]

1. Deviant behavior is learned according to the principles of operant conditioning.

2. Deviant behavior is learned both in nonsocial situations that are reinforcing or discriminating and through social interaction in which the behavior of others is reinforcing or discriminating for such behavior.

3. The principal part of the learning of deviant behavior occurs in those groups that comprise or control the individual's major source of reinforcements.

4. The learning of deviant behavior, including specific techniques, attitudes, and avoidance procedures, is a function of the effective and available reinforcers and the existing reinforcement contingencies.

5. The specific class of behavior learned and its frequency of occurrence are a function of the effective and available reinforcers and the deviant or nondeviant direction of the norms, rules, and definitions that in the past have accompanied the reinforcement.

6. The probability that a person will commit deviant behavior is increased in the presence of normative statements,

> Differential association theory says that criminality is learned through a process of association with criminal others.

■ **differential identification theory**   An explanation for crime and deviance that holds that people pursue criminal or deviant behavior to the extent that they identify themselves with real or imaginary people from whose perspective their criminal or deviant behavior seems acceptable.

definitions, and verbalizations that, in the process of differential reinforcement of such behavior over conforming behavior, have acquired discriminative value.

7. The strength of deviant behavior is a direct function of the amount, frequency, and probability of its reinforcement. The modalities of association with deviant patterns are important insofar as they affect the source, amount, and scheduling of reinforcement.

Akers's SSSL theory says that social learning is the social-psychological mediating process through which social structural aspects of the environment work to cause crime and that it integrates two levels of explanation—social structure and social learning—by specifying the links between the larger social context and the individual relationships that lead to criminal behavior.[11] Hence, a person's location in the social structure—defined by age, gender, ethnicity, place of residence, and so on—is seen as a major determinant of how that person is socialized and what he or she will learn.

Differential Identification Theory

Like Akers, **Daniel Glaser** built on Sutherland's notion of differential association, and Glaser offered a **differential identification theory**.[12] The central tenet of Glaser's differential identification theory is that "a person pursues criminal behavior to the extent that he identifies himself with real or imaginary persons from whose perspective his criminal behavior seems acceptable."[13] Glaser proposed that the process of differential association leads to an intimate personal identification with lawbreakers, resulting in criminal or delinquent acts. Glaser recognized that people will identify with various people and that some of these identifications will be relatively strong and others weaker—hence the term *differential identification*. According to Glaser, it is not the frequency or intensity of association that determines behavior (as Sutherland believed) but the symbolic process of identification. Identification with a person or with an abstract understanding of what that person might be like can be more important than actual associations with real people. Role models can consist of abstract ideas as well as actual people, so an individual might identify with a serial killer or a terrorist bomber even though he or she has never met that person. Glaser also recognized the role of economic conditions, frustrations with one's place in the social structure, learned moral creeds, and group participation in producing differential identifications. Alternatively, identification with noncriminals offers the possibility of rehabilitation.

> Identification with noncriminals offers the possibility of rehabilitation.

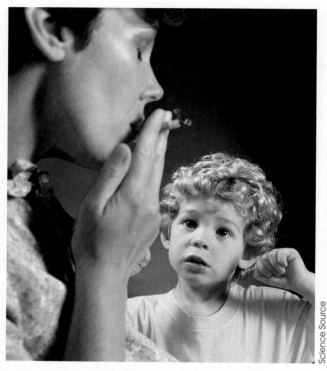

A child watching his mother smoke a cigarette. Social learning theory says that social behavior is learned. Will this child grow up to be a smoker?

A recent meta-analysis of 133 empirical studies of social learning theory that had been published in leading criminology journals between 1974 and 2003 found strong support for concepts such as differential association and "definitions favorable to law violations," but less support for ideas like differential reinforcement and modeling/imitation.[14] The authors concluded that "the empirical support for social learning theory stacks up well relative to the criminological other perspectives that have been subjected to metaanalysis." Learn more about social learning and adolescent development via **http://tinyurl.com/k9oywav** and **http://tinyurl.com/lh4j4ff**.

Social Control Theories

We mentioned earlier that theories of social control focus primarily on the strength of the bond that people share with the individuals and institutions around them, especially as those relationships shape their behavior. According to **Charles R. Tittle**, a prominent sociologist at Washington State University with a specialty in crime and deviance, social control theory emphasizes "the inhibiting effect of social and psychological integration with others whose potential negative response, surveillance, and expectations regulate or constrain criminal impulses."[15] In other

■ **containment theory** A form of control theory that suggests that a series of both internal and external factors contributes to law–abiding behavior.

words, social control theorists seek to identify those features of the personality (see Chapter 6) and the environment (see Chapter 7) that keep people from committing crimes. According to Tittle, social control theorists take a step beyond static aspects of the personality and physical features of the environment in order to focus on the process through which social integration develops. The extent of a person's integration with positive social institutions and with significant others determines that person's resistance to criminal temptations, and social control theorists focus on the process through which such integration develops. Rather than stressing causative factors in criminal behavior, social control theories tend to ask why people actually obey rules instead of breaking them.[16]

Containment Theory

In the 1950s, a student of the Chicago School of criminology, **Walter C. Reckless**, wrote *The Crime Problem*.[17] He tackled head–on the realization that most sociological theories, although conceptually enlightening, offered less–than–perfect predictability, being unable to predict which individuals (even those exposed to various "causes" of crime) would become criminal. Reckless thought that prevalent sociological perspectives offered only half of a comprehensive theoretical framework, writing that crime was the consequence of both social pressures to become involved in

violations of the law and failures to resist such pressures. Reckless called his approach **containment theory** and compared it with a biological immune response, saying that only some people exposed to a disease actually come down with it and that both sickness and crime result from the failure of control mechanisms, some internal and others external.

In the case of crime, Reckless wrote that external containment consists of "the holding power of the group."[18] Under most circumstances, Reckless said that "the society, the state, the tribe, the village, the family, and other nuclear groups are able to hold the individual within the bounds of the accepted norms and expectations."[19] In addition to setting limits, he saw society as providing individuals with meaningful roles and activities, also important factors of external containment.

Reckless stated that inner containment "represents the ability of the person to follow the expected norms, to direct himself."[20] For Reckless, this ability is enhanced by a positive self–image, a focus on socially approved goals, personal aspirations in line with reality, a tolerance for frustration, and a general adherence to society's norms and values.

In Figure 8–2 (a diagram of containment theory), "Pushes toward Crime" represents those factors in an individual's background that might propel him or her into criminal behavior, including a criminogenic background or upbringing involving

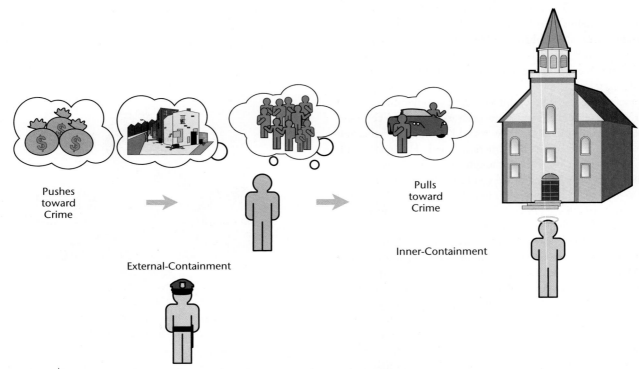

Pushes toward Crime

External-Containment

Pulls toward Crime

Inner-Containment

FIGURE 8-2 | A Diagrammatic Representation of Containment Theory

■ **containment**   An aspect of the social bond that acts as a stabilizing force to prevent individuals from committing crimes and that keeps them from engaging in deviance.

■ **social bond**   The link, created through socialization, between individuals and the society of which they are a part.

participation in a delinquent subculture, deprivation, biological propensities toward deviant behavior, and psychological maladjustment. "Pulls toward Crime" signifies all the perceived rewards, including financial gain, sexual satisfaction, and higher status, that crime may offer. **Containment** is a stabilizing force that blocks such pushes and pulls from leading the individual into crime.

Reckless believed that inner containment was far more effective than external containment in preventing law violations. "As social relations become more impersonal, as society becomes more diverse and alienated, as people participate more and more for longer periods of time away from a home base, the self becomes more and more important as a controlling agent."[21]

Delinquency and Self-Esteem

Social control theory predicts that when social constraints on antisocial behavior are weakened or absent, delinquent behavior will emerge. An innovative perspective on social control was offered by **Howard B. Kaplan** in the mid-1970s, when he proposed that people who are ridiculed by their peers suffer a loss of self-esteem, assess themselves poorly, and abandon the motivation to conform.[22] This approach has come to be known as the *self-derogation theory of delinquency*.

Numerous studies appear to support the idea that low self-esteem fosters delinquent behavior.[23] However, it appears that delinquency can also enhance self-esteem, at least for some delinquents;[24] for example, one study found that delinquent behavior enhances self-esteem in adolescents whose self-esteem is already very low.[25]

Some researchers have examined ethnic identification as both a factor in low self-esteem and a precursor to delinquent behavior. In 1986, K. Leung and F. Dragsow tested Kaplan's self-derogation theory using white, African American, and Hispanic youth groups.[26] They concluded that although all three groups reported low self-esteem, only among white youths low levels of self-esteem related to delinquent behavior were found. Other researchers found no differences in self-esteem and delinquency between white and African American delinquents and nondelinquents.[27]

In 1990, in an effort to explain some contradictory findings of self-derogation research, Daphna Oyserman and Hazel Rose Markus proposed that "possible selves," rather than self-esteem, might be a major explanatory factor in delinquency.[28] According to this approach, the degree of disjuncture between what people want to be and what they fear they might become is a good potential predictor of delinquency.[29] For example, an adolescent who is confused about what he or she wants to be or is fearful about what he or she could become may resort to delinquency in order to resolve the conflict. Oyserman and

Markus suggested that the highest levels of delinquency can be found among youths who lack balance between their expected selves and their feared selves.

Social Bond Theory

An important form of social control theory was popularized by **Travis Hirschi** in his 1969 book *Causes of Delinquency*.[30]

> A social bond forms between individuals and society; when that bond is weakened or broken, deviance and crime may result.

Hirschi's approach was well received by criminologists and "epitomized social control theorizing for nearly three decades."[31] Hirschi argued that through successful socialization, a bond forms between individuals and the social group, but when that bond is weakened or broken, deviance and crime may result. Hirschi described four components of the **social bond** (Figure 8–3):

1. Attachment (a person's shared interests with others)
2. Commitment (the amount of energy and effort put into activities with others)
3. Involvement (the amount of time spent with others in shared activities)
4. Belief (a shared value and moral system)

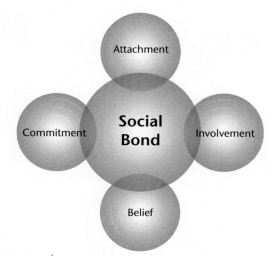

FIGURE 8-3 | The Four Components of the Social Bond

Source: Schmalleger, Frank, *Criminology*. Printed and electronically reproduced by permission of Pearson Education, Inc., Upper Saddle River, New Jersey.

■ **general theory of crime (GTC)**   The assertion that the operation of a single mechanism, low self-control, accounts for "all crime, at all times," including acts ranging from vandalism to homicide, from rape to white-collar crime.

The first component, attachment, refers to a person's shared interests with others. In his writings, Hirschi cites the psychopath as an example of the kind of person whose attachment to society is nearly nonexistent.[32] Other relatively normal individuals may find their attachment to society loosened through "the process of becoming alienated from others [which] often involves or is based on active interpersonal conflict," says Hirschi. "Such conflict could easily supply a reservoir of socially derived hostility sufficient to account for the aggressiveness of those whose attachments to others have been weakened."[33]

The second component of the social bond—commitment—reflects a person's investment of time and energies into conforming behavior and the potential loss of the rewards that he or she has already gained from that behavior. In Hirschi's words, "The idea, then, is that the person invests time, energy, himself, in a certain line of activity—say, getting an education, building up a business, acquiring a reputation for virtue. Whenever he considers deviant behavior, he must consider the costs of this deviant behavior, the risk he runs of losing the investment he has made in conventional behavior."[34] For such a traditionally successful person, committing petty theft is stupid because the potential loss far exceeds the possible gains. Recognizing that his approach applies primarily to individuals who have been successfully socialized into conventional society, Hirschi added, "The concept of commitment assumes that the organization of society is such that the interests of most persons would be endangered if they were to engage in criminal acts."[35]

Involvement, the third aspect, means "engrossment in conventional activities"[36] and is similar to Reckless's concept of meaningful roles. In explaining the importance of involvement in determining conformity, Hirschi cited the colloquial saying that "idle hands are the devil's workshop"—time and energy are limited, so if a person is busy with legitimate pursuits, he or she will have little opportunity for crime and deviance.

Belief (the last of his four aspects of the social bond) sets Hirschi's control theory apart from subcultural approaches because "control theory assumes the existence of a common value system within the society or group whose norms are being violated. We not only assume the deviant has believed the rules

> GTC holds that crime is a natural consequence of unrestrained human tendencies to seek pleasure and avoid pain.

[but also] assume he believes the rules even as he violates them."[37] How can a person simultaneously believe it is wrong to commit a crime and still commit it? Hirschi's answer would be that "many persons do not have an attitude of respect toward the rules of society."[38] Although they know the rules exist, they basically do not care and invest little of their sense of self in moral standards.

The General Theory of Crime

In 1990, **Michael Gottfredson**, in collaboration with Hirschi, proposed a **general theory of crime (GTC)** based on the concepts advanced earlier in control theory.[39] "Gottfredson and Hirschi's general theory of crime claims to be general, in part, due to its assertion that the operation of a single mechanism, low self-control, accounts for 'all crime, at all times'; acts ranging from vandalism to homicide, from rape to white-collar-crime."[40] Gottfredson and Hirschi defined self-control as the degree to which a person is vulnerable to temptations of the moment.[41] They proposed that self-control is acquired early in life and that low self-control combined with impulsivity is the premier individual-level cause of crime. It develops by the end of childhood and is fostered through parental emotional investment in the child, monitoring the child's behavior, recognizing deviance when it occurs, and punishing the child.

Gottfredson and Hirschi thought that it was important to ask, "What is crime?" Because nearly all crimes are mundane, simple, trivial, easy acts aimed at satisfying desires of the moment, their general theory is built on a classical or rational choice perspective—the belief that crime is a natural consequence of unrestrained human tendencies to seek pleasure and avoid pain. They concluded that crime is little more than a subset of general deviant behavior and bears little resemblance to the explanations offered in the media, by law enforcement officials, or by most academic thinkers on the subject.

■ **Follow the author's tweets about the latest crime and justice news @schmalleger.**

An example of a social bond forming early in life. What might this child be learning?

According to Gottfredson and Hirschi, the offender is neither the diabolical genius of fiction nor the ambitious seeker of the American Dream often portrayed by other social scientists. Offenders appear to have little control over their own desires, so when personal desires conflict with long-term interests, those who lack self-control often opt for the desires of the moment, thus contravening legal restrictions and becoming involved in crime.[42]

Central to Gottfredson and Hirschi's thesis is the belief that a well-developed social bond will result in the creation of effective mechanisms of self-control. "For Gottfredson and Hirschi, self-control is the key concept in the explanation of all forms of crime as well as other types of behavior. Indeed, they believe that all current differences in rates of crime between groups and categories may be explained by differences in the management of self-control."[43]

One recent Canadian study found that the effect of good parenting on the development of positive self-control was very strong, but that the role of factors such as household size and family structure also could make an important difference.[44] Families in which children lived with both biological parents seemed to be best at developing self-control in their children, whereas lower levels of self-control were found in single-parent families and in reconstituted families in which the parents had been divorced and remarried. The researchers concluded that "overall, regardless of family structure, it is evident that a nurturing, accepting family environment is positively associated with self-control."[45]

Some researchers have called the argument that self-control develops early in childhood and persists over time the *stability thesis*. In research reported in 2006, Florida State University criminologists Carter Hay and Walter Forrest conducted a test of the stability thesis, finding moderately strong support for it:[46] Levels of self-control that developed early in childhood tended to

persist, but not as strongly as the general theory of crime would suggest; 16% of the study population showed changes in levels of self-control over time, and those individuals demonstrating the greatest stability in self-control started at the highest levels.

More recent research appears to show that low self-control tends to lead to peer rejection and isolation—especially among juveniles.[47] Consequently, young people with low self-control tend to associate with their deviant peers, meaning that those with low levels of self-control are essentially self-selected into groups of people who share their characteristics. Constance L. Chapple of the University of Nebraska explained that "the delinquent peer group may provide increased opportunities for crime or exert situational pushes towards delinquency" because of the lack of self-control that characterizes its members.[48]

Gottfredson and Hirschi rejected the notion that some people have an enduring propensity to commit crime or that any such propensity compels people to do so.[49] Crimes require "no special capabilities, needs, or motivation; they are, in this sense, available to everyone."[50] However, some people have a tendency to ignore the long-term consequences of their behavior; they tend to be impulsive, reckless, and self-centered, and they often end up committing crime because of such tendencies.[51]

A meta-analysis (a summary analysis of other research) of 21 studies of self-control theory conducted by Travis Pratt and Francis Cullen in 2000 found considerable support for the thesis that lack of self-control plays a central role in crime and deviance.[52] Looking at various studies that explored self-control as a delinquency preventative—including those on self-reported juvenile delinquency, self-reported and projected crime and deviance among college students, adult criminal behavior, and official delinquency—Pratt and Cullen concluded that low self-control is "one of the strongest known correlates of crime."

Carter Hay of Washington State University studied the role that parenting plays in the development of self-control and concluded that effective parenting can contribute to the development of self-control in children.[53] He pointed out that although Gottfredson and Hirschi recognized the importance of parenting in the development of self-control, they failed to adequately consider the nature of effective parenting, which must involve fair and nonphysical forms of discipline; harsh or unfair discipline did not appear to contribute to the development of children's self-control. Hay stated, "The sort of discipline that teaches children to control their behavior is not simply that which consistently occurs in the wake of deviance; other factors may be consequential as well, including the extent to which discipline is perceived as fair and is not reliant on physical force."[54]

In 2002, Karen L. Hayslett-McCall and Thomas J. Bernard of Pennsylvania State University proposed a new theory of disproportionate male offending that combined elements of Gottfredson and Hirschi's theory of low self-control with ideas from attachment theory.[55] Hayslett-McCall and Bernard

Steve Rubin/The Image Works

■ **situational action theory (SAT)** A perspective on crime holding that criminal behavior is the result of human decision making based on personal morality when viewed within the context of the existing situation. SAT stresses the importance of moral interpretations over a person's ability to exercise self-control.

examined the strong relationship between gender and criminality (men are more likely than women to offend in almost all offense categories) and concluded that gender-based differences in offending are caused by disruptions in attachments to primary caregivers early in childhood and that such disruptions are more likely to occur in the lives of boys than girls because of cultural differences in the way boys are treated. Boys are held less, comforted less when they cry, and spoken to less than girls in their early years because of child-rearing patterns that are thoroughly ingrained in our culture—"boys disproportionately experience disruptions of early attachment and these disruptions are causally related to elements of what is often described as the masculine gender role." Low self-control among males, concluded Hayslett-McCall and Bernard, is the final result of gendered differences in attachment disruptions.

More recently, **Per-Olof H. Wikström** at the University of Cambridge proposed that self-control could best be analyzed as a situational concept rather than as an individual trait.[56] Wikström's **situational action theory (SAT)** suggests that an individual's ability to exercise self-control is an outcome of the interaction between his or her personal traits and the situation in which he or she is involved. SAT highlights the *situation* as the core unit of analysis and places emphasis on a person's sense of morality—which expresses itself when an individual is faced with a particular set of circumstances. In other words, Wikström proposes that acts of violence are essentially moral actions and that all such acts can be explained by a theory of moral action that takes into account both personal characteristics and the social setting. As one writer puts it, Wikström's theory contends that "personal morality and moral contexts provide a 'filter' prohibiting some people from perceiving and contemplating criminal actions as realistic possibilities."[57]

SAT argues that there is no fundamental difference between people who follow or break moral rules in general and those who follow or break rules defined by the law as criminal. The basic causal processes that operate in both cases are the same, it says—but the decision-making process is one in which moral interpretations are more important than degree of self-control.[58]

SAT says that explaining human moral action, such as acts of violence, has to do ultimately with understanding the interplay between common moral rules of conduct, an individual actor's personal moral rules, and the actor's interpretation of how his or her moral rules apply to the situation at hand.[59] The theory suggests that the particulars of a given situation, in combination with an actor's understanding of moral rules, determines what is right or wrong for that individual and, consequently, what that person will do.

Deterrence is seen as the "main causal mechanism through which formal and informal social controls influence a person's moral actions." Deterrence is defined by Wikström as "the felt worry about or fear of consequences when considering breaking a moral rule or committing an act of crime." Motivation and frictions are other important concepts in SAT. Motivation is defined as goal-directed attention, in which people are tempted to fill desires and commitments, and will seek out opportunities for fulfillment. Provocations, another important concept in SAT, can result from frictions, or unwanted interferences (i.e., verbal insults, physical interference), that arise in situation-specific circumstances.

For most people and in most circumstances, Wikström says that the decision as to whether or not to engage in acts of crime or deviance is not so much a question of a person's ability to exercise self-control, but rather a question of his or her morality. He argues that the ability to exercise self-control is only a relevant factor in crime causation in those situations where an individual actually deliberates about whether or not to engage in a criminal act. In his 2011 Presidential Address to the American Society of Criminology, Steven F. Messner applauded SAT, saying that it provided the "glimmer of a moral awakening in criminology."[60]

Wikström's theory was put to the test in 2016 by criminologists Jonathan R. Brauer and Charles R. Tittle. The pair examined the moral filtering hypothesis in Wikström's theory using household survey data from 573 people in the Dhaka District of Bangladesh. They concluded that "results suggest individuals with higher levels of personal morality (moral beliefs; guilt from contemplating violence; moral identity; emotional empathy) and exposure to strong moral settings are less likely to contemplate aggressive and violent actions in response to a provocation."[61]

Although Gottfredson and Hirschi's general theory of crime is well accepted today as an explanation for many forms of criminality, some writers note that the most powerful predictors of crime can be found when individuals with low self-control encounter criminal opportunities. They point out that the context of self-control is an important determining factor. In 2010, for example, two German researchers found support for the belief that the interaction between self-control and criminal opportunities is more effective at explaining criminal behavior than self-control alone.[62] Other contextual variables have also been explored. In 2008, for example, a group of researchers reported finding that "diminished language skills" are predictive of low self-control, and that the link between language and self-control had both a genetic and environmental basis.[63]

A few years ago, Gregory M. Zimmerman and colleagues explored the "contextual viability" of the relationship between self-control and offending—in other words, the influence of things like neighborhood variables and economic conditions on self-control.[64] They expected to find that the relationship between self-control and crime would "be amplified in disadvantaged neighborhoods where, due to low social control, opportunities for crime are presumed to be in abundance." In order to test that idea, the researchers looked at data from 1,431

■ **control ratio**   The amount of control to which a person is subject versus the amount of control that person exerts over others.

respondents across 41 neighborhoods in two Eastern European cities: one in Russia and the other in the Ukraine. Their findings showed that the morality of a neighborhood was more important than things like socioeconomic status (SES) and neighborhood opportunities for crime. Neighborhood morality was measured by examining the firmness of moral convictions within the community, using a set of questions that assessed the extent to which various acts would be morally acceptable to people living there. They found that the amount of crime in both rich and poor communities was primarily influenced by the strength of moral rules that characterized the community. The researchers explained their findings by noting that "the effects of neighborhood economic conditions are mediated, at least in part, by community social processes." The importance of their findings is to show that the relationship between self-control and crime may vary depending on the social context in which people find themselves.

Extending that notion further still, a number of studies have considered the potential role of an individual's expectation of an early death as it impacts self-control. Texas criminologist Alex R. Piquero, for example, found that a number of variables, including gender, race/ethnicity, and adverse neighborhood conditions, produce a "futureless" mindset among selected young people.[65] People who believe that they will not reach middle age because of their lifestyle, or because they are living in a dangerous or violent environment, may choose to exercise less self-control than those who believe that they will live longer—thus increasing their risk of offending. Piquero notes, however, that "The main message from the results is that an anticipated early death should not be considered deterministic but should instead be viewed as an opportunity for early prevention efforts and resiliency training where young children are taught that there are a variety of options even in the most constrained of circumstances."

Finally, it should be noted that some recent studies have found at least a partial biological basis for social control and suggest that previous criminological research has largely ignored this relationship. In examining two waves of data from the Add Health database, Kevin Beaver and others found that about half of the variance observed in self-control could be attributed to genetic factors—specifically the interaction of genes and the social environment.[66]

Control–Balance Theory

Traditional control theories posit that deviance and crime result from either weak social bonds or low levels of self-control, but a novel form of control theory can be found in the control–balance theory of Charles R. Tittle.[67] Tittle's control–balance approach resulted from blending the social bond and containment perspectives, and he argued that too much control can be just as dangerous as too little. The crucial concept in Tittle's approach is what he called the **control ratio**—the

CONTROL RATIO
(Ratio of Control Exercised to Control Experienced)

Control Surplus ◄———————— Balance ————————► Control Deficit

(controls others/has power)- - - - - - - -(is controlled/lacks power)

PROBABILITY OF CRIME/DEVIANCE

High ◄———————— Low ————————► High

- -

TYPE OF CRIME/DEVIANCE

Autonomous & Acquisitive ◄———————— Conformity ————————► Repressive & Predatory

(crime types: exploitation/plunder, white-collar, official deviance, police corruption)

(crime types: physical violence, rape, robbery, street crime)

FIGURE 8-4 | **Control–Balance Theory**
Source: Schmalleger, Frank, *Criminology*. Printed and electronically reproduced by permission of Pearson Education, Inc., Upper Saddle River, New Jersey.

amount of control to which a person is subject versus the amount of control that person exerts over others—which predicts not only the probability that a particular person will engage in deviance but also the specific form that deviance will take (Figure 8–4).

High levels of control (or overcontrol) are termed *control surplus*; low levels are called *control deficit*. Individuals with control surpluses are able to exercise a great deal of control over others and will work to extend their degree of control even further. Their efforts lead to deviant actions involving exploitation, plunder, and decadence—frequently seen in cases of white-collar crime and political corruption.[68] Tittle explained that control surpluses build on "the fundamental drive toward autonomy," which involves "a desire to extend control as far as possible" and results in forms of deviance that he called "autonomous."[69]

A control deficit exists for people unable to exercise much control over others (and who are hence overly controlled) and results in deviance as an attempt to escape repressive controls. Deviance engendered by control deficit takes the form of predation (physical violence, theft, sexual assault, robbery), defiance (challenges to conventional norms, including vandalism, curfew violations, and sullenness), or submission ("passive, unthinking, slavish obedience to the expectations, commands, or anticipated desires of others"[70]). According to Tittle, control imbalance only sets the stage for deviance: Deviance ultimately occurs once a person realizes, at some level, that acts of deviance can reset the control ratio in a favorable way. Opportunity also plays a significant role in Tittle's theory. "No matter how favorable the motivational and constraint configuration," said Tittle, "the actual likelihood of deviance occurring depends on there being an opportunity for it to happen."[71]

Labeling Theory

2018 was the first year in which students applying to a two or four-year school within the State University System of New York (SUNY) were no longer required to disclose whether they had ever been convicted of a felony.[72] In that landmark year, SUNY joined the popular "Ban the Box" movement and became the first public university system to no longer require that students reveal prior felony convictions. The Ban the Box movement had begun a few years earlier with efforts by organizers to remove what had, up until then, been a common checkbox on application forms—including those required for employment, the military, and education. Ban the Box advocates argued that elimination of the checkbox guaranteed "fair hiring policies to remove unfair barriers to employment of people with criminal records."

PUTTING CRIMINOLOGY TO WORK—Implementing Evidence-Based Policy

To make a difference in the real world, criminological theories must first be tested and evaluated. Once evidence has been developed that theory-based practices work, then programs based on them can be implemented to reduce or prevent crime, or to help make victims' lives better. One federal initiative, CrimeSolutions.Gov, strives to evaluate the effectiveness of theory-based practices, and then communicates its findings via the Web. Some of the most effective and promising programs are highlighted in boxes such as this one that appear throughout the text.

PROGRAM: Big Brothers/Big Sisters Community-based Mentoring

EVIDENCE RATINGS FOR OUTCOMES: Promising

PROFILE

The goal of Big Brother-Big Sisters of America (BBBS) Community-based Mentoring (CBM) is to support the development of healthy youths by addressing their need for positive adult contact, thereby reducing risk factors for negative behavior and enhancing protective factors for positive behavior.

BBBS CBM focuses on meeting the needs of communities that are facing hardship by helping youth withstand the many negative effects of adversity. The program is intended for youth between the ages of 6 and 18 who often come from single-parent households and low-income neighborhoods. In some cases, they are coping with the stress of parental incarceration. Youth targeted for this program are at high risk of exposure to violence and trauma at home and in the community.

The program involves one-to-one mentoring between a Big Brother or Big Sister (the mentor or adult) and a Little Brother or Little Sister (the mentee or youth) that takes place in a community setting. The match between the adult and youth is the most important part of the intervention, because this pairing can lead to a caring and supportive relationship, which can be crucial for youth at high risk.

Relevant Theory: Social Control

As with other mentoring programs, CBM is based on the theory of social control, where attachments to prosocial, supportive adults, a commitment to appropriate goals, and a mutually trusting relationship between the mentor and mentee (adult and youth) can allow the child to begin to feel more socially accepted and supported. The increased level of support from adults allows youths to view themselves in a more positive light and engage in more constructive behavior. Youth who are more socially bonded have more to lose from misbehavior.

Evidence-Based Review

These sources were used in the development of the program profile:

Study 1

Joseph P. Tierney, Jean Baldwin Grossman, and Nancy L. Resch, *Making a Difference: An Impact Study of Big Brothers/Big Sisters.* (Philadelphia, PA: Public/Private Ventures, 2000). http://ppv.issuelab.org/resource/making_a_difference_an_impact_study_of_big_brothersbig_sisters_re_issue_of_1995_study

Source: Adapted from https://www.crimesolutions.gov/ProgramDetails.aspx? ID=112

Notes: Putting Criminology to Work features are based on information published online by the National Institute of Justice's (NIJ) Crime Solutions Website. The program ratings shown are those provided by NIJ.

■ **tagging**   The process whereby an individual is negatively defined by agencies of justice.

■ **primary deviance**   The initial deviance often undertaken to deal with transient problems in living.

■ **secondary deviance**   The deviant behavior that results from official labeling and from association with others who have been so labeled.

■ **labeling theory**   An interactionist perspective that sees continued crime as a consequence of limited opportunities for acceptable behavior that follow from the negative responses of society to those defined as offenders; also called social reaction theory.

Even though the Ban the Box idea has been largely adopted, its success has been limited in scope. The old adage that while there are plenty of ex-cons, there is no such thing as an "ex-ex-con" ("once a con, always a con") still rings true. Society seems to never forget. Society's response to known or suspected offenders is important not only because it determines the future of those who are labeled as criminals but also because it may contribute to a heightened incidence of criminality by reducing the behavioral options available to labeled offenders.

Tagging

An early description of societal reaction to deviance can be found in the work of **Frank Tannenbaum**, whose 1938 book *Crime and the Community* popularized the term **tagging** to explain what happens to offenders following arrest, conviction, and sentencing. Tannenbaum told his readers that crime is essentially the result of two opposing views—those of the delinquent and those of the community at large. "This conflict over the situation is one that arises out of a divergence of values. As the problem develops, the situation gradually becomes redefined. The attitude of the community hardens definitely into a demand for suppression. There is a gradual shift from the definition of the specific acts as evil to a definition of the individual as evil, so that all his acts come to be looked upon with suspicion. From the community's point of view, the individual who used to do bad and mischievous things has now become a bad and unredeemable human being .... There is a persistent demand for consistency in character. The community cannot deal with people whom it cannot define."[73]

After the process whereby an offender comes to be seen as ultimately and irrevocably bad has been completed, Tannenbaum said, the offender "now lives in a different world. He has been tagged. The process of making the criminal, therefore, is a process of tagging."[74] Once the offender has been defined as bad, he or she finds that few legitimate opportunities remain open and that only other people who have been similarly defined by society as bad are available to associate with him or her, and this continued association with negatively defined others leads to continued crime.

Primary and Secondary Deviance

Using terminology developed by **Edwin M. Lemert**, it became fashionable to call an offender's initial acts of deviance **primary deviance** and his or her continued acts of deviance (especially those resulting from forced association with other offenders) **secondary deviance**. Primary deviance may be undertaken to solve some immediate problem or to meet the expectations of one's subcultural group. For example, the robbery of a convenience store by a college student temporarily desperate for tuition money may be the first serious criminal offense he or she has ever committed, and he or she may well intend for it to be the last, but if arrest ensues and the student is tagged with the status of a criminal, then secondary deviance may occur as a means of adjustment to the negative status. In Lemert's words, "When a person begins to employ his deviant behavior or a role based upon it as a means of defense, attack, or adjustment to the overt and covert problems created by the consequent societal reaction to him, his deviation is secondary."[75]

Secondary deviance is especially important due to the forceful role it plays in causing tagged individuals both to internalize the negative labels applied to them and to assume the role of the deviant. According to Lemert, "Objective evidences of this change will be found in the symbolic appurtenances of the new role, in clothes, speech, posture, and mannerisms, which in some cases heighten social visibility, and which in some cases serve as symbolic cues to professionalization."[76]

Labeling

The person most often associated with labeling theory is **Howard Becker**, who published *Outsiders: Studies in the Sociology of Deviance*, the work in which the perspective of **labeling theory** (the idea that society's response to the criminal and the process through which a person comes to be defined as a criminal and labeled "criminal" are significant contributory factors in future criminality) found its fullest development.[77] In *Outsiders*, Becker described the deviant subculture in which jazz musicians live and the process by which an individual becomes a marijuana user, but his primary focus was explaining how a person becomes labeled as an outsider, as "a special kind of person, one who cannot be trusted to live by the rules agreed on by the group."[78] The central fact

> Becker said that society creates both deviance and the deviant person by responding negatively to circumscribed behaviors.

■ **moral enterprise**   The efforts made by an interest group to have its sense of moral or ethical propriety enacted into law.

is that society creates both deviance and the deviant person by responding to circumscribed behaviors. In Becker's words, "Social groups create deviance by making the rules whose infraction constitutes deviance, and by applying those rules to particular people and labeling them as outsiders. From this point of view, deviance is not a quality of the act the person commits, but rather a consequence of the application by others of rules and sanctions. The deviant is one to whom that label has been successfully applied."[79] For Becker and other labeling theorists, no act is intrinsically deviant or criminal but must be defined as such by others; becoming deviant involves a sequence of steps that eventually leads to commitment to a deviant identity and participation in a deviant career.

In developing labeling theory, Becker attempted to explain how some rules carry the force of law whereas others have less weight or apply only within the context of marginal subcultures. His explanation centered on the concept of **moral enterprise**, meaning all the efforts a particular interest group makes to have its sense of propriety embodied in law. "Rules are the products of someone's initiative, and we can think of the people who exhibit such enterprise as moral entrepreneurs."[80]

An early example of moral enterprise can be found in the Women's Christian Temperance Union (WCTU), a group devoted to the prohibition of alcohol. From 1881 to 1919, the WCTU was highly visible in its nationwide fight against alcohol—holding marches and demonstrations, closing drinking establishments, and lobbying legislators. Press coverage of the WCTU's activities swayed many politicians into believing that the lawful prohibition of alcoholic beverages was inevitable, and an amendment to the U.S. Constitution soon followed, ushering in the age of prohibition.

A more contemporary example of moral enterprise is NORML—the National Organization for the Reform of Marijuana Laws. NORML says that its mission is "to move public opinion sufficiently to achieve the repeal of marijuana prohibition so that the responsible use of cannabis by adults is no longer subject to penalty."[81] Other recent examples of moral entrepreneurs can be found in those individuals and organizations that lobbied for the creation of Amber Alert systems and the passage of Megan's Laws (which authorize local law enforcement agencies to notify the public about convicted sex offenders living or working nearby) following the abduction and murder of young girls.

Moral enterprise is used, Becker claimed, by groups seeking to support their own interests with the weight of law. Often the group that is successful at moral enterprise does not represent a popular point of view. The group is simply more effective than others at maneuvering through the formal bureaucracy that accompanies legislation.

Becker was especially interested in describing deviant careers and the processes by which individuals become members of deviant subcultures and take on the attributes associated with the deviant role. Becker argued that most deviance is likely to be transitory but that transitory deviance can be effectively stabilized in a person's behavioral repertoire through the labeling process. Once a person is labeled deviant, opportunities for conforming behavior are seriously reduced and behavioral opportunities that remain open are primarily deviant ones; the budding deviant increasingly exhibits deviant behavior because his or her choices are restricted by society. Successful deviants must acquire the techniques and resources necessary to undertake the deviant act (drug use, bank robbery) and develop the mind-set characteristic of others like them. Near the end of a deviant career, the person labeled a deviant has internalized society's negative label, has assumed a deviant self-concept, and is likely a member of a deviant subgroup. "A drug addict once told me that the moment she felt she was really 'hooked' was when she realized she no longer had any friends who were not drug addicts."[82] In this way, explained Becker, deviance becomes a self-fulfilling prophecy, so labeling is a cause of crime insofar as the actions of society in defining the rule breaker as deviant push the person further in the direction of continued deviance.

Contributions of Labeling Theory

Labeling theory contributed a number of unique ideas to criminological literature:

- Deviance is the result of social processes involving the imposition of definitions rather than the consequence of any quality inherent in human activity itself.
- Deviant individuals achieve their status by virtue of social definition rather than inborn traits.
- The reaction of society to deviant behavior and to those who engage in such behavior is the major element in determining the criminality of the behavior and the person in question.
- Negative self-images follow processing by the formal criminal justice system rather than precede delinquency.
- Labeling by society and handling by the justice system tend to perpetuate crime and delinquency rather than reduce them.

Becker's typology of delinquents—the pure deviant, the falsely accused deviant, and the secret deviant—helped explain the labeling approach (Figure 8–5). The pure deviant is one who commits norm-breaking behavior and is accurately appraised by society, who is tried and convicted, and who gets what he or she deserves. The falsely accused individual is one who is not guilty but is labeled deviant nonetheless, who experiences the impact of conviction and of the experiences that attend prison life, and who is left with a negative self-concept and

Pure deviant   Falsely accused   Secret deviant

FIGURE 8-5 | Becker's Types of Delinquents

Source: Schmalleger, Frank, *Criminology*. Printed and electronically reproduced by permission of Pearson Education, Inc., Upper Saddle River, New Jersey.

with group associations practically indistinguishable from those of a true deviant. This person demonstrates the power of social definition—the life of the falsely accused is changed just as thoroughly as the life of the pure deviant by the process of labeling. The secret deviant violates social norms, but his or her behavior is not noticed, so negative societal reactions do not follow; a secret deviant again demonstrates the power of societal reaction, but in this case by the lack of consequences.

Although labeling theory fell into disregard during the late 1970s and early 1980s due to accusations that it was vague and ambiguous, some criminologists have recast the approach as a developmental theory of structural disadvantage.[83] The theory is now seen as one that points out the cumulative effects over time of official intervention on future life chances and opportunities for approved success. Robert J. Sampson and John H. Laub observed that labeling theory is "truly developmental in nature because of its explicit emphasis on processes over time."[84] Contemporary proponents of the labeling perspective generally see labeling as only one factor contributing to cumulative disadvantages in life chances. In 2003, Jon Gunnar Bernburg and Marvin D. Krohn studied the impact of negative official interventions on young men in Rochester, New York, from the time they were about 13.5 years old until they reached the age of 22. In keeping with what labeling theory would predict, Bernburg and Krohn found that official intervention during adolescence led to increased criminality in early adulthood because it reduced life chances for educational achievement and successful employment and that poor people were more negatively impacted by official processing, probably because they were already disadvantaged along other important social dimensions.[85]

Negative labels can carry significant visible liabilities as well as hidden ones. A 2004 study by the Legal Action Center, a crime and justice policy group, found that all 50 states have laws that hamper the ability of former offenders to reenter society.[86] Four states—Colorado, Georgia, South Carolina, and Virginia—were rated as places where ex-offenders have the least chance to become productive citizens. According to the center, many states prohibit ex-offenders from obtaining professional licenses to work in businesses as diverse as real estate, medicine, and law; 27 states,

in keeping with a requirement imposed by Congress on states seeking federal highway funds, revoke or refuse to issue driver's licenses to former drug felons, effectively prohibiting access to many job sites.

Mike S. Adams proposed a general sociological learning theory of crime and deviance that incorporated components of labeling theory and differential association.[87] Adams contended that "labeling effects are mediated by associations with delinquent peers," concluding that labeling is not a direct cause of delinquency and crime but "appears to cause delinquency indirectly via the effects of associations with delinquent peer groups" and that "the causal chain linking primary to secondary deviance must incorporate links that account for the effects of associations with delinquent [peers]."[88]

In 2013, Emily Restivo and her colleague Mark M. Lanier reported the results of a three-year study in which they randomly examined 677 juveniles selected from the Children at Risk study. They found that official intervention by the criminal justice system in the lives of those juveniles led to "an increased delinquent self-identity, decreased pro-social expectations, and an increased association with delinquent peers."[89] Further, those features were found to contribute to an increased likelihood of future offending. An important strength of labeling theory is that it is dynamic because it allows for changes in self-perception over time that may have important impacts on an individual's behavior. In 2014, criminologists Michael Rocque, Chad Posick, and Ray Paternoster studied the role of evolving identity in the desistance process using data derived from the Rutgers Health and Human Development Project (HHDP).[90] They found that positive changes in self-identity over time can lead to enhanced desistance to crime and increased resistance to the attractions of crime. The researchers termed their perspective an "identity desistance theory," and said that it clearly demonstrated the role of adult social bonds and identity change in the desistance process over time. Learn more about labeling theory at **http://tinyurl.com/l88fzru** and read about the post prison consequences of a criminal label at **http://www.lac.org/roadblocks-to-reentry/upload/lacreport/Roadblocks-to-Reentry-2009.pdf**.

CRIMINAL | PROFILES

Dr. Farid Fata—Prescribing Unneeded Chemotherapy

Some people argue that poverty leads to crime. While the relationship between crime and available financial resources is complex, social process theory suggests that greed can be a strong criminal motivator. Consider the case of 50-year-old Dr. Farid Fata, an oncologist who became wealthy administering unneeded or excessive chemotherapy to hundreds of patients, including some whom he knew did not have cancer.[i] Lebanese-born Fata, who practiced medicine in suburban Detroit, Michigan, intentionally misdiagnosed patients, telling many that they had multiple myeloma or other types of cancers. He even told dying patients that they had a "70% or more chance of remission" if they followed his treatment orders—often keeping them on chemotherapy until they died, all while knowing that continued treatment would only make them sicker. One patient was given 195 chemotherapy treatments, even though established medical protocol would have limited the number to only 18. Fata, a married father of three, ran an oncology practice out of seven locations, and owned a radiation treatment center, a pharmacy, and a diagnostic testing center. Each business provided substantial revenue, but Fata also embezzled funds from a fake charity that he founded.

Fata's downfall came after some of his current and former employees told federal investigators about the doctor's illegal activities. He was arrested in 2013 and plead guilty a year later to 13 counts of healthcare fraud, conspiracy to receive kickbacks from a hospice, and money laundering. All told, Fata victimized 553 patients and received more than $17 million from Medicare and private insurers, although some estimates ran as high as $35 million over a two-year period.[ii] Testimony at his 2015 sentencing hearing was heartbreaking. One patient told the judge that because of Fata's deliberate mistreatment of her, she now suffered from severe osteoporosis and neuropathy. "I have days where I cannot stand; most nights the pain is too great to allow me to sleep," she testified. Another said that Fata had overmedicated her father, causing him to suffer excruciating physical and psychological pain. "You are a monster. You are evil. You poisoned him. You tortured and murdered my dad," she told the court. In calling for a lengthy prison term, prosecutors cited the false hope that Fata gave to patients, and the loss of faith in the medical profession that his actions fostered.

At sentencing, Fata wept and asked for mercy from U.S. District Judge Paul Borman. "I misused my talents, yes, and permitted this sin to enter me because of power and greed," Fata said. "My quest for power is self-destructive." In reply, Borman told Fata that he had committed "a huge, horrific series of criminal acts. You practiced greed and shut down whatever compassion [you] had." When the hearing ended, Fata was sentenced to 45 years in federal prison.

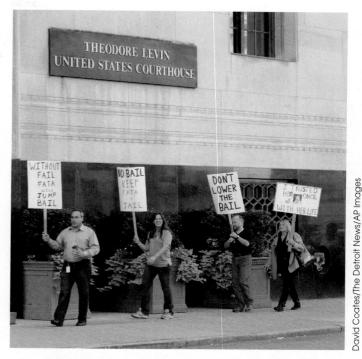

Demonstrators gather at the trial of Dr. Farid Fata, the Detroit cancer doctor who falsely diagnosed some patients with cancer and overtreated many others with powerful chemotherapy in order to enrich himself.

The case of Dr. Farid Fata raises a number of interesting questions. Among them are the following:

1. Wikström's situational action theory (SAT) suggests that an individual's ability to exercise self-control is an outcome of the interaction between his or her personal traits and the situation in which he or she is involved. Can SAT help explain Dr. Fata's actions?

2. How might Charles Tittle's control-balance theory be applicable in this case?

3. Do you think the sentence that Dr. Fata received was just? Might he have been effectively rehabilitated through the use of reintegrative shaming, without the need for prison time, or was prison time needed because of the seriousness of his crimes?

Notes

i. Robert Lowes, "Physician Who Gave Unneeded Chemo Gets 45 Years in Prison," *Medscape*, July 10, 2015, http://www.medscape.com/viewarticle/847791?nlid=84043_28.

ii. Kaitrease Stafford, "Cancer Doctor Was Really Just 'A Monster'," *Detroit Free Press*, July 7, 2015, http://www.freep.com/story/news/local/michigan/oakland/2015/07/06/farid-fata- court-sentencing/29762499.

■ **reintegrative shaming**   A form of shaming, imposed as a sanction by the criminal justice system, that is thought to strengthen the moral bond between the offender and the community.

■ **stigmatic shaming**   A form of shaming, imposed as a sanction by the criminal justice system, that is thought to destroy the moral bond between the offender and the community.

Reintegrative Shaming

In a contemporary offshoot of labeling theory, **John Braithwaite** and colleagues at the Australian National University (ANU) reported initial results of studies in 1997 on **reintegrative shaming**, which describes processes by which a deviant is labeled and sanctioned but then is brought back into a community of conformity through words, gestures, or rituals.[91]

Called RISE (for Reintegrative Shaming Experiments), the project assessed the efficacy of each approach using several criteria: (1) prevalence and frequency of repeat offending, (2) victim satisfaction with the process, (3) estimated cost savings within the justice process, (4) changes in drinking or drug use among offenders, and (5) perceptions of procedural justice, fairness, and protection of rights.[92]

At the core of the study was Braithwaite's belief that two different kinds of shame exist. **Stigmatic shaming** is thought to destroy the moral bond between the offender and the community, whereas reintegrative shaming is thought to strengthen the moral bond between the offender and the community. According to Braithwaite and co-author Heather Strang, "Stigmatic shaming is what American judges employ when they make an offender post a sign on his property saying 'a violent felon lives here,' or a bumper sticker on his car saying 'I am a drunk driver.' Stigmatic shaming sets the offender apart as an outcast—often for the rest of the offender's life. By labeling him or her as someone who cannot be trusted to obey the law, stigmatic shaming says the offender is expected to commit more crimes."[93]

Their alternative to stigmatic humiliation is "to condemn the crime, not the criminal."[94] Through carefully monitored diversionary conferences, Braithwaite and Strang hoped to give offenders the opportunity to rejoin the community as law-abiding citizens, but to earn the right to a fresh start, offenders must express remorse for their past conduct, apologize to any victims, and repair the harm caused by the crime.

Preliminary results from the RISE studies

> Reintegrative shaming is thought to strengthen the moral bond between the offender and the community.

Newscom

Minor offenders in Hillsborough County, Florida, performing court-ordered duties in public view. Some people believe that shaming can be an effective rehabilitative tool. What different kinds of shaming can you identify?

supported the claimed value of reintegrative shaming, but most of these results have been measured using interviews with offenders following diversionary conferences and consist primarily of anecdotal evidence based on the reported feelings of respondents. These findings showed that offenders are far more likely to feel ashamed of their crimes if they are handled through conferences rather than through formal court processing, and that both offenders and victims find conferences fairer than official court proceedings. Learn more about reintegrative shaming experiments at **http://www.aic .gov.au/criminal_justice_system/rjustice/rise.aspx** and **http://ssrn.com/abstract=938796** and **http://ssrn .com/abstract=914503**.

Dramaturgical Perspective

Another social process approach to the study of criminology can be found in the work of **Erving Goffman** in his 1959 book *The Presentation of Self in Everyday Life,* which introduced

■ **dramaturgical perspective**   A theoretical point of view that depicts human behavior as centered around the purposeful management of interpersonal impressions.

■ **impression management**   The intentional enactment of practiced behavior that is intended to convey to others one's desirable personal characteristics and social qualities.

students of criminology to dramaturgy.[95] The **dramaturgical perspective** says that individuals play a variety of nearly simultaneous social roles—such as mother, teacher, daughter, wife, and part-time real estate agent—and that such roles must be sustained in interactions with others. Goffman argued that social actors present themselves more or less effectively when acting out a particular role and that role performances basically consist of managed impressions. Criminals, through a similar process of managed impressions and by the fear engendered in their victims, may likewise achieve cooperation.

Impression management, according to Goffman, is a complex process involving a never-ending give-and-take of information. When it has been successful, said Goffman, dramatic realization has occurred: "Together, the participants contribute

PUTTING CRIMINOLOGY TO WORK—Implementing Evidence-Based Policy

To make a difference in the real world, criminological theories must first be tested and evaluated. Once evidence has been developed that theory-based practices work, then programs based on them can be implemented to reduce or prevent crime, or to help make victims' lives better. One federal initiative, CrimeSolutions.Gov, strives to evaluate the effectiveness of theory-based practices, and then communicates its findings via the Web. Some of the most effective and promising programs are highlighted in boxes such as this one that appear throughout the text.

PROGRAM: Juvenile Diversion

EVIDENCE RATINGS FOR OUTCOMES: Promising

PROFILE

Juvenile diversion is an intervention strategy that redirects youths away from formal processing in the juvenile justice system, while still holding them accountable for their actions. Diversion programs may vary from low-intensity warn-and-release programs to more-intensive treatment or therapeutic programming, all in lieu of formal court processing. Diversion programs are also designed to be less costly than formal court proceedings because they reduce the burden on the court system, reduce the caseload of juvenile probation officers, and free up limited resources and services for high-risk juvenile offenders. The goal of diversion programs is to reduce recidivism or the occurrence of problem behaviors without having to formally process youth in the justice system.

Generally, diversion programs attempt to remove low-risk youths, such as status offenders or first-time offenders, from traditional system processing. However, some diversion programs may target high-risk juvenile offenders, or youths with specific psychosocial needs (such as mentally ill offenders or

those with substance abuse issues). Diversion can occur at several different contact points in the juvenile justice system, but generally youths are diverted pre- or post-charging but before the initiation of formal court procedures.

Relevant Theory: Labeling Theory and Differential Association

Diversion is primarily grounded in two different theories: labeling theory and the theory of differential association. Labeling theory emphasizes the stigma and negative consequences that youths may experience if they are labeled delinquent at a young age. Differential association theory says that youths can learn antisocial attitudes and behaviors by associating with peers who exhibit such behavior. Diversion attempts to minimize the effects of labeling associated with offending and limit the opportunities youths have to associate with antisocial peers by reducing their contact and exposure to the juvenile justice system.

Evidence-Based Review

These sources were used in the development of this practice profile:

Meta-Analysis 1

Craig S. Schwalbe, Robin E. Gearing, Michael J. MacKenzie, Kathryne B. Brewer, and Rawan W. Ibrahim, "A Meta-Analysis of Experimental Studies of Diversion Programs for Juvenile Offenders," *Clinical Psychology Review*, Vol. 32 (2012), pp. 26–33.

Meta-Analysis 2

Holly A. Wilson and Robert D. Hoge, "The Effect of Youth Diversion Programs on Recidivism: A Meta-Analytic Review," *Criminal Justice and Behavior* (2012), (published online October 15, 2013).

Source: Adapted from https://www.crimesolutions.gov/PracticeDetails.aspx?ID=37

Notes: Putting Criminology to Work features are based on information published online by the National Institute of Justice's (NIJ) Crime Solutions Website. The program ratings shown are those provided by NIJ.

■ **discrediting information**   Any information that is inconsistent with the managed impressions being communicated in a given situation.

■ **total institution**   A facility from which individuals can rarely come and go and in which communal life is intense and circumscribed. Individuals in total institutions tend to eat, sleep, play, learn, and worship together.

■ **prosocial bond**   A bond between the individual and the social group that strengthens the likelihood of conformity. Prosocial bonds are characterized by attachment to conventional social institutions, values, and beliefs.

to a single overall definition of the situation which involves not so much a real agreement as to what exists but rather a real agreement as to whose claims concerning what issues will be temporarily honored."[96]

Deviant behavior finds its place in the dramaturgical perspective through the concept of discreditable disclosure. Some actors, said Goffman, may find themselves targeted by the introduction of **discrediting information**, information they have sought to hide that is inconsistent with managed impressions. The flow of interaction is then disrupted and the nature of the performance may be altered substantially.

Goffman's work takes on considerable relevance for criminology in his later writings, especially his book *Stigma: Notes on the Management of Spoiled Identity*, in which he advanced the notion that discredited or stigmatized individuals differ significantly from "normals" in the way that society responds to them.[97] By definition, he said that "we believe that a person with a stigma is not quite human. On this assumption, we exercise varieties of discrimination, through which we effectively, if often unthinkingly, reduce his life chances. We construct a stigma-theory, an ideology to explain his inferiority and account for the danger he represents. We tend to impute a wide range of imperfections on the basis of the original one."[98] A stigma may be physical (birthmarks), behavioral (theft), or ideational (low rank in the pecking order).

In *Stigma*, Goffman was primarily concerned with how "normals" and stigmatized individuals interact. At times, discredited individuals are known to others before they come in contact with them, and when that happens, normal people approach the stigmatized ones with expectations of encountering further stigmatizing behavior. When discrediting information does not precede interpersonal encounters, the stigmatized individuals may attempt to pass as normal by using various techniques of concealment, including aliases and misrepresentation.

According to Goffman, societal reactions, although they may forcibly create social identities, are also instrumental in the formation of group identities. When similarly discredited individuals come together in like-minded groups, they may align themselves against the larger society; in so reacting, they may justify their own deviant or criminal behavior. At the conclusion of *Stigma*, Goffman reminded us, "The normal and the stigmatized are not persons, but rather perspectives. These are generated in social situations during mixed contacts by virtue of the unrealized norms that are likely to play upon the encounter."[99]

In his book titled *Asylums*, Goffman described **total institutions**—facilities from which individuals can rarely come and go and in which communal life is intense and circumscribed.[100] Individuals in total institutions tend to eat,

sleep, play, learn, and worship together; military camps, seminaries, convents, prisons, rest homes, and mental hospitals are all types of total institutions. Goffman believed that residents of total institutions bring "presenting cultures" with them to their respective facilities, so some inmates would carry street culture into correctional facilities. However, residents undergo a period of "disculturation," during which they drop aspects of their native culture that are not consistent with existing institutional culture—a culture that they must acquire. Read about jails as total institutions at **http://tinyurl.com/lqwh3p3**.

Policy Implications of Social Process Theories

Social process theories suggest that crime-prevention programs should work to enhance self-control and to build **prosocial bonds** (bonds that strengthen conformity). One program that seeks to build strong prosocial bonds while attempting to teach positive values to young people is the Juvenile Mentoring Program (JUMP) of the Office of Juvenile Justice and Delinquency Prevention (OJJDP), funded by Congress in 1992 under an amendment to the Juvenile Justice and Delinquency Prevention Act of 1974.[101] JUMP programs, commencing in 1996, place at-risk youths (those at risk of delinquency, gang involvement, educational failure, or dropping out of school) in a one-on-one relationship with favorable adult role models.

The most recent data showed that 9,200 youths (average age just under 12) enrolled in more than 200 JUMP programs nationwide. Based on evaluation data, both youths and mentors were very positive when rating various aspects of their mentoring experiences.[102] Learn more about JUMP at **http://www.ncjrs.gov/pdffiles1/ojjdp/182209.pdf**.

Another social control–based program is Preparing for the Drug Free Years (PDFY), designed to increase effective parenting as part of the Strengthening America's Families Project.[103] PDFY works with parents of children in grades four to eight in an effort to reduce drug abuse and behavioral problems in adolescents, seeks to teach effective parenting skills as a way to decrease the risks that juveniles face, and incorporates both behavioral skills training and communication-centered approaches into parent training. Through a series of ten one-hour sessions, parents learn to (1) increase their children's opportunities for family involvement, (2) teach needed family participation and social skills, and (3) provide reinforcement for positive behavior and appropriate consequences for misbehavior. Early studies showed that program participation (session attendance) tends to

A scene from the Broadway musical *Jersey Boys*. Some criminologists suggest that people, like actors on a stage, intentionally present themselves to others in ways calculated to produce predictable social responses. How might criminals manipulate impressions?

be high and that the program is effective at improving general child-management skills among parents.[104] Learn more about PDFY at **http://www.ncjrs.gov/html/jjbulletin/9907/ contents.html**.

A program emphasizing the development of self-control is the Montreal Preventive Treatment Program, which addresses early-childhood risk factors for gang involvement by targeting boys from poor socioeconomic backgrounds who display disruptive behavior while in kindergarten.[105] The program offers training sessions for parents designed to teach family crisis management, disciplining techniques, and other parenting skills while the boys participate in training sessions emphasizing the development of prosocial skills and self-control. At least one evaluation of the program showed that it was effective at keeping boys from joining gangs.[106]

Critique of Social Process Theories

Criticisms of social process theories are many and varied. Perhaps the most potent criticism of differential association theory is the claim that Sutherland's initial formulation of differential association is not applicable at the individual level because even people who experience an excess of definitions favorable to law violation may still not become criminal and those who rarely associate with recognized deviants may still turn to crime. Also, the theory is untestable because most people experience a multitude of definitions—both favorable and unfavorable to law violation—and

it is up to them to interpret what those experiences mean, so classifying experiences as either favorable or unfavorable to crime commission is difficult at best.

Other critics suggest that differential association alone is not a sufficient explanation for crime. In effect, association theory does not seem to provide for free choice in individual circumstances, nor does it explain why some individuals, even when surrounded by associates committed to lives of crime, are still able to hold on to noncriminal values. Biosocial theorists John Paul Wright and Kevin M. Beaver, for example, suggest that there is a substantial genetic component to self-control and that impulsivity may be at least partially based in biology.[107] Expanding on that idea, it's clear that social process theories largely ignore individual differences, and mostly "assess outcomes averaged across all study participants," rather than examining whether the effectiveness of social interventions are based on individual differences within respondents. In other words, there may be some inherent differences in individuals—whether biological or not—that make some people more responsive to association with others, and influence the way in which (and the degree to) people learn from experiences of all kinds. Finally, differential association theory fails to account for the emergence of criminal values, addressing only the communication of those values.

> The labeling approach does little to explain the origin of crime and deviance.

Although the labeling approach successfully points to the labeling process as a reason for continued deviance and as a cause of stabilization in deviant identities, it does little to

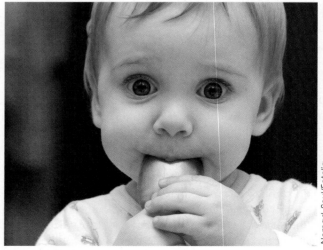

A baby holds on to a spoon. What concepts are key to the social development approach?

■ **human development**   The relationship between the maturing individual and his or her changing environment, as -well as the social processes that the relationship entails.

■ **social development perspective**   An integrated view of human development that examines multiple maturational levels, including psychological, biological, familial, interpersonal, cultural, societal, and ecological, simultaneously.

explain the origin of crime and deviance, and few studies seem to support the basic tenets of the theory. Critics of labeling have pointed to its "lack of firm empirical support for the notion of secondary deviance, [and] many studies have not found that delinquents or criminals have a delinquent or criminal self-image."[108] There is also a lack of empirical support for the claim that contact with the justice system is fundamentally detrimental to the personal lives of criminal perpetrators, but even if that were true, one must ask whether it would ultimately be better if offenders were not caught and forced to undergo the rigors of processing by the justice system. Although labeling theory hints that official processing makes a significant contribution to continued criminality, it seems unreasonable to expect that offenders untouched by the system would forgo the rewards of future criminality. Finally, labeling theory has little to say about secret deviants (people who engage in criminality but are never caught). Can they be expected to continue in lives of deviance if never caught?

Goffman's work has been criticized as providing a set of "linked concepts" rather than a consistent theoretical framework.[109] Other critics have faulted Goffman for failing to offer suggestions for institutional change or for not proposing treatment modalities based on his assumptions. Goffman's greatest failing may be taking the analogy of the theater too far and convincing readers that real life is but a form of playacting; according to George Psathas, "Performing and being are not identical."[110]

The Social Development Perspective

Over the past 25 years, an appreciation for the process of **human development** (the relationship between the maturing individual and his or her changing environment and the social processes that relationship entails) has played an increasingly important role in understanding criminality.[111] Students of human development recognize that the process of development occurs through reciprocal dynamic interactions that take place between individuals and various aspects of their environment, and the social development perspective posits that development, which begins at birth (and perhaps even earlier), occurs primarily within a social context. Unlike social learning theory (discussed earlier in this chapter), social development sees

socialization as only one feature of that context. If socialization were the primary determinant of criminality, then we might expect that all problem children would become criminals as adults, but because that doesn't happen, there must be other aspects to the developmental process that social learning theories don't fully cover.

According to the **social development perspective**, human development simultaneously occurs on many levels—psychological, biological, familial, interpersonal, cultural, societal, and ecological—so social development theories tend to be integrated theories combining various points of view. The rest of this chapter describes life course criminology, the major social development perspective; various ideas contributing to the life course perspective, along with other perspectives on social development, are also described.

Concepts in Social Development Theories

Most sociological explanations for crime involve the study of groups and the identification of differences among groups of offenders, but social development theories focus more on individual rates of offending and seek to understand both increases and decreases in rates of offending over the individual's lifetime. Social development theories generally employ longitudinal (over time) measurements of delinquency and offending, and they pay special attention to the transitions that people face as they move through the life cycle.

Most theories of social development recognize that a critical transitional period occurs as a person moves from childhood to adulthood, and life course theorists have identified at least seven developmental tasks that American adolescents must confront: (1) establishing identity, (2) cultivating symbiotic relationships, (3) defining physical attractiveness, (4) investing in a value system, (5) obtaining an education, (6) separating from family and achieving independence, and (7) obtaining and maintaining gainful employment.[112] Youths are confronted with many obstacles or risks in their attempts to resolve these issues as they work to make a successful transition to adulthood. Figure 8–6 provides a conceptual model of the developmental processes that a maturing youth experiences during adolescence. Learn more about the transitional process leading to adulthood at **https://www.egdstudy.org**.

■ **life course perspective** A perspective that draws attention to the fact that criminal behavior tends to follow a distinct pattern across the life cycle; also called life course criminology.

FIGURE 8-6 | A Conceptual Model of Adolescent Development

Source: Family and Youth Services Bureau, *Understanding Youth Development: Promoting Positive Pathways of Growth* (Washington, DC: U.S. Department of Health and Human Services, 2000).

The Life Course Perspective

Traditional explanations for crime and delinquency often lack a developmental perspective because they generally ignore developmental changes throughout the life course and frequently fail to distinguish between different phases of criminal careers.[113] By contrast, developmental theories draw attention to the fact that criminal behavior tends to follow a distinct pattern across the life cycle: Criminality is relatively uncommon during childhood, tends to begin as sporadic instances of delinquency during late adolescence and early adulthood, and then diminishes and sometimes completely disappears from a person's behavioral repertoire by age 30 or 40. Of course, some people never commit crimes or do so only rarely, whereas others become career criminals and persist in lives of crime.

The **life course perspective** (also called *life course criminology*) shifted the traditional focus away from the reasons why people begin offending to questions about what the dimensions of criminal offending are over the entire life course.[114] It has its roots in a 1986 National Academy of Sciences (NAS) panel report prepared by Alfred Blumstein, Jacqueline Cohen, Jeffrey

■ **criminal career**   The longitudinal sequence of crimes committed by an individual offender.

■ **life course**   The different pathways through the age-differentiated life span; the course of a person's life over time.

FIGURE 8-7 | **Aspects of Criminal Careers**
Source: Schmalleger, Frank, *Criminology*. Printed and electronically reproduced by permission of Pearson Education, Inc., Upper Saddle River, New Jersey.

Roth, and Christy Visher that emphasized the importance of the study of criminal careers and of crime over the life course.[115] The NAS panel defined a **criminal career** as "the longitudinal sequence of crimes committed by an individual offender."[116] The report was especially important for its analysis of "offending development," a concept that underlies the life course perspective (see the Theory in Perspective box in this chapter).

The panel noted (Figure 8–7) that criminal careers can be described in terms of four dimensions: participation, frequency, duration, and seriousness. *Participation*, which refers to the fraction of a population that is criminally active, depends on the scope of criminal acts considered and the length of the observation period.[117] *Frequency* refers to the number of crimes committed by an individual offender per unit of time. Hence, a burglar who commits one burglary a year has a much lower frequency than one who is active monthly or weekly. Frequency is generally not constant and varies over the life course—even for habitual offenders. *Duration* refers to the length of the criminal career. A criminal career can be very short, consisting of only one offense, or it can be quite long, as in the case of habitual or chronic criminals. *Seriousness* is relatively self-explanatory, although it is worthwhile to note that some offenders with long criminal careers commit only petty crimes, whereas others are serious habitual offenders, and still others commit offenses with a mixed degree of seriousness.

Life course criminology was given its name in a seminal book written by **Robert J. Sampson** and **John H. Laub** in 1993, entitled *Crime in the Making*.[118] Earlier, the concept of **life course** had been defined as "pathways through the life span involving a sequence of culturally defined, age-graded roles and social transitions enacted over time."[119] Life course theories, which build on social learning and social control principles, recognize that criminal careers may develop as the result of various criminogenic influences that affect individuals over the course of their lives.

Researchers who focus on the life course as it leads to delinquency, crime, and criminal identities are interested both in evaluating the prevalence, frequency, and onset of offending and in identifying different developmental pathways to delinquency. Life course researchers ask a variety of questions: How do early-childhood characteristics (e.g., antisocial behavior) lead to adult behavioral processes and outcomes? How do life transitions (e.g., shifts in relationships from parents to peers,

transitions from same-sex peers to opposite-sex peers, moves from school to work, marriage, divorce) influence behavior and behavioral choices? How do offending and victimization interact over the life cycle?[120]

Life course researchers examine "trajectories and transitions through the age-differentiated life span."[121] According to Sampson and Laub, "Trajectories refer to longer-term patterns and sequences of behavior, whereas transitions are marked by specific life events (e.g., first job or the onset of crime) that are embedded in trajectories and evolve over shorter time spans."[122] The concept of age differentiation (or age grading) recognizes the fact that certain forms of behavior and some experiences are more appropriate (in terms of their social consequences) in certain parts of the life cycle than in others. Life course theorists search for evidence of continuity between childhood or adolescent experiences and adult outcomes or lifestyles.

Three sets of dynamic concepts are important to the life course perspective: (1) activation, (2) aggravation, and (3) desistance.[123] *Activation*, the way that delinquent behaviors are stimulated and the processes by which the continuity, frequency, and diversity of delinquency are shaped, comes in three types: (1) acceleration (increased frequency of offending over time), (2) stabilization (increased continuity over time), and (3) diversification (propensity of individuals to become involved in more diverse delinquent activities). *Aggravation*, the second dynamic process, refers to the existence of a developmental sequence of activities that escalates or increases in seriousness over time. *Desistance*, the third process, which is discussed in greater detail later in this chapter, describes a slowing down in the frequency of offending (deceleration), a reduction in its variety (specialization), or a reduction in its seriousness (de-escalation).[124]

Glen H. Elder, Jr., has identified five important life course principles (Figure 8–8) that provide a concise summary of life course theory:[125]

> The life course perspective highlights the development of criminal careers.

1. **The principle of historical time and place.** The life course of individuals is embedded in and shaped by the historical times and places they experience over their lifetime.

■ **human agency**   The active role that people take in their lives; the fact that people are not merely subject to social and structural constraints but actively make choices and decisions based on the alternatives they see before them.

THEORY | in PERSPECTIVE
Social Development Theories

Social development theories are integrated theories of human development that simultaneously examine many different levels of development—psychological, biological, familial, interpersonal, cultural, societal, and ecological.

Life Course Perspective

The life course perspective highlights the development of criminal careers, which are seen as the result of various criminogenic influences that affect individuals throughout the course of their lives.

Period: 1980s–present

Theorists: Alfred Blumstein, John H. Laub, Robert J. Sampson, David P. Farrington, Donald J. West, Lawrence E. Cohen, Richard Machalek, Terence Thornberry

Concepts: Criminal career, life course, trajectory, turning points, age grading, social capital, human agency, developmental pathways, life course persisters, persistence, desistance, resilience, cohort, cohort analysis, longitudinal research, evolutionary ecology

FIGURE 8-8 | **Five Important Life Course Principles**

Source: Schmalleger, Frank, *Criminology*. Printed and electronically reproduced by permission of Pearson Education, Inc., Upper Saddle River, New Jersey. ISBN 0132966751

Hence, children born in the United States during the Great Depression or in Nazi Germany during World War II were no doubt strongly influenced by the conditions around them. Similarly, surviving children whose parents were lost in the Holocaust experienced trajectories in their life course that probably would have been far different had they been born in a different place or at a different time.

2. **The principle of timing in lives.** The developmental impact of a succession of life transitions or events is contingent on when they occur in a person's life. Early marriage, for example, or childbearing at an early age can significantly influence the course of people's lives through the long-term consequences of such events. People who start families early may find themselves excluded from further

schooling by the demands of parenthood, and those who leave home and marry at an early age may find that parental financial support is not as readily available to them as it might have been if they had continued to live at home.

3. **The principle of linked lives.** Lives are lived interdependently, and social and historical influences are expressed through a network of shared relationships across the life span. If a child or a spouse develops a serious illness, for example, the lives of other family members are likely to be affected. Caring for an ill family member is emotionally and financially costly, and it takes time. Because of such costs, opportunities that might have been otherwise available are likely to be lost.

4. **The principle of *human agency*.** Human agency refers to the fact that individuals construct their own life course through the choices they make and the actions they take within the opportunities and constraints of history and social circumstances. The example that Elder gives is of hard-pressed Depression-era parents who "moved their residence to cheaper quarters and sought alternative forms of income." In making such choices, they were involved in the process of building a new life course.

5. **The principle of life-long learning development.** Learning is not limited to youth, and individuals continue to acquire knowledge from the experiences they have at every stage in the life course.

Life course theories are supported by research dating back over three-quarters of a century. During the 1920s and 1930s, **Sheldon Glueck** and **Eleanor Glueck** studied the life cycles and careers of 500 nondelinquent and 500 known delinquent boys and another 500 girls in an effort to identify the causes of delinquency.[126] Study group participants were matched on age, intelligence, ethnicity, and neighborhood residence. Data were collected through psychiatric interviews with subjects, parent

■ **Turning point**   Crucial life-experiences that can change behavior.

and teacher reports, and official records obtained from police, court, and correctional files, and surviving subjects were interviewed again between 1949 and 1965.

Significantly, the Gluecks investigated possible contributions to crime causation on four levels: sociocultural (socioeconomic), somatic (physical), intellectual, and emotional-temperamental and concluded that family dynamics played an especially significant role in the development of criminality—"the deeper the roots of childhood maladjustment, the smaller the chance of adult adjustment."[127] Delinquent careers, said the Gluecks, tend to carry over into adulthood and frequently lead to criminal careers.

In 2012, in an interesting test of life course theory and turning points, David S. Kirk at the University of Texas at Austin showed that former prisoners returning home to New Orleans were far less likely to continue lives of crimes if they moved to new neighborhoods. Kirk found that the displacement produced by Hurricane Katrina generally led to lower rates of recidivism among those former prisoners because it resulted in a reduction of criminal opportunities and a loss of association with former criminal peers.[128]

Read more about the life course perspective at **http://www.westerncriminology.org/documents/WCR/v04n1/article_pdfs/wrightarticle.pdf** and review a paper comparing the life course perspective to other theories discussed in this book at **http://www.ncjrs.gov/pdffiles1/nij/grants/198827.pdf**.

Laub and Sampson's Age-Graded Theory

John H. Laub and Robert J. Sampson dusted off 60 cartons of nearly forgotten data that had been collected by the Gluecks and stored in the basement of the Harvard Law School.[129] Upon reanalysis of the data, Laub and Sampson found that children who turned to delinquency were frequently those who had trouble at school and at home and who had friends who were already involved in delinquency. They also discovered that two events in the life course—marriage and job stability—seemed to be especially important in reducing the frequency of offending in later life.

Using a sophisticated cyberanalysis of the Gluecks' original data, Laub and Sampson developed an "age-graded theory of informal social control."[130] Like Hirschi (discussed earlier), Laub and Sampson suggested that delinquency is more likely to occur when an individual's bond to society is weak or broken, but they also recognized that "social ties embedded in adult transitions (e.g., marital attachment, job stability) explain variations in crime unaccounted for by childhood deviance."[131] Hence, although it incorporated the concept of social bonds, Laub and Sampson's perspective also emphasized the significance of continuity and change over the life course.

> Delinquency is more likely to occur when an individual's bond to society is weak or broken.

Central to Laub and Sampson's approach is the idea of **turning points** in a criminal career—"the interlocking nature of trajectories and transitions may generate turning points or a change in the life course."[132] Turning points were first identified by G. B. Trasler in 1980 when he wrote, "As they grow older, most young men gain access to other sources of achievement and social satisfaction—a job, a girlfriend, a wife, a home and eventually children—and in doing so become gradually less dependent upon peer-group support."[133] Given the importance of turning points—which may turn a person toward or away from criminality and delinquency—a clear-cut relationship between early delinquency and criminality later in life cannot be assumed. Sampson and Laub also identified two significant turning points: employment and marriage. Other important turning points can occur in association with leaving home, having children, getting divorced, graduating from school, and receiving a financial windfall. According to Laub and Sampson, even chronic offenders can be reformed when they experience the requisite turning points, whereas individuals with histories of conventionality can begin offending in response to events and circumstances that undermine previously restraining social bonds.[134]

Because transitions in the life course are typically associated with age and because transitional events either enhance or weaken the social bond, Sampson and Laub contended that "age-graded changes in social bonds explain changes in crime"; because these events are not the result of "purposeful efforts to control," they are dubbed "informal social controls."[135]

In 2001, an examination of data from the Dunedin Study (referred to in Chapter 5) suggested the idea of life course interdependence, in which "the effects of social ties on crime vary as a function of criminal propensity."[136] In other words, prosocial ties that deter crime (education, marriage, steady employment) are more likely to discourage criminality among those who are already predisposed to avoid it than among those who are not; researchers dubbed this the "social-protection effect." Conversely, a "social-amplification effect" could be identified in antisocial ties (delinquent friends) that promote crime among individuals predisposed to criminality. The researchers concluded that certain features of the social environment could serve as positive turning points in the lives of antisocial individuals, but the social-amplification effect could produce negative turning points in the lives of the same people.

Similarly, in 2014, a combined research effort examined the importance of jobs and employment on desistance from

■ **social capital**   The degree of positive relationships with others and with social institutions that individuals build up over the course of their lives.

■ **life course–persistent offender**   An individual who displays more or less constant patterns of misbehavior throughout life.
■ **adolescence–limited offender**   An individual who goes through limited periods where they exhibit high probabilities of offending.

crime. The study found that transition to employment is largely a consequence of desistance rather than its cause, but that the most critical issue has to do with the timing of employment transitions in the life trajectory.[137] In other words, employment can be seen as the cement that holds together and finalizes positive changes that have already led to important turning points in offenders' lives.

Also in 2014, researchers examining the role that changes in personal identity have on desistance learned that people are more likely to refrain from crime commission as they move from a deviant to pro-social conception of self. They found that increases in "pro-social identity over time ... is a robust predictor of criminal behavior over the life course."[138]

Another important concept in Laub and Sampson's theory is **social capital**, which refers to the degree of positive relationships with other people and with social institutions that individuals build up over the course of their lives.[139] Social capital directly impacts life course trajectories: The greater a person's social capital, the less chance there is of criminal activity.[140]

A study of how two primary constituents of social capital— marriage and full-time employment—impact life course trajectories was reported by Matthew G. Yeager in 2003. He examined the lives of 773 adult male prisoners released from the Canadian federal prison system between 1983 and 1984, following them for a period of three years.[141] He found that being married reduced the likelihood of return to prison, but an even stronger indicator of postprison success was full-time employment, which Yeager described as having "a strong suppression effect on general criminal recidivism." Because employment is something for which prisoners can be prepared and because it can be offered by the state or federal government, Yeager suggested that it provides a rare opportunity for successful intervention in the lives of released prisoners.

In 2006, Sampson and Laub reported on the application of sophisticated data-analysis techniques to subjects from the Gluecks' original study group who were reinterviewed at age 70. The 2006 study supported the conclusion that "being married is associated with an average reduction of approximately 35 percent in the odds of crime compared to nonmarried status for the same man."[142]

An interesting evaluation of social capital—commitment to a romantic partner, strong job attachment, and nature of close friends among adult subjects—was reported by a group of criminologists in 2002.[143] They found that adolescent delinquency tended to result in involvement with an antisocial romantic partner for both males and females and that such a relationship tended to influence the nature of adult relationships and to increase the likelihood of later criminality. Conventional romantic partners and friends, along with strong job attachment, were found to be especially likely to reduce the chance of criminality

among young adult women, but only conventional adult friends had the same effect among males.

Finally, in 2006, Lisa M. Broidy and Elizabeth E. Cauffman reexamined the Glueck's early data on girls in order to determine how social capital contributed to desistance from crime among women.[144] Using data on 500 female offenders originally collected by the Gluecks, the researchers found that social capital in the form of marriage, motherhood, and positive work experiences led to desistance from crime "in a manner that transcends both gender and historical content." Because much of the data gathered by the Gluecks came from the 1920s, Broidy and Cauffman concluded that marriage, because it was regarded as a universal goal for women during that period of time and because it signified a commitment to conventional norms, represented a significant turning point in the life of young women that marked the start of the desistance process. Learn more about the concept of social capital via **http://westerncriminology.org/documents/WCR/v04n1/article_pdfs/katzarticle.pdf**.

Moffitt's Dual Taxonomic Theory

Criminologists have long noted that although adult criminality is usually preceded by antisocial behavior during adolescence, most antisocial children do not become adult criminals. Psychologist **Terrie E. Moffitt** developed a two-path (dual taxonomic) theory of criminality that helps to explain this observation.[145] Moffit's theory contends that as a result of neuropsychological deficits (specifically, early brain damage or chemical imbalances) combined with poverty and family dysfunction, some people come to display more or less constant patterns of misbehavior throughout life.[146] These people are called **life course–persistent offenders** or *life course persisters*. Life course persisters tend to fail in school and become involved in delinquency at an early age. As a consequence, their opportunities for legitimate success become increasingly limited with the passage of time.

Other teenagers, says Moffitt, go through limited periods where they exhibit high probabilities of offending. Probabilities of offending are generally highest for these people, says Moffitt, during the mid-teen years. This second group, called **adolescence-limited offenders**, is led to offending primarily by structural disadvantages, according to two-path theory. The most significant of these disadvantages is the status anxiety of teenagers that stems from modern society's inadequacy at easing the transition from adolescence to adulthood for significant numbers of young people. Moffitt hypothesizes that a significant source of adolescent strain arises from the fact that biological maturity occurs at a relatively early age (perhaps as early as 12) and brings with it the

■ **persistence**   A person's continuity in crime or continual involvement in offending.

■ **desistance**   A person's cessation of criminal activity or termination of a period of involvement in offending behavior.

desire for sexual and emotional relationships as well as personal autonomy.[147] Society, however, does not permit the assumption of autonomous adult roles until far later (around age 18). As adolescents begin to want autonomy, they are prevented from achieving it because of preexisting societal expectations and societally limited opportunities, resulting in what Moffitt calls a "maturity gap." They might be told, "You're too young for that," or "Wait until you grow up." Lacking the resources to achieve autonomy on their own, they are drawn into delinquent roles by lifelong deviants who have already achieved autonomy and serve as role models for others seeking early independence. At least an appearance of autonomy is achievable for adolescence-limited offenders by engaging in actions that mimic those routinely undertaken by life course–persistent offenders. Once adolescence-limited offenders realize the substantial costs of continuing misbehavior, however, they abandon such social mimicry and the participation in delinquent acts that characterizes it. As they mature, they begin to aspire toward achieving legitimate autonomy. Those who fail to make the transition successfully add to the ranks of the life course–persistent population.

Moffitt notes that adolescence-limited offenders display inconsistencies in antisocial behavior from one place to another. They might, for example, participate in illicit drug use with friends or shoplift in stores. They might also experiment sexually. Still, their school behavior is likely to remain within socially acceptable bounds, and they will probably act with respect toward teachers, employers, and adults. Life course–persistent offenders, on the other hand, consistently engage in antisocial behavior across a wide spectrum of social situations.

Research findings indicate that positive developmental pathways are fostered when adolescents are able to develop (1) a sense of industry and competency, (2) a feeling of connectedness to others and to society, (3) a belief in their ability to control their future, and (4) a stable identity.[148] Adolescents who develop these characteristics appear more likely than others to engage in prosocial behaviors, exhibit positive school performances, and be members of nondeviant peer groups. Competency, connectedness, control, and identity are outcomes of the developmental process. They develop through a person's interactions with his or her community, family, school, and peers. The following kinds of interactions appear to promote development of these characteristics:

- Interactions in which children engage in productive activities and win recognition for their productivity
- Interactions in which parents and other adults control and monitor adolescents' behaviors in a consistent and caring

manner while allowing them a substantial degree of psychological and emotional independence

- Interactions in which parents and other adults provide emotional support, encouragement, and practical advice to adolescents
- Interactions in which adolescents are accepted as individuals with unique experiences based on their temperament; gender; biosocial development; and family, cultural, and societal factors

Farrington's Delinquent Development Theory

Life course theorists use the term **persistence** to describe continuity in crime or continual involvement in offending; **desistance** refers to the cessation of criminal activity or the termination of a period of involvement in offending behavior. Desistance (mentioned briefly earlier in this chapter) can be unaided or aided: Unaided desistance refers to desistance that occurs without the formal intervention or assistance of criminal justice agencies like probation or parole agencies, the courts, or prison or jail, and aided desistance, involving agencies of the justice system, is generally referred to as rehabilitation. Delinquents often mature successfully and grow out of offending; even older persistent offenders may tire of justice system interventions, lose the personal energy required for continued offending, and "burn out."

A number of early criminologists noted the desistance phenomenon. Marvin Wolfgang described the process as one of "spontaneous remission,"[149] although it was recognized far earlier—in 1833, Adolphe Quetelet argued that the penchant for crime diminished with age "due to the enfeeblement of physical vitality and the passions."[150] The Gluecks later developed the concept of maturational reform to explain the phenomenon and suggested that the "sheer passage of time" caused delinquents to "grow out" of this transitory phase and to "burn out" physiologically, concluding, "Ageing is the only factor which emerges as significant in the reformative process."[151]

In 1985, Walter R. Grove proposed a maturational theory of biopsychosocial desistance that sees the desistance phenomenon as a natural or normal consequence of the aging process.[152] "As persons move through the life cycle, (1) they will shift from self-absorption to concern for others; (2) they will increasingly accept societal values and behave in socially appropriate ways; (3) they will become more comfortable with social relations;

■ **resilience** The psychological ability to successfully cope with severe stress and negative events.

■ **cohort analysis** A social scientific technique that studies a population with common characteristics over time. Cohort analysis usually begins at birth and traces the development of cohort members until they reach a certain age.

■ **Cambridge Study in Delinquent Development** A longitudinal (life course) study of crime and delinquency tracking a cohort of 411 boys born in London in 1953.

(4) their activities will increasingly reflect a concern for others in their community; and (5) they will become increasingly concerned with the issue of the meaning of life."[153] Some criminologists argued, however, that the claim that aging causes desistance is meaningless because it doesn't explain the actual mechanisms involved.

Longitudinal studies of crime over the life course conducted by **David P. Farrington** and **Donald J. West** have shown far greater diversity in the ages of desistance than in the ages of onset of criminal behavior.[154] In 1982, in an effort to explain the considerable heterogeneity of developmental pathways, Farrington and West began tracking a cohort of 411 boys born in London in 1953 in an ongoing study known as the **Cambridge Study in Delinquent Development**, which uses self-reports of delinquency as well as psychological tests and in-depth interviews. To date, participants have been interviewed nine times, with the earliest interviews being conducted at age eight.

The Cambridge study reveals that life course patterns found in the United States are also characteristic of English delinquents. Farrington found that the study's persistent offenders suffered from "hyperactivity, poor concentration, low achievement, an antisocial father, large family size, low family income, a broken family, poor parental supervision, and parental disharmony."[155] Other risk factors for delinquency included harsh discipline, negative peer influences, and parents with offense histories of their own. Chronic offenders were found to have friends and peers who were also offenders, and offending was found to begin with early antisocial behavior, including aggressiveness, dishonesty, problems in school, truancy, hyperactivity, impulsiveness, and restlessness. Consistent with other desistance studies, Farrington found that offending tends to peak around the age of 17 or 18 and then declines. By age 35, many subjects were found to have conforming lifestyles, although they were often separated or divorced and had poor employment records and patterns of residential instability. Many former offenders were also substance abusers and consequently served as very poor role models for their children.

Although studies of desistance are becoming increasingly common, one of the main methodological problems for researchers is determining when desistance has occurred. Some theorists conceptualize desistance as the complete or absolute stopping of criminal behavior of any kind, whereas others see it as the gradual cessation of criminal involvement.[156] In 1990, Rolf Loeber and Marc LeBlanc identified four components of desistance:[157] (1) deceleration—a slowing down in the frequency of offending, (2) specialization—a reduction in the variety of offenses, (3) de-escalation—a reduction in the seriousness of offending, and (4) reaching a ceiling—remaining at a certain level of offending and not committing more serious offenses.

Resilience, another important concept in life course research, refers to the psychological ability to successfully cope with severe stress and negative events and has important implications for the development of delinquency and criminal offending.[158] One recent study of resilience among teenage girls exposed to a number of risk factors associated with delinquency development (physical and sexual assault, neglect, poverty, unemployed parents, female-headed households) found a number of protective factors that could enhance resilience among girls. Included were things like religiosity, school connectedness and success, and presence of a caring adult; the latter offered the most protection against delinquency. "The most consistent protective effect … was the extent to which a girl felt she had caring adults in her life."[159]

> Resilience is the psychological ability to successfully cope with severe stress and negative events and has important implications for the development of delinquency and criminal offending.

Evolutionary Ecology

Because life course theory uses a developmental perspective in the study of criminal careers, life course researchers typically use longitudinal research designs involving **cohort analysis**, which usually begins at birth and traces the development of a population whose members share common characteristics until they reach a certain age. One well-known analysis of a birth cohort, undertaken by **Marvin Wolfgang** during the 1960s, found that a small nucleus of chronic juvenile offenders accounted for a disproportionately large share of all juvenile arrests.[160] Wolfgang studied male individuals born in Philadelphia in 1945 until they reached age 18 and concluded that a small number of violent offenders were responsible for most of the crimes committed by the cohort—6% of cohort members accounted for 52% of all arrests (Figure 8–9). A follow-up study found that the seriousness of the offenses among the cohort increased in adulthood but that the actual number of offenses decreased as the cohort aged.[161] Wolfgang's analysis has since been criticized for its lack of a second cohort, or control group, against which the experiences of the cohort under study could be compared.[162]

The ecological perspective on crime control, pioneered by **Lawrence E. Cohen** and **Richard Machalek**, provides a more contemporary example of a life course approach.[163]

■ **evolutionary ecology** An approach to understanding crime that draws attention to the ways people develop over the course of their lives.

■ **interactional theory** A theoretical approach to exploring crime and delinquency that blends social control and social learning perspectives.

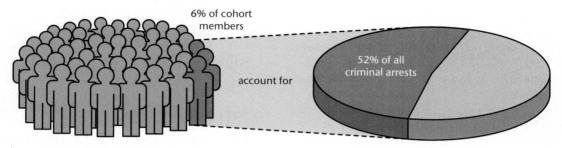

FIGURE 8-9 | The Nucleus of Chronic Offenders
Source: Schmalleger, Frank, *Criminology*. Printed and Electronically reproduced by permission of Pearson Education, Inc., Upper Saddle River, New Jersey.

Evolutionary ecology builds on the approach of social ecology while emphasizing developmental pathways encountered early in life. Criminologist Bryan Vila stated that "the evolutionary ecological approach draws attention to the ways people develop over the course of their lives. Experiences and environment early in life, especially those that affect child development and the transmission of biological traits and family management practices across generations, seem particularly important."[164] According to Vila, evolutionary ecology "attempts to explain how people acquire criminality—a predisposition that disproportionately favors criminal behavior—when and why they express it as crime, how individuals and groups respond to those crimes, and how all these phenomena interact as a dynamic self-reinforcing system that evolves over time."[165]

Thornberry's Interactional Theory

Terence Thornberry proposed what he calls an **interactional theory** regarding crime, which integrates social control and social learning explanations of delinquency.[166] In constructing his approach, Thornberry was attentive to the impact of social structure on behavior and noted how delinquency and crime seem to develop within the context of reciprocal social arrangements. Reciprocity was especially important to Thornberry because he believed that too many other theories were overly simplistic in their dependence on simple unidirectional causal relationships (see the Theory versus Reality box).

The fundamental cause of delinquency according to interactional theory is a weakening of a person's bond to conventional society.[167] Thornberry pointed out that adolescents who are strongly attached to their parents and family and who strive to achieve within the context of approved social arrangements, such as education, rarely turn to serious delinquency. It takes more than weak conventional bonds, however, for delinquency to develop; it requires the presence

of an environment in which delinquency can be learned and in which rule-violating behavior can be positively rewarded. Delinquent peers are especially important in providing the kind of environment necessary for criminal behavior to develop, and gang membership can play a highly significant role in the development and continuation of such behavior. Associating with delinquent peers, said Thornberry, leads to delinquent acts but also involves a causal loop such that those who commit delinquent acts are likely to continue associating with others like themselves—creating a mechanism of social reinforcement and resulting in ever-escalating levels of criminal behavior. Thornberry also predicted that delinquents will seek out association with ever-more delinquent groups if their delinquency continues to be rewarded, so delinquency is seen as a process that unfolds over the life course.

In a test of interactional theory, Thornberry used data drawn from the Rochester Youth Development Study, a multiwave panel study designed to examine drug use and delinquent behavior among adolescents in the Rochester, New York, area.[168] Study findings (discussed in more detail later) supported the loop-type aspects of interactional theory and showed that delinquency is part of a dynamic social process, not merely the end result of static conditions. The study also found that the development of beliefs supportive of delinquent behavior tends to follow that behavior in time. In other words, commitment to delinquent values may be more a product of delinquent behavior that is rewarded than an initial cause of such behavior.

Thornberry also found that childhood maltreatment (based on official records) could be an important element of the developmental process leading to delinquency and that the degree of maltreatment experienced in childhood bore some relationship to the extent of delinquent involvement later in life.[169] While maltreatment appears to weaken the bond to conventionality, it also weakens the family bond. Suman Kaker of Florida International University, in an extension of interactional theory, noted that delinquency also puts stress on the family, resulting in a further weakening of the familial bond.[170]

THEORY | versus REALITY

Social Influences on Developmental Pathways

A report by the Family and Youth Services Bureau (an agency of the U.S. Department of Health and Human Services) identified five "aspects of the social context" that can either promote or block the development of prosocial behavior among adolescents:

1. **Biophysical aspects of the individual.** Biophysical characteristics found to influence developmental pathways during adolescence include temperament, gender, cognitive development, and age of onset of puberty. The influence of these factors on development depends to a large extent on how others in the social context react to them. Individuals bring these aspects of self to the interactions in which they are engaged, and the reaction of the social context to these aspects determines the quality and nature of the interactions.

2. **Aspects of society.** Society may be understood as the economic and institutional structures, values, and mores that constitute a national identity. Some of the aspects of society that influence the development of a sense of competency, connectedness, control, and identity are current economic and employment conditions, discrimination and prejudice, and educational institutions. Societal factors influence adolescent development directly and indirectly through their effects on communities and families. The societal factors of prejudice and discrimination often present barriers to positive developmental pathways for minority and economically disadvantaged youths, so for these youths, community and family contexts are particularly important for moderating the potentially negative influences of societal factors.

3. **Aspects of the community.** The community context (neighborhood or town) incorporates where individuals spend their time and with whom they spend it. The aspects of the community context that have been studied with respect to their effects on adolescent development include community culture, availability of sources of support to parents and youths, and availability of quality community institutional or organizational resources for children and youths. As with societal factors, community factors have both direct and indirect influences on developmental pathways during adolescence. Formal and informal broad-based community institutions and organizations, in particular, influence adolescent development directly by teaching and encouraging prosocial behaviors and indirectly by supporting parents in their parenting efforts.

4. **Aspects of the family.** The following aspects of the family context have received considerable research attention with respect to their influences on developmental pathways: quality of the parent–child relationship, parenting styles or practices, family structure, and family dysfunction. In general, family practices that serve to monitor and control adolescents' behaviors in a caring and consistent manner, provide support and encouragement to adolescents, and allow them psychological and emotional independence appear to be most effective in fostering the development of a sense of competency, connectedness, control over one's fate in life, and identity.

5. **Aspects of peer relationships.** Research findings do not support the popular notion that adolescent problem behaviors are the result of peer pressure; instead, it has been shown that peers do not direct adolescents to new behaviors as much as they reinforce existing dispositions that helped direct the adolescent to a particular peer group in the first place. Close friendships with peers during adolescence have been found to promote positive growth because they foster the development of conceptions of fairness, mutual respect, empathy, and intimacy, through which youths are able to develop a sense of connectedness to others and a stable sense of identity.

The information in the Family and Youth Services Bureau report suggested that interventions designed to assist youths in making successful transitions to adulthood will need to provide adolescents, either directly or through parents and community resources, with opportunities to engage in interactions that foster the development of a sense of competency, connectedness, control, and identity and that interventions must address children, families, and communities as a unit if they are to be effective for large numbers of children and their families.

Discussion Questions

1. How would you rank the five aspects of the social context identified in this box as impacting the development of prosocial behavior among adolescents in order of relative importance? Why would you choose such a ranking?

2. How might the five aspects of the social context interact?

3. Are there other important aspects of the social context that can be identified? If so, what might they be?

Source: Family and Youth Services Bureau, *Understanding Youth Development: Promoting Positive Pathways of Growth* (Washington, DC: U.S. Department of Health and Human Services, January 1997).

Developmental Pathways

Researchers have found that manifestations of disruptive behaviors in childhood and adolescence are often age dependent, reflecting a developing capability to display different behaviors with age.[171] Budding behavioral problems can often be detected at an early age. In 1994, Rolf Loeber and Dale F. Hay described the emergence of opposition to parents and aggression toward siblings and peers as a natural developmental occurrence during the first two years of life.[172] As toddlers develop the ability

Childhood maltreatment is an important element of the developmental process leading to delinquency.

to speak, they become increasingly likely to use words to resolve conflicts, with oppositional behaviors declining between ages three and six as children acquire greater verbal skills for expressing their needs and for dealing with conflict, but children who

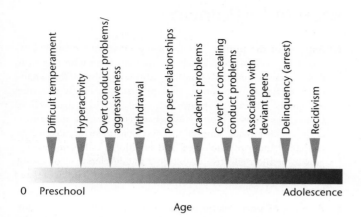

FIGURE 8-10 | Manifestations of Disruptive and Antisocial Behaviors in Childhood and Adolescence

Source: Barbara Tatem Kelley et al., *Developmental Pathways in Boys' Disruptive and Delinquent Behavior* (Washington, DC: Office of Juvenile Justice and Delinquency Prevention, December 1997).

are unable to develop adequate verbal coping skills commit acts of intense aggression, initiate hostile conflict, and are characterized by parents as having a difficult temperament.[173] Figure 8–10 shows the order in which disruptive and antisocial childhood behaviors tend to manifest between birth and late adolescence, and Figure 8–11 shows the order of learning of skills and attitudes deemed necessary for successful prosocial development during childhood and adolescence.

One of the most comprehensive studies to date attempting to detail life pathways leading to criminality, which began in 1986, is the Program of Research on the Causes and Correlates of Delinquency, sponsored by the U.S. Department of Justice's Office of Juvenile Justice and Delinquency Prevention. The program, a longitudinal study producing ongoing results, aims to better understand serious delinquency, violence, and drug use by examining how youths develop within the context of family,

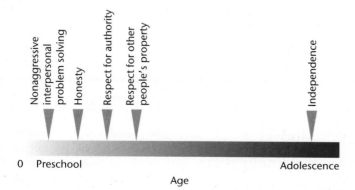

FIGURE 8-11 | The Order of Learning of Skills and Attitudes Necessary for Successful Prosocial Development

Source: Barbara Tatem Kelley et al., *Developmental Pathways in Boys' Disruptive and Delinquent Behavior* (Washington, DC: Office of Juvenile Justice and Delinquency Prevention, December 1997).

school, peers, and community.[174] It has compiled data on 4,500 youths from three distinct but coordinated projects: the Denver Youth Survey, conducted by the University of Colorado; the Pittsburgh Youth Study, undertaken by University of Pittsburgh researchers; and the Rochester Youth Development Study, fielded by professors at the University at Albany (New York).

The Causes and Correlates projects, using a similar research design, are longitudinal investigations involving repeated contacts with youths during a substantial portion of their developmental years. Researchers conduct individual face-to-face interviews with inner-city youths considered to be at high risk for involvement in delinquency and drug abuse. Multiple perspectives on each child's development and behavior were obtained through interviews with the child's primary caretakers and with teachers. In addition to interview data, the studies collect extensive information from official agencies, including police, courts, schools, and social services.[175] Following are some program results:

1. Delinquency is related to individual risk factors such as impulsivity.

2. The more seriously involved in drugs a youth is, the more seriously that juvenile will be involved in delinquency.

3. Children who are more attached to and involved with their parents are less involved in delinquency.

4. Greater risks exist for violent offending when a child is physically abused or neglected early in life.

5. Students who are not highly committed to school have higher rates of delinquency, and delinquency involvement reduces commitment to school.

6. Poor family life, especially poor parental supervision, exacerbates delinquency and drug use.

7. Affiliation with street gangs and illegal gun ownership are both predictive of delinquency.

8. Living in a bad neighborhood doubles the risk for delinquency.

9. A family being on public assistance (welfare) is associated with the highest risk of delinquency (followed by a family having low socioeconomic status).[176]

Results showed that "peers who were delinquent or used drugs had a great impact on [other] youth" and that "the best predictors of success were having conventional friends, having a stable family and good parental monitoring, having positive expectations for the future, and not having delinquent peers."[177]

Research findings indicated that positive developmental pathways are fostered when adolescents are able to develop (1) a sense of industry and competency, (2) a feeling of connectedness to others and to society, (3) a belief in their ability to control their future, and (4) a stable identity.[178] Competency, connectedness, control, and identity develop through youths' interactions with their community, family, school, and peers. Adolescents who develop these characteristics appear more likely than others to engage in prosocial behaviors, exhibit positive school performance,

■ **Pathways to Desistance study**   The largest longitudinal study of serious adolescent offenders ever conducted. The study analyzed data that was gathered on serious youthful offenders as they moved from adolescence into early adulthood.

and be members of nondeviant peer groups. The following inter-actions appear to promote these characteristics:

- Children engage in productive activities and win recognition for their productivity.
- Parents and other adults control and monitor adolescents' behaviors in a consistent and caring manner while allowing them a substantial degree of psychological and emotional independence.
- Parents and other adults provide emotional support, encouragement, and practical advice to adolescents.
- Adolescents are accepted as individuals with unique experiences based on their temperament, gender, and biosocial development as well as family, cultural, and societal factors.

Perhaps the most significant result of the Causes and Correlates study is the finding that three separate developmental pathways to delinquency (shown in Figure 8–12) exist:[179]

1. Authority conflict pathway. Subjects appear to begin quite young (three or four years of age) on the authority conflict pathway. "The first step," said the study authors, "was stubborn behavior, followed by defiance around age 11, and authority avoidance—truancy, staying out late at night, or running away."

2. Covert pathway. "Minor covert acts such as frequent lying and shoplifting usually [start] around age 10." Delinquents following the covert pathway quickly progress "to acts of property damage, such as fire starting or vandalism, around

age 11 or 12, followed by moderate and serious forms of delinquency."

3. Overt pathway. The first step on the overt pathway is minor aggression such as "annoying others and bullying—around age 11 or 12." Bullying was found to escalate into "physical fighting and violence as the juvenile progressed along this pathway." The overt pathway eventually leads to violent crimes like rape, robbery, and assault.

Researchers have found that these three different pathways are not necessarily mutually exclusive and can at times converge (see Figure 8–13). Self-report data have shown that simultaneous progression along two or more pathways leads to higher rates of delinquency.[180] Learn more about the Causes and Correlates study and view results from each study site at **http://www.ncjrs.gov/pdffiles1/fs99100.pdf**. Read more about the Program of Research on the Causes and Correlates of Delinquency at **http://www.ojjdp.gov/jjbulletin/9810_2/program.html** and review literature on developmental pathways at **http://www.britsoccrim.org/volume2/003.pdf** and **http://www.ncjrs.gov/html/ojjdp/jjbul9712–2/jjb1297.html**.

Pathways to Desistance

The **Pathways to Desistance study** is the largest longitudinal study of serious adolescent offenders ever conducted. The study, which involved multiple sites, gathered data on serious adolescent offenders as they transitioned from adolescence into early adulthood.

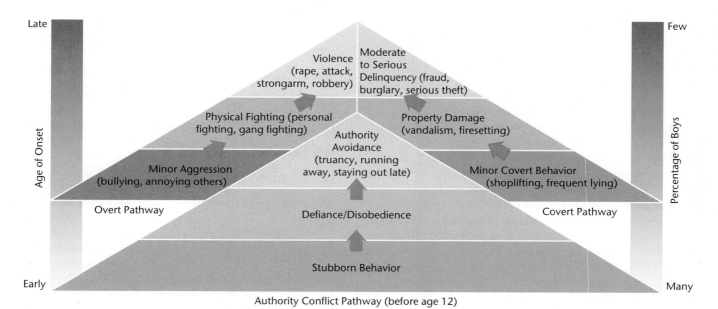

FIGURE 8-12 | **Three Pathways to Disruptive Behavior and Delinquency**

Source: Barbara Tatem Kelley et al., *Developmental Pathways in Boys' Disruptive and Delinquent Behavior* (Washington, DC: Office of Juvenile Justice and Delinquency Prevention, December 1997).

■ **Project on Human Development in Chicago Neighborhoods (PHDCN)** An intensive study of Chicago neighborhoods employing longitudinal evaluations to examine the changing circumstances of people's lives in an effort to identify personal characteristics leading toward or away from antisocial behavior.

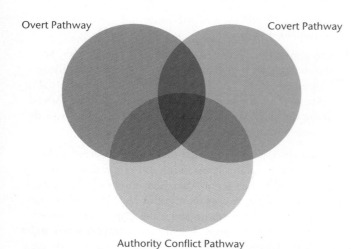

FIGURE 8-13 | **Single or Multiple Disruptive Pathways**

Source: Barbara Tatem Kelley et al., *Developmental Pathways in Boys' Disruptive and Delinquent Behavior* (Washington, DC: Office of Juvenile Justice and Delinquency Prevention, December 1997).

Between November 2000 and January 2003, 1,354 adjudicated youths from the juvenile and adult court systems in Maricopa County (Phoenix), Arizona, and Philadelphia County, Pennsylvania, were enrolled into the study. The youth were at least 14 years old and under 18 years old at the time of offense.

Each study participant was followed for a period of seven years past enrollment, and interviews were conducted regularly with the adolescents as well as with family members and friends, providing a comprehensive picture of life changes in a wide array of areas over the course of the study. Overall, more than 20,000 interviews were conducted. The study attempted to identify factors that lead youth who commit serious offenses to continue or desist from offending, including individual maturation, life changes, and involvement with the criminal justice system.

The primary findings of the study include (1) a decrease in self-reported offending over time by the most serious adolescent offenders, (2) the relative inefficacy of longer juvenile incarcerations and its lack of impact on decreasing recidivism, (3) the effectiveness of community-based supervision as a component of aftercare for incarcerated youth, and (4) the positive impact of substance abuse treatment in reducing both substance use and crime commission by serious adolescent offenders. Significantly, the study also found that most youth who commit felonies greatly reduce their offending over time—regardless of intervention, preventative efforts, earlier experiences, or the expectations of others. Longer stays in juvenile confinement facilities were not found to reduce recidivism.[181] Learn more about the Pathways to Desistance study at **www.justicestudies.com/pubs/pathways2015.pdf**.

Project on Human Development in Chicago Neighborhoods (PHDCN)

The **Project on Human Development in Chicago Neighborhoods** (PHDCN), begun in 1990, is jointly sponsored by the National Institute of Justice and the John D. and Catherine T. MacArthur Foundation.[182] The PHDCN is directed by physician Felton J. Earls, professor of human behavior and development at Harvard University's School of Public Health; also involved are Robert Sampson, professor of sociology at the University of Chicago, and Stephen Raudenbush, professor of education at Michigan State University. Earls and Albert J. Reiss described the ongoing research as "the major criminologic investigation of this century."[183]

The PHDCN, which consists of a longitudinal analysis of how individuals, families, institutions, and communities evolve together, is now "tracing how criminal behavior develops from birth to age 32."[184] It involves experts from a wide range of disciplines, including psychiatry, developmental and clinical psychology, sociology, criminology, public health and medicine, education, human behavior, and statistics.

The project is actually two studies combined into a single comprehensive design: One is an intensive study of Chicago's neighborhoods that evaluates the social, economic, organizational, political, and cultural components of each neighborhood and seeks to identify changes that have taken place in the neighborhoods over the study's eight-year data-gathering period. The second study consists of a series of coordinated longitudinal evaluations of 6,000 randomly selected children, adolescents, and young adults that looks at the changing circumstances of people's lives and attempts to identify personal characteristics leading toward or away from antisocial behavior (see the Who's to Blame box in this chapter). Researchers explore a wide range of variables—from prenatal drug exposure, lead poisoning, and nutrition to adolescent growth patterns, temperament, and self-image—as they try to identify which individuals might be most at risk for crime and delinquency. They also study children's exposure to violence and its consequences and evaluate child care and its impact on early

> The Project on Human Development in Chicago Neighborhoods (PHDCN) has been called "the major criminologic investigation of the century."

WHO'S TO BLAME—The Individual or Society?

Sexual Abuser Claims Victim Status

Mortimer Rataway was arrested after authorities received a report of a man struggling with a boy in a Short Stop food and beverage store. A police officer on nearby patrol arrived at the scene within minutes and observed Rataway forcing the boy, nine-year-old Justin, into an old sedan outside the convenience store. When the officer asked Rataway what was going on, the boy blurted out that he had been kidnapped.

The officer had heard reports on his radio describing the kidnapping of a nine-year-old boy from a school bus stop in an adjacent city two days earlier, and he quickly took Rataway into custody on suspicion of kidnapping.

Justin was taken to a special area reserved for juveniles in the local police station, where he told detectives that he was the boy who had been kidnapped. Although he was physically okay, he told police that Rataway had forced him to engage in repeated masturbation and that Rataway had taken many photographs of him naked.

A search of Rataway's apartment uncovered a number of digital cameras and a computer Web server hosting a child pornography site. The camera and computer contained photos of many other young boys; some of the photos had probably been purchased over the Internet, but Rataway later admitted taking others.

"I never hurt anybody," Rataway told investigators. "Most of the boys agreed to serve as models after I paid them. But I got carried away and grabbed Justin because I thought he'd make one of my best models.

"Yeah, I'm gay," Rataway told the police in a recorded statement. "And sure, I like boys. But it isn't my fault. When I was growing up as a young Catholic I was taught to enjoy my body and to like other men by the parish priest. Now I know that most priests are good men and that the crisis in the Church was way

Shutterstock

overblown by the media some time back. But if that hadn't happened to me, I know I would have been straight, and I'm sure I would have gotten married and had kids of my own. Because of what happened to me when I was a kid, I'm as much a victim as anybody. It doesn't matter how much you punish me, I'm never going to change my sexual orientation."

Think about it

1. Do you see Rataway as a criminal or a victim (as he claims)? Might he be both?

2. Some people describe child molesters as "sick." Is Rataway "sick"? If so, how can he be cured?

3. Will sending Rataway to prison rehabilitate him? Why or why not? How can you ensure that he won't pose a future threat if he is released back into society someday?

4. How does this case illustrate the way our understandings of criminal motivation and crime causality influence our notions of fairness and justice in the treatment of offenders?

Note: Who's to Blame boxes provide fictionalized critical thinking opportunities based on actual cases.

---

childhood development. Various study methodologies, including self-reports, individualized tests and examinations, direct observations, examination of existing records, and reports by informants, are being used. Following are some areas and questions being explored:[185]

- **Communities.** Why do some communities experience high rates of antisocial behavior whereas apparently similar communities are relatively safe?

- **Schools.** Some children have achievement problems early in school and others have behavioral or truancy problems; some exhibit both kinds of problems, and others neither kind. Why do these differences exist? What are their causes and effects?

- **Peers.** Delinquent youths tend to associate with delinquent peers and usually act in groups. Does this association lead to delinquency, or is it simply a case of "like finding like"? Are the influences of peers equally important for girls and for boys or are their developmental pathways entirely different?

- **Families.** Poor parenting practices are strongly associated with substance abuse and delinquency, but are they the cause of such behaviors? If so, then social programs in parenting skills could make a difference. But what if there are underlying factors, such as temperamental characteristics or social isolation, that cause problems in both parents and children?

■ **Comprehensive Strategy for Serious, Violent, and Chronic Juvenile Offenders program**   A National Institute of Justice initiative that provides participating communities with a framework for preventing delinquency, intervening in early delinquent behavior, and responding to serious, violent, and chronic offending.

A tug-of-war in Chicago during the annual Youth Fest. The Project on Human Development in Chicago Neighborhoods (PHDCN) is a multidisciplinary project, consisting of a longitudinal analysis of how individuals, families, institutions, and communities evolve together, jointly sponsored by the National Institute of Justice and the John D. and Catherine T. MacArthur Foundation. What results has the study produced?

- **Individual differences.** What health-related, cognitive, intellectual, and emotional factors in children promote positive social development? What factors put them at risk of developing antisocial behaviors?

PHDCN study results have led to targeted interventions intended to lower rates of offending. According to Sampson, "Instead of external actions (e.g., a police crackdown), we stress in this study the effectiveness of 'informal' mechanisms by which residents themselves achieve public order. In particular, we believe that collective expectations for intervening on behalf of neighborhood children [are] a crucial dimension of the public life of neighborhoods."[186] Life course perspectives, like the one informing the PHDCN, often point to the need for early intervention with nurturant strategies that build self-control through positive socialization. As Vila pointed out, "There are two main types of nurturant strategies: those that improve early life experiences to forestall the development of strategic styles based on criminality, and those that channel child and adolescent development in an effort to improve the match between individuals and their environment."[187] Learn more about the PHDCN at **http://www.icpsr.umich.edu/icpsrweb/PHDCN/. http://ssrn.com/abstract=1081894** discusses cultural mechanisms involved in neighborhood violence.

Policy Implications of Social Development Theories

Social development strategies have been widely applied to juvenile justice and human services settings. The OJJDP adopted the social development model as the foundation for its **Comprehensive Strategy for Serious, Violent, and Chronic Juvenile Offenders program**, which provides participating communities with a framework for preventing delinquency, intervening in early delinquent behavior, and responding to serious, violent, and chronic offending. It assists communities in establishing or modifying a juvenile justice continuum of care through risk-focused prevention, risk and needs assessment, structured decision making, and graduated sanctions training and technical assistance. The OJJDP's Comprehensive Strategy program centers around the following six components:

1. Strengthening families in their role of providing guidance and discipline and instilling sound values as the first and primary teacher of children

2. Supporting core social institutions, including schools, churches, and other community organizations, so that they can reduce risk factors and help children develop their full potential

3. Promoting prevention strategies that enhance protective factors and reduce the impact of negative risk factors affecting the lives of young people at risk for high delinquency

4. Intervening immediately and constructively when delinquent behavior first occurs

5. Identifying and controlling a small segment of violent and chronic juvenile offenders

6. Establishing a broad spectrum of sanctions that ensure accountability and a continuum of services

A few years ago, the OJJDP began a national evaluation of the Comprehensive Strategy Program. Learn more about the program via **http://www.ojjdp.gov/jjjournal/jjjournal997/plan.html** where you can keep abreast of the ongoing evaluation.

Another contemporary example of social intervention efforts tied to a developmental model is Targeted Outreach, a program operated by Boys and Girls Clubs of America.[188] The program has its origins in the 1972 implementation of a youth development strategy based on studies undertaken at the University of Colorado, which showed that at-risk youths could be effectively diverted from the juvenile justice

■ **Follow the author's tweets about the latest crime and justice news @schmalleger.**

system through the provision of positive alternatives. Using a wide referral network made up of local schools, police departments, and various youth services agencies, club officials work to end what they call the "inappropriate detention of juveniles."[189]

The program's primary goal is to provide a positive and productive alternative to gangs for the youths who are most vulnerable to their influences or are already entrenched in gang activity. It recruits at-risk youngsters (as young as seven years old) and diverts them into activities intended to promote a sense of belonging, competence, usefulness, and self-control: A sense of belonging is fostered through clubs that provide familiar settings where each child is accepted; competence and usefulness are developed through opportunities for meaningful activities, which young people in the club program can successfully undertake; and self-control is developed as youthful participants have a

> THE OJJDP adopted the social development model as the foundation for its Comprehensive Strategy for Serious, Violent, and Chronic Juvenile Offenders program.

chance to be heard and to influence decisions affecting their future. To date, Targeted Outreach has served more than 10,000 at-risk youths and hopes to eventually involve more than 1.5 million youngsters between the ages of seven and 17. Mobilization for Youth and Targeted Outreach are the kinds of programs that theorists who focus on the social structure typically seek to implement.

Critique of Social Development Theories

Social development theories have been criticized for definitional issues. What, for example, do life course concepts like turning point, pathway, risk factor, persistence, desistance, and criminal career really mean? Precise definitions of such concepts are necessary if hypotheses derived from life course theories are to be tested. Some writers have identified "associated problems of how to develop risk/needs assessment devices and how to use these both in fundamental research (to maximize the yield of serious offenders while still making it possible to draw conclusions about the general population) and in applied research (to decide which populations should be targeted by interventions)."[190]

CRIMINAL | PROFILES

Adam Lanza and the Sandy Hook School Shootings

On December 14, 2012, 20-year-old Adam Lanza, a socially awkward young man, went on a shooting rampage at Sandy Hook Elementary School in Newtown, Connecticut. In a matter of minutes, Lanza fired 155 bullets and shot to death 20 kindergarten students, four teachers, a principal, and the school's psychologist.[i] The shooting spree ended when Lanza turned one of his three guns on himself. Before the massacre, Lanza killed his mother at the house they shared only minutes from the school. The horrific shooting was covered by media services for days and reignited an intense national debate about gun control.

Although the Newtown shooting stood out as especially horrific because it ended so many innocent young lives, it is but one of a number of random mass shootings in the United States in recent years. In 2012 alone, there were 12 other random mass killings—including a July attack by a lone gunman in an Aurora, Colorado, movie theater where 12 people were killed and another 58 injured during a midnight showing of the movie *The Dark Knight Rises*.[ii] In that crime, the alleged shooter, 24-year-old James Eagan Holmes, who dressed as the Joker (a nefarious character from the film) during the shooting spree, was arrested outside the theater. He was found guilty of multiple counts of first-degree murder in 2015.

Experts tell us that the number of random mass shootings is on the increase. According to the *Wall Street Journal*, there "were 18 random mass shootings in the 1980s, 54 in the 1990s, and 87 in the 2000s."[iii] The journal's emphasis was on *random* shootings, and it noted that other mass killings—in which victims were in some way known to the shooter—had not significantly increased or decreased in number.

A fair question to ask would be "Why are the number of such random incidents increasing?" Some answers might be found in the personal characteristics of the shooters. Lanza and Holmes shared a number of things in common. Both were middle-class white males in their early twenties who were regarded by their peers as unnervingly intelligent. Holmes had been a former neuroscience graduate student at the University of Colorado's Anschutz Campus, whose academic career unraveled shortly before the movie theater shooting. Lanza, once a prominent member of his high school's technology club and an honors student, was said to have been extraordinarily bright by former teachers. Neither shooter had a previous criminal record.[iv]

What may have contributed to both incidents, however, was one additional feature the two men shared—a disordered personality.[v]

(Continued)

According to the American Psychiatric Association, most mentally ill people do not turn to violence, although some forms of mental illness have been associated with aggression and criminal activity, especially when combined with illegal drug use.[vi]

Questions about Lanza's mental health were quickly raised following the Sandy Hook shootings by former friends and family members who knew him to be painfully shy, reclusive, and psychologically troubled. Described by personal acquaintances as "very bright" but emotionally disturbed, Lanza may have suffered from a form of Asperger's syndrome and was said to be impervious to physical pain. He had been on numerous medications intended to lower the anxiety that he experienced in everyday social situations, and prior to the Newtown shootings, his mother had repeatedly sought help in controlling her increasingly unresponsive and emotionally withdrawn son. Months after the Sandy Hook shooting, investigators revealed that Lanza had compiled a detailed record to include a timeline of mass shootings across the nation and may have wanted to achieve a "record" of some kind—by killing more than any other attacker ever had.[vii] Holmes, the Colorado shooter, met with at least three mental health professionals prior to the movie theater shooting, and CBS news reports that the fact "adds to the picture of Holmes being clearly on [psychiatrists'] radar in the time period leading up to the shooting."[viii]

Once we understand that guns and certain forms of mental illness can prove to be a dangerous combination, it is important to ask whether something can be done to predict and prevent episodes of random mass violence. Two days after the Newtown shooting, President Obama, for example, told those gathered at a memorial service at the town's high school, "We can't tolerate this anymore,"[ix] and promised to examine federal gun-control options.[x]

Yet the answer may not be as simple as gun control. Lanza and Holmes were known to have serious mental health problems, yet they were able to live freely in society, to arm themselves, and to attack unprotected and innocent people in what should have been safe public places. As this chapter will later explain in some detail, U.S. society is built on a delicate balance between the demand for *personal freedoms* and the need for *public safety*. The tears that appear in the social and legal fabric woven from the attempt to achieve balance between these two contrasting goals is where crimes like random mass shootings can occur.

Kateleen Foy/Getty Images News/Getty Images

Adam Lanza, the Sandy Hook Elementary School shooter. Why do random mass shootings occur so frequently in the United States today?

In a footnote to this story, Peter Lanza, Adam Lanza's father, spoke to investigative reporters in 2014. He said that he's lived in a "state of sustained incomprehension about what happened" ever since the shooting. "But it's real," he said. "It doesn't have to be understood to be real."[xi]

The case of Adam Lanza raises a number of interesting questions. Among them are the following:

1. Is Lanza's father right that "it doesn't have to be understood to be real"? Is it possible to understand Adam Lanza's crime? If so, how?

2. What do you think led Lanza to attack an elementary school and take so many lives?

3. What role did biology, society, and his mental state play in contributing to Lanza's crime?

4. Can future random mass shootings be predicted or prevented? If so, how?

Notes

i. Michael Isikoff, Tom Winter, and Erin McClam, "Investigators: Adam Lanza Surrounded by Weapons at Home; Attack Took Less Than 5 Minutes," *NBC News*, March 28, 2013, http://openchannel.nbcnews.com/_news/2013/03/28/17501282-investigators-adam-lanza-surrounded-by-weapons-at-home-attack-took-less-than-5-minutes?lite (accessed March 29, 2014).

ii. "U.S. Mass Shootings in 2012," *The Washington Post*, December 14, 2012, http://professional.wsj.com/article/SB10001424127887323723104578185271857424036.html?mod=WSJ_hp_mostpop_read&mg=reno64-wsj; http://www.washingtonpost.com/wp-srv/special/nation/us-mass-shootings-2012 (accessed March 20, 2013). The same article, however, notes that there has been no long-term increase in mass shootings; only in *random* mass shootings.

iii. David Kopel, "Guns, Mental Illness and Newtown," *Wall Street Journal*, December 17, 2012 (accessed March 21, 2013).

iv. Holly Yan, "Gunman's Family at a Loss to Explain Connecticut Shooting," *CNN*, December 17, 2012, http://www.cnn.com/2012/12/16/justice/connecticut-shooting-suspect-profile/index.html (accessed March 20, 2013).

v. The Autism Research Institute's Autistic Global Initiative Project notes that autism and Asperger's syndrome are neurodevelopmental issues and does not consider them to be mental health disorders.

vi. American Psychiatric Association, Council on Law and Psychiatry, *Access to Firearms by People with Mental Illness: Resource Document* (Arlington, VA: American Psychiatric Association, 2009).

vii. Howard Koplowitz, "Adam Lanza Spreadsheet: Sandy Hook Shooter Compiled Extensive List of Mass Murderers," *International Business Times*, March 18, 2013, http://www.ibtimes.com/adam-lanza-spreadsheet-sandy-hook-shooter-compiled-extensive-list-mass-murderers-1133557# (accessed March 28, 2013).

viii. Rick Sallinger, "James Holmes Saw Three Mental Health Professionals Before Shooting," *CBS News*, August 21, 2012, http://www.cbsnews.com/8301-201_162-57497820/james-holmes-saw-three-mental-health-professionals-before-shooting/(accessed March 21, 2014).

ix. "Transcript: 'We Have Wept with You'; Obama Says in Newtown Speech," *CNN*, December 16, 2012, http://politicalticker.blogs.cnn.com/2012/12/16/breaking-we-have-wept-with-you-obama-says-in-newtown-speech (accessed March 20, 2013).

x. Jared A. Favole, "Obama Says All Gun Buyers Should Face Checks," *Wall Street Journal*, December 19, 2012, http://professional.wsj.com/article/SB10001424127887324461604578188680585236550.html?mod=WSJPRO_hps_MIDDLEThirdNews (accessed March 22, 2015).

xi. Andrew Solomon, "The Reckoning," *The New Yorker*, March 17, 2004, http://www.newyorker.com/magazine/2014/03/17/the-reckoning (accessed March 3, 2015).

Like the social structural approaches discussed in Chapter 7, social development theories are intimately associated with the first prong of this text theme—the social problems approach (described in Chapter 1). For policy makers, important questions include: What role (if any) does individual choice play in human development? Do people actively select components of the life course? Do they influence their own trajectories? Because so many important life course determinants are set in motion in early childhood and during adolescence, should those who make wrong choices be held accountable?

Finally, as is the case with social learning theories, social development theories tend to ignore differences between people—even though there may be some important personal characteristics that make some individuals more responsive to changes in the life course, or that cause some people to respond to risk factors differently than do others—and which may even influence responses to certain features of crime control programs.

SUMMARY

- According to social process theories, criminal behavior is learned in interaction with others. The socialization process occurring as the result of group membership—in families, peer groups, work groups, and reference groups—is seen as the primary route through which learning occurs. Social process theories suggest that individuals who have weak stakes in conformity are more likely to be influenced by the social processes and contingent experiences that lead to crime, and that criminal choices tend to persist because they are reinforced by the reaction of society to those whom it has identified as deviant.

- A number of theories can be classified under the social process umbrella: social learning theory, social control theory, labeling theory, reintegrative shaming, and dramaturgical perspective.

- Social process theories suggest that crime-prevention programs should enhance self-control and build prosocial bonds. Preparing for the Drug Free Years (PDFY) is designed to increase effective parenting and is part of the Strengthening America's Families Project.

- Criticisms of social process theories are many and varied. Differential association theory is not applicable at the individual level; in addition, the theory is untestable. The labeling approach does little to explain the origin of crime and deviance. Dramaturgical perspective's greatest failing may be in taking the analogy of the theater too far and convincing readers that real life is but a form of playacting.

- The life course perspective is the major social development perspective discussed in this chapter and emphasizes turning points in a criminal career. Age-graded theory incorporates the element of social bonds and also stresses the idea of turning points in a criminal career. The delinquent development approach places an emphasis on desistance and persistence over the life course, and interactional theory points to a weakening of a person's bond to conventional society as the fundamental cause of delinquency.

- The central concepts of social development theories include: criminal careers, the life course, trajectory, turning points, age grading, social capital, human agency, developmental pathways, life course persisters, persistence, desistance, resilience, cohort, cohort analysis, longitudinal research, and evolutionary ecology.

- Social development strategies have been widely applied to juvenile justice and human services settings. The OJJDP has adopted the social development model as the foundation for its Comprehensive Strategy for Serious, Violent, and Chronic Juvenile Offenders program, which provides participating communities with a framework for preventing delinquency, intervening in early delinquent behavior, and responding to serious, violent, and chronic offending.

- Social development theories have been criticized for definitional issues. What do life course concepts like turning point, pathway, risk factor, persistence, desistance, and criminal career really mean? Precise definitions of such concepts are necessary if hypotheses derived from life course theories are to be tested.

KEY TERMS

adolescence-limited offenders, 219

Cambridge Study in Delinquent Development, 221

cohort analysis, 221

Comprehensive Strategy for Serious, Violent, and Chronic Juvenile Offenders program, 228

containment, 200

containment theory, 199

control ratio, 204

criminal career, 216

desistance, 220

differential association, 195

differential identification theory, 198

discrediting information, 212

dramaturgical perspective, 211

evolutionary ecology, 222

general theory of crime (GTC), 201

human agency, 217

human development, 214

impression management, 211

interactional theory, 222

labeling theory, 206

life course, 215

life course–persistent offenders, 219

life course perspective, 215

moral enterprise, 207

Pathways to Desistance study, 225

persistence, 220

primary deviance, 206

Project on Human Development in Chicago Neighborhoods (PHDCN), 226 prosocial bond, 212

reintegrative shaming, 210

resilience, 221

secondary deviance, 206

situational action theory
     (SAT), 203

social bond, 200

social capital, 219

social control theory, 195

social development
     perspective, 214

social development theory, 194

social learning theory, 195

social process theory, 194

stigmatic shaming, 210

tagging, 206

total institution, 212

turning point, 218

KEY NAMES

Ronald L. Akers, 197

Howard Becker, 206

John Braithwaite, 210

Robert Burgess, 197

Lawrence E. Cohen, 221

David P. Farrington, 221

Daniel Glaser, 198

Eleanor Glueck, 217

Sheldon Glueck, 217

Erving Goffman, 210

Michael Gottfredson, 201

Travis Hirschi, 200

Howard B. Kaplan, 200

John H. Laub, 216

Edwin M. Lemert, 206

Richard Machalek, 221

Terrie E. Moffitt, 219

Walter C. Reckless, 199

Robert J. Sampson, 216

Edwin Sutherland, 195

Frank Tannenbaum, 206

Terence Thornberry, 222

Charles R. Tittle, 198

Donald J. West, 221

Per-Olof H. Wikström, 203

Marvin Wolfgang, 221

QUESTIONS FOR REVIEW

1. How does the perspective of social interaction contribute to understandings criminal behavior?

2. What are the various social process approaches discussed in this chapter? Describe each.

3. What kinds of social policy initiatives might be based on social process theories of crime causation?

4. What are the shortcomings of social process theories?

5. What are the various social development perspectives discussed in this chapter? Describe each.

6. What are the central concepts of social development theories? Explain each.

7. What kinds of social policy initiatives might be suggested by social development perspectives?

8. What are the shortcomings of social development theories of criminality?

QUESTIONS FOR REFLECTION

1. This chapter describes both social process and social development perspectives. What are the significant differences between these two perspectives? What kinds of theories characterize each?

2. This text emphasizes the theme of social problems versus individual responsibility. Which of the perspectives discussed in this chapter (if any) best support the social problems approach? Which (if any) support the individual responsibility approach? Why?

3. This chapter contains a discussion of the labeling process. What are a few examples of the everyday imposition of positive (rather than negative) labels? Why is it so difficult to impose positive labels on individuals who were previously labeled negatively?

4. Do you believe that Erving Goffman's dramaturgical perspective, which sees the world as a stage and individuals as actors on that stage, provides any valuable insights into crime and criminality? If so, what are they?

5. Examine your personal life course. What turning points did you experience that led to where you are today?

CHAPTER 9
SOCIAL CONFLICT THEORIES

It's How We Relate

LEARNING OUTCOMES

After reading this chapter, you should be able to answer the following questions:

- What three analytical perspectives on law and social order are described in this chapter?

- What are the central tenets of radical criminology?
- What six emerging conflict perspectives discussed in this chapter purport to explain crime and criminality?
- What are the crime-control implications of social conflict theories?

■ **Follow the author's tweets about the latest crime and justice news @schmalleger.**

■ **consensus perspective**   An analytical perspective on social organization that holds that most members of society agree about what is right and wrong and that the various elements of society work together toward a common vision of the greater good.

Introduction

One of the most interesting issues being debated today concerns the legal status of marijuana. Marijuana had long been used in this country by many musicians, artists, and Bohemians—a word used in the early 1900s to describe people engaged in nonconventional lifestyles. In the 1960s, however, the drug became popular among college students and other young people. Soon, it assumed a central role in the widespread movement against the Vietnam war, which featured many marijuana-fueled protests. The slogan "Flower Power"—a reference to the flowering and powerful part of the female marijuana plant—came to symbolize the antiwar movement and the protestors who participated in it.

Legislative initiatives at the federal government labeled marijuana a Category I substance under the 1970 Controlled Substances Act (CSA). Category I substances include the most "serious" illegal drugs, for which there is no known medicinal use. The CSA led to a nationwide War on Drugs, in which federal and local law enforcement officials sought to combat growing inner-city crime fed by illicit profits from the manufacture and distribution of cocaine, heroin, marijuana, and other drugs.

Today, public attitudes have changed, and a recent Gallup poll found 58% of Americans favoring the legalization of marijuana for personal recreational use.[1] Political action groups, formed over the past few years, are pushing for pot legalization, and social media campaigns are promoting wider social acceptance of the drug. A Cannabis Manifesto[2] has been adopted by many in the medical marijuana community, and is being circulated in a number of Western democracies (see **http://cista.org/manifesto**).

Today, the generation that embraced marijuana use 40 and 50 years ago is largely in control of legislatures throughout the nation; and many lawmakers at both the state and federal level are either members of that generation or their children. Consequently, the country is now in the midst of a widespread cannabis legalization movement with a strong political base. Whether, or to what extent, that movement succeeds depends on the American political process—a clear demonstration that criminal laws are the result of conflict between groups with varying interests.

Learn more about marijuana at **https://www.drugabuse .gov/publications/drugfacts/marijuana**.

Law and Social Order Perspectives

The focus of this chapter is on conflict theories, which are shared among social sciences generally and are not unique to criminology. Before describing conflict theories in more detail, however, it is important to understand the interplay between law and social order.

A young woman vaping marijuana. How do divergent attitudes toward marijuana use capture the essence of conflict theory?

Three analytical perspectives shed some light on this subject: the consensus perspective, the pluralist perspective, and—of course—conflict perspective.

The Consensus Perspective

The **consensus perspective** of social organization (described briefly in Chapter 1) posits that most members of society agree on what is right and wrong and that the various elements of society—including institutions such as churches, schools, government agencies, and businesses—work together toward a shared vision of the greater good. **Raymond J. Michalowski** notes that the consensus perspective is characterized by four principles:[3]

1. **Most members of a society believe in the existence of core values.** The consensus perspective holds that shared notions of right and wrong characterize the majority of society's members.

2. **Laws are a reflection of shared will.** Law is seen as the result of a consensus, achieved through legislative action, and represents a kind of social conscience.

3. **All persons are equal under the law.** From the consensus point of view, the law not only embodies a shared view of justice but also is perceived to be just in its application.

4. **Law violators represent a unique subgroup with distinguishing features.** The consensus approach holds that law violators must somehow be improperly socialized or psychologically defective or must suffer from some other lapse that leaves them unable to participate in what is otherwise widespread agreement on values and behavior.

The consensus perspective was operative in American politics and characterized social scientific thought in this country throughout much of the early 1900s and found its greatest champion in **Roscoe Pound**, former dean of Harvard School of Law and one of the greatest legal scholars of modern times. Pound developed

■ **pluralist perspective** An analytical approach to social organization that holds that a multiplicity of values and beliefs exists in any complex society but that most social actors agree on the usefulness of law as a formal means of dispute resolution.

■ **conflict perspective** An analytical perspective on social organization that holds that conflict is a fundamental aspect of social life and can never be fully resolved.

the notion that the law is a tool for engineering society, meets the needs of men and women living together in society, and can be used to fashion society's characteristics and major features. Pound distilled his ideas into a set of jural postulates explaining the existence and form of all laws insofar as laws reflect shared needs:[4]

- In civilized society, men and women must be able to assume that others will commit no intentional aggressions upon them.[5]

- In civilized society, men and women must be able to assume that they may control for beneficial purposes what they have discovered and appropriated to their own use, what they have created by their own labor, and what they have acquired under the existing social and economic order.

- In civilized society, men and women must be able to assume that those with whom they deal in the general intercourse of society will act in good faith....

- In civilized society, men and women must be able to assume that those who are engaged in some course of conduct will act with due care not to cause an unreasonable risk of injury upon others.

- In civilized society, men and women must be able to assume that those who maintain things likely to get out of hand or to escape and do damage will restrain them or keep them within their proper bounds.

The Pluralist Perspective

Contrary to the assumptions made by consensus thinkers, it has become quite plain to most observers of the contemporary social scene that not everyone agrees on what the law should say and that society is rife with examples of conflicting values and ideals—consensus is hard to find. Modern debates center on issues such as abortion, euthanasia, the death penalty, purposes of criminal justice agencies in a diverse society, social justice, rights and responsibilities of minorities and other underrepresented groups, women's issues, the proper role of education, economic policy, social welfare, functions of the military in a changing world, environmental concerns, and appropriate uses of high technology. There exists within America today a great diversity of social groups, each with its own point of view regarding right and wrong, each with its own agenda. Add to that the plethora of self-proclaimed individual experts busily touting their own points of view, and anything but a consensus of values seems characteristic of society today.

Such a situation is described by some writers as "pluralist." A **pluralistic perspective** (described briefly in Chapter 1) mirrors the thought that a multiplicity of values and beliefs exists in any complex society and that each different social group will have its own set of beliefs, interests, and values. A crucial element of this perspective is the assumption that although different viewpoints exist, most individuals agree on the usefulness of law as a formal means of dispute resolution, so from a pluralist perspective, the law exists as a peacekeeping tool that allows officials and agencies within the government to effectively settle disputes between individuals and among groups. It also assumes that whatever settlement is reached will be acceptable to all parties because of their agreement on the fundamental role of law in dispute settlement. Following are five basic principles of the pluralist perspective:[6]

1. Society consists of many distinct social groups. Differences in age, gender, sexual preference, ethnicity, and the like often provide the basis for much naturally occurring diversity.

2. Each group has its own set of values, beliefs, and interests. Variety in gender, sexual orientation, economic status, and ethnicity, as well as other forms of diversity, produces interests that may unite like-minded individuals but may also place them in natural opposition to other social groups.

3. A general agreement exists on the usefulness of formalized laws as a mechanism for dispute resolution. People and groups accept the role of law in the settlement of disputes and accord decisions reached within the legal framework at least a modicum of respect.

4. The legal system is free of petty disputes and above the level of general contentiousness that may characterize relationships among groups.

5. The best interests of society are represented in legal institutions. Legislators, judges, prosecutors, attorneys, police officers, and correctional officials are assumed to perform idealized functions beyond the reach of the everyday interests of self-serving groups, so official functionaries can be trusted to act in accordance with the greater good, to remain unbiased, and to maintain a value-free system for the enforcement of laws.

According to the pluralist perspective, conflict is essentially resolved through the peacekeeping activities of unbiased government officials exercising objective legal authority.

The Conflict Perspective

A third point of view, the **conflict perspective**, maintains that conflict is a fundamental aspect of social life that can never be fully resolved. Formal agencies of social control merely coerce the unempowered and disenfranchised to comply with the rules established by those in power. Laws are a tool of the powerful, useful

■ **bourgeoisie**   The "haves," or the class of people who own the means of production, in Marxist theory.

■ **proletariat**   The "have-nots," or the working class, in Marxist theory.

The conflict perspective maintains that conflict is a fundamental aspect of social life and can never be fully resolved.

in keeping others from wresting control over important social institutions. Rather than being the result of any consensus or process of dispute resolution, social order rests on the exercise of power through law. Those in power must work ceaselessly to remain there, although the structures they impose on society—including the patterns of wealth building that they define as acceptable and the circumstances under which they authorize the exercise of legal power and military might—give them all the advantages they are likely to need. Figure 9–1 lists the key elements of the conflict perspective, which is also known as the *social conflict perspective*. See the Criminal Profiles box on the Unabomber, someone who fits the conflict perspective. **http://www.washingtonpost.com/wp-srv/national/longterm/unabomber/manifesto.text.htm** provides related information.

One of the best-known writers on social conflict was **Karl Marx**, whose writings on the conflicts inherent in capitalism led to the formulation of communist ideals and the rise of communist societies in the twentieth century. According to Marx, two fundamental social classes exist in any capitalist society: the haves or the **bourgeoisie**, who are capitalists and wealthy owners of the means of production (factories, businesses, land, natural resources), and the have-nots or the **proletariat**, who are relatively uneducated workers without power.

According to Marx, members of the proletariat, possessing neither capital nor means of production, must earn their

Marx saw a struggle between classes as inevitable in the evolution of any capitalist society.

living by selling their labor, and the powerful bourgeoisie oppose the proletariat in an ongoing class struggle. Marx saw such a struggle between classes as inevitable in the evolution of any capitalist society and believed that the natural outcome of such a struggle would be the overthrow of the capitalist social order and the birth of a truly classless, or communist, society. Learn more about the life and writings of Karl Marx at **http://www.philosophypages.com/ph/marx.htm** and **https://www.biography.com/people/karl-marx-9401219**.

Conflict theory in the social sciences has a long history. In 1905, the writings of **Willem Bonger** echoed Marxist principles by describing the ongoing struggle between the haves and the have-nots as a natural consequence of capitalist society;[7] he

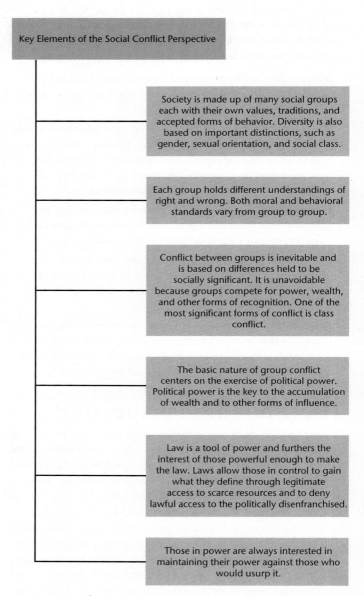

Key Elements of the Social Conflict Perspective

Society is made up of many social groups each with their own values, traditions, and accepted forms of behavior. Diversity is also based on important distinctions, such as gender, sexual orientation, and social class.

Each group holds different understandings of right and wrong. Both moral and behavioral standards vary from group to group.

Conflict between groups is inevitable and is based on differences held to be socially significant. It is unavoidable because groups compete for power, wealth, and other forms of recognition. One of the most significant forms of conflict is class conflict.

The basic nature of group conflict centers on the exercise of political power. Political power is the key to the accumulation of wealth and to other forms of influence.

Law is a tool of power and furthers the interest of those powerful enough to make the law. Laws allow those in control to gain what they define through legitimate access to scarce resources and to deny lawful access to the politically disenfranchised.

Those in power are always interested in maintaining their power against those who would usurp it.

FIGURE 9-1 | **Key Elements of the Social Conflict Perspective**

advanced the notion that in such societies only those who lack power are routinely subject to the criminal law. Georg Simmel's 1908 text *Conflict and the Web of Group Affiliations* highlighted the role of social conflict in two- and three-person groups, which Simmel called diads and triads.[8] Thorsten Sellin's notion of culture conflict (discussed in Chapter 6) also incorporated the notion of social conflict. Since Sellin's day, many other thinkers have

■ **social class**   A distinction made between individuals based on important social characteristics.

THEORY | in PERSPECTIVE
Social Conflict Theories

Social conflict theories emphasize the role of conflict within society, which is thought to be based largely on inequities between social classes.

Radical Criminology

Radical criminology holds that the causes of crime are rooted in social conditions empowering the wealthy and the politically well organized but disenfranchising those who are less successful.

> **Period:** 1960s–present
>
> **Theorists:** Karl Marx, Ralf Dahrendorf, George B. Vold, Richard Quinney, William J. Chambliss, Raymond J. Michalowski, Austin Turk
>
> **Concepts:** Social class, bourgeoisie, proletariat

Left-Realist Criminology

This branch of radical criminology posits that crime is a real social problem experienced by the lower classes.

> **Period:** 1980s–present
>
> **Theorists:** Walter DeKeseredy, Jock Young
>
> **Concepts:** Radical realism, critical realism, street crime, social justice, crime control

Feminist Criminology

This radical criminological approach to the explanation of crime sees the conflict and inequality present in society as being based primarily on gender.

> **Period:** 1970s–present
>
> **Theorists:** Freda Adler, Rita J. Simon, Kathleen Daly, Meda Chesney-Lind, John Hagan, Carol Smart, Susan Caufield, Nancy Wonders
>
> **Concepts:** Power-control issues, gender socialization, empowerment

Peacemaking Criminology

Peacemaking criminology holds that crime-control agencies and citizens must work together to alleviate social problems, including crime.

> **Period:** 1980s–present
>
> **Theorists:** Harold E. Pepinsky, Richard Quinney, Bo Lozoff, Michael Braswell
>
> **Concepts:** Compassionate criminology, restorative justice, inner corrections

Convict Criminology

Convict criminology consists of writings and musings on criminology by convicted felons and ex-inmates who have acquired academic credentials or are associated with credentialed others.

> **Period:** 2001–present
>
> **Theorists:** Jeffrey Ian Ross, Stephen J. Richards, John Irwin, K. C. Carceral, Thomas J. Bernard
>
> **Concepts:** Issues-based writings, personal experience as valid information, critical of system

---

contributed to the development of conflict theory, and we will discuss their approaches throughout this chapter.[9]

Central to the conflict perspective is the notion of **social class** (distinctions made between individuals based on characteristics such as race, religion, education, profession, income, wealth, family background, housing, artistic tastes, aspirations, cultural pursuits, child-rearing habits, speech, and accent). Some authors maintain that "class is nothing but an abbreviation to describe a way of living, thinking, and feeling."[10] Individuals are assigned to classes by others and by themselves on the basis of characteristics that are both ascribed and achieved: Ascribed characteristics are those a person is born with, such as race or gender; achieved characteristics are acquired through personal effort or chance over the course of a person's life and include level of education, income, place of residence, and profession.

Although Marx concerned himself with only two social classes, most social scientists today talk in terms of at least three groups—the upper, middle, and lower classes. Some, such as

Vance Packard, have distinguished among five hierarchically arranged classes (the real-upper, semiupper, limited-success, working, and real-lower classes) and further subdivided classes horizontally according to ascribed characteristics such as race and religion.[11]

In his 1958 book *Theoretical Criminology*, **George B. Vold** described crime as the product of political conflict between groups, an ongoing struggle for power, control, and material well-being.[12] Conflict is "a universal form of interaction," and groups are naturally in conflict because their interests and purposes "overlap, encroach on one another and [tend to] be competitive."[13] Vold's most succinct observation of the role conflict plays in contributing to crime stated: "The whole political process of law making, law breaking, and law enforcement becomes a direct reflection of deep-seated and fundamental conflicts between interest groups. Those who produce legislative majorities win control over the power and dominate the policies that decide who is likely to be involved in violation of the law."[14]

■ **radical criminology**   A perspective that holds that the causes of crime are rooted in social conditions empowering the wealthy and the politically well organized, but disenfranchising the less fortunate.

■ **Marxist criminology**   A perspective on crime and crime causation based on the writings of Karl Marx.

The tomb of Karl Marx in Highgate Cemetery, London. Marxist thought underpins the writings of many radical criminologists. How did Marxism influence criminology?

From Vold's point of view, the body of laws that characterizes any society is a political statement, and crime is a political definition imposed on those whose interests lie outside those that the powerful, through the law, define as acceptable.

Conflict theorists of the early and mid-1900s saw in the concept of social class the rudimentary ingredients of other important concepts like authority, power, and conflict. **Ralf Dahrendorf** wrote that "classes are social conflict groups the determinant of which can be found in the participation in or exclusion from the exercise of authority."[15] For Dahrendorf, conflict was ubiquitous, fundamental, and coextensive: "Not the presence but the absence of conflict is surprising and abnormal, and we have good reason to be suspicious if we find a society or social organization that displays no evidence of conflict."[16]

From Dahrendorf's perspective, power and authority were most at issue between groups and the cause of class conflicts. It is out of conflict that change—either destructive or constructive—arises. Destructive change brings a lessening of social order, whereas constructive change increases cohesiveness within society.

Another mid-twentieth-century conflict theorist, **Austin Turk**, said that in the search for an explanation of criminality, "one is led to investigate the tendency of laws to penalize persons whose behavior is more characteristic of the less powerful than of the more powerful and the extent to which some persons and groups can and do use legal processes and agencies to maintain and enhance their power position vis-à-vis other persons and groups."[17] In his 1969 seminal work, *Criminality and Legal Order*, Turk wrote that in any attempt to explain criminality, "it is more useful to view the social order as mainly a pattern of conflict" rather than to offer explanations for crime based on behavioral or psychological approaches.[18] Turk, like most other conflict criminologists, saw the law as a powerful tool of prominent social groups seeking continued control over others and crime as the natural consequence of such intergroup struggles, resulting from definitions imposed by the laws of the powerful on the disapproved strivings of the unempowered.

Radical Criminology

The conflict perspective is today thoroughly entrenched in **radical criminology**, which holds that the causes of crime are rooted in social conditions empowering the wealthy and the politically well organized but disenfranchising those less fortunate; it is also called *new criminology* and *critical criminology* as well as **Marxist criminology** (when based on Marx's writings). Radical criminology is the intellectual child of three important historical circumstances: (1) the ruminations of

> Radical criminology holds that the causes of crime are rooted in social conditions empowering the wealthy.

nineteenth-century social utopian thinkers, including Karl Marx, Friedrich Engels, Georg Wilhelm Friedrich Hegel, Georg Simmel, Willem Bonger, and Max Weber; (2) the rise of conflict theory in the social sciences; and (3) the dramatic radicalization of American academia in the 1960s and 1970s. **William J. Chambliss**, a well-known spokesperson for radical thinkers, succinctly summarized the modern perspective: "What makes the behavior of some criminal is the coercive power of the state to enforce the will of the ruling class."[19]

In 1971, Chambliss, along with Robert T. Seidman, published a critically acclaimed volume titled *Law, Order, and Power*, which represented a bridge between earlier conflict theorists and the more radical approach of the Marxists. Through its emphasis on social class, class interests, and class conflict, *Law, Order, and Power* presented a Marxist perspective stripped of any overt references to capitalism as the root cause of crime. "The more economically stratified a society becomes, the more it becomes necessary for the dominant groups in the society to enforce through coercion the norms of conduct which guarantee their supremacy."[20] Chambliss and Seidman outlined their position in four propositions:[21]

1. The conditions of one's life affect one's values and norms.

2. Complex societies are comprised of groups with widely different life conditions and highly disparate and conflicting sets of norms.

3. The probability of a given group having its particular normative system embodied in law is not distributed equally but is closely related to the political and economic position of that group.

4. The higher a group's political or economic position is, the greater the probability that its views will be reflected in laws.

Chambliss also believed that middle- and upper-class criminals are more apt to escape apprehension and punishment, not because they are any smarter or more capable of hiding their crimes than lower-class offenders but because of a "very rational choice on the part of the legal system to pursue those violators that the community will reward them for pursuing and to ignore those violators who have the capability for causing trouble for the agencies."[22]

By the 1970s, Chambliss's writings assumed a much more Marxist flavor. In a 1975 article, Chambliss once again recognized the huge power gap separating the

> Crime is created by members of the ruling class, who define as criminal any undertakings and activities contravening their interests, yet sometimes violate the criminal law with impunity because it is their own creation.

A deteriorating factory in Russia. Radical criminology has its origins in the writings of Karl Marx, whose thinking was strongly influenced by the social conditions of the industrial era. How did the downfall of the Soviet Union impact radical thought in criminology?

haves from the have-nots, saying that crime is created by the ruling class, who define as criminal any undertakings and activities contravening their interests yet sometimes violate the criminal law with impunity because it is their own creation.[23]

Soon the Marxist flavor of Chambliss's writing became undeniable: "As capitalist societies industrialize and the gap between the bourgeoisie and the proletariat widens, penal law will expand in an effort to coerce the proletariat into submission."[24] For Chambliss, the economic consequences of crime within a capitalist society were partially what perpetuated it. Socialist societies, he wrote, should reflect much lower crime rates than capitalist societies because a "less intense class struggle should reduce the forces leading to and the functions of crime."[25] Learn more about the writings of William J. Chambliss at **https://goedalaluci.wordpress.com/2011/12/06/the-saints-and-the-roughnecks**.

Although Chambliss provided much of the intellectual bedrock of contemporary radical criminology, that school of thought found its most eloquent expression in the writings of **Richard Quinney**, who attempted to challenge and change American social life for the better by setting forth in 1974 his six Marxist propositions for an understanding of crime:[26]

1. American society is based on an advanced capitalist economy.

2. The state is organized to serve the interests of the dominant economic class—that is, the capitalist ruling class.

3. Criminal law is an instrument of the state and ruling class used to maintain and perpetuate the existing social and economic order.

4. Crime control in a capitalist society is accomplished through a variety of institutions and agencies established

■ **structural Marxism**   A perspective that holds that the structural institutions of society influence the behavior of individuals and groups by virtue of the type of relationships created.

■ **instrumental Marxism**   A perspective that holds that those in power intentionally create laws and social institutions that serve their own interests and keep others from becoming powerful.

■ **critical criminology**   A perspective that holds that crime is the natural product of a capitalist system.

and administered by a governmental elite, representing ruling-class interests, for the purpose of establishing domestic order.

5. The contradictions of advanced capitalism—the disjunction between existence and essence—require that the subordinate classes remain oppressed by whatever means necessary, especially through the coercion and violence of the legal system.

6. Only with the collapse of the capitalist society and the creation of a new society, based on socialist principles, will there be a solution to the crime problem.

Later, Quinney published *Class, State, and Crime*, in which he argued that almost all crimes committed by members of the lower classes are necessary for the survival of individual members of those classes and are actually an attempt by the socially disenfranchised "to exist in a society where *survival* is not assured by other, collective means."[27] He concluded, "Crime is inevitable under capitalist conditions [because crime is] a response to the material conditions of life. Permanent unemployment—and the acceptance of that condition—can result in a form of life where criminality is an appropriate and consistent response."[28] The solution offered by Quinney to the problem of crime is the development of a socialist society: "The *ultimate meaning* of crime in the development of capitalism is the need for a socialist society."[29]

Contemporary radical criminology attributes much existing propensity toward criminality to differences in social class, especially those societal arrangements that maintain class differences. Quinney explained, "Classes are an expression of the underlying forces of the capitalist mode of production."[30]

Today's radical criminologies can be divided into two schools: structuralist and instrumentalist. **Structural Marxism** sees capitalism as a self-maintaining system in which the law and the justice system work to perpetuate the existing system of power relationships. Even the rich are subject to certain laws designed to prevent them from engaging in forms of behavior that might undermine the system of which they are a part, and laws regulating trade practices and monopolies regulate the behavior of the powerful and ensure survival of the capitalist system. **Instrumental Marxism** sees the criminal law and the justice system as tools that the powerful use to control the poor and to keep them disenfranchised. The legal system serves not only to perpetuate the power relationships that exist within society but also to keep control in the hands of those who are already powerful. A popular book by **Jeffrey H. Reiman** titled *The Rich Get Richer and the Poor Get Prison*

is built on this premise, contending that the criminal justice system is biased against the poor from start to finish and that well-to-do members of society control the criminal justice system from the definition of crime through the process of arrest, trial, and sentencing.[31]

Reiman also claimed that many actions undertaken by well-off people, such as refusal to make workplaces safe, refusal to curtail deadly industrial pollution, promotion of unnecessary surgery, and prescription of unnecessary drugs, should be defined as criminal but aren't. This kind of self-serving behavior creates occupational and environmental hazards for the poor and those less well-off and produces as much death, destruction, and financial loss as the so-called crimes of the poor. Learn more about radical criminology at **http://scholarlycommons.law .northwestern.edu/cgi/viewcontent.cgi?article=6223&c ontext=jclc**.

Critical Criminology

Many writers use the phrase *radical-critical criminology* to refer to all theoretical perspectives on crime that build on significant differences in economic, social, and political power between distinct social groups. This chapter follows that convention. Some theorists, however, distinguish between *critical criminology* and *radical criminology*. Those who do say that the former is simply a way of critiquing social relationships that lead to crime, whereas the latter constitutes a proactive call for radical change in the social conditions that lead to crime. That is, critical criminology provides a focused critique of current social and economic arrangements as they are related to crime, whereas radical criminology issues a call to action and asks for changes in political and economic systems that are responsible for fostering criminality.

Gresham M. Sykes further explained **critical criminology** this way: "It forces an inquiry into precisely how the normative content of the criminal law is internalized in different segments of society, and how norm-holding is actually related to behavior."[32] Sykes's use of the word *inquiry* reveals the central role of critical inquiry in critical criminology. See the Who's to Blame box for a present-day issue regarding whether something should be "criminal."

A cogent example of the critical perspective in contemporary criminology can be seen in the work of Elliott Currie, who claimed that "'market societies'—those in which the pursuit of private gain becomes the dominant organizing principle of social and economic life—are especially likely to breed high levels of violent crime."[33] Market societies are characterized by more

WHO'S TO BLAME—The Individual or Society?

Human Trafficking, Illegal Aliens, and the American Dream

Jose Gonzales, a naturalized U.S. citizen who worked for a Houston-based trucking company, was driving a tractor trailer through a U.S. Customs checkpoint on the Mexican border near San Diego when his truck was searched and found to contain 45 illegal immigrants concealed in Brazilian-made caskets that were being shipped to Los Angeles. Each of the immigrants had been supplied with plastic bottles containing water, and a few even had portable radios to keep them entertained on what had been planned as an hours-long trip.

The illegal immigrants were interrogated and fingerprinted and then taken back across the border to the Mexican border town of Tijuana in a U.S. Customs and Border Protection van. They were released into the custody of a Mexican Federal Investigative Agency official at a local police station, with instructions not to attempt an illegal return into the United States.

Gonzales's fate was quite different. Arrested and charged under the federal Immigration and Nationality Act with attempting to bring unauthorized aliens into the United States, he was held in a federal jail in southern California, where he met with his court-appointed lawyer. The lawyer, Felix Alverez, told Gonzales that agents had him cold, and that he might as well confess in return for a plea bargain that might get him only a brief stint in a federal correctional facility. "Why confess?" Gonzales replied. "I was only trying to help those people have better lives. Many of them were my friends. I didn't even take money for what I was doing."

"Why you were doing what you were doing doesn't matter," Alverez said. "You broke the law, and they are going to punish you."

"No," Gonzales replied. "I am a citizen. I want a trial. You can show them that I was only trying to help unfortunate

Alexandre Meneghini/AP Images

A border crossing between the USA and Mexico. Are illegal immigrants criminal?

people live the American Dream. Most of the people who live here and are going to be on a jury have immigrant ancestors. A lot of them were illegal. They won't dare find me guilty." **http://ssrn.com/abstract=1273726** and **http://ssrn.com/abstract=984927** relate to this box.

Think about it

1. Why did Gonzales attempt to smuggle illegal immigrants into the United States? Do you think it was primarily for money or for altruistic motives?

2. How likely would Gonzales have been to commit this offense if he had a different ancestry—say, African American or European?

3. What do you think of Gonzales's claim that a jury won't find him guilty? Should he be held responsible for violating the law? Why or why not?

Note: Who's to Blame boxes provide fictionalized critical thinking opportunities based on actual cases.

---

than free enterprise and a free market economy; they are societies in which striving after personal economic gain runs rampant and becomes the hallmark of social life, and this striving leads to high crime rates because it undercuts and overwhelms more traditional principles that "have historically sustained individuals, families, and communities." The United States is the world's premier market society, and its culture provides "a particularly fertile breeding ground for serious violent crime." According to Currie, seven "profoundly criminogenic and closely intertwined mechanisms" operate in a market society to produce crime:

1. "The progressive destruction of livelihood," which results from the long-term absence of opportunities for stable and rewarding work and is a consequence of the fact that market societies view labor "simply as a cost to be reduced" rather than as an asset with intrinsic value

2. "The growth of extremes of economic inequality and material deprivation," which causes many children to spend their developmental years in poverty

3. "The withdrawal of public services and supports, especially for families and children," which results from the fact that "it is a basic operating principle of market society to keep the public sector small"

4. "The erosion of informal and communal networks of mutual support, supervision, and care," which is brought about by the high mobility of the workforce characteristic of market societies

5. "The spread of a materialistic, neglectful, and 'hard' culture," which exalts brutal forms of individualized competition

6. "The unregulated marketing of the technology of violence," which includes ready availability of guns, emphasis on advancing technologies of destruction (such as the military), and mass-marketed violence on television and in other media

7. "The weakening of social and political alternatives," which leaves people unable to cope effectively with the forces of the market society, undermines their communities, and destroys valuable interpersonal relationships

Currie suggested that as more nations emulate the "market society" culture of the United States, crime rates throughout the world will rise, and that an increasing emphasis on punishment and the growth of huge prison systems will consequently characterize most of the world's nations in the twenty-first century.

Radical-Critical Criminology and Policy Issues

According to more contemporary writers on radical criminology, "Marxist criminology was once dismissed as a utopian perspective with no relevant policy implication except revolution. At best, revolution was considered an impractical approach to the problems at hand. Recently, however, many radicals have attempted to address the issues of what can be done under our current system."[34] Most radical-critical criminologists today have come to terms with the collapse of the Soviet Union, a society representing utopian Marxism in practice, and have recognized that a sudden and total reversal of existing political arrangements within the United States is highly unlikely. Such theorists have begun to focus instead on promoting a gradual transition to socialism and to socialized forms of government activity, including "equal justice in the bail system, the abolition of mandatory sentences, prosecution of corporate crimes, increased employment opportunities, and promoting community alternatives to imprisonment."[35] Programs to reduce prison overcrowding, efforts to highlight injustices in the current system, elimination of racism and other forms of inequality in handling both victims and offenders, and increased equality in criminal justice system employment are all frequently mentioned as midrange strategies for bringing about

a justice system that is more fair and closer to the radical ideal (Figure 9–2).

Michalowski summarized well the policy directions envisioned by today's radical-critical criminologists: "We cannot be free from the crimes of the poor until there are no more poor; we cannot be free from domination of the powerful until we reduce the inequalities that make domination possible; and we cannot live in harmony with others until we begin to limit the competition for material advantage over others that alienates us from one another."[36] Even so, few radical-critical criminologists seem to expect to see dramatic changes in the near future. Michael J. Lynch and W. Byron Groves explained, "In the end, the criminal justice system has failed as an agent of social change because its efforts are directed at an individual as opposed to social remedies. For these reasons, radicals suggest that we put our efforts into the creation of economic equality or employment opportunities to combat crime."[37]

Critique of Radical-Critical Criminology

Radical-critical criminology has been criticized for its nearly exclusive emphasis on methods of social change at the expense of well-developed theory. William V. Pelfrey stated, "It is in

- Equal justice in the bail system
- Abolition of mandatory sentences
- Prosecution of corporate crimes
- Increased employment opportunities
- Promotion of community alternatives to imprisonment
- Programs to reduce prison overcrowding
- Efforts to highlight current injustices
- Elimination of racism and other forms of inequality
- Increased equality in criminal justice system employment
- Raising the minimum wage
- Ensuring full and quality employment
- Enhanced social services and programs
- Use of social networking websites to achieve social justice

Minimum wage

FIGURE 9-2 | Conflict Criminology's Midrange Approaches to Crime Reduction

Source: Schmalleger, Frank, *Criminology*. Printed and Electronically reproduced by permission of Pearson Education, Inc., Upper Saddle River, New Jersey.

the Radical School of Criminology that theory is almost totally disregarded, except as something to criticize, and radical methods are seen as optimum."[38] Radical-critical criminology can also be criticized for failing to recognize what appears to be a fair degree of public consensus about the nature of crime—that crime is undesirable and that criminal activity should be controlled. If criminal activity was a true expression of the sentiments of the politically and economically disenfranchised, as some radical criminologists claim, then public opinion might be expected to offer support for at least certain forms of crime, but even the sale of illicit drugs (a type of crime that may provide an alternative path to riches for the otherwise disenfranchised) is frequently condemned by residents of working-class communities.[39]

An effective criticism of Marxist criminology centers on the fact that Marxist thinkers appear to confuse issues of personal politics with social reality, allowing personal values and political leanings to enter the criminological arena and sacrificing their objectivity. Jackson Toby claimed that Marxist and radical thinkers are simply building on an "old tradition of sentimentality toward those who break social rules."[40] Such sentimentality can be easily discounted when we realize that "color television sets and automobiles are stolen more often than food and blankets."[41] The Marxist perspective also fails to recognize that personal success in any society often comes as the result of hard work and preparation and is not merely the result of luck, so wording characterizing social failures as less "fortunate" than others does not take into account the efforts made by those who have succeeded and seems to blame them for the failures of others who have not expended equal effort.

Marxist criminology has also been refuted by contemporary thinkers who find that it falls short in appreciating the multiplicity of problems that contribute to the problem of crime. Astute criminologist Hermann Mannheim critiqued Marxian assumptions by showing how "subsequent developments" have shown that "Marx was wrong in [his] thinking" in several areas: (1) "that there could be only two classes in a capitalist society," (2) that "class struggle was entirely concerned with the question of private property in the means of production," (3) "that the only way in which fundamental social changes could be effected was by violent social revolution," and (4) "that all conflicts were class conflicts and all social change could be explained in terms of class conflicts."[42] Mannheim also pointed out that the development of a semi-skilled workforce along with the advent of highly skilled and well-educated workers has led to the creation of a multiplicity of classes within contemporary capitalist societies and that their growth effectively spreads the available wealth in those societies where such workers are employed and reduces the likelihood of revolution.

A now-classic critique of radical criminology was offered in 1979 by Carl Klockars.[43] Klockars charged that Marxists are unable to explain low crime rates in some capitalist countries, such as Japan, and seem equally unwilling to acknowledge or address the problems of communist countries, which often have terrible human rights records. Writing more than 20 years ago, Klockars claimed that Marxist criminologists behaved more like "true believers" in a "new religion" who were unwilling to objectively evaluate their beliefs.[44]

> Marxist criminologists are unable to explain low crime rates in some capitalist countries.

Marxist criminology has suffered a considerable loss of prestige among many would-be followers in the wake of the collapse of the former Soviet Union and its client states in Eastern Europe and other parts of the world. Many would argue that the work of writers like Quinney and Chambliss presaged the decline of Soviet influence and had already moved Marxist and radical criminology into new areas. The work of Currie and others has since led in a post-Marxist direction while retaining a critical emphasis on the principles out of which radical criminology was fashioned. Today's radical criminologists have largely rescinded calls for revolutionary change and escalated their demands for the eradication of gender, racial, and other inequalities in the criminal justice system; the elimination of prisons; the abolition of capital punishment; and an end to police misconduct.

Emerging Conflict Theories

The radical ideas associated with mid-twentieth-century Marxist criminology contributed to the formation of new and innovative approaches to crime and criminology, such as left-realist criminology, feminist criminology, postmodern criminology, peacemaking criminology, moral time, and convict criminology. It is to these perspectives that we now turn our attention.

Left-Realist Criminology

Left-realist criminology, a natural outgrowth of concerns with street crime, the fear of crime, and everyday victimization, approaches criminology based on the ideas of **left realism**, which uses a pragmatic assessment of crime and its problems. Left-realist criminology faults radical-critical criminologists for

■ **feminist criminology**   A corrective model intended to re-direct the thinking of mainstream criminologists to include gender awareness.

romanticizing street crime and the criminals who commit it. It does not reject the conflict perspective inherent in radical-critical criminology but shifts the focus to the assessment of crime and the needs of crime victims, seeking to portray crime in terms understandable to those most affected by it—victims and their families, offenders, and criminal justice personnel. The test insisted on by left-realist criminology is not whether a particular perspective on crime control or an explanation of crime causation complies with rigorous academic criteria but whether it speaks meaningfully to those faced with crime on a routine basis. "For realists crime is no less harmful to its victims because of its socially constructed origins."[45]

Left-realist criminology is generally considered synony-mous with left realism (also called *radical realism* or *critical realism*) but tends to distance itself from some of the more visionary claims of early radical and Marxist theory.[46] Daniel J. Curran and Claire M. Renzetti portrayed left realism as a natural con-sequence of increasingly conservative attitudes toward crime and criminals in both Europe and North America: "Though not successful in converting many radicals to the right, this new conservatism did lead a number of radical criminologists to temper their views a bit and to take what some might call a less romanticized look at street crime."[47]

Some authors credit **Walter DeKeseredy**[48] with popular-izing left-realist notions in North America, and **Jock Young**[49] is identified as a major source of left-realist writings in England. Prior to the writings of DeKeseredy and Young, radical crimi-nology, with its emphasis on the crime-inducing consequences of existing power structures, tended to portray the ruling class as the "real criminals" and saw street criminals as social rebels who were acting out of felt deprivation; DeKeseredy and Young were successful in refocusing leftist theories on the serious con-sequences of street crime and on the crimes of the lower classes. Left realists argued that victims of crime are often the poor and disenfranchised who fall prey to criminals with similar back-grounds and saw the criminal justice system and its agents not as pawns of the powerful but as institutions that could offer useful services if modifications were made to reduce their use of force and to increase their sensitivity toward the public.

A central tenet of left realism is that radical ideas must be translated into realistic social policies if contemporary criminol-ogy is to have any practical relevance. Concrete suggestions with respect to community policing models are indicative of the direction left realists are headed. Instead of seeing the police as oppressors working on behalf of the state, left realists recommend that the police work with, and answer to, the communities they serve.[50] The major goal of left realism is to achieve a just and orderly society through a practical emphasis on social justice.[51]

Critique of Left-Realist Criminology

Left-realist criminology has been convincingly criticized for be-ing more of an ideological emphasis than a theory. As Don C. Gibbons explained, "Left realism can best be described as a gen-eral perspective centered on injunctions to 'take crime seriously' and to 'take crime control seri-ously' rather than as a well-developed crimi-nological perspective."[52] Realist criminologists appear to build on preexisting theoretical frameworks but rarely offer new testable propositions or hypotheses, but they do sug-gest crime-control approaches in keeping with the needs of the victimized. Policies promulgated by left realists understandably include an emphasis on community policing, neighborhood justice centers, and dispute-resolution mechanisms, whereas right realists are more punitive in their policy suggestions. Piers Beirne and James W. Messerschmidt summarized the situa-tion this way: "What left realists have essentially accomplished is an attempt to theorize about conventional crime realisti-cally while simultaneously developing a 'radical law and order' program for curbing such behavior."[53] Read some original writings in the area of critical criminology via **http://www.guerrillalaw.com/left.html**, **http://www.critcrim.org/redfeather/crime/003socialist.html**, and **http://journal.radicalcriminology.org/index.php/rc**.

> Left-realist criminology has been criticized for being more of an ideology than a theory.

Feminist Criminology

As some have observed, "Women have been virtually invisible in criminological analysis until recently and much theorizing has proceeded as though criminality is restricted to men."[54] Others put it this way: "Criminological theory assumes a woman is like a man."[55] But beginning in the 1970s, advances in feminist theory were applied to criminology, resulting in what has been called a **feminist criminology** (a model redirecting criminologists' thinking to include gender awareness).

Feminism is a way of seeing the world, not a sexual ori-entation. To be a feminist is to "combine a female mental per-spective with a sensitivity for those social issues that influence primarily women."[56] Central to understanding feminist thought is the realization that feminism views gender in terms of power relationships. According to feminist approaches, men have tra-ditionally held much more power in the patriarchal structure of Western society than women and have excluded women from much decision making in socially significant areas, and sexist

■ **liberal feminism**   A feminist perspective in criminology that sees gender-role socialization as the primary source of women's oppression.

■ **radical feminism**   A perspective that sees patriarchy as the cause of women's oppression.

attitudes—deeply ingrained notions of male superiority—have perpetuated inequality between the sexes. The consequences of sexism and the unequal gender-based distribution of power have been far-reaching, affecting fundamental aspects of social roles and personal expectations at all levels.

Five strands of feminist thought inform feminist criminology today: liberal feminism, radical feminism, Marxist feminism, socialist feminism, and postmodern feminism. Each of these perspectives argues that conflict in society is based on inequalities focused around issues of gender. Learn more at **http://ssrn.com/abstract=1130587**.

Liberal Feminism

Liberal feminism sees gender-role socialization as the primary source of women's oppression.[57] Liberal feminists describe a power-based and traditional domination of women's bodies and minds by men throughout history and blame present

inequalities on the development within culture and society of "separate and distinct spheres of influence and traditional attitudes about the appropriate role of men and women."[58] Liberal feminists call for elimination of traditional divisions of power and labor between the sexes as a way of eliminating inequality and promoting social harmony.

Radical Feminism

Radical feminism sees patriarchy, or male dominance, as the cause of women's oppression, depicting men as being fundamentally brutish, aggressive, and violent and controlling women through sexuality by taking advantage of both women's biological dependence during childbearing years and their lack of physical strength relative to men. The exploitation of women by men triggers women's deviant behavior, because young women who are sexually or physically exploited may run away or abuse substances and become criminalized, so

PUTTING CRIMINOLOGY TO WORK—Implementing Evidence-Based Policy

To make a difference in the real world, criminological theories must first be tested and evaluated. Once evidence has been developed that theory-based practices work, then programs based on them can be implemented to reduce or prevent crime, or to help make victims' lives better. One federal initiative, CrimeSolutions.Gov, strives to evaluate the effectiveness of theory-based practices, and then communicates its findings via the Web. Some of the most effective and promising programs are highlighted in boxes such as this one that appear throughout the text.

PROGRAM: The Duluth Model of Interventions for Domestic Violence Offenders

EVIDENCE RATINGS FOR OUTCOMES: Effective

PROFILE

The Duluth Model provides treatment for domestic violence offenders, and employs a feminist psychoeducational approach. Originating in 1981 from the Duluth Domestic Abuse Intervention Project in Duluth, Minnesota, the program proposes that the principal cause of domestic violence is a social and cultural patriarchal ideology that historically has allowed men to control women through power and violence. Violence perpetrated on women and children originates from their relative positions of weakness and vulnerability socially, politically, economically, and culturally.

As such, the model does not assume that domestic violence is caused by mental or behavioral health problems, substance use, anger, stress, or dysfunctional relationships. The program concentrates on providing group facilitated exercises that challenge a male's perception of entitlement to control and dominate his partner. The program strives to provide an improved and broadened understanding of the causes and effects of the underlying problems experienced by the offender.

Relevant Theory: Feminist Criminology

Feminist theory is based upon an understanding of male power, control, and dominance as culturally and historically pervasive, and which allowed, if not encouraged, men to control women, sometimes through the use of violence.

Evidence-Based Review

These sources were used in the development of the practice profile:

Meta-Analysis 1

Julia C. Babcock, Charles E. Green, and Chet Robie, "Does Batterers' Treatment Work? A Meta-Analytic Review of Domestic Violence Treatment," *Clinical Psychology Review*, Vol. 23 (2004), pp. 1023–1053.

Source: Adapted from https://www.crimesolutions.gov/PracticeDetails.aspx?ID=17
Notes: Putting Criminology to Work features are based on information published online by the National Institute of Justice's (NIJ) Crime Solutions Website. The program ratings shown are those provided by NIJ.

■ **socialist feminism**   A perspective in modern criminology that sees gender oppression as a consequence of the interaction between the economic structure of society and gender-based roles.

■ **postmodern feminism**   A perspective in modern criminology that questions the social construction of concepts typically used in discussions of crime and justice.

■ **patriarchy**   The tradition of male dominance.

■ **androcentricity**   A male-dominated perspective, as in the case of criminologists who study only the criminality of males.

■ **Marxist feminism**   A perspective in feminist criminology that sees the oppression of women as caused by their subordinate class status within capitalist societies.

the elimination of male domination should reduce crime rates for women and "even precipitate a decrease in male violence against women."[59]

Marxist Feminism

The oppression of women caused by their subordinate working-class status in capitalist societies is the main tenet of **Marxist feminism**. Within capitalist society, women may be drawn into crime commission in an effort to support themselves and their children; men commit violent street crimes more often, whereas women commit property and vice crimes.[60]

Social Feminism

Socialist feminism, a fourth perspective, sees gender oppression as a consequence of the interaction between the economic structure of society and gender-based roles. Egalitarian societies would be built around socialist or Marxist principles with the aim of creating a society that is free of gender and class divisions.

Postmodern Feminism

The social construction of concepts typically used in any discussion of criminology—including concepts like justice and crime—are questioned by **postmodern feminism**. According to criminologist Amanda Burgess-Proctor, postmodern feminism departs from the other feminist perspectives by questioning the existence of any one "truth," including "women's oppression," and that "postmodern feminists reject fixed categories and universal concepts in favor of multiple truths and as such examine the effects of discourse and symbolic representation on claims about knowledge."[61]

Proponents of Feminist Criminology

Feminist criminology points out the inequities inherent in patriarchal forms of thought. According to James W. Messerschmidt, **patriarchy** (male dominance) is a "set of social relations of power in which the male gender appropriates the labor power of women and controls their sexuality."[62]

Early works in the field of feminist criminology include *Sisters in Crime* by **Freda Adler** [63] and *Women and Crime* by **Rita J. Simon**,[64] both published in 1975. In these books, the authors attempted to explain existing divergences in crime rates

between men and women as being due primarily to socialization rather than biology. Women were taught to believe in personal limitations, faced reduced socioeconomic opportunities, and suffered from lowered aspirations. As gender equality increased, they said, it could be expected that male and female criminality would take on similar characteristics, but such has not been the case, and the approach of Adler and Simon has not been validated by observations surrounding increased gender equality over the past few decades. One exception, however, comes from Mexico, where the number of women incarcerated for federal crimes grew 400% between 2007 and 2012.[65] Most of the crimes for which women are serving time in Mexican federal prisons are drug-related, and it may be that that country's crackdown on drug crime over the past several years has had more of an impact on the number of imprisoned women than actual changes in the rate of crime committed by Mexican women.

Another early work, *Women, Crime and Criminology*, was published in 1977 by British sociologist **Carol Smart**;[66] it sensitized criminologists to sexist traditions within the field and led to recognition of women's issues. Smart pointed out that men and women experience and perceive the world in different ways, and she showed how important it is for women to have a voice in interpreting the behavior of other women as opposed to having women's behavior interpreted from a man's standpoint.

Early feminist theorizing may not have borne the fruit that some researchers anticipated, but it has led to a heightened awareness of gender issues within criminology. Two of the most insightful contemporary proponents of the need to apply feminist thinking to criminological analysis are **Kathleen Daly** and **Meda Chesney-Lind**, who are concerned about the existence of an **androcentricity** (male-dominated) perspective in criminology and point out that "gender differences in crime suggest that crime

> Gender differences in crime suggest that crime may not be so normal after all.

may not be so normal after all."[67] Traditional understandings of what is typical about crime are derived from the study of men, especially that small

■ **power-control theory**   A perspective that holds that power relationships existing in the wider society are reflected in domestic settings and in everyday relationships among men, women, and children in the context of family life.

group of men who commit most crimes. The relative lack of criminality exhibited by women is rarely acknowledged as having criminological significance, which calls into question many traditional assumptions about crime—especially the assumption that crime is somehow a "normal" part of social life. Daly and Chesney-Lind have identified the following five elements of feminist thought that set it apart from other types of social and political thought:[68]

1. Gender is not a natural fact but a complex social, historical, and cultural product that is related to, not simply derived from, biological sex differences and reproductive capacities.

2. Gender and gender relations order social life and social institutions in fundamental ways.

3. Gender relations and constructs of masculinity and femininity are not symmetrical but are based on an organizing principle of men's superiority and their social, political, and economic dominance over women.

4. Systems of knowledge reflect men's views of the natural and social world; the production of knowledge is gendered.

5. Women should be at the center, not the periphery, of intellectual inquiry; they should not be invisible or treated as appendages to men.

In a more recent analysis of feminist criminology, **Susan Caulfield** and **Nancy Wonders** described "five major contributions that have been made by feminist scholarship and practice" to criminological thinking: (1) a focus on gender as a central organizing principle of contemporary life, (2) an awareness of the importance of power in shaping social relationships, (3) a heightened sensitivity to the way in which social context helps shape human relationships, (4) the recognition that social reality must be understood as a process and that the development of research methods should take this into account, and (5) a commitment to social change as a crucial part of feminist scholarship and practice.[69]

John Hagan built on defining features of power relationships in his book *Structural Criminology*, in which he explained that power relationships existing in the wider society are effectively "brought home" to domestic settings and are reflected in everyday relationships among men, women, and children within the context of family life.[70] Hagan's approach, termed **power-control theory**, suggested that "family class structure shapes the social reproduction of gender relations, and in turn the social distribution of delinquency."[71]

In a cogent analysis encompassing much of contemporary feminist theory, Daly and Chesney-Lind suggested that feminist thought is more important for the way it informs and challenges existing criminology than for the new theories it offers. Theories of crime causation and prevention must include

women, and more research on gender-related issues in the field is badly needed. Daly and Chesney-Lind explained that "criminologists should begin to appreciate that their discipline and its questions are a product of white, economically privileged men's experiences." They note that rates of female criminality, which are lower than those of males (Figure 9–3), may highlight the fact that criminal behavior is not as "normal" as once thought.[72] Because modern-day criminological perspectives were mostly developed by white middle-class men, the perspectives failed to take into consideration women's "ways of knowing."[73] Feminist criminologists Daly and Chesney-Lind asked: Given the current situation in theory development, do existing theories of crime causation apply as well to women as they do to men, or "do theories of men's crime apply to women?"[74]

Other feminists have analyzed the process by which laws are created and legislation passed and have concluded that modern-day statutes frequently represent characteristically masculine modes of thought and that existing criminal laws are overly rational and hierarchically structured, reflecting traditionally male ways of organizing the social world.[75] Until recently, many jurisdictions viewed assault victims differently based on the gendered relationships involved in the offense. *Assault* (or *battery*) is defined as an attack by one person on another, but until the last few decades of the twentieth century, domestic violence statutes tended to downplay the seriousness of the attacks involved, giving the impression that because they occurred within the home and the victims were typically women, they weren't as important to the justice system as other forms of assault. Some analysts have suggested that existing laws need to be replaced by "a system of justice based upon the specifically feminine principles of care, connection and community."[76]

In the area of social policy, feminist thinkers have pointed to the need for increased controls over men's violence toward women, the creation of alternatives (to supplement the home and traditional family structures) for women facing abuse, and the protection of children. They also questioned the role of government, culture, and the mass media in promulgating pornography, prostitution, and rape and portrayed ongoing crimes against women as characteristic of continuing traditions in which women are undervalued and controlled. Many radical feminists have suggested the replacement of men with women in positions of power, especially within justice system and government organizations, but others noted that replacement still would not address needed changes in the structure of the system itself, which is gender biased due to years of male domination. Centrists, on the other hand, have offered a more balanced approach, believing that individuals of both genders have much to contribute to a workable justice system.[77] Learn more about feminist criminology at **http://www.tulane.edu/~femtheory/journals/ paper8.html** and **http://www.historylearningsite.co.uk/ feminism_crime.htm**.

■ **gender gap** The observed differences between male and female rates of criminal offending in a given society.

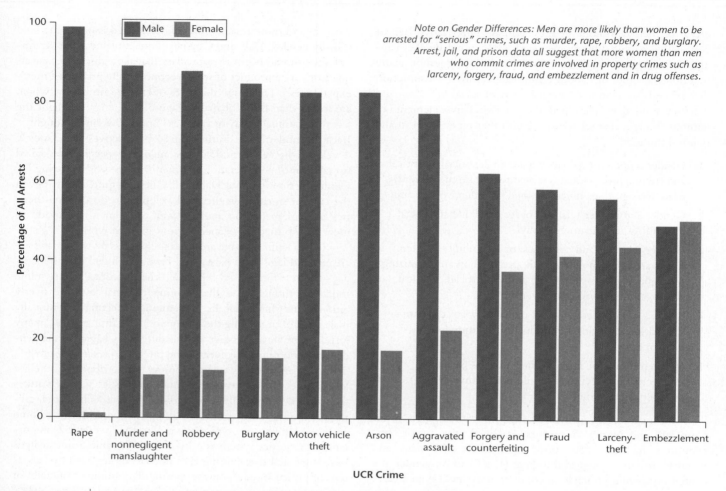

Note on Gender Differences: Men are more likely than women to be arrested for "serious" crimes, such as murder, rape, robbery, and burglary. Arrest, jail, and prison data all suggest that more women than men who commit crimes are involved in property crimes such as larceny, forgery, fraud, and embezzlement and in drug offenses.

FIGURE 9-3 | **Male and Female Involvement in Crime: Offense Patterns, 2015**

Source: Federal Bureau of Investigation, *Crime in the United States, 2015* (Washington, DC: U.S. Department of Justice, 2016).

Critique of Feminist Criminology

Some would argue that feminist criminology has yet to live up to its promise because few comprehensive feminist theories of crime were proposed; feminist criminology focused instead on descriptive studies of female involvement in crime.[78] Male violence against women was seen as adding support to the central tenet of feminist criminology (that the relationship between the sexes is primarily characterized by the exercise of power), but that did not make for broad theory building. As one writer explained, "Feminist theory is a theory in formation."[79]

> Some would argue that feminist criminology has yet to live up to its promise.

Feminist criminology has faced criticism from many other directions. Predicted increases in female crime rates have failed to materialize as social opportunities available to both genders have become more balanced, and the **gender gap** in crime—with males accounting for much more law violation than females—continues to exist. Criminologist Karen Heimer noted that the gender gap is "virtually a truism in criminology. The relationship holds, regardless of whether the data analyzed are arrest rates, victimization incidence reports on characteristics of offenders, or self-reports of criminal behavior.... [A]s far as we can tell, males have always been more criminal than females, and gender differences emerge in every society that has been studied systematically."[80] Other critics have pointed to fundamental flaws in feminist thought, asking such questions as "If men have more power than women, then why are so many more men arrested?"[81]

Some critics have even argued that a feminist criminology is impossible. Daly and Chesney-Lind agreed that although feminist thought may inform criminology, "a feminist criminology cannot exist because neither feminism nor criminology is

■ **postmodern criminology**   A brand of criminology that builds on the tenets inherent in postmodern social thought.

■ **deconstructionist theory**   A postmodern perspective that challenges existing criminological theories in order to debunk them and that works toward replacing traditional ideas with concepts seen as more appropriate to the postmodern era.

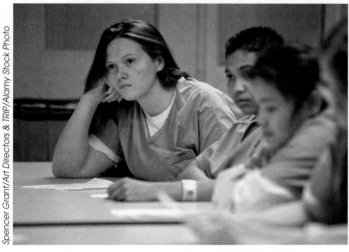

Female jail inmates participate in a drug treatment seminar in Santa Ana, California. Feminists claim that much of today's criminology is male-centered and that the special needs and interests of women are rarely considered when discussing crimes committed by females. What role do you think gender plays in research on crime and criminality?

a unified set of principles and practices."[82] A criminology built solely on feminist principles is unlikely because neither feminist thought nor criminology meets the strict requirements of formal theory building. Read more about feminist perspectives on crime and criminology at **http://www.springerlink.com/content/p1h9906602485822** and **http://critcrim.org/critpapers/chesney-lind1.htm**.

Postmodern Criminology

Some significant new approaches now emerging within criminology are largely the result of postmodern social thought and can be lumped together under the rubric **postmodern criminology**, which applies understandings of social change inherent in postmodern philosophy to criminological theorizing and to issues of crime control.

Postmodern thought, which developed primarily in Europe after World War II, represents "a rejection of the enlightenment belief in scientific rationality as the main vehicle to knowledge and progress."[83] One of its important aspects can be found in its efforts to demonstrate the systematic intrusion of sexist, racist, capitalist, colonialist, and professional interests into the very

content of science. Contemporary feminist scholar Joycelyn M. Pollock put it this way: "Post-modernism questions whether we can ever 'know' something objectively; so-called neutral science is considered a sham and criminology's search for causes is bankrupt because even the question is framed by androcentric, sexist, classist, and racist definitions of crime, criminals, and cause."[84]

All postmodern criminologies build on the feeling that past criminological approaches have failed to realistically assess the true causes of crime and have failed to offer workable solutions for crime control. Hence, much postmodern criminology is deconstructionist, and its theories are sometimes called **deconstructionist theories**, meaning approaches that challenge existing criminological perspectives to debunk them and to work toward replacing them with approaches more relevant to the postmodern era.

Two notable authors in the field of postmodern criminology are **Stuart Henry** and **Dragan Milovanovic**,[85] whose constitutive criminology, rooted in phenomenology, claimed that crime and crime control are not "object-like entities" but are constructions produced through a social process in which offender, victim, and society are all involved.[86] A central feature of their constitutive criminology is its assertion that individuals shape their world while also being shaped by it.

Semiotics, or the study of signs and symbols, is another important concept in constitutive criminology. Semiotics can be applied to the notion of crime, itself a socially constructed category or sign. In the words of Henry and Milovanovic, crime "is a categorization of the diversity of human conflicts and transgressions into a single category 'crime,' as though these were somehow all the same. It is a melting of differences reflecting the multitude of variously motivated acts of personal injury into a single entity."[87] Crime should be understood as an integral part of society, not as something separate from it.

From this perspective, a kind of false consciousness, or lack of awareness, gives rise to criminal activity. According to Werner Einstadter and Stuart Henry, crime is seen to be the culmination of certain processes that allow persons to believe they are somehow not connected to other humans and society, that place others in categories or stereotypes, and that make them different or alien, denying their humanity; this results in the denial of responsibility for other people and to other people.[88] Learn more about postmodern criminology at **http://www.critcrim.org/redfeather/journal-pomocrim/pomocrimindex.html** and read an interesting paper by Dragan Milovanovic at **http://critcrim.org/critpapers/milovanovic_postmod.htm**.

Critique of Postmodern Criminology

Ian Taylor is a British sociologist who lent focus to radical-critical criminology in the 1970s with the publication of two well-received books.[89] He criticized postmodern approaches to crime and deviance for their "increasing incoherence."[90] In other words, postmodern criminologists employ vaguely defined terminology. Taylor also explained that the "battle with orthodox criminology" has led postmodern approaches to increasingly obfuscate their most basic claims, so a second result of the postmodern influence on criminology "has been the development of a social account of crime that entirely lacks a value or ethical foundation."[91] Deconstructionism may challenge traditional theories, but unless it offers viable alternatives for crime control and prevention, it does little good.

Peacemaking Criminology

Throughout much of history, formal agencies of social control—the police, officials of the courts, and corrections personnel—have been seen as pitted against criminal perpetrators and would-be wrongdoers, and crime control has been depicted as an epic struggle in which diametrically opposed antagonists continuously engage one another but in which only one side can emerge victorious. Another point of view has come to the fore: **Peacemaking criminology** (also called *compassionate criminology*), a form of postmodern criminology with roots in Christian and Eastern philosophies, advances the notion that social control agencies and the citizens they serve should work together to alleviate social problems and human suffering and thus reduce crime.[92] Peacemaking criminology includes the notion of service and suggests that "compassion, wisdom, and love are essential for understanding the suffering of which we are all a part and for practicing a criminology of nonviolence."[93]

Peacemaking criminology is popularized by the works of **Harold E. Pepinsky**[94] and Richard Quinney.[95] Both Pepinsky and Quinney restated the problem of crime control from one of how to stop crime to one of how to make peace within society and between citizens and criminal justice agencies (see Figure 9–4). Peacemaking criminology draws attention to many issues: (1) perpetuation of violence through continuation of social policies based on dominant forms of criminological theory, (2) role of education in peacemaking, (3) commonsense theories of crime, (4) crime control as human rights enforcement, and (5) conflict resolution within community settings.[96]

Richard Quinney and John Wildeman summarized the underpinnings of peacemaking criminology by stating that "a criminology of peacemaking—a nonviolent criminology of

Roman/Fotolia

A homeless man in New York City. Peacemaking criminology holds that the alleviation of social problems and the reduction of human suffering will lead to a truly just world and thus reduce crime. What do you think?

compassion and service—seeks to end suffering and thereby eliminate crime."[97]

Other contributors to the peacemaking movement include **Bo Lozoff**, **Michael Braswell**, and Clemens Bartollas. In *Inner Corrections*, Lozoff and Braswell claimed that "we are fully aware by now that the criminal justice system in this country is founded on violence. It is a system which assumes that violence can be overcome by violence, evil by evil. Criminal justice at home and warfare abroad are of the same principle of violence. This principle sadly dominates much of our criminology."[98] *Inner Corrections* provides meditative techniques and prayers for those seeking to become more compassionate and includes a number of letters from convicts who demonstrate the book's philosophy.

In a work titled "Correctional Treatment, Peacemaking, and the New Age Movement," Bartollas and Braswell applied New Age principles to correctional treatment:[99] "Most offenders suffered abusive and deprived childhoods. Treatment that focuses on the inner child and such qualities as forgiveness and self-esteem could benefit offenders."[100] In a fundamental sense, peacemaking criminologists exhort their colleagues to transcend personal dichotomies to end the political and ideological divisiveness that separates people.

Participatory and Restorative Justice

Peacemaking criminology suggests that effective crime control can best be achieved by the adoption of a **peace model** of

■ **participatory justice**   An informal type of criminal justice case processing that makes use of local community resources rather than requiring traditional forms of official intervention.

■ **restorative justice**   A postmodern perspective that stresses solutions and restoration rather than imprisonment, punishment, and neglect of victims; also called reparative justice.

TRADITIONAL PUNISHMENT
Once an ex-con always an ex-con

I drew a circle that shut him out.

THE PEACEMAKING PROCESS
Reintegration into society

We drew a circle that drew him in.

FIGURE 9-4 | **The Differences between Peacemaking and Traditional Punishment**

Source: Schmalleger, Frank, *Criminology*. Printed and Electronically reproduced by permission of Pearson Education, Inc., Upper Saddle River, New Jersey.

crime control based on cooperation rather than retribution and focused on effective ways of developing a shared consensus on critical issues that could seriously affect people's quality of life. Major issues include crimes like murder and rape but also extend to property rights, rights to the use of new technologies, and ownership of information; minor issues, including sexual preference, nonviolent sexual deviance, gambling, drug use, noise, child-custody claims, and publicly offensive behavior, can be dealt with in ways that require few resources beyond those immediately available in the community.

Alternative dispute resolution plays an important role in peacemaking perspectives.[101] Mediation programs, such as dispute-resolution centers and neighborhood justice centers, are characterized by cooperative efforts to reach dispute resolution rather than the adversarial proceedings now characteristic of most American courts. Dispute-resolution programs, now operating in over 200 areas throughout the country, are based on **participatory justice**—all parties to a dispute accept a kind of binding arbitration by neutral parties, often utilize administrative hearings and ombudsmen, and are staffed by volunteers who work to resolve disputes without assigning blame.

Miami's drug court, a local judicial initiative begun in 1989, provides an example of dispute-resolution programs. It diverts nonviolent drug users from the traditional path of streets to court to jail. Officially called the Dade County Diversion and Treatment Program, the drug court "channels almost all nonviolent defendants arrested on drug possession charges into an innovative court-operated rehabilitation program as an alternative to prosecution."[102] Drug-court processing appears to be

successful at reducing the incidence of repeat offenses, does not result in a criminal record for those completing the program, and offers drug-dependent offenders a second chance at gaining control over substance-abuse problems.

Alternative dispute resolution is not without its critics, who charge that this type of program is often staffed by poorly qualified individuals who are ill-prepared to mediate disputes effectively. But as case-processing expenses continue to rise and minor cases continue to flood justice system agencies, we can expect that an emphasis on alternative dispute resolution will continue.

Many dispute-resolution strategies are really a form of **restorative justice** (also called *reparative justice*), "a new system based on remedies and restoration rather than on prison, punishment and victim neglect."[103] It is "a system rooted in the concept of a caring community," and adherents hope it leads to social and economic justice and increased concern and respect for both victims and victimizers.[104]

> Restorative justice is a modern social movement that stresses healing rather than retribution.

But restorative justice is more than a system—it is a modern social movement to reform the criminal justice system that stresses healing rather than retribution.[105]

Restoration (repairing the harm done by crime and rebuilding relationships in the community) is the primary goal of restorative justice, and its effectiveness is measured by how many relationships are healed rather than by how much

■ **Balanced and Restorative Justice (BARJ) model** A form of justice which holds that the community, victim, and offender should receive balanced attention and all three should gain tangible benefits from their interactions with the justice system.

TABLE 9–1 | Differences between Retributive and Restorative Justice

RETRIBUTIVE JUSTICE	RESTORATIVE JUSTICE
Crime is an act against the state, a violation of a law, an abstract idea.	Crime is an act against another person or the community.
The criminal justice system controls crime.	Crime control lies primarily with the community.
Offender accountability is defined as taking punishment.	Offender accountability is defined as assuming responsibility and taking action to repair harm.
Crime is an individual act with individual responsibility.	Crime has both individual and social dimensions of responsibility.
Victims are peripheral to the process of resolving a crime.	Victims are central to the process of resolving a crime.
The offender is defined by deficits.	The offender is defined by the capacity to make reparation.
The emphasis is on adversarial relationships.	The emphasis is on dialogue and negotiation.
Pain is imposed to punish, deter, and prevent.	Restitution is a means of restoring both parties; the goal is reconciliation.
The community is on the sidelines, represented abstractly.	The community is the facilitator in the restorative process by the state.
The response is focused on the offender's past behavior.	The response is focused on harmful consequences of the offender's behavior; the emphasis is on the future and on reparation.
There is dependence on proxy professionals.	There is direct involvement by both the offender and the victim.

Source: Adapted from Gordon Bazemore and Mark S. Umbreit, *Balanced and Restorative Justice: Program Summary* (Washington, DC: Office of Juvenile Justice and Delinquency Prevention, 1994), p. 7.

FIGURE 9–5 | The Balanced and Restorative Justice (BARJ) Model

Source: Office of Juvenile Justice and Delinquency Prevention, *Balanced and Restorative Justice: Program Summary* (Washington, DC: OJJDP, no date), p. 1.

this model, the community, victim, and offender should receive balanced attention and all three should gain tangible benefits from their interactions with the justice system. Its three components may be described as follows:[106]

● **Accountability.** When an offense occurs, an obligation to the victim results. Victims and communities should have their losses restored by the actions of offenders making reparation, and victims should be empowered as active participants in the justice process.

● **Community protection.** The public has a right to a safe and secure community and must be protected during the time the offender is under supervision. The justice system must provide a range of intervention alternatives geared to the varying risks presented by the offenders.

● **Competency development.** Offenders who come within the jurisdiction of the court should leave the system capable of being productive and responsible in the community. Rather than simply receiving treatment and services aimed at suppressing problem behavior, offenders should make measurable improvements in their ability to function as productive, responsible citizens.

Restorative justice programs make use of a number of techniques, but central to all of them is restorative conferencing, also called "community conferencing," in which victim, offender, and affected community members meet face-to-face in a safe setting with an impartial facilitator to discuss the facts and the impact of a particular offense.[107] The victim can ask

punishment is inflicted on the offender. Table 9–1 highlights some of the significant differences between traditional retributive justice and restorative justice.

The Balanced and Restorative Justice (BARJ) Model

One form of restorative justice is the **Balanced and Restorative Justice (BARJ) model**. (See Figure 9–5.) Under questions and express directly to the offender how the crime has affected his or her life. Conferencing provides the victim with greater access to the criminal justice process and a strong voice in the process.[108] Conferencing also humanizes the incident for the offender so that he or she may better understand the real human consequences of his or her wrongdoing. The offender can propose steps that he or she can take to help restore the harm caused to the victim and the community. Participation in conferences is voluntary for victims and offenders. In some cases, a victim unwilling to participate in a face-to-face meeting may make a written statement to be used in the conference, or a surrogate victim may take his or her place. Learn more about restorative justice at **http://www.cehd.umn.edu/ssw/rjp**.

Critique of Peacemaking Criminology

Peacemaking criminology has been criticized as being naïve and utopian and for failing to recognize the realities of crime control and law enforcement because few victims would expect to gain much

---

PUTTING CRIMINOLOGY TO WORK—Implementing Evidence-Based Policy

To make a difference in the real world, criminological theories must first be tested and evaluated. Once evidence has been developed that theory-based practices work, then programs based on them can be implemented to reduce or prevent crime, or to help make victims' lives better. One federal initiative, CrimeSolutions.Gov, strives to evaluate the effectiveness of theory-based practices, and then communicates its findings via the Web. Some of the most effective and promising programs are highlighted in boxes such as this one that appear throughout the text.

PROGRAM: Restorative Policing

EVIDENCE RATINGS FOR OUTCOMES: Promising

PROFILE

The Reintegrative Shaming Experiments (RISE) in Canberra, Australia, were designed to measure the impact of "restorative policing" on both victims and offenders' perceptions of justice, as well as overall satisfaction following the conference. The ultimate goal of the conference is to repair the harm caused by the offense by bringing together the offender, victim, and members of the community in a way that allows offenders to reintegrate into the community, and victims to return to their normal routines without fear of further victimization.

The program involves the offender, victim, and supportive individuals for both parties, who come together to discuss the crime and its impact, and to reach an agreement on how the offender can make amends. The aim of the project was to include "middle range" offenses, neither so trivial that they would normally be dealt with by a simple caution or warning, nor so serious that the police would be reluctant to bypass the court system.

Unlike some other programs, the conference coordinator and facilitator is a police officer, and the conference is held at a police station. The conferencing model involved also used a great deal of reintegrative shaming.

It is also believed that victims will have a more positive perception of justice and less fear of re-victimization by participating in restorative justice conferences, as they are able to have a voice in the process.

Program Theory: Restorative Justice

The RISE procedures are based on the restorative justice ideal, which is grounded in social control and community shaming. The focus of restorative justice is to heal those—both offender and victim—harmed by the offense rather than punish the offender for the sake of the victim. The idea is to make offenders aware of the potential pain their actions have caused, and to feel remorse. By forcing offenders to face the potential consequences of their actions, the belief is that they will be deterred from engaging in further law violation. The RISE experiments were reintegrative in nature because they avoided stigmatizing the offender as an "other," excluding him or her from the justice process and hindering the process of reintegration.

Evidence-Based Review

These sources were used in the development of the program profile:

Study 1

Lawrence W. Sherman, Heather Strang, and Daniel J. Woods, *Recidivism Patterns in Canberra Reintegrative Shaming Experiments (RISE)*. Canberra, Australia: Australian National University, Research School of Social Sciences, Centre for Restorative Justice, 2000.

Study 2

Tom R. Tyler, Lawrence Sherman, Heather Strang, Geoffrey C. Barnes, and Daniel Woods, "Reintegrative Shaming, Procedural Justice, and Recidivism: The Engagement of Offenders' Psychological Mechanisms in the Canberra RISE Drinking-and-Driving Experiment." *Law & Society Review*, Vol. 41, No. 3 (2007), pp. 553–585.

Source: Adapted from https://www.crimesolutions.gov/ProgramDetails.aspx?ID=325

Notes: Putting Criminology to Work features are based on information published online by the National Institute of Justice's (NIJ) Crime Solutions Website. The program ratings shown are those provided by NIJ.

■ **moral time**   A conflict perspective that highlights the clash between social understandings of right and wrong—especially as those understandings change over time and between groups—as the cause of human conflict. It sees conflict as a fundamental and inescapable feature of social life.

from attempting to make peace with their victimizers (although such strategies do occasionally work). Such criticisms may be improperly directed at a level of analysis that peacemaking criminologists have not assumed. Although it involves work with individual offenders, peacemaking criminology envisions positive change on the societal and institutional levels and does not suggest to victims that they attempt to effect personal changes in offenders.

Moral Time

A very different approach to conflict is offered by Donald Black in his book *Moral Time.*[109] Black uses the concept of social time to refer to specific events that alter relationships within what he refers to as *social space.* Black says that conflict is produced by changes in the amount of intimacy, inequality, or diversity that characterize human relationships. Rapid social change along any of these dimensions produces conflict. Such change in social space results from the movement of social time. The greater the speed and intensity of social time, the greater the conflict, says Black. He notes that crime is dynamic, and that it is an *event,* not a thing, or a condition. Although it may be people who commit crime, it is other events in social time that are the direct cause of crime. Black's use of the word "time" is meant to encompass change. Black would say that it is not poverty itself that causes crime, but rather that crime is more likely to result from a quick descent into poverty—an event that takes place in moral time because it alters a person's relationship with others as time passes. Seen this way involvement in crime can result from an attempt to compensate for one's changed economic relationship with others.

According to Black, conflict is everywhere. Black says that conflict "is inevitable and inescapable" and suggests that it is the result of a clash between what people view as right or wrong and the ability to apply that sense to events in social time. "The fundamental cause of conflict" says Black, "is the movement of social time." Social time, as Black conceives of it, "includes the fluctuations of every dimension of social space," and he identifies three dimensions: relational time, vertical time, and cultural time. Relational time is an increase or decrease in intimacy; vertical time is an increase or decrease of inequality; and cultural time is an increase or decrease of diversity. Seen this way, social events, and the personal experiences derived from them, are movements of social time. Black says that rape, divorce, achievement, loss, or the creation of something new is a movement in social time. As Black sees it:

Social time moves when someone increases or decreases intimacy with someone else, achieves more or less than someone else, or accepts or rejects an idea of someone else. It moves when someone allows a relationship to weaken, disobeys an authority, or converts to another religion. It moves when strangers become acquaintances, when a marriage begins or ends, when a business hires or fires an employee, and when a nation rises or falls. It moves when someone gains or loses wealth, gives birth or dies, commits a crime or punishes a criminal....

Movement in social space is what Black refers to as *social time.* Social norms and a group's sense of morality, however, seek to prevent social change. As Black sees it, morality "forbids the movement of social time." He adds, however, that "morality does not forbid every movement of social time, but everything morality forbids is a movement of social time."

Black emphasizes the idea that conflict is a social event and notes that social time causes conflict in human relationships. Every movement of social time that causes conflict, says Black, is an increase or decrease in social closeness. Seen this way, conflict is a direct function of closeness, and a change in closeness can result in overcloseness or undercloseness. Although crime results from a movement of social time, says Black, the seriousness of an offense varies with intimacy. For example, he says, the rape of a stranger is a greater offense than the rape of a spouse because strangers were not intimate before the encounter took place—resulting in a greater movement of social time than that produced by the rape of an intimate. Greater movements in social time, says Black, attract greater social control.

Static conditions cannot cause crime, says Black—only changes in intimacy, or movements in social time. Changes over time and between groups, especially as they impact and change values, are what Black calls **moral time.** Black uses the example of the loss of a job, which might lead to violence because of the loss of social status that it confers upon an individual, or the loss of intimacy that occurs when a woman leaves her husband, which might also result in a violent offense. When social time does not lead to crime, Black says, then the ripples in the fabric of society that it creates must be resolved in some other way—such as through mediation, the use of civil courts, or personal changes.

Black's ideas should be testable. One idea that he proposes, for example, is that it's not the *condition* of poverty that is criminogenic, but rather the process of becoming poor—that is, a person's downward movement in social space.

Moral Time is Black's attempt at a general theory of conflict, and with it he seeks to explain all conflicts, in all human relationships, "across the world and throughout history ... between relatives, friends, colleagues, strangers, groups, or nations."

Convict Criminology

One of the newest radical paradigms to emerge in the field of criminology is **convict criminology** (also called *alternative criminology*), which is not so much a school of thought as it is a body of writings and musings on criminology by convicted

■ **convict criminology** A radical paradigm consisting of writings on criminology by convicted felons and ex-inmates who have acquired academic credentials or who are associated with credentialed others; also called alternative criminology.

felons and ex-inmates who have acquired academic credentials or who are associated with credentialed others. It was formalized in 2001 with the publication of the article "Introducing the New School of Convict Criminology" by **Stephen C. Richards** in the journal *Social Justice*.[110] With the publication of "Convict Criminology" by **Jeffrey Ian Ross** and Stephen Richards in 2002,[111] the writings of convict criminologists went mainstream and began garnering attention from those in the discipline as well as the media. Today convict criminology (sometimes referred to as the New School of Convict Criminology) offers a blend of writings by credentialed ex-inmates and critical criminologists who have joined forces in distrust of mainstream criminology.[112] Convict criminology is largely issues based and personal; it has an agenda and tends to assume a critical perspective with regard to the justice system—especially corrections. The language of convict criminologists is different from that of academic criminologists who do not share their convict background (the latter use words like *convicts* instead of *offenders* and *inmates* instead of *prisoners*). The distinction is an important one, because the terminology used by academic criminologists is "managerial," consistent with the language of controlling agents in the justice system such as police officers, correctional officers, probation and parole officers, and court officials. By using the language of convict insiders, convict criminologists signify their allegiance to an insider's perspective and refer to traditional criminology as *managerial criminology*.[113]

> Convict criminology is largely issues based and personal.

The method used by convict criminologists is based in ethnography, a branch of anthropology that studies other cultures (in this case, inmate society). Ethnographers depend on lived experiences and oral communications about them (interviews, stories, conversations of study subjects). The advantage of convict criminologists is that they are their own subjects, so the long hours needed to gather experiences have already been spent—usually in prison or in personal interactions with the justice system.

The prototype convict criminologist was **John Irwin**, who spent five years in California's Soledad Prison in the 1950s for armed robbery. While imprisoned, Irwin earned college credits and after release went on to attend San Francisco State College and then UCLA. "The point is, I made my transition from the life of a thief, drug addict, and convict to one of a 'respectable' professional." Irwin went on to write *The Felon*, an academic work that shared the career criminal's point of view with interested readers.[114]

More recent works in convict criminology result from the collaboration between traditional criminologists and ex-convicts: *Behind Convict's Eyes*[115] and *Prison, Inc.: A Convict Exposes Life inside a Private Prison*,[116] both by the author team of **K. C. Carceral** (a convict serving life in prison who holds an associate's degree in paralegal studies), **Thomas J. Bernard** (a criminologist at Penn State University), and others.

Convict criminology is the source of a number of recommendations for improving the justice system that stem not from traditional forms of social scientific research but from "personal research" based on the lived experiences of the convict criminologists:[117]

1. Prisons hold far too many people, do not effectively reduce crime, and hold far too many people who have committed minor crimes.

2. Prison expansion has disproportionately and unfairly impacted the nation's poor—especially young men of color—who have made bad decisions in their lives and committed relatively harmless and bothersome crimes.

3. A substantial reduction in the number of federal and state prisoners is needed. Many of today's prisoners are nonviolent drug offenders who committed property crimes in support of drug habits or who were caught with drugs in their possession for either personal use or resale; diversion and treatment are viable alternatives to incarceration. The nation's "war on drugs"—seen as having a negative impact on all society—should be terminated.

4. Corrections today can benefit significantly from the use of smaller prisons instead of large institutions that now characterize many state facilities because they are less dangerous than large ones and tend to result in heightened rates of rehabilitation.

5. Treatment should be given precedence over security because most inmates will eventually return to society, and treatment offers the best hope for desistance from crime. Institutional priorities should be reversed—treatment programs need to receive top-level funding.

Critique of Convict Criminology

Not everyone agrees that convict criminology offers an edge over traditional criminology. Critics say that having been in prison might actually distort a criminologist's view of the field rather than enhance it and that personal experience rarely gives anyone the entire picture needed to understand a phenomenon. Focusing on the injustices of prison life might keep someone from appreciating the reformative effects of punishment. Read more about convict criminology at **http://tinyurl.com/kaf6twf**.

New Issues in Radical-Critical Thought

Some people have suggested that with the fall of the Soviet Union in the late twentieth century, and the decline of communist governments in Eastern Europe, radical-critical

CRIMINAL | PROFILES

Theodore John "Ted" Kaczynski—the Unabomber

Born in Chicago on May 22, 1942, Kaczynski recalled his childhood as "uneventful." (Interestingly, he claimed to have been the victim of verbal and emotional abuse—but those claims never surfaced until he was in his 20s.) An introspective child and youth, Ted Kaczynski did not socialize easily or well and periodically underwent episodes of intense brooding and withdrawal. As he grew older, the episodes were increasingly accompanied by a seething rage.[i] Consumed with obsessions and emotionally crippled, the reclusive Kaczynski would eventually resolve his contempt for society's technological advances by mounting a bombing campaign that killed three people and injured 29 others.

His academic abilities enabled him to skip both the 6th and 11th grades, start undergraduate studies at Harvard at age 16, and earn his doctoral degree at the age of 25, but the promise of his remarkable early academic achievements foundered quickly.[ii] Upon completing his PhD, Kaczynski accepted an assistant professorship in mathematics at the University of California–Berkeley in 1967, but in June 1969, declaring there was "no relevance" to what he was doing, he quit his teaching post and then worked only sporadically out of financial necessity, living off the land in a hermit's existence of self-exile in a ramshackle cabin in the remote Montana wilderness for almost 25 years.[iii]

Kaczynski also experienced lifelong difficulties with sexual relationships. He struggled with his own sexuality, came to believe he should undergo a sex-change operation, and initiated the process, but when finally seen by a doctor, he claimed to be there for an entirely different reason and then left in a rage; subsequently, he described the experience as shameful and humiliating.[iv] In the ensuing years, he attempted to establish meaningful relationships with women but was never able to do so.

As he retreated deeper into his isolationist lifestyle, Kaczynski handwrote a lengthy manifesto railing against contemporary life, stating "The Industrial Revolution and its consequences have been a disaster for the human race."[v]

Between May 25, 1978, and April 24, 1995, Kaczynski left or sent a total of 16 homemade pipe bombs to various targets, primarily associated with universities and airlines. (The Federal Bureau of Investigation's designation of the investigation as the "Unabomb" case derives from these early university targets.) The first ten bombs caused serious injuries to numerous people; the 11th resulted in the first death.[vi]

Kaczynski's intermittent attacks were anonymous, a trait inexplicably broken when he began sending letters to a newspaper threatening to bomb an airplane. He also stated that he would stop the bombings if his 35,000-word manifesto was published in the *Washington Post*,[vii] and its subsequent publication eventually led to his capture.

Upon reading the manifesto, David Kaczynski (Ted's younger brother) immediately realized that "the tone of the language ... almost had the feeling for me of one of Ted's angry letters over the years."[viii] The content and wording of the manifesto led David Kaczynski to contact the Federal Bureau of Investigation (FBI). The FBI went to Kaczynski's cabin in the isolated Montana wilderness and found overwhelming evidence that he was the Unabomber: a live bomb, meticulous notes of past bombings, bomb-making materials, and the original copy of his infamous manifesto.

Ralf-Finn Hestoft/Corbis/Getty Images

Former University of California-Berkeley math professor Theodore John Kaczynski—aka the Unabomber—being led to an interview at the Federal Administrative Maximum Prison in Florence, Colorado. What motivated Kaczynski?

On January 22, 1998, after reaching a plea agreement, Kaczynski pleaded guilty to four bombings that occurred in 1985, 1993, and 1995. Kaczynski also admitted to the three deaths his bombings had caused, and all other charges against him were resolved; he was sentenced to a life term without parole.[ix] Kaczynski remains imprisoned at the maximum-security federal prison in Florence, Colorado. Nine years after he entered prison, Kaczynski filed suit against the federal government and a group of his victims, seeking to prevent the sale of more than 40,000 pages of his original writings and correspondence.[x]

In 2012, Kaczynski responded to a standard Harvard University request for updated alumni information. In his reply, he listed his eight life sentences as "awards," and noted that his occupation is "prisoner."[xi]

The case of Ted Kaczynski raises a number of interesting questions. Among them are the following:

1. Although Kaczynski is not a criminologist, it is likely that he would agree with some of the principles of the social conflict perspective. With which of those principles do you think he would be most comfortable? Why?

2. How does Kaczynski being a loner fit with the crimes he committed? Might it indicate that he was in conflict with the wider society? Explain.

3. How might Kaczynski's difficulties with gender relationships provide further evidence of his difficulties with social life in general?

4. What similarities do you see between Kaczynski's writings and those of Karl Marx? (Learn more about Marx at http://www.philosophypages.com/ph/marx.htm.)

Notes:

i. Paul Ferguson, "A Loner from Youth," CNN Interactive, http://www.cnn.com/SPECIALS/1997/unabomb/accused/early (accessed May 28, 2007).

ii. Ted Ottley, "Ted Kaczynski: The Unabomber," CourtTV Crime Library, http://www.crimelibrary.com/terrorists_spies/terrorists/kaczynski/1.html (accessed May 28, 2007).

iii. CNN and Time Interactive, "The Unabomb Case," Cable News Network, http://www.cnn.com/SPECIALS/1997/unabomb/index.html (accessed May 28, 2007).

iv. Ottley, "Ted Kaczynski."

v. "The Unabomber's Manifesto: Industrial Society and Its Future," *Sacramento Bee*, http://www.unabombertrial.com/manifesto/index.html (accessed May 28, 2007).

vi. CNN and Time Interactive, "The Unabomb Case."

vii. Paul Ferguson, "Tracking the Unabomber: More Luck Than Computer Analysis," CNN Interactive, http://www.cnn.com/SPECIALS/1997/unabomb/investigation/puzzle/index.html (accessed May 28, 2007).

viii. "When Your Brother Is the Unabomber," MSNBC, December 29, 2006, http://www.msnbc.msn.com/id/16304477 (accessed May 28, 2007).

ix. "Kaczynski Admits He Is Unabomber, Sentenced to Life without Parole," CNN Interactive, January 22, 1998, http://www.cnn.com/US/9801/22/unabomb.plea (accessed June 16, 2007).

x. Serge F. Kovaleski, "Unabomber Wages Legal Battle to Halt Sale of Papers," *New York Times*, January 22, 2007, http://www.nytimes.com/2007/01/22/us/22unabomber.html?ex=1327122000&en=3fda08d949905a96&ei=5088&partner=rssnyt&emc=rss (accessed May 28, 2007).

xi. Michael Zennie, "Harvard Apologizes for Publishing 50-year Reunion Update from Unabomber Ted Kaczynski that Bragged about His 'Eight Life Sentences,'" *Daily Mail*, May 2012.

criminology had become largely irrelevant. While it may be true that the characteristic Marxist flavor of many early conflict theories has been dampened, radical-critical criminology today remains a vibrant and evolving field. In a recent paper presented to the American Society of Criminology, Walter S. DeKeseredy identified a number of new areas of concern for radical thinkers.[118] One important area, said DeKeseredy, is the study of indigenous populations that includes a need to describe their plight and struggle for change. Crime and social harms experienced by indigenous communities, said DeKeseredy, "cannot be adequately addressed without a thorough, sophisticated understanding of colonialism." DeKeseredy, borrowing from other authors, offered the following definition of colonialism: "the systematic oppression of people through a variety of assimilationist measures that are intended to eradicate the peoples and/or their sense of individual and cultural identify."[119]

A second area of exploration suggested by DeKeseredy is what he terms "the corporatization of institutions of higher learning." One of the dangers of such a process, he says, is the development of applied criminology programs modeled after conservative criminal justice programs that are already being offered nationwide. Such development threatens to marginalize the further development of theory in critical criminology and to limit critical thought within the field. To support his point

of view, DeKeseredy cites Canadian prime minister Stephen Harper, who recently said that criminologists are "ivory tower experts" and "part of society's crime problem." According to DeKeseredy, Harper notes that criminologists "are not criminals themselves, but ... are always making excuses for them, and when they aren't making excuses, they are denying that crime is even a problem."[120]

Policy Implications of Social Conflict Theories

The policy implications of social conflict theory are fairly clear: Bring about social change and redistribute the wealth in society, and crime rates will fall. At one extreme, radical-Marxist criminologists argue that the only effective way of reducing conflict is through a total dismantling of the existing capitalist system in the United States and its replacement by a socialist economic structure. At the other extreme are the calls of peacemaking criminologists for a practical application of the principles of conflict resolution. Between these two extremes lie left realism and feminist criminology, although the solutions they offer vary from the reduction of paternalism in all its forms to a practical recognition of the consequences of crime to victims.

SUMMARY

- Three analytical perspectives on law and social order are discussed in this chapter: the consensus perspective, the pluralist perspective, and the conflict perspective. The consensus perspective is built around the notion that most members of society agree on what is right and wrong and that various elements of society work together toward a

shared vision of the greater good. The pluralistic perspective holds that a multiplicity of values and beliefs exists in any complex society and that each different social group will have its own set of beliefs, interests, and values. The conflict perspective maintains that conflict is a fundamental aspect of social life itself that can never be fully resolved.

- Radical criminology holds that the root causes of crime are found in social conditions empowering the wealthy and the politically well organized but disenfranchising the less successful and that law is a tool of the powerful, who use it to control the less fortunate.

- Six perspectives offer explanations of crime and criminality: left-realist criminology, feminist criminology, postmodern criminology, peacemaking criminology, moral time, and convict criminology. Left-realist criminology is concerned with street crime, fear of crime, and everyday victimization and embraces radical and Marxist criminology. Feminist criminology believes that sexism and an unequal gender-based distribution of power in our patriarchal society affect both crime and its understanding in the field of criminology. Postmodernist criminologists doubt that an objective study of crime is possible and believe that criminology's search for the causes of crime is doomed because its questions are framed by sexist, class-specific, and racist assumptions. Peacemaking criminology restates the problem of crime control from how to stop crime to how to make peace within society and between citizens and criminal justice agencies. Convict criminology is a body of writings on criminology by convicted felons and ex-inmates who have acquired academic credentials or who are associated with credentialed others.

- Conflict theories hold that social conflict and its manifestations are the root causes of crime; the crime-control implications involve redressing injustices to end the marginalization of the politically and economically disadvantaged.

KEY TERMS

androcentricity, 246

Balanced and Restorative Justice (BARJ) model, 252

bourgeoisie, 236

conflict perspective, 235

consensus perspective, 234

convict criminology, 254

critical criminology, 240

deconstructionist theory, 249

feminist criminology, 244

gender gap, 248

instrumental Marxism, 240

left realism, 243

left-realist criminology, 243

liberal feminism, 245

Marxist criminology, 238

Marxist feminism, 246

moral time, 254

participatory justice, 251

patriarchy, 246

peace model, 250

peacemaking criminology, 250

pluralistic perspective, 235

postmodern criminology, 249

postmodern feminism, 246

power-control theory, 247

proletariat, 236

radical criminology, 238

radical feminism, 245

restorative justice, 251

social class, 237

socialist feminism, 246

structural Marxism, 240

KEY NAMES

Freda Adler, 246

Thomas J. Bernard, 255

Willem Bonger, 236

Michael Braswell, 250

K. C. Carceral, 255

Susan Caufield, 247

William J. Chambliss, 239

Meda Chesney-Lind, 246

Ralf Dahrendorf, 238

Kathleen Daly, 246

Walter DeKeseredy, 244

John Hagan, 247

Stuart Henry, 249

John Irwin, 255

Bo Lozoff, 250

Karl Marx, 236

Raymond J. Michalowski, 234

Dragan Milovanovic, 249

Harold E. Pepinsky, 250

Roscoe Pound, 234

Richard Quinney, 239

Jeffrey H. Reiman, 240

Stephen C. Richards, 255

Jeffrey Ian Ross, 255

Rita J. Simon, 246

Carol Smart, 246

Austin Turk, 238

George B. Vold, 237

Nancy Wonders, 247

Jock Young, 244

QUESTIONS FOR REVIEW

1. What three analytical perspectives on law and social order are described in this chapter?

2. What are the central tenets of radical criminology? What are its shortcomings?

3. What six emerging conflict perspectives discussed in this chapter purport to explain crime and criminality?

4. What are the crime-control implications of social conflict theories?

QUESTIONS FOR REFLECTION

1. This text emphasizes the theme of social problems versus individual responsibility. Which of the theoretical perspectives discussed in this chapter (if any) support the social problems approach? Which (if any) support the individual responsibility approach? Why?

2. What are the differences among the consensus, pluralist, and conflict perspectives? Which comes closest to your way of understanding society? Why?

3. What is Marxist criminology? How (if at all) does it differ from radical criminology? From critical criminology?

4. Does the Marxist perspective hold any significance for contemporary American society? Why?

5. What are the fundamental propositions of feminist criminology? How would feminists change the study of crime?

6. What does it mean to say that traditional theories of crime need to be "deconstructed"? What role does deconstructionist thinking play in postmodern criminology?

CHAPTER 10
CRIMINAL VICTIMIZATION

It's Personal

LEARNING OUTCOMES

After reading this chapter, you should be able to answer the following questions:

- What is meant by the *dark figure of crime*, and how is it related to self-report surveys?

- What do official statistics tell us about crime trends in the United States?

- Explain demographics. What kind of demographic features correlate with criminal victimization?

- How can the personal impact of victimization be assessed?

- What is victimology, and what theories of victimization does this chapter discuss?

- Describe the development of victims' rights in the United States, and tell how such rights are recognized.

- Describe restorative justice, and what it means to "make the victim whole again?"

■ **post-traumatic stress disorder (PTSD)** A serious condition that can develop in an individual who has undergone or witnessed traumatic and terrifying experiences, such as crime victimization. PTSD can be characterized by both psychological and physical symptoms, and people who suffer from it will generally experience impaired functioning in various aspects of their lives.

■ **dark figure of crime** The numerical total of unreported crimes not reflected in official crime statistics.
■ **self-report survey** A survey in which respondents, without fear of disclosure or arrest, are asked to confidentially report any violations of the criminal law that they have committed, or victimizations that they have experienced.

Introduction

Recently, the National Criminal Justice Reference Service (NCJRS) developed a special website feature called "Children Exposed to Violence."[1] The site's creation followed release of a special report by the U.S. Attorney's General's National Task Force on Children Exposed to Violence, entitled *Defending Childhood*.[2] In keeping with the report's findings, the website noted that "research suggests that witnessing violence can have detrimental effects similar to being a direct victim of violence." The report also noted that "While there may not always be clear physical signs of exposure to violence, such as bruises and cuts, children often suffer from invisible wounds that affect them emotionally or psychologically." Children who witness or experience violence, said the report, may subsequently suffer symptoms of **post-traumatic stress disorder (PTSD)** or depression that can lead to problems in educational attainment and psychological development.

Perhaps more surprisingly, the National Survey of Children's Exposure to Violence (NatSCEV) found that more than 60% of the children it surveyed were exposed to violence within the year preceding the survey.[3] Survey researchers noted that exposure to violence might have been either direct or indirect (i.e., witnessing a violent attack against a family member, neighbor, or close friend) and that the exposure might have occurred in their own homes, in schools, or elsewhere in their communities. To learn more about the effects of childhood violence, watch the federal Office for Victims of Crime video *Through Our Eyes: Children Violence and Trauma* at **http://www.youtube.com/watch?v=z8vZxDa2KPM**. The full 256-page written report from the U.S. Attorney General's Office can be accessed at **http://justicestudies.com/pubs/defending_childhood.pdf**.

Hidden Victims

Not all crimes are crimes of violence, and many crimes of all kinds never become known to authorities; some are not even uncovered by those who are victimized Figure 10-1 (**dark figure of crime** is a term used to describe the relatively large number of unreported crimes that never come to the attention of officials. Crime's dark figure is sometimes glimpsed through offender and victim self-reports, also known as **self-report surveys**, in which respondents, without fear of disclosure or arrest, are asked to confidentially report any violations of the

CRIME has a big impact often on the very small

Each year, more than half of our children are exposed to violence in their homes, schools, and communities.

They are more likely to suffer from depression and anxiety, abuse drugs and alcohol, or have difficulty in school. And they may go on to commit crimes themselves.

Learn how to take action to protect children. Visit the **Defending Childhood Initiative** at www.justice.gov/defendingchildhood/index.html.

SPONSORED BY: U.S. DEPARTMENT OF JUSTICE • OFFICE OF JUSTICE PROGRAMS • OFFICE FOR VICTIMS OF CRIME

US Department of Justice

An online poster showcasing findings from the National Task Force on Children Exposed to Violence. What are the long-term effects of violence on children who experience or witness it?

criminal law that they have committed, or victimizations that they have experienced.

A recent survey by the Centers for Disease Control and Prevention, for example, found 1.3 million women saying that they had been raped in the year preceding the survey, but only 83,425 of those rapes were reported to the police.[4] Similarly, a recent Canadian sexual assault survey conducted by independent researchers showed a rate more than 100 times higher than official reports of rape.[5] (Rape victimization will be discussed in greater detail in the next chapter.)

While the underreporting of rape is well known, almost all crimes are underreported to some degree. And although the number of *unreported crimes* may be large for at least some types of crime, the number of *undiscovered crimes* is likely larger still and is very difficult to estimate. Undiscovered crimes are those that are not known

■ **victimization** In National Crime Victimization Survey terminology, the harming of any single victim in a criminal incident.
■ **victim** A person who suffers direct or threatened physical, psychological, or financial harm as a result of the commission or attempted commission of a crime or delinquent act.

■ **National Crime Victimization Survey (NCVS)** A survey conducted annually by the Bureau of Justice Statistics that provides data on surveyed households reporting that they were affected by crime.

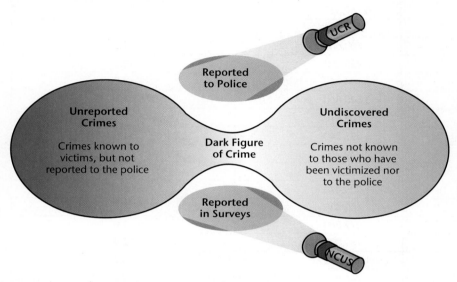

FIGURE 10-1 | The Dark Figure of Crime

even to those who have been victimized. Many undiscovered crimes are committed through the use of high technology and illegal access to digital information (and money) through social media or Internet-based transactions. Some notorious offenses, like the classic Nigerian e-mail scheme, in which a victim is promised huge sums of money after making a "small" initial investment, may even lead victims to think that they are fortunate to have participated. Other crimes, including white-collar pyramid schemes, in which early investors are paid off with proceeds from later participants, may never face law enforcement scrutiny as long as the nature of the **victimization** remains unknown. Bernie Madoff, a famous Ponzi schemer, bilked stock investors of as much as $18 billion, and might never have been caught but for economic circumstances that impacted the entire American economy—causing his scheme to spiral out of control. Undiscovered offenses are responsible for a significant level of victimization in the virtual world and can have very significant impacts on people's lives, although they frequently remain hidden or are found out only with the passage of time.

Victimization by the Numbers

As noted in Chapter 1, no study of crime would be complete without a consideration of victimization and of the role that victims play in the criminal event. To better understand

victims and victimization, it is necessary to gain an appreciation for how crime is measured. Consequently, this section examines how crime statistics are gathered, how they are accessed, and how they impact our view of crime and victimization.

The government-sponsored gathering of crime data for the nation as a whole began in the United States around 1930. Before then, the gathering of crime statistics was random at best, and most accounts of victimization were anecdotal and spread by word of mouth or were printed in local newspapers (or both).

Today, official U.S. crime statistics are available through two major sources. One, an annual survey-based self-reporting program conducted under the auspices of the Bureau of Justice Statistics (BJS), is the National Crime Victimization Survey (NCVS). The other, run by the Federal Bureau of Investigation (FBI), is known as the Uniform Crime Reporting (UCR) program. The UCR program also includes data from the newer National Incident-Based Reporting System (NIBRS), and we will refer to it as the UCR/NIBRS program. The major difference between the BJS's NCVS and the FBI's UCR/NIBRS can be found in the fact that the UCR/NIBRS program reports data on crimes that come to the attention of law enforcement authorities largely through victim complaints filed with the police, while the NCVS is survey-based, which means that it relies upon information collected by interviewers who gather data through the canvassing of randomly selected households.

The National Crime Victimization Survey (NCVS)

The Bureau of Justice Statistics' (BJS) **National Crime Victimization Survey (NCVS)** is the primary information source in the United States on the number and nature of criminal victimization incidents research.[6] As already mentioned, the NCVS uses self-report interviews to gather information on nonfatal personal crimes (rape or sexual assault, robbery, aggravated and simple assault, and personal larceny) and household property crimes (burglary, motor vehicle theft, and other theft). Interviewers gather

TABLE 10-1 | **NCVS: Violent Victimization by Type of Crime**

TYPE OF VIOLENT CRIME	NUMBER	RATE PER 1,000
Violent crime	5,749,330	21.1
Rape/sexual assault	323,450	1.2
Robbery	500,680	1.8
Assault	4,925,200	18.1
Aggravated assault	1,084,340	4.0
Simple assault	3,840,860	14.1
Domestic violence	1,109,610	4.1
Intimate partner violence	597,740	2.2
Stranger violence	2,232,260	8.2
Violent crime involving injury	1,366,250	5.0
Serious violent crime	1,908,470	7.0
Serious domestic violence	402,430	1.5
Serious intimate partner violence	272,380	1.0
Serious stranger violence	789,370	2.9
Serious violent crime involving weapons	1,267,810	4.7
Serious violent crime involving injury	746,850	2.7

Note: Rate per 1,000 persons ages 12 and older.
Source: Bureau of Justice Statistics, National Crime Victimization Survey, 2016.

data on crimes, whether or not those offenses have been reported to police. Consequently, a unique feature of the NCVS is that it collects data on both reported and unreported crimes.

Each year, BJS surveys a nationally representative sample of approximately 164,000 persons age 12 or older living in U.S. households. All first interviews are conducted in person, while subsequent interviews, if any, are conducted either in person or by phone. NCVS data provide information about the victim and the offender for each self-reported victimization incident (e.g., age, race/ethnicity, gender, and victim–offender relationship), characteristics of the crime (including time and place of occurrence, use of weapons, nature of injury, and economic consequences), whether the victimization was reported to police, reasons the offense was or was not reported, and victim experiences with the criminal justice system. Table 10-1 shows 2016 violent victimization rates using NCVS data, while Figure 10-2 shows NCVS victimization rates from 1993 to 2016.

NCVS data are available through a number of venues. One, a print and online publication called *Criminal Victimization*, takes the form of an annual report that covers the broad range of detailed information collected by the NCVS. The second, the *NCVS Victimization Analysis Tool*, is an online database through which users can explore victimization rates, crime counts, and percentages using a range of victim and offense characteristics. BJS also periodically publishes detailed reports on topics such as intimate partner violence, workplace violence, hate crime, and crime against persons with disabilities. The National Archive of Criminal Justice Data at the University of Michigan maintains the NCVS datafiles to enable researchers to perform independent analyses on newly collected and historical data. The NCVS Victimization Analysis Tool can be reached via **http://www.bjs.gov/index.cfm?ty=nvat**.

Critique of the NCVS

The NCVS can be criticized for possible overreporting because it is difficult to verify the actual occurrence of crimes reported to NCVS interviewers. Hence, no reliable measure exists as to the number of crimes that might be falsely reported or of the number of crimes that might be underreported in NCVS data. There are many likely causes of misreporting. Some individuals, when approached by NCVS interviewers, may be unable to resist embellishing victimization reports pertaining to their households and may even concoct victimization data for purposes of self-aggrandizement or in an attempt to please the interviewer by providing copious

■ **Uniform Crime Reporting (UCR) program**   A Federal Bureau of Investigation data-gathering initiative that provides an annual tally of statistics consisting primarily of information on crimes reported to the police and on arrests.

■ **National Incident-Based Reporting System (NIBRS)**   An enhanced statistical reporting system to collect data on each incident and arrest within 22 crime categories.
■ **Office for Victims of Crime (OVC)**   A federal office that administers the Crime Victims Fund and that provides funds and assistance to help victims of crime throughout the United States.

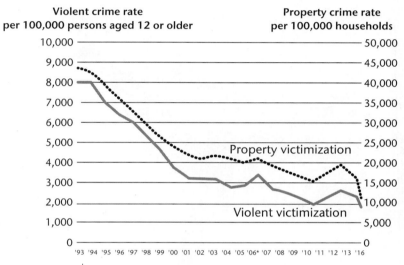

FIGURE 10-2 │ **Victimization Rates from the National Crime Victimization Survey, 1993–2016**

Source: Adapted from Bureau of Justice Statistics, National Crime Victimization Survey, 2016.

amounts of data. Similarly, certain subgroups are not contacted by NCVS surveyors, including anyone not living in a household. Homeless people and those living in institutions like hospitals, prisons, battered women's shelters, and so on are excluded from the sample. Also, the NCVS only interviews respondents aged 12 or older, so crimes against younger victims are not included.

The NCVS program is much newer than the FBI's UCR Program, and comparisons between the programs are not available before 1973. As with the UCR/NIBRS, definitions of crimes measured by the NCVS do not necessarily correspond to any federal or state statutes or to definitions used for other purposes, making comparisons with other state and federal crime records difficult. Similarly, the NCVS covers only a very small number of crimes—it doesn't include homicide, crimes against businesses, federal crimes or white-collar crime. Complicating matters still further, changes in NCVS categories have resulted in the inability to easily compare NCVS findings of even a decade ago with current NCVS data.[7] Finally, the NCVS does not attempt to verify the information in the surveys that it conducts and has to assume that respondents are being honest and forthright.

The Uniform Crime Reporting Program (UCR)

The FBI's **Uniform Crime Reporting program** had its start in 1929, when the International Association of Chiefs of Police (IACP) began publishing information on reported crimes. Since 1930, the FBI has administered the program, which currently collects information on murder and non-negligent manslaughter, rape, robbery, aggravated assault, burglary, larceny-theft, motor vehicle theft, arson, human trafficking, cargo theft, and hate crimes. Law enforcement agencies report arrest data for 24 offense categories through the program's **National Incident-Based Reporting System**. UCR/NIBRS data come from monthly law enforcement reports or individual crime incident records transmitted directly to the FBI or to centralized agencies that then report that information to the FBI.

The federal **Office for Victims of Crime (OVC)** says that NIBRS reporting, because of the additional detail contained in its reports, provides eight specific benefits to victim service providers that go beyond traditional UCR reports. They are as follows:

1. Provision of a broad range of crime data
2. Victimization data that are categorized by age and type of crime
3. Data on victim–offender relationships
4. Information on the timing of victimizations
5. Data on victimizations involving weapons
6. Data on co-occurring victimization in a given offense
7. Statistics on case clearances
8. A more complete picture of crime and victimization.[8]

Figure 10-3 shows combined rates of violent and property crime by county, using UCR/NIBRS data.

The FBI publishes its findings in a preliminary release in the spring of each year, followed by a detailed annual report called *Crime in the United States*, which is issued in the fall.

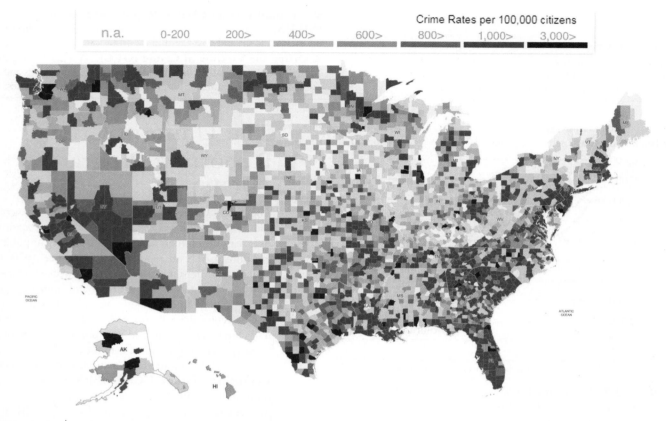

FIGURE 10-3 | Crime Rates by County

Source: FBI, Uniform Crime Reports.

In addition to crime counts and trends, the UCR report includes data on crimes cleared, persons arrested (by age, gender, and race), law enforcement personnel, and the characteristics of homicides (including age, gender, and race of victims and offenders; victim–offender relationships; weapons used; and circumstances surrounding the homicides). The UCR Program also generates other periodic reports, including an important series of documents describing the incidence of hate crimes.

Critique of UCR/NIBRS

The most significant feature of the UCR/NIBRS program is indicated by its name. It is a *reporting* program. In other words, only crimes that are reported to the police (or that are discovered by the police or by others who then report them to the police) are included in the victimization statistics compiled by the program. Most complaints are made by victims, and not all victims go to the police. Reasons for not doing so may include embarrassment, fear of the law (as in the case of undocumented aliens), fear of retaliation from victimizers, or even a simple inability to communicate.

Some experts say, for example, that rape is the most underreported crime in the FBI data, with four to five times as many rapes occurring each year as are reported. Reasons for not reporting a crime such as rape are numerous and include fear of the perpetrator, shame, fears the victim may have of not being believed, and fear of participation in the justice system.

Although rape is indeed seriously underreported (a conclusion drawn from comparison of NCVS and UCR/NIBRS rape statistics), many other crimes are likely underreported as well. The most seriously underreported crime may be larceny because the theft of small items never makes it into official police reports.

As with the NCVS, definitional problems exist within the UCR/NIBRS program. Attempts to address those problems can lead to difficulties in comparing data over time. A few years ago, for example, the URC/NIBRS definition of "rape," which had previously only included the rape of females, was changed to include all genders (see the next chapter for additional information).

Another problem can be found in the fact that only 5,000 of the nation's approximately 200,000 law enforcement agencies currently report *complete* crime data in NIBRS format—and many of those that do are small town or rural agencies. Agency participation in NIBRS was originally anticipated at much higher levels, but the current lack of participation has necessitated the creation of the National Crime Statistics Exchange (NCS-X). NCS-X is a BJS-led statistical sampling program that aims to collect complete crime data from 400 large city police departments (from among the approximately 15,000 non-NIBRS reporting police agencies), with the goal of providing detailed national estimates of the volume and characteristics of crimes known to law enforcement. NCS-X works by combining data from those 400 agencies with reported NIBRS data from law enforcement agencies that are already fully NIBRS compliant. Many of the compliant agencies are small, but the participation of 400 large agencies in the NCS-X program permits the application of statistical techniques that provide a more accurate national picture of crime than would be otherwise possible.

Comparing the UCR/NIBRS and the NCVS

The NCVS and the UCR/NIBRS share many similarities. Essentially, the two programs measure the same subset of serious crimes: rape, robbery, aggravated assault, burglary, theft, and motor vehicle theft, although the NCVS does not gather murder statistics. For data-gathering purposes, rape, robbery, theft, and motor vehicle theft are defined virtually identically by both the UCR/NIBRS and the NCVS. The major definitional exception is the crime of burglary which the UCR/NIBRS defines as the unlawful entry or attempted entry of a structure to commit a felony or theft. The NCVS defines burglary as the entry or attempted entry of a residence by a person who had no right to be there.

There are other significant differences between the programs. The UCR/NIBRS program's primary objective is to provide a reliable set of crime statistics for law enforcement administration, operation, and management. BJS, however, established the NCVS to provide researchers with previously unavailable information about victimization (including victimizations not reported to police) and victim and offender characteristics. Consequently, the two programs measure an overlapping but nonidentical set of crimes. The NCVS includes, but the UCR/NIBRS excludes, sexual assault (completed, attempted, and threatened), attempted robberies, verbal threats of rape, simple assault, and crimes not reported to law enforcement. The UCR/NIBRS includes, but the NCVS

excludes, homicide, arson, commercial crimes, and crimes against children under age 12.

Changing Offense Patterns

Since official crime statistics were first gathered around 1930, there have been three major shifts in victimization patterns.[9] The first occurred during the early 1940s at the outbreak of World War II, when crime decreased sharply due to the large number of young men who entered military service.

> Larcenies are the least likely crime to be reported.

Young males make up the most "crime-prone" segment of the population, and their participation in the war efforts abroad did much to lower rates of reported victimization at home. From 1933 to 1941, victimization rates declined from 770 to 508 offenses per every 100,000 members of the U.S. population.[10]

The second significant shift in victimization statistics was a dramatic increase in most forms of crime that began in the 1960s and ended in the 1990s. Many criminologists believe that this shift also had a link to World War II. With the end of the war and the return of millions of young men to civilian life, birth rates skyrocketed between 1945 and 1955, creating a postwar baby boom. By 1960, baby boomers were entering their teenage years. A disproportionate number of young people in the U.S. population produced a dramatic increase in most major crimes.

Other factors contributed to the increase in reported victimizations during the same period. Crimes that may have gone undetected in the past began to figure more prominently in official statistics. Similarly, the growing professionalization of some police departments resulted in more accurate and increased data collection, making some of the most progressive departments appear to be associated with the largest crime increases.[11] Finally, the 1960s were tumultuous years, punctuated by the Vietnam War, a vibrant civil rights struggle, the heady growth of secularism, dramatic increases in the divorce rate, diverse forms of "liberation," and the influx of psychedelic and other drugs. As a consequence, social norms were blurred and group control over individual behavior declined substantially. According to the FBI, from 1960 to 1980, victimization rates rose from 1,887 to 5,950 offenses per every 100,000 members of the U.S. population.

Victimization rates recorded by the FBI continued to remain high, with the exception of a brief decline in the early 1980s, when postwar boomers began to "age out" of the crime-prone years and U.S. society emerged from the cultural drift that had characterized the previous 20 years. At about the same time, however, an increase in drug-related criminal activity led victimization rates to soar once again, especially in the area of violent crime. UCR/NIBRS-reported victimizations peaked around 1991 and have since shown a third major shift, with decreases in the rates of most major crimes being reported since that time. Between 1991 and 2016, the victimization rate decreased from 5,898 to 2,837 offenses per every 100,000 citizens, sending it down to levels not seen since 1968.

Decreases in crime rates since the mid-1990s may have been largely due to an "aging out" of the post–World War II baby-boomer generation (members of which are now mostly too old to continue active criminal lifestyles), new strict laws, expanded justice system and police funding, changes in crime-fighting technologies, economic factors, and the increase in forms of crime not readily counted by official reporting programs. In 2013, in an article published in the journal *Crime Science*, Graham Farrell, Professor of International Comparative Criminology at the University of Leeds in England, examined fifteen hypotheses that have been proposed to explain the decrease in "street crime" that has occurred throughout much of the Western world since 1990.[12] Hypotheses that were tested included decreased lead poisoning among young people; abortion legalization; the decriminalization of drugs; changing immigration and migration patterns; increased policing and criminal punishments; use of the death penalty; changes in gun laws; improved security; and various aspects of changing demographics (Table 10-2). Farrell was able to reject fourteen of the fifteen hypotheses, and found that only the security hypothesis held true explanatory power. The security hypothesis, based on the notion of situational crime prevention, is a relatively simple explanation for crime's decline—and says that improved security measures that have been put in place since the early 1990s have reduced criminal opportunities, and have therefore lowered rates of street crime.

While the 25-year-long decline in reported victimization that took place in the United States beginning in 1991 is noteworthy, it did not even begin to bring the overall rate of street crime in this country anywhere close to the low crime rates characteristic of the early 1940s and the 1950s. From a long-term perspective, even with recent declines, rates of reported criminal victimizations in the United States remain more than seven times what they were in 1940.

Some evidence seems to indicate that the decline in U.S. crime is ending and that we may be on the cusp of a new cycle of increased criminal activity.[13] Part of that potential increase may come in the form of new and innovative forms of victimization that are not easily captured by official measures. Many types of crimes today are Internet-based or involve advanced technology. Neither the UCR nor the NCVS count computer crimes among the major crime categories that they report, although these types of offenses are sometimes subsumed under the category of "larceny" because they frequently involve the theft of money or other things of value. Additionally, the specter of random mass shootings, a high number of inner-city murders, and novel forms of criminal activity complicate today's victimization picture.

> The specter of random mass shootings, a high number of inner-city murders, and novel forms of criminal activity complicate today's victimization picture.

TABLE 10-2 | Fifteen Hypotheses Offered to Explain the Drop in Crime Rates That Began in the Early 1990s

NAME	MECHANISM
Strong economy	Wealthy offenders commit less crime
Concealed weapons laws	More defensive guns, less crime
Capital punishment	More death penalty deterred crime
Gun control laws	Less guns, less crime
Rising prison population	Incapacitation and deterrence reduce crime
Policing strategies	Policing focused on crime problems (Compstat, POP)
More police	More police detected and deterred crime
Legalization of abortion	More abortion since 1973, less offenders by 1990s
Immigration	Immigrants commit less crime, so crime fell as immigration rose
Consumer confidence	Wealthy buy less from stolen goods markets
Waning crack market	Second-generation youth deterred by violence and prison for elders
Childhood lead	Lead poisoning of children made them adolescent criminals
Changing demographics	Aging population means relatively less young offenders
Civilizing process	Social institutions more legitimate (1960s–80s = age of protest)
Improved security	Improved security, reduced crime opportunities

Source: Graham Farrell, "Five Tests for a Theory of the Crime Drop," *Crime Science*, Vol. 2, No. 5 (2013).

■ **demographics** The characteristics of population groups, usually expressed in statistical fashion.

Demographic Correlates of Victimization

Demographics describe the statistical qualities of a given population. While victims of crime may be of any gender, age, race, or ethnicity, demographic characteristics are significantly correlated with victimization risk (Table 10-3). Young single women, for example, are more likely to be sexually victimized than any other subgroup in the American population. In general, however, studies show that the "typical victim" of violent crime is a socioeconomically disadvantaged young black male, especially one living in the inner-city region of a large metropolitan area.[14] This is not to say that females and older people are not similarly victimized; they are, but the rate of violent victimization is notably higher for young African-American males than for other demographic groups.

In and of itself, demographic characteristics tell us nothing about why victimization occurs. Even so, a number of additional social factors can be identified that are associated with increased risk of victimization. They include the region of the country in which a person lives, and family factors including low socioeconomic status (SES), family criminal history (parental crime), single-parent household, and poor parental supervision.[15] According to information published by the Bureau of Justice Statistics in 2017, those living in urban locations were 150% more likely to be violently victimized than people in rural areas; while those in the South were considerably less likely to be violently victimized than people living in the Northeastern or Western parts of the United States. Risk of property crime, however, was highest in the West and South, but slightly lower in the Midwest, and lowest of all in the Northeast.

A recent BJS compilation of victimization data (Figure 10-4) shows that persons living in poor households at or below the Federal Poverty Level (FPL) (39.8 per 1,000) have more than double the rate of violent victimization as do persons in high-income

TABLE 10-3 | Violent Victimization Rates by Victim Demographic Characteristics, 2004, 2012, and 2016

VICTIM DEMOGRAPHIC CHARACTERISTIC	VIOLENT CRIME		
	2004	2012	2016
Total	27.8	26.1	21.1
Sex			
Male	30.2	29.1	21.4
Female	25.5	23.3	20.8
Race/Hispanic origin			
White	28.5	25.2	20.5
Black/African American	30.2	34.2	24.1
Hispanic/Latino	20.1	24.5	20.2
Other	34.1	25.1	23.0
Age			
12–17	49.7	48.4	30.9
18–24	55.4	41.0	31.0
25–34	31.2	34.2	31.8
35–49	28.0	29.1	22.9
50–64	15.4	15.0	16.1
65 or older	2.5	5.7	4.4
Marital status			
Never married	46.2	40.7	29.8
Married	13.8	13.5	12.4
Widowed	9.3	8.3	10.7
Divorced	36.7	37.0	30.1
Separated	110.7	83.1	67.5

Note: Rates shown are per 1,000 persons age 12 or older.
Source: Bureau of Justice Statistics, National Crime Victimization Survey, various years.

■ **polyvictimization**   Multiple victimizations of different kinds, such as sexual abuse, physical abuse, bullying, and exposure to family violence.

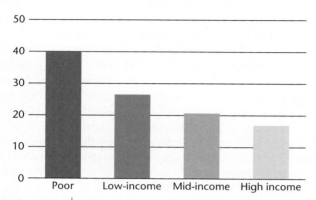

FIGURE 10-4 | **Rate of Violent Victimization, by Household Poverty Level (per 1,000 Persons Age 12 or Older)**

Note: "Poor" refers to households at 0% to 100% of the Federal Poverty Level (FPL). "Low income" refers to households at 101% to 200% of the FPL. "Mid-income" refers to households at 201% to 400% of the FPL. "High income" refers to households at 401% or higher than the FPL.
Source: Erika Harrell, Lynn Langton, Marcus Berzofsky, Lance Couzens, and Hope Smiley-McDonald, *Household Poverty and Nonfatal Violent Victimization, 2008–2012* (Washington, DC: Bureau of Justice Statistics, 2014), p. 1.

households (16.9 per 1,000).[16] The percentage of persons reporting violence to police is also higher among households at or below the FPL. More than half of victims of violence from poor households (51%) reported the victimization to police compared to 45% of victims from high-income households.

Finally, victimization risk varies considerably by type of crime. Young minority women, and especially those living with male partners, for example, are more likely than other demographic groups to experience domestic violence. Similarly, victims of white-collar crime are more likely to be older and to be of relatively high socioeconomic status.

Revictimization and Polyvictimization

People who are demographically situated in such a way as to be at high risk for victimization are often polyvictimized, meaning that they are likely to be repeatedly victimized. **Polyvictimization**, a concept that entered the criminological literature only a few years ago, recognizes the ripple effects of victimization.[17] It acknowledges that victimization can lead to more and continued victimization as people lose the ability to defend themselves or their property through loss of financial resources, livelihood, and psychological and physical health—all due to earlier instances of victimization.

Polyvictimization (also called *multiple victimization*) refers to multiple instances of *varied* victimizations, that is, to victimizations of different kinds, such as sexual abuse, physical

abuse, bullying (see Chapter 11), and exposure to family violence.[18] According to some writers, polyvictimization "appears to signal a more generalized vulnerability [than other kinds of victimizations]."[19] In a study of polyvictimized children, it was found that the demographic characteristics (Table 10-4) that distinguish polyvictims of violence from children who are less exposed to violence include (1) the more serious nature of their victimizations; (2) the greater range of victimizations they suffer; and (3) their overrepresentation among certain demographic groups (i.e., boys, older children, children of medium socioeconomic status, African-American children, and children in single-parent, stepparent, and other adult caregiver families).

TABLE 10-4 | **Polyvictimization Rates by Demographic Characteristics**

CHARACTERISTIC	POLYVICTIM (%)
Gender	
Female	7.5
Male	8.4
Age Group	
2–5 Years	5.2
6–9 Years	4.0
10–13 Years	9.5
14–17 Years	13.0
Socioeconomic Status	
Low	7.3
Middle	8.8
High	4.7
Race/Ethnicity	
White, non-Hispanic	7.7
Black, non-Hispanic	12.8
Other Race, non-Hispanic	7.9
Hispanic, Any Race	4.5
Family Structure	
Two-Parent Family	5.2
Stepparent or Partner Family	12.8
Single-Parent Family	12.4
Other Adult Caregiver	13.9
City Residence (300,000 + population)	
Yes	8.3
No	7.8

Source: David Finkelhor, Heather Turner, Sherry Hamby, and Richard Ormrod, *Polyvictimization: Children's Exposure to Multiple Types of Violence, Crime, and Abuse* (Washington, DC: Office of Juvenile Justice and Delinquency Prevention, 2011), p. 7.

WHO'S TO BLAME—The Individual or Society?

He Stood His Ground

In mid-2017, Walter Thorton of Misabella, Idaho, was app-roached by two strangers as he pumped gas into his pickup truck only a mile from his home. The men began a conversa-tion with Thorton, but it quickly became clear that they wanted money. Thorton told them that he didn't have anything to give them. The men became more aggressive and started to shove Thorton, pushing him up against his truck. "Who do you think you are, man?" They said. "Do you think you're better than us?" The shoving quickly turned into a scuffle when one of the men reached for Thorton's wallet. Thorton, feeling afraid that the men might hurt him, and not wanting to lose his wal-let, reached into his right front pants pocket for a snub-nosed .38-calibre revolver that he always carried. As Thorton reached into his pocket, one of the men—the rougher looking of the two—reached into his own pocket. Thorton didn't know what the man was reaching for, but thought that it must have been a gun or a knife. Before the man could remove it, however, Thorton fired a shot that hit the man in the chest. He fell to the ground with blood squirting out of his chest. Seeing what hap-pened, the other would-be-robber ran away.

The entire incident was captured on gas station security cameras, although they recorded only video and not sound. The gas station attendant called police and Thorton remained at the scene until they arrived. EMT personnel arrived quickly and took the wounded man to a hospital, where he later died.

Misabella is a small town, and news about the shooting quickly spread, causing the county prosecutor to hastily call a news conference. "Mr. Thorton," explained the prosecu-tor, "has been arrested and charged with second degree murder." He went on to say, "Our courts operate under a long-established castle doctrine, in which a person can use reasonable force to protect themselves, their friends and family, and their property, when someone attacks them when they are in their home or at their place of residence. Unlike some other states," he continued, "Idaho does not have what is commonly referred to as a 'stand-your ground' law. In Idaho, if you feel you are in danger, you have a duty

Pumping fuel at a gas station. What do you think of "stand-your-ground" laws?

Daniel Dillon/Alamy Stock Photo

to retreat—to move away from the threat or from those who are threatening you—until you no longer have a clear path of retreat. Then, and only then, are you permitted under our law to use deadly force to protect yourself. Mr. Thorton had a duty under law to retreat; but he did not retreat. He shot and killed a man who would likely still be alive today if he had."

Think about it

1. Who was the victim in this scenario? Thorton or the man whom he shot?

2. Should Thorton have tried to move away and put distance between himself and the men? Would doing so have been reasonable under the circumstances? Would it have in-creased the danger he was in?

3. Although the Idaho legislature has not passed a stand-your-ground law, some legal experts suggest that the right to stand your ground can be found in precedent-setting decisions by the state's courts (see, for example, State v. McGreevey, 105 P. 1047, ID Supreme Court 1909). If you were in Thorton's shoes, would you feel comfortable mak-ing an argument before a judge that was based on such case law?

Note: Who's to Blame boxes provide fictionalized critical thinking opportunities based on actual cases.

A notable characteristic of polyvictimization is the far greater level of additional lifetime adversities and levels of distress that polyvictimized children suffer. Polyvictims are more likely to have other kinds of lifetime adversities such as illnesses, accidents, family unemployment, parental substance abuse, and mental illness (an average of 4.7 ad-versities vs.2.1 for nonpolyvictims). Moreover, they are at a disadvantage when it comes to future life experiences and suffer from greater rates of poverty, incarceration, drug use, and mental illness later in life than do people who were not

victims of multiple crimes or of multiple offenders when they were children.

A study of polyvictimized children found that they "were considerably more distressed than the children who were vic-tims of one type of chronic victimization but did not have additional different kinds of victimization." The study noted that having multiple sexual victimizations, for example, was not associated with nearly as much distress as having any sexual victimization in combination with several other different kinds of victimization. Study authors wrote "that among children

■ **revictimization**   Multiple episodes of the same kind of victimization.

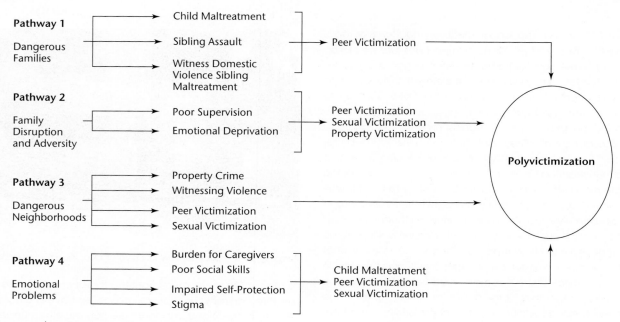

FIGURE 10-5 | Pathways to Polyvictimization

Source: David Finkelhor, Heather Turner, Sherry Hamby, and Richard Ormrod, *Polyvictimization: Children's Exposure to Multiple Types of Violence, Crime, and Abuse* (Washington, DC: Office of Juvenile Justice and Delinquency Prevention, 2011), p. 9.

identified with a single kind of victimization (such as sexual assault), the ones with the most distress will generally be those with other kinds of victimization as well."

A related term, **revictimization**, refers to continued victimization by the same offender committing the same type of crime. Revictimization, while still quite serious in its consequences, does not appear to create the same degree of lasting social and other handicaps as does polyvictimization. *Repeat victimization* and *chronic victimization* are other terms used by victimiologists to describe continued victimization of the same individual.

The Developmental Victimization Survey (DVS)

The Developmental Victimization Survey (DVS), conducted between December 2002 and February 2003 by American Sociologist David Finkelhor and colleagues, was based on a national telephone survey involving a sample of 2,030 children and youth between the ages of 10 and 17.[20] Children were interviewed about their own victimization experiences, and the parents or other caregivers of children ages 2 to 9 provided information about younger children. DVS researchers also conducted two follow-up surveys of the same population in the years that followed. A total of 989 respondents took part in all three survey waves.

Using the DVS, researchers developed and tested a conceptual model that specifies four distinct pathways for children culminating in polyvictimization (see Figure 10-5). The four pathways are: (1) living in a "dangerous family"—or one that experiences considerable violence and conflict (dangerous family); (2) having a family beset with problems around such things as money, employment, and substance abuse that might compromise a child's supervision or create unmet emotional needs (family disruption and adversity); (3) residing in or moving into a dangerous community (dangerous neighborhoods); and (4) being a child with preexisting emotional problems that increase risky behavior, create antagonism, and compromise the capacity for self-protection. The study confirmed that each of these pathways contributes independently to the onset of polyvictimization.[21] The emotional problems pathway was most prominent for children younger than 10 years old, while the other pathways appeared to be more associated with children aged 10 and older.

The Personal Impact of Criminal Victimization

In this section, we examine the personal effects of victimization, looking at things such as psychological, physical, economic, and social impacts of victimization.

The Socio-emotional Impact of Victimization

Researchers have long known that crime victims can be significantly impacted by the experience of victimization. One researcher who surveyed crime victims found that "Almost all respondents reported that their lives had changed forever."[22] Crime victims may have trouble sleeping or concentrating, may be easily startled, might fail to participate in activities they once enjoyed, and may develop lowered self-esteem.[23] In 2014, the Bureau of Justice Statistics (BJS) reported on a multiyear study of crime victims.[24] The study, which examined the personal impact of violent crime, found that 68% of victims of serious violence experienced socio-emotional problems as a result of their victimization.[25] Victims of intimate partner violence reported significantly greater feelings of distress than victims of stranger violence, and a greater percentage of female than male victims reported experiencing socio-emotional problems, regardless of the type of violence or victim–offender relationship. Although most of the stress symptoms experienced by victims were found to be emotional (i.e., feelings of being worried or anxious, angry, unsafe, violated, vulnerable, distrustful, sad or depressed), 61% of victims experienced one or more physical symptoms (i.e., trouble sleeping, fatigue, upset stomach, muscle tension, high blood pressure, headaches, problems with eating or drinking) for a month or more. Those symptoms are characteristic of PTSD, mentioned at the start of this chapter.

Figure 10-6 shows the level of distress experienced by violent crime victims in the BJS study, by type of problems experienced as a result of victimization, while Figure 10-7 displays the level of distress experienced by victims by type of crime. Although the type of crime made a significant difference in the number and degree of socio-emotional problems experienced by victims, BJS researchers found no consistent relationship between the presence or absence of a weapon or an injury with the degree of such problems. An exception was robbery, where a higher percentage of victims of robbery involving

A young female crime victim. Victimization often leaves people in a compromised socio-emotional state and can result in post-traumatic stress syndrome (PTSD). What can be done to help victims of crime?

both an injury and weapon (85%) experienced socio-emotional problems, compared to victims of robbery that did not involve an injury or weapon. Similarly, the location where violent victimizations occurred also affected the likelihood of victims experiencing socio-emotional problems. Overall, a greater percentage of victims who were victimized in their home (80%) reported socio-emotional problems than victims of violence in other locations. Finally, BJS researchers also found that experiencing socio-emotional problems may influence whether a victim chooses to seek formal help, such as reporting to police or seeking out victim services. Overall, a greater percentage of victims of violence who experienced socio-emotional problems (54%) reported their victimization to police than victims who did not experience socio-emotional problems (38%).

Finally, another study found that a large number of victims of personal crimes reported "drinking, smoking, using drugs more often since the offense." That study found that many victims were

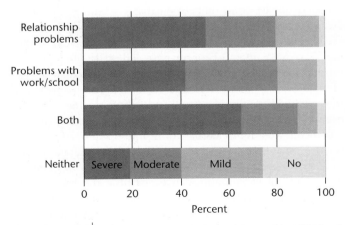

FIGURE 10-6 | Level of Distress Experienced by Violent Crime Victims, by Type of Problems Experienced as a Result of Victimization

Source: Lynn Langton and Jennifer Truman, "Socio-emotional Impact of Violent Crime," BJS Special Report, September 2014, p. 2.

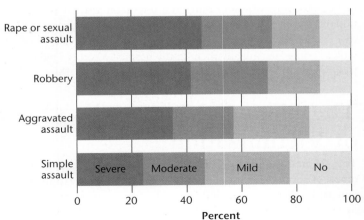

FIGURE 10-7 | Level of Distress Experienced by Violent Crime Victims, by Type of Crime

Source: Lynn Langton and Jennifer Truman, "Socio-emotional Impact of Violent Crime," BJS Special Report, September 2014, p. 3.

■ **secondary victimization**   Social injuries that occur, not as a direct result of a criminal act, but through the response of social institutions and individuals to the victim.

■ **secondary victims**   Persons not directly affected by a criminal event, but who suffer unintended consequences of the victimization of others to whom they are close, such as family members, friends, coworkers, and neighbors.

critical with themselves for having been victimized, and that many expressed a need to "understand why it happened." A large percentage felt isolated and alone, and even more wanted to inform the offender of how the crime affected them. Finally quite a few victims reported being afraid of retaliation by the offender.[26]

The Physical Impact of Victimization

While some crimes result in direct physical injury, others—particularly those that are violent and confrontational—produce other kinds of physical reactions in those who are victimized.[27] Physical impacts other than injury may include stimulation of the fight-or-flight response, which includes increases in blood-level adrenalin, increased heart rate, hyperventilation, shaking, numbness, crying, dryness of the mouth, loss of bowel control, and a sense that things are occurring in slow motion. Physical reactions can recur even after the danger has passed and victims have returned to safety.

Physical injuries can themselves be minor (bumps and scratches), or more serious (gunshot wounds, broken bones), or even deadly. Severe physical injuries can be life-threatening and may result in long-term disability or permanent disfigurement. Sometimes physical injuries that result from criminal victimization are not readily apparent, as is often the case in domestic violence situations where bruising and internal injuries may take time to manifest. Because injuries are not always obvious, law enforcement and other first responders may ask that victims of violent crimes accompany them to the hospital or other medical facility for further examination.

The Financial Impact of Victimization

The financial impact of victimization can be measured in terms of immediate loss resulting from the victimization itself, and other costs, including medical, repairs to property or possessions, mental health services, increased insurance premiums, and the costs associated with the installation of security systems. Participation in the justice system can also have substantial personal costs, including transportation, lost wages, child care, and so on. Likewise, costs associated with relocating a residence in order to move out of a high-crime

area or away from a home that holds fearful memories can be substantial.[28] Victims may find it difficult to concentrate on work and their economic productivity may suffer. Finally, funeral and burial expenses have to be borne by the surviving victims of a murdered family member or relative. The financial burdens of victimization may be especially difficult to bear for the economically marginalized, the young, and the disabled.

Secondary Victimization

Secondary victimization frequently occurs as a result of the initial, or primary, victimization. Secondary victimization, which sometimes blurs the line between victim and offender, refers to social injuries that occur, not as a direct result of the criminal act, but through the response of social institutions and individuals to the victim. A significant form of secondary victimization happens when the justice system imposes requirements on the victim that are difficult to meet, or which interfere with his or her ability to recover from the initial victimization. An overzealous investigator, for example, may be unrelenting in questioning the victim—leaving her with little time to emotionally adjust to the circumstances surrounding the victimization experience and keeping her emotionally and psychologically off balance. In other cases, members of the public may be unsympathetic to the victim, communicating messages via social media or in other ways that say "she got what she deserved"; or "she's the one who should be behind bars." Even friends can tire of hearing the victim's story, and avoid or shun her.[29] Likewise, members of the press and media photographers can intrude on the victim's privacy and file inaccurate reports of what actually took place. The victim may also come to feel frustrated with the justice system and believe that he or she has been extended fewer considerations than the victimizer, or is accorded fewer "rights" as the criminal justice process wends its way to conclusion. Cases that are plea-bargained are most likely to leave the victim feeling that justice has not been done and that additional victimization has occurred at the hands of the justice system. Finally, the social and financial burdens imposed by justice system participation (i.e., attending the trial of one's victimizer) can lead to lost time at work, the inability to fully participate in family life, added child care fees, Uber and taxi costs, and other kinds of expenses.

Secondary victimization should be distinguished from **secondary victims**, who are persons not directly affected by a

■ **victimology**   The scientific study of crime victims and the victimization process. Victimology is a field of study that grew out of criminology.

■ **victimologist**   One who studies victims and the process of criminal victimization.

criminal event, but suffer unintended consequences of the victimization of others whom they are close to, like family members, friends, coworkers, and neighbors.[30]

Art work intended to express the experience of victimization. What is that experience like for crime victims?

Victimization as a Risk Factor for Crime

In 2014, Dana D. DeHart, a social worker at the University of South Carolina, surveyed women at a maximum-security state women's correctional facility in the southeastern United States. Survey results showed that women's victimization can be a significant contributor to future criminal involvement. In a survey of incarcerated women, DeHart identified direct and indirect ways in which victimization can lead to criminality.

> Women in the sample were physically and sexually assaulted by strangers and acquaintances. Their property was vandalized or stolen. They were beaten, raped, tormented, and controlled by relationship partners. Their own children witnessed violence in the home and were subject to abuse. It is not necessary here to provide lurid examples of each type of act, as the focus here is on violence's impact, and readers will gain a fuller perspective throughout the report as we provide examples of impact as embedded in the women's lives.[31]

DeHart found, for example, that sexual abuse can lead to residential dislocation in the lives of many young women, with some running away from homes in which abuse occurs. Once these women are on the streets, they are forced to turn to prostitution, theft, and other forms of criminal activity in order to survive. Similarly, DeHart found that women who engaged in defensive or retaliatory efforts in an effort to end abuse, ended up being arrested and prosecuted for assault. She notes that "The victimization directly preceded the women's crime, and the women acted in response to being pushed, slapped, punched, beaten, choked, raped, or threatened with a weapon."

Other women reported being drawn into crime when forced (often by male partners) to commit crimes, such as shoplifting, check fraud, robbery, prostitution, or even murder. Finally, DeHart found that women's marginalization from mainstream lifestyles, which flowed from lowered self-esteem,

impaired physical and mental health, and poor psychosocial functioning following victimization, influenced their involvement in criminal activities. Sex abuse, for example, often led to unwanted pregnancies that left women with financial and other problems that led to drug abuse as a means of escape from psychological suffering and to offenses like prostitution and theft as an alternative means of support. The loss of jobs attributed to domestic abuse, stalking, and fear of continued victimization also heightened women's financial needs and pushed them into criminal activity. DeHart concluded that the justice system "de-contextualize women's criminal acts in a manner that ignores motivations and responsibilities," which means that women who are forced into crime as consequence of their own victimization are often seen as victimizers when their own victimization should be understood.

Victimology

As mentioned earlier, no study of crime would be complete without a consideration of the role that victims play in the criminal event. **Victimology**, a field of study that developed out of criminology, includes more than just theories and extends to all aspects of the scientific study of criminal victimization, including the process of victimization, the criminal, the victim, the justice system, and society. As such, **victimologists** study particularly vulnerable groups of people and attempt to understand the victimization process.[32] Victimologists can be members of various professional organizations. One of the largest is the World Society of Victimology. The International Victimology Institute at Tilburg University (INTERVICT) in the Netherlands promotes interdisciplinary research that contributes to a comprehensive, evidence-based body of knowledge on the status of victims. You can reach the The American Society of Criminology's Division of Victimology on the Web at **http://ascdov.com**.

■ **victimogenesis** The contributory background of a victim as a result of which he or she becomes prone to criminal victimization.

■ **victim precipitation** Any contribution made by the victim to the criminal event, especially one that led to its initiation.

■ **victim proneness** An individual's likelihood of victimization.

Blaming the Victim: Early Theories of Victim Precipitation

While theories of crime causation frequently focus on the offender, some consider the role of the victim in setting the stage leading up to the criminal event. As noted in Chapter 1, criminal victimization is a complex process involving many parties (the criminal, the victim, the justice system, members of society, and others). Theories that emphasize the role of the victim in crime causation were some of the earliest contributions to the study of victimology.

Victimogenesis is a term that refers to the origin or cause of victimization and includes a cluster of variables that ultimately lead to victimization. Some victims actively contribute to their own victimization by appearing defenseless (i.e., being old and frail, being intoxicated, or displaying a physical disability), by failing to take appropriate defensive measures (leaving doors unlocked or forgetting to remove the key from a vehicle), by displaying wealth (flashing large amounts of cash or other valuables in a public place), or simply by making other unwise choices (like walking down a dark alley off of New York City's Times Square at 3 o'clock in the morning). In any discussion of victimization, however, it is critically important to recognize that while a victim's actions may put him or her in jeopardy, that does not necessarily mean that any subsequent victimization was the victim's fault. In other words, victims should not be blamed for their own victimization, especially when their actions are innocent.

Victim–offender relationships were the focus of first-generation victimologists who classified victims according to the degree to which they contributed to their own victimization. These early victimologists developed the important notions of **victim precipitation** and **victim proneness**. The concept of victim precipitation examines the characteristics of victims, the nature of their surroundings, or the quality of their relationships, insofar as they play a role in precipitating victimization. Victim precipitation builds on observable correlates of victimization to explain why some people are more likely to be victimized than others. So, for example, individuals who live in inner-city high-crime areas are, generally speaking, more likely to become crime victims than those who reside in gated suburban communities. Similarly, those who work in certain occupations (i.e., late-night convenience store clerks) are more likely to become victims of crime than those in certain other occupations (i.e., medical

technologists). Two types of victim precipitation can be distinguished: active and passive. *Passive precipitation* occurs when the victim unknowingly encourages the offender toward criminal action, and *active precipitation* takes place when the victim literally provokes the victimization. First-generation victimologists also developed the term *victim proneness* to refer to an individual's likelihood of victimization.

In addition to this simple dichotomy, victimologists recognize three ways in which victims contribute to their own victimization. The first is *victim facilitation*, which can occur when potential victims fail to take simple precautions against being victimized. Facilitation of victimization may happen when home-owners leave their doors unlocked, when drivers leave keys in their cars, or when purses are left unattended in a restaurant or public place. Victim facilitation can be distinguished from *victim provocation*, in which the victim may be the initial aggressor who has the tables turned on him or her and ends up being injured or killed. Finally, *victim initiation* happens when the victim attracts the offender's attention through certain activities (i.e., hiking alone on an isolated mountain trail) or by visible displays of wealth or other things of interest.

The thrust of the concepts of victim precipitation and victim proneness is not to blame the victim for becoming a victim, but to examine both individual and situational factors that may have contributed to and initiated the crime. This is especially important in studying patterns of homicide, for example, because quite often a homicide begins as a fight or an argument between people who know each other. The circumstances of the particular encounter determine whether the event will end as some type of assault or as a homicide. **Marvin Wolfgang**, a famous pioneer in victim studies, was one of the first researchers to make an effort to assess the extent of victim participation in homicide events. Wolfgang studied Philadelphia homicides in the late 1940s to early 1950s and concluded that 26% were the result of active victim precipitation. Wolfgang found that causative factors in homicide victimization were a personal relationship between the victim and victimizer; a disagreement that careened out of control; and the consumption of alcohol. Wolfgang found that alcohol played an important role in homicide cases where the "victim is a direct, positive precipitator in the crime."[33] He concluded that the positive and significant association between alcohol and victim-precipitated homicides may be explained by the fact that the victim was the "first to slap, punch, stab, or in some other manner commit an assault" and that if the victim had not been drinking, he or she would have been less violent.[34] He also hypothesized that at least some victims of homicide were longing to commit suicide and provoked others to kill them as a way of satisfying that unconscious desire.

Other first-generation victimologists include **Benjamin (or "Beniamin" in his native language) Mendelsohn, Hans von Hentig, Stephen Schafer**, and **Menachem Amir**. Each developed a typology of victims.

Mendelsohn, a Romanian attorney who is often referred to as the *father of victimology*, coined the term *victimology* in 1947 and proposed the creation of a victimological research institute, a journal of victimology, and the establishment of a society for the study of victims.[35] He is best remembered for the creation of a six-part victimology typology based on degree of victim culpability. For the most part, Mendelsohn believed that victims had an unconscious aptitude for victimization. Mendelsohn's six types of victims ranged from the completely innocent victim (i.e., a completely unconscious person or an infant) to the imaginary or simulated victim (i.e., someone who, as a result of a psychological disorder, believes that they have been victimized when in fact they have not). In between were victims with minor guilt, victims as guilty as the offender, and victims with more guilt than the offender. Of his six types, only the completely innocent victim was truly blameless in Mendelsohn's scheme.

Von Hentig, who wrote in the late 1940s, published an important book, *The Criminal and His Victim*, in which he created a taxonomy describing how victims might be responsible for the harms that befell them.[36] Von Hentig classified victims into 13 categories depending on psychological, social, and biological factors, which he believed correlated with victimization risk. Von Hentig's typology of victims included categories such as lonesome and heartbroken, depressive, greedy, wonton, and tormentor. The depressive-type victim was seen as careless and unsuspecting; the greedy type was easily deceived; and the wonton type was needful and therefore vulnerable, while the tormentor type (or fighting victim) brought victimization upon himself.

Schafer, a Hungarian criminologist, published a book in 1968 that played on the title of von Hentig's work. It was called *The Victim and His Criminal*.[37] Schafer used the term "functional responsibility" in assigning victims to categories that he envisioned as based on the degree of provocation in which they engaged. His typology, which included victims with no functional responsibility (i.e., the completely innocent victim), to those with total responsibility (i.e., self-victimizing), included the following types:

1. Unrelated victims (with no victim responsibility)
2. Provocative victims (victim shares responsibility)
3. Precipitative victims (with some degree of victim responsibility)
4. Biologically weak victims (with no victim responsibility)
5. Socially weak victims (with no victim responsibility)
6. Self-victimizing (who has total victim responsibility)
7. Political victim (with no victim responsibility)

Amir, whose work was published in the early 1970s, focused largely on the crime of rape. He found that 19% of all forcible rapes involving female victims were caused by the use of alcohol (by both parties), seductive behavior or conversation on the part of the victim, and provocative clothing. Amir's research was intensely criticized by the feminist movement that began about the time he published his findings. Some said, however, that Amir's critics, failed to appreciate the fact that victim precipitation and victim blaming are not the same thing.

The idea that victims are somehow selected for victimization based on personal traits is still being explored. In 2013, for example, the results of a study published in the *Journal of Interpersonal Violence* suggested that people are sometimes mugged because of the way they walk. Researchers found that an unsteady or slow gait reveals to potential robbers that the victim is slow, unable to escape, and unable to defend him- or herself—and makes an ideal target for interpersonal crime.[38]

Victimization and Lifestyle

Theories of victimology, which developed in the late 1970s, moved the focus away from the role of victim characteristics as a central cause of victimization and examined the choices that people make that increase their availability to offenders and make them easier targets for crime.[39] Two major approaches embodying this approach are lifestyle theory and the routine activities approach, which are discussed in what follows.

Lifestyle Theory

Michael J. Hindelang, **Michael R. Gottfredson**, and **James Garofalo**, developed the *lifestyle exposure theory* (aka **lifestyle theory**) of victimization in 1978.[40] The theory originally attempted to explain crimes against persons, but it has since been expanded to include property crimes. **Lifestyle** refers to a style of life, or the way a person lives. Lifestyles are composed of repetitive, patterned, regular, and recurrent events that people engage in on an everyday basis. Because lifestyles are associated with exposure to people, places, and times with varying risk of victimization, they determine a person's vulnerability to

THEORY | in PERSPECTIVE
Types of Victimization Theories

Theories of victimization shift the focus away from the criminal and onto the victim. The shift is a critical one, for it emphasizes the role of the victim, or the victim's circumstances, as setting the stage for victimization to occur. Theories focusing on the victim and on the process of victimization are part of the criminological subfield known as *victimology*.

Victim Precipitation Theory

Theories of victim precipitation examine the relationship between victims and criminals and assess the likelihood that the victim may (in some ways, including those that are blame-free) have contributed to his or her own victimization.

> **Period:** 1940s–1970s
>
> **Theorists:** Benjamin Mendelsohn, Hans von Hentig, Stephen Schafer, Menachem Amir, and Marvin Wolfgang
>
> **Concepts:** victimogenesis, victim precipitation, victim facilitation, victim provocation, victim initiation, victim proneness

Lifestyle Exposure Theory

Lifestyle exposure theory, also called lifestyle theory, says that certain lifestyles favor victimization because they offer more opportunities for it.

> **Period:** 1970s–today

> **Theorists:** Michael J. Hindelang, Michael R. Gottfredson, and James Garofalo
>
> **Concepts:** lifestyles, lifestyle theory, elder abuse

Routine Activities Theory (RAT)

Routine activities theory (RAT) examines the interaction of motivated offenders, capable guardians, and suitable targets as an explanation for crime and suggests that an individual's everyday activities contribute significantly to the likelihood of his or her criminal victimization.

> **Period:** 1970s–today
>
> **Theorists:** Lawrence Cohen and Marcus Felson
>
> **Concepts:** motivated offenders, suitable targets, capable guardian

Deviant Places Theory

Deviant places theory is a spatially oriented perspective which suggests that victimization occurs most frequently in socially disorganized high-crime areas and that people become victims as a result of their exposure to such areas.

> **Period:** 1980s–today
>
> **Theorists:** Rodney Stark
>
> **Concepts:** stigmatized neighborhoods

---

criminal victimization.[41] Simply put, certain lifestyles favor victimization because they offer more opportunities for it.[42]

Lifestyle theory proposes that demographic variables, including things such as age, gender, race/ethnicity, and SES, influence lifestyles and hence determine victimization risk through their effect on lifestyle. Someone working a late-night shift in a crime-prone area, for example, is likely at higher risk of victimization than someone who is asleep at home. Similarly, a person who routinely withdraws large sums of cash from the same ATM machine on a regular basis is more likely to be victimized than one who conducts transactions at a teller's window in a bank, or who varies their routine—especially if they frequently visit ATMs in poorly lit areas late at night. Some authors use date rape as another example of crime associated with lifestyles, especially when young women engage in high-frequency dating with a relatively large number of men. A married lifestyle, they point out, is relatively safer, even though domestic abuse and family violence are not uncommon. Similarly, drug abusers, who sometimes share aspects of their lifestyle with strangers or acquaintances, may find themselves the target of robbery or theft, or may even end up being arrested as a consequence of the lifestyle choices they've made. Those who participate in a given lifestyle often make rational decisions about specific behaviors (such as in our earlier example of going to a given automated teller machine at a certain time). The same is true of criminal lifestyles. Hence, the meshing of choices made by both victims and criminals contributes significantly to both the frequency and the type of criminal activity observed in society.

Some groups of people—including the homeless, runaways, sex tourists, and heavy drinkers or alcoholics who visit public bars and nightclubs—participate in very risky lifestyles.[43] Likewise, unemployed youth who drop out of school are more likely to associate with others who get them into "trouble," and may find themselves faced with victimization.[44] In one recent study, Florida State University researchers Toya Like Haislip and Patricia Warren found that some situational features of a person's lifestyle (e.g., riding public transportation) and contextual features (e.g., residential stability) increased the risks of violent victimization among females of color.[45] Finally, criminal lifestyles themselves also increase the risk of victimization, or at least injury, especially during crime commission—a risk that is substantially increased in confrontational types of crime (i.e., robbery, home invasion, aggravated assault, etc.).

Some years after the original formulation of lifestyle theory, Garofalo, one of its founders, observed that "victimization is not evenly distributed randomly across space and time—there are high-risk locations and high-risk time periods."[46] He may have been thinking of special populations, many of whom are at heightened risk of victimization and for whom such risk is inherent in their status. These include the intellectually challenged, the physically disabled, the elderly, and children (as the story that opened this chapter showed). For a free 104-page National Academy Press report on the disproportionate victimization risk of persons with developmental disabilities visit **http://www.nap .edu/catalog/10042/crime-victims-with-developmental -disabilities-report-of-a-workshop**.

■ **elder abuse**   Intentional actions that cause harm or create a serious risk of harm to a vulnerable elder by a caregiver or other person who stands in a trust relationship to the elder; or failure by a caregiver to satisfy the elder's basic needs or to protect the elder from harm.

■ **routine activities theory (RAT)**   A theory that examines the interaction of motivated offenders, capable guardians, and suitable targets as an explanation for crime, and which suggests that an individual's everyday activities contribute significantly to the likelihood of his or her criminal victimization.

■ **motivated offenders**   The population of potential criminal offenders in a given area.
■ **suitable target**   Something or someone of value to offenders in a criminal offense.
■ **capable guardian**   One who effectively discourages crime; effective deterrents to criminal activity.

One of those special populations, the elderly, deserves special mention because the issue of elder mistreatment and abuse is garnering the attention of the law enforcement, medical, and research communities as more people are living longer than ever before. This trend is expected to increase, as the U.S. Census Bureau projects that more than 62 million Americans will be of age 65 or older in 2025, an increase of 78% from 2001, and more than 7.4 million will be of age 85 or older, an increase of nearly 68% from 2001.[47]

Because the elderly, like children, often do not have complete control over their own lives they are especially subject to victimization by caregivers, who may often be family members. The National Research Council defines **elder abuse** and mistreatment as "(a) intentional actions that cause harm or create a serious risk of harm to a vulnerable elder by a caregiver or other person who stands in a trust relationship to the elder, or (b) failure by a caregiver to satisfy the elder's basic needs or to protect the elder from harm."[48]

A 2014 study of crimes against the elderly found that from 2003 to 2013 rates of nonfatal violent crime against the elderly increased by 27%.[49] Nonfatal violent crime includes rape or sexual assault, robbery, aggravated assault, and simple assault. From 2003 to 2013, the elderly were victims in approximately 2% of all violent crimes and 2% of all serious violent crimes.

However, victimization rates for elderly persons were consistently lower than rates for persons in younger age groups. The study also found that the ratio of property crime to violent crime was higher for the elderly (13 to 1) than for younger persons ages 25 to 49 (3 to 1) and persons ages 50 to 64 (5 to 1). More than half (56%) of elderly violent crime victims reported their victimization to police, compared to only a third (38%) for persons ages 12 to 24. Among elderly violent crime victims, about 59% reported being victimized at or near their home.

According to the NIJ-funded National Elder Mistreatment Study, the risk of elder victimization is higher for individuals with the following demographic characteristics: low household income, unemployed or retired, reporting poor health, having experienced a prior traumatic event, or reporting low levels of social support.[50] Because elder abuse has been historically viewed as a social rather than a criminal problem, most states did not establish adult protective services units to address elder victimization until the mid-1980s.[51]

Finally, it should be noted that many studies have demonstrated the worth of lifestyle theory and have validated relationships between daily activities and the likelihood of criminal victimization.[52] The U.S. Department of Justice runs a Web-based elder justice initiative, which can be accessed at **http://www.justice.gov/elderjustice/**.

Routine Activities Theory (RAT)

Routine activities theory was proposed by **Lawrence Cohen** and **Marcus Felson** in 1979.[53] Writing shortly after the introduction of lifestyle theory, Cohen and Felson noted that "routine activities deliver easy crime opportunities to the offender."[54] They stated, "The risk of criminal victimization varies dramatically among the circumstances and locations in which people place themselves and their property." In other words, the nature or pattern of routine social interaction contributes significantly to both the volume and the type of crime found in society. Cohen and Felson were focused on explaining the rise in victimizations that had occurred in American cities following World War II, and they believed that postwar society had facilitated the convergence in space and time of (1) **motivated offenders** with the goal of committing crimes against (2) **suitable targets** in the absence of (3) a **capable guardian** (i.e., one who effectively discourages crime).[55] Figure 10-8 represents these concepts diagrammatically.

Charlie Neibergall/AP Images

Iowa Attorney General Tom Miller speaks to crime victims at the statehouse in Des Moines, Iowa. Many victims of crime are elderly. What is elder abuse?

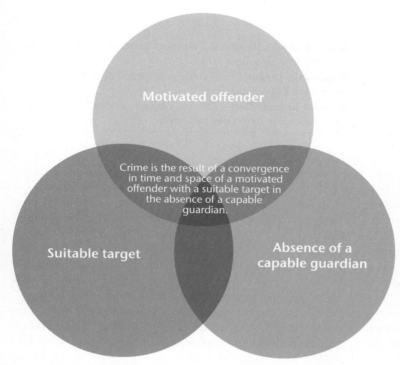

Crime is the result of a convergence in time and space of a motivated offender with a suitable target in the absence of a capable guardian.

FIGURE 10-8 | **Features of Routine Activities Theory**

For example, a person who routinely walks down a dark alleyway in a high-crime area on their way to work for an evening shift at a local pharmacy is far more likely to come into contact with motivated offenders (i.e., to be preyed upon by robbers) than someone who stays home after dark. Cohen and Felson assume that there will always be a substantial number of motivated offenders, but that suitable targets (either vulnerable people or unattended valuables) and capable guardians (watchful friends and neighbors, the police, and security personnel) vary with the place and over time. Social activities engaged in by potential victims who are suitable targets for robbery contribute substantially to criminal opportunities when they are undertaken in the absence of a capable guardian—as when someone wearing valuable jewelry fails to consider the potential threat of being out in public unaccompanied by others, Cohen and Felson also suggest that changes in American society during the 1960s and 1970s (which led to greater personal affluence and more involvement in social activities outside the home) increased the number of suitable targets and brought about heightened rates of household theft and personal victimization by strangers. Finally, they also recognized that victims oftentimes experience propinquity (e.g., similar sociodemographic characteristics) and relative physical proximity to violent perpetrators.

Combining the findings of victimization studies that employ lifestyle and routine activities theory, researchers have found that the risk of criminal victimization increases in a person's life if they (1) are a member of a racial or ethnic minority who (2) ventures out in public (3) at night (4) in dangerous areas (5) without friends or family, (6) while carrying valuables or (7) engages in risk-taking behavior.[56] As Felson notes, however, "potential victims of crime can be guided and channeled in their daily movements so as to minimize their risk."[57] Learn more about the routine activities approach, including its implications for crime control, via **http://www.popcenter.org/learning/pam/help/theory.cfm**.

> Central to the routine activities approach is the claim that crime is likely to occur when a motivated offender and a suitable target come together in the absence of a capable guardian.

The Situational Model

In a later work, Felson suggested that a number of "situational insights" combine to elicit a criminal response from individual actors enmeshed in a highly varied social world, pointing out that "individuals vary greatly in their behavior from one situation to another" and that criminality might flow from temptation, bad company, idleness, or provocation.[58] Retail stores, for example, create temptations toward theft when they display their merchandise within easy reach of customers.

Felson's situational model defines what constitutes an opportunity. As in earlier writings on routine activities theory, situations favoring victimization arise when a motivated offender, a suitable target, and the absence of a capable guardian all coalesce. Crime can be prevented, however, by changing a potential victim's routines, or by hardening targets. Christopher J. Schreck, for example, examined school victimization and concluded that target-hardening strategies such as the use of metal detectors, security guards, and school patrols do not prevent school crime. Rather, Schreck found that the risk of victimization is "associated with the presence of likely offenders at school as well as individual students who have delinquent characteristics and criminal associates."[59] Schreck pointed out that "victimization does not happen to just anyone"; but that "certain variables stand out as salient predictors." He concluded that students could reduce the risk of victimization by "increasing the level of guardianship around themselves and their belongings."

■ **deviant places theory**   A spatially oriented theory of victimization that suggests that victimization occurs most frequently in socially disorganized areas and that people become victims as a result of their exposure to such areas.

PUTTING CRIMINOLOGY TO WORK—Implementing Evidence-Based Policy

To make a difference in the real world, criminological theories must first be tested and evaluated. Once evidence has been developed that theory-based practices work, then programs based on them can be implemented to reduce or prevent crime, or to help make victims' lives better. One federal initiative, CrimeSolutions.Gov, strives to evaluate the effectiveness of theory-based practices, and then communicates its findings via the Web. Some of the most effective and promising programs are highlighted in boxes such as this one that appear throughout the text.

PROGRAM: Maryland Ignition Interlock Program

EVIDENCE RATINGS FOR OUTCOMES: Effective

PROFILE

Maryland introduced the Ignition Interlock Program for drivers with multiple alcohol offenses to decrease the number of subsequent alcohol-related traffic violations. The Maryland program targeted drivers applying for license reinstatements who had two or more alcohol-related traffic violations in their lifetime and who had been approved by the Medical Advisory Board in Maryland to apply for the reinstatement. Participating drivers were notified by letter that they were eligible for license reinstatement pending enrollment in the program. Participants had 30 days to install a Breath analyze ignition interlock system in their vehicle or face suspension of their driver's license for failure to comply. The interlock is a device that connects the vehicle's ignition system to a breath analyzer. Before the offender can start the car, the individual must breathe into the device, which is calibrated to "lock" the ignition if the breath-alcohol level exceeds a preprogrammed level. A "datalogger" device captures vehicle usage and records instances of noncompliance: The driver, his/her vehicle,

and other program information. Participating drivers are expected to pay for all costs associated with the program, including the installation of the ignition interlock, the monthly maintenance costs, the extra fee for obtaining a restricted driver's license, and the fee for obtaining a license without the restriction once the sentence has been completed.

Relevant Theory: Routine Activity Theory (RAT)

To the extent that a theory grounds the use of interlock devices, routine activity theory (RAT) applies. RAT predicts that crime increases when motivated offenders find suitable targets that lack capable guardians. Seen this way, the interlock device acts as a capable guardian to remove a suitable target (a drivable car) from a motivated offender (the alcohol-impaired driver).

Evidence-Based Review

These sources were used in the development of the program profile:

Study 1

Kenneth H. Beck, William J. Rauch, Elizabeth A. Baker, and Allan F. Williams, "Effects of Ignition Interlock License Restrictions on Drivers with Multiple Alcohol Offenses: A Randomized Trial in Maryland," *American Journal of Public Health*, Vol. 89 (1999), pp. 1696–1700.

Study 2

William J. Rauch, Eileen M. Ahlin, Paul L. Zador, Jan M. Howard, and G. Doug Duncan, "Effects of Administrative Ignition Interlock License Restrictions on Drivers with Multiple Alcohol Offenses," *Journal of Experimental Criminology*, Vol. 7, No. 2 (2011), pp. 127–148.

Source: Adapted from https://www.crimesolutions.gov/ProgramDetails.aspx?ID=63

Notes: Putting Criminology to Work features are based on information published online by the National Institute of Justice's (NIJ) Crime Solutions Website. The program ratings shown are those provided by NIJ.

Deviant Places Theory

Deviant places theory is spatially oriented. It suggests that victimization occurs most frequently in socially disorganized areas and that people become victims as a result of their exposure to such areas—by living there, transiting through them, or by visiting them. The theory focuses primarily on the geographically determined risk of coming into contact with

an offender, irrespective of lifestyle, behavior, or personal characteristics.

University of Washington sociologist **Rodney Stark** proposed deviant places theory in 1987, and called it "a theory of the ecology of crime."[60] Stark had observed that certain locations had high and unchanging victimization rates even after an almost complete turnover of the population—during which previous residents moved away and new ones moved in. He

■ **stigmatized neighborhoods**   Residential areas with bad reputations that hold little attraction for those that can afford to live elsewhere.

concluded that victimologists needed a "kinds of places" theory to supplement other theories, which he called "kinds of people" theories. Stark examined more than a century of ecological research on crime and integrated his findings into a set of thirty propositions. Those propositions focused on neighborhood conditions and, taken together, they form the crux of deviant places theory. Certain neighborhood conditions produce what Stark called **stigmatized neighborhoods**, that is, neighborhoods with bad reputations that hold little attraction for those that can afford to live elsewhere. Stigmatized neighborhoods are characterized by crowded homes, transience, dilapidation, and the lack of successful role models. A selected few of Stark's propositions follow:

- To the extent that neighborhoods are dense and poor, homes will be crowded.

- Where homes are more crowded, there will be a greater tendency to congregate outside the home in places and circumstances that raise levels of temptation and opportunity to deviate.

- Where homes are more crowded, there will be lower levels of supervision of children.

- Where homes are more crowded, there will be higher levels of conflict within families weakening attachments and thereby stakes in conformity.

Stark recognized that while stigmatized neighborhoods increase the chance of victimizations for those living or visiting there, most neighborhood residents do not become criminal. This, he said, happens because "the larger culture seems able to instill high levels of aspiration in people even in the worst ecological settings." He concludes by noting that "the fact that most slum residents aren't criminals is beside the point," because it is the nature and structure of the neighborhoods themselves that sustain high rates of crime and deviance.

Finally, Stark noted that his theory of deviant places depends entirely upon ecological features associated with a given location, and not upon racial, ethnic, or other personal characteristics of the people who live there. This was important, he said, because criminologists of the time had observed overly high rates of criminality among black communities, and Stark wanted to avoid the implications of associating race and ethnicity with crime and deviance. Addressing the disproportionate amount of black crime in the United States at the time, Stark wrote: "my answer is that high black crime rates are, in large measure, the result of *where* they live."

Recent research largely supports deviant places theory. The Moving to Opportunity for Fair Housing Demonstration Program (MTO), for example, was an ambitious multiyear antipoverty social experiment run by the U.S. Department of Housing and Urban Development (HUD) that combined tenant-based rental assistance with housing counseling to help 4,604 very low-income households move from poverty-stricken urban areas to low-poverty neighborhoods. As noted by program evaluators at the conclusion of the project, "there is a long-standing belief that living in a less economically and socially distressed neighborhood can improve people's well-being and long-term life chances, owing to some combination of better housing conditions, lower crime, less stress, greater job opportunities, more supportive schools, and role models who are more affirming of pro-social behaviors."[61] MTO demonstration projects took place in the mid-1990s in Baltimore, Boston, Chicago, Los Angeles, and New York City and were evaluated 10 to 15 years later.

A final post-project evaluation of MTO showed that the program had some positive outcomes and had helped families move into neighborhoods where neighbors were more willing to work together to support shared norms. It also resulted in increased social connections of adults to other people who were employed full-time or had completed college. Moreover, MTO moves did not appear to increase social isolation. Nonetheless, in the words of the final evaluation report, "few statistically significant differences in the number of arrests for violent crimes, property crimes, or other (nonviolent, non-property, non-drug) crimes" were noted.[62] These findings are something akin to the old saying that "You can move a person out of the city, but you can't move the city out of the person," which means that simply changing neighborhoods does little to change previously established ways of thinking or preexisting behavior patterns in those who move.

Other studies have similarly shown that moving young males and their families out of poverty-stricken areas did not lead to a significant decline in the likelihood of arrest for a violent crime, and actually may increase the level of risky behavior in which they engaged, perhaps because of the lack of social controls.[63]

Finally, in 2014, criminologists David S. Kirk and Margaret Hardy studied Chicago neighborhoods using data from the Project on Human Development in Chicago Neighborhoods (PHDCN).[64] They set out to examine "whether the effects of neighborhood context are situational *and* whether they endure over time," especially in youth exposed to violence. Their research demonstrated not only that the level of exposure to neighborhood violence had an enduring effect on levels of aggression among young males, but that levels of aggression remained high even after leaving the neighborhoods in which they had been raised. The findings were attributed to "changes in social cognitions brought on by [neighborhood] exposure…" In other words, learned patterns of social interaction that people acquired from troubled neighborhood tend to stay with them even after they have moved away from those neighborhoods. Kirk and Hardy conclude that "This finding is alarming, and speaks to the durable effect of past neighborhood conditions."[65] These findings suggest that changing individuals' neighborhood environment does not lead to healthier outcomes, at least not immediately.

Victims' Rights

In May of 2013, the federal Office for Victims of Crime (OVC) released a report called *Vision 21*, which focused on transforming victims' services. Victims' services have grown in this country along with an emphasis on the rights of victims that began in the 1960s and 1970s.[66] "The goal for Vision 21" said OVC, "is simple yet profound: to permanently alter the way we treat victims of crime in America." In fact, the treatment of victims in America has changed greatly since the mid-1900s, as described in the following section. Access the complete *Vision 21* report at **http://ovc.ncjrs.gov/vision21/**.

A History of the Victim

Less than 50 years ago, it was common for victims to testify at trial.[67] However, they rarely had any other role in the justice process, and the criminal justice system routinely downplayed the experience of victimization and largely disregarded the psychological trauma and financial problems engendered both by having been a victim and by having to endure the criminal proceedings intended to bring the criminal to justice. That changed in 1982, when the President's Task Force on Victims of Crime gave focus to a burgeoning victims' rights movement and urged the widespread expansion of victims' assistance programs during what was then their formative period.[68] Victims' assistance programs, which are common today, offer services in the areas of crisis intervention and follow-up counseling, and help victims secure their rights under the law.[69] Following successful prosecution, some victims' assistance programs also advise victims in the filing of civil suits to recoup financial losses directly from the offender.

About the same time, voters in California approved Proposition 8, a resolution that called for changes in the state's constitution to reflect concern for victims. A continuing goal

> A continuing goal of victims' advocacy groups is an amendment to the U.S. Constitution.

of victims' advocacy groups is an amendment to the U.S. Constitution, which such groups say is needed to provide the same kind of fairness to victims that is routinely accorded to defendants. In the past, for example, the National Victims' Constitutional Amendment Passage (NVCAP) has sought to add a phrase to the Sixth Amendment: "likewise, the victim, in every criminal prosecution, shall have the right to be present and to be heard at all critical stages of judicial proceedings." The NVCAP now advocates the addition of a separate amendment to the U.S. Constitution focused on victims' rights. Visit the NVCAP via **http://nvcap.org**.

In September 1996, a victims' rights constitutional amendment—Senate Joint Resolution 65—was proposed by a bipartisan committee in the U.S. Congress,[70] but problems of wording and terminology prevented its passage. A revised amendment was proposed in 1998,[71] and again in 1999, but none made it to the Senate floor. The legislation also lacked the support of then-President Bill Clinton and was officially withdrawn by its sponsors in 2000. Since that time, other victims' rights amendments have been introduced in the House and Senate, the latest having been a bi-partisan plan brought before the House Judiciary Committee's Subcommittee on the Constitution and Civil Justice by Rep. Trent Franks (R-AZ), Jim Costa (D-CA), and Rep. Edward Royce (R-CA) in 2013.[72]

Although a victims' rights amendment to the federal Constitution may not yet be a reality, more than 30 states have passed their own victims' rights amendments (Figure 10-9).[73] According to the NVCAP, California Proposition 9, or the Victims' Rights and Protection Act of 2008 (also known as Marsy's Law), is the most comprehensive victims' bill of rights of any state in the nation.[74] Proposition 9, which appeared on the November 4, 2008, ballot in California, passed with 53.8% of the vote. It amended the California Constitution by adding new provisions that provide victims in California with a number of specifically enforceable rights. The text of the California amendment can be seen in Exhibit 10-1.

■ **Victims of Crime Act (VOCA)** A federal law enacted in 1984 that established the federal Crime Victims Fund. The fund uses monies from fines and forfeitures collected from federal offenders to supplement state support of local victims' assistance programs and state victims' compensation programs.

■ **Violence against Women Act (VAWA)** A federal law enacted as a component of the 1994 Violent Crime Control and Law Enforcement Act and intended to address concerns about violence against women. The law focused on improving the interstate enforcement of protection orders, providing effective training for court personnel involved with women's issues, improving the training and collaboration of police and prosecutors with victim service providers, strengthening law enforcement efforts to reduce violence against women, and increasing services to victims of violence.

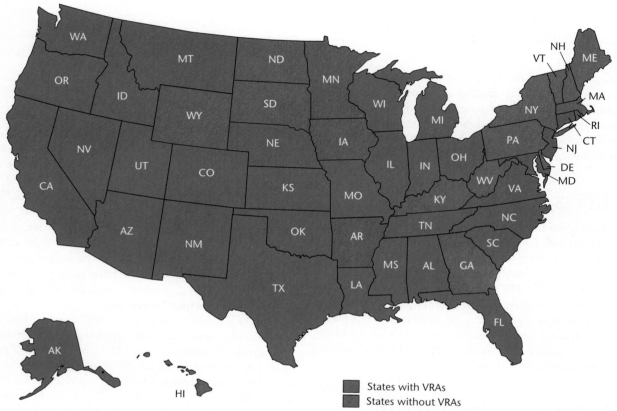

States with VRAs
States without VRAs

FIGURE 10-9 | The Status of Victim's Rights Amendments (VRA) in the States
Source: Office for Victims of Crime.

Victims' Rights Legislation

Although a federal victims' rights amendment to the U.S. Constitution has yet to be passed, a number of federal laws offer both protections and rights to victims of crime (Figure 10-10). The 1982 Victim and Witness Protection Act (VWPA),[75] for example, requires judges to consider victim-impact statements at federal sentencing hearings and places responsibility for their creation on federal probation officers. In 1984, the federal **Victims of Crime Act (VOCA)** was enacted with substantial bipartisan support. VOCA authorized federal funding to help states establish victims' assistance and victims' compensation programs. Under VOCA, the U.S. Department of Justice's Office for Victims of Crime provides a significant source of both funding and information for victims' assistance programs.

The rights of victims were further strengthened under the Violent Crime Control and Law Enforcement Act of 1994, which created a federal right of allocution, or right to speak, for victims of violent and sex crimes. This gave victims the right to speak at the sentencing of their assailants. The 1994 law also requires sex offenders and child molesters convicted under federal law to pay restitution to their victims and prohibits the diversion of federal victims' funds to other programs. Other provisions of the 1994 law provide civil rights remedies for victims of felonies motivated by gender bias and extend "rape shield law" protections to civil cases and to all criminal cases, prohibiting inquiries into a victim's sexual history.

A significant feature of the 1994 law can be found in a subsection titled the **Violence against Women Act (VAWA)**. The VAWA provides financial support for police, prosecutors, and victims' services in cases involving sexual violence or domestic

EXHIBIT 10-1 | Victims' Rights in California

In order to preserve and protect a victim's rights to justice and due process, a victim shall be entitled to the following rights:

1. To be treated with fairness and respect for his or her privacy and dignity, and to be free from intimidation, harassment, and abuse, throughout the criminal or juvenile justice process.

2. To be reasonably protected from the defendant and persons acting on behalf of the defendant.

3. To have the safety of the victim and the victim's family considered in fixing the amount of bail and release conditions for the defendant.

4. To prevent the disclosure of confidential information or records to the defendant, the defendant's attorney, or any other person acting on behalf of the defendant, which could be used to locate or harass the victim or the victim's family or which disclose confidential communications made in the course of medical or counseling treatment, or which are otherwise privileged or confidential by law.

5. To refuse an interview, deposition, or discovery request by the defendant, the defendant's attorney, or any other person acting on behalf of the defendant, and to set reasonable conditions on the conduct of any such interview to which the victim consents.

6. To reasonable notice of and to reasonably confer with the prosecuting agency, upon request, regarding the arrest of the defendant if known by the prosecutor, the charges filed, the determination whether to extradite the defendant, and, upon request, to be notified of and informed before any pretrial disposition of the case.

7. To reasonable notice of all public proceedings, including delinquency proceedings, upon request, at which the defendant and the prosecutor are entitled to be present and of all parole or other post-conviction release proceedings, and to be present at all such proceedings.

8. To be heard, upon request, at any proceeding, including any delinquency proceeding, involving a postarrest release decision, plea, sentencing, post-conviction release decision, or any proceeding in which a right of the victim is at issue.

9. To a speedy trial and a prompt and final conclusion of the case and any related post-judgment proceedings.

10. To provide information to a probation department official conducting a pre-sentence investigation concerning the impact of the offense on the victim and the victim's family and any sentencing recommendations before the sentencing of the defendant.

11. To receive, upon request, the pre-sentence report when available to the defendant, except for those portions made confidential by law.

12. To be informed, upon request, of the conviction, sentence, place and time of incarceration, or other disposition of the defendant, the scheduled release date of the defendant, and the release of or the escape by the defendant from custody.

13. To restitution.

14. To the prompt return of property when no longer needed as evidence.

15. To be informed of all parole procedures, to participate in the parole process, to provide information to the parole authority to be considered before the parole of the offender, and to be notified, upon request, of the parole or other release of the offender.

16. To have the safety of the victim, the victim's family, and the general public considered before any parole or other post-judgment release decision is made.

17. To be informed of the rights enumerated in paragraphs (1) through (16).

Reference: Section 28(e) of Article I of the California Constitution.

FIGURE 10-10 | Timeline of Federal Crime Victims Legislation

abuse. That act signified a major shift in our national response to domestic violence, stalking (which is often part of the domestic violence continuum), and sexual assault crimes. For the first time in our nation's history, violent crimes against women were addressed in relation to the more general problem of gender inequality. VAWA was reauthorized by Congress in 2000, 2005, and again in 2013.[76] The 2005 VAWA reauthorization included a new statute known as the International Marriage Broker Regulation Act (IMBRA), which provides potential life-saving protections to prospective foreign brides who may immigrate to the United States. Finally, the 2013 reauthorization made $659 million

Today, all 50 states and the federal government have passed legislation providing for monetary payments to victims of crime.

available each year for five years for programs that strengthen the justice system's response to crimes against women and some men, including protections for gays, lesbians, bisexual, and transgender Americans.

In 2001, the USA PATRIOT Act amended the Victims of Crime Act of 1984 to make victims of terrorism and their families eligible for victims' compensation payments.[77] It also created an antiterrorism emergency reserve fund to help provide compensation to victims of terrorism. A year earlier, in November 2000, the federal Office for Victims of Crime (OVC) created the Terrorism and International Victims Unit (TIVU) to develop and manage programs and initiatives that help victims of domestic and international terrorism, mass violence, and crimes that have transnational dimensions.[78]

In 2004, the U.S. Congress passed the Crime Victims' Rights Act[79] (CVRA) as part of the Justice for All Act. Some saw the legislation as at least a partial statutory alternative to a constitutional victims' rights amendment. The CVRA established statutory rights for victims of federal crimes and gave them the necessary legal authority to assert those rights in federal court. The act grants the following rights to victims of federal crimes:[80]

1. The right to be reasonably protected from the accused

2. The right to reasonable, accurate, and timely notice of any public proceeding involving the crime or of any release or escape of the accused

3. The right to be included in any such public proceeding

4. The right to be reasonably heard at any public proceeding involving release, plea, or sentencing

5. The right to confer with the federal prosecutor handling the case

6. The right to full and timely restitution as provided by law

7. The right to proceedings free from unreasonable delay

8. The right to be treated with fairness and with respect for the victim's dignity and privacy

In addition to establishing these rights, the legislation expressly requires federal courts to ensure that they are afforded to victims. In like manner, federal law enforcement officials are required to make their "best efforts to see that crime victims are notified of, and accorded," these rights. To teach citizens about the rights of victims of crime, the federal government created a website that you can access via **https://www.ovc.gov.** It includes an online directory of crime victims' services, which

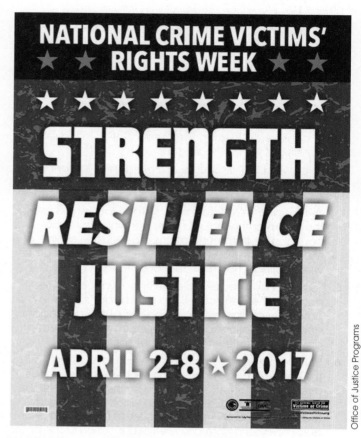

The 2017 National Crime Victims' Rights Week poster. Can you list some fundamental victims' rights?
Source: Office for Victims of Crime.

Office of Justice Programs

can be searched locally, nationally, and internationally. A user-friendly database of victims' rights laws can be found online at **https://www.victimlaw.org** and a U.S. Department of Justice Web page detailing victims' rights is at **http://www.doj.state. or.us/victims/rights.shtml**.

Restorative Justice: Making the Victim Whole Again

Much of the philosophical basis of today's victims' movement can be found in the restorative justice model. Restorative justice, which was discussed in the last chapter, emphasizes both offender accountability and victim reparation.

Restorative justice has both a community safety dimension and an offender accountability focus.[81] The community safety dimension of the RJ philosophy recognizes that the justice system has a responsibility to protect the public from crime and

■ **victim restitution**   Court-ordered payments to victims of crime, generally made by offenders, as reimbursement for damages and/or losses.

■ **victim compensation**   Payments to victims of crime, generally made by a government agency, as compensation for lost wages and medical expenses.

from offenders.[82] It also recognizes that the community can participate in ensuring its own safety. The accountability element defines criminal conduct in terms of obligations incurred by the offender, both to the victim and to the community.[83] RJ also has what some describe as a competency development element, which holds that offenders who enter the justice system should leave it more capable of participating successfully in the wider society than when they entered.

Victim Restitution and Victim Compensation

An important aspect of restorative justice is **victim restitution**. Sentencing options that seek to restore the victim frequently focus on restitution payments that offenders are ordered to make, either to their victims or to a general fund, which may then reimburse victims for damages, and/or losses. *Service restitution*, in which offenders are ordered to perform either a service to the victim or to the community, is another form of victim restitution. In support of these goals, the 1984 Federal Comprehensive Crime Control Act specifically requires that "[i]f sentenced to probation, the defendant must also be ordered to pay a fine, make restitution, and/or work in community service."[84]

Today, all 50 states and the federal government have passed legislation providing for monetary payments to victims of crime. Such payments are primarily designed to compensate victims for medical expenses and lost wages. All existing

victim compensation programs require that applicants meet certain eligibility criteria, and most set limits on the maximum amount of compensation that can be received. Generally disallowed are claims from victims who are significantly responsible for their own victimization, such as those who are injured in fights they provoke. The California Victim Compensation Program (CalVCP), for example, provides compensation for victims of violent crime who are injured or threatened with injury. Among the crimes covered are domestic violence, child abuse, sexual and physical assault, homicide, robbery, and vehicular manslaughter. If a victim meets eligibility criteria, CalVCP will compensate many types of services needed when the costs are not covered by other sources (such as insurance). Eligible services include medical and dental care, mental health services, income loss, funeral expenses, rehabilitation, and relocation.[85] Funding for CalVCP comes from restitution fines and orders, penalty assessments levied on persons convicted of crimes and traffic offenses, and matching federal funds. In 2016, the program received 37,600 applications, and provided more than $52 million in compensation to crime victims.[86] In that same year, the time period for filing a victim compensation application in California increased from one to three years, and new legislation authorized county social workers to file on behalf of a child or elder abuse victim if that victim is unable to file on his or her own behalf.[87] Both victim compensation and victim restitution programs have the goal of making the victim "whole again"—meaning that they work to restore the health, dignity, functioning, and financial integrity of victims of crime that have been compromised by the experience of criminal victimization.

CRIMINAL | PROFILES

Omar Mateen—American Monster

In 2016, the U.S. was rocked by what was then the worst mass shooting in recent history. The shooter, 29-year-old Floridian Omar Mateen, killed 49 people and wounded 53 more at the Pulse nightclub in Orlando, Florida, during a Latin Night celebration. The club, a popular gathering spot for the LGBT community, had been packed with party goers when shooting started around 2 AM on the morning of Sunday, June 12, 2016. Mateen had entered the club unchallenged carrying an AR-15 assault rifle and a 9 mm pistol. He started firing almost immediately. Off-duty police officers serving as club security personnel tried to stop the violence, but Mateen's superior fire power and crowded conditions forced them back. Mateen's life ended three hours later when a police SWAT team smashed through a wall at the rear of the building and killed him.

During the shooting, Mateen made three 911 calls to emergency operators, and one to an Orlando TV station, saying that he was a soldier of the Islamic State, and that his attack was a protest against U.S. actions in the Middle East. During the calls, he pledged loyalty to Abu Bakr al-Baghdadi, leader of the Islamic State.[i]

Although Mateen had made two trips to the Saudi Arabia on religious pilgrimages, later investigation by the CIA found "no direct link" between Mateen and terrorists.

Mateen was born in New York City to Seddique and Shahla Mateen, natives of Afghanistan. They moved to Florida when Mateen was still in grade school. The elder Mateen paid for and broadcast an occasional television show on a U.S.-based Afghan satellite channel for about three years. The show supported the Taliban in its border

Omar Mateen, AKA "The Pulze nightclub shooter." Mateen killed 49 people and wounded 53 more at the Pulse nightclub in Orlando, Florida, in 2016. How can his actions be explained?

struggle with Pakistan. The father even conducted a remote bid for the presidency of Afghanistan while living in Florida.

As a child, Mateen was difficult. In fifth grade, he was disciplined more than 15 times for misbehavior. A middle school teacher warned his family of his "inability to show self-control." In high school he was arrested for fighting, and later expelled. Schoolmates recalled that he openly celebrated the terrorist attacks of September 11, 2001.[ii]

As an adult, Mateen held a variety of jobs, including that of a prison guard at a Florida correctional facility. He was fired from that position in 2007 after becoming enraged that a piece of hamburger he was cooking at a barbecue with fellow workers touched a piece of pork. He told the others there that he out to kill of them, and that he would come back with a gun.[iii] By 2013, he was working as a security guard at the St. Lucie County Courthouse in Fort Pierce, Florida. While there he reportedly boasted of family ties to al-Qaeda, prompting the local sheriff to remove him from the job. The security company that he worked for, G4S, then transferred him to work at a residential golfing community in the area. At the time of the killings, he was still employed as an armed security officer for G4S — one of the largest private security companies in the world.

Prior to the shootings, Mateen had been interviewed by the FBI on two occasions for possible terrorist connections. At one point Mateen had reportedly been seen at a party in private conversation with Moner Muhammad Abu Salha, the man who became America's first suicide bomber in Syria.

During what became a ten-month long FBI investigation, Mateen's name was added to the federal Terrorist Identities Datamart Environment (TIDE), a classified repository that includes the names of suspected terrorists or their associates; as well as to the Terrorist Screening Database (TSDB), a sophisticated database that comprises the main terrorist "watch list" used by the FBI.[iv] He had even been placed on the domestic no-fly terrorist watch list before being removed from it in 2014 when the FBI closed its investigation of him; finding no credible evidence of his links to terrorist organizations.[v] After the shooting, however, the FBI concluded that Mateen had been radicalized by "Islamist propaganda," but found no evidence that the shooting had been coordinated from outside of the United States.[vi]

In what may be an important insight into his personality, coworkers and ex-wife, Sitora Yusufiy, described Mateen as bigoted, angry, and abusive. One coworker said that he quit his job after complaints to superiors about Mateen went unheeded, and Mateen harassed him with repeated disparaging telephone calls.

Yusufiy later told reporters that her husband had likely been gay, but was hiding the truth about his sexual orientation from his parents. She also said that, during their marriage, Mateen would become uncontrollably angry for no apparent reason, and became verbally and physically abusive toward her for not having the laundry done or dinner cooked when he got home. Yusufiy, who emigrated into the United States from Uzbekistan also said that Mateen would confiscate her paychecks, and forced her into social isolation from family and friends.

If, indeed Mateen was acting out a felt-identity with Islamic State, then the research of anthropologist Scott Atran of the University of Michigan in Ann Arbor could be relevant. Atran says that it is a mistake to dismiss people like Mateen as mentally ill or as lonely losers, arguing instead that Mateen's behavior can be explained by the concept of a "devoted actor." Devoted actors, says Atran, "will sacrifice themselves, their families and anyone or anything else" because of closely held personal values.[vii] These values are regarded as sacred and nonnegotiable, and to be defended at all costs. The question in Mateen's case, says Atran, is not *why* he did what he did, but rather *how* he acquired the values that motivated him to take the actions that he did.

Edited transcripts released by the FBI of phone calls between the Orlando Police Department and the shooter can be viewed at: justicestudies.com/pubs/FBI_Orlando.pdf.

The case of Omar Mateen raises some interesting questions. Among them are the following:

1. One of the learning objectives in this chapter focuses on the socio-emotional impact of victimization. What kind of impact did the Orlando shooting have? On whom?

2. What would the General Theory say about Mateen? How might it explain his behavior?

3. The story of Omar Mateen appears to blend the propaganda of terrorism, aspects of the LGBT community, and a difficult personality into a tragic event. How do the pieces fit?

4. What can the Orlando attack teach us? What can we do to prevent others like it?

Notes

i   "Orlando gunman raged against 'filthy ways of the west,'" CJBK radio, June 15, 2016, http://www.cjbk.com/WorldCP/Article.aspx?id=517722 (accessed June 15, 2016).

ii Damian Paletta, Alexandra Berzon, and John R. Emshwiller, *The Wall Street Journal*, June 16, 2016, http://www.wsj.com/articles/a-life-of-violent-threats-paved-way-for-orlando-attack-1466127324 (accessed June 20, 2016).

iii "Orlando Shooter Omar Mateen Was Fired for Bringing a Gun to Work in 2007: Report," June 15, 2016, http://www.usmagazine.com/celebrity-news/news/orlando-shooter-fired-for-bringing-gun-to-work-in-2007-report-w210285 (accessed June 16, 2016).

iv Nicholas Hautman, "This Is How Orlando Shooter Omar Mateen Evaded the FBI's Inquiries," *U.S. Weekly Magazine*, June 15, 2016, http://www.usmagazine.com/celebrity-news/news/this-is-how-the-orlando-shooter-evaded-the-fbis-inquires-w210184 (accessed June 16, 2016).

v   "FBI Tracked Orlando Killer Omar Mateen and Came up Empty," *The Daily Beast*, June 14, 2016, http://www.thedailybeast.com/articles/2016/06/14/fbi-tracked-orlando-killer-omar-mateen-and-came-up-empty.html (accessed June 16, 2016).

vi "Orlando shooting: FBI 'confident' gunman Omar Mateen was 'radicalized,'" First Post, June 15, 2016, http://www.firstpost.com/world/orlando-shooting-fbi-confident-gunman-omar-mateen-was-radicalised-2834122.html (accessed June 16, 2016).

vii Bruce Bower, "Deadly Devotion: New Studies Explore Why Ordinary People Turn Terrorist," *Science News*, July 9, 2016, pp. 18–21.

SUMMARY

- This chapter is about crime victims and the victimization process. It is important to know that many crimes of all kinds never come to the attention of authorities and some are not even discovered by those who are victimized. The *dark figure of crime* is a term used to refer to the relatively large number of unreported crimes that have not come to the attention of officials. Crime's dark figure is sometimes glimpsed through self-reports, in which anonymous respondents are asked to confidentially report any violations of the criminal law that they have committed, or any victimizations that they have experienced.

- Official crime statistics in the United States are available through two major sources. One, an annual survey-based self-reporting program conducted under the auspices of the Bureau of Justice Statistics (BJS), is called the National Crime Victimization Survey (NCVS). The other, run by the Federal Bureau of Investigation (FBI), is known as the Uniform Crime Reporting (UCR) program. The UCR includes data from the National Incident-Based Reporting System (NIBRS), and this chapter refers to it as the UCR/NIBRS program. The major difference between the BJS's NCVS and the FBI's UCR/NIBRS can be found in the fact that the UCR/NIBRS program reports data on crimes that come to the attention of law enforcement authorities, while the NCVS is survey based, which means that it relies upon the information collected by interviewers who collect victimization data through the canvassing of randomly selected households.

- Demographics describe the statistical qualities of a given population, and demographic characteristics are significantly correlated with victimization risk. While victims of crime may be of any gender, age, race, or ethnicity, demographics can be used to describe those who are most at risk of victimization. It is important to remember, however, that while demographic characteristics can tell us about the risk of victimization, they say nothing about why victimization occurs.

- The victimization experience significantly impacts victims of crime. Victims are impacted along personal, physical, financial, and social dimensions, and this chapter examines each.

- Victimology, a subfield of criminology, extends to all aspects of the scientific study of criminal victimization, including the process of victimization, the criminal, the victim, the justice system, and society. Victimologists study particularly vulnerable groups of people. While early theories of victimology tended to blame the victim for his or her own victimization, more recent victimological approaches examine lifestyles, routine activities, and the features of deviant places, as factors that contribute to criminal victimization.

- Since the 1960s and 1970s, victims' services have grown in this country, accompanied by an expanded emphasis on the rights of victims. More than 30 states have amended their constitutions with victims' rights amendments, and a number of other states have passed victims' rights legislation. While a federal victims' rights amendment is not yet a reality, a number of federal laws grant certain rights to victims of crime. Among those laws are the 1982 Victim and Witness Protection Act (VWPA), the 1984 federal Victims of Crime Act (VOCA), the Violent Crime Control and Law Enforcement Act of 1994, the USA PATRIOT Act of 2001, the 2004 Crime Victims' Rights Act, and the Violence against Women Act (VAWA). Many states operate victims' compensation programs, and the federal government is instrumental in funding victims' services programs nationwide.

- Restorative justice (RJ), a concept that underlies much of today's victims' movement, emphasizes both offender accountability and victim reparation. Restitution, which is typically conceived of as payments by the offender to the victim, is intended to make the offender "whole again."

KEY TERMS

capable guardian, 277

dark figure of crime, 260

demographics, 267

deviant places theory, 279

elder abuse, 277

lifestyle, 275

lifestyle theory, 275

motivated offenders, 277

National Crime Victimization Survey (NCVS), 261

National Incident-Based Reporting System (NIBRS), 263

Office for Victims of Crime (OVC), 263

polyvictimization, 268

post-traumatic stress disorder (PTSD), 260

revictimization, 270

routine activities theory (RAT), 277

secondary victimization, 272

secondary victims, 272

self-report survey, 260

stigmatized neighborhoods, 280

suitable target, 277

Uniform Crime Reporting (UCR) program, 263

victim, 261

victim compensation, 285

victimization, 261

victimogenesis, 274

victimologist, 273

victimology, 273

victim precipitation, 274

victim proneness, 274

victim restitution, 285

Victims of Crime Act (VOCA), 282

Violence against Women Act (VAWA), 282

KEY NAMES

Menachem Amir, 275

Lawrence Cohen, 277

Marcus Felson, 277

James Garofalo, 275

Michael R. Gottfredson, 275

Hans von Hentig, 275

Michael J. Hindelang, 275

Benjamin Mendelsohn, 275

Stephen Schafer, 275

Rodney Stark, 279

Marvin Wolfgang, 274

QUESTIONS FOR REVIEW

1. What is meant by the *dark figure of crime*, and how is it related to self-report surveys?

2. What do official statistics tell us about crime trends in the United States?

3. Explain demographics. What kind of demographic features correlate with criminal victimization?

4. What are the personal impacts of victimization?

5. What is victimology, and what theories of victimization does this chapter discuss?

6. Describe the development of victims' rights in the United States, and tell how such rights are recognized.

7. Describe restorative justice, and what it means to "make the victim whole again"?

QUESTIONS FOR REFLECTION

1. Why are certain demographic characteristics associated with, and fairly good predictors of, criminal victimization? What characteristics do you think are most likely to be associated with the risk of victimization? Why?

2. Early theories of victimization tended to blame the victim, shifting some of the responsibility for the criminal act away from the offender and onto the victim. How much truth do "blame the victim" theories hold? Might they be more applicable to some crimes than to others?

3. What's the difference between routine activities theory and lifestyle theory? Does "lifestyle" encompass the notion of "routine activities"?

4. What rights do you think all crime victims should have? Explain each of your choices.

CHAPTER 11
CRIMES AGAINST PERSONS

It's What We Fear

LEARNING OUTCOMES

After reading this chapter, you should be able to answer the following questions:

- What is criminal homicide, and what are the key issues involved in explaining patterns of homicide?

- How is the crime of rape defined, and what are the key issues involved in understanding the crime of rape?

- What does the term *child sexual abuse* encompass? What are the various types of child sex abusers?

- How is the crime of robbery defined, and what are the different kinds of robbery?

- How is the crime of assault defined, and what are the various kinds of assault?

- What additional forms of interpersonal violence does this chapter discuss?

■ **Follow the author's tweets about the latest crime and justice news @schmalleger.**

■ **homicide** The killing of one human being by another.
■ **murder** An unlawful homicide, also called *criminal homicide.*

Introduction

In 2016, South African Judge Thokozile Masipa, rejected an appeal by prosecutors in the case of "Blade Runner" Oscar Pistorius.[1] One year earlier, South Africa's Supreme Court of Appeal overturned the culpable homicide conviction of Pistorius and found him guilty of murder. Pistorius admitted shooting his 29-year-old girlfriend, model Reeva Steenkamp, to death through a closed bathroom door on Valentine's Day 2013.[2] The famed paralympian fired four shots into the bathroom after, he said, he was awakened at night to the sounds of what he thought was a prowler in his house. In 2014 Pistorius had been sentenced to serve five years in prison, but was paroled after having served only a year and then moved to house arrest. The 2016 appeal was an attempt by prosecutors to increase the length of his sentence.

This chapter discusses violent crimes, including murder, rape, robbery, and aggravated assault (Figure 11-1).

Homicide

The terms **homicide** and **murder** are often used interchangeably, although they are not the same. Homicide is the willful killing of one human being by another, whereas murder is an unlawful homicide. Some homicides, such as those committed in defense of oneself or one's family, may be justifiable and therefore legal. In legal parlance, *criminal homicide* means "the causing of the death of another person without legal justification or excuse."

According to the Uniform Crime Reports/National Incident Based Reporting System (UCR/NIBRS), 17,250 murders were committed throughout the United States in 2016.[3] The 2016 rate of criminal homicide was 5.3 people murdered for every 100,000 individuals in the U.S. population. As is the case with other major crimes, rates of criminal homicide in the United States increased between 1960 and the early 1990s, but then began decreasing until they reached levels not seen since

Murder and Nonnegligent Homicide	The willful (nonnegligent) killing of one human being by another. The UCR does not include deaths caused by negligence, suicide, or accident; justifiable homicides; or attempts to murder or assaults to murder, which are classified as aggravated assaults.
Rape	The penetration, no matter how slight, of the vagina or anus with any body part or object, or oral penetration by a sex organ of another person, without the consent of the victim. Attempts to commit rape by force or threat of force are also included; however, statutory rape (without force) and other sex offenses are excluded.
Robbery	Taking or attempting to take anything of value from the care, custody, or control of a person or persons by force or threat of force, or violence and/or by putting the victim in fear.
Aggravated Assault	An unlawful attack by one person upon another for the purpose of inflicting severe bodily injury. Aggravated assault is usually accompanied by the use of a weapon or by means likely to produce death or great bodily harm.

FIGURE 11-1 | Violent Crimes and Their Definitions
Source: FBI, Uniform Crime Reporting Program.

■ **first-degree murder**   The premeditated unlawful killing of a human being.

■ **second-degree murder**   The unlawful intentional killing of a human being without premeditation.

■ **negligent homicide**   The unlawful killing of a human being that occurs as a result of an unlawful or negligent action.

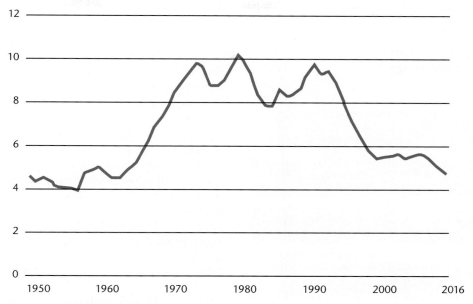

FIGURE 11-2 | Murder Rates, 1950–2016

Source: FBI, *Crime in the United States,* various years.

the 1960s (Figure 11-2). General features of criminal homicide in the United States today are shown in Figure 11-3.

Jurisdictions generally distinguish among various types of murder. Among the distinctions made are **first-degree murder**, also called "premeditated murder"; **second-degree murder**; and third-degree murder, or **negligent homicide**. First-degree

Oscar Pistorius, the South African Paralympic athlete known as the "blade runner," being escorted to a sentencing hearing in South Africa after his conviction in 2014 of negligent homicide in the shooting death of his model girlfriend, Reeva Steenkamp. Pistorius served 10 months in prison, but then was ordered to serve another six years after prosecutors appealed his original conviction. What is the difference between homicide and murder? What types of murder are distinguishable under law?

murder differs from the other two types of murder in that it is planned. It involves what some statutes call "malice aforethought," which may become evident by someone "lying in wait" for the victim, but can also be proved by a murderer's simple action of going into an adjacent room to find a weapon and returning with it to kill. In effect, any activity in preparation to kill that demonstrates the passage of time, however brief, between formation of the intent to kill and the act of killing itself is technically sufficient to establish the legal requirements needed for a first-degree murder prosecution.

Second-degree murder, on the other hand, is a true crime of passion. It is an unlawful killing in which the intent to kill and the killing itself happen almost simultaneously. Hence, a person who kills in a fit of anger is likely to be charged with second-degree murder, as is one who is provoked into killing by insults, physical abuse, and the like. For a murder to be second-degree, however, the killing must follow immediately upon the abuse. Time that elapses between abuse or insults and the murder itself allows the opportunity for thought to occur and hence for premeditation.

Both first- and second-degree murderers intend to kill. Third-degree murder, although it varies in meaning between jurisdictions, most often refers to homicides that are the result of some action that is unlawful or negligent. Hence, it is frequently called "negligent homicide," "negligent manslaughter," "manslaughter," or "involuntary manslaughter." Under negligent homicide statutes, for example, a drunk driver who causes a fatal accident may be charged with third-degree murder even though that person had not the slightest intent to kill.

■ **felony murder** An unlawful homicide that occurs during the commission or attempted commission of a felony, or certain felonies specified by law.

General Features of Criminal Homicide in the United States

Males are nearly four times more likely than females to be murdered.

Males are seven times more likely than females to commit murder.

The homicide victimization rate for blacks is 6 times higher than the rate for whites.

Young adults (18 to 24 years old) have the highest victimization rate in each racial and sex group.

Young adults (18 to 24 years old) have the highest offending rate in each racial and sex category.

Young males (14 to 24 years old), particularly young black males, are disproportionately involved in homicide compared to their proportion of the population.

Most homicides with known victim–offender relationships involve people who knew each other.

Female victims are substantially more likely than male victims to have been killed by an intimate.

Guns are the most frequently used type of weapon in intimate homicides, but weapon type varied by relationship.

FIGURE 11-3 | **General Features of Criminal Homicide in the United States**

Source: Alexis Cooper and Erica L. Smith, *Homicide Trends in the United States, 1980–2008: With Annual Rates for 2009 and 2010* (Washington, DC: Bureau of Justice Statistics, November 2011).

Some jurisdictions have created a special category of **felony murder**, whereby an offender who commits a crime during which someone dies can be found guilty of first-degree murder even though the person committing the crime had no intention of killing anyone. Bank robberies in which one of the robbers is shot to death by police, for example, or in which a bank patron succumbs to a fear-induced heart attack may

leave a surviving robber subject to the death penalty under the felony murder rule. Hence, felony murder is a special class of criminal homicide whereby an offender may be charged with first-degree murder when that person's criminal activity results in another person's death.

Significant contributions to the understanding of the crime of homicide are being made today by the Homicide Research Working Group (HRWG). The HRWG brings together researchers, academicians, and investigators working in the area of interpersonal violence from numerous disciplines. Prior to the creation of the HRWG, work in lethal violence had been scattered among numerous disciplines and was largely uncoordinated. To address this lack of coordination, homicide experts from various disciplines, including criminology, public health, demography, medicine, sociology, criminal justice, and other fields, joined together to create the HRWG.

> Homicide offending is very much patterned in terms of sociodemographics.

Although homicide offenders include men and women, young and old, rich and poor, homicide offending is very much patterned in terms of sociodemographics, with members of some groups being disproportionately represented as offenders. Distinctive patterns of homicide can be identified by such factors as individual characteristics, cultural norms, community characteristics, geographic region, availability of weapons and weapons used, gang activity and affiliation, and the victim–offender relationship. All of these sociodemographic features have been used to further our understanding of homicide patterns and to create typologies surrounding homicide.

The Subculture of Violence Theory

What causes some cities to have high rates of violence while others don't? High rates of unemployment, poverty, and low educational attainment are frequently associated with violence, although they might not necessarily be its cause. In Flint, Michigan, for example—a city with one of the highest rates in America—the poverty rate is over 40%, and only 80% of adults hold a high school degree and the median household income was just $23,380—the second lowest of all 555 cities in the United States measured by the U.S. Census Bureau.[4] Association is not the same thing as causation, however, and some say that although "it is very clear that poverty in particular is associated with higher crime rates," it's "very difficult to say whether crime makes places poorer, or poverty causes more crime."[5]

■ **subculture of violence theory**   The belief that certain groups or subcultures in society have values and attitudes that are conducive to crime and violence.

■ **primary homicide**   A murder involving a family member, friend, or acquaintance.

■ **expressive crime**   A criminal offense that results from acts of interpersonal hostility, such as jealousy, revenge, romantic triangles, and quarrels.

■ **nonprimary homicide**   A murder that involves a victim and an offender who have no prior relationship and that usually occurs during the course of another crime, such as robbery.

■ **instrumental crime**   A goal-directed offense that involves some degree of planning by the offender and little or no precipitation by the victim.

> The subculture of violence theory holds that certain groups share norms and values that contribute to lifestyles involving violence.

An alternative perspective is the subculture of violence theory that was originally formulated by Marvin Wolfgang and Franco Ferracuti,[6] and which was discussed in Chapter 7. These authors stressed that certain groups share norms and values in lifestyles of violence. Ethnic and racial differences in criminal activity rely on interaction with others, including a shared sense of history, language, values, and beliefs. A subculture requires a sufficient number of people who share not only values and beliefs but also a social forum that expresses membership. Such a forum may be something as elusive as a street corner. It is primarily the nature of this situation that makes it difficult to test empirically. The subculture of violence thesis has been the primary theoretical perspective used to explain the similarity between homicide victims and offenders. First, homicide statistics reveal that victims and offenders share similar sociodemographic characteristics such as age, gender, and race. African Americans are disproportionately represented in the homicide statistics as both victims and offenders.[7] Second, victims and offenders who know each other well are disproportionately represented in homicide statistics. An analysis of supplemental homicide reports shows that approximately 60% of victims and offenders have some prior relationship.[8]

The **subculture of violence theory** has also been explored at the community level, where the emphasis is on the importance of "critical masses" as support for the existence of subcultures.[9] Early research argued that the disproportionate rate at which African Americans commit homicide is associated with the presence of a large African American population, the "critical mass" necessary for the "transmission of violence-related models" and subcultural behavior patterns.[10] However, most of the research that found higher homicide rates to be associated with higher percentages of African Americans in the population did not take into consideration socioeconomic status, level of education, and so forth.[11] Research by Robert Sampson, using more sophisticated measures and stronger research designs, revealed that the racial composition of an area alone did not have a significant effect on the homicide rates for either whites or African Americans.[12]

Homicide: A Closer Look

Marvin Wolfgang's now-famous 1958 study of homicides in Philadelphia revealed that approximately 25% of all homicides were between family members and that women were far more likely than men to be both offenders and victims within this category than within any other.[13] Males are more likely to be killed by friends and strangers than by their family members, and very few women (relative to men) are murderers. However, when a male is killed by a female, the offender is most likely to be his spouse.[14] Other researchers have emphasized qualitative differences in the pattern of homicide within the victim–offender relationship. Figure 11-4 shows the relationship between killers and their victims.

The Victim–Offender Relationship

The work of **Robert Nash Parker** and Dwayne Smith represented the first systematic research that focused on differentiating homicide according to the victim–offender relationship (see Chapter 10 for more on this topic).[15] Their work used two classifications of homicide: primary and nonprimary. **Primary homicides** are the most frequent and involve family members, friends, and acquaintances, and they are usually characterized as **expressive crimes** because they often result from interpersonal hostility, based on jealousy, revenge, romantic triangles, and minor disagreements.[16]

Nonprimary homicides involve victims and offenders who have no prior relationship and usually occur in the course of another crime such as robbery; these are referred to as **instrumental crimes** because they involve some degree of premeditation by the offender and are less likely to be precipitated by the victim. The difference between expressive and instrumental motives for homicide continues to be important in criminological research, and we will return to this shortly.

Further attention to the heterogeneous nature of homicide is found in the work of K. R. Williams and R. L. Flewelling, who disaggregated homicide rates according to two criteria: (1) the nature of the circumstances surrounding the homicide, which included whether there was some indicator of a fight or argument precipitating the homicide and (2) the victim–offender relationship, distinguishing between victims and offenders who were family members, acquaintances, or strangers.[17] By comparing how factors like poverty and population size have different effects on different types of homicide,

■ **exposure-reduction theory**   A theory of intimate homicide that claims that a decline in domesticity, accompanied by
an improvement in the economic status of women and a growth
in domestic violence resources, explains observed decreases in
intimate-partner homicide.

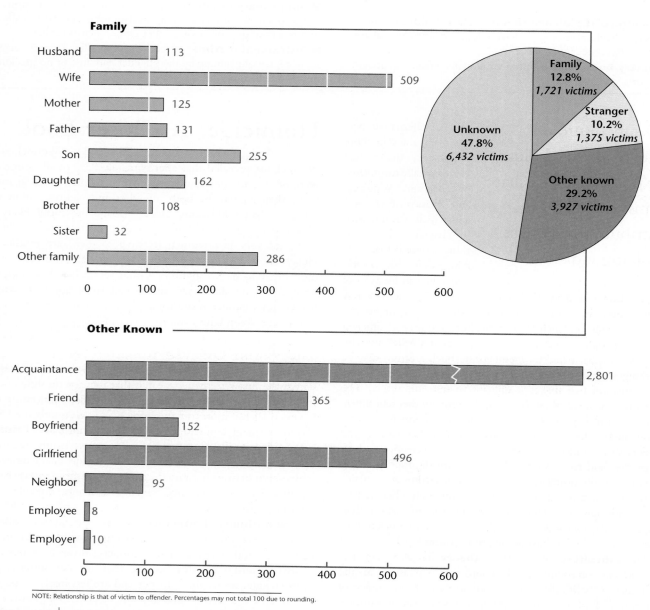

FIGURE 11-4 | **Murder by Relationship, 2016**
Source: Federal Bureau of Investigation, *Crime in the United States, 2016* (Washington, DC: FBI, 2017).

Williams and Flewelling found that some factors are more
important in explaining certain forms of homicide. Poverty
is a stronger predictor of family homicide, population size is
more important in explaining stranger homicide, and both the
victim–offender relationship and the context of the homicide
(e.g., the end result of a robbery) are crucial factors in explaining patterns of homicide.

Beginning in the 1980s, the intimate-partner homicide
rate began to decline, a decline that has continued to the
present day. Using homicide data from a sample of 29 large
cities in the United States from 1976 to 1992, Laura Dugan,
Daniel S. Nagin, and Richard Rosenfeld offered an **exposure-
reduction theory** of intimate-partner homicide.[18] These researchers examined the ability of the "decline in domesticity,

■ **sibling offense**   An offense or incident that culminates in homicide. The offense or incident may be a crime, such as robbery, or an incident with a less stringent criminal definition, such as a lovers' quarrel involving assault or battery.

■ **selective disinhibition**   A loss of self-control due either to the social setting or to drugs or alcohol, or a combination of both.

improved economic status of women, and growth in domestic violence resources" to explain decreases in intimate-partner homicide in urban areas.[19] Analysis of the data did support the major hypotheses offered by Dugan, Nagin, and Rosenfeld—as resources supporting a nonviolent exit from a violent relationship increase, rates of intimate-partner homicide decrease. Read more about intimate-partner violence at **http://www.apa.org/topics/violence/partner.aspx**.

Sibling Offenses

Not all homicide offenders intend to kill their victims. This may be the case when the incident begins as a robbery motivated by instrumental ends, such as getting money. An argument may also precede a homicide, but this circumstance is expressive rather than instrumental because "the dominant motivation is the violence itself," even if lethal violence is not planned in advance.[20] The importance of instigating incidents is explored in research by Carolyn Rebecca Block and Richard Block.[21] The Blocks use the term **sibling offense** to refer to the incident that begins the homicide. A sibling offense may be a crime, such as robbery, or another incident, such as a lover's quarrel. It is crucial to take these sibling offenses into account because they help explain why some robberies end in murder and others do not. The Blocks developed an elaborate typology of homicide to illustrate how an understanding of the patterns of nonlethal violence can assist in the prevention of lethal violence. For example, there are a great many incidents of street gang violence, most of which do not end in death, and understanding those nonlethal incidents can assist in preventing homicides.[22]

Weapon Use

There are different perspectives on the role that weapons play in crime, with most of the discussion centering on the role of firearms in homicide. In examining the relationship between guns and homicide, it is important to differentiate between instrumentality and availability. *Instrumentality* refers to the fact that the type of weapon used in a particular encounter has an effect on whether the encounter ends in death. For example, the involvement of a gun may mean the difference between a criminal event ending as an assault or a homicide. When guns are used in robberies, the fatality rate is "three times as high as for robberies with knives and 10 times as high as for robberies with other weapons."[23]

Availability refers to issues surrounding how access to guns may increase their presence in all types of interactions,

including criminal ones.[24] The ease of availability is important, given the relative spontaneity of some violent encounters. The availability of guns is important at the individual level as well as the community level because the greater the presence of guns in a particular neighborhood, the easier the access for individuals beyond their immediate households. Compared to gun instrumentality, then, gun availability may be a much stronger factor in explaining lethal violence.[25] See **http://www.justfacts.com/guncontrol.asp** for more information.

Alcohol and Drug Use

An important conceptual typology detailing the relationship between alcohol or drugs and crime was developed by Paul J. Goldstein in an article first published in 1985.[26] According to Goldstein, the association of alcohol and illicit drugs with violent offending generally takes one of three forms: psychopharmacological use, economic compulsion, and systemic violence. Drugs may be linked to violent offending through *psychopharmacological use*, whereby infrequent or chronic use of certain drugs produces violent behavior by lowering inhibitions or elevating aggressive tendencies; however, not all drugs produce such effects, and the relationship appears to hold only for people with certain types of personalities using certain substances in certain settings.

When crimes are committed to support a drug habit, Goldstein said that the concept of *economic compulsion* best describes the relationship between crime and drug use. He used the idea of *systemic violence* to describe the connection between drugs and trafficking, and it can take several forms, ranging from rival drug wars to robberies of drug dealers. Although distinct types of relationships between drugs and violence can be described, these are not necessarily mutually exclusive, with one or more relationships present in a single criminal incident.

Researchers from the Drug Relationships in Murder Project (DREIM), which analyzed incarcerated homicide offenders in New York State, found that in the majority of homicide cases involving both alcohol and illicit drugs, the primary basis for the connection with the crime was psychopharmacological.[27]

One theoretical approach focused on explaining the role that alcohol plays in homicide as social in nature rather than biochemical is **selective disinhibition**, advanced by Robert Nash Parker and others.[28] In particular situations or interactions, the "disinhibiting" effect of alcohol may operate to suspend certain factors that could restrain the occurrence of violence and may operate

■ **visionary serial killers** Serial killers motivated by auditory or visual hallucinations.

■ **comfort serial killers** Serial killers motivated by financial or material gain.

■ **hedonistic serial killers** Serial killers who derive pleasure from killing.

■ **power seekers** Serial killers who relish having power over another human being.

■ **serial murder** A type of criminal homicide that involves the killing of several victims in three or more separate events.

The selective nature of alcohol-related homicide is dependent on the interaction of an impaired rationality and the nature of the social situation.

to put into play certain factors that could increase the occurrence or degree of violence. This perspective relies on the existence of norms operating both to prohibit and to proscribe the use of violence in particular situations. Because alcohol can reduce both forms of constraint, "the selective nature of alcohol-related homicide is dependent on the interaction of an impaired rationality and the nature of the social situation."[29] Parker and his colleagues tested this model by analyzing data on homicides in several cities in 1980, in several cities between 1960 and 1980, and in several states from 1976 to 1983. One key finding from this research was the ability of alcohol to significantly predict primary homicide. In relationships between individuals who are known to each other, alcohol may operate to disinhibit restraints against violence, but the norms that operate to govern interactions between strangers are more rigid in terms of the type of conduct that is proscribed. The use of violence against those known to us is treated with greater tolerance—tolerance that can be increased even more in the presence of alcohol.[30]

In his research using state-level data, Parker tested several hypotheses derived from competing theoretical perspectives about the effect of alcohol on homicide.[31] Based on the victim-offender relationship, five types of homicides were identified: "robbery, other felony, family intimate, family other, and primary nonintimate."[32] Poverty had a stronger effect on both robbery and other felony homicides in states with "above average rates of alcohol consumption";[33] alcohol consumption had direct effects on two of the three types of primary homicide.

Serial Killers

Serial murder is a criminal homicide that "involves the killing of several victims in three or more separate events."[34] Criminologists **James Alan Fox** and **Jack Levin** have written extensively on both serial killing and mass murder.

Contrary to some commonly held beliefs, the vast majority of serial killers are not legally insane or medically psychotic. "They are more cruel than crazy," according to Fox and Levin. "Their crimes may be sickening but their minds are not necessarily sick."[35] Many serial killers are diagnosed as sociopaths, a term for those with antisocial personalities.

Sailson Jose das Gracas, of Brazil, who admitted in 2014 that he had killed at least 41 people "for fun." The 26-year-old, who said killing gave him "a buzz," was described as a "psychopath" by police. Are there other people like das Gracas?

Xinhua/Alamy Stock Photo

Because they lack a conscience, sociopaths do not consider the needs or basic humanity of others in their decision making or their view of the world. They do not see themselves as being bound by conventional rules or by the expectations of others. Sociopaths view other people as "tools to be manipulated for the purpose of maximizing their personal pleasure."[36] However, many sociopaths are neither serial killers nor involved in violent crime, even though "they may lie, cheat, or steal."[37]

Although not an exclusive characteristic of serial killers, sexual sadism is a strong pattern. In many of the typologies developed by researchers, this characteristic forms the basis for a type of serial killer. Typologies of serial killers are organized around different, but generally related, themes. Some criminologists identify four different types of serial killers: **Visionary serial killers** hear voices and have visions that are the basis for a compulsion to murder; **comfort serial killers** are motivated by financial or material gain; **hedonistic serial killers** murder because they find it enjoyable and derive psychological pleasure from killing; and **power seekers** operate from some position of authority over others, and their killings usually involve a period where the killer plays a kind of cat-and-mouse game with the victim.[38] Fox and Levin offer a three-part typology. They classify serial murderers as thrill-motivated, mission-oriented, or expedience-directed killers. *Thrill-motivated killers*, the most common type of serial killer, may be of two types: the sexual sadist and the dominance killer. *Mission-oriented killers* are not as common and generally have either a reformist or visionary orientation. Reformists want to rid the world of evil, and visionaries hear voices

■ **Violent Criminal Apprehension Program (VICAP)**
The program of the Federal Bureau of Investigation focusing on serial murder investigation and the apprehension of serial killers.

commanding them to do certain activities. Visionary killers are quite rare and tend to be genuinely psychotic. *Expedience-directed serial killers* are driven by either profit or protection. Profit-driven killers may kill for financial or material gain, and protection-oriented killers commit murder to mask other crimes, such as robbery.[39]

Female Serial Killers

Although the vast majority of serial killers are male, there have been female serial killers, and the patterns of their activities are sometimes distinct from those of male serialists.[40] Female serial killers typically select their victims from among people they know, unlike male serial killers, who tend to target strangers.[41] A type of serial killer found primarily among women is the *disciple killer*, who murders as the result of the influence of a charismatic personality. The women who killed at the behest of Charles Manson were of this type. Male serial killers often commit their crimes some distance from their homes, generally without regard to type of neighborhood. However,

Serial killer Aileen Wuornos who was executed by the state of Florida in 2002 after refusing further appeals. Although some women are moving into areas of traditional male criminality, the number of women committing violent crimes is still far smaller than the number of men. How does the criminality of women appear to differ from that of men?

geographic stability characterizes almost all of the known female serial killers.[42]

Michael D. Kelleher and C. L. Kelleher researched female serial killers from a historical perspective and developed a typology based on motivation. Arguing that there are two broad categories of female serial killers—those who act alone and those who work in partnership with others—Kelleher and Kelleher present a typology based on distinct motivation, selection of victim, and method of killing.[43] The categories include the *black widow*, who generally kills spouses and usually for economic profit, and the *angel of death*, who generally kills "those in her care or who rely on her for some form of medical attention or similar support."[44] The typical career of a female serial killer is longer than that of her male counterpart. Other than women who commit their crimes with others, usually men, female serial killers tend to approach their crimes in a systematic fashion—a characteristic that may explain their longer careers.[45]

Apprehending Serial Killers

Fox and Levin contended that it is extremely difficult to identify and apprehend serial killers because of the cautiousness and skill with which they operate—the very factors that allow them to kill often enough to be labeled *serial killers*. The FBI established the **Violent Criminal Apprehension Program (VICAP)** in 1985 to increase the efficiency and effectiveness of serial killer apprehension. Although Fox and Levin called VICAP an "excellent concept in theory," they noted several practical problems with the program.[46] First, the data complexity and the associated record keeping have limited reporting compliance by law enforcement officials, seriously affecting VICAP's potential usefulness; second, the recognition of patterns among serial killers, even with the assistance of powerful computers, is not easily achieved; and third, VICAP functions more as a detection tool than an apprehension tool.

In addition to VICAP, the FBI employs crime analysts who assist local law enforcement. Employing a classification system based on two prongs, FBI analysts distinguish between organized social killers and disorganized asocial killers. Organized social killers have a higher level of intelligence, better social skills, and a greater ability to function in all areas of life than do disorganized killers. These two types also differ in their method of killing—although variation exists among them, the "organized/disorganized continuum is used as an overall guideline for drawing inferences from the crime scene to the behavioral characteristics of the killer."[47] More recent attempts to identify serial killers rely on geo-mapping techniques to approximate the killer's probable location.[48]

■ **mass murder**   The illegal killing of three or more victims at one location within one event.

CRIME | in the NEWS

Why Mass Shootings Won't Go Away

Mass shootings by lone gunmen seem to be a uniquely American phenomenon. To date, the 2017 shooting of nearly 600 people (of whom 58 died) in Las Vegas by 64-year-old Stephen Paddock is the deadliest such attack. Paddock fired from a guest room on the 32nd floor of a nearby resort into a music festival crowd of more than 30,000 people. In 2016, Omar Marteen (who is featured in a Criminal Profile box elsewhere in this text) shot over 100 people at the Pulse nightclub in Orlando. Forty-nine of them died. Marteen, who was 29 years old at the time of the attack, was killed after a police SWAT team forced its way into the building.

In 2012, 20-year-old Adam Lanza, a mentally troubled young man, killed 25 people at an elementary school in Newtown, Connecticut—20 of them children.

Mass shootings show no signs of declining, despite an overall drop in the U.S. homicide rate. "The frequency of gun violence does not fluctuate much year to year," said James Alan Fox, a criminology professor at Northeastern University. Looking back 35 years, Fox counted 19 such shootings in 1976 and 18 in 2010, with a range of 7 in 1985 to 30 in 2003.

A study of past incidents reveals a portrait of the mass shooter. He tends to be a young man without friends and recently encountered some humiliation. He's aiming for a high body count. Sometimes he copies another mass shooter or a figure from the movies, as Colorado shooter James Holmes did when imitating the Joker, Batman's sworn enemy. Although many mass shooters are depressed, they rarely suffer psychosis, according to James L. Knoll, a psychiatrist at SUNY Upstate Medical Center.

Little in this portrait, however, can help predict future mass shootings. Mass shooters rarely talk about their exploits in advance. But many of them do undergo a personality change just before their crimes, as evidenced by Holmes dyeing his hair orange. Larry Burton, a professor at Bryn Mawr College in Pennsylvania, thinks people should notice these changes and report them to authorities.

Other ways to address mass shootings might be to ban assault rifles, which could reduce the carnage, and the imposition of stricter background checks for gun purchases. But a mass shooter, like Paddock, without a criminal record might not be identified and prevented from

A memorial to the victims of the October 1, 2017, Las Vegas mass shooting, which claimed the lives of 58 people, and injured 546 others. The shooter, 64-year-old Stephen Paddock fired thousands of rounds from the 32nd floor of the Mandalay Bay Resort and Casino into a nearby music festival crowd of over 30,000. How can mass killings be prevented?

buying weapons. Fox argues that preventing these calamities is pretty much impossible. "We're not going to turn our country into one big fortress," he said. "People hate it when I say this, but it's true. This kind of tragedy is one of the unfortunate prices we pay for our freedoms."

Discussion Questions

1. Why have random mass shootings become relatively commonplace in American society?

2. What can be done to prevent future incidents of random mass shootings?

Sources: Seth Cline, "Are Mass Shootings a Fact of Life in America?" *US News & World Report*, August 28, 2012, http://www.usnews.com/news/articles/2012/08/28/are-mass-shootings-a-fact-of-life-in-america; Lizette Alvarez, Richard Perez-Pena and Christine Hauser, "Orlando Gunman was 'Cool and Calm' after Massacre, Police Say," June 13, 2016, *The New York Times*, https://www.nytimes.com/2016/06/14/us/orlando-shooting.html (accessed March 3, 2017); and Doug Criss, "The Las Vegas Attack is the Deadliest Mass Shooting in Modern US History," CNN, http://www.cnn.com/2017/10/02/us/las-vegas-attack-deadliest-us-mass-shooting-trnd/index.html (accessed November 25, 2017).

Mass Murder

Mass murder is the illegal killing of three or more individuals at a single time.[49] Mass murder can follow the political motivations of the offenders, as was the case with the 1995 Oklahoma City bombing, in which 168 individuals, including children, were killed. The most notable politically motivated mass murder was the September 11, 2001, destruction of the World

Trade Center towers in New York City, in which approximately 2,700 people died.

Other mass murderers kill for more personal reasons. The mass killing of 32 people at the Virginia Polytechnic Institute and State University (Virginia Tech) campus in Blacksburg, Virginia, in 2007 by student gunman Seung-Hui Cho appears to have been at least partially motivated by a seething anger against those whom Cho perceived as being more successful

■ **rape** The penetration, no matter how slight, of the vagina or anus with any body part or object, or oral penetration by a sex organ of another person, without the consent of the victim.

than he, and the bombings carried out by two Chechen brothers at the 2013 Boston Marathon, in which three people died, was politically motivated.[50]

Mass murderers tend to surprise their victims because they often attack in everyday locales that are considered safe and because they erupt spontaneously. In 2016, for example, shooter Omar Marteen opened fire in the crowded Pulse nightclub in Orlando, Florida, killing or wounding more than 100 patrons.[51] Although mass murders do not occur with great frequency, they cause great concern because they shatter the sense of safety that characterizes everyday life. Given the number of mass shootings that have occurred over the past few years, however, many schools, hospitals, and businesses across the nation are taking steps to deal with such events.[52]

Fox and Levin offer a four-part typology of mass murder that differentiates these crimes by motive:[53]

- *Revenge* murderers represent the largest category of such killers. They are motivated by *revenge* against either particular individuals or groups of individuals. Other revenge-motivated murderers may be less specific in the selection of a target, as in the case of George Hennard, who hated "all of the residents of the county in which he lived." In 1991, Hennard drove his truck through the front window of Luby's Cafeteria in Killeen, Texas, and then "indiscriminately opened fire on customers as they ate their lunch, killing 23."[54]

- Mass murderers motivated by *love* have a sense of love that is distorted and obsessive. They often commit suicide after they murder, and in the case of a spouse killing, they may also kill their children.

- Mass murderers who kill for *profit* are usually trying to eliminate witnesses in an effort to cover up a major crime.

- Some mass murderers are motivated by *terror*, such as the individuals who participated in the Charles Manson killings. These people want to send a message to society.

Although most mass murders strike the public as senseless acts of a crazy person, Levin and Fox contend that "most massacres are not madmen."[55] Yet why would a person such as James Huberty, a former security guard, walk calmly into a fast-food restaurant in 1984 and fatally shoot 21 victims at random, most of whom were children? Why would Patrick Edward Purdy shoot and kill 5 children and wound 30 others at Cleveland Elementary School in Stockton, California, in 1989?[56] And what of the motivation of 20-year-old Adam Lanza, who shot and killed 20 children and 6 adults at the Sandy Hook Elementary School in Newton, Connecticut, in 2012? Levin and Fox argue that factors such as frustration, isolation, blame, loss, failure, and other external and internal motivations and situational elements contribute to the activities of mass murderers. They delineate three types of contributing factors: *predisposers*, "long-term and stable preconditions that become incorporated into the personality of the killer," which are nearly always present in his or her

biography; *precipitants*, "short-term and acute triggers," that is, catalysts; and *facilitators*, conditions, usually situational, that "increase the likelihood of a violent outburst but are not necessary to produce that response."[57] Using this typology to explain why, for example, most mass murderers are middle-aged, Levin and Fox contend that it takes a long time to accumulate the kind of rage and frustration that sets off some mass murderers. Mass murderers often select targets that have some significance for them, such as workers at a site of former employment. As Fox and Levin state, "A majority of mass killers target victims who are specially chosen, not just in the wrong place at the wrong time. The indiscriminate slaughter of strangers by a 'crazed' killer is the exception to the rule."[58] Unlike serial murderers, mass murderers are relatively easy to apprehend because they rarely leave the scene of the crime, either because they commit suicide after the killing or because they stay long enough to be detected and apprehended.

Rape

In early 2012, then-Attorney General Eric Holder announced a new gender-neutral definition of the word **rape** to be used by federal agencies.

The new definition of rape reads: "The penetration, no matter how slight, of the vagina or anus with any body part or object, or oral penetration by a sex organ of another person, without the consent of the victim."[59]

UCR/NIBRS statistics on rape, as currently reported, include cases of both rape and attempted rape. Statutory rape (sexual relations between an underage female minor and an adult male) and other sex offenses are excluded from the count of rape crimes. In 2016, 130,603 rapes were reported nationwide under the UCR Program. As Figure 11-5 shows, the risk of sexual assault victimization for both females and males varies

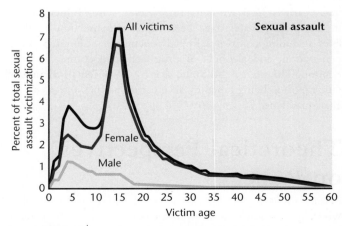

FIGURE 11-5 | Sexual Assault Victimization by Age and Sex

Source: Office of Juvenile Justice and Delinquency Prevention, *Juvenile Offenders and Victims: 2014 National Report* (Washington, DC: OJJDP, 2015), p. 44.

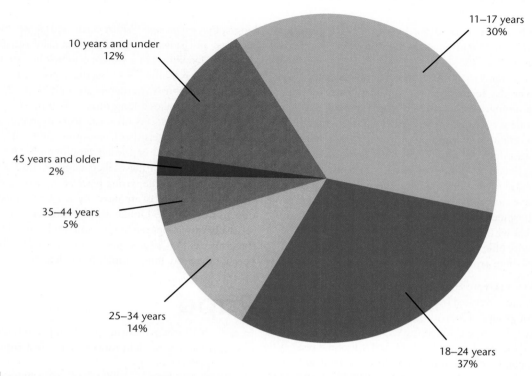

FIGURE 11-6 | **Age at Time of First Completed Rape Victimization among Female Victims**

Source: Centers for Disease Control, National Center for Injury Prevention and Control, *National Intimate Partner and Sexual Violence Survey Factsheet* (Atlanta, GA: Centers for Disease Control and Prevention, National Center for Injury Prevention and Control, November 2011).

greatly by age. Figure 11-6 details the age at the time of first rape victimization among females.

Reports to the police of the crime of rape rarely reveal its true incidence. Recently, the National Center for Injury Prevention and Control (a part of the federal Centers for Disease Control and Prevention) released its *National Intimate Partner and Sexual Violence Survey*. The most recent report shows that nearly 1 in 5 women (18.3%) and 1 in 71 men (1.4%) in the United States have been raped at some time in their lives, including completed forced penetration, attempted forced penetration, and alcohol- or drug-facilitated completed penetration. The survey also found that 51.1% of female victims of rape reported being raped by an intimate partner and 40.8% by an acquaintance.[60]

Theoretical Perspectives on Rape

Several theoretical perspectives have been offered to explain what the individual motivations for rape are, why rape is more prevalent in particular contexts, and how certain cultural values may reinforce rape. Many of these perspectives attempt to explain how rape is patterned according to the context, the victim–offender relationship, and the motivations of the rapist.

Feminist Perspectives

There is no single feminist perspective on rape, but some common elements run through the various feminist perspectives (also discussed in Chapter 9). Feminists view gender as a social construct rather than a biological given and regard as problematic the way in which gender is used to structure social relations and institutions. The patriarchal relations and structures within our society contributing to the privileged status of men are inseparable from rape itself because rape serves as a social control mechanism. Rape is viewed as an act of power or domination in which the "tool" used to subordinate is sexual—rape is a crime of violence that is sexual in nature, but this aspect is considered secondary to the power dynamics that occur in rapes.[61]

Socialization patterns, cultural practices, structural arrangements, media images, sexuality norms, and women's status in society all combine to create a rape culture in which both men and women come to view male aggression as normal, even in sexual relations.[62] Within this culture, women are blamed for their own rapes by virtue of the fact that males are naturally incapable of controlling their sexual desire. For feminists like **Catherine MacKinnon**[63] and **Andrea Dworkin**,[64] rape and sex are not easily distinguishable under patriarchy because the male dominance that characterizes patriarchy is inherent in both the act of rape and the social construction of sex. Who women are and what women choose for themselves become

CRIMINAL | PROFILES

Karla Homolka—A Woman Rapist?

On October 17, 1987, then-17-year-old Karla Homolka met then-23-year-old Paul Bernardo in an Ontario hotel restaurant.[i] Their physical attraction was immediate and intense, and two hours later the couple had sex in one of the hotel's rooms.

Unbeknownst to Homolka, the handsome boy-next-door Paul Bernardo had already embarked on a clandestine career as a serial rapist. In May of 1987, Bernardo raped a young woman in Scarborough, a small suburban town northeast of Toronto on the shores of Lake Ontario. Hers was to be the first of at least 14 rapes that the man dubbed the "Scarborough Rapist" would admit to committing during the next five years. Additionally, he was convicted of murdering two of his rape victims.[ii]

As the relationship between Bernardo and Homolka evolved, Bernardo began to assert increasingly outrageous sexual demands with which Homolka willingly complied. Eventually, he expressed his annoyance that she had not been a virgin when he first met her. To resolve the problem, Homolka arranged to present Bernardo her own virgin younger sister, Tammy, as a Christmas gift. On December 23, 1990, then-15-year-old Tammy was fed alcohol laced with the sedative Halcion. When Tammy passed out, Bernardo raped and sodomized her while Homolka kept a drug-laced rag over Tammy's face to maintain her unconscious state. Both Bernardo and Homolka videotaped the rape as it was occurring, including Tammy's death at the end of the incident.[iii]

When Bernardo later complained to Homolka that she had cost him future sexual opportunities with Tammy by allowing her to die, Homolka found a replacement virgin whom she offered to Bernardo as a prewedding gift. Homolka invited a 15-year-old family acquaintance to dinner at the house she had rented with Bernardo. As with Tammy, the girl was fed Halcion until she became unconscious. Bernardo then videotaped Homolka performing sexual acts on the sleeping girl, then raped and brutally sodomized the girl as Homolka videotaped his acts.[iv]

On June 14, 1991, Bernardo abducted 14-year-old Leslie Mahaffy and brought her back to the house he shared with Homolka. After stripping and blindfolding the terrified girl, Bernardo woke his future wife and proceeded to act as a movie director while videotaping Homolka performing lesbian sexual acts on Mahaffy. Homolka then took over the camera while Bernardo initiated a violent assault on the young girl, including brutal anal rape. Bernardo's violence continued to escalate until Mahaffy finally died. The two then dismembered her body and dumped the parts into Lake Ontario.[v]

Bernardo and Homolka married on June 29, 1991, and Bernardo continued his campaign of rape, often with Homolka's encouragement and assistance. At least one victim recalled seeing a woman videotaping her rape.

On April 16, 1992, the married rapists/killers abducted 16-year-old Kristen French from the parking lot outside of French's church. They then raped, tortured, and murdered the pretty young girl and left her nude body in a roadside ditch.

A courtroom photograph of notorious Canadian sex criminal Karla Homolka as she appeared in court in Joliette, Quebec, on June 3, 2005. She was set free after having served 12 years in prison for helping her former husband rape and murder three teenage girls, including her younger sister. Why are female sex killers so rare?

Frank Gunn/AP Images

DNA evidence finally led to Bernardo's arrest on February 17, 1993. Homolka agreed to testify against him in exchange for a sentence of just 12 years for her role as an accomplice.

In July 1993, Homolka pleaded guilty and her sentence, as agreed to in the plea bargain, was pronounced. Controversy exploded, however, when the numerous videotapes of the rapes and murders surfaced in September 1994, and the public became aware of the full extent of Homolka's willing participation in the atrocities.[vi]

Bernardo was convicted of the two murders on September 15, 1995, and was sentenced to life in prison without possibility of parole. Public ire again boiled over following Homolka's release from prison on parole on July 4, 2005, when it became known that Homolka was complaining about the postrelease restrictions to which she was subjected. In February 2007, the Canadian media reported that Homolka, with a new husband and a new name—Leanne Teale—had given birth to a baby boy.[vii]

By 2016, she was reported to have moved to Chateauguay—a Montreal suburb, where two of her children were said to be attending public school.[viii]

The case of Karla Homolka raises a number of interesting questions. Among them are the following:

1. Which of the theories discussed in previous chapters might best explain Homolka's behavior? Would any of them have helped authorities identify Homolka before she could kill again?

2. What motivated Homolka? Did she share the same motivation as her husband, killer Paul Bernardo?

Notes

i. Posted by Her Karma on Vancouver Forum, the Discover Vancouver Bulletin Board, July 3, 2005, http://www.discovervancouver.com/forum/topic.asp?TOPIC_ID521791&whichpage52 (accessed May 28, 2011).

ii. Marilyn Bardsley, "Paul Bernardo and Karla Homolka," CourtTV Crime Library, http://www.crimelibrary.com/serial_killers/notorious/bernardo/index_1.html (accessed May 28, 2007).

iii. Anne M. Griffy, "The Evil Within: The Twisted Minds of Paul Bernardo and Karla Homolka," Justice Junction, http://www.justicejunction.com/judicial_injustice_the_evil_within.htm (accessed May 27, 2010).

iv. Ibid.

v. Ibid.

vi. Linda Diebel, "Professor Alan Young on Karla Homolka's Deal," *Toronto Star*, May 28, 2005, http://osgoode.yorku.ca/media2.nsf/83303ffe5af03ed585256ae6005379c9/47f95c9ce0cae54385257011007096ca!OpenDocument (accessed May 28, 2007).

vii. "Victims' Families 'Distressed' over Homolka Baby: Lawyer," CBC News, February 13, 2007, http://www.cbc.ca/canada/montreal/story/2007/02/13/homolka-baby.html (accessed May 28, 2010).

viii. "Karla Homolka Found Living in the Montreal Suburb of Chateauguay," City News Canada, http://www.citynews.ca/2016/04/19/karla-homolka-found-living-in-the-montreal-suburb-of-chateauguay (accessed March 3, 2017).

problematic in the perspectives of these feminists because heterosexuality is "compulsory" under patriarchy. The views of feminists like MacKinnon and Dworkin are often met with resistance by others and are misunderstood as "male bashing." MacKinnon and Dworkin did not focus on individual males as somehow being either "good" or "bad" but on the construction of gender and all that flows from it under patriarchy. The work of Dworkin, MacKinnon, and others also stressed the existence of a rape culture that has the effect of equating sex with violence and objectifying women to the point that they lack an identity separate from that which is defined by men.

> ## Pornography and prostitution are institutions that support social patterns and responses to rape.

Pornography is often thought to contribute to the manner in which women are objectified because violence and sex are combined in a manner that makes the association normative. In an essay first published in 1974, Robin Morgan asserted that "pornography is the theory, and rape the practice."[65] Susan Brownmiller also discussed both pornography and prostitution as institutions that encourage and support social patterns and responses to rape.[66] Although not everyone shares the same view of the role of pornography in supporting the inequality of women and justifying violence against women, pornography is frequently associated with rape in the writings and research of many prominent feminists.

James W. Messerschmidt acknowledged the positive contributions of feminist thought but critiqued these perspectives for their often one-dimensional view of masculinity.[67] Ngaire Naffine also shared Messerschmidt's positive evaluation of this body of work, saying that "Dworkin is trying to shatter our complacency about everyday life for women, to get us to see the daily criminal violence and injustice done to women that has been rendered utterly ordinary and so invisible."[68] Messerschmidt also contended that the response of the state to violence against women is not monolithic; although there are limits to how the state will respond on behalf of women, the state is viable as a site for positive change in terms of women and feminist ideals, and the emergence of rape crisis centers and changes in institutional protocol regarding rape victims illustrate that a state that is basically patriarchal in nature can be pushed to respond to women in ways that are positive and that increase women's autonomy.

Psychopathological Perspective

The psychopathological perspective on rape is based on two assumptions: (1) Rape is the "result of idiosyncratic mental disease," and (2) "it often includes an uncontrollable sexual impulse."[69] Acknowledgment that rape is connected to issues like power and anger is found in the frequently cited work of

Nicholas Groth[70] (other works also contained elements of this psychopathological perspective).[71] Some researchers claimed that Groth's model does not appear to successfully characterize the majority of men who rape, yet this model has been applied as if that were the case.[72] However, Russell did find elements of Groth's model to be useful in developing her own typology for men who rape within marriage.[73] Several of the factors that Groth identifies as important to understanding the motivation and pattern of rapes are found in other typologies of rapists.

Integrated Theory of Rape

Larry Baron and **Murray A. Straus** offered what they termed an "integrated theory of rape."[74] They combined elements from other theoretical explanations of rape into one model positing that (1) support for legitimate violence, (2) higher levels of gender inequality, and (3) social disorganization combine to produce higher rates of rape at the state level. The phrase "support for legitimate violence" refers to norms and institutional arrangements that serve to justify the expression of violence in certain contexts as normative.

"Higher levels of gender inequality" are related to rates of rape because as women's status in society improves, rape is challenged as a mechanism of social control over women. This occurs as socialization patterns change and as women attain positions of power within society. The connection between gender inequality and rape is supported in cross-cultural and anthropological research.[75]

The wording "social disorganization" refers to the inability of communities to sustain viable social institutions—institutions that serve as a buffer to all sorts of social ills, including criminal activity. Poverty alone is not enough to directly produce crime, but in the absence of other factors that strengthen institutional structures within communities, poverty is linked to crime by virtue of its association with other factors.

In a test of their theory at the state level, Baron and Straus found support for the direct effect of gender inequality on rape rates: The higher the level of gender inequality—a combination of several measures relating to economic indicators—the higher was a state's rape rate. They examined the direct effect of pornography and found that higher rates of pornography were associated with higher rates of rape within the state; high levels of social disorganization, measured by such things as residential mobility, percentage of female-headed households, and divorce rates, were also tied to increased rates of rape.[76]

Evolutionary/Biological Perspectives

Within the evolutionary perspective, "humanity is a product of evolution in which both physical and social traits conducive to survival are selected and survive through a process of natural selection. Propagation is the key to survival of a trait, as a genetic predisposition can be passed on only through offspring."[77] Natural selection favors those traits that are most adaptive, and over several generations these traits survive. An evolutionary perspective does not identify rape as an adaptation but focuses on certain motives and ends that are conducive to rape. The environment is also thought to play a role because "genes cannot make traits without environmental causes acting in concert."[78] According to **Randy Thornhill** and **Craig T. Palmer**, "Selection favored different traits in females and males, especially when the traits were directly related to mating. Although some of these differences could have arisen from what Darwin called natural selection, most of them are now believed to have evolved through sexual selection."[79] *Sexual selection* refers to the observation that some traits appear to survive not because they are related to survival, but because they further the attainment of mates or defense against competition over mates; this is said to apply primarily to males because "male fitness is limited by access to the opposite sex much more directly than is female fitness, with the result that females compete for mates much less than do males."[80]

> Evolutionary perspectives have been criticized for justifying rape as "natural."

The specialized jargon and knowledge that inform evolutionary perspectives make it difficult to understand how they apply to social behaviors like rape, and these perspectives have been severely criticized for justifying rape as "natural." Proponents of the usefulness of evolutionary perspectives on rape contend that evolutionary perspectives can explain why rape is so prevalent and why it takes the forms that it does, arguing that "biology provides understanding, not justification, of human behavior."[81] Evolutionary perspectives contend that the feminist position on rape that equates it primarily with expressions of violence diminishes the fact that there is a biologically based sexual motivation and that ignoring this eliminates one avenue by which rape may be understood and prevented. Rather than being counter to the agenda of feminists, evolutionary psychologists offer their perspective as another avenue through which rape can be approached, understood, and thereby prevented.

Typologies of Rapists

Several researchers have attempted to develop typologies of rapists. Nicholas Groth's work represented one of the first systematic attempts to do this based on empirical evidence, gathered in his capacity as a prison psychologist. **Robert R. Hazelwood** and **Ann Burgess** developed a four-part typology of rapists based on the motivation of the offender and revolving around the themes of power, anger, and sadism:[82] power–assertive, power–reassurance, anger–retaliatory, and anger–excitation.

Based on interviews with 61 serial rapists (all incarcerated in a South Carolina maximum-security prison for the crime of

rape), Dennis J. Stevens offered a typology of his own based on motivations. Using Groth's "Protocol for the Clinical Assessment of the Offender's Sexual Behaviors" to structure the interview, Stevens explored the areas of premeditation, victim selection, style of attack, degree of violence associated with the rape, accompanying fantasies, and role of aggression. One of his major findings was the role of lust as a primary motive among a large proportion of the rapists (42%). Although acknowledging that "lust is not a new idea concerning predatory rape," Stevens believes it to be a primary rather than a secondary motive for rapists.[83] A constant theme emerging throughout Stevens's interviews with the rapists was that, for most of them, the amount of force that accompanied the rape was just enough to accomplish the victim's submission, but in cases in which extreme violence accompanied all stages of the rape, the violence would have been present regardless of the level of victim resistance. Therefore, one of the conclusions reached by Stevens is that advocating the idea that women should not resist their attackers is ill-advised.

Another way to approach a typology of men who rape is represented in the work of **Diana Scully**, a professor at Virginia Commonwealth University.[84] Scully's research involved intensive interviews with 114 convicted rapists in seven prisons, all of whom volunteered to be interviewed. Scully rejected the psychopathological perspective on rape and instead employed a feminist sociocultural perspective

In 2016, California Governor Jerry Brown signed a bill that imposes mandatory prison sentences on those convicted of sexually assaulting unconscious victims. The legislation was enacted after the infamous "Stanford rape case," in which a Stanford University student was sentenced to six months in jail after being convicted of three felony counts of sexual assault on an unconscious woman. The student was released after serving half of his sentence, causing public uproar over what many saw as only minor punishment for a serious crime.

WHO'S TO BLAME—The Individual or Society?

Exotic Dancer Claims Rape

Twenty-one-year-old Carla Lovejoy called 9-1-1 from her cell phone at 3:00 A.M. on a Sunday morning, telling the 9-1-1 operator who answered that she had just been raped.

"Ma'am, are you injured? Are you in need of immediate medical assistance?" the operator asked.

"No, no, I'm okay," Carla told her.

"Are you safe? Is anyone threatening you? Is anyone there with you?" the operator continued.

"I'm okay. I'm back home. Alone," Carla said.

Carla gave her address, and the operator dispatched a patrol car to the location.

The female officer who arrived encouraged Carla to go with her to the hospital for an examination and for evidence collection. Once Carla had been signed in at the emergency room, the officer took a report of the incident.

Carla described herself as an exotic dancer and for-hire personal companion, who spent her evenings entertaining men of all ages. "I show them a good time," she said, "and there's nothing illegal about that. But that don't give them the right to rape me," she told the officer.

Carla then went on to tell the officer how she had been hired by two men who were attending a local convention to come to their hotel room with a friend and put on a show. "Dancing, that's all we were supposed to do," she said. The men, she said, called a number of their friends into their room to watch the show. At some point, Carla told the officer, she had to go to the bathroom. That's when,

Micheal Kemp/Alamy Stock Photo

she said, a man followed her and pushed her into the small room, locking the door behind them. "That's when it happened," she said. "He put his hand around my throat, and he raped me."

Think about it

1. Assuming that Carla is telling the truth about what happened, how would you explain this crime? That is, why did it happen, and how might it have been prevented?

2. In your opinion, does Carla bear any responsibility for her own victimization? Why or why not?

Note: Who's to Blame boxes provide fictionalized critical thinking opportunities based on actual cases.

---

premised on several assumptions. First, rape is "socially learned behavior," involving "not only behavioral techniques, but also a host of values and beliefs, like rape myths, that are compatible with sexual aggression against women."[85] This premise is based on the assumption that both positive and negative forms of social behavior are learned "socially through direct association with others as well as indirectly through cultural context."[86] Second, Scully viewed rape not as a reflection of pathology but as a reflection of a continuum of normality in which it is important to understand "how sexual violence is made possible in a society [and] what men who rape gain from their sexually violent behavior."[87] Scully thus approached these interviews with convicted rapists from the feminist perspective of wanting to understand the explanations given by the rapists and their sociocultural beliefs about women and sexual violence. Scully identified several patterns in the rationalizations used by men who rape, and she organized these according to two broad types of rapists: admitters and deniers.

In the interviews, Scully explored how these two groups could operate from an understanding of reality that justified their behavior and tended to normalize it as well as what they gained from such behavior. Although some of the rapists in the admitter group relied on rape myth ideology, this was a more prevalent pattern among the deniers. The rape myths' definition of a very narrow group of individuals as legitimate rape victims was a common theme in the interviews given by these rapists. Although variations existed, the majority of rapists in both groups expressed little guilt or empathy for their victims. Read more about the violent criminal victimization of women in America via **http://tinyurl.com/mkzws9u** and **http://ag.ca.gov/publications/womansrights/ch7.htm**.

Rape: A Closer Look

Although rape can occur in almost any social context, certain social situations are characterized by a higher prevalence of rape and by a difference in the offender's motivation.

■ **acquaintance rape**   A rape characterized by a prior social, although not necessarily intimate or familial, relationship between the victim and the perpetrator.

■ **spousal rape**   A rape of one spouse by the other. The term usually refers to the rape of a woman by her husband.

Acquaintance Rape

The vast majority of rapes occur when the victim and the offender have some prior relationship—although not necessarily an intimate or familial one. Some researchers and activists who work with rape victims have stated that **acquaintance rape** is the most common scenario for rapes. Among adults, acquaintance rape usually occurs within the context of a dating relationship and is sometimes referred to as *date rape*.

Researchers have identified college campuses as places that typically have a high incidence of rape. Societal awareness and concern for rape on college campuses did not emerge until the 1980s. Helping to publicize the problem have been a number of high-profile rape cases on college campuses in which the victims not only went public with their experiences, but also grabbed headlines and the covers of major publications such as *Time*, *Newsweek*, and *People*.[88] Media publicity has emphasized the reality of the college setting as a site of rape, and in 1992, the Campus Sexual Assault Victims' Bill of Rights Act became law.[89] It requires campus authorities to "conduct appropriate disciplinary hearings, treat sexual assault victims and defendants with respect, making their rights and legal options clear, and cooperate with them in fully exercising those rights."[90]

A great deal of the research on rape in college settings has focused on identifying the unique factors of campus life that may be conducive to rape. Some researchers contend that college fraternities "create a sociocultural context in which the use of coercion in sexual relations with women is normative and in which the mechanisms to keep this pattern of behavior in check are minimal at best and absent at worst."[91] The increased awareness of campus rape has led to the development of services and programs that assist victims of sexual violence and present information that challenges rape myths.

Spousal Rape

Until the 1970s, under common law, a legally married husband could not be charged with raping his wife. Rape, as research indicates, happens to many women within marriage as part of a practice of *spousal abuse* that may involve beatings and other violence. Until 1976, **spousal rape** could not be prosecuted in any state. Today, it is illegal in every state in the United States.

The first researcher to systematically examine spousal rape was **Diana E. H. Russell**. Based on an analysis of interview data, Russell developed a four-part typology of men who rape their wives:

- Husbands who prefer raping their wives to having consensual sex with them

- Husbands who are able to enjoy both rape and consensual sex with their wives or who are indifferent to which it is

- Husbands who would prefer consensual sex with their wives but are willing to rape them when their sexual advances are refused

- Husbands who might like to rape their wives but do not act out these desires

Thus, rather than being one-dimensional, rape within marriage has several forms that reflect various motivational nuances on the part of offenders.

Rape in Prison

Prison rape, which is generally considered to involve physical assault, represents a special category of sexual victimization behind bars. In 2003, Congress mandated the collection of statistics on prison rape as part of the Prison Rape Elimination Act (PREA).[92] The purposes of the PREA are to[93]

- Establish a zero-tolerance standard for prison rape.

- Make prison rape prevention a top priority in correctional facilities and systems.

- Develop and implement national standards for the detection, prevention, reduction, and punishment of prison rape.

- Increase the availability of information on the incidence and prevalence of prison rape.

- Increase the accountability of corrections officials with regard to the issue of sexual violence in U.S. prisons.

The PREA requires the Bureau of Justice Statistics (BJS) to collect data in federal and state prisons, county and city jails, and juvenile institutions, with the U.S. Census Bureau acting as the official repository for collected data.

In 2016, the BJS published the results of its third annual national inmate survey (NIS).[94] The survey was conducted in 233 state and federal prisons, 358 local jails, and 15 special confinement facilities operated by Immigration and Customs Enforcement (ICE). A total of 92,449 inmates participated. The survey was also administered to 527 juveniles ages 16 to 17 held in state prisons and 1,211 juveniles of the same age held in local jails. Among the findings:

- An estimated 4.0% of state and federal prison inmates and 3.2% of jail inmates reported experiencing one or more incidents of sexual victimization by another inmate or facility staff in the past 12 months.

- Among state and federal prison inmates, 2.0% (or an estimated 29,300 prisoners) reported an incident involving another inmate, 2.4% (34,100) reported an incident involving facility staff, and 0.4% (5,500) reported both an incident by another inmate and staff.

- About 1.6% of jail inmates (11,900) reported an incident with another inmate, 1.8% (13,200) reported an incident with staff, and 0.2% (2,400) reported both an incident by another inmate and staff.

- An estimated 1.8% of juveniles ages 16 to 17 held in adult prisons and jails reported being victimized by another inmate, compared to 2.0% of adults in prisons and 1.6% of adults in jails; an estimated 3.2% of juveniles ages 16 to 17 held in adult prisons and jails reported experiencing staff sexual misconduct.

- Inmates who reported their sexual orientation as gay, lesbian, bisexual, or other were among those with the highest rates of sexual victimization. Among non-heterosexual inmates, 12.2% of prisoners and 8.5% of jail inmates reported being sexually victimized by another inmate; 5.4% of prisoners and 4.3% of jail inmates reported being victimized by staff.

PREA surveys are only a first step in understanding and eliminating prison rape. As the BJS notes, "Due to fear of reprisal from perpetrators, a code of silence among inmates, personal embarrassment, and lack of trust in staff, victims are often reluctant to report incidents to correctional authorities."[95]

Lee H. Bowker, a criminologist who specializes in studying life inside prisons, summarizes studies of sexual violence in prison with the following observations:[96]

- Most sexual aggressors do not consider themselves homosexuals.

- Sexual release is not the primary motivation for sexual attack.

- Many aggressors must continue to participate in gang rapes to avoid becoming victims themselves.

- The aggressors have themselves suffered much damage to their masculinity in the past.

As in cases of heterosexual rape, sexual assaults in prison are likely to leave psychological scars on the victim long after the physical event is over.[97] Victims of prison rape live in fear, may feel constantly threatened, and can turn to self-destructive activities.[98] Many victims question their masculinity and undergo a personal devaluation.

The Sexual Victimization of Men

Until recently, the sexual victimization of men in America was largely ignored. Recently, however, the *American Journal of Public Health* reported the results of a 12-month study of prevalence and incidence data on men's sexual victimization.[99] The data came from five federal surveys, including three from the Bureau of Justice Statistics, one from the Centers for Disease Control and Prevention, and one from the Federal Bureau of Investigation. Authors of the study noted that a "male perpetrator and female victim paradigm underlies assumptions about sexual victimization" in this country, and that the paradigm tends to obscure data that run counter to it. In other words, the entire concept of sexual victimization is rooted in normative understandings of gender roles. Moreover, the authors noted, sexually victimized men are often significantly stigmatized; and traditional data sources often overlook settings (such as prisons) in which men are likely to be victimized.

The study found that the sexual victimization of men is common, and that some forms of men's victimization equate to those experienced by women. For example, the Centers for Disease Control's National Intimate Partner and Sexual Violence Survey (NISVS) revealed that men and women were similarly victimized by nonconsensual sex (1.27 million women and 1.26 million men in the 12 months preceding the survey). As the study authors note, "This remarkable finding challenges stereotypical assumptions about the gender of victims of sexual violence." Even so, CDC's publications based on the NISVS highlight female sexual victimization and inadvertently reinforce "public perceptions that sexual victimization is primarily a women's issue." Part of the problem may stem from the fact that the incidence of female sexual victimization is frequently calculated using data from the UCR and the NCVS, while prison rape surveys (also discussed in this chapter) reveal that ten times the number of men than women report being sexually victimized in detention facilities. Such surveys are rarely cited in sexual victimization publications.

The study also found that traditional notions holding that men are virtually insatiable sexually, and the belief that male victims experience less physical force than do female victims, contribute to "dismissive attitudes toward male sexual victimization." Moreover, although laws concerning sexual victimization have become more gender-neutral over time, prosecutions for the sexual victimization of men remain rare. The study authors attribute this to "a lack of concern for male victims," based on inaccurate and inappropriate cultural stereotypes. They also note that 46% of male victims reported female perpetrators, but that traditional gender assumptions can "obscure sexual abuse perpetrated by women."

Authors of the study found that "reliance on the male perpetrator and female victim paradigm limits understandings, not only of male victimization but of all counter paradigmatic abuse." They conclude by calling for "the consistent use of gender inclusive terms for sexual victimization, objective reporting of data, and improved methodologies that account for institutionalized populations." In this way, they noted, "research and reporting on sexual victimization will more accurately reflect the experiences of both women and men." The entire study can be accessed online at **http://ajph.aphapublications.org/doi/pdf/10.2105/AJPH.2014.301946.**

■ **child sexual abuse (CSA)**   A term encompassing a variety of criminal and civil offenses in which an adult engages in sexual activity with a minor, exploits a minor for purposes of sexual gratification, or exploits a minor sexually for purposes of profit.

Child Sexual Abuse

Child sexual abuse (CSA) is a term encompassing a variety of criminal and civil offenses in which an adult engages in sexual activity with a minor, exploits a minor for purposes of sexual gratification, or exploits a minor sexually for purposes of profit. The term includes a variety of activities and motivations, including child molestation, child sexual exploitation (CSE), and the commercial sexual exploitation of children (CSEC).

The National Institute of Justice (NIJ) observes that "few criminal offenses are more despised than the sexual abuse of children, and few are so little understood in terms of incidence (the number of offenses committed), prevalence (the proportion of the population who commit offenses), and reoffense risk."[100]

The NIJ also notes that sexual offenses are more likely than other types of criminal conduct to elude the attention of the criminal justice system. Self-reports from both sex offenders and sexually abused children reveal far more abuse than officially reported.[101] The Child Molestation Research and Prevention Institute, based in Atlanta, Georgia, estimates that at least two out of every ten girls and one out of every ten boys have been sexually abused by the time they turn 14.[102]

One of the most informative offender self-report studies on the adult sexual victimization of children comes from research conducted slightly more than two decades ago.[103] In that study, investigators recruited 561 adult subjects who engaged in what the researchers described as "child-focused sexual behavior." The subjects, who were guaranteed anonymity, were recruited through health care workers, media advertising, presentations at meetings, and in other ways. All were free from confinement at the time of the interviews. The 561 adults interviewed reported a total of 291,737 "paraphiliac acts" over the course of their adult lives committed against 195,407 victims under the age of 18. The results of this study make it clear that in cases of CSA, a relatively small number of offenders can commit a large number of crimes.

> Self-reports from both sex offenders and sexually abused children reveal far more abuse than officially reported.

US Department of Justice

The home page of the U.S. Department of Justice's National Sex Offender Public Registry at **www.nsopr.gov**. Community notification laws frequently result in the posting of online offender databases. How do such databases help victims?

Types of Child Sex Abusers

Almost all pedophiles are male, with one study of more than 4,400 offenders finding fewer than 0.5% of convicted child sex offenses committed by females.[104] Other than that, little can be said about similarities among child sexual abusers. As individuals, they tend to be highly dissimilar from one another in terms of personal characteristics, life experiences, and criminal histories. No single "molester profile" exists.[105] Child molesters appear to arrive at deviancy via multiple pathways and engage in many different sexual and nonsexual "acting-out" behaviors (Table 11-1). Figure 11-7 shows the number of registered predatory child sex offenders by state.

In 1983, Nicholas Groth and his associates proposed a simple two-part distinction among pedophiles whereby offenders were classified as either "regressed" or "fixated."[106] Regressed offenders, said Groth, are attracted sexually primarily to members of their own age groups but are passively aroused by minors. Generally speaking, the use of alcohol, drugs, or other inhibition-lowering substances, combined with social circumstances providing opportunity, can cause the regressed offender to act out his or her interest in having sexual encounters with children. Fixated offenders, said Groth, are adult pedophiles who engage in planned sexual acts with children and whose behavior is not necessarily influenced by drugs or alcohol.

■ **child pornography**   A visual representation of any kind that depicts a minor engaging in sexually explicit conduct that is obscene and that lacks serious literary, artistic, political, or scientific value.

TABLE 11-1 | Hypothetical Profiles of Child Sex Predators

	INTERPERSONAL	NARCISSISTIC	EXPLOITATIVE	MUTED SADISTIC	NONSADISTIC AGGRESSIVE	SADISTIC
Amount of Contact with Children	High	High	Low	Low	Low	Low
Sexual Acts	Fondling, caressing, frottage (nonphallic sex)	Phallic nonsadistic sex	Phallic nonsadistic sex[a]	Sodomy, "sham" sadism[a]	Phallic nonsadistic sex	Sadism
Relationship of Offender to Victim	Known	Known or stranger	Stranger	Stranger	Stranger	Stranger
Amount of Physical Injury to Victim	Low	Low	Instrumental[b]	Instrumental	High	High
Amount of Planning in Offenses	High[c]	Moderate	Low	Moderate	Low	High

[a] "Sham" sadism implies behaviors or reported fantasies that reflect sadism without the high victim injury present in the sadistic type.

[b] Instrumental aggression implies only enough force to gain victim compliance.

[c] Interpersonal types know their victims and may spend a considerable amount of time "grooming" them (setting them up), but the offenses often appear to be unplanned or spontaneous.

Source: Adapted from Robert A. Prentky, Raymond A. Knight, and Austin F. S. Lee, *Child Sexual Molestation: Research Issues* (Washington, DC: National Institute of Justice, 1997).

A U.S. Department of Justice publication representing a compilation of studies produced by the NIJ shows that most victims of childhood sexual abuse do not go on to become child molesters.[107] However, the NIJ points out that sexual victimization as a child, if accompanied by other factors—such as the co-occurrence of physical and verbal abuse—may contribute to the child-victim's development as a perpetrator of CSA later in life. Similarly, says the NIJ, social competence deficits are significant in child molestation, but an individual's inadequate social and interpersonal skills do not, by themselves, make his or her sexual abuse of children inevitable.

> Some evidence exists to suggest that child molestation may be related to an offender's restaging of his or her own childhood sexual victimization.

Some evidence exists to suggest that child molestation may be related to an offender's restaging of his or her own childhood sexual victimization.[108] Tests of the restaging theory on a sample of 131 rapists and child molesters revealed that child molesters who committed their first

assault when they were 14 or younger were sexually victimized at a younger age than offenders who committed their first assault in adulthood; they also experienced more severe sexual abuse than offenders with adult onset of sexual aggression.[109]

Nonetheless, sexual victimization alone is unable to fully explain child molestation. Studies show that most victims of childhood sexual abuse do not go on to become perpetrators.[110] As is true for other kinds of maltreatment, childhood sexual victimization may be one critical element in the presence or absence of a variety of other factors (e.g., co-occurrence of other types of abuse, availability of supportive caregivers, ego strength of child-victim at the time of abuse, and availability of treatment), all of which appear to moderate the likelihood of becoming a child molester.

Not all adults involved in the sexual abuse of children pursue personal sexual gratification. Some have a profit motive, as is the case in instances of *commercial sexual exploitation of children*, or CSEC. CSEC refers to all offenses in which an adult victimizes a child sexually for profit, including the prostituting of a child and creating or trafficking in child pornography.

Awareness of **child pornography** exploded onto the American scene in the 1990s, as the advent of rapid transmission of high-quality images and video became possible through the

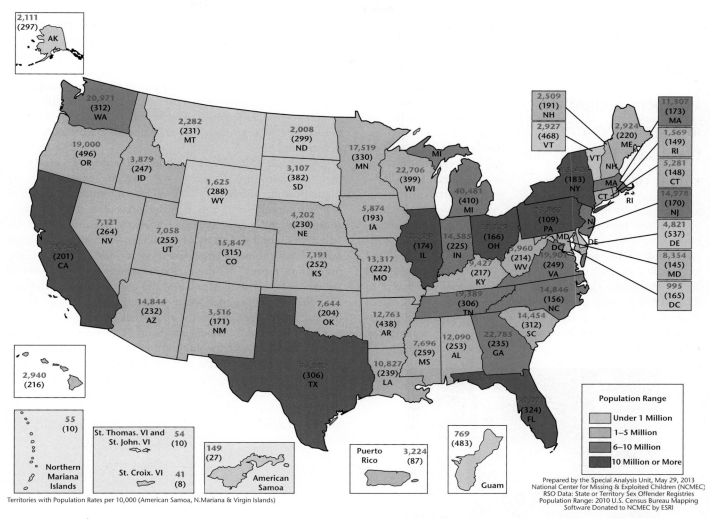

FIGURE 11-7 | **Registered Sex Offenders by State**

Source: National Center for Missing & Exploited Children, http://www.missingkids.com. Reprinted with permission.

growth of the Internet. Child pornography can be defined as a visual representation of any kind that depicts a minor engaging in sexually explicit conduct that is obscene and that lacks serious literary, artistic, political, or scientific value.

The Internet created special problems in enforcement of the laws designed to control pedophiles and child pornographers. Because it is an international medium, the Internet is hard to police, and activities through which information on the Internet is transmitted may be illegal in one jurisdiction and not so in another. Similarly, the relative anonymity of buyers and sellers of child pornography over the Internet provides both a sense of security and impersonality to those involved in such transactions.

According to the United Nations Children's Fund (UNICEF), tens of thousands of children in the United States and tens of millions of children worldwide are involved in CSEC.[111] UNICEF says the number of sexually

exploited children worldwide may exceed 100 million, not all of whom are located in "poor" or "developing" countries.

Read a comprehensive report on the commercial and sexual exploitation of children in the United States at **http://justicestudies.com/pubs/exploitation.pdf.**

Robbery

In 2016, media celebrity Kim Kardashian West, 36, was robbed at a French hotel by a group of men who tied her up in the bathroom and took millions of dollars worth of her jewelry—including a $4 million ring. Kardashian West had travelled to France to attend Paris Fashion Week with friends and her sister. In January, 2017, French authorities charged 10 men in connection with the robbrery.[112]

■ **personal robbery**   A robbery that occurs on a highway or a street or in a public place (also called a mugging) or a robbery that occurs in a residence.

■ **institutional robbery**   A robbery that occurs in a commercial setting, such as a convenience store, gas station, or bank.

Robbery is classified as a violent crime because it involves the threat or use of force, but it also involves a property component because its express purpose is to take the property of another.[113] Robberies can occur in different locations and are quite often categorized in this manner by both law enforcement agencies and social science researchers. Robberies that occur on the highway or street are often referred to as highway robberies or muggings; muggings and robberies that occur in residences are types of **personal robbery**. Although residential robberies are certainly deterred by the presence of security precautions, the effectiveness of deterrents depends on the type of neighborhood in which the residence is located. Terance D. Miethe and David McDowall found that security precautions that tend to be effective in neighborhoods characterized by a viable social control structure are ineffective in socially disorganized neighborhoods.[114] Security precautions, such as not leaving the home unoccupied, are not enough in socially disorganized neighborhoods to compensate for the strong effect that neighborhood context has on increasing the likelihood of robbery. Homes and persons do not exist as potential targets for motivated offenders in a vacuum but appear as more or less attractive targets based on their perceived vulnerability and the social context of the surrounding neighborhood in which they are found. The FBI reported that an estimated 332,198 robberies occurred in 2016.

> Robbery is classified as a violent crime because it involves the threat or use of force.

Robberies that occur in commercial settings (Figure 11-8), such as convenience stores, gas stations, and banks, are **institutional robberies**.[115] Several research studies have found that institutional robberies may be prevented through environmental and policy changes. Scott A. Hendricks and his colleagues found in a study of convenience store robberies that "the robber chooses a target based on various situational crime prevention factors";[116] these factors include staffing, hours of operation, cash-handling policies, and characteristics of the surrounding neighborhood. Many of the precautions that lower the risk of robbery are costly, so not all businesses can afford them. As Richard T. Wright and Scott H. Decker noted, "This puts businesses located in high-crime neighborhoods in a no-win situation because their clientele frequently are too poor to bear increased prices to support crime prevention measures."[117] Additionally, if the business fails as a result of robberies, the community loses again because the exodus of businesses that are forced to relocate makes the community less viable. Most of

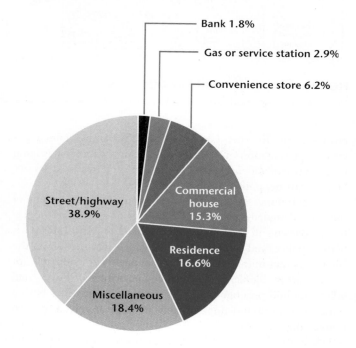

Kim Kardashian West, who was robbed by a group of men who tied her up in the bathroom of her Paris hotel room. The men fled with millions of dollars worth of jewelry, but were later arrested. What's the difference between robbery and theft?

FIGURE 11-8 | **Robbery Locations**

Bank 1.8%
Gas or service station 2.9%
Convenience store 6.2%
Commercial house 15.3%
Residence 16.6%
Miscellaneous 18.4%
Street/highway 38.9%

Source: Federal Bureau of Investigation, *Crime in the United States, 2016* (Washington, DC: U.S. Department of Justice, 2017).

the robbers interviewed by Wright and Decker in their ethnographic study of robbers who selected commercial targets generally selected liquor stores, taverns, and pawnshops, because of the large amount of cash available, and targeted businesses with low levels of customer activity, because they viewed customers as an unpredictable risk factor. The robbers interviewed as part of Floyd Feeney's research in California during the 1970s reported very little planning overall, but those who engaged in commercial robbery were much more likely to report planning than those who engaged in personal robberies (60% compared with 30%).[118]

The Lethal Potential of Robbery

Robbery carries the threat of injury—often lethal injury—for the victim. Reported injuries were found among one in every three robbery victims whose data were entered into the NIBRS.[119] Robbery provides the context for 6% of all homicides annually. Approximately 15% of all homicides occur during the commission of another felony, and among these cases, robbery is the most likely felony to result in homicide, accounting for 30% of all felony murders.[120] The weapon most often used in robbery homicides is a firearm, accounting for 78.5% of all cases; the type of firearm used in the vast majority of these cases (78.3%) is a handgun.[121] See **http://tinyurl.com/zb8y854**.

Criminal Careers of Robbers

Are robbers specialists (specialize in only robbery) or generalists (vary the types of crimes they commit)? The majority of robbery offenders are generalists who have fairly lengthy but varied criminal careers.[122] Research on a sample of inmates in California prisons found that less than 10% of convicted robbers could be labeled specialists who engaged solely in robbery to the exclusion of other offenses;[123] in a survey of inmates sponsored by RAND Corporation, approximately 18% of offenders were primarily involved in only one type of offense.[124] Diversity in offense type appears to be the norm for the vast majority of offenders, based on both ethnographic and survey data.

The majority of robbers are generalists who have fairly lengthy but varied criminal careers.

Robbery and Public Transportation

One setting in which crime-prevention strategies can be quite effective is public transportation. According to Martha J. Smith and Ronald V. Clarke, "Robbery on mass transit is a rare event, even in systems with relatively high numbers of incidents such as New York City."[125] Viewing instances of robbery on public transportation as reflecting a "lack of supervision," Smith and Clarke contended that the majority of these robberies follow one of three scenarios: (1) Offenders purposefully select their victims from among passengers in isolated areas of large subway stations, especially when the station is not crowded, meaning that security measures (such as using closed-circuit television and closing off unused parts of the station) may serve to effectively deter these offenders;[126] (2) offenders select their victims outside the station at particular locales and times that are relatively isolated; and (3) offenders act on opportunity and often lie in wait for passengers leaving public transportation.[127] Prevention strategies to deter these types of robberies include a variety of surveillance techniques. In addition to targeting public transportation customers, robbers also target the staff in order to steal the fare money; Smith and Clarke stated that policies such as exact fare and other similar changes "led to a dramatic fall in the number of bus robberies in New York City."[128]

According to Smith and Clarke, "Transit workers with perhaps the greatest risk of robbery are taxicab drivers, who carry cash, travel by themselves around cities with strangers, and do not choose their destinations."[129] Derek Cornish offered several strategies, ranging from having a weapon to screening passengers for potential threats, that taxicab drivers can use to prevent robberies.[130] Although "drivers can use informal passenger screening practices such as refusing to pick up fares at certain locations," such screening practices "can discriminate against those who live in poorer areas or are from certain racial or age groups, making it difficult for them to use the service."[131] These very practices have recently been the subject of debate because of claims of discrimination.

Other strategies, such as the installation of protection partitions between the driver and passenger, can be quite effective in deterring crime. Under the New York City Police Department's special Taxi-Livery Task Force, created in 1992, police in unmarked cars stop taxis in particular neighborhoods, often according to some strategy such as every fifth taxi. A similar strategy was also adopted in Boston, again as a response to the substantial number of violent crimes (especially robberies) experienced by cab drivers. Whereas the Boston statute withstood court review, the New York Court of Appeals ruled in

December 1999 that the policy of the police department "gave officers too much discretion to stop taxis carrying passengers when they had no reason to suspect any crime was afoot."[132] The U.S. Supreme Court was asked to review both rulings and declined, allowing the rulings of the lower courts to stand. Policies like those in New York and Boston clearly illustrate the tension involved in policing a democratic society; measures that might prevent certain forms of crime must be weighed against the potential violation of individual liberties.

The Motivation of Robbers

Research tends to support the idea that most robberies, of both people and places, involve very little planning on the part of the offender. Floyd Feeney's research in California during the early 1970s found little evidence that the majority of bank robbers had even been in the bank before the robbery.[133] Most of the robbers Feeney studied did very little planning, no matter what the target, and the planning that did occur was minor and "generally took place the same day as the robbery and frequently within a few hours of it."[134] The motivation and decision-making of street robbers were evaluated in a series of research studies conducted by Bruce A. Jacobs, Richard Wright, and others at the University of Missouri at St. Louis involving 86 active robbers in St. Louis. Jacobs and Wright found that the decision to offend occurs as part of ongoing social action that is "mediated by prevailing situations and subcultural conditions."[135] Fast cash was the direct need that robbery satisfied, but this need can be properly understood only against the backdrop of street culture. Jacobs and Wright hypothesized that street culture was the intervening force that connected background factors (such as low self-esteem, deviant peer relations, and weak social bonds) to the motivation to offend, and they found that the majority of robbers gave little thought to planning robberies until they found themselves needing money. For less than half the robbers, the financial need was for basic necessities; mostly, it was connected to a fairly hedonistic lifestyle.

Jacobs and Wright considered three alternatives that these individuals could have employed for money: (1) performing legitimate work; (2) borrowing; and (3) committing other crimes. Legitimate employment was not a viable option for these individuals for several reasons. Most of the robbers had neither the skills nor the education to obtain decent-wage jobs, and even if they did have such resources, their perceived need for cash was too immediate for legitimate work to satisfy; additionally, legitimate work was viewed as an impediment to their lifestyle of "every night is a Saturday night." Borrowing money was not a viable route because many had no one to turn to for a loan, and for those who did, borrowing was not part of the self-sufficient code of the streets. Robbery was preferable to committing other crimes because it was perceived to be safer than burglary and quicker than fencing stolen goods. Other research has found that some robberies do begin as another crime, such as burglary,

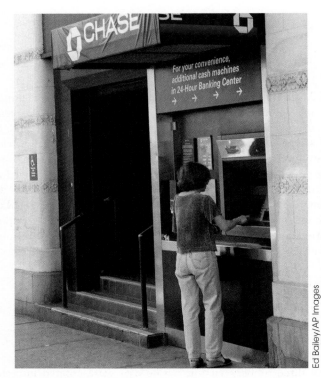

Ed Bailey/AP Images

A possible robbery victim. Some robbers seem to give little thought to planning their crimes until they need fast cash. Why might this person be an attractive target for such robbers?

> Being a street robber is a way of behaving, a way of thinking, an approach to life.

and become robberies more by accident than design.[136] Jacobs and Wright concluded that the economic motivation behind robbery should not be interpreted as "genuine financial hardship" but as an ongoing crisis situation experienced as a result of the logic of the street context of robbers' daily lives.[137] For the individuals whom Jacobs and Wright interviewed, "being a street robber ... is a way of behaving, a way of thinking, an approach to life."[138] Such individuals are unlikely to be easily deterred by legal sanctions, and the rationality of their decision making is unlikely to be adequately explained outside the context of their street culture.

In 2006, Trevor Bennett and Fiona Brookman interviewed 120 English robbery offenders in a study funded by Britain's Economic and Social Research Council (ESRC).[139] Bennett and Brookman found that financial gain was only one of many motivations reported by robbers. Others included having a "sheer desire to fight," desiring to set right a perceived injustice, enhancing one's street credibility, and doing it "just for kicks." Some offenders participating in the study had been arrested as many as 50 times and reported that they were addicted to robbery. One told the researchers, "I was more addicted to robbing than I was to drugs" (drug connections were mentioned in 60% of all robberies studied).

Drug Robberies

In their ethnographic research on armed robbers, Richard T. Wright and Scott H. Decker found that "six out of every ten offenders who specialized in street robbery—forty-three of seventy-three—said that they usually preyed on individuals who themselves were involved in lawbreaking."[140] These are generally not reflected in official statistics on crime because the victims do not report their victimization to the police due to their own illegal behavior, so they can be victimized with relative impunity. Because the overriding motivation behind the robberies for many offenders in Wright and Decker's research was to get high, it follows that drug dealers would be an obvious target. Among offenders who stated that they selected victims involved in crime, the vast majority targeted drug dealers, although rarely major drug dealers. "Almost all of these offenders targeted young, street-level dealers who sold quantities of crack cocaine directly to consumers."[141] According to one robber, the attraction of robbing drug dealers was twofold: "It satisfies two things for me; my thirst for drugs and the financial aspect."[142] The neighborhoods in which these robbers lived and conducted their routine activities were generally characterized by an abundance of drug dealers, which increased their suitability as targets. Because they were also unlikely to report their victimization to the police, drug customers were perceived as ideal targets. Additionally, offenders were well aware that the police did not take drug robberies seriously. However, these factors do not consider the one element that makes robbing drug dealers very risky: "There always is a possibility of violent retaliation."[143]

Further analysis of the ethnographic research on the armed robbers in St. Louis by Bruce A. Jacobs, Volkan Topalli, and Richard Wright explored the issue of retaliation by asking, "Why should offenders elect to reduce their chances of getting arrested at the cost of increasing their odds of being killed?"[144] To answer this, the researchers looked at the findings from 25 in-depth interviews with active drug robbers conducted as part of the larger study of robbers in St. Louis. The researchers conceptualized retaliation as an informal sanction "capable of deterrence in its own right; to be sure, it may be the sole sanction offenders face."[145] Drug dealers who are victimized are cut off from one avenue of redress, the formal sanctions provided by police, and "have a strong incentive to retaliate."[146]

The drug robbers interviewed in the St. Louis study were completely aware of the risk involved in targeting drug dealers and sought to minimize it by selecting one of three strategies: intimidation, anonymity, or hypervigilance. Drug robbers primarily targeted dealers "whose retributive potential was weak."[147] Some of the offenders stated that "some street corner dealers simply dismissed robberies as an occupational hazard and accepted their losses with equanimity."[148]

The second strategy used by robbers who targeted drug dealers, anonymity, involved robbing only those dealers with whom they were totally unfamiliar so that "retaliation becomes moot" because the victim does not know the robber.[149] Hypervigilance, the third strategy, refers to how offenders consciously "devoted a significant portion of their day-to-day cognitive resources to minimizing the prospect of postoffense victim contact."[150] For offenders engaged in a substantial volume of robberies, the chances of running into a victim were increased even if the victim was initially unknown to them, so offenders avoided the sites of previous robberies until they could be fairly sure that the threat of recognition or retaliation had subsided, and the nomadic lifestyle of drug robbers allowed them to easily do this.

Circumstances and situations bring offenders and victims together in unexpected ways—"the more members of a network there are, and the denser that network is, the more likely run-ins become. Bus stops, mini-malls, grocery stores, bars, theaters, and fast-food restaurants emerge as contexts fraught with potential risk."[151] This not only hinders the offender's ability to manage the risk of retaliation but also increases the potential for violence within the entire community itself, based on the extent of drug robberies. Jacobs and his colleagues concluded that this community effect represents the "contagion-like processes through which violence is contracted and contained," and if "street justice" is stronger than the formal justice represented by law enforcement, the community becomes increasingly unstable.[152] They explained, "The more entrenched informal justice becomes, and the more likely formal authorities will 'look the other way,'" the more the community becomes disorganized and violence spreads beyond robbers and their victims.[153] This becomes one set of dynamics that creates and sustains the "tangled web of violence we see in so many high-crime urban locales across the country."[154]

The Gendered Nature of Robbery

According to researcher **Jody Miller**, "With the exception of rape, robbery is perhaps the most gender differentiated serious crime in the United States."[155] Women represent robbery offenders in approximately 14.8% of all incidents.[156] Miller's research goal was to assess the extent to which gender impacts robbery offending, so she analyzed a subset of the interviews

■ **aggravated assault**   The unlawful, intentional inflicting, or attempted or threatened inflicting, of serious injury upon the person of another.

with active robbers from the research data used by Jacobs and Wright consisting of 37 robbers, 14 women and 23 men. The two groups were matched on current age and age at first robbery. In her examination of motivations for robbery, Miller found that economic incentives were the primary motivation for both men and women but that there were significant differences in the way in which men and women carried out street robberies. Men exhibited a fairly uniform pattern. Their robberies were characterized by "using physical violence and/or a gun placed on or at close proximity to the victim in a confrontational manner";[157] the presence of a gun was almost a constant in robberies conducted by men. While perceiving women to be easier targets, male robbers tended to rob other men rather than women because of another perception—that men tended to carry more money. The majority of males targeted as victims were those involved in "street life."

> With the exception of rape, robbery is the most gender differentiated serious crime in the United States.

Female robbers tended to fall into one of three patterns. The robbery of other women in a "physically confrontational manner" was the most prevalent way in which female robbers worked, but they also used their sexuality to attract male victims and acted as accomplices to male robbers in offenses against other men.[158] Except when they were robbing men, female robbers generally did not use guns. Although similar cultural and structural forces can drive men and women to offend in the same way, gender continues to exert an influence on shaping the nature of robbery incidents. Learn more about the crime of robbery at **http://bjs.ojp.usdoj.gov /index.cfm?ty=tp&tid=313**.

Aggravated Assault

On Christmas Eve, 2011, Jacquetta Simmons, 26, a Batavia, New York, resident was arrested after she punched a Walmart female greeter in the face and knocked her down, resulting in fractures to her facial bones.[159] The greeter had asked Simmons to see receipts for items she was carrying before she hit the greeter and ran out of the store. Employees and customers gave chase and held Simmons until police arrived. A state police spokesperson later told reporters that Simmons, who was charged with two counts of assault, had store receipts for everything in her possession.

There are two types of assault: simple and aggravated. **Aggravated assault**, which the FBI defines as "the unlawful attack by one person upon another wherein the offender uses a weapon or displays it in a threatening manner, or the victim suffers obvious or severe bodily injury,"[160] is the more serious type of assault and the one that concerns us here. According to the FBI, 803,007 aggravated assaults were reported to police agencies across the nation in 2016, producing an aggravated assault rate of 248.5 for every 100,000 people in the country.

The profile of a typical offender in aggravated assault mirrors that of homicide, with disproportionate involvement of males, African Americans, 15- to 34-year-olds, those of lower socioeconomic status, those with prior arrest records, and offenders demonstrating little evidence of offense specialization.[161] Also consistent with most homicides, aggravated assaults are "spontaneous, triggered by a trivial altercation or argument that quickly escalates in the heat of passion."[162]

Based on statistics from the National Crime Victimization Survey (NCVS), which tallies simple as well as aggravated assault, the majority of assaults reported by victims to NCVS interviewers are simple rather than aggravated assault. According to the NCVS, the overall decline in the nation's crime rate between 1993 and 2016 was mostly due to decreases in the rate of simple assault.

Aggravated assaults are distinguished according to those involving injury and those not involving injury. The victims and offenders in aggravated assault are, for the most part, equally likely to be strangers or nonstrangers to each other. When you look at the gender of the victim, a pattern emerges. A slight majority of male victims are assaulted by a stranger, whereas slightly more than one-third (39%) of female victims are assaulted by a stranger in aggravated assaults. Simple assaults, by contrast, are more likely to involve nonstrangers (58%). Almost one-half (47%) of male victims are assaulted by nonstrangers, whereas 71% of female victims are assaulted by nonstrangers in these cases. Whether it is an aggravated or simple assault, the largest category of nonstranger offenders of female victims is represented by friends and acquaintances followed by intimate partners. Weapons are present in less than one-fourth (23%) of all assaults, and when a weapon is present, it is most likely to be something other than a gun or a knife.[163]

Stranger Assault

The possibility of stranger violence elicits a great deal of fear and concern among most members of the population. But based on research using victimization data in both the United States and Great Britain, "the probability of suffering a serious personal crime by strangers is very low,"[164] with this likelihood varying by demographic characteristics such as gender, age, marital status, and lifestyle. For example, individuals who have an active social life away from home and in the evening are far more likely to be victimized by strangers, but this effect depends very much on the community context in which the individuals engage in their leisure pursuits.

Assault within Families

As the statistics from several sources reveal, the majority of assaults involve victims and offenders who are known to each other, quite often in a familial or an intimate relationship. In the sections that follow, the familial context of assault is examined, with a special emphasis on how key variables like weapons and alcohol help us understand the patterns of these crimes.

Family Privacy

Although statistics on homicide have long supported the violent potential of families, criminologists were not the pioneers in studies centered on the violent aspects of our society's most basic institution. Richard J. Gelles, a leading family-violence researcher, correctly asserted in the 1970s that violence within the family concerned criminologists only when someone was killed.[165] Criminology as a discipline began to give more attention to violent behavior within the family just as societal attention turned to viewing the halo of privacy that has long surrounded the family with a bit more scrutiny. Empirical research concerning the phenomenon of family violence encounters several problems. The family as a social institution is intensely private, and the discussion of physical, emotional, and sexual violence among family members violates this privacy; these types of abuse also represent extremely sensitive parts of a person's experience, which an individual may be reluctant to discuss. Michael Hindelang conducted research on crime-reporting behavior and found that two of the most common reasons for not reporting crimes to the police were that it was a private matter and that there might be reprisal from the offender.[166] Current research has shown that such rationales supporting nonreporting continue to characterize incidents involving violence among family members.

Early Studies of Family Violence

The initial research on violence within the family came from small clinical studies and official records, the latter consistently revealing that women were much more likely than men to become victims of domestic violence. Based on an examination of emergency room victims in the late 1970s, Evan Stark and colleagues found that approximately 25% of all women who had

been injured had been the victim of a spousal attack.[167] Murray Straus and colleagues at the University of New Hampshire were the first to develop a survey methodology for the study of family violence nationally and conducted the first National Survey on Family Violence (NSFV) in 1975 with a representative sample of 2,146 families; the second NSFV was conducted in 1985 with a sample of 4,032 households.[168] In both surveys, the key tool developed for measuring family violence was the Conflict Tactics Scale, containing a series of 18 items that range from calm discussion to the use of a potentially lethal weapon. By the time a respondent reaches the questions concerning spousal behavior, Straus reasoned that familiarity with the questions would diminish the respondent's uneasiness about answering whether he or she had ever hit a spouse.[169] The rate of violence between spouses in the 1985 NSFV was 161 per 1,000 couples.[170] Although this rate was lower than that reported in 1975, it still remained higher than estimates produced from other studies not specifically directed at family violence, such as the NCVS.

Survey Research on Family Violence

In the years since survey research was first used to estimate violence against family members, other surveys have emerged to assess this phenomenon, and existing data sources have improved. A few years ago the FBI released specialized reports on family violence based on available NIBRS data. Using a measure of violent crime that includes murder, rape, robbery, and assault, NIBRS data revealed that 51% of violent crimes involved victims and offenders who were related. Among all offenses involving family members that came to the attention of the police, the overwhelming majority (92%) were assaults.[171] Although assault is the most frequently occurring violent crime both among the general population and within the family, the percentage is even higher within the family.

Firearms are less likely to be used in family assaults; fists, hands, and knives are more common, and a slight majority of aggravated assaults involve some type of injury both in the general population (57.5%) and within the family (60.8%). Women are more likely to be the victims of both aggravated assaults and simple assaults within the family than in the general population (60% vs. 41% and 72% vs. 60%, respectively).[172] Learn more about family violence and the crimes it engenders via **http://www.phac-aspc.gc.ca/ncfv-cnivf/index-eng.php**.

Intimate-Partner Assault

Intimate-partner assault is a term used to characterize assaultive behavior that takes place between individuals involved in an intimate relationship. Based on research using various data sources, the overwhelming majority of victims of marital

■ **separation assault**   A type of violence inflicted by a partner on a significant other who attempts to leave an intimate relationship.

Intimate-partner assault refers to assaultive behavior that takes place between individuals involved in an intimate relationship.

violence within heterosexual relationships are women. This does not deny that men can be the victims of violence at the hands of their wives but merely states that based on official records, self-reports, emergency room records, and small clinical samples, it is women who emerge as victims. In line with this empirical reality, Neil Websdale titled his ethnographic exploration of violence in rural areas of Kentucky *Rural Woman Battering and the Justice System*.[173] However, the terms *woman battering* and *wife assault* are biased in terms of heterosexual relationships, so some researchers now use the term *intimate-partner assault* to avoid this bias. We will also use this term in our discussion because it now frequently appears in the literature on assault among intimates and because it reflects the changing nature of most sexual assault laws and mandatory arrest laws, which are becoming gender neutral and moving away from the legal relationship as the criterion that defines an intimate relationship.

For many individuals, the notion of assault between intimate partners gives rise to the response "If I was hit, I would leave," but this places the burden on the victim to justify why she stays and takes the burden off the offending partner. More crucially, this type of response ignores the reality that when most women do leave violent relationships, that behavior may trigger a particularly violent response by the male partner, labeled **separation assault** by Martha R. Mahoney.[174] A woman who attempts to leave a violent relationship is seen as violating the right of her husband to control her, and even if she does manage to leave, many times the husband will follow her and attempt to take her back.

Violent relationships between intimate partners are characterized by a cycle of violence in which numerous forms of social control may be used. Men in Websdale's research disconnected telephone lines, disabled cars, and threatened women at their place of work, actions that narrowed the abused partner's options to leave, especially in the case of women in rural settings where powerful notions of family loyalty and gender roles work against leaving as an option. As Websdale noted in his research, many women who are battered by their husbands must face the fact that if they leave their husbands, they will be leaving their communities. Physical assaults often involve other tactics of abuse, such as emotional abuse and attacks or threats against children—most women who have reported abuse by intimate partners also had dependent children.[175]

In analyzing the cases of women in two counties in Massachusetts who applied for restraining orders during 1992 and 1993, as well as observations in the courtroom, **James**

Ptacek developed a typology of the strategies men used to control women in violent relationships.[176] He analyzed both the types of abuse that women reported in their petitions for restraining orders and the rationales that women provided in their affidavits that "gave some indication of the objectives behind the men's violence and abuse."[177] In 18% of the cases, the woman reported that her male partner had used violence to prevent her from leaving, and in 22% of the cases, the woman reported that violence was used to get back at her for leaving. Ptacek argued that women are assaulted in the process of leaving their abusers, and some of the incidents of separation assault had occurred more than a year following legal separation or divorce. Men also used "punishment, coercion, and retaliation against women's actions concerning children," which could take several forms.[178] Some men attacked their wives during pregnancy, other men attacked women who challenged their parental authority over the children, and still others attacked partners who had requested child support through the courts. In about 12% of the cases, the affidavits of women revealed that men used violence in response to other types of legal action. Ptacek labeled this "retaliation or coercion against women's pursuit of court or police remedies," in which the men responded with violence to actions that women were thought to have taken, whether those actions were real or imaginary. The final motivation for the violence of males was "retaliation for other perceived challenges to authority." These challenges included comments that the woman made concerning her male partner's behavior, ranging from drinking behavior to financial matters. As with the other motivational categories, the challenge to male authority was viewed as actionable, and violence was considered a justified course of action.[179] Ethnographic research like that of Websdale and Ptacek is an important avenue for increasing our knowledge of intimate-partner violence.

Another source of information is the NVAW Survey (mentioned earlier), which had the goal of estimating both the extent and the nature of physical abuse among intimate partners. At some point during their lifetime, 22% of women and slightly more than 7% of men reported having been physically assaulted by an intimate partner, and during the study year, slightly more than 1% of women and less than 1% of men reported physical assault by an intimate partner. The vast majority of behaviors considered to be physical assault were acts like grabbing and shoving rather than acts using a gun or knife. In both same-sex and opposite-sex relationships, males more often perpetrate intimate-partner violence (Figure 11-9).

On the extent of injury in intimate-partner assaults, the NVAW Survey revealed that women are more likely than men to report injuries and that most of the injuries received are minor in nature. More findings from the NVAW Survey are presented in the section of this chapter examining stalking. Learn more about intimate-partner violence via **http://www .cdc.gov/ViolencePrevention/intimatepartnerviolence /definitions.html**.

■ **bullying**   Any unwanted aggressive behavior(s) by another youth or group of youths who are not siblings or current dating partners that involves an observed or perceived power imbalance and is repeated multiple times or is highly likely to be repeated.

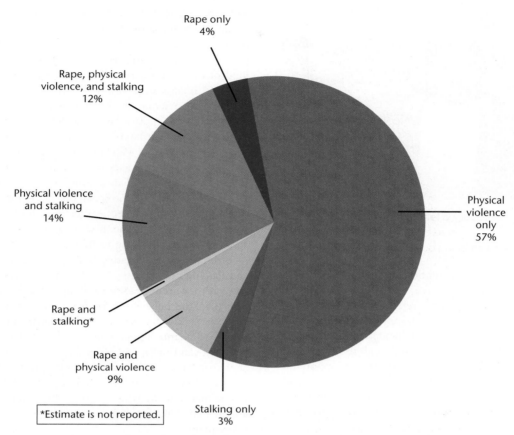

FIGURE 11-9 | **Overlap of Lifetime Intimate Partner Rape, Stalking, and Physical Victimization**

Source: Centers for Disease Control and Prevention, National Center for Injury Prevention and Control, The National Intimate Partner and Sexual Violence Survey: Factsheet 2010 (Atlanta, GA: Centers for Disease Control and Prevention, National Center for Injury Prevention and Control), p. 2.

Other Forms of Interpersonal Violence

This chapter concludes with an overview of four special forms of interpersonal violence and threatened violence: bullying, workplace violence, hate crimes, and stalking. We begin our discussion with the topic of bullying.

Bullying

By its very nature, bullying involves threats, and frequently includes threats of violence.[180] Society generally regards bullying as a form of undesirable adolescent behavior, although adults can be bullied, and often are, by other adults (and sometimes even by children). In this text, however, we use a definition of bullying developed by the Centers for Disease Control and Prevention in conjunction with the U.S. Department of Education. According to that definition, which focuses only on adolescent bullying, **bullying** is "any unwanted aggressive behavior(s) by another youth or group of youths who are not siblings or current dating partners that involves an observed or perceived power imbalance and is repeated multiple times or is highly likely to be repeated."[181]

Bullying is usually not a simple interaction between an adolescent who bullies and another who is bullied. Instead, it often involves groups of adolescents who support each other in bullying others. Moreover, there is not one profile of a young person involved in bullying that fits all bullies. Youth who bully can be either well connected socially or marginalized, and may be bullied by others as well. Similarly, those who are bullied sometimes bully others. Youth who both bully others and are also themselves bullied are at greatest risk for subsequent behavioral, mental health, and academic problems.

Prevalence studies show that between 1 out of 4, to 1 out of 3 students report having been bullied at school. Young people who are perceived as different from their peers are often at greatest risk for being bullied.

■ **Cyberbullying**   The willful and repeated use of cell phones, computers, and other electronic communication devices to harass and threaten others.

A group of male students bully a teenage boy wearing glasses. Young people who are perceived as different from their peers are often at greatest risk of being bullied. Why?

The Olweus Bullying Prevention Program, a widely-used school-based intervention initiative, identifies seven different types of participants within what is referred to as the "bullying circle": (1) students who want to bully and who initiate the action; (2) their followers or henchmen/henchwomen, who may take an active part in the bullying even though they don't initiate it; (3) supporters or passive bullies; (4) passive supporters or possible bullies, who enjoy the bullying they see, but exhibit few signs of it; (5) disengaged onlookers; (6) possible defenders; and (7) defenders who dislike the action of bullying and actively step in to help those who are victimized.[182]

Over the past two decades awareness of the problem of bullying has grown, which may lead some people to believe that bullying is increasing. However, studies suggest that rates of bullying may be declining, although bullying still remains a prevalent and serious problem in today's schools. The government website, **stopbullying.gov**, says that there is often a disconnect between young people's experience of bullying and what adults see. The website also notes that adults often don't know how to respond when they do recognize bullying.

In an interesting 2016 study of youth bullying, Justin W. Patchin and Sameer Hindjua sought to analyze the effectiveness of the threat of harsh penalties intended to dissuade bullying, and used the deterrence model as the basis for a study of around 1,000 students from two middle schools. Specifically, the researchers sought to determine whether "youth are actually being deterred" by threats of punishment. They concluded that potential bullies are more deterred by the threat of punishment from their parents and the school, and least deterred by the threat of punishment from the police.[183]

Cyberbullying

The twenty-first century has brought with it a new form of bullying, known as cyberbullying. **Cyberbullying** is the willful

and repeated use of cell phones, computers, and other electronic communication devices to harass and threaten others.[184] Instant messaging, Facebook, Snapchat, e-mail, and messages posted on websites are the most common methods of this new kind of bullying. Cyberbullies can quickly spread misinformation and images to a vast audience, while remaining anonymous, often making them difficult to trace.[185] Much of the information they post is fake, but their intent is to embarrass or socially isolate their target.

As Hinduja and Patchin point out, cyberbullying is easy to spot when it is extreme because "it involves repeated threats, multiple humiliating posts, and numerous cruel texts." Activities can include the spreading of rumors about someone, threatening to hurt someone, creating a hurtful or embarrassing web page about someone, posting embarrassing videos and images, or even pretending to be the target of the cyberbullying in order to incite negative sentiments against them. Hinduja and Patchin say that the core elements of cyberbullying are the same as they are in traditional bullying, and involve: (1) repetition (i.e., the behavior is far from accidental and occurs over and over), (2) intent (i.e., it's deliberately undertaken to cause harm), (3) harm (either physical, emotional, or psychological suffering can result), and (4) an imbalance of power (where the aggressor has power perceived to be greater than the victim). As these four characteristics demonstrate, bullying is quite different than assault, which is typically a one-time occurrence, and which may also have serious physical and psychological consequences.

In 2015, Hinduja and Patchin surveyed nearly 15,000 middle- and high-school students in over 100 schools across the United States. They found that cyberbullying behaviors are relatively common. Combining their research with that of other recent studies, they discovered that an average of 21.6% of respondents had been the victim of cyberbullying, while 15.2% reported that they had cyberbullied others.[186] Cyberbullying methods involved mean or hurtful comments posted online (14.3%), rumors online (13.3%), and threats through a cell phone text message (8.4%). Cell phones, however, were the most commonly used device in the perpetration of cyberbullying, followed by use of the school computers. Taken as a whole, about one out of every four teens has experienced cyberbullying, and about one out of every six teens has been a cyberbully.[187]

Cyberbullying varies greatly by gender. Based on a 2010 study involving a random sample of 2,212 teen males and 2,162 teen females, the male to female ratio varied the most in the following three areas: (1) victimization within a person's lifetime (16.6% for males vs. 25.1% for females); (2) admitted to a cyberbullying offense within a person's lifetime (17.5% for males vs. 21.3% for females); and (3) had a hurtful comment posted about oneself online (10.5% for males vs. 18.2% for females).[188]

■ **workplace violence**   Nonfatal violence (rape/sexual assault, robbery, and aggravated and simple assault) against employed persons age 16 or older.

Though many adolescents tend to deny the emotional harm caused by bullying tactics such as name- calling, rumor spreading, and teasing, research suggests that the opposite is true. In a study that utilized a sample of over 3,000 students, researchers found that "38% of bullying victims felt vengeful, 37% were angry and 24% felt helpless." Another study conducted by the Cyberbullying Research Center involved a sample of 468 students, and revealed that females are typically more emotionally affected by cyberbullying than males. The females in the study reported being frustrated (39.6%), angry (36%), and sad (25.2%)—more often than males who reported lower percentages in each category (27.5%, 24.3%, 17.9% respectively).

Some instances of cyberbullying have led to self-harming behaviors, including suicide. The relationship between bullying and suicide is complex. Many media reports oversimplify this relationship, by implying that bullying can cause suicide. Instead, research indicates that:

- persistent bullying can lead to or worsen feelings of isolation, rejection, exclusion, and despair, as well as depression and anxiety, which can contribute to suicidal behavior.

- the vast majority of young people who are bullied do not become suicidal.

- most young people who die by suicide have multiple risk factors, only one of which is bullying.

- some youth, such as LGBT youth, are at increased risk for suicide attempts even when bullying is not a factor.

View a recent CDC report at **www.cdc.gov /violenceprevention/pdf/bullying-suicide-translation -final-a.pdf**, which examines the relationship between bullying and suicide more closely.

Finally, while some bullying actions can fall into criminal categories, such as harassment, hazing, or assault, there is no federal anti-bullying law. Even though 49 states have anti-bullying legislation, bullying itself is not illegal. Existing laws don't criminalize the behavior, but instead are intended to encourage or require action by teachers and school administers to prevent or stop bullying and cyberbullying.

Workplace Violence

At 6:45 in the morning of August 26, 2015, a 24-year-old TV reporter and her 27-year-old cameraman were shot dead on live television while interviewing a woman at the Bridgewater Plaza in Franklin County, Virginia. The reporter, Alison Parker, and cameraman Adam Ward, were shot multiple times by a former co-worker, 41-year-old Vester Lee Flanagan. Flanagan, a disgruntled past employee of WDBJ-TV, used his cellphone to record a video of the killings, in which he fired 15 shots from a semiautomatic pistol. Within minutes, Flanagan, who later

took his own life while being pursued by police, had posted the video on social media.

Workplace violence (murder, rape, robbery, and assault committed against persons who are at work or on duty) is a significant problem in America today. The FBI says that "workplace violence is now recognized as a specific category of violent crime that calls for distinct responses from employers, law enforcement, and the community."[189] In a given year, approximately 570,000 nonfatal violent crimes (rape/sexual assault, robbery, and aggravated and simple assault) occur against persons age 16 or older while they are at work or on duty, based on findings from the National Crime Victimization Survey (NCVS).[190] This accounts for about 24% of nonfatal violence against employed persons age 16 or older. Nonfatal workplace violence is about 15% of all nonfatal violent crime against persons age 16 or older.

> Workplace violence is a significant problem in America today.

Today an estimated 4 violent crimes per 1,000 employed persons age 16 or older are committed while victims are at work or on duty, compared to 6 violent crimes per 1,000 employed persons age 16 or older in 2002. In 1993, the rate of nonfatal violence was 16 violent crimes per 1,000 employed persons while at work, a rate that was 75% higher than it is today.

As might be expected, police officers experience workplace violence at rates higher than persons employed in almost any other occupation (except bartenders), whereas college or university professors are among persons least likely to be victimized (Figure 11–10).

Workplace violence falls into four broad categories:

1. Violent acts by criminals who have no other connection with the workplace but who enter to commit robbery, acts of terrorism, or another crime

2. Violence directed at employees by customers, clients, patients, students, inmates, or any others for whom an organization provides services

3. Violence against coworkers, supervisors, or managers by a present or former employee

4. Violence committed in the workplace by someone who doesn't work there but who has a personal relationship with an employee, such as an abusive spouse or domestic partner

Violence committed by criminals otherwise unconnected to the workplace accounts for nearly 80% of all workplace homicides.[191] In such incidents, the motive is usually theft, and in a great many cases, the criminal is carrying a gun or other weapon, increasing the likelihood that the victim(s) will be killed or seriously wounded. This type of violence falls heavily

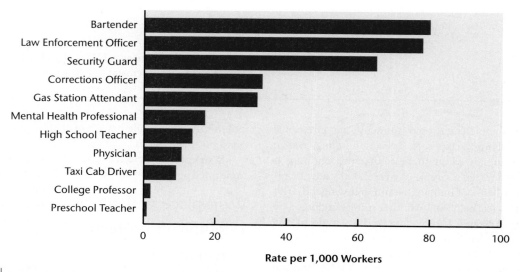

FIGURE 11-10 | Rate of Violent Workplace Victimization by Occupation

Source: Erika Harrell, *Workplace Violence, 1993–2009* (Washington, DC: Bureau of Justice Statistics, 2011), p. 4.

on particular occupational groups whose jobs make them vulnerable: taxi drivers, late-night retail or gas station clerks and others on duty at night, workers in isolated locations or dangerous neighborhoods, and workers with cash or access to it.

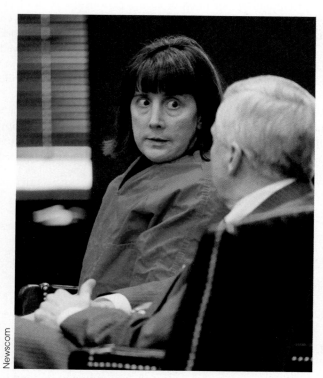

University of Alabama–Huntsville (UAH) shooter Amy Bishop conferring with her lawyer in Madison Circuit Court (Alabama). In 2012, Bishop, age 47, pled guilty to killing three fellow UAH biology faculty members and wounding three others during a shooting rampage at a faculty meeting on campus on February 12, 2010. She received a life sentence, although civil suits that had been filed against her were dismissed in 2014. Can anything be done to reduce the number of incidents of workplace violence?

The second type of workplace violence typically involves assaults on an employee by a customer, patient, or someone else receiving a service.[192] In general, the violent acts occur as workers are performing their daily tasks. In some occupations (police officers, correctional officers, security guards, and mental health workers), dealing with dangerous people is a part of the job. In other occupations, violent reactions by a customer or client are unpredictable, possibly triggered by an argument, anger at the quality of service or denial of service, a delay, or some other precipitating event. Employees experiencing the largest number of these assaults are those in health care occupations—nurses, in particular, as well as doctors and aides who deal with psychiatric patients; members of emergency medical response teams; and hospital employees working in admissions, emergency rooms, and crisis or acute care units.

The third and fourth types of violence—incidents of violence by past or present employees and acts committed by domestic abusers and other personal relational issues that follow an employee into the workplace—are often the kind of workplace violence reported in the media. Violence in these categories is no less damaging than any other violent act, but when the violence comes from an employee or someone close to an employee, there is a much greater chance that some warning sign will have reached the employer prior to the violent act.

A BJS study revealed the following facts about workplace violence:[193]

- Private-sector and federal government employees are victimized at similar rates.

- More than 80% of all workplace homicides are committed with a firearm.

- Rape and sexual assault, robbery, and homicide account for a small percentage (6%) of all workplace violent crime; the majority of workplace violent incidents (almost 19 of every 20) are aggravated or simple assaults.

- Males experience more workplace violence (except for rape and sexual assault) than females, with about

■ **hate crime** A criminal offense in which the motive is hatred, bias, or prejudice based on the actual or perceived race, color, religion, national origin, ethnicity, gender, or sexual orientation of another individual or group of individuals.

two-thirds of all robberies, aggravated assaults, and simple assaults in the workplace being committed against males.

- People ages 20–34 experience workplace violence at a rate higher than any other age group.

- The workplace violent crime rate for whites (13 per 1,000 in the workforce) is 25% higher than the rate for blacks (10 per 1,000) and 59% higher than the rate for other races (8 per 1,000); whites experience more than four-fifths of all rapes and sexual assaults (88%), robberies (81%), aggravated assaults (86%), and simple assaults (89%) occurring in the workplace, but blacks have the highest rates of overall violent crime (including both workplace and nonworkplace violence).

- Most workplace victimizations are intraracial—about six in ten white and black victims of workplace crime perceive their assailant to be of the same race.

- Almost four of every ten robberies occurring while the victim is at work or on duty are committed against someone in retail sales or transportation.

- About 12% of all workplace violence victims sustain injuries from the incident; of those injuries, about 10 out of 11 are minor injuries.

The National Institute for Occupational Safety and Health (NIOSH)[194] recommends a number of prevention strategies to lower the incidence of workplace violence, including environmental design factors that physically separate workers from customers: bullet-resistant barriers or enclosures, high counters to prevent customer access to workers and goods, and limited avenues of access and egress.[195] Also recommended are enhanced administrative controls such as staffing plans and work practices that include the prescreening of patients or customers and the training and education of employees in conflict-resolution strategies.

Visit NIOSH's Occupational Violence Center to learn more about workplace violence and techniques to prevent it at **https://www.cdc.gov/niosh/topics/violence.** Learn about recommendations for curtailing workplace violence from the FBI at **https://www.justicestudies.com/pubs/ workplaceviolence.pdf.**

Hate Crimes

In 2017, 22-year-old white supremacist Dylann Roof was sentenced to death by a federal jury. Roof is the infamous "Charleston church shooter" who walked into a Bible study class at the historically black Emanuel African Methodist Episcopal Church in Charleston, S.C., and shot twelve people, killing nine. Roof was convicted of 33 federal charges, including the commission of a violent **hate crime** (a crime

whose motive is hatred, bias, or prejudice). A Criminal Profiles box at the end of this chapter describes Roof's case in more detail.

The collection of hate-crime statistics was mandated by the U.S. Congress with passage of the Hate Crime Statistics Act of 1990.[196] Under the law, the FBI is required to serve as a repository for data collected on crimes motivated by religious, sexual orientation, ethnic, or racial prejudice. The Violent Crime Control and Law Enforcement Act of 1994 mandated the addition to the category of hate crimes any crimes motivated by biases against people with disabilities, and the UCR Program began reporting such crimes in 1997.[197]

> The collection of hate-crime statistics was mandated by the U.S. Congress in 1990.

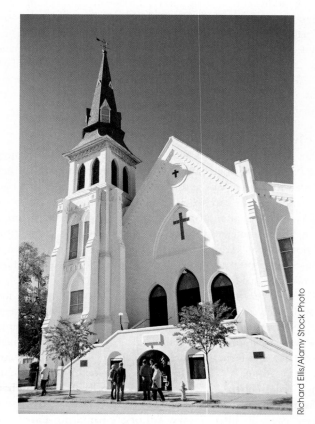

Richard Ellis/Alamy Stock Photo

Charleston's (South Carolina) historically black Emanuel African Methodist Episcopal Church. In mid-2015, the church became the scene of a violent crime in which 12 people were shot and nine killed by white supremacist Dylann Roof. What are hate crimes?

■ **stalking**   A course of conduct directed at a specific person that involves repeated visual or physical proximity; nonconsensual communication; verbal, written, or implied threats; or a combination thereof that would cause a reasonable person fear.

According to the BJS, hate crimes (also called *bias crimes*) are characterized by "manifest evidence of prejudice based on race, religion, sexual orientation, or ethnicity, including where appropriate the crimes of murder, non-negligent manslaughter, rape, aggravated assault, simple assault, intimidation, arson, and destruction, damage, or vandalism of property."[198] In 2009, President Barack Obama signed into law a bill that enhances the federal protection of gays by specifically adding acts of violence against gay, lesbian, bisexual, and transgender people to the list of federal hate crimes.[199]

Based on FBI statistics on hate crimes, 6,121 hate-crime incidents were reported in 2016.[200] Of all the incidents reported 57.5% were motivated by racial bias, 17.7% by a sexual-orientation bias, 21.0% by religious bias. Bias against a disability accounted for 1.2% of single-bias incidents. Of the 4,720 hate crime offenses classified as crimes against persons in 2016, intimidation accounted for 44.7%, simple assaults for 35.7%, and aggravated assaults for 18.5%. Nine murders and 24 rapes were reported as hate crimes.

In addition to violent crimes, 2,519 hate crime property offenses occurred in 2016. The majority of these (76%) were acts of vandalism. Robbery, burglary, larceny-theft, motor vehicle theft, arson, and other offenses accounted for the remaining 24% of crimes against property. Forty-six percent of the 5,770 known offenders were white; 26% were black. The race was unknown for 18%, and other races accounted for the remaining known offenders.

Role of Hate Groups

Hate groups like the Ku Klux Klan (KKK), the Aryan Nations, the National Alliance, and the Identity church movement have existed for many years and have long been associated with acts of violence. It is easy to classify groups in the hate-group category when their fundamental purpose is grounded in prejudice, but in the case of some other organizations, classification is not as easy. Are all militia groups hate groups? Given its anti-Semitic position, does the Nation of Islam, led by Louis Farrakhan, qualify as a hate group?

Are hate groups a necessary feature of hate crimes? Citing a wide array of research studies, James B. Jacobs and Kimberly A. Potter found that "the vast majority of reported hate crimes are not committed by organized hate groups and their members, but by teenagers, primarily white males, acting alone or in a group."[201] Visit the NCJRS Hate Crime Resources page via **http://www.ncjrs.gov/spotlight/Hate_Crimes /Summary.html** and the Anti-Defamation League's Combating Hate page at **http://www.adl.org/combating-hate/** and read **http://www.ncjrs.gov/pdffiles1/nij/jr000257c.pdf** and **http://www.ncjrs.gov/pdffiles1/nij/grants/210300.pdf** to learn more about hate crimes. View the latest FBI statistics on hate crimes via **http://www2.fbi.gov/ucr/hc2009/index.html**.

Stalking

In 2014, a woman identified as 30-year-old Genoveva Nunez-Figueroa was arrested after being rescued from a chimney in which she had become stuck while trying to shimmy into a residence in Thousand Oaks, California. The home belonged to a man she had met through an online dating service. Nunez-Figueroa was charged with illegal entry and giving false information to police, while the male homeowner was left with the bill to repair his chimney—which was destroyed during the rescue effort. The attempted chimney entry was Nunez-Figueroa's third effort to see the man, who had decided against dating her.[202] Several high-profile cases have illustrated the dangerous potential of **stalking** behavior. John Hinkley was obsessed with actress Jodie Foster and thought he could capture her attention and admiration by shooting President Ronald Reagan in 1981. Mark David Chapman, the man who shot John Lennon in 1980, considered himself to be one of Lennon's biggest fans. Talk-show host David Letterman was stalked from 1988 to 1993 by a woman who professed her love for him by breaking into his house repeatedly, trespassing on his property, and stealing his car. Michael David Barrett, a 47-year-old divorced Chicago-area man, pleaded guilty in 2009 to interstate stalking for filming ESPN reporter Erin Andrews through a peephole while she undressed in her neighboring hotel room.[203] That same year, Michael Lawrence Kozelka of Townsend, Maryland, was arrested on charges of stalking singer-songwriter Jewel at her Texas ranch; at the time of his arrest, Kozelka, age 50, told authorities that he had been on a mission from God.[204] Although these high-profile cases may capture media attention because they involve celebrities, stalking often involves average individuals as they go about their lives.

The first antistalking statute was passed in 1990 in California;[205] now all states and the federal government have antistalking laws. Rather than being an offense that occurs once, stalking is conceptualized as a pattern of behavior that causes victims to fear for their personal safety. The definition used in the Model Antistalking Code for States, developed by the NIJ, is "a course of conduct directed at a specific person that involves repeated visual or physical proximity, nonconsensual communication, or verbal, written or implied threats, or a combination thereof, that would cause a reasonable person fear"[206] (*repeated* is defined to mean at least two occasions).

Statutory definitions of *stalking* encompass a number of diverse but interrelated behaviors: making phone calls, following the victim, sending letters, making threats in some manner, vandalizing property, and watching the victim. Rather than viewing these behaviors in isolation from one another, antistalking laws take into account the totality of the circumstances so that seemingly benign behaviors are seen in light of how they are connected to other behaviors. For example, sending unwanted letters might be seen as innocuous behavior, but when this activity is combined with following the victim and standing outside his or her place of work or residence, the behavior takes on a more threatening tone and may be the precursor for more serious offenses like assault, rape, and murder.[207]

The Extent of Stalking

Recent data on stalking come from the BJS report *Stalking Victimization in the United States*, which shows that during a recent 12-month period, an estimated 3.4 million persons age 18 or older were victims of stalking.[208] The BJS report, derived from data accumulated under the NCVS, identified seven types of harassing or unwanted behaviors consistent with conduct experienced by stalking victims: (1) receiving unwanted phone calls; (2) receiving unsolicited or unwanted letters or e-mails; (3) being followed or spied upon; (4) having the stalker show up at places without a legitimate reason; (5) having the stalker wait at places for the victim; (6) receiving unwanted items, presents, or flowers; and (7) having the stalker post information or spread rumors about the victim on the Internet, in a public place, or by word of mouth. The BJS noted that these acts, taken individually, may not be criminal, but "collectively and repetitively these behaviors may cause a victim to fear for his or her safety or the safety of a family member."

The BJS report found the following during the 12-month data-gathering period:[209]

- An estimated 14 in every 1,000 persons age 18 or older were victims of stalking.
- About half (46%) of stalking victims experienced at least one unwanted contact per week, and 11% of victims said they had been stalked for five years or more.
- The risk of stalking victimization was highest for individuals who were divorced or separated—34 per 1,000 individuals.
- Women were at greater risk than men for stalking victimization; however, women and men were equally likely to experience harassment.
- A pattern of decreasing risk for stalking victimization existed for persons residing in households with higher incomes.
- Male (37%) and female (41%) stalking victimizations were equally likely to be reported to the police.
- Approximately one in four stalking victims reported some form of cyberstalking, such as through e-mail (83%) or instant messaging (35%).
- About 46% of stalking victims felt fear of not knowing what would happen next.
- Nearly three in four stalking victims knew their offender in some capacity.
- More than half of stalking victims lost five or more days from work as a result of experiencing stalking.

The most common reasons victims perceived as the cause of stalking behavior were retaliation, anger, spite (37%), or desire to control the victim (33%). About one in six victims believed the stalking started to keep him or her in the relationship with the offender, and one in ten reported that the stalking began while living with the offender. About a tenth of victims did not know why the stalking began.

For stalking victims, the most common fear cited was not knowing what would happen next; 9% of stalking victims reported their worst fear was death, 29% feared the behavior would never stop, and more than 50% feared bodily harm to themselves, their children, or another family member. More than seven in ten victims felt angry or annoyed at the beginning of the unwanted contacts or as they progressed. Stalking victims were about twice as likely as harassment victims to feel anxious or concerned at the beginning of the unwanted contacts (52.7% vs. 25.4%), and as the unwanted contacts progressed, about 15% of stalking victims felt depressed or sick, and 1% reported feeling suicidal.

About 139,000 stalking victims were attacked with a weapon, with stalkers equally likely to use a knife, blunt instrument, or other object; 23% used handguns. Of the 279,000 victims who were injured in an attack, nearly all (99%) sustained minor bruises and other injuries, and about 20% sustained serious injuries, including gunshot or knife wounds, internal injuries, or broken bones.

Examining the behaviors that stalkers engage in, Patricia Tjaden and Nancy Thoennes (principal investigators for the NVAW Survey) concluded that antistalking laws requiring that an overt threat be made against the victim before action can be taken against the stalker are ill-advised and that laws should be strengthened to allow for early action by the justice system to prevent later harm to stalking victims.[210]

Types of Stalkers

A psychiatric study of 145 Canadian stalkers who had been referred to a forensic psychiatry center for treatment found that most were men (79%) and that many were unemployed (39%).[211] Perhaps not surprisingly, most (52%) had never had an intimate relationship. Five types of stalkers were identified:

1. **Rejected stalkers.** Rejected stalkers pursue their victims in order to reverse, correct, or avenge a felt rejection (e.g., divorce, separation, and termination).

2. **Intimacy-seeking stalkers.** Wanting to establish an intimate, loving relationship with the victim, intimacy-seeking stalkers may see the victim as a soul mate, someone whom they are fated to be with.

3. **Incompetent suitors.** Incompetent suitors have a romantic or sexual interest in the victim despite having poor social or courting skills.

4. **Resentful vendetta-motivated stalkers.** Vendetta-motivated stalkers act out revenge based on a perceived

wrong or a grievance against the victim, and their intent is generally to frighten and distress the victim.

5. **Predatory stalkers.** Predatory stalkers spy on the victim in preparation for an attack, which is usually sexual in nature.

Delusional disorders were found to be common among the stalkers treated, and 30% were determined to suffer consistently from delusions about those they stalked. Stalking behavior among those studied lasted anywhere from four weeks to 20 years, with an average of 12 months. Rejected and intimacy-seeking stalkers tended to persist the longest in stalking behavior. About 63% of stalkers made threats toward their victims, and 36% were assaultive. The researchers concluded, "Stalkers have a range of motivations, from reasserting power over a partner who rejected them to the quest for a loving relationship."[212] Read more about the types of stalkers identified in the social scientific literature and their motivations at **http://www.jaapl.org/cgi/reprint/34/4/439**.

Victim–Offender Relationships in Stalking

The majority of stalking victims identified in the NVAW Survey are women (78%, or four out of every five victims), and the majority of individuals who stalk are men (94% of women and 60% of men identify a male as the stalker). The majority of stalking victims are young, with 52% between the ages of 18 and 29 and 22% between the ages of 30 and 39. Results from the NVAW Survey confirmed previous research showing that the majority of victims know their stalkers—a stranger was identified as the stalker in only 23% of the cases where a woman was stalked and 36% of the cases where a man was stalked. For women who are stalked, the majority (59%) are more likely to be stalked by an intimate partner than by a stranger, an acquaintance, or a relative other than the spouse, but the majority of men are stalked by strangers or acquaintances (70%), usually a male in both cases (90%). Tjaden and Thoennes stated that although there is no clear explanation for this finding, it may be related to a greater risk of stalking among homosexual as opposed to heterosexual men because the survey found that stalking was more often experienced by male respondents who indicated that they had lived as a couple with another male. The belief that stalkers suffer from mental illness or personality disorder was not confirmed by the survey findings, as only 7% of the victims stated that they were stalked by offenders who were "mentally ill or abusing drugs or alcohol."[213]

Stalking in Intimate-Partner Relationships

Almost one-fourth (21%) of female respondents in the NVAW Survey who had been stalked by an intimate partner stated that they were stalked before the end of the relationship, 43% indicated that the stalking occurred after the relationship had ended, and slightly over one-third (36%) reported that they were stalked both before and after the end of the relationship with their partner.[214] The survey found that other forms of violence often accompany stalking. For women stalked by an intimate partner, 81% were also physically assaulted, and about 33% were sexually assaulted by the stalker; the percentage of women experiencing assault of either kind by a current or former intimate partner who stalked them was higher than the percentage experiencing some form of assault but no stalking (20% of women who had ever married or lived with a male partner had experienced physical assault by that partner and 5% had experienced sexual assault).[215] Men who stalked their former wives were "significantly more likely than ex-husbands who did not stalk to engage in emotionally abusive and controlling behavior toward their wife."[216]

Consequences of Stalking

Respondents in the NVAW Survey reported a number of consequences of stalking that negatively affected their lives, with women who had been stalked reporting a significantly higher level of concern for their personal safety than those who had not been stalked. Almost one-third reported seeking counseling, and slightly more than one-fourth lost time from work. Women took a variety of extra self-protective measures as a response to the stalking: 17% stated they had bought a gun, 11% stated they had changed residences, and 11% stated they had moved out of state. Women who had been stalked were more likely than men to have obtained a protective order against the stalker (23% vs. 10%, respectively).[217]

> Women who had been stalked reported a significantly higher level of concern for their personal safety than those who had not been stalked.

Because the definition used in the NVAW Survey to assess stalking required high levels of fear on the part of victims, it is worthwhile to note the data on whether the victims reported stalking to the police—a higher percentage of women than men reported the stalking to police (55% vs. 48%, respectively). When asked their reasons for not reporting stalking to the police, victims consistently gave fairly general reasons: 20% defined it as not a police matter, 17% did not believe the police could do anything, 16% were afraid of reprisal from the stalker, 12% said they resolved it on their own, and smaller percentages reported that the police would not believe them or that it was a private matter.[218] Responses to questions on satisfaction with law enforcement's handling of the case indicated that about half of respondents approved of police procedure, but in cases where an arrest was made in the stalking, three-fourths of the victims were satisfied with the police handling of the case.[219] Learn more about the

■ **cyberstalking** An array of high-technology options, including e-mail and the Internet, that an offender uses to harass or "follow" another individual.

crime of stalking at the federal Stalking Resource Center at **http://www.victimsofcrime.org/our-programs/ stalking-resource-center**.

Cyberstalking

In 2016, Kassandra Cruz, 23, of Miami, Florida, was sentenced in federal court to 22 months in prison, followed by three years of supervised release stemming from her conviction on one count of cyberstalking—a violation of federal law.[220] Court documents show that Cruz sent a "friend" request to a woman identified as S.B., portraying herself as a man and saying that she was an active duty marine. S.B. grew suspicious when Cruz started following her other online friends. But when she attempted to end the online friendship, Cruz threatened to blackmail her using past social media postings. Cruz demanded $100,000 on multiple occasions in exchange for no further contact. In total, S.B. received over 900 unwanted calls and text messages. Cruz was eventually identified by the FBI and was taken into custody, ending S.B.'s social media nightmare.

Cyberstalking—the use of electronic communication like e-mail or the Internet to harass individuals—has received attention as efforts progress to better understand the consequences of our increased reliance on electronic communication and the Internet.[221] One federal government report made the following recommendations to help control cyberstalking:[222]

- A review of all stalking laws at the state level is needed to ensure that provisions for cyberstalking are included.
- An amendment to federal law is needed to make transmission of communication in specified forms of commerce actionable if the intent involves threatening behavior or causes the recipient fear.
- Training on cyberstalking should be offered at all levels of law enforcement.
- A website with information on cyberstalking should be created and made available to the public.

Learn more about the crime of cyberstalking from the Stalking Resource Center run by the National Center for Victims of Crime at **http://tinyurl.com/mgl64h9**, and read an article describing the growing use of technology and other menacing stalking behaviors at **http://www.victimsofcrime.org/our -programs/stalking-resource-center/stalking-information /the-use-of-technology-to-stalk**.

CRIMINAL | PROFILES

Dylann Storm Roof—The Charleston Church Shooter

Dylann Storm Roof was 21 years old when he walked into a Bible study class in the basement of Charleston's historically black Emanuel African Methodist Episcopal Church in mid-2015 and sat on a folding chair. Roof, a stranger to those gathered there, was warmly welcomed into the group. The church's pastor offered him a Bible and a printed study sheet so that he could participate in discussions. Roof remained seated quietly for 30 minutes before pulling a .45-calibre pistol from a fanny pack and yelling that he was there to kill black people. Over the next few minutes, he proceeded to murder nine of the twelve people in the room. The group's members had just closed their eyes to begin a final prayer when Roof started shooting. At one point he approached a woman who was hiding under a table, shouting that he would let her live so that she could tell the story of what happened to her friends. Before he slipped out of a side door and into the church's parking lot, Roof, a self-declared white supremacist, had fired more than 70 times, stopping periodically to re-load. Each of his victims had been shot at least five times.

A video camera recorded Roof as he left the church, but responding officers had not yet arrived, and he calmly strode away. He was arrested the next day in Shelby, North Carolina – a three and a half hour drive from his South Carolina home. During the police interrogation that followed Roof laughed while admitting to the killings, and told investigators that he had been trying to ignite a race war.

FBI agents found Roof's written ramblings at his home and in internet postings. On a Website that he owned, called "The Last Rhodesian," were photos of Roof surrounded by neo-Nazi symbolism. The site also contained a manifesto that Roof had written claiming that black men are "raping and killing our women." Roof also said

Dylann Roof shown entering the courthouse in Shelby, North Carolina.

that black-on-white crime had reached unacceptable levels. "Negroes have lower IQs, lower impulse control, and higher testosterone levels in general," Roof wrote. "These three things alone are a recipe for violent behavior." His writings also described his chosen target: a church. "I have no choice. I am not in a position to, alone, go into the ghetto and fight," he wrote.

Roof's writings also evidenced hatred for Hispanics, Jews, and the American flag. He wrote that Modern American patriotism is a joke," because, he said, white people are being murdered every day "in the streets" by blacks, while "pretending like they have something to be proud of."

Roof's admission of guilt was used at trial. Prosecutors told the jury that Roof had a "cold and hateful heart" while he pulled the trigger.

As Roof's trial began, a *New York Times* reporter asked the question that everyone seemed to want answered: "How did the silent young man with no record of violence in his past come to be accused of killing nine people who had gathered to pray?"

People who knew Roof before the shootings described him as struggling with school; he had attended ninth grade twice before dropping out. Papers filed with civic court during his parents' divorce proceedings said that he showed signs of obsessive-compulsive disorder, and was overly concerned about germs and cleanliness. As an adolescent, Roof moved a lot, and attended at least seven schools in nine years. Those schools were racially integrated, and Roof grew up with black friends. His grandfather was a well-known local lawyer. Neighbors said that Roof had drifted in and out of low-paying jobs, often sat on the curb in front of his house, and dabbled in drugs. He had a few minor run-ins with the police, and began visiting white supremacist websites. He boasted to his friends about wanting to start a race war. Roof's parents were divorced, and both had experienced financial hardship while sharing custody of their son. Roof's father was a building contractor with a passion for Harley-Davidson motorcycles.

Roof was tried on 33 federal charges, including: (1) nine counts of violating the federal Hate Crimes Act resulting in death; (2) nine counts of use of a firearm to commit murder during and in relation to a crime of violence; (3) nine counts of obstruction of exercise of religion resulting in death; (4) three counts of violating the federal Hate Crimes Act involving an attempt to kill; (5) three counts of obstruction of exercise of religion involving an attempt to kill and use of a dangerous weapon. On December 15, 2015, he was found guilty on all counts. The jury had taken only two hours to reach its verdict.

A separate sentencing phase of Roof's trial was held in January, 2017. At that hearing, Roof represented himself while a lawyer was available for him to consult with. Extracts from his white supremacist manifesto, which he had written while in jail, showed an unrepentant Roof and revealed the depth of his racial bias. "I would like to make it crystal clear," Roof wrote, "I do not regret what I did. I am not sorry." The manifesto continued, saying, "I do feel sorry for the innocent white children forced to live in this sick country and I do feel sorry for the innocent white people that are killed daily at the hands of the lower race. I have shed a tear of self-pity for myself. I feel pity that I had to do what I did in the first place. I feel pity that I had to give up my life because of a situation that should never have existed." When Roof spoke at sentencing, he told the court, "There's nothing wrong with me psychologically," but said little else. At the end of the hearing, a unanimous jury recommended that Roof be sentenced to death.

The Case of Dylann Roof raises a number of interesting questions. Among them are the following:

1. Roof seemed to be filled with hate – not just for black people, but for other groups as well. Where did those hateful feelings originate?

2. Was Roof's way of thinking the product of his prior socialization, or did he intentionally seek out a way of life that led him down the path of self-radicalization?

Sources: Alan Blinder and Kevin Sack, "Dylann Roof, Addressing Court, Offers No Apology or Explanation for Massacre," *The New York Times*, January 4, 2017, http://nytimes.com/2017/01/04/us/dylann-roof-sentencing.html (accessed January 4, 2017); "Dylann Roof Had 'Cold and Hateful Hear,' During Charleston Church Shooting, Prosecutor Says, CBS News, December 7, 2016, http://www.cbsnews.com/news/dylann-roof-death-penalty-trial-charleston-church-shooting (accessed January 17, 2017); "Dylann Roof Trial: Survivor Spared from Massacre Tells Her Story," CNN, December 14, 2016, http://www.cnn.com/2016/12/14/us/dylann-roof-murder-trial/index.html (accessed January 17, 2017); and Frances Robles and Nikita Stewart, "Dylann Roof's Past Reveals Trouble at Home and School," The New York Times, July 16, 2016, http://www.nytimes.com/2015/07/17/us/charleston-shooting-dylann-roof-troubled-past.htm (accessed January 17, 2017).

SUMMARY

- Criminal homicide, the illegal killing of one human being by another, ranges from serial killing and mass murder to murder in intimate settings. Patterns of murder vary along subcultural and social structural dimensions such as economic inequality and community social disorganization.

- The FBI defines rape as "The penetration, no matter how slight, of the vagina or anus with any body part or object, or oral penetration by a sex organ of another person, without the consent of the victim."

- The term *child sexual abuse* encompasses a variety of criminal and civil offenses in which an adult engages in sexual activity with a minor, exploits a minor for purposes of sexual gratification, or exploits a minor sexually for purposes of profit. The term includes a variety of activities and motivations, including child molestation, child sexual exploitation (CSE), and the commercial sexual exploitation of children (CSEC).

- The FBI defines robbery as the taking of or attempting to take anything of value from the care, custody, or control of someone by using force or threat of force or violence or by putting the victim in fear. Muggings and robberies in residences are personal robbery, and robberies in commercial settings are institutional robberies. The majority of robbery offenders are generalists with a fairly lengthy but varied criminal career who put very little planning into their robberies.

- Assaults are either simple or aggravated (violent unlawful attacks for the purpose of inflicting severe or aggravated bodily injury). Intimate-partner violence characterizes assaultive behavior between individuals involved in an intimate relationship.

- This chapter concludes with a discussion of four different forms of interpersonal violence: bullying, workplace violence, hate crimes, and stalking. Workplace violence is a widespread significant problem today and includes murder, rape, robbery, and assault committed against persons who are at work or on duty. Hate crimes are criminal offenses motivated by hatred, bias, or prejudice based on the race, religion, national origin, ethnicity, gender, or sexual orientation of another person. Stalking is repeated visual or physical proximity, nonconsensual communication, and/or threats that would cause someone to be fearful; cyberstalking is a special type of stalking that uses high technology to harass someone.

KEY TERMS

acquaintance rape, 305

aggravated assault, 314

bullying, 317

child pornography, 308

child sexual abuse (CSA), 307

comfort serial killers, 296

cyberbullying, 318

cyberstalking, 325

exposure-reduction theory, 294

expressive crime, 293

felony murder, 292

first-degree murder, 291

hate crime, 321

hedonistic serial killers, 296

homicide, 290

institutional robbery, 310

instrumental crime, 293

intimate-partner assault, 315

mass murder, 298

murder, 290

negligent homicide, 291

nonprimary homicide, 293

personal robbery, 310

power seekers, 296

primary homicide, 293

rape, 299

second-degree murder, 291

selective disinhibition, 295

separation assault, 316

serial murder, 296

sibling offense, 295

spousal rape, 305

stalking, 322

subculture of violence theory, 293

Violent Criminal Apprehension Program (VICAP), 297

visionary serial killers, 296

workplace violence, 319

KEY NAMES

Larry Baron, 302

Ann Burgess, 303

Andrea Dworkin, 300

James Alan Fox, 296

Nicholas Groth, 302

Robert R. Hazelwood, 303

Jack Levin, 296

Catherine MacKinnon, 300

Jody Miller, 313

Craig T. Palmer, 303

Robert Nash Parker, 293

James Ptacek, 316

Diana E. H. Russell, 305

Diana Scully, 303

Murray A. Straus, 302

Randy Thornhill, 303

QUESTIONS FOR REVIEW

1. What is criminal homicide, and what are the key issues involved in explaining patterns of homicide?

2. How is the crime of rape defined, and what are the key issues involved in understanding the crime of rape?

3. What does the term *child sexual abuse* encompass, and what are the various types of child sex abusers that this chapter identifies?

4. How is the crime of robbery defined, and what are the different kinds of robbery?

5. How is the crime of assault defined, and what are the various kinds of assault?

6. What additional forms of interpersonal violence does this chapter discuss?

QUESTIONS FOR REFLECTION

1. Are violent crimes primarily rational activities?

2. Why was the federal government's recent redefinition of the term "rape" necessary? How does the definition differ from statutory terminology?

3. Is robbery primarily a rational activity? Why or why not?

CRIMES AGAINST PROPERTY

It's What We Lose

LEARNING OUTCOMES

After reading this chapter, you should be able to answer the following questions:

- What are the major forms of property crime discussed in this chapter?
- What constitutes the crime of burglary? What are some of its characteristics?
- What constitutes the crime of larceny-theft? What forms does it take?
- What is motor vehicle theft? How prevalent is it?
- What constitutes the crime of arson?
- What are some characteristics of persistent and professional thieves?
- What are the typical activities of receivers of stolen property, and how are stolen goods distributed?

■ **property crime** According to the FBI's Uniform Crime Reporting program, a crime category that includes burglary, larceny, motor vehicle theft, and arson.
■ **burglary** The unlawful entry of a structure to commit a felony or a theft.

Introduction

In 2012, Pedro Antonio Marcuello Guzman, 46, and Maria Martha Elisa Ornelas Lazo, 50, were arrested and charged with possession of stolen goods when they tried to sell a painting created in 1925 by the French Impressionist Matisse.[1] The painting, titled *Odalisque a la culotte rouge*, depicts a bare-chested woman sitting cross-legged on the floor wearing a pair of scarlet trousers. It is estimated to be worth over $3 million, and had been stolen from the Caracas Museum of Contemporary Art in Venezuela a decade earlier. Guzman and Lazo, who admitted knowing that the painting was stolen, had offered to sell it for $740,000 to undercover agents of the Federal Bureau of Investigation (FBI) posing as art collectors.

Art theft can be a lucrative business. In May 2010, a lone thief stole five paintings from the Paris Museum of Modern Art, including works by Picasso and Matisse.[2] Estimates put the value of the art stolen at hundreds of millions of dollars. Two years prior to the Paris incident, armed robbers stole four paintings from a private museum in Zurich, Switzerland, with an estimated value of $163 million. The art included works by van Gogh and Monet, some of which were recovered. Similarly, in 2007, three paintings by Pablo Picasso were stolen in two separate incidents—one in Brazil and the other in Paris, France. The latter involved a nighttime burglary at the home of one of

Picasso's granddaughters. Art thefts are relatively common and occur with great regularity.

The largest art theft in U.S. history took place at the Isabella Stewart Gardner Museum in Boston in 1990, when thieves made off with several paintings worth more than $300 million. In that case, two people disguised as Boston police officers entered the museum, incapacitated security guards, and made off with the paintings as well as surveillance tapes.[3] The Boston art theft was atypical for several reasons. According to Lynne Chafinch, an expert in art theft with the FBI, the vast majority of "stolen art is lower value" and hence represents works that will not be easily recognized.[4] Even though the FBI maintains a listing of stolen art and cultural property in its National Stolen Art File, the bureau investigates such thefts only if they occur in a "museum as defined by federal statute, [and then] a stolen artwork has to be either more than 100 years old and worth more than $5,000 or less than 100 years old and worth more than $100,000."[5] According to Don Hrycyk, who leads the art theft unit of the Los Angeles Police Department, one of the few of its kind nationally, many people involved in art theft are common burglars who steal art along with any other goods available. Other art thieves do not fit a conventional criminal profile and instead come from the ranks of college professors, gallery owners, and individuals involved in insurance fraud.[6] In more than a decade of such investigation, Hrycyk noted that about the only type of crook that he hasn't come across is the sophisticated, debonair thief portrayed in movies like *Entrapment* and *The Thomas Crown Affair*.[7] Learn more about art theft at **http://www.saztv.com**.

Types of Property Crime

Both the Uniform Crime Reporting (UCR) Program and the National Crime Victimization Survey (NCVS) report data on property crimes. According to the FBI, the major **property crimes** are burglary, larceny, motor vehicle theft, and arson. Definitions used by the FBI for statistical data-gathering purposes are shown in Figure 12-1.

Burglary

Burglary is a common crime. The FBI defines **burglary** as the unlawful entry into a structure for the purpose of felony commission, generally a theft. The structure may be a business,

SuperStock/Glow Images

Henri Matisse's painting, "Pastoral" (1905), stolen from the National Museum of Modern Art in Paris in 2010. The painting remains unrecovered. Do you think that most art thieves know the value of the art that they steal?

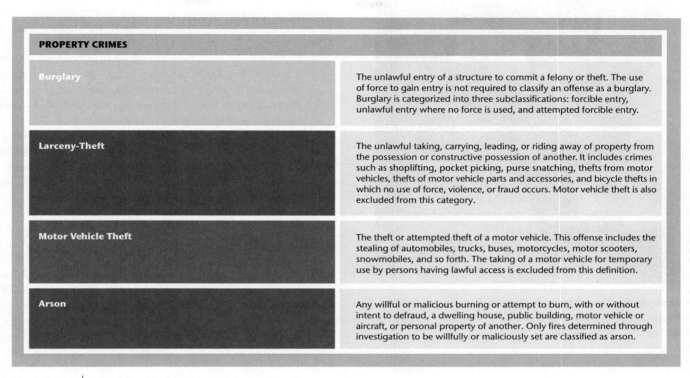

FIGURE 12-1 | Property Crimes and Their Definitions

Source: FBI, Uniform Crime Reporting Program.

a residence, or some other type of building. Force is not a necessary ingredient of burglary, but the FBI distinguishes between burglaries involving forcible entry, unlawful entry, and attempted forcible entry.[8] Based on an examination of victimization data, 72% of households within the United States are burglarized at least once.[9] In contrast to lifetime risk, however, the risk of burglary occurring within any given year is much lower. Even so, burglary is feared because the offense invades the sanctity of the home and threatens the existence of businesses.

In 2016, according to the FBI, there were an estimated 1,515,096 burglaries throughout the country. In that year, burglary accounted for 19.1% of the total number of property crimes committed. Burglary offenses cost victims an estimated $3.6 billion in lost property, and the average dollar loss per burglary offense was $2,361. Burglary of residential properties accounted for 69.5% of all burglary offenses, and 51.5% of residential burglaries occurred during the daytime, whereas 43% of nonresidential burglaries occurred during nighttime hours. Only about 18.3% of burglaries were cleared by arrest or other means in 2016.

In contrast to UCR/NIBRS reports, NCVS statistics on burglary paint quite a different picture. The NCVS reported 2,904,570 household burglaries and attempted burglaries in 2015—nearly 55% more than UCR/NIBRS estimates.[10] Rates of burglary were generally higher for African-American households than for white households, regardless of family income

levels, although wealthy African-American families had far lower burglary rates than did low-income white families.

According to UCR/NIBRS data for 2016, most burglaries involve forcible entry, followed in prevalence by unlawful entry and then by attempted forcible entry. Most residential burglaries are likely to occur during the day.[11] Most residential burglars commit their offenses at a time when residents are unlikely to be home. This is an important factor in their choice of target.

The consequences of both residential and commercial burglary can be profound for the victim. Residential burglaries, by definition, do not involve direct confrontation between the victims and the perpetrators, although the invasion of one's home produces a level of fear and apprehension beyond the dollar loss of the property taken. In cases of commercial burglary, because the targets are likely to be smaller, less stable businesses, the loss from burglaries can seriously affect the business's viability.[12]

The Social Ecology of Burglary

Rates of property crimes vary across cities, communities, and states, with higher burglary rates in large metropolitan areas and in particular regions, such as the South. Much research on variations in property crime at the aggregate level has examined how economics influences rates of crime. Lifestyle theory[13] and

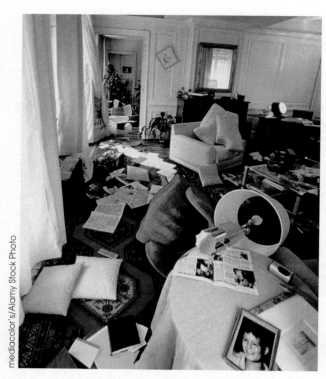

mediacolor's/Alamy Stock Photo

A ransacked home following a burglary. Burglary is a property crime that can turn violent if victims encounter the perpetrator. What are the characteristics of a professional burglar?

routine activities theory[14] (described in Chapter 10) have had a significant impact on explanations of how the nature and level of property crime have changed in response to alterations in the structures and routine activities of daily living. Both of these theoretical perspectives emphasize how criminal opportunity is affected by the everyday activities and environments experienced by victims and offenders. RAT says that for a property crime to occur, three ingredients are necessary: (1) someone who wants something (a *motivated offender*) coming in direct contact with (2) someone who has that thing (a *suitable target*) and (3) the lack of anything or anyone to inhibit the crime (a *capable guardian*). See Figure 12-2. The basic contention of both lifestyle theory and routine activities theory is that what people do, where they do it, how often they do it, and with whom they do it all influence the risk of criminal victimization, and the theories explore not why people commit crimes but rather "how the structure of social life makes it easy or difficult for people to carry out these inclinations," which are taken as a given.[15]

One 2017 study of decision making by burglars, found that, among other things, frequent local pedestrian traffic was associated with a lower level of burglary than in areas where pedestrians were few.[16] Researchers also found that burglars typically target locales close to their homes because they are familiar with the area, and that streets that are known to an offenders are more likely to be targeted.

In a study of residential burglary, Lawrence E. Cohen and David Cantor set out to test Michael Hindelang's hypothesis that household wealth was a more important factor in selection of burglary targets than was ease of access to the household because they wanted to resolve often contradictory findings of

> Both the highest- and the lowest-income households have the greatest victimization risk.

previous research on the relationship between the impact of income and race on burglary victimization.[17] Cohen and Cantor found that, independent of race, the highest-income households and the lowest-income households in areas both within and outside the central city had the greatest victimization risk, which meant that high-income households (with items of special value) and low-income households (with ease of access) were both targeted.

Using data from the British Crime Survey, Robert J. Sampson and John D. Wooldredge estimated the risk for crimes like burglary and personal theft.[18] Given the specific implications of two components of opportunity theory for victimization risk—the proximity of suitable targets and motivated offenders and the spatial structure of community organization—these researchers were concerned with the impact of community context on lifestyle. Sampson and Wooldredge's research revealed that the highest victimization risks for burglary were found in single-adult households, in households with younger adults as heads, and in households left unguarded. Of the seven community-level variables, all but one had moderate to strong effects: The highest victimization risks were for residents in areas characterized by high unemployment, high building density, primary individual households, and single-parent households with children. Even controlling for individual factors of single-person households, the community measure of percentage of single-adult households continues to have a significant effect on increasing the risk of burglary victimization.

Sampson and Wooldredge found that victimization risk for personal theft was less for those who were married, older, and male and higher for individuals with more education and for women.[19] The community factors of (1) the percentage of

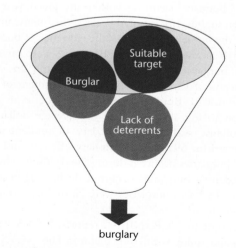

FIGURE 12-2 | **Routine Activities Theory Applied to Burglary**

Source: Schmalleger, Frank, *Criminology*. Printed and Electronically reproduced by permission of Pearson Education, Inc., Upper Saddle River, New Jersey.

THEORY | versus REALITY

Ethnographic Research on Active Burglars

Ethnographic research involving active burglars attempts to understand a burglar's way of life and hence offers a depth of insight rarely achieved in survey research or research using official data. However, ethnographic research is often dangerous, costly, and time-consuming.

The true benefit that comes from studying active burglars is related to an essential methodological issue common to all research endeavors: the classic issue of how individuals behave when they know they are being studied. In the case of studying burglars who are active versus those who are incarcerated, Richard T. Wright and Scott H. Decker note that individuals behave differently "in the wild" than in the jailhouse. The researchers point to statements made by two pioneers in criminology, Edwin Sutherland and Donald Cressey, more than 30 years ago: "Those who have had intimate contacts with criminals in the open know that criminals are not 'natural' in police stations, courts, and prisons, and that they must be studied in their everyday life outside of institutions if they are to be understood."[i] It is this concern for getting as close as possible to the social world one is studying that marks the tradition of ethnography.

Ethnographic research has already been described in Chapter 11, where research by Richard Wright and Scott Decker on armed robbers was discussed. This chapter presents further ethnographic research by Wright and Decker, this time on residential burglars. During 1989, the researchers located and interviewed 105 active residential burglars in St. Louis, Missouri. To qualify for inclusion in Wright and Decker's research, the offenders had to meet one of three criteria: they had to (1) have committed a residential burglary within two weeks prior to contact, (2) define themselves as residential burglars, or (3) be labeled as residential burglars by other offenders so identified. Research subjects were identified by the field workers whom Wright and Decker employed, most of whom were ex-offenders. The interviews with the subjects were all conducted in the field. Building on previous research on active offenders not currently incarcerated, Wright and Decker provide insight into various facets of the offending of burglars, including an examination of their motivation, target selection, entry method, search for valuable goods, and disposal of goods. In addition to answering questions, the offenders were asked to reconstruct their most recent residential burglary offense.

Defining the eligibility of subjects for research and using field workers are common practices in ethnographic research. Similar strategies were followed in other ethnographic research projects discussed in this chapter. They include research on 30 active burglars in an urban Texas setting by Paul F. Cromwell and his colleagues[ii] and research on the professional fence by Darrell J. Steffensmeier.[iii] As you read through the discussion of research in this chapter, keep in mind the strengths of ethnographic research and the insights to be gained by studying criminal offenders within their native social and cultural contexts.

Discussion Questions

1. What is ethnographic research? How does it differ from other types of research in the field of criminology?

2. Can criminologists learn anything special about burglary by focusing on active burglars who are not currently incarcerated—rather than on burglars who are imprisoned?

Notes

i. Edwin Sutherland and Donald Cressey, *Criminology*, 8th ed. (Philadelphia: Lippincott, 1970), p. 68, cited in Richard T. Wright and Scott H. Decker, *Burglars on the Job: Streetlife and Residential Break-Ins* (Boston: Northeastern University Press, 1994), p. 5.

ii. Paul F. Cromwell, James N. Olson, and D'Aunn Wester Avary, *Breaking and Entering: An Ethnographic Analysis of Burglary* (Newbury Park, CA: Sage, 1991).

iii. Darrell J. Steffensmeier, *The Fence: In the Shadow of Two Worlds* (Savage, MD: Rowman and Littlefield, 1986).

---

single adults with children, (2) social cohesion, and (3) street activity were significantly related to victimization risk—areas characterized by a high degree of family disruption, low social cohesion, and a large amount of street activity had higher victimization risks for personal theft. You can learn more about burglary trends by reading a special Bureau of Justice Statistics (BJS) report on household burglary via **http://www.justicestudies.com/pubs/householdburglary.pdf.** and read about the most common targets of burglars at **http://www.popcenter.org/problems/burglary_home**. See the Theory versus Reality box for ethnographic research on active burglars.

A Typology of Burglars

A three-part typology of burglary types was offered by **Mike Maguire**: low-level, middle-range, and high-level burglars (Figure 12-3).[20] **Neil Shover** determined how the social organization of burglary varied based on Maguire's three types. *Low-level burglars* (primarily juveniles) often commit their crimes "on the spur of the moment," usually work with others, and are

FIGURE 12-3 | Types of Burglars

Source: Schmalleger, Frank, *Criminology*. Printed and Electronically reproduced by permission of Pearson Education, Inc., Upper Saddle River, New Jersey.

easily dissuaded from a particular target by sound locks, alarms, and/or other such security devices, and the rewards are generally not significant, so many desist from burglary as they get older and feel "the pull of conventional relationships and fear of more severe adult sanctions."[21] Members of this group never develop connections that allow them to move large volumes of stolen goods.

Middle-range burglars are a bit older (although they may have begun their offending as juveniles) and go back and forth between legitimate pursuits and involvement in crime, and the use of alcohol and other drugs is more common. These offenders select targets that take into account both the potential payoff and the risk involved; however, they are not as easily dissuaded by security devices as the low-level burglars. Although their take from their crimes may be substantial at times, they lack the type of connections that would permit dealing in stolen goods on a large scale.

High-level burglars are professionals who work in organized crews and "are connected with reliable sources of information about targets."[22] Members of this group earn a good living from the proceeds of their crimes, which have carefully planned targets based on the assistance of outside sources (like the art theft described at the beginning of this chapter).

The Locales and Times of Burglary

Burglars may target residences and/or commercial buildings. Although most research has focused on residential burglary, many findings on offender patterns apply to both types. Police reports generally detail the time of the burglary, with nighttime residential burglary and daytime commercial burglary being considered the most serious. Evening hours are the time burglars are most likely to face homeowners, and daytime hours present the greatest risk of confrontation between offenders and customers or workers.[23] According to NCVS data, slightly more residential burglaries take place during the daytime than during the evening hours, but one-third of burglary reports do not contain information on when the burglary occurred, so those incidents could significantly change the temporal pattern of occurrence.[24]

Burglary is known as a "cold" crime because there is usually little physical evidence to link the offender to the offense. By the time the victim realizes there has been a burglary and calls the police, the burglar is long gone. However, commercial buildings are more likely to have alarms or other security devices.

The Motivation of Burglars

Rational choice perspectives (discussed in Chapter 3), which have guided a great deal of research on decision making among property offenders, contend that the decision-making process is not defined by only one objective or shared view of rationality but is guided by the logic and perspective of an individual offender. The way offenders justify their decisions may not make sense objectively, but their decisions have their own logic based on the offenders' social world and reflect the fact that many of them are "limited information processors with various simplifying strategies for resolving decisions."[25]

The most prevalent rationale behind residential burglary is economic: a need for fast cash.[26] Based on ethnographic research conducted in Texas[27] and in St. Louis,[28] active burglars do not have a conventional lifestyle, and most of their everyday concerns revolve around maintaining their street status and supporting a lifestyle of self-indulgence and often gratuitous consumption of drugs. Wright and Decker contended that the need to maintain a party lifestyle, to "keep up appearances," and to provide basic necessities for themselves and their families are all key factors that drive offenders' decisions to commit a burglary.[29]

> The most common rationale behind residential burglary is a need for fast cash.

As in the ethnographic research on the lifestyle of armed robbers (discussed in Chapter 11), Wright and Decker found that the vast majority of residential burglars they interviewed were committed to a lifestyle of "every night is a Saturday night," so when offenders discussed their offending as a means of survival, it had to be interpreted against the backdrop of this lifestyle, for it was only in this context that an understanding of what they meant by "survival" emerged. The vast majority of offenders were committed to street culture, and almost three-fourths of the money they obtained from burglary pursuits went to support their party lifestyle, which included illicit drugs, alcohol, and sexual pursuits. Keeping up appearances resulted in the need to buy things that assisted in maintaining street status (the right clothes, the right car). Although some offenders interviewed by Wright and Decker did use the proceeds from their burglaries to pay their bills, the researchers noted that "the bills were badly delinquent because the offenders avoided paying them for as long as possible—even when they had the cash—in favor of buying, most typically, drugs."[30] The lifestyle of these offenders all but guaranteed that "the crimes they commit will be economically motivated," but it is not an economic motivation that results from a desire to satisfy needs as opposed to wants.[31]

Burglaries of commercial establishments are generally thought to be even more associated with instrumental ends—usually economic gain—than residential burglaries. The same is true of professional burglars, who invest more planning and strategy into their offenses, calculating and carefully weighing risks and benefits.

What causes offenders to focus on burglary as their crime of choice? Some offenders selected burglary quite simply because "they regarded burglary as their 'main line.'"[32] Because most of the offenders interviewed by Wright and Decker regarded themselves as hustlers, "people who were always looking to get over by making some fast cash," they would commit offenses other than burglary if an opportunity presented itself; otherwise, they stayed with burglary.[33] For many, burglary was not as risky as selling drugs, which has carried increasingly stiffer penalties that offenders fear. Robbery was perceived as too risky because it involved direct confrontation with the victim and hence a higher likelihood of being injured, and some offenders stated they did not own guns. Because guns can be easily translated into cash in the street economy, "offenders who are in need of immediate cash often are tempted to sell their weapon instead of resorting to a difficult or risky crime."[34]

A small number of offenders in Wright and Decker's research in St. Louis indicated that "they did not typically commit burglaries as much for the money as for the psychic rewards."[35] This is consistent with Katz's concept of sneaky thrills: "If we looked more closely at how [offenders] define material needs, we might get a different image of these 'serious thieves.'"[36] Based on his ethnographic research with property offenders, **Kenneth D. Tunnell** concluded that "excitement was present but only as a latent benefit—a by product of the criminal act."[37]

Target Selection for Burglary

The sites for commercial burglaries are usually selected on the basis of suitability. Retail establishments are four times as likely to be burglarized as other types of establishments, such as wholesale or service businesses.

Residential burglary targets are selected somewhat differently. According to Wright and Decker, most residential burglars already have potential targets in mind before committing their offenses. Generally, burglars select a target by drawing on their knowledge of the occupants, "through receiving a tip," or "through observing a potential target."[38]

Whereas a prior relationship between offenders and victims has long characterized many violent crimes, property crimes generally do not involve known victims, and the pattern of the victim–offender relationship in property crimes does not mirror that of violent crimes; however, there are some interesting dynamics. The residential burglars interviewed by Wright and Decker rarely selected residences of close friends or relatives as targets, but they did quite often purposefully select as targets residences of individuals otherwise known to them.[39] An offender may also target known drug offenders because they can be victimized with relative impunity. A job provides offenders with the opportunity to get to know the occupants of a household and their daily routine as well as to determine their target suitability. When offenders did target residences of friends and loved ones, it was generally in two scenarios: One occurred when an argument or some type of wrongdoing on the victim's part had occurred, and the burglary was as much for revenge as for economic gain; the other involved the offender having such a desperate need for money that anyone was fair game. Although many offenders expressed remorse over having burglarized the homes of close family members, this was not universally the case, and burglars' expressions of remorse must be interpreted with the knowledge that "their allegiances seemed forever to be shifting to suit their own ends."[40]

Burglars may also select a target based on information from tipsters, who "regularly pass on intelligence about good burglary opportunities for a fee or a cut of the take."[41] Those who use tipsters do so in a variety of ways, including using individuals who work in service capacities in households and businesses and acting in collusion with insurance agents or other middle-class people who feed the offender information in exchange for money or for some stolen merchandise.

Approximately one-fourth of burglaries do not involve any type of forced entry, "the world affords abundant poorly protected opportunities for burglars."[42] Although offenders may not go out actively searching for potential targets, they are "continually 'half looking' for targets."[43]

Target selection is also influenced by other key elements such as signs of occupancy because "most offenders are reluctant to burglarize occupied dwellings," according to Wright and Decker.[44] Burglars have reported that they avoid occupied homes because they want to avoid injury to their victims and to themselves. For some offenders, the fear of their own injury was greater than the fear of apprehension: "I'd rather for the police to catch me versus a person catching me breaking in their house because the person will kill you."[45] To ensure that a residence was unoccupied, offenders would knock on the door (ready to offer some excuse if someone actually answered), phone the residence, or even phone the householder at work.

Most residential burglars also avoid residences with complex security devices because they generally lack the expertise to bypass such systems. Dogs also will deter an offender from a potential target because they make noise and could injure the offender. Offenders tended to stay in the same area, sometimes within walking distance, because of lack of a car. As one offender in Wright and Decker's research noted, "It's hard as hell getting on a bus carrying a big picture or a vase."[46]

The Costs of Burglary

According to the NCVS, well over three-fourths (86%) of all household burglaries involve some type of economic loss. Approximately 20% of household burglaries involve losses exceeding $1,000, 21% involve losses between $250 and $1,000, 24% involve losses between $50 and $249, and slightly more than 14% involve losses under $50.[47] One recent federal study found that the typical household burglary costs $5,489—including an average loss to victims of $1,362 and an additional $4,127 in justice system costs.[48] What do offenders steal from homes? According to self-reports of victims of household burglary, 29% of items stolen from homes are personal in nature, with the largest categories being jewelry and clothing; household furnishings represent 11% of all stolen items, followed by tools (6%) and cash (6%). Another type of crime cost can be gauged by looking at whether victims lose time from work as a result of their victimization: Among all victims of household burglaries, approximately 7% lose some time from work, with 33% of those losing less than one day, slightly over 50% losing from one to five days, and 7% losing six days or more.[49]

Using NCVS data to test the relationship between criminal victimization and a household's decision to move, researcher **Laura Dugan** revealed that property crimes like burglary have a greater effect on the decision to move than violent crimes.[50] Dugan had hypothesized that experiencing a violent crime would have a greater effect on the decision to move—a hypothesis not supported by the data. Instead, she found that a household's likelihood of moving increased after experiencing a criminal victimization near the home, an effect that was significant and strong for property crime but not for violent crime. Communities are also affected because the more affluent households are the ones most likely to relocate after experiencing victimization.

The Burglary–Drug Connection

During the 1980s, the parallel rates of robbery and burglary began to diverge, with robbery increasing and burglary decreasing. Using city-level data from 1984 to 1992, research by Eric Baumer and colleagues linked these changes to the effects of an increased demand for crack cocaine on altering structures of offending.[51] As a stimulant, crack use is characterized by short highs that are "followed by an intense desire for more crack."[52] If users are funding their drug habit through criminal pursuits, they need to rely on offenses that complement the demands of their drug of choice—offenses like robbery—that can net cash quickly, directly, anytime; burglary is more likely to net stolen goods than cash. As the illicit market for crack drove down the street value of stolen property, "dramatically enhancing the attractiveness of cash," burglary became an offense with diminishing rewards.[53] Ethnographic research on active burglars supported the claim that in areas with a strong crack cocaine trade, there was also a "preference for cash-intensive crimes like robbery and a corresponding reduced preference for burglary."[54] This is consistent with research that emphasized that most property offenders are generalists rather than strictly committed to one type of property offense.

The Sexualized Context of Burglary

Although economic gain is the primary motive for the vast majority of burglaries, some criminologists say that there is a category of burglaries with "hidden sexual forces lying at their root."[55] According to Louis B. Schlesinger and Eugene Revitch, the sexual dynamics associated with burglaries may be of two general interrelated types: One type of offender craves fetishes, stealing particular items as an outlet for sexual gratification rather than for their material value. A voyeuristic burglar has a more subtle sexual dynamic in which the goal may be just to "look around, to inspect the drawers," but not to actually take anything.[56] Schlesinger and Revitch analyzed the clinical records of 52 sexual murderers and found that the majority of these offenders had a history of burglaries, so burglary may serve as a precursor to more serious offenses and may constitute part of a pattern of sexual offending. A certain number of sexually motivated homicides begin as other offenses, such as burglary, and the ability to link the two early in the investigation is important for effective forensic assessment, so details of a burglary should be more purposefully evaluated because they could be related to a progression of events that could culminate in homicide.

> Some sexually motivated homicides begin as other offenses, such as burglary.

■ **larceny-theft** The unlawful taking, carrying, leading, or riding away of property (other than a motor vehicle) from the possession or constructive possession of another (attempts are included), according to the UCR/NIBRS.

Mark Warr investigated the connection of sexual offenses with property crimes from a different perspective.[57] Not only can sexual motives underlie property crimes, Warr argued, but the theoretical perspective of opportunity theory (discussed in Chapter 6) can explain patterns of rape and burglary. Warr said that "residential rape and burglary can be viewed as crimes of stealth that involve the unlawful entry of a structure [and] have very similar opportunity structures."[58] Using city arrest data, Warr found support for his contention that both the type of residence and the type of people victimized are similar enough in certain rape and burglary incidents to call into question the idea that rape shares a criminal etiology exclusively with violent offending.

For a certain category of rape termed *home-intrusion rape*, "the traditional distinction between violent crime and property crime may not apply," and such incidents represent a "hybrid offense"; they are "a violent crime with the opportunity structure of a property crime."[59] According to Warr, the correspondence in the opportunity structures of rape and burglary warrants consideration if research and investigative procedures are to identify the "proximate causes of rape."[60]

Larceny-Theft

Larceny-theft is defined by the UCR Program as "the unlawful taking, carrying, leading, or riding away of property from the possession, or constructive possession, of another."[61] Just about anything can be stolen. In California during November 2000, for example, thieves stole "more than 1,200 young orange trees during nightly raids at the San Joaquin Valley, heartland of the state's citrus crop."[62]

The FBI reports that during 2016, there were an estimated 5.6 million larceny-thefts nationwide and larceny-thefts accounted for an estimated 71% of all property crimes. The rate of larceny-theft is 1,745 per every 100,000 people living in the United States. The average value of property taken during larceny-thefts was $999 per offense. When the average value is multiplied by the estimated number of larceny-thefts, the loss to victims nationally was an estimated $5.6 billion.

Larceny is the most frequently occurring property offense according to official data compiled by the FBI and data from the NCVS. Within the offenses subsumed under the category of larceny in UCR/NIBRS data, the largest category is theft from motor vehicles, followed by shoplifting and theft from buildings (Figure 12-4).[63] Offenses such as pocket picking and purse snatching constitute a small percentage of all larcenies,

less than 1% each. Just as rates of different offenses within the category of larceny differ, so, too, do estimated losses to victims.

As a form of theft, larceny (as opposed to burglary) does not involve the use of force or other means of illegal entry. For this reason, among others, larceny is a crime "less frightening than burglary because to a large, perhaps even to a preponderant extent, it is a crime of opportunity, a matter of making off with whatever happens to be lying around loose: Christmas presents in an unlocked car, merchandise on a store counter, a bicycle in a front yard."[64]

Shoplifting and Employee Theft

Thefts cost U.S. retailers a staggering $45.2 billion in an average year.[65] Some retail theft is shoplifting, but other theft is committed by store employees. "The theft of merchandise by employees can range from the simple act of walking out the door with stolen goods to complex schemes requiring the manipulation of documents and/or involving several employees."[66] Most of the

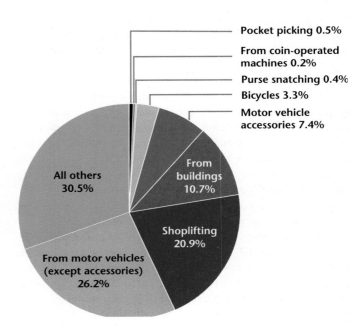

Pocket picking 0.5%

From coin-operated machines 0.2%

Purse snatching 0.4%

Bicycles 3.3%

Motor vehicle accessories 7.4%

All others 30.5%

From buildings 10.7%

Shoplifting 20.9%

From motor vehicles (except accessories) 26.2%

FIGURE 12-4 | **Larceny-Theft Distribution, 2016**

Source: Federal Bureau of Investigation, *Crime in the United States, 2016* (Washington, DC: FBI, 2017).

employees engaging in theft of either cash or merchandise are short-term workers. They are typically found in retail establishments with higher-than-average sales and a significant degree of turnover in management. Many retailers believe the issue of internal theft to be more serious than the economic loss caused by customer shoplifting.

Nonetheless, retailers must consider that efforts to combat shoplifting might impact sales. This concern was reflected by a marketing director who commented, "You don't want to hinder sales by intimidating the shopper. We used to think just about stopping shoplifting. We didn't think enough about selling more merchandise."[67]

Technology represents one of the best ways to address both shoplifting and employee theft. The use of computerized inventory counts to track merchandise is useful in quickly identifying thefts by employees. As will be discussed shortly, the widespread prevalence of shoplifting among youths who are fast and often operate together in small gangs means that increased security personnel in stores are less successful at detection than are electronic and other devices.

Shoplifting continues to be an offense that crosses class lines, although it is not an offense committed primarily by women. The dominant motivation used today to explain shoplifting does not rely on medical labels. Even though "respectable" people continue to be found among those who commit this offense, there is no evidence that these individuals constitute a significant segment of offenders.

Who Shoplifts?

On August 4, 2010, Caroline Giuliani, the 20-year-old daughter of former New York City Mayor Rudolph Giuliani, was arrested and placed in handcuffs after she stuffed makeup worth about $100 into her jacket pockets at a Sephora store in New York's Upper East Side.[68] The younger Giuliani, a Harvard University student, was caught on store security cameras and charged with larceny. Many people viewed the arrest as ironic because her father, a former presidential candidate, became famous as a strong law-and-order mayor. One month later, in a plea deal arranged in Manhattan Criminal Court, Giuliani was ordered to serve one day of community service working for the city's Sanitation Department.[69]

Giuliani is not the first well-known person to be charged with shoplifting. In another case, on December 6, 2002, actress Winona Ryder was sentenced to three years of probation and required to perform 480 hours of community service for shoplifting more than $5,500 in merchandise from a Beverly Hills, California, Saks Fifth Avenue store a year earlier; and in 2011, Lindsay Lohan was charged with felony grand theft for allegedly stealing a $2,500 necklace from a Venice, California, jewelry store.[70]

Neither the Ryder, Lohan, nor the Giuliani case, however, is that of a typical shoplifter. In self-reports of offending, official arrest data, and store records, juveniles are overrepresented as shoplifters. Variation exists in the frequency of offending among adolescents, but most offending patterns are fairly sporadic and are characterized by a greater prevalence among younger adolescents. The sporadic nature of shoplifting among adolescents is typical across all social classes even though the most serious and chronic forms are found among the economically disadvantaged. Although females represent the majority of offenders in some shoplifting data sources, this finding has been seriously challenged in research since the 1970s.[71]

Research by **Lloyd W. Klemke**, which used self-report techniques to assess juvenile shoplifting, revealed that almost two-thirds of the sample had shoplifted at some point in their lifetime.[72] Although previous research by **Mary Owen Cameron**, using department store records, had revealed that females were more likely than males to be apprehended for shoplifting,[73] Klemke found the reverse to be true. The difference in these findings may be attributed to the fact that Klemke's research included only adolescents, whereas Cameron's research also included adults.

Youths from lower-income households are more likely to shoplift than are their higher-income counterparts. However, this relationship is a moderate one at best, and the fact remains that shoplifting is reported by a solid majority of youths in several self-report studies. The relationship between social class and likelihood of shoplifting is stronger among adults.

Among Klemke's other findings was a "maturing out" pattern, whereby "shoplifting activity peaked in the under ten age category" and decreased considerably as the youths entered adolescence.[74] These findings are contrary to other research that supports escalation during late adolescence.

A young shoplifter in action. As the text points out, shoplifting is a common offense. Who shoplifts and why?

Lisa S./Shutterstock

CRIME | in the NEWS

"Flash Robs" Become a Troublesome Trend

"Flash robs," a crime akin to shoplifting, but on a massive scale, are a form of larceny. Although there were a few flash robs in the news as far back as 2002, these crimes have only become a nationwide phenomenon relatively recently, and are now being widely reported. Typically, a large group of teenagers files into a convenience store, takes low-priced candy and sodas, and exits immediately. The whole incident takes as little as one minute.

Flash robs are not technically robberies, because there is no threat of force. Filmed on a store's security video (and then posted later on the Internet), smiling participants form an orderly line and limit themselves to one or two goodies each. They don't brandish any weapons, but store employees are frightened and usually stay out of the way.

This new form of lawbreaking comes at a time when youth crime is relatively low. From 2008 to 2009, juvenile arrests for violent crime fell 10%, according to a Justice Department report. But the economy was still ailing and high percentages of teenagers didn't have jobs. In June 2012, the unemployment rate among blacks ages 16 to 19 was 39.3%—high for African-American rates and nearly double the 20.9% rate for whites the same age.

A youthful group dynamic takes hold in a flash rob. "Young people are risk-takers," said Scott Decker, a professor of criminology at Arizona State University. "They do things in groups far more than adults do." He believes they are proud rather than upset when they see themselves in the videos shown on the evening news. They feel protected by the power of numbers, said New York psychologist Jeff Gardere.

The store's security videos help authorities identify perpetrators, but prosecuting them can be frustrating. Many hundreds of dollars' worth of goods may be stolen, but one person's take is just a few bucks, which amounts to nothing more than a Class C misdemeanor. When prosecutors intercept messages on social media from kids planning the event, they can add conspiracy charges, but according to the National Retail Federation, social media is identified in less than half of apprehended cases of flash robs.

To aid prosecution, the Maryland Legislature has been considering a bill that would treat multiple acts of theft in unison as one crime. The measure would automatically define a flash rob as a conspiracy, and

Bruce Adams/Daily Mail/ZUMA Press/Newscom

A flash robbery in progress. How do social media facilitate such crimes?

charges against each person would depend on the total amount stolen, not on each person's take.

Discussion Questions

1. How do flash robberies differ from other kinds of larceny?
2. What kind of impact might this kind of crime, if it continues to expand, have on retailers?

Sources: Derek Valcourt, "Law Enforcement Frustrated with Growing Number of Flash Mob Crimes in Md.," *CBS Baltimore*, July 26, 2012, http://baltimore.cbslocal .com/2012/07/26/law-enforcement-frustrated-with-growing-number-of-flash-mob-crimes-in-md/; Ellen Arndt, "Fighting the Rising Tide of Flash Mobs in Retail," *Security*, July 24, 2012, http://www.securitymagazine.com/articles/83326-fighting-the-rising-tide-of-flash-mobs-in-retail; and Tim Dees, "Stay on Top of 'Flash Robs'," PoliceOne .com, June 12, 2012, http://www.policeone.com/police-products/communications/articles/5603418-Stay-on-top-of-flash-robs.

Flash Mobs and Larceny

Over the past few years, a new term has entered the popular lexicon—flash mobs. Flash mobs are purposeful crowds of people brought together on a moment's notice through the use of social media websites such as Twitter and Facebook. Sometimes the gatherings are peaceful and fun—as was the case a few years ago when a McDonald's restaurant in Chicago asked people to dress in beach attire and to converge on its location.[75] Other flash mobs, however, can have more insidious purposes and even involve organized criminal activity. In 2012, for example, three Chicago-area Sports Authority stores became the targets of flash mobs, who ransacked the retailers—even dragging entire racks of clothing out of the store and into waiting vehicles. Frantic employees tried to grab the apparel back as it was taken from shelves, but the crowd was too large. An online video of the events can be seen at **http:// www.nbcchicago.com/news/local/Video-Flash-Mob-Robberies-Chicago-Sports-Authority-230985451.html**.

■ **Identity Theft and Assumption Deterrence Act**   The first federal law to make identity theft a crime. The 1998 statute makes it a crime whenever anyone "knowingly transfers or uses, without lawful authority, a means of identification of another person with the intent to commit, or to aid or abet, any unlawful activity that constitutes a violation of federal law, or that constitutes a felony under any applicable state or local law."

■ **identity theft**   The unauthorized use of another individual's personal identity to fraudulently obtain money, goods, or services; to avoid the payment of debt; or to avoid criminal prosecution.

■ **Identity Theft Penalty Enhancement Act**   A 2004 federal law that added two years to federal prison sentences for criminals convicted of using stolen credit card numbers and other personal data to commit crimes.

Loss-prevention specialists refer to larcenies committed by flash mobs as multiple-offender crimes, and statistics show that 10% of retail establishments report being victimized by multiple offenders who formed flash mobs during a recent 12-month period.[76] Recently, in recognition of the problem, the National Retail Federation issued a report outlining steps that stores could take to combat criminal flash mobs.[77] Those steps include documenting the larceny, especially through the use of video recordings and store security cameras, and quickly reporting the events to law enforcement agencies. Some states have even considered criminalizing flash mobs in an effort to prevent the kinds of crimes to which they can lead.

Identity Theft

Identity theft—the misuse of another individual's personal information to commit fraud[78]—is a relatively new form of larceny that appears to be growing rapidly. Identity theft involves obtaining credit, merchandise, or services by fraudulent personal representation. Usually, individuals learn that they have become identity theft victims only after being denied credit or employment or when a debt collector seeks payment for a debt the victim did not incur. The most threatening aspects of identity theft are its potential relationship to international terrorism. Even where terrorism is not involved, identity theft can be used broadly by transnational crime rings.

The misuse of stolen personal information can be classified into two broad categories. *Existing account fraud* occurs when thieves obtain account information involving credit, brokerage, banking, or utility accounts that are already open. Existing account fraud is typically less costly, but more prevalent. A stolen credit card may lead to thousands of dollars in fraudulent charges, for example, but the card generally will not provide a thief with enough information to establish a false identity. Moreover, most credit card companies do not hold consumers liable for fraudulent charges, and federal law caps liability of victims of credit card theft at $50.

The second and more serious category is *new account fraud.* In new account fraud, identity thieves use personal information such as Social Security numbers, birth dates, and home addresses to open new accounts in the victim's name, make charges indiscriminately, and then disappear. Although this type of identity theft is less likely to occur, it imposes much greater costs and hardships on victims. In addition, identity thieves sometimes use stolen personal information to obtain government, medical, or other benefits to which the criminals are not legally entitled.

In addition to the losses that result when identity thieves fraudulently open accounts or misuse existing accounts, monetary costs of identity theft include indirect costs to businesses for fraud prevention and mitigation of the harm once it has occurred (e.g., for mailing notices to consumers and upgrading systems). Similarly, individual victims often suffer indirect financial costs, including the costs incurred in dealing with civil litigation initiated by creditors and in overcoming the many obstacles they face in obtaining or retaining credit. Victims of nonfinancial identity theft, for example, including health-related or criminal record fraud, face other types of harm and frustration.

Consumers' fears of becoming identity theft victims can also harm the digital economy. In a recent online survey conducted by the Business Software Alliance and Harris Interactive, nearly 30% of adults interviewed said that security fears caused them to shop online less or not at all.[79] Identity theft became a federal crime in 1998 with the passage of the **Identity Theft and Assumption Deterrence Act**.[80] The law makes it a crime whenever anyone "knowingly transfers or uses, without lawful authority, a means of identification of another person with the intent to commit, or to aid or abet, any unlawful activity that constitutes a violation of federal law, or that constitutes a felony under any applicable state or local law."

The 2004 **Identity Theft Penalty Enhancement Act**[81] added two years to federal prison sentences for criminals convicted of using stolen credit card numbers and other personal data to commit crimes. It also prescribed prison sentences for those who use identity theft to commit other crimes, including terrorism, and it increased penalties for defendants who exceed or abuse the authority of their position in unlawfully obtaining or misusing means of personal identification.

The Incidence of Identity Theft

Recently, the Bureau of Justice Statistics (BJS) provided information on the incidence of identity theft derived from the National Crime Victimization Survey (NCVS).[82] For statistical reporting purposes, the BJS defines *identity theft* to include the following three behaviors: (1) the unauthorized use or attempted use of existing credit cards; (2) the unauthorized use or attempted use of other existing accounts such as checking accounts; and (3) the misuse of personal information to obtain new accounts or loans or to commit other crimes.

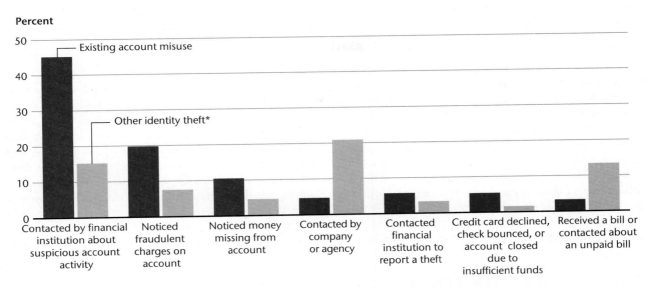

Percent

FIGURE 12-5 | **Most Common Ways Victims Discovered Identity Theft, by Type of Theft**

Source: Erika Harrell, *Victims of Identity Theft, 2014* (Washington, DC: Bureau of Justice Statistics, 2015), p. 5.

BJS surveyors found that approximately 17.6 million persons, or 8% of all U.S. residents age 16 or older, were victims of one or more incidents of identity theft in 2014. Among those victims, the misuse of existing bank (38%) or credit cards (42%) accounted for most victimization. Figure 12-5 shows the most common ways that victims discovered that their identity had been stolen.

BJS surveys also reveal that about one in six victimized households had to pay higher interest rates as the result of identity theft and that one in nine households was denied phone or utility service as a consequence of being victimized.[83] About 7% of victimized households were turned down for insurance or had to pay higher rates, 5% became the subject of a civil suit or judgment, 4% became the subject of a criminal investigation, and about 20% reported other kinds of problems.

Identity Thieves: Who They Are

Unlike some groups of criminals, identity thieves cannot be readily classified.[84] According to a survey of identity theft by the Federal Trade Commission (FTC), about 14% of victims claim to know the perpetrator, who may be a family member, a friend, or an in-home employee. Identity thieves can act alone or as part of a criminal enterprise. Each poses unique threats to the public.

Identity thieves often have no prior criminal background and sometimes have preexisting relationships with the victims. They have been known to prey on people they know, including coworkers, senior citizens for whom they may be serving as caretakers, and even family members. Some identity thieves use minimal sophistication, such as stealing mail from homeowners' mailboxes or trash containing

financial documents. In some jurisdictions, identity theft by illegal immigrants has resulted in passport, employment, and Social Security fraud. Occasionally, loosely knit groups of individuals with no significant criminal records work together to obtain personal information and even to create false or fraudulent documents.[85]

Paul Froggatt/FamousPix/Alamy Stock Photo

Rapper 50 Cent, who became a victim of identity theft in 2013. Two men from Hartford, Connecticut, were later arrested and charged with using the rapper's stolen identity to buy Cadillacs, Vespas, and jewelry from Tiffany's. The pair spent more than $500,000 before they were caught. Other famous victims of identity theft include Tiger Woods, Kim Kardashian, Will Smith, Steven Spielberg, and Oprah Winfrey. Could your identity be stolen? How would you know if it was?

■ **motor vehicle theft**   The theft or attempted theft of a motor vehicle, according to the UCR/NIBRS. In the FBI's definition, this offense category includes the stealing of automobiles, trucks, buses, motorcycles, motor scooters, and snowmobiles.

■ **joyriding**   An opportunistic car theft, often committed by a teenager, for fun or thrills.

Law enforcement agencies also have seen increased involvement of foreign organized criminal groups in computer- or Internet-related identity theft schemes. In Asia and Eastern Europe, for example, organized groups are increasingly sophisticated both in the techniques they use and in the complexity of their tools. According to law enforcement agencies, such groups also are demonstrating increasing levels of sophistication and specialization in their online crime, even selling goods and services—such as software templates for making counterfeit identification cards and payment card magnetic strip encoders—that make the stolen data even more valuable to those who have it.

Motor Vehicle Theft

The UCR Program defines **motor vehicle theft** as "the theft or attempted theft of a motor vehicle," where the term *motor vehicle* refers to various means of transportation, including automobiles, buses, motorcycles, and snowmobiles.[86] Automobiles are the type of vehicle most often stolen. Cars represent more than merely a possession; for many Americans, they are an extension of their identity. The type of car a person drives reflects social status and personal identity.

The theft of a car, then, violates the victim in a way that goes beyond financial loss. Auto theft also makes it difficult for many people to get to work and sometimes requires them to take time away from work to take care of the incident.[87]

Approximately, 765,484 vehicles were reported stolen in 2016 (for an auto theft rate of 236.9 per every 100,000 people), with an estimated total value in excess of $5.9 billion (or $7,680 per vehicle stolen). The largest percentage of thefts was vehicles stolen from a parking lot or garage.[88] A significant percentage of motor vehicle theft take place either at or quite near the victim's residence, with approximately 17% happening on a street near the home.[89] Depending on the neighborhood in which the victim resides, *near home* can mean different things, and the same distance from the residence in urban communities may be more of a risk for motor vehicle theft than in other communities. Marcus Felson contends that the risks posed by where one parks are related to population density.

Based on data from NCVS, on average, 75% of all motor vehicle thefts, both attempted and completed, are reported to the police. As is seen with other offenses, the reporting percentage is higher (90%) for completed motor vehicle thefts than for attempted incidents (54%).[90] Although the rate of motor vehicle victimization is the same for the lowest-income households (under $7,500 per year) as for the highest-income households ($75,000 or more per year), the rate of reporting increases with the income level of the household.[91] Based on available data, approximately 62% of stolen cars are recovered.[92] Both law

enforcement agencies and insurance companies keep records of recovered vehicles, but each uses its own definition of *recovery*, and some "recovered" cars may actually have been totally destroyed.

Cars are stolen for a variety of reasons, including joyriding, temporary transportation needs, use in a crime, and stripping. Each of these rationales is representative of a fairly distinctive offender profile. Given the wide variety of rationales supporting automobile theft, almost any type of car is a target. Some people suggest that thieves tend to prefer certain cars. According to Robert Bryant, chief executive officer of the National Insurance Crime Bureau, "Vehicle thieves follow market trends and target the most popular vehicles because they provide the best market for stolen vehicle parts and illegal export to other countries."[93]

One 2013 study of Los Angeles car thieves seemed to disprove that claim and demonstrated that "car types are stolen almost exclusively in response to their environmental availability."[94] In other words, study authors found that only occasionally are cars targeted because of their make and model, or because they have higher perceived payoffs. The study showed that if a neighborhood has mostly Chevys, for example, then it will be Chevys that are the type of car most often stolen.

Theft of Car Parts

Approximately one-third of stolen vehicles that are scored as "recovered" are completely stripped at chop shops, and another third are stripped of easy-to-sell accessories like radios, air bags, and seats.[95] The theft of car parts is variously motivated. Some car parts are worth a significant sum on the illegal market and can be sold easily by even the most inexperienced thieves. Novice thieves usually do not have access to the type of network required to sell "hot cars." Also, stolen car parts are more difficult to identify than entire cars.[96]

In the United States, the Motor Vehicle Theft Law Enforcement Act,[97] passed by Congress in 1984, "called for the marking of the major sheet metal parts of high-theft automobiles with Vehicle Identification Numbers (VINs). The point of the law was to enable detection of persons engaged in the presumably widespread sale of stolen parts to the auto body repair industry."[98] Although data are scarce on how many car thefts are carried out for stripping, some research has been conducted in this regard both in the United States and elsewhere.

Joyriders: Car Theft for Fun

Some car thefts are opportunistic in nature, committed by teenagers, usually in groups, for the purpose of fun or thrills. These offenses are referred to as **joyriding**. Because these thefts involve the temporary use of a vehicle primarily to satisfy

CRIMINAL | PROFILES

Frank W. Abagnale, Jr.—"Catch Me If You Can"

High school dropout Frank Abagnale never met a credential he couldn't cheerfully ignore. He simply assumed any role that needed a credential and let you assume that he had it—or helped you assume he had it by showing you convincing forgeries of qualifying documents. Airline pilot, attorney, pediatrician, college professor, stockbroker, and FBI agent were all roles that Abagnale convincingly assumed at one point or other in his criminal career.[i]

Born April 17, 1948, Abagnale started a life of crime by conning his father out of $2,500 just after the younger Abagnale's 16th birthday. Allowed to use his father's gas credit card, Abagnale schemed for spending money by using the card to buy tires from a gas station, then selling them back to the station owner at half price for cash.[ii] The scam was discovered at the same time that Abagnale's parents were divorcing, which gave him an excuse to run off to New York.

He was a 16-year-old runaway when he made his first big score—$40,000—by printing up a bunch of bank deposit slips with his own account number (obtained, of course, under a false name) printed on them in magnetic ink. He then placed them at the service desk in the bank's lobby in place of the generic deposit slips provided by the bank for customer use. Other customers used the slips to make deposits, thinking that the deposit would be credited to their own account. In reality, the automated processing equipment would read Abagnale's account number magnetically encoded on the slip and credit his account for the amount of the deposit. When the account balance reached $40,000, he simply withdrew the funds and closed the account.

After five years of tricking people around the world, Abagnale was arrested while pretending to be a licensed commercial airline pilot when an Air France flight attendant recognized him from a wanted poster on the bulletin board in the employee lounge. Abagnale subsequently served time in prisons in France (six months) and Sweden (six months) before he was finally extradited to the United States. Convicted of federal forgery charges, he received a 12-year sentence to federal prison.[iii]

Abagnale's exploits during that infamous five-year period of nonstop cons were the subject of Steven Spielberg's highly successful film *Catch Me If You Can*, released in 2002.

After Abagnale had served four years of his sentence, he received an offer from the U.S. government that changed his life. Wanting to learn how to prevent future Abagnale-like scams, the U.S. government asked Abagnale to teach them how he carried out the frauds, and how to prevent others from doing them in the future. Specifically, they wanted to explore his ability to manipulate official documents so as to virtually eliminate any chance of detection. In exchange, the government offered him immediate release from prison.[iv]

And that is how Frank Abagnale, the most successful con man of the twentieth century, morphed into a world-renowned expert on forgery, embezzlement, and document security. Today, he heads Abagnale and Associates, a highly respected secure document consultancy. Abagnale has become an extraordinarily successful author and lecturer whose speeches, according to multiple-Oscar–winner Tom

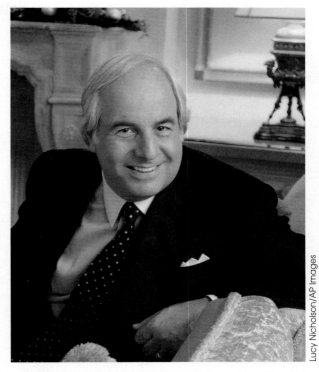

Lucy Nicholson/AP Images

Frank Abagnale, Jr., posing for a photo at the Four Seasons Hotel in Beverly Hills, California. Abagnale, portrayed by actor Leonardo DiCaprio in the film *Catch Me If You Can,* is the real-life subject of a book he wrote about his time as a successful con artist. How does Abagnale differ from most other property offenders?

Hanks, "may be the best one-man show you will ever see."[v] Visit Abagnale's website at **www.abagnale.com**.

The case of Frank Abagnale raises a number of questions. Among them are the following:

1. Abagnale pretended to be someone he wasn't. But is the phrase *identity theft* applicable to Abagnale, or should his crimes be described in other ways?

2. What might life course theory say about Abagnale's early deviance? How did his behavior differ from others who commit property crimes?

3. Why did Abagnale persist in criminal behavior even though he knew he'd probably get caught?

4. Today Abagnale runs a fraud-prevention business. How do you think his criminal experience aided his new professional career?

Notes

i Bernie Alexander, "Frank Abagnale: From Fraud to FBI," AskMen.com, http://www.askmen.com/toys/special_feature/36_special_feature.html (accessed July 10, 2007).

ii Norman Swan, "Frank Abagnale–New Life," *Life Matters*, March 17, 2000, http://www.abc.net.au/rn/talks/lm/stories/s111098.htm (accessed July 10, 2007).

iii Rachael Bell, "Skywayman: The Story of Frank W. Abagnale Jr.," CourtTV Crime Library, http://www.crimelibrary.com/criminal_mind/scams/frank_abagnale/index.html (accessed July 10, 2007).

iv Ibid.

v Frank W. Abagnale, personal website, http://www.abagnale.com (accessed March 10, 2017).

WHO'S TO BLAME—The Individual or Society?

Body Parts for Sale

On March 20, 2015, Dr. Paul Sutter, a Palm Beach, Florida, plastic surgeon, was arrested and charged with a federal crime after he allegedly purchased facial bones that he knew had been illegally removed from a cadaver and implanted them into a wealthy female patient undergoing elective facial reconstructive surgery following a car accident. The doctor and a mortician, who sold him the bones, were both charged with violating the National Organ Transplant Act of 1984, which expressly prohibits interstate trafficking in human tissue for profit.

In an interview the doctor gave after posting bail, Sutter told reporters, "I understand that there's a law against what I did. But it's not my fault that the materials I need to work with are frequently so hard to acquire. There needs to be a better system in place for the distribution of bones and other tissues that are so desperately needed by patients like the woman whose face I reconstructed in this case."

Lily/Fotolia

Think about it

1. Why did Sutter violate the law? What do you think was his primary motivation for what he did?

2. Do you think it would have mattered to Sutter's patient had she known that the bones used in her surgery had been acquired illegally?

3. Can body parts be considered items of property, like a person's other possessions? If so, should he or she have the right to sell them—perhaps to the highest bidder?

Learn more about the illegal trade in body parts at **https://papers.ssrn.com/sol3/papers.cfm?abstract_id=1089229.**

Note: Who's to Blame boxes provide fictionalized critical thinking opportunities based on actual cases.

needs ranging from excitement to personal autonomy, joyriding is often characterized as an "expressive act with little or no extrinsic value."[99] This motivation for auto theft is not characterized by planning and quite often involves an unlocked car left in a public place, frequently with the keys in the ignition.[100]

Most vehicles stolen for purposes of joyriding are recovered, usually found abandoned, often after they have been crashed. Although adolescents may select a vehicle for joyriding that belongs to strangers, they are more likely to select the car of a known owner.[101]

Research offers no definite answer as to whether there is a distinctive social class profile of the joyriding offender.

Some research indicates that higher social class can be associated with greater involvement in auto theft because of greater access to cars and an earlier association of cars as status symbols. On the other hand, the "disadvantaged-group hypothesis" contends that youths from lower socioeconomic classes are more likely to be involved in car thefts because conventional means of acquiring status symbols such as cars are blocked, and they are left with only the avenue of illegitimate acquisition.[102] Although some support has been found for each of these perspectives, other research has failed to find a link between social class and involvement in auto theft among adolescents.[103]

■ **arson**   The willful or malicious burning (or attempt to burn), with or without intent to defraud, of a house, public building, motor vehicle or aircraft, or personal property of another.

Professional Car Theft

Although representing the most costly and most serious form of auto theft, professional thefts are not as common as thefts for other uses, such as joyriding. Like joyriders, professional auto thieves operate in groups, but their groups are characterized by a great deal more planning and calculation in target selection. The cars targeted by professional thieves are luxury cars that may be driven across national borders or shipped overseas. Professional thefts have the lowest recovery rates. Still, professionals are only a small part of the vehicle theft problem.

Arson

The FBI defines **arson** as "any willful or malicious burning or attempt to burn, with or without intent to defraud, a dwelling house, public building, motor vehicle or aircraft, personal property of another, etc."[104] It is only after a fire has been investigated and officially classified as arson by the proper investigative authorities that the FBI records the incident as an arson. Fires that are suspicious or of unknown origin are not included in the FBI's arson statistics.[105]

In 2016, the FBI received reports of 43,249 arsons that occurred throughout the country, for an arson rate of 13.9 offenses for every 100,000 inhabitants. Arsons involving structures (e.g., residential, storage, and public) accounted for 45.7% of the total number of arson offenses. Mobile property was involved in 24.4% of arsons, and other types of property, such as crops, timber, and fences, accounted for 29.8% of reported arsons. The average dollar loss due to arson was $14,182 per offense, whereas arson involving industrial/manufacturing structures resulted in the highest average dollar losses (an average of $270,462 per arson). In 2016, arson offenses increased when compared with arson data reported in 2015. Nationally, the clearance rate for arson was only 20.8% in 2016. Of all arson arrests, 32% involve juveniles—a higher percentage than for any other major crime. In addition, 73.2% of arson arrestees are white and 80.2% are male.

Several diverse motives may underlie arson, from profit to thrill seeking. On August 1, 2003, for example, a 206-unit San Diego condominium complex burned down while under construction. A 12-foot banner found at the scene declared, "If you build it, we will burn it." The banner was signed with the letters *ELF*, which stand for the Earth Liberation Front. Less than a month later, ELF arsonists attacked a number of car dealerships in Los Angeles, targeting those that sold gas-guzzling SUVs such as Hummers. Although one person was arrested, he was soon released.

The ELF, described as an ecoterrorist group by law enforcement officials, may have begun in California as the Environmental Life Force in 1977. The present-day ELF targets what it deems to be threats to the environment—including residential and commercial construction in environmentally sensitive areas, certain types of animal research facilities, and sometimes Starbucks restaurants.

Fire Setters

Whatever the motive, the vast majority of those involved in arson are juveniles. According to UCR/NIBRS data, juveniles represent the offenders in arson incidents at a much higher rate than is found in any other index offense; 49% of all arsons that are cleared are found to have involved a juvenile offender. Juveniles are a bit more likely to be involved in arsons in cities than in suburbs or rural areas. Overall, among the arson types, "juveniles account for 21 percent of the clearances for arsons of mobile property, 40 percent of structural arson clearances and 41 percent of clearances for arsons of all other property."[106] According to Jay K. Bradish, editor of *Firehouse* magazine, "Arson is the third leading cause of residential fires and the second-leading cause of residential fire deaths nationwide. Arson is the leading cause of deaths and injuries and accounts for the highest dollar loss in commercial fires."[107] In both residential and commercial arson, juveniles are involved more often than adults.

Three general groups of juvenile fire setters can be identified.[108] The first consists of children younger than seven who generally start fires by accident or out of curiosity. The second group is children between the ages of 8 and 12 who may start fires out of curiosity, but "a greater proportion of their fire setting represents underlying psychosocial conflicts."[109] The final group, youths between the ages of 13 and 18, has had a history of fire setting, usually undetected. It is believed that many of the fires started by juveniles go undetected by law enforcement officials because they are started on school property, perhaps even accidentally, and are discovered early by janitors or other school staff who do not report the incidents. In response to a growing awareness of the problem created by juvenile fire setters, several agencies and organizations, including the U.S. Fire Administration, have developed model programs to mobilize community agencies across the nation to deal more effectively with juvenile fire setters.

For more information on the problem of fire setting among juveniles, as well as the prevalence of and issues surrounding arson

■ **professional criminal**   A criminal offender who makes a living from criminal pursuits, is recognized by other offenders as professional, and engages in offending that is planned and calculated.
■ **persistent thief**   One who continues in common law property crimes despite no better than an ordinary level of success.

■ **offense specialization**   A preference for engaging in a certain type of offense to the exclusion of others.
■ **occasional offender**   A criminal offender whose offending patterns are guided primarily by opportunity.

in the United States, visit the National Fire Data Center online via **https://www.usfa.fema.gov.** Learn more about the crime of arson from **http://ssrn.com/abstract=1272616** and **http://www.ncjrs.gov/pdffiles/fs9751.pdf.**

Understanding Property Crimes

Criminologists have identified various types of property criminals and examined the motivation behind property crimes. In the final section of this chapter, we will explore some of these dimensions.

Persistent and Professional Thieves

Although legal distinctions separate the offenses of larceny and burglary, both are basically property crimes of theft, and those who commit such offenses are thieves. Willie Sutton, a famous bank robber, saw himself as a professional and defined a professional thief quite simply as "a man who wakes up every morning thinking about committing a crime, the same way another man gets up and goes to his job."[110] In a classic study of the professional thief, Edwin H. Sutherland defined this offender as one who "makes a regular business of stealing," plans carefully, possesses "technical skills and methods which are different from those of other professional criminals," and moves from locale to locale in offending pursuits.[111] Neil Shover defined **professional criminals** as those "who commit crime with some degree of skill, earn reasonably well from their crimes, and despite stealing over long periods of time, spend rather little time incarcerated."[112] This is certainly not the profile of most offenders, who continue to commit crimes but never exhibit signs of a professional approach to lawbreaking; instead of being viewed as professional, they are best understood as persistent.

> Professional criminals commit crime with some degree of skill, earn reasonably well from their crimes, and spend little time incarcerated.

Persistent thieves are those who continue in "common-law property crimes despite their, at best, ordinary level of success."[113] Rather than specializing to any significant degree, the vast majority of persistent thieves alternate between a variety of crimes like burglary, robbery, car theft, and confidence games. Even though they exhibit a generalist approach to offending, persistent thieves may have "crime preferences" that take the form of characteristics such as "whether to avoid or to confront their victim(s)."[114]

Similarly, **offense specialization**, a preference for a certain type of offense, is quite limited among property offenders and does not allow the classification of most offenders as professionals or specialists. Significant numbers of property offenders are fully immersed in a street culture and lifestyle characterized by a hedonistic approach to life and a disregard for conventional pursuits, and their everyday lives are filled with a wide array of petty crimes, including confidence games, gambling, and minor thefts.[115]

Malcolm W. Klein used the term *cafeteria-style offending* in his research to refer to the heterogeneous and unplanned nature of offending among gang members.[116] In analyzing offending among gang members for possible patterns, he likened it to "a cafeteria display with [several] choices of food. Imagine the gang member walking along the display, choosing to try a little petty theft, then a group assault, then some truancy, then two varieties of malicious mischief, and so on."[117] Research using data sources ranging from official crime statistics to offenders' self-reports to ethnographies confirms that a minimal level of specialization exists among property offenders.[118] Shover, who has studied burglary and professional thieves for more than two decades, suggested that terms like *burglar* have little utility if conceived of in a strict sense of exclusive offending within that crime type. Many offenders engaged in burglary prefer this type of offending to offenses like robbery because burglary does not involve direct contact with victims.[119]

Because of the short-term, sporadic nature of their offending, property offenders are also known as **occasional offenders**[120] (the label "occasional" refers not to the frequency of offending but to the nature and character of offending), whom **John R. Hepburn** defined as those whose crimes "occur on those occasions in which there is an opportunity or situational inducement to commit the crime."[121] This observation (which fits well with rational choice theory discussed in Chapter 3) has been confirmed in subsequent research, such as the work of Richard T. Wright and Scott H. Decker, who stated that the burglars they interviewed are not a "continually motivated group of criminals;

Warren (Ohio) Police Detective Jeff Hoolihan (left) and Canfield (Ohio) Police Detective Sergeant Andy Bodzar standing in front of items seized from members of a theft-to-order burglary ring that operated in and around Youngstown, Ohio. What's the difference between larceny and burglary?

the motivation for them to offend is closely tied to their assessment of current circumstances and prospects."[122] This does not mean that offenders plan their crimes carefully or accurately assess a situation; it means only that they are seeking to achieve some personal benefit through criminal activity. Often offenders don't succeed because they rarely have all the information they need, they do not devote enough time to planning their actions, they take risks, and they make mistakes. This is how we all behave in everyday decision making and is what theorists call *limited* or *bounded rationality*.[123] So although some degree of rationality characterizes the criminal activity of most property offenders, it is only a limited or bounded rationality.

The Criminal Careers of Property Offenders

Criminologists have long studied the criminal careers of offenders, both violent offenders and property offenders. Neil Alan Weiner defined a criminal career as "criminal behavior [that] is an integrated, dynamic structure of sequential unlawful acts that advances within a wider context of causal and correlative influences, including among others, those of biological, psychological, and informal social and formal criminal justice origins."[124]

According to Alfred Blumstein and colleagues, a criminal career in property offending consisted of three distinct phases.[125] The first phase is the "break-in" period, which characterizes the early years of an offender's career, a time when young offenders become increasingly committed to criminal careers and explore

various kinds of criminality; this initial phase generally lasts for the first 10 to 12 years. The second phase, the "stable" period, is the time of highest commitment, the period in an offender's career when he or she identifies most closely with a criminal lifestyle and probably also the period when rehabilitation efforts are most likely to fail. The final phase of a criminal career, the "burnout" period, begins around age 40 and is characterized by increasing dropout rates and a lowered commitment to criminal lifestyles.

In a study of violent offending, D. S. Elliott and fellow researchers examined data from the National Youth Survey and found that the careers of violent offenders were typically quite short—averaging just 1.58 years.[126] Only about 4% of subjects studied by Elliott and others had a violent criminal career of five years or more. However, they defined *career length* as the maximum number of consecutive years the individual was classified as a serious violent offender during the study period.

It was long assumed that offending becomes more serious and more frequent over time, but that assumption was strongly challenged by Michael R. Gottfredson and Travis Hirschi.[127] They posited that although the idea of deviance and crime as an orderly process similar to the rationality of conventional activities may be appealing for social policy purposes, evidence on offense specialization and the trajectories associated with chronic offending offer more support for crime as a fragmented pursuit than as a "career." Other researchers have found that although there is a certain logic to offenders' lifestyles, it is not one that easily complies with "a concept appropriate in a distinctly different culture (lawful society)."[128]

Based on ethnographic research on street criminals in urban settings, **Mark S. Fleisher** argued that the "social maturation" of the street life cycle "allows hustlers at any age to speak and act like adolescents and never acquire responsibilities similar to those marking social maturation in lawful society. In the sociocultural world of hustlers, youth is marked by gang membership, 'kids' crimes,' the onset of drug and alcohol addictions, and juvenile detention."[129] From the cradle to the grave, the lifestyle of street criminals is "created less by design than by default."[130] Fleisher explained that street criminals do not have careers, so thinking of their offenses or the pattern of their lives as following a series of life events similar to those outside this sociocultural environment will do little to increase understanding of the patterns of property offending because there is not enough planning in how the street criminal approaches life and crime to constitute a career. The type of offense specialization existing among property offenders is a loosely based preference for certain types of offending but not necessarily for a particular offense.

> The lifestyle of street criminals is created less by design than by default.

■ **fence**   An individual or a group involved in the buying, selling, and distributing of stolen goods.

Property Offenders and Rational Choice

Property crimes are often investigated from the perspective of rational choice theories (discussed in Chapter 3). One definition of *rationality* offered by Dermot Walsh was "activities identified by their impersonal, methodical, efficient, and logical components";[131] however, the rationality of the typical criminal offender is not the same as "the rationality used by the civil engineer."[132] Thomas Bennett and Richard Wright researched the rationality surrounding decision making by burglars.[133] Walsh's conclusions agreed with theirs—that offenders employ a "limited, temporal rationality.... Not all these men are highly intelligent, and few are equipped to calculate Bentham-style, even supposing the information were available. Yet it is very common for rationality to be used. Of course it is partial and limited rather than total, but at the time, the actor feels he has planned enough and weighed enough data."[134] Although some offenders (especially those closer to the end of the continuum marked professional) use a higher degree of rationality and others may exhibit totally senseless behavior, most expressions of rationality are not dramatically clear. As Neil Shover and David Honaker explained, "Rationality is not a dichotomous variable," so given the extent to which it is shaped by the social context of offenders' lives, researchers must "learn more about the daily worlds that comprise the immediate contexts of criminal decision making behavior."[135] The extent to which property crimes are rational pursuits for either expressive or instrumental gains is a question that can be addressed by examining a wide variety of research on typologies of property crimes. Learn more about trends in property crimes from **http://bjs.ojp.usdoj.gov/content/glance/house2.cfm**.

Receivers of Stolen Property

Darrell J. Steffensmeier posited that "the 1827 English statute—'a person receiving stolen property knowing the same to be stolen is deemed guilty of a felony'—is the prototype of subsequent American law. The exact wording may vary from one state to another, but the basic elements of the crime— 'buying and receiving,' 'stolen property,' and 'knowing it to be stolen'—have remained essentially intact."[136] Only small numbers of thieves steal for their own consumption, steal mostly cash, and have no need to translate the goods into cash. In other cases, it is necessary for stolen goods to be translated into cash, and "there are many paths that stolen property may take from

thieves to eventual customers."[137] Receiving stolen property is engaged in for profit by individuals and groups with varying skill levels. Some burglars commit their offenses specifically to get something they know someone wants and sell their merchandise directly to a waiting customer.[138] Burglars may sell to people they know or may take stolen goods to places like flea markets or auctions. Other options for disposing of stolen goods "involve the thief and dabbling 'middlemen' who buy and sell stolen property under the cover of a bar, a luncheonette, or an auto service station with the encouragement, if not the active participation, of the proprietor."[139] Some burglars also sell their merchandise to merchants by representing it as legal goods. The most complicated path from the thief to customers is through a **fence** (someone involved in buying, selling, and/or distributing stolen goods); the use of a fence is the least common method of disposing of stolen goods for the majority of thieves but the most common method used by professional burglars.

Steffensmeier linked the rise of fences to industrialization and the availability of mass-produced goods, which made fencing profitable for significant numbers of people.[140] Steffensmeier used case studies to research the fence, as did **Carl Klockars** in his classic work.[141] Klockars detailed the career of Vincent Swaggi, a successful fence for more than 20 years; Steffensmeier profiled Sam Goodman, a 60-year-old white male whom he began interviewing in early 1980.[142] Building on Klockars's definition, Steffensmeier defined a *fence* as one who "purchases stolen goods both on a regular basis, and for resale."[143] The defining characteristics of the professional fence are that he or she "[has] direct contact with thieves,... buys and resells stolen goods regularly and persistently,... [and is a] public dealer—recognized as a fence by thieves, the police, and others acquainted with the criminal community."[144] Other variations and distinguishing characteristics exist for those who are part of the puzzle of how stolen goods move from the original owner to the open market.

The Role of Criminal Receivers

In their ethnographic research on residential burglars, **Paul F. Cromwell** and his colleagues offered a three-part typology of criminal receivers: professional receivers, avocational receivers, and amateur receivers.[145] *Professional receivers* fit the definition of *fences* provided by Steffensmeier: those who purchase stolen goods on a regular basis for resale. The use of a professional fence to dispose of stolen goods is uncommon for most residential burglars, who lack "sophisticated underworld connections."[146] Such connections often distinguish "high-level burglars" from the more typical and prevalent residential burglars.[147] Burglars and other thieves who develop access to fences have cited a number of advantages to disposing of stolen goods this way. First, the professional fence offers a safe and quick means of disposing of goods, especially for burglars who commit high-visibility crimes and have easily recognizable goods. In Wright and Decker's ethnographic research on residential burglars, one burglar who had stolen from a local celebrity's house stated, "We couldn't just sell [the jewelry] on the street, it was like too hot to handle."[148] Second, fences are the best outlet for a large volume of stolen goods. Some professional fences are "generalists" who deal in a wide variety of stolen goods,

> The professional fence offers a safe and quick means of disposing of goods.

and others are "specialists" who deal only in certain types of goods. Goodman (the professional fence described in Steffensmeier's research) started as a specialist but evolved into a generalist as a "function of greater capital and a growing knowledge of varied merchandise."[149] The vast majority of professional fences are involved in a legitimate business that serves as a cover for their criminal activity and facilitates it. For example, Goodman operated a secondhand store whose inventory partially matched the stolen goods he received, a characteristic that made him quasi-legitimate, a "partly covered fence." Fences who are "fully covered" do not deal in stolen goods that are outside their inventory in the legitimate business, and "noncovered" fences are those whose "illicit lines of goods are distinct from the legitimate commerce."[150] The more a fence is able to cover illicit activities by incorporating them into

legitimate enterprises, the safer the fence is from criminal detection and prosecution.

There is a great deal of variety in the businesses that fences use as a front for their criminal activity, ranging from those viewed by the "community-at-large as strictly clean," like restaurants, to businesses that "are perceived as clean but somewhat suspect," like auto parts shops and antique shops, to businesses that are viewed as "quasi-legitimate or marginal," like pawnshops.[151] Some of the residential burglars interviewed by Wright and Decker stated that they avoided marginal businesses like pawnshops when disposing of stolen goods because, given the increasingly strict regulations of pawnshops, owners must often demand identification and take photos of those selling to them, and they have "hot sheets" of recently stolen goods. In addition, pawnshops generally do not provide the greatest return on the merchandise. Given the fact that many residential burglars commit their offenses for fast cash, "pawnshops almost always [have] the upper hand in negotiations."[152] The residential burglars who did regularly use pawnshops reported having an established relationship with the owner that enabled them "to pawn stolen property 'off camera'" because they had made transactions with the owner previously that had not resulted in "bringing additional police pressure to bear on his business."[153]

A second type of fence is *avocational receivers*, who buy stolen property as a part-time endeavor "secondary to, but usually associated with, their primary business activity."[154] This is a fairly diverse group that can include individuals involved in respectable occupations, such as lawyers or bail bondsmen who "provide legitimate professional services to property offenders who cannot pay for these services with anything but stolen property."[155] Others involved in illegitimate occupations, such as drug dealers, may also accept stolen goods.

Amateur receivers are those "otherwise honest citizens who buy stolen property on a relatively small scale, primarily, but not exclusively, for personal consumption. Crime is peripheral rather than central to their lives."[156] These individuals are quite sporadic in their involvement in activities that generate stolen goods. Cromwell and colleagues cited as an example a "public-school teacher who began her part-time fencing when she was approached by a student who offered her a 'really good deal' on certain items."[157] Although these individuals do not engage in receiving stolen property at the same level as professional or avocational fences, "they represent a large market for stolen goods" because they "compensate for lack of volume with their sheer numbers."[158] Stuart Henry's study of property crime among ordinary people, which he termed "hidden-economy crime," described the involvement of ordinary citizens in a wide variety of property offenses, including receiving stolen property.[159] Learn more about how fences operate at **bjc.oxford journals.org/content/45/2/129.full.pdf**.

Michael Hanson/National Geographic Image Collection/Alamy Stock Photo

A Las Vegas pawnshop owner displays goods acquired from clients. Could this shop serve as a front for a fencing operation?

CRIMINAL | PROFILES

Colton Harris-Moore—the Barefoot Bandit

On January 27, 2012, Colton Harris-Moore, 21, was sentenced to six and one-half years in federal prison for dozens of crimes he had committed in three different countries. Harris-Moore, who gained celebrity for his widely publicized attempts to evade arrest, came to be known as the "Barefoot Bandit" because he reportedly committed some of his crimes while barefoot.[i]

Harris-Moore began living a survivalist lifestyle in his home state of Washington at age seven and would break into homes and businesses to steal food, blankets, and other supplies. At 12, he was convicted of possessing stolen property, and he quickly built a record of continued juvenile offenses. Diagnosed with attention deficit disorder and depression, he was ordered to community service or brief stays in a detention facility following each offense. By 2008, then-17-year-old Harris-Moore was stealing evermore-expensive items and was sentenced to spend three years in a halfway house. He fled soon after arriving at the home.[ii]

His criminal career eventually expanded to include more than 100 larcenies, involving thefts of cars, bicycles, boats, and airplanes. Eventually, Harris-Moore went on the run, leaving a trail of thefts and stolen vehicles from the state of Washington to Indiana. He became a sensation on Facebook when a fan page was created to follow his exploits. On July 4, 2010, he stole a Cessna single-engine airplane from the Bloomington, Indiana, airport and, using skills he had learned from flight simulation software and airplane manuals, flew it to Great Abaco Island in the Bahamas, where he crash-landed in water. After drinking beer in a local bar, Harris-Moore stole a 44-foot power boat from a marina on Great Abaco and used it to travel to nearby Eleuthera Island. Spotted by authorities, he attempted to flee, but officers shot out the engine and captured him.

On December 16, 2011, Harris-Moore was sentenced in Island County, Washington, to more than seven years in prison on charges ranging from identity theft and theft of a firearm to residential burglary. His lawyers had argued that he was abused as a child, suffered from prenatal alcohol exposure, and was raised by a drunken mother. In a statement provided to the judge, Harris-Moore said that his childhood was one he wouldn't wish on his "darkest enemies." Judge Vickie Churchill apparently agreed, saying, "This case is a tragedy in many ways, but it's a triumph of the human spirit in other ways." Describing Harris-Moore's childhood as a "mind numbing absence of hope," she stated that the 20-year-old was genuinely remorseful for his crimes.[iii]

In an e-mail a few days after his sentencing in state court, Harris-Moore wrote to his supporters, saying, "When all the acting and spreading of high propaganda on the part of the state was over and my lawyers argued the true facts, the judge gave me a much-appreciated recognition and validation, calling my story a 'triumph of the human spirit.' She wasn't having none of the weak argument the prosecution tried to peddle, and ended up handing down a sentence that was the lowest possible within the range.... Once again, I made it through a situation I shouldn't have."[iv]

Colton Harris-Moore, the "Barefoot Bandit," under arrest. Harris-Moore committed dozens of crimes in three different countries and became something of a folk hero before his arrest. Why did Harris-Moore turn to crime?

Harris-Moore has said that he plans to spend his prison time studying in preparation for applying to college to earn a degree in aeronautical engineering. Fox bought the movie rights in a deal that could be worth $1.3 million, with the money earmarked for victims. When it was released in 2015, the movie, titled *The Barefoot Bandit Documentary*, failed to attract significant numbers of movie goers.

The case of the Barefoot Bandit raises a number of interesting questions. Among them are the following:

1. What led Harris-Moore to embark on a crime spree?

2. What role did his mother and father (or his mother's boyfriends) play in contributing to Harris-Moore's criminal lifestyle?

3. Would Harris-Moore have turned to crime had he been raised under different circumstances? Explain.

Notes

i. Laura L. Myers, " 'Barefoot Bandit' Gets 6.5 Years of Federal Time," *Chicago Tribune* via Reuters, January 27, 2012, http://www.chicagotribune.com/news/sns-rt-us-barefoot-bandit-sentencingtre80q1tm-20120127,0,4418476.story (accessed March 1, 2012).

ii. Manual Valdes, "'Barefoot Bandit' Sentenced to 6½ Years," Pantagraph.com via AP, January 31, 2012, http://www.pantagraph.com/news/weird-news/barefoot-bandit-sentenced-to-years/article_e671e808-4c28-11e1-81c6-0019bb2963f4.html (accessed May 2, 2012).

iii. Charles Montaldo, "'Barefoot Bandit' Gets 6½ Federal Years," About.com/Crime and Punishment, January 28, 2012, http://crime.about.com/b/2012/01/28/barefoot-bandit-gets-7-federal-years.htm (accessed March 2, 2012).

iv. Gene Johnson, "'Barefoot Bandit' Emails Ridicule Law Enforcement," *Associated Press*, January 25, 2012, http://abcnews.go.com/US/wireStory/barefoot-bandit-emails-ridicule-law-enforcement-15432245#.TyIn_mNSRak (accessed May 1, 2014).

SUMMARY

- The major forms of property crime discussed in this chapter are larceny-theft, motor vehicle theft, burglary, and arson.

- Burglary is the unlawful entry of a structure (residential or commercial) with intent to commit a felony or a theft. Burglars often cross the line to more serious violent crimes like homicide, rape, and robbery, but even in the absence of violent crime, the social costs of burglary to victims and to society are numerous.

- Larceny-theft is the unlawful taking or attempted taking, carrying, leading, or riding away of property from the possession or constructive possession of another (motor vehicles are excluded). The largest category is theft from motor vehicles, followed by shoplifting and theft from buildings; pocket picking and purse snatching are much less common.

- Motor vehicle theft is the theft of a motor vehicle and does not include farm equipment, bulldozers, airplanes, construction equipment, or motorboats; almost 1 million motor vehicles are stolen in the United States each year.

- Arson, the burning or attempted burning of property with or without intent to defraud, has the potential to result in both great economic loss and loss of life. Although arson for profit and for protest certainly occurs, most arsons involve adolescents with various motives for fire setting.

- Professional thieves commit thefts with some degree of skill, earn reasonably good money from their crimes, and spend relatively little time incarcerated. Persistent thieves continue in property crimes despite their ordinary level of success; professional thieves are characterized by greater planning and financial reward. Strict specialization is rarely found among property offenders.

- Property crimes usually involve stolen goods that need to be turned into cash. Those who receive stolen goods range from the amateur receiver, who is occasionally involved in fencing, to the professional fence, who buys and sells stolen goods in volume and offers a safe, quick means of disposing of goods, especially for burglars who have committed high-visibility crimes and have easily recognizable goods. Most professional fences are also involved in legitimate businesses that serve as a cover for their criminal activity and facilitate it.

KEY TERMS

arson, 345

burglary, 330

fence, 348

identity theft, 340

Identity Theft and Assumption Deterrence Act, 340

Identity Theft Penalty Enhancement Act, 340

joyriding, 342

larceny-theft, 337

motor vehicle theft, 342

occasional offender, 346

offense specialization, 346

persistent thief, 346

professional criminal, 346

property crime, 330

KEY NAMES

Mary Owen Cameron, 338

Paul F. Cromwell, 348

Laura Dugan, 336

Mark S. Fleisher, 347

John R. Hepburn, 346

Malcolm W. Klein, 346

Lloyd W. Klemke, 338

Carl Klockars, 348

Mike Maguire, 333

Neil Shover, 333

Darrell J. Steffensmeier, 348

Kenneth D. Tunnell, 335

QUESTIONS FOR REVIEW

1. What are the major forms of property crime discussed in this chapter?

2. What constitutes the crime of burglary? What are some of its characteristics?

3. What constitutes the crime of larceny-theft? What forms does it take?

4. What is motor vehicle theft? How prevalent is it?

5. What constitutes the crime of arson?

6. What are some characteristics of persistent and professional thieves?

7. What are the typical activities of receivers of stolen property, and how are stolen goods distributed?

QUESTIONS FOR REFLECTION

1. To what extent is thrill seeking a motivation behind certain types of property offenses? How might it contribute to the crime of shoplifting?

2. Why is so much attention given to shoplifting among adolescents? Should it be? Why or why not?

3. How are "honest" citizens and professional criminal receivers connected?

4. To what extent are property offenders rational actors? Use examples from larceny, burglary, and receipt of stolen property to illustrate your answer.

5. What does the phrase "sexualized context of burglary" mean? How can burglary have a sexual component or motivation?

6. How are drugs involved in the offending patterns of some burglars? Might effective drug-treatment programs reduce the number of burglaries committed? Why or why not?

WHITE-COLLAR AND ORGANIZED CRIME

Crime as a Job

LEARNING OUTCOMES

After reading this chapter, you should be able to answer the following questions:

- What is the history of white-collar crime in this country?

- What is white-collar crime? What are the various kinds of white-collar crimes?

- What is corporate crime? How does it differ from more traditional forms of white-collar crime? Can businesses be charged with corporate crime?

- What are the causes of white-collar crime? How do the motivations of white-collar criminals differ from those of other criminals?

- How can white-collar and corporate crime be controlled?

- What is organized crime and how does it differ from white-collar crime?

- Identify some international criminal organizations.

- What is transnational organized crime?

- What is the RICO statute and how does it enable the use of asset forfeiture as an enforcement technique.

- How can organized crime be controlled?

Introduction

In 2015, the U.S. Department of Justice announced a nationwide sweep led by its Medicare Fraud Strike Force.[1] The operation resulted in charges against 243 individuals, including 46 doctors, nurses, and other licensed medical professionals, for their alleged participation in Medicare fraud schemes involving approximately $712 million in false billings. According to court documents, the defendants participated in schemes to submit claims to Medicare and Medicaid for treatments that were medically unnecessary and often never provided. The coordinated takedown was the largest in Strike Force history in terms of both the number of defendants charged and dollar amounts.

Those arrested were charged with various health-care fraud-related crimes, including conspiracy to commit health-care fraud, violations of anti-kickback statutes, money laundering and aggravated identity theft. The charges were based on a variety of fraud schemes involving various medical treatments and services, including home health care, psychotherapy, physical and occupational therapy, durable medical equipment (DME) and pharmacy fraud. More than 44 of the defendants arrested were charged with fraud related to the Medicare prescription drug benefit program known as Part D, which is the fastest growing component of the Medicare program.

Since the Medicare Fraud Strike force began operations about ten years ago, nearly 900 individuals have been charged in national investigations, which have involved more than $2.5 billion in fraudulent billings.

A Brief History of White-Collar Crime

White-collar crime is not unique to the twenty-first century. Financial scandals have a long and ubiquitous history in the United States, sometimes even involving government regulators. In 1929, the Teapot Dome scandal, which embroiled the administration of President Warren Harding, began in 1921 when Secretary of the Interior Albert B. Fall secretly leased naval oil reserves at Teapot Dome, Wyoming, and Elk Hills, California, to developers without asking for competitive bids. A Senate investigation later revealed that large sums of federal money had been loaned to developers without interest. Fall was eventually fined and sent to prison, and a 1927 U.S. Supreme Court decision ordered the fields restored to the U.S. government.

The insider-trading scam of stock market tycoon Ivan Boesky and the securities fraud conviction of junk-bond king Michael Milken in the 1980s demonstrated again how fortunes could be amassed through white-collar law violations. Boesky was estimated to have netted a profit of $250 million for himself and a few close friends; Milken paid a $600 million fine—far less than the amount he is estimated to have reaped from illegal bond trading.

The nationwide savings and loan (S&L) disaster of the 1980s, which some have called the "biggest white-collar crime in history," serves as another example of white-collar crime. The S&L fiasco was the result of years of intentional mismanagement and personal appropriation of depositors' funds by institutional executives. Although the actual amount of money lost or stolen during the scandal may never be known, it has been estimated to run into the hundreds of billions of dollars. The collapse of just one such institution, Charles Keating's California-based Lincoln Savings and Loan Association, cost taxpayers—who were left to redeem the insolvent institution—approximately $2.5 billion, and the collapse of Neil Bush's Silverado Banking Savings and Loan in Denver cost nearly $1 billion.

> Today, it's easier to steal money with a computer than it is with a gun.

Mario beauregard/Fotolia

Medical records. Medicare fraud is a major area of criminal activity in the United States. What kinds of fraudulent activities would be included?

- **securities fraud**   The theft of money resulting from intentional manipulation of the value of equities, including stocks and bonds. Securities fraud also includes theft from securities accounts and wire fraud.
- **insider trading**   A type of equity trading based on confidential information about important events that may affect the price of the issue being traded.
- **bank fraud**   Any fraud or embezzlement that occurs within or against financial institutions that are insured or regulated by the U.S. government. Fraud of financial institutions includes commercial-loan fraud, check fraud, counterfeit negotiable instruments, mortgage fraud, and false credit applications.
- **white-collar crime**   A violation of the criminal law committed by a person of respectability and high social status in the course of his or her occupation.

Another type of white-collar crime sprang from the low interest rates characteristic of the early and mid-1990s. Sham banking operations flourished by offering high interest rates and double-digit rates of return on investments, but such "phantom banks" evaporated as quickly as they were formed, leaving investors stunned and sometimes penniless.

The past two decades have seen a number of infamous white-collar crime prosecutions, including those involving executives at the former energy-trading giant Enron Corporation, which had used complex off-balance-sheet partnerships to hide losses and inflate revenues. The company's collapse in 2001 set the stage both for massive reforms in the business and financial world and for federal and state investigations into the accounting practices and business dealings of all publicly traded companies in the United States. Enron's bankruptcy wiped out at least $24 billion in retirement plans, stock accounts, and mutual funds as the company's stock plummeted.

On July 21, 2002—less than a year after the collapse of Enron—WorldCom, Inc., a huge telecommunications company, filed for what was then the largest-ever U.S. bankruptcy. At least $11 billion of the company's money had been lost in an accounting fraud intended to save the failing company.

One month later, a federal grand jury indicted former WorldCom top executives Buford Yates and Scott Sullivan on charges of conspiracy, **securities fraud**, and false filings with the Securities and Exchange Commission (SEC).

Yates pleaded guilty and helped federal prosecutors build cases against others at the company; he was sentenced in 2005 to a year and a day in prison. Sullivan became the government's star witness at the criminal trial of former WorldCom CEO Bernard Ebbers. Sullivan received a five-year sentence, but Ebbers was found guilty of nine counts of conspiracy, securities fraud, and false regulatory filings and was sent to prison for 25 years. For a list of *Time* magazine's "Top 10 Crooked CEOs" of recent years, visit **http://www.time.com/time/specials/packages/completelist/0,29569,1903155,00.html**.

Allegations of criminal wrongdoing spread to other companies. In 2002, ImClone founder Dr. Sam Waksal pleaded guilty to six federal charges of bank fraud and conspiracy involving **insider trading** (equity trading based on confidential information that could affect stocks being traded) that threatened the home-decorating

In 2002, insider trading threatened the home-decorating empire of Martha Stewart.

empire of Martha Stewart. Prosecutors alleged that Waksal had tipped off family members and friends, including Stewart and her stockbroker, that the Food and Drug Administration (FDA) would not approve his company's experimental cancer drug, Erbitux.

Waksal, who admitted to **bank fraud** for forging the name of ImClone's chief attorney to a document securing a line of credit, was sentenced to seven years in prison, and Martha Stewart was ordered to spend five months behind bars.

More recently, in 2017 Volkswagen, AG agreed to plead guilty to three criminal felony charges and to pay $4.3 billion in criminal and civil penalties for conspiring to defraud customers by rigging computers on its vehicle's to report false exhaust emission readings.[2] The company had been charged with violations of the federal Clean Air Act, customs fraud, and obstructing justice. A federal grand jury also indicted six VW executives and employees for their roles in the nearly 10-year-long conspiracy. Table 13-1 describes the terminology of financial crimes.

Understanding White-Collar Crime

In 1939, **Edwin H. Sutherland** defined **white-collar crime** as violations of the criminal law "committed by a person of respectability and high social status in the course of his occupation."[3] Many criminologists do not properly understand crime, Sutherland claimed, because they fail to recognize that the secretive violations of public and corporate trust by those in positions of authority are just as criminal as predatory acts committed by people of lower social standing.

According to Sutherland, the criminality of upper-class persons has been demonstrated again and again.

Sutherland also noted that white-collar criminals are far less likely to be investigated, arrested, or prosecuted than are other types of offenders. In Sutherland's day, when they were convicted, white-collar offenders were much less likely to receive active prison terms than were "common criminals." The deference shown to white-collar criminals, said Sutherland, is due primarily to their social standing. Many white-collar criminals have been well respected in their communities, and many have taken part in national affairs.

TABLE 13-1 | The Terminology of Financial Crimes

Antitrust violation: Any activity that illegally inhibits competition between companies within an industry, such as price fixing and monopolies in restraint of trade. Antitrust violations are infractions of the Sherman Act (15 U.S.C. Sections 1–7) and the Clayton Act (15 U.S.C. Sections 12–27).

Bank fraud (also financial fraud or financial institution fraud): Fraud or embezzlement that occurs within or against financial institutions that are insured or regulated by the U.S. government. Financial institution fraud includes commercial loan fraud, check fraud, counterfeit negotiable instruments, mortgage fraud, and false credit applications.

Bankruptcy fraud: The misleading of creditors through the concealment and misstatement of assets. Bankruptcy fraud also involves illegal pressure on bankruptcy petitioners.

Economic espionage/trade secret theft: The theft or misappropriation of proprietary economic information (i.e., trade secrets) from an individual, a business, or an industry.

Embezzlement: The unlawful misappropriation for personal use of money, property, or other thing of value entrusted to the offender's care, custody, or control.

Environmental law violation: Any business activity in violation of federal and state environmental laws, including the discharge of toxic substances into the air, water, or soil, especially when those substances pose a significant threat of harm to people, property, or the environment.

Government fraud: Fraud against the government, especially in connection with federal government contracting and fraud in connection with federal and/or federally funded programs. Such programs include public housing, agricultural programs, defense procurement, and government-funded educational programs. Fraudulent activities involving government contracting include bribery in contracts or procurement, collusion among contractors, false or double billing, false certification of the quality of parts or of test results, and substitution of bogus or otherwise inferior parts.

Health-care fraud: Fraudulent billing practices by health-care providers, including hospitals, home health care, ambulance services, doctors, chiropractors, psychiatric hospitals, laboratories, pharmacies, and nursing homes, that affect health-care consumers, insurance providers, and government-funded payment providers such as Medicare and Medicaid. Fraudulent activities include receiving kickbacks, billing for services not rendered, billing for unnecessary equipment, and billing for services performed by a less qualified person.

Insider trading: Equity trading based on confidential information about important events that may affect the price of the issue being traded. Because confidential information confers advantages on those who possess it, federal law prohibits them from using that knowledge to reap profits or to avoid losses in the stock market.

Insurance fraud: Fraudulent activity committed by insurance applicants, policyholders, third-party claimants, or professionals who provide insurance services to claimants. Such fraudulent activities include inflating, or "padding," actual claims and fraudulent inducements to issue policies and/or establish a lower premium rate.

Kickbacks: The return of a certain amount of money from seller to buyer as a result of a collusive agreement.

Mail fraud: The use of the U.S. mail in furtherance of criminal activity.

Money laundering: The process of converting illegally earned assets, originating as cash, to one or more alternative forms to conceal such incriminating factors as illegal origin and true ownership.

Securities fraud: The theft of money resulting from intentional manipulation of the value of equities, including stocks and bonds. Securities fraud also includes theft from securities accounts and wire fraud.

Tax evasion: Fraud committed by filing false tax returns or not filing tax returns at all.

Welfare fraud: The use of deceitful statements, practices, or devices to unlawfully obtain welfare benefits.

Wire fraud: The use of an electric or electronic communications facility to intentionally transmit a false and/or deceptive message in furtherance of a fraudulent activity.

Sources: Cynthia Barnett, *The Measurement of White-Collar Crime Using Uniform Crime Reporting Data*, Federal Bureau of Investigation, Criminal Justice Information Services Division, http://www.fbi.gov/ucr/whitecollarforweb.pdf (accessed June 18, 2009); Clifford Karchmer and Douglas Ruch, "State and Local Money Laundering Control Strategies," *NIJ Research in Brief* (Washington, DC: National Institute of Justice, 1992); and Legal Information Institute, "White-Collar Crime: An Overview," http://www.law.cornell.edu/topics/white_collar.html (accessed July 1, 2017).

■ **occupational crime**   An act punishable by law that is committed through opportunity created in the course of a legal occupation.

Given these kinds of sentiments, criminologists felt compelled for years to address the question "Is white-collar crime really crime?" As recently as 1987, writers on the subject were still asking, "Do persons of high standing commit crimes?"[4] Although most criminologists today would answer the question with a resounding *yes*, members of the public were slower to accept the notion that violations of the criminal law by businesspeople share conceptual similarities with street crime. Attitudes, however, have quickly changed during the past few years as headline-making charges have been filed against a number of corporate scam artists and financial managers who duped investors out of billions of dollars.

Definitional Evolution of White-Collar Crime

Between the early and later definitions of *white-collar crime*, many investigators refined its conceptual boundaries. **Herbert Edelhertz** defined *white-collar crime* as any "illegal act or series of illegal acts committed by nonphysical means and by concealment or guile, to obtain money or property, to avoid the payment or loss of money or property, or to obtain business or personal advantages."

Gilbert Geis grappled with the notion of "upperworld crime," which he called "a label designed to call attention to the violation of a variety of criminal statutes by persons who at the moment are generally not considered, in connection with such violations, to be the 'usual' kind of underworld and/or psychologically aberrant offenders."

Many writers were quick to realize that "upperworld," or white-collar, crime might have its counterpart in certain forms of blue-collar crime committed by members of less prestigious occupational groups, so the term *blue-collar crime* emerged as a way of classifying the law-violating behavior of people involved in appliance and automobile repair, yard maintenance, house cleaning, and general installation services. See the Theory versus Reality box for more on definitions of white-collar crime.

In an effort to bring closure to the concept of work-related crime, the term **occupational crime**—"any act punishable by law that is committed through opportunity created in the course of an occupation which is legal"—emerged as a kind of catchall category that included the job-related law violations of both white- and blue-collar workers. An excellent four-part typology of occupational crime is offered by **Gary S. Green** in his book *Occupational Crime*:

1. **Organizational occupational crime.** An organizational occupational crime is committed for the benefit of an employer or organization, but only the employer or organization—not individual employees—benefits.

2. **State authority occupational crime.** A state authority occupational crime is committed by people exercising their state-based authority, is occupation specific, and can be committed only by officials in public office or those working for them.

3. **Professional occupational crime.** A professional occupational crime is committed by professionals while in their occupational capacity (such as physicians, attorneys, and psychologists).

4. **Individual occupational crime.** An individual occupational crime, committed by an individual acting alone, is a kind of catchall category that includes personal-income-tax evasion, theft of goods and services by employees, and filing of false expense reports.

> The idea of occupational crime became a kind of catchall category.

For an interesting presentation of white-collar and occupational crime typologies, visit the National Check Fraud Center and Cornell Law School's white-collar crime page via **http://www.ckfraud .org/whitecollar.html** and **http://topics.law.cornell.edu /wex/White-collar_crime**. Learn more about white-collar crime and its measurement from **http://topics.law.cornell .edu/wex/White-collar_crime**.

White-Collar Crime Today

The chief criterion for a crime to be "white collar" is that "it occurs as a part of, or a deviation from, the violator's occupational role."[5] This focus on the violator, rather than on the offense, in deciding whether to classify a crime as white collar was accepted by the 1967 Presidential Commission on Law Enforcement and Administration of Justice. In its classic report *The Challenge of Crime in a Free Society*, members of the commission wrote, "The 'white-collar' criminal is the broker who distributes fraudulent securities, the builder who deliberately uses defective material, the corporation executive who conspires to fix prices, the legislator who peddles his influence and votes for private gain, or the banker who misappropriates funds in his keeping."[6]

Over the past few decades, the concept of white-collar crime has undergone considerable refinement.[7] The reason, according to the U.S. DOJ, is that "the focus has shifted to the nature of the crime instead of the persons or occupations involved."[7] The methods used to commit white-collar crime, such as the use of a computer and the Internet, and the special skills and knowledge necessary for attempted law violation have resulted in a contemporary understanding of white-collar crime

■ **corporate crime**   A violation of a criminal statute either by a corporate entity or by its executives, employees, or agents acting on behalf of and for the benefit of the corporation, partnership, or other form of business entity.

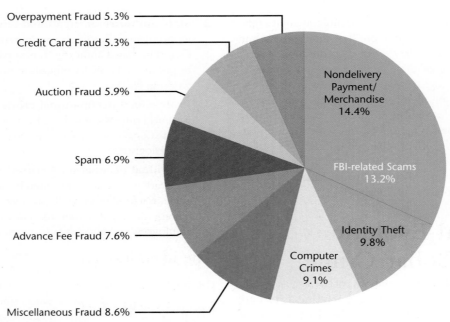

Overpayment Fraud 5.3%
Credit Card Fraud 5.3%
Auction Fraud 5.9%
Spam 6.9%
Advance Fee Fraud 7.6%
Miscellaneous Fraud 8.6%
Nondelivery Payment/ Merchandise 14.4%
FBI-related Scams 13.2%
Identity Theft 9.8%
Computer Crimes 9.1%

FIGURE 13-1 | **Top Ten Internet Crime Complaint Categories**

that emphasizes the type of offense being committed rather than the social standing or occupational role of the person committing it. Some reasons for this shift are changes in the work environment and in the business world itself. Other reasons are pragmatic. In the words of the Justice Department, "The categorization of 'white-collar crime' as crime having a particular modus operandi [committed in a manner that utilizes deception and special knowledge of business practices and committed in a particular kind of economic environment] is of use in coordinating the resources of the appropriate agencies for purposes of investigation and prosecution."[9]

Visit the National White Collar Crime Center and the Internet Crime Complaint Center (ICC3) at **http://www.NW3C.org** and **http://www.IC3.gov**. Both report on white-collar crimes committed via the Internet. Figure 13–1 shows the top ten Internet crime complaint categories recorded by the IC3.

Corporate Crime

Corporate malfeasance, which is essentially another form of white-collar crime, has been dubbed "corporate crime." **Corporate crime** can be defined as "a violation of a criminal statute ether by a corporate entity or by its executives, employees, or agents acting on behalf of and for the benefit of the corporation, partnership, or other form of business entity."[10] Corporate crimes come in

> Corporate crime is a violation of a criminal statute by a corporate entity or by its executives, acting on behalf of the corporation.

many forms, ranging from prior knowledge about automobile defects to price fixing and insider securities trading. Culpability, which often results in civil suits against the corporation along with possible criminal prosecutions, is greatest where company officials can be shown to have had advance knowledge about product defects, dangerous conditions, or illegal behavior on the part of employees.

In 1909, in the case of *New York Central and Hudson River Railroad Co.* v. *United States*,[11] the U.S. Supreme Court reasoned that the criminal acts and intentions of a company's employees can extend to the company itself. The Court said that because corporations could be held liable for civil wrongs involving their employees' bad conduct, it would be appropriate to hold them criminally liable as well. In a precedent-setting decision assigning legal liability to a corporate entity, the justices wrote, "Since a corporation acts by its officers and agents, their purposes, motives, and intent are just as much those of the corporation as are the things done."

In 2002, in an example of how corporations can be held criminally responsible for the acts of their officials, the

■ **corporate fraud**   A type of organizational fraud, such as accounting schemes, self-dealing by corporate executives, obstruction of justice, insider trading, kickbacks, and misuse of corporate property for personal use.

THEORY | versus REALITY

White-Collar Crime: The Initial Statement

At least one eminent criminologist has called the concept of white-collar crime "the most significant development in criminology, especially since World War II."[1] The roots of the concept go back to 1939, when Edwin Sutherland first coined the term *white-collar crime* in his presidential address to the American Sociological Society. Details of that address are discussed elsewhere in this chapter. His speech concluded with the following five points:

1. White-collar criminality is real criminality, being in all cases in violation of the criminal law.

2. White-collar criminality differs from lower-class criminality principally in implementation of the criminal law, which segregates white-collar criminals administratively from other criminals.

3. The theories of the criminologists that crime is due to poverty or to psychopathic and sociopathic conditions statistically associated with poverty are invalid because, first, they are derived from samples

that are grossly biased with respect to socioeconomic status; second, they do not apply to the white-collar criminals; and third, they do not even explain the criminality of the lower class, as the factors are not related to a general process characteristic of all criminality.

4. A theory of criminal behavior that will explain both white-collar criminality and lower-class criminality is needed.

5. A hypothesis of this nature is suggested in terms of differential association and social disorganization.

Discussion Questions

1. Why is white-collar crime possibly the most significant development in criminology since World War II?

2. Why did Sutherland have to remind people that "white-collar criminality is real criminality"? Why might some have thought otherwise?

Note
[1] Donald J. Newman, "White-Collar Crime: An Overview and Analysis," *Law and Contemporary Problems*, Vol. 23, No. 4 (Autumn 1958).
Source: Edwin Sutherland, "White-Collar Criminality," *American Sociological Review*, Vol. 5 (February 1940), pp. 1–12.

accounting firm of Arthur Andersen was convicted of obstruction of justice after its employees destroyed documents related to Enron Corporation audits. Arthur Andersen, which had served as Enron's auditor, was forced to relinquish its U.S. licenses and closed its American offices. The company also paid more than $130 million to settle issues relating to questionable accounting practices in its work with another company, Waste Management, in the late 1990s. The company had provided accounting services for WorldCom, Inc., prior to the arrest of that company's chief financial officer and other executives.[11] In 2005, however, the firm was at least partially vindicated when its conviction was overturned by the U.S. Supreme Court, which found that the instructions given to the jury in the 2002 trial had been flawed.[13]

Power Fasteners, Inc., of Brewster, New York, was indicted in 2007 on charges of manslaughter by Massachusetts prosecutors after the epoxy products it manufactured failed in Boston's "Big Dig" tunnel in 2006, allowing 20 tons of concrete ceiling panels to collapse onto a car below, killing the passenger.[14] In 2008, the company agreed to pay $16 million to settle a civil lawsuit brought against it in exchange for a promise by prosecutors to drop manslaughter charges.[15]

Finally, in 2012, British Petroleum (BP) pleaded guilty to criminal charges and agreed to pay a $4.5 billion in fines—in addition to the tens of billions of dollars it had already agreed to pay for cleanup and to reimburse victims whose livelihood had been affected by the oil spill from the company's Deepwater Horizon oil rig in 2010 in the Gulf of Mexico.[16]

It should be noted that corporate criminal liability is what some have called a unique form of "American exceptionalism," as few other countries hold corporations criminally accountable.[17]

Financial Crime

Most white-collar crimes are financial crimes, meaning illegal activities generally committed for monetary profit by businesses and those who run them. The FBI classifies the following types of activities as financial crimes: corporate fraud, securities and commodities fraud, health-care fraud, mortgage fraud, insurance fraud, mass-marketing fraud, welfare fraud, theft or piracy of intellectual property, and money laundering (Figure 13–2).[18] Many of these categories are discussed in the pages that follow.

Corporate Fraud

The term **corporate fraud** refers to accounting schemes, self-dealing by corporate executives, and obstruction of justice as well as insider trading, kickbacks, and misuse of corporate property for personal gain. The majority of these cases pursued at the federal level are built on accounting schemes intended to deceive investors, auditors, and analysts about the financial health of a corporation; in addition to significant financial losses to investors, corporate fraud has the potential to cause damage to both investor confidence and the U.S. economy.

Corporate fraud sometimes involves the backdating of executive stock options under which the date of options is set

■ **securities and commodities fraud** A crime involving investments, such as stock-market manipulation, high-yield-investment fraud (Ponzi schemes, pyramid schemes, and prime bank schemes), advance fee fraud, hedge fund fraud, commodities fraud, foreign exchange fraud, and broker embezzlement.

■ **Ponzi scheme** A form of high-yield-investment fraud that uses money collected from new investors, rather than profits from the purported underlying business venture, to pay high rates of return promised to earlier investors.

FIGURE 13-2 | Types of Financial Crime

Source: Derived from Federal Bureau of Investigation, *Financial Crimes Report to the Public, Fiscal Year 2007,* http://www.fbi.gov/publications/financial/fcs_report2007/financial_crime_2007.htm#financial.

low-volume stock in the over-the-counter securities market, that is largely controlled by the fraud perpetrators. This artificially increased trading volume unfairly increases the price of the targeted security (the "pump"), which is rapidly sold off into the inflated market created for the security by the fraud perpetrators (the "dump"), resulting in illicit gains for the perpetrators and losses for innocent third-party investors.

High-yield-investment fraud takes various forms, all of which are characterized by offers of low- or no-risk investments that guarantee unusually high rates of return. **Ponzi schemes** use money collected from new investors, rather than business profits, to pay high rates of return promised to earlier investors, giving them the impression that this is a legitimate money-making enterprise when, in reality, investors' money is the only source of funding. The term *pyramid scheme* refers to money collected from newer victims of the fraud to pay earlier victims to provide a veneer of legitimacy; the victims themselves are induced to recruit more victims through the payment of recruitment commissions. *Prime bank schemes* (another form of high-yield-investment fraud) induce victims to invest in financial instruments, allegedly issued by well-known institutions, offering risk-free opportunities for high rates of return. The benefits are supposedly the result of access to a secret worldwide exchange ordinarily open only to the world's largest financial institutions, but such networks don't exist or the perpetrators don't have access to them, and the perpetrators keep the money with which they've been entrusted.

Advance fee fraud encompasses a broad variety of schemes designed to induce victims into remitting upfront payments in exchange for the promise of goods, services, and/or prizes; victims are informed that to participate in this promising investment opportunity, they must first pay various taxes and/or fees—which go directly to the perpetrators.

Hedge fund fraud uses private investment partnerships that have generally experienced a relative lack of regulatory scrutiny, and the fraud perpetrated by fund managers can involve the overstatement or misappropriation of fund assets overcharges for fund management fees, insider trading, market timing, and late trading.

Commodities fraud typically involves the deceptive or fraudulent sale of commodities investments (e.g., gold, silver, oil, copper, and natural gas); false or deceptive sales practices are used to solicit victim funds for commodities transactions that either never occur or are inconsistent with the original sales promises. Commodities market participants may also attempt to illegally manipulate the market for a commodity by fraudulently reporting price information or cornering the market to artificially increase the price of the targeted commodity.

to a time in the past when the price of the stock was lower than on the date the options were actually issued. Backdating stock options inflates the value of the options to the holder at the expense of regular shareholders.

Obstruction of justice occurs when activities are undertaken that are designed to conceal any of the types of criminal conduct noted here, particularly when the obstruction impedes the inquiries of the SEC, other regulatory agencies, and/or law enforcement agencies.

Securities and Commodities Fraud

Securities and commodities fraud includes crimes such as stock market manipulation, high-yield-investment fraud (Ponzi schemes, pyramid schemes, and prime bank schemes), advance fee fraud, hedge fund fraud, commodities fraud, foreign exchange fraud, and broker embezzlement.

Stock market manipulation schemes (commonly referred to as "pump and dumps") create artificial buying pressure for a targeted security, generally a

Foreign exchange fraud uses false or deceptive sales practices alleging high rates of return for minimal risk to induce victims to invest in the foreign currency exchange market. The transactions never occur or are executed for the sole purpose of generating excessive trading commission—in breach of the trader's responsibilities to the client. Alternatively, individual currency traders employed by large financial institutions may illegally attempt to manipulate foreign currency exchange prices to generate illicit trading profits for their own enrichment.

Schemes using *broker embezzlement* involve illicit, unauthorized actions by brokers to steal directly from their clients; these may be facilitated by the forging of client documents, the doctoring of account statements, or unauthorized trading and fund transfers in violation of the broker's legal obligations to the client.

According to the FBI, the losses associated with these types of fraud range from the macroeconomic (erosion of investor confidence in capital markets) to the corporate (reduction in the economic health of corporations/industries due to decreased market capitalization) to the intensely personal (devastation of retirement and investment portfolios).[19] Victims of these kinds of fraud include government entities, corporations, financial institutions, pension funds, and individual investors.

Health-Care Fraud

All health-care programs are subject to fraud, with Medicare and Medicaid being most victimized. Estimates of fraudulent billings to health-care programs (public and private) are said to be between 3 and 10% of all health-care expenditures. According to the FBI, health-care fraud is not limited to any particular geographic area, targets large health-care programs (public and private) as well as beneficiaries, has become more sophisticated and complex over time, and is even being perpetrated by a number of organized crime groups.

The FBI stated that "one of the most significant trends in recent health-care fraud cases includes the willingness of medical professionals to risk patient harm in their schemes."[20] These cases involve health-care providers who conduct unnecessary surgeries, prescribe dangerous drugs without medical necessity, and engage in abusive or substandard care practices. Other schemes involve fraudulent billing for services not rendered and upcoding of charges for services provided.[21]

Mortgage Fraud

The federal government has reported a spike in the number of corporate fraud cases involving subprime-mortgage-lending companies[22] (businesses that lend to borrowers who do not qualify for loans from mainstream loan companies). The subprime market grew from 2% of all home mortgages in 1998 to 20% of mortgages in 2006, but as the housing market declined, subprime lenders were forced to buy back a number of nonperforming loans. Many of these subprime lenders had relied on a continuous increase in real estate values to allow borrowers to refinance or sell their properties before defaulting, but due to the slowdown in the housing market, loan defaults increased.

As subprime lenders suffered financial difficulties due to rising defaults, analyses of company financials by regulators identified instances of false accounting entries and fraudulently inflated assets and revenues. Federal investigations then determined that many now-bankrupt subprime lenders manipulated their reported loan portfolio risks and used various accounting schemes to inflate and falsify their financial reports; in addition, before the value of these subprime lenders' stocks rapidly declined, some executives with insider information sold their equity positions and made illegal profits.

Mortgage fraud, which is not confined to the subprime market, involves material misstatements, misrepresentations, and/or omissions relating to the property or potential mortgage relied on by an underwriter or lender to fund, purchase, or insure a loan. As initial mortgage products are repackaged and sold on secondary markets, the process can conceal or distort the original fraud so that it is not reported, leading the FBI to explain that "the true level of mortgage fraud is largely unknown."[23]

Current mortgage fraud, according to the FBI, includes equity skimming, property flipping, and mortgage debt elimination. *Equity skimming* uses corporate shell companies, corporate identity theft, and bankruptcy/foreclosure (or the threat of it) to dupe homeowners and investors. *Property flipping* involves purchasing properties and artificially inflating their value through false appraisals; the overvalued properties are then repurchased several times for a higher price by associates of the "flipper." After three or four sham sales, the properties are foreclosed on by victim lenders. Often flipped properties are ultimately repurchased for 50 to 100% of their original value. *Mortgage debt elimination* uses e-mail or Web-based ads to promote the elimination of mortgage loans, credit card debt, and other debt for an up-front fee to prepare documents to satisfy the debt, but these documents (typically referred to as Declaration of Voidance, Bond for Discharge of Debt, Bill of Exchange, Due Bill, or Redemption

■ **welfare fraud**   The use of deceitful statements, practices, or devices to unlawfully obtain public assistance benefits.

Certificate) do not achieve debt-elimination goals; they only gain profit for the scammers.

Insurance Fraud

The U.S. insurance industry consists of thousands of companies and collects nearly $1 trillion in premiums each year, so its size makes it a prime target for criminal activity.[24] The Coalition Against Insurance Fraud (CAIF) estimated that the cost of fraud in the industry is as high as $80 billion each year, a cost passed on to consumers in the form of higher premiums. The National Insurance Crime Bureau (NICB) calculated that insurance fraud raises the yearly cost of premiums by $300 for the average household.

Insurance fraud involving arson is also related to the mortgage crisis. Some distressed homeowners, property flippers, and other real estate investors have resorted to committing arson to avoid real estate foreclosure; the insurance policyholders for these properties receive otherwise-unobtainable proceeds/profits through the filing of false insurance claims.

With the downturn in the American and worldwide economies that started in the first decade of this century, workers' compensation fraud has soared. Workers' compensation insurance accounts for as much as 46% of small-business owners' operating expenses, so small-business owners have an incentive to shop for workers' compensation insurance on a regular basis. This has created an illicit opportunity for entities purporting to provide workers' compensation insurance to enter the marketplace, offer reduced premiums, and misappropriate funds without providing insurance, leaving injured and deceased victims without workers' compensation coverage to pay medical bills.

Mass-Marketing Fraud

Mass-marketing fraud is a general term for any fraud connected with communications media such as telemarketing, mass mailings, and the Internet. Mass-marketing fraud takes a variety of forms that share a common theme: use of false and/or deceptive representations to induce potential victims to make advance-fee-type payments to fraud perpetrators. Although there are no comprehensive statistics on the subject, it is estimated that mass-marketing frauds victimize millions of Americans each year and generate losses in the hundreds of millions of dollars. Following is a brief description of three key concepts and schemes associated with mass-marketing fraud:

1. **Nigerian letter fraud.** Victims of Nigerian letter fraud are contacted regarding substantial sums of money held in foreign accounts that they are told is owed to them, and they are requested to pay various fees to secure the transfer of these monies to the United States; these fees are kept by the perpetrators. Victims also may be asked to act as U.S. agents in securing the release of such funds and are provided with counterfeit instruments to be cashed to pay any required fees, only to discover that they must reimburse their financial institutions for cashing counterfeit instruments.

2. **Foreign lottery/sweepstakes fraud.** Victims are informed that they have won a substantial prize in a foreign lottery or sweepstakes but must remit payment for various taxes/fees to receive their winnings; the taxes/fees are paid to the perpetrators. Victims may be given financial documents, supposedly representing a portion of the winnings, to be cashed to pay the required fees, only to discover that they must reimburse their financial institutions for cashing counterfeit instruments.

3. **Overpayment fraud.** Victims who have advertised some item for sale are contacted by buyers who remit counterfeit instruments in excess of the purchase price for payment; the victims are told to cash the instruments, deduct any expenses, and return or forward the excess funds to an individual identified by the buyer, only to discover that they must reimburse their financial institution for cashing counterfeit instruments.

Welfare Fraud

Welfare fraud refers to the use of deceitful statements, practices, or devices to unlawfully obtain public assistance benefits. Such benefits may include social security payments, food stamps (from the Supplemental Nutrition Assistance Program), unemployment benefits, housing assistance, and workers' compensation payments. Welfare fraud, while thought to be quite large in scope, is typically committed by an individual whose social and occupational status is unlikely to easily permit their categorization as a white-collar or occupational offender. Nonetheless, it is an important type of financial crime whose extent is estimated to be in the billions of dollars. Welfare fraud occurs when applicants or recipients of public assistance moneys intentionally withhold information or provide false or incomplete information to obtain benefits and services. Oftentimes, welfare fraud recipients are receiving duplicate forms of assistance, benefits to which they are not entitled, or assistance in amounts for which they are not eligible. Twenty-five years ago, for example, 38-year-old Pasadena, California, resident Dorothy Woods made headlines as the nation's largest fraudulent welfare recipient. Woods, who was reported to have owned a Rolls-Royce, Mercedes Benz, and Cadillac, was alleged to have bilked the county of Los Angeles out of more than $400,000 in public assistance funds over seven years by claiming benefits for 38 imaginary children.[25]

Although the amount of welfare fraud that occurs in the United States each year is difficult to estimate, one early study by the Government Accounting Office found that about $1.1 billion in Aid to Families with Dependent Children (AFDC) went to ineligible families headed by undocumented

■ **money laundering**   The process of converting illegally earned assets from cash to one or more alternative forms to conceal factors such as illegal origin and true ownership.

■ **environmental crime**   A violation of the criminal law committed by businesses, business officials, organizational entities, and/or individuals that damages some protected or otherwise significant aspect of the natural environment.

(illegal alien) parents.[26] Moreover, the U.S. Department of Labor reports that approximately 2 to 3% of unemployment benefits are attributable to fraud or abuse.

Money Laundering

Money laundering is the process by which illegal gains are disguised as legal income. A more formal definition is offered by the National Institute of Justice for *money laundering*: "the process of converting illegally earned assets, originating as cash, to one or more alternative forms to conceal such incriminating factors as illegal origin and true ownership."[27] In 2010, Wachovia Corporation (now part of Wells Fargo & Company) agreed to pay $160 million to settle federal charges that it failed to establish an adequate program to prevent money laundering through its facilities.[28] The plea resulted from transactions involving Wachovia and Mexican money exchanges between 2004 and 2007 that facilitated money transfers between the United States and Mexico; a federal investigation found that drug dealers routinely used them to move funds between the two countries.

> In money laundering, illegal gains are disguised as legal income.

Title 18, Section 1956, of the U.S. Criminal Code specifically prohibited what it called the "laundering of monetary instruments" and defined *money laundering* as "[efforts] to conceal or disguise the nature, the location, the source, the ownership, or the control of the proceeds of specified unlawful activity."[29] To assist in the identification of money launderers, a provision of the 1986 federal Money Laundering Control Act required that banks report to the government all currency transactions in excess of $10,000. The Bank Secrecy Act (BSA), formally known as the Currency and Foreign Transactions Reporting Act, required financial institutions to assist government agencies in detecting and preventing activities related to money laundering, to report cash transactions exceeding an aggregate amount of $10,000 daily per account, and to report suspicious financial activity. However, high-end money launderers know these requirements and routinely evade them by dealing in commodities such as gold, using foreign banks, or making a series of smaller deposits and transfers, often involving numerous financial institutions. Reliable official estimates of the amount of money laundered in the United States are hard to establish. However, the Drug Enforcement Administration reported that estimates provided by the International Monetary Fund pegged worldwide money-laundering activities at between 2 and 5% of the world's gross domestic product, or about $600 billion annually.[30]

The problem of money laundering may be getting worse: A 2010 report by the Senate Permanent Subcommittee on Investigations found that billions of dollars are leaving the United States every year to be put into the flow of commerce and returned to this country as laundered capital.[31] The report also identified a number of individuals and organizations suspected of bringing millions of dollars from illegal activities into the country by funneling it through offshore accounts.

Environmental Crimes and Green Criminology

A relatively new area of corporate and white-collar criminality, which is defined solely in terms of violations of the criminal law, is that of crimes against the environment.[32] **Environmental crimes** are violations of the criminal law that, although typically committed by businesses or business officials, may also be committed by other individuals or organizational entities and that damage some protected or otherwise significant aspect of the natural environment.

Whaling in violation of international conventions, for example, constitutes a form of environmental crime. So, too, does intentional pollution, especially when state or federal law contravenes the practice. Sometimes negligence contributes to environmental criminality, as in the case of the 1,000-foot *Valdez* supertanker owned by Exxon Corporation, which ran aground off the coast of Alaska in 1989, spilling 11 million gallons of crude oil over 1,700 miles of pristine coastline. In September 1994, an Alaskan jury ordered Exxon to pay $5 billion in punitive damages to 14,000 people affected by the 1989 spill and another $287 million in actual damages to commercial fishermen in the region. Exxon also agreed to pay $100 million in criminal fines.[33]

> Crimes against the environment constitute a relatively new area of corporate and white-collar criminality.

In a more recent example, mentioned earlier in this chapter, Volkswagen AG, plead guilty and agreed to pay $4.3 billion in criminal and civil penalties for conspiring to cheat U.S. emissions tests in violation of the federal Clean Air Act. In 2017, when the plea was entered the U.S. Department of Justice called the company's actions "an egregious violation of our nation's environmental, consumer protection and financial laws."[34]

Yet another example comes from British Petroleum (BP) that, as mentioned earlier, has agreed to pay billions of dollars in compensation stemming from the Gulf oil spill that began on April 20, 2010. The disaster occurred when the company's deep-water

■ **green criminology**   The study of environmental harm, crime, law, regulation, victimization, and justice.

Cleanup workers at an illegal dump site wash off at the end of their shift. Environmental crimes have recently become an area of special concern to criminologists. Why have such offenses only recently been recognized as crimes?

drilling platform Deepwater Horizon suffered an explosion and fire and sank, releasing 206 million gallons of oil into the Gulf of Mexico from a wellhead 5,000 feet below the surface.[35]

The devastating fires set in oil fields throughout Kuwait by retreating Iraqi Army troops during the Gulf War in 1991 provide an example of arson that resulted in global pollution while negatively affecting fossil fuel reserves throughout much of the Middle East. These intentional fires, although properly classified as environmental criminality, also serve as an example of ecological terrorism because they were set for the purpose of political intimidation.

Green criminology is the study of environmental harm, crime, law, regulation, victimization, and justice. The term was recently introduced by Michael J. Lynch at the University of South Florida and Paul B. Stretesky at the University of Colorado, Denver. According to Lynch and Stretesky, green criminology has increasing relevance to contemporary problems at local, national, and international levels.

Learn more about environmental crimes from the Duke Environmental Law and Policy Forum and the FBI at **http:// www.law.duke.edu/journals/delpf/** and **http://www.fbi .gov/news/stories/2004/april/earth_042204**; read about the conviction and sentencing of some defendants in environmental-crime prosecutions at **http://www.justice.gov/opa/pr/2000/ April/239enrd.htm.**

Terrorism and White-Collar Crime

Terrorist activity frequently involves some form of white-collar crime because terrorists need money for daily living expenses and for weapons, travel, and communications. Terrorist groups also frequently send a portion of the money acquired from illegal activities back to their home country or pass it along to those higher up in the chain of command. Involvement in white-collar crime allows terrorist groups to maintain a significantly lower profile than if they raised funds through other crimes such as bank robberies and illegal drug sales.

> Involvement in white-collar crime allows terrorist groups to maintain a low profile.

John Kane and April Wall, in a report prepared for the White Collar Crime Center, pointed out that "curtailing terrorist activity may be achieved through the combined efforts of nations, through legislation that criminalizes the financing of terrorism, modifications to regulations that govern nonprofit or charity-based corporations, international cooperation, and a willingness of the international banking community to adhere to reporting rules designed to detect money laundering and suspicious activity" and that shell companies have been used by terrorist groups to receive and distribute money.[36] The term *shell companies* refers to entities engaged in legitimate activities to establish a good reputation in the business community and provide a veneer of legitimacy; they can launder funds by creating invoices for nonexistent products or services that then appear to be paid by another company to provide a channel for profits from illegal activities (such as insurance fraud and identity theft) so that the money enters the legitimate flow of cash disguised as revenue from legitimate activities. In 2001, for example, an American telecommunications company was indicted on charges of aiding members of al-Qaeda in preparation for the 9/11 terrorist attacks by handling more than $500,000 in monthly money transfers. Table 13-2 provides examples of the kinds of white-collar crimes associated with terrorism in recent years, along with information on federal criminal statutes that these kinds of activities violate.

Causes of White-Collar Crime

When Edwin H. Sutherland first coined the term *white-collar crime*, he wrote, "A hypothesis is needed that will explain both white-collar criminality and lower-class criminality."[37] The answer Sutherland gave to his own challenge was that "white-collar criminality, just as other systematic criminality, is learned."[38] He went on to apply elements of his famous theory of differential association (discussed in Chapter 7) to white-collar crime, saying that "it is learned in

> Edwin Sutherland said that white-collar criminality is learned, just like other forms of criminal activity.

TABLE 13-2 | White-Collar Crimes Associated with Terrorism Cases

TYPE OF OFFENSE	DESCRIPTION OF OFFENSE	STATUTE
Identification Document Fraud	Fraud in connection with identification documents	18 USC 1028
	Forgery or false use of passports	18 USC 1543
	Misuse of passports	18 USC 1544
	Fraud and misuse of visas, permits, and other documents	18 USC 1546
	Social Security fraud	42 USC 408
Financial Fraud	Bribery of public officials and witnesses	18 USC 201
	Counterfeited or forged securities of states and private entities	18 USC 513
	False statements on credit application	18 USC 1014
	Bank fraud	18 USC 1344
	Money laundering	18 USC 1956
	Unlicensed money-transmitting business	18 USC 1960
	Racketeering	18 USC 1962
	Transactions structured to evade reporting requirements	31 USC 5324
Mail and Wire Fraud	Mail fraud	18 USC 1341
	Fraud by wire, radio, or television	18 USC 1343
Credit Card Fraud	Fraud in connection with access devices	18 USC 1029
Tax Fraud	Materially false income tax returns	26 USC 7206
	Corrupt endeavors to impede IRS laws	26 USC 7212
Immigration Fraud	Deportable alien	8 USC 1227
	Alien failing to report address change	8 USC 1305
	Alien smuggling	8 USC 1324
	Evasion of immigration laws	8 USC 1325
	False representations as U.S. citizen	18 USC 911
	Illegal alien	18 USC 922
	False statements regarding naturalization, citizenship, or alien registry	18 USC 1015
	Unlawful procurement of citizenship or naturalization	18 USC 1425
Other Related Charges	Aiding and abetting	18 USC 2
	Conspiracy to commit offenses against or defraud the U.S.	18 USC 371
	Materially false statements	18 USC 1001
	Perjury	18 USC 1621
	Provision of material support to terrorists	18 USC 2339
	Conspiracy to give or receive funds, goods, or services for designated terrorist	50 USC 595

Source: John Kane and April Wall, *Identifying the Links between White-Collar Crime and Terrorism* (Glen Allen, VA: National White Collar Crime Center, September 2004), p. 13.

direct or indirect association with those who already practice the behavior."[39]

In 1968, Gary S. Becker was awarded the Nobel Prize for using mathematical models to show the trade-offs involved in rational decision making—including the decision making of white-collar criminals.[40] Becker assumed that white-collar offenders act rationally in perpetrating their crimes and that they apply their enterprenureal and management skills to schemes designed to produce illicit rewards.

More recently, other authors have offered integrative perspectives. **Travis Hirschi** and **Michael Gottfredson,** for example, in an issue of the journal *Criminology* published half a century after Sutherland's initial work, wrote, "In this paper we outline a general theory of crime capable of organizing the facts about white-collar crime at the same time it is capable of organizing the facts about all forms of crime."[41] Their analysis of white-collar crime focuses squarely on the development of the concept itself. Hirschi and Gottfredson suggest that if we were not aware of the fact that the concept of white-collar crime arose "as a reaction to the idea that crime is concentrated in the lower class, there would be nothing to distinguish it from other" forms of crime.[42] "It may be, then," they write, "that the discovery of white-collar criminals is important only in a context in which their existence is denied by theory or policy."[43] In other words, nothing is unusual about the idea of white-collar crime other than the fact that many people are loath to admit that high-status individuals commit crimes just as people of lower status do.

In fact, say Hirschi and Gottfredson, white-collar criminals are motivated by the same forces that drive other criminals: self-interest, the pursuit of pleasure, and the avoidance of pain. White-collar crimes certainly have special characteristics. They generally involve more intellectual complexity than street criminals, they often involve some form of fraudulent representation, they provide relatively large rewards, the rewards they produce may follow quickly from their commission, sanctions associated with them may be vague or only rarely imposed, and they may require only minimal effort from those with the requisite skills to engage in them.

Hirschi and Gottfredson conclude, however, that criminologists err in assuming that white-collar criminality is common or that it is as common as the forms of criminality found among the lower classes. They reason that the personal characteristics of most white-collar workers are precisely those we would expect to produce conformity in behavior. High educational levels, a commitment to the status quo, personal motivation to succeed, deference to others, attention to conventional appearance, and other inherent aspects of social conformity—all of which tend to characterize those who operate at the white-collar level—are not the kinds of personal characteristics associated with crime commission. "In other words," say Hirschi and Gottfredson, "selection processes inherent to the high end of the occupational structure tend to recruit people with relatively low propensity to crime."[44]

One other reason most criminologists are mistaken about the assumed high rate of white-collar criminality is because "white-collar researchers often take organizations as the unit of analysis" and confuse the crimes committed by organizational entities with those of individuals within those organizations.[45] Similarly, rates of white-collar offending tend to lump together the crimes of corporations with crimes committed by individual representatives of those organizations when making comparisons with the rate of criminal activity among blue-collar and other groups.

A complementary perspective by Australian criminologist **John Braithwaite** says that white-collar criminals are frequently motivated by a disparity between corporate goals and the limited opportunities available to businesspeople through conventional business practices.[46] When pressured to achieve goals that may be unattainable within the existing framework of laws and regulations surrounding their business's area of endeavor, innovative corporate officers may turn to crime to meet organizational demands.[47]

Braithwaite believes that a general theory covering both white-collar and other forms of crime can be developed by focusing on inequality as the central explanatory variable in all criminal activity.[48] Although alienation from legitimate paths to success may lead lower-class offenders to criminal activity in an effort to acquire the material possessions necessary for survival, greed can similarly motivate relatively successful individuals to violate the law to acquire even more power and more wealth.[49] New types of criminal opportunities and new paths to immunity from accountability arise from inequitable concentrations of wealth and power. Inequality thus worsens crimes of poverty motivated by the need to survive as well as crimes of wealth motivated by greed.

Braithwaite also suggests that corporate culture socializes budding executives into clandestine and frequently illegal behavioral modalities, making it easier for them to violate the law when pressures to perform mount. The hostile relationship that frequently exists between businesses and the government agencies that regulate them may further spur corporate officers to evade the law. Braithwaite emphasizes his belief that the potential for shame associated with discovery—whether by enforcement agencies, the public, or internal corporate regulators—can have a powerful deterrent effect on most corporate executives because they are fundamentally conservative individuals who are otherwise seeking success through legitimate means.[50]

Braithwaite also recommends implementation of an "accountability model," which would hold all those responsible for corporate crimes accountable.[51] Rather than merely punishing corporations through fines, personal punishment meted out to corporate lawbreakers, says Braithwaite, should have the potential to substantially reduce white-collar offending.[52]

In sum, Braithwaite contends that an integrated theory of organizational crime would include insights garnered from (1) strain theories, as to the distribution of legitimate and illegitimate opportunities; (2) subcultural theory, as applied to

■ **Sarbanes-Oxley Act** Officially known as the Public Company Accounting Reform and Investor Protection Act, requires chief executive officers and chief financial officers to personally vouch for the truth and fairness of their companies' financial disclosures and establishes an independent oversight board to regulate the accounting profession. The law also gives the federal Securities and Exchange Commission the authority to bar dishonest corporate directors and officers from ever again serving in positions of corporate responsibility and increases the maximum federal prison term for common types of corporate fraud from 5 to 20 years.

business subcultures; (3) labeling theory, or the way stigmatization can foster criminal subculture formation; and (4) control theory, as to how potential white-collar offenders can be made accountable.[53]

Finally, in 2016, in the book *Why They Do It*, Harvard Business School professor Eugene Soltes published the results of seven years of research and correspondence with 50 convicted white-collar criminals.[54] Soltes concluded that the men and women he studied had not planned out their crimes, nor weighed the consequences in any rational way, but rather acted with little conscious thought, and often got caught up in circumstances from which they could not escape. Small missteps snowballed into illegal dealings that went beyond their control. Many felt that what they did wasn't really wrong, or that they had been selectively prosecuted for actions that are common in the industries that they represented.

Curtailing White-Collar and Corporate Crime

It is far easier to convict street criminals than white-collar criminals, and it may even be difficult for prosecutors to show that a white-collar crime has occurred. "When someone breaks into a house and takes the TV and VCR," says Harvard University criminal law professor William Stuntz, "it's a matter of proving who did it. With white-collar crime it's usually not even clear what happened."[55]

White-collar crimes are often difficult to investigate and prosecute for a number of other reasons. For one thing, white-collar criminals are generally better educated compared to other offenders and are therefore better able to conceal their activities.[56] Similarly, cases against white-collar offenders must often be built on evidence of a continuing series of offenses, not a single crime, such as a bank robbery. Often the evidence involved is only understandable to financial or legal experts and can be difficult to explain to jurors. Finally, business executives, because they often have the financial resources of an entire corporation at their disposal and because they sometimes earn salaries and bonuses in the millions of dollars, are able to hire excellent defense attorneys and can tie up the courts with motions and appeals that might not be as readily available to defendants with fewer resources.

Events such as the 2001 collapse of Enron Corporation left investors around the world leery of American stock markets and forced federal legislators to enact sweeping financial reform. At the same time, the Securities and Exchange Commission (SEC) renewed efforts to enforce existing regulations and mandated new rules for investment bankers. By the start of 2001, the atmosphere of distrust that had been created by corporate criminals had become so severe that President George W. Bush believed it was necessary to make significant efforts to help restore investor confidence and to bring order to American financial markets. Consequently, the president created a federal Corporate Fraud Task Force within the U.S. DOJ, and on July 30, 2002, he signed the **Sarbanes-Oxley Act** (officially known as the Public Company Accounting Reform and Investor Protection Act), which set stiff penalties for corporate wrongdoers.[57]

In 2007, the U.S. DOJ announced that activities of the task force had resulted in 1,236 fraud convictions, including those of 214 chief executive officers and 53 chief financial officers, since 2002.[58] In announcing the convictions, then-Attorney General Alberto Gonzales noted that "perhaps the most important accomplishment is the criminal conduct that never occurred because of the widespread deterrent effect" of the task force.[59]

In 2009, President Barack Obama replaced President Bush's Corporate Fraud Task Force with an interagency task force targeting financial crimes. Called the Financial Fraud Enforcement Task Force, the organization consists of senior-level officials from more than 20 federal departments, agencies, and offices.[60] The new task force, which was given a wider mandate than its predecessor, was charged with combating mortgage fraud, securities fraud, Recovery Act fraud, and discrimination by financial institutions in the making of loans and in other financial activities. The task force also aimed to fully enforce the Fraud Enforcement and Recovery Act of 2009,[61] which targeted the recovery of federal funds spent on fraudulent claims made under the American Recovery and Reinvestment Act of 2009 (also known as the Financial Stimulus Act),[62] fraudulent claims under the Troubled Assets Relief Program (TARP),[63] and financial fraud related to any "other form of Federal assistance."

In his 2012 State of the Union Address to Congress, President Obama announced the creation of two more enforcement initiatives—one of which will be charged with targeting financial crimes; the other, with fighting unfair trade practices. The first, the Residential Mortgage-Backed Securities Working Group, will operate under the previously created Financial Fraud Enforcement Task Force; the second, which

■ **organized crime**   The unlawful activity of members of a highly organized association engaged in supplying illegal goods and services, including gambling, prostitution, loan-sharking, narcotics, and racketeering.

will investigate unfair trade practices in countries such as China, will likely be run from the White House under the Deputy National Security Advisor for International Affairs.[64]

The Sarbanes-Oxley Act, referred to earlier, has been called the most far-reaching reform of U.S. business practices since the time of Franklin Delano Roosevelt. The law authorizes funding for investigators and for the development of new technologies at the SEC targeted at uncovering corporate wrongdoing. Under the Sarbanes-Oxley Act, the SEC has the authority to bar dishonest corporate directors and officers from ever again serving in positions of corporate responsibility. Similarly, penalties for obstructing justice and shredding documents are greatly increased, corporate officers who profit illegally can be forced to return their gains to investors, and the maximum federal prison term for common types of corporate fraud has been increased from 5 to 20 years.

The Sarbanes-Oxley Act also requires chief executive officers and chief financial officers to personally vouch for the truth and fairness of their companies' financial disclosures and establishes an independent oversight board to regulate the accounting profession. The board is required to set clear standards to uphold the integrity of public audits and has the authority to investigate abuses and discipline offenders. Similarly, the Sarbanes-Oxley Act prohibits auditing firms from providing consulting services that create conflicts of interest. Finally, under the law, officials in public corporations are barred from buying or selling stock during periods when employees are prevented from making stock transactions in their retirement or 401(k) accounts.

The Sarbanes-Oxley Act was the latest in a long line of federal legislation relating to the conduct of U.S. business that extends back more than 100 years. Some of the earliest such legislation can be found in the federal Sherman Act,[65] which became law in 1890. The Sherman Act was passed to eliminate restraints on trade and competition and specifically to prevent the development of trusts and monopolies in restraint of trade. The Clayton Act,[66] passed in 1914, prohibits mergers and acquisitions in which the effect "may be substantially to lessen competition, or to tend to create a monopoly."

The Securities Act of 1933[67] and the Securities Exchange Act of 1934[68] were enacted by federal legislators reeling from the effects of the Great Depression, which began with the stock market crash of 1929. Often referred to as the "truth-in-securities" law, the Securities Act of 1933 has two basic objectives: (1) to require that investors receive financial and other significant information concerning securities being offered for public sale and (2) to prohibit deceit, misrepresentations, and other fraud in the sale of securities.

The Securities Exchange Act of 1934 gave birth to the SEC and conferred upon the SEC broad authority over all aspects of the securities industry. This includes the power to register, regulate, and oversee brokerage firms, transfer agents, and clearing agencies as well as the nation's stock exchanges. The act also identified and prohibited certain types of conduct in the markets and provides the SEC with disciplinary powers over regulated entities and people associated with them. Finally, the act empowered the SEC to require periodic reporting of information by companies with publicly traded securities.

Certain forms of occupational crime may be easier to address than others. Individual occupational crimes especially may be reduced by concerted enforcement and protective efforts, including enhanced IRS auditing programs, theft-deterrent systems, and good internal financial procedures. Consumer information services can help eliminate fraudulent business practices, and increases in both victim awareness and reporting can help target businesses and individuals responsible for various forms of white-collar or occupational crime.

Learn more about corporate responsibility and ethical business practices from the Interfaith Center on Corporate Responsibility and the Center for Business Ethics and Social Responsibility at **http://www.iccr.org** and **http://centers.scb.rit.edu/ethics/**; similar resources, including many government links, the American Institute of Certified Public Accountants' Antifraud and Corporate Responsibility Center, and the Carnegie Mellon Center for International Corporate Responsibility, can be found at **http://www.aicpa.org/interestareas/forensicandvaluation/resources/fraudpreventiondetectionresponse/pages/fraud-prevention-detection-response.aspx**. Links to various corporate codes of ethics can be found online at **http://www.ethicsweb.ca/resources/business/codes.html**. A discussion about deterring white-collar crime can be found at **http://ssrn.com/abstract=1001707**.

Organized Crime

Organized crime specifically refers to unlawful activities of the members of a highly organized, disciplined association engaged in supplying illegal goods and services, including prostitution, gambling, loan-sharking, narcotics, and labor racketeering. In 1967, the President's Commission on Law Enforcement and Administration of Justice investigated organized crime in the United States and found that—at the time—many organized crime families were of Italian descent. The Commission depicted the structure of a typical Italian American organized crime family as shown in Figure 13–3.

- **Mafia**   A criminal organization of Sicilian origin; also called La Cosa Nostra.
- **La Cosa Nostra**   A criminal organization of Sicilian origin; also call the Mafia. The term literally means "our thing."
- **ethnic succession**   The continuing process whereby one immigrant or ethnic group succeeds another by assuming its position in society.

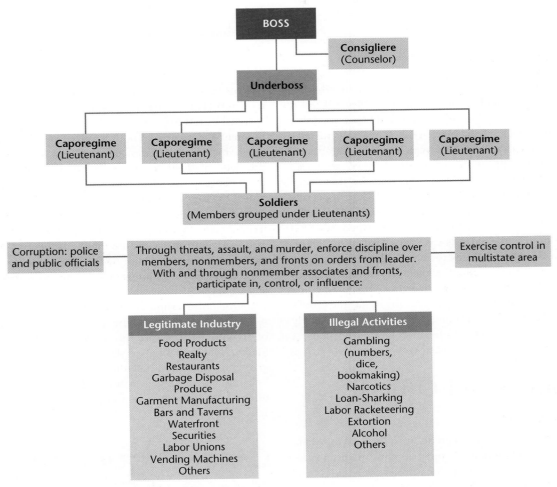

FIGURE 13-3 | A Typical Italian American Organized Crime Family

Source: Adapted from the President's Commission on Law Enforcement and Administration of Justice, *The Challenge of Crime in a Free Society* (Washington, DC: U.S. Government Printing Office, 1967), p. 47.

Much of what most Americans traditionally think of today as organized crime—sometimes called the **Mafia** or **La Cosa Nostra**—has roots that predate the establishment of the United States. For hundreds of years, secret societies have flourished in Italy.[69] Italian criminal organizations that came to the United States with the wave of European immigrants during the late nineteenth and early twentieth centuries included the Mafia and the Black Hand. The Black Hand (in Italian, *La Mano Negro*) "specialized in the intimidation of Italian immigrants,"[70] typically extorting protection money and valuables.

The Mafia worked to become a quasi-police organization in the Italian ghetto areas of the burgeoning American cities of the industrial era—often enforcing its own set of laws and codes. Secret societies in Italy were all but expunged during the 1930s and early 1940s under Fascist dictator Benito Mussolini. Surviving Mafia members became vehemently anti-Fascist, sentiments that endeared them to American and Allied intelligence services during World War II. Following the war, *mafioso* leaders resumed their traditional positions of power within Italian society, and links grew between American criminal organizations and those in Italy.

Other organized criminal groups, including Jewish and Irish gangs, flourished in New York City prior to the arrival of large numbers of Italian immigrants in the late 1800s. Ethnic succession has been as much a reality in organized crime as in most other aspects of American life. **Ethnic succession** refers to the continuing process whereby one immigrant or ethnic group succeeds another through assumption of a particular position in society.

■ **criminal enterprise**   A group of individuals with an identified hierarchy who are engaged in significant criminal activities.

Throughout the late nineteenth and early twentieth centuries, for example, Jewish gangsters such as Meyer Lansky, Benjamin "Bugsy" Siegel, "Dutch" Schultz, and Lepke Buchalter ran many of the "rackets" in New York City, only to have Italian immigrants who arrived a few years later take their places.

Around the middle of the twentieth century, organized criminal activity in the United States became the domain of Italian American immigrants and their descendants, especially those of Sicilian descent. Keep in mind that most Sicilians who immigrated to this country did not have ties or experience with Mafia organizations in the old country. Many Sicilian Americans immigrated to the United States to escape Mafia despotism at home, and most became productive members of their adopted society. The few who did involve themselves in organized crime created an organization known variously as the Mafia, the Outfit, the Mob, La Cosa Nostra ("our thing"), the syndicate, or simply the organization. Because *Mafia* is used most often, we will use it to describe Sicilian American organized criminal groups.

Prohibition and Official Corruption

In many ways, the advent of Prohibition was a godsend for Mafia leaders. Prior to Prohibition, Mafia operations in American cities were concerned mostly with gambling, protection rackets, and loan-sharking. Many *mafiosi*, however, were well versed in the manufacture of low-cost, high-proof, untaxed alcohol,[71] an expertise they had brought from their native country. In addition, the existing infrastructure of organized crime permitted easy and efficient entry into the running and sale of contraband liquor. The huge profits to be had from bootlegging led to the wholesale bribery of government officials and to the quick corruption of many law enforcement officers throughout the country. Nowhere was corruption more complete than in Chicago, where runners working for organized crime distributed illegal alcohol under police protection[72] and corrupt city government officials received regular payoffs from criminal cartels.

Activities of Organized Crime

The 1976 federal Task Force on Organized Crime identified five types of activity that may qualify as organized crime:

racketeering, vice operations, theft/fence rings, gangs, and terrorism. Throughout the past half century, Sicilian American criminal cartels have continued to be involved in (1) the establishment and control of both legalized and illicit forms of gambling, including lotteries, bookmaking, horse race wagering, and bets on athletic contests; (2) loan-sharking, which involves the lending of money at rates far higher than legally prescribed limits; (3) large-scale drug trafficking; (4) the fencing of stolen goods, including securities; (5) infiltration of legitimate businesses, including labor unions and corporations that can be used as quasi-legitimate fronts for money laundering and other activities; and (6) labor union racketeering through which legitimate businesses are intimidated by threats of strikes, walkouts, and sabotage.

Organized crime is involved in many kinds of rackets, including gambling and the illegal copying and distribution of copyrighted software, music, and other forms of recorded media. The provision of elaborately staged recorded pornographic productions, including "snuff movies" (in which a sex "star" is actually killed in front of the camera), and elements of child pornography can also be traced to organized criminal activity.

Other Organized Criminal Groups

The FBI defines a **criminal enterprise** as "a group of individuals with an identifiable hierarchy, and extensive supporting networks, engaged in significant criminal activity."[73] According to **Howard Abadinsky**, the hallmark of true criminal organizations is that they function independently of any of their members, including their leaders, and have continuity over time as personnel within them change.[74] Abadinsky mentioned the James Gang, which dissolved with the death of its leader, Jesse James. By contrast, says Abadinsky, "When Al Capone was imprisoned fifty years later, the 'Capone Organization' continued, and in its more modern form (the 'Outfit') it continues to operate in Chicago."[75]

The terms *organized crime* and *criminal enterprise* are closely related and are often used interchangeably, but various federal criminal statutes have specifically defined the elements of a criminal enterprise that need to be proven to convict

The terms *organized crime* and *criminal enterprise* are often used interchangeably. individuals or groups of individuals under those statutes. The federal Continuing Criminal Enterprise statute defines a *criminal enterprise* as any group of six or more people—with one of the six occupying an organizing, supervisory, or management position—that generates substantial income or resources and is engaged in a continuing series of violations of Subchapters I and II of Chapter 13 of Title 21 of the U.S. Code (Chapter 13 is that portion of federal law concerned with drug-abuse prevention and control).[76]

State laws defining criminal enterprise are generally more inclusive than federal statutes. The laws of New York, for example, stated that "the concept of criminal enterprise should not be limited to traditional criminal syndicates or crime families, and may include persons who join together in a criminal enterprise … for the purpose of corrupting … legitimate enterprises or infiltrating and illicitly influencing industries."[77] New York criminal statutes have defined *criminal enterprise* as "a group of persons sharing a common purpose of engaging in criminal conduct, associated in an ascertainable structure distinct from a pattern of criminal activity, and with a continuity of existence, structure and criminal purpose beyond the scope of individual criminal incidents."[78]

When people think of criminal enterprises, they often picture the Italian and Sicilian *mafioso* of popular television shows and movies, but the face of organized crime in the United States has changed, and its threat is broader and more complex than ever, with criminal enterprises of different origins. Some especially noteworthy groups include the following:

- Russian mobsters who fled to the United States in the wake of the Soviet Union's collapse
- Groups from African countries such as Nigeria that engage in drug trafficking and financial scams
- Chinese tongs, Japanese *Boryokudan*, and other Asian crime rings
- Enterprises based in Eastern European nations such as Hungary and Romania

Many organized crime groups of different nationalities currently operate in the United States. Many organized crime groups of different nationalities—including Eurasian, Balkan, Asian, African, and Middle Eastern—currently operate in the United States or are targeting U.S. citizens from afar using the Internet and other technologies; we will describe each of these (Figure 13–4).

FIGURE 13-4 | International Organized Criminal Groups Whose Activities Impact the United States

Eurasian Criminal Enterprises

The term *Eurasian organized crime* refers to organized crime groups comprising criminals born in or with family ties to the former Soviet Union or Central or Eastern Europe.[79] Eurasian organized crime in the United States is rooted in the *Vory V Zakone* (meaning "thieves in law"), career criminals who banded together for support and profit in the Soviet prison system; their leaders operated outside the official Soviet system and were illegally paid to acquire scarce consumer goods and to divert raw materials and finished goods from production lines for the benefit of *Nomenklatura* (the educated elite) and criminals.

With the collapse of the Soviet Union in 1991, members of the *Vory V Zakone* joined with corrupt public officials to acquire control of industries and resources that were being privatized, which gave the criminal syndicate a one-time infusion of wealth and supplied the infrastructure with continuing cash flows and opportunities to launder criminal proceeds. In February 1993, Boris Yeltsin, the first elected president of the Federation of Russian States, said, "Organized crime has become the No. 1 threat to Russia's strategic interests and to national security .... Corrupted structures on the highest level have no interest in reform."

Organized crime members first emerged in the West in the 1970s when so-called Soviet *Refuseniks* were allowed to immigrate to Europe, Israel, and the United States. Secreted among the *Refuseniks* were criminals who sought to exploit their newfound freedoms and helped major criminal groups expand to the West; when the Soviet Union collapsed, the people of the region were able to move about freely, many coming to join their criminal colleagues already in the United States and Western Europe.

In the United States, Eurasian criminal organizations are heavily involved in health-care fraud, auto insurance fraud, securities and investment fraud, money laundering, drug trafficking, extortion, auto theft, and interstate transportation of stolen property as well as human smuggling and prostitution.

Balkan Criminal Enterprises

The term *Balkan organized crime* applies to criminal enterprises originating from or operating in Albania, Bosnia-Herzegovina, Bulgaria, Croatia, Greece, Kosovo, the former Yugoslav Republic of Macedonia, Romania, and Serbia and Montenegro and is an emerging threat in the United States today. The FBI noted that although several of these groups are active in various cities across the country, "they do not yet exhibit the established criminal sophistication of traditional Eurasian or La Cosa Nostra (LCN) organizations."

Organized crime in the rural areas of the Balkans sprang from traditional clan structures, which had large familial ties for protection and mutual assistance. Starting in the fifteenth century, clan relationships operated under the *kanun* (code), which values loyalty and *besa*, or secrecy. Each clan established itself in specific territories and controlled the criminal activities and illicit interests there; the protection of these interests often led to violence between clans.

Years of communist rule led to black market activities in the Balkans, but the impact of those activities was mostly limited to the region. However, when Soviet-style communism collapsed in the late 1980s and early 1990s, Balkan organized crime activities expanded. Within the Balkans, organized crime groups infiltrated newly established democratic institutions, further expanding opportunities for criminal profits. Criminal markets once closed to Balkan groups suddenly opened, which led to the creation of an international criminal network.

Balkan criminal organizations have been active in the United States since the mid-1980s.[80] Initially, they were involved in low-level crimes, such as bank robberies, ATM burglaries, and home invasions. Later, ethnic Albanians affiliated themselves with established Mafia families in New York and acted as low-level participants; as their communities and presence became more established, they expanded their own organizations.

Balkan organized crime is not structured like the traditional Sicilian Mafia. The members brought their clanlike structure to the United States, meaning they are not clearly defined or organized, but instead are grouped around central leaders who maintain ties with the Balkan region while establishing close-knit communities in many cities across the nation. According to the FBI, "Albanian organized crime activities in the United States include gambling, money laundering, drug trafficking, human smuggling, extortion, violent witness intimidation, robbery, attempted murder, and murder" and are said to "have recently expanded into more sophisticated crimes including real estate fraud."[81] Learn more about Albanian organized crime in the United States at **http://www.justicestudies.com/pubs /albanian.pdf.**

Asian Criminal Enterprises

Asian criminal enterprises have been active in the United States since the early 1900s.[82] The first of these groups evolved from Chinese tongs—social organizations formed by early Chinese American immigrants. A century later, the criminalized tongs continue to thrive and have been joined by similar organizations with ties to East and Southeast Asia. The FBI has stated that "members of the most dominant Asian criminal enterprises affecting the United States have ties—either directly or culturally—to China, Korea, Japan, Thailand, the Philippines, Cambodia, Laos, and Vietnam."[83] Groups from the South Pacific island nations are also emerging as a threat.

Asian organized criminal groups rely on extensive networks of national and international criminal associates that are fluid and mobile, easily adapt to changes, have multilingual abilities, are sophisticated in their criminal operations, and have extensive financial capabilities. Some enterprises have commercialized their criminal activities and can be considered business firms, ranging from small family-run operations to large corporations.

Asian criminal enterprises have prospered due to communications technology, international travel, and the globalization of world economies. The FBI explained that "generous immigration policies have provided many members of Asian criminal enterprises the ability to enter and live on every populated continent in the world today undetected."[84]

Two categories of Asian criminal enterprises have been identified. Traditional criminal enterprises include the Chinese triads (or underground societies) based in Hong Kong, Taiwan, and Macau, as well as the Japanese *Yakuza* or *Boryokudan*; nontraditional criminal enterprises comprise criminally influenced Chinese tongs, triad affiliates, and other ethnic Asian street gangs found in several countries with sizable Asian communities.

Today's Asian criminal enterprises conduct traditional racketeering activities: extortion, murder, kidnapping, illegal gambling, prostitution, and loan-sharking. They also smuggle aliens, traffic in heroin and methamphetamine, commit financial fraud, steal automobiles and computer chips, produce counterfeit computer and clothing products, and launder money.

In this country, Asian criminal enterprises have been identified in more than 50 metropolitan areas but are more prevalent in Boston; Chicago; Honolulu; Las Vegas; Los Angeles; Newark; New Orleans; New York; Philadelphia; Portland; San Francisco; Seattle; and Washington, DC.

African Criminal Enterprises

African criminal enterprises have developed quickly since the 1980s due to advances in communications technology and the globalization of the world's economies.[85] Easier international travel, expanded world trade, and transnational financial transactions have enabled these groups to target international victims and to develop criminal networks within prosperous countries and regions. The political, social, and economic conditions in African countries such as Ghana, Liberia, and Nigeria also have helped some enterprises expand globally.

African criminal enterprises actively operate in several major metropolitan areas in the United States but are most prevalent in Atlanta; Baltimore; Chicago; Dallas; Houston; Milwaukee; Newark; New York; and Washington, DC. Nigerian criminal enterprises are the most significant group and operate in more than 80 countries around the world. The FBI stated that "they are among the most aggressive and expansionist international criminal groups and are primarily engaged in drug trafficking and financial frauds."[86]

The most profitable activity for Nigerian groups is drug trafficking, primarily the delivery of cocaine from South America into Europe and South Africa and heroin from Southeast and Southwest Asia into Europe and the United States. (Large populations of ethnic Nigerians in India, Pakistan, and Thailand have given them direct access to 90% of the world's heroin production.) Money laundering has also helped establish Nigerian criminal enterprises around the world.

Nigerian groups are famous for their financial frauds, which cost U.S. citizens, businesses, and government offices an estimated $1 billion to $2 billion each year. Their schemes are diverse: "insurance fraud involving auto accidents; health-care billing scams; life insurance schemes; bank, check, and credit card fraud; advance-fee schemes known as 4-1-9 letters; and document fraud to develop false identities." The Internet and e-mail have made such crimes even more profitable and prevalent.

Middle Eastern Criminal Enterprises

The FBI has pointed out "that some Middle Eastern criminal groups have no nexus to terror. Instead, these groups have the same goals as any traditional organized crime ring—to make

Kansas City pharmacist Robert R. Courtney, age 48, speaks to the court while partially obscured by his lawyer. In 2002, Courtney pleaded guilty to 20 felony counts charging him with the fraudulent distribution of diluted intravenous chemotherapy drugs to at least 34 patients. Other charges included tampering with consumer products, adulteration of drugs, and misbranding of drugs. Courtney, who is estimated to have made hundreds of thousands of dollars in the scheme, was caught when a drug salesman noticed that he was billing doctors for more medication than he was buying. His thirty-year prison sentence was upheld by the U.S. Court of Appeals for the Eighth Circuit. How does Sutherland's definition of *white-collar crime* apply in a case like this?

L. Eric Craven/Newscom

■ **transnational organized crime**   An unlawful activity undertaken and supported by organized criminal groups operating across national boundaries.

money through illegal activities."[87] Middle Eastern criminal enterprises originate from Afghanistan, Algeria, Bahrain, Egypt, India, Iran, Iraq, Israel, Jordan, Kuwait, Lebanon, Libya, Morocco, Oman, Pakistan, Qatar, Saudi Arabia, Syria, Tunisia, Turkey, United Arab Emirates, and Yemen.

Middle Eastern criminal groups have been active in the United States since the 1970s, tending to operate in areas with significant Middle Eastern or Southwest Asian populations; according to the FBI, they are most active in Illinois, Ohio, New Jersey, and New York.

The FBI explains that these enterprises engage in "automobile theft, financial fraud, money laundering, interstate transportation of stolen property, smuggling, drug trafficking, document fraud, health-care fraud, identity fraud, cigarette smuggling, and the theft and redistribution of infant formula."[88] They rely on extensive networks of international criminal associates and can be highly sophisticated in their criminal operations; internationally, they thrive in Afghanistan, Canada, Iran, Pakistan, Turkey, and the United Arab Emirates.

Suzanne Plunkett/AP Images

Georgiy Gleyzer being escorted from the federal building in New York City. Gleyzer was arrested in connection with Russian mob activities and charged with terrorizing citizens of Russian communities in New York. What is the likely future of Russian organized crime in the United States?

Transnational Organized Crime

Transnational organized crime, which refers to unlawful activity undertaken and supported by organized criminal groups operating across national boundaries, is emerging as one of the most pressing challenges of the early twenty-first century.[89]

Russian organized crime is of special interest because it has grown quickly following the collapse of the Soviet Union and because it has taken root in the United States and other countries outside the former Soviet sphere of influence.

With the dissolution of Soviet-style controls between 1992 and 1994, the Russian Mafia quickly seized control of the country's banking system through the investment of ill-gotten gains, money laundering, intimidation, fraud, murder, and the outright purchase of financial institutions. Ninety-five Russian bankers were murdered by *Mafiya* operatives between 1995 and 2000, and hundreds of reform-minded business leaders and investigative journalists have been assassinated or kidnapped.[90] In September 2006, Russian Central Bank deputy chairman Andrei Kozlov was fatally shot as he left a soccer stadium in Moscow. Kozlov had been a crusader against money laundering and had suspended or withdrawn the licenses of dozens of banks. After Kozlov's death, President Vladimir Putin created a task force to combat financial crime.

The Analytical Center for Social and Economic Policies, a Russian think tank, estimates that four out of every five Russian businesses pay protection money to the mob.[91] In response to the wave of organized crime that Russia is currently experiencing, more than 25,000 private security firms have sprung up throughout the country. Analysts say, however, that few of these firms are legitimate, with many being fronts for Russian gangsters.[92]

Russian organized criminals differ from their counterparts in the United States because their ranks consist largely of ex-KGB officers, veterans of the 1979–1989 war in Afghanistan, underpaid military officers, and former Communist Party operatives who formed powerful economic alliances with traditional gangsters and black marketers years ago. As some observers note, Russian organized crime seems to be a natural outgrowth of the corrupt practices of officials who operated in the days of strict Soviet control, combined with a huge underground criminal black market that had already developed a complex organizational structure long before the Soviet Union fell apart.[93]

While Russian organized crime profits from American-style activities such as narcotics, prostitution, racketeering, and illicit gambling, it is also heavily involved in human trafficking,

CRIME | in the NEWS

U.S. Authorities Grapple with the Rise of Transnational Criminal Organizations

A Few years ago, the National Intelligence Council completed a comprehensive assessment of transnational organized crime. The report concluded that transnational criminal activities had expanded dramatically in size, scope, and influence, and had begun to pose a significant threat to U.S. and international security.

Following up on the assessment, then-president Obama issued an executive order creating a new threat category, transnational criminal organizations (TCOs). It named four TCOs and directed the Treasury Department to freeze their U.S. assets. The acronym "TCO" is patterned after that for FTOs, the U.S. government's designation for foreign terrorist organizations. After the September 11, 2001, attacks, President George W. Bush used the same executive powers to block assets of persons aiding terrorists.

The four TCOs that were named are the Brothers' Circle in the former Soviet Union, the Camorra in Italy, the Yakuza in Japan, and the Los Zetas drug cartel in Mexico. The Treasury Department was authorized to add more TCOs to the list, and in 2012 the Treasury added MS-13, originally a Los Angeles street gang founded by immigrants from El Salvador. "These organizations facilitate and aggravate violent civil conflicts and increasingly facilitate the activities of other dangerous persons," the president said. "They are increasingly entrenched in the operations of foreign governments and the international financial system."

The National Strategy to Combat Transnational Organized Crime, a background document released along with the executive order, acknowledged that international criminal organizations had been around for years, but they were "largely regional in scope, hierarchically structured and had only occasional links to terrorism. Today's criminal networks are fluid, striking new alliances with other networks around the world and engaging in a wide range of illicit activities, including cybercrime, and providing support for terrorism."

By freezing the assets of TCOs, the U.S. government aimed "to squeeze them out of the global financial system and protect the U.S. financial system from laundering of its criminal proceeds," the department stated.

Discussion Questions

1. What are TCOs? How do they differ from traditional criminal organizations?

2. What kinds of international cooperation are needed to combat TCOs?

MS-13 gang members. In 2012, MS-13 was added to the list of large-scale transnational criminal organizations (TCOs) — allowing the U.S. Treasury Department to freeze the group's assets. What is a transnational criminal organization?

Neil Marriott/Photodisc/Getty Images

Sources: Howard LaFranchi, "MS-13 Gang Labeled Transnational Criminal Group, a First for US Street Gang," *Christian Science Monitor*, October 12, 2012, http://www.csmonitor.com/USA/Foreign-Policy/2012/1012/MS-13-gang-labeled-transnational-criminal-group-a-first-for-US-street-gang; Adam R. Pearlman, "Sanctions, Transnational Organized Crime," *The Federalist Society*, October 3, 2011, http://www.fed-soc.org/publications/detail/sanctions-transnational-organized-crime; and Robert Chesney, "Material Support to ... Transnational Criminal Organizations?" Lawfare Blog, July 25, 2011, http://www.lawfareblog.com/2011/07/material-support-to-transnational-criminal-organizations.

---

product diversion and counterfeiting of popular Western goods (including software, video, and music duplication), and illicit arms sales and smuggling on a massive scale.

Over the past decade or two, hundreds of thousands of Russian citizens have immigrated to the United States. As U.S. officials have now discovered, many of these people were former black market profiteers and hard-core offenders who had been released by the KGB from the Soviet gulag.[94]

Russian organized criminal groups today operate out of 17 American cities in 14 states. According to one source, "The FBI believes there are 15 separate organized crime groups and 4,000 hard-core Mafia criminals from the former Soviet Union at work in the United States They are engaged in money laundering, automobile theft, smuggling, contract murder, loan-sharking, medical insurance fraud, narcotics, and credit card and telecommunications fraud. The theft of electronic serial numbers

> The globalization of crime has necessitated the enhanced coordination of law enforcement efforts in different parts of the world.

from cellular phones and the duplication (cloning) of these PIN numbers have grown into a multimillion-dollar industry."[95]

The globalization of crime has necessitated the enhanced coordination of law enforcement efforts in different parts of the world and the expansion of American law enforcement activities beyond national borders. U.S. police agencies routinely send agents to assist law enforcement officers in other countries who are involved in transnational investigations.

■ **Racketeer Influenced and Corrupt Organizations (RICO) Act** A statute that is part of the federal Organized Crime Control Act of 1970 whose goal is to combat criminal conspiracies.

Organized Crime and the Law

For many years, American law enforcement agencies had few special weapons in the fight against organized crime. Instead, they prosecuted organized criminal operatives under statutes directed at solitary offenders, using laws such as those against theft, robbery, assault, gambling, prostitution, drug abuse, and murder. Innovative prosecutors at times drew upon other statutory resources in the drive to indict leaders of organized crime. On October 17, 1931, for example, Al Capone was convicted on various charges of income tax evasion after federal investigators were able to show that he had paid no taxes on an income in excess of $1 million. Laws regulating the sale of alcohol and drugs and statutes circumscribing acts of prostitution have also been used against organized criminals, although with varying degrees of success.

The first federal legislation aimed specifically at curtailing the activities of organized crime was the Hobbs Act, which encompassed a series of statutes that were passed beginning in 1946. In essence, the Hobbs Act made it a violation of federal law to engage in any form of criminal behavior that interferes with interstate commerce. It also criminalized interstate or foreign travel in furtherance of criminal activity and made it a crime to use the highways, telephone, or mail in support of activities such as gambling, drug trafficking, loan-sharking, and other forms of racketeering.

The single most important piece of federal legislation ever passed that specifically targets the activities of organized crime is the **Racketeer Influenced and Corrupt Organizations (RICO) Act**, which was part of the federal Organized Crime Control Act of 1970. The Organized Crime Control Act defines *organized crime* as "the unlawful activities of the members of a highly organized, disciplined association engaged in supplying illegal goods and services, including but not limited to gambling, prostitution, loansharking, narcotics, labor racketeering, and other unlawful activities of members of such organizations."[96] The RICO portion of the act brought under one single piece of legislation the many and diverse activities of American organized crime and made each punishable in a variety of new ways. RICO did not make racketeering itself illegal but, rather, focused on the ill-gotten gains derived from such activity, specifying that it will be unlawful for anyone involved in a pattern of racketeering to derive any income or proceeds from that activity.

Punishments provided for under RICO include **asset forfeiture**, which makes it possible for federal officials to seize the proceeds of those involved in racketeering. In the words of the statute, "Whoever violates any provision of this chapter shall be fined or imprisoned not more than 20 years (or for life if the violation is based on a racketeering activity for which the maximum penalty includes life imprisonment), or both, and shall forfeit to the United States, irrespective of any provision of State law any property derived from any proceeds that the person obtained, directly or indirectly, from racketeering activity or unlawful debt collection."[97] Hence, as a result of RICO, federal agents are empowered to seize the financial and other tangible fruits of organized criminal activity, including businesses, real estate, money, equities, gold and other commodities, vehicles (including airplanes and boats), and just about anything else that can be shown to have been acquired through a pattern of racketeering activity.

Policy Issues: The Control of Organized Crime

In a cogent analysis of organized crime, **Gary W. Potter** tells us that "the question of what we [should] do about organized crime is largely predicated on how we conceptualize [of] organized crime."[98] To understand organized crime and to deal effectively with it, according to Potter, we must study the social context in which it occurs. Such study reveals "that organized crime is simply an integral part of the social, political, and economic system,"[99] says Potter. Any effective attack on organized crime, therefore, would involve either meeting or eliminating the demands of the consumers of organized crime's products and services. Potter suggests that this can be accomplished by punishing the consumers more effectively and/or by educating them about the perils of their own behavior.

Fighting corruption in politics and among law enforcement personnel and administrators is another track Potter suggests in the battle against organized crime. If organized crime has been successful at least partially because it has been able to corrupt local politicians and enforcement agents, then, Potter asks, why not work to reduce corruption at the local level?

Howard Abadinsky recommends four approaches to the control of organized crime, each involving changes at the policy-making level:[100]

- Increase the risk of involvement in organized crime by increasing the resources available to law enforcement agencies that are useful in fighting organized crime.

- Increase law enforcement authority so as to increase the risks of involvement in organized crime. Money-laundering statutes that expand the scope of law enforcement authority, racketeering laws, and forfeiture statutes may be helpful in this regard.[101]

■ **asset forfeiture** The authorized seizure of money, negotiable instruments, securities, or other things of value. In federal antidrug laws, it is the authorization of judicial representatives to seize all monies, negotiable instruments, securities, and other things of value furnished or intended to be furnished by any person in exchange for a controlled substance, as well as all proceeds traceable to such an exchange.

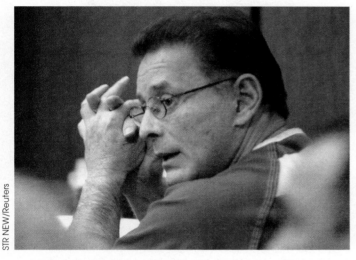

Salvatore "Sammy the Bull" Gravano, shown in court. He admitted to 19 murders and has been called the "most significant witness in the history of organized crime." How has La Cosa Nostra been impacted by witnesses like Gravano?

- Reduce the economic lure of involvement in organized crime by making legitimate opportunities more readily available. Educational programs, scholarships, job-training initiatives, and so on, might play a role in such a strategy.

- Decrease organized criminal opportunity through de-criminalization or legalization. This last strategy is perhaps the most controversial. It would decriminalize or legalize many of the activities from which organized crime now draws income, such as through state-run gambling and the ready and legitimate availability of narcotics.

Strict enforcement of existing laws is another option. This strategy has been used with considerable success by a number of federal and state law enforcement operations that have targeted organized crime. One of the most spectacular mob trials was that of John "Dapper Don" Gotti, who took over control of New York's Gambino crime family after orchestrating the murder of "Big Paul" Castellano in 1985. Over the years, Gotti had been arrested on many occasions and had been prosecuted at least five times for various offenses. His ability to escape conviction earned him the title

"Teflon Don." That changed on April 2, 1992, when Gotti was convicted on 13 federal charges, including murder and racketeering, and was sentenced to life in prison without the possibility of parole. Gotti's major mistake was personally participating in several executions, including that of Castellano. After Gotti went to prison, his son, John, Jr., took over control of the family, but in 1999, he pleaded guilty to charges of bribery, extortion, gambling, fraud, tax evasion, and loan-sharking and was sentenced to six and a half years in prison.[102] After being released from prison, John, Jr., was tried on a number of racketeering charges, resulting in three hung juries, and following his last trial, he vowed to leave New York, saying he might move his family to the Midwest or to Florida; his father died of cancer at a federal prison hospital in 2002 at the age of 61.

The senior Gotti's downfall came at the hands of Salvatore "Sammy the Bull" Gravano, a former underboss in the Gambino crime family. Gravano, who admitted to 19 murders, shared family secrets with federal investigators in return for leniency and succor through the federal witness protection program. Gravano spent days on the witness stand testifying against his former boss, and federal prosecutor Zachary Carter later called Gravano "the most significant witness in the history of organized crime."[103]

In 1997, Gravano again assumed center stage when he testified in federal district court in Brooklyn as the star prosecution witness in the murder and racketeering trial of Vincent Gigante, reputed head of the powerful Genovese crime family. Gravano was assailed by defense lawyers for being a notorious liar and for leading "a life of lies," facts he largely admitted in his best-selling book *Underboss*.[104] Although Gravano was sent to Phoenix, Arizona, under the witness protection program, he found it hard to lead a straight life. In 2000, he was arrested on three separate occasions on drug-running and money-laundering charges and was indicted by a New York federal grand jury and charged with financing and running a major Ecstasy drug ring in conjunction with an Israeli organized crime syndicate.[105]

Finally, in 2015, in a sign that traditional American organized crime remains active, "Goodfellas" mobster Vinny Asaro was acquitted of charges in the infamous 1978 Lufthansa heist. A jury also found Asaro, who had been known as "the ultimate tough guy," not guilty of murder and other serious charges.[106]

CRIMINAL | PROFILES

Bernie Madoff—Disgraced Financier

On July 24, 2009, convicted Ponzi schemer and formerly wealthy investment counselor Bernard (Bernie) Madoff arrived by prison bus at the federal correctional institution in Butner, North Carolina, to begin serving a 150-year sentence.[i] The 71-year-old Madoff had been convicted only days earlier of multiple fraud and securities violations stemming from a scheme in which he exploited thousands of clients who had entrusted him with their money for over 20 years. Among his victims were very wealthy people from places as diverse as New York City and Palm Beach, Florida.[ii]

Some estimates put losses to investors as high as $65 billion dollars—money that seemed to evaporate into thin air and that investigators struggled to recover. By the time Madoff went to prison, only about $1.2 billion had been found and insurance payments of around $500,000 had been made to investors.[iii] Madoff's scheme has been called "the largest investor fraud ever committed by a single person."[iv]

In fact, Madoff may not have invested any of his clients' money, instead paying off redemptions from his fund with money from new clients. The false account statements that Madoff issued to "investors" showed their accounts rapidly growing in value—outpacing the investment results of even the most savvy investment managers. The stock market downturn of 2008, however, led to a record number of redemption requests—and when Madoff was unable to meet them, the game was up.

Born Bernard Lawrence Madoff on April 29, 1938, in Queens, New York, Madoff began his adult life as a plumber; he also worked as a lifeguard and a landscaper. He soon went to college, graduating from New York's Hofstra University in 1960 with a degree in political science. A year later, he dropped out of Brooklyn Law School to become a stockbroker, eventually rising through the financial ranks to serve as a chairman of the NASDAQ stock exchange. In 1960, Madoff founded his own firm, Bernard L. Madoff Investment Securities, LLC. He served as chairman of that company until his arrest on December 11, 2008.

Doubts about Madoff preceded his arrest by at least ten years, as his firm had faced a number of investigations by the SEC, some of which had apparently been dropped by the SEC for lack of money. At the time of this writing, only one other person—Madoff's longtime accountant, David Friehling—has been charged in connection with the fraud, although authorities suspect that others must have been involved. Madoff refused to cooperate in the investigation, claiming that he was the only person with knowledge of the scam. Federal prosecutors reached a settlement with Madoff's wife under which she abandoned claims to $85 million in assets that the couple had owned, leaving her with $2.5 million in cash. The couple's sons, Mark and Andrew, both of whom had worked with their father, denied any claims of any wrongdoing. On the second anniversary of the day his father was arrested in the worst investment fraud in American history, Mark Madoff, 46, was found dead in the living room of his SoHo loft. He was hanging from a black dog leash while his two-year-old son slept nearby.

During the sentencing stage of the proceedings against him, the elder Madoff apologized to his victims, saying, "I have left a legacy of shame...to my family and my grandchildren. This is something I will live with for the rest of my life. I'm sorry."[v]

Disgraced financier Bernard Madoff leaving the federal court in Manhattan after appearing at a bail hearing on January 5, 2009, in New York City. Madoff was convicted of operating a Ponzi scheme that bilked investors out of $50 billion. He is currently serving a 150-year sentence at the medium-security Federal Correctional Institution in Butner, North Carolina. Some people thought that his sentence was too harsh; others that it was too lenient. What do you think?

Kristin Callahan/Everett Collection/Alamy Stock Photo

The case of Bernie Madoff raises a number of interesting questions. Among them are the following:

1. Do you think that Madoff originally set out to build a Ponzi scheme? If not, how might the scheme have evolved?

2. How do the crimes of Madoff differ from the criminal activities of other offenders discussed in criminal profile boxes throughout this book? In what way might they be the same?

3. Do the theories of criminal behavior that this book discusses seem as applicable to white-collar criminals, like Bernie Madoff, as they do to other offenders who commit crimes of violence? If so, what theoretical approach might explain Madoff's behavior?

4. How would you compare Madoff to other white-collar criminals? What do they have in common?

Notes

i. Zachery Kouwe, "Madoff Arrives at Federal Prison in North Carolina," New York Times, July 14, 2009, http://www.nytimes.com/2009/07/15/business/15madoff.html (accessed July 21, 2009).

ii. Michael Moore, "Bernie Madoff," The 2009 TIME 100, http://www.time.com/time/specials/packages/article/0,28804,1894410_1893837_1894189,00.html (accessed July 20, 2009).

iii. "The Ticker," Washington Post, July 14, 2009; and Elizabeth Dwoskin, "Bernie Madoff's Accountant Charged, Pleads Not Guilty," The Village Voice, July 17, 2009, http://blogs.villagevoice.com/runninscared/archives/2009/07/bernie_madoffs.php (accessed July 21, 2009).

iv. "Topic: Bernard Madoff," New York Post (various dates), http://www.nypost.com/topics/topic.php?t=Bernard_Madoff (accessed August 12, 2009). During the sentencing stage of the proceedings against him, the elder Madoff apologized to his victims, saying, "I have left a legacy of shame...to my family and my grandchildren. This is something I will live with for the rest of my life. I'm sorry."[v]

v. "Transcript of Madoff's Sentencing Statement," New York Post, June 29, 2009, http://www.nypost.com/seven/06292009/news/regionalnews/partial_transcript_of_madoffs_sentencing_176718.htm (accessed August 12, 2009).

SUMMARY

- White-collar crime is not unique to the twenty-first century. Financial scandals have a long and ubiquitous history in the United States, sometimes even involving government regulators. The insider-trading scam of stock market tycoon Ivan Boesky and the securities fraud conviction of junk-bond king Michael Milken in the 1980s demonstrated again how fortunes could be amassed through white-collar law violations. The past two decades have seen a number of infamous white-collar crime prosecutions, including those involving executives at the former energy-trading giant Enron Corporation, which had used complex off-balance-sheet partnerships to hide losses and inflate revenues.

- This chapter distinguishes between white-collar, occupational, corporate, and organized crime. White-collar crimes can be further broken down into antitrust violations, bank fraud, bankruptcy fraud, economic espionage, embezzlement, environmental law violations, government fraud, health-care fraud, insider trading, insurance fraud, kickbacks, mail fraud, securities fraud, tax evasion, and wire fraud.

- Corporate crimes, or corporate malfeasance, come in many forms, ranging from prior knowledge about dangerous automobile defects to price fixing and insider securities trading. Businesses may be charged with corporate crimes for the acts of their corporate officers, as can individuals for legal wrongs committed in their corporate capacity.

- White-collar criminals have many of the same motivations as do other criminals, and criminologists generally agree that white-collar crime, like other crime, is learned. Although white-collar criminals may not be directly dangerous to the health and physical well-being of their victims, they are motivated by the same forces that drive other criminals: self-interest, the pursuit of pleasure, and the avoidance of pain. Other authors have held that white-collar criminals are motivated by a disparity between corporate goals and the limited opportunities available to businesspeople through conventional business practices.

- White-collar and organized crimes are often difficult to investigate and prosecute. Nonetheless, the U.S. SEC has renewed efforts to enforce existing regulations and has mandated new rules for investment bankers. The now-defunct U.S. DOJ's Corporate Fraud Task Force, the Obama administration's Financial Fraud Enforcement Task Force, the 2002 Sarbanes-Oxley Act, and RICO statutes all provided law enforcers with new tools to fight white-collar and organized crime.

- Much of what most Americans traditionally think of today as organized crime—sometimes called the Mafia or La Cosa Nostra—has roots that predate the establishment of the United States and extend to secret societies that have flourished in Italy for hundreds of years. Other organized criminal groups, including Jewish and Irish gangs, flourished in New York City prior to the arrival of large numbers of Italian immigrants in the late 1800s, and ethnic succession has been as much a reality in organized crime as it has in most other aspects of American life. The huge profits to be had from bootlegging under Prohibition in the United States led to the wholesale bribery of government officials and to the quick corruption of many law enforcement officers throughout the country. The activities of organized crime include the establishment and control of both legalized and illicit forms of gambling; loan-sharking; large-scale drug trafficking; the fencing of stolen goods (including securities); the infiltration of legitimate businesses, including labor unions and corporations; labor union racketeering; and other crimes.

- A criminal enterprise is a group of individuals with an identifiable hierarchy, and extensive supporting networks, engaged in significant criminal activity. Some of the most important criminal gangs operating in the United States today are Eurasian criminal enterprises such as the *Vory V Zakone*, Balkan organized criminal groups, Asian criminal enterprises such as the *Yakuza*, African criminal groups, and Middle Eastern criminal enterprises.

- Transnational organized crime refers to unlawful activity undertaken and supported by organized criminal groups operating across national boundaries. Transnational organized crime is emerging as one of the most pressing challenges of the twenty-first century.

- The first federal legislation aimed specifically at curtailing the activities of organized crime was the Hobbs Act, which encompassed a series of statutes that were passed beginning in 1946. The single most important piece of federal legislation ever passed that specifically targets the activities of organized crime, however, is the Racketeer Influenced and Corrupt Organizations (RICO) Act, which was part of the federal Organized Crime Control Act of 1970.

- Organized crime is an integral part of the social, political, and economic systems in our society. As such, any effective attack on organized crime would involve meeting or eliminating the demands of the consumers of organized crime's products and services.

KEY TERMS

asset forfeiture, 376	insider trading, 355
bank fraud, 355	La Cosa Nostra, 369
corporate crime, 358	Mafia, 369
corporate fraud, 359	money laundering, 363
criminal enterprise, 370	occupational crime, 357
environmental crimes, 363	organized crime, 368
ethnic succession, 369	Ponzi scheme, 360
green criminology, 364	

Racketeer Influenced and
Corrupt Organizations
(RICO) Act, 376

Sarbanes–Oxley Act, 367

securities and commodities
fraud, 360

securities fraud, 355

transnational organized
crime, 374

welfare fraud, 362

white-collar crime, 355

KEY NAMES

Howard Abadinsky, 370

John Braithwaite, 366

Herbert Edelhertz, 357

Gilbert Geis, 357

Michael Gottfredson, 366

Gary S. Green, 357

Travis Hirschi, 366

Gary W. Potter, 376

Edwin H. Sutherland, 355

QUESTIONS FOR REVIEW

1. What are some examples of white-collar crime in American history?

2. What is white-collar crime? How did the idea of white-collar crime develop in the criminological literature?

3. What is corporate crime? How does corporate crime differ from white-collar crime, if at all?

4. What are some of the causes of white-collar crime? How do white-collar criminals differ from other offenders?

5. How can white-collar and corporate crime be controlled?

6. What is organized crime? How does it differ from white-collar crime?

7. What are some international criminal enterprises that this chapter discusses? What kinds of activities do they engage in?

8. What transnational organized criminal groups does this chapter identify? How do their activities differ from those of traditional organized crime families?

9. Identify federal statutes and other initiatives that target organized crime.

10. What strategies does this chapter discuss for combating the activities of organized crime?

QUESTIONS FOR REFLECTION

1. What linkages, if any, might exist between white-collar and organized crime?

2. What types of white-collar crime has this chapter identified? Is corporate crime a form of white-collar crime? Is occupational crime a form of white-collar crime?

3. How would you describe a typical "traditional" organized crime family, as outlined in this chapter? Why does a crime family contain so many different "levels"?

4. What is money laundering? How might money laundering be reduced or prevented? Can you think of any strategies this chapter does not discuss for the reduction of money-laundering activities in the United States? If so, what are they?

CHAPTER 14

DRUG AND SEX CRIMES

Recreational Offenses

LEARNING OUTCOMES

After reading this chapter, you should be able to answer the following questions:

- What can be said about the history of drugs, and drug abuse, in the United States?
- What are the various categories of controlled substances described by federal law, and what is a dangerous drug?

- How can drug addiction be understood?
- What is drug trafficking, and what efforts are being made to curtail it?
- What government strategies have been used to reduce the incidence of drug use in the United States?
- What is prostitution, and what are the various types of prostitutes identified in this chapter?

■ **victimless crimes**   Illegal activities that involve willing participants. Although direct and immediate victimization may not occur in victimless crimes, social and personal costs are frequently associated with such activities.

■ **Follow the author's tweets about the latest crime and justice news @schmalleger.**
■ **psychoactive substance**   A substance that affects the mind, mental processes, or emotions.

Introduction

In 2016, the Drug Enforcement Administration released it's Heroin Threat Assessment report.[1] That document showed that deaths from heroin overdose have increased more than 300% over the past few years—with the largest increases occurring in both rural and urban areas of the Mid-Atlantic, New England, and the midwest. Reasons for the dramatic upswing in deaths are thought to include an overall increase in heroin users; high purity batches of heroin now being sold in certain markets; an increase in new heroin initiates; the abuse of prescription opioids; and the use of highly toxic heroin adulterants such as fentanyl. In response to increased heroin and opiod overdoses, many law enforcement agencies now offer training in the administration of Naloxone—a drug that can reverse the effects of opioid overdose.

  This chapter is about drug and sex crimes—particularly those where the people involved are voluntary participants. Such crimes have sometimes been called victimless. **Victimless crimes** are, however, not necessarily without victims, as in the case of a child who suffers because his or her parents are too drug-involved to provide proper care. Just such a thing happened in 2017 to a 9-year-old Cincinnati, Ohio, girl who found herself in a locked car with parents who had passed out from heroin overdoses. Although too small to disable the child locks on the car's doors, she was able to use her cellphone to call her grandmother who sent rescuers to the scene.

History of Drug Abuse in the United States

The rampant, widespread use and abuse of mind- and mood-altering drugs, so commonplace in the United States today, is of relatively recent origin. Throughout the 1800s and early 1900s, the use of illegal drugs in America was mostly associated with artistic individuals and fringe groups and was almost exclusively confined to small groups of musicians, painters, poets, and other highly imaginative individuals seeking to enhance their creativity. One significant exception existed in the form of opium dens, which flourished in West Coast cities and eventually made their way across the country as a result of increased Asian immigration; some Chinese immigrants had brought

ZUMA Archive/ZUMAPRESS/Newscom

The herbal marijuana substitute Spice, or K2. Why are illegal drugs so pervasive in American society?

opium products with them and introduced other segments of the American population to opium smoking.

  Psychoactive substances (substances affecting mental processes and emotions) gained widespread acceptance during the hippie movement during the late 1960s and early 1970s, which was characterized by slogans like "If it feels good, do it" and "Tune in, turn on, drop out," promoting free love, personal freedom, experimentation with subjective states of consciousness, and "mind expansion."

  One influential figure in the drug-inspired movement of the times was Harvard professor Timothy Leary, who formed the League of Spiritual Discovery in the mid-1960s, "an orthodox, psychedelic religion that permits the use of LSD and marijuana as sacraments by League members."[2] With the advent of the hippie era, marijuana, lysergic acid diethylamide (LSD), hashish, psilocybin, and peyote burst on the national scene as an ever-growing number of individuals began to view drugs as recreational substances and as more and more young people identified with the tenor of the period.

Extent of Drug Abuse

Data on drug abuse in the United States are available through a variety of sources, such as the *Monitoring the Future* (MTF) study, conducted by the University of Michigan's Institute for Social

■ **National Survey on Drug Use and Health (NSDUH)** A national survey of illicit drug use among people 12 years of age and older that is conducted annually by the Substance Abuse and Mental Health Services Administration.

A smoker in an opium den in Chinatown, San Francisco, circa 1925. How have American attitudes toward drugs changed over time?

Research with funding from the National Institute on Drug Abuse at the National Institutes of Health; the **National Survey on Drug Use and Health (NSDUH)**, conducted annually by the Substance Abuse and Mental Health Services Administration (SAMHSA); the National Narcotics Intelligence Consumers Committee *NNICC Report*, published

> The annual National Survey on Drug Use and Health is conducted by the Substance Abuse and Mental Health Services Administration.

in conjunction with the Drug Enforcement Administration (DEA); the National Institute of Justice (NIJ) quarterly Arrestee Drug Abuse Monitoring Program report; the Office of National Drug Control Policy (ONDCP) *Pulse Check: National Trends in Drug Abuse*, which reports at least once a year on drug-use trends; and annual reports published by SAMHSA's Drug Abuse Warning Network.

According to NSDUH data released in 2017, an estimated 28.6 million Americans aged 12 or older were current (past month) illicit drug users, meaning they had used an illicit drug during the month prior to the survey interview (Figure 14-1). This estimate represents 10.6% of the population aged 12 or older. Illicit drugs include marijuana/hashish, cocaine (including crack), heroin, hallucinogens, inhalants, or prescription-type psychotherapeutics used nonmedically. The report describes the

number and percentage of persons aged 12 or older who were current users of specific drugs in 2016 as follows:[3]

- Marijuana was the most commonly used illicit drug, with 24 million current users (or 8.9% of the American population aged 12 or older).
- About 475,000 people aged 12 or older were current heroin users in 2016.
- 6.2 million persons (2.3% of the population) were nonmedical users of prescription-type psychotherapeutic drugs, including 3.3 million users of pain relievers, 2.0 million users of tranquilizers, 1.7 million users of stimulants, and 497,000 users of sedatives (Figure 14-2).
- 3.3 million misused prescription pain relievers.
- 2.0 million (0.7%) were current users of cocaine.
- Hallucinogens were used in the past month by 1.4 million persons (0.5%) aged 12 or older.
- The overall rate of current illicit drug use among persons aged 12 or older in 2016 was 10.6%.
- In 2016, the rate of illicit drug use was highest among young adults aged 18 to 25 (23.2%).

The amount and type of drug used varies by region of the country. Figure 14-3 shows the percent of the population that regularly uses marijuana by state. Similarly, the NSDUH survey found that substance-abuse rates are highly correlated with

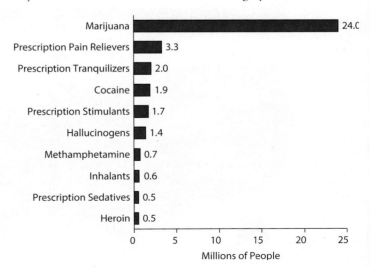

FIGURE 14-1 | **Past-Month Illicit Drug Use among Persons Ages 12 and Older by Type of Drug, 2016**

Source: Substance Abuse and Mental Health Services Administration, *2016 National Survey on Drug Use and Health* (Rockville, MD: SAMHSA, 2017).

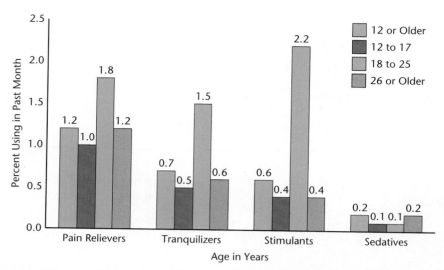

FIGURE 14-2 | Past-Month Misuse of Prescription Pain Relievers, Tranquilizers, Stimulants, and Sedatives among People Aged 12 or Older, by Age Group, 2016

Source: Substance Abuse and Mental Health Services Administration, *2016 National Survey on Drug Use and Health* (Rockville, MD: SAMHSA, 2017).

educational status: Among young adults 18 years and older, those who had not completed high school had the highest rate of abuse (11.8%), whereas college graduates had the lowest rate of abuse (6.7%), despite the fact that adults who had completed four years of college were more likely to have tried illicit drugs in their lifetime than adults who had not completed high school. Hence, it appears that the more education a person receives, the more likely he or she is to discontinue using drugs with age.

If NSDUH results are accurate, they would seem to indicate that drug abuse is now somewhat less of a problem than it was two decades ago. In 1979, the number of current illicit drug users was at its highest level, when estimates of current users reached 25 million; the largest ever annual estimate of marijuana use put routine users at 22.5 million in 1979,

and the greatest cocaine use was estimated at 5.3 million in 1985—figures that are greater than those of today. Growth of the American population over time gives the estimated decline even greater weight.

There are some methodological problems associated with any nationwide survey, and in recognition of these problems, NSDUH authors wrote, "Sample size, coverage, and validity problems are likely to be more pronounced for NSDUH estimates of heavy users than for other measures generated by the survey. Therefore, estimates of heavy use are considered conservative, and changes over time are generally not statistically significant.... Clearly there is considerable uncertainty about the size of the heavy drug-using population."[4] Read the latest NSDUH report at **www.justicestudies.com/pubs/nsduh2016.pdf**.

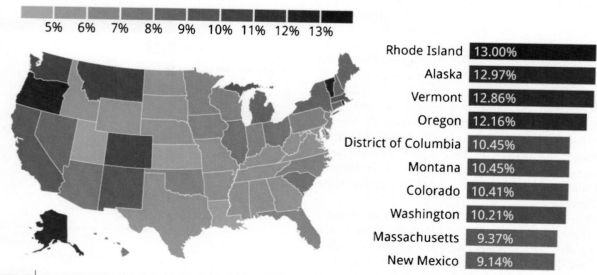

FIGURE 14-3 | The Percentage of the Population Using Marijuana in the Past Month, by State

Source: Niall McCarthy, "Tiny Rhode Island is America's Marijuana Capital," Statista, August 7, 2014. http:// www.statista.com/chart /2545/americas-marijuana-capital.

MTF researchers noted that in the late twentieth century, illicit drug use among young Americans had reached very high levels. In 1975, when the MTF survey began, the majority of young people (55%) reported having used an illicit drug by the time they left high school, and this figure rose to two-thirds (66%) by 1981 before a long and gradual decline to 41% by 1992, the low point. After 1992, the proportion rose again, reaching a high of 55% in 1999 and stood at 50% in 2013.[5]

> In the late twentieth century, drug use among young Americans reached very high levels.

Because marijuana use is much more common than that of any other illicit drug, trends in marijuana use significantly influence the index of "any illicit drug use" reported by the survey. In 1975, over one-third (36%) of 12th-graders had tried some illicit drug other than marijuana, a figure that rose to 43% by 1981 and then declined for a long period to a low of 25% in 1992. Some increases followed in the 1990s as the use of a number of drugs rose steadily, reaching 30% by 1997; then the rate fell to around 14% in 2016. Although the use of marijuana declined in 2016, marijuana attitudes among students continued to move toward greater acceptance.

Perhaps the most striking finding in 2016 was that across the broad spectrum of drugs (more than 50 classes and subclasses), most decreased and hardly any exhibited a statistically significant increase. In many cases, these decreases in use were continuing the declines seen in 2014 and 2015. Cigarettes and alcohol continued to show significant declines, reaching their lowest levels in the history of the study. With regard to illicit drugs, annual prevalence declined in all three grades that were studied (8th, 10th, and 12th). The same was true for the combined use of any illicit drug, including marijuana, synthetic marijuana, MDMA (ecstasy, Molly), cocaine, crack, amphetamines, methamphetamine, heroin, Rohypnol, some psychotherapeutic drugs used without medical supervision (Vicodin, tranquilizers), and steroids.

Since the MTF survey began in 1975, between 83 and 90% of the members of every senior class have said they could get marijuana "fairly easily" or "very easily" if they wanted some, so marijuana has remained a highly accessible drug. Since 1991, when data became available for 8th- and 10th-graders, marijuana has become considerably less accessible to younger adolescents; however, in 2016, one-third of 8th graders, two-thirds of 10th graders, and 86% of 12th graders reported it as being easy or very easy to get.

Walt Weis/AP Images

Dr. Timothy Leary, guru of the 1960s psychedelic movement. Leary died in 1996, and his ashes were shot into space a year later. What was Leary's message?

Young People and Drugs

While NSDUH data provided a picture of drug abuse among all those 12 years of age and older, the National Institute on Drug Abuse's MTF study supplied data on drug abuse among junior high school and high school students, tracking 12th-graders' illicit drug use, their perceived availability of drugs, and their attitudes toward drugs since 1975; in 1991, 8th- and 10th-graders were added to the survey. The 2016 survey gathered responses from about 45,000 students in close to 400 schools across the nation about lifetime use, past-year use, past-month use, and daily use of drugs, alcohol, cigarettes, and smokeless tobacco. For access to the full 2016 MTF data describing the use of many other drugs, including inhalants, visit **http:// monitoringthefuture.org//pubs/monographs/mtf -overview2016.pdf**. Similarly, the Harvard School of Public Health's College Alcohol Study provides a great deal of information on alcohol and abuse—especially about college students and binge drinking. Publications produced by the study can be found at **http://archive.sph.harvard.edu/cas.**

■ **Office of National Drug Control Policy (ONDCP)**   A national office charged by Congress with establishing policies, priorities, and objectives for the nation's drug-control program. The ONDCP is responsible for annually developing and disseminating the National Drug-Control Strategy.

Costs of Drug Abuse

The **Office of National Drug Control Policy (ONDCP)** estimates that Americans annually spend around $103 billion to purchase illegal drugs. (See Figure 14-4.) The true costs of drug abuse, however, are difficult to measure, but a 2011 report by the National Drug Intelligence Center (NDIC) placed the total annual cost of illicit drug abuse in the United States at $193 billion.[6] As Figures 14-5, 14-6, and 14-7 show, the NDIC breaks down that amount into direct and indirect costs, including direct justice system costs ($109,498,643,000), indirect health-care costs ($11,416,232,000), and indirect costs of lost productivity due to drug abuse ($72,182,055,000).

Although the NDIC report is comprehensive, it still might not include all of the social costs associated with drug abuse. Many cases of acquired immunodeficiency syndrome (AIDS), for example, can be traced to intravenous drug use, and AIDS/HIV has proved to be a costly disease in social terms. Researchers at the Centers for Disease Control and Prevention (CDC) say that AIDS/HIV is the leading cause of death of black and Hispanic men aged 25 to 44. AIDS/HIV, says the CDC, has become the second leading cause of death among black women aged 25 to 44. The CDC says that 47% of HIV infection among minority women is traceable

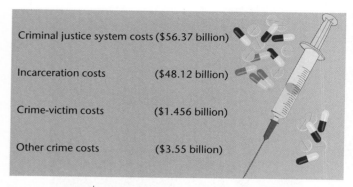

FIGURE 14-5 | **Annual Direct Costs of Illegal Drug Use in the United States: Justice System and Victimization**

Note: Annual criminal justice system amounts due to drug abuse total $109,498,643,000. They include the costs associated with investigation, arrest, adjudication, and parole and probation, plus the costs of incarceration, which are shown separately.
Source: National Drug Intelligence Center, *The Economic Impact of Illicit Drug Use on American Society* (Washington, DC: U.S. Department of Justice, 2011).

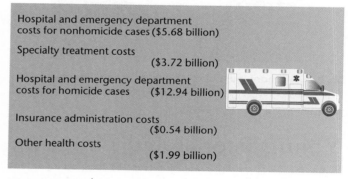

FIGURE 14-6 | **Annual Indirect Costs of Illegal Drug Use in the United States: Health Care**

Note: Annual health-care costs due to drug abuse total $11,416,232,000.
Source: National Drug Intelligence Center, *The Economic Impact of Illicit Drug Use on American Society* (Washington, DC: U.S. Department of Justice, 2011).

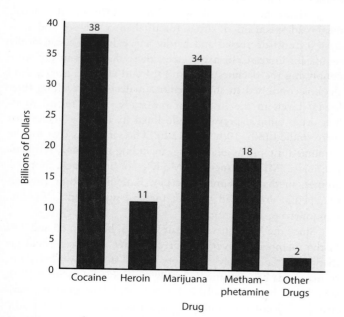

FIGURE 14-4 | **The Annual Amount Spent on Illegal Drugs in the United States**

Source: Office of National Drug Control Policy, *Drug Data Summary* (Washington, DC: ONDCP, 2012). Figures are estimates due to difficulty in obtaining current and accurate data from illicit users.

to intravenous drug use, whereas 37% appears to be due to heterosexual intercourse. Still, the hidden impact of sexual intercourse with intravenous drug users is not entirely clear. In the words of the CDC: "Sharing syringes and other equipment for drug injection is a well known route of HIV transmission, yet injection drug use contributes to the epidemic's spread far beyond the

The proportion of HIV infection among minority women traceable to intravenous drug use is 47%.

■ **controlled substances** Chemical substances or drugs as defined under the 1970 federal Controlled Substances Act.

■ **dangerous drug** A controlled substance other than cocaine, opiates, and cannabis products. Amphetamines, LSD, methamphetamines, methcathinone, and phencyclidine (PCP), as well as synthetic drugs, are all considered dangerous drugs.

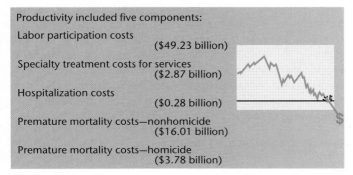

Productivity included five components:

Labor participation costs
($49.23 billion)

Specialty treatment costs for services
($2.87 billion)

Hospitalization costs
($0.28 billion)

Premature mortality costs—nonhomicide
($16.01 billion)

Premature mortality costs—homicide
($3.78 billion)

FIGURE 14-7 | **Annual Indirect Costs of Illegal Drug Use in the United States: Lost Productivity**

Note: Annual costs of lost productivity due to drug abuse total $72,182,055,000. Source: National Drug Intelligence Center, The Economic Impact of Illicit Drug Use on American Society (Washington, DC: U.S. Department of Justice).

circle of those who inject. People who have sex with an injection drug user (IDU) also are at risk for infection through the sexual transmission of HIV. Children born to mothers who contracted HIV through sharing needles or having sex with an IDU may become infected as well."[7]

Types of Illegal Drugs

The DEA identifies seven major categories of "dangerous drugs": stimulants, depressants, cannabis, narcotics, hallucinogens, anabolic steroids, and inhalants, while the 1970 Controlled Substances Act (CSA) includes five "schedules" of illegal drugs. Table 14-1 shows the five schedules of **controlled substances**, the criteria for inclusion of a drug under each schedule, a list of drugs in each schedule, and street names for drugs.

TABLE 14-1 | Controlled Substances under the Federal Controlled Substances Act

SCHEDULE	DESCRIPTION OF SCHEDULE	DRUGS IN SCHEDULE	STREET NAMES
I	• high potential for abuse • no currently accepted medical use in the United States • lacks accepted safety standards for use under medical supervision	marijuana, heroin, opioids, hallucinogenic substances, peyote, mescaline, gamma-hydroxybutyric acid (GHB), and others	pot, weed, grass, reefer, joint, angel dust, horse
II	• high potential for abuse • currently accepted for medical use • may lead to severe psychological or physical dependence	cocaine, opium, oxycodone, methadone, morphine, Seconal, methamphetamine, Adderall, and other amphetamines	snow, crack, coke, meth, speed, uppers
III	• potential for abuse less than the drugs or other substances in Schedules I and II • currently accepted for medical use • may lead to moderate or low physical dependence or high psychological dependence	anabolic steroids, ketamine, hydrocodone, and a number of barbiturates and sedatives	downers, goof balls, yellow jackets
IV	• lower potential for abuse relative to the drugs or other substances in Schedule III • currently accepted for medical use • may lead to limited physical dependence or psychological dependence relative to the drugs or other substances in Schedule III	some antidiarrheal drugs; some partial opioid analgesics; some sleeping pills such as Zolpidem; long-acting barbiturates; and benzodiazepines such as Xanax, Librium, and Valium	blues, peaches, bars, zombie pills, no-go-pills, A-minus
V	• low potential for abuse relative to the drugs or other substances in Schedule IV • currently accepted for medical use • may lead to limited physical dependence or psychological dependence relative to the drugs or other substances in Schedule IV	some cough suppressants, anticonvulsants, and selected prescription pain pills	

PUTTING CRIMINOLOGY TO WORK—Implementing Evidence-Based Policy

Throughout this text there are a number of boxes like this one. Each of them describes a program or practice that has been found effective at fighting crime—or which appears to hold future promise. The programs and practices identified in these boxes have been evaluated by the National Institute of Justice (NIJ), and details about them can be found on the NIJ's Website at CrimeSolutions.Gov.

This box is different in that it describes a website devoted to identifying what works in drug prevention and drug intervention, as well as programs that have been evaluated for their effectiveness in the mental health arena. That site, the National Registry of Evidence-based Programs and Practices (NREPP), is run and maintained by the Substance Abuse and Mental Health Services Administration (SAMHSA)—a federal agency dedicated to helping people with mental health, substance abuse, and drug addiction issues.

To date, over 400 programs have been listed on the NREPP site, and each is rated as "effective," "promising," or "ineffective." One such program is described in the remainder of this box.

PROGRAM: AlcoholEdu for College

EVIDENCE RATING FOR OUTCOMES: Effective for alcohol use disorders.

PROFILE

AlcoholEdu for College is an online alcohol education, misuse prevention, and harm reduction course for undergraduate students in colleges and universities. The course takes 2 to 3 hours to complete and is delivered in two parts. The course uses a multimedia approach, including text with graphics, video streaming, and interactive Web pages to deliver course material.

The first part of the course includes a baseline survey and four modules: Introduction, Getting the Facts, Deciding for Yourself, and Review and Exam. Some of these interactive modules adapt the information being provided to students, based on student responses. The first module gives an overview of the course and illustrates standard sizes of alcoholic drinks. The second module reviews students' perception of college-drinking norms; analyzes the effects of alcohol on the brain and body, including blood-alcohol concentration; and provides information on local alcohol laws and policies. In the third module, students develop a personal plan with academic, social, and health-related goals for the next year

Source: Adapted from **http://nrepp.samhsa.gov/ProgramProfile.aspx?id=9**

and select from various harm-reduction approaches to help achieve those goals. The final module reviews course material and includes a course exam that provides students with feedback on their answers.

Students are emailed the second part of the course 30–45 days later, which includes a review of the previous material, a module for revising the student's personal plan, material on managing stress and recognizing alcohol misuse, and a follow-up survey. Learn more about the program at **http://everfi.com/higher-education-old/alcoholedu**. A recorded Webinar that features eight studies demonstrating the effectiveness of AlcoholEdu can be viewed at **https://vimeo.com/168264054**.

Relevant Theory: Learning Theory

Social learning theory (discussed in Chapter 8) says that all behavior is learned. That's true for conforming, deviant, and criminal behavior. Because most learning occurs through association with others, human behavior is a product of the social environment, not an innate characteristic of particular individuals. The AlcoholEdu program facilitates learning by teaching students to understand the personal and social consequences of alcohol use and abuse. That teaching includes strategies that can be applied to avoid overindulgence in alcohol.

Evidence-Based Review

After a one-month assessment period, students in the AlcoholEdu group reported a statistically significant reduction in alcohol use involvement compared with students in the assessment-only control group. The following sources were used in the development of this practice profile:

J. T. P. Hustad, N. P. Barnett., B. Borsari, and K. M. Jackson, "Web-based alcohol prevention for incoming college students: A randomized controlled trial," *Addictive Behaviors*, Vol. 35 (2010), pp. 183–189.

M. J. Paschall, T. Antin, C. L. Ringwalt, and R. F. Saltz, "Effects of AlcoholEdu for College on alcohol-related problems among freshmen: A randomized multicampus trial," *Journal of Studies on Alcohol and Drugs*, Vol. 72 (2011), pp. 642–650.

M. J. Paschall, T. Antin, C. L. Ringwalt, and R. F. Saltz, "Evaluation of an Internet-based alcohol misuse prevention course for college freshmen: Findings of a randomized multi-campus trial," *American Journal of Preventive Medicine*, Vol. 41, No. 3 (2011), pp. 300–308.

Federal law also allows for the control of other **dangerous drugs**, a term used by the DEA to refer to "broad categories or classes of controlled substances."[8] The availability of precursor chemicals, such as the popular decongestant pseudoephedrine used in the manufacture of methamphetamine, is also limited under the Combat Methamphetamine Epidemic Act of 2005.

One category of drugs that deserves special mention is inhalants. Nitrous oxide, carbon tetrachloride, amyl nitrite, butyl nitrite, chloroform, Freon, acetate, and toluene, as well as other volatile solvents, are all in the inhalant category. Inhalants are found in fast-drying glues, nail polish remover, room and car deodorizers, lighter fluid, paint thinner, kerosene, cleaning fluids,

■ **drug trafficking**   The manufacturing, distributing, dispensing, importing, and/or exporting of a controlled substance or a counterfeit substance.

■ **Heroin Signature Program (HSP)**   A Drug Enforcement Administration program that identifies the geographic source of a heroin sample through the detection of specific chemical characteristics in the sample peculiar to the source area.

■ **addiction**   A chronic brain disease characterized by compulsive drug seeking and use despite harmful consequences.

The DEA identifies seven categories of "dangerous drugs": stimulants, depressants, cannabis, narcotics, hallucinogens, anabolic steroids, and inhalants, while the 1970 Controlled Substances Act includes five "schedules" of illegal drugs.

household sealants, and gasoline. Although some of these substances (e.g., ether, nitrous oxide, amyl nitrate, and chloroform) have legitimate medical uses, others are employed only to produce a sense of light-headedness often described in colloquial terms as a "rush." Inhalants are generally sniffed, inhaled, huffed, or snorted. It has been estimated that there are over 1,000 substances that are abused. The use of inhalants "can disturb vision, impair judgment, and reduce muscle and reflex control."[9]

Drug Addiction

The term *drug addiction* is widely used but often not well understood. The National Institute on Drug Abuse (NIDA), a part of the National Institutes of Health, defines **addiction** as "a chronic, relapsing brain disease that is characterized by compulsive drug seeking and use, despite harmful consequences."[10] NIDA notes that people often underestimate the complexity of drug addiction, which leads to physical changes in the brain, resulting in modified structure and functioning of this crucial organ. NIDA researchers explained that brain imaging studies of drug-addicted individuals showed changes in areas of the brain that are critical to judgment, decision making, learning and memory, and behavior control.[11] Because it is a disease that impacts the brain, said NIDA, "stopping drug abuse is not simply a matter of willpower." Whether a person becomes addicted to drugs depends on a number of factors: the age at first use; the frequency of initial use, with genetic and environmental factors interacting with critical developmental stages; gender, ethnicity, and preexisting mental disorders; and social influences

in the environment, such as peer pressure, physical and sexual abuse, stress, and parental involvement.[12] See the first Who's to Blame box in this chapter for a creative example of how drugs can affect two brothers differently.

Drug Trafficking

The term *drug trafficking* has a variety of meanings. On one hand, it refers to the illegal shipment of controlled substances across state and national boundaries. On the other hand, it means the sale of controlled substances. Hence, in colloquial usage, a person who "traffics" in drugs may simply sell them. Technically speaking, **drug trafficking** includes manufacturing, distributing, dispensing, importing, and exporting (or possessing with intent to do the same) a controlled or counterfeit substance.[13] Federal law enforcement agencies, in their effort to reduce trafficking, focus largely on the prevention of smuggling and on the apprehension of smugglers.

Drugs such as cocaine, heroin, and LSD are especially easy to smuggle because relatively small quantities of these drugs can be adulterated with other substances to provide large amounts of illicit commodities for sale on the street. Figures 14-8 and 14-9 provide maps of major cocaine and heroin trafficking routes (sometimes called "pipelines"), respectively, worldwide. Most cocaine that enters the United States originates in the Western Hemisphere, especially in the South American nations of Colombia, Peru, and Bolivia. Transportation routes into the United States include (1) shipment overland from South America through Central America and Mexico, (2) direct shipments to U.S. ports while concealed in containers or packed with legitimate products, (3) flights into the United States via commercial airplanes or in private aircraft, and (4) airdrops to vessels waiting offshore for smuggling into the United States.

The DEA follows heroin trafficking through its **Heroin Signature Program (HSP)**, which identifies the geographic source area of a heroin sample through the laboratory detection of specific chemical characteristics in the sample that are peculiar to that area. The HSP employs special chemical analyses to identify and measure chemical constituents of a sample of seized heroin. Results of the HSP show that 62% of heroin in

FIGURE 14-8 | **Global Cocaine Trafficking: Source Countries and Pipelines**

Source: Adapted from the Office of National Drug Control Policy, *The National Drug Control Strategy: 2000 Annual Report* (Washington, DC: U.S. Government Printing Office, 2000), p. 78.

FIGURE 14-9 | **Global Heroin Trafficking: Source Countries and Pipelines**

Source: Adapted from the Office of National Drug Control Policy, *The National Drug Control Strategy: 2000 Annual Report* (Washington, DC: U.S. Government Printing Office, 2000), p. 81.

the United States originates in South America, 17% in Southeast Asia, 16% in Southwest Asia, and 5% in Mexico. According to the DEA, most heroin originating in Southeast Asia is produced in the Golden Triangle area, which encompasses Burma, Laos, and Thailand. Shipments are "controlled by ethnic Chinese criminal groups...while U.S.-based ethnic Chinese traffickers with links to these international criminal groups [are] the most prolific importers and distributors of Southeast Asian heroin" within the United States.[14] HSP data were based on examination of over 800 random samples, including some obtained through undercover purchases, domestic seizures, and seizures made at

U.S. ports of entry. In the 2016 report that opened this chapter, however, the DEA notes, that heroin in the United States, regardless of its point of origin, is largely controlled by Mexican traffickers.

Pharmaceutical Diversion and Synthetic Drugs

The pharmaceutical diversion and subsequent abuse of legitimately manufactured controlled substances are a major source

■ **pharmaceutical diversion**   The process by which legitimately manufactured controlled substances are diverted for illicit use by illegal prescribing (physicians) and/or illegal dispensing (pharmacists).

WHO'S TO BLAME—The Individual or Society?

His Brother's Keeper

In March 2017, Nicole Smithfield received a letter from her former boyfriend, Derek Little. Derek proclaimed his love for Nicole, and said that he wanted to get back together with her. The letter came from the state's maximum-security prison where Derek was serving life without possibility of parole for the murder of his older brother, Hamilton. The brothers had grown up together and attended school in the same small town where Nicole lived. Derek began dealing drugs at age 13, bringing in a few dollars selling marijuana to some friends at school. By the time he was 24, Derek was operating one of the largest drug distribution networks in the county and bringing in thousands of dollars a week. He drove an expensive car, had the best clothes and high-tech gadgets, and carried a lot of cash with him wherever he went. People who knew him said that he also carried a nine-shot semiautomatic pistol strapped to his waist.

Hamilton took a different path and joined the army. He went to Afghanistan and then to Iraq for two tours of duty. One night, when he was home on leave, Hamilton stopped by his brother's house and an argument ensued. Hamilton wanted Derek to get out of the drug business and to turn his life around. "It's only a matter of time before you get arrested," Hamilton told his brother. "Do you want to spend the rest of your life in prison?"

"I'm too smart for that," Derek responded. "I've got too many layers (of dealers) protecting me. They'll never get anything on me."

"Yeah—but what about all the lives you're affecting? What about all the kids from our neighborhood who are getting strung out on drugs because of you? You're preying on society," Hamilton said, angry now. "And if you don't quit, I'll make you."

"What do you mean by that?" Derek asked, jumping out of his chair.

"I just think you need to stop, and if I have to, then I'll find a way to make you," Hamilton said, and left, beginning the walk home to his mother's mobile home less than a mile away.

An American flag being folded at a military funeral. How can we control the drug problem?

According to evidence presented at his trial, that's when Derek got into his pickup truck and started down the road, accelerating to 80 mph before swerving onto the shoulder and hitting his brother. Hamilton's body flew 40 feet through the air before hitting the ground and then tumbled another 30 feet through the brush.

Prosecutors tried to present additional evidence showing that Derek was likely responsible for the deaths of three other people who had threatened him during the past two years, or who had said that they would turn him in to authorities—but the judge would not allow the jury to hear those claims. When the trial concluded, Derek was found guilty of killing his brother and sentenced to life in prison without the possibility of parole. Nicole never replied to Derek's letter.

Think about it

1. How is it that two brothers raised in the same environment might choose such different paths? What might explain their choices?

2. How would you explain the attraction that the drug trade seems to have for so many people in this country?

3. If you were able to set crime-control policies for the nation, how would you address the drug problem? Would you consider the decriminalization of any substances? If so, which ones and why? (See **http://ssrn.com/abstract=1403506.**)

Note: Who's to Blame boxes provide fictionalized critical thinking opportunities based on actual cases.

of drug-related addiction or dependence, medical emergencies, and death. **Pharmaceutical diversion** occurs through illegal prescribing by physicians and illegal dispensing by pharmacists. "Doctor shopping," the process of finding a physician who is liberal in prescribing types and amounts of certain drugs, and visits to numerous physicians for the purpose of collecting large quantities of prescribed medicines exacerbate the problem. Depressants, including sedatives, tranquilizers, and antianxiety drugs (especially Xanax and Valium), along with stimulants and anabolic steroids, constitute the types of drugs most often diverted.

■ **synthetic drug**   A new substance designed by slightly altering the chemical makeup of other illegal or tightly controlled drugs.

■ **drug-defined crime**   A violation of the laws prohibiting or regulating the possession, use, or distribution of illegal drugs.

■ **drug-related crime**   A crime in which drugs contribute to the offense (excluding violations of drug laws).

■ **narcoterrorism**   The distribution of a controlled substance in order to provide something of pecuniary value to a person or group that has engaged or is engaging in terrorist activity.

A number of drugs, especially those that fall into the "synthetic" category, are manufactured in drug facilities that are sometimes called "basement laboratories" because they are operated by individuals out of their homes. **Synthetic drugs** are so named because "they are new substances designed by slightly altering the chemical makeup of other illegal or tightly controlled drugs."[15] Synthetic drugs such as Nexus (a reputed aphrodisiac), Spice (or K2), bath salts, fentanyl, or Smiles (also known as N–Bomb) usually fall under the rubric "synthetic narcotic" or "synthetic hallucinogen."

Drugs and Crime

While the manufacture, sale, transportation, and use of controlled substances are themselves criminal, drugs and crime are also linked in other ways. The addict who is so habituated to the use of illegal drugs that he or she steals to support a "habit," the drug importer who kills a rival dealer, and the offender who commits a criminal act due to the stimulation provided by drugs are examples of how drug abuse may be linked to other forms of criminal activity.

Recognizing these differences, the Bureau of Justice Statistics (BJS) distinguishes between drug-defined and drug-related crimes. **Drug-defined crimes** are "violations of laws prohibiting or regulating the possession, use, or distribution of illegal drugs."[16] The costs of all drug-defined crime, says the BJS, are directly attributable to illegal drug use. **Drug-related crimes**, on the other hand, "are not violations of drug laws but are crimes in which drugs contribute to the offense."[17] Illegal drug use, says the BJS, "is related to offenses against people and property in three major ways: (1) pharmacologically drugs can induce violent behavior, (2) the cost of drugs induces some users to commit crimes to support their drug habits, [and] (3) violence often characterizes relations among participants in the drug distribution system."[18]

According to the U.S. Department of Justice (DOJ), "There is extensive evidence of the strong relationship between drug use and crime." This relationship can be summarized in the following three points, each of which, the department says, is supported "by a review of the evidence":[19]

> Extensive evidence shows the strong relationship between drug use and crime.

- Drug users report greater involvement in crime and are more likely than nonusers to have criminal records.
- People with criminal records are much more likely than others to report being drug users.
- Crimes rise in number as drug use increases.

Narcoterrorism

In 2012, a U.S. Circuit Court of Appeals upheld the 2008 conviction of Khan Mohammed, 38, a member of an Afghan Taliban terrorism cell, on **narcoterrorism** charges. Following conviction, Mohammed had been ordered by U.S. District Judge Colleen Kollar-Kotelly to serve two life sentences as well as 60 months of supervised release.[20] His conviction followed a seven-day jury trial on one count of distribution of heroin knowing and intending that it be imported into the United States, and one count of narcoterrorism. During the trial, Judge Kollar-Kotelly told the jury that narcoterrorism consisted of "the distribution of a controlled substance...in order to provide something of pecuniary value to a person or group that has engaged or is engaging in terrorist activity." The conviction represented the first time a defendant had been convicted in federal court of narcoterrorism charges since the enactment of a narcoterrorism statute in March 2006.[21] At Mohammed's trial, DEA agents testified that the Taliban has played a central role in

A Taliban militant holding an automatic weapon (right) as farmers collect resin from poppies in an opium poppy field in Helmand province, southwest Afghanistan. Helmand province is one of the world's top opium-producing regions. How does this photo illustrate the link between illegal drugs and terrorism?

Anonymous/AP Images

every stage of opium/heroin production and transportation, relying on it as a principal source of funding for its activities. One agent testified that more than 50% of current DEA cases have a definitive Taliban component.

Social Policy and Drug Abuse

Prior to 1907, any and all drugs could be bought and sold in the United States without restriction. Manufacturers were not required to disclose the contents of their products. Patent medicines of the time were trade secrets. This came to an end with the federal Pure Food and Drug Act of 1906, which required manufacturers to list their ingredients and specifically targeted mood-changing chemicals.

The Harrison Act, passed by Congress in 1914, was the first major piece of federal antidrug legislation. It required anyone dealing in opium, morphine, heroin, cocaine, or their derivatives to register with the federal government and to pay a tax of $1 per year. The act, however, only authorized the registration of physicians, pharmacists, and other medical professionals, effectively outlawing street use of these drugs. However, by 1920, court rulings severely curtailed the use of heroin for medical purposes, claiming that it only caused addiction.

In 1919, the Eighteenth Amendment to the U.S. Constitution, which prohibited the manufacture, sale, and transportation of alcoholic beverages, was ratified. Support for Prohibition began to wane not long after the amendment was enacted. Objections to Prohibition included the claims that it gave the government too much power over people's personal lives, was impossible to enforce, corrupted agents of enforcement, and made many bootleggers wealthy. The coming of the Great Depression, which began in 1929, magnified the effect of lost alcohol tax revenues on the federal government, and in 1933, Congress proposed and the states ratified the Twenty-first Amendment, which repealed Prohibition.

In 1937, passage of the Marijuana Tax Act effectively outlawed marijuana, a federal stance that was reinforced by the Boggs Act of 1951. The Boggs Act also mandated deletion of heroin from the list of medically useful substances and required its complete removal from all medicines.

In 1970, the federal government enacted the Comprehensive Drug Abuse Prevention and Control Act. Title II of that Act is known as the Controlled Substances Act (CSA) and established "schedules" or categories for controlled substances, some of which were described earlier. The CSA is the most important piece of federal antidrug legislation to date.

In 1991, steroids were added to the list of Schedule III controlled substances by congressional action, and in 1996, the Drug-Induced Rape Prevention Act[22] increased penalties for trafficking in the drug Rohypnol, which is known as the "date rape drug" because of its use by "young men [who] put doses of the drug in women's drinks without their consent in order to lower their inhibitions."[23] The drug is variously known as "roples," "roche," "ruffles," "roofies," and "rophies" on the street.

Another date rape drug, gamma hydroxybutyrate (GHB), has effects similar to those of Rohypnol, but was once sold in health food stores as a supplement to enhance body building. In 1990, the FDA banned the use of GHB except under the supervision of a physician. Table 14-2 provides a timeline of federal drug-control legislation.

Recent Legislation

On the federal level, recent drug-control legislation includes the Comprehensive Methamphetamine Control Act (CMCA) of 1996 and relevant portions of the Violent Crime Control and Law Enforcement Act of 1994. The CMCA, which contains provisions for the seizure of chemicals used in the manufacture of methamphetamine, regulated the use of iodine (used in meth labs); created new reporting requirements for distributors of combination products containing ephedrine, pseudoephedrine (a common decongestant), and phenylpropanolamine; and increased penalties for the manufacture and possession of equipment used to make controlled substances.

The far-reaching Violent Crime Control and Law Enforcement Act of 1994 included a number of drug-related provisions. Specifically, the act allocated other drug-treatment moneys for the creation of state and federal programs to treat drug-addicted prisoners and provided $1 billion for drug court programs for nonviolent offenders with substance abuse problems. The law also expanded the federal death penalty to include large-scale drug trafficking and mandated life imprisonment for criminals convicted of three drug-related felonies.

Some states, however, have legalized the personal use of marijuana, or allow the use of marijuana for medical purposes. Medical marijuana, or the use of physician-prescribed marijuana to alleviate pain and nausea associated with various physical ailments, is legal in 28 states.[24] California, Massachusetts, Nevada, Maine, Colorado, Washington, Oregon, Alaska, and the District of Columbia were the first states to have legalized the possession and use of small amounts of marijuana for recreational use in private. On April 20–21, 2012, the nation's first Cannabis Cup held in Denver, Colorado, drew more than 50,000 people—many of whom openly smoked marijuana in

TABLE 14-2 | Timeline of Federal Drug-Control Legislation

1906	1914	1937	1938	1956	1970
Food and Drug Act	Harrison Narcotics Act	Marijuana Tax Act	Food, Drug and Cosmetic Act	Narcotics Control Act	Comprehensive Drug Abuse Prevention and Control Act
Required the proper and accurate labeling of "patent medicines"	Taxed and regulated the use of "narcotics" including coca and cocaine	Regulated the buying and selling of cannabis	Required that new drugs be proven safe before marketing	Increased penalties for drug law violations	Title II of the law, known as the Controlled Substances (CSA) created federal drug schedules and associated penalties

violation of that state's privacy requirement.[25] Most recently, California, Maine, Massachusetts, and Nevada enacted legislation that legalized recreational marijuana use.

In response to state action, the U.S. Department of Justice issued a memorandum to all federal prosecutors providing

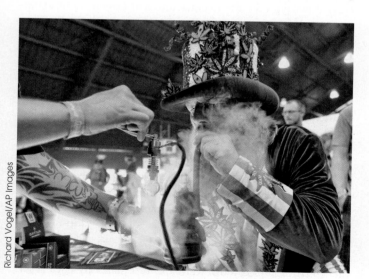

The 2017 Las Vegas Cannabis Cup celebration. Why have some states moved to legalize small amounts of marijuana for private recreational or medical use? Why does the drug remain illegal elsewhere?

guidance on enforcement of the Controlled Substances Act in those jurisdictions. The memorandum took a "hands-off" approach and established federal enforcement priorities with regard to marijuana distribution and use in states that legalized the drug. Those priorities include preventing the distribution of marijuana to minors and preventing marijuana sales revenue from going to criminal enterprises and cartels.[26] Also in 2014, the U.S. Attorney General announced new regulations that would open banking services to state-sanctioned marijuana businesses. Prior to the new regulations, most state-licensed marijuana distributors had to pay employees, purchase inventories, and conduct sales in cash.

Finally, in 2016, the 21st Century Cures Act was signed into law. The act, whose primary target is mainstream health issues, addresses drug addiction by providing $1 billion in state grants to assist in drug treatment, prevention, and prescription drug monitoring. Sponsors were primarily concerned about the rapid spread in the use of opiates—particularly heroin and related substances. The act also funded federal drug courts—or courts which specialize in the handling of drug offenders utilizing community resources in an effort to divert offenders from prison.[27]

Drug-Control Strategies

Major policy initiatives in the battle against illicit drugs have included antidrug legislation and strict enforcement,

Richard Vogel/AP Images

■ **interdiction**   An international drug-control policy whose goal is to stop drugs from entering the country illegally.

■ **forfeiture**   A legal procedure that authorizes judicial representatives to seize "all moneys, negotiable instruments, securities, or other things of value furnished or intended to be furnished by any person in exchange for a controlled substance and all proceeds traceable to such an exchange."

1973	1984	1988	1996	2006	2016
Heroin Trafficking Act	Analogue Act	Anti-Drug Abuse Act	Comprehensive Methamphetamine Control Act	Combat Methamphetamine Epidemic Act	The 21st Century Cures Act
Increased criminal penalties for the distribution of heroin	Criminalized designer drugs	Established the Office of National Drug Control Policy and increased penalties for recreational drug use	Restricted access to chemicals and equipment used in the manufacture of methamphetamine	Made it harder to obtain pseudo-ephedrine, ephedrine, and phenylpropanol-amine (chemicals used in the manufacture of methamphetamine)	Authorized $1 billion in grants to the states to address drug problems through treatment, prevention, and prescription drug monitoring. It also funded the expansion of federal drug courts.

interdiction, crop control, forfeiture, and antidrug education and drug treatment.[28] Much legislative emphasis in recent years has shifted from targeting users to arresting, prosecuting, and incarcerating the distributors of controlled substances. Similar shifts have occurred among employers requiring routine drug testing as a condition of employment and retention.

Interdiction is an international drug-control policy designed to stop drugs from entering the country illegally. Another antidrug strategy, crop control, has both international and domestic aspects. During 2015, for example, the DEA's Domestic Cannabis Eradication and Suppression Program was responsible for the eradication of 3,904,213 cultivated outdoor cannabis plants and 396,620 indoor plants for a total of 4,300,833 marijuana plants. In addition, the same program was responsible for 6,310 arrests, and agents seized 4,989 weapons and $27.3 million in assets.[29]

Forfeiture, or asset forfeiture, is another strategy in the battle against illegal drugs. **Forfeiture** is a legal procedure that authorizes judicial representatives to seize "all moneys, negotiable instruments, securities, or other things of value furnished or intended to be furnished by any person in exchange for a controlled substance…[and] all proceeds traceable to such an exchange."[30]

Another strategy, antidrug education and drug treatment, has gained significant popularity over the past decade. Those favoring educational attacks on the problem of

> Those who favor educational attacks on the problem of drug abuse claim that other techniques have not been effective.

drug abuse are quick to claim that other measures have not been effective in reducing the incidence of abuse. Antidrug education programs often reach targeted individuals through schools, corporations, and media campaigns.

The Drug Legalization/ Decriminalization Debate

The war on drugs has been costly. Domestic law enforcement activities (including all federal law enforcement programs within the nation's borders) account for the lion's share of federal antidrug expenditures, whereas demand-reduction programs (i.e., educational activities) absorb the smallest part of the antidrug budget. Figure 14-10 depicts federal drug-control spending by functional area for fiscal years 2013–2017. When state moneys are added in, the total cost of the war on drugs has been enormous.

The drug war has been costly in other ways as well. Court resources must be diverted to deal with the enormous influx of drug prosecutions. In some jurisdictions, drug cases account

■ **decriminalization**   The redefinition of certain previously criminal behaviors as regulated activities that become "ticketable" instead of "arrestable."

■ **legalization**   The elimination of laws and criminal penalties associated with certain behaviors—usually the production, sale, distribution, and possession of a controlled substance.

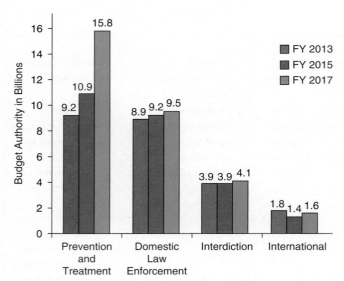

FIGURE 14-10 | **Federal Drug-Control Spending, Fiscal Years 2013–2017**

Source: Executive Office of the President of the United States, *National Drug Control Budget: FY 2017 Funding Highlights* (Washington, DC: April 2016).

for as much as two-thirds of the criminal case filings. America's major cities have been especially affected. Strict enforcement has combined with a lock 'em-up philosophy to produce astonishingly high rates of imprisonment for drug offenders. The proportion of federal prisoners who are sentenced drug offenders rose from 38% to over 46% today.[31]

Part of the increase was due to congressional action that required high mandatory minimum sentences in drug cases, so that even first-time offenders were sentenced to long prison terms instead of probation. Approximately 70% of all first-time offenders in federal prisons are serving drug sentences. This is also true of 85% of illegal immigrants who are federal prisoners and 66% of female federal prisoners.[32]

Alternative Drug Policies

Decriminalization and legalization have both been suggested as drug-control policies at the state and local levels. Both strategies are based on the assumption that drug abuse can never be eliminated. Whereas **decriminalization** typically reduces criminal penalties associated with the personal possession of a controlled substance, **legalization** eliminates "the laws and associated criminal penalties that prohibit its production, sale, distribution, and possession."[33]

Decriminalization enhances personal freedoms in the face of state control, whereas legalization "is aimed," in part, "at reducing the control that criminals have over the drug trade."[34] Other arguments in favor of legalization include the following notions:

- In a free society, people should be permitted to do what they want as long as they don't harm others.
- Keeping drugs illegal means that they will continue to be high-priced commodities. Legalizing them could greatly lower the price and make them taxable—providing the states with much-needed revenue.
- The expense of illicit drugs, kept artificially high by their illegal status, encourages the commission of many drug-related crimes, including prostitution, robbery, and burglary, by users seeking to feed their habits.
- Legalizing drugs would reduce the influence of criminal cartels.
- The illegal status and associated high cost of drugs indirectly victimize others, such as property owners in drug-infested areas and taxpayers who foot the enforcement bill.
- Drug legalization would dramatically reduce the opportunity for official corruption, which is now frequently associated with the illicit drug trade.
- The legalization of drugs would allow for better control over public health issues related to drug use. Drug quality and potency, for example, could be monitored and ensured.

Opponents of drug legalization argue the following:

- Reducing official control over psychoactive substances is immoral, is socially irresponsible, and would result in heightened costs to society from drug abuse.
- Drug legalization would simply increase the types of problems now associated with alcohol abuse, such as lost time from work, drug-induced criminality, the loss of personal self-control, and the severing of important social relationships.
- The fact that laws are not easily enforceable is no reason to eliminate them.

WHO'S TO BLAME—The Individual or Society?

Gangs, Teenagers, and Peer Pressure

Fourteen-year-old Lakisha Jackson found herself in trouble with the law at her junior high school prom when her 18-year-old boyfriend, Jamal Carter, was caught smoking pot behind the curtain covering the school's stage. Jamal told off-duty police officers working the dance that the marijuana wasn't his, but that Lakisha had given it to him.

Jamal was known to the officers as a member of the Top 6 gang and bore a number of tattoos indicating his gang affiliation. Officers from the police department's juvenile division were called to the school, and both Lakisha and Jamal were taken to the police station for questioning. No additional drugs were found on either youth.

What bothered officers, however, was Lakisha's hostile attitude. While they expected that Jamal would refuse to say more than he already had about the source of the marijuana, they had hoped that Lakisha would either refute Jamal's story or tell them where she had gotten the substance. Lakisha, however, refused to say anything about the incident, calling the officers "pigs" and telling them to mind their own business. "I don't rat on nobody," was all she would volunteer.

A police psychologist who was present during the interviews later explained the youth's behavior in terms of gang and subcultural loyalties. "Even if this case involved a serious crime like a murder—maybe even especially then—you wouldn't get any cooperation from these kids," he said. "You can be sure that if they knew who committed a crime they wouldn't talk. It's not only part and parcel of their gang loyalties, but pretty much a value inherent in the subculture in which they've been raised. Maybe in another neighborhood things would be different—but not here."

Tracy Whiteside/Shutterstock

Young men hanging out in a culvert. Why is it so difficult for the police to gain the cooperation of members of youth subcultures when investigating crimes?

Think about it

1. Do you agree with the police psychologist? Is his explanation for why these youngsters won't talk to the police a plausible one, or is there likely to be some other explanation?

2. If the psychologist is correct in his assessment of the situation, then do you think that Lakisha and Jamal should "know better" than to let subcultural values influence them? Why or why not?

3. Are the police likely to get any more information from Lakisha or her boyfriend? Why or why not?

Note: Who's to Blame boxes provide fictionalized critical thinking opportunities based on actual cases.

Prostitution

A few years ago, the small town of Kennebunk, Maine, was shaken by a prostitution scandal that involved a Zumba fitness instructor who was charged with running a sex-for-hire business out of her downtown studio.[35] Twenty-nine-year-old fitness instructor Alexis Wright was arrested after her landlord called police, complaining of strange sounds coming from her office. Following Wright's arrest, a judge ordered the release of 21 names of an estimated 150 johns found on a list of customers that she had maintained. The list included the names of prominent Maine businessmen and professionals, along with men from Massachusetts and New Hampshire. Wright also faced charges of invasion of privacy for allegedly creating secret video recordings of her sexual encounters. Prosecutors announced that they would charge not only Wright, but the men to whom she sold sexual services, who were charged with soliciting a prostitute—a misdemeanor under Maine law. In 2013, Wright

■ **prostitution**   The act of engaging in sexual activity for money or its equivalent.

pled guilty to 20 misdemeanor counts and was sentenced to 10 months in jail, although the original indictment against her had charged her with 106 counts of prostitution, tax evasion, and other things.[36]

Prostitution can be defined as the act of engaging in sexual activity for money. In heterosexual prostitution involving men as clients (or "johns") and women as sexual "service providers," the men can also be charged with and found guilty of the offense of prostitution. Same-sex prostitution, which generally involves male prostitutes serving male clients, is also illegal when the exchange of money or other valuables is involved. Except for in parts of Nevada, all forms of prostitution are criminal acts in the United States and are generally classified as misdemeanors.

In the United States, over 48,620 men, women, and juveniles are arrested yearly for the crime of prostitution.[37] The number of juveniles engaging in prostitution is estimated to be between 100,000 and 300,000 annually.

Robert F. Bukaty/AP Images

Zumba instructor Alexis Wright, jailed in 2013 in the town of Kennebunk, Maine, following a prostitution conviction. Why is prostitution illegal in most parts of the United States? Why is it legal in other parts?

Morals Legislation

Laws against prostitution have a long and varied history in the United States, and have largely focused on traditional forms of prostitution, which involve women servicing men; and that is the form of prostitution that this chapter focuses on. Underlying statutes forbidding prostitution are fundamental questions about legislating morality. Whether and to what extent the criminal law should reflect and enforce the morality of the society it represents is one of the classic debates in criminal law literature. Most people agree that actions that harm others, as in the case of child prostitution, should be controlled, but not everyone sees prostitution, especially when willingly undertaken, as harmful (see **http://ssrn.com/abstract=1105409**).

Some people argue that every organized society is permitted—even obligated—to enforce morality by means of criminal and other legal sanctions. Arguments in favor of criminalizing street prostitution can be seen in Table 14-3.

The classic statement that the law should not unnecessarily criminalize what are personal moral decisions that harm no one (other than possibly the person making them) was offered by the nineteenth-century English philosopher John Stuart Mill, who argued that society should interfere with an individual's freedom of action only "to prevent harm to others. His own good, either physical or moral, is not a sufficient warrant" for interference.[38]

A Typology of Prostitutes

There are many different venues where sexual services are sold: so-called red-light districts, commercial houses of prostitution, massage parlors, studios for nude photography, strip clubs, stag parties, theaters for erotic dance, and last but certainly not least, the Internet.[39] Using location as the basis for a typology of prostitutes produces the categories of streetwalkers, bar/hotel prostitutes, club girls, online escrots/call girls, and brothel prostitutes; and others who don't clearly fit any of these categories (Figure 14-11).

Streetwalkers, whose numbers are dwindling due to the widespread use of the Internet in today's sex trade, are generally seen as the lowest class of prostitute because they solicit customers in public—often on foot and from curbside. They tend to be highly visible, and their dress is revealing, both of which advertise their services and entice customers. Streetwalkers, who perform their services in customers' cars, alleyways, nearby hotels, and darkened doorways, command the lowest prices and have little bargaining power over things like condom use and choice of sexual practices; they face the highest risk of harm from customers or others and run the highest risk of arrest.

TABLE 14-3 | **Harms Caused by Street Prostitution**

Moral and Nuisance Concerns
- Prostitution offends some citizens' moral standards.
- Prostitution is a nuisance to passersby and nearby residents and businesses.
- Prostitutes and clients offend uninvolved people when they solicit them.
- Juveniles who are less capable of making informed choices may become prostitutes.

Public Health Concerns
- Prostitutes and clients may spread sexually transmitted diseases such as syphilis, herpes, and AIDS.
- Used condoms, syringes, and other paraphernalia left on the ground are unsightly and potentially hazardous.
- Prostitutes without access to proper facilities may relieve themselves or bathe in public.

Personal Safety Concerns
- Clients may harm prostitutes.
- Clients or prostitutes may be defrauded, robbed, or assaulted.
- Pimps may financially and physically exploit prostitutes and clients.

Spillover-Effect Concerns
- Street prostitution and drug markets are often linked.
- Prostitution may provide a seedbed for organized crime.
- Prostitutes create parking and traffic problems where they congregate.
- Prostitution attracts strangers and criminals to a neighborhood.

Economic Concerns
- Legitimate businesses may lose customers who avoid the area because of prostitution.
- Prostitutes' presence may negatively affect the area's economy, reducing property values and limiting property use.

Civil Rights Concerns
- Prostitutes have rights that need to be protected.

Police-Integrity Concerns
- Policing prostitution creates special opportunities for police officers to engage in unethical conduct, such as taking payments in exchange for nonenforcement, because prostitutes, pimps, and clients are in weak positions to complain about police misconduct.

Source: Adapted from Michael S. Scott and Kelly Dedel, *Street Prostitution*, 2nd ed. (Washington, DC: Office of Community Oriented Policing Services, U.S. Department of Justice, 2006).

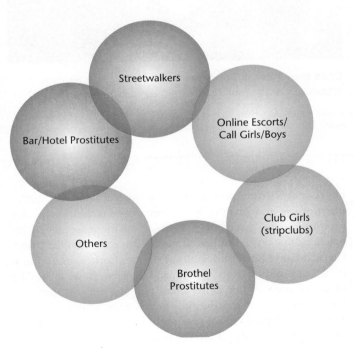

FIGURE 14-11 | **Types of Prostitutes**

Bar/hotel prostitutes work in bars, clubs, and hotels and may have a standing relationship with managers, bartenders, and security personnel, with whom they share their profits or for whom they provide "free" services. They tend to "work" conventions, sporting events, and business meetings. Desk clerks, valets, and even discreet concierges sometimes refer clients to prostitutes, whose services are typically provided in the establishment, perhaps in a dark corner, a back room, or a hotel room rented by the customer or prostitute; the prices charged by bar/hotel prostitutes vary considerably according to the prestige of the establishment with which they are associated. A prostitute's risk of harm and arrest is low to moderate as long as the collaborative relationship with the establishment is maintained.

Club girls operate much the same way as bar/hotel prostitutes, except that the settings in which they work are strip clubs (often referred to as "gentlemen's clubs"), and the sex workers do double duty as on-stage performers and prostitutes. A girl's performance on stage often acts as an enticement for customers to "book" her for private performances and sexual intercourse.

Most call girls see well-to-do clients who prefer the anonymity of a referral service.

Online escorts and outcall girls work for escort services—which advertise in flyers, in newspapers, in the yellow pages, on TV, and via the Internet (sometimes referred to as "cyberprostitution")—on an "outcall" basis and are not restricted to specific locales. Most call girls see relatively well-to-do clients who prefer the anonymity of a referral service, and many customers are regulars who maintain a standing relationship with the service. Prostitutes are typically assigned by the agency to customers who may select them from pictures printed in brochures or posted on the Internet. Fees are often charged to credit cards by the customer before the girl is dispatched; on site, prostitutes may negotiate with the customer for specific services. Through this arrangement, the escort service tends to insulate itself from

CRIME | in the NEWS

International Sex Traffickers Turn Girls into Slaves

According to wide-ranging estimates from the United Nations (UN) and the FBI, hundreds of thousands of girls around the world are in bondage to sex traffickers, and the numbers are rising. The victims are typically aged 8 to 18, and some are as young as 4 or 5.

In poor countries like Cambodia, families reportedly sell a young daughter to sex traffickers for the equivalent of $10. Some of these girls are later rescued and sent to shelters. Then-Secretary of State Hillary Clinton visited one such shelter in Cambodia in 2010. "I met with dozens of girls, most of them very young, who had been sexually exploited and abused," she recalled. "They had been given refuge at the shelter and they were learning valuable skills to help them reenter society."

Sex traffickers are most active within their own countries, but many of them cross borders and even enter the United States. In some cases, they lure their victims with promises of a legitimate job, and then keep them in bondage until they pay off excessively high debts for their transportation. The Department of Justice reports about 2,000 instances of sex trafficking annually. Although most involve girls and young women, some involve boys.

Victims of sex trafficking are often afraid to contact authorities for fear of being identified as illegal immigrants, the State Department reports. They have justification, the department explained in a 2016 report. When they are discovered, they are often arrested, incarcerated, and deported, rather than given aid and shelter.

To address this rising international crime, in 2000 the U.S. Congress passed the Trafficking Victims Protection Act (TVPA), which also addresses indentured laborers. On the international level, the law authorizes the State Department to create public awareness programs, assess trafficking in each foreign country, and develop sanctions against countries that fail to take action.

Within the United States, the TVPA increased prosecution of traffickers based on federal charges and heightened penalties. U.S.

Immigration and Customs Enforcement (ICE) oversees prosecution, and victims can be protected from deportation through a new type of visa intended to shield victims of sex trafficking.

Discussion Questions

1. How might transnational criminal organizations be involved in prostitution?

2. What is the goal of the Trafficking Victims Protection Act (TVPA)? How can it be used to combat the types of crime described in this box?

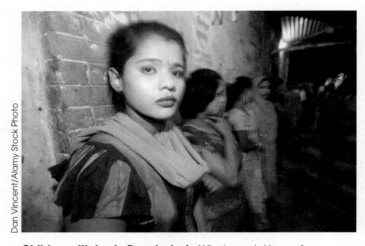

Child prostitutes in Bangladesh. What special issues face trafficked children who have been rescued from prostitution?

Sources: Amanda Walker-Rodriguez and Rodney Hill, "Human Sex Trafficking," *Law Enforcement Bulletin*, March 2011, http://www.fbi.gov/stats-services/publications/law-enforcement-bulletin/march_2011/human_sex_trafficking.Trafficking in Persons Report," Department of State, June 2016, https://www.state.gov/documents/organization/258876.pdf.

---

legal action, claiming that it simply arranged for companionship. Call girls depend on the agency to screen customers, which can be done by referrals from other agencies or by established clients with connections to the agency. Prices in this market segment reach the highest levels, and escorts have considerable bargaining power over such things as use of condoms and kinds of sexual services provided; call girls face the lowest risk of harm or arrest.

House or brothel prostitutes ply their trade in legal environments, which are limited to a few venues in the United States. Legalized prostitution, however, is common in a number of other countries, including Australia (where laws vary by state), New Zealand, the Netherlands (which outlaws pimping and trafficking of human beings), and Germany (where advertising sex services remains illegal). In countries where prostitution is legal, it is still subject to health and locality controls as well as age and other restrictions. In such locales, prostitutes are generally licensed sex workers who pay taxes, belong to unions, and are eligible for government benefits such as unemployment wages and medical services. Some countries tolerate prostitution

but restrict activities associated with it, such as pimping, operating brothels, and advertising services; others technically permit prostitution but have other kinds of restrictions making its practice difficult. In this latter category are countries like Brazil, Canada, Costa Rica, and Scotland. In Denmark, prostitution is legal, but profiting from it is not, and Sweden allows the selling of sexual services but criminalizes pimping and the purchasing of sex services (on the theory that such activity demeans women). In Japan, vaginal prostitution is illegal, but fellatio for money is not considered prostitution.

In the United States, brothel prostitution is an option in some rural counties in Nevada. Nevada's house prostitutes operate with posted fees and generally earn 40 to 60% of the revenue they generate. State law requires that they be fingerprinted, undergo regular health examinations, and keep financial records for tax purposes. All forms of prostitution are illegal in Nevada's Clark County (which contains Las Vegas). See the Criminal Profiles box on Heidi Fleiss, who ran a prostitution business in Hollywood and Los Angeles.

Commercial Sexual Exploitation of Children

Sex trafficking is a form of human trafficking. Human trafficking is discussed in greater detail in Chapter 16. When discussing prostitution, however, it is important to know that the commercial sexual exploitation of children (CSEC) plays a significant and growing role in the sex trade. The average age of entry into the sex industry in America is 14–16 years old.[40] Child prostitutes are typically lured into sex work by pimps promising a better life, drugs, companionship, or even small things like a puppy or toy. Sexually exploited children are victims in need of help–not criminal offenders. Unfortunately, however, undercover law enforcement operations targeting the sex industry frequently lead to the arrest of girls and boys who are caught up in police raids and sweeps of commercial sex establishments. Those children run the risk of being formally processed by the justice system and may end up in residential confinement facilities. Many states and local police agencies, however, are making significant progress in identifying child victims of sex trafficking and are diverting them to shelters and community service agencies, rather than taking them to jail and sending them to court. Under federal law, anyone under the age of 18 who is induced into the commercial sex trade is classified as a victim of sex trafficking—regardless of whether the trafficker used force, fraud, or coercion to gain their compliance.

In 2016, more than 3,500 sex trafficking cases were reported to the National Human Trafficking Resource Center, and estimates are that as many as 325,000 children are at risk for becoming victims of sexual exploitation in America. The commercial sexual exploitation of children includes the production of child pornography, juvenile prostitution, trafficking in children for sexual purposes, and child sex tourism. Studies show that some sex traffickers can earn as much as $200,000 per child each year, and the average number of young girls that a pimp exploits is between 4 and 6.

One study conducted by members of the School of Social Work at the University of Pennsylvania identified three discrete groups of factors that contribute to the commercial sexual exploitation of children.[41] They range from external factors over which individuals can exert little control to factors that are internal to the psychological makeup of exploited children and their families. Study authors grouped these factors into three categories: (1) macro/contextual factors; (2) micro/situational factors; and (3) individual/internal factors.

The first category, macro/contextual factors, includes social processes that exist in the larger environment over which individuals can exercise only minimal control but which, nonetheless, exert powerful influences on their lives. Contributing factors in this category are poverty; negative societal attitudes toward children and youth; a lack of direction and connectedness among youth; child criminal and sexual victimization; inadequate societal responses to crimes committed against children; the presence of preexisting adult prostitution markets; and the number of unattached and transient young males, including those in the military, seasonal workers, motorcycle gangs, conventioneers, etc.

The second category, micro/situational factors, includes external processes and events that impact individuals directly and over which they can exert *some* measure of control. Factors found in this category are active recruitment into prostitution by peers, family members, gangs, and other criminal organizations; and social-behavioral factors such as parental drug use, family dysfunction, personal drug dependency, school failure, gang membership, and a history of physical or sexual assault. The third category, individual/internal factors, includes cognitive factors that influence a person's sense of mastery over his own personal environment and future. This category includes things like poor self-esteem, ongoing depression, limited personal opportunities, and a negative "external locus of control." Visit Project Safe Childhood at **https://www.justice.gov/psc**, which seeks to combat the growing epidemic of child sexual exploitation and abuse.

Clients of Prostitutes

Some years ago, the NIJ undertook sponsorship of an extensive study conducted by Martin A. Monto of prostitutes' clients—commonly known as "johns"—that explored the sex-related behavior characteristic of men who solicited prostitutes.[42] The study, whose results were published in 2000, examined the effects of the First Offender Prostitution Program (FOPP) in San Francisco and similar programs in other cities.[43] These programs offered johns an opportunity to pay a fine and attend a daylong seminar rather than go to jail, and participants were advised that no further legal action would be taken against them if they successfully avoided rearrest for a year, but if there was a subsequent offense, they would be prosecuted for the new offense and the original charge would be reinstated.

Monto surveyed 1,291 men arrested for soliciting street prostitutes before they participated in FOPP or similar programs in Las Vegas, Nevada; Portland, Oregon; and Santa Clara, California. He collected data on their reasons for use of prostitutes, their attitudes regarding violence against women, and the consequences of their views of sex as a commodity. Monto found that 72% of the men, who ranged in age from 18 to 84 years (median age of 37), had attended some college and were less likely to be married than other men. Although their motives for seeking sex with a prostitute differed, there were similarities among certain groups: Married clients and college graduates more often wanted a different kind of sex than they had with their regular partners; unmarried clients and those without college degrees felt shy and awkward when trying to meet women but did not feel intimidated by prostitutes.

Researcher Monto also explored men's attitudes toward rape myths (discussed in Chapter 11). Less than 0.5% of the men surveyed indicated acceptance of the majority of rape myths, but 20% demonstrated acceptance of four or more of them. Although the evidence wasn't clear, researchers believed that it was this latter group that may be responsible for perpetrating violent acts against women for hire.

Concerning the degree to which clients regarded sexuality as a commercial commodity, Monto found that the greater a client's belief that women and sex were commercial products, the more frequently he would visit prostitutes. This mind-set was also a strong predictor of the acceptance of rape myths, less frequent condom use with prostitutes, and a disinclination to view prostitution as a demeaning profession for women.

> The greater a man's belief that women and sex were commercial products, the more frequently he would visit prostitutes.

Monto and his colleagues also studied the recidivism of those clients who participated in the San Francisco and Portland FOPPs. Although both programs had a recidivism rate of about 2%, researchers acknowledged that conclusions about the programs' efficacy in reducing recidivism were hampered by a lack of available baseline data for comparative purposes. Read Monto's entire 80-page report on street prostitution at **http://www.ncjrs.gov/pdffiles1/nij/grants/182860.pdf**.

Prostitution: A Changing Business

In 2010, the National Institute of Justice (NIJ) funded the Washington-based Urban Institute to measure the size and structure of the underground commercial sex economy (UCSE) in the United States. The resulting Urban Institute report, which was published in 2014, found that "The UCSE has changed significantly over time—it used to mainly consist of street prostitution, whereas over the last decade, a majority of the business takes place on the Internet."[44] The shift from street prostitution to Internet-based "escort" services not only removed many prostitutes from the streets, but has also changed the structure of prostitution, including how "dates" are arranged, the nature of recruitment efforts (for new girls), solicitation of new customers (or "Johns"), the advertisement of services, fee setting, and other forms of communications between prostitutes, their clients, and their pimps. The Urban Institute report notes that "The Internet has become a powerful tool for employee recruitment," used by many pimps nationwide. It concludes by saying that "The widespread availability and rapid expansion of the Internet has redefined the spatial and social limitations of the sex market by introducing new markets for both recruitment and advertisement."

Exiting the Sex Trade

Once people have become involved in the sex trade, it can be very difficult for them to leave. One 2014 study found that "exiting is a long and complex process that requires a tremendous amount of internal drive and social support."[45] Other findings showed that current social service systems are not meeting the unique needs of those wanting to leave.

Sex workers are often motivated to return to a more conventional lifestyle by family and friends—especially their own children, for whom they want to offer a wholesome role model. Similarly, dangers associated with the trade, including violent clients, drug use, and criminal victimization, provide additional motivation for lifestyle changes. In any case, exiting the trade is often more of a process than a one-time decision. That process can take years, and includes building the inner strength needed to move forward, and identifying resources that can support the transition. Finding a job, stopping the use of drugs, disassociating from former friends and partners, and even finding spirituality are steps along the way to making a successful move toward conventional lifestyles.

Feminist Perspectives on Prostitution

Prostitution represents a significant issue in today's feminist thought. Some feminist thinkers argue that prostitution exploits and demeans women and subjects them to the dangers of violence and disease. Andrea Dworkin, an ex-prostitute and anti-pornography crusader, wrote that commercial sex is a form of rape perpetrated by poverty and frequent overt violence (often by pimps).[46]

Others take a different approach, saying that selling sex need not be inherently exploitative and might actually be liberating because it fulfills a woman's rights to control her body and her sexuality; they see prostitution as legitimate sex work and argue for the legalization of prostitution (with added protections for those who choose sex work as a trade). The redefinition of prostitution as sex work has been accompanied by the development of an activist movement comprising organizations such as Call Off Your Old Tired Ethics (COYOTE). COYOTE, founded in 1973, advocates for the repeal of prostitution laws and an end to the stigma associated with sex work.

CRIMINAL | PROFILES

Heidi Lynne Fleiss—Madame to the Stars

Heidi Fleiss's notorious high-priced prostitution ring was the stuff of Hollywood lore, but no more so than her arrest, trial, incarceration, and postrelease emergence as an unrepentant sex entrepreneur.[i] Fleiss was initially arrested in June 1993 on state charges that included five counts of pandering and one count of narcotics possession. On July 28, 1994, during her California trial, she was indicted by a federal grand jury on charges of income tax evasion, money laundering, and conspiracy.

Fleiss was convicted in federal court of income tax evasion, money laundering, and eight counts of conspiracy in August 1995. She also pled guilty in state court to the pandering charges. The combined sentences resulted in her serving three years in prison.

Born in Los Angeles on December 30, 1965, Heidi Fleiss showed a precocious flair for business as early as age 12. A popular and responsible babysitter, she soon found herself with more job offers than she could handle herself, so she established a babysitting service by hiring her friends from school to handle some of the jobs. She, of course, got a cut of all the fees.[ii]

Her school performance, however, did not keep pace with her business enterprise. Low grades in junior high and high school ultimately led to her dropping out in the tenth grade. For the next few years, she held a variety of low-wage jobs. Fleiss's aspirations never wavered, however, and she was constantly on the lookout for the right opportunity.

That opportunity came when she and a friend attended a party at 61-year-old millionaire financier Bernie Cornfeld's estate. Impressed with Fleiss, Cornfeld hired her as his personal secretary, an arrangement that, in short order, evolved into a personal relationship. Fleiss sought to deepen the relationship to a live-in level, which she hoped would result in her enjoying a financially secure life of privilege and hedonistic pursuits. Cornfeld, however, had a well-known appetite for classical beauties, which he enthusiastically indulged. His continued dalliances signaled an unwillingness to remain in a monogamous relationship, and the couple eventually broke up.

Still, Fleiss walked away with newly acquired business skills learned from associating with Cornfeld and his friends. A chance meeting with the reigning queen madam of the Los Angeles area, Madam Alex, gave Fleiss entrée to the sex industry.

Madam Alex was, at that time, looking for a replacement to take over her business operations so that she could live a privileged retirement. Fleiss's business acumen fit the bill so well that she increased Madam Alex's profits by more than 400%. But when Madam Alex proved to be less than generous in sharing her largess, Fleiss went off on her own.

And the rest is sex industry history. Ultimately, Fleiss's client base included top producers, directors, and movie stars from the Hollywood scene, as well as some of the world's most famous (and wealthiest) men. Business tycoons, Middle Eastern sheiks, members of royalty, and various heads of state are counted among those to whom she provided women for sexual services.[iii]

Since her release from prison, Fleiss has parlayed her notoriety into a series of successful business ventures, including a men's apparel store in Los Angeles called "Heidi's Wear." A book (*Pandering*), a DVD

Regis Martin/Getty Images

Renowned Hollywood Madame Heidi Fleiss at the Melbourne, Australia, Stock Exchange for the start of trading of "The Daily Planet" bordello—the first brothel in the world to be listed on a national stock exchange. For years, Fleiss's prostitution business had catered to the rich and famous in Hollywood and Los Angeles, but she spent 20 months in prison after being convicted in 1995 on federal charges of conspiracy, tax evasion, and money laundering. Should Fleiss have received a longer sentence?

(*Sex Tips*), a website, an Animal Planet TV show called *Prostitutes to Parrots*, and repeated appearances on late-night talk shows kept her in the public eye for years. Ever the sensationalist, tried to open a Nevada "stud farm,"[iv] staffed by male prostitutes to service Fleiss's hoped-for female customers.[v]

The case of Heidi Fleiss raises a number of interesting questions. Among them are the following:

1. Did the crimes that Fleiss committed hurt anyone? If so, what kind of damage did they cause?

2. How did Fleiss get involved in prostitution? What makes her different from other women who might not have taken advantage of the criminal opportunities that presented themselves to her?

3. Will Fleiss ever get out of the sex business? If so, what kind of work might she pursue?

Notes

i. "Then & Now: Heidi Fleiss," CNN, June 19, 2005, http://www.cnn.com/2005/US/02/28/cnn25.tan.fleiss (accessed September 2, 2015).

ii. Rachael Bell, "Heidi Fleiss: The Million Dollar Madam," CourtTV Crime Library, http://www.crimelibrary.com/notorious_murders/celebrity/heidi_fleiss/index.html (accessed June 1, 2010).

iii. Ibid.

iv. "Fleiss Plans Makeover for Nevada Brothel," *USA Today*, November 16, 2005, http://www.usatoday.com/life/people/2005-11-16-fleiss_x.htm (accessed September 2, 2015).

v. Steve Friess, "Betting on the Studs," *Newsweek*, December 12, 2005, http://www.msnbc.msn.com/id/10313009/site/newsweek (accessed June 1, 2007).

Feminists who believe that prostitution is inherently exploitative reject the idea that prostitution can be reformed. The assumptions that women exist for men's sexual enjoyment, that all men need sex, and that women's bodily integrity and sexual pleasure are irrelevant underlie the whole idea of prostitution, making it an inherently exploitative sexist practice. One feminist argument against Dworkin's position is that prostitution is exploiting men more than it exploits women.

In an interesting critique of what he calls "extreme radical feminist theory," as represented by the writings of Dworkin and others, sociologist Ronald Weitzer of George Washington University listed four core claims characterizing this body of literature:[47]

1. Prostitution involves male domination and exploitation of women regardless of historical time period, societal context, or legal status.
2. Violence is omnipresent in prostitution.
3. Female prostitutes lack agency (they cannot actively make choices about whether or not to stay in prostitution).
4. Legalization or decriminalization would only make the situation worse.

Weitzer saw these claims as counterproductive because they tend to stifle debate over prostitution and effectively divert research programs through what he calls "considerable ideological contamination of our understanding of prostitution."[48] Extreme feminists have contributed to a growing moral panic over prostitution by tying it to sex trafficking and the trafficking of children for sex. Many of the radicals' claims, explained Weitzer, are simply false; violence is not inevitably associated with prostitution, some prostitutes (especially those engaged in legal prostitution) see themselves positively, and prostitution can be lawfully organized in ways that protect the prostitutes' health, rights, and freedoms.

Legalization and Decriminalization of Prostitution

Numerous arguments have been made in favor of legalizing or decriminalizing prostitution. Under legalization, women beyond a specified age would be able to offer paid sexual services with few restrictions (as in parts of Nevada). Decriminalization would significantly reduce the criminal penalties associated with prostitution but would still regulate the practice and might require counseling and alternative employment programs for women in that line of work in an effort to curtail the practice (see **http://ssrn.com/abstract=1451044**).

> Legalization of prostitution would free up law enforcement resources to be used in the investigation of more serious types of crime.

Those who argue in favor of legalization say that keeping prostitution illegal tends to force prostitution out of areas where it might naturally be found (certain hotels, massage parlors) and onto the streets and into other parts of the community and that prostitutes will continue to be viewed as easy targets for pimps, sex offenders, and violent predators. Legalization of prostitution would free up law enforcement resources to be used in the prevention and investigation of more serious types of crime.

Those who argue for keeping prostitution illegal point out that it is regarded as morally and ethically wrong, that it is often not a line of work that is freely chosen, and that it is dangerous for sex workers as well as for their clients because of the disease and violence often associated with it.[49]

SUMMARY

- Drug abuse has a long and varied history in American society, from the use of illegal drugs by artistic individuals seeking to enhance their creativity to citizens using medicinal elixirs containing cocaine, alcohol, and opium.

- Controlled substances are grouped into seven categories: stimulants, depressants, cannabis, narcotics, hallucinogens, anabolic steroids, and inhalants. A separate eighth category, dangerous drugs, provides a kind of legal and definitional catchall. The Controlled Substances Act established five schedules of federally controlled substances based on the effects of a drug and its potential for abuse.

- The National Institute on Drug Abuse (NIDA), a part of the National Institutes of Health, defines addiction as "a chronic, relapsing brain disease that is characterized by compulsive drug seeking and use, despite harmful consequences." Brain-imaging studies of drug-addicted individuals showed changes in areas of the brain that are critical to judgment, decision making, learning and memory, and behavior control. Whether a person becomes addicted to drugs depends on a number of factors: the age at first use;

the frequency of initial use, with genetic and environmental factors interacting with critical developmental stages; gender, ethnicity, and preexisting mental disorders; and social influences in the environment, such as peer pressure, physical and sexual abuse, stress, and parental involvement.

- Drug trafficking includes manufacturing, distributing, dispensing, importing, and exporting (or possessing with intent to do the same) a controlled substance or a counterfeit substance. Federal law enforcement agencies focus on the prevention of smuggling and the apprehension of smugglers.

- Strategies to reduce the flow of illegal drugs into this country are supplemented with programs of education and treatment to reduce the demand for controlled substances. Major policy initiatives have included (1) antidrug legislation and strict enforcement, (2) interdiction, (3) crop control, (4) forfeiture, and (5) antidrug education and drug treatment. Decriminalization and legalization are alternative policies that can be used to address the drug problem.

- Prostitution is a morals offense. Using location as the basis for a typology of prostitutes results in the categories of streetwalkers, bar/hotel prostitutes, online escorts/call girls, club girls, and brothel prostitutes, as well as others who don't fit any of these categories.

KEY TERMS

addiction, 389

controlled substances, 387

dangerous drug, 388

decriminalization, 396

drug-defined crime, 392

drug-related crime, 392

drug trafficking, 389

forfeiture, 395

Heroin Signature Program (HSP), 389

interdiction, 395

legalization, 396

narcoterrorism, 392

National Survey on Drug Use and Health (NSDUH), 383

Office of National Drug Control Policy (ONDCP), 386

pharmaceutical diversion, 391

prostitution, 398

psychoactive substance, 382

synthetic drug, 392

victimless crimes, 382

QUESTIONS FOR REVIEW

1. What can be said about the history of drugs, and drug abuse, in the United States?

2. What are the various categories of controlled substances described by federal law? What is a dangerous drug?

3. What is drug addiction? How does it affect the brain?

4. What is drug trafficking? How do drugs like cocaine and heroin enter the United States?

5. What government strategies have been used to reduce the incidence of drug use in the United States?

6. What is prostitution? What are the various types of prostitutes identified in this chapter?

QUESTIONS FOR REFLECTION

1. This book emphasizes the theme of social problems versus individual responsibility. Which of the social policy approaches to controlling drug abuse discussed in this chapter (if any) appear to be predicated on a social problems approach? Which (if any) are predicated on an individual responsibility approach? Explain the nature of the relationship.

2. What are some of the costs of illicit drug use in the United States today? Which costs can be more easily reduced than others? How would you reduce the costs of illegal drug use?

3. What is the difference between decriminalization and legalization? Should drug use remain illegal? What do you think of the arguments in favor of legalization? Those against?

4. How is prostitution like other crimes? How does it differ?

5. Do you think that prostitution should be legalized? Why or why not?

Golden-I/Rex Features/AP Images

CHAPTER 15
TECHNOLOGY AND CRIME

It's a Double-Edged Sword

LEARNING OUTCOMES

After reading this chapter, you should be able to answer the following questions:

- How does advancing technology produce new forms of crime?
- How does high technology provide new criminal opportunities?
- What is the extent of cybercrime today?

- Name some of the federal laws targeting cybercriminals.
- Describe the characteristics of cybercriminals.
- What new technologies are being used in today's fight against crime?
- What is being done today to combat cybercrime and to secure the Internet?
- What are some of the personal freedoms that are threatened by today's need for advanced security?

Introduction

In 2017, the Senate Select Committee on Intelligence, along with the House Permanent Select Committee on Intelligence, began separate probes on claims that Russian hacking may have influenced the 2016 presidential election.[1] Only a few months earlier, Yahoo! disclosed that the online accounts of around 1 billion of its users had been compromised by a data breach that exposed personal information.[2] This chapter discusses technology and crime, and it is clear that the number of crimes committed through the use of high technology has rapidly increased in the past decade or two.

Technology and Crime

Technology and crime have always been closely linked. The con artist who uses a telephone in a financial scam, the robber who uses a firearm and drives a getaway car, even the murderer who wields a knife—all employ at least rudimentary forms of technology in the crimes they commit. Technology can be employed by both crime fighters and lawbreakers. Early forms of technology, including the telegraph, telephone, and automobile, were embraced by agents of law enforcement as soon as they became available. Evidence derived from fingerprint and ballistics analysis is routinely employed by prosecutors; and emerging technologies promise to keep criminologists and law enforcement agents in step with high-tech offenders.

> **Technology and crime have always been closely linked.**

As technology advances, it facilitates new forms of behavior, so we can be certain that tomorrow's crimes will differ from those of today. Personal crimes of violence and traditional property crimes will continue to occur, but advancing technology will create new and as-yet-unimaginable opportunities for criminals and other international actors positioned to take advantage of it and of the power it will afford.

A frightening and early preview of such possibilities was seen during the collapse of the Soviet Union when the resulting social disorganization made the acquisition of fissionable materials, stolen from Soviet stockpiles, simple for even relatively small outlaw organizations. In what is a nightmare for authorities throughout the world, Middle Eastern terrorist groups are still making efforts to acquire former Soviet nuclear weapons and the raw materials necessary to manufacture their own

The Kremlin in Moscow, Russia. In 2017, both chambers of the U.S. Congress conducted investigations into claims that Russian hackers had influenced the November 2016 presidential elections. How are technology and crime related?

Pearl-diver/Shutterstock

bombs, and some evidence suggests that nuclear weapons parts may have already been sold to wealthy international drug cartels and organized criminal groups, who could hoard them to use as bargaining chips against possible government prosecution.

About five years ago, the White House identified the Chinese military as the source of cyberintrusions into public and private websites throughout the United States; and in 2014, a federal grand jury returned indictments charging five Chinese military officers with economic espionage and conspiracy to hack into computers located in the United States. Federal prosecutors said that the men had stolen trade secrets and other sensitive business information.[3] Since that time, other large American companies, including Yahoo! corporation, Bank of America, J.P. Morgan, and Sony Pictures, have been the victim of similar attacks by other parties.

U.S. companies are not the sole victims of cyberattacks, of course, and in a 2017 example, Ruslan Stoyanov, a key cybercrime investigator at Russia's biggest cybersecurity firm, Kaspersky Labs, was arrested in his home country and charged with treason. Stoyanov was taken into custody along with a senior Russian FSB intelligence officer, Sergei Mikhailov, who also faced treason charges. Mikhailov was the deputy head of the information security department of the Russian national security service (FSB). Both men were accused of taking bribes from foreign entities to facilitate computer intrusions in various places around the world.[4]

■ **hacker** A person who uses computers for exploration and exploitation.
■ **cybercrime** Any crime that involves the use of computers or the manipulation of digital data, as well as any violation of a federal or state cybercrime statute.

High Technology and Criminal Opportunity

The twenty-first century has been termed the postindustrial information age. Information is vital to the success of any endeavor, and certain forms of information hold nearly incalculable value for those who possess it. Patents on new products, pharmaceutical formulations, corporate strategies, and the financial resources of corporations all represent competitive and corporate trade secrets. Government databases, if infiltrated, can offer terrorists easy paths to destruction and mayhem.

Some criminal perpetrators intend simply to destroy or alter data without otherwise accessing or copying the information. Disgruntled employees, mischievous computer **hackers**, business competitors, and others may have varied degrees of interest in destroying the records or computer capabilities of others.

High-tech criminals seeking illegitimate access to computerized information take a number of routes. One is the path of direct access, wherein office workers or corporate spies, planted as seemingly innocuous employees, use otherwise legitimate work-related entry to a company's computer resources to acquire wanted information.

Another path of illegal access, called *computer trespass*, involves remote access to targeted machines. Anyone equipped with a computer and Internet access has potential access to numerous computer systems. Many such systems have few, if any, security procedures in place. Similarly, electromagnetic field (EMF) decoders can scan radio frequency emanations generated by all types of computers. Keystroke activity, internal chip-processed computations, and disk reads, for example, can be detected and interpreted at a distance by such sophisticated devices. Computers secured against such passively invasive practices are rarely found in the commercial marketplace, although the military had adopted them for many applications. Within the last decade, wireless networking has heightened fears of data theft, and cell phones, handheld devices, and other forms of radio communication offer opportunities for data interception.

The realities of today's digital world have led to a form of crime called cybercrime, and to new laws intended to combat it. Simply put, **cybercrime**, or *computer crime*, is any violation of a federal or state computer-crime statute. Many argue that only those crimes that use computer technology as central to their commission may properly be called "cybercrimes." However, a number of other kinds of offenses can also be described as cybercrimes. A Federal Bureau of Investigation (FBI) typology distinguishes between five types of cyber-crimes: (1) internal cybercrimes, such as viruses; (2) Internet and telecommunications crimes, including illegal hacking; (3) support of criminal enterprises, such as databases supporting drug distribution; (4) computer-manipulation crimes, such as embezzlement; and (5) hardware, software, and information theft.[5] Table 15-1 lists these five categories, with additional examples of each. Learn more about cybercrime typologies by reading **http://www.lectlaw.com/files/cri14.htm**.

TABLE 15-1 | Categories of Cybercrime

Internal Cybercrimes (Malware)
Trojan horses
Logic bombs
Trap doors
Viruses
Ransomware
Internet and Telecommunications Crimes
Hacking
Denial of service attacks
Illegal websites
Dissemination of illegal material (e.g., child pornography)
Misuse of telecommunications systems
Theft of telecommunications services
Illegal eavesdropping
Illegal Internet-based gambling
Support of Criminal Enterprises
Databases to support drug distribution
Databases to support loan-sharking
Databases to support illegal gambling
Databases to keep records of illegal client transactions
Electronic money laundering
Communications in furtherance of criminal conspiracies
Computer-Manipulation Crimes (aka Computer Fraud)
Embezzlement
Electronic fund transfer fraud
Other fraud/phishing
Extortion threats/electronic terrorism
Cyberbullying
Hardware, Software, and Information Theft
Software piracy (warez)
Thefts of computers
Thefts of microprocessor chips
Thefts of trade secrets and proprietary information
Identity theft

■ **software piracy**   The unauthorized and illegal copying of software programs.

■ **phishing**   An Internet-based scam to steal valuable information such as credit card numbers, Social Security numbers, user IDs, and passwords.

When discussing cybercrime, it is important to realize that a huge number of today's financial transactions are computerized.

The person most likely to invade your computer is currently on your payroll.

Although most people probably think of money as bills and coins, money today is really just information—information stored in a computer network, possibly located within the physical confines of a bank, but more likely existing as bits and bytes of data on service providers' machines. Typical financial customers give little thought to the fact that very little "real" money is held by their bank, brokerage house, mutual fund, or commodities dealer. Nor do they often consider the threats to their financial well-being by activities such as electronic theft or the sabotage of existing accounts. Unfortunately, however, the threat is very real. Computer criminals equipped with enough information (or able to find the data they need) can quickly and easily locate, steal, and send vast amounts of money anywhere in the world.

No reliable estimates exist as to the losses suffered in such transactions due to the activities of technologically adept criminal perpetrators. Accurate estimates are lacking largely because sophisticated high-tech thieves are so effective at eluding apprehension.

The Extent of Cybercrime

A recent CSO (Chief Security Officer) Cyber Security Watch Survey, a cooperative effort between the U.S. Secret Service, Deloitte & Touche, Carnegie Mellon's Software Engineering Institute (CERT), and *CSO* magazine, found that a sophisticated cybercrime-fueled underground economy exists in America and that its members continue to develop a sophisticated arsenal of damaging software tools with which most companies cannot keep pace while remaining focused on their core businesses. One recent global report on the cost of cybercrime found the following:

1. Cybercrimes continue to be on the rise and so do the costs associated with them.
2. The most costly cybercrimes are those caused by malicious insiders.
3. Business disruption represents the highest cost, followed by the costs associated with information loss.[6]

Another industry group, the Ponemon Institute, surveyed 383 business organizations in 7 countries in 2016 and found that the typical company lost $4 million in each cyberattack. The average cost paid for each lost or stolen record containing sensitive and confidential information was put at $158.[7] **Software piracy**, or the unauthorized and illegal copying of software, is also rampant. According to the Business Software Alliance, global losses from pirated software (known as *warez* in the computer underground) totaled over $70 billion in 2017.[8] The Alliance found that 1 out of 5 pieces of installed software in the United States was unlicensed in 2017.

Phishing (pronounced "fishing") is a relatively new scam that uses official-looking e-mail to steal valuable information such as credit card numbers, Social Security numbers, user IDs, and passwords from victims. The e-mails appear to come from a user's bank, credit card company, retail store, or Internet service provider (ISP) and generally inform the recipients that some vital information in their account urgently needs to be updated. Those who respond are provided with an official-looking Web form on which they can enter their private financial information. Once the information is submitted, it enters the phisher's database.

The Anti-Phishing Working Group (APWG), a coalition of banks and ISPs, says that a typical phishing scheme reaches up to 1 million e-mail in-boxes. The watchdog group has identified more than 277,000 different phishing websites.[9] Although servers that run those sites can be anywhere in the world, the APGW found that 46% of them are located in the United States.

Phishing has the potential to threaten the viability of e-commerce and to call into question the safety of all Web-based financial transactions.

Phishing sites often attempt to hijack brand names, and some phishers are capable of sending e-mails that are difficult to distinguish from legitimate ones. When that happens and customers respond to those e-mails in significant numbers, a brand (such as the name of a bank or credit card company) is said to have been hijacked. Some observers have noted that in addition to losses suffered by individuals and institutions, phishing has the potential to threaten the viability of e-commerce and to call into question the safety of all Web-based financial transactions.[10]

Not all cybercrime is committed for financial gain. Some types of computer crime, including the creation and transmission

■ **computer virus**   A set of computer instructions that propagates copies or versions of itself into computer programs or data when it is executed.

■ **ransomware**   A type of malware that prevents legitimate access to user data stored on computers, and demands payments, often in Bitcoins, to renable access.

■ **Communications Decency Act (CDA)**   A federal statute labeled Title 5 of the federal Telecommunications Act of 1996 (Public Law 104–104, 110 Stat. 56) that sought to protect minors from harmful material on the Internet and that criminalizes the knowing transmission of obscene or indecent messages to any recipient under 18 years of age. In 1997, in *Reno* v. *ACLU* (521 U.S. 844), the U.S. Supreme Court found the bulk of the CDA to be unconstitutional, ruling that it contravenes First Amendment free speech guarantees.

Dr. Ali-Reza Ghasemi and his wife, Shahla Ghasemi, of Tampa (Florida). They lost $400,000 to an advance fee scheme on the Internet. Advance fee schemes (often called Nigerian e-mail fraud because many of the messages appear to come from Nigeria) promise victims a lot of money in return for advancing fees to cover legal services and transfer of funds. How can you tell when an e-mail message is likely to be a fraud?

of destructive computer viruses, "worms," spyware, and other malicious forms of programming code (often called *malware*), might better be classified as "criminal mischief." Perhaps not surprisingly, these types of activities are typically associated with young, technologically sophisticated male miscreants seeking a kind of clandestine recognition from their computer-savvy peers. Computer crimes committed by youthful and idealistic offenders may represent a novel form of juvenile delinquency—one aimed at expressing dissatisfaction with the status quo.

Computer viruses have shown signs of becoming effective terrorist-like tools in the hands of young, disaffected "technonerds" intent on attacking or destroying existing social institutions. A **computer virus** is a computer program that is designed to secretly invade computer systems to modify the way in which they operate or to alter the information they store.[11] Other types of destructive programs are logic bombs, ransomware worms, and Trojan horse routines. Distinctions among these programs are based on the way in which they infect targeted machines or on the way in which they behave once they have found their way into a computer. Not all malware is created by disaffected programmers. Recently, computer security company Symantec announced the discovery of what it called the "world's most sophisticated computer malware."[12] The software code, named Reign, is a highly sophisticated worm designed to provide

backdoor access to computers that it infects. It is virtually undetectable and can modify its own code or simply disappear from infected systems in order to avoid discovery. Cybersecurity experts suspect that it was developed by a Western intelligence agency to target foreign governments and that it may have been in operation for years before its discovery. Reign follows in the footsteps of Stuxnet, a hacking software that was apparently created by Western governments in 2010 to disrupt Iranian computers in that country's nuclear facilities. Similarly, in 2017, a stealth email virus called *WannaCry* made headlines when it disabled millions of computers around the world. WannaCry fell into the category of "**ransomware**", and its creators demanded payments in Bitcoins to "free" affected machines, and to allow their users to access important data that the ransomware had effectively encrypted. While some experts claimed that the ransomware attacks originated in North Korea, others said that they used software exploits developed by the National Security Agency—which, although highly classified, had been exposed by the hacker group known as Shadow Brokers. Another ransomware program called Adylkuzz, began infecting computers shortly after the *WannaCry* outbreak had been contained. Figure 15-1 provides an overview of some of the most damaging computer viruses of all time. Learn more about botnets, computer viruses, and malware at **http://antivirus.about.com/od/virusdescriptions/ Latest_Malware_and_Vulnerabilities.htm.**

Cybercrime and the Law

In the early years of computer-based information systems, most U.S. jurisdictions tried to prosecute unauthorized computer access under preexisting property crime statutes, including burglary and larceny laws. Unfortunately, because the actual carrying off of a computer is quite different from copying or altering some of the information it contains, juries were confused by how such laws apply to high-tech crimes and computer criminals were often let free. As a result, all states and the federal government developed computer-crime statutes specifically applicable to invasive activities that illegally access stored information.

In 1996, President Bill Clinton signed into law the **Communications Decency Act (CDA)**,[13] which sought to protect minors from harmful material on the Internet. A portion of the CDA criminalized the knowing transmission of

■ **No Electronic Theft Act (NETA)**   A 1997 federal law (Public Law 105–147) that criminalizes the willful infringement of copyrighted works, including by electronic means, even when the infringing party derives no direct financial benefit from the infringement (such as when pirated software is freely distributed online).

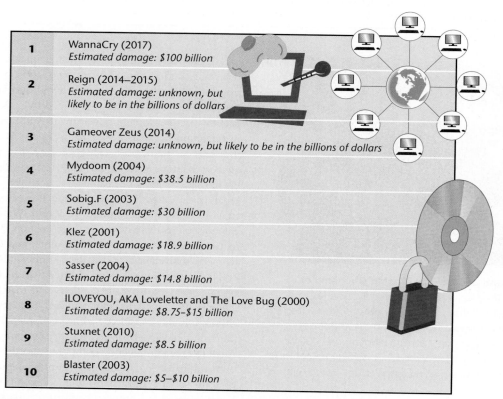

1	**WannaCry (2017)** *Estimated damage: $100 billion*	
2	**Reign (2014–2015)** *Estimated damage: unknown, but likely to be in the billions of dollars*	
3	**Gameover Zeus (2014)** *Estimated damage: unknown, but likely to be in the billions of dollars*	
4	**Mydoom (2004)** *Estimated damage: $38.5 billion*	
5	**Sobig.F (2003)** *Estimated damage: $30 billion*	
6	**Klez (2001)** *Estimated damage: $18.9 billion*	
7	**Sasser (2004)** *Estimated damage: $14.8 billion*	
8	**ILOVEYOU, AKA Loveletter and The Love Bug (2000)** *Estimated damage: $8.75–$15 billion*	
9	**Stuxnet (2010)** *Estimated damage: $8.5 billion*	
10	**Blaster (2003)** *Estimated damage: $5–$10 billion*	

FIGURE 15-1 | **The Ten Most Damaging Computer Viruses and Worms of All Time**

Sources: *Smithsonian Magazine*, "Top Ten Most-Destructive Computer Viruses," http://www.smithsonianmag.com/science-nature/Top-Ten-Most-Destructive-Computer-Viruses.html#ixzz2SNIYZ0Tz (accessed September 6, 2015); "Computer Invaders," http://safeandsavvy.f-secure.com/2011/03/21/25-infamous-viruse/ (accessed September 6, 2015); Buzzle.com, "The Most Damage Causing Computer Viruses Revealed," http://www.buzzle.com/articles/the-most-damage-causing-computer-viruses-revealed.html (accessed October 22, 2013); and others.

obscene or indecent messages to any recipient under 18 years of age. Another section prohibited the knowing sending or displaying to a person under 18 any message "that, in context, depicts or describes, in terms patently offensive as measured by contemporary community standards, sexual or excretory activities or organs." Shortly after the law was passed, however, the American Civil Liberties Union (ACLU) and a number of other plaintiffs filed suit against the federal government, challenging the constitutionality of the law's two provisions relating to the transmission of obscene materials to minors.

In 1996, a three-judge federal district court entered a preliminary injunction against enforcement of both challenged provisions, ruling that they contravened First Amendment guarantees of free speech. The government then appealed to the U.S. Supreme Court. The Court's 1997 decision *Reno* v. *ACLU*[14] upheld the lower court's ruling and found that the CDA's "indecent transmission" and "patently offensive display" provisions abridge "the freedom of speech" protected by the First Amendment. Most other federal legislation aimed at keeping online pornography away from the eyes of children has not fared any better when reviewed by the Court. Although the Children's Internet Protection Act (CIPA), which requires public and school libraries receiving certain kinds of federal funding to install pornography filters on their Internet-linked computers, was approved by the justices, most observers acknowledge that the Court has placed the Internet in the same category as newspapers and other print media, where almost no regulation is permitted.

Enacted in 1997, the **No Electronic Theft Act (NETA, or NET Act)** criminalizes the willful infringement of copyrighted works, including by electronic means, even when the infringing party derives no direct financial benefit from the infringement (such as when pirated software is freely distributed online). In keeping with requirements of the NETA, the U.S. Sentencing Commission enacted amendments to its guidelines to increase penalties associated with electronic theft.

■ **Digital Theft Deterrence and Copyright Damages Improvement Act**   A 1999 federal law (Public Law 106–160) that amends Section 504(c) of the Copyright Act by increasing the amount of damages that could be awarded in cases of copyright infringement.

■ **Cyber Security Enhancement Act (CSEA)**   A federal law found in the Homeland Security Act of 2002 that directs the U.S. Sentencing Commission to take specific factors into account in creating new sentencing guidelines for cybercriminals.

■ **computer-related crime**   An illegal act using computer technology in its perpetration, investigation, or prosecution.

■ **computer abuse**   An unlawful incident associated with computer technology in which a victim suffers loss or a perpetrator reaps benefit.

■ **Cybersecurity Information Sharing Act (CISA)**   A 2015 federal law that is designed to facilitate the sharing of information about cybersecurity threats between the U.S. government and technology companies.

The **Digital Theft Deterrence and Copyright Damages Improvement Act** of 1999 increased the amount of damages that could be awarded in cases of copyright infringement—a crime that is intimately associated with software piracy. The **Cyber Security Enhancement Act (CSEA)** of 2002,[15] which is part of the Homeland Security Act of 2002, directed the U.S. Sentencing Commission to take several factors into account in creating new sentencing guidelines for computer criminals. The law told the commission to consider not only what financial loss was caused by computer crime, but also what level of planning was involved in the offense, whether the crime was committed for commercial or private advantage and whether malicious intent existed on the part of the perpetrator. Under the law, computer criminals can face life in prison if they put human lives in jeopardy. Certain future illegitimate activities using computer equipment may not be adequately covered by existing law. On the other hand, some crimes committed with the use of a computer may be more appropriately prosecuted under "traditional" laws. For that reason, some experts distinguish between computer crime, computer-related crime, and computer abuse. **Computer-related crime** is "any illegal act for which knowledge of computer technology is involved for its investigation, perpetration, or prosecution," whereas **computer abuse** is said to be "any incident without color of right associated with computer technology in which a victim suffered or could have suffered loss and/or a perpetrator by intention made or could have made gain."[16] The Cybersecurity Enhancement Act of 2014 (whose name is almost identical to the 2002 legislation described earlier) provides for "an ongoing, voluntary

> Money today is really only information stored in a computer network as bits and bytes of data.

public-private partnership to improve cybersecurity, and to strengthen cybersecurity research and development, workforce development and education, and public awareness and preparedness, and for other purposes."

The **Cybersecurity Information Sharing Act of 2015 (CISA)** is designed to improve cybersecurity in the United States by facilitating the sharing of information about cybersecurity threats. It allows for the easy sharing of Internet traffic information between the U.S. government and technology and manufacturing companies.

The purpose of the law is to make it easier for private companies to quickly and directly share personal information with the government, especially in cases involving specific cybersecurity threats.

The law also creates a portal for a variety of federal agencies, including the FBI and the National Security Agency, to receive threat information directly from private companies, without the need for the involvement of the Department of Homeland Security. Critics of the legislation say that it facilitates mass surveillance of private communications via the sharing of information between companies and the government, most notably the National Security Agency. Significant federal cybersecurity legislation is shown in Figure 15-2.

FIGURE 15-2 | Significant Federal Cybersecurity Legislation

■ **phone phreak**   A person who uses switched, dialed-access telephone services for exploration and exploitation.

■ **cyberspace**   The compuuter-created matrix of virtual possibilities, including online services, in which human beings interact with one another and with the technology itself.

The History and Nature of Hacking

Some authors suggest that computer hacking began with the creation of the interstate phone system and direct distance dialing implemented by AT&T in the late 1950s.[17] Early switching devices used audible tones that were easily duplicated by electronics hobbyists and "blue boxes" capable of emulating such tones quickly entered the illicit marketplace. **Phone phreaks** used special telecommunications access codes and other restricted technical information to avoid paying long-distance charges. Some were able to place calls from pay phones and others fooled telephone equipment into billing other callers.

Recently, the U.S. Department of Homeland Security (DHS) identified a number of contemporary threats to mobile phones and other handheld devices. According to DHS, "Smartphones' popularity and relatively lax security have made them attractive targets for attackers."[18] As DHS notes, smartphone security has not kept pace with traditional computer security, and security measures, such as firewalls, antivirus, and encryption, are relatively uncommon on mobile phones. Moreover, mobile phone operating systems are not updated as frequently as those on personal computers, and mobile social networking applications often lack the privacy controls of their PC counterparts. Unfortunately, says DHS, many smartphone users do not recognize these security shortcomings, and so they fail to enable the security software that comes with their phones. Users believe that surfing the Internet on their phones is as safe as or safer than surfing on their computers. Increasing the threat, DHS notes, are "recent innovations in mobile commerce that have enabled users to conduct many transactions from their smartphone, such as purchasing goods and applications over wireless networks, redeeming coupons and tickets, banking, processing point-of-sale payments, and even paying at cash registers."[19]

See **http://ssrn.com/abstract=1363932** for a discussion of self-defense in cyberspace.

A Profile of Cybercriminals

Cybercriminals come from a diverse background and cybercrime can run the gamut from simple computer hacking to far more malicious activities. In 2014, for example, Tevon Harris aka "Da Kidd" and "King Kidd," 22, of Houston, was convicted of trafficking children under the age of 18 for commercial sex and sentenced to 40 years in federal prison. Harris was also ordered to spend the rest of his life on supervised release and must register as a sex offender.[20]

Prior to his 2012 arrest, Harris forced young girls, whom he met on social networking sites, into prostitution. His scheme involved promises of a modeling career. Instead Harris arranged to pick them up, then took them to motel rooms where he forced them to have sex with him. He used violence to keep the girls compliant and deprived them of food, while supplying them with drugs and alcohol. The victims were photographed and their images were posted in online ads for prostitution.

A less violent, but still serious, offense led to the 2014 indictment of Evgeniy Mikhailovich Bogachev of Anapa (part of the Russian Federation). Bogachev was charged by U.S. officials with administering the GameOver Zeus botnet.[21] A botnet is a global network of infected computers that can be used for illegal purposes (Figure 15-3). Bogachev used personal cyberskills that he had acquired during his youth to steal banking credentials from financial institutions and then wired as much as $100 million to overseas accounts.

The indictment of Bogachev illustrates both the potential for high-technology offenders to thwart government efforts at prosecution by operating internationally as well as the transnational nature of hacker subculture. It is from hacker subculture that cybercriminals tend to come because hackers and hacker identities are the products of **cyberspace**, a realm that exists only within electronic networks where computer technology and human psychology meet. For many hackers, cyberspace provides the opportunity for impersonal interpersonal contact, technological challenges, and game playing. Fantasy

FIGURE 15-3 | Botnet Architecture

Source: Federal Bureau of Investigation, http://www.fbi.gov/news/stories/2014/june/gameover-zeus-botnet-disrupted/documents/gameover-zeus-and-cryptolocker-poster-pdf.

role-playing games are popular among hackers and may engross many "wave riders," who appear to prefer what is called "virtual reality" to the external physical and social worlds around them: "Cyberspace is hacker heaven."[22]

No one knows the actual identity of many of these people, but computer-security experts have come up with a rough profile of the average hacker.[23] He is a male between the ages of 16 and 25 who lives in the United States, is a computer user but not a programmer, and hacks with software written by others; his primary motivation is to gain access to websites and computer networks, not to profit financially (see the Who's to Blame box in this chapter).

Hackers can be distinguished both by their purpose and by their method of operation, but such categorization is descriptive; distinctions can also be made on the basis of personality and lifestyle. Some experts have suggested that hackers can be grouped according to psychological characteristics:[24]

- **Pioneers.** Individuals who are fascinated by the evolving technology of telecommunications and explore it without knowing exactly what they are going to find are called pioneers; few hard-core criminals are found among this group.

- **Scamps.** Hackers with a sense of fun, with no intention to harm, are referred to as scamps.

- **Explorers.** Explorers are hackers motivated by their delight in discoveries associated with breaking into new computer systems—the farther away geographically such systems are from the hackers' physical locations or the more secure such systems are, the greater the excitement associated with breaking into them.

- **Game players.** Game players enjoy defeating software or system copy protection and may seek to illegally access computer systems with games to play. Hacking itself becomes a game for this sort of hacker.

- **Vandals.** Malicious hackers who deliberately cause damage with no apparent gain for themselves are called vandals. The original 414 Gang in Milwaukee, which broke into the Sloan-Kettering Cancer Institute's computers and wiped out patient records, is an example of this type of hacker.

- **Addicts.** Classic computer nerds who are addicted to hacking and to computer technology are addicts. They may also be addicted to illicit drugs (some hacker bulletin board systems post information on drugs as well as on modems, passwords, and vulnerable systems).

Psychologist Percy Black argued for the existence of an underlying theme in all cases of hacking, calling it "the search for a feeling of power, possibly stemming from a deep-seated sense of powerlessness."[25] Hacking may serve as compensation for feelings of personal inferiority; by challenging the machine and by winning against machine culture, hackers go through a kind of rite of passage into adulthood, whereby they prove themselves capable of success.

Because most hackers are young adolescent males, it is important to realize that "their other favorite risky business is the time-honored adolescent sport of trespassing. They insist on going where they don't belong. But then teen-age boys have been proceeding uninvited since the dawn of human puberty. It seems hard-wired. The only innovation is in the new form of the forbidden zone and the means of getting in it."[26]

CRIME | in the NEWS

Cyberbanging

Recently, a new term, *cyberbanging*—referring to the use of the Internet and social networking websites by street gangs to tout their exploits, recruit new members, post threats, and socialize—entered the law enforcement lexicon. Videos and lyrics glorifying gang activities can be found on Facebook, MySpace, and Twitter, and some gangs have their own home pages and even run their own servers. "Gangs are going to use any form of communication they can," stated George W. Knox, director of the National Gang Crime Research Center, "including Twitter, including Facebook." Law enforcement experts have said that gangs sometimes use social networking sites to circumvent court injunctions forbidding members from meeting face-to-face.

One study of Internet gang activity, however, found that gangs are not using the Web to recruit new members or to commit cybercrimes. Instead, they "are doing online what they are doing on the street," the study found. That means that they are using sites like Facebook, Twitter, and YouTube for self-promotion, bragging, and making territorial claims. According to study authors, the virtual world is viewed by gang members as another territory, or turf, on which to post electronic graffiti, gang signs, and images. The study was based on interviews with 585 young adult gang members from five cities.

Police agencies and criminal prosecutors have begun scouring social networking sites looking for evidence they can use to disrupt gang activities or to prosecute gang members for crimes they've committed. "Five years ago we would find evidence in a gang case on the Internet and say, 'Wow!'" Bruce Riordan, director of antigang operations for the Los Angeles City Attorney's office commented. "Well, there's no more 'Wow' anymore. It's much more routine."

Discussion Questions

1. What is cyberbanging? What purpose does it serve?

2. Can you imagine any new and innovative ways in which gangs might make use of the Internet and social media?

Splash News/Newscom

A prisoner charged with murdering a corrections officer who took him to a hospital appointment in Utah. Curtis Allgier, a neo-Nazi affiliated with the Aryan Brotherhood, is alleged to have wrestled the guard's gun from him and shot him; he then carjacked a vehicle and led police on a chase before being apprehended. Why are street gangs turning to the Internet?

Sources: Tony Castro, "Valley Gangs Leave Trail on Web," *Los Angeles Daily News*, December 5, 2009, http://www.dailynews.com/news/ci_13931149 (accessed May 12, 2012); "Study Explores Gang Activity on the Internet," *Science Codex*, March 26, 2013, http://www.sciencecodex.com/study_explores_gang_activity_on_the _internet-109243 (accessed May 22, 2013); and David C. Pyrooz, Scott H. Decker, and Richard K. Moule, "Criminal and Routine Activities in Online Settings: Gangs, Offenders, and the Internet," *Justice Quarterly*, Spring 2013.

Unfortunately, not all computer hackers are simply kids trying their hand at beating technological challenges. Many are "high-tech computer operators using computers to engage in unlawful conduct."[27] Learn more about hackers and information security at the CERT Coordination Center, which can be reached via **http://www.cert.org/**.

Cybercrime as a Form of White-Collar Crime

Numerous analysts have suggested that cybercrime is merely a new form of white-collar crime or maybe its ultimate expression (white-collar crime is discussed in detail in Chapter 13). Donn B. Parker, author of the National Institute of Justice (NIJ) *Computer Crime: Criminal Justice Research Manual,* compared white-collar criminals with computer criminals, stating that both share certain "common criminal behavior-related issues":[28]

- Both types of acts are often committed through non-violent means, although certain industrial, consumer, and environment-related crimes have life-threatening consequences.

- Access to computers or computer storage media, through employment-related knowledge or technical skills, is often needed.

WHO'S TO BLAME—The Individual or Society?

Criminal Activity or Mischievous Gaming?

Late last year, Calvin Mutchnak was arrested and charged under federal law with interfering with the operation of computers owned by the federal government. The computers, mostly Apple iMacs, ran Apple's latest operating system, popularly referred to as Mac OS X Yosemite, and were located in Veterans Administration (VA) hospitals across the country.

Mutchnak was especially taken with the long-standing popular impression that Apple's operating system was secure and impenetrable—a myth that computer hackers had long known was untrue, but that Apple corporate officials had done little to dispel. The feeling of those who worked for Apple, Mutchnak concluded, was that the popular myth could help sell computers. Nonetheless, most hackers continued to focus their efforts on Microsoft's Windows operating system because of its greater popularity, and because it was easier to hack. After the advent of Windows 10 in 2015, however, and with the introduction of Macintosh computers able to dual-boot both Windows and OS X, and able to run both simultaneously, attention in the hacker community had increasingly turned to identifying backdoors into the Apple operating system.

Soon Mutchnak was devoting all of his spare time to dispelling Apple's myth of invincibility, and to writing malware—malicious software code—that could successfully invade almost any of Apple's higher-end computers that were connected to the Internet.

After writing a malicious script that he could insert into a tiny QuickTime video, Mutchnak sent the video as an e-mail attachment to VA hospital computers, making the e-mail look as though it contained administrative data that would be of significance to people in charge of the facilities. Although the e-mail had to be opened and the video file clicked on, and although the person reading the e-mail had to be logged in under an administrative account (most, he found, were), Mutchnak's plan was very successful, and soon most Apple computers in federally run hospitals across the country

A computer laboratory. What motivates computer hackers?

were infected. Unfortunately for Mutchnak, however, federal anticyberterrorism officials had been running a drill responding to a mock cyberterrorism attack when his e-mail made its way onto the Net. Within minutes of its release, Mutchnak's malicious e-mail had been traced to the IP address assigned to his home by his ISP.

A warrant for his arrest was drawn up, and Mutchnak was arrested by federal agents who charged him with violating various federal computer crime laws, including one meant to deter terrorists.

Think about it

1. Do you believe that Mutchnak saw his activity as criminal? As terrorist activity? If not, how did he perceive it?

2. Was Mutchnak, as he claimed, doing a service by showing weaknesses in parts of the nation's computer infrastructure?

3. Might there have been other ways for Mutchnak to make his point? Would those ways have been as effective as the computer mischief in which he engaged? Why or why not?

Note: Who's to Blame boxes provide fictionalized critical thinking opportunities based on actual cases.

- These acts generally involve information manipulations that either directly or indirectly create profits or losses.
- These crimes can be committed by an individual, by several individuals working in collusion, or by organizations, with the victims in the last case ranging from individual clients to customers to employees in other organizations.

See the Criminal Profiles box for the story of a convicted hacker who became an author.

According to Parker, cybercrime and white-collar crime also share the following similarities:

- These crimes are difficult to detect, with discovery often started by accident or by customer complaint rather than as the result of direct investigation.
- The general public views many of these acts as less serious than crimes involving physical violence.
- These crimes cost individuals, organizations, and society large amounts of money and other resources.
- Prevention of these crimes requires a combination of legal, technical, managerial, security, and audit–monitoring controls.

Technology in the Fight against Crime

Technology is a double-edged sword: It arms evildoers with potent new weapons of crime commission, yet it provides police agencies and criminal justice personnel with powerful tools useful in the battle against crime. Criminally useful or evasive technologies and law enforcement capabilities commonly leapfrog one another. Consider traffic radar, which has gone from early always-on units through trigger-operated radar devices to today's sophisticated laser-based speed-measuring apparatus—each change being an attempt by enforcement agencies to keep a step ahead of increasingly sophisticated radar-detection devices marketed to drivers. Radar-jamming devices and laser jammers are also now used by people apparently intent on breaking speed-limit laws. Not to be outdone, suppliers to law enforcement agencies have created radar- detector detectors, which are used by authorities in states where radar detectors have been outlawed.[29]

Criminal technologies and law enforcement capabilities leapfrog one another.

Other potent technologies in law enforcement today are computer databases of known offenders (including public access to sex-offender databases), machine-based expert systems, cellular communications, video surveillance (often combined with face-recognition technology), electronic eavesdropping, deoxyribonucleic acid (DNA) analysis, and less-lethal weapons. Transponder-based automated vehicle location (AVL) systems now use patrol car–based transmitters in tandem with orbiting global positioning system (GPS) satellites to pinpoint locations of police vehicles to within 50 feet so that dispatchers can better allocate available resources on a given shift and be able to substantially reduce police response times in crisis situations. (Chip-based transponders are also installed in private vehicles to deter thieves and to help trace stolen automobiles.)

In jurisdictions with computer-aided dispatch (CAD) systems, police dispatchers are prompted by computers for important information that allows them to distinguish a location (such as a particular McDonald's). CAD systems also quickly provide information about how often officers have been called to a given site and can tell responding officers what they might expect to find based on past calls from that location.

More innovative crime-fighting technologies are becoming available. The "Spiderman snare," being tested for its usefulness in incapacitating fleeing suspects, is a 16-foot-wide net that is compressed into a small shotgun-like shell. The net has small weights at its circumference and wraps itself around its target after being fired. The snare's impact is harmless, and test subjects report being able to watch with open eyes as the net wraps around them. Another example is a special-frequency disco-like strobe light which quickly disorients human targets by causing intense dizziness, leaving subjects unable to resist cuffing and arrest (operators wear special glasses designed to counter the influence of the light). Because high-speed chases pose a substantial danger to the public, scientists have developed an electromagnetic pulsing device that can be used to temporarily disable a vehicle's electrical system, causing the engine to stall. The prototype is said to be safe enough to use on vehicles driven by those wearing pacemakers.

As new technologies are developed, their potential usefulness in law enforcement activities is evaluated by the FBI, the NIJ, and other agencies. The NIJ's Technology Assessment Program (TAP) focuses on four areas of advancing technology: protective equipment, such as bulletproof vests and other body armor; forensic sciences, including advances in DNA technology; transportation and weapons, such as electronic stun guns and other less-lethal weapons; and communications and electronics, including computer security and electronic eavesdropping.

Recently, the U.S. Department of Justice's National Law Enforcement and Corrections Technology Center (NLECTC) began testing a high-power compact microwave source designed for vehicle immobilization.[30] The microwave beam emitted by the device can interfere with an automobile's computer circuitry, effectively shutting down a car's engine from up to 35 feet away. As the technology is improved, the device will likely become operable over longer distances, and it may soon become a routine tool in police work.

Other groups, such as the National Computer Security Association, the American Cryptography Association, and the American Society for Industrial Security, bring more specialized high-tech expertise to the private-security and public law enforcement professions.

DNA Technology

On January 16, 2001, Christopher Ochoa, age 34, was released from a Texas prison after serving 13 years for a murder he did not commit.[31] Ochoa had confessed to the rape and murder of 20-year-old Nancy DePriest at a Pizza Hut in Austin in 1988; although Ochoa later said he had been coerced by homicide detectives into confessing, no one believed him. A decade after he began serving a life sentence, law students at the Wisconsin

CRIMINAL | PROFILES

Kevin Mitnick—Hacker Turned Security Expert

At the time of his arrest in February 1995, Kevin Mitnick was the most-wanted computer criminal in U.S. history. His crimes included wire fraud, computer fraud, and wire communication interception, and the cost to his victims included millions of dollars in lost licensing fees, marketing delays, lost research and development, and the costs of repairing compromised computer systems.[i]

Cloned cellular telephones, hacker software programs, "sniffer" devices, and so-called social engineering were the tools Mitnick used to conduct the computer crime spree that launched a lengthy investigation beginning in 1992. The evidence amassed by the FBI during its three-year probe was sufficient to force Mitnick to accept a plea bargain rather than risk more severe penalties by going to trial.[ii] His corporate victims included a number of Fortune 500 companies, and he used University of Southern California computer systems to hide software code and obscure his identity.

Born August 6, 1963, and a product of a blue-collar upbringing in California's San Fernando Valley, Mitnick's 1981 juvenile arrest for stealing computer manuals led to his being placed on probation. The experience had little deterrent effect, however, as evidenced by his subsequent arrests in 1989 (for possession of unauthorized access devices) and in 1992 (for allegedly hacking into California Department of Motor Vehicles computers).[iii]

An intriguing element of Mitnick's case was the manner in which he was finally caught. Computer expert Tsutomu Shimomura, infuriated after Mitnick hacked into and stole information from his home computer, employed a dramatic cybersleuthing effort to track Mitnick down, resulting in Mitnick's arrest by the FBI in a Raleigh, North Carolina, apartment complex.

As a result of his 1995 arrest, Mitnick spent more than five years in prison, with more than eight months of it in solitary confinement. Now, in his 50's, a significantly matured Mitnick has done a 180-degree turnaround in his approach to computer security. On March 1, 2000, he testified before the U.S. Senate's Governmental Affairs Committee, during which he suggested that the millions of dollars corporations spend on firewalls and secure access devices are negated by the "the weakest link in the security chain: the people who use, administer and operate computer systems."[v] Mitnick regaled the committee with tales of his use of "social engineering" (what he defines as "using manipulation, influence, and deception to get a trusted insider to release information and to perform some sort of action item") that enables a hacker to successfully attack the insider's own computer system.

Mitnick now oversees a highly successful computer consulting firm that specializes in advising on computer security issues. Disturbingly,

Joe Cavaretta/AP Images

Hacker-turned-author Kevin Mitnick posing for a portrait in 2002 in Las Vegas. Barred by the terms of his probation from using computers, ex-convict Mitnick turned to writing about them, baring the tricks of his former trade of hacking in a book titled *The Art of Deception.* Mitnick was granted an exemption to use a computer to write his book. What is he doing today?

he suggests that it is easier to hack today than it was years ago, citing social engineering as still an extraordinarily effective technique for computer exploit. Mitnick's message is clear: Notwithstanding tremendous advances in both hardware and software security measures, the weak link is still the human element.[vi]

The case of Kevin Mitnick raises a number of interesting questions. Among them are the following:

1. What theoretical perspectives might explain Mitnick's involvement in crime?

2. What does Mitnick mean by "social engineering"? Does the concept of social engineering apply to other types of crimes?

Notes:

i. "Kevin Mitnick Sentenced to Nearly Four Years in Prison," U.S. Department of Justice Press Release, August 9, 1999; and "Computer Hacker Ordered to Pay Restitution to Victim Companies Whose Systems Were Compromised," U.S. Attorney's Office, Central District of California, August 9, 1999, http://www.cybercrime.gov /mitnick.htm (accessed June 2, 2010).

ii. Ibid.

iii. John Christensen, "The Trials of Kevin Mitnick," CNN, March 18, 1999, http://www.cnn.com/SPECIALS/1999/mitnick.background (accessed September 6, 2015). It is said that Mitnick served as the inspiration for the 1983 film War Games by breaking into the U.S. Department of Defense's North American Defense Command (NORAD) computers in 1982.[iv]

iv. Ibid.

v. Elizabeth Wasserman, "Mitnick Schools Feds on Hacking 101," CNN, March 3, 2000, http://archives.cnn.com/2000/TECH/computing/03/03/mitnick.the.prof/mitnick .the.prof.html (accessed June 2, 2007).

vi. "A Convicted Hacker Debunks Some Myths," CNN, October 13, 2005, http://www.cnn.com/2005/TECH/internet/10/07/kevin.mitnick.cnna (accessed September 6, 2015).

■ **DNA profiling**   The use of biological residue found at a crime scene for genetic comparisons in aiding the identification of criminal suspects.

■ ***Daubert* standard**   A test of scientific acceptability applicable to the gathering of evidence in criminal cases.

Innocence Project at the University of Wisconsin–Madison took an interest in his case, studied surviving information, and concluded that DNA evidence conclusively proved that someone else had killed DePriest. The students and their law professor took the evidence to District Judge Bob Perkins, who called the case "a fundamental miscarriage of justice" and ordered Ochoa set free. According to authorities, evidence of DePriest's murder implicated Texas inmate Achim Joseph Marino, who confessed to her murder in 1996 following a religious conversion. Marino, currently serving three life sentences for other crimes, has provided investigators with the gun and handcuffs used to commit the crime.

The law students involved in the case used **DNA profiling**, matching DNA samples taken from mouth swabs of Marino with the DNA found in semen taken from the victim's body. Without DNA profiling, Ochoa would still be in prison, and DePriest's real killer would be unknown. You can watch a video in which Ochoa discusses his case on YouTube at **https://www.youtube.com/watch?v=0xJlsxCGw9w.**

A person's genetic code is contained in his or her DNA, whose composition is unique to each individual (except in the case of identical twins). DNA samples can be taken from blood, hair, semen, saliva, or even small flakes of skin left at the scene of a crime. After processing, DNA profiles appear like bar codes on film negatives, codes that can exonerate a suspect or provide nearly irrefutable evidence of guilt.

DNA evidence is long lasting—fossilized DNA is now being used to reconstruct genetic maps of long-extinct plant and animal species. Although DNA analysis is theoretically possible using only a single cell, most reputable DNA laboratories require a considerably greater quantity of material to conduct an effective analysis, but that could change. Using a Nobel Prize–winning technique called "polymerase chain-reaction technology," minute strands of DNA can be effectively amplified so that even the identity of a person taking a single puff from a cigarette can be accurately established from the trace DNA left on the cigarette. With costs dropping, these technological advances are expected to soon be available to a range of forensic analysts.

The National Research Council has called DNA profiling "a highly reliable forensic tool" but admits that it is not infallible.[32] Obvious differences in scrutinized DNA samples can easily eliminate a suspect, but testing provides less certainty with positive identification, with human error in conducting the tests being perhaps the greatest threat to reliable results. More than 20 states and the federal government generally accept DNA evidence in criminal trials. Other jurisdictions, including California, are less clear in their recognition of DNA testing,

and trial judges in those states may offhandedly exclude the use of such evidence when experts disagree as to its validity.

In 1993, the U.S. Supreme Court, in the civil case of *Daubert* v. *Merrell Dow Pharmaceuticals, Inc.*, revised the criteria for the admissibility of scientific evidence;[33] the ruling rejected the previous admissibility standard established in the 1923 case of *Frye* v. *United States*.[34] The *Daubert* Court ruled that the older *Frye* standard, requiring "general acceptance" of a test or procedure by the relevant scientific community, "is not a necessary precondition to the admissibility of scientific evidence," which is established by Rule 402 of the *Federal Rules of Evidence*, published after *Frye* and superseding it. Rule 402 says that "all relevant evidence is admissible [in a trial], except as otherwise provided by the Constitution of the United States, by Act of Congress, by these Rules, or by other rules prescribed by the Supreme Court pursuant to statutory authority."[35] The Court said that although "the *Frye* test was displaced by the Rules of Evidence, [it] does not mean that the Rules themselves place no limits on the admissibility of purportedly scientific evidence. Nor is the trial judge disabled from screening such evidence. To the contrary, under the Rules the trial judge must ensure that any and all scientific testimony or evidence admitted is not only relevant, but reliable." The real test for the admissibility of scientific expert testimony is for the trial judge to decide "at the outset whether the expert is proposing to testify to (1) scientific knowledge that (2) will assist the trier of fact to understand or determine a fact in issue." The Court concluded that the trial judge's task is one of "ensuring that an expert's testimony both rests on a reliable foundation and is relevant to the task at hand. Pertinent evidence based on scientifically valid principles will satisfy those demands."

The plaintiffs in *Daubert* were not arguing the merits of DNA testing but were claiming that the drug Bendectin caused birth defects, but the ***Daubert* standard** eased the criteria for the introduction of scientific evidence at both civil and criminal trials—and effectively cleared the way for the use of DNA evidence in the courtroom.[36] The *Daubert* Court found that the following factors may be used to determine whether a form of scientific evidence is reliable:

● It has been subjected to testing.

● It has been subjected to peer review.

● It has known or potential rates of error.

● It has standards controlling application of the techniques involved.

One observer, discussing the quality of DNA identification methods, noted, "The challenges today are no longer technical; instead they lie in taking the technology and building a meaningful legal infrastructure around it."[37] As DNA evidence is accepted throughout jurisdictions nationwide and worldwide, digitized forensic DNA databases (similar to widely used fingerprint archives) are useful at the state and national levels, and most of the states and the federal government (through the FBI laboratory) already have them. In 1998 the FBI announced that its National DNA Index System (NDIS)—which enables U.S. forensic laboratories to exchange and compare DNA profiles electronically, thereby linking unsolved serial violent crimes to each other and to known offenders—had begun operation.[38] Shortly thereafter, all 50 states had passed legislation requiring convicted offenders to provide samples for DNA databases, and all states have been invited to participate in NDIS. The federal DNA Identification Act of 1994 authorized the FBI to establish DNA indexes for (1) offenders convicted of crimes, (2) samples recovered from crime scenes, and (3) samples recovered from unidentified human remains.[39] Today, the National DNA Index System is administered under the FBI's Combined DNA Index System (CODIS) and the combined database is known as the CODIS/NDIS. CODIS/NDIS contained around 13 million offender profiles at the start of 2017. The Web-available CODIS/NDIS interactive map with available statistical tables are found in Figure 15-4.

In 1995 the British police, operating under a new nationwide crime bill, became the first national police force in the world to begin routine collection of DNA samples from anyone involved in a "recordable" offense (a serious crime).[40] It appears that genetic profiling will become one of the most significant crime-fighting technologies of

> ### Genetic profiling will become one of the most significant crime-fighting technologies of the twenty-first century.

the twenty-first century. "Genetic profiling—the use of biotechnology to identify the unique characteristics of an individual's DNA—is about to become as prevalent as the Breathalyzer and more important than the fingerprint."[41]

In 1996, the NIJ released a comprehensive report, titled *Convicted by Juries, Exonerated by Science*, on the applicability of DNA testing to criminal case processing, calling DNA testing "the most important technological breakthrough of twentieth-century forensic science" and providing a detailed review of 28 cases in which postconviction DNA evidence exonerated defendants who had been sentenced to lengthy prison terms.[42] The 28 cases were selected on the basis of a detailed examination of records that indicated the convicted defendants might have actually been innocent. The men in the study had served, on average, seven years in prison, and most had been tried and sentenced prior to the widespread availability of reliable DNA testing. More and more defense attorneys in court-appointed cases are filing motions for DNA testing and requesting that states pay for the tests.[43]

Finally, it is important to note that a growing number of jurisdictions are requiring the gathering of DNA information from arrestees, and in 2013 the U.S. Supreme Court held, in the case of *Maryland* v. *King*, that "When officers make an arrest supported by probable cause … and bring the suspect to the station to be detained in custody, taking and analyzing a cheek swab of the arrestee's DNA is, like fingerprinting and photographing, a legitimate police booking procedure that is reasonable under the Fourth Amendment."[44]

Learn more about the science behind forensic DNA testing and how it has been used to convict as well as exonerate criminal defendants at **http://science.howstuffworks.com/life/genetic/dna-evidence.htm**. An assessment of its likely future is available at **http://www.ojp.usdoj.gov/nij/pubs-sum/183697.htm**.

Computers as Crime-Fighting Tools

Computers are used to keep records of every imaginable sort—from point-of-sale contacts to inventory maintenance and production schedules. Computers also control everyday items like Fitbits, smart home devices (like thermostats), and vending machines.

Computers connect people and things. The Internet contains a large number of law-oriented and law enforcement–oriented newsgroups and provides access to the United Nations and worldwide crime data through its link to the United Nations Criminal Justice Information Network. Other computer services provide access to security information and to software useful in law enforcement administration. Innovative computer technologies facilitate the work of enforcement agents. Among them are automated fingerprint

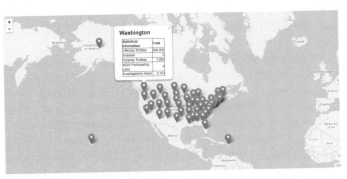

FIGURE 15-4 | A Map-based Interface Allowing Access to the FBI's CODIS/NDIS statistics.

Source: FBI Headquarters. https://www.fbi.gov/services/laboratory/biometric-analysis/codis/ndis-statistics#Map

■ **expert system**   A system of computer hardware and software that attempts to duplicate the decision-making processes used by skilled investigators in the analysis of evidence and in the recognition of patterns that such evidence might represent.

■ **Internet of Things**   The computer-based multiple simultaneous communications between devices with embedded information processors.

■ **data encryption**   The process by which information is encoded, making it unreadable to all but its intended recipients.

■ **threat analysis**   A complete and thorough assessment of the kinds of perils facing an organization.

■ **audit trail**   A sequential record of system activities that enables auditors to reconstruct, review, and examine the sequence of states and activities surrounding each event in one or more related transactions from inception to output of final results back to inception.

identification systems, or AFISs (often with interstate and even international links); computerized crime-scene simulations and reenactments; expert systems; and online clearinghouses containing data on criminal activity and offenders. AFISs allow investigators to complete in a matter of minutes what would otherwise consume weeks or months of work manually matching a suspect's fingerprints against stored records. AFIS computers are able to compare and eliminate from consideration many thousands of fingerprints per second, sometimes leading to the identification of a suspect in a short time. Once crime-related information or profiles of criminal offenders have been generated, they are typically stored in a database and often made accessible to law enforcement agencies at other sites. Other specialized database programs now track inner-city gang activity and gang membership, contain information on known sexual predators, and describe missing children.

Forensic expert systems deploy machine-based artificial intelligence to draw conclusions and to make recommendations to investigators and others interested in solving problems related to crime and its commission. **Expert systems**, developed by professional "knowledge engineers" who work with "knowledge bases" and computer software called "inference engines," attempt to duplicate the decision-making processes used by skilled investigators in the analysis of evidence and in the recognition of patterns that such evidence might represent. One such system is currently being perfected by the FBI's National Center for the Analysis of Violent Crime (NCAVC). The NCAVC expert system attempts to profile serial killers by matching clues left at a crime scene with individual personality characteristics.

A number of specialized software programs, such as ImAger, which is produced by Face Software, Inc., and Compu-Sketch, a product of Visatex Corporation, can assist police artists in rendering composite images of suspects and missing victims.[45] Finally, the **Internet of Things**, or the computer-based multiple simultaneous communications between devices with embedded information processors, including automobiles, airplanes, household appliances, manufacturing facilities, distribution chains, and almost anything else that generates information, can provide real time data on billions of ongoing activities, and the information it generates can be used by law enforcement agencies and criminal enterprises alike.

Combating Cybercrime

Today's global market for information security software, information security hardware, and information security services is in the billions of dollars and will grow far larger still by 2020.[46] Among the products in use today are **data encryption**, key log detectors, and Web servers supporting major security protocols. Data encryption is the process by which information is encoded, making it unreadable to all but its intended recipients.

Any effective program intended to secure a company or business operation against the threat of high-tech crime must be built on a realistic threat analysis. **Threat analysis**, sometimes called "risk analysis," involves a complete and thorough assessment of the potential disasters facing an organization. Some risks, such as floods, tornadoes, hurricanes, and earthquakes, arise from natural events and are often unpredictable. Others, including fire, electrical outages, and disruptions in public services, may be of human origin—but equally difficult to predict. Theft, employee sabotage, and terrorist attacks constitute yet another category of risk. Responses to unpredictable threats can nonetheless be planned, and strategies for dealing with almost any kind of risk can be implemented.

> Any program intended to secure a company against high-tech crime must be built on a realistic threat analysis.

Once specific threats are identified, strategies tailored to dealing with them can be introduced. For example, one powerful tool useful to identify instances of computer crime when they occur is the audit trail. Formally defined, an **audit trail** is "a sequential record of system activities that enables auditors to reconstruct, review, and examine the sequence of states and activities surrounding each event in one or more related transactions from inception to output of final results back to inception."[47] In other words, audit trails, which (once implemented) are recorded in some form of computer memory, trace and record the activities of computer operators and facilitate the apprehension of computer criminals.

■ **DCS–3000** An FBI-developed network diagnostic tool that is capable of assisting in criminal investigations by monitoring and capturing large amounts of Internet traffic. It was originally called Carnivore.

Police Investigation of Computer Crime

Many state and local police departments do not have personnel skilled in the investigation of computer crimes. Most officers know little about tracing the activities of computer criminals, and some police investigators find it difficult to understand how a crime can actually have occurred when nothing at the scene appears to be missing or damaged. Horror stories of botched police investigations are plentiful. They include tales of officers standing by while high-tech offenders perform seemingly innocuous activities that destroy evidence, of seized magnetic or optical media allowed to bake in the sun on the dashboards of police vehicles, and of the loss of evidence stored on magnetic media due to exposure to police clipboards and evidence lockers containing magnets.

Police departments also may intentionally avoid computer-crime investigations because they are complex and demanding. The amount of time and money spent on computer-crime investigations, it is often believed, could better be spent elsewhere. In addition, investigators who spend a great deal of time on crimes involving computers tend not to be promoted

> Police departments sometimes intentionally avoid cybercrime investigations because they can be complex and demanding.

as readily as their more glamorous counterparts in the homicide and property crime divisions, and personnel who are skilled in computer applications are apt to take jobs with private industries, where pay scales are far higher than in police work. As a consequence of these considerations and others, many police departments and their investigators make cybercrime a low priority.

But the situation has been changing due to federal intervention. In 1992, the FBI formed a National Computer Crime Squad (NCCS)[48] to investigate violations of the federal Computer Fraud and Abuse Act of 1984[49] and other federal computer-crime laws. Prior to the creation of the Department of Homeland Security (DHS), the FBI's Washington Field Office housed the agency's Computer Crime and Intellectual Property Section (CCIPS). The squad, whose duties have

been transferred to the DHS, investigated the illegal interception of signals (especially cable and satellite signal theft) and the infringement of copyright laws related to software. Visit the CCIPS via **https://www.justice.gov/criminal-ccips**.

Automated monitoring of network traffic is an area of considerable interest to law enforcement officials. One network "sniffer" created by the FBI called DCS–1000 (previously known as "Carnivore") was a diagnostic tool intended to assist in criminal investigations by monitoring and capturing large amounts of Internet traffic. DCS–1000 was to be installed by FBI agents in ISP data centers as necessary to monitor the electronic communications of individuals suspected of federal crimes such as terrorism. The Carnivore/DCS–1000 initiative was later retitled **DCS–3000**, and its focus was changed to intercepting suspect personal communications delivered via wireless services.[50]

As privacy activist Edward Snowden showed the world in 2013, information is a precious commodity. Nations that can effectively manage valuable information and make it accessible to their citizens will receive enhanced productivity and greater wealth as a reward. Moving information safely and securely is also important; today, a large part of that responsibility falls to the Internet. The Internet provides amazing and constantly growing capabilities. Unfortunately, as the Internet has grown, it has been targeted by hackers and computer criminals, some of whom have introduced rogue computer programs into the network's machines.

Cybercrime and Internet Security

America is a service-oriented, information-rich society. John Naisbitt, author of *Megatrends*, explained it this way: "The transition from an industrial to an information society does not mean manufacturing will cease to exist or become unimportant. Did farming end with the industrial era? Ninety percent of us produced 100% of the food in the agricultural era; now 3% of us produce 100%. In the information age, the focus of manufacturing will shift from the physical to more intellectual functions on which the physical depends."[51]

Although goods and materials will always need to be created, transported, and distributed, it is information that forms the lifeblood of the new world order and is a very valuable resource, comparable to (or exceeding) natural resources like

■ **Internet**   The world's largest computer network for moving data and making information accessible.

oil, gas, coal, and gold. According to Naisbitt, "Information is an economic entity because it costs something to produce and because people are willing to pay for it."[52] Moving information safely and securely is important, and today a large part of that is done on the **Internet**, the world's largest computer network. It began with the linkage of military and scientific computer facilities already existing on the Arpanet and Milnet and today consists of a vast resource of tens of thousands of computers around the world all linked together as a way of moving data quickly and making information accessible to masses of citizens.

The Internet is used by almost everyone today, and provides services such as websites, e-mail, mailing lists, newsgroups, and file-transfer capability. Internet access was originally restricted to commercial users, researchers, and university personnel, but access to the Internet is now routinely available through ISPs that furnish Internet access to anyone able to pay the monthly fee. Web browsers combine with search engines like Google to make it easy to search the tremendous amount of information on the Web and to interact with other Internet users.

As mentioned earlier, the Internet is not immune to attack. In 1988, the infamous Internet "worm" written by Cornell University graduate student Robert T. Morris, Jr., circulated through computers connected to the Internet, effectively disabling many of them. Morris was later arrested, sentenced to 400 hours of community service and three years of probation, and was fined $10,000. Since then, many other hackers have exploited loopholes in the software and hardware supporting the Internet.

In response to the growing threat to the nation's information systems, President Clinton created the Commission on Critical Infrastructure Protection, which was charged with assessing threats to the nation's computer networks and recommending policies to protect them.[53] Security issues related to information systems that control the nation's telecommunications, electric power, oil and gas, banking and finance, transportation, water supply, emergency services, and government operations were studied by the commission. Its October 1997 report proposed (1) establishing an Information Analysis and Warning Center to collect information on computer security breaches in industry and government; (2) creating legislation to permit private companies to conduct special background checks when hiring computer experts for sensitive positions; (3) creating a White House office to coordinate the information security roles of government, including the departments of Commerce, Defense, Energy, Justice, Treasury, and Transportation; and (4) quadrupling research on cyberspace security to $1 billion by the year 2004.[54]

The National Infrastructure Protection Center (NIPC), created in 1998 and located at the FBI's headquarters in Washington, DC, served as the federal government's center for threat assessment, warnings, investigation, and response for threats or attacks against the nation's critical infrastructures. Its successor, the Office of Infrastructure Protection (IP Office), operates today within the DHS. Visit the IP Office via **http://www.dhs.gov/xabout/structure/gc_1185203138955.shtm**.

In February 2000, the President's Working Group on Unlawful Conduct on the Internet released a report titled *The Electronic Frontier: The Challenge of Unlawful Conduct Involving the Use of the Internet*.[55] The group reported that "similar to the technologies that have preceded it, the Internet provides a new tool for wrongdoers to commit crimes, such as fraud, the sale or distribution of child pornography, the sale of guns or drugs or other regulated substances without regulatory protections, or the unlawful distribution of computer software or other creative material protected by intellectual property rights."

The group said that "although the precise extent of unlawful conduct involving the use of computers is unclear, the rapid growth of the Internet and e-commerce has made such unlawful conduct a critical priority for legislators, policymakers, industry, and law enforcement agencies." Because of the Internet's potential to reach vast audiences easily, the potential scale of unlawful conduct is equally wide.

Cybercriminals are no longer hampered by the existence of national or international boundaries because information and property can be easily transmitted through communications and data networks. A computer server running a Web page designed to defraud senior citizens might be located in Thailand, but victims of the scam could be scattered throughout the world. Evidence of a crime can be stored at a remote location, either for concealment of the crime from law enforcement or due to the design of the network. "A cyberstalker in Brooklyn, New York, may send a threatening e-mail to a person in Manhattan. If the stalker routes his communication through Argentina, France, and Norway before reaching his victim, the New York Police Department may have to get assistance from the Office of International Affairs at the Department of Justice in Washington, DC, which, in turn, may have to get assistance from law enforcement in (say) Buenos Aires, Paris, and Oslo just to learn that the suspect is in New York." In this example, the working group points out, the perpetrator needs no passport and passes through no checkpoints as he commits his crime, while law enforcement agencies are burdened with cumbersome mechanisms for international cooperation—mechanisms that often derail or slow investigations. Because the gathering of information in other jurisdictions and internationally is crucial to investigating and prosecuting cybercrimes, the President's Working Group concluded that "all levels of government will need to develop concrete and reliable mechanisms for cooperating with each other." Read the entire text of *The Electronic Frontier* via **http://www.justice.gov/opa/pr/2000/March/111ag.htm**.

■ **First and Fourth Amendments to the U.S. Constitution**   The amendments that guarantee each person freedom of speech and security in his or her "persons, houses, papers, and effects, against unreasonable searches and seizures."

■ **Electronic Frontier Foundation (EFF)**   A nonprofit organization formed in July 1990 to help ensure that the principles embodied in the Constitution and the Bill of Rights are protected as new communications technologies emerge.

In September 2003, the U.S. government established the United States Computer Emergency Readiness Team (US–CERT), a partnership between the DHS and public and private sectors to protect the nation's Internet infrastructure and to coordinate defenses against cyberattacks across the nation. US–CERT is in charge of the National Cyber Alert System: "America's first cohesive national cyber security system for identifying, analyzing, and prioritizing emerging vulnerabilities and threats."[56] The Cyber Alert System relays computer security updates and warning information to anyone who subscribes to its bulletins and provides all citizens—from computer security professionals to home-computer users with basic skills—with free, timely, actionable information to better secure their computer systems. Visit US–CERT at **http://www.us-cert.gov**.

After taking office, President Barack Obama identified cybersecurity as one of the most serious economic and national-security challenges facing the United States and noted that the country was not adequately prepared to counter cybersecurity threats. In May 2009, the president decided to implement recommendations from the Comprehensive National Cybersecurity Initiative (CNCI), which had been launched by President George W. Bush in January 2008.[57] More recently, the Department of Homeland Security's Cyber Security Division was tasked with (1) developing and transitioning new technologies, tools, and techniques to protect and secure systems, networks, infrastructure, and users and (2) providing coordination and research and development leadership across federal, state, and municipal governments, and working with international partners, the private sector, and academia in order to improve cybersecurity.[58] Read about new legislation to address the problem of cybercrime at **http://papers.ssrn.com/sol3/papers.cfm?abstract_id=1555232**. The White House's *Cyberspace Policy Review* is available at **http://www.justicestudies.com/pubs/cyspace.pdf**.

Policy Issues: Personal Freedoms in the Information Age

The continued development of telecommunications resources has led not only to concerns about security and data integrity, but also to an expanding interest in privacy, free speech, and personal freedoms. Although the **First and Fourth Amendments to the U.S. Constitution** guarantee each person freedom of speech and security in his or her "persons,

houses, papers, and effects, against unreasonable searches and seizures," the Constitution is understandably silent on the subject of electronic documents and advanced forms of communication facilitated by technologies that did not exist at the time of the Constitutional Convention.

Within the context of contemporary society we are left to ask these questions: What is speech? What are papers? Do electronic communications qualify for protection under the First Amendment, as does the spoken word? In an era when most houses are wired for telephones and many support data links that extend well beyond voice capabilities, it becomes necessary to ask what constitutes one's "speech" or one's "home." Does e-mail qualify as speech? Where does the concept of a home begin and end for purposes of constitutional guarantees? Do activities within the home that can be accessed from without (as when a computer web site is run out of a home) fall under the same constitutional guarantees as a private conversation held within the physical confines of a house?

Complicating matters still further are today's "supersnoop" technologies, which provide investigators with the ability to literally hear through walls (using vibration detectors), listen to conversations over great distances (with parabolic audio receivers), record voices in distant rooms (via laser readings of windowpane vibrations), and even look through walls using forward-looking infrared (FLIR) devices, which can detect temperature differences of as little as two-tenths of a degree.

In 1990, concerned individuals banded together to form the **Electronic Frontier Foundation (EFF)**, a citizens' group funded by private contributions that set for itself the task of actively assisting in refining notions of privacy and legality as they relate to telecommunications and other computer-based media. In the foundation's own words, "The Electronic Frontier Foundation (EFF) was founded in July of 1990 to ensure that the principles embodied in the Constitution and the Bill of Rights are protected as new communications technologies emerge. From the beginning, EFF has worked to shape our nation's communications infrastructure and the policies that govern it in order to maintain and enhance First Amendment, privacy and other democratic values. We believe that our overriding public goal must be the creation of Electronic Democracy."[59]

The EFF, which also supports litigation in the public interest, has been an active supporter of the public advocacy group Computer Professionals for Social Responsibility (CPSR). The CPSR maintains a Computing and Civil Liberties Project in keeping with the EFF's purpose. The EFF also supported challenges to the CDA that resulted in the 1997 Supreme Court ruling in *Reno v. ACLU*, which found key provisions of the act unconstitutional. Visit the EFF on the Web via **http://www.eff.org**.

SUMMARY

Technology and criminology have always been closely linked—as technology advances, it facilitates new forms of criminal behavior.

- High-technology offenses can dramatically change our understanding of crime. Some forms of high-tech crime, committed without regard for national borders or even the need for physical travel, hold dangers never before imagined.

- High technology provides new criminal opportunities by making available to perpetrators new tools and advanced techniques useful in the commission of crime, and by contributing to the development of items of value, such as computer codes, that did not previously exist.

- Cybercrime is serious, widespread, aggressive, growing, and increasingly sophisticated, and it poses major implications for national and economic security.

- Federal laws targeting cybercriminals include the No Electronic Theft Act (NETA), the Digital Theft Deterrence and Copyright Damages Improvement Act, the Cyber Security Enhancement Act, and the Cybersecurity Information Sharing Act (CISA). The 2015 CISA makes it easier for private companies to quickly and directly share personal information with the government, especially in cases involving specific cybersecurity threats.

- Cybercriminals, including hackers, can be pioneers (those fascinated by the evolving technology of telecommunications and its exploration), scamps (those with a sense of fun and no intent to harm), explorers (those motivated by personal delight in discoveries associated with breaking into new systems), game players (those whose joy is in defeating software or copyright protection), vandals (those with the goal of intentional damage without personal apparent gain), and/or addicts (those computer nerds addicted to hacking and computer technology).

- Technology in law enforcement today involves computer databases of known offenders, expert systems, cellular communications, video surveillance and face-recognition technology, electronic eavesdropping, DNA analysis, and less-lethal weapons.

- Any effective program to combat cybercrime and secure an organization against the threat of high-tech crime must use threat analysis. Once specific threats are identified, strategies tailored to dealing with them can be implemented.

- Efforts to control high-tech crime through criminal investigation and prosecution impact issues of individual rights, from free speech to technological privacy in the context of digital interconnectedness. There will need to be an acceptable balance between constitutional guarantees of continued freedom of access to legitimate high-tech activities and effective enforcement initiatives for the massive threat high-tech crimes represent.

KEY TERMS

audit trail, 422

Communications Decency Act (CDA), 411

computer abuse, 413

computer-related crime, 413

computer virus, 411

cybercrime, 409

Cyber Security Enhancement Act (CSEA), 413

Cybersecurity Information Sharing Act (CISA), 413

cyberspace, 414

data encryption, 422

Daubert standard, 420

DCS–3000, 423

Digital Theft Deterrence and Copyright Damages Improvement Act, 413

DNA profiling, 420

Electronic Frontier Foundation (EFF), 425

expert system, 422

First and Fourth Amendments to the U.S. Constitution, 425

hacker, 409

Internet, 424

Internet of Things, 422

No Electronic Theft Act (NETA), 412

phishing, 410

phone phreak, 414

ransomware, 411

software piracy, 410

threat analysis, 422

QUESTIONS FOR REVIEW

1. How does advancing technology produce new forms of crime?

2. How does high technology provide new criminal opportunities?

3. What is the extent of cybercrime today?

4. Name some of the federal laws targeting cybercriminals.

5. Describe the characteristics of cybercriminals.

6. What new technologies are being used in today's fight against crime?

7. What is being done today to combat cybercrime and to secure the Internet?

8. What are some of the personal freedoms that are threatened by today's need for advanced security?

QUESTIONS FOR REFLECTION

1. This book emphasizes the theme of social problems versus individual responsibility. Which perspective better explains the involvement of capable individuals in criminal activity necessitating high-tech skills? What is the best way to deal with such criminals?

2. What is the difference between high-tech crime and traditional forms of criminal activity? Will the high-tech crimes of today continue to be the high-tech crimes of tomorrow? Why or why not?

3. What forms of high-tech crime can you imagine that this chapter has not discussed? Describe each briefly.

4. Do you believe that high-tech crimes will eventually surpass the abilities of enforcement agents to prevent or solve them? Why or why not?

5. What different kinds of high-tech offenders can you imagine? What is the best way to deal with each type of offender? Give reasons for your answers.

Luis Soriano/Notimex/Newscom

CHAPTER 16

GLOBALIZATION AND TERRORISM

Our Small World

LEARNING OUTCOMES

After reading this chapter, you should be able to answer the following questions:

- What is comparative criminology, and what role does globalization play in understanding criminal activities today?
- What are the differences between human smuggling and human trafficking?

- What is terrorism, and what are the various types of terrorism that this chapter discusses?
- What is known about the radicalization process of homegrown American al-Qaeda-inspired terrorists?
- What efforts are being made to counter the terrorist threat?
- What international crime-fighting organizations does this chapter discuss?

■ **comparative criminology**   The cross-national study of crime.

■ **comparative criminologist**   A criminologist involved in the cross-national study of crime.

■ **globalization**   A process of social homogenization by which the experiences of everyday life, marked by the diffusion of commodities and ideas, can foster a standardization of cultural expressions around the world.

■ **Follow the author's tweets about the latest crime and justice news @schmalleger.**

Introduction

In 2017, the Russian Duma (the Russian parliament) considered a bill to decriminalize some forms of domestic violence throughout the country. The legislation would decriminalize intimate partner violence for first offenders who "inflict physical pain but do not cause serious bodily injury."[1] The Duma created the bill in response to an earlier ruling from the country's supreme court, which held that battery that does not cause bodily harm is not criminal. The court's action, however, did not extend to domestic violence, which is a separate offense under Russian law. Olga Batalina, one of the bill's coauthors, told state television that "The criminal code still carries criminal responsibility for battery, but now it will be applicable only for repeat offenders." All those "who terrorize their family members," she said, and "who do it repeatedly … will face criminal responsibility."

A few years before the Russian legislation was proposed, the president of the Philippines asked the country's legislative arm to lower the age of criminal responsibility from 15 to 10 years of age. A compromise between the president and proponents of youth rehabilitation led to a lowering of the age to 13.[2] Both the Russian and Philippines legislation point to significant cultural differences between the United States, Russia, and the Philippines with regard to attitudes toward domestic violence and adolescence.

Comparative Criminology

Comparative criminology is the study of crime on a cross-national level. When crime patterns in one country are compared with those in another, theories and policies that have been taken for granted in one place can be reevaluated in the light of world experience. As some noted **comparative criminologists** have observed, "The challenge for comparative criminologists is to develop theories with increased specificity while managing to construct them in such a way that they can be applied across more than one culture or nation-state. This eventually must demand that theories be developed to conceptualize societies as totalities and that theories that manage to provide a world context in which total societies behave be further constructed."[3]

An important force in the modern world is **globalization**, which can be defined as a process of social homogenization by

A meeting of the Russian Duma, or parliament. In 2017, Russian legislators acted to decriminalize some forms of domestic violence. Why is it important to study the crime rates and criminal laws of other countries?

Sergei Fadeichev/ITAR-TASS Photo Agency/Alamy Stock Photo

which the experiences of everyday life, marked by the diffusion of commodities and ideas, can foster a standardization of cultural expressions around the world.[4] The increasing integration of previously isolated events and their impact is an important aspect of globalization, and the idea of globalization encompasses the increasingly interconnectedness of people, ideas, and things on a worldwide scale.

Some have used the term *globalization of knowledge* to describe the increase in understanding that results from a sharing of information between cultures. The globalization of knowledge is beginning to play a significant role in both the process of theory formation within criminology and the development of American crime control policies.

> The term *globalization of knowledge* describes the increase in understanding that results from a sharing of information between cultures.

According to some, "Globalization will make it increasingly difficult for nation-states to ignore the criminal justice information of other countries." A few years ago, as recipient of the prestigious Vollmer Award in Criminology, **Franklin E. Zimring,** of the University of California, Berkeley, addressed the American Society of Criminology, complaining about the

■ **ethnocentrism**   The phenomenon of "culture-centeredness" by which one uses one's own culture as a benchmark against which to judge all other patterns of behavior.

fact that American criminology had been self-obsessed and "particularly inattentive to the value and necessity of transnational comparisons." Zimring sees comparative efforts as providing a context for evaluating knowledge and reviewing observations. Using this perspective, Zimring demonstrated that the crime decline in the United States during the 1990s was not unique to America—and that the same decline occurred in Canada at the same time.

Ethnocentrism

One important issue facing comparative criminologists is **ethnocentrism**. Ethnocentrism, or culture-centeredness, can interfere with the work of comparative criminologists in a number of ways, including the ways in which crime statistics are gathered, analyzed, and presented.

Only in recent years have American specialists in criminology begun to closely examine crime in other cultures. Not all societies are equally open, and it is not always easy to explore them. In some societies, even the *study* of crime is taboo. As a result, data-gathering strategies taken for granted in Western culture may not be well received elsewhere. One author, for example, has observed that in China, "the seeking of criminal justice information through face-to-face questioning takes on a different meaning than it does generally in the Western world. While we accept this method of inquiry because we prize thinking on our feet and quick answers, it is offensive in China because it shows lack of respect and appreciation for the information given through the preferred means of prepared questions and formal briefings."[5] Most of the information available about Chinese crime rates comes by way of officialdom, and routine Western social science practices such as door-to-door interviews, participant observation, and random surveys might not produce results in China.

Similar difficulties arise in the comparison of crime rates from one country to another. The crime rates of different nations are difficult to compare because of (1) differences in the way a given crime is defined; (2) diverse crime-reporting practices; and (3) political, social, economic, and other influences on the reporting of statistics to international agencies.[6]

> Definitional differences create the biggest problem in reporting crime.

Definitional differences create what may be the biggest problem in reporting crime (see the Theory versus Reality box). For cross-national comparisons of crime data to be meaningful, it is essential that the reported data share conceptual similarities, but that is often not the case because nations report offenses according to the legal criteria by which their arrests are made and under which their prosecution can occur. Switzerland includes bicycle thefts in its reported data on what we call "auto theft" because Swiss data gathering focuses more on the concept of personal transportation than on the type of stolen vehicle; the Netherlands has no crime category for robberies, counting them as thefts; Japan classifies an assault resulting in death as an assault or an aggravated assault, not as a homicide; Greek rape statistics include crimes of sodomy, lewdness, seduction of a child, incest, and prostitution, and China reports only robberies and thefts that involve citizens' property, using crimes against state-owned property as a separate category.

Reporting practices vary substantially among nations. The International Criminal Police Organization (INTERPOL) and the United Nations (UN) are the only international organizations that regularly collect crime statistics from a large number of countries, and both can only request data and have no way of checking on the accuracy of those data. Many countries do not disclose the requested information, and those that do sometimes make only partial reports; in general, small countries are more likely to report than large ones, and nonsocialist countries are more likely to report than are socialist nations.

International comparisons are also difficult because complete up-to-date data are not easy to acquire, as the information made available to agencies like INTERPOL and the UN is reported at different times and according to schedules varying from nation to nation. In addition, official UN crime surveys are conducted infrequently at the international level (as of 2015, twelve such surveys had been undertaken).[7]

Economic differences among countries compound these difficulties. Auto-theft statistics between countries like the United States and Bangladesh need, for example, to be placed into an economic as well as a demographic context. Whereas the United States has two automobiles for every 3 people, Bangladesh has only one car per every 2,600 of its citizens.[8] For the auto theft rate in Bangladesh to equal that of the United States, every automobile in the country would have to be stolen over 100 times each year!

Crime statistics also reflect social and political contexts, with some nations not accurately reporting the frequency of certain kinds of culturally reprehensible crimes. Communist countries appear loathe to report crimes like theft, burglary, and robbery because the very existence of such offenses might appear to demonstrate felt inequities within the communist system, and the social norms in some societies may make it

TABLE 16-1 | World Homicide Rates for Selected Countries

COUNTRY	NUMBER OF MURDERS	RATE PER 100,000
Denmark	47	0.8
Italy	530	0.9
Canada	543	1.6
United States	*14,827*	*4.7*
Russia Federation	13,120	9.2
Nicaragua	675	11.3
Mexico	26,037	21.5
Belize	145	44.7
Hondouras	7,172	90.4

Source: United Nations Office on Drugs and Crime, 2013 Global Study on Homicide (Vienna: UNDOC, 2014) http://www.unodc.org/documents/gsh/pdfs/2014_GLOBAL_hOMICIDe_BOOK_web.pdf. Used by permission.

almost impossible for women to report cases of rape or sexual abuse, whereas in others, women are encouraged to come forward.

With all these caveats in mind, it can still be instructive to look at crime rates in other countries and attempt comparisons with U.S. crime rates. A useful tool for international crime rate comparisons is *The United Nations Survey on Crime Trends and the Operations of Criminal Justice Systems*. To some, U.S. violent crime rates seem high compared with violent crime rates of other developed countries, but American crime rates are far from the highest in the world, and UN surveys typically place U.S. crime rates well below world highs (see Table 16-1 for comparative murder rates). Figure 16-1 shows worldwide homicide rates by country.

Lawless areas without strong central governments and countries experiencing strong social upheaval might be expected to have high violent crime rates, but some other parts of the world do as well. Murder rates in Colombia and South Africa are more than 12 times that of the United States, Russia has a murder rate that is almost four times the U.S. rate, and homicide rates in Mexico are more than twice that of those in the United States. The rate of reported rape in South Africa is four times that of the United States,

whereas Canada and Australia have rape rates more than double the U.S. figure. Spain has a robbery rate many times higher than that of the United States, and many countries have rates of assault that are greater than that reported in the United States.

See more international crime statistics at **http://www.nationmaster.com/graph/cri_tot_cri-crime-total-crimes**, and visit the National Institute of Justice (NIJ) International Center at **http://www.bjs.gov/content/ijs.cfm**. Read an intriguing paper on comparative criminology at **http://www.justicestudies.com/pubs/comparative.pdf**. The *United Nations Survey on Crime Trends*, covering 64 countries, is available at **http://www.unodc.org/unodc/en/data-and-analysis/statistics/crime.html,** and the *European Sourcebook of Crime and Criminal Justice Statistics* can be accessed via **http://wp.unil.ch/europeansourcebook**.

Transnational Crimes

Globalization is making it impossible to ignore criminal activity in other parts of the world, especially where that crime is perpetrated by transnational criminal and terrorist organizations.

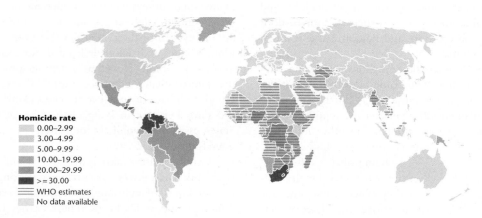

FIGURE 16-1 | Homicide Rates by Country

Source: United Nations Office on Drugs and Crime (UNDOC), 2013 Global Study on Homicide: Trends, Contexts, Data (Vienna: UNODC, 2014), p. 25. http://www.unodc.org/documents/gsh/pdfs/2014_GLOBAL_hOMICIDe_BOOK_web.pdf. Used by permission.

■ **human smuggling**   A type of illegal immigration in which an agent is paid to help a person cross a border clandestinely.

THEORY | versus REALITY
UN Offense Definitions

The UN Office on Drugs and Crime regularly conducts a survey of international crime trends. Data are still being collected for the latest such survey, the 2016 United Nations Survey on Crime Trends and Operations of Criminal Justice Systems (2016 UN-CTS). In an effort to standardize reporting practices, the UN provides the following crime definitions to guide survey participants:

Intentional homicide means unlawful death inflicted upon a person with the intent to cause death or serious injury.

Honor killing is the unlawful killing of a person by relatives or other closely associated persons as a result of avenging a perceived dishonor brought on the family, or with the intent of restoring the honor of the family, related to an actual or assumed sexual or behavioral transgression, including adultery, sexual intercourse or pregnancy outside marriage.

Assault means the intentional or reckless application of physical force inflicted upon the body of a person. Assault leading to death should be excluded.

Rape means sexual penetration without valid consent or with consent as a result of intimidation, force, fraud, coercion, threat, deception, use of drugs or alcohol, abuse of power or of a position of vulnerability, or the giving or receiving of benefits.

Robbery means unlawfully taking or obtaining property with the use of force or threat of force against a person with intent to permanently or temporarily withhold it from a person or organization.

Theft means unlawfully taking or obtaining of property with the intent to permanently withhold it from a person or organization without consent and without the use of force, threat of force or violence, coercion or deception.

Burglary means unauthorized access to a part of a building/dwelling or other premises with or without the use of force against the building/dwelling, with intent to commit theft or when actually committing theft.

Learn more about the United Nations Office on Drugs and Crime, including it's data-gathering program on drugs, crime and criminal justice at the international level at **https://www.unodc.org/unodc/en/data-and-analysis/statistics.html.**

Source: United Nations Office on Drugs and Crime, *The 2016 United Nations Survey of Crime Trends and Operations of Criminal Justice Systems (2016 UN-CTS).* Reprinted by permission.

No one is immune to the economic effects of transnational crime.

Transnational organized crime, which is also discussed in Chapter 11, has emerged as one of the most pressing challenges of the early twenty-first century. The growing globalization of crime has required the coordination of law enforcement efforts in different parts of the world and the expansion of U.S. law enforcement activities internationally. Transnational crimes range from relatively simple fraudulent e-mail and phishing schemes to the more dangerous and threatening illegal trafficking in human beings, human organs, and illicit drugs. It includes the activities of multinational drug cartels, the support of terrorist groups by criminal organizations seeking armed protection, and well-funded and sophisticated efforts by organized criminal groups looking to overthrow the ruling regime in regions with others sympathetic to their operations.

Human Smuggling and Trafficking

According to the United Nations,[9] trafficking in persons and human smuggling are some of the fastest-growing areas of international criminal activity today. There are important distinctions between the two. The U.S. State Department defines **human smuggling** as "the facilitation, transportation, attempted transportation or illegal entry of a person(s) across an international border, in violation of one or more country's laws, either clandestinely or through deception, such as the use of fraudulent documents."[10] In other words, human smuggling refers to illegal immigration in which an agent is involved for payment to

Comparative criminologists compare crime patterns in one country with those in another.

■ **trafficking in persons (TIP)**   The exploitation of unwilling or unwitting people through force, coercion, threat, or deception.

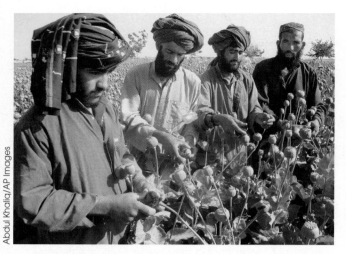

Afghans collecting resin from a poppy field in Lashkar Gah, south of Kabul, Afghanistan. Afghanistan is one of the top producers of opium in the world, where its growth is largely controlled by Taliban militia who either befriend or intimidate local poppy growers. Much of the heroin manufactured from opium produced in Afghanistan is sold in the United States, completing an international cycle that forms one aspect of globalization and serves as a source of funds for the ongoing Taliban resistance in Afghanistan. How can the cycle be broken?

help a person cross a border clandestinely.[11] Human smuggling may be conducted to obtain financial or other benefits for the smuggler, although sometimes people smuggle others to reunite their families. Human smuggling generally occurs with the consent of the people being smuggled, who often pay for the services.

Once in the country they've paid to enter, they usually are no longer in contact with the smuggler. The State Department notes that the vast majority of people who are assisted in illegally entering the United States annually are smuggled rather than trafficked.

Although smuggling might not involve active coercion, it can be deadly. In January 2007, for example, truck driver Tyrone Williams, 36, a Jamaican citizen living in Schenectady, New York, was sentenced to life in prison for causing the deaths of 19 illegal immigrants in the nation's deadliest known human smuggling attempt.[12]

The Intelligence Reform and Terrorism Prevention Act of 2004[13] established the Human Smuggling and Trafficking Center (HSTC) within the Department of Homeland Security (DHS). U.S. Immigration and Customs Enforcement (ICE), the largest investigative agency within the DHS, has primary responsibility for enforcing laws related to human smuggling and trafficking. As a result, ICE plays a leading role in the fight against human smuggling and trafficking.

In contrast to smuggling, **trafficking in persons (TIP)** can be compared to a modern-day form of slavery. Trafficking involves the exploitation of unwilling people through force, coercion, threat, or deception and includes human rights abuses such as debt bondage, deprivation of liberty, or lack of control over freedom and labor. Trafficking is often undertaken for purposes of sexual exploitation or labor exploitation. The primary destination countries for trafficking victims are the United States, Italy, Japan, Canada, Australia, and other First World nations. The map from UNDOC in Figure 16-2 shows countries of both origin and destination for victims of trafficking.

A recent report says that "The term trafficking in persons can be misleading [because] it places emphasis on the

The arrows show the flows that represent 5% and above of the total victims detected in destination subregions

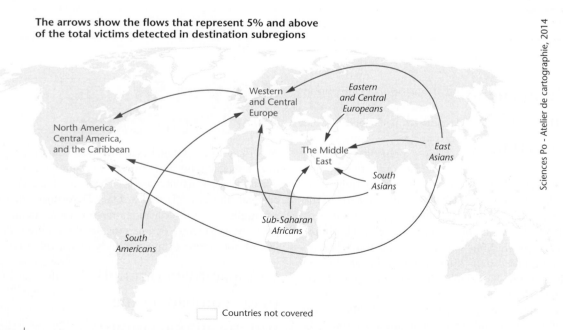

Sciences Po - Atelier de cartographie, 2014

Countries not covered

FIGURE 16-2 | **Main Destination Areas of Human Trafficking Flows and Their Origins, 2010–2012**

Source: United Nations Office on Drugs and Crime (UNODC), page 40, Global Report on Trafficking in Persons 2014, http://www.unodc.org/documents/data-and-analysis/glotip/GLOTIP_2014_full_report.pdf.

TABLE 16-2 | **Distinguishing between Human Trafficking and Smuggling**

TRAFFICKING	SMUGGLING
Must contain an element of force, fraud, or coercion (actual, perceived, or implied), unless the victim is under 18 years of age and is involved in commercial sex acts	The person being smuggled is generally cooperating
Forced labor and/or exploitation	No forced labor or other exploitation
Persons trafficked are victims	Persons smuggled are violating the law. They are not victims
Enslaved, subjected to limited movement or isolation, or had documents confiscated	Persons are free to leave, change jobs, and so forth
Need not involve the actual movement of the victim	Facilitates the illegal entry of person(s) from one country into another
No requirement to cross an international border	Smuggling always crosses an international border
Person must be involved in labor/services or commercial sex acts (i.e., must be "working")	Person must only be in the country or attempting entry illegally

Note: This table is meant to be conceptual and is not intended to provide precise legal distinctions between smuggling and trafficking.
Source: Adapted from U.S. Department of State, Bureau for International Narcotics and Law Enforcement Affairs, Human Smuggling and Trafficking Center, *Distinctions between Human Smuggling and Human Trafficking* (Washington, DC: January 1, 2005).

transaction aspects of a crime that is more accurately described as enslavement. Exploitation of people, day after day. For years on end."[14]

Practically speaking, it is sometimes difficult to distinguish between a smuggling case and a trafficking case because trafficking often includes an element of smuggling (i.e., the illegal crossing of a national border.) Some trafficking victims may believe they are being smuggled when they are really being trafficked, but are unaware of their eventual fate. This happens, for example, when women trafficked for sexual exploitation may have thought they were agreeing to work in legitimate industries for decent wages—part of which they may have agreed to pay to the trafficker who smuggled them. They didn't know that upon arrival, the traffickers would keep them in bondage, subject them to physical force or sexual violence, force them to work in the sex trade, and take most or all of their income. Table 16-2 draws some important distinctions between human trafficking and smuggling.

Human Trafficking

U.S. government officials estimate that 800,000 to 900,000 victims are trafficked globally each year and that 17,500 to 18,500 are trafficked into the United States. Women and children comprise the largest group of victims, and they are often physically and emotionally abused (see Figure 16-3). Although TIP is often an international crime that involves the crossing of borders, it is important to note that TIP victims can be trafficked within their own country and community. Traffickers can move victims between locations within the same country and often sell them to other trafficking organizations.

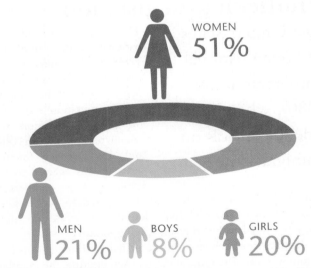

FIGURE 16-3 | **Profile of Worldwide Trafficking Victims**
Source: United Nations Office on Drugs and Crime (UNDOC), *Global Report on Trafficking in Persons 2016*, http://reliefweb.int/sites/reliefweb.int/files/resources/2016_Global_Report_on_Trafficking_in_Persons.pdf. Used by permission of United Nations Office on Drugs and Crime.

The International Labour Organization (ILO), the United Nations agency charged with addressing labor standards, employment, and social protection issues, estimates that 12.3 million people are in forced labor, bonded labor, forced child labor, and sexual servitude throughout the world today (Figure 16-4).[15] Other estimates range as high as 27 million. Worldwide, however, fewer than 10,000 prosecutions for human trafficking occur annually.

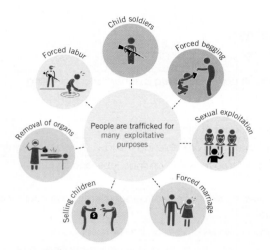

FIGURE 16-4 | **Types of Trafficking**

Source: UNODC, Global Report on Trafficking in Persons 2016 p. 8. Used by permission.

Federal Immigration and Trafficking Legislation

The United States had open national borders until the 1880s, when limited federal controls on immigration began.

The United States had open national borders until the 1880s, when limited federal controls on immigration began. One of the nation's first immigration laws was the Chinese Exclusion Act, which became law in 1882 and was enforced for ten years; it was enacted in response to large numbers of Chinese male laborers who had immigrated to the western United States in the mid-1800s looking for work and often took jobs on railroads and in the mining industry.

A more comprehensive piece of federal immigration legislation was the 1924 Immigration Act limiting the number of immigrants who could be admitted from any one country to 2% of the number of people from that country who were already living here (calculated using the Census of 1890). The law also barred immigration from specific parts of the Asia-Pacific Triangle, including Cambodia, China, Japan, Korea, Laos, the Philippines, and Thailand. The Immigration and Nationality Act (INA) of 1952, establishing the Immigration and Naturalization Service (INS) while continuing numerical ethnic quotas, provided criminal penalties for anyone bringing or attempting to bring unauthorized aliens into the United States;[16] years later, the INA amendments of 1965 abolished quotas based on ethnicity.[17] The Homeland Security Act of 2002 (HSA) dissolved the INS and transferred most of its functions to three branches of the DHS: Citizenship and

Immigration Services (CIS), Customs and Border Protection (CBP), and ICE.

Recognizing that human smuggling and TIP were serious social issues, Congress passed the Trafficking Victims Protection Act of 2000 (TVPA), which addressed the significant problem of TIP for the purposes of having people commit commercial sex acts (termed *sex trafficking*) and of subjecting them to involuntary servitude, peonage, or debt bondage and increased the protections afforded victims of trafficking.[18] The TVPA specified severe forms of trafficking: "a.) sex trafficking in which a commercial sex act is induced by force, fraud, or coercion, or in which the person induced to perform such an act has not attained 18 years of age; or b.) the recruitment, harboring, transportation, provision, or obtaining of a person for labor or services, through the use of force, fraud, or coercion for the purpose of subjection to involuntary servitude, peonage, debt bondage, or slavery."[19]

Under the TVPA, human trafficking does not require the crossing of an international border or even the transportation of victims from one locale to another because victims of certain forms of trafficking are not just illegal aliens, but also U.S. citizens, legal residents, or visitors. Victims do not have to be women or children; they may also be adult males.

The Trafficking Victims Protection Reauthorization Act (TVPRA) of 2003 added a new initiative to the original law to collect foreign data on trafficking investigations, prosecutions, convictions, and sentences. Its 2006 data showed that reporting jurisdictions prosecuted 5,808 people for trafficking-related

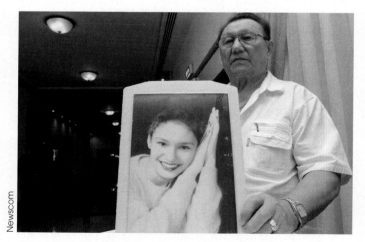

Russian father Nikolai Rantchev holding up a portrait of his dead daughter, Oxana, at a hotel in Nicosia during a conference on human trafficking. Only days after Oxana left Russia for the Mediterranean island of Cyprus, duped into thinking she would work as a translator, her body was found slumped at the foot of a building. Her father, a former Soviet army officer, believes she was killed by human traffickers who wanted to turn her into a sex slave. What different forms does human trafficking take?

■ **terrorism**   An act of premeditated, politically motivated violence perpetrated against a noncombatant target by a subnational group or clandestine agent.

■ **domestic terrorism**   The unlawful use of force or violence by an individual or group based and operating entirely within the United States and its territories, without foreign influence, directed at the U.S. government, the civilian population, or any segment thereof for political or social objectives.

offenses and secured 3,160 convictions, the lowest number of reported foreign prosecutions since reporting began in 2003.[20] TVPA was again reauthorized in 2005, 2008, and 2013. The latest reauthorization improved the original legislation by, among other things, authorizing the TIP Office to negotiate child protection compacts with designated focus countries to increase resources to eradicate child trafficking.

Section 7202 of the Intelligence Reform and Terrorism Prevention Act of 2004 established the HSTC within the U.S. State Department, and the secretary of state, the secretary of the DHS, the attorney general, and members of the National Intelligence Community oversee it. The center was created to achieve greater integration and overall effectiveness in the U.S. government's enforcement of issues related to human smuggling, TIP, and criminal support of clandestine terrorist travel. Read the U.S. State Department's Trafficking in Persons Report for 2016 at **http://www.justicestudies.com/pubs/tiprpt.pdf.**

Terrorism

The U.S. Department of State defines **terrorism** as "premeditated, politically motivated violence perpetrated against noncombatant targets by subnational groups or clandestine agents, usually intended to influence an audience."[21] Europol says that "[t]errorism is not an ideology or movement, but a tactic or a method for attaining political goals."[22] Paul Pillar, former deputy chief of the Counterterrorist Center of the Central Intelligence Agency (CIA), has identified four key features of terrorism that distinguish it from other forms of violence.[23] Those features are shown in Table 16-3.

> Terrorist acts are inherently criminal because they violate the law, involve criminal activity, and produce criminal results.

Terrorist acts are criminal because they violate the criminal law, because they involve criminal activity, and because they produce criminal results. The primary distinction between violent criminal acts and acts of terrorism, however, has to do with the political motivation or social ideology of the offender.[24]

TABLE 16-3 | Characteristics of Terrorism

TERRORISM USUALLY IS	TERRORISM USUALLY IS NOT
Premeditated or planned	Impulsive or an act of rage
Politically motivated (i.e., intended to change the existing political order)	Perpetrated for criminal gain (i.e., illicit personal or financial benefit)
Aimed at civilians	Aimed at military targets or combat-ready troops
Carried out by subnational groups	Perpetrated by the army of a country

Terrorist organizations vary in their goals and can be categorized as follows:

1. **Nationalist terrorists** seek to change the entire political, social, and economic system to an extreme right, or ultraconservative, model.

2. **Religious terrorists** use violence to bring about social and cultural changes that are in keeping with their religious views.

3. **State-sponsored terrorists** are deliberately employed by radical nations as foreign policy tools.

4. **Left-wing terrorists** seek to replace economies based on free enterprise with socialist or communist economic systems.

5. **Right-wing terrorists** are motivated by fascist ideals and work toward the dissolution of democratic governments.

6. **Anarchist terrorists** are revolutionary, anticapitalist, and antiauthoritarian. Although these groups are often motivated by domestic politics, they also are usually part of wider international campaigns and may fight against free-trade agreements, what they see as ecologically damaging practices, and so forth.

Figure 16-5 lists examples of contemporary terrorist groups according to the categories listed here.

The United States is faced today with three major types of terrorism: domestic, international, and cyber. **Domestic terrorism** is unlawful force or violence by a group or an individual who is based and operates entirely within the United States and its territories without foreign direction and whose acts are

■ **international terrorism** The unlawful use of force or violence by an individual or group with a connection to a foreign power or whose activities transcend national boundaries against people or property to intimidate or coerce a government, the civilian population, or any segment thereof for political or social objectives.

Nationalist
Irish Republican Army
Basque Fatherland and Liberty
Kurdistan Workers' Party
Hizballah (Middle East)
al-Shabaab (Africa)

Left Wing
Red Brigades (Italy)
Baader-Meinhof Gang (Germany)

State Sponsored
Hezbollah (backed by Iran)
Abu Nidal Organization (Syria, Libya)

Religious
Al-Qaeda
Hamas
Hezbollah
Aum Shinrikyo (Japan)
ISIS aka ISIL (Middle East)
Taliban (Middle East)
al-Nusrah Front (Middle East)
Boko Haram (Africa)

Anarchist
Sovereign citizen movement
Some contemporary
antiglobalization groups

Right Wing
Neo-Nazis
Skinheads
White supremacists

FIGURE 16-5 | **Types of Terrorist Groups**

Source: Derived from information provided by the Council on Foreign Relations and the Markle Foundation, "Types of Terrorism," http://www.terrorismanswers.com/terrorism/types.html (accessed January 10, 2010) and http://www.cfr.org/issue/135/ (accessed July 10, 2012).

directed at elements of the U.S. government or population.[25] **International terrorism** is unlawful force or violence by a group or an individual who has a connection to a foreign power or whose activities transcend national boundaries against persons or property to intimidate or coerce a government, the civilian population, or any segment thereof, in furtherance of political or social objectives.[26] International terrorism is sometimes incorrectly called *foreign terrorism*, a term that, strictly speaking, refers only to acts of terrorism that occur outside the United States. Cyberterrorism makes use of high technology in planning and carrying out terrorist attacks.

> The United States has to deal with three types of terrorism: domestic, international, and cyber.

Domestic Terrorism

More than 20 years ago, the 1995 terrorist bombing of the Alfred P. Murrah Federal Building in downtown Oklahoma City, Oklahoma, which killed 168 people and wounded hundreds more, showed just how vulnerable the United States is to domestic terrorist attacks. The nine-story building was devastated by a homemade bomb. The fertilizer and diesel fuel device used in the attack was left in a parked rental truck beside the building, and the blast left a crater 30 feet wide and 8 feet deep and spread debris over a ten-block area.

In June 1997, a federal jury found 29-year-old Timothy McVeigh guilty of 11 counts ranging from conspiracy to first-degree murder in the bombing. Jurors concluded that McVeigh had conspired with Terry Nichols, a friend he had met while both were in the army, and with unknown others to use a truck bomb to destroy the Murrah building. More recent examples of domestic terrorism abound, and they include a shooting by Omar Mateen in an Orlando, Florida, nightclub in 2016 that killed 49 people; an attack on a business-related Christmas party in San Bernardino, California, that killed 14 and seriously wounded 22; and the killing of 9 members of a Bible study group by Dylann Roof in Charleston, S.C., in 2015. Roof, a white supremacist, is described elsewhere in a Criminal Profiles box in this text.

Today, the activities of numerous groups in the United States fall under the heading of domestic terrorism. One of the largest and fastest growing is the sovereign citizen movement, a group of loosely affiliated individuals who argue that they are not subject to local, state, or federal laws. Many do

FIGURE 16-6 | Hate Groups in the United Sates

Source: Southern Poverty Law Center, https://www.splcenter.org/hate-map. Used by permission.

not recognize the authority of the justice system, including the courts and police. Recently, the DHS and the National Counterterrorism Center (NCTC) listed the sovereign citizen movement as a major threat, placing it alongside white supremacists and homegrown Islamic terrorists.[27] The FBI classifies the organization as an "extremist antigovernment group." According to Mark Potok, a senior fellow at the Southern Poverty Law Center, more than 100,000 Americans "have aligned themselves" with the sovereign citizens movement.[28] Many other hate groups exist throughout the United States, as shown by the map in Figure 16-6.

International Terrorism

In 2016, a Gallup poll found that 79% of Americans identified international terrorism as the greatest threat facing the United States.[29] International terrorism was the top threat identified by the poll.

According to the U.S. Department of State, more than 220 separate organizations were perpetrators of terrorist attacks in 2013, including 38 groups that had not previously been identified.[30] In that same year, more than 9,700 terrorist attacks occurred throughout the world. Those attacks resulted in 17,891 deaths and left 32,577 more people wounded. Another 2,990 individuals were kidnapped or taken hostage.

Among the countries reporting the most attacks in 2013, were Iraq, followed by Pakistan. According to the State Department, patterns of global terrorism in 2013 were influenced by trends in several key locations. In particular, terrorist violence increased coinciding with the onset of the spring "fighting season" in Afghanistan. Between February and July

2013, the number of attacks in Afghanistan more than doubled, and the number of people killed in that country increased by 253%. Pakistan and Iraq experienced similar increases in attacks during this time period, although the number of attacks and fatalities reported in Iraq continued to increase throughout the rest of the year.

Of the attacks for which perpetrator information was reported, more than 20% were attributed to the Taliban, operating primarily in Afghanistan. That group was responsible for the greatest number of fatalities in 2013. Along with the Taliban in Afghanistan, five other groups carried out attacks that were more lethal than the global average. They included Boko Haram, al-Qa'ida in Iraq (AQI), Islamic State of Iraq and the Levant (ISIL), Tehrik-i-Taliban Pakistan (TTP), and al-Qa'ida in the Arabian Peninsula.

Although terrorist attacks occurred in 93 different countries in 2013, they were heavily concentrated geographically. More than half of all attacks and fatalities, and nearly three-quarters of all injuries occurred in three countries: Iraq, Pakistan, and Afghanistan. The highest numbers of attacks, fatalities, and injuries took place in Iraq. The average lethality of attacks in Iraq was nearly 40% higher than the global average (1.84 killed per attack). The most lethal single attack in 2013 took place in September in Nigeria, where members of Boko Haram set up illegal checkpoints and killed at least 142 civilians.

Nearly half of all terrorist attacks in 2013 caused no fatalities and 53% caused no injuries. The majority of the nonlethal attacks were bombings and approximately one-quarter of them were unsuccessful attacks (e.g., an explosive was planted but defused or failed to detonate). Nearly 3,000 people were

■ **lone-wolf terrorist**   A domestic terrorist who perpetrates political violence by acting alone; who does not belong to an organized terrorist group or network; who acts without the direct influence of a leader; and whose tactics and methods are self-directed.

kidnapped or taken hostage in 552 terrorist attacks in 2013. More than 1,800 hostages were released, rescued, or escaped from their captors. The remaining hostages were either killed or the outcome of the event was not reported.

Each terrorist attack can involve one or more tactics in a continuous sequence of actions. The most commonly used tactic involved explosives, followed by armed assaults. In addition, there were 31 unarmed assaults in 2013, ten of which involved

CRIME | in the NEWS

"Lone-Wolf" Terrorists Remain Difficult to Track Down

"Lone-wolf" terrorists defy the traditional definition of terrorism. Terrorism tends to be a collective enterprise—replete with recruiters, cells of fighters, and its own hierarchy—whereas lone wolves choose their own path, standing outside organizations. But like any terrorists, these solitary fighters are totally dedicated to their cause and can be extremely violent.

The Internet would seem to be a boon for lone wolves, because it makes it easier to communicate extremist messages and acquire terrorist ideologies without having to join a group. But there has been a significant increase in lone-wolf activities in the past 10 years, according to a study by the Southern Poverty Law Center. That study, which surveyed terrorist attacks in the United States between 2009 and 2015 found that a domestic terrorist attack or foiled attack occurs, on average, every 34 days. It also found that 74% of those attacks were carried out, or planned, by a lone wolf; and a total of 90% of all attacks were the "work of just one or two persons…"

That study, limited to a dozen European countries plus Australia, Canada, and the United States, found that lone-wolf attacks represented just over 1% of all terrorist incidents in these countries. But in the United States alone, the study found that lone wolves made up almost 42% of the total. Moreover, 80% of U.S. lone wolves were involved in domestic issues, rather than international issues like Muslim fundamentalism.

U.S. lone wolves' objectives vary widely. Theodore Kaczynski, the Unabomber, protested advances in technology by mailing package bombs that killed three people and injured 23 between 1978 and 1995. In 2009, Nidal Malik Hassan, a military psychiatrist at Fort Hood, Texas, killed 13 soldiers and wounded 43 more in the name of Islam. Wade Michael Page, who in August 2012 killed six and injured three at a Sikh temple in Oak Creek, Wisconsin, advocated white power. And finally, Omar Seddique Mateen, 29, profiled elsewhere in this text, killed 49 people and wounded 53 in an Orlando, Florida, nightclub in 2016. During the attack, Mateen called 911 to proclaim his allegiance to ISIS.

Lone wolves can be motivated by a variety of ideologies. White supremacist writers have championed lone-wolf tactics. Louis Beam, a former Ku Klux Klan and Aryan Nations member, advocated "leaderless resistance" in the 1980s. A decade later, Tom Metzger encouraged fellow extremists to commit violent acts on their own, so that they

David Swanson/McClatchy-Tribune/Tribune Content Agency LLC/Alamy Stock Photo

Edward Archer, dressed in a long white robe, shoots at Philadelphia police officer Jesse Hartnett in 2016. Hartnett, while shot three times, was able to return fire and injure Archer. Archer vowed allegiance to the Islamic State. Was Archer a "lone-wolf" terrorist?

could not easily be detected. It is very difficult for authorities to track down terrorists who don't communicate with anybody, which explains why the Unabomber could wreak havoc for 17 years.

In 2009, the FBI created the Lone Wolf Initiative. The initiative involves studying past lone-wolf attacks and developing new tactics. One tactic others have identified is reaching out to communities of disgruntled Americans that might inspire lone wolves and delegitimizing the lone wolf's extreme approach.

When the initiative was launched, Michael Heimbach, the FBI's assistant director for counterterrorism, said lone-wolf terrorism "will only be prevented by good intelligence, the seamless exchange of information among law enforcement at every level and vigilant citizens reporting suspicious activity."

Discussion Questions

1. What are lone-wolf terrorists? Why are they of concern to criminologists?

2. How can lone-wolf terrorists be identified before they strike?

Sources: Randall Law, "Lone Wolf Terrorism: Understanding the Motives behind Mass Shootings," *The Hill*, September 5, 2012, http://thehill.com/blogs/congress-blog/homeland-security/247633-lone-wolf-terrorism-understanding-the-motives-behind-mass-shootings; George Michael, "What's to Stop a 'Lone Wolf' Terrorist?" Southern Poverty Law Center, *Age of the Wolf: A Study of the Rise of Lone Wolf and Leaderless Resistance Terrorism*, February 12, 2016, http://www.splcenter.org/sites/default/files/downloads/publication/lone_wolf_special_report.pdf (accessed March 2, 1017).

■ **cyberterrorism** A form of terrorism that makes use of high technology, especially computer technology and the Internet, in planning and carrying out terrorist attacks.

■ **infrastructure** The basic facilities, services, and installations needed for the functioning of a community or society, such as its transportation and communications systems, water and power lines, and public institutions.

chemical or biological agents. Thirteen hijackings were also carried out, all involving cars, trucks, buses, and one ambulance, but no aircraft or ships.

Worldwide, 510 suicide attacks took place in 2013, resulting in more than 3,800 deaths and more than 7,700 injuries. Suicide attacks in 2013 were almost five times as lethal as non-suicide attacks.[31]

Cyberterrorism

Another type of terrorism, called **cyberterrorism**, can be either domestic or international in origin. Cyberterrorism is terrorism that makes use of high technology, especially computers, the Internet, and the World Wide Web, for planning and carrying out terrorist attacks. Most common forms of terrorism target people and things—the physical world; cyberterrorism targets software, information, and communications—the virtual world. The term *cyberterrorism* was coined in the 1980s by Barry Collin, a senior research fellow at the Institute for Security and Intelligence in California, who used it to refer to the convergence of cyberspace and terrorism.[32] It was later popularized by a 1996 RAND report that warned of an emerging "new terrorism" being implemented by terrorist groups organizing and using technology; it warned of a coming "netwar," or "infowar," consisting of coordinated cyberattacks on our nation's economic, business, and military infrastructures.[33] A country's **infrastructure** consists of the basic facilities, services, and installations needed for its functioning, such as transportation and communications systems, water and power lines, and institutions serving the public (banks, schools, post offices, prisons).[34]

> Cyberterrorism makes use of high technology in planning and carrying out terrorist attacks.

Following the RAND report, (then) President Bill Clinton announced the formation of the President's Commission on Critical Infrastructure Protection (PCCIP) to study the critical components of the support systems of the nation, determine their vulnerabilities to a wide range of threats, and propose a strategy for protecting them in the future.[35] Eight critical infrastructure components were identified: telecommunications, banking and finance, electrical power, oil and gas distribution and storage, water supply, transportation, emergency services, and government services.[36] The PCCIP was the first national effort to address the vulnerabilities created by the information age.[37]

Earlier in 1998, the federal National Infrastructure Protection Center (NIPC) was created to serve as a focal point within the U.S. government for threat assessment, warning, investigation, and response to threats or attacks against the nation's critical infrastructure. NIPC functions have since been assumed by various groups within the DHS Information Analysis and Infrastructure Protection (IAIP) Directorate.

The Critical Infrastructure Assurance Office (CIAO) was created by a Presidential Decision Directive in May 1998 to coordinate the federal government's initiatives on critical infrastructure protection, and its responsibilities expanded in 2001 when (then) President George W. Bush signed an executive order establishing the President's Critical Infrastructure Protection Board (PCIPB).[38] In September 2002, the board released a study called *The National Strategy to Secure Cyberspace*, which stated that "for the United States, the Information Technology Revolution quietly changed the way business and government operate. Without a great deal of thought about security, the nation shifted the control of essential processes in manufacturing, utilities, banking, and communications to networked computers. As a result, the cost of doing business dropped and productivity skyrocketed."[39] The board found that "our economy and national security are fully dependent upon information technology and the information infrastructure. A network of networks directly supports the operation of all sectors of our economy—energy (electric power, oil and gas), transportation (rail, air, merchant marine), finance and banking, information and telecommunications, public health, emergency services, water, chemical, defense industrial base, food, agriculture, and postal and shipping. The reach of these computer networks exceeds the bounds of cyberspace. They also control physical objects such as electrical transformers, trains, pipeline pumps, chemical vats, radars, and stock markets."[40] In 2003, the functions of the CIAO were transferred to the National Cyber Security Division (NCSD) of the then-newly created DHS; the creation of NCSD improved protection of critical cyberassets by "maximizing and leveraging the resources" of previously separate offices; and in 2009 President Obama created the position of Cybersecurity Czar in his cabinet to address national issues of cybersecurity (see Chapter 15).[41]

Scenarios describing cyberterrorism possibilities are imaginative and diverse, ranging from a successful cyberterrorist attack on the nation's air traffic control system, causing multiple airplanes to collide in midair, to an attack on food and cereal processing plants, drastically altering the levels of certain nutritional supplements to sicken or kill a large proportion of our nation's young children. Other terrorist attacks could cause the country's power grid to collapse or could muddle the records and transactions of banks and stock exchanges. The possibilities are almost endless.

CRIMINAL | PROFILES

Mohammed Atta—Leader of the 9/11 Attacks

This profile box is somewhat different from those in previous chapters. Background information regarding Mohammed Atta, the subject of this box, is sparse, unreliable, and rife with conflicting claims. Given that Atta trained as a terrorist, came from the Middle East, and likely made efforts to live a life "under the radar," it is unsurprising that extensive research into Atta's pre-9/11 life yields little information about which one can feel confident. Although some facts about Atta's life are verifiable, many of the available sources appear to be speculative or outright rumor.

We know, for example, that Atta was born in Kafr El Sheikh in Egypt's Nile Delta, grew up in Cairo, and received an undergraduate degree in architecture from Cairo University. He is known to have resided in Germany from 1993 to 1999, where he pursued an urban planning degree at the University of Hamburg. Reliable records also show that he was a licensed pilot who moved to Venice, Florida, in 2000 to pursue additional flight training at Huffman Aviation International. Records and witness information tell us that he was a committed fundamentalist Muslim.[i] We can conclude that he was intensely motivated by personal ideals and zealous spiritual beliefs, most of which were acquired through his life experiences.

Other claims, however, cannot be as readily confirmed. For example, England's *Telegraph* online daily newspaper reported on December 13, 2003, that documents it had obtained showed that during the summer of 2001 Atta underwent an intensive three-day "work programme" in Baghdad under the tutelage of notorious Palestinian terrorist Abu Nidal. The handwritten, top secret memo the *Telegraph* had acquired was, ostensibly, prepared by the former head of Iraq's Intelligence Service and submitted to then-president Saddam Hussein. The memo purportedly lauds Atta's "extraordinary effort" in preparing to lead the team that would be "responsible for attacking the targets that we have agreed to destroy."[ii] Numerous subsequent investigations, however—including the U.S. government's own 9/11 Commission—have failed to confirm a direct link between Hussein's Iraqi government and the al-Qaeda terrorist group of which Atta was a member and that later claimed responsibility for the 2001 World Trade Center attacks.[iii]

In Atta's case, extensive scrutiny of existing information sources reveals a confusing and often conflicting profile of a man whose movements and activities during the period immediately preceding the World Trade Center attacks cannot be reliably confirmed. Available news reports starkly conflict with official documents. Some government agency documents conflict with the documentary evidence provided by other government agencies. "Highly reliable" information reported by reputable news sources in the period immediately following the attacks has subsequently proven to be almost completely inaccurate. It is the nature of the terrorists' nether world. Secrecy,

September 11 hijacker Mohammed Atta. Why do we know so little about him?

Portland Police Department/AP Images

disinformation, obfuscation, and orchestrated confusion are tools of the trade in such an environment.

The life experiences and complex motivations of terrorists do not fit the motivational patterns of the (for lack of a better word) *ordinary* criminals described in previous chapters. Those seeking to understand terrorist behavior would probably be best served by examining the cultural, educational, ideological, and religious influences that shape the terrorists' worldviews, as those same views also serve to justify in the terrorist's mind even the most horrendous behavior in their pursuit of "correcting" perceived wrongs.

The case of Mohammed Atta raises a number of interesting questions. Among them are the following:

1. Is terrorism a crime so different in form that it requires a separate explanation than other crimes? If not, how can it be explained within the theoretical frameworks offered by this text?

2. Does conflict theory offer an adequate explanation for most acts of terrorism?

3. How can future acts of terrorism be prevented? Would prevention measures involve primarily security measures, or social initiatives designed to reduce the attraction that radical political ideas hold for some people?

Notes:

i.   John Hooper, "The Shy, Caring, Deadly Fanatic," The Observer (Hamburg), September 23, 2001, http://observer.guardian.co.uk/waronterrorism/story/0,,556630,00 .html (accessed June 3, 2007).

ii.   Con Coughlin, "Terrorist behind September 11 Strike Was Trained by Saddam," Telegraph (United Kingdom), December 13, 2003, http://www.telegraph.co.uk/ news/main.jhtml?xml=/news/2003/12/14/wterr14.xml&sSheet=/portal/2003/12/14/ixportaltop.html (accessed June 3, 2007).

iii. Walter Pincus and Dana Milbank, "Al-Qaeda-Hussein Link Is Dismissed," Washington Post, June 17, 2004, http://www.washingtonpost.com/wp-dyn/articles/A47812 -2004Jun16.html (accessed June 3, 2007).

WHO'S TO BLAME—The Individual or Society?

The Making of a Suicide Bomber

Khaled Al-Rasheed was born in New York City to Egyptian parents and repeatedly visited the Middle East with his father. His last trip was in 2010 when Khaled spent part of the summer with his grandparents near the world-famous Aswan dam. Although his American passport didn't show it, Khaled, a Muslim, had traveled extensively throughout the Arab world while he was growing up, sometimes in the company of his father, and sometimes with his grandfather.

He had seen firsthand the damage done by the first Gulf War in 1991, much of which hadn't been repaired by the time he first visited the region. He had also experienced the resentment festering among the huge non-Arab populations in Saudi Arabia and Kuwait, where oil money paid for the extravagant lifestyles of the royal families but didn't find its way into the hands of the working class.

By the time he was 15, he had befriended a group of radical young Islamists living in Jordan, who blamed the problems in the Middle East on the Great Satan—their name for America. "Americans are stealing our region's wealth," he was told, "and polluting the holy land with their vice and nonbelief."

Returning to the United States in the fall of 2015, Khaled had become radicalized and was ready to strike a blow in what he saw as a worldwide holy war against nonbelievers. As a U.S. citizen, he could travel easily in and out of the country, and on one of his trips he was able to smuggle in the equipment necessary to manufacture a new kind of explosive—one that could be packed into condoms and swallowed like the heroin and cocaine that often crossed the country's southern borders. Equipped with a small blasting-cap whose thin wire ran up the esophagus and into his mouth, the last charge to be swallowed could be set off by simply biting down on a tiny switch clenched between Khaled's molars. The device, which used very little metal, was virtually undetectable.

One day, Khaled swallowed six explosive-filled condoms, passed through security, and boarded a plane at New York's John F. Kennedy airport. Once the plane, bound for Los

Mariusz Blach/Fotolia

Angeles, was airborne, Khaled bit down on the detonator. To his surprise, nothing happened. An hour into the flight, however, one of the swallowed condoms ruptured, and Khaled became violently ill as its contents entered his digestive system. Removed from the plane when it landed in Los Angeles, he was taken to a hospital where the explosives were discovered. An operation saved his life, and he recovered in the medical wing of the Los Angeles County Men's Central Jail.

Think about it

1. What does it mean to say, as this scenario does, that "Khaled had become radicalized"? Might the term be applied to other kinds of offenders? If so, which ones?

2. How could someone like Khaled, born in America, be so taken with a foreign ideology?

3. If you were in charge of policy making for America's "War on Terror," what would you want to see happen to Khaled?

4. If you were a judge in charge of sentencing Khaled for his attempted terrorist attack, what kind of sentence would you give him? Is there any chance that he might be rehabilitated? What does "rehabilitation" mean in this context?

Note: Who's to Blame boxes provide fictionalized critical thinking opportunities based on actual cases.

In an effort to protect its vital interests from future acts of terrorism, the U.S. government planned to build a whole new Internet of its own. Dubbed "GovNet" (govnet.net), the service was planned to be a voice and data network based on the Internet Protocol (IP) that had very limited connectivity with commercial or public networks and was to be physically and electronically separate from existing Internet routers and gateways. The idea was to create a network that could performs its functions with very minimal risk of penetration or disruption from users on other networks.[42] The idea for GovNet was first offered by Richard Clarke, President Bush's cybersecurity adviser, in late 2001: "We'll be working to secure our cyberspace from a range of possible threats, from hackers to criminals to terrorist groups, to foreign nations, which might use cyber war against us."[43]

The system that eventually developed, however, was quite different from what was originally planned. Today's federal Critical Infrastructure Warning Information Network (CWIN) is still being developed, with plans to let government insiders share data on critical infrastructure sectors without risk of intrusion from outside sources.[44] In the words of the developers, "CWIN is DHS' only survivable, critical communications tool not dependent on the Public Switch Network (PSN) or the public Internet that can communicate both data and voice information in a collaborative environment in support of infrastructure restoration." The CWIN provides a survivable, dependable method of communication allowing DHS to communicate with other federal agencies, state and local government, the private sector, and international organizations in the event that primary methods of communication are unavailable. **http://ssrn.com/abstract=1452803** provides additional insight into the issue of cyberterrorism, and **http://www.dhs.gov/xlibrary/assets/privacy/privacy_pia_cwin.pdf** is a Department of Homeland Security document describing the CWIN.

Terrorism and Technology

The technological sophistication of state-sponsored terrorist organizations is rapidly increasing. Handguns and even

> **The technological sophistication of state-sponsored terrorist organizations is rapidly increasing.**

larger weapons are now being manufactured out of plastic polymers and ceramics; they are capable of firing Teflon-coated, armor-piercing hardened ceramic bullets and are extremely powerful as well as impossible to discern with metal detectors. The black market makes available other sinister items, including liquid metal embrittlement (LME), a chemical that slowly weakens any metal it contacts, which some experts say could be applied with a felt-tipped marker to fuselage components in domestic aircraft, causing delayed structural failure.[45] Backpack-type electromagnetic pulse generators may be used by terrorists who would carry them into major cities, set them up next to important computer installations, and activate them to wipe out billions of items of financial, military, or other information now stored on magnetic media. International terrorists, along with the general public, have easy access to maps and other information that could be used to cripple the nation. The approximately 500 extremely high-voltage (EHV) transformers on which the nation's electric grid depends, for example, are largely undefended but have been specified with extreme geographic accuracy on easily available Web-based power-network maps.

It is clear that at least some terrorist organizations are seeking to obtain weapons of mass destruction (WMDs) and chemical, biological, radiological, nuclear and explosive weapons

(CBRNE) for possible threats. A CIA report made public in 2003 warned that al-Qaeda's end goal is to use WMDs and noted that the group had "openly expressed its desire to produce nuclear weapons" and that sketches and documents recovered from an al-Qaeda facility in Afghanistan contained plans for a crude nuclear device.[46] A 2008 report by the federal Commission on the Prevention of Weapons of Mass Destruction Proliferation and Terrorism contained the frightening conclusion that "unless the world community acts decisively and with great urgency, it is more likely than not that a weapon of mass destruction will be used in a terrorist attack somewhere in the world by the end of 2013."[47] In fact, in 2013 and 2014, Syrian forces are alleged to have used chemical weapons against rebels in the country fighting to unseat President Assad.[48]

One study by Harvard University researchers found that the United States and other countries were moving too slowly in efforts to help Russia and other former Soviet-bloc nations destroy poorly protected nuclear material and warheads left over from the cold war; the study also warned that most civilian nuclear reactors in Eastern Europe are "dangerously insecure."[49] Experts said the amount of plutonium needed to make one bomb can be smuggled out of a supposedly secure area in a briefcase or even in the pocket of an overcoat. Although the Harvard study is now more than ten years old, no one really knows how much bomb-grade nuclear material is available on the black market today.

Biological weapons were banned by the 1975 international Biological Weapons Convention (BWC),[50] but a biocrime called *bioterrorism*—defined by the Centers for Disease Control and Prevention (CDC) as the "intentional or threatened use of viruses, bacteria, fungi, or toxins from living organisms to produce death or disease in humans, animals, or plants"[51]—is of considerable concern today. The infamous anthrax letters mailed to at least four people in the United States in 2001 (discussed earlier) provide an example of a bioterrorism incident intended to create widespread fear among Americans; five people (including mail handlers) died, and 23 others were infected.[52] Other possible bioterrorism agents include botulism toxin, brucellosis, cholera, glanders, plague, ricin, smallpox, and tularemia Q fever as well as a number of viral agents such as viral hemorrhagic fevers and severe acute respiratory syndrome (SARS). Experts fear that technologically savvy terrorists could create their own novel bioweapons through bioengineering, a process that uses snippets of made-to-order DNA, the molecular code on which life is based.[53] Learn more about biological agents via the CDC website at **http://emergency.cdc.gov/agent/agentlist.asp**, and visit the Center for the Study of Bioterrorism via **http://biosecurity.slu.edu**. The Centers for Disease Control and Prevention bioterrorism agents/diseases is available at: **https://emergency.cdc.gov/agent/agentlist.asp**.

The Radicalization Process

In early 2017, the U.S. Department of Justice released four federally funded reports on the radicalization of homegrown terrorists. The first report involved a behavioral study of the radicalization trajectories of 135 American "homegrown" al-Qaeda-inspired terrorists. Authored by Jytte Klausen of Brandeis University, the report sought to "develop a new approach to the assessment of individuals who are suspected of posing a risk to public safety or attempting to engage in criminal behaviors in support of terrorism at home or abroad."[54] Klausen studied the life histories of convicted American homegrown terrorism offenders who had been motivated by the Salafi-jihadist system of beliefs. Her research showed that individuals who are in the process of becoming dangerously radicalized "will exhibit overt and detectable behaviors that are somewhat predictable." Klausen's pathways to terrorism model helps in understanding the radicalization process by focusing on the use of behavioral indicators that are known to be associated with belief systems advocating violent extremism. Klausen's model differs from those of other researchers by focusing on tracking ongoing radicalization through observations of changes in ideology and behavior. Klausen found that most offenders in the study exhibited signs of progressing through four phases of radicalization in a fairly predictable trajectory. This progression moved the offenders from learning about the extremist belief system to changing their lifestyle and then on to criminal action or to making plans for such action. Klausen's four stages of progression in the development of radicalization include:

1. **Pre-radicalization**. This first stage is highlighted by searching behaviors, in which the individual looks for "cognitive openings" into the radicalization process. The pre-radicalization stage might begin with a personal or family crisis, and often involves "expressions of disillusionment with world affairs" or with political and religious authorities.

2. **Detachment**. In this second stage, the budding terrorist seeks out new authority figures—often doing so online. He or she may experience a personal revelation that leads to further changes in lifestyle. Those changes frequently involve dropping out of work or quitting a job.

3. **Peer-Immersion and Training**. The behaviors characteristic of this stage include leaving home, or leaving one's family, and sometimes attempting to go abroad in efforts to "officially" join a radical organization.

4. **Planning and Execution of Violent Action**. This final stage is indicated by joining a terrorist group abroad or attempting to join such a group. It may end with actions that support others in carrying out terrorist activities, or with the now radicalized individual initiating a terrorist attack.

Klausen also found that among offenders radicalized in 2010 and after, 50% were radicalized through online contacts, while the other half was radicalized through offline connections with radicalized individuals.

The second DOJ report, also written by Klausen, concerned itself with the role of social networks in the evolution of al-Qaeda-inspired violent extremism in the United States.[55] In it, Klausen sought to determine how and why foreign terrorist organizations recruit Americans to their cause. Specifically, Klausen focused on the Hezbollah, Hamas, and jihadist networks operating in the United States over the past twenty-five years. She used a technique known as social network analysis (SNA), which had been developed by sociologists to study the dynamics of informal networks. The technique produced a number of results, of which one of the most interesting was a clearer understanding of Internet recruitment. Beginning in 2007, a number of websites and blogs appeared with names like RevolutionMuslim.com and evolution4muslim.com. These sites, many of which portrayed themselves as ministries, linked to file sharing sites like YouTube and Scribd. Facebook and other social networking sites were also drawn into the mix. Through social networking, prospective radicals could share ideas and learn extreme ideology. Klausen found a common thread running through the lives of radicalized homegrown American militants, and that was that they always wanted "to go abroad to fight." In late 2014 and in 2015, however, she found that the dynamic changed, and many radicalized individuals started to plot to "do something" at home, rather than abroad.

The third DOJ report, conducted by Michael Jensen and Gary LaFree, both at the University of Maryland, was part of the National Consortium for the Study of Terrorism and Responses to Terrorism (START) project.[56] It employed a database known as PIRUS, which stands for "Profiles of Individual Radicalization in the United States." The database includes 147 variables covering demographics, personal background, group affiliation, and ideological information for 1,473 violent and nonviolent extremists from across the ideological spectrum. Through a set of robust statistical models, the project identified a number of factors that indicate which extremists are most likely to engage in violent acts. All other things being equal, the report found, pre-radicalization criminal activity and post-radicalization clique membership are strongly associated with violent outcomes among radicalized individuals. Because law enforcement agencies and countering violent extremism (CVE) programs prioritize potentially violent individuals when resources are constrained, this finding suggests that they should place their focus on individuals with prior interactions with the criminal justice system, and on those who are known to associate with others holding extreme views.

The fourth report attempted to identify differences between lone-wolf terrorists and mass murderers.[57] It found that mass murderers lack a motivating ideology, and that most commit their crimes because of personal feelings of having been wronged. Lone-wolf terrorists, on the other hand, are ideologically motivated and can be distinguished from mass murderers by three categories: (1) the degree to which they interact with co-conspirators; (2) the behaviors they engage in before acting, and (3) the degree "to which they leak information prior to the attack.

Specifically, lone wolves could be distinguished from mass murderers by the fact that they more often tried to recruit others; more frequently interacted with members of a wider network; used social media tools to communicate with other like-minded individuals; joined a wider movement; and made public statements prior to attacking. They also were more likely to attempt "dry runs" before attacking; were more likely to verbalize their intent to family and friends; and to be socially isolated. They were less likely, however, to have problems with personal relationships, to be under chronic stress, to abuse substances, or to have a personal history with the event location. See the FBI's most wanted terrorists at **https://www.fbi.gov/wanted/wanted_terrorists.**

Finally, in 2017, a University of Chicago study analyzed 112 people who had been indicted for ISIS-related crimes over the past three years and found that 85% were American citizens, 64% were American born, and only 4% were foreign nationals.[58] The average age of the indicted individuals was 27; two-thirds had been to college; three-quarters had jobs or were in school; and more than 40% were in a relationship. Eighty-three percent had watched ISIS propaganda before becoming radicalized, leading report authors to conclude that "The strength of ISIS is in the videos with which it can basically recruit ordinary Americans to its cause."[59] The report concluded that American officials "need to understand ISIS's propaganda strategy in the U.S. and target its methods for driving recruitment and radicalization."

Countering the Terrorist Threat

The U.S. Department of State, in its publication *Patterns of Global Terrorism*, made a number of policy recommendations for use in the fight against international terrorism. One of the most significant was that "Money is like oxygen to terrorists, and it must be choked-off."[60] In September 2001, (then) President George W. Bush issued an executive order imposing stiff penalties on anyone providing financial support to terrorists or their organizations.[61] The order also blocked the assets of designated individuals and organizations linked to global terrorism; prohibited financial transactions with the terrorist groups, leaders, and corporate and charitable fronts listed in the order; and established America's ability to block the U.S. assets of (and deny access to U.S. markets to) any foreign banks refusing to freeze terrorists' assets.

In 2003, the White House released its official *National Strategy for Combating Terrorism*, which included a multipronged initiative aimed at reducing both the threat severity and international reach of international terrorist organizations.[62] The strategy had as goals: (1) defeating terrorists and their organizations

The FBI's Most Wanted Terrorists Web page. How many Americans are on the page?

■ **foreign terrorist organization (FTO)** A foreign organization that engages in terrorist activity threatening the security of U.S. nationals or the national security of the United States and that is so designated by the U.S. secretary of state.

by identifying, locating, and destroying them; (2) diminishing the underlying conditions that terrorists seek to exploit by resolving regional disputes; by fostering economic, social, and political development; by encouraging market-based economies; by supporting good governance and the rule of law; and by "winning the war of ideas" to ensure that ideologies that promote terrorism do not find fertile ground in any nation; and (3) defending U.S. citizens and interests at home and abroad by implementing strong and effective security measures and by enhancing measures intended to ensure the integrity, reliability, and availability of critical physical and information-based infrastructures (including transportation and information systems).

The July 2004 report of the 9/11 Commission proposed sweeping changes within the U.S. intelligence community, including the creation of the position of a national intelligence director (NID), and then the Intelligence Reform and Terrorism Prevention Act of 2004 (IRTPA) facilitated the creation of the NCTC under the newly created position of NID.[63] The NID would act as the principal adviser to the president, the National Security Council, and the Homeland Security Council for intelligence matters related to national security, and the NCTC would serve as the primary organization for integrating and analyzing all intelligence pertaining to terrorism and counterterrorism and for conducting strategic counterterrorism operational planning.[64]

Finally, in 2011, the White House released its official National Strategy for Counterterrorism.[65] The strategy maintained a focus on deterring Islamic-inspired terrorism and promised to pressure "al-Qa'ida's core while emphasizing the need to build foreign partnerships and capacity … to strengthen our resilience." The authors of the strategy noted that it "augments our focus on confronting the al-Qa'ida-linked threats that continue to emerge from beyond its core safehaven in South Asia." At the time, the strategy said that "The preeminent security threat to the United States continues to be from *al-Qa'ida and its affiliate and adherents*," although ISIS (aka ISIL) may have now assumed that role.

Learn more about countering terrorist threats at **http://www.flashpoints.info/Flashpoints/IB%20Counter-Terrorism.html**, and the *National Strategy* is available in its entirety at **http://www.whitehouse.gov/sites/default/files/rss_viewer/national_security_strategy.pdf**. Visit the Global Terrorism Database at **http://www.start.umd.edu/gtd/globe/index.html**.

Foreign Terrorist Organizations

From the late 1970s to the mid-1990s, U.S. antiterrorism policy focused largely on deterring and punishing state sponsors of terrorism as opposed to terrorist groups themselves.[66]

In 1996, passage of the federal Anti-Terrorism and Effective Death Penalty Act signaled an important shift in policy:[67] It recognized the transnationalism of many terrorist organizations, created a legal category of **foreign terrorist organizations (FTOs)**, and banned funding, granting of visas, and other material support to such organizations and their members. The USA PATRIOT Act extended and strengthened the provisions of that legislation.[68]

Federal law has required that any organization considered for FTO designation must be *foreign* and engage in terrorist activity as defined in Section 212(a)(3)(B) of the Immigration and Nationality Act;[69] it must also threaten the security of U.S. nationals *or* the national security (national defense, foreign relations, *or* economic interests) of the United States. The U.S. Department of State has the authority to designate any group external to the United States as an FTO based on an exhaustive interagency review in which all evidence of a group's activity, from both classified and open sources, is scrutinized; the State Department, working closely with the Justice and Treasury Departments and the intelligence community, would prepare a detailed "administrative record" documenting the terrorist activity of the designated FTO. Under federal law, FTO designations are subject to judicial review, and in the event of a challenge to a group's FTO designation in federal court, the U.S. government would rely on the administrative records containing classified intelligence

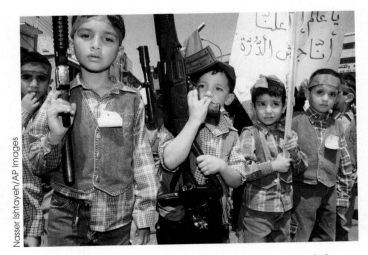

Nasser Ishtayeh/AP Images

Palestinian boys wearing green ribbons on their heads in support of Hamas and brandishing plastic rifles as they march through the streets of the West Bank town of Nablus in a protest rally against what their elders see as Israeli aggression. Some argue that terrorists already control the hearts and minds of young people in many parts of the world. What can be done to change that?

information to defend the designation decision. FTO designations expire in two years unless renewed.

Once an organization has been designated an FTO, a number of legal consequences ensue. It becomes unlawful for a person in the United States or subject to the jurisdiction of the United States to provide funds or other material support to a designated FTO, and representatives and certain members of a designated FTO can be denied visas or kept from entering the United States if they are aliens. Also, U.S. financial institutions must block funds of designated FTOs and their agents and report the blockage to the Office of Foreign Assets Control in the U.S. Department of the Treasury. Designated FTOs can be found in Table 16-4.

The State Department also has the authority to designate selected foreign governments as *state sponsors of international terrorism*, and four countries currently are so designated: Iran, North Korea, Sudan, and Syria. Iran remains the most active state sponsor of terrorism in the world: Iran's Islamic Revolutionary Guard Corps (IRGC) and the Ministry of Intelligence and Security (MOIS) continue to be involved in the planning and support of terrorist acts and aid a variety of groups that use terrorism to pursue their goals, and the

TABLE 16-4 | Designated Foreign Terrorist Organizations as of Mid-2017

DATE DESIGNATED	NAME	DATE DESIGNATED	NAME
10/8/1997	Abu Nidal Organization (ANO)	3/22/2004	Ansar al-Islam (AAI)
10/8/1997	Abu Sayyaf Group (ASG)	7/13/2004	Continuity Irish Republican Army (CIRA)
10/8/1997	Aum Shinrikyo (AUM)	12/17/2004	Islamic State of Iraq and the Levant (formerly al-Qa'ida in Iraq)
10/8/1997	Basque Fatherland and Liberty (ETA)		
10/8/1997	Gama'a al-Islamiyya (Islamic Group) (IG)	6/17/2005	Islamic Jihad Union (IJU)
10/8/1997	HAMAS	3/5/2008	Harakat ul-Jihad-i-Islami/Bangladesh (HUJI-B)
10/8/1997	Harakat ul-Mujahidin (HUM)	3/18/2008	al-Shabaab
10/8/1997	Hizballah	5/18/2009	Revolutionary Struggle (RS)
10/8/1997	Kahane Chai (Kach)	7/2/2009	Kata'ib Hizballah (KH)
10/8/1997	Kurdistan Workers Party (PKK) (Kongra-Gel)	1/19/2010	al-Qa'ida in the Arabian Peninsula (AQAP)
10/8/1997	Liberation Tigers of Tamil Eelam (LTTE)	8/6/2010	Harakat ul-Jihad-i-Islami (HUJI)
10/8/1997	National Liberation Army (ELN)	9/1/2010	Tehrik-e Taliban Pakistan (TTP)
10/8/1997	Palestine Liberation Front (PLF)	11/4/2010	Jundallah
10/8/1997	Palestinian Islamic Jihad (PIJ)	5/23/2011	Army of Islam (AOI)
10/8/1997	Popular Front for the Liberation of Palestine (PFLP)	9/19/2011	Indian Mujahedeen (IM)
		3/13/2012	Jemaah Anshorut Tauhid (JAT)
10/8/1997	PFLP-General Command (PFLP-GC)	5/30/2012	Abdallah Azzam Brigades (AAB)
10/8/1997	Revolutionary Armed Forces of Colombia (FARC)	9/19/2012	Haqqani Network (HQN)
		3/22/2013	Ansar al-Dine (AAD)
10/8/1997	Revolutionary People's Liberation Party/Front (DHKP/C)	11/14/2013	Boko Haram
		11/14/2013	Ansaru
10/8/1997	Shining Path (SL)	12/19/2013	al-Mulathamun Battalion
10/8/1999	al-Qa'ida (AQ)	1/13/2014	Ansar al-Shari'a in Benghazi
9/25/2000	Islamic Movement of Uzbekistan (IMU)	1/13/2014	Ansar al-Shari'a in Darnah
5/16/2001	Real Irish Republican Army (RIRA)	1/13/2014	Ansar al-Shari'a in Tunisia
12/26/2001	Jaish-e-Mohammed (JEM)	4/10/2014	ISIL Sinai Province (formally Ansar Bayt al-Maqdis)
12/26/2001	Lashkar-e Tayyiba (LeT)		
3/27/2002	Al-Aqsa Martyrs Brigade (AAMB)	5/15/2014	al-Nusrah Front
3/27/2002	Asbat al-Ansar (AAA)	8/20/2014	Mujahidin Shura Council in the Environs of Jerusalem (MSC)
3/27/2002	al-Qaida in the Islamic Maghreb (AQIM)		
		9/30/2015	Jaysh Rijal al-Tariq al Naqshabandi (JRTN)
8/9/2002	Communist Party of the Philippines/New People's Army (CPP/NPA)	1/14/2016	ISIL-Khorasan (ISIL-K)
		5/20/2016	Islamic State of Iraq and the Levant's Branch in Libya (ISIL-Libya)
10/23/2002	Jemaah Islamiya (JI)		
1/30/2003	Lashkar i Jhangvi (LJ)	6/30/2016	al-Qa'ida in the Indian Subcontinent

Source: U.S. Department of State, Office of the Coordinator for Counterterrorism. Current as of March, 2017.

The State Department has the authority to designate foreign governments as *state sponsors of international terrorism.* Iranian government continues to provide support to numerous terrorist groups, including the Lebanese Hezbollah, Hamas, and the Palestine Islamic Jihad (PIJ), all of which seek to undermine Middle East peace negotiations through the use of terrorism. Since 2007, Sudan has provided shelter for members of al-Qaeda, the Lebanese Hezbollah, al-Gama'a al-Islamiyya, Egyptian Islamic Jihad, the PIJ, and Hamas, in spite of being engaged in a counterterrorism dialogue with the United States since mid-2000. Syria offers safe haven and support to several terrorist groups, some of which oppose the Middle East peace negotiations. Learn more about terrorist activities in individual countries from the Department of State's Country Reports on Terrorism via **http://www.state .gov/j/ct/rls/crt/**.

The 2001 USA PATRIOT Act created a Terrorist Exclusion List (TEL) with immigration consequences for groups on the list.[70] The federal government may deport aliens living in the United States who provide material assistance to organizations listed on the TEL and may refuse entry to the country to anyone who assists or solicits assistance from those organizations.

At the individual level, the U.S. government's Terrorist Identities Datamart Environment (TIDE) serves as a central repository of information on international terrorist identities.[71] TIDE supports the federal government's various terrorist screening systems or "watchlists" and the U.S. Intelligence Community's overall counterterrorism efforts. The Terrorist Identities Group (TIG), located in NCTC's Information Sharing and Knowledge Development Directorate (ISKD), is responsible for building and maintaining TIDE, whose database includes all information the U.S. government has on the identities of individuals who are known or lawfully suspected to be or who have been involved in terrorism-related activities. Federal agencies nominate individuals based on evaluations of available intelligence and law enforcement antiterrorism information; then federal data analysts create and enhance TIDE records based on their review of those nominations and daily transmit those data to the Terrorist Screening Center (TSC) for use in the government's consolidated watchlist. The watchlist supports screening processes to detect and interdict known and suspected terrorists at home and abroad and is used to create and maintain the Transportation Security Administration's "no-fly list," the Department of State's visa database, and other similar databases.

Present U.S. policy focuses largely on terrorist organizations like al-Qaeda and their affiliated networks and state supporters.[72] New brands of terrorists—individuals who are not affiliated with any established terrorist organization and are apparently not agents of any state sponsor—represent a significant new threat. For example, the terrorist Ramzi Ahmed Yousef, believed to have masterminded the 1993 World Trade Center bombing, apparently did not belong to any larger established terrorist group, although he may have had some ties to al-Qaeda operatives. The worldwide threat of individual or "lone wolf terrorism" (discussed in a box earlier in this chapter) is substantial and was recognized by outgoing FBI director Robert Mueller in 2013 when he told reporters affiliated with National Public Radio that "the core of al-Qaida has been decimated, and the accused Boston bombers and the Army psychiatrist who carried out a massacre at Fort Hood, Texas, to support the Taliban exemplify the new face of terrorism." Mueller continued, saying, "You have individuals that are not aligned with any particular group who can be radicalized and find a weapon of choice and then kill American innocent civilians.... and unfortunately, we have to be prepared for that. It's much more difficult to discern, but we could anticipate that there may be more in the future."[73]

Another problem that surfaced in the wake of incidents associated with Islamic fundamentalist groups was how to condemn and combat such terrorist activity—and the extreme and violent ideology of specific radical groups—without appearing to be anti-Islamic in general. A desire to punish a state for supporting international terrorism may also conflict with other foreign policy objectives involving that nation. Learn more about terrorism from the Terrorism Research Center via **http://trc.uark.edu** and the NIJ Research on Domestic Radicalization and Terrorism at **https://www. nij.gov/topics/crime/terrorism/Pages/welcome .aspx** or visit the NCTC via **http://www.nctc.gov**.

The Future of Terrorism

The Congressional Research Service (CRS) identified three trends in modern terrorism.[74] The first trend—one that makes terrorism especially difficult to combat—is toward loosely organized, self-financed international terrorist networks. The second is toward terrorism that is religiously or ideologically motivated, and groups using religion as a pretext (such as radical Islamic fundamentalist groups) pose serious terrorist threats of varying kinds to U.S. interests and call upon other like-minded people throughout the world to join their causes. The third trend is the recent growth of cross-national links among different terrorist organizations, which may involve combinations of military training, funding, technology transfer, and political advice. The CRS cited intelligence reports showing, for example, that Chechen rebels have been trained in al-Qaeda terrorist camps in Afghanistan and even in Chechnya itself; al-Qaeda funding reputedly helped establish the Islamic separatist group Abu Sayyaf in the Philippines; and some intelligence reports have suggested the possibility of mid- and low-level cooperation between al-Qaeda and the Lebanese Hezbollah in weapons

■ **INTERPOL**   The International Criminal Police Organization (INTERPOL) An international law enforcement support organization that today has 190 member nations.

■ **europol**   The European Police Office, an integrated police intelligence-gathering and dissemination arm of the member nations of the European Union.

smuggling, money laundering, and training for terrorist operations.

Looming over the entire issue of international terrorism is a trend toward proliferation of WMDs. Iran has been aggressively seeking nuclear arms capability; Iraq is thought to be stockpiling chemical and biological agents and rebuilding its nuclear weapons program. North Korea has admitted to having a clandestine program for uranium enrichment, and indications have also surfaced that al-Qaeda has attempted to acquire chemical, biological, radiological, and nuclear weapons. Stakes in the war against international terrorism are increasing, and margins for error in selecting appropriate policy instruments or combinations of them to prevent terrorist attacks are diminishing.

> Looming over the issue of international terrorism is the proliferation of WMDs.

International Crime-Fighting Organizations

Cross-jurisdictional crimes can be especially difficult to combat. Imagine how a cyberthief in Kiev might buy confidential personal information from a Dark Web server hosted in Africa, and then use that information to illicitly transfer funds from a bank in Boston to one in Beijing. Not only would it be unclear what laws had been violated, and in what nation, but investigation of the crime would be difficult to coordinate between the law enforcement agencies of the affected countries. To meet the challenges involved in such a scenario, two international information-sharing agencies now work to assist in the investigation and prosecution of international crime. They are described in the paragraphs that follow.

INTERPOL

The International Criminal Police Organization (**INTERPOL**), headquartered in Lyons, France, traces its origins back to the first International Criminal Police Congress of 1914, which met in Monaco.[75] The theme of that meeting was international cooperation in the investigation of crimes and the apprehension of

fugitives. INTERPOL, however, did not officially begin operations until 1946, when the end of World War II brought about a new spirit of international harmony.

Today, 190 nations belong to INTERPOL.[76] The U.S. INTERPOL unit is called the U.S. National Central Bureau (USNCB) and is a separate agency within the U.S. Department of Justice.

INTERPOL's primary purpose is to act as a clearinghouse for information on offenses and suspects who are believed to operate across national boundaries. The organization is committed to promoting "the widest possible mutual assistance between all criminal police authorities within the limits of laws existing in … different countries and in the spirit of the Universal Declaration of Human Rights."[77]

INTERPOL does not have its own field investigators. The agency has no powers of arrest or of search and seizure in member countries. Instead, INTERPOL's purpose is to facilitate, coordinate, and encourage police cooperation as a means of combating international crime. It draws on the willingness of local and national police forces to lend support to its activities. The headquarters staff of INTERPOL consists of about 250 individuals, many with prior police experience, who direct data-gathering efforts around the world and who serve to alert law enforcement organizations to the movement of suspected offenders within their jurisdiction.

Today, INTERPOL provides a range of policing expertise and capabilities, supporting three main crime programs: counterterrorism, cybercrime, and organized and emerging crime. The agency continues to expand its activities and is in the process of developing a centralized international forensic DNA database. It has also created an international framework for disaster victim identification.[78] Visit INTERPOL headquarters via **http://www.interpol.int**.

Europol

In the Maastricht Treaty of February 7, 1992, members of the European Union (EU) agreed to the establishment of the European Police Office (**Europol**). Based in The Hague, the Netherlands, Europol started limited operations in 1994 in the form of the Europol Drugs Unit. Over time, other important law enforcement activities were added to the Europol agenda. The Europol Convention was ratified by all member states in 1998, and Europol commenced full operations the next year.

CRIMINAL | PROFILES
The Tsarnaev Brothers—The Boston Bombers

In early 2014, attorneys with the U.S. Department of Justice announced that they would ask a federal trial jury to recommend the death penalty for surviving Boston Marathon bombing suspect Dzhokhar Tsarnaev.[i] A year earlier, Tsarnaev, 19, had been shot by police and arrested, while his brother, Tamerlan, 26, was killed during a massive manhunt launched by authorities who used public video recordings of the crime scene that showed the brothers placing the explosive devices. The blasts, which came from home-made pressure-cooker bombs, killed three people near the marathon's finish line and injured more than 260 others—many of them seriously. During the Tsarnaevs' flight to avoid capture, they hijacked a Mercedes, killed an M.I.T. police officer, threw bombs at pursuing police cars, and engaged in a shootout with Boston law enforcement officers. After Tamerlan was killed, the manhunt ended when Dzhokhar was found hiding in a dry-docked boat in the backyard of a Watertown, Massachusetts, home.[ii]

Shortly after the arrest of Dzhokhar, relatives of the brothers were located by media representatives and interviewed. "You put a shame on our entire family ... and you put a shame on the entire Chechen ethnicity," said Ruslan Tsarni, the brothers' uncle.[iii]

Investigators soon learned that the Tsarnaevs had emigrated in 2002 from the former Russian Republic of Chechnya, apparently fleeing from the brutal war that had engulfed the country after the fall of the Soviet Union. The family of six had come to America in 2002, settling in Cambridge, Massachusetts. With few financial resources at their disposal, they rented a crowded third-floor apartment in an aging home in an old neighborhood. The mother, Zubeidat, and father, Anzor, claimed to have been well educated in Chechnya and to have held prestigious jobs before emigrating. A *Boston Globe* exposé, however, later disclosed that both parents had few professional skills.

Although the Tsarnaevs had hoped to participate in the "American dream," they found themselves living in near poverty when their desire for steady work, college educations for their sons, and a successful career in boxing for Tamerlan didn't materialize. One of the Tsarnaev daughters became pregnant, marrying only a short time before her baby was born, thus sabotaging her parents' plans for an arranged marriage. Dzhokhar's college career fell apart after he became a popular marijuana dealer on the campus of the University of Massachusetts at Dartmouth. He apparently made a good deal of money selling drugs, causing him to lose academic focus. Friends said that he often carried a handgun to protect his "stash" of drugs and the large sums of money that he carried on his person.

By the time of the bombings, the two Tsarnaevs daughters, both of whom had divorced after brief marriages, returned home with their infant children, crowding the family's 800-square-foot residence even further. Under the familial strain, Zubeidat and Anzor divorced, and Anzor moved to Dagestan in the Northern Caucasuses. Before his father left, however, Tamerlan told friends that he was hearing voices inside of his head directing him to do things. One doctor suggested that he was suffering from schizophrenia, and that constant marijuana smoking, combined with head injuries received from years of boxing, had caused him to become delusional.

Tamerlan's mother, Zubeidat, could not accept the idea that her son might be mentally ill, and attempted to immerse him in religion, hoping that it would relieve the mental strain he was suffering. As economic problems mounted, the family began to disintegrate and Tamerlan turned to radical Islam with mounting fervor. Friends later said that Tamerlan, unable to find steady work, and with his boxing

Dzhokhar Tsarnaev, the surviving Boston Marathon bomber. Was Dzhokhar merely following his brother in an attempt to terrorize the American public?

Tamerlan Tsarnaev, killed in a shoot-out with Boston police officers following the bombing of the Boston Marathon. What led him to attack the marathon?

career in tatters, spent much of his time on the Internet, reading radical Islamist literature. He soon began attending a local mosque, but was thrown out after interrupting services by shouting his disagreement with the imam's sermons.

Shortly before the bombings, Tamerlan visited Dagestan, where his father lived. Once there, he fell in with members of a radical Muslim group known as the Union of the Just. The group strongly condemned U.S. intervention in Muslim countries. Reports say that Tamerlan spent much of his time in Dagestan studying the Koran and praying with other members of the Union. The Russian Federal Security Service (FSB) later told American intelligence officers that Tamerlan met with members of the Muslim insurgency fighting for independence from the Russian Republic. Although FSB reports were sent to U.S. authorities in 2011 and 2012, FBI officers who investigated them didn't find them alarming enough to interrogate Tamerlan after he returned to the United States. Friends who knew him said that Tamerlan had come home a changed man, and railed against American intervention in the Middle East. Shortly after his return, he opened a YouTube account using the name of muazseyfullah, which can be translated as "The Sword of God."

As Tamerlan grew more and more obsessed with radical Islam, the family's disintegration continued. The oldest Tsarnaev sister, Bella, was arrested in New Jersey and charged with marijuana distribution; and Zubeidat was attempting to evade arrest on an outstanding warrant for a shoplifting charge. Dzhokhar, now failing out of college, and with more than $20,000 of unpaid debts, came back to a troubled household. Making matters worse, the building's landlord forced the Tsarnaevs to leave their Cambridge residence after raising the rent to a level they could not afford. As one source put it, "It was a time of great family upheaval."

After the bombings, it was discovered that the Tsarnaev brothers had read an online al-Qaeda English publication entitled "Make a Bomb in the Kitchen of Your Mom." The article explained how to make pressure-cooker bombs, and how to fill them with shrapnel in order to make them more destructive.

A *Boston Globe* investigative reporter who studied the Tsarnaev family history concluded that "the motivation for the Tsarnaev brothers' violent acts is more likely rooted in the turbulent collapse of their family and their escalating personal and collective failures than, as federal investigators have suggested, on the other side of the globe."[iv]

The case of the Tsarnaev brothers raises a number of interesting questions. Among them are the following:

1. Why did the Tsarnaev brothers attack spectators and participants at the 2013 Boston Marathon? What were they hoping to accomplish with those attacks?

2. What might policymakers and law enforcement officials have done to prevent the attacks?

Notes:

i   Katharine Q. Seelye, "U.S. Weighs Pursuit of Death Penalty for Suspect in Boston Bombings," The New York Times, January 24, 2014, http://www.nytimes.com/2014/01/24/us/us-weighs-pursuit-of-death-penalty-in-boston-bombing.html?_r=0 (accessed June 5, 2014).

ii Chelsea J. Carter, "Official: Boston Bombing Suspect 'Sedated,'" CNN, April 20, 2013, http://www.cnn.com/2013/04/20/us/boston-attack/index.html (accessed July 5, 2014).

iii Alan Cullison, "A Family Terror: The Tsarnaevs and the Boston Bombing," The Wall Street Journal, December 13, 2013, http://online.wsj.com/news/articles/SB10001424052702304477704579254482254699674 (accessed May 30, 2014).

iv Sally Jacobs, David Filipov, and Patricia Wen, "The Fall of the House of Tsarnaev," The Boston Globe, December 2013, http://www.bostonglobe.com/Page/Boston/2011-2020/WebGraphics/Metro/BostonGlobe.com/2013/12/15tsarnaev/tsarnaev.html (accessed January 26, 2014).

Europol's mission is to improve the effectiveness and cooperation of law enforcement agencies within the member states of the EU with the ultimate goal of preventing and combating terrorism, illegal drug trafficking, illicit trafficking in radioactive and nuclear substances, illegal money laundering, trafficking in human beings, and other serious forms of international organized crime. Europol is sometimes described as the "European Union police clearing house."[79]

In 2013, the European Commission established a European Cybercrime Center (EC3) at Europol. The center has become the focal point in the European Union's fight against cybercrime. Europol and INTERPOL work together to develop information on international terrorism, drug trafficking, and trafficking in human beings. Visit Europol on the Web at **http://www.europol.europa.eu.**

The International Criminal Court

On April 12, 2000, the International Criminal Court (ICC) was created under the auspices of the United Nations. The ICC is intended to be a permanent criminal court for trying individuals (not countries) who commit the most serious crimes of concern to the international community, such as genocide, war crimes, and crimes against humanity—including the wholesale murder of civilians, torture, and mass rape. The goal of the ICC is to be a global judicial institution with international jurisdiction complementing national legal systems around the world. The court is headquartered in The Hague, the Netherlands, and has over 800 staff members working in approximately 100 countries.

Support for the ICC was developed through the UN, where more than 70 countries approved the court's creation by ratifying the Rome Statute of the International Criminal Court.

Today, the court has more than 120 member countries.

In 2012, in the first verdict ever reached by the ICC, judges found Thomas Lubanga, a rebel leader in eastern Congo, guilty of conscripting child soldiers. His conviction was upheld by appeals judges at the ICC in 2014.[80]

The International Criminal Court (ICC) in The Hague, Netherlands.
What is the jurisdiction of the ICC?

On January 3, 2017, the ICC determined that it has jurisdiction over the alleged war crimes of rape and sexual slavery of child soldiers by Bosco Ntaganda, former Deputy Chief of the General Staff of the Patriotic Force for the Liberation of Congo (FPLC). Ntaganda is accused of 13 counts of war crimes, and five crimes against humanity, all of which were allegedly committed in the Democratic Republic of the Congo. Ntaganda has been in the custody of the court since 2015.

Learn more about this case and other activities of the ICC by visiting the Coalition for an International Criminal Court via **http://www.iccnow.org**.

SUMMARY

- Comparative criminology is the study of crime on a cross-national level. By comparing crime patterns in one country with those in another, accepted local theories can be reevaluated in light of world experiences. *Globalization of knowledge*, a term describing the increased understanding due to sharing of information among cultures, plays a significant role in both criminological theory formation and American crime-control policies. Ethnocentrism, or culture-centeredness, can interfere with the work of comparative criminologists in gathering, analyzing, and presenting crime statistics by causing those statistics to only reflect the social and political arenas in which they were generated. Globalization refers to the increasing integration of previously isolated events in all areas of life and to its effects on people throughout the world. Globalization makes it impossible for U.S. policy makers to ignore criminal activity in other parts of the world. Transnational crime refers to unlawful activity undertaken and supported by organized criminal groups operating across national boundaries whose activities include fraudulent e-mail and phishing schemes, drug running, sex tourism, illegal trafficking in human beings and human organs, and international trade in weapons of mass destruction.

- The United Nations tells us that human smuggling and human trafficking are two of the fastest-growing areas of international criminal activity today. Human smuggling involves illegal border crossings, either clandestinely or through deception, such as the use of fraudulent documents. Human trafficking, on the other hand, involves the exploitation of unwilling people through force, coercion, threat, or deception and includes human rights abuses such as debt bondage, deprivation of liberty, or lack of control over freedom and labor. Trafficking is often undertaken for purposes of sexual exploitation or labor exploitation, while smuggling usually involves direct payment to the smugglers by the people being smuggled.

- Terrorism is politically motivated violence planned and perpetrated against noncombatant targets by subnational groups or clandestine agents to bring about change in an existing social order, often with the threat of massive destruction and large numbers of casualties. Domestic, international, and cyber are three main forms of terrorism; specific terrorist activities include cyberterrorism and attacks on information-management segments of our nation's critical infrastructure. The vigilance required to prevent both domestic and international terrorism has resulted in new laws restricting some freedoms that many Americans had previously taken for granted.

- Studies of the radicalization process of American home-grown terrorists show that the process involves four steps, and that individuals undergoing the radicalization process often exhibit important behavioral cues.

- Strategies for fighting terrorism include cutting off funding to radical organization, U.S. government designation of international terrorist groups as Foreign Terrorist Organizations, and changes in U.S. law, including the 2001 USA PATRIOT Act.

- Two international crime fighting organizations, INTERPOL and Europol were discussed in this chapter. Both organizations provide information to member law enforcement agencies from the European Union and around the world. The International Criminal Court (ICC), based in the Hague, Netherlands, has limited global authority to prosecute war criminals and others who commit crimes against humanity.

KEY TERMS

comparative criminologist, 428

comparative criminology, 428

cyberterrorism, 439

domestic terrorism, 435

ethnocentrism, 429

Europol, 448

foreign terrorist organization (FTO), 445

globalization, 428

human smuggling, 431

infrastructure, 439

International Criminal Court, 450

international terrorism, 436

INTERPOL, 448

lone-wolf terrorist, 438

terrorism, 435

trafficking in persons (TIP), 432

KEY NAME

Franklin E. Zimring, 428

QUESTIONS FOR REVIEW

1. What is comparative criminology and what role does globalization play in understanding criminal activities today?

2. What are the differences between human smuggling and human trafficking?

3. What is terrorism? What types of terrorism does this chapter discuss?

4. What is known about the radicalization process of home-grown American al-Qaeda-inspired terrorists? What efforts are being made to counter the terrorist threat?

5. What organizations exist today to assist in the fight against international crimes?

QUESTIONS FOR REFLECTION

1. What are the advantages of a comparative perspective in criminology? Are there any disadvantages? If so, what are they?

2. Do you think that many Americans are victims of human trafficking? If so, how might they become involved?

3. Has the "war against terror" affected you personally? If so, how?

4. Has the average American had to sacrifice any rights or freedoms in the fight against terrorism? If so, what rights or freedoms have been sacrificed?

5. Is it true that the only way to secure freedom is to curtail it during times of national crisis? Why or why not?

Glossary

acquaintance rape A rape characterized by a prior social, although not necessarily intimate or familial, relationship between the victim and the perpetrator.

addiction A chronic brain disease characterized by compulsive drug seeking and use despite harmful consequences.

administrative law Law that regulates many daily business activities. Violations of these regulations generally result in warnings or fines, depending on their adjudged severity.

adolescence-limited offender A juvenile offender who abandons delinquency upon maturity.

Age of Reason *See* Enlightenment.

aggravated assault (UCR) An unlawful attack by one person upon another for the purpose of inflicting severe or aggravated bodily injury. *See also* simple assault.

allele Variation of a gene.

alloplastic adaptation A form of adjustment that results from changes in the environment surrounding an individual.

altruism Selfless, helping behavior.

androcentricity A male-dominated perspective, as in the case of criminologists who study only the criminality of males.

anomie A social condition in which norms are uncertain or lacking.

anomie theory *See* strain theory.

Anti-Drug Abuse Act A federal law (Public Law 99–570) enacted in 1986 that established new federal mandatory minimum sentences for drug offenses.

antisocial (asocial) personality An individual who is unsocialized and whose behavior pattern brings him or her into repeated conflict with society.

antisocial personality disorder (ASPD) A psychological condition exhibited by an individual who is unsocialized and whose behavior pattern brings him or her into conflict with society.

applied research Any research based on scientific inquiry that is designed and carried out with practical applications in mind.

arson The willful or malicious burning (or attempt to burn), with or without intent to defraud, of a house, public building, motor vehicle or aircraft, or personal property of another.

asocial personality *See* antisocial (asocial) personality.

assault *See* aggravated assault; simple assault

asset forfeiture The authorized seizure of money, negotiable instruments, securities, or other things of value. In federal antidrug laws, it is the authorization of judicial representatives to seize all monies, negotiable instruments, securities, or other things of value furnished or intended to be furnished by any person in exchange for a controlled substance, as well as all proceeds traceable to such an exchange.

atavism A term used by Cesare Lombroso to suggest that criminals are physiological throwbacks to earlier stages of human evolution. The term is derived from the Latin term *atavus*, which means "ancestor."

attachment theory A social-psychological perspective on delinquent and criminal behavior holding that the successful development of secure attachment between a child and his or her primary caregiver provides the basic foundation for all future psychological development.

audit trail A record of computer activities that enables auditors to reconstruct and review the sequence of activities surrounding each event in one or more related transactions from inception to output of final results back to inception.

autoplastic adaptation A form of adjustment that results from changes within an individual.

Balanced and Restorative Justice (BARJ) Model A form of justice which holds that the community, victim, and offender should receive balanced attention and all three should gain tangible benefits from their interactions with the justice system.

bank fraud Any fraud or embezzlement that occurs within or against financial institutions that are insured or regulated by the U.S. government. Fraud of financial institutions includes commercial-loan fraud, check fraud, counterfeit negotiable instruments, mortgage fraud, and false credit applications.

behavioral genetics The study of genetic and environmental contributions to individual variations in human behavior.

behaviorism A psychological perspective that stresses observable behavior and disregards unobservable events that occur in the mind.

behavior theory A psychological perspective positing that behavior that is rewarded will increase in frequency and behavior that is punished will decrease in frequency.

bias crime *See* hate crime.

biological theories Theories that maintain that the basic determinants of human behavior, including criminality, are constitutionally or physiologically based and often inherited.

biopsychology A field of study that combines the principles of psychology with those of neuroscience and biology. It examines how thoughts and behavior are mediated by interaction between the brain (especially neurotransmitters) and the environment; also known as *behavioral psychology* and *behavioral neuroscience*.

biosocial criminology A theoretical perspective that sees the interaction between biology and the environment as key to understanding human behavior, including criminality.

booster A frequent shoplifter.

born criminal An individual who is born with a genetic predilection toward criminality.

bourgeoisie The "haves," or the class of people who own the means of production in the Marxist theory.

Brady Handgun Violence Prevention Act A federal law (Public Law 103–159) enacted in 1993 that initiated a national background checking system for all potential gun purchasers.

Brawner rule A somewhat vague rule for determining insanity created in the 1972 federal court case of *United States* v. *Brawner* (471 F.2d 969), since superseded by statute, that asks the jury to decide whether the defendant could be justly held responsible for the criminal act with which he or she stands charged in the face of any claims of insanity or mental incapacity.

broken windows theory A perspective on crime causation that holds that physical deterioration in an area leads to increased concerns for personal safety among area residents and to higher crime rates in that area.

Buck v. Bell A U.S. Supreme Court case decided in 1927 that upheld state statutes authorizing the sterilization of individuals who were determined to have "bad genes," and which supported the eugenics movement of the early twentieth century.

bullying Any unwanted aggressive behavior(s) by another youth or group of youths who are not siblings or current dating partners that involves an observed or perceived power imbalance and is repeated multiple times or is highly likely to be repeated.

burglary The trespassory breaking and entering of the dwelling house of another in the nighttime with the intent to commit a felony; also the unlawful entry of a structure to commit a felony or a theft.

burglary (UCR) The unlawful entry of a structure to commit a felony or a theft.

Cambridge Study in Delinquent Development A longitudinal (life course) study of crime and delinquency tracking a cohort of 411 boys born in London in 1953.

capable guardian One who effectively discourages crime; effective deterrents to criminal activity.

capital punishment The legal imposition of a sentence of death upon a convicted offender; also known as the *death penalty*.

carjacking The stealing of a car while it is occupied.

case study A form of research that employs detailed analysis of a person, group, or situation—often over a period of time.

Chicago Area Project A program originating at the University of Chicago during the 1930s that focused on urban ecology and that attempted to reduce delinquency, crime, and social disorganization in transitional neighborhoods.

Chicago School of criminology An ecological approach to explaining crime that examines how social disorganization contributes to social pathology.

child pornography A visual representation of any kind that depicts a minor engaging in sexually explicit conduct that is obscene and that lacks serious literary, artistic, political, or scientific value.

child sexual abuse (CSA) A term encompassing a variety of criminal and civil offenses in which an adult engages in sexual activity with a minor, exploits a minor for purposes of sexual gratification, or exploits a minor sexually for purposes of profit.

chromosomes Bundles of genes.

civil law The body of law that regulates arrangements between individuals, such as contracts and claims to property.

Classical School A criminological perspective of the late 1700s and early 1800s that had its roots in the Enlightenment and that held that humans are rational beings, that crime is the result of the exercise of free will, and that punishment can be effective in reducing the incidence of crime to the degree it negates the pleasure to be derived from crime commission.

clearance rate The proportion of reported or discovered crimes within a given offense category that are solved.

Code of Hammurabi An early set of laws established by the Babylonian king Hammurabi, who ruled the ancient city from 1792 to 1750 B.C.

cognitive information-processing theory (CIP) A psychological perspective that involves the study of human perceptions, information processing, and decision making.

cohort A group of individuals having certain significant social characteristics in common, such as gender and date and place of birth.

cohort analysis A social scientific technique that studies a population with common characteristics over time. Cohort analysis usually begins at birth and traces the development of cohort members until they reach a certain age.

collective efficacy The collective ability of residents to produce social action to meet common goals and preserve shared values.

comfort serial killers Serial killers motivated by financial or material gain.

Commission on Law Observance and Enforcement *See* Wickersham Commission.

common law Law originating from usage and custom rather than from written statutes. The term refers to nonstatutory customs, traditions, and precedents that help guide judicial decision making.

Communications Decency Act (CDA) A 1996 federal statute labeled Title 5 of the federal Telecommunications Act of 1996 (Public Law 104–104, 110 Stat. 56) that seeks to protect minors from harmful material on the Internet and that criminalizes the knowing transmission of obscene or indecent messages to any recipient under 18 years of age. In 1997, in *Reno* v. *ACLU* (521 U.S. 844), the U.S. Supreme Court found the bulk of the CDA to be unconstitutional, ruling that it contravenes First Amendment free speech guarantees.

comparative criminologist A criminologist involved in the cross-national study of crime.

comparative criminology The cross-national study of crime.

Comprehensive Crime Control Act A far-reaching federal law (Public Law 98–473) enacted in 1984 that mandated new federal sentencing guidelines, eliminated parole at the federal level, limited the use of the insanity defense in federal criminal courts, and increased federal penalties associated with drug dealing.

Comprehensive Strategy for Serious, Violent, and Chronic Juvenile Offenders program A National Institute of Justice initiative that provides participating communities with a framework for preventing delinquency, intervening in early delinquent behavior, and responding to serious, violent, and chronic offending. The strategy is based on a social development model.

computer abuse An unlawful incident associated with computer technology in which a victim suffers loss or a perpetrator reaps benefit.

computer crime Any violation of a federal or state computer crime statute. The term is now being replaced with *cybercrime*.

computer-related crime An illegal act using computer technology in its perpetration, investigation, or prosecution.

computer virus A program designed to invade computer systems and either modify the way they operate or alter the information they store.

conditioning A psychological principle that holds that the frequency of any behavior can be increased or decreased through reward, punishment, or association with other stimuli.

conduct norm A shared expectation of a social group relative to personal conduct.

confidentiality *See* data confidentiality.

conflict perspective An analytical perspective on social organization that holds that conflict is a fundamental aspect of social life and can never be fully resolved.

confounding effect A rival explanation or competing hypothesis that is a threat to the internal or external validity of a research design.

consensus perspective An analytical perspective on social organization that holds that most members of society agree about what is right and wrong and that the various elements of society work together toward a common vision of the greater good.

constitutional theories Theories that explain criminality by reference to offenders' body types, inheritance, genetics, or external observable physical characteristics.

constitutive criminology The study of the process by which human beings create an ideology of crime that sustains the notion of crime as a concrete reality.

containment An aspect of the social bond that acts as a stabilizing force to prevent individuals from committing crimes and that keeps them from engaging in deviance.

containment theory A form of control theory that suggests that a series of both internal and external factors contributes to law-abiding behavior.

control group A group of experimental subjects that, although the subject of measurement and observation, is not exposed to the experimental intervention.

controlled experiment An experiment that attempts to hold conditions (other than the intentionally introduced experimental intervention) constant.

control ratio The amount of control to which a person is subject versus the amount of control that person exerts over others.

control theory *See* social control theory.

controlled substances Chemical substances or drugs as defined under the 1970 federal Controlled Substances Act.

convict criminology A radical paradigm consisting of writings on criminology by convicted felons and ex-inmates who have acquired academic credentials or who are associated with credentialed others; also known as *alternative criminology*.

corporate crime A violation of a criminal statute by an organization or its executives, employees, or agents acting on its behalf and for its benefit.

corporate fraud A type of organizational fraud, such as accounting schemes, self-dealing by corporate executives, obstruction of justice, insider trading, kickbacks, and misuse of corporate property for personal use.

correctional psychology The branch of forensic psychology concerned with the diagnosis and classification of offenders, the treatment of correctional populations, and the rehabilitation of inmates and other law violators.

correlation A causal, complementary, or reciprocal relationship between two measurable variables. *See also* statistical correlation.

Cosa Nostra *See* La Cosa Nostra.

crime Any human conduct in violation of the criminal laws of the federal government or a local jurisdiction with the power to make such laws.

Crime Prevention Through Environmental Design (CPTED) A crime prevention technique that modifies features of the physical environment to accomplish its goals.

crime typology A classification of crimes along a particular dimension, such as legal categories, offender motivation, victim behavior, or characteristics of individual offenders.

Crime Victims' Rights Act A 2004 federal law that establishes statutory rights for victims of federal crimes and gives victims the necessary legal authority to assert those rights in federal courts.

criminal anthropology The scientific study of the relationship between human physical characteristics and criminality.

criminal behavior Human activity, both intentional and negligent, that violates the criminal law. It may include a failure to act when there is a legal obligation to do so.

criminal career The longitudinal sequence of crimes committed by an individual offender.

criminal enterprise A group of individuals with an identified hierarchy engaged in significant criminal activities.

criminal homicide The illegal killing of one human being by another.

criminal homicide (UCR) The UCR category that includes and is limited to all offenses of causing the death of another person without justification or excuse.

criminal street gangs Locally-run organizations of three or more persons, whether formal or informal, having as one of their primary activities the commission of criminal activity, and sharing a common name or common identifying signs or symbols.

criminalist A specialist in the collection and examination of the physical evidence of crime.

criminality A behavioral predisposition that disproportionately favors criminal activity.

criminality index The actual extent of the crime problem in a society. The criminality index is computed by adding the actual crime rate and the latent crime rate.

criminalize To make illegal.

criminal justice The scientific study of crime, the criminal law, and components of the criminal justice system, including the police, courts, and corrections.

criminal justice system The various agencies of justice, especially the police, courts, and corrections, whose goal it is to apprehend, convict, punish, and rehabilitate law violators.

criminal law The body of law that regulates actions that have the potential to harm the interests of the state or the federal government.

criminaloid A term used by Cesare Lombroso to describe the occasional criminal who is enticed into criminality primarily by environmental influences.

criminal psychology The application of the science and profession of psychology to questions and issues relating to law and the legal system; also known as *forensic psychology*.

criminal receiver *See* fence.

criminogenic needs Dynamic attributes (also known as *dynamic risk factors*) of offenders and their circumstances that are associated with rates of recidivism.

criminologist One who is trained in the field of criminology; also one who studies crime, criminals, and criminal behavior.

criminology An interdisciplinary profession built around the scientific study of crime and criminal behavior, including their forms, causes, legal aspects, and control.

criminology of place A perspective that emphasizes the importance of geographic location and architectural features as they are associated with the prevalence of criminal victimization; also known as *environmental criminology*.

critical criminology A perspective that holds that crime is the natural product of a capitalist system.

cross-impact analysis A technique of futures research that attempts to analyze one trend or event in light of the occurrence or nonoccurrence of a series of related events.

cultural transmission The idea that delinquency is transmitted through successive generations of people living in an area through the same process of social communication as languages, roles, and attitudes are transmitted.

culture conflict theory A sociological perspective on crime that suggests that the root cause of criminality can be found in a clash of values between variously socialized groups over what is acceptable or proper behavior; also known as *cultural deviance theory*.

cyberbullying xxx

cybercrime Any crime that involves the use of computers or the manipulation of digital data as well as any violation of a federal or state cybercrime statute.

Cyber Security Enhancement Act (CSEA) A federal law found in the Homeland Security Act of 2002 that directs the U.S. Sentencing Commission to take specific factors into account in creating new sentencing guidelines for cybercriminals.

Cybersecurity Information Sharing Act (CISA)   A 2015 federal law that is designed to facilitate the sharing of information about cybersecurity threats between the U.S. government and technology companies.

cyberspace   The computer-created matrix of virtual possibilities, including online services, in which human beings interact with one another and with the technology itself.

cyberstalking   An array of high-technology options, including e-mail and the Internet, that an offender uses to harass or "follow" another individual.

cyberterrorism   A form of terrorism that makes use of high technology, especially computer technology and the Internet, in planning and carrying out terrorist attacks.

cycloid   A term developed by Ernst Kretschmer to describe a particular relationship between body build and personality type. The cycloid personality, which was associated with a heavyset, soft type of body, was said to vacillate between normality and abnormality.

dangerous drug   A controlled substance other than cocaine, opiates, and cannabis products. Amphetamines, LSD, methamphetamines, methcathinone, and phencyclidine (PCP), as well as designer drugs, are all considered dangerous drugs.

dangerousness   The likelihood that a given individual will later harm society or others. Dangerousness is often measured in terms of recidivism, or the likelihood of new crime commission or rearrest for a new crime within a five-year period following arrest or release from confinement.

dark figure of crime   The numerical total of unreported crimes not reflected in official crime statistics.

data confidentiality   The ethical requirement of social scientific research to protect the confidentiality of individual research participants while preserving justified research access to the information participants provide.

data encryption   The process by which information is encoded, making it unreadable to all but its intended recipients.

date rape   The unlawful forced sexual intercourse with a woman against her will that occurs within the context of a dating relationship.

***Daubert* standard**   A test of scientific acceptability applicable to the gathering of evidence in criminal cases.

DCS–3000   An FBI-developed network diagnostic tool that is capable of assisting in criminal investigations by monitoring and capturing large amounts of Internet traffic.

death penalty   *See* capital punishment.

deconstructionist theory   A postmodern perspective that challenges existing criminological theories in order to debunk them and that works toward replacing traditional ideas with concepts seen as more appropriate to the postmodern era.

decriminalization   The redefinition of certain previously criminal behaviors as regulated activities that become "ticketable" instead of "arrestable."

defensible space   The range of mechanisms that combine to bring an environment under the control of its residents.

delinquency   Violations of the criminal law and other misbehavior committed by young people.

Delphi Method   A technique of futures research that uses repetitive questioning of experts to refine predictions.

demographics   The characteristics of population groups, usually expressed in statistical fashion.

demography   The study of the characteristics of population groups.

descriptive statistics   The statistics that describe, summarize, or highlight the relationships within data that have been gathered.

designer drug   A new substance designed by slightly altering the chemical makeup of other illegal or tightly controlled drugs.

desistance   A person's cessation of criminal activity or termination of a period of involvement in offending behavior. Also, the cessation of criminal offender or other antisocial behavior.

desistance phenomenon   The observable decrease in crime rates that is invariably associated with age.

determinate sentencing   A criminal punishment strategy that mandates a specified and fixed amount of time to be served for every offense category. Under the strategy, for example, all offenders convicted of the same degree of burglary would be sentenced to the same length of time behind bars. It is also known as *fixed sentencing*.

deterrence   The prevention of crime. *See also* general deterrence; specific deterrence.

deterrence strategy   A crime-control strategy whose goal is to lessen motivation for a crime by increasing the perceived sureness or severity of its penalty.

deviant behavior   Any human activity that violates social norms.

deviant places theory   A spatially oriented theory of victimization that suggests that victimization occurs most frequently in socially disorganized areas and that people become victims as a result of their exposure to such areas.

differential association   The sociological thesis that criminality, like any other form of behavior, is learned through a process of association with others who communicate criminal values.

differential identification theory   An explanation for crime and deviance that holds that people pursue criminal or deviant behavior to the extent that they identify themselves with real or imaginary people from whose perspective their criminal or deviant behavior seems acceptable.

digit ratio   The comparative length of index and ring fingers; also known as the 2D-4D ratio.

Digital Theft Deterrence and Copyright Damages Improvement Act   A 1999 federal law (Public Law 106–160) that amends Section 504(c) of the Copyright Act increasing the amount of damages that could be awarded in cases of copyright infringement.

disclosure (of research methods)   The provision of information to potential subjects informing them of the nature of the research methods to be used by the social scientific study in which their involvement is planned.

discrediting information   Any information that is inconsistent with the managed impressions being communicated in a given situation.

displacement   A shift of criminal activity from one location to another.

distributive justice   The rightful, equitable, and just distribution of rewards within a society.

dizygotic (DZ) twin   A twin who develops from a separate ovum and who carries the genetic material shared by siblings.

DNA fingerprinting   *See* DNA profiling.

DNA profiling   The use of biological residue found at a crime scene for genetic comparisons in aiding the identification of criminal suspects.

domestic terrorism   The unlawful use of force or violence by an individual or group based and operating entirely within the United States and its territories, without foreign influence, directed at the U.S. government, the civilian population, or any segment thereof for political or social objectives.

dramaturgical perspective   A theoretical point of view that depicts human behavior as centered around the purposeful management of interpersonal impressions; also known as *dramaturgy*.

dramaturgy *See* dramaturgical perspective.

drug-defined crime A violation of the laws prohibiting or regulating the possession, use, or distribution of illegal drugs.

drug-related crime A crime in which drugs contribute to the offense (excluding violations of drug laws).

drug trafficking The manufacturing, distributing, dispensing, importing, and/or exporting of a controlled substance or a counterfeit substance.

Durham rule A standard for judging legal insanity that holds that an accused is not criminally responsible if his or her unlawful act was the product of mental disease or mental defect.

ecological theory A type of sociological approach that emphasizes demographics (the characteristics of population groups) and geographics (the mapped location of such groups relative to one another) and that sees the social disorganization that characterizes delinquency areas as a major cause of criminality and victimization.

ectomorph A body type originally described as thin and fragile, with long, slender, poorly muscled extremities and delicate bones.

ego The reality-testing part of the personality; also known as the *reality principle*. More formally, it is the personality component that is conscious, most immediately controls behavior, and is most in touch with external reality.

elder abuse Intentional actions that cause harm or create a serious risk of harm to a vulnerable elder by a caregiver or other person who stands in a trust relationship to the elder; or failure by a caregiver to satisfy the elder's basic needs or to protect the elder from harm.

electroencephalogram (EEG) The electrical measurement of brain wave activity.

Electronic Frontier Foundation (EFF) A nonprofit organization formed in July 1990 to help ensure that the principles embodied in the Constitution and the Bill of Rights are protected as new communications technologies emerge.

encryption *See* data encryption.

endomorph A body type originally described as soft and round or overweight.

Enlightenment A social movement that arose during the eighteenth century and that built upon ideas like empiricism, rationality, free will, humanism, and natural law; also known as *Age of Reason*.

environmental crime A violation of the criminal law committed by businesses, business officials, organizational entities, and/or individuals that damages some protected or otherwise significant aspect of the natural environment.

environmental criminology A perspective that emphasizes the importance of geographic location and architectural features as they are associated with the prevalence of criminal victimization; also known as *criminology of place*.

environmental scanning A technique of futures research. It is a "systematic effort to identify in an elemental way future developments (trends or events) that could plausibly occur over the time horizon of interest."

epigenetics The study of the chemical reactions that occur within a genome, and that switch parts of the genome on or off at strategic times and locations.

ethnic succession The continuing process whereby one immigrant or ethnic group succeeds another by assuming its position in society.

ethnocentrism The phenomenon of "culture-centeredness" by which one uses one's own culture as a benchmark against which to judge all other patterns of behavior.

eugenic criminology A perspective that holds that the root causes of criminality are passed from generation to generation in the form of "bad genes."

eugenics The study of hereditary improvement by genetic control.

Europol The European Police Office, an integrated police intelligence-gathering and dissemination arm of the member nations of the European Union.

evidence based Any evidence built on scientific findings, especially practices and policies founded on the results of randomized, controlled experiments.

evidence-based criminology A form of contemporary criminology that makes use of rigorous social scientific techniques, especially randomized, controlled experiments and the systematic review of research results; also known as *knowledge-based criminology*.

evolutionary ecology An approach to understanding crime that draws attention to the ways people develop over the course of their lives.

evolutionary neuroandrogenic (ENA) theory A perspective that holds that (1) the propensity for crime commission evolved among humans beings as part of the male reproductive strategy and (2) a particular neu-

rochemistry, which is characteristic of males, increases the probability of criminality among males relative to females.

evolutionary perspective A theoretical approach that (1) seeks to explain behavior with reference to human evolutionary history and (2) recognizes the influence that genes have over human traits.

experiment *See* controlled experiment; quasi-experimental design.

experimental criminology *See* evidence-based criminology.

expert system A system of computer hardware and software that attempts to duplicate the decision-making processes used by skilled investigators in the analysis of evidence and in the recognition of patterns that such evidence might represent.

exposure-reduction theory A theory of intimate homicide that claims that a decline in domesticity, accompanied by an improvement in the economic status of women and a growth in domestic violence resources, explains observed decreases in intimate-partner homicide.

expressive crime A criminal offense that results from acts of interpersonal hostility, such as jealousy, revenge, romantic triangles, and quarrels.

external validity The ability to generalize research findings to other settings.

felony A serious criminal offense, specifically one punishable by death or by incarceration in a prison facility for a year or more.

felony murder An unlawful homicide that occurs during the commission or attempted commission of a felony or certain felonies specified by law.

feminist criminology A corrective model intended to redirect the thinking of mainstream criminologists to include gender awareness.

fence An individual or a group involved in the buying, selling, and distribution of stolen goods.

First and Fourth Amendments to the U.S. Constitution The amendments that guarantee each person freedom of speech and security in his or her "persons, houses, papers, and effects, against unreasonable searches and seizures."

first-degree murder A criminal homicide that is planned or involves premeditation.

Five Factor Model A psychological perspective that builds on the Big Five core traits of personality.

focal concern   A key value of any culture, especially a delinquent subculture.

folkways   A time-honored custom. Although folkways carry the force of tradition, their violation is unlikely to threaten the survival of the group. *See also* mores.

forcible rape   The carnal knowledge of a person forcibly and against his or her will.

foreign terrorist organization (FTO)   A foreign organization that engages in terrorist activity threatening the security of U.S. nationals or the national security of the United States and that is so designated by the U.S. secretary of state.

forensic psychiatry   A branch of psychiatry having to do with the study of crime and criminality.

forensic psychology   The application of the science and profession of psychology to questions and issues relating to law and the legal system; also known as *criminal psychology*.

forfeiture   *See* asset forfeiture.

frontal brain hypothesis   A perspective that references physical changes in certain parts of the brain to explain criminality.

frustration–aggression theory   A theory that holds that frustration, which is a natural consequence of living, is a root cause of crime. Criminal behavior can be a form of adaptation when it results in stress reduction.

future criminology   The study of likely futures as they impinge on crime and its control.

futures research   "A multidisciplinary branch of operations research [whose principal aim] is to facilitate long-range planning based on (1) forecasting from the past supported by mathematical models, (2) cross-disciplinary treatment of its subject matter, (3) systematic use of expert judgments, and (4) a systems-analytical approach to its problems."

futurist   One who studies the future.

galvanic skin response (GSR)   A measure of the skin's resistance to electrical current, detectable through simple test instruments. Variations in GSR are often caused by an emotional reaction to stimuli.

gateway offense   An offense, usually fairly minor in nature, that leads to more serious offenses.

gender gap   The observed differences between male and female rates of criminal offending in a given society.

gender ratio problem   The need for an explanation of the fact that the number of crimes committed by men far exceeds the number of crimes committed by women in almost all categories.

gene   A segment of DNA.

gene expression   The process by which the coded information that is stored within a gene is used to create a biological product, usually a protein. Also, the manifestation of a trait in an individual carrying the gene or genes that determine that trait.

gene pool   The total genetic information of all the individuals in a breeding population.

general deterrence   A goal of criminal sentencing that seeks to prevent others from committing crimes similar to the one for which a particular offender is being sentenced.

general strain theory (GST)   A perspective that suggests that law-breaking behavior is a coping mechanism enabling those who engage in it to deal with the socioemotional problems generated by negative social relations.

general theory   A theory that attempts to explain all (or at least most) forms of criminal conduct through a single overarching approach.

general theory of crime (GTC)   A perspective on crime, developed by Travis Hirschi and Michael Gottfredson, that asserts "that the operation of a single mechanism, low self-control, accounts for 'all crime, at all times,' [including] acts ranging from vandalism to homicide, from rape to white-collar crime."

genes   Parts of the human genome. They are made of DNA and carry coded instructions for making everything the body needs.

genetic determinism   The belief that genes are the major determining factor in human behavior.

genetic memory   or *transgenerational memory*, is inherited memory present from birth that exists in the absence of learned experience, and which is incorporated into the genome over long periods of time. Also referred to as *ancestral memory*, it is passed down through generations in the absence of socialization or training, and may provide the basis for phobias, anxiety, and other psychological states.

globalization   A process of social homogenization that everyday experiences can foster by standardized cultural expressions through the diffusion of goods and ideas around the world.

green criminology   The study of environmental harm, crime, law, regulation, victimization, and justice.

guilty but mentally ill (GBMI)   A finding that offenders are guilty of the criminal offense with which they are charged, but because of their prevailing mental condition, they are generally sent to psychiatric hospitals for treatment rather than to prison. Once they have been declared cured, such offenders can be transferred to correctional facilities to serve out their sentences.

GxE   A simple formula intended to highlight the fact that neither genes nor the environments are sufficient by themselves to explain antisocial behavior, but that it is the interaction between the two that determines what happens in most circumstances.

habitual offender statute   A law intended to keep repeat criminal offenders behind bars. These laws sometimes come under the rubric of "three strikes and you're out."

hacker   A person who uses computers for exploration and exploitation.

hard determinism   The belief that crime results from forces beyond the control of the individual.

hate crime   A criminal offense in which the motive is hatred, bias, or prejudice based on the actual or perceived race, color, religion, national origin, ethnicity, gender, or sexual orientation of another individual or group of individuals.

Hate Crimes Sentencing Enhancement Act   A federal law (28 U.S. Code, Section 994) enacted in 1994 as part of the Violent Crime Control and Law Enforcement Act that required the U.S. Sentencing Commission to increase penalties for crimes in which the victim was chosen due to actual or perceived color, ethnicity, religion, gender, disability, or sexual orientation.

hedonistic calculus   The belief, first proposed by Jeremy Bentham, that behavior holds value to any individual undertaking it according to the amount of pleasure or pain it can be expected to produce for that person. *See also* utilitarianism.

hedonistic serial killers   Serial killers who derive pleasure from killing.

heredity   The passing of traits from parent to child.

heritability   A statistical construct that estimates the amount of variation in the traits of a population that is attributable to genetic factors.

Heroin Signature Program (HSP)   A Drug Enforcement Administration program that identifies the geographic source of a heroin sample through the detection of specific chemical characteristics in the sample peculiar to the source area.

homicide   The killing of one human being by another.

hormone   A chemical substance produced by the body that regulates and controls the activity of certain cells or organs.

household crime (NCVS) An attempted or completed crime that does not involve confrontation, such as burglary, motor vehicle theft, and household larceny.

human agency The active role that people take in their lives; the fact that people are not merely subject to social and structural constraints but actively make choices and decisions based on the alternatives they see before them.

human development The relationship between the maturing individual and his or her changing environment, as well as the social processes that the relationship entails.

human ecology The interrelationship between human beings and the physical and cultural environments in which they live.

human genome A complete copy of the entire set of human gene instructions.

human smuggling A type of illegal immigration in which an agent is paid to help a person cross a border clandestinely.

human trafficking *See* trafficking in persons (TIP).

hypoglycemia A medical condition characterized by low blood sugar.

hypothesis An explanation accounting for a set of facts that can be tested by further investigation.

id The aspect of the personality from which drives, wishes, urges, and desires emanate. More formally, this division of the psyche is associated with instinctual impulses and demands for immediate satisfaction of primitive needs.

identity theft The unauthorized use of another individual's personal information to commit fraud.

Identity Theft and Assumption Deterrence Act The first federal law to make identity theft a crime. The 1998 statute makes it a crime whenever anyone "knowingly transfers or uses, without lawful authority, a means of identification of another person with the intent to commit, or to aid or abet, any unlawful activity that constitutes a violation of federal law, or that constitutes a felony under any applicable state or local law."

Identity Theft Penalty Enhancement Act A 2004 federal law that added two years to federal prison sentences for criminals convicted of using stolen credit card numbers and other personal data to commit crimes.

illegitimate opportunity structure A subcultural pathway to success that the wider society disapproves of.

impression management The intentional enactment of practiced behavior that is intended to convey to others one's desirable personal characteristics and social qualities.

incapacitation The use of imprisonment or other means to reduce the likelihood that an offender will be capable of committing future offenses.

individual-rights advocate One who seeks to protect personal freedoms in the face of criminal prosecution.

individual responsibility perspective The belief that individuals are fundamentally responsible for their own behavior and that they choose crime over other, more law-abiding courses of action.

inferential statistics Any statistics that specify how likely findings are to be true for other populations or in other locales.

informed consent The ethical requirement of social scientific research that research subjects be informed about the nature of the research to be conducted, their anticipated role in it, and the uses to which the data they provide will be put.

infrastructure The basic facilities, services, and installations needed for the functioning of a community or society, such as its transportation and communications systems, water and power lines, and public institutions.

insanity (legal) A legally established inability to understand right from wrong or to conform one's behavior to the requirements of the law.

insanity (psychological) A persistent mental disorder.

insider trading A type of equity trading based on confidential information about important events that may affect the price of the issue being traded.

institutional robbery A robbery that occurs in a commercial setting, such as a convenience store, gas station, and bank.

instrumental crime A goal-directed offense that involves some degree of planning by the offender and little or no precipitation by the victim.

instrumental marxism A perspective that holds that those in power intentionally create laws and social institutions that serve their own interests and keep others from becoming powerful.

integrated theory An explanatory perspective that merges (or attempts to merge) concepts drawn from different sources.

interactional theory A theoretical approach to exploring crime and delinquency that blends social control and social learning perspectives.

interactionist perspective *See* social process theory.

interdiction An international drug-control policy whose goal is to stop drugs from entering the country illegally.

internal validity The certainty that experimental interventions did indeed cause the changes observed in the study group; also the control over confounding factors that tend to invalidate the results of an experiment.

interpol The International Criminal Police Organization (Interpol) An international law enforcement support organization that today has 190 member nations.

international terrorism The unlawful use of force or violence by an individual or group with a connection to a foreign power or whose activities transcend national boundaries against people or property to intimidate or coerce a government, the civilian population, or any segment thereof for political or social objectives.

Internet The world's largest computer network for moving data and making information accessible.

Internet of Things The computer-based multiple simultaneous communications between devices with embedded information processors.

intersubjectivity A scientific principle that requires that independent observers see the same thing under the same circumstances for observations to be regarded as valid.

intimate-partner assault A gender-neutral term used to characterize assaultive behavior that takes place between individuals involved in an intimate relationship.

irresistible-impulse test A standard for judging legal insanity that holds that a defendant is not guilty of a criminal offense if the person, by virtue of his or her mental state or psychological condition, was not able to resist committing the crime.

Italian School of Criminology A perspective on criminology developed in the late 1800s that held that criminals can be identified by physical features and are throwbacks to earlier stages of human evolution. The Italian School was largely based on studies of criminal anthropology.

jockey A professional car thief involved in calculated steal-to-order car thefts.

joyriding An opportunistic car theft, often committed by a teenager, for fun or thrills.

Juke family A well-known "criminal family" studied by Richard L. Dugdale.

just deserts model The notion that criminal offenders deserve the punishment they receive at the hands of the law and that punishments should be appropriate to the type and severity of crime committed.

justice model A contemporary model of imprisonment in which the principle of just deserts forms the underlying social philosophy.

Kallikak family A well-known "criminal family" studied by Henry H. Goddard.

Kefauver Committee The popular name for the federal Special Committee to Investigate Organized Crime in Interstate Commerce, formed in 1951.

Kriminalpolitik The political handling of crime; also a criminology-based social policy.

labeling theory An interactionist perspective that sees continued crime as a consequence of limited opportunities for acceptable behavior that follow from the negative responses of society to those defined as offenders; also known as *social reaction theory*.

La Cosa Nostra A criminal organization of Sicilian origin; also known as *Mafia*. The term literally means "our thing."

larceny The unlawful taking or attempted taking of property (other than a motor vehicle) from the possession of another, by stealth, without force or deceit, with intent to permanently deprive the owner of the property.

larceny-theft (UCR) The unlawful taking, carrying, leading, or riding away of property (other than a motor vehicle) from the possession or constructive possession of another (attempts are included).

latent crime rate A rate of crime calculated on the basis of crimes that would likely be committed by those who are in prison or jail or who are otherwise incapacitated by the justice system.

law-and-order advocate One who suggests that under certain circumstances involving criminal threats to public safety, the interests of society should take precedence over individual rights.

Law Enforcement Assistance Administration (LEAA) A federal program, established under Title 1 of the Omnibus Crime Control and Safe Streets Act of 1967, designed to provide assistance to police agencies.

learning theory *See* social learning theory.

left realism A conflict perspective that insists on a pragmatic assessment of crime and its associated problems; also known as *radical realism* or *critical realism*.

left-realist criminology An approach to criminology based on ideas inherent in the perspective of left realism.

legalization The elimination of laws and criminal penalties associated with certain behaviors—usually the production, sale, distribution, and possession of a controlled substance.

liberal feminism A feminist perspective in criminology that sees gender-role socialization as the primary source of women's oppression.

life course The different pathways through the age-differentiated life span; also the course of a person's life over time.

life course–persistent offender An offender who, as a result of neuropsychological deficits combined with poverty and family dysfunction, displays patterns of misbehavior throughout life.

life course perspective A perspective that draws attention to the fact that criminal behavior tends to follow a distinct pattern across the life cycle; also known as *life course criminology*.

lifestyle A style of life, or the way a person lives.

lifestyle exposure theory See lifestyle theory.

lone-wolf terrorist A domestic terrorist who perpetrates political violence by acting alone; who does not belong to an organized terrorist group or network; who acts without the direct influence of a leader; and whose tactics and methods are self-directed.

lifestyle theory A perspective that holds that an individual's lifestyle contributes significantly to the likelihood of his or her criminal victimization. Also known as *lifestyle exposure theory*.

Mafia A criminal organization of Sicilian origin, also known as *La Cosa Nostra*.

mala in se An act that is thought to be wrong in and of itself.

mala prohibita An act that is wrong only because it is prohibited.

Marxist criminology A perspective on crime and crime causation based on the writings of Karl Marx.

Marxist feminism A perspective in feminist criminology that sees the oppression of women as caused by their subordinate class status within capitalist societies.

masculinity hypothesis An early belief in the field of criminology that criminal women exhibit masculine features and mannerisms.

mass murder The illegal killing of three or more victims at one location within one event.

mesomorph A body type described as athletic and muscular.

meta-analysis A study that combines the results of other studies about a particular topic of interest; a comprehensive and systematic review of other studies.

metatheory A theory about theories and the theorizing process.

misdemeanor A criminal offense that is less serious than a felony and is punishable by incarceration, usually in a local confinement facility, typically for a year or less.

M'Naughten rule A standard for judging legal insanity that requires that offenders did not know what they were doing, or if they did, that they did not know it was wrong.

modeling A form of social learning in which people learn how to act by observing others.

money laundering The process of converting illegally earned assets from cash to one or more alternative forms to conceal factors such as illegal origin and true ownership.

Monitoring the Future A national self-report survey on drug use that has been conducted since 1975.

monozygotic (MZ) twin One of two twins who develop from the same egg and who carry virtually the same genetic material.

moral development theory A perspective on crime causation holding that individuals become criminal when they have not successfully completed their intellectual development from childhood to adulthood.

moral enterprise The efforts made by an interest group to have its sense of moral or ethical propriety enacted into law.

moral time A conflict perspective that highlights the clash between social understandings of right and wrong—especially as those understandings change over time and between groups—as the cause of human conflict. It sees conflict as a fundamental and inescapable feature of social life.

mores The behavioral proscriptions covering potentially serious violations of a group's values. Examples include strictures against murder, rape, and robbery. *See also* folkways.

motivated offenders The population of potential criminal offenders in a given area.

motor vehicle theft (UCR) The theft or attempted theft of a motor vehicle. In the FBI's definition, this offense category includes the stealing of automobiles, trucks, buses, motorcycles, motor scooters, and snowmobiles.

murder An unlawful homicide.

narcoterrorism The distribution of a controlled substance in order to provide something of pecuniary value to a person or group that has engaged or is engaging in terrorist activity.

National Advisory Commission on Criminal Justice Standards and Goals A federal body commissioned in 1971 by President Richard Nixon to examine the nation's criminal justice system and to set standards and goals to direct the development of the nation's criminal justice agencies.

National Crime Victimization Survey (NCVS) A survey conducted annually by the Bureau of Justice Statistics that provides data on surveyed households reporting they were affected by crime.

National Incident-Based Reporting System (NIBRS) An enhanced statistical-reporting system to collect data on each incident and arrest within 22 crime categories.

National Survey on Drug Use and Health (NSDUH) A national survey of illicit drug use among people 12 years of age and older that is conducted annually by the Substance Abuse and Mental Health Services Administration.

National Violence against Women (NVAW) Survey A national survey of the extent and nature of violence against women conducted between November 1995 and May 1996 funded through grants from the National Institute of Justice and the U.S. Department of Health and Human Services National Center for Injury Prevention and Control.

National Youth Survey (NYS) A longitudinal panel study of a national sample of 1,725 individuals that measured self-reports of delinquency and other types of behavior.

natural law The philosophical perspective that certain immutable laws are fundamental to human nature and can be readily ascertained through reason. Human-made laws, in contrast, are said to derive from human experience and history—both of which are subject to continual change.

natural rights The rights that, according to natural law theorists, individuals retain in the face of government action and interests.

negative affective state An adverse emotion such as anger, fear, depression, and disappointment that derives from the experience of strain.

negligent homicide The act of causing the death of another person by recklessness or gross negligence.

neoclassical criminology A contemporary version of classical criminology that emphasizes deterrence and retribution, with reduced emphasis on rehabilitation.

neurocriminology A perspective that examines the neurological links between the organism, social factors, and criminal behavior.

neuroplasticity The ability of the brain to alter its structure and function in response to experience.

neurosis A functional disorder of the mind or of the emotions involving anxiety, phobia, or other abnormal behavior.

neurotransmitters Chemical substances that facilitate the flow of electrical impulses from one neuron to the next across nerve synapses.

No Electronic Theft Act (NETA) A 1997 federal law (Public Law 105–147) that criminalizes the willful infringement of copyrighted works, including by electronic means, even when the infringing party derives no direct financial benefit from the infringement (such as when pirated software is freely distributed online). In keeping with requirements of the NETA, the U.S. Sentencing Commission enacted amendments to its guidelines on April 6, 2000, to increase penalties associated with electronic theft.

nonprimary homicide A murder that involves victims and offenders who have no prior relationship and that usually occurs during the course of another crime such as robbery.

nothing-works doctrine The belief popularized by Robert Martinson in the 1970s that correctional treatment programs have little success in rehabilitating offenders.

nurturant strategy A crime-control strategy that attempts "to forestall development of criminality by improving early life experiences and channeling child and adolescent development" in desirable directions.

occasional offender A criminal offender whose offending patterns are guided primarily by opportunity.

occupational crime Any act punishable by law that is committed in the course of an individual's legal occupation.

offense A violation of the criminal law or, in some jurisdictions, a minor crime, such as jaywalking, sometimes described as "ticketable."

offense specialization A preference for engaging in a certain type of offense to the exclusion of others.

Office for Victims of Crime (OVC) A federal office that administers the Crime Victims Fund and that provides funds and assistance to help victims of crime throughout the United States.

Office of Juvenile Justice and Delinquency Prevention (OJJDP) A national office that provides monetary assistance and direct victim-service programs for juvenile courts.

Office of National Drug Control Policy (ONDCP) A national office charged by Congress with establishing policies, priorities, and objectives for the nation's drug-control program. The ONDCP is responsible for developing and disseminating the *National Drug-Control Strategy.*

omertà The informal unwritten code of organized crime, which demands silence and loyalty, among other things, of family members.

Omnibus Anti-Drug Abuse Act A federal law (Public Law 100–690) enacted in 1988 that substantially increased federal penalties for recreational drug users and created a new cabinet-level position (known unofficially as the drug czar) to coordinate the drug-fighting efforts of the federal government.

Omnibus Crime Control and Safe Streets Act A federal law enacted in 1967 to eliminate the social conditions that create crime and to fund many anticrime initiatives nationwide.

operant behavior Any behavior that affects the environment in such a way as to produce responses or further behavioral cues.

operationalization The process by which concepts are made measurable.

opportunity structure A path to success. Opportunity structures may be of two types: legitimate and illegitimate.

organized crime The unlawful activities of the members of a highly organized, disciplined association engaged in supplying illegal goods and services, including gambling, prostitution, loan-sharking, narcotics, and labor racketeering.

Panopticon A prison designed by Jeremy Bentham that was to be a circular building with cells along the circumference, each clearly visible from a central location staffed by guards.

paradigm An example, a model, or a theory.

paranoid schizophrenic A schizophrenic individual who suffers from delusions and hallucinations.

Part I offenses The crimes of murder, rape, robbery, aggravated assault, burglary, larceny, and motor vehicle theft, as defined under the FBI's Uniform Crime Reporting Program; also known as *major crimes.*

Part II offenses The less serious offenses as identified by the FBI for the purpose of reporting arrest data.

participant observation A strategy in data gathering in which the researcher observes a group by participating, to varying degrees, in the activities of the group.

participatory justice A relatively informal type of criminal justice case processing that makes use of local community resources rather than requiring traditional forms of official intervention.

patriarchy The tradition of male dominance.

Pathways to Desistance study The largest longitudinal study of serious adolescent offenders ever conducted. The study analyzed data that was gathered on serious youthful offenders as they moved from adolescence into early adulthood.

pattern theory The idea that specific types of crime are associated with certain areas—and that it is the characteristics of those areas that contribute to crime's concentration.

peacemaking criminology A perspective that holds that crime-control agencies and the citizens they serve should work together to alleviate social problems and human suffering and thus reduce crime.

peace model An approach to crime control that focuses on effective ways for developing a shared consensus on critical issues that could seriously affect the quality of life.

penal couple A term that describes the relationship between offender and victim; also the two individuals most involved in the criminal act: the offender and the victim.

persistence The act of continuing in crime; also continual involvement in offending.

persistent thief One who continues in common law types of property crimes despite no better than an ordinary level of success.

personality The characteristic patterns of thoughts, feelings, and behaviors that make a person unique and that tend to remain stable over time. Personality influences an individual's thoughts, behavior, and emotions.

personal robbery A robbery that occurs on the highway or street or in a public place (also known as *mugging*) or that occurs in a residence.

pharmaceutical diversion The process by which legitimately manufactured controlled substances are diverted for illicit use.

phenomenological criminology The study of crime as a social phenomenon that is created through a process of social interaction.

phenomenology The study of the contents of human consciousness without regard to xternal conventions or prior assumptions.

phishing An Internet-based scam whose goal is to steal valuable personal information such as credit card or Social Security numbers, user IDs, and passwords.

phone phreak A person who uses switched, dialed-access telephone services for exploration and exploitation.

phrenology The study of the shape of the head to determine anatomical correlates of human behavior.

piracy *See* software piracy.

pluralist perspective An analytical approach to social organization that holds that a multiplicity of values and beliefs exists in any complex society but that most social actors agree on the usefulness of law as a formal means of dispute resolution.

polyvictimization Multiple victimizations of different kinds, such as sexual abuse, physical abuse, bullying, and exposure to family violence.

Ponzi scheme A form of high-yield-investment fraud that uses money collected from new investors, rather than profits from the purported underlying business venture, to pay high rates of return promised to earlier investors.

positivism The application of scientific techniques to the study of crime and criminals.

Positivist School An early criminological perspective that employ scientific objectivity, measurement, and observation in the study of crime and its causation.

postcrime victimization Any problem that tends to follow from initial victimization; also known as *secondary victimization.*

postmodern criminology A brand of criminology that developed following World War II and that builds on the tenets inherent in postmodern social thought.

postmodern feminism A perspective within modern criminology that questions the social construction of concepts that are typically used in any discussion of crime and justice.

post-traumatic stress disorder (PTSD) A serious condition that can develop in an individual who has undergone or witnessed traumatic and terrifying experiences, such as crime victimization. PTSD can be characterized by both psychological and physical symptoms, and people who suffer from it will generally experience impaired functioning in various aspects of their lives.

power-control theory A perspective that holds that the distribution of crime and delinquency within society is to some degree founded upon the consequences that power relationships within the wider society hold for domestic settings and for the everyday relationships among men, women, and children within the context of family life.

power seekers Serial killers who relish having power over another human being.

prefrontal cortex dysfunction A condition of the brain that may negatively impact social skills and moral reasoning. Such dysfunction may occur as the result of physical injuries to the brain, disease, or other factors.

prenatal substance exposure Fetal exposure to maternal drug and alcohol use. Prenatal substance exposure can significantly increase a child's risk for developmental and neurological disorders.

primary deviance The initial deviance often undertaken to deal with transient problems in living.

primary homicide A murder involving a family member, friend, or acquaintance.

primary research Any research characterized by original and direct investigation.

professional criminal A criminal offender who makes a living from criminal pursuits, is recognized by other offenders as professional, and engages in offending that is planned and calculated.

Project on Human Development in Chicago Neighborhoods (PHDCN) An intensive study of Chicago neighborhoods employing longitudinal evaluations to examine the changing circumstances of people's lives in an effort to identify personal characteristics that may lead toward or away from antisocial behavior.

proletariat The "have-nots," or the working class, in Marxist theory.

property crime According to the FBI's Uniform Crime Reporting program, a crime category that includes burglary, larceny, motor vehicle theft, and arson.

prosocial bond A bond between the individual and the social group that strengthens the likelihood of conformity. Prosocial bonds are characterized by attachment to conventional social institutions, values, and beliefs.

prostitution The offering of one's self for hire for the purpose of engaging in sexual relations, or the act or practice of engaging in sexual activity for money or its equivalent.

protection/avoidance strategy A crime-control strategy whose goal is to reduce criminal opportunities by changing people's routine activities, increasing guardianship, or incapacitating convicted offenders.

psychiatric criminology Any theory that is derived from the medical sciences, including neurology, and that, like other psychological theories, focuses on the individual as the unit of analysis. Psychiatric theories form the basis of psychiatric criminology. *See also* forensic psychiatry.

psychiatric theory A theory derived from the medical sciences, including neurology, and that, like other psychological theories, focuses on the individual as the unit of analysis.

psychoactive substance A substance that affects the mind, mental processes, or emotions.

psychoanalysis The theory of human psychology founded by Sigmund Freud on the concepts of the unconscious, resistance, repression, sexuality, and the Oedipus complex.

psychoanalytic theory A psychiatric approach developed by Sigmund Freud that emphasizes the role of personality in human behavior and that sees deviant behavior as the result of dysfunctional personalities.

psychobiotics The study of the psychological and behavioral effects that bacteria can have on the mind, feelings, emotions, and behavior.

psychological profiling The attempt to categorize, understand, and predict the behavior of certain types of offenders based on behavioral clues they provide.

psychological autopsy A procedure for investigating a person's death by reconstructing what the person thought, felt, and did before death, based on information gathered from personal documents, police reports, medical and coroner's records, and face-to-face interviews with families, friends, and others who had contact with the person before the death. Used primarily in cases of suicide, or murder-suicide.

psychological theory A theory derived from the behavioral sciences that focuses on the individual as the unit of analysis. Psychological theories place the locus of crime causation within the personality of the individual offender.

psychopath An individual who has a personality disorder, especially one manifested in aggressively antisocial behavior, and who is lacking in empathy. Psychopaths are thought to have been born that way.

psychopathology A psychological disorder that causes distress for either the individual or someone in the individual's life. It is also the study of pathological mental conditions (mental illness).

psychopathy A personality disorder characterized by antisocial behavior and lack of affect.

psychosis A form of mental illness in which sufferers are said to be out of touch with reality.

psychotherapy A form of psychiatric treatment based on psychoanalytical principles and techniques.

public policy A course of action that government takes in an effort to solve a problem or to achieve an end.

punishment An undesirable behavioral consequence likely to decrease the frequency of occurrence of that behavior.

pure research Any research undertaken simply for the sake of advancing scientific knowledge.

qualitative method A research technique that produces subjective results or results that are difficult to quantify.

quantitative method A research technique that produces measurable results.

quasi-experimental design An approach to research that, although less powerful than experimental designs, is deemed worthy of use when better designs are not feasible.

Racketeer Influenced and Corrupt Organizations (RICO) Act A statute that was part of the federal Organized Crime Control Act of 1970 and that is intended to combat criminal conspiracies.

radical criminology A perspective that holds that the causes of crime are rooted in social conditions that empower the wealthy and the politically well organized but disenfranchise the less fortunate; also known as *critical criminology* and *Marxist criminology*.

radical feminism A perspective that holds that any significant change in the social status of women can be accomplished only through substantial changes in social institutions such as the family, law, and medicine. Radical feminism argues, for example, that the structure of current legal thinking involves what is fundamentally a male perspective, which should be changed to incorporate women's social experiences and points of view.

randomization The process whereby individuals are assigned to study groups without biases or differences resulting from selection.

ransomware A type of malware that prevents legitimate access to user data stored on computers, and demands payments, often in Bitcoins, to renable access.

rape (NCVS) Carnal knowledge through the use of force or the threat of force, including attempts. Statutory rape (without force) is excluded. Both heterosexual and homosexual rape are included.

rape The penetration, no matter how slight, of the vagina or anus with any body part or object, or oral penetration by a sex organ of another person, without the consent of the victim. *See also* forcible rape.

rape myth A false assumption about rape, such as "When a woman says no, she really means yes." Rape myths characterize much of the discourse surrounding sexual violence.

rape-shield law A statute providing for the protection of rape victims by ensuring that defendants do not introduce irrelevant facts about the victim's sexual history into evidence.

rational choice theory A perspective that holds that criminality is the result of conscious choice and that predicts that individuals choose to commit crime when the benefits outweigh the costs of disobeying the law.

reaction formation The process by which a person openly rejects that which he or she wants or aspires to but cannot obtain or achieve.

realist criminology *See* left realism.

recidivism The repetition of criminal behavior.

recidivism rate The percentage of convicted offenders who have been released from prison and who are later rearrested for a new crime, generally within five years following release. *See also* dangerousness.

reintegrative shaming A form of shaming, imposed as a sanction by the criminal justice system, that is thought to strengthen the moral bond between the offender and the community.

relative deprivation A sense of social or economic inequality experienced by those who are unable, for whatever reason, to achieve legitimate success within the surrounding society.

replicability A scientific principle that holds that valid observations made at one time can be made again later if all other conditions are the same.

repression The psychological process through which a person rejects his or her own desires and impulses toward pleasurable instincts by excluding them from consciousness, thereby removing them from awareness and rendering them unconscious.

research The use of standardized, systematic procedures in the search for knowledge.

research design The logic and structure inherent in an approach to data gathering.

resilience The psychological ability to successfully cope with severe stress and negative events.

restitution A criminal sanction, especially the payment of compensation by the offender to the victim.

restorative justice A form of justice which holds that the community, victim, and offender should receive balanced attention and all three should gain tangible benefits from their interactions with the justice system. Also referred to as *balanced and restorative justice.*

retribution The act of taking revenge on a criminal perpetrator.

revictimization Multiple episodes of the same kind of victimization.

reward A desirable behavioral consequence likely to increase the frequency of occurrence of that behavior.

risk analysis *See* threat analysis.

risk assessment The practice of using a structured instrument that combines information about individuals in order to classify them as being low, moderate, or high risk for violent behavior, reoffending, or continued criminal activity.

robbery (UCR) The taking of or attempting to take anything of value from the care, custody, or control of a person or persons by force or threat of force or violence or by putting the victim in fear.

routine activities theory (RAT) A theory that examines the interaction of motivated offenders, capable guardians, and suitable targets as an explanation for crime, and which suggests that an individual's everyday activities contribute significantly to the likelihood of his or her criminal victimization.

Sarbanes–Oxley Act Officially known as the Public Company Accounting Reform and Investor Protection Act, requires chief executive officers and chief financial officers to personally vouch for the truth and fairness of their companies' financial disclosures and establishes an independent oversight board to regulate the accounting profession. The law also gives the federal Securities and Exchange Commission the authority to bar dishonest corporate directors and officers from ever again serving in positions of corporate responsibility, and increases the maximum federal prison term for common types of corporate fraud from 5 to 20 years.

scenario writing A technique intended to predict future outcomes that builds on environmental scanning by attempting to assess the likelihood of a variety of possible outcomes once important trends have been identified.

schizoid A person characterized by schizoid personality disorder. Such disordered personalities appear to be aloof, withdrawn, unresponsive, humorless, dull, and solitary to an abnormal degree.

schizophrenia A serious mental illness that distorts the way a person thinks, feels, and behaves. Primary features of schizophrenia include the inability to distinguish between real and imagined experiences and the inability to think logically.

script Generalized knowledge about specific types of situations that is stored in the mind.

secondary deviance Any deviant behavior that results from official labeling and from association with others who have been so labeled.

secondary research A new evaluation of existing information that had been collected by other researchers.

secondary victims Persons not directly affected by a criminal event, but who suffer unintended consequences of the victimization of others to whom they are close, such as family members, friends, co-workers, and neighbors.

secondary victimization secondary victimization Social injuries that occur, not as a direct result of a criminal act, but through the response of social institutions and individuals to the victim. *See also* postcrime victimization.

second-degree murder A criminal homicide that is unplanned and that is often described as a "crime of passion."

securities and commodities fraud A crime involving investments, such as stock-market manipulation, high-yield-investment fraud (Ponzi schemes, pyramid schemes, and prime bank schemes), advance fee fraud, hedge fund fraud, commodities fraud, foreign exchange fraud, and broker embezzlement.

securities fraud The theft of money resulting from intentional manipulation of the value of equities, including stocks and bonds. Securities fraud also includes theft from securities accounts and wire fraud.

selective disinhibition A loss of self-control due to the characteristics of the social setting, drugs or alcohol, or a combination of both.

selective incapacitation A social policy that seeks to protect society by incarcerating those individuals deemed to be the most dangerous.

self-control A person's ability to alter his or her own mental and emotional states and behavioral responses.

self-report A test or measure about one own's behavior, feelings, or other personal knowledge and characteristics.

self-report survey A survey in which anonymous respondents, without fear of disclosure or arrest, are asked to confidentially report any violations of the criminal law that they have committed, or victimizations that they have experienced.

separation assault Any violence inflicted by partners on significant others who attempt to leave an intimate relationship.

serial murder A criminal homicide that involves the killing of several victims in three or more separate events.

serotonin A neurotransmitter that is commonly found in the pineal gland, the digestive tract, the central nervous system, and blood platelets.

sex trafficking The recruitment, harboring, transportation, provision, or obtaining of a person for the purpose of a commercial sex act.

sexual selection A form of natural selection that influences an individual's ability to find or choose a mate.

sibling offense An offense or incident that culminates in homicide. The offense or incident may be a crime, such as robbery, or an incident that meets a less stringent criminal definition, such as a lover's quarrel involving assault or battery.

simple assault (NCVS) An attack without a weapon, resulting either in minor injury or in undetermined injury requiring less than two days of hospitalization. *See also* aggravated assault.

situational action theory (SAT) A perspective on crime holding that criminal behavior is the result of human decision making based on personal morality when viewed within the context of the existing situation. SAT stresses the importance of moral interpretations over a person's ability to exercise self-control.

situational choice theory A brand of rational choice theory that views criminal behavior "as a function of choices and decisions made within a context of situational constraints and opportunities."

situational crime prevention A social policy approach whose goal is to develop greater understanding of crime as well as more effective crime-prevention strategies by focusing on physical, organizational, and social environments that make crime possible.

snitch An amateur shoplifter.

social bond The link, created through socialization, between individuals and the society of which they are a part.

social capital The degree of positive relationships with others and with social institutions that individuals build up over the course of their lives.

social class A distinction made between individuals on the basis of important defining social characteristics.

social cognition theory A perspective which holds that people learn how to act by observing others.

social cohesion An emotional and social investment in a neighborhood and sense of shared destiny among residents.

social contract The Enlightenment-era concept that human beings abandon their natural state of individual freedom to join together and form society. In the process of forming a social contract, individuals surrender some freedoms to society as a whole, and government, once formed, is obligated to assume responsibilities toward its citizens and to provide for their protection and welfare.

social control theory A perspective that predicts that when social constraints on antisocial behavior are weakened or absent, delinquent behavior emerges. Rather than stressing causative factors in criminal behavior, social control theory asks why people actually obey rules instead of breaking them.

social development perspective An integrated view of human development that examines multiple levels of maturation simultaneously, including the psychological, biological, familial, interpersonal, cultural, societal, and ecological levels. Also known as *social development theory*.

social disorganization A condition said to exist when a group is faced with social change, uneven development of culture, maladaptiveness, disharmony, conflict, and lack of consensus.

social disorganization theory A perspective on crime and deviance that sees society as a kind of organism and crime and deviance as a kind of disease or social pathology. Theories of social disorganization are often associated with the perspective of social ecology and with the Chicago School of criminology, which developed during the 1920s and 1930s.

social ecology An approach to criminological theorizing that attempts to link the structure and organization of a human community to interactions with its localized environment.

social epidemiology The study of social epidemics and diseases of the social order.

socialist feminism A perspective within modern criminology that sees gender oppression as a consequence of the interaction between the economic structure of society and gender-based roles.

socialization The lifelong process of social experience whereby individuals acquire the cultural patterns of their society.

social learning theory A perspective that places primary emphasis on the role of communication and socialization in the acquisition of learned patterns of criminal behavior and the values that support that behavior; also known as *learning theory*.

social life The ongoing and (typically) structured interaction that occurs between persons in a society, including socialization and social behavior in general.

social pathology A concept that compares society to a physical organism and that sees criminality as an illness.

social policy A government initiative, program, or plan intended to address problems in society. The "war on crime," for example, is a kind of generic (large-scale) social policy—one consisting of many smaller programs.

social problems perspective The belief that crime is a manifestation of underlying social problems, such as poverty, discrimination, pervasive family violence, inadequate socialization practices, and the breakdown of traditional social institutions.

social process The interaction between and among social institutions, individuals, and groups.

social process theory A theory that asserts that criminal behavior is learned in interaction with others and that socialization processes that occur as the result of group membership are the primary route through which learning occurs; also known as the *interactionist perspective*.

social relativity The notion that social events are differently interpreted according to the cultural experiences and personal interests of the initiator, the observer, or the recipient of that behavior.

social structure The pattern of social organization and the interrelationships among institutions characteristic of a society.

social structure theory A theory that explains crime by reference to some aspect of the social fabric. These theories emphasize relationships among social institutions and describe the types of behavior that tend to characterize groups of people rather than individuals.

sociobiology "The systematic study of the biological basis of all social behavior."

sociological theory A perspective that focuses on the nature of the power relationships that exist between social groups and on the influences that various social phenomena bring to bear on the types of behaviors that tend to characterize groups of people.

sociopath An individual who has a personality disorder, especially one manifested in aggressively antisocial behavior, and who is lacking in empathy. Psychopaths are thought to have been born that way.

soft determinism The belief that human behavior is the result of choices and decisions made within a context of situational constraints and opportunities.

software piracy The unauthorized and illegal copying of software programs.

somatotyping The classification of human beings into types according to body build and other physical characteristics.

specific deterrence A goal of criminal sentencing that seeks to prevent a particular offender from engaging in repeat criminality.

spousal rape The rape of one spouse by the other. The term usually refers to the rape of a woman by her husband.

stalking A course of conduct directed at a specific person that involves repeated visual or physical proximity; nonconsensual communication; verbal, written, or implied threats; or a combination thereof that would cause a reasonable person fear as well as a constellation of behaviors involving repeated and persistent attempts to impose on another person unwanted communication and/or contact.

state-organized crime Any act defined by law as criminal that is committed by a state official during his or her work as a representative of the state.

statistical correlation The simultaneous increase or decrease in value of two numerically valued random variables.

statistical school A criminological perspective with roots in the early 1800s that seeks to uncover correlations between crime rates and other types of demographic data.

statute A formal written enactment by a legislative body.

statutory law Law in the form of statutes or formal written strictures made by a legislature or governing body with the power to make law.

stigmatic shaming A form of shaming, imposed as a sanction by the criminal justice system, that is thought to destroy the moral bond between the offender and the community.

stigmatized neighborhoods Residential areas with bad reputations that hold little attraction for those that can afford to live elsewhere.

strain theory A sociological approach that posits a disjuncture between socially and subculturally sanctioned means and goals as the cause of criminal behavior; also known as *anomie theory*.

strategic assessment A technique that assesses the risks and opportunities facing those who plan for the future.

structural Marxism A perspective that holds that the structural institutions of society influence the behavior of individuals and groups by virtue of the type of relationships created. The criminal law, for example, reflects class relationships and serves to reinforce those relationships.

subcultural theory A sociological perspective that emphasizes the contribution made by variously socialized cultural groups to the phenomenon of crime.

subculture A collection of values and preferences that is communicated to subcultural participants through a process of socialization.

subculture of violence theory The belief that certain groups or subcultures in society have values and attitudes that are conducive to crime and violence.

sublimation The psychological process whereby one aspect of consciousness comes to be symbolically substituted for another.

substantial-capacity test A standard for judging legal insanity that requires that a person lack the mental capacity needed to understand the wrongfulness of his or her act or to conform his or her behavior to the requirements of the law.

suitable target Something or someone of value to offenders in a criminal offense.

superego The moral aspect of the personality; much like the conscience. According to Freud, this part of the psyche develops by incorporating the community's (perceived) moral standards, is mainly unconscious, and includes the conscience.

supermale A male individual displaying the XYY chromosome structure.

superpredator A member of a new generation of juveniles "who [is] coming of age in actual and 'moral poverty' without the benefits of parents, teachers, coaches and clergy to teach [him or her] right from wrong and show [him or her] 'unconditional love.'" The term is often applied to inner-city youths.

survey research A social science data-gathering technique that involves the use of questionnaires.

tagging The process whereby an individual is negatively defined by agencies of justice; also known as *labeling*.

target hardening The reduction in criminal opportunity for a particular location, generally through the use of physical barriers, architectural design, and enhanced security measures.

technique of neutralization A culturally available justification that can provide criminal offenders with the means to disavow responsibility for their behavior.

TEMPEST A standard developed by the U.S. government that requires that electromagnetic emanations from computers designated as "secure" be below levels that would allow radio receiving equipment to read the data being computed.

terrorism Any premeditated, politically motivated violence perpetrated against noncombatant targets by subnational groups or clandestine agents, usually intended to influence an audience.

test of significance A statistical technique intended to provide researchers with confidence that their results are, in fact, true and not the result of sampling error.

testosterone The primary male sex hormone produced in the testes. Its function is to control secondary sex characteristics and sexual drive.

Thanatos A death wish.

theoretical criminology A subfield of general criminology, it posits explanations for criminal behavior.

theory A series of interrelated propositions that attempt to describe, explain, predict, and ultimately control some class of events. A theory gains explanatory power from inherent logical consistency and is "tested" by how well it describes and predicts reality.

threat analysis A complete and thorough assessment of the kinds of perils facing an organization; also known as *risk analysis*.

three-strikes legislation A criminal statute that mandates life imprisonment for criminals convicted of three violent felonies or serious drug offenses.

total institution A facility from which individuals can rarely come and go and in which communal life is intense and circumscribed. Individuals in total institutions tend to eat, sleep, play, learn, and worship together.

trafficking in persons (TIP) The exploitation of unwilling or unwitting people through force, coercion, threat, or deception.

traits Notable features or qualities of a biological entity. Traits may be classified as physical, behavioral, or psychological. Traits are passed from generation to the next.

translational criminology A form of criminology whose purpose it is to translate the results of research into workable social policy.

transnational organized crime Any unlawful activity undertaken and supported by organized criminal groups operating across national boundaries.

trend extrapolation A technique of futures research that makes future predictions based on the projection of existing trends.

tribalism The attitudes and behavior that result from strong feelings of identification with one's own social group.

truth in sentencing A close correspondence between the incarceration sentence given the offender and the time actually served prior to prison release.

turning point A crucial life experience that can change behavior.

Twelve Tables Early Roman laws written circa 450 B.C. that regulated family, religious, and economic life.

unicausal The characteristic of having one cause. Unicausal theories posit only one source for all that they attempt to explain.

Uniform Crime Reporting (UCR) Program A Federal Bureau of Investigation data-gathering initiative that provides an annual tally of statistics consisting primarily of information on crimes reported to the police and on arrests.

USA PATRIOT Act A federal law (Public Law 107–56) enacted in response to terrorist attacks on the World Trade Center and the Pentagon on September 11, 2001. The law, officially titled the Uniting and Strengthening America by Providing Appropriate Tools Required to Intercept and Obstruct Terrorism Act, substantially broadened the investigative authority of law enforcement agencies throughout America and is applicable to many crimes other than terrorism. The law was slightly revised and reauthorized by Congress in 2006. Also called *Antiterrorism Act*.

utilitarianism *See* hedonistic calculus.

variable A concept that can undergo measurable changes.

verstehen The kind of subjective understanding that can be achieved by criminologists who immerse themselves in the everyday world of the criminals they study.

victim A person who suffers direct or threatened physical, psychological, or financial harm as a result of the commission or attempted commission of a crime or delinquent act.

victim compensation Payments to victims of crime, generally made by a government agency, as compensation for lost wages and medical expenses.

victim restitution Court-ordered payments to victims of crime, generally made by offenders, as reimbursement for damages and/or losses.

victimization In National Crime Victimization Survey terminology, the harming of any single victim in a criminal incident.

victimless crimes Illegal activities that involve willing participants. Although direct and immediate victimization may not occur in victimless crimes, social and personal costs are frequently associated with such activities.

victimogenesis The contributory background of a victim as a result of which he or she becomes prone to criminal victimization.

victimologist One who studies victims and the process of criminal victimization.

victimology The scientific study of crime victims and the victimization process. Victimology is a field of study that grew out of criminology.

victim precipitation Any contribution made by the victim to the criminal event, especially one that led to its initiation.

victim proneness An individual's likelihood of victimization.

victim restitution Court-ordered payments to victims of crime, generally made by offenders as reimbursement for suffering, damages and/or financial losses.

victimization rate (NCVS) A measure of the occurrence of victimizations among a specified population group. For personal crimes, the rate is based on the number of victimizations per 1,000 residents age 12 or older. For household crimes, the victimization rates are calculated using the number of incidents per 1,000 households.

victim-impact statement A written document that describes the losses, suffering, and trauma experienced by the crime victim or by the victim's survivors. In jurisdictions where victim-impact statements are used, judges are expected to consider them in arriving at an appropriate sentence for the offender.

victim-precipitated homicide A killing in which the victim was the first to commence the interaction or was the first to resort to physical violence.

Victims of Crime Act (VOCA) A federal law enacted in 1984 that established the federal Crime Victims Fund. The fund uses monies from fines and forfeitures collected from federal offenders to supplement state support of local victims' assistance programs and state victims' compensation programs.

victim-witness assistance program A program that counsels victims, orients them to the justice process, and provides a variety of other services, such as transportation to court, child care during court appearances, and referrals to social services agencies.

Violence against Women Act (VAWA) A federal law enacted as a component of the 1994 Violent Crime Control and Law Enforcement Act and intended to address concerns about violence against women. The law focused on improving the interstate enforcement of protection orders, providing effective training for court personnel involved with women's issues, improving the training

and collaboration of police and prosecutors with victim service providers, strengthening law enforcement efforts to reduce violence against women, and increasing services to victims of violence.

Violent Crime Control and Law Enforcement Act A federal law (Public Law 103–322) enacted in 1994 that authorized spending billions of dollars on crime prevention, law enforcement, and prison construction. It also outlawed the sale of certain types of assault weapons and enhanced federal death-penalty provisions.

Violent Criminal Apprehension Program (VICAP) The program of the Federal Bureau of Investigation focusing on serial murder investigations and the apprehension of serial killers.

virus *See* computer virus.

visionary serial killers Serial killers motivated by auditory or visual hallucinations.

welfare fraud The use of deceitful statements, practices, or devices to unlawfully obtain public assistance benefits.

white-collar crime Any violation of the criminal law committed by a person of respectability and high social status in the course of his or her occupation.

Wickersham Commission A commission (officially known as the Commission on Law Observance and Enforcement) created by President Herbert Hoover in 1931 whose mandate was to improve justice system practices and to reinstate law's role in civilized governance. The commission made recommendations concerning the nation's police forces and described how to improve policing throughout America.

workplace violence The crimes of murder, rape, robbery, and assault committed against persons who are at work or on duty.

Notes

CHAPTER 1: WHAT IS CRIMINOLOGY?

1. "'NCIS, S.H.I.E.L.D.' and 'Sleepy Hollow' all Earn Noms in the 2014 PCA's," The Examiner, http://www.examiner.com/article/ncis-s-h-i-e-l-d-and-sleepyhollow-all-earn-noms-the-2014-pca-s (accessed May 12, 2015).

2. "NCIS Audience Ratings," NCIS Fan Site, http://www.ncis-fanwiki.com/page/NCIS+Audience+Ratings (accessed May 26, 2015).

3. Sara Bibel, "'CSI: Crime Scene Investigation' Is the Most-Watched Show in the World," TV by the Numbers, June 14, 2012, http://tvbythenumbers.zap2it.com/2012/06/14/csi-crime-scene-investigation-is-the-most-watched-show-in-the-world-2/138212/ (accessed July 26, 2012).

4. From the standpoint of the law, the proper word is *conduct* rather than *behavior* because the term *conduct* implies intentional and willful activity, whereas *behavior* refers to any human activity—even that which occurs while a person is unconscious as well as that which is unintended.

5. Paul W. Tappan, "Who Is the Criminal?" *American Sociological Review,* Vol. 12 (1947), pp. 96–102.

6. Edwin Sutherland, *Principles of Criminology,* 4th ed. (New York: Lippincott, 1947).

7. Jeffrey H. Reiman, *The Rich Get Richer and the Poor Get Prison,* 4th ed. (Boston: Allyn & Bacon, 1997).

8. C. D. Shearing, "Criminologists Must Broaden Their Field of Study beyond Crime and Criminals," in R. Boostrom, ed., *Enduring Issues in Criminology* (San Diego, CA: Greenhaven, 1995).

9. Ezzat Fattah, *Introduction to Criminology* (Burnaby, British Columbia: School of Criminology, Simon Fraser University, 1989).

10. Hermann Mannheim, *Comparative Criminology* (Boston: Houghton Mifflin, 1965).

11. Ron Claassen, "Restorative Justice: Fundamental Principles," http://www.fresno.edu/pacs/rjprinc.htm (accessed May 5, 2007).

12. H. Schwendinger and J. Schwendinger, "Defenders of Order or Guardians of Human Rights?" in I. Taylor, P. Walton, and J. Young, eds., *Critical Criminology* (London: Routledge and Kegan Paul, 1975).

13. Ibid.

14. Jeffrey H. Reiman, *The Rich Get Richer and the Poor Get Prison,* 4th ed. (Boston: Allyn & Bacon, 1997).

15. Ezzat Fattah, *Introduction to Criminology* (Burnaby, British Columbia: School of Criminology, Simon Fraser University, 1989).

16. Matthew Robinson, "Defining 'Crime,'" http://www.appstate.edu/~robinsnmb/smokeharms.htm (accessed November 4, 2006).

17. Laura A. Baker, Catherine Tuvblad, and Adrian Raine, "Genetics and Crime," in E. McLoughlin and T. Newburn, eds., *The SAGE Handbook of Criminological Theory* (London: SAGE, 2010), pp. 21–40.

18. Edwin H. Sutherland, Principles of Criminology (Chicago: University of Chicago Press, 1934).

19. Susan Spencer-Wendel, "Let 'Em Sag, Judge Rules on Riviera Beach's No-Baggy-Pants Law," *Palm Beach Post,* April 22, 2009, http://www.palmbeachpost.com/localnews/content/local_news/epaper/2009/04/22/0422saggy.html (accessed March 24, 2010).

20. Neal J. Riley, "S.F. Barely Passes Public-Nudity Ban," *San Francisco Chronicle,* November 21, 2012, http://www.chron.com/bayarea/article/S-F-barely-passes-public-nudity-ban-4055606.php#photo-3732744 (accessed February 1, 2013).

21. Lotteries exist in 44 U.S. states, the District of Columbia, Puerto Rico, and the U.S. Virgin Islands.

22. John Wagner, "Trump Suggests Loss of Citizenship or Jail for Those Who Burn U.S. Flags," *The Washington Post,* November 29, 2016, https://www.washingtonpost.com/news/post-politics/wp/2016/11/29/trump-suggests-loss-of-citizenship-or-jail-for-those-who-burn-u-s-flags/?utm_term=.235d47035724 (accessed January 5, 2017).

23. Piers Beirne, *Inventing Criminology* (Albany: State University of New York Press, 1993).

24. See also Paul Topinard, *Anthropology* (London: Chapman and Hall, 1894).

25. Joseph F. Sheley, *Criminology: A Contemporary Handbook* (Belmont, CA: Wadsworth, 1991), p. xxiii.

26. Edwin H. Sutherland, *Criminology* (Philadelphia: Lippincott, 1924), p. 11.

27. Edwin H. Sutherland, *Principles of Criminology* (Chicago: University of Chicago Press, 1934).

28. Sutherland, Edwin H., *Encyclopedia of Criminology,* http://www.fitzroydearborn.com/chicago/criminology/sample-sutherlandedwin.asp (accessed November 15, 2007).

29. Edwin H. Sutherland and Donald R. Cressey, *Criminology,* 9th ed. (Philadelphia: Lippincott, 1974), p. 3.

30. Gennaro F. Vito and Ronald M. Holmes, *Criminology: Theory, Research, and Policy* (Belmont, CA: Wadsworth, 1994), p. 3.

31. Clemens Bartollas and Simon Dinitz, *Introduction to Criminology: Order and Disorder* (New York: Harper & Row, 1989), p. 548.

32. Marvin E. Wolfgang and Franco Ferracuti, *The Subculture of Violence: Towards an Integrated Theory in Criminology* (London: Tavistock, 1967).

33. European Society of Criminology, Constitution, Section 1 (d), http://www.esc-eurocrim.org/constitution.shtml (accessed July 10, 2007).

34. Jack p. Gibbs, "The State of Criminological Theory," *Criminology,* Vol. 25, No. 4 (November 1987), pp. 822–823.

35. Jim Short, "President's Message: On Communicating, Crossing Boundaries and Building Bridges," *The Criminologist,* Vol. 22, No. 5 (September/October 1997), p. 1.

36. Available through Sage Publications, Thousand Oaks, CA.

37. Piers Beirne and Colin Sumner, "Editorial Statement," *Theoretical Criminology,* Vol. 1, No. 1 (February 1997), pp. 5–11.

38. There are those who deny, however, that criminology deserves the name *discipline.* See, for example, Don C. Gibbons, *Talking about Crime and Criminals: Problems and Issues in Theory Devel-*

opment in Criminology (Upper Saddle River, NJ: Prentice Hall, 1994), p. 3.

39. Charles F. Wellford, "Controlling Crime and Achieving Justice: The American Society of Criminology 1996 Presidential Address," *Criminology*, Vol. 35, No. 1 (1997), p. 1.

40. Don C. Gibbons, *Talking about Crime and Criminals: Problems and Issues in Theory Development in Criminology* (Upper Saddle River, NJ: Prentice Hall, 1994), p. 3.

41. *The American Heritage Dictionary* on CD-ROM (Boston: Houghton Mifflin, 1992).

42. *The American Heritage Dictionary of the English Language,* 3rd ed. (Boston: Houghton Mifflin, 1996).

43. This list is not meant to be exclusive. There are many other journals in the field, too many to list here.

44. Edwin Sutherland, *Principles of Criminology*, 4th ed. (New York: Lippincott, 1947).

45. Don M. Gottfredson, "Criminological Theories: The Truth as Told by Mark Twain," in William S. Laufer and Freda Adler, eds., *Advances in Criminological Theory*, Vol. 1 (New Brunswick, NJ: Transaction, 1989), p. 1.

46. Gregg Barak, *Integrating Criminologies* (Boston: Allyn & Bacon, 1998), p. 5.

47. Don C. Gibbons, "Talking about Crime: Observations on the Prospects for Causal Theory in Criminology," *Criminal Justice Research Bulletin* (Sam Houston State University), Vol. 7, No. 6 (1992).

48. Ibid.

49. American Society of Criminology, "The ASC Announces a New Division: The Division of Experimental Criminology," https://www.asc41.com/DECannouncement.html (accessed April 7, 2010).

50. David Weisburd, "Editor's Introduction," *Journal of Experimental Criminology*, Vol. 1 (2005), p. 3.

51. National Institute of Justice, "What Is Translational Criminology?," *NIJ Journal,* No. 268 (November 3, 2011), http://www.nij.gov/nij/journals/268/criminology.htm (accessed May 1, 2012).

52. Editorial, "In Denial about On-Screen Violence," *New Scientist,* April 21, 2007, p. 5.

53. Congressional Public Health Summit, Joint Statement on the Impact of Entertainment Violence on Children, July 26, 2000.

54. Federal Trade Commission, *Marketing Violent Entertainment to Children* (Washington, DC: U.S. Government Printing Office, 2000).

55. Sue Pleming, "U.S. Report Says Hollywood Aims Violence at Kids," Reuters wire service, September 11, 2000.

56. "Editorial: In Denial about On-Screen Violence," *New Scientist,* April 21, 2007, http://www.newscientist.com/channel/opinion/mg19426003.600-editorial-in-denial-about-onscreen-violence.html (accessed August 1, 2007).

57. Lydia Saad, "Crime Tops List of Americans' Local Concerns," Gallup Organization, June 21, 2000, http://www.gallup.com/poll/releases/pr000621.asp (accessed February 20, 2004).

58. National Institute of Justice, "What Is Translational Criminology?" *NIJ Journal,* No. 268 (November 3, 2011), http://www.nij.gov/nij/journals/268/criminology.htm (accessed May 1, 2012).

59. Alfred Blumstein, "Making Rationality Relevant: The American Society of Criminology 1992 Presidential Address," *Criminology*, Vol. 31, No. 1 (February 1993), p. 1.

60. Ibid.

61. John P. Crank, *Understanding Police Culture* (Cincinnati, OH: Anderson, 1998), p. 15.

62. Public Law 103–322.

63. For a good overview of this issue, see Wesley G. Skogan, ed., *Reactions to Crime and Violence: The Annals of the American Academy of Political and Social Science* (Thousand Oaks, CA: Sage, 1995).

64. For an excellent discussion of crime as a social event, see Leslie W. Kennedy and Vincent F. Sacco, *Crime Counts: A Criminal Event Analysis* (Toronto: Nelson Canada, 1996).

65. For a good discussion of the social construction of crime, see Leslie T. Wilkins, "On Crime and Its Social Construction: Observations on the Social Construction of Crime," *Social Pathology,* Vol. 1, No. 1 (January 1995), pp. 1–11.

66. For a parallel approach, see Terance D. Miethe and Robert F. Meier, *Crime and Its Social Context: Toward an Integrated Theory of Offenders, Victims, and Situations* (Albany: State University of New York Press, 1995).

67. Joan McCord, "Family Relationships, Juvenile Delinquency, and Adult Criminality," *Criminology,* Vol. 29, No. 3 (August 1991), pp. 397–417.

68. Elizabeth Candle and Sarnoff A. Mednick, "Perinatal Complications Predict Violent Offending," *Criminology,* Vol. 29, No. 3 (August 1991), pp. 519–529.

69. Carol W. Kohfeld and John Sprague, "Demography, Police Behavior, and Deterrence," *Criminology,* Vol. 28, No. 1 (February 1990), pp. 111–136.

70. Leslie W. Kennedy and David R. Forde, "Routine Activities and Crime: An Analysis of Victimization in Canada," *Criminology,* Vol. 28, No. 1 (February 1990), p. 137.

71. William G. Doerner, "The Impact of Medical Resources on Criminally Induced Lethality: A Further Examination," *Criminology,* Vol. 26, No. 1 (February 1988), pp. 171–177.

72. Ibid., p. 177.

73. Jeff Ferrell, "Criminological Verstehen: Inside the Immediacy of Crime," *Justice Quarterly,* Vol. 14, No. 1 (1997), p. 11.

74. James F. Gilsinan, "They Is Clowning Tough: 911 and the Social Construction of Reality," *Criminology,* Vol. 27, No. 2 (May 1989), pp. 329–344.

75. See, for example, Miethe and Meier, *Crime and Its Social Context.*

76. For a good discussion of the historical development of criminology, see Leon Radzinowicz, *In Search of Criminology* (Cambridge: Harvard University Press, 1962).

77. As quoted in W. Wayt Gibbs, "Trends in Behavioral Science: Seeking the Criminal Element," *Scientific American,* Vol. 272, No. 3 (March 1995), pp. 100–107.

78. Charles F. Wellford, "Controlling Crime and Achieving Justice: The American Society of Criminology 1996 Presidential Address," *Criminology*, Vol. 35, No. 1 (1997), p. 4.

CHAPTER 2: WHERE DO THEORIES COME FROM?

1. Although witnesses agreed that Eugene gnawed on his victim's face, autopsy results showed no human remains in Eugene's stomach.

2. Some of the details for this story come from Seniboye Tienabeso, "Miami Cannibal Told Victim, 'I'm Going to Kill You,'" ABC News, August 9, 2012, http://abcnews.go.com/US/miami-cannibal-victimattacker-ripped-ribbons/story?id=16967183 (accessed January 4, 2013).

3. "Medical Examiner: Causeway Cannibal Not High on Bath Salts," *CBS Miami*, June 27, 2012, http://miami.cbslocal.com/2012/06/27/medical-examiner-causeway-cannibal-not-high-on-bath-salts (accessed February 2, 2017).

4. "Girlfriend Recalls Rudy Eugene's Final Day," *CBS Miami*, May 31, 2012, http://miami.cbslocal.com/2012/05/31/girlfriend-recalls-rudy-eugenes-final-day (accessed February 2, 2017).

5. Lawrence W. Sherman, *Evidence-Based Policing* (Washington, DC: Police Foundation, 1998), p. 4.

6. David Weisburd, Lorraine Mazerolle, and Anthony Petrosino, "The Academy of Experimental Criminology: Advancing Randomized Trials in Crime and Justice," http://www.crim.upenn.edu/aec/AECCriminologist417.doc (accessed May 20, 2010).

7. David P. Farrington, Lloyd Ohlin, and James Q. Wilson, *Understanding and Controlling Crime* (New York: Springer-Verlag, 1986).

8. Lawrence W. Sherman, *Policing Domestic Violence* (New York: Free Press, 1992).

9. Anthony Petrosino et al., "Toward Evidence-Based Criminology and Criminal Justice," *International Journal of Comparative Criminology*, Vol. 3 (2003), 191–213.

10. John H. Laub, "The Life Course of Criminology in the United States: The American Society of Criminology 2003 Presidential Address," *Criminology*, Vol. 42, No. 1 (February 2004), pp. 1–26.

11. Ibid., p. 7.

12. Ibid.

13. As discussed by Piers Beirne and Colin Summer, "Editorial Statement," *Theoretical Criminology: An International Journal*, Vol. 1, No. 1 (February 1997), pp. 5–11.

14. Hermann Mannheim, *Comparative Criminology* (Boston, MA: Houghton Mifflin, 1967), p. 20.

15. Paul Stokes, "Extra Police Put on the Beat for Full Moon," *The Telegraph*, June 7, 2006, http://www.telegraph.co.uk/news/main.jhtml?xml=/news/2007/06/06/nmoon106.xml (accessed July 12, 2007).

16. Don M. Gottfredson, "Criminology Theories: The Truth as Told by Mark Twain," in William S. Laufer and Freda Adler, eds., *Advances in Criminological Theory*, Vol. 1 (New Brunswick, NJ: Transaction, 1989), p. 3.

17. Kenneth R. Hoover, *The Elements of Social Scientific Thinking*, 5th ed. (New York: St. Martin's, 1992), p. 34.

18. Ibid.

19. Todd Clear, "Policy and Evidence: The Challenge to the American Society of Criminology—2009 Presidential Address to the American Society of Criminology," *Criminology*, Vol. 48, No. 1 (2010), p. 6.

20. Ibid.

21. Susette M. Talarico, *Criminal Justice Research: Approaches, Problems and Policy* (Cincinnati, OH: Anderson, 1980), p. 3.

22. Ibid.

23. For a good review of secondary research, see J. H. Laub, R. J. Sampson, and K. Kiger, "Assessing the Potential of Secondary Data Analysis: A New Look at the Gluecks' Unraveling Juvenile Delinquency Data," in Kimberly L. Kempf, ed., *Measurement Issues in Criminology* (New York: Springer-Verlag, 1990), pp. 241–257; and Robert J. Sampson and John H. Laub, *Crime in the Making* (Cambridge, MA: Harvard University Press, 1993).

24. Sampson and Laub, *Crime in the Making*, p. 3.

25. Larry S. Miller and John T. Whitehead, *Introduction to Criminal Justice Research and Methods* (Cincinnati, OH: Anderson, 1996).

26. The Free Oxford English Dictionary, https://en.oxforddictionaries.com, Oxford University Press.

27. Donald T. Campbell and Julian C. Stanley, *Experimental and Quasi-Experimental Designs for Research* (Chicago: Rand-McNally, 1966), p. 35.

28. Ibid., p. 5, from which many of the descriptions that follow are adapted.

29. Ibid., p. 34.

30. According to Denise C. Gottfredson, "[M]idnight basketball programs are not likely to reduce crime." Gottfredson cites research (J. G. Ross et al., "The Effectiveness of an After-School Program for Primary Grade Latchkey Students on Precursors of Substance Abuse," *Journal of Community Psychology*, OSAP Special Issue [1992], pp. 22–38) showing that such programs may actually increase the risk for delinquency by increasing risk taking and impulsiveness. See Denise C. Gottfredson, "School-Based Crime Prevention," in Lawrence W. Sherman et al., *Preventing Crime: What Works, What Doesn't, What's Promising* (Washington, DC: National Institute of Justice, 1998), http://www.ncjrs.org/works/chapter5.htm (accessed June 15, 2004).

31. Shawn Bushway and David Weisburd, "Acknowledging the Centrality of Quantitative Criminology in Criminology and Criminal Justice," *The Criminologist*, Vol. 31, No. 4 (2006), p. 1.

32. Lawrence W. Sherman et al., *Evidence-Based Crime Prevention* (New York: Routledge, 2002).

33. Frank E. Hagan, *Research Methods in Criminal Justice and Criminology*, 6th ed. (New York: Allyn & Bacon, 2003).

34. Jeff Ferrell, "Criminological Verstehen: Inside the Immediacy of Crime," *Justice Quarterly*, Vol. 14, No. 1 (1997), p. 11.

35. William Foote Whyte, *Street Corner Society: The Social Structure of an Italian Slum* (Chicago: University of Chicago Press, 1943), pp. v–vii.

36. Ibid., p. vii.

37. Hagan, *Research Methods in Criminal Justice and Criminology*.

38. Nicole Vanden Heuvel, *Directory of Criminal Justice Information* (Washington, DC: National Institute of Justice, 1992), p. 145.

39. Hagan, *Research Methods in Criminal Justice and Criminology*.

40. Hoover, *The Elements of Social Scientific Thinking*, p. 34.

41. Abraham Kaplan, *The Conduct of Inquiry: Methodology for Behavioral Science* (San Francisco: Chandler, 1964), p. 134.

42. Ibid.

43. See American Society of Criminology, "Critical Criminal Justice Issues," 1994; available from the National Institute of Justice via http://www.ncjrs.gov/App/AbstractDB/AbstractDBDetails.aspx?id=158837.

44. Avshalom Caspim et al., "Are Some People Crime-Prone? Replications of the Personality-Crime Relationship across Countries, Genders, Races, and Methods," *Criminology*, Vol. 32, No. 2 (May 1994), pp. 162–195.

45. Abraham Kaplan, *The Conduct of Inquiry: Methodology for Behavioral Science* (San Francisco: Chandler, 1964), p. 134.

46. As with almost anything else, qualitative data can be assigned to categories and the categories can be numbered. Hence, qualitative data can be quantified, although the worth of such effort is subject to debate.

47. Sanyika Shakur, *Monster: The Autobiography of an L.A. Gang Member* (New York: Penguin, 1993), pp. 45–46.

48. Ibid., p. xiv.

49. Jeff Ferrell, "Criminological Verstehen: Inside the Immediacy of Crime," *Justice Quarterly*, Vol. 14, No. 1 (1997), p. 11.

50. Academy of Criminal Justice Sciences, *Code of Ethics*, Section 18.

51. Ibid., Section 19.

52. National Institute of Justice, *Human Subjects and Privacy Protection*, http://www.nij.gov/funding/humansubjects/welcome.htm (accessed January 31, 2017).

53. Jeff Ferrell, "Criminological Verstehen: Inside the Immediacy of Crime," *Justice Quarterly*, Vol. 14, No. 1 (1997), p. 8.

54. Frank E. Hagan, *Research Methods in Criminal Justice and Criminology*, 6th ed. (New York: Allyn & Bacon, 2003).

55. Ibid.

56. See Dennis Cauchon, "Study Critical of D.A.R.E. Rejected," *USA Today*, October 4, 1994, p. 2A.

57. See Susan T. Ennett et al., "How Effective Is Drug Abuse Resistance Education? A Meta-Analysis of Project DARE Outcome Evaluations," *American Journal of Public Health*, Vol. 84, No. 9 (September 1994), pp. 1394–1401.

58. Susan T. Ennett et al., "Long-Term Evaluation of Drug Abuse Resistance Education," *Addictive Behaviors*, Vol. 19, No. 2 (1994), pp. 112–125.

59. Donald R. Lynam and Richard Milich, "Project DARE: No Effects at 10-Year Follow-Up," *Journal of Consulting and Clinical Psychology*, Vol. 67, No. 4 (August 1999), pp. 590–593.

60. Kevin Helliker, "The Case for Alcoholics Anonymous: It Works Even If the Science Is Lacking," *Wall Street Journal*, October 17, 2006, p. D1.

61. American Society of Criminology, "Draft Code of Ethics," Section II, paragraph 7 (unpublished manuscript).

62. Faye S. Taxman, "Research and Relevance: Lessons from the Past, Thoughts for the Future," *Criminology and Public Policy*, Vol. 3, No. 2 (March 2004), p. 170.

63. Julian Leigh, "Mandatory Arrest Laws Can Reduce Domestic Violence," in Tamara L. Roleff, ed., *Domestic Violence: Opposing Viewpoints* (San Diego, CA: Greenhaven Press, 2000).

64. James Austin, "Why Criminology Is Irrelevant," *Criminology and Public Policy*, Vol. 2, No. 3 (July 2003), pp. 557–564.

65. The Campaign for an Effective Crime Policy, *The Impact of Three Strikes and You're Out Laws: What Have We Learned?* (Washington, DC: CECP, 1997).

66. Fox Butterfield, no headline, New York Times News Service Online, April 16, 1997.

67. Sherman et al., *Preventing Crime*.

68. "Solving Crime Problems with Research," *NIJ Journal*, No. 269, March 26, 2012; http://www.nij.gov/journals/269/pages/research.aspx.

69. Patricia Van Voorhis et al., "The Impact of Family Structure and Quality on Delinquency: A Comparative Assessment of Structural and Functional Factors," *Criminology*, Vol. 26, No. 2 (May 1988), pp. 235–261.

70. David F. Greenberg, "Comparing Criminal Career Models," *Criminology*, Vol. 30, No. 1 (February 1992), pp. 132–140.

71. This list of journals is representative at best. For a much more complete list, see Michael S. Vaughn et al., "Journals in Criminal Justice and Criminology: An Updated and Expanded Guide for Authors," *Journal of Criminal Justice Education*, Vol. 15, No. 1 (Spring 2004), pp. 61–192.

72. American Psychological Association, *Publication Manual of the American Psychological Association*, 5th ed. (Washington, DC: APA, 2001).

73. William Strunk, Jr., and E. B. White, *The Elements of Style*, 4th ed. (New York: Longman, 2000).

74. Mary-Claire van Leunen, *A Handbook for Scholars*, rev. ed. (Oxford: Oxford University Press, 1992).

CHAPTER 3: CLASSICAL AND NEOCLASSICAL THOUGHT

1. "About Listverse" (accessed February 10, 2012).

2. "Top 10 Tips to Commit the Perfect Crime," http://listverse.com/2007/08/16/top-10-tips-to-commit-the-perfect-crime/ (accessed January 31, 2017).

3. Ibid.

4. William Graham Sumner, *Folkways* (New York: Dover, 1906).

5. Marvin Wolfgang, "The Key Reporter," *Phi Beta Kappa*, Vol. 52, No. 1.

6. Roman influence in England had ended by A.D. 442, according to Crane Brinton, John B. Christopher, and Robert L. Wolff, *A History of Civilization*, 3rd ed., Vol. 1 (Upper Saddle River, NJ: Prentice Hall, 1967), p. 180.

7. Howard Abadinsky, *Law and Justice* (Chicago: Nelson-Hall, 1988), p. 6.

8. Edward McNall Burns, *Western Civilization*, 7th ed. (New York: W. W. Norton, 1969).

9. Ibid.

10. Brinton, Christopher, and Wolff, *A History of Civilization*, p. 274.

11. Harry V. Jaffa and Ernest van den Haag, "Of Men, Hogs, and Law: If Natural Law Does Not Permit Us to Distinguish between Men and Hogs, What Does?" *National Review*, February 3, 1992, p. 40.

12. Abraham Lincoln, Speech on the Kansas-Nebraska Act, October 16, 1854.

13. Referred to in official transcripts as Rudolf Franz Ferdinand Hoess.

14. International Military Tribunal, "One Hundred and Eighth Day, Monday, 4/15/1946, Part 3," in Trial of the Major War Criminals before the International Military Tribunal, Vol. XI. Proceedings: 4/8/1946–4/17/1946 (Nuremberg: International Military Tribunal, 1943), pp. 398–400.

15. The quotations attributed to Beccaria in this section are from Cesare Beccaria, *Essay on Crimes and Punishments* (Livorno, Italy: Tipografia Coltellini, 1764).

16. Bentham, *An Introduction to the Principles of Morals and Legislation* (Oxford: Clarendon Press, 1907); reprint of the 1823 edition, first printed 1780.

17. R. Martinson, "What Works: Questions and Answers about Prison Reform," *Public Interest*, No. 35 (1974), pp. 22–54.

18. James Q. Wilson, *Thinking about Crime* (New York: Vintage, 1975).

19. David Fogel, *We Are the Living Proof: The Justice Model of Corrections* (Cincinnati, OH: Anderson, 1975).

20. Conrad P. Rutkowski, "Fogel's 'Justice Model': Stop Trying to Reform. Punish, but Treat All Alike," *Illinois Issues*, February 1976.

21. Felton M. Earls and Albert J. Reiss, *Breaking the Cycle: Predicting and Preventing Crime* (Washington, DC: National Institute of Justice, 1994), p. 49.

22. D. B. Cornish and R. V. Clarke, eds., *The Reasoning Criminal: Rational Choice Perspectives on Offending* (New York: Springer-Verlag, 1986).

23. Ronald V. Clarke and Derek B. Cornish, eds., *Crime Control in Britain: A Review of Police and Research* (Albany: State University of New York Press, 1985), p. 8.

24. Ronald V. Clarke, "Situational Crime Prevention—Everybody's Business," paper presented at the 1995 Australian Crime Prevention Council conference, http://barney.webace.com.au/~austcpc/conf95/clarke.htm (accessed December 2, 2000).

25. See Derek B. Cornish and Ronald V. Clarke, "Understanding Crime Displacement: An Application of Rational Choice Theory," *Criminology,* Vol. 25, No. 4 (November 1987), p. 933.

26. See Tomislav V. Kovandzic, Lynne M. Vieraitis, and Denise Paquette Boots, "Does the Death Penalty Save Lives? New Evidence from State Panel Data, 1977 to 2006," *Criminology and Public Policy,* Vol. 8, No. 4 (2009), pp. 803–843.

27. Werner Einstadter and Stuart Henry, *Criminological Theory: An Analysis of Its Underlying Assumptions* (Fort Worth, TX: Harcourt Brace, 1995), p. 70.

28. Daniel J. Curran and Claire M. Renzetti, *Theories of Crime* (Boston: Allyn & Bacon, 1994), p. 18.

29. "Waves of Car Burning Crimes Across Sweden Moves to Stockholm Ghetto," *Reuters,* August 16, 2016, https://www.yahoo.com/news/wave-car-burning-crimes-across-sweden-moves-stockholm-160817759.html (accessed January 20, 2017).

30. Jack Katz, *Seductions of Crime: Moral and Sensual Attractions in Doing Evil* (New York: Basic Books, 1988), p. 8.

31. Ibid., p. 3.

32. Ibid., p. 76.

33. Ibid., p. 71.

34. Bill McCarthy, "Not Just 'for the Thrill of It': An Instrumentalist Elaboration of Katz's Explanation of Sneaky Thrill Property Crimes," *Criminology,* Vol. 33, No. 4 (1995), pp. 519–538.

35. David Weisburd, "Reorienting Crime Prevention Research and Policy: From the Causes of Criminality to the Context of Crime," *NIJ Research Report* (Washington, DC: National Institute of Justice, June 1997).

36. See P. Brantingham and P. Brantingham, "Situational Crime Prevention in Practice," *Canadian Journal of Criminology* (January 1990), pp. 17–40; and R. V. Clarke, "Situational Crime Prevention: Achievements and Challenges," in M. Tonry and D. Farrington, eds., *Building a Safer Society: Strategic Approaches to Crime Prevention, Crime and Justice: A Review of Research,* Vol. 19 (Chicago: University of Chicago Press, 1995).

37. Quotes in this paragraph and the next are taken from Weisburd, "Reorienting Crime Prevention Research and Policy."

38. See, for example, J. E. Eck and D. Weisburd, eds., *Crime and Place: Crime Prevention Studies,* Vol. 4 (Monsey, NY: Willow Tree Press, 1995).

39. M. Lyn Exum, "The Application and Robustness of the Rational Choice Perspective in the Study of Angry Intentions to Aggress," *Criminology,* Vol. 40, No. 4 (2002), p. 933, citing Allen E. Liska and Stephen F. Messner, *Perspectives on Crime and Deviance,* 3rd ed. (Upper Saddle River, NJ: Prentice Hall, 1999).

40. Dolf Zillman, *Hostility and Aggression* (Hillsdale, NJ: Lawrence Erlbaum Associates, 1979), p. 279.

41. David Lee and Justin McCrary, "Crime, Punishment, and Myopia," NBER Working Paper No. W11491 (Cambridge, MA: National Bureau of Economic Research, 2005). Available at SSRN: http://ssrn.com/abstract=762770.

42. Ibid

43. Francesco Drago, Roberto Galbiati, and Pietro Vertova, "The Deterrent Effects of Prison: Evidence from a Natural Experiment," *Journal of Political Economy,* Vol. 117 (2009), pp. 257–280.

44. Kenneth D. Tunnell, "Choosing Crime: Close Your Eyes and Take Your Chances," *Justice Quarterly,* Vol. 7 (1990), pp. 673–690.

45. See R. Barr and K. Pease, "Crime Placement, Displacement and Deflection," in M. Tonry and N. Morris, eds., *Crime and Justice: A Review of Research,* Vol. 12 (Chicago: University of Chicago Press, 1990).

46. For a good summation of target hardening, see Ronald V. Clarke, *Situational Crime Prevention* (New York: Harrow and Heston, 1992).

47. For a good summation of studies on displacement, see R. Hesseling, "Displacement: A Review of the Empirical Literature," in R. V. Clarke, ed., *Crime Prevention Studies,* Vol. 3 (Monsey, NY: Willow Tree Press, 1994).

48. C. S. Lewis, "The Humanitarian Theory of Punishment," *Res Judicatae,* Vol. 6 (1953), pp. 224–225.

49. Tracey L. Snell, *Capital Punishment, 1999* (Washington, DC: Bureau of Justice Statistics, 2000).

50. See, for example, W. C. Bailey, "Deterrence and the Death Penalty for Murders in Utah: A Time Series Analysis," *Journal of Contemporary Law,* Vol. 5, No. 1 (1978), pp. 1–20; and William Bailey, "An Analysis of the Deterrent Effects of the Death Penalty for Murder in California," *Southern California Law Review,* Vol. 52, No. 3 (1979), pp. 743–764.

51. See, for example, B. E. Forst, "The Deterrent Effect of Capital Punishment: A Cross-State Analysis of the 1960s," *Minnesota Law Review,* Vol. 61 (1977), pp. 743–764.

52. Scott H. Decker and Carol W. Kohfeld, "Capital Punishment and Executions in the Lone Star State: A Deterrence Study," *Criminal Justice Research Bulletin* (Criminal Justice Center, Sam Houston State University), Vol. 3, No. 12 (1988).

53. Tomislav V. Kovandzic, Lynne M. Vieraitis, and Denise Paquette Boots, "Does the Death Penalty Save Lives? New Evidence from State Panel Data, 1977 to 2006," *Crime and Public Policy,* Vol. 8, No. 4 (2009), p. 803.

54. Committee on Law and Justice, *Deterrence and the Death Penalty* (Washington, DC: National Academy of Sciences, 2012).

55. Information and quotes in this paragraph are from the Death Penalty Information Center's Web site, http://www.deathpenaltyinfo.org.

56. As some of the evidence presented before the Supreme Court in *Furman* v. *Georgia,* 408 U.S. 238 (1972), suggested.

57. *McCleskey* v. *Kemp,* 481 U.S. 279 (1987).

58. Formerly known as the National Committee to Prevent Wrongful Executions.

59. The Constitution Project, *Mandatory Justice: Eighteen Reforms to the Death Penalty* (Washington, DC: The Constitution Project, 2001). The Constitution Project, www.constitutionproject.org

60. E. Ann Carson, *Prisoners in 2015* (Washington, DC Bureau of Justice Statistics, 2016).

61. Marvin Wolfgang, Thorsten Sellin, and Robert Figlio, *Delinquency in a Birth Cohort* (Chicago: University of Chicago Press, 1972).

62. Z. Hamilton, C. M. Campbell, J. van Wormer, A. Kigerl, and B. Posey, "Impact of Swift and Certain Sanctions: Evaluation of Washington State's Policy for Offenders on Community Supervision," *Criminology and Public Policy,* Vol. 15, No. 4 (2016), pp. 1009–1072.

63. Randy Martin, Robert J. Mutchnick, and W. Timothy Austin, *Criminological Thought: Pioneers Past and Present* (New York: Macmillan, 1990), p. 17.

64. Ibid., p. 18.

65. Walter Moore, "An Alternative Take on the State of Los Angeles," *Press-Telegram*, April 26, 2012, http://www.presstelegram.com/opinions/ci_20461647/oped-an-alternate-take-state-los-angeles (accessed February 2, 2017).

66. Ibid.

CHAPTER 4: EARLY BIOLOGICAL PERSPECTIVES ON CRIMINAL BEHAVIOR

1. Marco Visscher, "How Food Can Cut Crime," *Ode Magazine*, February 9, 2010, http://www.care2.com/greenliving/how-food-can-cut-crime.html/4 (accessed February 3, 2017).

2. C. B. Gesch, S. M. Hammond, S. E. Hampson, A. Eves, and M. J. Crowder, "Influence of Supplementary Vitamins, Minerals and Essential Fatty Acids on the Antisocial Behavior of Young Adult Prisoners: Randomized, Placebo-Controlled Trial," *British Journal of Psychiatry*, Vol. 181 (July 2002), pp. 22–28.

3. Visscher, op. cit.

4. C. Ray Jeffery, "Biological Perspectives," *Journal of Criminal Justice Education*, Vol. 4, No. 2 (Fall 1993), pp. 292–293.

5. Anthony Walsh and Craig Hemmens, eds., *Introduction to Criminology: A Text/Reader*, 2nd ed. (Thousand Oaks, CA: Sage, 2011), p. 272.

6. Auguste Comte, *A System of Positive Polity*, trans. John Henry Bridges (New York: Franklin, 1875; originally published in four volumes, 1851–1854).

7. See K. L. Henwood and N. F. Pidgeon, "Qualitative Research and Psychological Theorising," *British Journal of Psychology*, Vol. 83 (1992), pp. 97–111.

8. Cesare Lombroso, "Introduction," in Gina Lombroso-Ferrero, *Criminal Man According to the Classification of Cesare Lombroso* (1911; reprint, Montclair, NJ: Patterson Smith, 1972), p. xiv.

9. Robert Fletcher, "The New School of Criminal Anthropology," *The American Anthropologist*, Vol. IV, No. 3 (July 1891), pp. 201–236.

10. Cesare Lombroso, "Introduction," in Lombroso-Ferrero, *Criminal Man According to the Classification of Cesare Lombroso*, p. xv. 1911.

11. Charles Darwin, *Descent of Man: And Selection in Relation to Sex*, rev. ed. (London: John Murray, 1874), p. 137.

12. The English-language version appeared in 1895 as Cesare Lombroso, *The Female Offender* (New York: D. Appleton, 1895).

13. Marvin Wolfgang, "Cesare Lombroso," in Hermann Mannheim, *Pioneers in Criminology*, 2nd ed. (Montclair, NJ: Patterson Smith, 1972), p. 254.

14. Charles Goring, *The English Convict: A Statistical Study* (London: His Majesty's Stationery Office, 1913; reprint, Montclair, NJ: Patterson Smith, 1972), p. 15.

15. Ibid.

16. Earnest A. Hooton, *Crime and the Man* (Cambridge, MA: Harvard University Press, 1939; reprint, Westport, CT: Greenwood Press, 1972).

17. Earnest A. Hooton, *The American Criminal: An Anthropological Study* (Cambridge, MA: Harvard University Press, 1939).

18. Nichole Hahn Rafter, "Criminal Anthropology in the United States," *Criminology*, Vol. 30, No. 4 (1992), p. 525.

19. L. Arseneault et al., "Minor Physical Anomalies and Family Adversity as Risk Factors for Violent Delinquency in Adolescence," *American Journal of Psychiatry*, Vol. 157, No. 6 (June 2000), pp. 917–923.

20. William H. Sheldon, *Varieties of Delinquent Youth* (New York: Harper & Brothers, 1949).

21. Ibid.

22. See Joseph D. McInerney, "Genes and Behavior: A Complex Relationship," *Judicature*, Vol. 83, No. 3 (November–December 1999).

23. Sir Francis Galton, *Inquiry into Human Faculty and Its Development*, 2nd ed. (London: J. M. Dent and Sons, 1907).

24. Richard Louis Dugdale, *The Jukes: A Study in Crime, Pauperism, Disease, and Heredity*, 3rd ed. (New York: G. P. Putnam's Sons, 1895).

25. Arthur H. Estabrook, *The Jukes in 1915* (Washington, DC: Carnegie Institute of Washington, 1916).

26. Henry Herbert Goddard, *The Kallikak Family: A Study in the Heredity of Feeblemindedness* (New York: Macmillan, 1912).

27. See Nicole Hahn Rafter, *Creating Born Criminals* (Urbana: University of Illinois Press, 1997).

28. See Nicole Hahn Rafter, ed., *White Trash: The Eugenics Family Studies, 1877–1919* (Boston: Northeastern University Press, 1988).

29. *Buck v. Bell*, 274 U.S. 200, 207 (1927).

30. P. A. Jacobs, M. Brunton, and M. Melville, "Aggressive Behavior, Mental Subnormality, and the XYY Male," *Nature*, Vol. 208 (1965), p. 1351.

31. Webster's defines *karyotype* as "a photomicrograph of metaphase chromosomes in a standard array" (*Webster's II New College Dictionary* [Chicago, IL: Houghton Mifflin Harcourt, 2005], p. 618).

32. Anthony Walsh, *Biology and Criminology: The Biosocial Synthesis* (New York: Routledge, 2009), p. 268.

33. See David A. Jones, *History of Criminology: A Philosophical Perspective* (Westport, CT: Greenwood Press, 1986), p. 124.

34. As reported by S. A. Mednick and J. Volavka, "Biology and Crime," in N. Morris and M. Tonry, *Crime and Justice: An Annual Review of Research*, Vol. 2 (Chicago: University of Chicago Press, 1980), pp. 85–158; and D. A. Andrews and James Bonta, *The Psychology of Criminal Conduct* (Cincinnati, OH: Anderson, 1994), pp. 126–127.

35. T. Sarbin and J. Miller, "Demonism Revisited: The XYY Chromosomal Anomaly," *Issues in Criminology*, Vol. 5 (1970), p. 199.

36. Johannes Lange, *Verbrechen als Schicksal* (Leipzig: Georg Thieme, 1929).

37. Karl O. Christiansen, "A Preliminary Study of Criminality among Twins," in Sarnoff Mednick and Karl Christiansen, eds., *Biosocial Bases of Criminal Behavior* (New York: Gardner Press, 1977).

38. The Minnesota Twin Family Study, http://www.psych.umn.edu/psylabs/mtfs (accessed August 10, 2007).

39. T. J. Bouchard et al., "Sources of Human Psychological Differences: The Minnesota Study of Twins Reared Apart," *Science*, Vol. 250, No. 4978 (1990), pp. 223–228.

40. Peter McGuffin and Anita Thapar, "Genetic Basis of Bad Behaviour in Adolescents," *Lancet*, Vol. 350 (August 9, 1997), pp. 411–412.

41. Wendy Slutske et al., "Modeling Genetic and Environmental Influences in the Etiology of Conduct Disorder: A Study of 2,682 Adult Twin Pairs," *Journal of Abnormal Psychology*, Vol. 106, No. 2 (1997), pp. 266–279.

42. Louise Arseneault et al., "Strong Genetic Effects on Cross-Situational Antisocial Behaviour among 5-Year-Old Children

According to Mothers, Teachers, Examiner-Observers, and Twins' Self-Reports," *Journal of Child Psychology and Psychiatry,* Vol. 44, No. 6 (September 2003), pp. 832–848.

43. Ibid.

44. Jeanette Taylor et al., "Genetic and Environmental Influences on Psychopathy Trait Dimensions in a Community Sample of Male Twins," *Journal of Abnormal Child Psychology,* Vol. 31, No. 6 (December 2003), pp. 633–645.

45. S. H. Rhee, and I. D. Waldman, "Genetic and Environmental Influences on Antisocial Behavior: A Meta-Analysis of Twin and Adoption Studies," *Psychological Bulletin,* Vol. 128 (2002), 490–529.

46. Konrad Lorenz, *On Aggression* (New York: Harcourt, Brace and World, 1966).

47. Ibid., p. 23.

48. Ibid., p. 38.

49. Ibid., p. 249.

50. Ibid.

51. Edward O. Wilson, *Sociobiology: The New Synthesis* (Cambridge, MA: Harvard Univ. Press, 1980).

52. Arthur Fisher, "Sociobiology: Science or Ideology?" *Society,* July/August 1992, pp. 67–79.

53. John H. Beckstrom, *Evolutionary Jurisprudence: Prospects and Limitations on the Use of Modern Darwinism Throughout the Legal Process* (Champaign, IL: Univ. of Illinois Press, 1989).

54. Michael Ruse, "Edward O. Wilson on Sociobiology," *The Chronicle of Higher Education,* March 31, 2010.

55. Kevin M. Beaver, John Paul Wright, Matt DeLisi, and Michael G. Vaughn, "Genetic Influences on the Stability of Law Self-Control: Results from a Longitudinal Sample of Twins," *Journal of Criminal Justice,* Vol. 36 (2008), pp. 478–485.

56. Taken from "Hope for the 'Hopeless,'" *Crime Times,* Vol. 10, No. 2 (2004), p. 2.

CHAPTER 5: BIOSOCIAL AND OTHER CONTEMPORARY PERSPECTIVES

1. Marc Lallianilla, "Genetics May Provide Clues to Newtown Shooting," *Livescience,* http://www.livescience.com/25853-newtown-shooter-dna.html December 28, 2012 (accessed February 3, 2017).

2. Rick Weiss, "Genome Project Completed," *Washington Post,* April 15, 2003, p. A6.

3. James Watson and Francis Crick, "Molecular Structure of Nucleic Acids: A Structure for Deoxyribose Nucleic Acid," *Nature,* Vol. 171 (April 1953), p. 737.

4. Mary Kugler, "What Are Genes, DNA and Chromosomes?" About.com, http://rarediseases.about.com/od/geneticdisorders/a/genesbasics.htm (accessed February 12, 2017).

5. Ibid.

6. McKusick-Nathans Institute of Genetic Medicine, "The 1,000 Genomes Project," The Johns Hopkins University, 2010, http://www.hopkinsmedicine.org/geneticmedicine/news/NewsletterStories/2010_12/2010_12_1000_genomes.html (accessed January 3, 2013).

7. Much of the information and some of the wording in this section come from the National Human Genome Research Institute's Web page, http://www.nhgri.nih.gov/HGP (accessed November 16, 2007).

8. Geoffrey Cowley and Carol Hallin, "The Genetics of Bad Behavior: A Study Links Violence to Heredity," *Newsweek,* November 1, 1993, p. 57.

9. H. G. Brunner, M. Nelen, X. O. Breakefield, H. H. Ropers, B. A. van Oost, "Abnormal Behavior Associated with a Point Mutation in the Structural Gene for Monoamine Oxidase A," *Science,* Vol. 262, No. 5133 (Oct. 22, 1993), pp. 578–580.

10. Quoted in Tim Friend, "Violence Linked to Gene Defect: Pleasure Deficit May Be the Spark," *USA Today,* May 9, 1996. See the original research at Kenneth Blum et al., "Reward Deficiency Syndrome," *American Scientist,* Vol. 84 (March/April 1996), pp. 132–145, http://www.sigmaxi.org/amsci/Articles/96Articles/Blum-full.html (accessed January 5, 2005).

11. See, for example, M. Rutter, H. Giller, and A. Hagell, *Antisocial Behavior by Young People* (Cambridge: Cambridge University Press, 1998).

12. Avshalom Caspi et al., "Role of Genotype in the Cycle of Violence in Maltreated Children," *Science,* Vol. 298, No. 2 (August 2002), p. 851.

13. For more information on the Dunedin Multidisciplinary Health and Development Study, see T. E. Moffitt et al., *Sex Differences in Antisocial Behavior: Conduct Disorder, Delinquency and Violence in the Dunedin Longitudinal Study* (Cambridge: Cambridge University Press, 2001). Visit the Dunedin Multidisciplinary Health and Development Research Unit on the Web at http://healthsci.otago.ac.nz/dsm/dmhdru.

14. Ibid.

15. Nilsson Oreland et al., "Monoamine Oxidases: Activities, Genotypes and the Shaping of Behaviour," *Journal of Neural Transmission,* April 12, 2007; and Rickard L. Sjöberg et al., "Adolescent Girls and Criminal Activity: Role of MAOA-LPR Genotype and Psychosocial Factor," *American Journal of Medical Genetics Part B: Neuropsychiatric Genetics,* Vol. 144B, No. 2 (October 2006), pp. 159–164.

16. Kevin M. Beaver, Matt DeLisi, Michael G. Vaughn, and John Paul Wright, "The Intersection of Genes and Neuropsychological Deficits in the Prediction of Adolescent Delinquency and Low Self-Control," *International Journal of Offender Therapy and Comparative Criminology,* Vol. 20, No. 10 (2008), p. 17.

17. National Geographic Television, "Inside the Warrior Gene," http://natgeotv.com/ca/inside-the-warrior-gene/about (accessed February 3, 2017).

18. A. E. Baum et al., "A Genome-Wide Association Study Implicates Diacylglycerol Kinase Eta (DGKH) and Several Other Genes in the Etiology of Bipolar Disorder," *Molecular Psychiatry,* advance online publication, http://doi:10.1038/sj.mp.4002012 (accessed May 8, 2007).

19. National Institute on Drug Abuse, "Genetics of Addiction: A Research Update from the National Institute on Drug Abuse," http://www.drugabuse.gov/tib/genetics.html (accessed May 1, 2010).

20. Nathalie M. G. Fontaine, Eamon J. P. McCory et al., "Predictors and Outcomes of Joint Trajectories of Callous–Unemotional Traits and Conduct Problems in Childhood," *Journal of Abnormal Psychology,* Vol. 123, No. 3 (August 2011), pp. 740–741.

21. Twins Early Development Study, "TEDS," http://www.teds.ac.uk/about.html (accessed January 27, 2012).

22. Danielle Boisvert, John Paul Wright, Valerie Knopik, and Jamie Vaske, "A Twin Study of Sex Differences in Self-Control," *Justice Quarterly,* Vol. 30, No. 3 (2013), pp. 529–559.

23. Anthony Walsh, "Behavior Genetics and Anomic/Strain Theory," in Anthony Walsh and CaigCraig Hemmens, eds., *Introduction to Criminology: A Text/Reader* (Thousand Oaks, CA: Sage, 2010), p. 284.

24. "2017 Winner of the Stockholm Prize in Criminology," Stockholm University, http://www.su.se/english/about/prizes-awards/the-stockholm-prize-in-criminology/2017-winner-of-the-stockholm-prize-in-criminology-1.309600 (accessed January 19, 2017).

25. The University of Utah, Genetic Science Learning Center, "Epigenetics," http://learn.genetics.utah.edu/content/epigenetics (accessed February 12, 2017).

26. J. D. McInerney, "Genes and Behavior: A Complex Relationship," *Judicature*, Vol. 80, No. 3 (1999), pp. 112–115.

27. See "The Genome Changes Everything: A Talk with Matt Ridley," http://www.edge.org/3rd_culture/ridley03/ridley_print.html (accessed February 12, 2017).

28. Ananya Mandal, "What Is DNA Methylation?" *Medical News*, http://www.news-medical.net/health/DNA-Methylation-What-is-DNA-Methylation.aspx (accessed February 12, 2017).

29. Theresa Phillips, "The Role of Methylation in Gene Expression," *Nature Education*, Vol. 1, No. 1 (2008), p. 116.

30. Alison Gopnik, "Can Poverty Affect Our Genes? Poverty's Vicious Cycle Can Affect our Genes," *Wall Street Journal*, September 25, 2014, http://www.wsj.com/video/povertys-vicious-cycle-can-affect-our-genes/807808BA-C792-49E0-8A72-5C265201ABF9.html?mod=djemTEW_h (accessed February 12, 2017).

31. Robert Kumsta, Elisabeth Hummel, Frances S. Chen, and Markus Heinrichs, "Epigenetic Regulation of the Oxytocin Receptor Gene: Implications for Behavioral Neuroscience," *Frontiers in Neuroscience*, Vol. 7 (2013), p. 83.

32. Carsten K. W. De Dreu, "Oxytocin Modulates Cooperation within and Competition between Groups: An Integrative Review and Research Agenda," *Hormones and Behavior*, Vol. 61, No. 3 (March 2012), pp. 491–428.

33. Virginia Hughes, "Mice Inherit Specific Memories, Because Epigenetics?", National Geographic, December 1, 2013, http://phenomena.nationalgeographic.com/2013/12/01/mice-inherit-specific-memories-because-epigenetics/ (accessed May 1, 2017).

34. Matt Ridley, "What Makes You Who You Are?" *Time*, June 2, 2003, pp. 55–63.

35. See Adrian Raine et al., "Prefrontal Glucose Deficits in Murderers Lacking Psychosocial Deprivation," *Neuropsychiatry, Neuropsychology, and Behavioral Neurology*, Vol. 11, No. 1 (1998), pp. 1–7; and Adrian Raine et al., "Selective Reductions in Prefrontal Glucose Metabolism in Murderers," *Biological Psychiatry*, Vol. 36 (September 1, 1994), pp. 319–332.

36. "PET Study: Looking inside the Minds of Murderers," *Crime Times*, Vol. 1, No. 1–2 (1995), http://www.crime-times.org/95a/w95ap1.htm (accessed November 15, 2006).

37. Ibid.

38. Raine et al., "Selective Reductions in Prefrontal Glucose Metabolism in Murderers."

39. Adrian Raine, Monte Buchsbaum, and Lori LaCasse, "Brain Abnormalities in Murderers Indicated by Positron Emission Tomography," in Kevin M. Beaver and Anthony Walsh, eds., *Biosocial Theories of Crime* (Burlington, VT: Ashgate, 2010), pp. 465–478.

40. Adrian Raine, J. Reid Meloy, Susan Bihrle, Jackie Stoddard, Lori LaCasse, and Monte S. Buchsbaum, "Reduced Prefrontal and Increased Subcortical Brain Functioning Assessed Using Positron Emission Tomography in Predatory and Affective Murderers," in Kevin M. Beaver and Anthony Walsh, eds., *Biosocial Theories of Crime* (Burlington, VT: Ashgate, 2010), pp. 479–492.

41. "Researchers Explore the Brain for Clues to the Causes of Anti-Social Behavior," AAAS 2011 Annual Meeting News, February 25, 2011, http://news.aaas.org/2011_annual_meeting/0225nature-nurture-in-antisocial-behavior.shtml (accessed January 27, 2011).

42. "Kids' Brains May Hold Clues to Future Criminals," CNN Health, February 21, 2011, http://thechart.blogs.cnn.com/2011/02/21/kids-brains-may-hold-clues-to-future-criminals (accessed January 27, 2012).

43. James H. Fallon, "Neuroanatomical Background to Understanding the Brain of the Young Psychopath," *Ohio State Journal of Criminal Law*, Vol. 3 (2006), pp. 340–367.

44. Daniel Strueber, Monika Lueck, and Gerhard Roth, "The Violent Brain," *Scientific American*, November 29, 2006, http://www.scientificamerican.com/article.cfm?id=the-violent-brain (accessed February 21, 2012).

45. Katie Moisse, "Communication Breakdown in Brain Caused by a Gene Defect May Contribute to Schizophrenia," *Scientific American*, April 1, 2010, http://www.scientificamerican.com/article.cfm?id=schizophrenia-gene-mechanism (accessed May 20, 2010). See also Torfi Sigurdsson et al., "Impaired Hippocampal-Prefrontal Synchrony in a Genetic Mouse Model of Schizophrenia," *Nature*, Vol. 464, No. 7289 (2010), pp. 763–667.

46. See, for example, A. R. Mawson and K. J. Jacobs, "Corn Consumption, Tryptophan, and Cross National Homicide Rates," *Journal of Orthomolecular Psychiatry*, Vol. 7 (1978), pp. 227–230; and A. Hoffer, "The Relation of Crime to Nutrition," *Humanist in Canada*, Vol. 8 (1975), p. 8.

47. "Flu in Pregnancy Changes Fetal Brain," *New Scientist*, January 30, 2010, p. 15.

48. Douglas S. Massey, "Segregation and Stratification: A Biosocial Perspective," in Kevin M. Beaver and Anthony Walsh, eds., *Biosocial Theories of Crime* (Burlington, VT: Ashgate, 2010), p. 62.

49. "Childhood Abuse Hurts the Brain," *Harvard University Gazette*, May 22, 2003, http://www.news.harvard.edu/gazette/2003/05.22/01-brain.html (accessed June 4, 2010).

50. Ibid.

51. Violence Makes a Kid's Brain Like That of a Soldier," *New Scientist*, December 10, 2011, p. 12.

52. Christian Jarrett, "Predicting Reoffending?" *The Psychologist*, April 23, 2013.

53. See Proceedings of the National Academy of Sciences of the United States of America, *Biological Embedding of Early Social Adversity: From Fruit Flies to Kindergartners—the Sackler Colloquium*, October 16, 2012, http://www.pnas.org/content/109/suppl.2 (accessed February 2, 2017).

54. Marla B. Sokolowski, W. Thomas Boyce, and Bruce S. McEwen, "Scarred for Life?," *New Scientist*, January 26, 2013, p. 28.

55. Antoine Lutz et al., "Long-Term Meditators Self-Induce High-Amplitude Gamma Synchrony during Mental Practice," *Proceedings of the National Academy of Sciences*, Vol. 101, No. 46 (November 16, 2004), pp. 16369–16373.

56. Jeffrey M. Schwartz and Sharon Begley, *The Mind and the Brain: Neuroplasticity and the Power of Mental Force* (New York: Regan Books, 2002).

57. Anthony Walsh, *Biosocial Criminology: Introduction and Integration* (Cincinnati, OH: Anderson, 2002), p. ix.

58. Ibid.

59. D. Hill and W. Sargent, "A Case of Matricide," *Lancet*, Vol. 244 (1943), pp. 526–527.

60. William Dufty, *Sugar Blues* (Pandor, PA: Chilton, 1975).

61. See *Court TV*'s Crime Library, "Twinkies as a Defense," http://www.crimelibrary.com/criminal_mind/psychology/insanity/7.html (accessed August 8, 2007).

62. Nanci Hellmich, "Sweets May Not Be Culprit in Hyper Kids," *USA Today*, February 3, 1994, p. 1A (reporting on a study published in the *New England Journal of Medicine*).

63. Ibid., p. 1A.

64. See, for example, C. Hawley and R. E. Buckley, "Food Dyes and Hyperkinetic Children," *Academy Therapy*, Vol. 10 (1974), pp. 27–32; and Alexander Schauss, *Diet, Crime and Delinquency* (Berkeley, CA: Parker House, 1980).

65. "Special Report: Measuring Your Life with Coffee Spoons," *Tufts University Diet and Nutrition Letter*, Vol. 2, No. 2 (April 1984), pp. 3–6.

66. See, for example, "Special Report: Does What You Eat Affect Your Mood and Actions?," *Tufts University Diet and Nutrition Letter*, Vol. 2, No. 12 (February 1985), pp. 4–6.

67. See *Tufts University Diet and Nutrition Newsletter*, Vol. 2, No. 11 (January 1985), p. 2; and "Special Report: Why Sugar Continues to Concern Nutritionists," *Tufts University Diet and Nutrition Letter*, Vol. 3, No. 3 (May 1985), pp. 3–6.

68. "School Study: Supplementation Decreases Delinquent Behaviors, Raises IQ," *Crime Times*, Vol. 6, No. 2 (2000), p. 3, http://www.crimetimes.org/00b/w00bp3.htm (accessed March 10, 2012).

69. S. J. Schoenthaler and D. Bier, "The Effect of Vitamin-Mineral Supplementation on Juvenile Delinquency among American Schoolchildren: A Randomized, Double-blind Placebo-controlled Trial," *Journal of Alternative Complementary Medicine*, Vol. 6, No. 1 (February 2000), pp. 31–35.

70. I. B. Helland et al., "Maternal Supplements with Very-Long-Chain Omega-3 Fatty Acids during Pregnancy and Lactation Augment Children's IQ at 4 Years of Age," *Pediatrics*, Vol. 111, No. 1 (January 2003), pp. 39–44.

71. C. Iribarren et al., "Dietary Intake of Omega-3, Omega-6 Fatty Acids and Fish: Relationship with Hostility in Young Adults—The CARDIA Study," *European Journal of Clinical Nutrition*, Vol. 50, No. 1 (January 2004), pp. 24–31.

72. David Benton, "The Impact of Diet on Anti-Social, Violent and Criminal Behaviour," *Neuroscience and Biobehavioral Reviews*, Vol. 31 (2007), pp. 752–774.

73. Avery Johnson, "Links Tighten between IQ, Breast-Feeding," *The Wall Street Journal*, July 29, 2013, http://online.wsj.com/article/SB10001424127887324809004578635783141433600.html (accessed February 3, 2017).

74. Roger D. Masters, Brian Hone, and Anil Doshi, "Environmental Pollution, Neurotoxicity, and Criminal Violence," in J. Rose, ed., *Environmental Toxicology* (London and New York: Gordon and Breach, 1997).

75. Peter Montague, "Toxics and Violent Crime," *Rachel's Environment and Health Weekly*, No. 551 (June 19, 1997).

76. See, for example, Rick Nevin, "How Lead Exposure Relates to Temporal Changes in IQ, Violent Crime, and Unwed Pregnancy," *Environmental Research*, Vol. 83, No.1 (May 2000), pp. 1–22.

77. Quoted in Alison Motluck, "Pollution May Lead to a Life of Crime," *New Scientist*, Vol. 154, No. 2084 (May 31, 1997), p. 4.

78. L. Goldschmidt, N. L. Day, and G. A. Richardson, "Effects of Prenatal Marijuana Exposure on Child Behavior Problems at Age 10," *Neurotoxicology and Teratology*, Vol. 22, No. 3 (May/June 2000), pp. 325–336.

79. David Fergusson, Lianne Woodward, and L. John Horwood, "Maternal Smoking during Pregnancy and Psychiatric Adjustment in Late Adolescence," *Archives of General Psychiatry*, Vol. 55 (August 1998), pp. 721–727.

80. Jacob F. Orlebeke, Dirk L. Knol, and Frank C. Verhulst, "Increase in Child Behavior Problems Resulting from Maternal Smoking during Pregnancy," *Archives of Environmental Health*, Vol. 52, No. 4 (July/August 1997), pp. 317–321.

81. Travis C. Pratt, Jean Marie McGloin, and Noelle E. Fearn, "Maternal Cigarette Smoking during Pregnancy and Criminal/Deviant Behavior: A Meta-Analysis," *International Journal of Offender Therapy and Comparative Criminology*, Vol. 50, No. 6 (2006), pp. 672–690.

82. See, for example, Ann Pytkowicz Streissguth et al., "Fetal Alcohol Syndrome in Adolescents and Adults," *Journal of the American Medical Association*, Vol. 265, No. 15 (April 17, 1991).

83. Ibid.

84. Ibid, p. 29.

85. Laura Sanders, "Microbes and the Mind," *New Scientist*, April 2, 2016, p. 23-John Cryan and Timothy Dinan, "A Light on Psychobiotics," *New Scientist*, January 25, 2014, pp. 28–29.

86. "Wiping Out Gut Bacteria Impairs Brain," *Science News*, June 25, 2016, p. 14.

87. Tresa M. Roebuck, Sarah N. Mattson, and Edward P. Riley, "Behavioral and Psychosocial Profiles of Alcohol-Exposed Children," *Alcoholism: Clinical and Experimental Research*, Vol. 23, No. 6 (June 1999), pp. 1070–1076.

88. See, for example, D. H. Fishbein, "The Psychobiology of Female Aggression," *Criminal Justice and Behavior*, Vol. 19 (1992), pp. 99–126.

89. T. I. Paus et al., "Sexual Dimorphism in the Adolescent Brain: Role of Testosterone and Androgen Receptor in Global and Local White Matter," *Hormones and Behavior*, Vol. 57 (2010), pp. 63–75.

90. See, for example, R. T. Rada, D. R. Laws, and R. Kellner, "Plasma Testosterone Levels in the Rapist," *Psychosomatic Medicine*, Vol. 38 (1976), pp. 257–268.

91. "The Insanity of Steroid Abuse," *Newsweek*, May 23, 1988, p. 75.

92. Dan Olweus et al., "Testosterone, Aggression, Physical and Personality Dimensions in Normal Adolescent Males," *Psychosomatic Medicine*, Vol. 42 (1980), pp. 253–269.

93. Richard Udry, "Biosocial Models of Adolescent Problem Behaviors," *Social Biology*, Vol. 37 (1990), pp. 1–10.

94. Dan Olweus, "Testosterone and Adrenaline: Aggressive Antisocial Behavior in Normal Adolescent Males," in Sarnoff A. Mednick, Terrie E. Moffitt, and Susan A. Stack, eds., *The Causes of Crime: New Biological Approaches* (Cambridge: Cambridge University Press, 1987), pp. 263–282.

95. Alan Booth and D. Wayne Osgood, "The Influence of Testosterone on Deviance in Adulthood: Assessing and Explaining the Relationship," *Criminology*, Vol. 31, No. 1 (1993), p. 93.

96. E. G. Stalenheim et al., "Testosterone as a Biological Marker in Psychopathy and Alcoholism," *Psychiatry Research*, Vol. 77, No. 2 (February 1998), pp. 79–88.

97. Michelle M. Wirth and Oliver C. Schultheiss, "Basal Testosterone Moderates Responses to Anger Faces in Humans," *Physiology and Behavior*, Vol. 90 (2007), pp. 496–505.

98. Ibid., p. 502.

99. Richard Udry, Luther Talbert, and Naomi Morris, "Biosocial Foundations for Adolescent Female Sexuality," *Demography*, Vol. 23 (1986), pp. 217–227.

100. James M. Dabbs, Jr., and Marian F. Hargrove, "Age, Testosterone, and Behavior among Female Prison Inmates," *Psychosomatic Medicine*, Vol. 59 (1997), pp. 447–480.

101. A. Maras et al., "Association of Testosterone and Dihydrotestosterone with Externalizing Behavior in Adolescent Boys and Girls," *Psychoneuroendocrinology*, Vol. 28, No. 7 (October 2003), pp. 932–940.

102. *Regina* v. *English*, unreported, Norwich Crown Court, November 10, 1981.

103. Paul C. Bernhardt, "Influences of Serotonin and Testosterone in Aggression and Dominance: Convergence with Social Psychology," *Current Directions in Psychological Science*, Vol. 6, No. 2 (April 1997), pp. 44–48.

104. Don Cherek and Scott Lane, "Effects of d,1-Fenfluramine on Aggressive and Impulsive Responding in Adult Males with a History of Conduct Disorder," *Psychopharmacology*, Vol. 146 (1999), pp. 473–481.

105. Ibid.

106. Anastasia Toufexis, "Seeking the Roots of Violence," *Time*, April 19, 1993.

107. See, for example, Jeffrey Halperin et al., "Serotonergic Function in Aggressive and Nonaggressive Boys with ADHD," *American Journal of Psychiatry*, Vol. 151, No. 2 (February 1994), pp. 243–248.

108. Roger D. Masters, Brian Hone, and Anil Doshi, "Environmental Pollution, Neurotoxicity, and Criminal Violence," in J. Rose, ed., *Environmental Toxicology* (London and New York: Gordon and Breach, 1997).

109. Terrie E. Moffitt et al., "Whole Blood Serotonin Relates to Violence in an Epidemiological Study," *Biological Psychiatry*, Vol. 43, No. 6 (March 15, 1998), pp. 446–457.

110. Ibid.

111. H. Soderstrom et al., "New Evidence for an Association between the CSF HVA:5–HIAA Ratio and Psychopathic Traits," *Journal of Neurology, Neurosurgery and Psychiatry*, Vol. 74 (2003), pp. 918–921.

112. Angela D. Crews, "Biological Theory," in J. Mitchell Miller, ed., *21st Century Criminology: A Reference Handbook* (Thousand Oaks, CA: Sage, 2009), p. 196.

113. Keith McBurnett et al., "Low Salivary Cortisol and Persistent Aggression in Boys Referred for Disruptive Behavior," *Archives of General Psychiatry*, Vol. 57, No. 1 (January 2000), pp. 38–43.

114. Ibid.

115. See E. G. Stalenheim, L. von Knorring, and L. Wide, "Serum Levels of Thyroid Hormones as Biological Markers in a Swedish Forensic Psychiatric Population," *Biological Psychiatry*, Vol. 43, No. 10 (May 15, 1998), pp. 755–761; and P. O. Alm et al., "Criminality and Psychopathy as Related to Thyroid Activity in Former Juvenile Delinquents," *Acta Psychiatrica Scandinavica*, Vol. 94, No. 2 (August 1996), pp. 112–117.

116. Paul J. Zak, "The Trust Molecule," WSJ.com, April 27, 2012, http://professional.wsj.com/article/SB100014240527023048113045773657829953203 66.html?mod=WSJPRO_hps_MIDDLESecondNews#printMode (accessed February 4, 2017).

117. Michale F. Lorber, "Psychophysiology of Aggression, Psychopathy, and Conduct Problems: A Meta-Analysis," *Psychological Bulletin*, Vol. 130 (2004), pp. 531–552; and Jame Ortiz and Adrian Raine, "Heart Rate Level and Antisocial Behavior in Children and Adolescents: A Meta-Analysis," *Journal of the American Academy of Child and Adolescent Psychiatry*, Vol. 43 (2004), pp. 154–162.

118. Adrian Raine, Annis Lai-Chu Fung, Jill Portnoy, Olivia Choy, and Victoria L. Spring, "Low Heart Rate as a Risk Factor for Child and Adolescent Proactive Aggressive and Impulsive Pyschopathic Behavior," *Aggressive Behavior* (2014), doi: 10.1002/ab.21523.

119. Jill Portnoy, Adrian Raine, Frances R. Chen, Dustin Pardini, Rolf Loeber, and J. Richards Jennings, "Heart Rate and Antisocial Behavior: The Mediating Role of Impulsive Sensation Seeking," *Criminology*, 2014, early electronic release; doi: 10.1111/1745-9125.12038.

120. Adriane Raine, "Biosocial Studies of Antisocial and Violent Behavior in Children and Adults: A Review," *Journal of Abnormal Child Psychology*, Vol. 30 No. 4 (2002), pp. 311–326.

121. Marvin Zuckerman, *Sensation Seeking and Risky Behavior* (Washington, DC: American Psychological Association, 2007).

122. Adrian Raine, "The Role of Prefrontal Deficits, Low Autonomic Arousal, and Early Health Factors in the Development of Antisocial and Aggressive Behavior in Children," *Journal of Child Psychology and Psychiatry*, Vol. 43 (2002), pp. 417–434.

123. Olivia Choy, et al., "Explaining the Gender Gap in Crime: The Role of Heart Rate," *Criminology*, 2017, doi: 10.1111/1745-9125.12138 (accessed November 25, 2017).

124. Ibid., p. 14.

125. Ibid., p. 15.

126. Neil Carlson, *Physiology of Behavior* (Upper Saddle River, New Jersey: Pearson, 2013).

127. H. Kurnlawman, A. V. Maslov, M. Penchenizkly, "Stress Detection from Speech and Galvanic Skin Response Signals," paper presented at the 26th International Symposium on Computer-Based Medical Systems (2013).

128. Jonathan Jackson and Ioanna Gouseti, "Fear of Crime," in J. Mitchell Miller, ed., *The Encyclopedia of Theoretical Criminology* (Blackwell, 2014).

129. Nanucha Teixeira da Silvaa, Pedro Schestatskya, Pablo Brea Wincklerc, Giovanni Abrahão Saluma, Alana Wypyszynski Petrocelid, and Elizeth Paz da Silva Heldta, "Oppositionality and Sympathetic Skin Response in Adolescents: Specific Associations with the Headstrong/Hurtful Dimension," *Biological Psychology*, Vol. 103 (December 2014), pp. 242–247.

130. C. Iria, F. Barbosa, and R. Paixao, "Reduced Galvanic Skin Responses to Facial Expressions of Emotions in Psychopaths: An Exploratory Study," *International Journal of Psychophysiology*, Vol. 1 (2008), p. 268.

131. Oshumi, T and Ohira, H. "The Positive Side of Psychopathy: Emotional Detachment in Psychopathy and Rational Decision-Making in the Ultimatum Game," *Personality and Individual Differences*, Vol. 49 (2010), pp. 451–456.

132. Leah E. Daigle, "Biochemical Theories of Criminal Behavior," in Richard A Wright and J. Mitchell Miler, eds., *Encyclopedia of Criminology*, Vol. 1 (London: Routledge, 2005), p. 103.

133. D.S. Moskowitz, Rachel Sutton, David C. Zuroffa, and Simon N. Young, "Fetal exposure to androgens, as indicated by digit ratios (2D:4D), increases men's agreeableness with women," *Personality and Individual Differences*, Volume 75, March 2015, Pages 97–101.

134. Lee Ellis and Anthony W. Hoskins, "Criminality and the 2D:4D Ratio: Testing the Prenatal Androgen Hypothesis,"

International Journal of Offender Therapy and Comparative Criminology, Vol. 59, No. 3 (2015).

135. Joseph Goldstein, "It Has Been Frigid Outside, but Also a Lot Less Dangerous," *New York Times,* January 25, 2013, http://www.nytimes.com/2013/01/26/nyregion/cold-wave-cut-murders-in-new-york-city-significantly.html (accessed February 4, 2017).

136. J. Rotton and E. G. Cohn, "Weather, Climate, and Crime," in R. Bechtel and E. Churchman, eds., *The 2002 Handbook of Environmental Psychology* (New York: Wiley, 2002), pp. 461–498.

137. E. G. Cohn and J. Rotton, "Assault as a Function of Time and Temperature: A Moderator-Variable Time-Series Analysis," *Journal of Personality and Social Psychology,* Vol. 72 (1997), pp. 1322–1334.

138. J. Rotton and E. G. Cohn, "Violence as a Curvilinear Function of Temperature in Dallas: A Replication," *Journal of Personality and Social Psychology,* Vol. 78 (2000), pp. 1074–1081.

139. E. G. Cohn and J. Rotton, "Weather, Seasonal Trends, and Property Crimes in Minneapolis, 1987–1988: A Moderator-Variable Time-Series Analysis of Routine Activities," *Journal of Environmental Psychology,* Vol. 20 (2000), pp. 257–272.

140. J. Rotton and E. G. Cohn, "Temperature, Routine Activities, and Domestic Violence: A Reanalysis," *Victims and Violence,* Vol. 16 (2001), pp. 203–215.

141. J. Rotton and E. G. Cohn, "Weather, Disorderly Conduct, and Assaults: From Social Contact to Social Avoidance," *Environment and Behavior,* Vol. 32 (2000), pp. 649–671.

142. Thomas J. Schory et al., "Barometric Pressure, Emergency Psychiatric Visits, and Violent Acts," *Canadian Journal of Psychiatry,* Vol. 48 (October 2003), pp. 624–627.

143. Monte Morin, "Violence Will Rise as Climate Changes, Scientists Predict," *The Los Angeles Times,* August 1, 2013, http://www.latimes.com/science/la-sci-climate-change-conflict-20130802-story.html (accessed February 5, 2017).

144. James Q. Wilson and Richard J. Herrnstein, *Crime and Human Nature* (New York: Simon & Schuster, 1985).

145. Quoted in Karen J. Winkler, "Criminals Are Born as well as Made, Authors of Controversial Book Assert," *Chronicle of Higher Education,* January 16, 1986, p. 5.

146. Wilson and Herrnstein, *Crime and Human Nature.*

147. Winkler, "Criminals Are Born as well as Made," p. 8.

148. Anthony Walsh, *Biosocial Criminology: Introduction and Integration* (Cincinnati, OH: Anderson, 2002), p. vii.

149. Anthony Walsh, "Biological Theories of Criminal Behavior," in Richard A. Wright and J. Mitchell Miller, eds., *Encyclopedia of Criminology,* Vol. 1 (New York: Routledge, 2005), p. 106.

150. Ibid.

151. Ibid.

152. Diana Fishbein, *Biobehavioral Perspectives in Criminology* (Belmont, CA: Wadsworth, 2001), pp. 2–3.

153. C. Ray Jeffery, "Biological Perspectives," *Journal of Criminal Justice Education,* Vol. 4 (1993), p. 300.

154. Leanne Fiftal Alarid et al., "Women's Roles in Serious Offenses: A Study of Adult Felons," *Justice Quarterly,* Vol. 13, No. 3 (September 1996), pp. 432–454.

155. Kevin Beaver, "Foreword," in Anthony Walsh, ed., *Feminist Criminology through a Biosocial Lens* (Durham, NC: Carolina Academic Press, 2011), p. 11.

156. Federal Bureau of Investigation, *Crime in the United States, 2012* (Washington, DC: U.S. Department of Justice, 2013).

157. Freda Adler, *Sisters in Crime: The Rise of the New Female Criminal* (New York: McGraw-Hill, 1975).

158. Darrell J. Steffensmeier, "Sex Differences in Patterns of Adult Crime, 1965–1977: A Review and Assessment," *Social Forces,* Vol. 58 (1980), pp. 1098–1099.

159. T. Bernard, J. Snipes, and A. Gerould, *Vold's Theoretical Criminology* (New York: Oxford University Press, 2010), cited in Anthony Walsh, ed., *Feminist Criminology through a Biosocial Lens* (Durham, NC: Carolina Academic Press, 2011), p. xi.

160. Anthony Walsh, ed., *Feminist Criminology through a Biosocial Lens* (Durham, NC: Carolina Academic Press, 2011), p. 22.

161. Ibid.

162. Laura Klappenbach, "Sexual Selection," About.com, 2 (accessed January 10, 2012).

163. I. Silverman, J. Choi, and M. Peters, "The Hunter-Gatherer Theory of Sex Differences in Spatial Abilities: Data from 40 Countries," *Archives of Sexual Behavior,* Vol. 36 (2007), pp. 261–268.

164. A. Walsh and L. Ellis, *Criminology: An Interdisciplinary Approach* (Thousand Oaks, CA: Sage, 2007).

165. Walsh, ed., *Feminist Criminology,* p. 125.

166. Kevin M. Beaver, John Paul Wright, and Anthony Walsh, "A Gene-Based Evolutionary Explanation for the Association between Criminal Involvement and Number of Sex Partners," in Kevin M. Beaver and Anthony Walsh, eds., *Biosocial Theories of Crime* (Burlington, VT: Ashgate, 2010), p. 351.

167. Anthony Walsh and Craig Hemmens, *Introduction to Criminology: A Text/Reader,* 2nd ed. (Thousand Oaks, CA: Sage, 2011), p. 269.

168. Anthony W. Hoskin and Lee Ellis, "Fetal Testosterone and Criminality: Test of Evolutionary Neuroandrogenic Theory," *Criminology,* Vol. 53, No. 1 (2015), http://onlinelibrary.wiley.com/doi/10.1111/crim.2015.53.issue-1/issuetoc.

169. Ibid.

170. Lee Ellis, "A Theory Explaining Biological Correlates of Criminality," in Anthony Walsh and Craig Hemmens, eds., *Introduction to Criminology: A Text/Reader,* 2nd ed. (Thousand Oaks, CA: Sage, 2011), pp. 299–306.

171. Jerome H. Barkow, Leda Cosmides, and John Tooby, eds., *The Adapted Mind: Evolutionary Psychology and the Generation of Culture* (New York: Oxford University Press, 1992).

172. Steven Pinker, *The Blank Slate: The Modern Denial of Human Nature* (New York: Viking, 2002).

173. Lee Ellis and Anthony Walsh, "Gene-Based Evolutionary Theories in Criminology," *Criminology,* Vol. 35, No. 2 (1997), pp. 229–230.

174. Terrie E. Moffitt, "The New Look of Behavioral Genetics in Developmental Psychopathology: Gene-Environment Interplay in Antisocial Behaviors," in Kevin M. Beaver and Anthony Walsh, eds., *Biosocial Theories of Crime* (Burlington, VT: Ashgate, 2010), p. 185.

175. Elizabeth Englander, *Understanding Violence,* 3rd ed. (Mahwah, NJ: Lawrence Erlbaum Associates, 2007).

176. Lee Ellis, Lee. (2005). "Theory Explaining the Biological Correlates of Criminality," *European Journal of Criminology,* Vol. 2, No. 3, pp. 287–314.

177. Julian Roberts and T. Gabor, "Lombrosian Wine in a New Bottle: Research on Crime and Race," *Canadian Journal of Criminology,* Vol. 32, pp. 291–313.

CHAPTER 6: PSYCHOLOGICAL AND PSYCHIATRIC FOUNDATIONS OF CRIMINAL BEHAVIOR

1. J. K. Peterson, J. Skeem, P. Kennealy, B. Bray, and A. Zvonkovic, A, "How Often and How Consistently Do Symptoms Directly Precede Criminal Behavior among Offenders with Mental Illness?" *Law and Human Behavior*. Advance online publication (April 14, 2014; http://dx.doi.org/10.1037/lhb0000075.

2. E. Fuller Torrey et al., *The Treatment of Persons with Mental Illness in Prisons and Jails: A State Survey* (Arlington, VA: Treatment Advocacy Center, 2014).

3. Christopher Hoffman, "Court Document: Wethersfield Man Confessed to Killing 86-Year-Old Mom," *Hartford Courant*, June 22, 2016, http://www.courant.com/community/wethersfield/hc-wethersfield-elderly-mother-slaying-0623-20160622-story.html (accessed September 1, 2017).

4. Ibid.

5. Ibid.

6. American Board of Forensic Psychology, http://www.abfp.com/brochure.html (accessed November 22, 2007).

7. See the American Academy of Psychiatry and the Law, http://www.aapl.org (accessed September 2, 2017).

8. Laurence Steinberg, "The Juvenile Psychopath: Fads, Fictions, and Facts," *National Institute of Justice Perspectives on Crime and Justice: 2001 Lecture Series,* Vol. V (Washington, DC: NIJ, 2002), pp. 35–64.

9. Ibid.

10. Nicole Hahn Rafter, "Psychopathy and the Evolution of Criminological Knowledge," *Theoretical Criminology*, Vol. 1, No. 2 (May 1997), p. 236.

11. Nolan D. C. Lewis, "Foreword," in David Abrahamsen, *Crime and the Human Mind* (New York: Columbia University Press, 1944; reprint, Montclair, NJ: Patterson Smith, 1969), p. vii.

12. As noted by Rafter, "Psychopathy and the Evolution of Criminological Knowledge." See Richard von Krafft-Ebing, *Psychopathia Sexualis* (1886; reprint, New York: Stein and Day, 1965); and Richard von Krafft-Ebing, *Textbook of Insanity* (Germany, 1879; reprint, Philadelphia: F. A. Davis, 1904).

13. Bernard H. Glueck, *Studies in Forensic Psychiatry* (Boston: Little, Brown, 1916).

14. William Healy, *The Individual Delinquent* (Boston: Little, Brown, 1915).

15. Early writings about the psychopathic personality focused almost exclusively on men, and most psychiatrists appeared to believe that very few women (if any) possessed such traits.

16. Hervey M. Cleckley, *The Mask of Sanity*, 4th ed. (St. Louis, MO: C. V. Mosby, 1964).

17. "Charles Manson," Research This Stuff, http://www.research-thisstuff.com/Charles_Manson_001.htm (accessed July 3, 2009).

18. Quoted in Joseph P. Newman and Chad A. Brinkley, "Psychopathy: Rediscovering Cleckley's Construct," *Psychopathology Research*, Vol. 9, No. 1 (March 1998).

19. Gwynn Nettler, *Killing One Another* (Cincinnati: Anderson, 1982), p. 179.

20. Ralph Serin, "Can Criminal Psychopaths Be Identified?" Correctional Service of Canada, October 22, 1999, http://www.csc-scc.gc.ca/text/pblct/forum/e012/e0121.shtml (accessed December 20, 2006).

21. David T. Lykken, *The Antisocial Personalities* (Hillsdale, NJ: Lawrence Erlbaum, 1995).

22. Robert D. Hare, "Checklist for the Assessment of Psychopathy in Criminal Populations," in M. H. Ben-Aron, S. J. Hucker, and C. D. Webster, eds., *Clinical Criminology* (Toronto: University of Toronto, Clarke Institute of Psychiatry, 1985), pp. 157–167. Hare developed this checklist on Cleckley's characteristics commonly found in psychopaths.

23. See Steinberg, "The Juvenile Psychopath," from which some of the wording in this paragraph is adapted.

24. Robert J. McMahon, Katie Witkiewitz, Julie S. Kotler, and The Conduct Problems Prevention Research Group, "Predictive Validity of Callous-Unemotional Traits Measured in Early Adolescence with respect to Multiple Antisocial Outcomes," *Journal of Abnormal Psychology,* Vol. 119 (2010), pp. 752–763.

25. Kent A. Kiehl et al., "Temporal Lobe Abnormalities in Semantic Processing by Criminal Psychopaths as Revealed by Functional Magnetic Resonance Imaging," *Psychiatry Research: Neuroimaging*, Vol. 130 (2004), pp. 27–42.

26. Ibid.

27. Julia C. Keller, "Aha! Study Finds Eureka Moments Light Up Brain," *Science and Theology News*, June 2004, http://www.stnews.org/feat_aha_0604.html (accessed December 12, 2006).

28. Bertine Lahuis, Chantal Kemmer, and Herman Van Engeland, "Magnetic Resonance Imaging Studies on Autism and Childhood-Onset Schizophrenia in Children and Adolescents," *Acta Neuropsychiatrica*, Vol. 15, No. 3 (June 2003), p. 140.

29. Ivan Semeniuk, "How We Tell Right from Wrong: An Interview with Marc Hauser," *New Scientist*, March 3, 2007, p. 44.

30. Michael Caldwell et al., "Treatment Response of Adolescent Offenders with Psychopathy Features: A 2-Year Follow-Up," *Criminal Justice and Behavior*, Vol. 33, No. 5 (2006), pp. 571–576.

31. Peter Aldhous, "Violent, Antisocial, Past Redemption?" *New Scientist*, April 14, 2007, pp. 8–9.

32. American Psychiatric Association, *Diagnostic and Statistical Manual of Mental Disorders*, 2nd ed. (Washington, DC: American Psychiatric Association, 1968).

33. Ibid., p. 43.

34. Paul Moran, "The Epidemiology of Antisocial Personality Disorder," *Social Psychiatry and Psychiatric Epidemiology,* Vol. 34 (1999), pp. 231–242.

35. American Psychiatric Association, *Diagnostic and Statistical Manual of Mental Disorders,* 4e Text Revision (Washington, DC: American Psychiatric Association, 2000); see also Jeffrey G. Johnson et al., "Adolescent Personality Disorders associated with Violence and Criminal Behavior during Adolescence and Early Adulthood," *American Journal of Psychiatry,* Vol. 157 (2000), pp.1406–1412.

36. Daniel Martins De Barros and Antonio de Padua Serafim, "Association between Personality Disorder and Violent Behavior Pattern," *Forensic Science International,* Vol. 179 (2008), pp. 19–22; and Adrian Raine, Adrian, "Features of Borderline Personality and Violence," *Journal of Clinical Psychology,* Vol. 49 (1993), pp. 277–281.

37. R. D. Hare, *Psychopathy: Theory and Research* (New York: John Wiley and Sons, 1970).

38. L. N. Robins, *Deviant Children Grow Up* (Baltimore: Williams and Wilkins, 1966).

39. S. B. Guze, *Criminality and Psychiatric Disorders* (New York: Oxford University Press, 1976).

40. Hans J. Eysenck, *Crime and Personality* (Boston: Houghton Mifflin, 1964).

41. Intelligence may also be seen as an ability. See, for example, Colin G. DeYoung, "Intelligence and Personality," in R. J. Sternberg and S. B. Kaufman, eds., *The Cambridge Handbook of Intelligence* (New York: Cambridge University Press, 2011), p. 2.

42. Some early personality theorists considered intelligence to be part of personality. See, for example, R. B. Cattell, *Personality* (New York: McGraw-Hill, 1950); and J. P. Guilford, *Personality* (New York: McGraw-Hill, 1959).

43. Ibid., p. 92.

44. Hans J. Eysenck, "Personality and Criminality: A Dispositional Analysis," in William S. Laufer and Freda Adler, eds., *Advances in Criminology Theory*, Vol. 1 (New Brunswick, NJ: Transaction, 1989), p. 90.

45. Eysenck, *Crime and Personality*, pp. 35–36.

46. Colin G. DeYoung, "Intelligence and Personality," in R. J. Sternberg and S. B. Kaufman, eds., *The Cambridge Handbook of Intelligence* (New York: Cambridge University Press, 2011), pp. 711–737.

47. Jean Piaget, *The Moral Judgment of the Child*, Routledge and Kegan Paul, 1955.

48. Cited in Holly K. Craig and Tanya M. Gallagher, "The Structural Characteristics of Monologues in the Speech of Normal Children: Syntactic Nonconversational Aspects," *Journal of Speech, Language, and Hearing Research*, Vol. 22 (March 1979), pp. 46–62.

49. Lawrence Kohlberg, *Stages in the Development of Moral Thought and Action* (New York: Holt, Rinehart and Winston, 1969).

50. Sergio Herzog, "Moral Judgment, Crime Seriousness, and the Relations between Them: An Exploratory Study," *Crime and Delinquency*, December 27, 2012.

51. K. Dodge, "A Social Information Processing Model of Social Competence in Children," *Minnesota Symposium in Child Psychology*, Vol. 8 (1986), pp. 77–125.

52. J. Lochman, Self and Peer Perceptions of Attributional Biases of Aggressive and Non-aggressive Boys in Dyadic Interactions," *Journal of Consulting and Clinical Psychology*, Vol. 55 (1987), pp. 404–410.

53. Calvin Langton and W. Marshall. "Contagion in Rapists: Theoretical Patterns by Typological Breakdown," *Aggression and Violent Behaviour*, Vol. 6 (2001), pp. 499–518.

54. R. C. Schank and R. P. Abelson, *Scripts, Plans, Goals and Understanding, an Inquiry into Human Knowledge Structures* (Hillsdale, NJ: Lawrence Erlbaum, 1977).

55. Helen Gavin and David Hockey, "Criminal Careers and Cognitive Scripts: An Investigation into Criminal Versatility," *The Qualitative Report*, Vol. 15, No. 2 (March 2010), pp. 389–410.

56. Ibid.

57. Samuel Yochelson and Stanton E. Samenow, *The Criminal Personality*, Vols. I, II, and III (New York, Aronson, 1976 and 1977).

58. Ibid.

59. Stanton E. Samenow, *Inside the Criminal Mind*, 2nd ed. (New York: Crown Publishers, 2004), p. xxi.

60. Ibid., p. 212.

61. Glenn D. Walters, "The Psychological Inventory of Criminal Thinking Styles, Part 1: Reliability and Preliminary Validity," *Criminal Justice and Behavior*, Vol. 22 (1995), pp. 307–325.

62. August Aichorn, *Wayward Youth* (New York: Viking Press, 1935).

63. Marti Ol. Laney, *The Hidden Gifts of the Introverted Child* (New York: Workman Publishing, 2006).

64. Mark Solms, "Freud Returns," *Scientific American*, Vol. 290, No. 5 (May 2004), pp. 82–90.

65. Eric R. Kandel, "Biology and the Future of Psychoanalysis: A New Intellectual Framework for Psychiatry Revisited," *American Journal of Psychiatry*, Vol. 156 (April 1999), pp. 505–524.

66. Gwynn Nettler, Killing One Another (Cincinnati: Anderson, 1982), p. 159.

67. Ibid., p. 155.

68. Runa Munkner, Soeren Haastrup, Torben Joergensen, and Peter Kramp, "The Temporal Relationship between Schizophrenia and Crime," *Social Psychiatry and Psychiatric Epidemiology*, Vol. 38, No. 7 (July 2003), pp. 347–353.

69. Elizabeth Walsh, Alec Buchanan, and Thomas Fahy, "Violence and Schizophrenia: Examining the Evidence," *The British Journal of Psychiatry*, Vol. 180 (2002), pp. 490–495.

70. Seena Fazel, Niklas Långström, Anders Hjern, Martin Grann, and Paul Lichtenstein, "Schizophrenia, Substance Abuse, and Violent Crime," *Journal of the American Medical Association*, Vol. 301, No. 19 (2009), pp. 2016–2023.

71. J. Dollard et al., *Frustration and Aggression* (New Haven, CT: Yale University Press, 1939).

72. Andrew F. Henry and James F. Short, Jr., *Suicide and Homicide: Economic, Sociological, and Psychological Aspects of Aggression* (Glencoe, IL: Free Press, 1954).

73. Stewart Palmer, *A Study of Murder* (New York: Crowell, 1960).

74. Seymour L. Halleck, *Psychiatry and the Dilemmas of Crime: A Study of Causes, Punishment and Treatment* (Berkeley: University of California Press, 1971).

75. Ibid., p. 78.

76. Ibid., p. 80.

77. Ibid.

78. Ibid.

79. Arnold S. Linsky, Ronet Bachman, and Murray A. Straus, *Stress, Culture, and Aggression* (New Haven, CT: Yale University Press, 1995).

80. Ibid., p. 7.

81. D. A. Andrews and J. Bonta, *The Psychology of Criminal Conduct*, 2nd ed. (Cincinnati, OH: Anderson Publishing Co., 1998).

82. D. A. Andrews and J. Bonta, "Rehabilitating Criminal Justice Policy and Practice," *Psychology, Public Policy, and Law*, Vol. 16, No. 1 (2010), pp. 39–55.

83. Adapted from Tony Ward and Claire Stewart, "Criminogenic Needs and Human Needs: A Theoretical Model," *Psychology, Crime and Law*, Vol. 9, No. 2 (2003), pp. 125–143.

84. Andrews and Bonta, "Rehabilitating Criminal Justice Policy and Practice," p. 46.

85. See Mary D. Salter Ainsworth, "John Bowlby, 1907–1990," *American Psychologist*, Vol. 47 (1992), p. 668.

86. John Bowlby, "The Nature of the Child's Tie to Its Mother," *International Journal of Psycho-Analysis*, Vol. 39 (1958), pp. 350–373.

87. See John Bowlby, *Maternal Care and Mental Health*, World Health Organization Monograph (1951); and John Bowlby, *A Secure Base* (New York: Basic Books, 1988).

88. Bowlby, *A Secure Base*, p. 11.

89. David P. Farrington and Donald J. West, "Effects of Marriage, Separation, and Children on Offending by Adult Males," *Current Perspectives on Aging and the Life Cycle*, Vol. 4 (1995), pp. 249–281.

90. Stephen A. Cernkovich and Peggy C. Giordano, "Family Relationships and Delinquency," *Criminology*, Vol. 25 (1987), pp. 295–313.

91. Gabriel Tarde, *The Laws of Imitation*, trans. E. C. Parsons (1890; reprint, Gloucester, MA: Peter Smith, 1962).

92. Albert Bandura, "The Social Learning Perspective: Mechanisms of Aggression," in Hans Toch, ed., *Psychology of Crime and Criminal Justice* (Prospect Heights, IL: Waveland, 1979), p. 198.

93. Albert Bandura, *Social Learning Theory* (Englewood Cliffs, NJ: Prentice Hall, 1977).

94. Ibid., p. 199.

95. M. M. Lefkowitz et al., "Television Violence and Child Aggression: A Follow-up Study," in G. A. Comstock and E. A. Rubinstein, eds., *Television and Social Behavior*, Vol. 3 (Washington, DC: U.S. Government Printing Office, 1972), pp. 35–135.

96. John C. Norcross, Gerald P. Koocher, and Ariele Garofalo, "Discredited Psychological Treatments and Tests: A Delphi Poll," *Professional Psychology: Research and Practice*, Vol. 37, No. 5 (2006), pp. 515–522.

97. North Carolina Department of Public Safety, *Cognitive Behavioral Interventions (CBI): Standard Operating Procedures* (December 2001).

98. Friedrich Losel, "Treatment and Management of Psychopaths," *NATO ASI Series*, Vol. 88 (1998), pp. 303–354.

99. *Brown* v. *Entertainment Merchants Association*, U.S. Supreme Court, No. 08-1448 (decided June 27, 2011).

100. For one of the first and still definitive works in the area of selective incapacitation, see Peter Greenwood and Allan Abrahamsen, *Selective Incapacitation* (Santa Monica, CA: Rand, 1982).

101. M. A. Peterson, H. B. Braiker, and S. M. Polich, *Who Commits Crimes?* (Cambridge, MA: Oelgeschlager, Gunn & Hain, 1981).

102. Jeremy Travis, "But They All Come Back," papers from the Executive Session on Sentencing and Corrections, No. 7 (Washington, DC: National Institute of Justice, 2000).

103. James L. Johnson et al., "The Construction and Validation of the Federal Post Conviction Risk Assessment (PCRA)," *Federal Probation* (September 2011), http://www.uscourts.gov/uscourts/FederalCourts/PPS/Fedprob/2011/construction.html.

104. Tracy L. Fass, "The LSI-R and the COMPAS: Validation Data on Two Risk-Needs Tools," *Criminal Justice and Behavior*, July 8, 2008, doi:10.1177/0093854808320497 (accessed August 10, 2013).

105. Christopher T. Lowenkamp and Kristin Bechtel, "Predictive Validity of the LSI-R on a Sample of Offenders Drawn from the Records of the Iowa Department of Corrections Data Management System," *Federal Probation*, Vol. 71, No. 3 (December 2007), pp. 25–29.

106. Ibid.

107. See, for example, A. M. Holsinger, C. T. Lowenkamp, and E. J. Latessa, "Ethnicity, Gender, and the Level of Service Inventory–Revised," *Journal of Criminal Justice*, Vol. 31 (2003), pp. 309–320; and D. G. Kroner and J. F. Mills, "The Accuracy of Five Risk Appraisal Instruments in Predicting Institutional Misconduct and New Convictions," *Criminal Justice and Behavior*, Vol. 28 (2001), pp. 471–489.

108. For further discussion of the risk-needs-responsivity model, see Andrews and Bonta, *The Psychology of Criminal Conduct*; for discussion of the Good Lives Model, see T. Ward and T. Gannon, "Rehabilitation, Etiology, and Self-Regulation: The Good Lives Model of Sexual Offender Treatment," *Aggression and Violent Behavior*, Vol. 11 (2006), pp. 77–94.

109. Robin J. Wilson and Pamela M. Yates, "Effective Interventions and the Good Lives Model: Maximizing Treatment Gains for Sexual Offenders," *Aggression and Violent Behavior*, Vol. 14 (2009), pp. 157–161.

110. Andrews and Bonta, "Rehabilitating Criminal Justice Policy and Practice," pp. 39–55.

111. Seena Fazel, Jay P. Singh, Helen Doll, and Martin Grann, "Use of Risk Assessment Instruments to Predict Violence and Antisocial Behavior in 73 Samples Involving 24,827 People: Systematic Review and Meta-Analysis," BMJ 2012;345:e4692 doi: 10.1136/bmj.e4692 (Published 24 July 2012).

112. The 1984 Amendment to § 200 of Title II (§ 200–2304) of Pub. L. 98–473 is popularly referred to as the "1984 Comprehensive Crime Control Act."

113. U.S. Sentencing Commission, *Federal Sentencing Guidelines Manual* (Washington, DC: U.S. Government Printing Office, 1987), p. 10.

114. John Paul Wright and Kevin M. Beaver, "Do Parents Matter in Creating Self-Control in Their Children? A Genetically Informed Test of Gottfredson and Hirschi's Theory of Low Self-Control," *Criminology* Vol. 43 (2005), pp. 1169–1202.

115. Jill Peay, "Dangerousness—Ascription or Description," in M. P. Feldman, ed., *Developments in the Study of Criminal Behavior*, Vol. 2, *Violence* (New York: John Wiley and Sons, 1982), p. 211, citing N. Walker, "Dangerous People," *International Journal of Law and Psychiatry*, Vol. 1 (1978), pp. 37–50.

116. See, for example, Michael Gottfredson and Travis Hirschi, *A General Theory of Crime* (Stanford, CA: Stanford University Press, 1990); and Travis Hirschi and Michael Gottfredson, "Age and the Explanation of Crime," *American Journal of Sociology*, Vol. 89 (1983), pp. 552–584.

117. MacArthur Research Network on Mental Health and the Law, "The MacArthur Violence Risk Assessment Study," September 2005, p. 4, http://www.macarthur.virginia.edu/risk.html (accessed February 22, 2017).

118. Ibid.

119. Lia Ahonen, Rolf Loeber, and Dustin Pardini, "The Prediction of Young Homicide and Violent Offenders," *Justice Quarterly*, Vol. 33, No. 7, pp. 1265–1291.

120. Jennifer L. White et al., "How Early Can We Tell? Predictors of Childhood Conduct Disorder and Adolescent Delinquency," *Criminology*, Vol. 28, No. 4 (1990), pp. 507–528.

121. David P. Farrington et al., "Advancing Knowledge about the Onset of Delinquency and Crime," in B. B. Lahey and A. E. Kazdin, eds., *Advances in Clinical Child Psychology*, Vol. 13 (New York: Plenum, 1990), pp. 283–342.

122. Paul C. Vitz, "The Use and Abuse of Freud," a review of *Freudian Fraud: The Malignant Effect of Freud's Theory on American Thought and Culture* by E. Fuller Torrey (Leadership U., 1993), p. 52.

123. J. Bonta, M. Law, and R. K. Hanson, "The Prediction of Criminal and Violent Recidivism among Mentally Disordered Offenders: A Meta-Analysis," *Psychological Bulletin*, Vol. 123 (1998), pp. 123–142.

124. Mark Solms, "Freud Returns," *Scientific American*, Vol. 290, No. 5 (May 2004), pp. 82–90.

125. Cathy Spatz Widom and Hans Toch, "The Contribution of Psychology to Criminal Justice Education," *Journal of Criminal Justice Education*, Vol. 4, No. 2 (Fall 1993), p. 253.

126. Interview by Amy Goldman, February 27, 1998, http://www.serialkillers.net/interviews/jdouglas2bak.html (accessed December 20, 2000).

127. See John Douglas and Alan Burgess, "Criminal Profiling: A Viable Investigative Tool against Violent Crime," *FBI Law Enforcement Bulletin,* December 1986.

128. Robert R. Hazelwood and John E. Douglas, "The Lust Murderer," *FBI Law Enforcement Bulletin,* April 1980.

129. Ibid.

130. Ibid.

131. Lea Winerman, "Criminal Profiling: The Reality behind the Myth," Monitor on Psychology, July/August 2004, http://www.apa.org/monitor/julaug04/criminal.aspx (accessed May 4, 2013).

132. University of Liverpool, School of Psychology, "Centre for Investigative Psychology," http://www.liv.ac.uk/psychology/centres/centre-for-investigative-psychology/about (accessed May 2, 2013).

133. Scott O. Lilienfeld, Steven Jay Lynn, John Ruscio, and Barry L. Beyerstein, *50 Great Myths of Popular Psychology* (Malden, MA: Wiley-Blackwell, 2010), p. 215.

134. B. Snook, J. Eastwood, P. Gendreau, C. Goggin, and R. M. Cullen, "Taking Stock of Criminal Profiling: A Narrative Review and Meta-Analysis, *Criminal Justice and Behavior,* Vol. 34 (2007), pp. 437–453.

135. *Segen's Medical Dictionary*, "Psychological Autopsy," http://medical-dictionary.thefreedictionary.com/Psychological+Autopsy (accessed January 28, 2017).

136. Some of the information in this section is derived from Matt Logan, "Case Study: No More Bagpiges—The Threat of the Psychopath," *FBI Law Enforcement Bulletin,* July 2012.

137. In civil proceedings, however, the state may confine a mentally ill person if it shows "by clear and convincing evidence that the individual is mentally ill and dangerous" (*Jones v. United States,* 463 U.S. 354 [1983]).

138. Seymour L. Halleck, *Psychiatry and the Dilemmas of Crime: A Study of Causes, Punishment and Treatment* (Berkeley: University of California Press, 1971), p. 213.

139. M. Phillips, A. Wolf, and D. Coons, "Psychiatry and the Criminal Justice System: Testing the Myths," *American Journal of Psychiatry,* Vol. 145 (1988), pp. 605–610.

140. Ibid.

141. E. Silver, C. Cirincoine, and H. J. Steadman, "Demythologizing Inaccurate Perceptions of the Insanity Defense," *Law and Human Behavior,* Vol. 18, pp. 63–70.

142. M. Kimberly MacLin, "Psychological Theories of Criminal Behavior," in Richard A. Wright and J. Mitchell Miller, eds., *Encyclopedia of Criminology,* Vol. 2 (New York: Routledge, 2005), p. 1337.

CHAPTER 7: SOCIAL STRUCTURE THEORIES

1. Charles R. Tittle, "Theoretical Developments in Criminology," *Criminal Justice 2000* (Washington, DC: National Institute of Justice, 2000), p. 70.

2. See Anthony Walsh, *Biosocial Criminology: Introduction and Integration* (Cincinnati: Anderson, 2002).

3. Emile Durkheim, *The Division of Labor in Society,* trans. George Simpson (1893; reprint, New York: Free Press, 1947).

4. Ferdinand Toennies, *Community and Society,* trans. Charles P. Loomis (1887; reprint, East Lansing: Michigan State University Press, 1957).

5. Georg Simmel, "The Metropolis and Mental Life," in Donald N. Levine, ed., *On Individuality and Social Forms* (Chicago: University of Chicago Press, 1903).

6. Durkheim, *The Division of Labor in Society,* p. 80.

7. W. I. Thomas and Florian Znaniecki, *The Polish Peasant in Europe and America* (Boston: Gorham, 1920).

8. Robert Park and Ernest Burgess, *The City* (Chicago: University of Chicago Press, 1925).

9. "Human Ecology," *Encyclopaedia Britannica* online, http://britannica.com (accessed March 7, 2007).

10. Peter Haggett, "Human Ecology," in Alan Bullock and Oliver Stallybrass, eds., *The Fontana Dictionary of Modern Social Thought* (London: Fontana, 1977), p. 187.

11. For an excellent contemporary review of measuring the extent of social disorganization, see Barbara D. Warner and Glenn L. Pierce, "Reexamining Social Disorganization Theory Using Calls to the Police as a Measure of Crime," *Criminology,* Vol. 31, No. 4 (November 1993), pp. 493–513.

12. Edwin M. Lemert, *Social Pathology* (New York: McGraw-Hill, 1951), p. 3.

13. Ibid., p. 7.

14. Clifford R. Shaw et al., *Delinquency Areas* (Chicago: University of Chicago Press, 1929).

15. David Matza, *Becoming Deviant* (Upper Saddle River, NJ: Prentice Hall, 1969).

16. Lawrence W. Sherman, Patrick R. Gartin, and Michael E. Buerger, "Hot Spots of Predatory Crime: Routine Activities and the Criminology of Place," *Criminology,* Vol. 27, No. 1 (1989), pp. 27–55.

17. P. Jeffrey Brantingham, "Crime Diversity," *Criminology,* doi: 10.1111/1745-9125.12116, 2016.

18. See, for example, David Weisburd et al., *Putting Crime in Its Place: Units of Analysis in Geographic Criminology* (New York: Springer Science+Business Media, 2009); John E. Eck and David Weisburd, eds., *Crime and Place* (Monsey, NY: Criminal Justice Press, 1995); and Anthony A. Braga, "The Effects of Hot Spots Policing on Crime," *Annals of the American Academy of Political and Social Science,* Vol. 578 (2001), pp. 104–125.

19. National Research Council, Committee to Review Research on Police Policy and Practices, *Fairness and Effectiveness in Policing: The Evidence,* edited by Wesley Skogan and Kathleen Frydl (Washington, DC: The National Academies Press, 2004), p. 35.

20. Rodney Stark, "Deviant Places: A Theory of the Ecology of Crime," *Criminology,* Vol. 25, No. 4 (1987), p. 893.

21. Ibid.

22. James Q. Wilson and George Kelling, "Broken Windows," *Atlantic Monthly,* March 1982, pp. 1–11.

23. David Thacher, "Order Maintenance Reconsidered: Moving beyond Strong Causal Reasoning," *Journal of Criminal Law and Criminology,* Vol. 94, No. 2 (2004), pp. 381–414.

24. James Q. Wilson and George L. Kelling, "Broken Windows: The Police and Neighborhood Safety," *Atlantic Monthly,* March 1982, http://www.theatlantic.com/politics/crime/windows.htm (accessed January 10, 2005).

25. Oscar Newman, *Architectural Design for Crime Prevention* (Washington, DC: U.S. Department of Justice, 1973). See also Oscar Newman, *Creating Defensible Space* (Washington, DC: Office of Housing and Urban Development, 1996).

26. Oscar Newman, *Defensible Space: Crime Prevention through Urban Design* (New York: Macmillan, 1972), p. 3. See also Ralph B. Taylor and Adele V. Harrell, *Physical Environment and Crime* (Washington, DC: National Institute of Justice, May 1996).

27. Sherman, Gartin, and Buerger, "Hot Spots of Predatory Crime," p. 31.

28. *Defensible Space*, op. cit.

29. Peter Hermann, "District Police Embrace Concept of Preventing Crime through Design," *The Washington Post*, September 3, 2012, http://www.washingtonpost.com/local/crime/district-police-embrace-concept-of-preventing-crime-through-design/2012/09/03/ebe49518-e621-11e1-8741-940e3f6dbf48_story.html?hpid=z6 (accessed May 1, 2013).

30. Bernard E. Harcourt, *Illusion of Order: The False Promise of Broken Windows Policing* (Cambridge: Harvard University Press, 2001).

31. Robert J. Sampson and Stephen W. Radenbush, "Systematic Social Observation of Public Spaces: A New Look at Disorder in Urban Neighborhoods," *American Journal of Sociology*, Vol. 105 (1999), p. 603.

32. Thacher, "Order Maintenance Reconsidered," p. 386.

33. Craig D. Uchida, Marc L. Swatt, Shellie E. Solomon, and Sean Varano, *Neighborhoods and Crime: Collective Efficacy and Social Cohesion in Miami-Dade County: Executive Summary* (Washington, DC: US Dept. of Justice, 2014).

34. Ibid.

35. David R. Schaefer, Nancy Rodriguez, and Scott H. Decker, "The Role of Neighborhood Context in Youth Co-Offending," *Criminology*, 2013, doi:10.1111/1745-9125.12032.

36. Thomas M. Arvanites and Robert H. Defina, "Business Cycles and Street Crime," *Criminology*, Vol. 44, No. 1 (2006), p. 141.

37. Emile Durkheim, *Suicide: A Study in Sociology* (New York: Free Press, 1897).

38. Robert K. Merton, "Social Structure and Anomie," *American Sociological Review*, Vol. 3, No. 5 (October 1938), pp. 672–682; and Robert K. Merton, *Social Theory and Social Structure*, rev. ed. (New York: Free Press, 1957).

39. Merton, "Social Structure and Anomie," p. 681.

40. Thomas M. Arvanites and Robert H. Defina, "Business Cycles and Street Crime," *Criminology*, Vol. 44, No. 1 (2006), pp. 139–164.

41. Steven F. Messner and Richard Rosenfeld, *Crime and the American Dream* (Belmont, CA: Wadsworth, 1994), p. 68.

42. J. Blau and P. Blau, "The Cost of Inequality: Metropolitan Structure and Violent Crime," *American Sociological Review*, Vol. 147 (1982), pp. 114–129.

43. Masahiro Tsushima, "Economic Structure and Crime: The Case of Japan," *Journal of Socio-Economics*, Vol. 25, No. 4 (Winter 1996), p. 497.

44. Thomas F. Pettigrew, "Applying Social Psychology to International Social Issues," *Journal of Social Issues* (Winter 1998), pp. 663–676.

45. Robert Agnew, "Foundation for a General Strain Theory of Crime and Delinquency," *Criminology*, Vol. 30, No. 1 (February 1992), pp. 47–87.

46. Adapted from Robert Agnew, *Pressured into Crime: An Overview of General Strain Theory* (Los Angeles: Roxbury, 2006), pp. 193–196.

47. Ibid., p. 60.

48. Agnew, "Foundation for a General Strain Theory of Crime and Delinquency."

49. Ibid., p. 48.

50. Raymond Paternoster and Paul Mazerolle, "General Strain Theory and Delinquency: A Replication and Extension," *Journal of Research in Crime and Delinquency*, Vol. 31, No. 3 (1994), pp. 235–263.

51. Robert Agnew and Helene Raskin White, "An Empirical Test of General Strain Theory," *Criminology*, Vol. 30, No. 4 (1992), pp. 475–499.

52. Lisa M. Broidy, "A Test of General Strain Theory," *Criminology*, Vol. 39, No. 1 (2002), pp. 9–35.

53. Ibid., p. 29.

54. Ibid.

55. Robert Agnew et al., "Strain, Personality Traits, and Delinquency: Extending General Strain Theory," *Criminology*, Vol. 40, No. 1 (2002), pp. 43–71.

56. Ibid., p. 47.

57. Joan R. Hipp, "Spreading the Wealth: The Effect of the Distribution of Income and Race/Ethnicity across Households and Neighborhoods on City Crime Trajectories," National Institute of Justice unpublished research report, May 27, 2010.

58. Arnold S. Linsky and Murray A. Straus, *Social Stress in The United States: Links to Regional Patterns in Crime and Illness* (Dover, Massachusetts: Auburn House Publishing Company, 1986).

59. James Austin and Gregory D. Squires, "The 'Startling' Link Between Low Interest Rates and Low Crime," The Crime Report, December 6, 2016, http://thecrimereport.org/2016/12/06/the-startling-link-between-low-interest-rates-and-low-crime/ (accessed January 5, 2017).

60. Thorsten Sellin, *Culture Conflict and Crime* (New York: Social Science Research Council, 1938).

61. Sellin, *Culture Conflict and Crime*, p. 68.

62. Frederic M. Thrasher, *The Gang* (Chicago: University of Chicago Press, 1927).

63. William F. Whyte, *Street Corner Society: The Social Structure of an Italian Slum* (Chicago: University of Chicago Press, 1943).

64. The quotations attributed to Miller in these paragraphs are from Walter Miller, "Lower Class Culture as a Generating Milieu of Gang Delinquency," *Journal of Social Issues*, Vol. 14, No. 3 (1958), pp. 5–19.

65. Gresham Sykes and David Matza, "Techniques of Neutralization: A Theory of Delinquency," *American Sociological Review*, Vol. 22 (December 1957), pp. 664–670.

66. See Volkan Topalli, "When Being Good Is Bad: An Expansion of Neutralization Theory," *Criminology*, Vol. 43 (2005), p. 797.

67. As cited in Topalli, "When Being Good Is Bad," p. 797.

68. David Matza, *Delinquency and Drift* (Piscataway, New Jersey: Transaction, 1990), p. 28.

69. Robert Agnew, "The Techniques of Neutralization and Violence," *Criminology*, Vol. 32, No. 4 (1994), p. 555.

70. Ibid.

71. Topalli, "When Being Good Is Bad."

72. Ken Levi, "Becoming a Hit Man: Neutralization in a Very Deviant Career," *Urban Life*, Vol. 10 (1981), pp. 47–63.

73. Lois Presser, "Remorse and Neutralization among Violent Male Offenders," *Justice Quarterly*, Vol. 20, No. 4 (2003), pp. 801–825.

74. Orly Turgeman-Goldschmidt, "The Rhetoric of Hackers' Neutralizations," in Frank Schmalleger and Michale Pittaro, eds., *Crimes of the Internet* (Upper Saddle River, NJ: Prentice Hall, 2008).

75. See, for example, Dorothy E. Denning, "Activism, Hacktivism, and Cyberterrorism: The Internet as a Tool for Influencing Foreign Policy," *Computer Security Journal*, Vol. 16 (2000), pp. 15–35; and Tim Jordan and Paul Taylor, *Hacktivism and Cyberwars: Rebels with a Cause?* (New York: Routledge, 2004).

76. Franco Ferracuti and Marvin Wolfgang, *The Subculture of Violence: Toward an Integrated Theory of Criminology* (London: Tavistock, 1967).

77. Ibid.

78. Ibid., p. 151.

79. Ibid., pp. 159–160.

80. For an excellent review of the literature, see F. Frederick Hawley, "The Southern Violence Construct: A Skeleton in the Criminological Closet," paper presented at the annual meeting of the American Society of Criminology, 1988.

81. Bertram Wyatt-Brown, *Southern Honor: Ethics and Behavior in the Old South* (Oxford: Oxford University Press, 1983).

82. James W. Clarke, *The Lineaments of Wrath: Race, Violent Crime, and American Culture* (New Brunswick, NJ: Transaction, 1998), p. 4.

83. Ibid.

84. Franklin Zimring et al., "Punishing Homicide in Philadelphia: Perspectives on the Death Penalty," *University of Chicago Law Review*, Vol. 43 (1976), pp. 227–252.

85. Richard A. Cloward and Lloyd E. Ohlin, *Delinquency and Opportunity: A Theory of Delinquent Gangs* (Glencoe, IL: Free Press, 1960).

86. Ibid., p. 7.

87. Ibid., p. 13.

88. Ibid., p. 16.

89. Ibid., p. 19.

90. Ibid., p. 3.

91. Ibid., p. 37.

92. Ibid., pp. 12–13.

93. Albert Cohen, *Delinquent Boys: The Culture of the Gang* (New York: Free Press, 1955), p. 13.

94. Ibid.

95. Donald J. Shoemaker, *Theories of Delinquency: An Examination of Explanations of Delinquent Behavior* (New York: Oxford University Press, 1984), p. 102, citing Cohen.

96. Albert Cohen, *Delinquent Boys: The Culture of the Gang* (New York: Free Press, 1955), p. 13.

97. Ibid., p. 121.

98. Shoemaker, *Theories of Delinquency*, p. 105.

99. Elijah Anderson, *The Code of the Street: Decency, Violence, and the Moral Life of the Inner City* (New York: W. W. Norton, 1990).

100. Arlen Egley, Jr., James C. Howell, and Meena Harris, *Highlights of the 2012 National Youth Gang Survey* (Washington, DC: Office of Juvenile Justice and Delinquency Prevention, 2014).

101. National Gang Crime Research Center, *Achieving Justice and Reversing the Problem of Gang Crime and Gang Violence in America Today: Preliminary Results of the Project Gangfact Study* (Chicago: National Gang Crime Research Center, 1996).

102. Carl Rogers, "Children in Gangs," in *Criminal Justice, 1993–94* (Guilford, CT: Dushkin, 1993), pp. 197–199.

103. "Youths Match Power, Fear, Guns," *Fayetteville (NC) Observer-Times*, September 6, 1993, p. 2A.

104. The quotations attributed to Curry and Spergel in this section are from G. David Curry and Irving A. Spergel, "Gang Homicide, Delinquency, and Community," *Criminology*, Vol. 26, No. 3 (1988), pp. 381–405.

105. Ibid., p. 401.

106. Finn-Aage Esbensen, "A National Gang Strategy," in J. Mitchell Miller and Jeffrey P. Rush, eds., *Gangs: A Criminal Justice Approach* (Cincinnati: Anderson, 1996).

107. Cited in Mary H. Glazier, review of J. Mitchell Miller and Jeffrey P. Rush, eds., *Gangs: A Criminal Justice Approach*, in *Criminologist* (July/August 1996), p. 29.

108. Joan McCord and Kevin P. Conway, *Co-Offending and Patterns of Juvenile Crime* (Washington, DC: National Institute of Justice), p. 1.

109. Steven Schlossman et al., *Delinquency Prevention in South Chicago: A Fifty-Year Assessment of the Chicago Area Project* (Santa Monica, CA: RAND, 1984).

110. J. Robert Lilly, Francis T. Cullen, and Richard A. Ball, *Criminological Theory: Context and Consequences* (Newbury Park, CA: Sage, 1989), p. 80.

111. Lamar T. Empey, *American Delinquency: Its Meaning and Construction* (Homewood, IL: Dorsey, 1982), p. 243.

112. See James DeFronzo, "Welfare and Burglary," *Crime and Delinquency*, Vol. 42 (1996), pp. 223–230.

113. Because overall rates of crime rose throughout much of the 1970s and 1980s, the effectiveness of such programs remains very much in doubt.

114. Public Law 104–193 (August 22, 1996).

115. Section 103 of the Welfare Reform Act of 1996.

116. See, for example, George L. Kelling, "Crime Control, the Police, and Culture Wars: Broken Windows and Cultural Pluralism," in National Institute of Justice, *Perspectives on Crime and Justice: 1997–1998 Lecture Series* (Washington, DC: National Institute of Justice, 1998).

117. Robert J. Bursik, "Social Disorganization and Theories of Crime and Delinquency: Problems and Prospects," *Criminology*, Vol. 26, No. 4 (1988), p. 519.

118. Stephen J. Pfohl, *Images of Deviance and Social Control* (New York: McGraw-Hill, 1985), p. 167.

119. Travis Hirschi, in review of Delbert S. Elliott, David Huizinga, and Suzanne S. Ageton, *Explaining Delinquency and Drug Use*, in *Criminology*, Vol. 25, No. 1 (February 1987), p. 195.

120. John Hagan, "Defiance and Despair: Subcultural and Structural Linkages between Delinquency and Despair in Life Course," *Social Forces*, Vol. 76, No. 1 (September 1997), p. 119.

121. Ibid.

122. Gwynn Nettler, *Killing One Another* (Cincinnati: Anderson, 1982), p. 67.

123. Margaret Anderson, "Review Essay: Rape Theories, Myths, and Social Change," *Contemporary Crises*, Vol. 5 (1983), p. 237.

124. Bradley R. Entner Wright et al., "Reconsidering the Relationship between SES and Delinquency: Causation But Not Correlation," *Criminology*, Vol. 37, No. 1 (February 1999), pp. 175–194.

125. R. Larzelre and G. R. Patterson, "Parental Management: Mediator of the Effect of Socioeconomic Status on Early Delinquency," *Criminology*, Vol. 28 (1990), pp. 301–323.

126. Nettler, *Killing One Another*, p. 54.

127. James Q. Wilson, *The Moral Sense* (New York: Free Press, 1993).

CHAPTER 8: THEORIES OF SOCIAL PROCESS AND SOCIAL DEVELOPMENT

1. Chris Jansing, "Natalee Holloway Suspect Joran van der Sloot Admits Killing Woman in Peru," MSNBC TV, January 12, 2012, http://www.msnbc.msn.com/id/45954171/ns/world_news-americas/#.Tw-fJiO5dhE (accessed March 12, 2012).

2. Frank Bajak, "Peru Court Sentences Van der Sloot to 28 Years," Associated Press, January 13, 2012, http://www.google.com/hostednews/ap/article/ALeqM5jajjHkBVW2klSZb2fTAdyV1sRsOA?docId=b61a4dfc829e429a942854d33b86cde5 (accessed March 12, 2012).

3. Edwin Sutherland, *Principles of Criminology*, 3rd ed. (New York: Lippincott, 1939).

4. Edwin H. Sutherland and Donald R. Cressey, *Criminology* (New York: Lippincott, 1978).

5. Robert Burgess and Ronald L. Akers, "A Differential Association–Reinforcement Theory of Criminal Behavior," *Social Problems*, Vol. 14 (1966), pp. 363–383.

6. Ibid., p. 364.

7. Ronald L. Akers, *Deviant Behavior: A Social Learning Approach* (Belmont, CA: Wadsworth, 1973).

8. Ibid.

9. Ronald L. Akers, *Social Learning and Social Structure: A General Theory of Crime and Deviance* (Boston: Northeastern University Press, 1998).

10. Ronald L. Akers, *Deviant Behavior: A Social Learning Approach*, 3rd ed. (Belmont, CA: Wadsworth, 1985), pp. 40–41.

11. Gang Lee, Ronald L. Akers, and Marian J. Borg, "Social Learning and Structural Factors in Adolescent Substance Use," *Western Criminology Review*, Vol. 5, No. 1 (2004), p. 17.

12. Daniel Glaser, "Differential Association and Criminological Prediction," *Social Problems*, Vol. 8 (1960), pp. 6–14.

13. Daniel Glaser, "Differential Identification," in Henry N. Pontel, ed., *Social Deviance: Readings in Theory and Research*, 3rd ed. (Upper Saddle River, NJ: Prentice Hall 1999), p. 146.

14. Travis C. Pratt, Francis T. Cullen, Christine S. Sellers, L. Thomas Winfree, Jr., Tamara D. Madensen, Leah E. Daigle, Noelle E. Fearn, and Jacinta M. Gau, "The Empirical Status of Social Learning Theory: A Meta-Analysis," *Justice Quarterly*, Vol. 27, No. 6 (December 2010), pp. 765–802.

15. Charles R. Tittle, "Theoretical Developments in Criminology," in National Institute of Justice, ed., *The Nature of Crime: Continuity and Change*, Vol. 1 of *Criminal Justice 2000* (Washington, DC: National Institute of Justice, 2000), p. 65.

16. For a good overview of social control approaches, see George S. Bridges and Martha Myers, eds., *Inequality, Crime, and Social Control* (Boulder, CO: Westview Press, 1994).

17. Walter C. Reckless, *The Crime Problem*, 4th ed. (New York: Appleton-Century-Crofts, 1967).

18. Ibid., p. 470.

19. Ibid.

20. Ibid., p. 475.

21. Ibid.

22. Howard B. Kaplan, "Self-Derogation and Violence," paper presented at the first meeting of the International Society for Research on Aggression, Toronto, 1974. See also Howard B. Kaplan and A. D. Pokorny, "Self-Derogation as an Antecedent of Suicidal Responses," paper presented at the Eighth International Congress on Suicide Prevention and Crisis Intervention, Jerusalem, October 19–22, 1975.

23. Howard B. Kaplan, *Deviant Behavior in Defense of Self* (New York: Academic Press, 1980).

24. M. Rosenberg, C. Schooler, and C. Schoenbach, "Self-Esteem and Adolescent Problems: Modeling Reciprocal Effects," *American Sociological Review*, Vol. 54 (1989), pp. 1004–1018.

25. L. E. Wells, "Self-Enhancement through Delinquency: A Conditional Test of Self-Derogation Theory," *Journal of Research in Crime and Delinquency*, Vol. 26, No. 3 (1989), pp. 226–252.

26. K. Leung and F. Drasgow, "Relation between Self-Esteem and Delinquent Behavior in Three Ethnic Groups: An Application of Item Response Theory," *Journal of Cross-Cultural Psychology*, Vol. 17, No. 2 (1986), pp. 151–167.

27. G. Calhoun, Jr., S. Connley, and J. A. Bolton, "Comparison of Delinquents and Non-Delinquents in Ethnicity, Ordinal Position and Self-Perception," *Journal of Clinical Psychology*, Vol. 40, No. 1 (1984), pp. 323–328.

28. D. Oyserman and H. R. Markus, "Possible Selves in Balance: Implications for Delinquency," *Journal of Social Issues*, Vol. 46, No. 2 (1990), pp. 141–157.

29. Daphna Oyserman and Hazel Markus, "The Sociocultural Self," in J. Suls, ed., *Psychological Perspectives on the Self*, Vol. 4 (Hillsdale, NJ: Erlbaum, 1993), pp. 187–220.

30. Travis Hirschi, *Causes of Delinquency* (Berkeley: University of California Press, 1969).

31. Tittle, "Theoretical Developments in Criminology," p. 65.

32. Ibid.

33. Ibid.

34. Ibid.

35. Ibid.

36. Ibid.

37. Ibid.

38. Ibid.

39. Michael Gottfredson and Travis Hirschi, *A General Theory of Crime* (Stanford, CA: Stanford University Press, 1990).

40. Teresa C. LaGrange and Robert A. Silverman, "Low Self-Control and Opportunity: Testing the General Theory of Crime as an Explanation for Gender Differences in Delinquency," *Criminology*, Vol. 37, No. 1 (1999), p. 41.

41. Gottfredson and Hirschi, *A General Theory of Crime*.

42. See also Michael R. Gottfredson and Travis Hirschi, "Criminality and Low Self-Control," in John E. Conklin, ed., *New Perspectives in Criminology* (Boston: Allyn & Bacon, 1996).

43. Werner Einstadter and Stuart Henry, *Criminological Theory: An Analysis of Its Underlying Assumptions* (Fort Worth, TX: Harcourt Brace, 1995), p. 189.

44. Kelli Phythian, Carl Keane, and Catherine Krull, "Family Structure and Parental Behavior: Identifying the Sources of Adolescent Self-Control," *Western Criminology Review*, Vol. 9, No. 2 (2008), pp. 73–87.

45. Ibid., p. 73.

46. Carter Hay and Walter Forrest, "The Development of Self-Control: Examining Self-Control Theory's Stability Thesis," *Criminology*, Vol. 44, No. 4 (November 2006), pp. 739–772.

47. Constance L. Chapple, "Self-Control, Peer Relations, and Delinquency," *Justice Quarterly*, Vol. 22, No. 1 (March 2005), pp. 89–106.

48. Ibid., p. 101.

49. Douglas Longshore, "Self-Control and Criminal Opportunity: A Prospective Test of the General Theory of Crime," *Social Problems*, Vol. 45, No. 1 (February 1998), pp. 102–114.

50. Gottfredson and Hirschi, *A General Theory of Crime*, p. 88.

51. Longshore, "Self-Control and Criminal Opportunity."

52. Travis C. Pratt and Francis T. Cullen, "The Empirical Status of Gottfredson and Hirschi's General Theory of Crime: A Meta-Analysis," *Criminology*, Vol. 38, No. 3 (2000), pp. 931–964.

53. Carter Hay, "Parenting, Self-Control, and Delinquency: A Test of Self-Control Theory," *Criminology*, Vol. 39, No. 3 (2001), pp. 707–736.

54. Ibid., p. 725.

55. Karen L. Hayslett-McCall and Thomas J. Bernard, "Attachment, Masculinity, and Self-Control: A Theory of Male Crime Rates," *Theoretical Criminology*, Vol. 6, No. 1 (February 2002), pp. 5–33.

56. Per-Olof H. Wikström and Kyle H. Treiber, "Violence as Situational Action," *International Journal of Conflict and Violence*, Vol. 3, No. 1 (2009), pp. 75–96.

57. Jonathan R. Brauer and Charles R. Tittle, "When Crime in Not an Option: Inspecting the Moral Filtering of Criminal Action Alternatives," *Justice Quarterly*, 2016.

58. Per-Olof H. Wikström and Kyle Treiber, "The Role of Self-Control in Crime Causation beyond Gottfredson and Hirschi's General Theory of Crime," *European Journal of Criminology*, Vol. 4, No. 237 (2007), pp. 237–264.

59. Ibid., p. 77.

60. Steven F. Messner, "Morality, Markets, and the ASC: 2011 Presidential Address to the American Society of Criminology," *Criminology*, Vol. 50, No. 1 (2012), p. 8.

61. Brauer and Tittle, "When Crime is Not an Option," p. 1.

62. Christian Seipel and Stefanie Eifler, "Opportunities, Rational Choice, and Self-Control on the Interaction of Person and Situation in a General Theory of Crime," *Crime and Delinquency*, Vol. 56, No. 2 (April 2010), pp. 167–197. doi: 10.1177/0011128707312525.

63. Kevin M. Beaver et al., "The Relationship between Self-Control and Language: Evidence of a Shared Etiological Pathway," *Criminology*, Vol. 46, No. 4 (2008), pp. 939–970.

64. Gregory M. Zimmerman, Ekaterina V. Botchkovar, Olena Antonaccio, and Lorine A. Hughes, "Low Self-Control in 'Bad' Neighborhoods: Assessing the Role of Context on the Relationship between Self-Control and Crime," *Justice Quarterly*, 2012.

65. Alex R. Piquero, "Take My License n' All That Jive, I Can't See... 35: Little Hope for the Future Encourages Offending Over time," *Justice Quarterly*, March 2014, doi: 10.1080/07418825.2014.896396.

66. Social Support or Biosocial Support?: A Genetically Informative Analysis of Social Support and Its Relation to Self-Control, *Criminal Justice and Behavior*, Vol. 41 (2014), available online at http://cjb.sagepub.com/content/41/4/453.

67. Charles R. Tittle, *Control Balance: Toward a General Theory of Deviance* (Boulder, CO: Westview Press, 1995).

68. For an excellent summation of control–balance theory, see Alex R. Piquero and Matthew Hickman, "An Empirical Test of Tittle's Control Balance Theory," *Criminology*, Vol. 37, No. 2 (1999), pp. 319–341.

69. Tittle, *Control Balance*, p. 181.

70. Piquero and Hickman, "An Empirical Test of Tittle's Control Balance Theory," p. 327.

71. Tittle, *Control Balance*, p. 95. For a good critique of control–balance theory, see Joachim J. Savelsberg, "Human Nature and Social Control in Complex Society: A Critique of Charles Tittle's Control Balance," *Theoretical Criminology*, Vol. 3, No. 3 (August 1999), pp. 331–338.

72. The Marshall Project, "The Obstacle Course," September 14, 2016, https://www.themarshallproject.org/2015/03/02/the-obstacle-course (accessed March 20, 2017).

73. Frank Tannenbaum, *Crime and the Community* (New York: Atheneum Press, 1938), pp. 17–18.

74. Ibid., p. 19.

75. Edwin M. Lemert, *Social Pathology: A Systematic Approach to the Theory of Sociopathic Behavior* (New York: McGraw-Hill, 1951), p. 76.

76. Ibid.

77. Howard Becker, *Outsiders: Studies in the Sociology of Deviance* (New York: Free Press, 1963).

78. Ibid., p. 1.

79. Ibid., p. 9.

80. Ibid., p. 147.

81. NORML, "About NORML," http://norml.org/about (accessed February 27, 2017).

82. Ibid., pp. 37–38.

83. Jon Gunnar Bernburg and Marvin D. Krohn, "Labeling, Life Chances, and Adult Crime: The Direct and Indirect Effects of Official Intervention in Adolescence on Crime in Early Adulthood," *Criminology*, Vol. 41, No. 4 (2003), pp. 1287–1318.

84. Robert J. Sampson and John H. Laub, "A Life-Course Theory of Cumulative Disadvantage and the Stability of Delinquency," in Terence P. Thornberry, ed., *Developmental Theories of Crime and Delinquency* (New Brunswick, NJ: Transaction, 1997).

85. Bernburg and Krohn, "Labeling, Life Chances, and Adult Crime."

86. Legal Action Center, "After Prison: Roadblocks to Reentry," 2008, http://lac.org/roadblocks-to-reentry.

87. Mike S. Adams, "Labeling and Differential Association: Towards a General Social Learning Theory of Crime and Deviance," *American Journal of Criminal Justice*, Vol. 20, No. 2 (1996), pp. 147–164.

88. Ibid., p. 160.

89. Emily Restivo and Mark M. Lanier, "Measuring the Contextual Effects and Mitigating Factors of Labeling Theory," *Justice Quarterly*, 2013, http://dx.doi.org/10.1080/07418825.2012.756115.

90. Michael Rocque, Chad Posick, and Ray Paternoster, "Identities through Time: An Exploration of Identity Change as a Cause of Desistance," *Justice Quarterly*, 2014, http://dx.doi.org/10.1080/07418825.2014.894111 (accessed May 5, 2015).

91. John Braithwaite and Heather Strang, *The Right Kind of Shame for Crime Prevention*, RISE Working Papers, Number 1 (Australian National University, 1997), http://www.aic.gov.au/rjustice/rise/working/risepap1.html (accessed March 11, 2005).

92. A number of papers have been released in the Reintegrative Shaming Experiments (RISE) series. They include Braithwaite and Strang, *The Right Kind of Shame for Crime Prevention*; Heather Strang and Lawrence W. Sherman, *The Victim's Perspective* (Canberra: Australian National University, 1997); Lawrence W. Sherman and Geoffrey C. Barnes, *Restorative Justice and Offenders' Respect for the Law* (Canberra: Australian National University,

1997); and Lawrence W. Sherman and Heather Strang, *Restorative Justice and Deterring Crime* (Canberra: Australian National University, 1997).

93. John Braithwaite and Heather Strang, *Restorative Justice and Offenders' Respect for the Law*, RISE Working Papers, Number 3 (Australian National University, 1997), http://www.aic.gov.au/rjustice/rise/working/risepap3.html (accessed March 11, 2005).

94. Ibid.

95. Erving Goffman, *The Presentation of Self in Everyday Life* (Garden City, NY: Doubleday, 1959).

96. Goffman, *The Presentation of Self in Everyday Life*, pp. 9–10.

97. Erving Goffman, *Stigma: Notes on the Management of Spoiled Identity* (Upper Saddle River, NJ: Prentice Hall, 1963).

98. Ibid., p. 5.

99. Ibid., p. 138.

100. Erving Goffman, *Asylums: Essays on the Social Situation of Mental Patients and Other Inmates* (Garden City, NY: Anchor, 1961).

101. P.L. 93–415; 42 U.S. Code Section 5667e.

102. See, for example, Information Technology International's initial report data at http://www.itiincorporated.com/showpage.asp?sect=proj&pid=6 (accessed June 8, 2007).

103. See Kevin Haggerty et al., *Preparing for the Drug Free Years* (Washington, DC: Office of Juvenile Justice and Delinquency Prevention, 1999), http://www.ncjrs.org/html/jjbulletin/9907/theo.html (accessed March 11, 2005).

104. Haggerty et al., *Preparing for the Drug Free Years*.

105. Material in this paragraph is adapted from Finn-Aage Esbensen, "Preventing Adolescent Gang Involvement," *OJJDP Juvenile Justice Bulletin* (Washington, DC: Office of Juvenile Justice and Delinquency Prevention, September 2000).

106. See R. E. Tremblay et al., "From Childhood Physical Aggression to Adolescent Maladjustment: The Montreal Prevention Experiment," in R. D. Peters and R. J. McMahon, eds., *Preventing Childhood Disorders, Substance Abuse, and Delinquency* (Thousand Oaks, CA: Sage, 1996), pp. 268–298.

107. John Paul Wright and Kevin M. Beaver, "Do Parents Matter in Creating Self-Control in Their Children? A Genetically Informed Test of Gottfredson and Hirschi's Theory of Low Self-Control," *Criminology*. Vol. 43 (2005), pp. 1169–1202.

108. Randy Martin, Robert J. Mutchnick, and W. Timothy Austin, *Criminological Thought: Pioneers Past and Present* (New York: Macmillan, 1990), p. 368.

109. Laurie Taylor, "Erving Goffman," *New Society*, December 1968, p. 836.

110. George Psathas, "Ethnomethods and Phenomenology," in Donald McQuarie, ed., *Readings in Contemporary Sociological Theory: From Modernity to Post-Modernity* (Toronto: Prentice Hall Canada, 1999).

111. For some influential writings of the period, see K. F. Riegel, "Toward a Dialectical Theory of Development," *Human Development*, Vol. 18 (1975), pp. 50–64; and U. Bronfenbrenner, *The Ecology of Human Development* (Cambridge: Harvard University Press, 1979).

112. R. M. Lerner, "Early Adolescence: Towards an Agenda for the Integration of Research, Policy and Intervention," in R. M. Lerner, ed., *Early Adolescence: Perspectives on Research, Policy, and Intervention* (Hillsdale, NJ: Erlbaum, 1993), pp. 1–13.

113. See T. P. Thornberry, *Developmental Theories of Crime and Delinquency* (Piscataway, NJ: Transaction, 1997).

114. Elaine Eggleston Doherty, "Self-Control, Social Bonds, and Desistance," *Criminology*, Vol. 44, No. 4 (November 2006), pp. 807–808.

115. A. Blumstein et al., eds., *Criminal Careers and Career Criminals* (Washington, DC: National Academy Press, 1986).

116. See Alfred Blumstein et al., "Introduction: Studying Criminal Careers," in Blumstein et al., eds., *Criminal Careers and Career Criminals*, p. 12.

117. Blumstein et al., *Criminal Careers and Career Criminals*, pp. 12–30.

118. Robert J. Sampson and John H. Laub, *Crime in the Making: Pathways and Turning Points through the Life Course* (Cambridge: Harvard University Press, 1993).

119. G. H. Elder, Jr., "Perspectives on the Life-Course," in G. H. Elder, Jr., ed., *Life-Course Dynamics* (Ithaca, NY: Cornell University Press, 1985).

120. Philip W. Harris, Wayne N. Welsh, and Frank Butler, "A Century of Juvenile Justice," in *Criminal Justice 2000*, Vol. 1 (Washington, DC: National Institute of Justice, 2000).

121. Elder, *Life-Course Dynamics*.

122. Robert J. Sampson and John H. Laub, "Understanding Variability in Lives through Time: Contributions of Life-Course Criminology," in Alex Piquero and Paul Mazerolle, eds., *Life-Course Criminology: Contemporary and Classic Readings* (Belmont, CA: Wadsworth, 2001), p. 243.

123. Marc LeBlanc and Rolf Loeber, "Developmental Criminology Updated," in Michael Tonry, ed., *Crime and Justice: A Review of Research*, Vol. 23 (Chicago: University of Chicago Press, 1998).

124. Adapted from Harris, Welsh, and Butler, "A Century of Juvenile Justice," p. 379.

125. Glen H. Elder, Jr. and Monica Kirkpatrick Johnson, "The Life Course and Aging: Challenges, Lessons, and New Directions," in Richard A. Settersten, Jr., ed., *Invitation to the Life Course: Toward New Understandings of Later Life* (Amityville, NY: Baywood Publishing, 2002), pp. 49–84.

126. See, for example, the collected papers of Sheldon Glueck, 1916–1972, which are part of the David L. Bazelon collection at Harvard University Law School (Cambridge, MA); Sheldon and Eleanor Glueck, *500 Delinquent Women* (New York: Alfred A. Knopf, 1934); and Sheldon and Eleanor Glueck, *500 Criminal Careers* (New York: Alfred A. Knopf, 1930). Results of the Gluecks' work were also reported in S. Glueck and E. Glueck, *Unraveling Juvenile Delinquency* (New York: The Commonwealth Fund, 1950).

127. Sheldon Glueck and Eleanor Glueck, *Delinquents and Nondelinquents in Perspective* (Cambridge: Harvard University Press, 1968).

128. David S. Kirk, "Residential Change as a Turning Point in the Life Course of Crime: Desistance or Temporary Cessation?" *Criminology*, Vol. 50, No. 2 (2012), p. 1.

129. John H. Laub and Robert J. Sampson, "Urban Poverty and the Family Context of Delinquency: A New Look at Structure and Process in a Classic Study," *Child Development*, Vol. 65 (1994), pp. 523–540. See also John H. Laub and Robert J. Sampson, "Turning Points in the Life Course: Why Change Matters to the Study of Crime," *Criminology*, Vol. 31, No. 3 (1993), pp. 301–325; and Robert J. Sampson and John H. Laub, "Crime and Deviance in the Life Course," *Annual Review of Sociology*, Vol. 18 (1992), pp. 63–84.

130. See John H. Laub and Leana C. Allen, "Life Course Criminology and Community Corrections," *Perspectives*, Vol. 24, No. 2 (Spring 2000), pp. 20–29.

131. Sampson and Laub, "Crime and Deviance in the Life Course," pp. 63–84.

132. John H. Laub, "The Life Course of Criminology in the United States: The American Society of Criminology 2003 Presidential Address," *Criminology*, Vol. 42, No. 1 (2004), pp. 1–26.

133. G. B. Trasler, "Aspects of Causality, Culture, and Crime," paper presented at the Fourth International Seminar at the International Centre of Sociological, Penal and Penitentiary Research and Studies, Messina, Italy, 1980.

134. Laub and Sampson, "Turning Points in the Life Course."

135. Ibid.

136. Bradley R. Entner Wright et al., "The Effects of Social Ties on Crime Vary by Criminal Propensity: A Life-Course Model of Interdependence," *Criminology*, Vol. 39, No. 2 (2001), pp. 321–348.

137. Torbjørn Skardhamar and Jukka Savolainen, "Changes in Criminal Offending Around the Time of Job Entry: A Study of Employment and Desistance," *Criminology*, 2014; doi: 10.1111/1745-9125.12037 (accessed May 1, 2015).

138. Michael Rocque, Chad Posick and Ray Paternoster, "Identities through Time: An Exploration of Identity Changes as a Cause of Desistance," *Justice Quarterly*, 2014, doi: 10.1080/07418825.2014.894111 (accessed May 1, 2015).

139. See Laub and Allen, "Life Course Criminology and Community Corrections," pp. 20–29.

140. Sampson and Laub, *Crime in the Making*.

141. Matthew G. Yeager, "Life-Course Study of Released Prisoners Suggests Importance of Employment for Offender Reintegration and Community Safety," *Offender Programs Report*, Vol. 7, No. 2 (July–August 2003), pp. 1, 28–32.

142. Robert J. Sampson, John H. Laub, and Christopher Wimer, "Does Marriage Reduce Crime? A Counterfactual Approach to Within-Individual Causal Effects," *Criminology*, Vol. 44, No. 3 (2006), pp. 465–508.

143. Ronald L. Simons et al., "A Test of Life-Course Explanations for Stability and Change in Antisocial Behavior from Adolescence to Young Adulthood," *Criminology*, Vol. 40, No. 2 (2002), pp. 401–434.

144. Lisa M. Broidy and Elizabeth E. Cauffman, "Understanding the Female Offender," National Institute of Justice, unpublished report, 2006.

145. Terrie E. Moffitt, "Adolescence-Limited and Life-Course-Persistent Antisocial Behavior," *Psychological Review* (1993), Vol. 100, pp. 674–701.

146. Adapted from Tittle, "Theoretical Developments in Criminology."

147. Moffitt, "Adolescence-Limited and Life-Course-Persistent Antisocial Behavior."

148. Family and Youth Services Bureau, *Understanding Youth Development: Promoting Positive Pathways of Growth* (Washington, DC: U.S. Department of Health and Human Services, 2000).

149. Marvin E. Wolfgang, "Crime in a Birth Cohort," Proceedings of the American Philosophical Society, Vol. 117, No. 5 (October 25, 1973), pp. 404–411.

150. A. Quetelet, *A Treatise on Man and the Development of His Facilities* (Gainesville, FL: Scholars Facsimiles and Reprints, 1969).

151. Sheldon Glueck and Eleanor Glueck, *Later Criminal Careers* (New York: The Commonwealth Fund, 1937), p. 105.

152. Walter R. Grove, "The Effect of Age and Gender on Deviant Behavior: A Biopsychosocial Perspective," in Alice S. Rossi, ed., *Gender and the Life Course* (New York: Aldine, 1985).

153. Ibid., p. 128.

154. See David P. Farrington, "The Twelfth Jack Tizard Memorial Lecture: The Development of Offending and Antisocial Behavior from Childhood—Key Findings from the Cambridge Study in Delinquent Development," *Journal of Child Psychology and Psychiatry*, Vol. 360 (1995), pp. 929–964; and Donald J. West and David P. Farrington, *The Delinquent Way of Life: Third Report of the Cambridge Study in Delinquent Development* (London: Heinemann, 1977).

155. David P. Farrington, "Explaining and Preventing Crime: The Globalization of Knowledge—The American Society of Criminology 1999 Presidential Address," *Criminology*, Vol. 38, No. 1 (February 2000), pp. 1–24.

156. Piquero and Mazerolle, *Life-Course Criminology*, p. xv.

157. Rolf Loeber and Marc LeBlanc, "Toward a Developmental Criminology," in M. Tonry and N. Morris, eds., *Crime and Justice: A Review of Research*, Vol. 12 (Chicago: University of Chicago Press, 1990).

158. Stephanie R. Hawkins et al., *Resilient Girls: Factors That Protect against Delinquency* (Washington, DC: Office of Justice Programs, 2009), p. 1.

159. Ibid., p. 9.

160. Marvin Wolfgang, Robert Figlio, and Thorsten Sellin, *Delinquency in a Birth Cohort* (Chicago: University of Chicago Press, 1972).

161. Marvin Wolfgang, Terence Thornberry, and Robert Figlio, *From Boy to Man, from Delinquency to Crime* (Chicago: University of Chicago Press, 1987).

162. Steven P. Lab, "Analyzing Change in Crime and Delinquency Rates: The Case for Cohort Analysis," *Criminal Justice Research Bulletin*, Vol. 3, No. 10 (Huntsville, TX: Sam Houston State University, 1988), p. 2.

163. Lawrence E. Cohen and Richard Machalek, "A General Theory of Expropriative Crime: An Evolutionary Ecological Approach," *American Journal of Sociology*, Vol. 94, No. 3 (1988), pp. 465–501; and Lawrence E. Cohen and Richard Machalek, "The Normalcy of Crime: From Durkheim to Evolutionary Ecology," *Rationality and Society*, Vol. 6 (1994), pp. 286–308.

164. Bryan Vila, "Human Nature and Crime Control: Improving the Feasibility of Nurturant Strategies," *Politics and the Life Sciences*, Vol. 16, No. 1 (March 1997), pp. 3–21.

165. Ibid.

166. Terence Thornberry, "Toward an Interactional Theory of Delinquency," *Criminology*, Vol. 25 (1987), pp. 863–891.

167. See Terence P. Thornberry et al., "Delinquent Peers, Beliefs, and Delinquent Behavior: A Longitudinal Test of Interactional Theory," *Criminology*, Vol. 32, No. 1 (1994), pp. 47–53.

168. Terence P. Thornberry et al., "Testing Interactional Theory: An Examination of Reciprocal Causal Relationships among Family, School and Delinquency," *Journal of Criminal Law and Criminology*, Vol. 82 (1991), pp. 3–35.

169. Carolyn Smith and Terence P. Thornberry, "The Relationship between Childhood Maltreatment and Adolescent Involvement in Delinquency," *Criminology*, Vol. 33, No. 4 (1995), pp. 451–477.

170. Suman Kakar, "Youth Gangs and Their Families: Effects of Gang Membership on Their Families' Subjective Well-Being," *Journal of Crime and Justice*, Vol. 21 (1998), pp. 157–171.

171. Barbara Tatem Kelley et al., *Developmental Pathways in Boys' Disruptive and Delinquent Behavior* (Washington, DC: Office of Juvenile Justice and Delinquency Prevention, December 1997).

172. R. Loeber and D. F. Hay, "Developmental Approaches to Aggression and Conduct Problems," in M. Rutter and D. F. Hay, eds., *Development through Life: A Handbook for Clinicians* (Oxford, England: Blackwell Scientific, 1994).

173. Ibid.

174. The Causes and Correlates of Delinquency study is being conducted by Terence P. Thornberry of the Rochester Youth Development Study at the State University of New York at Albany, New York; Rolf Loeber of the Pittsburgh Youth Study at the University of Pittsburgh; and David Huizinga of the Denver Youth Survey at the University of Colorado.

175. Adapted from Katharine Browning et al., "Causes and Correlates of Delinquency Program," OJJDP Fact Sheet (Washington, DC: U.S. Department of Justice, April 1999).

176. Compiled from Katharine Browning and Rolf Loeber, "Highlights of Findings from the Pittsburgh Youth Study," OJJDP Fact Sheet (Washington, DC: U.S. Department of Justice, February 1999); Katharine Browning, Terence P. Thornberry, and Pamela K. Porter, "Highlights of Findings from the Rochester Youth Development Study," OJJDP Fact Sheet (Washington, DC: U.S. Department of Justice, April 1999); and Katharine Browning and David Huizinga, "Highlights of Findings from the Denver Youth Survey," OJJDP Fact Sheet (Washington, DC: U.S. Department of Justice, April 1999).

177. Browning and Huizinga, "Highlights of Findings from the Denver Youth Survey."

178. Family and Youth Services Bureau, *Understanding Youth Development: Promoting Positive Pathways of Growth.*

179. Quotations in the following list are taken from Kelley et al., *Developmental Pathways in Boys' Disruptive and Delinquent Behavior.*

180. Ibid., p. 14.

181. Thomas A. Loughran, Robert Brame, Jeffrey Fagan, Alex R. Piquero, Edward P. Mulvey, and Carol A. Schubert, *Studying Deterrence among High-Risk Adolescents* (Washington, DC: OJJDP, 2015).

182. See Felton J. Earls and Albert J. Reiss, *Breaking the Cycle: Predicting and Preventing Crime* (Washington, DC: National Institute of Justice, 1994), http://www.ncjrs.org/txtfiles/break.txt (accessed March 12, 2006).

183. Ibid.

184. Ibid.

185. Adapted from the MacArthur Foundation, "The Project on Human Development in Chicago Neighborhoods," http://www.macfound.org/research/hcd/hcd_5.htm (accessed January 5, 2006).

186. "Study of Chicago Finds Neighborhood Efficacy Explains Reductions in Violence," Project on Human Development in Chicago Neighborhoods press release, http://phdcn.harvard.edu/press/index.htm (accessed January 5, 2006).

187. Vila, "Human Nature and Crime Control," p. 10.

188. Robert W. Sweet, Jr., "Preserving Families to Prevent Delinquency," *Office of Juvenile Justice and Delinquency Prevention Model Programs, 1990* (Washington, DC: U.S. Department of Justice, April 1992).

189. Ibid.

190. David P. Farrington, "The Twelfth Jack Tizard Memorial Lecture: The Development of Offending and Antisocial Behavior from Childhood—Key Findings from the Cambridge Study in Delinquent Development," *Journal of Child Psychology and Psychiatry,* Vol. 360 (1995), pp. 929–964.

CHAPTER 9: SOCIAL CONFLICT THEORIES

1. Gallup, "For First Time, Americans Favor Legalizing Marijuana," http://www.gallup.com/poll/165539/first-time-americans-favor-legalizing-marijuana.aspx (accessed February 28, 2017).

2. Steve DeAngelo, *The Cannabis Manifesto: A New Paradigm for Wellness* (North Atlantic Books, 2015).

3. For additional information, see Raymond J. Michalowski, "Perspectives and Paradigm: Structuring Criminological Thought," in Robert F. Meier, ed., *Theory in Criminology* (Beverly Hills, CA: Sage, 1977), pp. 17–39.

4. Roscoe Pound, *Social Control through the Law: The Powell Lectures* (Hamden, CT: Archon, 1968), pp. 113–114.

5. Although Pound's postulates originally referred only to men, we have here used the now-conventional phrase "men and women" throughout the postulates to indicate that Pound was speaking of everyone within the social group. No other changes to the original postulates have been made.

6. For more information, see Michalowski, "Perspectives and Paradigm."

7. William Bonger, *Criminality and Economic Conditions* (Bloomington: Indiana University Press, 1969). It was originally published in Amsterdam as *Criminalite et Conditions Economiques* (1905) and was translated into English in 1916.

8. Georg Simmel, *Conflict and the Web of Group Affiliations* (New York: Free Press, 1964). It was originally published in 1908.

9. Adapted from Michalowski, "Perspectives and Paradigm."

10. Richard Quinney, *Class, State, and Crime: On the Theory and Practice of Criminal Justice* (New York: David McKay, 1977).

11. Vance Packard, *The Status Seekers* (London: Harmondsworth, 1961).

12. George B. Vold, *Theoretical Criminology* (New York: Oxford University Press, 1958).

13. Ibid., p. 205.

14. Ibid., pp. 208–209.

15. Ralf Dahrendorf, *Class and Class Conflict in Industrial Society* (Stanford, CA: Stanford University Press, 1959).

16. Ralf Dahrendorf, "Out of Utopia: Toward a Reorientation of Sociological Analysis," *American Journal of Sociology,* Vol. 64 (1958), pp. 115–127.

17. Austin Turk, *Criminality and Legal Order* (Chicago: Rand McNally, 1969), p. vii.

18. Ibid.

19. William J. Chambliss, "Toward a Political Economy of Crime," in C. Reasons and R. Rich, eds., *The Sociology of Law* (Toronto: Butterworth, 1978), p. 193.

20. William Chambliss and Robert T. Seidman, *Law, Order, and Power* (Reading, MA: Addison-Wesley, 1971), p. 33.

21. Adapted from ibid., pp. 473–474.

22. William J. Chambliss, *Crime and the Legal Process* (New York: McGraw-Hill, 1969), p. 88.

23. Chambliss, "Toward a Political Economy of Crime."

24. Ibid.

25. Ibid.

26. Richard Quinney, *Critique of the Legal Order: Crime Control in Capitalist Society* (Boston: Little, Brown, 1974), p. 16.

27. Richard Quinney, *Class, State, and Crime: On the Theory and Practice of Criminal Justice* (New York: David McKay, 1977), p. 58.

28. Ibid.

29. Ibid., p. 61.

30. Ibid., p. 65.

31. Jeffrey H. Reiman, *The Rich Get Richer and the Poor Get Prison: Ideology, Class and Criminal Justice*, 6th ed. (Boston: Allyn & Bacon, 2000).

32. Gresham M. Sykes, "Critical Criminology," *Journal of Criminal Law and Criminology*, Vol. 65 (1974), pp. 206–213.

33. The quotations attributed to Currie in this section are from Elliott Currie, "Market, Crime, and Community," *Theoretical Criminology*, Vol. 1, No. 2 (May 1997), pp. 147–172.

34. Michael J. Lynch and W. Byron Groves, *A Primer in Radical Criminology*, 2nd ed. (Albany, NY: Harrow & Heston, 1989), p. 126.

35. Ibid., p. 128.

36. Raymond J. Michalowski, *Order, Law, and Crime: An Introduction to Criminology* (New York: Random House, 1985), p. 410.

37. Michael J. Lynch and W. Byron Groves, *A Primer in Radical Criminology* (Monsey, NY: Willow Tree Press, 1990), p. 130.

38. William V. Pelfrey, *The Evolution of Criminology* (Cincinnati: Anderson, 1980), p. 86.

39. For a good overview of critiques of radical criminology, see J. F. Galliher, "Life and Death of Liberal Criminology," *Contemporary Crisis*, Vol. 2, No. 3 (July 1978), pp. 245–263.

40. Jackson Toby, "The New Criminology Is the Old Sentimentality," *Criminology*, Vol. 16 (1979), pp. 516–526.

41. Ibid.

42. Hermann Mannheim, *Comparative Criminology* (Boston: Houghton Mifflin, 1965), p. 445.

43. Carl Klockars, "The Contemporary Crisis of Marxist Criminology," *Criminology*, Vol. 16 (1979), pp. 477–515.

44. Ibid.

45. Werner Einstadter and Stuart Henry, *Criminological Theory: An Analysis of Its Underlying Assumptions* (Toronto: Harcourt, 1995), p. 233.

46. For an excellent review of critical realism in a Canadian context, see John Lowman and Brian D. MacLean, eds., *Realist Criminology: Crime Control and Policing in the 1990s* (Toronto: University of Toronto Press, 1994).

47. Daniel J. Curran and Claire M. Renzetti, *Theories of Crime* (Boston: Allyn & Bacon, 1994), p. 283.

48. See M. D. Schwartz and W. S. DeKeseredy, "Left Realist Criminology: Strengths, Weaknesses, and the Feminist Critique," *Crime, Law, and Social Change*, Vol. 15, No. 1 (January 1991), pp. 51–72; W. S. DeKeseredy and B. D. MacLean, "Exploring the Gender, Race, and Class Dimensions of Victimization: A Left Realist Critique of the Canadian Urban Victimization Survey," *International Journal of Offender Therapy and Comparative Criminology*, Vol. 35, No. 2 (Summer 1991), pp. 143–161; and W. S. DeKeseredy and M. D. Schwartz, "British and U.S. Left Realism: A Critical Comparison," *International Journal of Offender Therapy and Comparative Criminology*, Vol. 35, No. 3 (Fall 1991), pp. 248–262.

49. See Jock Young, "The Failure of Criminology: The Need for a Radical Realism," in R. Matthews and J. Young, eds., *Confronting Crime* (Beverly Hills, CA: Sage, 1986), pp. 4–30; Jock Young, "The Tasks of a Realist Criminology," *Contemporary Crisis*, Vol. 11, No. 4 (1987), pp. 337–356; and Jock Young, "Radical Criminology in Britain: The Emergence of a Competing Paradigm," *British Journal of Criminology*, Vol. 28 (1988), pp. 159–183.

50. D. Brown and R. Hogg, "Essentialism, Racial Criminology, and Left Realism," *Australian and New Zealand Journal of Criminology*, Vol. 25 (1992), pp. 195–230.

51. Roger Matthews and Jock Young, "Reflections on Realism," in Jock Young and Roger Matthews, eds., *Rethinking Criminology: The Realist Debate* (Newbury Park, CA: Sage, 1992).

52. Don C. Gibbons, *Talking about Crime and Criminals: Problems and Issues in Theory Development in Criminology* (Upper Saddle River, NJ: Prentice Hall, 1994), p. 170.

53. Piers Beirne and James W. Messerschmidt, *Criminology* (New York: Harcourt Brace Jovanovich, 1991), p. 501.

54. Gibbons, *Talking about Crime and Criminals*, p. 165, citing Loraine Gelsthorpe and Alison Morris, "Feminism and Criminology in Britain," *British Journal of Criminology* (Spring 1988), pp. 93–110.

55. Sally S. Simpson, "Feminist Theory, Crime and Justice," *Criminology*, Vol. 27, No. 4 (1989), p. 605.

56. Roslyn Muraskin and Ted Alleman, eds., *It's a Crime: Women and Justice* (Upper Saddle River, NJ: Prentice Hall, 1993), p. 1.

57. As stated in Amanda Burgess-Proctor, "Intersections of Race, Class, Gender, and Crime: Future Directions for Feminist Criminology," *Feminist Criminology*, Vol. 1, No. 27 (2006), p. 29.

58. Carol Pateman, "Feminist Critiques of the Public/Private Dichotomy," in Anne Phillips, ed., *Feminism and Equality* (Oxford, England: Blackwell, 1987).

59. F. P. Williams III and M. D. McShane, *Criminological Theory* (Upper Saddle River, NJ: Prentice Hall, 1994), p. 238.

60. Ibid.

61. Amanda Burgess-Proctor, "Intersections of Race, Class, Gender, and Crime," p. 29.

62. James W. Messerschmidt, *Capitalism, Patriarchy and Crime: Toward a Socialist Feminist Criminology* (Totowa, NJ: Rowman and Littlefield, 1986).

63. Freda Adler, *Sisters in Crime: The Rise of the New Female Criminal* (New York: McGraw-Hill, 1975).

64. Rita J. Simon, *Women and Crime* (Lexington, MA: Lexington Books, 1975).

65. Damien Cave, "Mexico's Drug War, Feminized," *New York Times*, August 13, 2011.

66. Carol Smart, *Women, Crime and Criminology: A Feminist Critique* (London: Routledge, 1977).

67. Kathleen Daly and Meda Chesney-Lind, "Feminism and Criminology," *Justice Quarterly*, Vol. 5, No. 5 (December 1988), p. 527.

68. The following list is adapted from ibid., pp. 497–535.

69. Susan Caulfield and Nancy Wonders, "Gender and Justice: Feminist Contributions to Criminology," in Gregg Barak, ed., *Varieties of Criminology: Readings from a Dynamic Discipline* (Westport, CT: Praeger, 1994), pp. 213–229.

70. John Hagan, *Structural Criminology* (New Brunswick, NJ: Rutgers University Press, 1989), p. 130.

71. Ibid.

72. Daly and Chesney-Lind, "Feminism and Criminology," p. 506.

73. Ibid.

74. Ibid., p. 514.

75. For an intriguing analysis of how existing laws tend to criminalize women and their reproductive activities, see Susan O. Reed, "The Criminalization of Pregnancy: Drugs, Alcohol, and AIDS," in Muraskin and Alleman, eds., *It's a Crime*, pp. 92–117; and Drew Humphries, "Mothers and Children, Drugs and Crack: Reactions to Maternal Drug Dependency," in Muraskin and Alleman, eds., *It's a Crime*, pp. 131–145.

76. Dawn H. Currie, "Feminist Encounters with Postmodernism: Exploring the Impasse of the Debates on Patriarchy and Law," *Canadian Journal of Women and Law*, Vol. 5, No. 1 (1992), p. 10.

77. For an excellent overview of feminist theory in criminology and for a comprehensive review of research regarding female offenders, see Joanne Belknap, *The Invisible Woman: Gender, Crime and Justice* (Belmont, CA: Wadsworth, 1996).

78. Such studies are still ongoing and continue to add to the descriptive literature of feminist criminology. See, for example, Deborah R. Baskin and Ira Sommers, "Female Initiation into Violent Street Crime," *Justice Quarterly*, Vol. 10, No. 4 (December 1993), pp. 559–583; Scott Decker et al., "A Woman's Place Is in the Home: Females and Residential Burglary," *Justice Quarterly*, Vol. 10, No. 1 (March 1993), pp. 143–162; and Jill L. Rosenbaum, "The Female Delinquent: Another Look at the Role of the Family," in Muraskin and Alleman, eds., *It's a Crime*, pp. 399–420.

79. Ronald L. Akers, *Criminological Theories: Introduction and Evaluation* (Los Angeles: Roxbury, 1994), p. 39.

80. Karen Heimer, "Changes in the Gender Gap in Crime and Women's Economic Marginalization," in *The Nature of Crime: Continuity and Change,* Vol. 1 of *Criminal Justice 2000* (Washington, DC: National Institute of Justice, 2000), p. 428.

81. Ibid.

82. Citing Allison Morris, *Women, Crime and Criminal Justice* (New York: Blackwell, 1987).

83. Gregg Barak, "Introduction: Criminological Theory in the 'Postmodernist' Era," in Gregg Barak, ed., *Varieties of Criminology*, pp. 1–11.

84. Joycelyn M. Pollock, *Criminal Women* (Cincinnati: Anderson, 1999), p. 146.

85. See, for example, Stuart Henry and Dragan Milovanovic, *Constitutive Criminology: Beyond Postmodernism* (London: Sage, 1995); and Milovanovic, *Postmodern Criminology* (New York: Routledge, 1997).

86. Milovanovic, *Postmodern Criminology*.

87. Henry and Milovanovic, *Constitutive Criminology*, p. 118.

88. Werner Einstadter and Stuart Henry, *Criminological Theory: An Analysis of Its Underlying Assumptions* (Fort Worth, TX: Harcourt Brace, 1995).

89. Ian Taylor, Paul Walton, and Jock Young, *The New Criminology: For a Social Theory of Deviance* (London: Routledge, 1973); and Ian Taylor, Paul Walton, and Jock Young, *Critical Criminology* (London: Routledge, 1975).

90. Ian Taylor, "Crime and Social Criticism," *Social Justice*, Vol. 26, No. 2 (1999), p. 150.

91. Ibid.

92. For examples of how this might be accomplished, see F. H. Knopp, "Community Solutions to Sexual Violence: Feminist/Abolitionist Perspectives," in Harold E. Pepinsky and Richard Quinney, eds., *Criminology as Peacemaking* (Bloomington: Indiana University Press, 1991), pp. 181–193; and S. Caringella-MacDonald and D. Humphries, "Sexual Assault, Women, and the Community: Organizing to Prevent Sexual Violence," in Pepinsky and Quinney, eds., *Criminology as Peacemaking*, pp. 98–113.

93. Richard Quinney, "Life of Crime: Criminology and Public Policy as Peacemaking," *Journal of Crime and Justice*, Vol. 16, No. 2 (1993), pp. 3–9.

94. See, for example, Harold E. Pepinsky, "This Can't Be Peace: A Pessimist Looks at Punishment," in W. B. Groves and G. Newman, eds., *Punishment and Privilege* (Albany, NY: Harrow and Heston, 1986); Harold E. Pepinsky, "Violence as Unresponsiveness: Toward a New Conception of Crime," *Justice Quarterly*, Vol. 5 (1988), pp. 539–563; and Pepinsky and Quinney, eds., *Criminology as Peacemaking*.

95. See, for example, Richard Quinney, "Crime, Suffering, Service: Toward a Criminology of Peacemaking," *Quest*, Vol. 1 (1988), pp. 66–75; Richard Quinney, "The Theory and Practice of Peacemaking in the Development of Radical Criminology," *Critical Criminologist*, Vol. 1, No. 5 (1989), p. 5; and Richard Quinney and John Wildeman, *The Problem of Crime: A Peace and Social Justice Perspective*, 3rd ed. (Mayfield, CA: Mountain View Press, 1991)—originally published as *The Problem of Crime: A Critical Introduction to Criminology* (New York: Bantam, 1977).

96. All of these themes are addressed, for example, in Pepinsky and Quinney, eds., *Criminology as Peacemaking*.

97. Quinney and Wildeman, *The Problem of Crime*, pp. vii–viii.

98. Bo Lozoff and Michael Braswell, *Inner Corrections: Finding Peace and Peace Making* (Cincinnati: Anderson, 1989).

99. Clemens Bartollas and Michael Braswell, "Correctional Treatment, Peacemaking, and the New Age Movement," *Journal of Crime and Justice*, Vol. 16, No. 2 (1993), pp. 43–58.

100. Ibid.

101. For a good overview of such programs, see Thomas E. Carbonneau, *Alternative Dispute Resolution: Melting the Lances and Dismounting the Steeds* (Chicago: University of Illinois Press, 1989).

102. Peter Finn and Andrea K. Newlyn, *Miami's "Drug Court": A Different Approach* (Washington, DC: National Institute of Justice, June 1993), p. 2.

103. Fay Honey Knopp, "Community Solutions to Sexual Violence: Feminist-Abolitionist Perspectives," in Pepinsky and Quinney, eds., *Criminology as Peacemaking*, p. 183.

104. Ibid.

105. Daniel Van Ness and Karen Heetderks Strong, *Restoring Justice* (Cincinnati: Anderson, 1997), p. 31.

106. Office of Juvenile Justice and Delinquency Prevention, *Balanced and Restorative Justice: Program Summary* (Washington, DC: OJJDP, no date), p. 2, from which some of the wording in this section is adapted.

107. Milwaukee County District Attorney's Office, "Community Conferencing Program," no date.

108. Ibid.

109. Donald Black, *Moral Time* (New York: Oxford University Press, 2011).

110. Stephen C. Richards, "Introducing the New School of Convict Criminology," *Social Justice,* Vol. 28, No. 1 (2001), p. 177.

111. J. I. Ross and S. C. Richards, *Convict Criminology* (Belmont, CA: Thomson Wadsworth, 2002).

112. Stephen C. Richards and Jeffrey Ian Ross, "Convict Criminology," in Richard A. Wright and J. Mitchell Miller, eds., *Encyclopedia of Criminology*, Vol. 1 (New York: Routledge, 2005), pp. 232–236.

113. Ibid.

114. John Irwin, *The Felon* (Upper Saddle River, NJ: Prentice Hall, 1970).

115. K. C. Carceral et al., *Behind a Convict's Eyes: Doing Time in a Modern Prison* (New York: Wadsworth, 2003).

116. K. C. Carceral and Thomas J. Bernard, *Prison, Inc.: A Convict Exposes Life inside a Private Prison* (New York: New York University Press, 2006).

117. The following list is adapted from Richards and Ross, "Convict Criminology"; and Matthew B. Robinson, *Justice Blind: Ideals and Realities of American Criminal Justice*, 2nd ed. (Upper Saddle River, NJ: Prentice Hall, 2005).

118. Walter S. DeKeseredy, "Pushing the Envelope: The Current State of North American Critical Criminology," paper presented at the 2013 American Society of Criminology annual meeting in Atlanta, GA.

119. Ibid., p. 13.

120. Ibid., p. 16.

CHAPTER 10: CRIMINAL VICTIMIZATION

1. National Criminal Justice Reference Service, "Special Feature: Children Exposed to Violence," https://ncjrs.gov/childrenexposedtoviolence (accessed May 4, 2017).

2. *National Task Force on Children Exposed to Violence, Defending Childhood* (Washington, DC: U.S. Department of Justice, 2012).

3. David Finkelhor, Heather Turner, Richard Ormrod, Sherry Hamby, and Kristen Kracke, *Children's Exposure to Violence: A Comprehensive National Survey* (Washington, DC: Office of Juvenile Justice and Delinquency Prevention, 2009).

4. Carl Bialik, "Statistics Shed Little Light on Rape Rates," *Wall Street Journal*, August 30, 2013, http://www.wsj.com/articles/SB10001424127887324324404579043623106927570 (accessed February 12, 2017).

5. Ibid.

6. Much of the information in this section comes from Bureau of Justice Statistics, *The Nation's Two Crime Measures* (Washington, DC: U.S. Dept. of Justice, 2014); and Jennifer L. Truman and Rachel Morgan, *Criminal Victimization 2015* (Washington, DC: U.S. Dept. of Justice, 2016); from which some of the wording is taken.

7. For further information, see Ronet Bachman and Bruce Taylor, "The Measurement of Family Violence and Rape by the Redesigned National Crime Victimization Survey," *Justice Quarterly*, Vol. 11, No. 3 (September 1994); Bureau of Justice Statistics, "National Crime Victimization Survey Redesign," *BJS Fact Sheet*, October 19, 1994; and BJS, "Questions and Answers about the Redesign," October 30, 1994.

8. National Incident-Based Reporting System: Eight Benefits of NIBRS to Victim Service Providers," http://www.ovc.gov/pubs/NIBRS/index.html (accessed February 4, 2017).

9. Some of the material in this section is derived from Frank Schmalleger, *Criminal Justice Today*, 14th ed. (Pearson, Upper Saddle River, NJ: Pearson, 2016).

10. The President's Commission on Law Enforcement and Administration of Justice, *The Challenge of Crime in a Free Society* (Washington, DC: U.S. Government Printing Office, 1967). The President's Commission relied on *Uniform Crime Reports* data, and the other crime statistics reported in this section come from the UCR Program for various years.

11. Frank E. Hagan, *Research Methods in Criminal Justice and Criminology*, 5th ed. (Boston: Allyn & Bacon, 2000).

12. Graham Farrell, "Five Tests for a Theory of the Crime Drop," *Crime Science*, Vol. 2, No. 5 (2013).

13. John J. DiIulio, Jr., "The Question of Black Crime," *Public Interest* (Fall 1994), pp. 3–12.

14. Christopher J. Schreck, J. Mitchell Miller, and Chris L. Gibson, "Trouble in the School Yard: A Study of the Risk Factors of Victimization at School," *Crime and Delinquency*, Vol. 49, No. 3 (July 2003), p. 464.

15. R. Loeber, L. Kalb, and D. Huizinga, "Juvenile Delinquency and Serious Injury Victimization," *Juvenile Justice Bulletin*, 2001; and T. M. Achenbach & C. S. Edelbrock, *Manual for Child Behavior Checklist* (Burlington, VT: University of Vermont Press, 1987).

16. Erika Harrell, Lynn Langton, Marcus Berzofsky, Lance Couzens, and Hope Smiley-McDonald, *Household Poverty and Nonfatal Violent Victimization, 2008–2012* (Washington, DC: Bureau of Justice Statistics, 2014).

17. Finkelhor, D., Ormrod, R. K., Turner, H. A., and M. A. Holt,. Pathways to Poly-Victimization. *Child Maltreatment,* Vol. 14, No. 4 (2009), pp. 316–329.

18. M. Outlaw, B. Ruback, and C. Britt, "Repeat and Multiple Victimizations: The Role of Individual and Contextual Factors," *Violence and Victims*, Vol. 17, No. 2 (2002), pp. 187–204.

19. David Finkelhor, Heather Turner, Sherry Hamby, and Richard Ormrod, *Polyvictimization: Children's Exposure to Multiple Types of Violence, Crime, and Abuse* (Washington, DC: Office of Juvenile Justice and Delinquency Prevention, 2011), p. 7.

20. David Finkelhor, Richard Ormrod, H. A. Turner, and S. L. Hamby, "The Victimization of Children and Youth: A Comprehensive, National Survey," *Child Maltreatment,* Vol. 10, No. 1 (2005), pp. 5–25.

21. D. Finkelhor, R. K. Ormrod, H. A. Turner, and M.A. Holt, "Pathways to Poly-Victimization," *Child Maltreatment*, Vol. 14, No. 4 (2009), pp. 316–329.

22. Elizabeth Quinn DeValve, "A Qualitative Exploration of the Effects of Crime Victimization for Victims of Personal Crime," *Applied Psychology in Criminal Justice*, Vol. 1, No. 2 (2005), p. 84.

23. D. L. Petersen and S.D. Walker, The Psychological and Physiological Impact of Stress. In T.L. Underwood & C. Edmunds (Eds.), *Victim Assistance: Exploring Individual Practice, Organizational Policy, and Societal Responses* (New York: Springer Publishing Company, 2003), pp. 66–94.

24. Lynn Langton and Jennifer Truman, "Socio-Emotional Impact of Violent Crime," *BJS Special Report* (September 2014), from which much of the material in this section is adapted.

25. The study defined *socio-emotional problems* as "the experience of one or more of the following: feelings of moderate to severe distress; significant problems with work or school, such as trouble with a boss, coworkers, or peers; or significant problems with family members or friends, including more arguments than before the victimization, an inability to trust, or not feeling as close after the victimization."

26. DeValve, "A Qualitative Exploration of the Effects of Crime Victimization for Victims of Crime," p. 81.

27. Some of the information in this section is adapted from Canadian Resource Centre for Victims of Crime, "The Impact of Victimization," October 2005, http://www.crcvc.ca/docs/victimization.pdf (accessed January 3, 2015).

28. L. Dugan, "The Effect of Criminal Victimization On a Household's Moving Decision," *Criminology*, Vol. 37, No. 4 (1999), pp. 903–930.

29. B. Williams, *Working with Victims of Crime: Policies, Politics and Practice* (London: Jessica Kingsley Publishers, 1999).

30. A. Karmen, *Crime Victims: An Introduction to Victimology*, 4th ed. (Belmont, CA: Wadsworth/Thomson Learning, 2001).

31. Dana D. DeHart, *Pathways to Prison: Impact of Victimization in the Lives of Incarcerated Women* (Washington, DC: National Institute of Justice, January 2005).

32. Karola Dillenburger, "A Behavior Analytic Perspective on Victimology," *International Journal of Behavioral Consultation and Therapy*, Vol. 3, No. 3 (2007), pp. 433–448.

33. Marvin E. Wolfgang, *Patterns in Criminal Homicide* (New York: Wiley, 1958).

34. Ibid., p. 9.

35. John P. J. Dussich, "The Challenges of Victimology: Past, Present and Future," 144th International Senior Seminar, Visiting Experts' Papers, Resource Material Series, No. 81.

36. Hans von Hentig, *The Criminal and His Victim: Studies in the Sociobiology of Crime* (New York: Archon Books, 1948).

37. Stephen Schafer, *The Victim and His Criminal* (New York: Random House, 1968).

38. Angela Book, Kimberly Costello, and Joseph A. Camilleri, "Psychopathy and Victim Selection: The Use of Gait as a Cue to Vulnerability," *Journal of Interpersonal Violence*, February 2013.

39. Elizabeth Ehrhardt Mustaine, "Lifestyle Theory," in Bonnie S. Fisher and Stephen P. Lab, eds., *Encyclopedia of Victimology and Crime Prevention* (Thousand Oaks, CA: Sage, 2010).

40. Michael J. Hindelang, Michael R. Gottfredson, and James Garofalo, *Victims of Personal Crime: An Empirical Foundation for a Theory of Personal Victimization* (Cambridge, MA: Ballinger, 1978).

41. L. W. Kenedy and D. R. Forde, "Routine Activities and Crime: An Analysis of Victimization in Canada," *Criminology*, Vol. 28, No. 1 (1990), pp. 137–152.

42. Fernando Miro, "Routine Activity Theory," in J. Mitchell Miller, ed., *The Encyclopedia of Theoretical Criminology* (Maiden, MA: Blackwell Publishing, 2014), p. 5.

43. See, for example, Barrett A. Lee and Christopher J. Schreck, "Danger on the Streets: Marginality and Victimization among Homeless People," *American Behavioral Scientist,* Vol. 48, No. 8 (April 2005), pp. 1055–1081; and James R. Lasley, "Drinking Routines/Lifestyles and Predatory Victimization: A Causal Analysis," *Justice Quarterly*, Vol. 6, No. 4 (1989), pp. 529–542.

44. See, for example, Lee and Schreck, "Danger on the Streets."

45. Toya Z. Like-Haislip and Patricia Y. Warren, "Routine Inequality: Violent Victimization at the Intersection of Race and Ethnicity among Females," *Violence and Victims*, Vol. 26, No. 1 (2011), pp. 88–102.

46. James Garofalo, "Reassessing the Lifestyle Model of Criminal Victimization," in Michael Gottfredson and Travis Hirschi, eds., *Positive Criminology* (Newbury Park, CA: Sage, 1987), p. 26.

47. National Institute of Justice, "Elder Abuse," http://nij.gov/topics/crime/elderabuse/Pages/welcome.aspx (January 25, 2015).

48. R. Bonnie and R. Wallace, eds., *Elder Mistreatment: Abuse, Neglect and Exploitation in an Aging America* (Washington, DC: The National Academies Press, 2003).

49. Britney J. Mason and Rachel E. Morgan, *Crimes against the Elderly, 2003–2013,* (Washington, DC: Bureau of Justice Statistics, 2014), http://www.bjs.gov/index.cfm?ty=pbdetail&iid=5136 (accessed January 26, 2017); from which the information in this paragraph is taken.

50. National Institute of Justice, "Extent of Elder Abuse Victimization," http://nij.gov/topics/crime/elder-abuse/pages/extent.aspx (accessed January 10, 2017).

51. Office of Justice Programs, "Elder Abuse and Mistreatment," November 2011, http://ojp.gov/newsroom/factsheets/ojpfs_elderabuse.html (accessed January 25, 2017).

52. See, for example, David Riley, "Time and Crime: The Link between Teenager Lifestyle and Delinquency," *Journal of Quantitative Criminology*, Vol. 3, No. 4 (1987), pp. 339–354.

53. L. Cohen and M. Felson,. "Social Change and Crime Rate Trends: A Routine Activity Approach," *American Sociological Review*, Vol. 44, No. 4 (1979), pp. 588–608.

54. Marcus Felson, "Routine Activities and Crime Prevention in the Developing Metropolis," *Criminology*, Vol. 25, No. 4 (1987), pp. 911–931.

55. Fernando Miro, "Routine Activity Theory," in J. Mitchell Miller, ed., *The Encyclopedia of Theoretical Criminology* (Maiden, MA: Blackwell Publishing, 2014).

56. Richard Felson, "Routine Activities and Involvement in Violence as Actor, Witness, or Target," *Violence and Victimization*, Vol. 12 (1997), pp. 209–223.

57. Lawrence E. Cohen and Marcus Felson, "Social Change and Crime Rate Trends: A Routine Activity Approach," *American Sociological Review*, Vol. 44 (August, 1979), pp. 588–608.

58. Marcus Felson and L. E. Cohen, "Human Ecology and Crime: A Routine Activity Approach," *Human Ecology*, Vol. 8 (1980), pp. 389–406.

59. Christopher J. Schreck, J. Mitchell Miller, and Chris L. Gibson, "A Study of the Risk Factors of Victimization at School," *Crime and Delinquency*, Vol. 49, No. 3 (July 2003), pp. 460–484.

60. Rodney Stark, "Deviant Places: A Theory of the Ecology of Crime," *Criminology*, Vol. 25, No. 4 (1987), pp. 893–909.

61. Lisa Sanbonmatsu, et al., *Moving to Opportunity for Fair Housing Demonstration Program: Final Impacts Evaluation* (Washington, DC: U.S. Dept. of Housing and Urban Development, 2011).

62. Ibid., p. 30.

63. D. S. Kirk and A. V. Papachristos, "Cultural Mechanisms and the Persistence of Neighborhood Violence," *American Journal of Sociology*, Vol. 116 (2011), pp. 1190–1233; and J. R. Kling, J. S. Liebman, J. B., and L. F. Katz, "Experimental Analysis of Neighborhood Effects," *Econometrica*, Vol. 75 (2007), pp. 83–119.

64. David S. Kirk and Margaret Hardy, "The Acute and Enduring Consequences of Exposure to Violence on Youth Mental Health and Aggression," *Justice Quarterly*, Vol. 31, No. 3 (2014), pp. 539–567.

65. Ibid., p. 562.

66. Office for Victims of Crime, *Vision 21: Transforming Victim Services* (Washington, DC: USDOJ, May 2013).

67. Some of the materials in this section are adapted from Frank Schmalleger, *Criminal Justice Today*, 14th ed. (Upper Saddle River, NJ: Pearson, 2015).

68. "President's Task Force on Victims of Crime," *Final Report* (Washington, DC: U.S. Government Printing Office, 1982).

69. Peter Finn and Beverly N. W. Lee, *Establishing and Expanding Victim-Witness Assistance Programs* (Washington, DC: National Institute of Justice, 1988).

70. Senate Joint Resolution (SJR) 65 is a major revision of an initial proposal, SJR 52, which Senators Kyl and Feinstein introduced on April 22, 1996. Representative Henry Hyde introduced House Joint Resolution 174, a companion to SJR 52, and a similar proposal, House Joint Resolution 173, on April 22, 1996.

71. Senate Joint Resolution 44, 105th Congress.

72. House Joint Resolution 40, Introduced April 23, 2013.

73. See the National Victims' Constitutional Amendment Network News Page, http://www.nvcan.org/news.htm (accessed January 10, 2007).

74. National Victims' Constitutional Amendment Passage, http://www.nvcap.org (accessed June 9, 2009).

75. Pub. L., 97–291.

76. VAWA 2013 was signed into law by President Obama on March 7, 2013. It is officially known as the Violence against Women Reauthorization Act of 2013.

77. USA PATRIOT Act of 2001, Section 624.

78. Office for Victims of Crime, *Report to the Nation, 2003* (Washington, DC: OVC, 2003).

79. 18 U.S.C. § 3771.

80. U.S. Senate, Republican Policy Committee, Legislative Notice No. 63, April 22, 2004.

81. Shay Bilchik, *Balanced and Restorative Justice for Juveniles: A Framework for Juvenile Justice in the 21st Century* (Washington, DC: Office of Juvenile Justice and Delinquency Prevention, 1997), p. ii.

82. Ibid., p. 14.

83. Ibid.

84. U.S. Code, Title 18, Section 3563(a)(2).

85. California Victim Compensation Program, "California Victim Compensation Program Awards $2 Million to Help Victims through Local Programs," http://www.vcgcb.ca.gov/media/pressrelease/2014/pressrelease-10-17-14.aspx (accessed January 20, 2015). California Victim Compensation and Government Claims Board, "2013 CalVCP Program Changes (no date), http://www.vcgcb.ca.gov/docs/law/2013CalVCPChanges.pdf (accessed January 20, 2017).

86. CalVCB, "CalVCB Annual Report: Fiscal Year 2015–16," http://www.vcgcb.ca.gov/board/annualreport/15-16.aspx#stats (accessed March 12, 2017).

87. California Victim Compensation and Government Claims Board, "California Victim Compensation Program Awards $2 Million to Help Victims through Local Programs," http://www.vcgcb.ca.gov/media/pressrelease/2014/pressrelease-10-17-14.aspx (accessed January 20, 2017).

CHAPTER 11: CRIMES AGAINST PERSONS

1. Tanisha Heiberg, "Judge Crushes Efforts To Appeal Oscar Pistorius' Lenient Sentence," *Huffington Post*, August 26, 2016, http://www.huffingtonpost.com/entry/oscar-pistorius-appeal-rejected_us_57c00e79e4b04193420ea0cf (accessed January 25, 2017).

2. Brent Swails and Holly Yan, "Oscar Pistorius granted bail after murder conviction," CNN, December 8, 2015, http://www.cnn.com/2015/12/08/africa/oscar-pistorius-bail-hearing/index.html (accessed January 10, 2017).

3. This and other UCR statistics in this chapter are taken from Federal Bureau of Investigation, *Crime in the United States, 2016* (Washington, DC: FBI, 2017).

4. Information in this paragraph comes from: Samuel Weigley, Alexander E. M. Hess, and Michael B. Sauter, "The Most Dangerous Cities in America," 247 Wall Street, June 11, 2012, http://247wallst.com/special-report/2012/06/11/the-most-dangerous-cities-in-america-2 (accessed August 23, 2013).

5. Ibid., citing John Roman, senior fellow at the Urban Institute.

6. Marvin Wolfgang and Franco Ferracuti, *The Subculture of Violence: Towards an Integrated Theory in Criminology* (1967; reprint, Beverly Hills, CA: Sage, 1982).

7. Marc Reidel and Margaret A. Zahn, *The Nature and Patterns of American Homicide* (Washington, DC: U.S. Government Printing Office, 1985). See also Margaret A. Zahn and P. C. Sagi, "Stranger Homicide in Nine American Cities," *Journal of Criminal Law and Criminology*, Vol. 78, No. 2 (1987), pp. 377–397.

8. Kirk R. Williams and Robert L. Flewelling, "The Social Production of Criminal Homicide: A Comparative Study of Disaggregated Rates in American Cities," *American Sociological Review*, Vol. 53, No. 3 (1988), pp. 421–431.

9. Lynne A. Curtis, *American Violence and Public Policy* (New Haven, CT: Yale University Press, 1985); and Lynne A. Curtis, *Violence, Race and Culture* (Lexington, MA: Lexington Books, 1975).

10. Claude S. Fisher, "Toward a Subcultural Theory of Urbanism," *American Journal of Sociology*, Vol. 80 (1975), p. 1335.

11. Steven Messner, "Poverty, Inequality and Urban Homicide Rate," *Criminology*, Vol. 20 (1982), pp. 103–114; and Steven Messner, "Regional and Racial Effects on the Urban Homicide Rate," *American Journal of Sociology*, Vol. 88 (1983), pp. 997–1007.

12. Robert Sampson, "Neighborhood Family Structure and the Risk of Personal Victimization," in James Byrne and Robert J. Sampson, eds., *The Social Ecology of Crime* (New York: Springer-Verlag, 1985); and Robert J. Sampson, "Structural Sources in Variation in Race-Age Specific Rates of Offending across Major U.S. Cities," *Criminology*, Vol. 23, No. 4 (1985), pp. 647–673.

13. Marvin E. Wolfgang, *Patterns in Criminal Homicide* (New York: Wiley, 1958).

14. Ibid.

15. Rosert Nash Parker and Dwayne M. Smith, "Deterrence, Poverty and Type of Homicide" *American Journal of Sociology*, Vol. 85 (1979), pp. 614–624; and M. Dwayne Smith and Robert Nash Parker, "Types of Homicide and Variation in Regional Rates," *Social Forces*, Vol. 59 (1980), pp. 136–147.

16. The distinction between expressive and instrumental crimes has been incorporated into much research on different crimes. This approach has originated in the work of Richard Block and Franklin Zimring, "Homicide in Chicago, 1965–1970," *Journal of Research in Crime and Delinquency*, Vol. 10 (1973), pp. 1–12.

17. Williams and Flewelling, "The Social Production of Criminal Homicide."

18. Laura Dugan, Daniel S. Nagin, and Richard Rosenfeld, "Explaining the Decline in Intimate Partner Homicide," *Homicide Studies*, Vol. 3, No. 3 (1999), p. 189.

19. Ibid., p. 208.

20. Terance D. Miethe and Kriss A. Drass, "Exploring the Social Context of Instrumental and Expressive Homicides: An Application of Qualitative Comparative Analysis," *Journal of Quantitative Criminology*, Vol. 15, No. 1 (1999), p. 3.

21. Carolyn Rebecca Block and Richard Block, "Beginning with Wolfgang: An Agenda for Homicide Research," *Journal of Crime and Justice*, Vol. 24, No. 2 (1991), p. 42.

22. Ibid., p. 54.

23. Philip J. Cook and Mark H. Moore, "Guns, Gun Control, and Homicide," in M. Dwayne Smith and Margaret A. Zahn, eds., *Studying and Preventing Homicide: Issues and Challenges* (Thousand Oaks, CA: Sage, 1999), p. 252.

24. Ibid., p. 254.

25. Ibid., p. 266.

26. Reprinted as Paul J. Goldstein, "The Drugs/Violence Nexus: A Tripartite Conceptual Framework," in James A. Inciardi and

Karen McElrath, eds., *The American Drug Scene* (Los Angeles: Roxbury, 1995).

27. R. N. Parker and K. Auerhahn. "Drugs, Alcohol, and Homicide: Issues in Theory and Research," in M. D. Smith and M. Zahn, eds. *Homicide: A Sourcebook of Social Research* (Thousand Oaks, CA: Sage Publications, 1998), pp. 176–194.

28. Ibid.

29. Ibid., p. 108.

30. Ibid.

31. Robert Nash Parker, "Bringing 'Booze' Back In: The Relationship between Alcohol and Homicide," *Journal of Research in Crime and Delinquency*, Vol. 32, No. 1 (1995), pp. 3–38.

32. Ibid., p. 4.

33. Ibid., p. 25.

34. Bureau of Justice Statistics, *Report to the Nation on Crime and Justice*, 2nd ed. (Washington, DC: U.S. Government Printing Office, 1988), p. 4.

35. James Alan Fox and Jack Levin, "Serial Murder: Myths and Realities," in Smith and Zahn, eds., *Studying and Preventing Homicide: Issues and Challenges* (Thousand Oaks, CA: Sage, 1999), p. 84.

36. Ibid.

37. Ibid.

38. Ronald Holmes and J. DeBurger, "Profiles in Terror: The Serial Murderer," *Federal Probation*, Vol. 49, No. 3 (1985), pp. 29–34.

39. Fox and Levin, "Serial Murder."

40. Stephen T. Holmes, Eric Hickey, and Ronald M. Holmes, "Female Serial Murderesses: Constructing Different Typologies," *Journal of Contemporary Criminal Justice*, Vol. 7, No. 4 (1991), pp. 245–256.

41. Ibid.

42. Ibid.

43. Michael D. Kelleher and C. L. Kelleher, *Murder Most Rare: The Female Serial Killer* (Westport, CT: Praeger, 1998).

44. Ibid., p. 11.

45. Ibid., p. 7.

46. James Alan Fox and Jack Levin, "Multiple Homicide: Patterns of Serial and Mass Murder," *Crime and Justice*, Vol. 23 (1998), pp. 407–455.

47. Ibid., p. 428.

48. Ibid.

49. Thomas O'Reilly-Fleming, "The Evolution of Multiple Murder in Historical Perspective," in Thomas O'Reilly-Fleming, ed., *Serial and Mass Murder: Theory, Research, and Policy* (Toronto: Canadian Scholars' Press, 1996).

50. Stephanie Simon and Aaron Pressman, "Boston Marathon Bombing Investigation Turns to Motive," Reuters, April 20, 2013, http://www.reuters.com/article/2013/04/20/us-usa-explosions-boston-shooting-idUSBRE93I0GQ20130420 (accessed May 20, 2013).

51. Lizette Alvarez Richard Perez-Pena and Christine Hauser, "Orlando Gunman was 'Cool and Calm' After Massacre, Police Say," June 13, 2016, The New York Times, https://www.nytimes.com/2016/06/14/us/orlando-shooting.html (accessed March 3, 2017).

52. Joe Taschler, Security Experts Prepare Steps to Deal with 'Active Shooters,'" *Journal Sentinel*, August 13, 2012, http://www.jsonline.com/business/security-experts-prepare-steps-to-deal-with-active-shooters-9t6d08i-166029386.html (accessed February 12, 2017).

53. Jack Levin and James Alan Fox, "A Psycho-Social Analysis of Mass Murder," in O'Reilly-Fleming, ed., *Serial and Mass Murder*, p. 65.

54. Ibid., p. 66.

55. Ibid., p. 69.

56. Ibid., p. 71.

57. Ibid., p. 69.

58. James Alan Fox and Jack Levin, *Overkill: Mass Murder and Serial Killing Exposed* (New York: Dell, 1996), p. 149.

59. U.S. Department of Justice, Office of Public Affairs, news release, "Attorney General Eric Holder Announces Revisions to the Uniform Crime Report's Definition of Rape," January 6, 2012, http://www.justice.gov/opa/pr/2012/January/12-ag-018.html (accessed March 12, 2012).

60. Centers for Disease Control, National Center for Injury Prevention and Control, *National Intimate Partner and Sexual Violence Survey Factsheet*, (Atlanta, GA: Centers for Disease Control, National Center for Injury Prevention and Control, November 2011).

61. Susan Brownmiller, *Against Our Will: Men, Women, and Rape* (New York: Simon & Schuster, 1975).

62. Dianne Herman, "The Rape Culture," in Jo Freeman, ed., *Women: A Feminist Perspective* (Palo Alto, CA: Mayfield, 1984).

63. Catherine MacKinnon, *Toward a Feminist Theory of the State* (Cambridge: Harvard University Press, 1989); and Catherine MacKinnon, *Only Words* (Cambridge: Harvard University Press, 1993).

64. See Andrea Dworkin, *Pornography: Men Possessing Women* (New York: Plenum, 1981); Andrea Dworkin, "Questions and Answers," in Diana E. H. Russell, ed., *Making Violence Sexy: Feminist Views on Pornography* (New York: Teachers College Press, 1993); and Andrea Dworkin, "Against the Male Flood: Censorship, Pornography, and Equality," in Patricia Smith, ed., *Feminist Jurisprudence* (New York: Oxford University Press, 1993).

65. Robin Morgan, *The Word of a Woman: Feminist Dispatches, 1968–1992* (New York: W. W. Norton, 1992), p. 88.

66. Brownmiller, *Against Our Will*.

67. James W. Messerschmidt, *Masculinities and Crime: Critique and Reconceptualization of Theory* (Lanham, MD: Rowman and Littlefield, 1993).

68. Ngaire Naffine, *Feminism and Criminology* (Philadelphia: Temple University Press, 1996), p. 101.

69. Diana Scully and Joseph Marolla, "Riding the Bull at Gilley's: Convicted Rapists Describe the Rewards of Rape," *Social Problems*, Vol. 32, No. 2 (1985), p. 252.

70. Nicholas Groth, *Men Who Rape: The Psychology of the Offender* (New York: Plenum, 1979).

71. Scully and Marolla, "Riding the Bull at Gilley's."

72. Ibid.

73. Diana E. H. Russell, *Rape in Marriage* (Bloomington, Indiana: Indiana University Press, 1990).

74. Larry Baron and Murray A. Straus, *Four Theories of Rape in American Society: A State-Level Analysis* (New Haven, CT: Yale University Press, 1989).

75. For examples, see Peggy Reeves Sanday, "The Socio-Cultural Context of Rape: A Cross-Cultural Study," *Journal of Social Issues*, Vol. 37 (1981), pp. 5–27.

76. Baron and Straus, *Four Theories of Rape in American Society*.

77. Robert T. Sigler, Ida M. Johnson, and Etta F. Morgan, "Forced Sexual Intercourse: Contemporary Views," in Roslyn Muraskin,

ed., *It's a Crime: Women and Justice* (Upper Saddle River, NJ: Prentice Hall, 2000), p. 352.

78. Randy Thornhill, "The Biology of Human Rape," *Jurimetrics*, Vol. 39, No. 2 (1999), p. 138.

79. Randy Thornhill and Craig T. Palmer, *A Natural History of Rape* (Cambridge: MIT Press, 2000), p. 53.

80. Martin Daly and Margo Wilson, *Homicide* (New York: Aldine De Gruyter, 1988), p. 140.

81. Thornhill and Palmer, *A Natural History of Rape*, p. 199. See also Katharine K. Baker, "What Rape Is and What It Ought Not to Be," *Jurimetrics*, Vol. 30, No. 3 (1999), p. 233.

82. R. R. Hazelwood and A. N. Burgess, eds., *Practical Aspects of Rape Investigation: A Multidisciplinary Approach* (New York: CRC Press, 1995).

83. Dennis J. Stevens, *Inside the Mind of a Serial Rapist* (San Francisco: Austin and Winfield, 1999), p. 39.

84. Diana Scully, *Understanding Sexual Violence: A Study of Convicted Rapists* (New York: Routledge, 1990).

85. Ibid., p. 59.

86. Ibid.

87. Ibid.

88. See Frances P. Bernat, "Rape Law Reform," in James F. Hodgson and Debra S. Kelley, eds., *Sexual Violence: Policies, Practices, and Challenges in the United States and Canada* (New Brunswick, CT: Praeger, 2001).

89. Pub. L. 102–325, section 486(c).

90. Carol Bohmer and Andrea Parrot, *Sexual Assault on Campus: The Problem and the Solution* (New York: Lexington Books, 1993), pp. 15–16.

91. Patricia Yancey Martin and Robert A. Hummer, "Fraternities and Rape on Campus," *Gender and Society*, Vol. 3, No. 4 (1989), p. 462.

92. Pub. L. 108–79.

93. Dee Halley, "The Prison Rape Elimination Act of 2003: Addressing Sexual Assault in Correctional Settings," *Corrections Today* (June 2005), pp. 30, 100.

94. Office of Justice Programs, *PREA Data Collection Activities, 2016* (Washington, DC: Bureau of Justice Statistics, June 2016). https://www.bjs.gov/content/pub/pdf/pdca16.pdf (accessed January 27, 2017).

95. Dee Halley, "The Prison Rape Elimination Act of 2003: Addressing Sexual Assault in Correctional Settings," *Corrections Today* (June 2005), p. 2.

96. Ibid., p. 42.

97. Ibid., p. 1.

98. Hans Toch, *Living in Prison: The Ecology of Survival* (New York: Free Press, 1977), p. 151.

99. Lara Stemple and Iian H. Meyers, "The Sexual Victimization of Men in America: New Data Challenge Old Assumptions," *American Journal of Public Health*, Vol. 104, No. 6 (June 2014).

100. Robert A. Prentky, Raymond A. Knight, and Austin F. S. Lee, *Child Sexual Molestation: Research Issues* (Washington, DC: National Institute of Justice, 1997), p. 1.

101. G. G. Abel, J. V. Becker, M. S. Mittelman, J. Cunningham-Rathner, J. L. Rouleau, and W. D. Murphy, "Self-Reported Sex Crimes of Nonincarcerated Paraphiliacs," *Journal of Interpersonal Violence*, Vol. 2 (1987), pp. 3–25.

102. Child Molestation Research and Prevention Institute, "Some Facts," http://www.childmolestationprevention.org (accessed June 5, 2007).

103. Abel et al., "Self-Reported Sex Crimes of Nonincarcerated Paraphilics."

104. B. M. Maletzky, "Factors Associated with Success and Failure in the Behavioral and Cognitive Treatment of Sexual Offenders," *Annals of Sex Research*, Vol. 6 (1993), pp. 241–258.

105. Robert A. Prentky, Raymond A. Knight, and Austin F. S. Lee, *Child Sexual Molestation: Research Issues* (Washington, DC: National Institute of Justice, 1997), from which much of the information and some of the wording in this section is taken.

106. A. Nicholas Groth, W. F. Hobson, and T. S. Gary, "The Child Molester: Clinical Observations," *Journal of Social Work and Child Sexual Abuse*, Vol. 1, No. 2 (1982), pp. 129–144.

107. Prentky et al., *Child Sexual Molestation: Research Issues.*

108. Ibid., p. 3.

109. R. A. Prentky and R. A. Knight, "Age of Onset of Sexual Assault: Criminal and Life History Correlates," in G. C. N. Hall, R. Hirschman, J. R. Graham, and M. S. Zaragoza, eds., *Sexual Aggression: Issues in Etiology, Assessment, and Treatment* (Washington, DC: Taylor & Francis, 1993), pp. 43–62.

110. Prentky et al., *Child Sexual Molestation: Research Issues.*

111. Charlotte Bunch, "The Intolerable Status Quo: Violence against Women and Children," in UNICEF, *The Progress of Nations* (1997).

112. Aurelie Corinthios, "Kim Kardashian West Meets with French Authorities in New York City to Testify in Paris Robbery Case," *People*, February 1, 2017, http://people.com/celebrity/kim-kardashian-testifies-paris-robbery-case-french-judge-in-new-york-city/ (accessed March 12, 2017).

113. Note that although purse snatching and pocket picking involve the express goal of taking someone's property, they are classified as property crimes because they do not involve the same type of direct contact with the victim as does robbery.

114. Terance D. Miethe and David McDowall, "Contextual Effects in Models of Criminal Victimization," *Social Forces*, Vol. 71, No. 3 (1993), pp. 741–760.

115. Terance D. Miethe and Richard C. McCorkle, *Crime Profiles: The Anatomy of Dangerous Persons, Places, and Situations* (Los Angeles: Roxbury, 1998).

116. Scott A. Hendricks et al., "A Matched Case-Control Study of Convenience Store Robbery Risk Factors," *Journal of Occupational and Environmental Medicine*, Vol. 41, No. 11 (1999), p. 995.

117. Richard T. Wright and Scott H. Decker, *Armed Robbers in Action: Stickups and Street Culture* (Boston: Northeastern University Press, 1997), p. 88.

118. Floyd Feeney, "Robbers as Decision Makers," in Derek B. Cornish and Ronald V. Clarke, eds., *The Reasoning Criminal* (New York: Springer-Verlag, 2009).

119. Brian A. Reaves, *Using NIBRS Data to Analyze Violent Crime* (Washington, DC: U.S. Department of Justice, Office of Justice Programs, Bureau of Justice Statistics, 1993).

120. FBI, *Crime in the United States, 2016.*

121. Ibid.

122. Thomas Gabor et al., *Armed Robbery: Cops, Robbers, and Victims* (Springfield, IL: Charles C. Thomas, 1987).

123. Mark A. Peterson and Harriet B. Braiker, *Doing Crime: A Survey of California Prison Inmates* (Santa Monica, CA: RAND Corporation, 1980).

124. Mark A. Peterson and Harriet B. Braiker, *Who Commits Crimes: A Survey of Prison Inmates* (Boston: Oelgeschlager, Gunn, and Hain, 1981).

125. Martha J. Smith and Ronald V. Clarke, "Crime and Public Transport," in Michael Tonry, ed., *Crime and Justice: A Review of Research*, Vol. 27 (Chicago: University of Chicago Press, 2000), pp. 169–234.

126. Ibid.

127. Ibid.

128. Ibid., p. 181.

129. Ibid., p. 182.

130. Derek Cornish, "The Procedural Analysis of Offending and Its Relevance for Situational Prevention," in Ronald V. Clarke, ed., *Crime Prevention Studies*, Vol. 3 (Monsey, NY: Criminal Justice Press, 1994), cited in Smith and Clarke, "Crime and Public Transport," in Tonry, ed., *Crime and Justice*, p. 181.

131. Smith and Clarke, "Crime and Public Transport," p. 181.

132. "Supreme Court Lets Taxi-Stop Rulings Stand: NYC Searchers Too Intrusive, But Boston Sweeps Legal," APBnews.com, December 4, 2000, http://www.apbnews.com/newscenter/breaking-news/2000/12/04/taxi1204_01.html (accessed January 14, 2001).

133. Feeney, "Robbers as Decision Makers."

134. Ibid., p. 59.

135. Bruce A. Jacobs and Richard Wright, "Stick-Up, Street Culture, and Offender Motivation," *Criminology*, Vol. 37, No. 1 (1999), p. 150.

136. S. Morrison and I. O'Donnell, "An Analysis of the Decision Making Processes of Armed Robbers," in R. Homel, ed., *The Politics and Practice of Situational Crime Prevention*, Vol. 5 of *Crime Prevention Studies* (Monsey, NY: Criminal Justice Press, 1996). See also Gabor et al., *Armed Robbery*.

137. Jacobs and Wright, "Stick-Up, Street Culture, and Offender Motivation."

138. Ibid., pp. 167–168.

139. Trevor Bennett and Fiona Brookman, "A Qualitative Study of the Role of Violence in Street Crime," reported in Annika Howard, "Street Robbery Is Not Just about Money," *Medical News Today*, http://www.medicalnewstoday.com/printerfriend-lynews.php?newsid=57730, December 1, 2006 (accessed August 24, 2007).

140. Richard T. Wright and Scott H. Decker, *Armed Robbers in Action: Stickups and Street Culture* (Boston: Northeastern University Press, 1997), p. 62.

141. Ibid., p. 63.

142. Ibid.

143. Ibid., p. 66.

144. Bruce A. Jacobs, Volkan Topalli, and Richard Wright, "Managing Retaliation: Drug Robbery and Informal Sanction Threats," *Criminology*, Vol. 38, No. 1 (2000), p. 173.

145. Ibid.

146. Ibid., p. 177.

147. Ibid.

148. Wright and Decker, *Armed Robbers in Action*, p. 67.

149. Jacobs, Topalli, and Wright, "Managing Retaliation," p. 180.

150. Ibid., p. 185.

151. Ibid.

152. Ibid., p. 172.

153. Ibid., p. 194.

154. Ibid.

155. J. Miller, "Up It Up: Gender and the Accomplishment of Street Robbery," *Criminology*, Vol. 36 (1998), p. 37.

156. FBI, *Crime in the United States, 2016*, based on arrests.

157. Miller, "Up It Up."

158. Ibid.

159. Bennett Loudon, "Woman Accused of Punching Walmart Greeter," *Rochester Democrat and Chronicle*, http://www.democra-tandchronicle.com/article/20111226/NEWS01/112260313/Jacquetta-Simmons-accused-hitting-elderly-Walmart-worker December 25, 2011.

160. Bureau of Justice Statistics, *Criminal Victimization 2006* (Washington, DC: U.S. Department of Justice, Office of Justice Programs, 2007), p. 172.

161. Miethe and McCorkle, *Crime Profiles*, p. 25.

162. Ibid., p. 27.

163. Callie Marie Rennison, *Criminal Victimization, 1999: Changes 1998–1999 with Trends 1993–1999* (Washington, DC: U.S. Department of Justice, Office of Justice Programs, 2000).

164. Robert J. Sampson, "Personal Violence by Strangers: An Extension and Test of Predatory Victimization," *Journal of Criminal Law and Criminology*, Vol. 78, No. 2 (1987), p. 342.

165. Richard J. Gelles, *The Violent Home: A Study of Physical Aggression between Husbands and Wives* (Beverly Hills, CA: Sage, 1974).

166. Michael Hindelang, *Criminal Victimization in Eight American Cities* (Cambridge, MA: Ballinger, 1976).

167. Evan Stark, A. Flitcraft, and W. Frazier, "Medicine and Patriarchal Violence: The Social Construction of a Private Event," *International Journal of Health Service*, Vol. 9, No. 3 (1979), pp. 461–493.

168. Murray A. Straus, "The National Family Violence Surveys," in Murray A. Straus and Richard J. Gelles, eds., *Physical Violence in American Families: Risk Factors and Adaptations to Violence in 8,145 Families* (New Brunswick, NJ: Transaction, 1990).

169. Murray A. Straus, "The Conflict Tactics Scales and Its Critics: An Evaluation and New Data on Validity and Reliability," in Straus and Gelles, eds., *Physical Violence in American Families*.

170. Murray A. Straus and Richard J. Gelles, "How Violent Are American Families? Estimates from the National Family Violence Research and Other Studies," in G. Hotaling, ed., *New Directions in Family Violence Research* (Newbury Park, CA: Sage, 1988).

171. FBI, NIBRS, 2015, https://ucr.fbi.gov/nibrs/2015/tables/data-tables (accessed January 29, 2017).

172. Ibid.

173. Neil Websdale, *Rural Woman Battering and the Justice System* (Thousand Oaks, CA: Sage, 1997).

174. Martha R. Mahoney, "Legal Issues of Battered Women: Redefining the Issue of Separation," *Michigan Law Review*, Vol. 90, No. 1 (1991), p. 6.

175. Websdale, *Rural Woman Battering and the Justice System*.

176. James Ptacek, *Battered Women in the Courtroom* (Boston: Northeastern University Press, 1999).

177. Ibid., p. 29.

178. Ibid., p. 82.

179. Ibid.

180. Much of the information in this section comes from "Facts About Bullying," stopbullying.gov (accessed March 2, 2017).

181. Gladden, R. M., Vivolo-Kantor, A. M., Hamburger, M. E., and Lumpkin, C. D. *Bullying Surveillance Among Youths: Uniform Definitions for Public Health and Recommended Data Elements, Version 1.0.* (Atlanta, GA: National Center for Injury Prevention and Control, Centers for Disease Control and Prevention and U.S. Department of Education, 2014).

182. Olweus Bullying Prevention Program, "Violence Prevention Works," http://www.violencepreventionworks.org/public/bullying_effects.page (accessed March 1, 2017).

183. Justin W. Patchin and Sameer Hinduja, "Deterring Teen Bullying: Assessing the Impact of Perceived Punishment From Police, Schools, and Parents," *Youth Violence and Juvenile Justice*, Vol. 1, No. 18 (2016).

184. National Conference of State Legislatures, "Cyberbullying," December 14, 2010, http://www.ncsl.org/research/education/cyberbullying.aspx (accessed March 20, 2017).

185. Ibid.

186. Justin W. Patchin and Sameer Hinduja, "Measuring Cyberbullying: Implications for Research," *Aggression and Violent Behavior* (2015).

187. Cyberbullying Research Center, "Cyberbullying Facts," http://cyberbullying.org/facts (accessed March 2, 2017).

188. Hinduja, S. and Patchin, J. W. Bullying, Cyberbullying, and Suicide. *Archives of Suicide Research*, Vol.14, pp. 206–221. doi:10.1080/13811118.2010.494133.

189. Federal Bureau of Investigation, *Workplace Violence: Issues in Response* (Quantico, VA: FBI, 2004), from which the quotes and information in this section are taken.

190. Erika Harrell, *Workplace Violence, 1993–2009* (Washington, DC: Bureau of Justice Statistics, 2011).

191. Ibid., p. 13.

192. Ibid., p. 14.

193. Harrell, *Workplace Violence, 1993–2009*; see also Detis T. Duhart, *Violence in the Workplace, 1993–99* (Washington, DC: Bureau of Justice Statistics, 2001).

194. Centers for Disease Control, "Workplace Safety and Health Topics: Occupational Violence," http://www.cdc.gov/niosh/topics/violence (accessed February 2, 2015).

195. Ibid.

196. 28 U.S.C.A., Section 534.

197. Public Law 103–322.

198. Bureau of Justice Assistance, *Addressing Hate Crimes: Six Initiatives That Are Enhancing the Efforts of Criminal Justice Practitioners* (Washington, DC: U.S. Department of Justice, 2000).

199. Matthew Shepard and James Byrd, Jr., Hate Crimes Prevention Act, H.R. 2647.

200. FBI, *Crime in the United States, 2015*.

201. James B. Jacobs and Kimberly A. Potter, "Hate Crimes: A Critical Perspective," in Michael Tonry, ed., *Crime and Justice: A Review of Research* (Chicago: University of Chicago Press, 1997), p. 19.

202. "Woman Rescued from Thousand Oaks Chimney Belonging to Man She Met Online," *KFSN-TV*, http://news.yahoo.com/video/woman-rescued-thousand-oaks-chimney-055642336.html (accessed October 28, 2014).

203. "FBI: Man Arrested in ESPN Reporter Nude Video Case Has Buffalo Connection," *WKBW-TV News*, http://www.msnbc.com/id/33152457 (accessed May 4, 2010).

204. "Sheriff: Accused Jewel Stalker Says God Led Him," Associated Press, September 22, 2009.

205. Violence against Women Grants Office, *Stalking and Domestic Violence: The Third Annual Report to Congress under the Violence against Women Act* (Washington, DC: Violence against Women Grants Office, 1998).

206. Ibid., p. 6.

207. Ibid.

208. Katrina Baum, Shannan Catalano, and Michael Rand, *Stalking Victimization in the United States* (Washington, DC: Bureau of Justice Statistics, 2009).

209. Ibid.

210. Patricia Tjaden and Nancy Thoennes, *Stalking in America: Findings from the National Violence against Women Survey* (Washington, DC: National Institute of Justice, 1998).

211. Paul E. Mullen et al., "Assessing and Managing the Risks in the Stalking Situation," *Journal of the American Academy of Psychiatry and Law*, Vol. 34 (2006), pp. 439–450; and Paul E. Mullen et al., "Study of Stalkers," *American Journal of Psychiatry*, Vol. 156 (August 1999), pp. 1244–1249.

212. Ibid.

213. Ibid., p. 8.

214. Ibid. See also P. Tjaden and N. Thoennes, *Extent, Nature, and Consequences of Intimate Partner Violence: Findings from the National Violence against Women Survey* (Washington, DC: U.S. Department of Justice, 2000).

215. Tjaden and Thoennes, *Stalking in America*.

216. Ibid., p. 8.

217. Ibid., p. 10.

218. Ibid.

219. Ibid.

220. U.S. Attorney's Office, Southern District of Florida, "Miami Student Sentenced for Cyberstalking on Facebook and Instagram," https://www.justice.gov/usao-sdfl/pr/miami-student-sentenced-cyberstalking-facebook-and-instagram August 31, 2016 (accessed March 1, 2017).

221. T. Gregorie, *Cyberstalking: Dangers on the Information Highway* (Arlington, VA: National Center for Victims of Crime, 2000).

222. Janet Reno, *Cyberstalking: A New Challenge for Law Enforcement and Industry—A Report from the U.S. Attorney General to the Vice President* (Washington, DC: U.S. Department of Justice, 1999).

CHAPTER 12: CRIMES AGAINST PROPERTY

1. "Stolen Matisse Recovered in US," BBC, http://www.bbc.co.uk/news/entertainment-arts-18898804 (accessed March 5, 2013).

2. "Some of the Biggest Art Thefts in Recent Times," Associated Press, May 20, 2010, http://www.boston.com/news/world/europe/articles/2010/05/20/some_of_the_biggest_art_thefts_in_recent_times/ (accessed May 3, 2013).

3. William Spain, "Art Crime of the Century Still Frustrates: Empty Frames Still Hang in Boston Museum," APB News, June 16, 2000, http://apbnews.com/newscenter/breakingnews/2000/06/16/artcrime_gardner0161_01.html (accessed December 1, 2000).

4. William Spain, "Inside the World of Art Theft: Trade Ranks Third after Drugs, Arms Sales," APB News, June 16, 2000, http://apbnews.com/newscenter/breakingnews/2000/06/16/artcrime0616_01.html (accessed September 3, 2004).

5. Ibid.

6. Ibid.

7. Ibid.

8. Federal Bureau of Investigation, *Crime in the United States, 2016* (Washington, DC: FBI, 2017).

9. Herbert Koppel, *Lifetime Likelihood of Victimization* (Washington, DC: Bureau of Justice Statistics, 1987).

10. Bureau of Justice Statistics, *Criminal Victimization, 2016* (Washington, DC: BJS, 2017)

11. FBI, *Crime in the United States, 2016.*

12. Neil Shover, "Burglary," in Michael Tonry, ed., *Crime and Justice: A Review of Research* (Chicago: University of Chicago Press, 1991).

13. For representative examples of this perspective, see Michael J. Hindelang, *Criminal Victimization in Eight American Cities* (Cambridge, MA: Ballinger, 1978); and Michael J. Hindelang, Michael R. Gottfredson, and James Garolfalo, *Victims of Personal Crime: An Empirical Foundation for a Theory of Personal Victimization* (Cambridge, MA: Ballinger, 1978).

14. For representative discussions of this perspective, see Lawrence E. Cohen and Marcus Felson, "Social Change and Crime Rate Trends: A Routine Activity Approach," *American Sociological Review*, Vol. 44 (1979), pp. 588–607; and Marcus Felson and Lawrence E. Cohen, "Human Ecology and Crime: A Routine Activity Approach," *Human Ecology*, Vol. 8 (1980), pp. 398–405.

15. Marcus Felson, "Linking Criminal Choices, Routine Activities, Informal Control, and Criminal Outcomes," in Derek B. Cornish and Ronald V. Clarke, eds., *The Reasoning Criminal: Rational Choice Perspectives on Offending* (New York: Springer-Verlag, 1986), p. 127.

16. Michael J. Frith, Shane D. Johnson and Hannah M. Fry, "Role of the Street Network in Burglars' Spatial Decision-Making," Criminology, 2017; doi http://onlinelibrary.wiley.com/doi/10.1111/crim.2017.55.issue-2/issuetoc (accessed May 18, 2017).

17. Lawrence E. Cohen and David Cantor, "Residential Burglary in the United States: Life-Style and Demographic Factors Associated with the Probability of Victimization," *Journal of Research in Crime and Delinquency*, Vol. 18, No. 1 (1981), pp. 113–127.

18. Robert J. Sampson and John D. Wooldredge, "Linking the Micro- and Macro-Level Dimensions of Lifestyle-Routine Activity and Opportunity Models of Predatory Victimization," *Journal of Quantitative Criminology*, Vol. 3 (1987), pp. 371–393.

19. Ibid.

20. Mike Maguire, *Burglary in a Dwelling* (London: Heinemann, 1982), cited in Shover, "Burglary," p. 89.

21. Shover, "Burglary," p. 90.

22. Ibid., p. 91.

23. Terance D. Miethe and Richard C. McCorkle, *Crime Profiles: The Anatomy of Dangerous Persons, Places, and Situations* (Los Angeles: Roxbury, 1998).

24. Jennifer L. Truman and Michael Planty, *Criminal Victimization, 2015* (Washington, DC: BJS, 2016).

25. Kenneth D. Tunnell, *Choosing Crime: The Criminal Calculus of Property Offenders* (Beverly, MA: Wadsworth, 1992), p. 5.

26. See Paul F. Cromwell, James N. Olson, and D'Aunn Wester Avary, *Breaking and Entering: An Ethnographic Analysis of Burglary* (Newbury Park, CA: Sage, 1991); and Richard T. Wright and Scott H. Decker, *Burglars on the Job: Streetlife and Residential Break-Ins* (Boston: Northeastern University Press, 1994), p. 35.

27. Cromwell, Olson, and Avary, *Breaking and Entering.*

28. Wright and Decker, *Burglars on the Job.*

29. Ibid., p. 38.

30. Ibid., pp. 45–46.

31. Ibid., p. 47.

32. Wright and Decker, *Burglars on the Job*, p. 51.

33. Ibid.

34. Ibid., p. 56.

35. Ibid.

36. Jack Katz, *Seductions of Crime: Moral and Sensual Attractions in Doing Evil* (New York: Basic Books, 1990), p. 79.

37. Tunnell, *Choosing Crime*, p. 41.

38. Wright and Decker, *Burglars on the Job*, p. 63.

39. Ibid.

40. Ibid., p. 72.

41. Ibid., p. 73.

42. Neil Shover, "Burglary," in Michael Tonry, ed., Crime and Justice: A Review of Research (Chicago: University of Chicago Press, 1991), p. 83.

43. Ibid., p. 80.

44. Ibid., p. 110.

45. Ibid., p. 113.

46. Ibid., p. 86.

47. Bureau of Justice Statistics, *Criminal Victimization, 1999*, Tables 81 and 83.

48. Kathryn E. McCollister, Michael T. French, and Hai Fang, "The Cost of Crime to Society: New Crime-Specific Estimates for Policy and Program Evaluation," *Drug and Alcohol Dependence*, Vol. 108, No. 1-2 (April 1, 2010), p. 23.

49. Ibid., Tables 87 and 89.

50. Laura Dugan, "The Effect of Criminal Victimization on a Household's Moving Decision," *Criminology*, Vol. 37, No. 4 (1999), pp. 903–930.

51. Eric Baumer et al., "The Influence of Crack Cocaine on Robbery, Burglary, and Homicide Rates: A Cross-City, Longitudinal Analysis," *Journal of Research in Crime and Delinquency*, Vol. 35, No. 3 (1998), pp. 316–340.

52. Ibid., p. 317.

53. Ibid.

54. Ibid., p. 319.

55. Louis B. Schlesinger and Eugene Revitch, "Sexual Burglaries and Sexual Homicide: Clinical, Forensic, and Investigative Considerations," *Journal of the American Academy of Psychiatry and the Law*, Vol. 27, No. 2 (1999), p. 228.

56. Ibid., p. 232.

57. Mark Warr, "Rape, Burglary, and Opportunity," *Journal of Quantitative Criminology*, Vol. 4, No. 3 (1988), pp. 275–288.

58. Ibid., pp. 217–218.

59. Ibid., p. 287.

60. Ibid., p. 286.

61. Ramona R. Rantala and Thomas J. Edwards, *Effects of NIBRS on Crime Statistics* (Washington, DC: Office of Justice Programs, 2000), p. 12.

62. David Barry, "Thieves Peel Off with 1,200 Orange Trees: Culprits Strike California Groves at Night," APB News, November 27, 2000, http://www.apbnews.com/newscenter/breakingnews/2000/11/27/trees1127_01.html (accessed December 1, 2000).

63. Federal Bureau of Investigation, *Crime in the United States, 2016* (Washington, DC: FBI, 2017).

64. President's Commission on Law Enforcement and Administration of Justice, *The Challenge of Crime in a Free Society* (New York: Avon, 1968), p. 64.

65. National Retail Federation, *The 2016 National Retail Security Survey.*

66. Thomas Gabor, *Everybody Does It! Crime by the Public* (Toronto: University of Toronto Press), p. 80.

67. Dick Silverman, "Crime and Punishment," *Footwear News*, November 1999, http://www.allbusiness.com/crime-law/criminal-offenses-property/9030609-1.html (accessed July 28, 2009).

68. Sheila Marikar, "Caroline Giuliani, Daughter of Ex-NYC Mayor, Arrested for Shoplifting," ABC News, August 4, 2010, http://abcnews.go.com/Entertainment/TheLaw/caroline-giuliani-daughter-rudy-giuliani-arrested-shoplifting/story?id=11326577#.Ty7OkV2WZyo (accessed March 3, 2012).

69. "Caroline Giuliani Makes Deal in Shoplifting Case," Associated Press, August 31, 2010, http://abclocal.go.com/wabc/story?section=news/local&id=7641361 (accessed March 3, 2012).

70. Brandi Fowler, "Lindsay Lohan: Images of Missing Necklace Surveillance Video Surface on the Web," E! News, March 6, 2011, http://www.eonline.com/news/229566/lindsay-lohan-images-of-missing-necklace-surveillance-video-surface-on-the-web (accessed April 21, 2013).

71. Lloyd W. Klemke, *The Sociology of Shoplifting* (Westport, CT: Praeger, 1992).

72. Lloyd W. Klemke, "Exploring Juvenile Shoplifting," *Sociology and Social Research*, Vol. 67, No. 1 (1982), pp. 59–75.

73. Mary Owen Cameron, *The Booster and the Snitch: Department Store Shoplifting* (New York: Free Press of Glencoe, 1964).

74. Klemke, "Exploring Juvenile Shoplifting," p. 71.

75. Eric Tucker and Thomas Watkins, "For Flash Mobsters, Crowd Size a Tempting Cover," Associated Press, August 9, 2011 (accessed February 21, 2012).

76. Joe Larocca, "NRF Issues Guidelines for Retailers in Handling 'Criminal Flash Mobs,'" National Retail Federation, Retail's Big Blog, http://blog.nrf.com/2011/08/02/nrf-issues-guidelines-for-retailers-in-handling-criminal-flash-mobs/ (accessed February 21, 2012).

77. National Retail Federation, "Multiple Offender Crimes: Preparing for and Understanding the Impact of Their Tactics," http://www.nrf.com/modules.php?name=Documents&op=viewlive&sp_id=6788 (accessed February 21, 2012).

78. The President's Identity Theft Task Force, *Combating Identity Theft: A Strategic Plan* (Washington, DC: U.S. Department of Justice, 2007), from which much of the information comes from and which some of the wording is taken or adapted.

79. See Business Software Alliance, "Consumer Confidence in Online Shopping Buoyed by Security Software Protection, BSA Survey Suggests," January 12, 2006, http://www.bsacybersafety.com/news/2005-Online-Shopping-Confidence.cfm.

80. U.S. Code, Title 18, Section 1028.

81. H.R. 1731 (2004).

82. Erika Harrell, *Victims of Identity Theft, 2014* (Bureau of Justice Statistics, September 2015), https://www.bjs.gov/content/pub/pdf/vit14.pdf (accessed March 11, 2017).

83. Lynn Langton, *Identity Theft Reported by Households, 2005–2010* (Washington, DC: Bureau of Justice Statistics, 2011).

84. The information and some of the wording in this section is taken from The President's Identity Theft Task Force, *Combating Identity Theft: A Strategic Plan*.

85. See U.S. Attorney's Office, Southern District of Florida, press release, July 19, 2006, http://www.usdoj.gov/usao/fls/PressReleases/060719-01.html.

86. FBI, *Crime in the United States, 2016*.

87. BJS, *Criminal Victimization, 2016*.

88. FBI, *Crime in the United States, 2016*.

89. Ibid.

90. Shannan M. Catalano and Michael R. Rand, *Criminal Victimization, 2006* (Washington, DC: Bureau of Justice Statistics, 2007).

91. Ibid.

92. Caroline Wolf Harlow, *Motor Vehicle Theft* (Washington, DC: Bureau of Justice Statistics, 1988).

93. Ibid.

94. P. Jeffrey Brantingham, "Prey Selection Among Los Angeles Car Thieves," *Crime Science*, Vol. 2, No. 3 (2013).

95. Kevin Blake, "What You Should Know about Car Theft," *Consumer's Research*, October 1995, cited in Miethe and McCorkle, eds., *Crime Profiles*, p. 156.

96. Ibid.

97. Pub. L. 98–547, 98 Stat. 2754 (1984).

98. Patricia M. Harris and Ronald V. Clarke, "Car Chopping, Parts Marking and the Motor Vehicle Theft Law Enforcement Act of 1984," *Sociology and Social Research*, Vol. 75 (1991).

99. Miethe and McCorkle, *Crime Profiles*, p. 156.

100. Michael Gottfredson and Travis Hirschi, *A General Theory of Crime* (Stanford, CA: Stanford University Press, 1990), p. 35.

101. Miethe and McCorkle, *Crime Profiles*; and Ronald V. Clarke and Patricia M. Harris, "Auto Theft and Its Prevention," in Tonry, ed., *Crime and Justice*.

102. Miethe and McCorkle, *Crime Profiles*.

103. For research reporting on effect of social class, see Charles H. McCaghy, Peggy C. Giordano, and Trudy Knicely Henson, "Auto Theft: Offender and Offense Characteristics," *Criminology*, Vol. 15 (1977), pp. 367–385.

104. FBI, *Crime in the United States, 2016*.

105. Ibid.

106. Federal Bureau of Investigation, *Crime in the United States, 2016* (Washington, DC: FBI, 2017).

107. Ken Brownlee, "Ignoring Juvenile Arson Is Like Playing with Fire," *Claims*, Vol. 48, No. 3 (March 2000), p. 106.

108. Eileen M. Garry, *Juvenile Firesetting and Arson*, Office of Juvenile Justice and Delinquency Prevention Fact Sheet 51 (Washington, DC: Office of Juvenile Justice and Delinquency Prevention, 1997).

109. Ibid., p. 1.

110. Cited in Gabor, *Everybody Does It!*, p. 11.

111. Edwin Sutherland, *The Professional Thief* (Chicago, IL: University of Chicago Press, 1937), p. 172.

112. Neal Shover, *Great Pretenders: Pursuits and Careers of Persistent Thieves* (Boulder, CO: Westview, 1996), p. xiii.

113. Ibid., pp. xii–xiii.

114. Ibid., p. 63.

115. Mark S. Fleisher, *Beggars and Thieves: Lives of Urban Street Criminals* (Madison: University of Wisconsin Press, 1995).

116. Malcolm W. Klein, "Offense Specialization and Versatility among Juveniles," *British Journal of Criminology*, Vol. 24 (1984), pp. 185–194.

117. Ibid., p. 186.

118. Shover, "Burglary," in Tonry, ed., *Crime and Justice*.

119. See Shover, *Great Pretenders*; and Shover, "Burglary," in Tonry, ed., *Crime and Justice*.

120. John R. Hepburn, "Occasional Property Crime," in Robert F. Meier, ed., *Major Forms of Crime* (Beverly Hills, CA: Sage, 1984).

121. Ibid., p. 76.

122. Richard T. Wright and Scott H. Decker, *Burglars on the Job: Streetlife and Residential Break-Ins* (Boston: Northeastern University Press, 1994), p. 35.

123. See Center for Problem-Oriented Policing, "Crime Analysis for Problem Solvers in 60 Small Steps," from which the wording for this definition is taken, http://www.popcenter.org/learning/60steps/index.cfm?stepNum=10 (accessed May 31, 2007).

124. Neil Alan Weiner, "Violent Criminal Careers and 'Violent Career Criminals': An Overview of the Research Literature," in Neil Alan Weiner and Marvin E. Wolfgang, eds., *Violent Crime, Violent Criminals* (Newbury Park, CA: Sage, 1989), p. 39.

125. A. Blumstein et al., eds., *Criminal Careers and "Career Criminals,"* 2 vols. (Washington, DC: National Academy Press, 1986).

126. D. S. Elliott, "Serious Violent Offenders: Onset, Developmental Course, and Termination: 1993 Presidential Address," *Criminology*, Vol. 32, No. 1 (1994), pp. 1–22. See also D. S. Elliott, D. Huizinga, and B. Morse, "Self-Reported Violent Offending: A Descriptive Analysis of Juvenile Violent Offenders and Their Offending Careers," *Journal of Interpersonal Violence*, Vol. 1, No. 4 (1987), pp. 472–514.

127. Michael R. Gottfredson and Travis Hirschi, "Science, Public Policy, and the Career Paradigm," *Criminology*, Vol. 26 (1988), pp. 37–55.

128. Mark S. Fleisher, *Beggars and Thieves: Lives of Urban Street Criminals* (Madison: University of Wisconsin Press, 1995).

129. Ibid., p. 10.

130. Ibid., p. 11.

131. Dermot Walsh, "Victim Selection Procedures among Economic Criminals: The Rational Choice Perspective," in Derek B. Cornish and Ronald V. Clarke, eds., *The Reasoning Criminal: Rational Choice Perspectives on Offending* (New York: Springer-Verlag, 1986), p. 40.

132. Ibid., p. 50.

133. Thomas Bennett and Richard Wright, *Burglars on Burglary* (Aldershot, Hants, England: Gower, 1984).

134. Dermot Walsh, "Victim Selection Procedures among Economic Criminals: The Rational Choice Perspective," in Derek B. Cornish and Ronald V. Clarke, eds., *The Reasoning Criminal: Rational Choice Perspectives on Offending* (New York: Springer-Verlag, 1986), p. 40.

135. Neil Shover and David Honaker, "The Socially Bounded Decision Making of Persistent Property Offenders," *Howard Journal*, Vol. 31, No. 4 (1992), p. 290.

136. Darrell J. Steffensmeier, *The Fence: In the Shadow of Two Worlds* (Savage, MD: Rowman and Littlefield, 1986), p. 10.

137. Ibid., p. 9.

138. Ibid. See also Wright and Decker, *Burglars on the Job.*

139. Steffensmeier, *The Fence*, p. 9.

140. Ibid.

141. Carl B. Klockars, *The Professional Fence* (New York: Free Press, 1974).

142. Steffensmeier, *The Fence.*

143. Ibid., p. 13.

144. Ibid.

145. Cromwell, Olson, and Avary, *Breaking and Entering.*

146. Wright and Decker, *Burglars on the Job*, p. 167.

147. Shover, "Burglary," in Tonry, ed., *Crime and Justice*, p. 103.

148. Wright and Decker, *Burglars on the Job*, p. 169.

149. Steffensmeier, *The Fence*, p. 25.

150. Ibid., p. 23.

151. Ibid., p. 21.

152. Wright and Decker, *Burglars on the Job*, p. 179.

153. Ibid., pp. 175–176.

154. Cromwell, Olson, and Avary, *Breaking and Entering*, p. 74.

155. Ibid., p. 75.

156. Richard T. Wright and Scott H. Decker, *Burglars on the Job: Streetlife and Residential Break-Ins* (Boston: Northeastern University Press, 1994), p. 76.

157. Cromwell, Olson, and Avary, Breaking and Entering.

158. Ibid.

159. Stuart Henry, *The Hidden Economy: The Context and Control of Borderline Crime* (Oxford, England: Martin Robertson, 1978).

CHAPTER 13: WHITE-COLLAR AND ORGANIZED CRIME

1. FBI, National Press Release, "National Medicare Fraud Takedown Results in Charges Against 243 Individuals for Approximately $712 Million in False Billing," June 18, 2015.

2. U.S. Department of Justice news release, "Volkswagen AG Agrees to Plead Guilty and Pay $4.3 Billion in Criminal and Civil Penalties; Six Volkswagen Executives and Employees are Indicted in Connection with Conspiracy to Cheat U.S. Emissions Tests," January 11, 2017, https://www.justice.gov/opa/pr/volkswagen-ag-agrees-plead-guilty-and-pay-43-billion-criminal-and-civil-penalties-six (accessed January 11, 2017).

3. Edwin H. Sutherland, "White-Collar Criminality," *American Sociological Review*, Vol. 5, No. 1 (February 1940), pp. 2–10.

4. Travis Hirschi and Michael Gottfredson, "Causes of White-Collar Crime," *Criminology*, Vol. 25, No. 4 (1987), p. 952.

5. Donald J. Newman, "White-Collar Crime: An Overview and Analysis," *Law and Contemporary Problems*, Vol. 23, No. 4 (Autumn 1958).

6. President's Commission on Law Enforcement and Administration of Justice, *The Challenge of Crime in a Free Society* (Washington, DC: U.S. Government Printing Office, 1967), p. 47.

7. For excellent reviews of the evolution of the concept of white-collar crime, see K. Schlegel and D. Weisburd, "White-Collar Crime: The Parallax View," in Kip Schlegel and David Weisburd, eds., *White-Collar Crime Reconsidered* (Boston: Northeastern University Press, 1992), pp. 3–27; and K. Schlegel and D. Weisburd, "Returning to the Mainstream: Reflections on Past and Future White-Collar Crime Study," in Schlegel and Weisburd, eds., *White-Collar Crime Reconsidered*, pp. 352–365.

8. Task Force on Organized Crime, *Organized Crime* (Washington, DC: U.S. Government Printing Office, 1976).

9. Ibid.

10. Michael L. Benson, Francis T. Cullen, and William J. Maakestad, *Local Prosecutors and Corporate Crime* (Washington, DC: National Institute of Justice, 1993).

11. *New York Central and Hudson River Railroad Co. v. United States*, 212 U.S. 481 (1909).

12. Jonathan D. Glater and Kurt Eichenwald, "Audit Lapse at WorldCom Puzzles Some," *New York Times*, June 28, 2002, p. 1C.

13. *Arthur Andersen LLP v. United States*, 544 U.S. 696 (2005).

14. "Epoxy Company Indicted for Manslaughter in Big Dig Death," *Tollroads News*, August 8, 2007, http://www.tollroadsnews.com/node/3063 (accessed April 10, 2010).

15. "Epoxy Company to Pay Millions in Big Dig Collapse," WBZ-TV, December 17, 2008, http://wbztv.com/bigdig/big.dig.agreement.2.889425.html (accessed April 9, 2010).

16. Charles Kennedy, "BP Pleads Guilty to Criminal Charges in Deepwater Horizon Case," Oil Price, November 15, 2012, http://oilprice.com/Latest-Energy-News/World-News/BP-Pleads-Guilty-to-Criminal-Charges-in-Deepwater-Horizon-Case.html (accessed August 29, 2013).

17. Brandon L. Garrett, "Globalized Corporate Prosecutions," Vol. 97 (December 2011), Virginia Law Review, p. 1775.

18. Federal Bureau of Investigation, "Financial Crimes Report to the Public, Fiscal Year 2007," http://www.fbi.gov/publications/financial/fcs_report2007/financial_crime_2007.htm#financial (accessed May 10, 2012), from which much of the material in this section is derived.

19. Ibid.

20. Ibid.

21. Ibid.

22. Ibid.

23. Ibid.

24. Ibid.

25. "Woman's Aid Claims for 38 Children Are Examined," The New York Times, December 21, 1980.

26. USGAO, Report to Congressional Committees, "Illegal Aliens: Extent of Welfare Benefits Received on Behalf of U.S. Citizen Children," November, 1997.

27. Clifford Karchmer and Douglas Ruch, "State and Local Money Laundering Control Strategies," NIJ Research in Brief (Washington, DC: National Institute of Justice, 1992), p. 1.

28. "Wachovia to Pay $160M Settlement," Business Journal, March 18, 2010, http://www.bizjournals.com/triad/stories/2010/03/15/daily30.html (accessed May 2, 2010).

29. U.S. Code, Title 18, Section 1956.

30. U.S. Drug Enforcement Administration, "Money Laundering," http://www.usdoj.gov/dea/programs/money.htm (accessed June 18, 2007).

31. See Bernie Becker, "U.S. Report Details Money Laundering," New York Times, February 4, 2010, http://dealbook.blogs.nytimes.com/2010/02/04/us-report-details-money-laundering (accessed August 24, 2010).

32. Of course, environmental damage inflicted by corporations can result in civil liability as well as violate criminal statutes.

33. "Alaska Hit by 'Massive' Oil Spill," BBC News, March 11, 2006, http://news.bbc.co.uk/2/hi/americas/4795866.stm (accessed May 2, 2010).

34. U.S. Department of Justice news release, "Volkswagen AG Agrees to Plead Guilty and Pay $4.3 Billion in Criminal and Civil Penalties; Six Volkswagen Executives and Employees are Indicted in Connection with Conspiracy to Cheat U.S. Emissions Tests," January 11, 2017, https://www.justice.gov/opa/pr/volkswagen-ag-agrees-plead-guilty-and-pay-43-billion-criminal-and-civil-penalties-six (accessed February 4, 2017).

35. "BP Could Pay U.S. $25 Billion for Gulf Oil Spill: Analyst," Google News, January 19, 2012, http://www.google.com/hostednews/afp/article/ALeqM5if9Va_XAcDMrIPE7x6ppzdy8YMSw?docId=CNG.cb899fe5256d3216e8a921771e991d78.301 (accessed May 10, 2013).

36. John Kane and April Wall, "Identifying the Links between White-Collar Crime and Terrorism," National White Collar Crime Center, September 2004.

37. Edwin H. Sutherland, "White-Collar Criminality."

38. Ibid.

39. Ibid.

40. Gary S. Becker, "Crime and Punishment: An Economic Approach," The Journal of Political Economy, Vol. 76, No. 2 (March-April, 1968), pp. 169–217.

41. Travis Hirschi and Michael Gottfredson, "Causes of White-Collar Crime," Criminology, Vol. 25, No. 4 (1987), p. 952.

42. Ibid., p. 951.

43. Ibid., p. 956.

44. Ibid., p. 960.

45. Ibid.

46. Braithwaite began many of his studies of white-collar crime with investigations into the criminal activities of pharmaceutical company executives. See, for example, John Braithwaite, Corporate Crime in the Pharmaceutical Industry (London: Routledge and Kegan Paul, 1984).

47. For a test of this thesis, see Anne Jenkins and John Braithwaite, "Profits, Pressure and Corporate Lawbreaking," Crime, Law, and Social Change, Vol. 20, No. 3 (1993), pp. 221–232.

48. John Braithwaite, "Poverty, Power, White-Collar Crime and the Paradoxes of Criminological Theory," Australian and New Zealand Journal of Criminology, Vol. 24, No. 1 (1991), pp. 40–48.

49. Toni Makkai and John Braithwaite, "Criminological Theories and Regulatory Compliance," Criminology, Vol. 29, No. 2 (1991), pp. 191–217.

50. John Braithwaite and Gilbert Geis, "On Theory and Action for Corporate Crime Control," Crime and Delinquency, Vol. 28, No. 2 (1982), pp. 292–314. See also Brent Fisse and John Braithwaite, The Impact of Publicity on Corporate Offenders (Albany: State University of New York Press, 1983).

51. Brent Fisse and John Braithwaite, "Accountability and the Control of Corporate Crime: Making the Buck Stop," in Mark Findlay and Russell Hogg, eds., Understanding Crime and Criminal Justice (North Ryde, Australia: Law, 1988), pp. 93–127.

52. Brent Fisse and John Braithwaite, Corporations, Crime and Accountability (New York: Cambridge University Press, 1994).

53. John Braithwaite, "Criminological Theory and Organizational Crime," Justice Quarterly, Vol. 6, No. 3 (1989), pp. 333–358.

54. Eugene Soltes, Why They Do It: Inside the Mind of the White-Collar Criminal (Public Affairs Press, 2016).

55. Joan Biskupic, "Why It's Tough to Indict CEOs," USA Today, July 24, 2002, p. 1A.

56. Ibid.

57. See "Executive Order Establishment of the Corporate Fraud Task Force," July 9, 2002, http://www.whitehouse.gov/news/releases/2002/07/20020709-2.html (accessed January 2, 2005).

58. John R. Wilke, The Wall Street Journal Online, July 17, 2007, http://online.wsj.com/article/SB118469845609569168.html (accessed September 1, 2007).

59. Ibid.

60. Joe Palazzolo, "DOJ Unveils Financial Crime Task Force," Main Justice, November 17, 2009 (accessed May 8, 2012).

61. Pub. L. 111–21.

62. Pub. L. 111–5.

63. Pub. L. 110–343.

64. "Financial Crimes, Trade Enforcement Targeted in State of the Union," The Blog of Legal Times, January 25, 2012,

http://legaltimes.typepad.com/blt/2012/01/financial-crime strade-enforcement-targeted-in-state-of-the-union-.html (accessed January 25, 2012).

65. 15 U.S.C. Section 1.

66. 15 U.S.C. Sections 12–27.

67. 15 U.S.C. Section 77.

68. 15 U.S.C. Section 78.

69. Much of the information in this section comes from Julian Symons, *A Pictorial History of Crime* (New York: Bonanza, 1966).

70. Ibid.

71. Howard Abadinsky, *Organized Crime*, 9th ed. (New York: Wadsworth, 2010), p. 132.

72. John Kilber, *Capone: The Life and World of Al Capone* (Greenwich, CT: Fawcett, 1971).

73. William R. Schroeder, "Money Laundering," *FBI Law Enforcement Bulletin*, May 2001, p. 1.

74. Abadinsky, *Organized Crime*.

75. Ibid., p. 5.

76. U.S. Code, Title 21, Section 848(c)(2).

77. New York Penal Law, Section 460.00.

78. New York Penal Law, Section 460.10(3).

79. Much of the information and the quotes in this section come from Federal Bureau of Investigation, "Organized Crime: Eurasian Organized Crime," http://www.fbi.gov/hq/cid/orgcrime/eocindex.htm (accessed May 20, 2013).

80. Ibid.

81. Ibid.

82. Much of the information and the quotes in this section come from Federal Bureau of Investigation, "Organized Crime: Asian Criminal Enterprises," http://www.fbi.gov/hq/cid/orgcrime/asiancrim.htm (accessed May 20, 2015).

83. Ibid.

84. Ibid.

85. Much of the information and the quotes in this section come from Federal Bureau of Investigation, "Organized Crime: African Criminal Enterprise," http://www.fbi.gov/hq/cid/orgcrime/africancrim.htm (accessed May 20, 2015).

86. Ibid.

87. Much of the information and the quotes in this section come from Federal Bureau of Investigation, "Organized Crime: Middle Eastern Criminal Enterprises," http://www.fbi.gov/hq/cid/orgcrime/middle_eastern.htm (accessed May 20, 2013).

88. Ibid.

89. John T. Picarelli, "Responding to Transnational Organized Crime: Supporting Research, Improving Practice," *NIJ Journal*, No. 268 (October 2011), pp. 4–9.

90. Gary T. Dempsey, "Is Russia Controlled by Organized Crime?" *USA Today* magazine, May 1999.

91. Richard Lindberg and Vesna Markovic, "Organized Crime Outlook in the New Russia: Russia Is Paying the Price of a Market Economy in Blood," Search International, http://www.searchinternational.com/Articles/crime/russiacrime.htm (accessed January 24, 2009).

92. Ibid.

93. Dempsey, "Is Russia Controlled by Organized Crime?"

94. Richard Lindberg and Vesna Markovic, "*Organized Crime Outlook in the New Russia: Russia Is Paying the Price of a Market Economy in Blood,*" Search International, http://www .searchinter

national.com/Articles/crime/russiacrime.htm (accessed January 24, 2009).

95. Ibid.

96. The Organized Crime Control Act of 1970, Pub. L. 91–452, 84 Stat. 922 (October 15, 1970).

97. United States Code, Title 18, Chapter 96, Section 1961.

98. Gary W. Potter, *Criminal Organizations: Vice, Racketeering, and Politics in an American City* (Prospect Heights, IL: Waveland, 1994), p. 183.

99. Ibid.

100. Howard Abadinsky, *Organized Crime*, 9th ed. (New York: Wadsworth, 2010), p. 132.

101. Ibid., p. 508.

102. "'Junior' Gotti Gets Nearly 6 1/2 Years," Associated Press, September 3, 1999.

103. "5-Year Prison Term for Mafia Turncoat," *USA Today*, September 27, 1994, p. 3A.

104. Peter Maas, *Underboss: Sammy the Bull Gravano's Story of Life in the Mafia* (New York: HarperCollins, 1997). According to Ronald Kuby, an attorney suing Gravano to reclaim book royalties under New York's Son of Sam law, to avoid provisions of the law, a roundabout method had been used to pay Gravano. Kuby claimed that documents would show that author Peter Maas, Gravano, HarperCollins, and International Creative Management (the agent for the book) had conspired to hide payments made to Gravano. To learn more about the case, visit http://www.crimelibrary.com/gangsters2/gravano/24.htm.

105. "'Sammy the Bull' Faces More Drug Charges," Associated Press, December 21, 2000.

106. Selim Algar, "Mobster Acquitted of all Charges in 'Goddfellas' Heist," *New York Post*, November 12, 2015, http://nypost.com/2015/11/12/mobster-acquitted-of-all-charges-in-goodfellas-heist (accessed November 14, 2015).

CHAPTER 14: DRUG AND SEX CRIMES

1. Drug Enforcement Administration, *The National Heroin Threat Assessment* (Washington, DC: DEA, 2016).

2. This quote is taken from http://librearts.com/wsn8439.html (accessed September 21, 2007).

3. Data in this section are derived from Substance Abuse and Mental Health Services Administration, *2016 National Survey on Drug Use and Health* (Rockville, MD: SAMHSA, 2017).

4. Ibid.

5. L. D. Johnston, P. M. O'Malley, R. A. Miech, J. G. Bachman, & J. E. Schulenberg, *Monitoring the Future National Survey Results on Drug Use, 1975–2016* (Ann Arbor: Institute for Social Research, The University of Michigan, 2017).

6. National Drug Intelligence Center, *The Economic Impact of Illicit Drug Use on American Society* (Washington, DC: U.S. Department of Justice, 2011).

7. Centers for Disease Control and Prevention, "Drug-Associated HIV Transmission Continues in the United States," http://www.cdc.gov/hiv/resources/factsheets/idu.htm, (accessed March 12, 2015).

8. National Narcotics Intelligence Consumers Committee, *The NNICC Report, 1996: The Supply of Illicit Drugs to the United States* (Arlington, VA: Drug Enforcement Administration, 1997), p. 69.

9. Michael D. Lyman and Gary W. Potter, *Drugs in Society: Causes, Concepts and Control* (Cincinnati: Anderson, 1991), p. 45.

10. National Institute on Drug Abuse, *Drugs, Brains, and Behavior: The Science of Addiction*, July 2014, https://www.drugabuse.gov/publications/drugs-brains-behavior-science-addiction/preface (accessed September 3, 2017).

11. National Institute on Drug Abuse, "NIDA InfoFacts: Understanding Drug Abuse and Addiction," http://www.drugabuse.gov/infofacts/understand.html (accessed September 3, 2017).

12. Ibid.

13. As defined by federal law and precedent.

14. National Narcotics Intelligence Consumers Committee, *The NNICC Report* (Washington DC: USGPO, 1994).

15. U.S. Department of State, Bureau of International Narcotics and Law Enforcement Affairs, *2017 International Narcotics Control Strategy Report (INCSR)*, March 2017, https://www.state.gov/j/inl/rls/nrcrpt/2017 (accessed September 3, 2017).

16. Bureau of Justice Statistics, *Drugs, Crime and the Justice System* (Washington, DC: U.S. Government Printing Office, 1992), p. 2.

17. Ibid.

18. Ibid., p. 126.

19. Ibid., p. 2.

20. U.S. Department of Justice, "Member of Afghan Taliban Sentenced to Life in Prison in Nation's First Conviction on Narcoterror Charges," press release, December 22, 2008.

21. The federal narcoterrorism statute is found at 21 U.S.C. § 960a, which reads that anyone who "attempts or conspires to do so, knowing or intending to provide, directly or indirectly, anything of pecuniary value to any person or organization that has engaged or engages in terrorist activity."

22. Pub. L. 104–305.

23. "'Rophies' Reported Spreading Quickly throughout the South," *Drug Enforcement Report*, June 23, 1995, pp. 1–5.

24. Mike O'Sullivan, "Washington State Gears Up for Marijuana Industry," Voice of America, April 22, 2013, http://www.voanews.com/content/washington_state_gears_up_for_marijuana_industry/1646461.html (accessed May 30, 2013).

25. Kristen Wyatt, "Legal Weed Draws Tourists to Colorado, Washington, for 4/20 Marijuana Holiday," *Huffington Post*, April 15, 2013, http://www.huffingtonpost.com/2013/04/15/legal-pot-draws-tourists-_0_n_3084301.html (accessed May 30, 2013).

26. U.S. Dept. of Justice, Memorandum for all United States Attorneys, "Guidance Regarding Marijuana Enforcement," August 29, 2013.

27. The 21st Century Cures Act.

28. For an excellent overview of policy initiatives in the area of drug control, see Doris Layton MacKenzie and Craig D. Uchida, *Drugs and Crime: Evaluating Public Policy Initiatives* (Thousand Oaks, CA: Sage, 1994).

29. DEA, "Domestic Cannabis Eradication-Suppression Program," http://www.dea.gov/ops/cannabis.shtml (accessed March 21, 2017).

30. 21 U.S.C. Section 881(a)(6).

31. Federal Bureau of Prisons, "Offenses," https://www.bop.gov/about/statistics/statistics_inmate_offenses.jsp (accessed February 5, 2017).

32. "Who Is in Federal Prison?" *Washington Post*, October 3, 1994.

33. James Inciardi, *The War on Drugs II* (New York: McGraw-Hill, 1992), p. 239.

34. Michael D. Lyman and Gary W. Potter, *Drugs in Society: Causes, Concepts and Control* (Cincinnati: Anderson, 1991), p. 316.

35. Jason McLure, "Maine Town Is Shaken by Zumba Prostitution Scandal," Yahoo! News, October 17, 2012, http://en-maktoob.news.yahoo.com/maine-town-shaken-zumba-prostitution-scandal-222159193–sector.html (accessed May 20, 2013).

36. John Schriffen, "Zumba Sex Scandal: Alexis Wright Pleads Guilty to 20 Counts," ABC News, March 29, 2013, http://abcnews.go.com/US/zumba-sex-scandal-alexis-wright-pleads-guilty-20/story?id=18842770#.UXW3Xat4bYg (accessed May 20, 2013).

37. Federal Bureau of Investigation, *Crime in the United States, 2016* (Washington, DC: FBI, 2017).

38. John Stuart Mill, *On Liberty* (1859), chapter 1.

39. Much of the information in this section is derived from the Law Library: American Law and Legal Information, "Typology of Prostitution," *Crime and Justice*, Vol. 3, http://law.jrank.org/pages/1879/Prostitution-Typology-prostitution.html (accessed July 10, 2007).

40. "April M. Rand, "Exiting the Commercial Sex Trade," University of Kansas doctoral dissertation, 2014.

41. Richard J. Estes and Neil Alan Weiner, "The Commercial Sexual Exploitation of Children in the U.S., Canada and Mexico," February 20, 2002, https://maggiemcneill.files.wordpress.com/2011/04/estes-weiner-2001.pdf (accessed January 11, 2017).

42. Martin A. Monto, "Focusing on the Clients of Street Prostitutes: A Creative Approach to Reducing Violence against Women," final report submitted to the National Institute of Justice, Washington, DC: June 9, 2000, http://www.ncjrs.gov/pdffiles1/nij/grants/182860.pdf (accessed July 25, 2007).

43. Ibid.

44. Meredith Dank, et al, *Estimating the Size and Structure of the Underground Commercial Sex Economy in Eight Major US Cities* (Washington, DC: The Urban Institute, 2014).

45. "Exiting the Commercial Sex Trade."

46. Andrea Dworkin, Intercourse (New York: Free Press, 1987).

47. Ronald Weitzer, "The Growing Moral Panic over Prostitution and Sex Trafficking," The Criminologist, Vol. 30, No. 5 (September/October, 2005), pp. 1 and 3.

48. Ibid.

49. Janice G. Raymond, "10 Reasons for Not Legalizing Prostitution," Coalition against Trafficking in Women International, March 25, 2003, http://www.rapereliefshelter.bc.ca/issues/prostitution_legalizing.html (accessed July 25, 2007).

CHAPTER 15: TECHNOLOGY AND CRIME

1. Karoun Demirjian, "Senate's Investigation into Alleged Russian Hacking Begins Without End in Sight," The Washington Post, January 25, 2017, https://www.washingtonpost.com/news/powerpost/wp/2017/01/25/senates-investigation-into-alleged-russian-hacking-begins-without-end-in-sight/?utm_term=.369b712e68bc (accessed March 3, 2017).

2. Robert McMillan, Ryan Knutson, and Deepa Seetharaman, "Yahoo Discloses New Breach of 1 Billion User Accounts," *The Wall Street Journal*, December 14, 2016, http://www.wsj.com/articles/yahoo-discloses-new-breach-of-1-billion-user-accounts-1481753131 (accessed January 20, 2017).

3. U.S. Department of Justice, press release, "Attorney General Eric Holder Speaks at the Press Conference Announcing U.S.

Charges against Five Chinese Military Hackers for Cyber Espionage," May 19, 2014.

4. Natasha Bertrand, "A Top Hacker-Hunter at Russia's Largest Cybersecurity Firm has been Arrested on Charges of Treason," Business Insider, January 25, 2017, http://www.businessinsider.com/ap-top-manager-at-russian-cybersecurity-firm-arrested-in-moscow-2017-1 (accessed March 1, 2017).

5. Catherine H. Conly and J. Thomas McEwen, "Computer Crime," NIJ Reports.

6. Ponemon Institute, 2016 Cost of Data Breach Study: Global Analysis (IBM, 2016).

7. Ibid.

8. Business Software Alliance, "1 in 5 Pieces of Software in the U.S. Are Unlicensed." https://reporting.bsa.org/r/report/add.aspx?src=us&ln=en-us (accessed May 2, 2017).

9. The Anti-Phishing Working Group, Global Phishing Survey: Trends and Domain Name Use in 1H 2014, http://docs.apwg.org/reports/APWG_Global_Phishing_Report_1H_2014.pdf (accessed February 15, 2017).

10. Gregg Keizer, "Gartner: Phishing Attacks Threaten E-Commerce," Security Pipeline.com, http://www.securitypipeline.com/news/20000036 (accessed July 30, 2007).

11. This and most other definitions related to computer crime in this chapter are taken from Donn B. Parker, Computer Crime: Criminal Justice Resource Manual (Washington, DC: National Institute of Justice, 1989).

12. Sam Jones and Hannah Kuchler, "World's Most Advanced Hacking Spyware Let Loose," Financial Times, November 23, 2014.

13. Pub. L. 104–104, 110 Stat. 56.

14. Reno v. ACLU, 521 U.S. 844 (1997).

15. Enacted as Section 225 of the Homeland Security Act of 2002, H.R. 5710.

16. Parker, Computer Crime.

17. J. Bloombecker, "A Security Manager's Guide to Hacking," DATAPRO Reports on Information Security, Report IS35–450–101, 1986.

18. Paul Ruggiero and Jon Foote, "Cyber Threats to Mobile Phones" (Washington, DC Department of Homeland Security, United States Computer Emergency Readiness Team, 2011).

19. Ibid.

20. FBI press release, "Houston Man Gets 40 Years for Sex Trafficking of Children," August 14, 2014.

21. FBI, GameOver Zeus Botnet Disrupted," July 11, 2014, http://www.fbi.gov/news/stories/2014/june/gameover-zeus-botnet-disrupted/gameover-zeus-botnet-disrupted (accessed May 5, 2015).

22. Paul Saffo, "Desperately Seeking Cyberspace," Personal Computing, May 1989, p. 247.

23. John Markoff, "Cyberpunks," New York Times Upfront, Vol. 132, No. 15 (March 27, 2000), pp. 10–14.

24. J. Maxfield, "Computer Bulletin Boards and the Hacker Problem," EDPACS: The Electric Data Processing Audit, Control and Security Newsletter (Arlington, VA: Automation Training Center, October 1985).

25. Percy Black, personal communication, 1991, as cited in M. E. Kabay, "Computer Crime: Hackers" (undated electronic manuscript).

26. John Perry Barlow, "Crime and Puzzlement: In Advance of the Law on the Electronic Frontier," Whole Earth Review (fall 1990), p. 44.

27. Ibid.

28. Donn B. Parker, Computer Crime: Criminal Justice Resource Manual (Washington, DC: National Institute of Justice, 1989).

29. For insight into how security techniques often lag behind the abilities of criminal perpetrators in the high-technology arena, see James A. Fagin, "Computer Crime: A Technology Gap," International Journal of Comparative and Applied Criminal Justice, Vol. 15, Nos. 1 and 2 (spring/fall 1991), pp. 285–297.

30. Eureka Aerospace, "High-Power Compact Microwave Source for Vehicle Immobilization: Final Report," U.S. Department of Justice, National Institute of Justice, April 20, 2006, https://www.ncjrs.gov/pdffiles1/nij/grants/236756.pdf.

31. "DNA Frees Man Sentenced to Life," Associated Press, January 16, 2001, http://www.msnbc.com/news/517172.asp (accessed January 17, 2005).

32. Michael Schrage, "Today, It Takes a Scientist to Catch a Thief," Washington Post, March 18, 1994.

33. Daubert v. Merrell Dow Pharmaceuticals, Inc., 509 U.S. 579 (1993).

34. Frye v. United States, 54 App. D.C. 46, 47, 293 F. 1013, 1014 (1923).

35. Federal Rules of Evidence, Article IV, Rule 402.

36. For the application of Daubert to DNA technology, see Barry Sheck, "DNA and Daubert," Cardozo Law Review, Vol. 15 (1994), p. 1959.

37. Michael Schrage, "Today, It Takes a Scientist to Catch a Thief," Washington Post, March 18, 1994.

38. FBI press release, October 13, 1998, http://www.fbi.gov/pressrm/pressrel/pressrel98/dna.htm (accessed January 22, 2003).

39. U.S. Code, Title 42, Section 14132.

40. "British Police to Use DNA to Catch Burglars," Reuters, June 16, 1994.

41. Michael Schrage, "Today, It Takes a Scientist to Catch a Thief," Washington Post, March 18, 1994.

42. Edward Connors et al., Convicted by Juries, Exonerated by Science: Case Studies in the Use of DNA Evidence to Establish Innocence after Trial (Washington, DC: National Institute of Justice, 1996).

43. Ibid.

44. Maryland v. King, U.S. Supreme Court, No. 12-207 (decided June 3, 2013).

45. See, for example, FACES for Law Enforcement at http://www.facesid.com/products_faces_le.html.

46. Information Security Products and Services: Market Research Report (Dublin, Ireland: Research and Markets, 2014).

47. Parker, Computer Crime, p. xiii.

48. The FBI's contemporary cyberinvestigations Web page is available at https://www.fbi.gov/investigate/cyber.

49. As modified in 1986, 1988, and later years.

50. The Liberty Coalition, "Carnivore/DCS–1000," http://www.libertycoalition.net/backgrounders/carnivore-dcs-1000 (accessed June 17, 2007).

51. John Naisbitt, Megatrends: Ten New Directions Transforming Our Lives (New York: Warner, 1982), p. 36.

52. Ibid.

53. Gary H. Anthes, "White House Launches Cybershield," Computerworld, July 22, 1996, p. 29.

54. M. J. Zuckerman, "Clinton to Get Cyberterror Plan," USA Today, October 9, 1997, p. 1A.

55. The quotations attributed to the President's Working Group in this section are from President's Working Group on Unlawful Conduct on the Internet, *The Electronic Frontier: The Challenge of Unlawful Conduct Involving the Use of the Internet* (Washington, DC: White House, 2000), http://www.usdoj.gov/criminal/cybercrime/unlawful.htm (accessed April 16, 2007).

56. United States Computer Emergency Readiness Team, "About Us," http://www.us-cert.gov/aboutus.html (accessed August 1, 2007).

57. National Security Presidential Directive 54; Homeland Security Presidential Directive 23 (NSPD-54/HSPD-23).

58. U.S. Department of Homeland Security, *Cyber Security Division FY 2012 Annual Report* (Washington, DC: 2013), http://www.dhs.gov/sites/default/files/publications/csd-annual-report-fy12.pdf (accessed February 12, 2017), p. 1.

59. Original EFF "Statement of Purpose," from the EFF Web site, http://eff.org/abouteff.html (accessed April 20, 2001). For the EFF's most recent statement of purpose, see http://www.eff.org/about (accessed February 12, 2017).

CHAPTER 16: GLOBALIZATION AND TERRORISM

1. "Russia to Decriminalize Some Forms of Domestic Violence," Fox News, http://www.foxnews.com/world/2017/01/25/russia-to-decriminalize-some-forms-domestic-violence.html (accessed March 3, 2017).

2. "Statement of the Department of Social Welfare and Development on the Lowering of the Minimum Age of Criminal Responsibility in the New Penal Code of the Philippines," September 2, 2014, http://www.gov.ph/2014/09/02/statement-dswd-on-the-lowering-of-the-minimum-age-of-criminal-responsibility (accessed March 2, 2017).

3. Gregory J. Howard, Graeme Newman, and William Alex Pridemore, "Theory, Method, and Data in Comparative Criminology," in David Duffee, ed., *Criminal Justice 2000: Volume IV—Measurement and Analysis of Criminal Justice* (Washington, DC: NIJ, 2000), p. 189.

4. Adapted from "Globalization," *Encyclopedia Britannica, 2007*, Encyclopedia Britannica Premium Service, http://www.britannica.com/eb/article?eu5369857 (accessed July 23, 2007).

5. Robert Lilly, "Forks and Chopsticks: Understanding Criminal Justice in the PRC," *Criminal Justice International* (March/April 1986), p. 15.

6. See United Nations Office on Drugs and Crime, "Compiling and Comparing International Crime Statistics," http://www.unodc.org/en/crime_cicp_surveys_3.html (accessed June 5, 2007).

7. For information about the latest survey, see "United Nations Surveys on Crime Trends and the Operations of Criminal Justice Systems (CTS)," http://www.unodc.org/unodc/en/data-and-analysis/United-Nations-Surveys-on-Crime-Trends-and-the-Operations-of-Criminal-Justice-Systems.html (accessed February 12, 2017).

8. "Which Country Has the Fewest Cars," Big Site of Amazing Facts, http://www.bigsiteofamazingfacts.com/which-country-has-the-fewest-cars (accessed February 12, 2017).

9. Human Smuggling and Trafficking Center, *Distinctions between Human Smuggling and Human Trafficking* (Washington, DC: January 2005).

10. Ibid., p. 2.

11. Raimo Väyrynen, "Illegal Immigration, Human Trafficking, and Organized Crime," United Nations University/World Institute for Development Economics Research, Discussion Paper No. 2003/72 (October 2003), p. 16.

12. Details for this story come from "Immigrant Smuggler Faulted in 19 Deaths Sentenced to Life in Prison," Associated Press, January 18, 2007, http://www.usatoday.com/news/nation/2007-01-18-smuggler_x.htm.

13. Pub. L. 108–458, December 17, 2004.

14. United Nations Office on Drugs and Crime, *Global Report on Trafficking in Persons* (New York: United Nations, 2009), p. 6.

15. International Labor Organization, "Fact Sheet: Trafficking of Children, a Worst Form of Child Labour," http://www.ilo.org/public/english/region/asro/bangkok/child/trafficking/downloads/fact_sheet_november_01_tdm.pdf (accessed August 1, 2009).

16. U.S. Code, Title 8, Section 1324.

17. Pub. L. 89–236.

18. Trafficking Victims Protection Act of 2000, Division A of Pub. L. 106–386, Section 108, as amended.

19. United Nations Office on Drugs and Crime, *Global Report on Trafficking in Persons* (New York: United Nations, 2009), p. 6.

20. Ibid.

21. U.S. Department of State, *Patterns of Global Terrorism, 2001* (Washington, DC: U.S. Government Printing Office, 2002), http://www.state.gov/s/ct/rls/pgtrpt/2001/ (accessed January 2, 2003). Note: Until 2004, the U.S. Department of State made *Patterns of Global Terrorism* available to the public annually. As of 2004, however, the report became unavailable after its methodology was challenged by the Bush administration.

22. TE-SAT. p. 9.

23. Paul R. Pillar, *Terrorism and U.S. Foreign Policy* (Washington, DC: The Brookings Institution, 2001).

24. See Michael J. Lynch and W. Byron Groves, *A Primer in Radical Criminology* (Monsey, NY: Willow Tree Press, 1990), p. 39; and Michael J. Lynch et al., *The New Primer in Radical Criminology: Critical Perspectives on Crime, Power & Identity* (Monsey, NY: Willow Tree Press, 2000).

25. Adapted from "FBI Policy and Guidelines: Counterterrorism," http://www.fbi.gov/contact/fo/jackson/cntrterr.htm (accessed March 4, 2008).

26. Ibid.

27. Brian Bennett, "'Sovereign Citizen' Movement Now on FBI's Radar," *Los Angeles Times*, February 23, 2012, http://www.latimes.com/news/nationworld/nation/la-na-terror-cop-killers-20120224,0,5474022.story (accessed February 28, 2017).

28. Ibid.

29. Justin McCarthy, "Americans Cite Cyberterrorism Among Top Three Threats to U.S.," Gallup, February 10, 2016, http://www.gallup.com/poll/189161/americans-cite-cyberterrorism-among-top-three-threats.aspx?g_source=Politics&g_medium=newsfeed&g_campaign=tiles (accessed August 21, 2016).

30. U.S. Department of State, *Country Reports on Terrorism 2013: Annex of Statistical Information* (Washington, DC: 2013).

31. Ibid.

32. See Barry Collin, "The Future of Cyberterrorism," *Crime and Justice International* (March 1997), pp. 15–18.

33. John Arquilla and David Ronfeldt, *The Advent of Netwar* (Santa Monica, CA: RAND, 1996).

34. Adapted from Dictionary.com, http://dictionary.reference.com/search?q=infrastructure (accessed January 10, 2007).

35. The PCCIP was established by Executive Order 13010.

36. Dorothy E. Denning, "Activism, Hactivism, and Cyberterrorism: The Internet as a Tool for Influencing Foreign Policy," paper presented at the Internet and International Systems: Information Technology and American Foreign Policy Decisionmaking Workshop, San Francisco, CA, December 10, 2001.

37. Critical Infrastructure Assurance Office, "Resource Library," http://www.ciao.gov/resource/index.html (accessed January 10, 2002).

38. Executive Order 13231 (Critical Infrastructure Protection in the Information Age), October 16, 2001.

39. President's Critical Infrastructure Protection Board, *The National Strategy to Secure Cyberspace* (Washington, DC: U.S. Government Printing Office, September 18, 2002), p. 3.

40. Ibid.

41. "Ridge Creates New Division to Combat Cyber Threats," Department of Homeland Security press release, June 6, 2003, http://www.dhs.gov/dhspublic/display?content=916 (accessed September 20, 2006).

42. U.S. General Services Administration, "GovNet Planned to Protect Critical Government IT Functions from Cyber Attacks," GSA news release number 9890, October 10, 2001, http://w3.gsa.gov/web/x/publicaffairs.nsf/dea168abbe828fe9852565c600519794/1c10e9ac670553b885256ae100668beb?OpenDocument (accessed January 21, 2005).

43. "U.S. Plans New Secure Government Internet," Associated Press, October 11, 2001.

44. "Government Creates Its Own Private Cyber Network," Fox News, http://www.foxnews.com/story/0,2933,82273,00.html March 26, 2003 (accessed May 2, 2013).

45. The technological devices described in this section are discussed in G. Gordon Liddy, "Rules of the Game," *Omni*, January 1989, pp. 43–47, 78–80.

46. CIA Directorate of Intelligence, *Terrorist CBRN: Materials and Effects* (Washington, DC: CIA, 2003).

47. Commission on the Prevention of Weapons of Mass Destruction Proliferation and Terrorism, *World at Risk: The Report of the Commission on the Prevention of WMD Proliferation and Terrorism* (Washington, DC: The Commission, 2008), p. xv.

48. Human Rights Watch, "Syria: Strong Evidence Government Used Chemicals as a Weapon," May 13, 2014, http://www.hrw.org/news/2014/05/13/syria-strong-evidence-government-used-chemicals-weapon (accessed February 12, 2017).

49. Matthew Bunn, Anthony Wier, and John P. Holden, *Controlling Nuclear Warheads and Materials: A Report Card and Action Plan* (Cambridge: Nuclear Threat Initiative and Harvard University, 2003).

50. *Fact Sheet: The Biological Weapons Convention* (Washington, DC: Bureau of Arms Control, 2002), http://www.state.gov/t/ac/rls/fs/10401.htm (accessed August 8, 2006).

51. Ali S. Kahn et al., *Biological and Chemical Terrorism: Strategic Plan for Preparedness and Response* (Atlanta, GA: Centers for Disease Control, April 21, 2000), http://www.cdc.gov/mmwr/preview/mmwrhtml/rr4904a1.htm (accessed August 2, 2007).

52. Council on Foreign Relations, "Terrorism: Questions and Answers—The Anthrax Letters," http://www.terrorismanswers.com/weapons/anthraxletters.html (accessed August 3, 2006).

53. See Rick Weiss, "DNA by Mail: A Terror Risk," *Washington Post*, July 18, 2002.

54. Jytte Klausen, "A Behavioral Study of the Radicalization Trajectories of American "Homegrown" Al Qaeda-Inspired Terrorist Offenders," National Criminal Justice Reference Service, November 2016.

55. Jytte Klausen, "The Role of Social Networks in the Evolution of Al Qaeda-Inspired Violent Extremism in the United States, 1990–2015," National Criminal Justice Reference Service, June 2016.

56. Michael Jensen and Gary LaFree, "Final Report: Empirical Assessment of Domestic Radicalization (EADR)," National Criminal Justice Reference Service, December 2016.

57. John G. Horgan et al., "Across the Universe? A Comparative Analysis of Violent Behavior and Radicalization Across Three Offender Types with Implications for Criminal Justice Training and Education," National Criminal Justice Reference Service, June 2016.

58. Robert Pape et al., *The American Face of ISIS: Analysis of ISIS-related Terrorism in the US March 2014–August 2016* (Chicago, IL: The Chicago Project on Security and Threats, 2017), https://www.aspi.org.au/publications/the-american-face-of-isis-analysis-of-isis-related-terrorism-in-the-us-march-2014august-2016/ASPI_CPOST_ISIS_Indictees.pdf (accessed March 17, 2017).

59. "Study Reports Biggest Terror Threat Is Homegrown," *Security Newswire*, February 5, 2017, http://www.securitymagazine.com/articles/87780-biggest-terror-threat-is-homegrown (accessed March 17, 2017).

60. U.S. Department of State, *Patterns of Global Terrorism 2001* (Washington, DC: U.S. Government Printing Office, 2002), http://www.state.gov/s/ct/rls/pgtrpt/2001 (accessed January 2, 2003). Previously available annually, *Patterns of Global Terrorism* has been superseded by the National Counterterrorism Center's yearly *Report on Terrorist Incidents*, http://www.terrorisminfo.mipt.org/pdf/Country-Reports-Terrorism-2006-NCTC-Annex.pdf.

61. Executive Order 13224.

62. National Security Council, *National Strategy for Combating Terrorism* (Washington, DC: The White House, 2006).

63. The NCTC was established by Executive Order in 2004, although Congress codified the NCTC in the Intelligence Reform and Terrorism Prevention Act of 2004 (IRTPA) and placed the NCTC within the Office of the Director of National Intelligence.

64. National Counterterrorism Center, *NCTC and Information Sharing* (Washington, DC: NCTC, 2006), p. I, from which some of the wording in this paragraph is taken.

65. *National Strategy for Counterterrorism* (Washington, DC: The White House, June 2011).

66. Congressional Research Service, *Terrorism, the Future, and U.S. Foreign Policy* (Washington, DC: Library of Congress, April 11, 2003), from which the material in this section is derived.

67. Pub. L. 104–132.

68. Pub. L. 107–56.

69. U.S. Code, Title 8, Section 1–1599.

70. Pub. L. 107–56.

71. Information in this paragraph is taken from National Counterterrorism Center, "Terrorist Identities Datamart Environment (TIDE)," May 20, 2007, http://www.nctc.gov/docs/Tide_Fact_Sheet.pdf (accessed June 11, 2007).

72. Information in this paragraph comes from Congressional Research Service, *Terrorism, the Future, and U.S. Foreign Policy*, p. 6.

73. Carrie Johnson, "Outgoing FBI Boss on His Legacy and What Kept Him up at Night," National Public Radio, August 22, 2013, http://www.npr.org/2013/08/23/214549458/outgoing-fbi-boss-on-his-legacy-and-what-kept-him-up-at-night (accessed February 12, 2017).

74. Congressional Research Service, *Terrorism, the Future, and U.S. Foreign Policy*, p. 5.

75. See "Interpol: Extending Law Enforcement's Reach around the World," *FBI Law Enforcement Bulletin* (December 1998), pp. 10–16.

76. Interpol, "Member Countries," http://www.interpol.int/Member-countries/World (accessed April 21, 2017).

77. "Interpol at Forty," *Criminal Justice International*, November/December 1986, pp. 1, 22.

78. Interpol General Secretariat, *Interpol at Work: 2003 Activity Report* (Lyons, France, 2004).

79. Ibid.

80. "ICC Appeals Judges Uphold Conviction of Congolese Warlord Lubanga," December 1, 2014, http://blink.htcsense.com/web/articleweb.aspx?regionid=1&articleid=32624116 (accessed March 1, 2017).

Name Index

A

Abadinsky, Howard, 56, 370, 376
Abagnale, Frank W., Jr., 343
Abelson, Robert P., 139, 147
Adams, Mike S., 208
Adler, Freda, 123, 237, 246
Agnew, Robert, 166, 176, 177
Aichorn, August, 144, 147
Akers, Ronald L., 196, 197–198
Alexander, Travis, 126
Allgier, Curtis, 416
Al-Rasheed, Khaled, 441
Alverez, Felix, 241
Amir, Menachem, 275
Amurao, Corazon, 98
Anderson, Elijah, 185
Anderson, Margaret, 189
Andrade, Leandro, 63
Andrews, Donald A., 146
Andrews, Erin, 322
Aquinas, Thomas, 58
Arias, Jodi, 126
Arsenault, L., 88
Arvanites, Thomas M., 174
Atta, Mohammed, 440
Austin, James, 46
Austin, W. Timothy, 76

B

Bachman, Nicole, 117
Bachman, Ronet, 146
Bandura, Albert, 145, 147, 149–150
Barak, Gregg, 14
Barfield, Reginald, 184
Barkow, Jerome H., 125
Barnes, J. C., 107
Baron, Larry, 302
Barrett, Michael David, 322
Bartollas, Clemens, 9, 250
Baumer, Eric, 336
Beam, Louis, 438
Beaver, Kevin M., 104, 110, 123, 124
Beccaria, Cesare, 60, 61, 67, 76, 79
Becker, Howard, 196, 206–207
Beckstrom, John H., 96
Beirne, Piers, 5, 244
Bennett, Thomas, 348
Bennett, Trevor, 312
Bentham, Jeremy, 60–61, 62, 67, 79
Bernard, Thomas J., 110, 123, 203, 255
Bernardo, Paul, 301
Bernburg, Jon Gunnar, 208
Bernhardt, Paul C., 110, 116
Bishop, Amy, 320
Black, Donald, 254
Black, Percy, 415

Blau, Judith, 166, 175
Blau, Peter, 166, 175
Block, Carolyn Rebecca, 295
Block, Richard, 295
Bloodsworth, Kirk Noble, 73
Blum, Kenneth, 104
Blumstein, Alfred, 16, 215, 347
Bobbitt, Lorena, 159
Bodzar, Andy, 347
Boesky, Ivan, 354, 379
Bogle, Dale Vincent (Rooster), 107
Bonger, Willem, 236, 239
Bonta, James, 146
Booth, Alan, 110, 115
Bowker, Lee H., 306
Bowlby, John, 146, 147
Bradish, Jay K., 345
Braga, Anthony, 169
Braithwaite, John, 196, 210, 366
Braswell, Michael, 250
Bratton, William J., 76
Breivik, Anders Behring, 32, 140
Broidy, Lisa M., 177, 219
Brookman, Fiona, 312
Brownmiller, Susan, 302
Brunner, Hans, 103, 110
Bryant, Robert, 342
Buchalter, Lepke, 370
Bulger, James (Whitey), 107
Bulger, William (Billy), 107
Burgess, Ann, 303
Burgess, Ernest, 166, 167
Burgess, Robert, 196
Burgess-Proctor, Amanda, 246
Bush, George W., 375, 367, 425, 441, 444
Bush, Neil, 354
Bushway, Shawn, 37

C

Cameron, Mary Owen, 338
Cantor, David, 332
Capone, Al, 370, 376
Carceral, K. C., 255
Carlie, Mike, 188
Carter, Jamal, 397
Carter, Zachary, 377
Carver, H. Wayne, 102
Caspi, Avshalom, 104, 110
Castellano, "Big Paul," 377
Catherine the Great, 60
Cauffman, Elizabeth E., 219
Caulfield, Susan, 247
Chafinch, Lynne, 330
Chambliss, William J., 237, 239–240, 243
Chapman, Mark David, 322
Chapple, Constance L., 202
Charles R. Tittle, 203

Chesney-Lind, Meda, 237, 247
Cho, Seung-Hui, 298
Christiansen, Karl O., 85, 93
Churchill, Vickie, 350
Clarke, James W., 182
Clarke, Richard, 441
Clarke, Ronald V., 64, 67, 311
Claudius I, 56
Clear, Todd, 33
Cleckley, Hervey M., 134, 147
Clinton, Bill, 411, 424, 439
Clinton, Hillary, 400
Cloward, Richard A., 166, 183, 185, 188
Cohen, Albert, 166, 184–185
Cohen, Jacqueline, 215
Cohen, Lawrence E., 196, 215, 221, 332
Cohn, Ellen G., 121
Coke, Sir Edward, 57
Collin, Barry, 439
Collins, Francis, 102
Comte, Auguste, 84
Cook, John H., 95
Cornfeld, Bernie, 403
Cornish, Derek B., 64, 67, 311
Courtney, Robert R., 373
Cressey, Donald R., 9, 195, 333
Crick, Francis, 102
Cromwell, Paul F., 333, 348, 349
Cullen, Francis, 202
Curran, Daniel J., 244
Currie, Elliott, 240–241, 243
Curry, G. David, 186

D

Dahrendorf, Ralf, 237, 238
Daigle, Leah E., 118
Dailey, Rodney, 186
Dalton, Katharina, 116
Daly, Kathleen, 237, 247
Darwin, Charles, 87, 95, 124, 303
Deacon, George, 77
Decker, Scott H., 313, 333, 334–336, 339, 346, 349
Defina, Robert H., 174
DeKeseredy, Walter, 237, 244
DePriest, Nancy, 418
Dinitz, Simon, 9
Doerner, William G., 21
Dollard, J., 145, 147
Doshi, Anil, 112
Douglas, John E., 156
Doyle, Arthur Conan, 86
Drasgow, F., 200
Drummond, Edward, 157
Dugan, Laura, 295, 336
Dugdale, Richard Louis, 85, 90
Durkheim, Emile, 167, 172
Dworkin, Andrea, 300, 402

E

Earls, Felton J., 226
Ebbers, Bernard, 355
Eck, John, 169
Edelhertz, Herbert, 357
Edward the Confessor, 56
Edwards, Jonathan, 90
Einstadter, Werner, 246
Elder, Glen H., Jr., 196, 216, 217
Elliott, D. S., 347
Ellis, Lee, 110, 127
Engels, Friedrich, 239
English, Christine, 116
Ennett, Susan T., 45
Esbensen, Finn-Aage, 186
Estabrook, Arthur H., 85, 90
Eugene, Rudy, 28
Ewing, Gary, 63
Eysenck, Hans J., 110, 137, 147

F

Fall, Albert B., 354
Faris, Ellsworth, 125
Farrakhan, Louis, 322
Farrington, David P., 29, 196, 217, 221
Feeney, Floyd, 311,
Felson, Marcus, 277–278
Fergusson, David, 110, 114
Ferracuti, Franco, 9, 166, 182, 293
Ferrell, Jeff, 44
Ferri, Enrico, 85, 87, 89
Fishbein, Diana, 24, 122
Fisher, Arthur, 95
Fleisher, Mark S., 347
Fleiss, Heidi Lynne, 400, 403
Flewelling, R. L., 294
Flores, Stephany, 194
Fogel, David, 63
Fontaine, Nathalie, 105, 110
Forde, David R., 21
Forrest, Walter, 202
Foster, Jodie, 322
Fox, James Alan, 296, 297, 298, 299
Frederick the Great, 60
French, Kristen, 301
Freud, Sigmund, 133, 142–143, 144, 147, 160
Friehling, David, 378

G

Gall, Franz Joseph, 85–87
Galliher, John F., 4
Galton, Sir Francis, 85, 90
Gardere, Jeff, 339
Garofalo, James, 275
Garofalo, Raffael, 85, 87
Gavin, Helen, 140
Geis, Gilbert, 357
Gelles, Richard J., 315
Gerould, Alexander, 123
Gesch, C. Bernard, 82
Ghasemi, Ali-Reza, 411
Ghasemi, Shahla, 411
Gibbons, Don C., 14, 244
Gibbs, Jack P., 10

Giffords, Gabrielle, 132
Gigante, Vincent, 377
Gilsinan, James F., 22
Giuliani, Caroline, 338
Giuliani, Rudolph (Rudy), 76, 170, 174, 338
Glaser, Daniel, 196, 198
Glenn, Scott, 155
Gleyzer, Georgiy, 374
Glueck, Bernard H., 134
Glueck, Eleanor, 90, 196, 218, 219, 220
Glueck, Sheldon, 196, 218, 219, 220
Goddard, Henry Herbert, 85, 91–92
Goffman, Erving, 196, 212, 214, 232
Goldschmidt, L., 114
Goldstein, Paul J., 295
Gonzales, Alberto, 367
Gonzales, Jose, 241
Goodman, Sam, 348, 349
Goring, Charles Buckman, 85, 88
Gottesman, Irving, 107
Gottfredson, Don M., 13, 31
Gottfredson, Michael R., 196, 201, 347, 366
Gotti, John (Dapper Don), 377
Gotti, John, Jr., 377
Gravano, Salvatore (Sammy the Bull), 377
Green, Gary S., 357
Gross, Mortimer, 112
Groth, Nicholas, 302, 303, 307
Grove, Walter R., 220
Groves, W. Byron, 242
Guzman, Pedro Antonio Marcuello, 330

H

Hagan, Frank E., 45
Hagan, John, 237, 247
Halleck, Seymour L., 146, 147
Hammurabi, 56
Hannell, Lawrence E., 92
Harding, Warren, 354
Hare, Robert, 135
Harris-Moore, Colton, 350
Hassan, Nidal Malik, 438
Hay, Carter, 202
Hay, Dale F., 223
Hayslett-McCall, Karen L., 202
Hazelwood, Robert R., 156, 303
Healy, William, 134
Hegel, Georg Wilhelm Friedrich, 239
Heimbach, Michael, 438
Heimer, Karen, 248
Helland, Ingrid Bergliot, 112
Hendricks, Scott A., 310
Hennard, George, 299
Henry, Andrew F., 145
Henry, Stuart, 249, 349
Hepburn, John R., 346
Herrnstein, Richard J., 110, 121
Hess, Rudolf, 58
Himmler, Heinrich, 58
Hindelang, Michael, 275, 315, 332
Hinkley, John, 322
Hipp, Joan R., 178
Hirschi, Travis, 189, 196, 200–203, 218, 347, 366
Hitler, Adolf, 58–59, 155
Hmangte, Chungneijang Mary Kom, 124
Hobbes, Thomas, 57, 79

Hockey, David, 140
Holder, Eric, 299
Holloway, Natalee, 194
Holmes, James Eagan, 229, 230, 298
Holmes, Oliver Wendell, Jr., 91
Holmes, Ronald M., 9
Holmes, Sherlock, 86
Homolka, Karla, 301
Homolka, Tammy, 301
Honaker, David, 348
Hone, Brian, 112
Hoolihan, Jeff, 347
Hooton, Earnest A., 85, 88, 107
Hoover, Kenneth R., 32
Hrycyk, Don, 330
Huberty, James, 299
Humbolt, Roy, 18
Hussein, Saddam, 440
Huxley. Sir Julian, 95

I

Irwin, John, 255

J

Jackson, Lakisha, 397
Jacobs, Bruce A., 312, 313
Jacobs, James B., 322
Jacobs, Patricia A., 91, 110
Jaffa, Harry V., 58
James, Jesse, 370
James I, 57
Jefferson, Thomas, 58
Jeffery, C. Ray, 83, 129
Jewel, 322
John (King of England), 57
Johnson, Laura, 6
Johnson, Lyndon B., 189
Jonathan R. Brauer, 203Joseph II, 60
Juke family, 85, 90
Justinian I, 56

K

Kaczynski, David, 256
Kaczynski, Theodore John (Ted), 256–257, 438
Kaker, Susan, 222
Kallikak, Martin, 91
Kallikak family, 85, 90–91
Kandel, Eric R., 144
Kane, John, 364
Kaplan, Howard B., 196, 200
Karayiorgou, Maria, 109
Katz, Jack, 65–66, 67, 335
Keating, Charles, 354
Kelleher, C. L., 297
Kelleher, Michael D., 297
Kelling, George L., 170, 171, 174
Kennedy, Leslie W., 21
Kirk, David S., 218
Kittaro, Moonbeam, 75
Kleiman, Mark A. R., 113
Klein, Malcolm W., 346
Klemke, Lloyd W., 338
Klockars, Carl, 243, 348

Knoll, James L., 298
Knox, George W., 416
Kohfeld, Carol W., 20
Kohlberg, Lawrence, 138, 147
Kollar-Kotelly, Colleen, 392
Kovandzic, Tomislav V., 71
Kozelka, Michael Lawrence, 322
Kozlov, Andrei, 374
Krafft-Ebing, Richard von, 134
Kretschmer, Ernst, 85, 89
Krist, Gary Steven, 77
Krist, Gordon, 77
Krohn, Marvin D., 208

L

Laney, Marti Olsen, 144
Lange, Johannes, 93
Lanier, Mark M., 208
Lansky, Meyer, 370
Lanza, Adam, 229, 230, 102, 298, 299
Laub, John H., 30, 196, 208, 216, 217, 218, 219
Lazo, Martha Elisa Ornelas, 330
Leary, Timothy, 382, 385
LeBlanc, Marc, 221
Lee, David, 68
Lemert, Edwin M., 196, 206
Lennon, John, 322
Leno, Jay, 87
Letterman, David, 322
Leung, K., 200
Levi, Ken, 181
Levin, Jack, 296, 297, 299
Lewis, C. S., 69
Lewis, Nolan D. C., 134
Lincoln, Abraham, 58
Linsky, Arnold S., 146
Little, Derek, 391
Little, Hamilton, 391
Locke, John, 57–58, 79
Lockman, Joe, 151
Loeber, Rolf, 221, 223
Lohan, Lindsay, 338
Lombroso, Cesare, 85, 86–88, 149
Lorenz, Konrad, 95–96
Losel, Frederick, 151
Lozoff, Bo, 250
Luckenbill, David F., 9
Lykken, David, 135
Lynch, Michael J., 242, 364

M

Machalek, Richard, 196, 217, 221
MacKinnon, Catherine, 300
Mackle, Barbara Jane, 77
Madoff, Andrew, 378
Madoff, Bernard Lawrence (Bernie), 378
Madoff, Mark, 378
Maguire, Mike, 333
Mahaffy, Leslie, 301
Mahoney, Martha R., 316
Malone, Shirley, 98
Mannheim, Hermann, 243
Manson, Charles, 134, 297
Marino, Achim Joseph, 420

Markus, Hazel Rose, 200
Martin, Randy, 76
Martinson, Robert, 62
Marx, Karl, 236, 237, 239, 257
Massey, Douglas S., 109–110
Masters, Roger D., 113, 116
Matisse, Henri, 330
Matza, David, 166, 180
Mazerolle, Paul, 177
McBurnett, Keith, 118
McCord, Joan, 20, 188
McCrary, Justin, 68
McCrory, Eamon, 110
McDowall, David, 310
McKay, Henry, 168
McMahon, Francis, 105
McVeigh, Timothy, 436
Mead, Margaret, 125
Mednick, Sarnoff, 85, 93
Mendelsohn, Benjamin (Beniamin), 275
Merton, Robert K., 166, 172–173, 174
Messerschmidt, James W., 5, 244, 246, 302
Messner, Steven F., 166, 174, 203
Metzger, Tom, 438
Michalowski, Raymond J., 234, 237, 242
Miethe, Terance D., 310
Mikkelsen, Mads, 135
Milk, Harvey, 111
Milken, Michael, 354, 379
Mill, John Stuart, 398
Miller, Jody, 313
Miller, Larry S., 33
Miller, Walter B., 166, 180
Milovanovic, Dragan, 249
Mitnick, Kevin, 419
M'naughten (McNaughten, M'Naghton), Daniel, 157–158
Moffitt, Terrie E., 104, 110, 127, 196, 219–220
Mohammed, Khan, 392–393
Monet, Claude, 330
Monster Kody Scott (Sanyika Shakur), 43, 185, 187
Montesquieu, Charles-Louis de Secondat, 58, 79
Monto, Martin A., 401
Morgan, Robin, 302
Morris, Robert T., Jr., 424
Mueller, Robert, 447
Mussolini, Benito, 155, 369
Mutchnak, Kevin, 417
Mutchnick, Robert J., 76

N

Naffine, Ngaire, 302
Nagin, Danield S., 294
Naisbitt, John, 423, 424
Nettler, Gwynn, 144, 189, 190
Nichols, Terry, 436
Nidal, Abu, 440
Norcross, John C., 150

O

Obama, Barack, 103, 230, 322, 367, 375, 425, 439
Ochoa, Christopher, 418
O'Connor, Sandra Day, 63
Ohlin, Lloyd E., 29, 166, 183, 185, 188

Olweus, Dan, 115
Osgood, D. Wayne, 110, 115
Oyserman, Daphna, 200

P

Packard, Vance, 237
Page, Wade Michael, 438
Paine, Thomas, 58–59, 79
Palmer, Craig T., 303
Palmer, Stewart, 145
Park, Robert, 166, 167
Parker, Donn B., 416
Parker, Robert Nash, 293, 295–296
Parr, Andy, 30–31
Paternoster, Raymond, 177
Pavlov, Ivan, 148
Peel, Robert, 157
Pelfrey, William V., 242
Pepinsky, Harold E., 237, 250
Perkins, Bob, 420
Petrosino, Anthony, 29
Pfohl, Stephen J., 189
Piaget, Jean, 138
Picasso, Pablo, 330
Pillar, Paul, 435
Pinel, Philippe, 134
Pinker, Steven, 125
Pollock, Joycelyn M., 249
Poppo, Ronald, 28
Potok, Mark, 437
Potter, Gary W., 376
Potter, Kimberly A., 322
Pound, Roscoe, 234
Pratt, Travis, 202
Presser, Lois, 181
Psathas, George, 214
Ptacek, James, 316–317
Purdy, Patrick Edward, 299
Putin, Vladimir, 374

Q

Quetelet, Adolphe, 220
Quinney, Richard, 237, 240, 243, 250–251

R

Rafter, Nichole Hahn, 88
Raine, Adrian, 107, 110
Rantchev, Nikolai, 434
Rantcheva, Oxana, 434
Rataway, Mortimer, 227
Raudenbush, Stephen, 226
Reagan, Ronald, 322
Reckless, Walter C., 196, 199–200
Reiman, Jeffery H., 5, 240
Reiss, Albert J., 226
Reno, Janet, 42
Renzetti, Claire M., 244
Restivo, Emily, 208
Revitch, Eugene, 336
Richards, Stephen C., 255
Ridgeway, Lamont, 117
Rigas, John J., 355
Riordan, Bruce, 416

Robinson, Matthew B., 5
Roebuck, Tresa M., 114
Roosevelt, Franklin Delano, 368
Ropers, H. Hilger, 103, 110
Rosenfeld, Richard, 166, 174, 294
Ross, Ian, 237, 255
Roth, Jeffrey, 216
Rotton, James, 121–122
Rousseau, Jean-Jacques, 58, 79
Russell, Diana E. H., 302, 305
Ryder, Winona, 338

S

Saeed, Mohammed, 158
Samenow, Stanton E., 140, 147, 150
Sampson, Robert J., 196, 208, 216, 217, 218, 219, 226, 228, 293, 332
Scalia, Antonin, 32
Schafer, Stephen, 275
Schank, Roger C., 139, 147
Schauss, Alexander G., 110
Schier, Ruth Eisemann, 77
Schlesinger, Louis B., 336
Schoenthaler, Stephen, 110, 112
Schory, Thomas J., 121
Schultz, "Dutch," 370
Schuman, Alan, 63
Schwartz, Jeffrey M., 111
Schwendinger, Herman, 4
Schwendinger, Julia, 4
Scott, Monster Kody (Sanyika Shakur), 43, 185
Scully, Diana, 303–304
Seidman, Robert T., 239
Sellin, Thorsten, 166, 179, 236–237
Shakur, Sanyika (Monster Kody Scott), 43, 185, 187
Shakur, Tupac, 185
Shaw, Clifford, 166, 168, 188
Sheldon, William H., 85, 89–90
Sheley, Joseph F., 9
Sherman, Lawrence W., 29, 37, 169
Shimomura, Tsutomu, 419
Shoemaker, Donald J., 185
Short, James F., Jr., 145
Short, Jim, 10
Shover, Neil, 333, 346, 348
Siegel, Benjamin (Bugsy), 370
Simmel, Georg, 167, 236, 239
Simmons, Jacquetta, 314
Simon, Rita J., 237, 246
Skinner, B. F., 147, 148
Smart, Carol, 237
Smith, Dwayne, 293
Smith, Martha J., 311
Smithfield, Nicole, 391
Snipes, Jeffrey, 123
Speck, Richard Benjamin, 92, 98
Spergel, Irving A., 186
Spinoza, Baruch, 58
Sprague, John, 20
Spurzheim, Johann Gaspar, 85, 86
Stark, Evan, 315
Stark, Rodney, 170
Steffensmeier, Darrell J., 110, 123, 333, 348, 349

Stevens, Dennis J., 303
Stewart, James C., 29
Stewart, Martha, 355
Strang, Heather, 210
Straus, Murray A., 146, 302, 315
Stretesky, Paul B., 364
Strunk, William, Jr., 50
Stuntz, William, 367
Sullivan, Scott, 355
Sumner, William Graham, 54
Sutherland, Edwin H., 3, 9, 13, 195, 196, 198, 333, 346, 355, 359, 364, 380
Sutter, Jason, 151
Sutter, Paul, 344
Sutton, Willie, 346
Swaggi, Vincent, 348
Sykes, Gresham M., 166, 180, 240

T

Tannenbaum, Frank, 196, 206
Tappan, Paul W., 3
Tarde, Gabriel, 147, 149
Taxman, Faye S., 46
Taylor, Ian, 250
Taylor, Jeanette, 95
Teale, Leanne, 301
Teicher, Martin, 109
Teten, Howard, 155
Thacher, David, 171
Thoennes, Nancy, 323
Thomas, Clarence, 59
Thomas, W. I., 166, 167
Thornberry, Terrence, 196, 217, 222–224
Thornhill, Randy, 303
Thrasher, Frederic M., 166, 179, 185
Tittle, Charles R., 196, 198–199, 204–205
Tjaden, Patricia, 323
Toby, Jackson, 243
Toennies, Ferdinand, 167
Tojo, Hideki, 155
Topalli, Volkan, 313
Topinard, Paul, 9
Trasler, G. B., 218
Tremblay, Richard E., 88
Tsarnaev, Dzhokhar, 449
Tsarnaev, Tamerlan, 449
Tunnell, Kenneth D., 335
Turgeman-Goldschmidt, Orly, 182
Turk, Austin, 237, 238

V

van der Sloot, Joran, 194
van Gogh, Vincent, 330
van Leunen, Mary-Claire, 50
Vila, Bryan, 222, 228
Villariagosa, Antonio, 76
Visher, Christy, 216
Vito, Gennaro F., 9
Voit, Ann, 45
Vold, George B., 237, 238
von Hentig, Hans, 275

W

Waksal, Sam, 355
Wall, April, 364
Walsh, Anthony, 110, 121, 122, 124
Walsh, Dermot, 348–349
Walters, Richard H., 142, 145
Warr, Mark, 337–338
Watson, James, 102
Weber, Max, 44, 239
Websdale, Neil, 316
Weiner, Neil Alan, 347
Weisburd, David, 37, 66–67, 169
Weitzer, Ronald, 404
Wellford, Charles F., 11, 24
West, Donald J., 196, 217, 221
White, Dan, 111
White, E. B., 50
Whitehead, John T., 33
Whyte, William Foote, 39, 166, 179
Wiggins, David Lee, 73
Wikström, Per-Olof H., 196, 203–204
Wildeman, John, 250
William the Conqueror, 56
Williams, K. R., 293
Williams, Tyrone, 432
Wilson, Edward O., 85, 96, 99
Wilson, James Q., 29, 63, 110, 121, 166, 170, 174, 190
Wilson, Pete, 63
Winerman, Lea, 156
Wolfgang, Marvin E., 9, 56, 74, 166, 182, 196, 220, 221, 274, 276
Wonders, Nancy, 247
Wooldredge, John D., 332
Wright, Alexis, 397
Wright, Billy, 187
Wright, John P., 124
Wright, Richard T., 310, 312,, 313, 333, 334–336, 346, 349,
Wuornos, Aileen, 297

Y

Yates, Andrea Pia (Kennedy), 158
Yates, Buford, 355
Yates, Rusty, 158
Yeager, Matthew G., 219
Yeltsin, Boris, 372
Yochelson, Samuel, 140, 147
Young, Jock, 237, 244
Young Jeezy, 185
Yousef, Ramzi Ahmed, 447

Z

Zaalberg, Ap, 82
Zimmerman, Gregory M., 203
Zimring, Franklin E., 182, 428
Znaniecki, Florian, 166, 167

Subject Index

9/11 Commission, 440, 445

A

abnormality, 6
abortion, 59
abstract (research reports), 48
Academy of Criminal Justice Sciences (ACJS), 44
Academy of Experimental Criminology, 15
accounting fraud, 355
acknowledgments (research reports), 48
acquaintance rape, 305
activation, in life course perspective, 216
adaptation, crime as, 145–146
addiction, 389
adolescence, 214, 223. *See also* children; juveniles
adolescence-limited offenders, 220
advance fee fraud, 358, 360
African Americans, homicide and, 293
age, 117, 121
age-graded theory, 218–219
Age of Reason, 57
agencies, federal, 12
aggravated assault, 314–317
aggravation, in life course perspective, 216
aggression, 145
　biological roots of, 95–96
　brain mechanisms in, 109
　causes of, 32
　hormones and, 115–116
　modeling and, 149
　psychobiotics, 114
　serotonin and, 116–118
　toxic exposure and, 113
agreeableness, 137
Aid to Families with Dependent Children (AFDC), 188
aiding and abetting, 365
AIDS (acquired immunodeficiency syndrome), 386
alcohol use, 67
　prenatal exposure, 110
　violent crimes and, 297–298
Alcoholics Anonymous (AA), 45
aliens, illegal, 241, 434
allele, 104, 125
allergies, 109
alloplastic adaptation, 145
alternative criminology, 254
alternative dispute resolution, 251
alternative drug policies, 396
altruism, 96
amateur receivers, 348–349
American Civil Liberties Union (ACLU), 412
American Psychiatric Association, 229–230
American Recovery and Reinvestment Act of 2009, 367

American Society of Criminology (ASC), 15
Amir, Menachem, 275
analysis of data, 41–42
analysis (research reports), 49
analysis, secondary, 40
anarchist terrorists, 435
androcentricity, 246
angel of death, 297
anger, 298
anomie, 166
Anti-Phishing Working Group (APWG), 410
antisocial personality, 136
antisocial personality disorder (APD, ASPD, ANPD), 136–137
antitrust violation, 356
appendixes (research reports), 49
applied research, 33
aptitude-treatment interaction, 37
armchair criminology, 30
arson, 331, 345, 362
art theft, 330
Asian criminal enterprises, 372–373
assault, 247, 429
　aggravated, 314–317
　within families, 315–317
　intimate-partner, 315–317
　separation, 316
　simple, 314
asset forfeiture, 376
atavism, 86, 87–88
attachment, in social bond theory, 201
attachment theory, 147
attempted rape, 299
auction fraud, 358
audit trail, 422
authority conflict pathway, 225
autism, 135
automobile theft, 429
autonomic nervous system (ANS), 118
autonomy, 180
autoplastic adaptation, 145
availability of guns, 295
avocational receivers, 348

B

Balanced and Restorative Justice (BARJ) Model, 252–253
Balkan organized crime, 372–373
bank fraud, 355, 356
Bank Secrecy Act (BSA), 363
bankruptcy fraud, 356
bar/hotel prostitutes, 399
basketball, 36
battery, 247
behavior

adapted instinctive, 95
antisocial, 4
conditioned, 148
criminal, 7, 9
deviant. *See* deviant behavior
diet and, 82, 111–112
genetics and, 102, 105
maladaptive, 5, 142–148
operant, 148
survival instinct as determinant of, 96
behavior theory, 133, 148–150
behavioral conditioning, 148
behavioral genetics, 90
behavioral profiling, 155
Behavioral Science Unit (FBI), 155
behaviorism, 133
belief, in social bond theory, 201
bias, 44, 127
　experimenter's, 36
bias crimes, 322
bibliography (research reports), 49
binge drinking, 385
biological theories of crime, 24, 81–127
　assumptions of, 84
　biosocial criminology, 110, 121–125
　body chemistry theories, 111–114, 122
　body types, 121
　brain dysfunction, 107–111
　climate and weather, 120–121
　constitutional theories, 85, 88–90
　criminal families, 85, 90–91, 103, 202
　critiques of, 97–99, 127
　early theories, 84–95
　evolutionary theory, 124–125
　gender differences in criminality, 88, 122–124, 314
　genetics and heritability, 103–106, 110, 122
　heredity, 93–95
　hormones and criminality, 110, 115–121, 127
　physical features theories, 84–90
　policy implications of, 125
　principles of, 83–84
　sociobiology, 85, 95–99
　XYY supermale, 91–93
biosocial criminology, 110, 121–125
bioterrorism, 442
Black Hand (*La Mano Negro*), 369
black widow, 297
blank slate myth, 125
blue-collar crime, 357
body chemistry and criminality, 111–121
body parts, theft of, 344
body types, 89–90, 121, 122
Boggs Act, 393
bootlegging, 370
born criminals, 87
bounded rationality, 347

bourgeoisie, 236
Boys and Girls Clubs of America, 228
Brain Activity Map, 103, 105
brain dysfunction, 107–111, 122
brain plasticity, 109
breastfeeding, 112
British Petroleum (BP), 359, 363
broken windows theory, 170, 171, 174
broker embezzlement, 360
Bureau of Justice Statistics (BJS), 38, 261, 305
burglary, 330–337, 429
    costs of, 336
    disposing of stolen goods, 348–350
    drugs and, 334, 336
    ethnographic research on burglars, 333
    locales and times of, 334
    motivation of burglars, 334–335
    sexualized content of, 336–337
    social ecology of, 331–333
    target selection, 335–336
    typology of burglars, 333–334

C

cafeteria-style offending, 346
call girls, 398, 399
Call Off Your Old Tired Ethics
    (COYOTE), 402
Cambridge Study in Delinquent Development, 221
Campus Sexual Assault Victims' Bill of Rights Act,
    305
Cannabis Manifesto, 234
cannibalism, 28
capable guardian, 276
capital punishment, 17, 68, 70–74
    race and, 72–74
car parts, theft of, 342
career criminals, 152. See also criminal career
case studies, 33
causality, 30, 33
causative definitions, 9
causative factors, 2
causes of crime, 19. See also causality
    individual choice, 54, 59, 60, 61, 67, 79
    psychological and psychiatric theories, 133,
        154–155
    social factors, 67–68
    sociological approaches to, 164
    white-collar crime, 367–368
charismatic psychopaths, 135
chemical precursors of crime, 127
Chicago Area Project, 188
Chicago School of criminology, 167–168
child molestation, 307–309
Child Molestation Research and Prevention Insti-
    tute, 307
child pornography, 308
child-rearing practices, 20
child sex predator profiles, 308
child sexual abuse (CSA), 227, 307–309
child sexual exploitation (CSE), 307
children. See also adolescence; juveniles
    antisocial, 94
    maltreatment of, 104, 110, 222
    prostitution of, 400, 404
    protection from obscene Internet materials, 412
    sexual exploitation of, 307–309
    as victims, 307–309

    as violence witnesses, 15
Children's Internet Protection Act
    (CIPA), 412
choices, 54, 59, 61, 67, 79. See also rational choice
    theory (RCT)
    property offenders, 348
chop shops, 342
chromosomes, 102
cities, 167–168
class and class structure, 4
class struggle, 165, 236
classical conditioning, 147
Classical School of criminological thought, 54, 55,
    59–61, 67
    critique of, 76–79
    forerunners of, 54–59
    major figures in, 59–61
    policy implications, 74–76
Clayton Act, 356, 368
climate and crime, 120
co-offending, 186–188
Coalition Against Insurance Fraud
    (CAIF), 362
cocaine, 373
Code of Ethics, Academy of Criminal Justice Sci-
    ences, 44
Code of Hammurabi, 56
code of the street, 185
cognitive behavioral intervention (CBI), 150
cognitive information-processing theory (CIP),
    139–140
Cohen, Lawrence, 276
cohort analysis, 221
collective efficacy, 166
collective incapacitation, 74
College Alcohol Study (CAS), 385
comfort serial killers, 296
commercial sexual exploitation of children (CSEC),
    307, 308
Commission on Law Enforcement and Administra-
    tion of Justice, 188
Commission on the Prevention of Weapons of Mass
    Destruction Proliferation and Terrorism, 442
commitment, in social bond theory, 201
Committee on Law and Justice, National Academies
    of Sciences, 72
commodities fraud, 360–361
common law, 56–57
Communications Decency Act (CDA), 411
communism, 372
community, 167
comparative criminologists, 428
comparative criminology, 428–431
    ethnocentrism, 429–430
compassionate criminology, 250
competing cause, 36
Comprehensive Crime Control Act
    (1984), 153
Comprehensive Methamphetamine Control Act
    (CMCA), 393
Comprehensive National Cybersecurity Initiative
    (CNCI), 425
Comprehensive Strategy for Serious, Violent, and
    Chronic Juvenile Offenders program, 228
computer abuse, 413
computer crime. See cybercrime
Computer Fraud and Abuse Act of 1984, 423
computer games, 15, 414
computer-manipulation crimes, 409

Computer Professionals for Social Responsibility
    (CPSR), 425
computer-related crime, 413
computer trespass, 409
computer viruses and worms, 411, 412
conclusions, 40
conclusions (research reports), 49
conditioning, 133, 137, 147, 197
conduct norms, 179
conferencing, 252
conflict perspective, 235–238
Conflict Tactics Scale, 315
conformity, 172
confounding effects, 35
conscientiousness, 137
consensus perspective, 7, 234–235
consequences of crime, 19, 22
    in Classical School thought, 60–61
conspiracy, 365
Constitution, 6
Constitution Project, 73
constitutional theories, 85, 88–90
containment, 200
containment theory, 199–200
contributions (background causes of crime), 19
control–balance theory, 204–205
control deficit, 204
control group, 36
control ratio, 205
control surplus, 204
control theory, 367
controlled experiment, 35
controlled substances, 387, 389
Controlled Substances Act (CSA), 234, 387
convict criminology, 237, 254–255
copper, 113
copyright violations, 412, 423
corporate criminal liability, 358–359, 367–368
corporate fraud, 359
Corporate Fraud Task Force, 367
correctional psychology, 150
correlation, 41, 42
corruption, 370, 376
cortical plasticity, 109
cortisol, 118
covert pathway, 225
crack cocaine, 336
CREB genes, 106
credit card fraud, 358, 365
crime
    defined, 2, 121
    future, 408
    popular fascination with, 2
crime categories, 3
crime-control efforts, 24
crime-control policy, 2, 46
    situational, 66–67
crime-control strategies, nurturant, 227–228
crime families in organized crime, 368–370
crime funnel, 70
crime gene, 107
Crime in the United States (FBI publication), 291
crime planning, 54, 312, 346–347
crime prevention, 60
    genetic information supporting, 102
    public transportation and, 311
    situational approach to, 64–67
crime rates, 4, 178, 292
    declines in, 75–79

murder, 292
rape, 299, 301
transnational comparisons, 430–431
crime reduction, conflict criminology approaches
    to, 242
crime reporting, 429
crimes against humanity, 58–59
criminal anthropology, 85, 87
criminal behavior, 7, 9
criminal career, 216, 311, 347
criminal enterprise, 370–371
    technological support of, 409
    transnational, 429, 430–431
criminal families, 85, 90–91, 103, 107
criminal groups, 430–431
    auto theft, 344
    identity theft, 341
criminal homicide, 292. *See also* murder
criminal justice, 10, 11
criminal justice system, 20
criminal law, early sources of, 56–57
criminal mind-set, 140–142
criminal mischief, 411
criminal opportunity, 332
criminal profiling, 155
criminal psychological profiling, 155–157
criminal psychology, 132
criminal victimization, 259–288
    demographic correlates of, 267–270
    hidden victims, 260–261
    by the numbers, 261–266
    offense patterns, changing, 265–266
    restorative justice, 284–285
    socio-emotional impact of, 270–273
    victimology, 273–281
    victim's rights, 281–284
criminalist, 11
criminality, 10, 121
    predicting, 154
    of women, 246
criminalization, process of, 3
criminaloids, 87–88
criminogenic domains, 146
criminogenic environments, 106
criminogenic needs, 146
criminologists, 9, 12–14
criminology, 9–11
    definitions of terms used in, 9–11
    eras of, 29
    evidence-based, 29
    evolving science of, 29
    interdisciplinary nature of, 10, 24, 83
    roots of, 10
    scientific evidence for, 28–29
    social policy and, 15–16
    theoretical, 13–14
    translational, 15
criminology of place, 66, 168–171
critical criminology, 238, 240
Critical Infrastructure Assurance Office (CIAO),
    439
Critical Infrastructure Warning Information Net-
    work (CWIN), 441–442
critical realism, 244
cultural deviance theory, 166, 179
cultural transmission, 168
culture conflict theory, 166, 179–188, 236
    code of the street, 185
    delinquency and drift, 180–182

differential opportunity theory, 183
focal concerns, 180
reaction formation, 184–185
subcultural theory, 179
violent subcultures, 182–183
Currency and Foreign Transactions Reporting Act,
    363
cyberbanging, 416
cybercrime, 407–425. *See also* Internet, technology
    combating, 422–425
    computer access, 411
    cybercriminal profile, 414–417
    cyberprostitution, 399
    cybersecurity, 423–425
    cyberterrorism, 439–442
    data interception, 409
    extent of, 410–411
    federal research reports on, 413
    hijacking, 410
    Internet security and, 423–425
    law, 411–414
    typologies, 409
    as white-collar crime, 416
cyberprostitution, 399
cybersecurity, 423–425
cyberspace, 414
cyberstalking, 323
cyberterrorism, 439–442

D

Dade County Diversion and Treatment Program,
    251
danger seeking, 99
dangerous drugs, 388
Dangerous People with Severe Personality Disorder
    (DPSPD), 135
dangerousness, 78–79
    assessing, 152–154
D.A.R.E. (Drug Abuse Resistance Education), 45,
    46
dark figure of crime, 260–261
data, interpretation of, 32
data analysis, 41–42
data collection
    problems in, 40–41
    techniques, 38–40
data confidentiality, 44
data encryption, 422
data theft, 409
date rape, 305, 393
Daubert standard, 420
DCS-3000, 423
death penalty. *See* capital punishment
Death Penalty Information Center, 72
deconstructionist theories, 249
decriminalization, 396, 404
defensible space, 170, 173
definitions, types of, 9
delinquency, 6, 104, 180–182
    Chicago School study of, 168
    cybercrime and, 411
    hormones and, 118
    in strain theory, 172, 175, 176
delinquency and self-esteem, 200
delinquent development theory, 220–221
delinquent subcultures, 180–188
delinquents, typology of, 207

demographics, 267
demonic era, 55–56
Denver Youth Survey, 224
Department of Homeland Security (DHS), 414
deprivation, relative, 175
description of existing situation (research reports),
    48
description of research plan (research reports),
    48–49
descriptive criminology, 30
descriptive statistics, 41
designer drugs, 390
desistance, 216, 220–221
detachment, 443
determinate sentencing, 74
determinism, 61, 84
    genetic, 91, 97
deterrence, 60, 67–68, 69, 203
developmental pathways, 223–226
The Developmental Victimization Survey (DVS),
    270
deviance, 5–6
deviant behavior, 5–6, 183
    crime as subset of, 201
    explanations for, 9
    learning, 197–198
deviant neighborhoods, theory of, 170
deviant places theory, 279–280
devil, 28
diet, 35, 82, 111–112, 122
differential association, 195–197
differential association–reinforcement theory,
    197–198
differential attrition, 36
differential identification theory, 198
differential opportunity theory, 183
differential reinforcement theory, 197
differential selection, 36
Digital Theft Deterrence and Copyright Damages
    Improvement Act, 413
disciple killer, 297
disciplinary definitions, 9
disclaimers (research reports), 49
discrediting information, 212
discussion (research reports), 49
disease model, 133
disengagement, 150
disinhibition, selective, 295
disorganized social killers, 297
displacement, 145
displacement of crime, 68
distempered psychopaths, 135
distributive justice, 175
diversity, 7, 235
dizygotic (DZ) twins, 93
DNA, 54, 102
    exoneration using, 73
    profiling, 418
    technology, 24
domestic terrorism, 435, 436
dopamine, 104
dramaturgical perspective, 195, 196, 210
drug abuse
    costs of, 386–387
    extent of, 382–385
    illicit drugs, 383–384
    social policy and, 393–397
    U.S. history of, 382
    young people and, 385

Drug Abuse Resistance Education (D.A.R.E.), 45, 46
drug addiction, 389
drug-control legislation, 394–395
drug-control strategies, 394
drug-defined crimes, 392
Drug-Induced Rape Prevention Act, 393
drug-related crimes, 28, 392, 431
Drug Relationships in Murder Project (DREIM), 295
drug robberies, 313
drug trafficking, 370, 389–393
drugs and drug crimes, 70
    decriminalization debate, 395–397
    designer drugs, 390
    drug trafficking, 389–393
    gangs and, 186
    illegal drug types, 387
    legalization, 395–397
    narcoterrorism, 392–393
    pharmaceutical diversion, 390
    social policy and, 393–397
    violent crimes and, 295–296
dual taxonomic theory, 219–220
due process, 57
Dunedin Multidisciplinary Health and Development Study, 104, 218
duration, in criminal careers, 216
DVS. see The Developmental Victimization Survey (DVS)

E

Earth Liberation Front (ELF), 345
ecological theories, 164, 166, 168, 179
economic compulsion, 295
economic espionage, 356
ecoterrorism, 345
ectomorph, 89, 90
ego, 143
elder abuse, 277
electroencephalogram (EEG), 136
Electronic Frontier Foundation (EFF), 425
The Eleventh United Nations Survey on Crime Trends and the Operations of Criminal Justice Systems, 430
embedding, 110
embezzlement, 356, 360
emotional abuse, 316
empathy, 134, 135, 148
employee theft, 337–338
endnotes (research reports), 49
endomorph, 89, 90
The Enlightenment, 57–59
Enron Corporation, 355, 359, 367
entertainment, crime-related, 2, 16
entry, forcible, 331
environmental crimes, 363–364
environmental criminology, 170
environmental law violation, 356
environmental pollution, 112–114, 122
epigenetics, 105
equity skimming, 361
ethics, 44–45
ethnic succession, 369
ethnocentrism, 429–430
ethnography, 255
ethnology, 95
eugenic criminology, 91

eugenics, 91
European Cybercrime Center (EC3), 450
European Society of Criminology (ESC), 9
Europol, 449–450
event decisions, 65
evidence, 15
evidence-based criminology, 15
evidence-based policy, 71, 94, 141, 171, 205, 211, 245, 253, 279, 388
evil, 55–56, 59
evolutionary ecology, 221–222
evolutionary neuroandrogenic (ENA) theory, 125
evolutionary perspective, 125
evolutionary theory, 124–125
excitement, 180
excitement of crime, 75, 142
existing account fraud, 340
expedience-directed serial killers, 297
experimental intervention, 35
experimental method, 29
experimental mortality, 36
experimental research designs, 35–38
experimenter bias, 36
expert systems, 422
explanations for crime, 2, 13
exposure-reduction theory, 294
expressive crime, 293
external containment, 199, 200
external validity, 35, 37
extortion, 409
extraversion, 137
extroverts, 137
Exxon Valdez oil spill, 363

F

facilitators, 299
fact finding, 33
facts, 40
family violence, 315–317
Federal Bureau of Investigation (FBI), 31
Federal Trade Commission (FTC), 16
feeblemindedness, 91
felony murder, 292, 311
Felson, Marcus, 277
female serial killers, 297
feminist criminology, 237, 244–249
feminist perspectives on rape, 300, 302
fence, 348–349
financial crime, 355, 359–363
financial fraud, 356, 365
Financial Fraud Enforcement Task Force, 367
financial institution fraud, 356
Financial Stimulus Act, 367
findings (research reports), 49
findings review, 41–42
fire setters, 345
First Amendment, 412, 425
first-degree murder, 291
First Offender Prostitution Program (FOPP), 401
Five Factor Model, 137
flash mobs, 339–340
folkways, 54
footnotes (research reports), 49
forcible rape, 275
foreign exchange fraud, 360
foreign lottery/sweepstakes fraud, 362

foreign terrorist organizations (FTOs), 445–447
forensic psychiatry, 133, 142
forensic psychology, 132
forfeiture, 395
forgery, 343
Fourteenth Amendment, 6
Fourth Amendment, 425
FOXP2 gene, 106
fraud, 340, 354–355, 356
    Internet, 357
Fraud Enforcement and Recovery Act of 2009, 367
free will, 17, 59, 61
    biological theories of crime and, 97
freedom, personal. See personal freedoms
freedom of speech, 412
frequency, in criminal careers, 216
frictions, 203
frontal brain hypothesis, 109
frustration–aggression theory, 145, 147
full-moon hypothesis, 30–31
funding, 45
future criminology, 442

G

galvanic skin response (GSR), 119–120
gambling, 6, 55, 370
Gang Peace, 186
gangs, 179, 184, 185–188, 213
    crimes by, 346
    organized crime and, 370
    peer pressure and, 397
    technology use, 415
Garofalo, James, 275
gender, 121, 300. See also women
gender differences in criminality, 122–124, 203
    robbery, 314
gender gap, 123, 248
gender ratio problem, 123
gene-environment interaction, 104
gene expression, 105
gene pool, 96
general deterrence, 69
general strain theory (GST), 175–179
general theory of crime (GTC), 13, 201–204
generalizability, 43
genes, 102, 107
genetic determinism, 91, 97
genetic profiling, 421
genetics, 83, 103–106
    predispositions, 125
genome mapping, 24
geographic distribution of crime, 164
"get tough on crime" strategies, 74–79
Ghost in the Machine myth, 125
globalization, 428
    transnational crimes, 430–431
good, 55
Gottfredson, Michael R., 275
government, responsibilities of, 58
government fraud, 356
green criminology, 364
GSR. see galvanic skin response (GSR)
guardians, capable, 278
guilt, 97
guilty but mentally ill (GBMI), 159
gun laws, 7, 229–230

H

habitual offenders, 152
hackers, 182, 409, 415
    profile of, 414–417
    transnational, 414
hacking, 411
Hammurabi Code, 56
hard determinism, 61
hardware, software, and information theft, 409
Hare Psychopathy Checklist, 135
Harrison Act, 393
Hate Crime Statistics Act of 1990, 321
hate crimes, 321–322
Health and Human Development Project (HHDP),
    208
health-care fraud, 356, 360, 361
hedge fund fraud, 360
hedonistic calculus, 61
hedonistic serial killers, 296
heredity, 85, 90–91, 93–95
heritability, 106
Heroin Signature Program (HSP), 389–390
heterosexuality, 302
HHDP. see Health and Human Development Pro-
    ject (HHDP)
Hindelang, Michael J., 275
history, 36
HIV (human immunodeficiency virus) infection,
    386–387
Hobbs Act, 376
home-intrusion rape, 337
homicide. See also murder
    gang-related, 186
    violent subcultures and, 182–183
Homicide Research Working Group (HRWG), 292
homosexuality, 306
hormones, 110, 115–121, 127
hotel/brothel prostitutes, 398, 400
human agency, 217
human development, 214
human ecology, 167
human genome, 102
Human Genome Project (HGP), 102, 106
human smuggling, 431–435
Human Smuggling and Trafficking Center (HSTC), 432
human trafficking, 241, 400, 404, 431–435
    legislation, 434–435
    smuggling distinguished, 433
hypoglycemia, 111
hypothesis, 34–35
    defined, 31
    statement of, 48

I

id, 143
identification document fraud, 365
identity theft, 340–342, 358
    assumed identities, 343
Identity Theft and Assumption Deterrence Act, 340
Identity Theft Penalty Enhancement Act, 340
illegal aliens, 241
illegitimate opportunity structure, 183
imitation, 149, 152
immigration, illegal, 241, 431
immigration fraud, 365
immigration legislation, 434–435

impression management, 211
incapacitation, 74, 152
individual responsibility perspective, 17
inferential statistics, 41
information, 422, 433
Information Sharing and Knowledge Development
    Directorate (ISKD), 447
information theft, 409
informed consent, 44
infrastructure, 439
inhalants, 388
inner containment199, 200
Innocence Project, 73
innovation, 172–173
inputs, 19, 20
insanity, 92, 133, 157–159
insider trading, 354, 355, 356
Institute for Social Research (University of
    Michigan), 40
Institute of Criminology, 37
institutional review boards, 45
institutional robberies, 310
instrumental conditioning, 197
instrumental crime, 293
instrumental Marxism, 240
instrumentality, in weapon use, 295
instrumentation, internal validity and, 36
insurance fraud, 356, 359, 362
integrated theory, 13–14
integrated theory of rape, 302
integrative perspective, 22, 366
intelligence, 77, 114, 121, 122
Intelligence Reform and Terrorism Prevention Act
    of 2004, 432
intentional homicide, 431
interactional theory, 222
interactionist theories. See social process theories
interest rates, 178
interdiction, 395
internal cybercrimes (malware), 409
internal validity, 35
International Criminal Court (ICC), 450–451
International Criminal Police Organization
    (INTERPOL), 429, 448
international terrorism, 436, 437
Internet, 423–425. See also cybercrime; technology
    automated monitoring of, 423
    child pornography and, 308
    crimes, 358, 409, 410
    security, 423–425
    terrorism and, 439
interpersonal violence. See violent crime
interpretations, 19, 20
intersubjectivity, 40
intimate-partner assault, 315–316
intimate-partner homicide, 294
intimate-partner stalking, 324
introduction (research reports), 48
investor fraud, 378
involvement decisions, 65
involvement, in social bond theory, 202
irresistible-impulse test, 158–159
Italian School of Criminology, 86–88

J

James Gang, 370
johns (in prostitution), 397, 401

Journal of Experimental Criminology, 29
journals, 12, 49–50
joyriders, 342
Juke family, 90
just deserts, 69
just deserts model, 69
justice, 65–67
    criminal, 10, 12, 20
    distributive, 175
    interpersonal, 139
    justice model, 63
    obstruction of, 360
    participatory, 250–252
    reparative, 251
    restorative, 4, 251–252
    retributive, 252
justice system, 20, 22, 76
Justinian Code, 56
Juvenile Justice and Delinquency Prevention Act of
    1974, 212
Juvenile Mentoring Program (JUMP), 212
juveniles. *See also* adolescence; children
    drugs and, 385
    fire setters, 345
    shoplifting by, 338

K

Kallikak family, 91
kickbacks, 356
Klinefelter's syndrome, 91
knowledge-based criminology, 15
knowledge, globalization of, 428

L

La Cosa Nostra, 369, 370
labeling theory, 195, 205–208, 367
labor union racketeering, 370
larceny-theft, 322, 337–341
law, 3, 54, 234–236
    common, 56–57
    criminal, 56–57
    cybercrime, 411–414
    early Roman, 56
    insanity and, 157–159
    natural, 58–59
    public vs. private, 56
    re organized crime, 376
    re guns, 7, 229–230
    state, 17, 372, 393
law enforcement
    international cooperation, 424, 431
    technology use, 418–420, 422
lead exposure, 112, 113
learning theory, 194, 195
left realism, 243
left-realist criminology, 237, 243
left-wing terrorists, 435
legal system, 235
legalistic approach to crime, 3
legalization, 396, 404
liberal feminism, 245
life course, 218
life course–persistent offenders, 219, 220
life course criminology, 216
life course persisters, 219

life course perspective, 215–218
life histories, 38
lifestyle theory, 64, 275–277, 332
limitations (research reports), 49
limited rationality, 347
linguistic definitions, 9
linked lives, 217
list of references (research reports), 50
loan-sharking, 370
lone wolf terrorist, 438
love-motivated mass murderers, 299
lust murderers, 31, 156

M

MacArthur Violence Risk Assessment
    Study, 153
macro approach, 17
Mafia, 369–370
Magna Carta, 57
mala in se, 54–55
mala prohibita, 55
maladaptation, criminal behavior as, 142–148
malware, 410, 411
managerial criminology, 255
manganese, 112, 113, 116
Manhattan Institute, 174
manuscript submission, 50
marijuana, 383, 385
    legislation re, 393, 395
Marijuana Tax Act, 393
martyrs, 155
Marxist criminology, 238
Marxist feminism, 246
masculinity hypothesis, 88
mass-marketing fraud, 359, 362
mass murder, 230, 298–300
mass shootings, 21, 32, 298–300
maturation, internal validity and, 36
mean, 41, 42
measurement, 34
measurement of crimes, 3
media violence, 15, 21
median, 41
Medicare Fraud Strike Force, 354
Mendelsohn, Benjamin, 275
mental illness, 159
mercury, 113
mesomorph, 89, 90
meta-analysis, 47
micro approach, 17
midnight basketball, 36
Miller, Tom, 277
mind-set, criminal, 140–142
Minnesota Twin Family Study, 93
minor physical abnormalities (MPAs), 88
mission-oriented serial killers, 296
M'Naughten rule, 157
Mobilization for Youth, 188, 229
mode, 41
Model Antistalking Code for States, 322
modeling, 149
modeling theory, 147, 149–150
money laundering, 356, 360, 363
Money Laundering Control Act, 363
Monitoring the Future (MTF) study, 382
monoamine oxidase A (MAOA), 104
monozygotic (MZ) twins, 93
Montreal Preventive Treatment Program, 213

moral development theory, 138–139, 147
moral enterprise, 196
Moral Sense Test (MST), 131
moral time, 254
morality, 11, 54, 190
    in SAT, 203
morals legislation, 398
mores, 54
mortgage debt elimination, 361
mortgage fraud, 360, 361–362
motivated offenders, 278
motivation, 2, 203
motivation of criminals, 19
    robbers, 211–212
motor vehicle theft, 322, 342–345
Motor Vehicle Theft Law Enforcement
    Act, 342
muggings, 310
multiple-treatment interference, 37
murder
    mass, 229, 298–299
    serial, 296–297
murder (criminal homicide), 290–299, 325
    alcohol and drug use, 295–296
    felony murder, 292
    gender and, 119–120
    general features of, 292
    international statistics on, 431
    rates, 290, 291
    sibling offenses, 295
    subculture of violence thesis, 292–293
    victim–offender relationship,
        293–295, 300
    weapon use in, 295
mystique of quantity, 42–43

N

narcoterrorism, 392–393
National Archive of Criminal Justice, 39
National Center for Injury Prevention and Control,
    301
National Center for the Analysis of Violent Crime
    (NCAVC), 155, 422
National Computer Crime Squad
    (NCCS), 423
National Crime Victimization Survey (NCVS), 38,
    261–263, 314, 319
    critiques of, 262–263
    property crimes data, 330
    UCR and, 164
National Criminal Justice Reference Service
    (NCJRS), 260
National Cyber Security Division
    (NCSD), 439
National DNA Index System (NDIS), 421
National Gang Center (NGC), 185
National Gang Crime Research Center, 186
National Incident-Based Reporting
    System(NIBRS), 261, 263
National Infrastructure Protection Center(NIPC),
    424, 439
National Institute for Occupational Safety and
    Health (NIOSH), 321
National Institute of Justice (NIJ), 15, 29, 307
National Institute on Drug Abuse, 105
National Insurance Crime Bureau (NICB), 362
National Longitudinal Study of Adolescent
    Health(Add Health), 104, 125

National Strategy to Combat Transnational Organ-
    ized Crime, 375
National Survey on Drug Use and
    Health(NSDUH), 383
National Survey on Family Violence
    (NSFV), 315
National Violence against Women (NVAW) survey,
    316
National Youth Gang Survey (NYGS), 185
National Youth Survey, 177
nationalist terrorists, 435
natural law, 58–59
natural rights, 58–59
natural selection, 96, 302
NCVS. *see* National Crime Victimization Survey
    (NCVS)
needs, criminogenic, 146
negative affective states, 176
negligent homicide, 291
neoclassical criminology, 54, 61–68
    defined, 62
    policy implications, 74
    punishment and, 68–74
net effects, 37
neuroplasticity, 111
neuroscience, 103
neurosis, 143
neuroticism, 137
neurotoxicity hypothesis, 112
neurotransmitters, 103–104
neutralization techniques, 181–182
new account fraud, 340
new criminology, 238
New School of Convict Criminology, 255
New Scientist (magazine), 15
NIBRS. *see* National Incident-Based Reporting
    System (NIBRS)
Nigerian letter fraud, 362, 411
No Electronic Theft Act (NETA, NET Act),
    412–413
Noble Savage myth, 125
nonprimary homicide, 293
norepinephrine, 118
normality, 133
NORML (National Organization for the Reform
    of Marijuana Laws), 207
norms, social, 5
not guilty by reason of insanity (NGRI), 108
nothing-works doctrine, 62
nudity, 6
nutrition, 111–112

O

objectivity, 30, 39
obscenity, 412
observation, 31, 38, 84
    participant, 39, 44
    scientific, 40
obstruction of justice, 359
occasional offender, 346–347
occupational crime, 357
offenders, 20, 22
offense definitions, 431
offense specialization, 346, 347
Office for Victims of Crime (OVC), 263
Office of Justice Programs, 46
Office of Juvenile Justice and Delinquency
    Prevention (OJJDP), 212, 224, 226

Office of National Drug Control Policy (ONDCP), 383
omega-3 and -6 fatty acids, 112
operant behavior, 147
operationalization, 34
opportunity reduction, 66
opportunity theory, 332
organized crime, 368–370
African criminal enterprises, 371, 373
Asian criminal enterprises, 371, 372–373
Balkan criminal enterprises, 372
Eastern European criminal enterprises, 372
ethnic criminal groups, 368–370
Eurasian criminal enterprises, 372
law and, 376
Middle Eastern criminal enterprises, 371, 373–374
policy issues, 376–378
Russian criminal enterprises, 374, 373–374
transnational, 375, 374–375, 429
Organized Crime Control Act of 1970, 376
organized social killers, 297
outputs, 20, 22
OVC. see Office for Victims of Crime (OVC)
overpayment fraud, 358, 362
overt pathway, 225, 226
oxytocin, 118

P

Panopticon, 61, 62
paradigm, 95
paranoid schizophrenic, 144
parenting, 202
participant observation, 39, 44
participation, in criminal careers, 216
participatory justice, 251
patriarchy, 246, 300
pawnshops, 349
peace model, 250
peacemaking criminology, 237, 250–254
pedophiles, 307–308
peer-immersion and training, 443
perjury, 365
persistence, 220
persistent thief, 346
personal freedoms, 230, 55, 57–58
technology and, 424–425
Personal Responsibility and Work Opportunity Reconciliation Act of 1996, 188
personal robbery, 310
personal theft, 332
personality, 85–86, 122, 133
body types and, 89–90
disturbances, 133–138
in trait theory, 137–138
pharmaceutical diversion, 390
phishing, 410
phone phreaks, 414
phrenology, 85
physical features theories, 84–93
physiological theories, 88–90
Pittsburgh Youth Study, 224
place, 170
place-based crime prevention, 169
pluralist perspective, 7–8, 235
political perspective on crime, 2, 4
pollution, environmental, 108–110

polymorphism, 125
polyvictimization, 268
pathways to, 270
Ponzi schemes, 360–361, 378
pornography, 302, 370
child, 308
positive criminology, 89
positivism, 61, 84, 85, 89
positron emission tomography (PET) scans, 107
post-traumatic stress disorder (PTSD), 260
postmodern criminology, 249–250
postmodern feminism, 246
posttest, 35
poverty, 31
power-control theory, 247
power seekers, 296
precipitants, 299
prediction, 127, 154
predisposers, 299
preface (research reports), 48
premeditation, 293
premenstrual syndrome (PMS), 116
prenatal substance exposure, 114, 122
Preparing for Drug Free Years (PDFY), 212
pre-radicalization, 443
President's Commission on Critical Infrastructure Protection (PCCIP), 439
pretest, 35
pretest effects, 37
primary conflict, 179
primary deviance, 206
primary homicide, 293
primary psychopaths, 135
primary research, 33
prime bank schemes, 360
prison populations, 74
Prison Rape Elimination Act (PREA), 305
prisons, 61, 255
rape in, 305–306
private security, 12
problem identification, 33–34
professional criminals, 346
professional receivers, 348
profiling, 155–157
profit-driven serial killers, 297
profit-motivated mass murderers, 299
program effectiveness, 33, 48
Program of Research on the Causes and Correlates of Delinquency, 224–225
Prohibition, 370, 393
Project D.A.R.E. (Drug Abuse Resistance Education), 45, 46
Project Gangfact, 186, 188
Project on Human Development in Chicago Neighborhoods (PHDCN), 226–228, 280
proletariat, 236
proof, 60
property crimes, 330, 331
force in, 331, 337
hate crimes, 321
sexual content of, 336
understanding, 346–348
property flipping, 361
propriety, 54
prosocial bonds, 212
prostitutes, 88
prostitution, 397–404
changing business, 402
clients, 402

feminist perspectives on, 402–404
human trafficking and, 433
legal, 8, 54, 401
legalization/decriminalization of, 404
morals legislation, 398
typology of prostitutes, 398–400
protection rackets, 370
provocations, 203
psychiatric criminology, 142
psychoactive substances, 382
psychoanalysis, 142
psychoanalytic criminology, 147
psychoanalytic theory, 133
psychobiotics, 114
psychological and psychiatric theories, 132–159. See also insanity
behavior theory, 148–150
cognitive theories, 138–142
criminal psychological profiling, 155–157
critiques of, 155–157
history of, 133
maladaptation, criminal behavior as, 142–148
moral development theory, 138–139, 147
personality disturbances, 133–138
personality theory, 147
policy implications, 150–154
principles of, 132–133
psychological autopsy, 157
treatment implications, 150–154
psychological autopsy, 157
psychological development, 138
psychological (maladaptive) perspective on crime, 2
psychological profiling, 155–157
psychopathological perspective on rape, 302
psychopathology, 133
psychopaths, 134–135, 201
psychopathy, 134–135
Psychopathy Checklist (PCL), 135
psychopharmacological use, 295
psychosis, 143, 144
psychotherapy, 143
psychotic offenders, 144
psychoticism, 137–138
PTSD. See post-traumatic stress disorder (PTSD)
public safety, 230
public transportation, robbery and, 311
publication, writing for, 49–50
punishment, 54, 147, 251
capital, 68, 70–74
deterrence by, 69
just deserts model, 69
need for, 144
in neoclassical criminology, 68–74
Pure Food and Drug Act of 1906, 393
pure research, defined, 33
pyramid scheme, 360

Q

qualitative methods, 42–44
quantitative methods, 42
quasi-experimental research designs, 35–38

R

race, capital punishment and, 70–74
Racketeer Influenced and Corrupt Organizations (RICO) Act, 376

racketeering, 358
radar, 418
radical criminology, 237, 238–239
radical-critical criminology, 240–242
radical feminism, 245
radicalization process, 443-444
radical realism, 244
randomization, 36
rape, 299–306, 337, 431
  acquaintance rape, 305
  date rape, 305, 393
  definition change, 299
  evolutionary/biological perspectives on, 302
  feminist perspectives on, 302, 303
  integrated theory of, 302
  intimate-partner, 316
  in prison, 305–306
  sexual victimization of men, 306
  spousal, 305
  statistics, 299, 305
  theoretical perspectives on, 300–303
  typologies of rapists, 303–304
rape myths, 304, 305, 402
rational choice theory (RCT), 17,
    64–65, 348
  critique of, 67–69
rational thought, 59
rationalism, 59
rationality, 348
reaction formation, 184–185
reactions to crime, 18
reactive effects of experimental
    arrangements, 37
reactive effects of testing, 37
reactivity, 37
rebellion, 172, 174
receivers of stolen property, 348
recidivism, 69
recidivism rate, 69
reference list (research reports), 49
regression toward the mean, 36
rehabilitation, 62–63
reinforcements, 148
reintegrative shaming, 194, 210
relative deprivation, 175
religion and religious practices, 28, 55
religious terrorists, 435
reparative justice, 251
replicability, 40–41
repression, 144
research, 33–42
  data collection problems, 40–41
  data collection techniques, 38–40
  defined, 33
  design development, 34–38
  problem identification, 33–34
  quantitative versus qualitative methods, 42–44
  report, 48–49
  review of findings, 41–42
  social policy and, 46–47
  stages of, 33
  values and ethics in, 44–45
research designs
  development of, 34–38
  experimental and quasi-experimental, 35–37
research report, 48–49
researchers, 12–13
resilience, 221
responsibility, social, 17
restorative justice, 4, 252–253

results (research reports), 49
retaliation, 313, 316
retreatism, 172, 173
retribution, 56, 60, 68
retributive justice, 252
revenge-motivated mass murderers, 299
revictimization, 270
review of existing literature (research reports),
    48–49
review of findings, 41–42
reward, 149
rewards of crime, 54, 65
right-wing terrorists, 435
rights, natural, 58–59
RISE (Reintegrative Shaming Experiments), 210
risk assessment, 145
risk taking, 99
ritualism, 172, 173
robbery, 309–314, 335, 359
  flash mobs, 339–340
Rochester Youth Development Study, 222–223,
    224
Rohypnol, 393
Roman law, early, 56
routine activities theory, 64–65, 121, 277–278
  burglary and, 332

S

sample size, 42
sampling error, 41
Sandy Hook (Newtown, Connecticut) school
    shootings, 7, 229
Sarbanes-Oxley Act, 367, 368
Schafer, Stephen, 275
schizophrenia, 107–109, 133, 144
  childhood, 135
scientific criminology, 29
scientific definitions, 10
scientific evidence, 420
scientific method, 30
script theory, 139
scripts, 140
second-degree murder, 291
secondary analysis, 40
secondary conflict, 179
secondary deviance, 206, 207
secondary psychopaths, 135
secondary research, 33
Securities Act of 1933, 368
Securities and Exchange Commission
    (SEC), 367
Securities Exchange Act of 1934, 368
securities fraud, 354, 355, 356, 360–361
security devices, 334, 336
seductions of crime, 65
selective disinhibition, 295
selective incapacitation, 74, 152
self-control, 201–204
self-derogation theory of delinquency, 200
self-esteem, 200
self-report surveys, 260
self-reporting, 39–40
self-selection, 37
semiotics, 249
separation assault, 315
separation of powers, 58
serial murder, 296–297

seriousness, in criminal careers, 216
serotonin, 104, 116
sex hormone-binding globulin (SHBG), 115
sex industry, 401
sex trafficking, 400
sex work, 402, 434–435
sexual selection, 124–125, 303
shell companies, 364
Sherman Act, 356, 368
shoplifting, 122, 337–338
sibling offense, 295
simple assault, 314
situational action theory (SAT), 203–204
situational choice theory, 64
situational crime control, 64
situational crime-control policy, 66–67
situational crime prevention, 68, 168
situational model, 278
slavery, 432, 434
smartness, 180
smoking, 114
smuggling, 434–435
social bond, 200
social bond theory, 200–201
social capital, 219
social characteristics, change in, 423
social class, 237–238
social cognition theory, 149–150
social conflict theories, 165, 166, 233–257
  conflict perspective, 235–238
  consensus perspective, 234–235
  convict criminology, 237, 254–255
  critical criminology, 240–241
  elements of, 236
  emerging conflict theories, 243–257
  feminist criminology, 237, 244–249
  left-realist criminology, 237, 243
  moral time, 254
  peacemaking criminology, 237, 250
  pluralist perspective, 235
  policy implications of, 257
  postmodern criminology, 249–250
  radical criminology, 237, 238–239
  radical-critical criminology, 240–241
  radical-critical thought, 255–257
social context of crime, 18–21
social contract, 57–58, 60
social control policies, 54
social control theory, 194, 195, 198–204
social determinism, 84
social development theories, 165, 194, 196, 211,
    214
  age-graded theory, 218–220
  concepts in, 214
  critiques of, 229
  delinquent development theory,
      220–221
  developmental pathways, 223–225
  dual taxonomic theory, 219–220
  evolutionary ecology, 221–222
  interactional theory, 222–223
  life course perspective, 215–218
  pathways to desistance, 226
  policy implications of, 228–229
  principles of, 194
social disorganization, 166
social disorganization theory, 166–172
  Chicago School, 167–168
  collective efficacy, 171
  criminology of place, 168–172

social ecology, 167
social event, crime as, 119–20
social interaction perspective, 194
social learning, 194
social learning theory, 149, 196–198
social life, 165
social media, 339
social norms, 6
social order perspectives, 234
social pathology, 167
social policy, 10
    criminology and, 15–16
social problems perspective, 17, 188
social process theories, 165, 166, 194
    containment theory, 199–200
    control–balance theory, 204
    critiques of, 213–214
    delinquency and self-esteem, 200
    differential association, 195–197
    differential association–reinforcement theory,
        197–198
    differential identification theory, 198
    dramaturgical perspective, 195, 210–211
    general theory of crime, 201–203
    labeling theory, 195, 205–206
    policy implications of, 212
    principles of, 195
    reintegrative shaming, 185, 210
    social bond theory, 200–201
    social control theory, 198–205
    social learning theory, 196–198
    types of, 194–195
social processes, 165
social reaction theory, 196
social relativity, 19
social responsibility perspective, 17, 189
social space, 254
social structure, 165
social structure–social learning model
        (SSSL), 197
social structure theories, 163–190
    critiques of, 188–190
    culture conflict theory, 166, 179–188
    policy implications of, 188
    principles of, 164–165
    social disorganization theory, 166–172
    strain theory, 166, 172–179
    types of, 166–188
social time, 254
socialist feminism, 246
socialization, 21, 165, 194, 214
    gender-role, 245
    problems in, 88
society, 21
sociobiology, 85, 95–99
socioeconomic status, 189
sociological learning theory, 197
sociological (sociolegal) perspective on crime, 2, 23
sociological theories, 165–166
sociology, 23, 230
sociopaths, 134, 135, 296
soft determinism, 64, 181
software piracy, 410
Sourcebook of Criminal Justice Statistics, 70
sovereign citizen movement, 436
spam, 358
specific deterrence, 69
speech, 425
Spice, 382
"Spiderman snare," 418

spirit possession, 40
spousal abuse, 305
spousal rape, 305
stability thesis, 202
stalking, 322–326
standard deviation, 41
standard social science model (SSSM), 125
state laws, 17, 371, 393
state-sponsored terrorists, 435
state sponsors of international terrorism, 446
statement of hypothesis (research
        reports), 48
statistical analysis, 41
statistical regression, 36
statistics on crime, 3, 429
statutory rape, 299
sterilization, 91
stigma, 212
stigmata of degeneration, 87
stigmatic shaming, 210
Stark, Rodney, 280
stigmatized neighborhoods, 280
Stockholm Prize in Criminology, 47
strain, 172
strain theory, 166, 172–179, 367
stranger assault, 314
streetwalkers, 398–399
Strengthening America's Families Project, 212
stress, 106, 109
structural Marxism, 240
style guides, 50
subcultural theory, 366
subculture, 179
subculture of violence thesis, 292–293
subjectivity, 38
sublimation, 143
sugar hypothesis, 35, 112
suitable target, 278
summary (research reports), 49
superego, 144
supermale, 91–93, 98
supermax, 91–93, 98
supertraits, 137
survey research, 38
surveys, 38, 39
systemic violence, 295

table of contents (research reports), 48
tagging, 196
Taliban, 392
target hardening, 67, 68
Targeted Outreach, 228–229
tax evasion, 356
tax fraud, 365
techniques of neutralization, 181–182
technology, 407–425. See also cybercrime; Internet
    dependence on, 439
    for fighting crime, 418
    personal freedoms and, 425
    for property crime prevention, 338
    terrorism and, 439, 442
Technology Assessment Program (TAP), 418
telecommunications crimes, 409
telephones, 414
television shows, 2
temperature, 121
territoriality, 95

terror-motivated mass murderers, 299
terrorism, 435–442
    cybercrime and, 409
    cyberterrorism, 439–442
    domestic, 436
    future of, 447–448
    identity theft and, 341
    international, 437–438
    "lone-wolf" terrorists, 438, 447
    motivations for, 440
    organized crime and, 370
    radicalization and, 441
    state sponsors of, 435, 445
    technology and, 442
    terrorist group types, 435–436
    trends in, 447–448
    types of terrorists, 435
    white-collar crime and, 365–367
Terrorist Exclusion List (TEL), 447
Terrorist Identities Datamart Environment (TIDE),
        447
Terrorist Identities Group (TIG), 447
terrorist organizations, 431
Terrorist Screening Center (TSC), 447
test of significance, 43
testing
    repeated, 36
    of theories, 29
testing effects, 36
testosterone, 115–116
theft, 431
    categories, 337
    personal, 332
theft/fence rings, 370
theme of book, 16–17
theoretical criminology, 13–14
Theoretical Criminology (journal), 12
theory (-ies), 13–14
    building, 30–33
    defined, 30–33
    purposes and uses of, 31–32
thieves, persistent and professional, 346–347
third-degree murder, 291
Thorton, Walter, 269
threat analysis, 422
three-strikes legislation, 17, 46–47, 63
thrill-motivated serial killers, 296
thyroid hormone T3, 118
thyroid hormone T4 (thyroxine), 118
tipsters, 335
title page (research reports), 48
torture, 60
total institutions, 212
toughness, 180
Toxic Release Inventory, 112
trade secret theft, 356, 409
trafficking in persons (TIP), 434. See also
        human trafficking
Trafficking Victims Protection Act,
        400, 434
Trafficking Victims Protection Reauthorization Act
        (TVPRA), 434
trait theory, 137–138
traits, 137
translational criminology, 15
transnational criminal organizations
        (TCOs), 375
transnational organized crime, 374–375
tribalism, 96
trouble, as lower-class culture feature, 180

T

Troubled Assets Relief Program (TARP), 369
truth in sentencing, 74
turning points, 218
Twelve Tables, 56
Twin Early Development Study (TEDS), 105
twin studies, 93–94, 105
"Twinkie defense," 111

U

unemployment rates, 178
UN Office on Drugs and Crime
    (UNODC), 431
Unabomber, 256–257, 438
understanding, 31, 32–33
Uniform Crime Reporting (UCR)
    Program, 112, 261, 263–265, 299
    NCVS and, 265
Uniform Crime Reports/National Incident-Based
    Reporting System (UCR/NIBRS), 299
United Nations (UN), 429
United Nations Children's Fund
    (UNICEF), 309
United States Computer Emergency Readiness Test
    (US-CERT), 425
U.S. Immigration and Customs Enforcement (ICE),
    400, 432
U.S. Sentencing Commission, 153
USA PATRIOT Act, 17, 447
utilitarianism, 61

V

validity of research design, 34–35
values, 44–45
    criminal, 214
variable, 34
VAWA. See Violence against Women Act (VAWA)
Vehicle Identification Numbers (VINs), 342
verstehen, 44
vice operations, 370
victim, 261
victim–offender relationship, 293–294
    assault, 314–315
    burglary, 335
    identity theft, 341
    stalking, 322–323
victim precipitation, 274
victim proneness, 274
victim restitution, 285
victimization, 261. See also criminal victimization
    economic impact of, 272
    lifestyle and, 275–276

physical impact of, 272
psychological impact of, 271–272
as risk factor for crime, 273–274
secondary, 273
theories, types of, 274
victimization, risk of, 64
    burglary and, 332–333
victimogenesis, 274
victimologist, 274
victimology, 273–281
victims, 19, 22
    children as, 307–309
Victims of Crime Act (VOCA), 282
victim's rights amendments (VRAs), 282
victims' rights legislation, 282–284
video games, 32, 151, 152
violence
    displacement of, 145
    within group, 96
    interpersonal. See violent crime
    media, 15, 149
    random, 229–230
    risk factors for, 152
    subculture of violence thesis, 292–293
    subcultures of, 182–183
    systemic, 295
    video games and, 32, 151
    witnessing acts of, 15
Violence against Women Act
    (VAWA), 282
violent action, planning and execution
    of, 443
violent crime, 315–316
    aggravated assault, 314–316
    bullying, 317–319
    child sexual abuse, 307–309
    cyberbullying, 318–319
    definitions of, 431
    hate crimes, 321–322
    international statistics on, 429–430
    intimate-partner violence, 294
    murder (criminal homicide), 290–304
    nonlethal, 294
    rape, 304–306
    robbery, 309–314
    stalking, 322–326
    workplace violence, 319–320
Violent Crime Control and Law Enforcement Act
    of 1994, 17, 36, 393
violent crimes, 290
Violent Criminal Apprehension Program (VICAP),
    297
visionary serial killers, 296
vitamins, 112
VOCA. see Victims of Crime Act (VOCA)

von Hentig, Hans, 275
Vory V Zakone, 372

W

War on Poverty, 188
warez, 410
warrior gene, 104
weapon use, 295, 314
    family violence, 316
    stalking, 322
weapons, 311, 442
    availability of, 295
    of mass destruction (WMDs), 448
weather and crime, 120–121, 122
welfare fraud, 362
Welfare Reform Reconciliation Act of 1996, 188
Welfare-to-Work program, 188
whaling, 363
white-collar crime, 354–355
    causes of, 364–365
    corporate crime, 358–362
    curtailing, 367–368
    environmental crimes, 363–364
    evolution of, 357–358
    financial crime, 359–363
    history of, 354–355
    terminology, 356
    terrorism and, 364
    understanding, 340
Wikström's theory, 203
wire fraud, 356, 365
Wolfgang, Marvin, 274
women
    with ASPD, 136
    criminality of, 247
    rapists, 301
    serial killers, 296–297
    shoplifting by, 337
    testosterone and, 115, 116
Women's Christian Temperance Union (WCTU),
    207
workplace violence, 319–320
WorldCom, Inc., 355

X

XYY supermale, 91–92

Y

youth, violence and, 32. See also adolescence;
    children; juveniles